MANAGEMENT
ACCOUNTING

MANAGEMENT ACCOUNTING

DON R. HANSEN
Oklahoma State University

MARYANNE M. MOWEN
Oklahoma State University

SOUTH-WESTERN College Publishing

An International Thomson Publishing Company

Accounting Team Director: Mary H. Draper
Sponsoring Editor: Elizabeth A. Bowers
Developmental Editor: Leslie Kauffman
Production Editors: Laurie Merz, Jason M. Fisher
Production House: Matrix Productions
Internal Design: Joe Devine
Cover Design: Fusion Design/Kellie Schroeder
Photo Researcher: Jennifer Mayhall
Marketing Manager: Steve Hazelwood

AQ61DA
Copyright © 1997
by South-Western College Publishing
Cincinnati, Ohio

Library of Congress Cataloging-in-Publication Data
Hansen, Don R.
    Management accounting / Don R. Hansen, Maryanne M. Mowen.
        p.   cm.
    Includes index.
    ISBN 0-538-85630-0
    1. Managerial accounting. I. Mowen, Maryanne M. II. Title.
HF 5657.4.H36   1996   95-26788
658.15'11—dc20   CIP

International Thomson Publishing

South-Western College Publishing is an ITP Company.
The ITP trademark is used under license.

ISBN 0-538-85630-0

1 2 3 4 5 6 7 VH 2 1 0 9 8 7 6

Printed in the United States of America

Management Accounting, fourth edition, introduces students to the fundamentals of management accounting. It assumes that students have been introduced to the basics of financial accounting; however, extensive knowledge of financial accounting is not needed. Our emphasis is on the use of accounting information. Thus, the text should be of value to students with a variety of backgrounds. Although written to serve undergraduates, the text has been used successfully at the graduate level. The assignment material has sufficient variety to accommodate both undergraduate and graduate students.

Many business school students who are required to take a course in management accounting are not accounting majors. For these students, it is often difficult to appreciate the value of the concepts being taught. This text overcomes this attitude by using introductory chapter scenarios based on real-world settings, photos illustrating practical applications of management accounting concepts, and realistic examples illustrating the concepts within the chapters. Seeing that effective management requires a sound understanding of how to use accounting information should enhance the interest of both accounting and nonaccounting majors.

ACTIVITY-BASED MANAGEMENT

Management accounting continues to evolve and respond to changes in the manufacturing and service sectors of today's business world. One significant response has been the development of activity-based management. The effect of the activity-based management model on management accounting has been dramatic. The widespread acceptance and practice of activity concepts demands treatment of activity-based methods in an integrated, comprehensive framework. To respond to this need, we have developed such a framework. Within this framework we continue to offer extensive coverage of such topics as activity-based costing, process value analysis, quality, productivity, life-cycle cost management, target costing, and international management accounting issues.

TRADITIONAL COVERAGE

In a balanced approach to contemporary and traditional concepts, the fourth edition also continues to cover the traditional topics of management accounting. There is still widespread usage of the traditional management accounting models. Some of these traditional models and concepts can be adapted to an activity-based framework. Furthermore, it is fairly easy to see that traditional product-costing procedures are simply a special case of the more general activity-based costing approach. This insight lessens students' discomfort as they work with both traditional and activity-based costing models. Using an activity-based framework and integrating activity concepts throughout the text also helps students see the limitations of traditional procedures and the advantages of the activity-based approach. This understanding will help future managers to bring about change when it is merited. Perhaps understanding that management accounting is not a static discipline will itself contribute to additional innovative developments.

Take a few minutes to review the Table of Contents. You will see a balanced, integrative presentation of contemporary and traditional management accounting concepts. The Table of Contents is coded to help you quickly identify contemporary, traditional, and integrated coverage. Chapters covering contemporary topics are highlighted in green, traditional chapters are blue, and integrated chapters are purple.

ORGANIZATION OF THE TEXT

The sequence of chapters in the fourth edition of *Management Accounting* is significantly different. This is to facilitate the integration of activity-based costing concepts throughout the text. ABC concepts are presented much earlier than in the previous edition, allowing their integration into subsequent chapters. A detailed explanation of specific changes in chapter organization and topic coverage follows.

- In **Chapter 1**, more discussion of new management accounting concepts has been added. Students are introduced to the concepts of value chain, employee empowerment, and customer value.
- In **Chapter 2**, the following changes were made:
    a. The introduction to variable-costing income statements was removed. (Chapter 14 covers this topic thoroughly.)
    b. A discussion of value-chain product costing is added.
    c. The basic concepts of cost traceability are discussed, including direct tracing and driver tracing. Basic definitions of resource and activity drivers are provided.
    d. Services are defined and differences between services and tangible products are presented.
    e. Cost behavior is discussed totally within an activity framework.
    f. An overview and comparison of contemporary and traditional management accounting systems is provided. This overview is much more extensive than in the prior edition.
- **Chapter 3** (formerly Chapter 7) has been moved to allow an earlier introduction of cost behavior. Furthermore, the chapter now focuses on activity cost behavior and uses examples that involve both unit-level and nonunit-level drivers to explain cost behavior. The chapter also introduces the activity resource usage model with its insights regarding cost behavior.
- **Chapter 4** (formerly Chapter 6 and part of Chapter 3) now introduces normal costing and develops the activity-based costing model. Plantwide, departmental, and ABC approaches are defined and discussed. A new section has been added dealing with ABC assignment of costs to customers.
- In **Chapters 5 through 7** (formerly Chapters 3, 4, and 5), ABC applications have been integrated within the coverage of the traditional concepts of job-order costing, process costing, and allocation. Exercises and problems associated with these ABC applications have been added. Chapter 5 deals only with job-order costing since the overhead costing material is now found in Chapter 4.
- **Chapters 8 through 13**, the planning and control chapters, now appear in Part II, preceding the decision-making chapters. This reorganization allows additional concepts, such as budgeting, quality costs, and responsibility accounting to be developed before entering the world of decision making.
- **Chapter 10** (formerly Chapter 16) adds new material concerning the contemporary control model. It also more fully develops the process view of activity-based management. A section on driver analysis is added.
- **Chapters 14 through 18** are now fully integrated with contemporary approaches to decision making. For example, the role of the activity resource usage model in rele-

vant costing decisions is developed in Chapter 14. Similarly, Chapter 15 now presents both traditional and ABC approaches to CVP analysis.

- **Chapter 18,** covering inventory management, has been expanded to include a brief introduction to the Theory of Constraints.

CHAPTER ORGANIZATION AND STRUCTURE

Each chapter is carefully structured to help students focus on important concepts and remember them. Components found in each chapter include:

Learning Objectives. Each chapter begins with a set of learning objectives to guide students in their study of the chapter. These objectives outline the organizational flow of the chapter and serve as points of comprehension and evaluation. Learning objectives are tied to specific sections of topic coverage within the chapter. They are repeated in the margin at the beginning of the corresponding chapter coverage and are summarized at the end of the chapter.

Scenario. An interesting, real-world scenario opens each chapter. The scenario ties directly to concepts covered in the chapter and helps students relate chapter topics to actual business happenings. "Questions to Think About," a new feature in the fourth edition, has been added at the end of the scenarios. These critical-thinking questions are designed to pique student interest in the chapter and stimulate class discussion.

Summary of Learning Objectives. Each chapter concludes with a comprehensive summary of the learning objectives. Students can review and test their knowledge of key concepts and evaluate their ability to complete chapter objectives.

Key Terms. Throughout each chapter, key terms are highlighted and repeated in the margin for quick identification. A list of key terms, with page references, is presented at the end of each chapter to provide additional reinforcement. All key terms are defined in a comprehensive glossary at the end of the text.

Review Problems. Each chapter contains at least one review problem with the accompanying solution provided. These review problems demonstrate the application of major concepts and procedures covered in the chapter. Pages with review problems are shaded with a blue background, allowing for quick location.

Questions for Writing and Discussion. Approximately 15 to 25 short-answer questions appear at the end of each chapter to test students' knowledge of chapter concepts.

Many of the questions call for students to use critical thinking and written and oral communication skills. Several questions can be used to stimulate class participation and discussion.

Warm-up Exercises. This new end-of-chapter section has been added to the fourth edition. It provides exercises that duplicate the logic and structure of numerical examples within the chapter. Page references are provided so that students can easily refer to the chapter examples and use them as templates for developing their solutions. These Warm-up Exercises will help students learn to apply basic chapter concepts, providing a framework of knowledge to expand and build upon when completing more comprehensive exercises and problems.

Exercises. Exercises usually emphasize one or two chapter concepts and can be completed fairly quickly (30 minutes maximum). Exercises require basic application and computation and often ask students to interpret and explain their results.

Problems. Each chapter contains many end-of-chapter problems, with varying degrees of length and difficulty. Problems generally take longer to complete than exercises and probe for a deeper level of understanding. Problems usually have more than one issue, challenging situations, complex computations, and interpretations.

Managerial Decision Cases. Each chapter (except Chapter 1, due to its introductory nature) contains at least two cases. Cases have greater depth and complexity than problems. They are designed to help students integrate multiple concepts and further develop their analytical skills. At least one case in each chapter deals with ethical behavior. A research assignment case also appears in many chapters, allowing students to expand their research and communication skills beyond the classroom.

ADDITIONAL FEATURES OF THE FOURTH EDITION

International Coverage

See pages 9, 526–546

To emphasize the importance of international issues, we provide a full chapter on this topic (Chapter 13) as well as examples integrated throughout the text.

Ethics

See pages 15–18

See page 545

See pages 64, 196, 334

We continue to emphasize the study of ethical conduct for management accountants in the fourth edition. The role of ethics is discussed in Chapter 1, and the code of ethics developed by the Institute of Management Accountants is introduced. Examples of ethical conduct relative to management accounting issues are provided in other chapters as well. Chapter 13, dealing with international issues in management accounting, also has a section that discusses ethics in the international environment. Chapter 1 has several substantive problems on ethics, and subsequent chapters have at least one problem or case involving an ethical dilemma. These problems allow the instructor to introduce value judgments into management accounting decision making.

Real-World Emphasis

See pages 26, 286

See pages 9, 48, 132

The fourth edition incorporates many real-world applications of management accounting concepts, making the study of these concepts more familiar and interesting to the student. Opening scenarios introduce chapter topics within the context of realistic business examples. Real-company examples are incorporated throughout many chapters. Names of real companies are highlighted throughout the text for easy identification and

See pages 32, 166, 308 are listed in a company index at the back of the text. Photos have been added in individual chapters to help students relate to the real-world nature of management accounting.

See pages 281–284 A photo essay, following Chapter 7, uses scenes from an actual company (Panasonic) to depict management accounting concepts in action.

Increased Coverage of Service Industry

See pages 13, 107, 123, 310 Service businesses are experiencing unprecedented growth in today's economy. Managers of service businesses often use the same management accounting models as manufacturers, but must adapt them to their own unique situations of providing intangibles to consumers. To address this need, we have increased the coverage of service industry applications in the fourth edition. In addition, many real-company examples of service businesses are given. Service companies are highlighted in the company index at the end of the text.

ANCILLARIES

Check Figures. Key figures for solutions to selected problems and cases are provided at the end of the text as an aid to students as they prepare their answers.

Study Guide (Prepared by Donna Ulmer, St. Louis Community College at Meramec). The study guide provides a detailed review of each chapter and allows students to check their understanding of the material through quizzes and exercises. Specifically, students are provided with a Key Terms Test, a Chapter Quiz, and Practice Exercises. Answers are provided for all assignment material. New to this edition are Learning Organizers, developed to compare and contrast key concepts and aid in visual learning.

Instructor's Manual (Prepared by Marvin Bouillon, Iowa State University). The instructor's manual contains a complete set of lecture notes for each chapter, a listing of all exercises and problems with estimated difficulty and time required for solution, and a transition guide for the third edition of *Management Accounting* as well as other widely used management accounting texts. The manual also includes the section, "Cooperative Learning Techniques," written by Philip G. Cottell, Jr., Miami University, and Barbara J. Millis, University of Maryland.

Solutions Manual. The solutions manual contains the solutions for all end-of-chapter exercises, problems, and cases. Solutions have been error-checked to ensure their accuracy and reliability.

Solutions Transparencies. Acetate transparencies for selected solutions are also available.

Test Bank (Prepared by Anne Wessely and Donna Ulmer, St. Louis Community College at Meramec). The test bank offers multiple-choice problems, short problems, and essay problems. Designed to make exam preparation as convenient as possible for the instructor, each test bank chapter contains enough questions and problems to permit the preparation of several exams without repetition of material. The test bank is available in both printed and computerized (MicroExam III) versions.

Spreadsheet Templates (Prepared by John Palipchak). Template disks, using Lotus 1-2-3®,[1] provide outlined formats of solutions for selected end-of-chapter exercises and problems. These exercises and problems are identified with a margin symbol. The

1. Lotus 1-2-3 is a registered trademark of Lotus Development Corporation. Any reference to Lotus 1-2-3 refers to this footnote.

templates allow students to develop spreadsheet and "what-if" analysis skills. These disks are provided free of charge to instructors at educational institutions that adopt this text.

PowerPoint Slides and Student Study Notes (Prepared by Ted Compton, Ohio University). Selected transparencies of key concepts and exhibits from the text are available in PowerPoint®[2] presentation software. These slides integrate spreadsheets and video to provide a comprehensive multimedia outline of each chapter. Printouts of the slides, with accompanying notes, provide students with an individualized note-taking and study device.

Video Supplements. Three videos from the third edition will again be available for the fourth edition of the text. In a light, but highly demonstrative video, *GE Lighting Systems*, GE employees, in a mock setting, test the effectiveness of the contemporary manufacturing concepts of JIT, total production maintenance, and total quality control against traditional manufacturing methods and compare the results. A second video, *Activity-Based Costing: The Next Generation*, presents a joint teleconference from the Public Broadcasting System and Robert Morris College in which three partners from Big Six firms discuss their experiences in implementing ABC systems for clients. The third video is a series of segments featuring interviews with management accountants from various companies and footage of their operations. Included are segments that show the new manufacturing environment and how such concepts as JIT and ABC are applied in real situations.

In addition, a series of five videos is currently under development by LEARNet, a Michigan-based educational video company. These videos will incorporate footage of actual companies to illustrate key management accounting concepts, including activity-based costing, product costing, value-chain analysis, and total quality management.

Cases in Cost Management: A Strategic Emphasis (Written by John K. Shank, Dartmouth College). This set of cases is offered for those instructors who want to augment their management accounting course with richer, longer "fun" problems. Each case includes specific numerical questions to challenge and help develop the students' calculation skills with management accounting techniques. Each case also includes broader discussion questions to sharpen the controversial aspects of the calculations and emphasize the managerial issues behind the numbers. Accompanying the book is an instructor's manual, which contains comprehensive teaching commentaries for each of the cases.

Readings and Issues in Cost Management (Edited by James Reeve, University of Tennessee). This text is designed to expose students to the concepts and information they need to become responsive and flexible managers. Articles in the text cover topics such as TQM, employee empowerment, reengineering, continuous improvement, and short-cycle management.

ACKNOWLEDGMENTS

We would like to express our appreciation for all who have provided helpful comments and suggestions. The reviewers of the prior editions helped make it a successful product. Many valuable comments from instructors and students have helped us make significant improvements in the fourth edition. In particular, we would like to thank the following individuals who provided formal comments. Their input was deeply appreciated.

---

2. PowerPoint is a registered trademark of Microsoft Corporation. Any reference to PowerPoint refers to this footnote.

James F. Brown, Jr.
University of Nebraska—Lincoln

Jeffrey W. Schatzberg
University of Arizona

Darrel I. Gosse
Ball State University

Stephen V. Senge
Western Washington University

Dolan R. Hinson
University of North Carolina—Charlotte

Don Stone
University of Massachusetts

Richard E. McDermott
Weber State University

W. Joey Styron
Augusta College

Larry Paquette
Westfield State College

Monte R. Swain
Brigham Young University

Robert R. Picard
Idaho State University

James H. Thompson
Oklahoma City University

C. Douglas Poe
University of Kentucky

Tim West
Iowa State University

Jane Saly
University of Minnesota

We also would like to thank our verifiers. Cathy Xanthaky Larson, Middlesex Community College, served as the error-checker for the solutions manual. Patrick Berry, Oglethorpe University, verified the study guide and test bank. Their careful editing helped us produce a text and ancillary package of higher quality and accuracy.

We also want to express our gratitude to the Institute of Management Accountants for their permission to use adapted problems from past CMA examinations. They have also given us permission to reprint the ethical standards of conduct for management accountants.

Finally, we should offer special thanks to all the South-Western College Publishing staff. They have been most helpful and have carried out their tasks with impressive expertise and professionalism. We especially wish to thank Leslie Kauffman who has provided exceptionally insightful comments and who has exhibited courtesy and patience.

Don R. Hansen
Maryanne M. Mowen

DON R. HANSEN

Dr. Don R. Hansen is Professor of Accounting at Oklahoma State University. He received his Ph.D.from the University of Arizona in 1977. He has an undergraduate degree in mathematics from Brigham Young University. His research interests include productivity measurement, activity-based costing, and mathematical modeling. He has published articles in both accounting and engineering journals including *The Accounting Review, The Journal of Management Accounting Research, Accounting Horizons*, and *IIE Transactions*. He has served on the editorial board of *The Accounting Review* and is currently serving as an associate editor of the *Journal of Accounting Education*. His outside interests include playing basketball, watching sports, and studying Spanish and Portuguese.

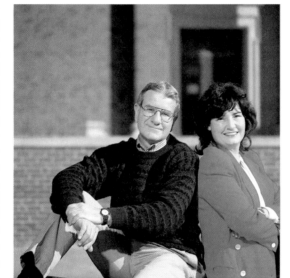

MARYANNE M. MOWEN

Dr. Maryanne M. Mowen is Associate Professor of Accounting at Oklahoma State University. She received her Ph.D. from Arizona State University in 1979. Dr. Mowen brings an interdisciplinary perspective to teaching and writing in cost and management accounting, with degrees in history and economics. In addition, she does scholarly research in behavioral decision theory. Dr. Mowen's interests outside the classroom include reading, playing golf, traveling, and working crossword puzzles.

CONTENTS IN BRIEF

Note: Chapters covering contemporary topics are highlighted in green, traditional chapters are blue, and integrated chapters are purple.

CONTENTS

Contemporary

10 Activity-based Management 384

Contemporary

11 Quality Costs and Productivity: Measurement, Reporting, and Control 432

PART 3
MANAGERIAL DECISION MAKING

Trad/Contemporary

16 Tactical Decision Making: Relevant Costing, the Activity Resource Usage Model, and Pricing 646

PHOTO CREDITS

Page 484   Courtesy of Kentucky Fried Chicken
Page 527   © Tony Stone Images/Kalunzy/Thatcher
Page 539   © Gamma Liaison/Ron McMillan
Page 557   © Tony Stone Images/Bob Torrez
Page 559   © The Stock Market/William Taufic
Page 572   © Gamma Liaison/E. deMalgaive
Page 601   © Index Stock Photography, Inc.
Page 611   © Tony Stone Images/Tom Tracy
Page 655   © Tony Stone Images/Steven Peters
Page 697   © Tony Stone Images/Chuck Keeler
Page 702   © John Madere
Page 749   © Tony Stone Images/Walter Hodges
Page 753   © Gamma Liaison

MANAGEMENT
ACCOUNTING

1. Explain the need for management accounting information.

2. Explain the differences between management accounting and financial accounting.

3. Provide a brief historical description of management accounting.

4. Identify and explain the emerging themes of management accounting.

5. Describe the role of management accountants in an organization.

6. Explain the importance of ethical behavior for managers and management accountants.

7. Identify three forms of certification available to management accountants.

CHAPTER

Introduction: The Role, History, and Direction of Management Accounting

SCENARIO

Consider the following comments made by individuals from several different organizations:

A. Manager: "I have just received a request to bid on the production of three specially constructed drill presses. The competition for this job is intense. Given the specifications described in the written request and the level of competition we are facing, I need to know the design costs, the expected manufacturing costs, and any other associated costs, and I need to know them with a high degree of accuracy. Knowing the costs of the job will reveal to me the minimum bid that I can submit that will assure us of a reasonable dollar return." (Product costing and pricing decision)

B. Local Operator(s): "I am confident that replacing the tooling in our machines and redesigning the decrease coupled with an increase in advertising costs and passenger volume is profitable." (Cost-volume-profit decision)

E. Manager: "I am not at all pleased with the performance of the emergency room. This latest performance report seems to reveal a total disregard for cost control. The actual costs incurred for almost every category are higher than the planned costs. Additionally, the revenues are lower than they should be for the number of patients treated. I think I need to meet with the assistant administrator of that area." (Managerial control)

F. Manager: "We must soon decide whether the acquisition of the robotic manufacturing equipment is in our best interests or not. This is a critical decision involving enormous amounts of capital and carries with it some long-run implications regarding the type of labor that we employ. To help us in that decision, our controller has estimated the cost of capital and the increase in after-tax cash flow that would be expected over the life of the equipment." (Capital investment decision and long-range planning)

grinding process will improve quality and decrease the time required to perform the operation. However, I would like to know if the number of defective units really drops and by how much. I also need to know if cycle time really decreases because of the changes. Furthermore, do these changes reduce the cost of performing the work we do? I also need to know the cost of resources used before and after the proposed changes to see if cost improvement really is taking place." (Continuous improvement)

C. Manager: "This is incredible! This job was supposed to cost $100,000. Yet, this final report shows a cost of $150,000. What happened? Were materials more expensive than expected? Did we use more labor than we should have? I need a report that identifies which costs overran their expected amounts, and I need someone to explain why! Even more important—why was I not informed about how the job was unfolding? It took two months to complete this job, and I received a report on final costs more than two weeks after it was completed. I need progress reports and on a timely basis. Perhaps we could have done something to correct the overruns before they became excessive." (Operational control)

D. Chief Executive Officer: "Our profits are being squeezed by the intense competition we are facing. My marketing vice-president argues that we can improve our financial position by reducing our airfares. She claims that if we reduce fares by 20 percent and simultaneously increase advertising expenditures by $500,000, we can increase the number of passengers by 20 percent. I need to decide whether the price

Questions to Think About:

1. *Who are the users of management accounting information?*
2. *What is management accounting information used for?*
3. *Should a management accounting system provide both financial and nonfinancial information?*
4. *What organizations need management accounting information systems?*

MANAGEMENT ACCOUNTING INFORMATION SYSTEM

Objective 1
Explain the need for management accounting information.

**management
   accounting
   information
   system**

The management accounting information system is an information system that produces outputs using inputs and processes needed to satisfy specific management objectives. *Processes* are the heart of a management accounting information system and are used to transform the inputs into outputs that satisfy the system's objectives. Processes are described by activities such as collecting, measuring, storing, analyzing, reporting, and managing information. Outputs include special reports, product costs, customer costs, budgets, performance reports, and even personal communication. The operational model of a management accounting information system is illustrated in Exhibit 1-1.

The management accounting information system is not bound by any formal criteria that define the nature of the inputs or processes—or even the output. The criteria are flexible and based on management objectives. The management accounting system has three broad objectives:

1. To provide information for costing out services, products, and other objects of interest to management
2. To provide information for planning, control, and evaluation
3. To provide information for decision making

These three objectives reveal that managers and other users need management accounting information and need to know how to use it. Management accounting information can help managers identify problems, solve problems, and evaluate performance (accounting information is needed and used in all phases of management, including planning, controlling, and decision making). Furthermore, the need for the information is not limited to manufacturing organizations. Management accounting information is used in all organizations: manufacturing, merchandising, and service.

Information Needs of Managers and Other Users

The scenarios can be used to illustrate each of the management accounting system objectives. Scenario A, for example, shows the importance of determining the cost of products and processes (illustrating objective 1). Scenario B emphasizes the importance of tracking costs and *nonfinancial* measures of performance over time. Thus, scenario A emphasizes the importance of *accuracy* in product costing and scenario B underscores the importance of tracking efficiency measures—both financial and nonfinancial (illustrating objective 2). Trends in these measures can suggest ways of improving a company's operations. For example, Milliken & Company, a leading textile manufacturer, began to use trend charts to track the change time for its dye nozzles. These charts provided the incentive for engineering and production personnel to reduce change time

Exhibit
Operational Model:
Management Accounting
Information System

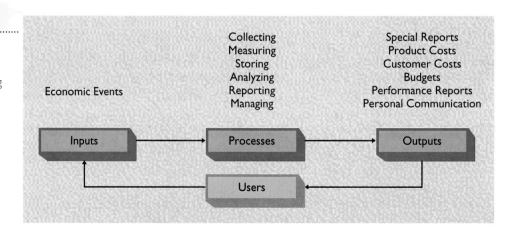

from 22 minutes to 8.2 minutes—a dramatic improvement.[1] Accuracy in costing assignments and the use of nonfinancial information (by both managers and nonmanagers) have emerged as key issues in recent years. These and other related issues have led to the development of new and more useful management accounting information. In fact, the need for greater accuracy has produced a new and improved management accounting information system—a system that will be referred to as a *contemporary management accounting information system* (to distinguish it from a traditional management accounting system).

Planning, control, and evaluation (objective 2) are illustrated by scenarios B, C, E, and F. Managers, executives, and workers need an information system that will identify problems, such as the possibility of cost overruns (scenario C) or the inability of a manager in a subunit to implement a plan properly (scenario E). Once problems are known, actions can be taken to identify and implement solutions. Scenario B also illustrates that both financial and nonfinancial information are needed so that workers can *evaluate* and *monitor* the effects of decisions that are intended to improve operational and unit performance. *Informing* workers about operational and financial performance allows workers to assess the effectiveness of their efforts to improve their work. Workers and managers should be committed to continuously improving the activities they perform. Continuous improvement means searching for ways of increasing the overall efficiency and productivity of activities by reducing waste, increasing quality, and reducing costs. Thus, information is needed to help identify opportunities for improvement and to evaluate the progress made in implementing actions designed to create improvement.

continuous improvement

The third objective, providing information for decision making, is intertwined with the first two. For example, information about the costs of products, customers, processes, and other objects of interest to management can be the basis for identifying problems and alternative solutions. Similar observations can be made about information pertaining to planning, control, and evaluation. Examples include using product cost to prepare a bid (scenario A), helping a manager decide whether to reduce prices and increase advertising to improve profitability (scenario D), or helping a manager decide whether to automate (scenario F).

The Management Process

The management process is defined by the following activities: (1) planning, (2) controlling, and (3) decision making. The management process describes the functions carried out by managers and *empowered workers*. Empowering workers to participate in the management process means giving them a greater say in how the plant operates. Thus, employee empowerment is simply authorizing operational personnel to plan, control, and make decisions without explicit authorization from middle and higher-level management.

employee empowerment

Employee empowerment is justified by the belief that the employees closest to the work can provide valuable input in terms of ideas, plans, and problem solving. Workers are allowed to shut down production to identify and correct problems, and their input is sought and used to improve production processes. For example, empowered workers at Duffy Tool and Stamping saved $14,300 per year by redesigning a press operation.[2] In one department, completed parts (made by a press) came down a chute and fell into a parts tub. When the tub became full, press operators had to stop operation while the stock operator removed the full tub and replaced it with an empty one. Empowered workers redesigned the operation so that each press had a chute with two branches—each leading to a tub. Now completed parts are routed into one branch of the chute. When the tub associated with the active branch becomes full, the completed parts are routed to the other branch and its tub while the full tub is being removed and replaced

1. James Don Edwards, "How Milliken Stays on Top," *Journal of Accountancy* (April 1989): 63–74 (see especially 72–74).
2. George F. Hanks, "Excellence Teams in Action," *Management Accounting* (February 1995): 35.

with an empty tub. This new design avoids machine downtime and produces significant savings. Clearly, employee empowerment is a key element in achieving continuous improvement.

planning

Planning The detailed formulation of action to achieve a particular end is the management activity called planning. Planning, therefore, requires setting objectives and identifying methods to achieve those objectives. For example, a firm may have the objective of increasing its short-term and long-term profitability by improving the overall quality of its products. By improving product quality, the firm should be able to reduce scrap and rework, decrease the number of customer complaints and warranty work, reduce the resources currently assigned to inspection, and so on, thus increasing profitability. But how is this to be accomplished? Management must develop some specific methods that, when implemented, will lead to the achievement of the desired objective. A plant manager, for example, may initiate a supplier evaluation program that has the objective of identifying and selecting suppliers that are willing and able to supply defect-free parts. Empowered workers, on the other hand, may be able to identify production causes of defects and create new methods for producing a product that will reduce scrap and rework and the need for inspection. The new methods should be clearly specified and detailed.

**controlling
feedback**

Controlling Planning is only half the battle. Once a plan is created, it must be implemented, and managers and workers must monitor its implementation to ensure that the plan is being carried out as intended. The managerial activity of monitoring a plan's implementation and taking corrective action as needed is referred to as controlling. Control is usually achieved with the use of feedback. Feedback is information that can be used to evaluate or correct the steps being taken to implement a plan. Based on the feedback, a manager (or worker) may decide to let the implementation continue as is, take corrective action of some type to put the actions back in harmony with the original plan, or do some midstream replanning.

Feedback is a critical facet of the control function. It is here that management accounting once again plays a vital role. Feedback can be financial or nonfinancial in nature. For example, the chute redesign at Duffy Tool and Stamping saved more than $14,000 per year—financial feedback. But the redesign also eliminated machine downtime and increased the number of units produced per hour (operational feedback). Both measures convey important information. Often financial and nonfinancial feedback is in the form of formal reports that compare the actual data with planned data. These reports are referred to as performance reports.

**performance
reports**

decision making

Decision Making The process of choosing among competing alternatives is decision making. This pervasive managerial function is intertwined with planning and control. A manager cannot plan without making decisions. Managers must choose among competing objectives and methods to carry out the chosen objectives. Only one of numerous competing plans can be chosen. Similar comments can be made concerning the control function.

Decisions can be improved if information about the alternatives is gathered and made available to managers. One of the major roles of the management accounting information system is to supply information that facilitates decision making. For example, the manager in scenario A was faced with the prospect of submitting a bid on the production of three drill presses. A large number of possible bids could be submitted, but the manager must choose one and only one to submit to the prospective customer. The manager requested information concerning the expected manufacturing costs of the three drill presses. This cost information, along with the manager's knowledge of competitive conditions, should improve his or her ability to select a bid price. Imagine having to submit a bid without some idea of the manufacturing costs.

Organization Type

The use of accounting information by managers is not limited to manufacturing organizations. Regardless of the organizational form, managers must be proficient in using accounting information. The basic concepts taught in this text are applicable to a variety of settings. The six scenarios at the beginning of this chapter involved manufacturing, health care, transportation, profit, and nonprofit organizations. Hospital administrators, presidents of corporations, dentists, educational administrators, and city managers all can improve their managerial skills by being well-grounded in the basic concepts and use of accounting information.

MANAGEMENT ACCOUNTING AND FINANCIAL ACCOUNTING

Objective 2

Explain the differences between management accounting and financial accounting.

financial accounting information system

Internal vs External Reporting

The accounting information system within an organization has two major subsystems: a management accounting system and a financial accounting system. (The accounting information system is a subsystem of a firm's overall management information system.) The two accounting subsystems differ in their objectives, the nature of their inputs, and the type of processes used to transform inputs into outputs. The financial accounting information system is primarily concerned with producing outputs for *external users*. It uses well-specified economic events as inputs and processes that meet certain rules and conventions. For financial accounting, the nature of the inputs and the rules and conventions governing processes are defined by the Securities Exchange Commission (SEC) and the Financial Accounting Standards Board (FASB). The overall objective is the preparation of external reports (financial statements) for investors, creditors, government agencies, and other outside users. This information is used for such things as investment decisions, stewardship evaluation, monitoring activity, and regulatory measures.

The management accounting system produces information for *internal users*, such as managers, executives, and workers. Thus, management accounting could be properly called *internal accounting*, and financial accounting could be called *external accounting*. Specifically, management accounting identifies, collects, measures, classifies, and reports information that is useful to internal users in planning, controlling, and decision making.

When comparing management accounting to financial accounting, several differences can be identified. Some of the more important differences follow and are summarized in Exhibit 1-2.

- *Targeted users.* As mentioned, management accounting focuses on providing information for internal users while financial accounting focuses on providing information for external users.
- *Restrictions on inputs and processes.* Management accounting is not subject to the requirements of generally accepted accounting principles. The Securities and Exchange Commission (SEC) and the Financial Accounting Standards Board (FASB) set the

1-2

Exhibit
Comparison of Management and Financial Accounting

Management Accounting	Financial Accounting
1. Internally focused	1. Externally focused
2. No mandatory rules	2. Must follow externally imposed rules
3. Financial and nonfinancial information; subjective information possible	3. Objective (financial) information / *verifiable*
4. Emphasis on the future	4. Historical orientation
5. Internal evaluation and decisions based on very detailed information	5. Information about the firm as a whole
6. Broad, multidisciplinary	6. More self-contained

Input & Processes are restricted

Information used

Subj to cost benefit justification

accounting procedures that must be followed for financial reporting. The inputs and processes of financial accounting are well-defined and, in fact, restricted. Only certain kinds of economic events qualify as inputs, and processes must follow generally accepted methods. Unlike financial accounting, management accounting has no official body that prescribes the format, content, and rules for selecting inputs and processes and preparing financial reports. Managers are free to choose whatever information they want—provided it can be justified on a cost-benefit basis.

- *Type of information.* The restrictions imposed by financial accounting tend to produce objective and verifiable financial information. For management accounting, information may be financial or nonfinancial and may be much more subjective in nature.

- *Time orientation.* Financial accounting has an historical orientation. It records and reports events that have already happened. Although management accounting also records and reports events that have already occurred, there is also a very strong emphasis on providing information about future events. Management, for example, may not only want to know what it cost to produce a product, it may also want to know what it *will* cost to produce a product. Knowing what it will cost helps in planning material purchases and making pricing decisions, among other things. This future-orientation is demanded because of the need to support the managerial functions of planning and decision making.

- *Degree of aggregation.* Management accounting provides measures and internal reports used to evaluate the performance of entities, product lines, departments, and managers. Essentially, very detailed information is needed and provided. Financial accounting, on the other hand, focuses on overall firm performance, providing a more aggregated viewpoint.

- *Breadth.* Management accounting is much broader than financial accounting. It includes aspects of managerial economics, industrial engineering, and management science, as well as numerous other areas.

It should be emphasized, however, that both the management accounting information system and the financial accounting information system are part of the total accounting information system. Unfortunately, all too often the content of the management accounting system is driven by the needs of the financial accounting system. The reports of both management and financial accounting are frequently derived from the same database, which usually was originally established to support the reporting requirements of financial accounting. Many organizations need to redesign this database in order to satisfy more fully the needs of the internal users. For example, a firm's profitability is of interest to investors, but managers need to know the profitability of individual products. The accounting system should be designed to provide both total profits and profits for individual products. The key point here is flexibility—the accounting system should be able to supply different information for different purposes.

A BRIEF HISTORICAL PERSPECTIVE OF MANAGEMENT ACCOUNTING

Objective 3

Provide a brief historical description of management accounting.

Most of the product-costing and management accounting procedures used in the twentieth century were developed between 1880 and 1925.[3] Interestingly, many of the early developments (until about 1914) concerned managerial product costing—tracing a firm's profitability to individual products and using this information for strategic decision making. By 1925, however, most of this emphasis had been abandoned in favor of inventory costing—assigning manufacturing costs to products so that the cost of inventories could be reported to external users of a firm's financial statements.

3. The historical information in this section is based on H. Thomas Johnson and Robert Kaplan, *Relevance Lost: The Rise and Fall of Management Accounting* (Boston: Harvard Business School Press, 1987).

Financial reporting became the driving force for the design of cost accounting systems. Managers and firms were willing to accept aggregated average cost information about individual products. Apparently, more detailed and accurate cost information about individual products was not needed. As long as a company had relatively homogeneous products that consumed resources at about the same rate, the average cost information supplied by a financially driven cost system was good enough. Furthermore, for some firms, even as product diversity increased, the need to have more accurate cost information was offset by the high cost of the processing required to provide the information. For many firms, the cost of a more detailed cost system apparently exceeded its benefits.

Some effort to improve the managerial usefulness of conventional cost systems took place in the 1950s and 1960s. Users discussed the shortcomings of information supplied by a system designed to prepare financial reports. Efforts to improve the system, however, essentially centered on making the financial accounting information more useful to users rather than on producing an entirely new set of information and procedures apart from the external reporting system.

In the 1980s and 1990s, many recognized that the traditional management accounting practices were no longer serving managerial needs. Some claimed that existing management accounting systems were obsolete and virtually useless. More accurate product costing and more useful and detailed input were needed to allow managers to improve quality, productivity, and reduce costs. In response to the perceived failure of the traditional management accounting system, efforts were made to develop a new management accounting system—one that satisfied the demands of the current economic environment.

EMERGING THEMES OF MANAGEMENT ACCOUNTING

Objective 4

Identify and explain the emerging themes of management accounting.

Thus, the economic environment many firms are facing today has required the development of innovative and relevant management accounting practices. In recent years, worldwide competitive pressures have changed the nature of our economy, forcing many U.S. manufacturers to change dramatically the way in which they operate their businesses. These changes are creating a new environment for management accounting—at least for a significant number of organizations. As the environment changes, the traditional management accounting system may no longer apply. For many firms, the benefits of a *contemporary* management accounting system which provides greater detail and more accurate cost assignments may now exceed its costs. The key factors that are bringing about these changes follow:

1. Customer orientation
2. Cross-functional perspective
3. Global competition
4. Total quality management
5. Time as a competitive element
6. Advances in information technology
7. Advances in the manufacturing environment
8. Growth and deregulation in the service industry
9. Activity-based management

A brief discussion of these themes is needed to understand fully the impact on management accounting.

Customer Orientation

customer value

Firms are focusing on creating a competitive advantage by creating better customer value for the same or lower cost than that of competitors or creating equivalent value for lower cost than that of competitors. Customer value is the difference between what a customer receives (customer realization) and what the customer gives up (customer

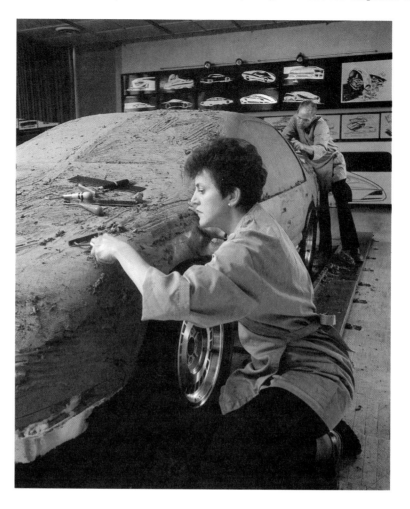

Designing a product that meets customer needs is a critical link in the value chain. Here, designers apply clay to a car, demonstrating prototype design styling.

total product

sacrifice). What is received is called the total product. The total product is the complete range of tangible and intangible benefits that a customer receives from a purchased product. Thus, customer realization includes basic and special product features, service, quality, instructions for use, reputation, brand name, and any other factors deemed important by customers. Customer sacrifice includes the cost of purchasing the product, the time and effort spent acquiring and learning to use the product, and postpurchase costs, which are defined as the costs of using, maintaining, and disposing of the product. Increasing customer value means increasing customer realization, or decreasing customer sacrifice, or both.

postpurchase costs

A focus on customer value means that the management accounting system should produce information about both realization and sacrifice. Collecting information about customer sacrifice means gathering information *outside* the firm, a practice not usually found within traditional management accounting systems. But there are even deeper implications. Effective management of the *value chain* is fundamental to increasing customer value, especially if maximizing customer realization at the lowest possible cost (to the firm) is a goal. The value chain is the set of activities required to design, develop, produce, market, and deliver products and services to customers. Thus, emphasizing customer value forces managers to determine which activities in the value chain are important to customers. A contemporary management accounting system should track information about a wide variety of activities that span the value chain. Consider, for example, the delivery segment. Timely delivery of a product or service is part of the total product, and, thus, of value to the customer. Customer value can be increased by increasing the speed of delivery and response. Federal Express exploited this part of the value chain and successfully developed a service that was not being offered by the U.S. Postal

value chain

Crucial element-Time PS 11

Service. Today, many customers believe that a delivery delayed is a delivery denied. This seems to indicate that a good management accounting system ought to develop and measure indicators of customer satisfaction.

It is important to note that companies have internal customers as well. The support (staff) functions of a company exist to serve the line functions. For example, the procurement process acquires and delivers parts and materials to producing departments. Providing high-quality parts on a timely basis to producing departments is just as vital for procurement as it is for a company to provide high-quality goods to external customers.

Cross-Functional Perspective

Emphasis on the value chain means that today's management accountant must understand many functions of the business, from manufacturing to marketing to distribution to customer service. This need is magnified when the company is involved in international trade. We see this, for example, in the varying definitions of product cost. Contemporary management accounting has moved beyond the traditional manufacturing cost definition of product cost to more inclusive definitions. These contemporary approaches to product costing may include initial design and engineering costs, as well as manufacturing costs, and the costs of distribution, sales, and service. An individual well-schooled in the various definitions of product cost, who understands the shifting definitions of cost from the short-run to the long-run, can be invaluable in determining what information is relevant in decision making. For example, strategic decisions may require a product cost definition that assigns the costs of all value-chain activities, whereas a short-run decision that is concerned with whether a special order should be accepted or rejected may require a product cost that assigns only marginal or incremental costs.

Why try to relate management accounting to marketing, management, engineering, finance, and other business functions? Can't management accountants just continue measuring manufacturing costs in the traditional way? No. When a value-chain approach is taken and customer value is emphasized, we see that these disciplines are interrelated; a decision affecting one affects the others. For example, many manufacturing companies engage in frequent trade loading, the practice of encouraging (often by offering huge discounts) wholesalers and retailers to buy more product than they can quickly resell. As a result, inventories become bloated and the wholesalers and retailers stop purchasing for a time. This looks like a marketing problem, but it is not—at least not entirely. When selling stops, so does production. As a result, trade-loading companies like Procter & Gamble, Bristol-Myers Squibb, and Duracell found themselves with wild swings in production. Sometimes the factories were producing around the clock to meet demand for the heavily discounted product; other times the factories were idle and workers were laid off. In effect, the sales were costing the companies millions of dollars of added production cost.[4] A cross-functional perspective lets us see the forest, not just one or two of the trees.

Global Competition

Vastly improved transportation and communications have led to a global market for many manufacturing and service firms. Several decades ago, firms neither knew nor cared what similar firms in places like Japan, France, Germany, and Singapore were making. These foreign firms were not competitors, since the markets were separated by large geographic distances. Now automobiles made in Japan can be in the United States in two weeks. Investment bankers and management consultants can communicate with foreign offices instantly. Improved transportation and communication have upped the ante for all firms. At the same time, major improvements in productivity and quality by foreign firms have placed tremendous competitive pressures on U.S. firms. Kodak, for

4. Patricia Sellers, "The Dumbest Marketing Ploy," *Fortune*, (5 October 1992), 88–94.

Modernizations in transportation and communication have led to increased global competition.

example, is developing Photo CD, a high-tech way to transfer photographs to CDs for use in electronic documents. However, the company has nearly six hundred competitors in optical storage technology. To succeed, Kodak will have to be at the cutting edge of technology and work to be a low-cost producer.[5] Because of these intense competitive pressures, the cost of making bad decisions based on low-quality information has increased significantly. Thus, increasing global competition has created a demand for improved management accounting information.

Total Quality Management

total quality management

Continuous improvement is fundamental for establishing a state of manufacturing excellence. Manufacturing excellence is the key to survival in today's world-class competitive environment. Producing products with little waste that actually perform according to specifications are the twin objectives of world-class firms. A philosophy of total quality management, in which manufacturers strive to create an environment that will enable workers to manufacture perfect (zero-defect) products, is replacing the "acceptable quality" attitudes of the past. This increased emphasis on quality has also created a demand for a management accounting system that provides financial and nonfinancial information about quality.

Service industries are also dedicated to improving quality. Service firms present special problems because quality may differ from employee to employee. As a result, service firms are emphasizing consistency through the development of systems to support employee efforts. For example, USAA, a financial services company specializing in insurance for current and former military officers, invested heavily in information technology in the mid-1980s. Incoming documents (for example, policy applications, checks, and appraisals) are scanned electronically and stored on optical disks. When a customer calls

5. Mark Maremont, "Kodak's New Focus: An Inside Look at George Fisher's Strategy," *Business Week*, (30 January 1995), 62–68.

USAA to see if a policy application for a new house has been received, a service representative can check the customer's file on the computer and answer the question immediately. This is in contrast to the old system, which required USAA reps to search a warehouse or other reps' desks for the relevant files—a process that could take up to two weeks.[6]

Quality cost measurement and reporting are key features of the contemporary management accounting system for both manufacturing and service industries. In both cases, the management accounting system should be able to provide both operational and financial information about quality, including information such as the number of defects, quality cost reports, quality cost trend reports, and quality cost performance reports.

Time as a Competitive Element

Time is a crucial element in all phases of the value chain.[7] World-class firms reduce time to market by compressing design, implementation, and production cycles. These firms deliver products or services quickly by eliminating nonvalue-added time, time of no value to the customer (for example, the time a product spends on the loading dock). Interestingly, *decreasing* nonvalue-added time appears to go hand in hand with *increasing* quality. The USAA example given in the previous section demonstrates the improvement in service quality that resulted from the insightful management of time. The overall objective, of course, is to increase customer responsiveness.

What about the relationship between time and product life cycles? The rate of technological innovation has increased for many industries, and the life of a particular product can be quite short. Managers must be able to respond quickly and decisively to changing market conditions. Information to allow them to accomplish this must be available. For example, Hewlett-Packard has found that it is better to be 50 percent over budget in new product development than to be six months late. This correlation between cost and time is the kind of information that should be available from a management accounting information system.

Advances in Information Technology

Two significant advances relate to information technology. One is intimately connected with computer-integrated manufacturing. With automated manufacturing, computers are used to monitor and control operations. Because a computer is being used, a considerable amount of useful information can be collected and reported to managers about what is happening on the floor almost as it happens. It is now possible to track products continuously as they move through the factory and to report (on a real-time basis) such things as units produced, material used, scrap, and product cost. The outcome is an information system that fully integrates manufacturing with marketing and accounting data.

Automation increases both the quantity and the timeliness of information. For managers to exploit the value of the more complex information system fully, they must have access to the data of the system and be able to extract and analyze it quickly and efficiently. This, in turn, implies that the tools for analysis must be powerful.

The second major advance supplies the required tools: the availability of personal computers (PCs), spreadsheet software, and graphics packages. The PC serves as a communications link to the company's information system, and spreadsheet and graphics programs supply managers with the analytical capability to use that information. PCs and software aids are available to managers in all types of organizations. PCs and user-

---

6. Myron Magnet, "Who's Winning the Information Revolution?" *Fortune,* (30 November 1992), 110–117.
7. An excellent analysis of time as a competitive element is contained in A. Faye Borthick and Harold P. Roth, "Accounting for Time: Reengineering Business Processes to Improve Responsiveness," *Journal of Cost Management* (Fall 1993): 4–14.

friendly software packages allow managers to do much of their own analysis and to decrease their dependence on a centralized information systems department. If a PC also acts as a terminal and is connected to an organization's database, managers can access information more quickly and prepare many of their own reports. Management accountants now have the flexibility to respond to the managerial need for more complex product costing. In addition, the vast computing capability now available makes it possible to generate reports on an as-needed basis. Many firms have found that the increased responsiveness of a contemporary management accounting system allows them to realize significant cost savings by eliminating the huge volume of internally generated monthly reports.

Advances in the Manufacturing Environment

Improving technology and processes is having a dramatic effect on the manufacturing environment. These changes, in turn, are affecting product-costing systems, control systems, cost behavior and traceability, capital budgeting, and many other management accounting practices.

Just-in-Time (JIT)

Just-in-Time Manufacturing Traditional manufacturing systems are *push-through systems*, meaning production is "pushed through" the system and efforts are then made to sell as many units as are produced. If production is greater than demand, then inventories of finished goods are created. A *demand-pull* system such as Just-in-Time (JIT) strives to produce a product only when it is needed and only in the quantities demanded by customers. Demand pulls products through the manufacturing process. Each operation produces only what is necessary to satisfy the demand of the succeeding operation. No production takes place until a signal from a succeeding process indicates the need to produce. Parts and materials arrive just in time to be used in production.

JIT manufacturing typically reduces inventories to much lower levels than found in conventional systems, increases the emphasis on quality control, and produces fundamental changes in the way production is organized and carried out. Basically, JIT manufacturing focuses on continual improvement by reducing inventory costs and dealing with other economic problems. Reducing inventories frees up capital that can be used for more productive investment. Increasing quality enhances the competitive ability of the firm. Finally, changing from a traditional manufacturing setup to JIT manufacturing allows the firm to focus more on quality and productivity and, at the same time, allows a more accurate assessment of what it costs to produce products. The increase in costing accuracy occurs because the ability to trace products in a JIT system increases.

Computer-Integrated Manufacturing Automation of the manufacturing environment allows firms to reduce inventory, increase productive capacity, improve quality and service, decrease processing time, and increase output. In other words, automation can produce a competitive advantage for a firm. The implementation of automated manufacturing typically follows JIT and is a response to the increased needs for quality and shorter response times. As more firms automate, competitive pressures will force other firms to do likewise. For many manufacturing firms, automation may be equivalent to survival.

There are three possible levels of automation: the stand-alone piece of equipment, the cell, and the completely integrated factory. However, before firms attempt any level of automation, they should do all they can to produce a more focused, simplified manufacturing process. Experience indicates that about 80 percent of the benefits of going to a completely integrated factory can be achieved simply by implementing JIT manufacturing.[8]

---

8. Steven M. Hronec, "The Effects of Manufacturing Productivity on Cost Accounting and Management Reporting," *Cost Accounting for the 90s,* 117–125.

If automation is justified, it may mean installation of a computer-integrated manufacturing (CIM) system. CIM implies the following capabilities: (1) the products are designed through the use of a computer-assisted design (CAD) system; (2) a computer-assisted engineering (CAE) system is used to test the design; (3) the product is manufactured using a computer-assisted manufacturing (CAM) system (CAMs use computer-controlled machines and robots); and (4) an information system connects the various automated components.

One particular type of CAM is the flexible manufacturing system. Flexible manufacturing systems are capable of producing a family of products from start to finish using robots and other automated equipment under the control of a mainframe computer. This ability to produce a variety of products with the same set of equipment is clearly advantageous.

Growth and Deregulation in the Service Industry

As the traditional smokestack industries have declined in importance, the service sector of the economy has increased in importance. The service sector makes up about three-fourths of the U.S. economy and employment. Many services are exported; these accounted for a $59 billion trade surplus in 1992. Experts predict that this sector will continue to grow as service productivity grows. Deregulation of many services (for example, airlines, financial services, and telecommunications) has increased competition in the service industry. Many service organizations are scrambling to survive. In the deregulated environment, many of the same issues facing manufacturers began to emerge: quality, productivity, cost efficiency, customer satisfaction, and time-based competition. These competitive issues have made managers of service companies more conscious of the need to use management accounting information for planning, controlling, and decision making. With its demand for better information and productivity, the service sector will increase its demand for management accounting information.

The central issue of the service-sector trend is the need for an increased awareness of management accounting's usefulness. Meeting this objective can be achieved to a large extent by illustrating the applicability of management accounting concepts to service-based settings. Additionally, the unique characteristics of service firms require us to extend and adapt management accounting techniques to their particular circumstances.

Activity-based Management

activity-based management

The demand for more accurate and relevant management accounting information has led to the development of *activity-based management*. Activity-based management is a systemwide, integrated approach that focuses management's attention on activities with the objective of improving customer value and the resulting profit. Activity-based management emphasizes *activity-based costing* (ABC) and *process value analysis*. Activity-based costing improves the accuracy of assigning costs by first tracing costs to activities and then to products or customers that consume these activities. Process value analysis, on the other hand, emphasizes activity analysis, trying to determine why activities are performed and how well they are performed. The objective is to find ways to perform necessary activities more efficiently and to eliminate those that do not create customer value. Peter Drucker, internationally respected management guru, points out the growing importance of activity-based costing (management):

Traditional cost accounting in manufacturing does not record the cost of nonproducing such as the cost of faulty quality, or of a machine being out of order, or of needed parts not being on hand. Yet these unrecorded and uncontrolled costs in some plants run as high as the costs that traditional accounting does record. By contrast, a new method of cost accounting developed in the last ten years—called "activity-based" accounting records all costs. And it relates them, as traditional accounting cannot, to value-added.

Within the next 10 years it should be in general use, and then we will have operational control in manufacturing.[9]

Activity-based management is the heart of the contemporary management accounting system. If Peter Drucker is correct in his viewpoint, the study of contemporary management accounting is crucial. Accordingly, the activity-based management model is strongly emphasized. However, at the same time traditional management accounting systems are not ignored—nor should they be. For some settings, traditional systems continue to work well and are much cheaper to use. Additionally, the transition from traditional management accounting to activity-based management accounting is not instantaneous. Time is required for firms to adopt new procedures. Furthermore, as new procedures are placed in the crucible of actual experience, we can expect more modifications.

THE ROLE OF THE MANAGEMENT ACCOUNTANT

Objective 5

Describe the role of management accountants in an organization.

Today's business press writes about world-class firms. These are firms that are at the cutting edge of customer support. They know their market and their product. They strive to continually improve product design, manufacture, and delivery. These companies can compete with the best of the best in a global environment. Management accountants must also be world-class. They must be intelligent, well-prepared, and stay current with new developments. They also must be familiar with the customs and practices of countries in which their firm operates.

The role of management accountants in an organization is one of support. They assist those individuals who are responsible for carrying out an organization's basic objectives. Positions that have direct responsibility for the basic objectives of an organization are referred to as **line positions**. Positions that are supportive in nature and have only indirect responsibility for an organization's basic objectives are called **staff positions**.

line positions
staff positions

For example, assume that the basic mission of an organization is to produce and sell laser printers. The vice-presidents of manufacturing and marketing, the factory manager, and the assemblers are all line positions. The vice-presidents of finance and human resources, the cost accountant, and the purchasing manager are all staff positions.

The partial organization chart shown in Exhibit 1-3 illustrates the organizational positions for production and finance. Because one of the basic objectives of the organization is to produce, those directly involved in production hold line positions. Although management accountants, such as controllers and cost accounting managers, may wield considerable influence in the organization, they have no authority over the managers in the production area. The managers in line positions are the ones who set policy and make the decisions that impact production. However, by supplying and interpreting accounting information, management accountants can have significant input into policies and decisions.

controller

The **controller**, the chief accounting officer, supervises all accounting departments. Because of the critical role that management accounting plays in the operation of an organization, the controller is often viewed as a member of the top management team and encouraged to participate in planning, control, and decision-making activities. As the chief accounting officer, the controller has responsibility for both internal and external accounting requirements. This charge may include direct responsibility for internal auditing, cost accounting, financial accounting (including SEC reports and financial statements), systems accounting (including analysis, design, and internal controls), and taxes. The duties and organization of the controller's office vary from firm to firm. For example, in some firms the internal audit department may report directly to the financial vice-president; similarly, the systems department may report directly to the financial

9. Peter F. Drucker, "We Need to Measure, Not Count," *The Wall Street Journal*, (13 April 1993), A14.

Exhibit 1-3 .... Partial Organization Chart, Manufacturing Company

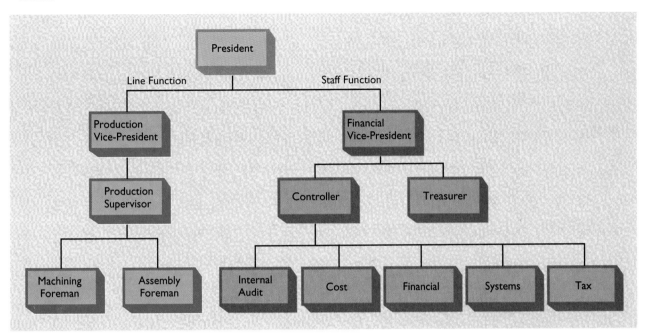

vice-president or some other vice-president. A possible organization of a controller's office is also shown in Exhibit 1-3.

treasurer   The treasurer is responsible for the finance function. Specifically, the treasurer raises capital and manages cash and investments. The treasurer may also be in charge of credit and collection and insurance. As shown in Exhibit 1-3, the treasurer reports to the financial vice-president.

MANAGEMENT ACCOUNTING AND ETHICAL CONDUCT

Objective 6

Explain the importance of ethical behavior for managers and management accountants.

Virtually all management accounting practices were developed to assist managers in maximizing profits. Traditionally, the economic performance of the firm has been the overriding concern. Yet, managers and management accountants should not become so focused on profits that they develop a belief that the *only* goal of a business is maximizing its net worth. The objective of profit maximization should be constrained by the requirement that profits be achieved through legal and ethical means. While this has always been an implicit assumption of management accounting, the assumption should be made explicit. To help achieve this objective, many of the problems in this text force explicit consideration of ethical issues.

Ethical Behavior

ethical behavior   Ethical behavior involves choosing actions that are "right" and "proper" and "just." Our behavior can be right or wrong; it can be proper or improper; and the decisions we make can be fair or unfair. People often differ in their views of the meaning of the ethical terms cited; however, there seems to be a common principle underlying all ethical systems. This principle is expressed by the belief that each member of a group bears some responsibility for the well-being of other members. Willingness to sacrifice one's self-interest for the well-being of the group is the heart of ethical action.[10]

10. For a detailed discussion of ethical behavior, see LaRue Tone Hosmer, *The Ethics of Management* (Homewood, Ill.: Irwin, 1987).

This notion of sacrificing one's self-interest for the well-being of others produces some core values—values that describe what is meant by right and wrong in more concrete terms. James W. Brackner, writing for the "Ethics Column" in *Management Accounting*, made the following observation:

For moral or ethical education to have meaning, there must be agreement on the values that are considered "right." Ten of these values are identified and described by Michael Josephson in, "Teaching Ethical Decision Making and Principled Reasoning." The study of history, philosophy, and religion reveals a strong consensus as to certain universal and timeless values essential to the ethical life.

These ten core values yield a series of principles that delineate right and wrong in general terms. Therefore, they provide a guide to behavior. . . [11]

The ten core values referred to in the quotation follow:

1. Honesty
2. Integrity
3. Promise keeping
4. Fidelity
5. Fairness
6. Caring for others
7. Respect for others
8. Responsible citizenship
9. Pursuit of excellence
10. Accountability

Although it may seem contradictory, sacrificing one's self-interest for the collective good may not only be right and bring a sense of individual worth but may also be good business sense. Companies with a strong code of ethics can create strong customer and employee loyalty. While liars and cheats may win on occasion, their victories are often short-term. Companies in business for the long term find that it pays to treat all of their constituents honestly and loyally.

Standards of Ethical Conduct for Management Accountants

Organizations commonly establish standards of conduct for their managers and employees. Professional associations also establish ethical standards. For example, the Institute of Management Accountants has established ethical standards for management accountants. On June 1, 1983, the Management Accounting Practices Committee of the IMA issued a statement outlining standards of ethical conduct for management accountants.[12] In this statement, management accountants are told that "they shall not commit acts contrary to these standards nor shall they condone the commission of such acts by others in their organizations." The standards and the recommended resolution of ethical conflicts are presented in Exhibit 1-4.

To illustrate an application of the code, suppose a manager's bonus is linked to reported profits, with the bonus increasing as profits increase. Thus, the manager has an incentive to find ways to increase profits, including unethical approaches. For example, a manager could increase profits by delaying promotions of deserving employees or by using cheaper parts to produce a product. In either case, if the motive is simply to increase the bonus, the behavior could be labeled as unethical. Neither action is in the best interest of the company or its employees. Yet, where should the blame be assigned?

---

11. James W. Brackner, "Consensus Values Should Be Taught," *Management Accounting* (August 1992): 19. For a more complete discussion of the ten core values, see also Michael Josephson, "Teaching Ethical Decision Making and Principled Reasoning," *Ethics Easier Said Than Done* (Los Angeles, Ca.: The Josephson Institute, Winter 1988), 29–30.

12. "Standards of Ethical Conduct for Management Accountants," *Statement on Management Accounting No. 1C* (Montvale, NJ: Institute of Management Accountants, 1983).

1-4

Exhibit
Standards of Ethical
Conduct for
Management
Accountants

I. Competence

Management accountants have a responsibility to:
1. Maintain an appropriate level of professional competence by ongoing development of their knowledge and skills.
2. Perform their professional duties in accordance with relevant laws, regulations, and technical standards.
3. Prepare complete and clear reports and recommendations after appropriate analyses of relevant and reliable information.

II. Confidentiality

Management accountants have a responsibility to:
1. Refrain from disclosing confidential information acquired in the course of their work except when authorized, unless legally obligated to do so.
2. Inform subordinates as appropriate regarding the confidentiality of information acquired in the course of their work and monitor their activities to ensure the maintenance of that confidentiality.
3. Refrain from using or appearing to use confidential information acquired in the course of their work for unethical or illegal advantage either personally or through a third party.

III. Integrity

Management accountants have a responsibility to:
1. Avoid actual or apparent conflicts of interest and advise all appropriate parties of any potential conflict.
2. Refrain from engaging in any activity that would prejudice their abilities to carry out their duties ethically.
3. Refuse any gift, favor, or hospitality that would influence their actions.
4. Refrain from either actively or passively subverting the attainment of the organization's legitimate and ethical objectives.
5. Recognize and communicate professional limitations or other constraints that would preclude responsible judgment or successful performance of an activity.
6. Communicate unfavorable as well as favorable information and professional judgments or opinions.
7. Refrain from engaging in or supporting any activity that would discredit the profession.

IV. Objectivity

Management accountants have a responsibility to:
1. Communicate information fairly and objectively.
2. Disclose fully all relevant information that could reasonably be expected to influence an intended user's understanding of the reports, comments, and recommendations presented.

Resolution of Ethical Conflict

In applying the standards of ethical conduct, management accountants may encounter problems in identifying unethical behavior or in resolving ethical conflict. When faced with significant ethical issues, management accountants should follow the established policies of the organization bearing on the resolution of such conflict. If these policies do not resolve the ethical conflict, management accountants should consider the following courses of action:
1. Discuss such problems with the immediate supervisor except when it appears that the superior is involved, in which case the problem should be presented initially to the next higher management level. If satisfactory resolution cannot be achieved when the problem is initially presented, submit the issues to the next higher management level.
2. If the immediate superior is the chief executive officer, or equivalent, the acceptable reviewing authority may be a group such as the audit committee, executive committee,

(continued)

board of directors, board of trustees, or owners. Contact with levels above the immediate superior should be initiated only with the superior's knowledge, assuming the superior is not involved.

3. Clarify relevant concepts by confidential discussion with an objective advisor to obtain an understanding of possible courses of action.

4. If the ethical conflict still exists after exhausting all levels of internal review, the management accountant may have no other recourse on significant matters than to resign from the organization and to submit an informative memorandum to an appropriate representative of the organization.

5. Except where legally prescribed, communication of such problems to authorities or individuals not employed or engaged by the organization is not considered appropriate.

Source: *Statement on Management Accounting No. 1C,* "Standards of Ethical Conduct for Management Accountants." Copyright © 1983, Institute of Management Accountants, 10 Paragon Drive, Montvale, NJ. Reprinted with permission.

After all, the reward system strongly encourages the manager to increase profits. Is the reward system at fault or is the manager who chooses to increase profits? Or both?

In reality, both probably are at fault. It is important to design the evaluation and reward system so that incentives to pursue undesirable behavior are minimized. Yet, designing a perfect reward system is not a realistic expectation. Managers also have an obligation to avoid abusing the system. Standard III-3 of the code makes this clear: "Management accountants have a responsibility to refuse any gift, favor, or hospitality that would influence their actions." Manipulating income to increase a bonus can be interpreted as a violation of this standard. Basically, the prospect of an increased bonus (for example, a favor) should not influence a manager to engage in unethical actions.

CERTIFICATION

Objective 7

Identify three forms of certification available to management accountants.

There are numerous forms of certification available to management accountants. Three of the major types will be briefly described: a Certificate in Management Accounting (CMA), a Certificate in Public Accounting (CPA), and a Certificate in Internal Auditing (CIA). Each certification offers particular advantages to a management accountant. In each case, an applicant must meet specific educational and experience requirements and pass a qualifying examination to become certified. Thus, all three certifications offer evidence that the holder has achieved a minimum level of professional competence.

Furthermore, all three certifications require the holders to engage in continuing professional education in order to maintain certification. Because certification reveals a commitment to professional competency, most organizations encourage their management accountants to become certified.

The CMA

Certified Management Accountant (CMA)

In 1974, the Institute of Management Accountants (IMA) sponsored a new certification, called the Certificate in Management Accounting. This certificate was designed to meet the specific needs of management accountants. A Certified Management Accountant (CMA) has passed a rigorous qualifying examination, has met an experience requirement, and participates in continuing education.

One of the key requirements for obtaining the CMA is passing a qualifying examination. Four areas are emphasized: (1) economics, finance, and management; (2) financial accounting and reporting; (3) management reporting, analysis, and behavioral issues; and (4) decision analysis and information systems. The parts to the examination reflect the needs of management accounting and underscore the earlier observation that management accounting has more of an interdisciplinary flavor than other areas of accounting.

One of the main purposes of the CMA was to establish management accounting as a recognized, professional discipline, separate from the profession of public accounting. Since its inception, the CMA program has been very successful. Many firms now sponsor and pay for classes that prepare their management accountants for the qualifying examination, as well as provide other financial incentives to encourage acquisition of the CMA.

The CPA

Certified Public Accountants (CPAs)

The Certificate in Public Accounting is the oldest and most well-known certification in accounting. The purpose of the Certificate in Public Accounting is to provide minimal professional qualification for external auditors. The responsibility of external auditors is to provide assurance concerning the reliability of a firm's financial statements. Only Certified Public Accountants (CPAs) are permitted (by law) to serve as external auditors. CPAs must pass a national examination and be licensed by the state in which they practice. Although the CPA does not have a management accounting–orientation, it is held by many management accountants.

The CIA

Certified Internal Auditor (CIA)

The other certification available to internal accountants is the Certificate in Internal Auditing (CIA). The forces that led to the creation of this certification in 1974 are similar to those that resulted in the CMA. Internal auditing is different from both external auditing and management accounting, and many internal auditors felt a need for a specialized certification. The Certified Internal Auditor (CIA) has passed a comprehensive examination designed to ensure technical competence and has two years' experience.

SUMMARY OF LEARNING OBJECTIVES

1. Explain the need for management accounting information.

Managers, workers, and executives use management accounting information to identify problems, solve problems, and evaluate performance. Essentially, management accounting information helps managers carry out their roles of planning, controlling, and decision making. Planning is the detailed formulation of action to achieve a particular end. Controlling is the monitoring of a plan's implementation. Decision making is choosing among competing alternatives.

2. Explain the differences between management accounting and financial accounting.

Management accounting differs from financial accounting in several ways. Management accounting information is intended for internal users, whereas financial accounting information is directed toward external users. Management accounting is not bound by the externally imposed rules of financial reporting. Furthermore, it tends to be more subjective and uses both financial and nonfinancial measures, whereas financial accounting provides audited, objective financial information. Finally, management accounting provides more detail than financial accounting, and it tends to be broader and multidisciplinary.

3. Provide a brief historical description of management accounting.

Most of the product-costing and internal accounting procedures used in this century were developed between 1880 and 1925. By 1925, the emphasis of management accounting procedures had become inventory costing, stemming from the emphasis on external reporting. In the 1950s and 1960s some effort was made to improve the managerial usefulness of traditional cost systems. In recent years, there have been significant efforts to radically change the nature and practice of management accounting, largely in response to some dramatic changes in the competitive environment.

4. Identify and explain the emerging themes of management accounting.

Management accounting must provide information that allows managers to focus on customer value, total quality management, and time-based competition. This implies that information about value-chain activities and customer sacrifice (such as postpurchase costs) must be collected and made available. JIT and automation have changed the nature and behavior of cost information. Also, factors such as global competition, deregulation of the service industry, and advances in information technology have significantly increased the demand for accurate and relevant management accounting information. Activity-based management is a major innovative response to the demand for more accurate and relevant management accounting information.

5. Describe the role of management accountants in an organization.

Management accountants are responsible for identifying, collecting, measuring, analyzing, preparing, interpreting, and communicating information used by management to achieve the basic objectives of the organization. Management accountants need to be sensitive to the information needs of managers. Management accountants serve as staff members of the organization and are responsible for providing information; they are usually intimately involved in the management process as valued members of the management team.

6. Explain the importance of ethical behavior for managers and management accountants.

Management accounting aids managers in their efforts to improve the economic performance of the firm. Unfortunately, some managers have overemphasized the economic dimension and have engaged in unethical and illegal actions. Many of these actions have relied on the management accounting system to bring about and even support that unethical behavior. To emphasize the importance of the ever-present constraint of ethical behavior on profit-maximizing behavior, this text presents ethical issues in many of the problems appearing at the end of each chapter.

7. Identify three forms of certification available to management accountants.

Three of the major types of certifications are the CMA, the CPA, and the CIA. The CMA is a certification designed especially for management accountants. The prestige of the CMA has increased significantly over the years and is now well regarded by the industrial world. The CPA is primarily intended for those practicing public accounting; however, because this certification is highly regarded many management accountants also hold it. The CIA serves internal auditors and is also well regarded.

KEY TERMS

Activity-based management *13*

Certified Internal Auditor (CIA) *19*

Certified Management Accountant (CMA) *18*

Certified Public Accountant (CPA) *19*

Continuous improvement *3*

Controller *14*

Controlling *4*

Customer value *7*

Decision making *4*

Employee empowerment *3*

Ethical behavior *15*

Feedback *4*

Financial accounting information system *5*

JIT manufacturing *12*

Line positions *14*

Management accounting information system *2*

Performance reports *4*

Planning *4*

Postpurchase costs *8*

Staff positions *14*

Total product *8*

Total quality management *10*

Treasurer *15*

Value chain *8*

QUESTIONS FOR WRITING AND DISCUSSION

1. What is a management accounting information system?
2. Describe the inputs, processes, and outputs of a management accounting information system.
3. What are the three objectives of a management accounting information system?
4. What organizations need management accounting information systems?
5. Who are the users of management accounting information?
6. What is management accounting information used for?
7. Should a management accounting system provide both financial and nonfinancial information? Explain.
8. What is meant by continuous improvement?
9. Describe what is meant by employee empowerment.
10. Explain why operational workers need management accounting information.
11. Describe the connection between planning, controlling, and feedback.
12. What role do performance reports play with respect to the control function?
13. How do management accounting and financial accounting differ?
14. Explain the role of financial reporting in the development of management accounting. Why has this changed in recent years?
15. Explain the meaning of customer value. How is focusing on customer value changing management accounting?
16. What is the value chain? Why is it important?
17. Explain why today's management accountant must have a cross-functional perspective.
18. Discuss the relationship of time-based competition and management accounting information.
19. Explain how advances in information technology have affected management accounting.
20. What is JIT? What is a flexible manufacturing system?
21. Deregulation of service industries (for example, airlines) has increased the demand for management accounting information. Why is this so?
22. What is activity-based management? Why is it important?
23. What is the difference between a staff position and a line position?
24. The controller should be a member of the top management staff. Do you agree or disagree? Explain.
25. What is the role of the controller in an organization? Describe some of the activities over which he or she has control.
26. What is ethical behavior? Is it possible to teach ethical behavior in a management accounting course?
27. Firms with higher ethical standards will experience a higher level of economic performance than firms with lower or poor ethical standards. Do you agree? Why or why not?
28. Review the code of ethical conduct for management accountants. Do you believe that the code will have an effect on the ethical behavior of management accountants? Explain.

29. Identify the three forms of accounting certification discussed. Which form of certification do you believe is best for a management accountant? Why?

30. What are the four parts to the CMA examination? What do they indicate about management accounting versus financial accounting?

PROBLEMS

P1-1

Management Accounting Information System

LO 1

The items that follow are associated with a management accounting information system.

a. Surveying customers to assess postpurchase costs
b. Incurrence of postpurchase costs
c. To cost out products
d. Assigning the cost of labor to a product
e. Report showing the cost of a product
f. Measuring the cost of quality
g. Repairing a defective part
h. Providing information for planning and control
i. Designing a product
j. Measuring the cost of design
k. A budget that shows how much should be spent on design activity
l. Using output information to make a decision
m. Usage of materials
n. A report comparing the actual costs of quality with the expected costs of quality

REQUIRED: Classify the items into one of the following categories:

a. Inputs
b. Processes
c. Outputs
d. System objectives

P1-2

Employee Empowerment

LO 1

Duffy Tool and Stamping has formed "excellence teams" made up of production line employees. These teams have been given the charge to improve production processes and enhance employee safety. The teams follow a very structured problem-solving methodology and have managed to make numerous improvements in production as well as safety. During a six-year period, pre-tax profits increased each year. Duffy's management credits much of the cost reductions and increased profits to the excellence teams.

Another company, Grand Rapids Spring and Wire Products, has formed minicompanies within their factory. The objective of minicompanies is to have each employee assume ownership of his or her work. Each minicompany has its own suppliers and customers (all within the factory). Furthermore, each minicompany is assigned its own support people: accountants, engineers, marketing people, and so on. The individuals within the minicompany are given responsibility for developing and maintaining good relations with its suppliers and customers and identifying problems, and developing and implementing solutions to those problems. The focus of each minicompany is on quality, cost, delivery, safety, and morale. The company has successfully created a quality culture, achieved a reputation for being a competitive, world-class manufacturer, and has become a "learning" organization.

REQUIRED:

1. What are the objectives of excellence teams and minicompanies? Did the companies achieve these objectives?
2. Do you think that employee empowerment is a good idea? Explain your answer. If yes, do you see any disadvantages? Explain.
3. What role, if any, does management accounting information have in employee empowerment?
4. What do you suppose is meant by the phrase "quality culture"? What is meant by a learning organization?

P1-3

The Managerial Process

LO 1

Each of the following scenarios requires the use of accounting information to carry out one or more of the following managerial activities: planning, control (including performance evaluation), or decision making. Identify the managerial activity or activities that are applicable for each scenario and indicate the role of accounting information in the activity.

A. Manager: "A supplier approached me recently and offered to sell our company vacuum hoses for $20 each. We currently manufacture our own hoses. I need to know what costs we will avoid if we buy the vacuum hoses."

B. Manager: "This report indicates that we have spent 20 percent more on materials than originally planned. An investigation into the cause has revealed the problem. We were using a lower-quality material than expected and the waste has been higher than normal. By switching to the quality level originally specified, we can cut the excess cost to 10 percent."

C. Manager: "Our salespeople indicate that they expect to sell 15 percent more units than last year. I want a projection of the effect this increase in sales will have on profits. I also want to know our expected cash receipts and cash expenditures on a month-by-month basis. I have a feeling that some short-term borrowing may be necessary."

D. Manager: "Given the intensity of competition, we need to do something about increasing the efficiency of our manufacturing process. Currently, we are considering the implementation of two different automated manufacturing systems. I need to know the future cash flows associated with each system."

E. Manager: "At the last board meeting, we established an objective of earning a 25 percent return on sales. I need to know how many units of our product we need to sell to meet this objective. Once I have the estimated sales in units, we need to outline a promotional campaign that will take us where we want to be. However, in order to compute the targeted sales in units, I need to know the expected unit price and a lot of cost information."

F. Manager: "Perhaps the Harrison Medical Clinic should not offer a full range of medical services. Some services seem to be having a difficult time showing any kind of profit. I am particularly concerned about the mental health service. It has not shown a profit since the clinic opened. I want to know what costs can be avoided if I drop the service. I also want some assessment of the impact on the other services we offer. Some of our patients may choose this clinic because we offer a full range of services."

P1-4
Emerging Themes
LO 4

Wilson McDonald has decided to purchase a personal computer. He has narrowed the choices to two: Quiknet and Reliable. Both brands have the same processing speed, the same hard-disk capacity, a 3.5-inch disk drive, and come with the same basic software support package. Both come from mail-order companies with good reputations. The selling price for each is identical. After some review, Wilson discovers that the cost of operating and maintaining Quiknet over a three-year period is estimated to be $200. For Reliable, the operating and maintenance cost is $600. The sales agent for Quiknet emphasized the lower operating and maintenance costs. The agent for Reliable, however, emphasized the service reputation of the product and the faster delivery time (Reliable can be purchased and delivered one week sooner than Quiknet). Based on all the information, Wilson has decided to buy Reliable.

REQUIRED:
1. What is the total product purchased by Wilson?
2. When asked why he decided to buy Reliable, Wilson responded, "I think that Reliable offers more value than Quiknet." What are the possible sources of this greater value? What implications does this have for the management accounting information system?
3. Suppose that Wilson's decision was prompted mostly by the desire to receive the computer quickly. Informed that they were losing sales because of the longer time to produce and deliver their products, the management of the company producing Quiknet decided process value analysis was the key to improving delivery performance. After adopting an activity-based costing system, they also discovered that they could lower their prices on Quiknet. Explain why management's view about process value analysis is correct. Also, explain why activity-based costing may have led management to lower the selling price of Quiknet.

P1-5
Role of Management Accountants
LO 5

Management accountants are actively involved in the process of managing the entity. This process includes making strategic, tactical, and operating decisions while helping to coordinate the efforts of the entire organization. To fulfill these objectives, the management accountant accepts certain responsibilities that can be identified as (1) planning, (2) controlling, (3) evaluating performance, (4) assuring accountability of resources, and (5) external reporting.

REQUIRED: Describe each of these responsibilities of the management accountant and identify examples of practices and techniques. (CMA adapted)

P1-6
Line versus Staff
LO 5

The job responsibilities of two employees of Barney Manufacturing follow.

Joan Dennison, Cost Accounting Manager Joan is responsible for measuring and collecting costs associated with the manufacture of the garden hose product line. She is also responsible for preparing periodic reports comparing the actual costs with planned costs. These reports are provided to the production line managers and the plant manager. Joan helps explain and interpret the reports.

Steven Swasey, Production Manager Steven is responsible for the manufacture of the high-quality garden hose. He supervises the line workers, helps develop the production schedule, and is responsible for seeing that production quotas are met. He is also held accountable for controlling manufacturing costs.

REQUIRED: Identify Joan and Steven as line or staff and explain your reasons.

P1-7
Ethical Behavior
LO 6

Consider the following scenario:

Manager: "If I can reduce my costs by $40,000 during this last quarter, my division will show a profit that is 10 percent above the planned level, and I will receive a $10,000 bonus. However, given the projections for the fourth quarter, it does not look promising. I really need that $10,000. I know one way I can qualify. All I have to do is lay off my three most expensive salespeople. After all, most of the orders are in for the fourth quarter, and I can always hire new sales personnel at the beginning of the next year."

REQUIRED: What is the right choice for the manager to make? Why did the ethical dilemma arise? Is there any way to redesign the accounting reporting system to discourage the type of behavior the manager is contemplating?

P1-8
Ethical Issues
LO 6

Assess and comment on each of the following statements that have appeared in newspaper editorials:

a. Business students come from all segments of society. If they have not been taught ethics by their families and by their elementary and secondary schools, there is little effect a business school can have.
b. Sacrificing self-interest for the collective good won't happen unless a majority of Americans also accept this premise.
c. Competent executives manage people and resources for the good of society. Monetary benefits and titles are simply the by-products of doing a good job.
d. Unethical firms and individuals, like high rollers in Las Vegas, are eventually wiped out financially.

P1-9
Ethical Issues
LO 6

The Alert Company is a closely held investment service group that has been very successful over the past five years, consistently providing most members of the top management group with 50 percent bonuses. In addition, both the chief financial officer and the chief executive officer have received 100 percent bonuses. Alert expects this trend to continue.

Recently, Alert's top management group, which holds 35 percent of the outstanding shares of common stock, has learned that a major corporation is interested in acquiring Alert. Alert's management is concerned that this corporation may make an attractive offer to the other share-holders and management would be unable to prevent the takeover. If the acquisition occurs, this executive group is uncertain about continued employment in the new corporate structure. As a consequence, the management group is considering changes to several accounting policies and practices that, although not in accordance with generally accepted accounting principles, would make the company a less attractive acquisition. Management has told Roger Deerling, Alert's controller, to implement some of these changes. Roger has also been informed that Alert's management does not intend to disclose these changes immediately to anyone outside the top management group.

REQUIRED: Using the code of ethics for management accountants, evaluate the changes that Roger's management is considering and discuss the specific steps that he should take to resolve the situation. (CMA adapted)

P1-10
Ethical Behavior
LO 6

Webson Manufacturing Company produces component parts for the airline industry and has recently undergone a major computer system conversion. Michael Darwin, the controller, has established a troubleshooting team to alleviate accounting problems that have occurred since the conversion. Michael has chosen Maureen Hughes, assistant controller, to head the team that will include Bob Randolph, cost accountant; Cynthia Wells, financial analyst; Marjorie Park, general accounting supervisor; and George Crandall, financial accountant.

The team has been meeting weekly for the last month. Maureen insists on being part of all the team conversations in order to gather information, make the final decision on any ideas or actions that the team develops, and prepare a weekly report for Michael. She has also used this team as a forum to discuss issues and disputes about him and other members of Webson's top management team. At last week's meeting, Maureen told the team that she thought a competitor might purchase Webson's common stock because she had overheard Michael talking about this on the telephone. As a result, most of Webson's employees now informally discuss the sale of Webson's common stock and how it will affect their jobs.

REQUIRED: Is Maureen Hughes's discussion with the team about the prospective sale of Webson unethical? Discuss, citing specific standards from the code of ethical conduct to support your position. (CMA adapted)

P1-11
Ethical
Responsibilities
LO 6

JLA Electronics is a U.S.-based, high-tech company that manufactures and distributes computer and telecommunications equipment. JLA has developed a handheld, lightweight fax system, Porto-Fax, that will allow the user total freedom in receiving and transmitting information. Marketing research studies indicate that the potential market for this item is large, and immediate action in test marketing the product is recommended.

Although JLA has excess capacity at its current manufacturing facility, the company has decided to build a new manufacturing plant to accommodate the Porto-Fax and is in the process of deciding where to locate the plant. The current unionized employees believe this move is being made to eliminate union involvement in the Porto-Fax manufacturing process. The management team that was formed to oversee the site selection process has already received bids from several locales, both domestic and foreign, offering a wide range of incentives to encourage the company to select particular sites.

Some of the incentives are personal in nature, such as housing at reduced cost for the selection team, reduced property taxes, open accounts at certain restaurants, and free tickets to local sporting events. Other incentives offered affect corporate profitability and include reduced tax rates, low-interest or no-interest loans, outright grants, and low-cost property. The marketing research team has reported that product price will have a major effect on the sale of Porto-Fax and recommends that the selection team pick a site that minimizes costs.

REQUIRED:
1. What is meant by the term *corporate social responsibility*?
2. Should JLA Electronics consider its social responsibility when making the final decision regarding the site selection?
3. Describe the ethical responsibilities of the individuals on the site selection team.
4. Discuss the responsibilities that the union at the current manufacturing facility may have in this situation. (CMA adapted)

1

PART

Cost Accumulation and Product Costing

Learning Objectives

After studying Chapter 2, you should be able to:

1. Explain the cost assignment process.

2. Define tangible and intangible products and explain why there are different product cost definitions.

3. Prepare income statements for manufacturing and service organizations.

4. Describe the relationship between activity drivers and cost behavior.

5. Explain the differences between traditional and contemporary management accounting systems.

CHAPTER

Basic Cost Concepts

SCENARIO

Kaylin Johnson, manager of Perry Electronics Division, scheduled a visit with the division's controller, Randy McManus, to address some issues recently brought to her attention. The following conversation was recorded.

Kaylin: Randy, you've been my controller for ten years. You, more than anyone, should be able to respond to some of the concerns that are surfacing in our company. Specifically, I have engineers, production managers, and marketing managers who are no longer comfortable with the product costs being reported by our system. I look at our reports and I see product costs reported to the fourth decimal place, which seems to imply great accuracy. Yet, I have managers who are saying that these costs are almost useless. In fact, I have been told that the engineering department has developed its own support our continuous improvement goal. But it will take commitment and significant effort by everyone to increase accuracy and then use the information for strategic analysis.

Questions to Think About

1. *What is meant by product-costing accuracy?*
2. *How will increasing accuracy of product costing improve decisions?*
3. *Why does Randy feel that the division's product costs are not very accurate?*
4. *Is assigning costs accurately as important for services as it is for tangible products?*

system for assessing costs of new and old products. What's happening here?

Randy: Well, I am pretty comfortable that in the aggregate our product costs are accurate. What we report on our balance sheet and income statements is pretty much on target.

Kaylin: That part is good—but are the individual product costs accurate? Can we rely on the individual costs for decision making? For example, can we use them to help us price our products or to bid on potential jobs? Can they be used to help us improve product designs? Or are my managers correct and we simply cannot rely on our current reported product costs?

Randy: To be honest, I am not confident that the individual product costs are that accurate. After all,

many costs we have are simply assigned to products based on an assumed relationship and this allocation may not reflect any actual cause-and-effect relationship.

Kaylin: Well, Randy, something must be done here. Can we improve the accuracy of our product costing? We must know how much each product is costing. It seems to me that we need to learn more about costs and then make decisions that bear directly on the costs. Understanding the nature of costs is fundamental to good management, and I need your help. After all, if we are going to pursue continuous improvement we must know where we are and what we can do to make things better.

Randy: I understand and I agree totally. There are some measures we can take to improve accuracy and to

COST ASSIGNMENT: DIRECT TRACING, DRIVER TRACING, AND ALLOCATION

Objective I

Explain the cost assignment process.

To study management accounting, it is necessary to understand the meaning of *cost* and the associated cost terminology. Assigning costs to products, services, and other objects of managerial interest is one of the principal objectives of a management accounting information system. Improving the cost assignment process has been one of the major developments in the management accounting field in recent years. The goal has been to increase the accuracy of assignments, producing higher-quality information, which can then be used to make better decisions. For example, Lord Corporation, a producer of products that reduce vibration and noise, found that more accurate cost assignments produced better pricing decisions and significant increases in profits.[1] However, before discussing the cost assignment process, we first need to define what we mean by "cost" and more fully describe its managerial importance.

Cost

cost

Cost is the cash or cash-equivalent value sacrificed for goods and services that are expected to bring a current or future benefit to the organization. We say *cash equivalent* because noncash resources can be exchanged for the desired goods or services. For example, it may be possible to exchange equipment for materials used in production. In effect, we can think of cost as a dollar measure of the resources used to achieve a given benefit. In striving to produce a current or future benefit, managers should make every effort to minimize the cost required to achieve this benefit. Reducing the cost required to achieve a given benefit means that a firm is becoming more efficient. Managers should have the objective of providing the same (or greater) customer value for a lower cost than their competitors. Why? Doing so means that a firm has achieved a competitive advantage.

opportunity cost

Managers should also understand what is meant by *opportunity cost*. Opportunity cost is the benefit given up or sacrificed when one alternative is chosen over another. For example, a firm may invest $100,000 in inventory for a year instead of investing the capital in a productive investment that would yield a 12 percent rate of return. The opportunity cost of the capital tied up in inventory is $12,000 ($0.12 \times \$100,000$) and is part of the cost of carrying the inventory.

expenses

Costs are incurred to produce future benefits. In a profit-making firm, future benefits usually mean revenues. As costs are used up in the production of revenues, they are said to expire. Expired costs are called expenses. In each period, expenses are deducted from revenues in the income statement to determine the period's profit. For a company to remain in business, revenues must consistently exceed expenses; moreover, the income earned must be large enough to satisfy the owners of the firm. Thus, cost and price are related in the sense that price must exceed cost such that sufficient income is earned. Furthermore, lowering price increases customer value by lowering customer sacrifice; and, the ability to lower price is connected to the ability to lower costs. Hence, managers need to know cost and trends in cost. Usually, however, knowing cost really means knowing what *something* or some *object* costs. Assigning costs to determine the cost of this object is therefore critical in providing this information to managers.

Cost Objects

cost object

Management accounting systems are structured to measure and assign costs to entities, called *cost objects*. A cost object is any item such as products, customers, departments, projects, activities, and so on, for which costs are measured and assigned. For example, if we want to determine what it costs to produce a bicycle, then the cost object is the bicycle. If we want to determine the cost of operating a maintenance department within

---

1. Alan W. Rupp, "ABC: A Pilot Approach," *Management Accounting* (January 1995): 50–55.

a plant, then the cost object is the maintenance department. If the objective is to determine the cost of developing a new toy, then the cost object is the new toy development project.

activity

In recent years, *activities* have emerged as important cost objects. An activity is a basic unit of work performed within an organization. It can also be defined as an aggregation of actions within an organization useful to managers for purposes of planning, controlling, and decision making. Activities play a prominent role in assigning costs to other cost objects and are essential elements of a contemporary management accounting system. Examples of activities include setting up equipment for production, moving materials and goods, purchasing parts, billing customers, paying bills, maintaining equipment, expediting orders, designing products, and inspecting products. Notice that an activity is described by an action verb (for example, paying and designing) joined with an object (for example, bills and products) that receives the action. Notice also that the action verb and object reveal very specific goals.

Accuracy of Assignments

Assigning costs *accurately* to cost objects is crucial. Our notion of accuracy is not evaluated based on knowledge of some underlying "true" cost. Rather, it is a relative concept and has to do with the reasonableness and logic of the cost assignment methods used. The objective is to measure and assign as well as possible the cost of the resources consumed by a cost object. Some cost assignment methods are clearly more accurate than others. For example, suppose you want to determine the cost of lunch for Elaine Day, a student that frequents Hideaway, an off-campus pizza parlor. One cost assignment approach is to count the number of customers Hideaway has between 12:00 P.M. and 1:00 P.M. and then divide the total receipts earned during this period. Suppose that this comes out to $4.50 per lunchtime customer. Thus, based on this approach we would conclude that Elaine spends $4.50 per day for lunch. Another approach is go with Elaine and *observe* how much she spends. Suppose that she has a slice of pizza and a medium drink each day, costing $2.50. It is not difficult to see which cost assignment is more accurate. The $4.50 cost assignment is distorted by the consumption patterns of other customers (cost objects). As it turns out, most lunchtime clients order the luncheon special for $4.99 (a minipizza, salad, and medium drink).

Distorted cost assignments can produce erroneous decisions and bad evaluations. For example, if a plant manager is trying to decide whether to continue producing power internally or to buy it from a local utility company, then an accurate assessment of how much it is costing to produce the power is fundamental to the analysis. An overstatement of the cost of power production could suggest to the manager that the internal power department should be shut down in favor of external purchase, whereas a more accurate cost assignment might suggest the opposite. It is easy to see that bad cost assignments can prove to be costly.

indirect costs
direct costs

traceability

Traceability The relationship of costs to cost objects can be exploited to help increase the accuracy of cost assignments. Costs are directly or indirectly associated with cost objects. Indirect costs are costs that cannot be easily and accurately traced to a cost object. Direct costs are those costs that can be easily and accurately traced to a cost object.[2] "Easily traced" means that the costs can be assigned in an economically feasible way and "accurately traced" means that the costs are assigned using a *cause-and-effect relationship*. Thus, traceability is simply the ability to assign a cost to a cost object in an economically feasible way by means of a cause-and-effect relationship. The more costs

2. This definition of direct costs is based on the glossary of terms prepared by Computer Aided Manufacturing-International, Inc. (CAM-I). See Norm Raffish and Peter B. B. Turney, "Glossary of Activity-Based Management," *Journal of Cost Management* (Fall 1991): 53–63. Other terms defined in this chapter and in the text also follow the CAM-I glossary.

that can be traced to the object, the greater the accuracy of the cost assignments. Establishing traceability is a key element in building accurate cost assignments.

It is possible for a particular cost item to be classified as both a direct cost and an indirect cost. Management accounting systems typically deal with many cost objects. It all depends on which cost object is the point of reference. For example, if the plant is the cost object, then the cost of heating and cooling the plant is a direct cost; however, if the cost object is a product produced in the plant, then this utility cost is an indirect cost.

tracing

direct tracing

Methods of Tracing Traceability means that costs can be assigned easily and accurately, whereas tracing is the actual assignment of costs to a cost object using an *observable* measure of the resources consumed by the cost object. Tracing costs to cost objects can occur in one of two ways: (1) direct tracing or (2) driver tracing. Direct tracing is the process of identifying and assigning costs that are specifically or physically associated with a cost object to that cost object. This is most often accomplished by *physical observation*. For example, assume that the cost object is the activity "maintaining equipment." The cost of parts, tools, and maintenance equipment are examples of costs that can be specifically identified by physical observation with the cost object. As a second example, let the cost object be a product: bicycles. The product uses both materials and labor. It is easy to observe how many wheels and other parts are used by the product and how many hours of labor it takes to produce bicycles. Both material and labor usage are physically observable and, therefore, their costs can be directly charged to the cost object. Ideally, all costs should be charged to cost objects using direct tracing. Unfortunately, it is often not possible or practical to physically observe the exact amount of resources being consumed by a cost object.

drivers

driver tracing

The next best approach is to use cause-and-effect reasoning to identify factors, called *drivers*, which are observable and which measure a cost object's resource consumption. Drivers are factors that *cause* changes in resource usage, activity usage, costs, and revenues. Driver tracing is the use of drivers to assign costs to cost objects. Although less precise than direct tracing, if the cause-and-effect relationship is sound, then a high degree of accuracy can be expected.

resource drivers

Driver tracing uses two types of drivers for tracing costs to cost objects: resource drivers and activity drivers. Resource drivers measure the demands placed on resources by activities, and are used to assign the cost of resources to activities. Consider the activity "maintaining equipment." This activity consumes resources such as parts, equipment, tools, labor, and energy (power to run the equipment and tools). Some of these resources such as equipment, tools, and materials are directly traceable to the activity. Other resources such as power and labor may not be directly traceable. Physically observing how much power is used would require a meter to measure the power consumption of the maintenance equipment. Metering may not be practical. Thus, a resource driver such as "machine hours" could be used to assign the cost of power. For example, if the power cost per machine hour is $0.50 and the activity, maintaining equipment, uses 20,000 machine hours, then $10,000 of the power cost ($0.50 × 20,000) would be assigned to the activity. The total cost of the activity is the sum of the directly traceable resource costs and the resource driver assigned costs.

activity drivers

Once the total cost of maintaining equipment is determined, then the cost of this activity can be assigned to objects that consume the activity by using activity drivers. Activity drivers measure the demands placed on activities by cost objects and are used to assign the cost of activities to cost objects. For example, the activity driver "number of maintenance hours worked" might be used to assign the cost of the activity "maintaining equipment" to the cost object "production departments." Thus, if the cost of providing the activity, maintaining equipment, is $20 per maintenance hour and a production department (say, grinding) uses 2,000 maintenance hours, then $40,000 of the activity's cost ($20 × 2,000 maintenance hours) would be assigned to grinding. A list of sample activities and their potential activity drivers is provided in Exhibit 2-1.

2-1 ....

Exhibit
Sample of Activities with
Potential Activity Drivers

Activity	Potential Activity Driver
Setting up equipment	Number of setups
Moving materials	Number of moves
Ordering materials	Number of purchase orders placed
Drilling holes	Number of machine hours
Redesigning products	Number of engineering orders
Paying bills	Number of invoices
Inspecting finished goods	Number of batches produced
Maintaining equipment	Number of maintenance hours
Providing power	Number of kilowatt-hours
Packing goods	Number of boxes
Scheduling production	Number of different products

**activity-based
costing**

The driver-tracing model just described is summarized in Exhibit 2-2. The driver-tracing model is the heart of a cost-assignment approach known as activity-based costing. Activity-based costing assigns costs to cost objects by first tracing costs to activities and then tracing costs to cost objects. The computational procedures for tracing costs to activities and other cost objects are described in detail in later chapters. At this point, the important thing to understand is that it is possible to assign costs to cost objects through the use of direct tracing, resource drivers, and activity drivers.

③ allocation

Assigning Indirect Costs Indirect costs cannot be traced to cost objects. This means that no causal relationship exists between the cost and the cost object or that tracing is not economically feasible. Assignment of indirect costs to cost objects is called allocation. Since no causal relationship exists, allocating indirect costs is based on *convenience* or some *assumed* linkage. For example, consider the cost of heating and lighting a plant in which five products are manufactured. Suppose that this utility cost is to be assigned to the five products. Clearly, it is difficult to see any causal relationship. A convenient way to allocate this cost is simply to assign it in proportion to the direct labor hours

2-2 ....

Exhibit
Assignment of Costs
Using Driver Tracing

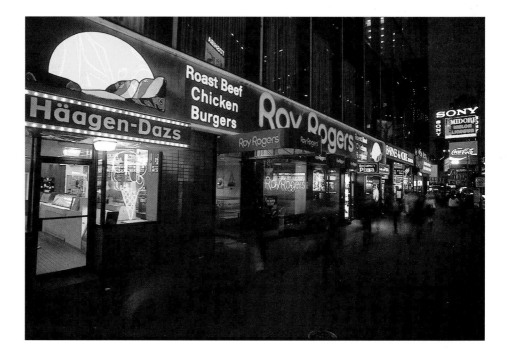

There is often no clear distinction between products and services. These fast food restaurants contain aspects of both. Roy Rogers, for example, produces hamburgers and french fries. It also provides take-out and dine-in service. Häagen-Dazs provides more service than production, as the ice cream is purchased, not made on the premises.

used by each product. Arbitrarily assigning indirect costs to cost objects reduces the overall accuracy of the cost assignments. Accordingly, the best costing policy may be assigning only direct (traceable) costs to cost objects. However, allocations of indirect costs may serve other purposes besides accuracy. For example, allocating indirect costs to products (a cost object) may be required to satisfy external reporting conventions. Nonetheless, most managerial uses of cost assignments are better served by accuracy; thus, at the very least direct and indirect cost assignments should be reported separately.

Cost Assignment Summarized The foregoing discussion reveals three methods of assigning costs to cost objects: direct tracing, driver tracing, and allocation. These methods are illustrated in Exhibit 2-3. Of the three methods, direct tracing is the most precise; it relies on physically observable causal relationships. Direct tracing is followed by driver tracing in terms of cost assignment accuracy. Driver tracing relies on causal factors, called drivers, to assign costs to cost objects. The precision of driver tracing depends on the quality of the casual relationship described by the driver. Identifying drivers and assessing the quality of the causal relationship is much more costly than either direct

2-3 ....

Exhibit
Cost Assignment
Methods

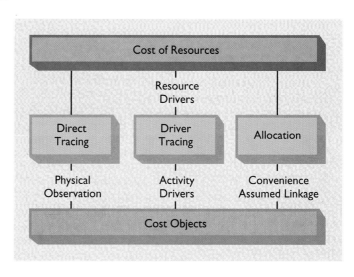

tracing or allocation. In fact, one advantage of allocation is its simplicity and low cost of implementation. However, allocation is the least accurate cost assignment method and its use should be minimized (avoided where possible). In many cases (maybe most) the benefits of increased accuracy outweigh the additional measurement cost associated with driver tracing. This cost-benefit issue is discussed more fully later in the chapter. What it really entails is choosing among competing management accounting information systems.

PRODUCT AND SERVICE COSTS

Objective 2

Define tangible and intangible products and explain why there are different product cost definitions.

tangible products

services

The output of organizations represents one of the most important cost objects. There are two types of output: tangible products and services. Tangible products are goods produced by converting raw materials through the use of labor and capital inputs, such as plant, land, and machinery. Televisions, hamburgers, automobiles, computers, clothes, and furniture are examples of tangible products. Services are tasks or activities performed for a customer or an activity performed by a customer using an organization's products or facilities. Services are also produced using materials, labor, and capital inputs. Insurance coverage, medical care, dental care, funeral care, and accounting are examples of service activities performed for customers. Car rental, video rental, and skiing are examples of services where the customer uses an organization's products or facilities.

intangibility

perishability

inseparability

heterogeneity

Services differ from tangible products on four important dimensions: intangibility, perishability, inseparability, and heterogeneity. Intangibility means that buyers of services cannot see, feel, hear, or taste a service before it is bought. Thus, services are *intangible products*. Perishability means that services cannot be stored for future use by a consumer (there are a few unusual cases where tangible goods cannot be stored) but must be consumed when performed. Although services cannot be stored, some services, like plastic surgery, have long-term effects and need not be repeated for a given customer. Other services have short-term effects and generate repeat customers. Examples of repetitive services are checking services, janitorial services, and dry cleaning. Inseparability means that producers of services and buyers of services must usually be in direct contact for an exchange to take place. In effect, services are often inseparable from their producers. For example, an eye examination requires both the patient and the optometrist to be present. However, producers of tangible products need not have direct contact with the buyers of their goods. Thus, buyers of automobiles never need to have contact with the engineers and assembly line workers that produced their automobiles. Heterogeneity means that there is a greater chance of variation in the performance of services than in the production of products. Service workers can be affected by the job undertaken, the mix of other individuals with whom they work, their education and experience, and personal factors such as home life.

These factors make providing a consistent level of service more difficult. The measurement of productivity and quality in a service company must be ongoing and sensitive to these factors. These differences affect the types of information needed for planning, control, and decision making. Exhibit 2-4 illustrates the features associated with services, some of their derived properties, and how they interface with the management accounting system. Notice that accurate cost assignments, quality, and productivity are concerns shared by producers of services with producers of tangible products.

Organizations that produce tangible products are called *manufacturing* organizations. Those that produce intangible products are called *service* organizations. Managers of both types of organizations need to know how much individual products cost. Accurate product costs are vital for profitability analysis and strategic decisions concerning product design, pricing, and product mix. Individual product cost can refer to either a tangible or an intangible product. Thus, when we discuss product costs, we are referring to both intangible and tangible products.

Feature	Derived Properties	Impact on Management Accounting
Intangibility	Services cannot be stored	No inventories
	No patent protection	Strong ethical code*
	Cannot display or communicate services	
	Prices difficult to set	Demand for more accurate cost assignment*
Perishability	Service benefits expire quickly	No inventories
	Services may be repeated often for one customer	Need for standards and consistent high quality*
Inseparability	Customer directly involved with production of service	Costs often accounted for by customer type*
	Centralized mass production of services difficult	Demand for measurement and control of quality to maintain consistency*
Heterogeneity	Wide variation in service product possible	Productivity and quality measurement and control must be ongoing*
		Total quality management critical*

*Many of these effects are also true of tangible products.

Different Costs for Different Purposes

product cost

Product cost is a cost assignment that supports a well-specified managerial objective. Thus, what "product cost" means depends on the managerial objective being served. The product cost definition illustrates a fundamental cost management principle: "different costs for different purposes." As a first example, suppose that management is interested in strategic profitability analysis. To support this objective, management needs information about all the revenues and costs associated with a product. In this case, a *value-chain product cost* is appropriate because it accounts for all the costs necessary to assess strategic profitability. Recall that the value chain is the set of all activities required to design, develop, produce, market, distribute, and service a product. The value chain is illustrated in Exhibit 2-5. A value-chain product cost is obtained by first assigning costs to the set of activities that define the value chain and then assigning the cost of these activities to products. As a second example, suppose that the managerial objective is short-run or tactical profitability analysis. In this case, the costs of designing and developing may not be relevant—especially for existing products. A decision, for example, to accept or reject an order for an existing product would depend on the price offered by the potential customer and the costs of producing, marketing, distributing, and servicing the special order. Thus, only the operating activities within the value chain would be important and the assignment of the costs of these activities to the product defines an *operating product cost.* As a third example, suppose that the managerial objective is external financial reporting. In this case, *traditional product costs* are needed. The rules and conventions that govern external financial reporting mandate that only production costs can be used in calculating product costs. Exhibit 2-6 summarizes the three product cost examples. Other objectives may use still other product cost definitions.

value chain

Exhibit
Value-Chain Activities

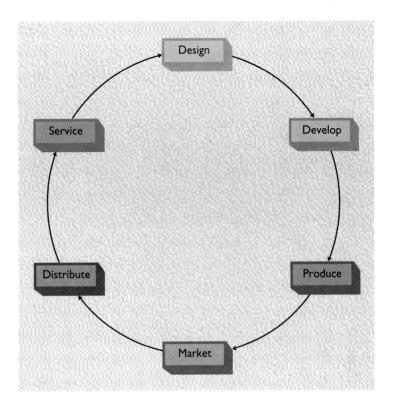

Product Costs and External Financial Reporting

One of the central objectives of a cost management system is the calculation of product costs for external financial reporting. For product-costing purposes, externally imposed conventions dictate that costs be classified in terms of the special purposes, or functions, they serve. Costs are subdivided into two major functional categories: production and

Exhibit

Examples of Product Cost Definitions

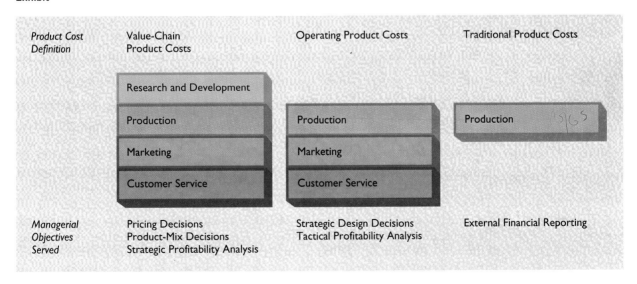

Product Cost Definition	Value-Chain Product Costs	Operating Product Costs	Traditional Product Costs
	Research and Development		
	Production	Production	Production
	Marketing	Marketing	
	Customer Service	Customer Service	
Managerial Objectives Served	Pricing Decisions Product-Mix Decisions Strategic Profitability Analysis	Strategic Design Decisions Tactical Profitability Analysis	External Financial Reporting

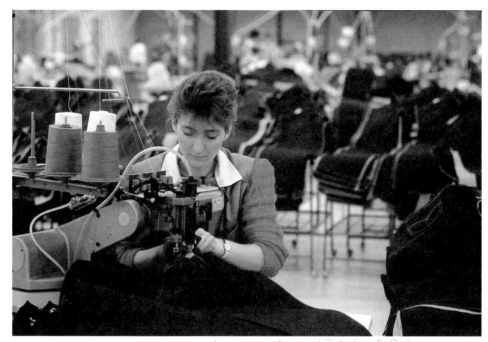

At this Levi's' jeans manufacturing plant, we see examples of many product costs. The woman sewing jeans is direct labor. Her sewing machine is part of overhead. The denim is direct materials and the thread may be direct or indirect materials. Notice also the pattern pieces stacked on carts—we can easily imagine the activity "materials handling" from these.

production costs
nonproduction costs

nonproduction. Production costs are those costs associated with the manufacture of goods or the provision of services. Nonproduction costs are those costs associated with the functions of designing, developing, marketing, distribution, customer service, and general administration. The costs of marketing, distribution, and customer service are often placed into one general category called *selling costs*. The costs of designing, developing, and general administration are placed into a second general category called *administrative costs*. For tangible goods, production and nonproduction costs are often referred to as *manufacturing costs* and *nonmanufacturing costs*, respectively. Production costs can be further classified as *direct materials*, *direct labor*, and *overhead*. Only these three cost elements can be assigned to products for external financial reporting.

direct materials

Direct Materials Direct materials are those materials that are traceable to the goods or services being produced. The cost of these materials can be directly charged to products because physical observation can be used to measure the quantity consumed by each product. Materials that become part of a tangible product or those that are used in providing a service are usually classified as direct materials. For example, steel in an automobile, wood in furniture, alcohol in cologne, denim in jeans, braces for correcting teeth, surgical gauze and anesthesia for an operation, a casket for a funeral service, and food on an airline are all direct materials.

direct labor

Direct Labor Direct labor is the labor that is traceable to the goods or services being produced. As with direct materials, physical observation can be used to measure the quantity of labor used to produce a product or service. Those employees who convert raw materials into a product or who provide a service to customers are classified as direct labor. Workers on an assembly line at Chrysler, a chef in a restaurant, a surgical nurse attending an open heart operation, and a pilot for Delta Airlines are examples of direct laborers.

overhead

Overhead All production costs other than direct materials and direct labor are lumped into one category called overhead. In a manufacturing firm, overhead is also known as *factory burden* or *manufacturing overhead*. The overhead cost category contains a wide variety of items. Many inputs other than direct labor and direct materials are needed to

supplies

produce products. Examples include depreciation on buildings and equipment, maintenance, supplies, supervision, material handling, power, property taxes, landscaping of factory grounds, and plant security. Supplies are generally those materials necessary for production that do not become part of the finished product or which are not used in providing a service. Dishwasher detergent in a fast-food restaurant and oil for production equipment are examples of supplies.

[handwritten margin note: MS, Direct but Indirect ex.]

Direct materials that form an insignificant part of the final product are usually lumped into the overhead category as a special kind of indirect material. This is justified on the basis of cost and convenience. The cost of the tracing is greater than the benefit of increased accuracy. The glue used in furniture or toys is an example.

The cost of overtime for direct laborers is usually assigned to overhead as well. The rationale is that typically no particular production run can be identified as the cause of the overtime. Accordingly, overtime cost is common to all production runs and is therefore an indirect manufacturing cost. Note that only the overtime cost is treated this way. If workers are paid an $8 regular rate and a $4 overtime premium, then only the $4 overtime premium is assigned to overhead. The $8 regular rate is still regarded as a direct labor cost. In certain cases, however, overtime is associated with a particular production run; for example, a special order is taken when production is at 100 percent capacity. In these special cases, it is appropriate to treat overtime premiums as a direct labor cost.

noninventoriable (period) costs

Selling and Administrative Costs There are two broad categories of nonproduction costs: selling costs and administrative costs. For external financial reporting, selling and administrative costs are *noninventoriable* or *period costs*. Noninventoriable (period) costs are expensed in the period in which they are incurred. Thus, none of these costs can be assigned to products or appear as part of the reported values of inventories on the balance sheet. In a manufacturing organization, the level of these costs can be significant (often greater than 25 percent of sales revenue), and controlling them may bring greater cost savings than the same effort exercised in controlling production costs. For service organizations, the relative importance of selling and administrative costs depends on the nature of the service produced. Physicians and dentists, for example, do very little marketing and thus have very low selling costs. A grocery chain, on the other hand, may incur substantial marketing costs, especially if the companies experiment with alternative shopping and delivery technologies. For example, Netherlands-based Albert Heijn implemented a home-shopping program in which consumers order products via fax, telephone, or interactive-CD technology. For a small charge, the orders are delivered to the customers' homes.[3]

marketing (selling) costs

Those costs necessary to market, distribute, and service a product or service are marketing (selling) costs. They are often referred to as *order-getting* and *order-filling costs*. Examples of selling costs include: salaries and commissions of sales personnel, advertising, warehousing, shipping, and customer service. The first two items are examples of order-getting costs; the last three are order-filling costs.

administrative costs

All costs associated with research, development, and general administration of the organization that cannot be reasonably assigned to either marketing or production are administrative costs. General administration has the responsibility of ensuring that the various activities of the organization are properly integrated so that the overall mission of the firm is realized. The president of the firm, for example, is concerned with the efficiency of selling, production, and research and development as they carry out their respective roles. Proper integration of these functions is essential to maximize the overall profits of a firm. Examples, then, of general administrative costs are top executive salaries, legal fees, printing the annual report, and general accounting. Research and development costs are the costs associated with designing and developing new products.

[handwritten margin note: R+D]

3. James Fallon, "Worldwide Connections," *Supermarket News* (25 September 1995): 15–16.

Prime and Conversion Costs The production and nonproduction classifications give rise to some related cost concepts. The functional delineation between nonmanufacturing and manufacturing costs is essentially the basis for the concepts of noninventoriable costs and inventoriable costs—at least for purposes of external reporting. Combinations of different production costs also produce the concepts of conversion costs and prime costs.

prime cost

conversion cost

Prime cost is the sum of direct materials cost and direct labor cost. Conversion cost is the sum of direct labor cost and overhead cost. For a manufacturing firm, conversion cost can be interpreted as the cost of converting raw materials into a final product.

EXTERNAL FINANCIAL STATEMENTS

Objective 3

Prepare income statements for manufacturing and service organizations.

To meet external reporting requirements, costs must be classified according to function. In preparing an income statement, production costs and selling and administrative costs are segregated. They are segregated because production costs are viewed as product costs, and selling and administrative costs are viewed as period costs. Thus, production costs attached to the products sold are recognized as an expense (cost of sales) on the income statement. Production costs that are attached to products that are not sold are reported as inventory on the balance sheet. Selling and administrative expenses are viewed as costs of the period and must be deducted each and every period as expenses; they would not appear on the balance sheet.

Income Statement: Manufacturing Firm

The income statement based on a functional classification for a manufacturing firm is displayed in Exhibit 2-7. This income statement follows the traditional format taught in an introductory financial accounting course. Income computed by following a functional classification is frequently referred to as absorption-costing (full-costing) income because all manufacturing costs are fully assigned to the product.

absorption-costing (full-costing) income

Under the absorption-costing approach, expenses are segregated according to function and then deducted from revenues to arrive at income before taxes. As can be seen in Exhibit 2-7, there are two major functional categories of expense: cost of goods sold and operating expenses. These categories correspond, respectively, to a firm's manufacturing and nonmanufacturing expenses. Cost of goods sold is the cost of direct materials, direct labor, and overhead attached to the units sold. To compute the cost of goods sold, it is first necessary to determine the cost of goods manufactured.

cost of goods sold

cost of goods manufactured

Cost of Goods Manufactured The cost of goods manufactured represents the total cost of goods completed during the current period. The only costs assigned to goods com-

2-7

Exhibit

Income Statement: Manufacturing Organization For the Year Ended December 31, 1998		
Sales		$2,800,000
Less cost of goods sold:		
Beginning finished goods inventory	$ 500,000	
Add: Cost of goods manufactured	1,200,000	
Goods available for sale	$1,700,000	
Less: Ending finished goods inventory	(300,000)	1,400,000
Gross margin		$1,400,000
Less operating expenses:		
Selling expenses	$600,000	
Administrative expenses	300,000	(900,000)
Income before taxes		$ 500,000

pleted are the manufacturing costs of direct materials, direct labor, and overhead. The details of this cost assignment are given in a supporting schedule, called the *statement of cost of goods manufactured.* An example of this supporting schedule for the income statement in Exhibit 2-7 is shown in Exhibit 2-8.

Notice in Exhibit 2-8 that the total manufacturing costs added during the period are added to the manufacturing costs found in beginning work in process, yielding total manufacturing costs to account for. The costs found in ending work in process are then deducted from total manufacturing costs to arrive at the cost of goods manufactured. If the cost of goods manufactured is for a single product, then the average unit cost can be computed by dividing the cost of goods manufactured by the units produced. For example, assume that the statement in Exhibit 2-8 was prepared for the production of bottles of perfume and that 480,000 bottles were completed during the period. The average unit cost is $2.50 per bottle ($1,200,000/480,000).

work in process   Work in process consists of all partially completed units found in production at a given point in time. Beginning work in process consists of the partially completed units on hand at the beginning of a period. Ending work in process consists of those on hand at the period's end. In the statement of cost of goods manufactured, the cost of these partially completed units is reported as the cost of beginning work in process and the cost of ending work in process. The cost of beginning work in process represents the manufacturing costs carried over from the prior period; the cost of ending work in process represents the manufacturing costs that will be carried over to the next period. In both cases, additional manufacturing costs must be incurred to complete the units in work in process.

Income Statement: Service Organization

An income statement for a service firm is shown in Exhibit 2-9. In a service organization, the cost of services sold is computed differently from the cost of goods sold in a manufacturing firm. As the income statement reveals, there are no beginning or ending finished goods inventories. Unlike a manufacturing firm, the service firm has no finished

2-8 ·······························

Exhibit

Statement of Cost of Goods Manufactured For the Year Ended December 31, 1998		
Direct materials:		
Beginning inventory	$200,000	
Add: Purchases	450,000	
Materials available	$650,000	
Less: Ending inventory	(50,000)	
Direct materials used		$ 600,000
Direct labor		350,000
Manufacturing overhead:		
Indirect labor	$122,500	
Depreciation	177,500	
Rent	50,000	
Utilities	37,500	
Property taxes	12,500	
Maintenance	50,000	450,000
Total manufacturing costs added		$1,400,000
Add: Beginning work in process		200,000
Total manufacturing costs		$1,600,000
Less: Ending work in process		(400,000)
Cost of goods manufactured		$1,200,000

How determ.?

Income Statement: Service Organization For the Year Ended December 31, 1998		
Sales		$300,000
Less expenses:		
Cost of services sold:		
Beginning work in process	$ 5,000	
Service costs added:		
Direct materials	$ 40,000	
Direct labor	80,000	
Overhead	100,000	220,000
Total		$225,000
Less: Ending work in process		(10,000) 215,000
Gross margin		$ 85,000
Less operating expenses:		
Selling expenses	$ 8,000	
Administrative expenses	22,000	(30,000)
Income before taxes		$ 55,000

goods inventories—it is not possible to store services. Thus, in a direct comparison with manufacturing firms, cost of services sold would always correspond to cost of goods manufactured. Furthermore, as Exhibit 2-9 reveals, the cost of services sold during a period (equivalent to cost of goods manufactured) can be computed following the same format shown in Exhibit 2-8. Exhibit 2-9 reveals that it is possible to have work in process for services. For example, an architect may have drawings in process and an orthodontist may have numerous patients in various stages of process for braces.

ACTIVITY DRIVERS AND COST BEHAVIOR

Objective 4

Describe the relationship between activity drivers and cost behavior.

Although preparing cost information for external financial reporting is important, providing cost information for other product-costing objectives and for operational control is also vital. Understanding cost behavior is fundamental to satisfying these additional objectives. In particular, understanding the behavior of activity costs is critical. Knowing how activity costs behave facilitates product-costing assignments and provides important input for such activities as budgeting and make or buy decisions. To understand cost behavior, some additional activity terminology is needed.

Cost Behavior Concepts

activity inputs

activity output

activity output measure

cost behavior

Every activity has inputs and outputs. Activity inputs are the resources consumed by an activity in producing its output. Activity inputs are the factors that enable the activity to be performed and can be classified into four categories: materials, energy, labor, and capital. Activities transform the inputs to produce an output. Activity output is the result or product of an activity. For example, if the activity is moving materials, the inputs would be such things as crates (materials), fuel (energy), a forklift operator (labor), and a forklift (capital). The output would be material movement. An activity output measure provides an assessment of the number of times the activity is performed. It is the quantifiable measure of the output. For example, number of moves is a possible output measure of moving materials. The output measure effectively is a measure of the demands placed on an activity and therefore corresponds to an activity driver. Cost behavior describes how the costs of activity inputs change with respect to changes in activity output. Exhibit 2-10 illustrates the relationship between inputs, activities, activity output, and cost behavior. Thus, to assess cost behavior, the activity must be defined, its

Exhibit
Activity Cost Behavior
Model

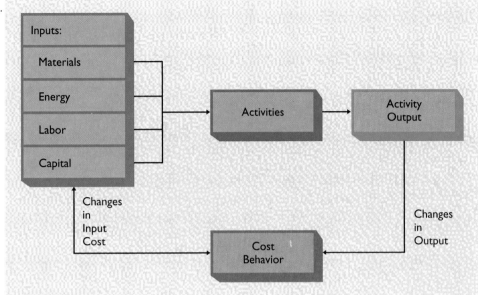

inputs and outputs must be identified and measured, and the effect on the cost of inputs as activity output changes must be calculated. Perhaps the most difficult task in assessing cost behavior is identifying good activity output measures.

We can simplify identification of activity output measures by classifying activities into one of four general categories: (1) unit level (2) batch level (3) product level, and (4) facility level.[4] Classifying activities into these general categories is useful because the costs of activities associated with the different levels respond to different types of activity drivers. The definition of the activities belonging to each general category clearly illustrates this feature. Unit-level activities are those performed each time a unit is produced. Grinding, polishing, and assembly are examples of unit-level activities. Output measures for unit-level activities, referred to as unit-level drivers, include such possibilities as units of product, direct labor hours, and machine hours. Batch-level activities are those performed each time a batch of goods is produced. The costs of batch-level activities vary with the number of batches but are fixed with respect to the number of units in each batch. Setups, inspections, production scheduling, and material handling are examples of batch-level activities. Output measures for batch-level activities are called batch-level drivers. Possible batch-level drivers are number of batches, inspection hours, number of production orders, and number of moves. Product-level (sustaining) activities are those performed as needed to support the various products produced by a company. These activities consume inputs that develop products or allow products to be produced and sold. These activities and their costs tend to increase as the number of different products increases. Engineering changes, developing product-testing procedures, marketing products, engineering processes, and expediting goods are examples of product-level activities. Activity output measures for product-level activities are product-level drivers and include number of change orders, number of products, number of processes, and number of expediting orders. Facility-level activities are those that sustain a factory's general manufacturing processes. Providing facilities, maintaining grounds, and providing plant security are examples. Useful output measures, or facility-level drivers, are difficult to define for this category of activities but might include such things as plant size (square feet), acres of ground maintained, and number of security personnel.

unit-level activities

unit-level drivers

batch-level activities

batch-level drivers

product-level (sustaining) activities

product-level drivers

facility-level activities

facility-level drivers

4. This classification and the associated definitions are taken from Robin Cooper, "Cost Classification in Unit-Based and Activity-Based Manufacturing Cost Systems." *Journal of Cost Management* (Fall 1990): 4–14.

Knowing the behavior of activity costs can be very useful information that can help in budgeting, supporting continuous improvement efforts, tactical decision making, and product costing. Generally, cost behavior can be described as fixed, variable, or mixed.

Fixed Costs

fixed (activity) costs

Fixed (activity) costs are costs that, *in total*, are constant within a relevant range as the level of activity output changes. To illustrate fixed-cost behavior, consider Reddy Heaters, a company that produces insert heaters for coffee pots. Although there are many activities performed within the plant, we will look at only one: the pipe cutting activity. This activity uses cutting machines to cut lengths of metal pipe into 3-inch segments, which are then used as a component for the insert heaters (one 3-inch pipe per heater). Thus, activity output can be measured by the number of 3-inch segments produced. Since this activity is performed each and every time an insert heater is produced, the number of insert heaters produced could also be used as the activity output measure (activity driver). For simplicity, assume that the cutting activity uses two inputs (resources): the cutting machine and power to operate the cutting machines. Focus for the moment on the cutting machine resource. Cutting machines are leased for $60,000 per year and have the capacity of producing up to 240,000 three-inch segments. The cost of leasing the cutting machines is a fixed cost as it remains unchanged in total as activity output changes. This behavior is illustrated by the following example:

Reddy Heaters

Lease of Machines	Number of 3-Inch Segments	Unit Cost
$60,000	0	N/A
60,000	60,000	$1.00
60,000	120,000	0.50
60,000	180,000	0.33
60,000	240,000	0.25

relevant range

Two components of the fixed-cost definition need further discussion: relevant range and the phrase "in total." Relevant range is the range over which the assumed fixed-cost relationship is valid. For the cutting activity, the cutting machines currently leased have the capability of producing up to 240,000 units of 3-inch pipe per year. Notice that the total cost of leasing remains constant within the 0 to 240,000-unit range. Reddy Heaters pays $60,000 per year for leasing the equipment regardless of whether it produces 0, 60,000, 120,000, or 240,000 units. While the total cost of leasing remains unchanged, as more segments are produced the cost per segment (the unit cost) does change. As the table shows, within the range of 60,000 to 240,000 units, the unit cost of leasing the pipe-cutting machines decreases from $1 to $0.25. Thus, while fixed costs remain unchanged *in total* as output increases, the *unit cost* will change because the fixed costs are being spread out over more output.

We can gain additional insight into the nature of fixed costs by portraying them graphically (Exhibit 2-11). As can be seen, for the relevant range, fixed-cost behavior is described by a horizontal line. Notice that at 120,000 units produced, leasing cost is $60,000; at 240,000 units produced, leasing cost is also $60,000. This line visually demonstrates that cost remains unchanged as the level of the driver varies. Total fixed costs can be represented by the following simple linear equation:

$$F = \text{Total fixed costs}$$

For our example, $F = \$60,000$.

Variable Costs

variable costs

Variable costs are defined as costs that, in total, vary in direct proportion to changes in activity output. To illustrate, let's expand the Reddy Heaters example to include the

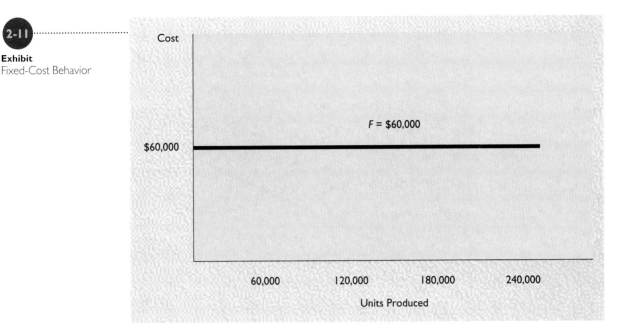

other resource used by the cutting activity: power. Power is also a cost of performing the cutting activity. The cost of this resource, however, behaves differently from that of the cutting machine resource. Power is consumed only if output is produced and as more output is produced, more power is consumed. Power is an input that is used only as needed by the cutting activity. Assume that cutting each segment uses 0.1 kilowatt-hour at $2.00 per kilowatt-hour. Thus, the cost of power per 3-inch segment is $0.20. The cost of power for various levels of activity output follows:

Reddy Heaters

Cost of Power	Number of 3-Inch Segments	Unit Cost
$ 0	0	$0.20
12,000	60,000	0.20
24,000	120,000	0.20
36,000	180,000	0.20
48,000	240,000	0.20

As more 3-inch segments are produced, the total cost of power increases in direct proportion. For example, as activity output doubles from 60,000 to 120,000 units, the total cost of power doubles from $12,000 to $24,000. Notice also that the unit cost of power is constant.

Variable costs can also be represented by a linear equation. Here total variable costs depend on the level of the driver. This relationship can be described by the following:

$$Y_v = VX$$

where Y_v = Total variable costs
        V = Variable cost per unit
        X = Number of units of driver (output measure)

In our example for Reddy Heaters, the relationship that describes the cost of power is $Y_v = \$0.20X$, where X = the number of 3-inch segments produced. Exhibit 2-12 graphically illustrates a variable cost. Variable-cost behavior is represented as a straight line coming out of the origin. Notice that at zero units processed, total variable cost is zero. However, as units produced increase, the total variable cost also increases. For example, at X = 120,000 units, the total variable cost is $24,000. Here it can be seen

2-12

Exhibit
Variable-Cost Behavior

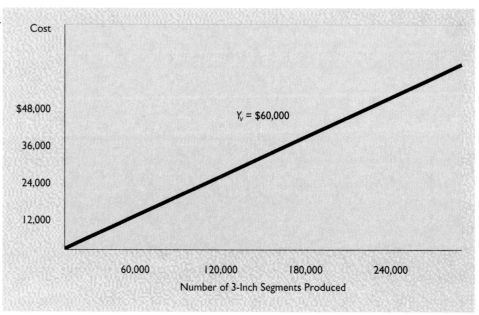

that total cost increases in direct proportion to increases in the number of segments produced (the activity output measure is a unit-level driver); the rate of increase is measured by the slope of the line.

Mixed Costs

mixed costs

Mixed costs are costs that have both a fixed and a variable component. For example, sales representatives are often paid a salary plus a commission on the sales. Suppose that Reddy Heaters has three sales representatives, each earning a salary of $10,000 per year plus a commission of $0.50 per heater insert sold. The activity is selling inserts and the activity driver is units sold. If 100,000 heater inserts are sold, then the total selling cost (associated with the sales representatives) is $80,000—the sum of the fixed salary cost of $30,000 ($3 \times \$10,000$) and the variable cost of $50,000 ($0.50 \times 100,000$).

The linear equation for a mixed cost is given by

$$Y = \text{Fixed cost} + \text{Total variable cost}$$
$$Y = F + VX$$

where Y = Total cost. For Reddy Heaters, the selling cost is represented by the following equation:

$$Y = \$30,000 + \$0.50X$$

The following table shows the selling cost for different levels of sales activity:

Reddy Heaters				
Fixed Cost of Selling	Variable Cost of Selling	Total Cost	Inserts Sold	Selling Cost per Unit
$30,000	$ 20,000	$ 50,000	40,000	$1.25
30,000	40,000	70,000	80,000	0.88
30,000	60,000	90,000	120,000	0.75
30,000	80,000	110,000	160,000	0.69
30,000	100,000	130,000	200,000	0.65

The graph for our mixed-cost example given in Exhibit 2-13 assumes that the relevant range is 0 to 200,000 units. Mixed costs are represented by a line that intercepts

Exhibit
Mixed-Cost Behavior

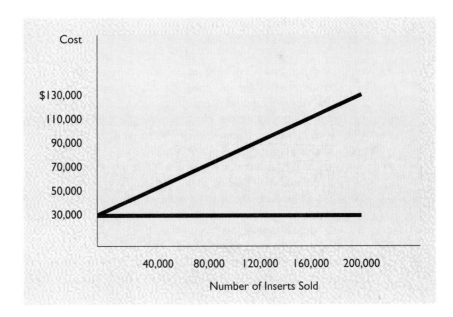

the vertical axis (at $30,000 for this example). The intercept corresponds to the fixed-cost component, and the slope of the line gives the variable cost per unit of cost driver (slope is $0.50 for the example portrayed).

TRADITIONAL AND CONTEMPORARY MANAGEMENT ACCOUNTING SYSTEMS

Objective 5

Explain the differences between traditional and contemporary management accounting systems.

Cost management systems can be broadly classified as *traditional* and *contemporary.* Both traditional and contemporary approaches are found in practice. Traditional cost management systems currently are more widely used than contemporary systems. The use of contemporary cost management systems, however, is increasing—particularly among organizations faced with increased product diversity, more product complexity, shorter product life cycles, increased quality requirements, and intense competitive pressures. These organizations often adopt a just-in-time manufacturing approach and implement contemporary manufacturing technology. For firms operating in this contemporary manufacturing environment, a traditional cost management system may not work well. More relevant and timely cost information is needed for these organizations to build a sustainable long-term competitive advantage. Organizations must improve the value received by their customers while increasing their profits at the same time. Better assessment of cost behavior, increased accuracy in product costing, and striving for continuous cost improvement are all critical for the contemporary manufacturing environment.

Traditional Management Accounting Systems: A Brief Overview

Traditional management accounting systems focus only on production\volume–based activity output measures. The traditional approach *assumes* that all costs can be classified as fixed or variable with respect to changes in the units or *volume* of product produced. Thus, units of product or other drivers that are highly correlated with units produced such as direct labor hours and machine-hours are the only activity drivers assumed to be of importance. These unit-level or volume-based drivers are used to assign production costs to products. Since unit-based cost drivers usually are not the only drivers that explain cause-and-effect relationships, much of the product cost assignment activity must be classified as allocation (recall that allocation is cost assignment based on *assumed* linkages or convenience). We can say, therefore, that traditional cost assignment tends to be allocation-intensive.

The product-costing objective of a traditional cost accounting system is typically satisfied by assigning production costs to inventories and cost of goods sold for purposes of external financial reporting. More comprehensive product cost definitions, such as the value-chain and operating cost definitions illustrated in Exhibit 2-6, are not available for management use. However, traditional cost accounting systems often furnish useful variants of the traditional product cost definition. For example, prime costs and variable manufacturing costs per unit may be reported (variable manufacturing costs are usually defined as direct materials, direct labor, and variable overhead, where variable behavior is defined with respect to a unit-based cost driver).

Providing information for planning and control is another objective of management accounting. The traditional management accounting approach to control assigns costs to organizational units and then holds the organizational unit manager responsible for controlling the assigned costs. Performance is measured by comparing actual outcomes with standard or budgeted outcomes. The emphasis is on financial measures of performance (nonfinancial measures are usually ignored). Managers are rewarded based on their ability to control costs. Thus, the traditional approach traces costs to individuals who are responsible for incurring costs. The reward system is used to motivate these individuals to manage costs. The approach assumes that maximizing the performance of the overall organization is achieved by maximizing the performance of individual organizational subunits (referred to as responsibility centers).

Contemporary Management Accounting Systems: A Brief Overview

Contemporary management accounting has evolved in response to significant changes in the competitive business environment faced by both service and manufacturing firms. The overall objective of a contemporary cost management system is to improve the quality, content, relevance, and timing of cost information.[5] Generally, more managerial objectives can be met with a contemporary system than with a traditional system.

Contemporary management accounting emphasizes tracing over allocation; in fact, it could be called tracing-intensive. The role of driver tracing is significantly expanded by identifying drivers unrelated to the volume of product produced (called *nonunit-based activity drivers*, they include the use of batch-level and product-level drivers). The use of both unit and nonunit-based activity drivers increases the accuracy of cost assignments and the overall quality and relevance of cost information. For example, consider the activity "moving raw materials and partially finished goods from one point to another within a factory." The number of moves required for a product is a much better measure of the product's demand for the material-handling activity than the number of units produced. In fact, the number of units produced may have nothing to do with measuring products' demands for material handling. (A batch of 10 units could require as much material-handling activity as a batch of 100 units.)

Product costing in contemporary management accounting tends to be flexible. Cost information is produced to support a variety of managerial objectives, including the financial reporting objective. More comprehensive product-costing definitions are emphasized for better planning, control, and decision making. For example, a more flexible accounting system, with its wealth of information on costs, activities, and drivers, could act as an early warning system of ethical problems. Metropolitan Life Insurance Company was dismayed to learn that some of its agents were selling policies as retirement plans. This practice is illegal, and cost the company more than $20 million in fines as well as $50 million in refunds to policyholders.[6] Comprehensive data on sales, individual agents, types of policies, and policyholders could have alerted Metropolitan Life to

---

5. Steven C. Schnoebelen, "Integrating an Advanced Cost Management System into Operating Systems (Part 1)." *Journal of Cost Management* (Winter 1993): 50–54.
6. Chris Roush, "Fields of Green—and Disaster Areas," *Business Week*, 9 January 1995, 94.

a potential problem. Thus, the maxim of "different costs for different purposes" takes on real meaning.

Contemporary control subsystems also differ significantly from traditional systems. The traditional emphasis is on managing costs. The emerging consensus, however, is that management of activities, not costs, is the key to successful control in the contemporary manufacturing environment. Thus, activity-based management is the heart and soul of contemporary control. Activity-based management focuses on the management of activities with the objective of improving the value received by the customer and the profit received by providing this value. It includes driver analysis, activity analysis, and performance evaluation and draws on activity-based costing as a major source of information (see Exhibit 2-14).[7] Notice from Exhibit 2-14 that the vertical dimension emphasizes tracing costs to cost objects—by tracing the cost of resources to activities and then to the cost objects. This is the activity-based costing dimension (referred to as the *cost view*); it serves as important input to the control dimension, which is called the *process view*. The process view is concerned with identifying factors that cause an activity's cost (explains *why* costs are incurred), assessing *what* work is done (identifies activities), and evaluating the work performed and the results achieved (*how well* the activity is performed). Thus, contemporary control requires detailed information on activities.

This new approach focuses on accountability for activities rather than costs and emphasizes the maximization of systemwide performance instead of individual performance. Activities cut across functional and departmental lines, are systemwide in focus, and require a global approach to control. Essentially, this form of control admits that maximizing the efficiency of individual subunits does not necessarily lead to maximum efficiency for the system as a whole. Another significant difference also should be mentioned. In a contemporary management accounting information system, both financial and nonfinancial measures of performance are important. Exhibit 2-15 compares the characteristics of the traditional and contemporary cost management systems.

Choice of a Management Accounting System

Contemporary management accounting offers significant benefits, including: improved product-costing accuracy, improved decision making, enhanced strategic planning, and

activity-based management

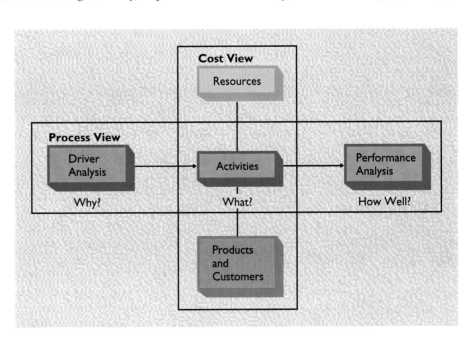

2-14

Exhibit
Activity-Based
Management Model

---

7. This definition of activity-based management and the illustrative model in Exhibit 2-14 are based on Norm Raffish and Peter B. B. Turney, "Glossary of Activity-Based Management," *Journal of Cost Management* (Fall 1991): 53–63. Many other terms throughout the text relating to activity-based management are also drawn from this source.

2-15

Exhibit
Comparison of
Traditional and
Contemporary Cost
Management Systems

Traditional	Contemporary
1. Unit-based drivers	1. Unit and nonunit-based drivers
2. Allocation-intensive	2. Tracing-intensive
3. Narrow and rigid product costing	3. Broad, flexible product costing
4. Focus on managing costs	4. Focus on managing activities
5. Sparse activity information	5. Detailed activity information
6. Maximization of individual unit performance	6. Systemwide performance maximization
7. Use of financial measures of performance	7. Use of both financial and nonfinancial measures of performance

better ability to manage activities. Furthermore, the contemporary system is particularly suited for supporting the goal of continuous improvement—an objective that is critical for firms competing on a global basis. These benefits, however, are not obtained without costs. A contemporary management accounting system is more complex, and it requires a significant increase in measurement activity—and measurement can be costly. However, with the advances in information technology, the costs of measurement have declined, making contemporary systems more attractive. Simultaneously, the cost of making bad decisions has increased (because of more intense competition resulting from the emergence of a worldwide economy, deregulation of services, and so on). The need to improve the quality of decision making has also increased the appeal of contemporary approaches.

For many firms the benefits of moving to a new management accounting system outweigh the costs. Thus, the use of activity-based costing and activity-based management is spreading and the interest in contemporary management accounting is high. Firms like Hughes Aircraft, Caterpillar, Xerox, National Semiconductor, Tektronix, Dayton Extruded Plastics, Armistead Insurance, and Zytec have adopted activity-based costing and management systems.[8] Furthermore, this is only a very small listing of firms that are using more contemporary systems.

S UMMARY OF LEARNING OBJECTIVES

1. Explain the cost assignment process.

Costs are assigned to cost objects such as products, projects, plants, and customers. There are three methods of cost assignment: direct tracing, driver tracing, and allocation. Direct and driver tracing offer more accuracy because they are based on cause-and-effect relationships. Direct tracing relies on physical observation to assign costs. Driver tracing relies on the use of causal factors called drivers to assign costs. Generally, driver tracing means that costs are first traced to activities using direct tracing and resource drivers and then assigned to products using activity drivers. Allocation relies on assumed relationships and convenience to assign costs. Allocation is essentially an arbitrary assignment and should be avoided as much as possible.

2. Define tangible and intangible products and explain why there are different product cost definitions.

There are two types of output: tangible products and services.

Tangible products are goods that are produced by converting raw materials through the use of labor and capital inputs such as plant, land, and machinery. Services are tasks or activities performed for a customer or an activity performed by a customer using an organization's products or facilities. Product cost is defined as cost assigned to a product that satisfies a particular managerial objective. Since managerial objectives can differ, product cost definitions can differ—each depending on the managerial objective being served.

3. Prepare income statements for manufacturing and service organizations.

If expenses are grouped according to function and then deducted from revenues, we have absorption-costing income statements. Absorption-costing income statements are required for external financial reporting. For manufacturing firms, the major functional classifications are manufacturing and nonmanufacturing; for service

8. Peter B. B. Turney, "Activity-Based Management," *Management Accounting* (January 1992): 20–25; Jack Hedicke and David Feil, "Hughes Aircraft," *Management Accounting* (February 1991): 29–33; and Lou F. Jones, "Product Costing at Caterpillar," *Management Accounting* (February 1991): 34–42.

organizations, the categories are production and nonproduction. For manufacturing firms, the cost of goods manufactured must be calculated. No such requirement exists for a services firm.

4. Describe the relationship between activity drivers and cost behavior.

Cost behavior is concerned with how the cost of activity inputs changes with changes in the amount of activity output. Activity output is measured by activity drivers. If input cost remains unchanged as output changes, then the cost is fixed; if input cost changes in direct proportion to activity output changes, then the cost is variable.

5. Explain the differences between traditional and contemporary management accounting systems.

Traditional management accounting uses unit-based drivers only, tends to be more allocation-intensive, uses narrow product cost definitions, focuses on managing costs, provides little activity information, emphasizes individual organizational unit performance, and uses financial measures of performance. Contemporary management accounting uses both unit-level and nonunit-level drivers, is tracing-intensive, allows flexible product-costing definitions, focuses on managing activities, provides detailed activity information, emphasizes systemwide performance, and uses both financial and nonfinancial measures of performance.

K EY TERMS

Absorption-costing (full-costing) income 38	Cost behavior 40	Indirect costs 29	Product-level (sustaining) activities 41
Activity 29	Cost object 28	Inseparability 33	Product-level drivers 41
Activity-based costing 31	Cost of goods manufactured 38	Intangibility 33	Relevant range 42
Activity-based management 47	Cost of goods sold 38	Marketing (selling) costs 37	Resource drivers 30
Activity drivers 30	Direct costs 29	Mixed costs 44	Service 33
Activity inputs 40	Direct labor 36	Noninventoriable (period) costs 37	Supplies 37
Activity output 40	Direct materials 36	Nonproduction costs 36	Tangible products 33
Activity output measure 40	Direct tracing 30	Overhead 36	Traceability 29
Administrative costs 37	Drivers 30	Opportunity cost 28	Tracing 30
Allocation 31	Driver tracing 30	Perishability 33	Unit-level activities 41
Batch-level activities 41	Expenses 28	Prime cost 38	Unit-level drivers 41
Batch-level drivers 41	Facility-level activities 41	Product cost 34	Work in process 39
Conversion cost 38	Facility-level drivers 41	Production costs 36	Value chain 34
Cost 28	Fixed (activity) costs 42		Variable costs 42
	Heterogeneity 33		

R EVIEW PROBLEMS

I. Manufacturing, Cost Classification, and Income Statement Pop's Burger Heaven produces and sells quarter-pound hamburgers. Each burger sells for $1.50. During December, Pop's sold 10,000 burgers (the average amount sold each month). The restaurant employs cooks, servers, and one supervisor (the owner, John Peterson). All cooks and servers are part-time employees. Pop's maintains a pool of part-time employees so that the number of employees scheduled can be adjusted to the changes in demand. Demand varies on a weekly as well as a monthly basis.

A janitor is hired to clean the building on a weekly basis. The building is leased from a local real estate company. The building has no seating capabilities. All orders are filled on a drive-through basis.

The supervisor schedules work, opens the building, counts the cash, advertises, and is responsible for hiring and firing. The following costs were incurred during December:

Hamburger meat	$1,600
Lettuce	300
Tomatoes	250
Buns	300
Other ingredients	20
Cooks' wages	2,550
Servers' wages	2,032
Supervisor's salary	2,000
Utilities	500

Depreciation:	
Cooking equipment	$ 200
Cash register	50
Advertising	100
Rent	800
Janitorial supplies	50
Janitor's wages	120

The only mixed cost is for utilities. The fixed component is $50.

REQUIRED:

1. Classify the costs for Pop's December operations in one of the following categories: direct materials, direct labor, overhead, or selling and administrative.
2. Prepare an absorption-costing income statement for the month of December.

Solution

1. Direct materials: Hamburger meat, lettuce, tomatoes, and buns
   Direct labor: Cooks' wages
   Overhead: Utilities, depreciation on the cooking equipment, rent, janitor's wages, janitorial supplies, and other ingredients
   Selling and administrative: Servers' wages, supervisor's salary, depreciation on the cash register, and advertising

Explanation of Classification

Cooks are direct laborers because they make the hamburgers. "Other ingredients" are overhead because of cost and convenience, even though technically they are direct materials. Because the primary purpose of the building is production (cooking hamburgers), all of the rent and building-related costs are classified as indirect production costs. (An argument could be made that the building also supports the selling and administrative functions and, consequently, a portion of the rent and building-related costs should be classified as selling and administrative costs.) Servers are responsible for taking and filling orders and are, therefore, classified as sales personnel. The cash register is used to support the sales function. The supervisor is responsible for overseeing the business as a whole and coordinating the sales and production functions. Thus, his salary is an administrative cost.

2.

Sales ($1.50 × 10,000)		$15,000
Cost of goods sold:		
Direct materials	$2,450	
Direct labor	2,550	
Overhead	1,690	(6,690)
Gross profit		$ 8,310
Less operating expenses:		
Selling expenses	$2,182	
Administrative expenses	2,000	(4,182)
Net income		$ 4,128

II. Services, Cost Behavior, and Income Statement Celestial Funeral Home offers a full range of services. Based on past experience, Celestial uses the following formula to describe its total overhead costs: $Y = \$100,000 + \$25X$, where Y = total overhead costs and X = number of funerals. Overhead costs are assigned by dividing the total overhead by the number of funerals. For a given funeral, the cost of direct materials ranges from $750 to $5,000 depending on the family's selection of a coffin. The average is $2,000. Direct labor averages $500 per funeral. During 1998, Celestial conducted 1,000 funerals. The average price charged for each funeral is $3,500. Celestial incurs annual selling expenses of $25,000 and administrative expenses of $75,000.

REQUIRED:

1. Does Celestial sell a tangible or intangible product? Explain.
2. Does Celestial use a traditional or contemporary management accounting system? Explain. Do you think this is a good choice? Explain.

3. What is the total overhead cost incurred by Celestial for the year?
4. What is the total fixed overhead cost for the year?
5. What is the total variable overhead cost for the year?
6. What is the overhead cost per funeral for the year?
7. Calculate the unit product cost for the year.
8. Prepare an income statement for Celestial.

Solution

1. Funerals are intangible products. They are services and cannot be stored and are connected to the producer (inseparability).
2. The use of a unit-based driver (number of funerals) to assign overhead costs (and apparently direct materials and direct labor) suggests a traditional system. A traditional system probably will work quite well for a local funeral home business. There is very little product diversity, selling and administrative expenses represent a small portion of total costs, and there are virtually no preproduction costs (research and development costs are absent). Thus, product cost is essentially defined by production costs. Furthermore, the absence of a great variety of products coupled with the fact that overhead costs represent a small percentage of product costs makes driver tracing much less important (direct materials and direct labor can be assigned using direct tracing).

3.
$$Y = \$100,000 + \$25(1,000)$$
$$Y = \$100,000 + \$25,000$$
$$Y = \$125,000$$

4. $100,000
5. $25,000
6. $125,000/1,000 = $125

7.

Unit product cost:	
Direct materials	$2,000
Direct labor	500
Overhead	125
	$2,625

8.

Celestial Funeral Home		
Income Statement		
For the Year Ended 1998		
Sales		$3,500,000
Cost of services sold:		
Direct materials	$2,000,000	
Direct labor	500,000	
Overhead	125,000	(2,625,000)
Gross margin		$ 875,000
Less operating expenses:		
Selling expenses	$ 25,000	
Administrative expenses	75,000	(100,000)
Income before taxes		$ 775,000

QUESTIONS FOR WRITING AND DISCUSSION

1. What is meant by "product-costing accuracy"?
2. What is a cost object? Give some examples.
3. What is an activity? Give some examples of activities within a manufacturing firm.
4. What is a direct cost? an indirect cost?

5. What does traceability mean? What is tracing?
6. What is allocation?
7. What are drivers? resource drivers? activity drivers? Give an example of a resource driver and an example of an activity driver.

8. Explain the difference between direct tracing and driver tracing.
9. Explain how driver tracing works.
10. What is a tangible product?
11. What is a service?
12. Explain how services differ from tangible products.
13. Give three examples of product cost definitions. Why do we need different product cost definitions?
14. Identify the three cost elements that determine the cost of making a product (for external reporting).
15. How do the income statements of a manufacturing firm and a service firm differ?
16. Explain why knowledge of cost behavior is useful information for a manager to have.

17. What are activity inputs?
18. What are activity outputs?
19. What is meant by "cost behavior"?
20. What role does the relevant range play in the definition of a fixed cost? a variable cost?
21. On a per-unit basis, fixed costs are variable and variable costs are fixed. Do you agree? Explain your reasoning.
22. Describe some of the major differences between a traditional cost management system and a contemporary cost management system.
23. When would a company choose a contemporary cost management system over a traditional system? What forces are moving firms to implement contemporary cost management systems?

W ARM-UP EXERCISES

This section provides short warm-up exercises based on the examples in the chapter. Each warm-up exercise gives the page number on which the text example can be found. You may want to refer to the text example to see how the exercise can be set up and solved.

W2-1
Activities and Drivers
LO 1
pp. 30 & 31

REQUIRED:
1. What is an activity driver?
2. Select an activity driver for each of the following activities:
   a. Setting up equipment
   b. Moving materials
   c. Grinding parts
   d. Shipping goods
   e. Repairing equipment
   f. Inspecting incoming parts
   g. Ordering parts
   h. Welding subassemblies

W2-2
Cost of Goods Sold
LO 3
p. 38

During the year, Norton Company manufactured goods costing $300,000. The beginning finished goods inventory was $25,000 and the ending finished goods inventory was $50,000.

REQUIRED: Prepare a statement of cost of goods sold.

W2-3
Cost of Goods Manufactured
LO 3
p. 39

During the year, Norton Company accumulated the following information:

Beginning inventory, raw materials	$ 20,000
Materials purchased	40,000
Ending inventory, raw materials	10,000
Direct labor cost	150,000
Overhead costs	125,000
Beginning work in process	10,000
Ending work in process	35,000

REQUIRED: Prepare a statement of cost of goods manufactured.

W2-4
Cost Behavior
LO 4
p. 42

The salary paid to a plant supervisor is $80,000 per year. The plant is capable of producing 80,000 pounds of a chemical per year.

REQUIRED: Prepare a table that shows how the cost of plant supervision behaves in total and on a per-unit basis as production increases from 0 to 80,000 pounds, using 20,000-pound increments. How would you classify this cost behavior?

W2-5
Cost Behavior
LO 4
p. 43

Kilroy Company has determined that the best driver for its material-moving activity is "miles traveled." They also discovered that the cost of fuel for forklifts doubled as the miles traveled doubled. The cost for 10,000 miles was $20,000 and for 20,000 miles was $40,000.

REQUIRED: Prepare a table that shows the total cost of fuel and unit cost for miles traveled ranging from 0 to 80,000 miles, using increments of 20,000 miles. How would you describe this cost behavior?

EXERCISES

E2-1
Cost Assignment Methods
LO 1

Hummer Company uses manufacturing cells to produce its products (a cell is a manufacturing unit dedicated to the production of subassemblies or products). One manufacturing cell produces small motors for lawn mowers. Suppose that the motor manufacturing cell is the cost object. Assume that all or a portion of the following costs must be assigned to the cell.

a. Salary of cell supervisor
b. Power to heat and cool the plant in which the cell is located
c. Materials used to produce the motors
d. Maintenance for the cell's equipment (provided by the maintenance department)
e. Labor used to produce motors
f. Cafeteria that services the plant's employees
g. Depreciation on the plant
h. Depreciation on equipment used to produce the motors
i. Ordering costs for materials used in production
j. Engineering support (provided by the engineering department)
k. Cost of maintaining the plant and grounds
l. Cost of the plant's personnel office
m. Property tax on the plant and land

REQUIRED: Identify which cost assignment method would likely be used to assign the costs of each activity to the small motor manufacturing cell: direct tracing, driver tracing, or allocation. When driver tracing is selected, identify a potential activity driver that could be used for the tracing.

E2-2
Value-Chain Activity
LO 2

The following activities are performed within a manufacturing firm. Classify each activity according to its value-chain activity category (for example, activity: grinding parts; value-chain activity category: producing).

a. Advertising products
b. Repairing goods under warranty
c. Designing a new process
d. Assembling parts
e. Shipping goods to a wholesaler
f. Inspecting incoming raw materials and parts
g. Storing finished goods in a warehouse
h. Creating a new computer chip
i. Answering product-use questions using a customer "hot line"
j. Moving partially finished goods from one department to another
k. Building a prototype of a new product
l. Creating plans for a new model of an automobile
m. Conducting a phone-sales campaign
n. Picking goods from a warehouse
o. Setting up equipment

E2-3
Product Cost Definitions
LO 2

Three possible product cost definitions were introduced: value-chain, operating, and traditional. Identify which of the three best fits the following situations (justify your choice):

a. Setting the price for a new product
b. Valuation of finished goods inventories for external reporting

c. Choosing among different products in order to maintain a product mix that will provide the company with a long-term sustainable competitive advantage
d. Choosing among competing product designs
e. Calculating cost of goods sold for external reporting
f. Deciding whether to increase the price of an existing product
g. Deciding whether to accept or reject a special order, where the price offered is lower than the normal selling price
h. Determining which of several potential new products should be developed, produced, and sold

E2-4
Cost of Goods Manufactured and Sold
LO 3

Lawton Company manufactures sleeping bags. At the beginning of September, the following information was supplied by their accountant:

Raw materials inventory	$37,000
Work-in-process inventory	18,000
Finished goods inventory	20,200

During September, direct labor cost was $40,500, raw materials' purchases were $61,500, and the total overhead cost was $105,750. The inventories at the end of September were:

Raw materials inventory	$16,800
Work-in-process inventory	29,500
Finished goods inventory	19,100

REQUIRED:
1. Prepare a statement of cost of goods manufactured for September.
2. Prepare a statement of cost of goods sold for September.

E2-5
Preparation of Income Statement: Manufacturing Firm
LO 3

SPREADSHEET

Bohanan manufactures a stuffed bear called Smokee. Last year 100,000 bears were made and sold for $30 each. The actual unit cost for the stuffed bear follows:

Direct materials	$ 4.00
Direct labor	6.00
Variable overhead	5.00
Fixed overhead	8.00
Total unit cost	$23.00

The only selling expenses were a commission of $2 per unit sold and advertising totaling $50,000. Administrative expenses, all fixed, equaled $150,000. There were no beginning or ending finished goods inventories.

REQUIRED: Prepare an income statement for external users.

E2-6
Cost Behavior
LO 4

Jackson Company manufactures air-conditioning compressors. Based on past experience, Jackson has found that its total cost of moving materials can be represented by the following formula: Cost of moving materials $= \$90,000 + \$0.20X$, where $X =$ pounds of material moved. The activity of moving materials uses forklifts, forklift operators, crates, and fuel (for the forklift). During 1998, Jackson moved 200,000 pounds of materials.

REQUIRED:
1. Identify the activity, its inputs, and its output measure (activity driver).
2. Identify which inputs are likely to vary with activity output over the relevant range. Assume the relevant range is 150,000 to 250,000 pounds of materials.

3. What is the total cost of moving materials incurred by Jackson in 1998? total fixed cost? total variable cost?
4. What is the cost of moving materials per pound moved?
5. What is the fixed cost per pound moved?
6. What is the variable cost of moving materials per pound moved?
7. Recalculate requirements 4, 5, and 6 for the following levels of activity: (a) 150,000 pounds moved and (b) 250,000 pounds moved. Explain this outcome.

E2-7
Traditional versus Contemporary Management Accounting Systems
LO 5

Iquitos Manufacturing produces two different models of cameras. One model has an automatic focus; the other requires the user to determine the focus. The two products are produced in batches. Each time a batch is produced, the equipment must be configured (setup) for the specifications of the camera model being produced. The manual focus camera requires more parts than the automatic focus model. The manual focus model is also more labor-intensive, requiring much more assembly time and less machine time. Although the manual model is more labor-intensive, the machine configuration required for this product is more complex and the manual model consumes more of the setup activity resources than the automatic camera. Many, but not all, of the parts for the two cameras are purchased from external suppliers. Because it has more parts, the manual model makes more demands on the purchasing and receiving activities than does the automatic camera. Iquitos currently assigns only manufacturing costs to the two products. Overhead costs are collected in one plantwide pool and are assigned to the two products in proportion to the direct labor hours used by each product. All other costs are viewed as period costs.

Iquitos budgets costs for all departments within the plant—both support departments like maintenance and purchasing, as well as production departments like machining and assembly. Departmental managers are evaluated and rewarded on their ability to control costs. Individual managerial performance is assessed by comparing actual costs with budgeted costs.

REQUIRED:
1. Is Iquitos using a traditional or contemporary management accounting system? Explain.
2. Assume that you want to increase accuracy of cost assignments. What changes would you need to make? Be specific. Explain why the changes you make will improve the accuracy of cost assignments.
3. What changes would need to be made to improve control? Be specific. Explain why you believe the changes will offer improvement.

E2-8
Cost of Goods Manufactured and Sold
LO 3

Hayward Company, a manufacturing firm, has supplied the following information from its accounting records for 1998:

Direct labor cost	$10,500
Purchases of raw materials	15,000
Supplies used	675
Factory insurance	350
Commissions paid	2,500
Factory supervision	2,225
Advertising	800
Material handling	3,745
Work-in-process inventory, December 31, 1997	12,500
Work-in-process inventory, December 31, 1998	14,250
Materials inventory, December 31, 1997	3,475
Materials inventory, December 31, 1998	9,500
Finished goods inventory, December 31, 1997	6,685
Finished goods inventory, December 31, 1998	4,250

REQUIRED:
1. Prepare a statement of cost of goods manufactured.
2. Prepare a statement of cost of goods sold.

E2-9
Income Statement;
Cost Concepts;
Service Company
LO 2, LO 3

Lance Peckam owns and operates three Confiable Muffler outlets in Tucson, Arizona. Confiable Muffler specializes in replacing mufflers—replacing them with mufflers that have a lifetime guarantee. Confiable is a franchise popular throughout the Southwest. In April, purchases of materials equaled $200,000, the beginning inventory of material was $26,300, and the ending inventory of material was $14,250. Payments to direct labor during the month totaled $53,000. Overhead incurred was $120,000. The Tucson outlets also spent $15,000 on advertising during the month. A franchise fee of $3,000 per outlet is paid every month. Revenues for May were $500,000.

REQUIRED:
1. What was the cost of materials used for muffler-changing services during April?
2. What was the prime cost for April?
3. What was the conversion cost for April?
4. What was the total service cost for April?
5. Prepare an income statement for the month of April.
6. Confiable purchases all its mufflers from Remington Company, a manufacturer of mufflers. Discuss the differences between the products offered by Remington and Confiable.

E2-10
Product Cost
Definitions
LO 2

Halverson Company produces chemicals used in the mining industry. Each plant is dedicated to producing a single industrial chemical. One of its plants produces an electrolyte used in the copper industry's solvent extraction process. During the most recent year, the electrolyte plant produced 1,000,000 pounds of electrolyte. For the same year, the following costs were assigned to the electrolyte plant:

Research and development	$ 250,000
Production	800,000
Marketing	150,000
Distribution	50,000
Servicing	100,000
Total costs assigned	$1,350,000

All costs, except for research and development, are assigned using only direct tracing.

REQUIRED:
1. Compute the unit product cost that must be used for external financial reporting purposes (cost per pound of electrolyte). How would the other costs be treated for external financial reporting?
2. Compute the unit value-chain product cost. Why would management want to know this product cost?
3. Compute the unit operating product cost. What purpose might this cost serve?
4. The research and development costs represent only a share of the company's total research and development costs. Discuss the importance of accurately assigning these costs to individual plants within the company.

E2-11
Activity
Classification
LO 4

Classify the following activities as unit level, batch level, product level, or facility level. Also, identify a potential activity driver (output measure) for each activity.

a. Setting up equipment
b. Processing checks in a bank
c. Unloading shipments of raw materials
d. Desalinizing water (water treatment facility)
e. Shipping goods
f. Ordering supplies
g. Reworking products
h. Administering parts

i. Moving materials
j. Testing for blood type prior to an operation
k. Providing plantwide security
l. Processing insurance claims
m. Providing space for production
n. Special product testing
o. Providing heating and air conditioning for the plant
p. Expediting batches of goods
q. Product support engineering

E2-12
Accuracy of Cost Assignments and Cost Behavior
LO 1, LO 4

Redland Paper Products is a small company that specialized in the production of paper towels until several years ago. The company had generally prospered, but five years ago, the market for towels became very competitive and profits dropped sharply. The output of the one plant owned by the company was exclusively devoted to towels. Two years ago, a decision to add a product line was made. Management determined that existing idle capacity could easily be adapted to produce paper napkins. Moreover, the variable cost of producing a package of napkins was virtually identical to that of a package of towels. Since the fixed expenses would not change, the new product was forecast to increase profits significantly.

Two years after the addition of the new product line, profits had not improved—in fact, they had actually dropped. Upon investigation, the president of the company discovered that profits had not increased as expected because the so-called fixed-cost pool had increased dramatically. The president interviewed the manager of each support department. Typical responses from three of those managers follow:

Purchasing: The new line increased the number of purchase orders. We had to use more resources to handle this increased volume.
Accounting: There were more transactions to process than before. We had to increase our staff.
Setups: There are two styles of napkins, each requiring a different setup. The increased number of setups required us to increase our expenditures.

REQUIRED:
1. Explain why the results of adding the new product line were not accurately projected.
2. Could this problem have been avoided with a contemporary management accounting system? If so, would you recommend that the company adopt a contemporary system? Explain and discuss the differences between a contemporary approach and a traditional approach.

PROBLEMS

P2-1
Cost Behavior, Accuracy of Assignment, Unit-Level and Nonunit-Level Drivers
LO 1, LO 4

Anderson Company currently produces an electronic circuit board for stereo units. A manufacturing cost formula based on direct labor hours for this product follows:

$$\text{Total manufacturing costs} = \$300,000 + \$15X$$

where X is direct labor hours. The plant is producing 10,000 units per year but has the capacity to produce 15,000. Market conditions will likely not permit any expansion of production for the stereo circuit board. The company, however, is planning to add a new product, a circuit board for small television sets. Existing equipment can be adapted to produce the product. Engineers estimate that the same direct labor hours will be used per unit. In fact, the same variable cost per direct labor hour will be incurred. The controller has argued that the fixed costs will remain at $300,000—after all, these costs should not change as production activity increases. Thus, the manufacturing cost formula will not change for the two-product setting.

Of the fixed costs, $100,000 represents depreciation, $100,000 is the cost of operating the purchasing department, and $100,000 is the cost of operating the engineering department. Currently, there is no unused capacity for either the purchasing department or the engineering department. Before making a final decision on the new product, a consultant was hired to assess the impact of the new product on the costs of the firm. The consultant developed the following cost formulas, using three different drivers:

Cost Formula	Activity Driver
Purchasing department cost:	
$40,000 + 30X_1$	X_1 = Number of purchase orders
Engineering department cost:	
$50,000 + \$100X_2$	X_2 = Number of engineering orders
Remaining overhead cost:	
$100,000 + \$15X_3$	X_3 = Direct labor hours

The consultant also provided the following estimates of activity for each product:

	Stereo Board	Television Board
Units of product	10,000	5,000
Direct labor hours	20,000	10,000
Purchase orders	2,000	2,000
Engineering orders	500	1,000

REQUIRED:
1. Calculate the total cost of producing the stereo circuit boards without the new product. Do you think this cost is accurate? Explain.
2. Using only the direct-labor-hour cost formula, calculate the total cost of producing both products.
3. Using the cost formulas developed by the consultant, calculate the total cost of producing both products. Explain why the two numbers differ. Which approach do you think provides the more accurate prediction? Why?
4. Using only the variable cost portion of the unit-based formula, calculate the variable cost per unit for each product. Now calculate the cost per unit for each product using only the variable elements from each of the consultant's formulas. Which method do you think provides the more accurate product costing? Explain.

P2-2
Cost Behavior
LO 4

Classify the following activity input costs as variable, fixed, or mixed. Identify the activity and the associated activity driver (output measure) that allows you to define the cost behavior. For example, assume that the resource input is "amalgam." The activity is "filling cavities," the behavior is variable, and the driver is "number of teeth repaired." Prepare your answer in the following format:

Activity	Cost Behavior	Activity Driver
Filling cavities	Variable	Number of teeth repaired

a. Wages of machinists
b. Tires placed on a car during assembly
c. Advertising
d. Sales commissions
e. Fuel for a forklift used to move materials
f. Depreciation on a warehouse
g. Depreciation on a forklift used to move partially completed goods
h. X-ray film used in a radiology department of a hospital
i. Rental car provided for a client
j. Crowns used by a dentist
k. Salaries, equipment, and materials used for setting up production equipment

l. Forms used to file insurance claims

m. Equipment, labor, and parts used to maintain production equipment

n. Printing and postage for advertising circulars

o. Salaries, forms, and postage associated with paying bills

P2-3

Cost Identification

LO 2, LO 4

Following is a list of cost items described in the chapter and a list of brief descriptive settings where the items are described. Match the items with the settings. There may be more than one cost classification associated with each setting; however, select the setting that seems to fit the item best.

Cost terms:

a. Variable cost

b. Fixed cost

c. Opportunity cost

d. Period cost

e. Product cost

f. Direct labor cost

g. Selling cost

h. Conversion cost *dir Lab/over*

i. Mixed cost

j. Prime cost *dir mat/lab*

k. Direct materials cost

l. Overhead cost

m. Administrative cost

Settings:

1. Marcus Armstrong, manager of Timmins Optical, estimated that the cost of plastic, wages of the technician producing the lenses, and overhead, totaled $30 per pair of single-vision lenses.

2. Linda was having a hard time deciding whether to return to school. She was concerned about the good salary she would have to give up for the next four years.

3. Randy Harris is the finished goods warehouse manager for a medium-size manufacturing firm. He is paid a salary of $90,000 per year. As he studied the financial statement prepared by the local CPA firm, he wondered how his salary was treated.

4. Jamie Young is in charge of the legal department at company headquarters. Her salary is $95,000 per year. She reports to the chief executive officer.

5. All factory costs that are not classified as direct materials or direct labor.

6. Gary Sorenson was trying to reduce the cost of the material-handling activity. He discovered that material-handling costs increased in direct proportion to the number of moves made. Accordingly, he initiated a study to see whether manufacturing operations could be redesigned to reduce the number of moves.

7. The new product required machining, assembly, and painting. The design engineer requested the accounting department to estimate the labor cost of each of the three operations. The engineer supplied the estimated labor hours for each operation.

8. After obtaining the estimate of direct labor cost, the design engineer estimated the cost of the materials that would be used for the new product.

9. The design engineer totaled the costs of materials and direct labor for the new product.

10. The design engineer also estimated the cost of converting the raw materials into its final form.

11. The rental agreement on the company car called for a payment of $200 per month plus $0.20 per mile driven. There was no penalty for excess use. At the end of the agreement, however, ownership of the car reverted to the lessor.

12. The auditor pointed out that the depreciation on the corporate jet had been incorrectly assigned to Finished Goods inventory (the jet was primarily used to fly the CEO and other staff to various company sites). Accordingly, the depreciation charge was reallocated to the income statement.

13. The salary of the director of radiology did not change as the number of X rays increased.

P2-4

Cost Behavior; Classification and Graphing

LO 4

Smith Concrete Company owns ten ready-mix trucks. Each truck can deliver (on average) 10,000 cubic yards of concrete per year (considering the truck's capacity, weather, and distance to each job). One driver per truck is needed. The labor cost of each driver is $25,000 per year. Depreciation on each truck averages $20,000. Raw materials (cement, gravel, and so on) cost about $25 per cubic yard of cement.

REQUIRED:

1. Prepare a graph for each of three costs: truck drivers' wages, truck depreciation, and raw materials. Use the vertical axis for cost and the horizontal axis for cubic yards of cement. Assume that concrete sales range from 0 to 100,000 cubic yards.
2. Assume that the normal operating range for the company is 80,000 to 90,000 cubic yards per year. How would you classify each of the three types of cost?

P2-5

Activity Levels and Drivers

LO 4, LO 5

A traditional cost accounting system relies on unit-level cost drivers to assign costs to cost objects. These drivers explain changes in cost attributable to changes in units produced. A unit-level driver measures usage of activity each and every time a unit is produced. Identify which of the following drivers explain changes in cost attributable to changes in the number of units produced. For those drivers that are not unit-based, classify them as batch level, product level, or facility level.

a. Number of setups
b. Direct labor hours
c. Number of purchase orders
d. Kilowatt-hours (machine-intensive production setting)
e. Machine hours
f. Number of material moves
g. Direct labor dollars
h. Direct material dollars
i. Number of inspection hours
j. Number of rework hours (labor hours used to correct a defective or faulty product)
k. Square feet for the plant
l. Number of engineering change orders (a document that tells engineering that a product must be redesigned)

P2-6

Contemporary versus Traditional Management Accounting Systems

LO 5

The following actions are associated with either contemporary management accounting or traditional management accounting.

a. Budgeted costs for the maintenance department are compared with the actual costs of the maintenance department.
b. The maintenance department manager receives a bonus for "beating" the budget.
c. The costs of resources are traced to activities and then to products.
d. The purchasing department is evaluated on a departmental basis.
e. Activities are identified and listed.
f. Activities are categorized as adding value or not adding value to the organization.
g. A standard for a product's material usage cost is set and compared against the product's actual material usage cost.
h. The cost of performing an activity is tracked over time.
i. The distance between moves is identified as the cause of material-handling cost.
j. A purchasing agent is rewarded for buying parts below the standard price set by the company.
k. The cost of the material-handling activity is reduced dramatically by redesigning the plant layout.
l. An investigation is undertaken to find out why the actual labor cost for the production of 1,000 units is greater than the labor standard allowed.
m. The percentage of defective units is calculated and tracked over time.
n. Engineering has been given the charge to find a way to reduce setup time by 75 percent.
o. The manager of the receiving department lays off two receiving clerks so that the fourth-quarter budget can be met.

REQUIRED: Classify these actions as belonging to either a contemporary management accounting system or a traditional management accounting system. Explain your classification.

P2-7

Income Statement: Cost of Goods Manufactured

LO 3

W. W. Phillips Company produced 4,000 leather recliners during 1998. These recliners sell for $400 each. Phillips had 500 recliners in finished goods inventory at the beginning of the year. At the end of the year there were 700 recliners in finished goods inventory. Phillip's accounting records provide the following information:

Purchases of raw materials	$320,000
Raw materials inventory, January 1, 1998	46,800
Raw materials inventory, December 31, 1998	66,800
Direct labor	200,000
Indirect labor	40,000
Rent, factory building	42,000
Depreciation, factory equipment	60,000
Utilities, factory	11,956
Salary, sales supervisor	90,000
Commissions, salespersons	180,000
General administration	300,000
Work-in-process inventory, January 1, 1998	13,040
Work-in-process inventory, December 31, 1998	14,996
Finished goods inventory, January 1, 1998	80,000
Finished goods inventory, December 31, 1998	114,100

REQUIRED:
1. Prepare a statement of cost of goods manufactured.
2. Compute the average cost of producing one unit of product in 1998.
3. Prepare an income statement for external users.

P2-8

Cost of Goods Manufactured; Cost Identification; Contribution Margin; Solving for Unknowns

LO 2, LO 3, LO 4

Winn Company creates, produces, and markets games of strategy. Before any employee is hired, a puzzle of some sort must be successfully solved.

You are applying for a job as an entry-level accountant. The controller of the firm wishes to test your knowledge of basic cost terms and concepts, and, at the same time, evaluate your analytical skills. To do so, he gives you the following information for 1998:

a. Total fixed overhead is $190,000.
b. Per-unit variable manufacturing cost, $25. There are no other variable costs.
c. Total current variable manufacturing costs equal 125 percent of current conversion cost.
d. The number of units produced is 10,000.
e. Beginning work in process is one-half the cost of ending work in process.
f. There are no beginning or ending inventories for raw materials or finished goods.
g. The cost of goods sold is $400,000.
h. Variable overhead equals 133 percent of direct labor costs.

REQUIRED:
1. Prepare a statement of cost of goods manufactured for 1998.
2. If the selling price is $50 per unit, what is the gross margin? What is the total contribution margin?
3. If you were operating below capacity and someone offered to buy 1,000 units for a price of $29 per unit, what is the change in profits (incremental profits) assuming the order is accepted? (Assume that the 1,000 units will be produced using the extra capacity available.)

P2-9

Income Statement; Cost of Services Provided; Service Attributes

LO 2, LO 3

Berry Company is an architectural firm. The firm is located in Detroit, Michigan, and employs ten professionals and five staff. The firm does design work for small and medium-size construction businesses. The following data are provided for the year ended July 31, 1998:

Designs processed	2,000
Designs in process, August 1, 1997	$ 60,000
Designs in process, July 31, 1998	100,000
Cost of services sold	890,000
Beginning direct materials inventory	20,000
Purchases, direct materials	40,000
Direct labor	800,000
Overhead	100,000
Administrative	50,000
Selling	60,000

REQUIRED:

1. Prepare a statement of cost of services sold.
2. Refer to the statement prepared in requirement 1. What is the dominant cost? Will this always be true of service organizations? If not, provide an example of an exception.
3. Assume that the average fee for a design is $700. Prepare an income statement for Berry Company.
4. Discuss three differences between services and tangible products. How do these differences affect the computations in requirement 1?

P2-10

Cost Identification and Analysis; Income Statement

LO 2, LO 3

Melissa Scothern has decided to open a printing shop. She has secured a five-year contract to print a popular regional magazine. The contract calls for 5,000 copies each month.

Melissa has rented a building for $800 per month. Her printing equipment was purchased for $40,000 and has a life expectancy of eight years with no salvage value. Straight-line depreciation will be used.

Insurance costs for the building and equipment are $75 per month. Utilities are directly related to output and are expected to cost $250 for an output of 5,000 copies.

Materials to print the magazine will cost $0.50 per copy. Melissa will supervise the operation and will hire workers to run the presses as needed. She must pay $10 per hour. Each worker can produce 20 copies of the magazine per hour. Melissa will receive a salary of $1,200 per month.

A salesperson has been hired for $500 per month plus a 20 percent commission on all new sales. Advertising on the local radio station will cost $330 per month.

REQUIRED:

1. What is the full manufacturing cost per unit for the regional magazine?
2. How many workers will Melissa need to hire for the first month (assume 40 hours per week equals one worker; there are four weeks in a month)?
3. What is the variable manufacturing cost per unit (considering only unit-level variable costs)?
4. What is the prime cost per unit? the conversion cost per unit?
5. In a single-product business, are there any indirect product costs? Explain.
6. If Melissa receives $1.80 per copy, how much will her income be for the first month of operations?

Ⓜ ANAGERIAL DECISION CASES

C2-1

Cost Classification; Income Statement; Unit-based Cost Behavior; Service Organization

LO 2, LO 3, LO 4

Gateway Construction Company is a family-operated business, founded in 1950 by Samuel Gateway. In the beginning, the company consisted of Gateway and three employees laying gas, water, and sewage pipelines as subcontractors. Currently, the company employs 25 to 30 people; it is directed by Jack Gateway, Samuel's son. The main line of business continues to be laying pipeline.

Most of Gateway's work comes from contracts with city and state agencies. All of the company's work is located in Nebraska. The company's sales volume averages $3 million, and profits vary between 0 and 10 percent of sales.

Sales and profits have been somewhat below average for the past three years due to a recession and intense competition. Because of this competition, Jack Gateway is constantly reviewing the prices that other companies bid for jobs; when a bid is lost, he makes every attempt to analyze the reasons for the differences between his bid and that of his competitors. He uses this information to increase the competitiveness of future bids.

Exhibit

Gateway Construction Income Statement For the Year Ended December 31, 1998		
Sales (18,200 equipment hours at $165)		$3,003,000
Less expenses:		
Utilities	$ 24,000	
Machine operators	218,000	
Rent (office building)	24,000	
CPA fees	20,000	
Other direct labor	265,700	
Administrative salaries	114,000	
Supervisor salaries	70,000	
Pipe	1,401,340	
Tires and fuel	418,600	
Depreciation, equipment	198,000	
Salaries of mechanics	50,000	
Advertising	15,000	
Total expenses		2,818,640
Net income		$ 184,360

Jack has become convinced that Gateway's current accounting system is deficient. Currently, all expenses are simply deducted from revenues to arrive at net income. No effort is made to distinguish among the costs of laying pipe, obtaining contracts, and administering the company. Yet, all bids are based on the costs of laying pipe.

Jack also knows that knowledge of cost behavior is important. He is certain that the company could offer more competitive bids if he knew which costs were variable and which were fixed. For example, Gateway often has idle equipment (the company needs more equipment than is often necessary so that it can bid on larger projects). If Gateway could bid enough to cover its variable costs and use the idle equipment, equipment operators could be more productively utilized and have more job stability. In fact, if the bid covered more than variable costs, profits would increase as well, since the fixed costs remain unchanged for increased activity.

With these thoughts in mind, Jack began a careful review of the income statement for the previous year (see Exhibit 2-16). First, he noted that jobs were priced on the basis of equipment hours, with an average price of $165 per equipment hour. However, when it came to classifying costs and identifying their behavior, he decided that he needed some help. One thing that really puzzled him was how to classify his own salary of $114,000. About half of his time was spent in bidding and securing contracts, and the other half was spent in general administrative matters.

REQUIRED:
1. Classify the costs in Exhibit 2-16 as (1) costs of laying pipe (production costs); (2) costs of securing contracts (selling costs); or, (3) costs of general administration. For production costs, identify direct materials, direct labor, and overhead costs. The company never has significant work in process (most jobs are started and completed within a day).
2. Using the functional classification developed in requirement 1, prepare an absorption-costing income statement. What is the average cost per equipment-hour for laying pipe?
3. Assume that the only significant cost driver is equipment-hours. Also assume that costs are either strictly fixed or strictly variable. Classify the costs as fixed or variable. Build a cost formula that describes Gateway's cost structure.
4. Suppose that Jack Gateway has idle equipment and wants to prepare a bid for a prospective job. He is confident that a bid of $140 will win the job. Describe how knowledge of cost behavior (see requirement 3) can help him with the bidding decision.

C2-2

Cost Information and Ethical Behavior; Service Organization

LO 1

Jean Erickson, manager and owner of an advertising company in Charlotte, North Carolina, had arranged a meeting with Leroy Gee, the chief accountant of a large, local competitor. The two were lifelong friends. They had grown up together in a small town and attended the same university.

Leroy was a competent, successful accountant but currently was experiencing some personal financial difficulties. The problems were created by some investments that had turned sour, leaving him with a $15,000 personal loan to pay off—just at the time that his oldest son was scheduled to enter college.

Jean, on the other hand, was struggling to establish a successful advertising business. She had recently acquired the rights to open a branch office of a large regional advertising firm headquartered in Atlanta, Georgia. During her first two years, she had managed to build a small, profitable practice; however, the chance to gain a significant foothold in the Charlotte advertising community hinged on the success of winning a bid to represent the state of North Carolina in a major campaign to attract new industry and tourism. The meeting she had scheduled with Leroy concerned the bid she planned to submit.

"Leroy, I'm at a critical point in my business venture. If I can win the bid for the state's advertising dollars, I'll be set. Winning the bid will bring $600,000 to $700,000 of revenues into the firm. On top of that, I estimate that the publicity will bring another $200,000 to $300,000 of new business."

"I understand," replied Leroy. "My boss is anxious to win that business as well. It would mean a huge increase in profits for my firm. It's a competitive business, though. As new as you are, I doubt that you'll have much chance of winning."

"You may be wrong. You're forgetting two very important considerations. First, I have the backing of all the resources and talent of a regional firm. Second, I have some political connections. Last year, I was hired to run the publicity side of the governor's campaign. He was impressed with my work and would like me to have this business. I am confident that the proposals I submit will be very competitive. My only concern is to submit a bid that beats your firm. If I come in with a lower bid and with good proposals, the governor can see to it that I get the work."

"Sounds promising. If you do win, however, there will be a lot of upset people. After all, they are going to claim that the business should have been given to local advertisers, not to some out-of-state firm. Given the size of your office, you'll have to get support from Atlanta. You could take a lot of heat."

"True. But I am the owner of the branch office. That fact alone should blunt most of the criticism. Who can argue that I'm not a local? Listen, with your help, I think I can win this bid. Furthermore, if I do win it, you can reap some direct benefits. With that kind of business, I can afford to hire an accountant, and I'll make it worthwhile for you to transfer jobs. I can offer you an up-front bonus of $15,000. On top of that, I'll increase your annual salary by 20 percent. That should solve most of your financial difficulties. After all, we have been friends since day one—and what are friends for?"

"Jean, my wife would be ecstatic if I were able to improve our financial position as quickly as this opportunity affords. I certainly hope that you win the bid. What kind of help can I provide?"

"Simple. To win, all I have to do is beat the bid of your firm. Before I submit my bid, I would like you to review it. With the financial skills you have, it should be easy for you to spot any excessive costs that I may have included. Or perhaps I included the wrong kind of costs. By cutting excessive costs and eliminating costs that may not be directly related to the project, my bid should be competitive enough to meet or beat your firm's bid."

REQUIRED:

1. What would you do if you were Leroy? Fully explain the reasons for your choice.
2. What is the likely outcome if Leroy agrees to review the bid? Is there much risk to him personally if he reviews the bid? Should the degree of risk have any bearing on his decision?
3. Apply the code of ethics for management accountants to the proposal given Leroy (see Chapter 1). What standards would be violated if he agrees to review the bid? Assume that Leroy is a member of the IMA and holds a CMA.

C2-3

Research Assignment

LO 1, LO 3, LO 4

Using the resources in your library, obtain copies of financial statements for a manufacturing firm and a service firm. Write a memo discussing the differences and similarities of the two statements.

C2-4
Research Assignment
LO 1, LO 3, LO 5

Interview an accountant who works for a manufacturing firm (preferably one who works in cost accounting). Ask that person the following questions and write up his or her responses:

a. What product or products does your firm produce?
b. What costs are assigned to the product or products produced?
c. For a particular product, what direct materials are used?
d. What percentage of total manufacturing costs is direct labor? materials? overhead?
e. How is overhead assigned to the products?
f. What are some examples of costs that vary with units produced? (Obtain at least five examples.)
g. What are some examples of costs that vary with other factors?
h. Does your accounting system separate fixed and variable costs? Why or why not?

CHAPTER 3

Activity Cost Behavior

Learning Objectives

After studying Chapter 3, you should be able to:

1. Define and describe cost behavior and explain the role of the resource usage model in understanding cost behavior.

2. Separate mixed costs into their fixed and variable components using the high-low method, the scatterplot method, and the method of least squares.

3. Evaluate the reliability of a cost equation.

4. Explain the role of multiple regression in assessing cost behavior.

5. Describe the use of managerial judgment in determining cost behavior.

SCENARIO

I have just been told that our quality costs make up about 20 percent of divisional sales revenues. I was also told that quality costs are incurred because poor quality exists or may exist. Twenty percent seems high to me. All this time I thought that we were spending money to create better quality not because we had poor quality. Rick, what am I missing here?" asked Patricia Fernandez, manager of a small appliance division. "What do we need to do to increase our efficiency?"

Rick Anderson, divisional controller, pondered the questions a moment and then responded. "Patricia, based on some recent seminars that I have attended, I now realize that managing costs and increasing efficiency has a lot to do with managing the activities that we perform inside the division. But to manage activities, we really need to under-

2. *Suppose that I know the total cost of rework activity and the total number of units reworked. Given this information, can I determine how much of this total cost is variable? How much is fixed? Is knowing fixed- and variable-cost behavior important?*

3. *What role does management play in determining cost behavior?*

4. *Can you think of reasons other than those suggested by the scenario that make it important for managers to understand cost behavior?*

stand how the costs of activities change as activity output changes. Consider our rework activity. When our inspection activity detects a bad appliance, we tear it apart and redo the work so that the product functions as it should. Some costs such as the depreciation on the equipment used do not change as the number of reworked products increases. Other costs like materials and power do increase with the number of units reworked. And some costs will change only with fairly large changes in activity output."

"This is interesting, but how will understanding this cost behavior help me increase my division's efficiency?"

"Simple. If it is really true that the cost of the rework activity is a function of the number of units reworked, then you can manage costs by focusing on what drives rework costs: reworked units. If we can find ways to reduce the number of defective units, then the cost of the rework activity should decrease, increasing our overall efficiency. And it would be interesting—in fact, essential—to know how the cost of resources used changes as the activity output changes. For example, we may need to spend more in preventing bad units to reduce rework. If the increase in prevention costs is less than the reduction in rework costs, then we would want to increase our prevention activity."

Questions to Think About

1. *Suppose that the division reduces the demand for the rework activity. Will resource spending be reduced by the same proportion for this activity? Is there a difference between resource spending and resource usage?*

COST BEHAVIOR AND THE RESOURCE USAGE MODEL

Objective 1

Define and describe cost behavior and explain the role of the resource usage model in understanding cost behavior.

cost behavior

Cost behavior is the general term for describing whether the costs of activity inputs are fixed or variable in relation to changes in activity output. Activity output changes as the usage of the activity changes. Thus, a cost that remains the same in total as activity usage increases or decreases is a fixed cost. A variable cost, on the other hand, changes in direct proportion to changes in activity output. In economics, it is usually assumed that fixed and variable costs are known. Management accountants must deal with the requirements to assess—that is, to estimate fixed and variable costs. Practical assessment of cost behavior requires consideration of time horizon, resource usage, and activity output measurement.

Time Horizon

long run
short run

Determining whether a cost is fixed or variable depends on the time horizon. According to economics, in the long run, all costs are variable; in the short run at least one cost is fixed. But how long is the short run? The length of the short run may differ from one cost to another cost. Consider a process that takes materials and molds them into the shape of a garden hose. The activity output is molded materials. As the number of molded units changes, the direct materials used are relatively easy to adjust (acquiring more as the output increases and less as it decreases). For all practical purposes, the firm may treat direct materials as strictly variable even though for the next few hours the amount of materials already purchased may be fixed. Now consider the cost of direct labor. In some settings, a company may have the ability to hire and lay off its labor in relatively short time intervals—in which case it could be treated as a variable cost. In other cases, circumstances may prohibit laying off labor for short-term drops in production. For example, there may exist formal contractual agreements with labor unions that make such layoffs impossible. Such agreements may make layoffs impossible in the short-run even when there have been permanent changes in the need for labor. Only when the contract is renegotiated can the level of labor be adjusted. At best, we can call these medium-run adjustments and thus characterize direct labor as a fixed cost rather than a variable cost. The same observation can be made for other forms of labor. For example, salaries of molding production line supervisors are also difficult to adjust as the activity output fluctuates. It could take months, or even a year or two, to determine whether a drop in production output is permanent, thus leading to a reduction in one or more supervisory jobs. Accordingly, this cost is typically seen as fixed.

The length of the short-run period depends to some extent on management judgment and the purpose for which cost behavior is being estimated. For example, submitting a bid on a one-time, special order may span only a month, long enough to create a bid and produce the order. Other types of decisions, such as product discontinuance or product-mix decisions, will affect a much longer period of time. In this case, the costs that must be considered are long-run variable costs, including product design and development, market development, and market penetration. Short-run costs often do not adequately reflect all the costs necessary to design, produce, market, distribute, and support a product. Recently, there have been some new insights into the nature of long-run and short-run cost behavior.[1] These insights relate to activities and the resources needed to enable an activity to be performed.

Activities, Resource Usage, and Cost Behavior

activity capacity

Activity capacity is simply the ability to perform activities. To perform an activity, capacity must be acquired. How much capacity is needed depends on the level of per-

---

1. The concepts presented in the remainder of this section are based on Alfred M. King, "The Current Status of Activity-Based Costing: An Interview with Robin Cooper and Robert S. Kaplan," *Management Accounting* (September 1991): 22–26, and Robin Cooper and Robert S. Kaplan, "Activity-Based Systems: Measuring the Costs of Resource Usage," *Accounting Horizons* (September 1992): 1–13.

practical capacity resources

formance required for each activity. Usually, we can assume that the activity capacity needed corresponds to the level where the activity is performed efficiently. This efficient level of activity performance is called practical capacity. *Resources* are needed to enable activities to be performed. Resources are simply economic inputs that are consumed in performing activities. Capital, labor, energy, and materials are examples of resources needed to perform an activity. For example, the activity of inspecting personal computers may require diagnostic equipment (capital), an inspector (labor), power to run the equipment (energy), and disks (materials). Resource spending is the cost of acquiring capacity to perform an activity. Resource usage is the amount of activity capacity used in producing the activity output. Thus, resource usage is equivalent to activity usage. If all of the activity capacity acquired is not used, then we have unused capacity, which is the difference between the acquired capacity and the actual activity usage. The relationship between resource spending and resource usage can be used to define variable- and fixed-cost behavior. To see how, we need to understand how resources are supplied.

resource spending resource usage

unused capacity

Resources are supplied in one of two ways: (1) as used (and needed) and (2) in advance of usage. Resources supplied as used and needed are those that are acquired from outside sources, where the terms of acquisition do not require any long-term commitment for any given amount of the resource. Thus, the organization is free to buy only the quantity of resource needed. As a result, the quantity of the resource supplied equals the quantity demanded. Materials and energy are examples. There is no unused activity capacity for this category of resources (resource usage = resource supplied). Resources supplied in advance of usage are those acquired by the use of either an explicit or implicit contract to obtain a given quantity of resource, regardless of whether the quantity of the resource available is fully used or not. Resources supplied in advance may exceed the demand for their usage; thus, unused capacity is possible. Equipment and supervision are examples.

resources supplied as used and needed

resources supplied in advance of usage

Resources Supplied as Needed and Cost Behavior Since the cost of the resources supplied as needed equals the cost of resources used, the total cost of the resource increases as demand for the resource increases. Thus, generally, we can treat the cost of resources supplied as needed as a variable cost. For example, in a just-in-time manufacturing environment, materials are acquired and used as needed for production activities. Using "units produced" as the activity driver, it is clear that as the units produced increase, the usage (and cost) of raw materials would increase proportionately. Similarly, power is acquired and used as needed. For example, a machining activity will use more power as more machine hours are used; thus, the cost of power will increase with an increase in machine hours (the output measure). Note that in both examples, resource supply and usage are measured by an activity driver.

Resources Supplied in Advance and Cost Behavior Many resources are acquired before the actual demands for the resource are realized. There are two examples of this category of resource acquisition. First, organizations acquire many *multiperiod service capacities* by paying cash up front or by entering into an explicit contract that requires periodic cash payments. Buying or leasing buildings and equipment is an example of this form of advance resource acquisition. The annual expense associated with the multiperiod category is independent of actual usage of the resource; thus, these expenses can be defined as fixed expenses. They essentially correspond to committed fixed expenses, costs incurred that provide long-term activity capacity. A second and more important example concerns organizations that acquire resources in advance through implicit contracts, usually with its salaried and hourly employees. The implicit understanding is that the organization will maintain employment levels even though there may be temporary downturns in the quantity of activity used. This outcome implies that the expense associated with this category of resources is independent of the quantity used—at least in the short run. Thus, in the short run, the amount of resource expense remains unchanged even though the quantity used may vary, and this resource cost

committed fixed expenses

discretionary fixed expenses

category can be treated (cautiously) as a fixed expense. Resource spending for this category essentially corresponds to discretionary fixed expenses, costs incurred for the acquisition of short-term activity capacity. Hiring three receiving clerks for $90,000 who can supply the capacity of processing 9,000 receiving orders is an example of implicit contracting ("receiving orders" is the driver used to measure the receiving activity's capacity and usage).[2] Certainly, none of the three clerks would expect to be laid off if only 6,000 orders were actually processed—unless, of course, the downturn in demand is viewed as permanent. This implicit contracting raises ethical issues. Many companies today are turning to contingent employment to handle variation in demand for labor services. A key reason for the increase in contingent employment includes "buffering core workers against job loss." Apparently, many companies attempt to shield long-time workers from market fluctuations.[3] Suppose that the drop is permanent. In this case, we have an activity with too much capacity and until we reduce the capacity, resource spending will not be reduced. Thus, resource spending changes *lag* changes in permanent activity output demands.

Implications for Control and Decision Making The activity-based resource usage model just described can improve both managerial control and decision making. Operational control systems encourage managers to pay more attention to controlling resource usage and spending. For example, a well-designed operational control system would allow managers to assess the changes in resource demands that will occur from new product-mix decisions. Adding new, customized products may increase the demands for various overhead activities; and, if sufficient unused activity capacity does not exist, then resource spending must increase. Similarly, if activity management brings about excess activity capacity (by finding ways to reduce resource usage), managers must carefully consider what is to be done with the excess capacity. Eliminating the excess capacity may decrease resource spending and thus improve overall profits. Alternatively, using the excess capacity to increase products produced and sold could increase revenues without a corresponding increase in resource spending. How resource usage and spending is affected by managing activities is more fully explored in Chapter 10.

The activity-based resource usage model also allows managers to calculate the changes in resource supply and demand resulting from implementing such decisions as make or buy a part, accept or reject special orders, and keep or drop product lines. Additionally, the model increases the power of a number of traditional management accounting decision-making models. The impact on decision making is explored in the decision-making chapters found in Part 3 (Chapters 14 through 18). Most of the decision-making models in those chapters depend heavily on knowledge of cost behavior.

Measures of Activity Output

Variable costs move in total with changes in activity output. Fixed costs, however, remain unchanged as activity output changes. Thus, describing cost behavior requires measurement of activity output. From Chapter 2, we know that activity output is measured by activity drivers. Therefore, in order to understand the behavior of costs we must first determine the underlying activities and the associated drivers that measure activity capacity and usage. The need to understand this cost-activity relationship leads us to the determination of an appropriate measure of activity output, or activity driver. For example, material-handling output may be measured by number of moves, shipping goods output by the units sold, and laundering hospital-bedding output by pounds of laundry. The choice of driver is tailored not only to the particular firm but also to the particular activity or cost being measured.

2. Receiving refers to the activities involved in bringing purchased materials into the plant. These activities may include inspecting, unpacking, creating a receiving order to match to the invoice, and moving the materials to the storeroom.
3. "Contingent Employment on the Rise," *Deloitte & Touche Review* (4 September 1995): 1–2.

These young entrepreneurs have one of the simplest businesses possible. They take Mom's pitcher and mix lemons, sugar, and water to make lemonade. The activities are simple and easily identifiable. Can you list the manufacturing and selling activities suggested by this picture? Which costs are variable? Fixed?

This juice processing plant is far more complex than the lemonade stand. The capital requirements are far higher, as are the unseen engineering and design costs. Can you list the manufacturing activities suggested by this picture? Don't forget the behind-the-scenes activities such as purchasing and setups. Compare the degree to which costs are fixed or variable with the cost behavior of the lemonade stand.

Activity drivers explain changes in activity costs by measuring changes in activity usage (output). There are two general categories of activity drivers: unit-level drivers and nonunit-level drivers. Unit-level drivers explain changes in cost as units produced change. Pounds of direct materials, kilowatt-hours used to run production machinery, and direct labor hours are examples of unit-based activity drivers. Nonunit-level drivers explain changes in cost as factors other than units change. There are three nonunit-level categories: batch level, product level, and facility level. Batch-level costs tend to vary as the number of batches changes. Product-level costs tend to change as the number of different products changes. Facility-level costs tend to stay constant and can be viewed as globally fixed costs—at least for the short run. Examples of nonunit-based cost drivers include setups, work orders, engineering change orders, inspection hours, and material moves.

In a traditional management accounting system, cost behavior is assumed to be described by unit-based drivers only. In a contemporary management accounting system, both unit- and nonunit-based drivers are used. Thus, the contemporary system produces a much richer view of cost behavior than a traditional system.

Linearity Assumption

The definition of variable cost assumes a linear relationship between activity cost and the associated activity driver. For example, suppose that Star Company produces personal computers. Each personal computer uses one floppy disk drive, which has a cost of $40. The total variable cost of disk drives can be expressed as:

$$TVC = \$40 \times \text{units produced}$$
$$= \$40X$$

where TVC = Total variable cost of disk drives
  X = Number of personal computers produced

If 100 computers are produced, the total cost of floppy drives is $4,000 ($40 × 100). If 200 computers are produced, the total cost is $8,000 ($40 × 200). As production doubles, the cost of the drives doubles. In other words, cost increases in direct proportion to the number of units produced. The linear relationship for the computer example is portrayed in Exhibit 3-1. How reasonable is this assumption that costs are linear? Do variable activity costs really increase in direct proportion to increases in the level of the

Exhibit 3-1
Linearity of Variable Costs

activity driver? If not, then how well does this assumed linear cost function approximate the underlying cost function?

Economists usually argue that variable costs increase at a decreasing rate up to a certain volume, at which point they increase at an increasing rate. This type of *nonlinear behavior* is displayed in Exhibit 3-2. Here variable costs increase as the number of units increases, but not in direct proportion. For example, a power supplier that initially has ample capacity may offer prices that decrease per kilowatt-hour to encourage consumption; yet, once the power plant capacity has been met, any further demands may produce higher prices to ration a now scarce input among users. What if the nonlinear view more accurately portrays reality? What do we do then? One possibility is to determine the actual cost function. But, every activity could have a different cost function, and this approach could be very time consuming and expensive (if it can even be done). It is much simpler to assume a linear relationship.

Exhibit 3-2
Nonlinearity of Variable Costs

Exhibit
Linear Approximation

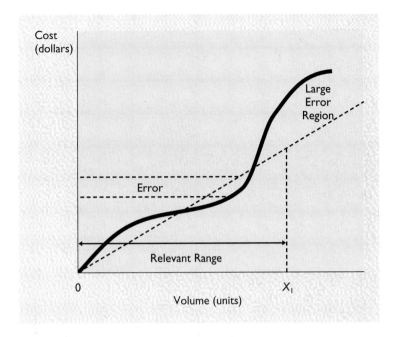

If the linear relationship is assumed, then the main concern is how well this assumption approximates the underlying cost function. Exhibit 3-3 gives us some idea of the consequences of assuming a linear cost function. As with fixed costs, we can define the *relevant range* as the range of activity output for which the assumed cost relationships are valid. Here validity refers to how closely the linear cost function approximates the underlying cost function. Note that for units of the activity driver beyond X_1 the approximation appears to break down.

Step-Cost Behavior

step-cost function

In our discussion of cost behavior, we have assumed that the cost function (be it linear or nonlinear) is continuous. In reality, some cost functions may be discontinuous, as shown in Exhibit 3-4. This type of cost function is known as a step function. A step-cost function has the property of displaying a constant level of cost for a range of activity usage (output) and then jumping to a higher level of cost at some point, where it remains for a similar range of activity. In Exhibit 3-4, the cost is $100 as long as activity output is between 0 and 10 units. If the output is between 10 and 20 units, the cost jumps to $200.

Step-Variable Costs Items that display a step-cost behavior must be purchased in chunks. The width of the step defines the range of activity usage for which a quantity of the resource must be acquired. The width of the step in Exhibit 3-4 is ten units of activity. If the width of the step is narrow, as in Exhibit 3-4, the cost of the resource changes in response to fairly small changes in resource usage (as measured by activity usage). Costs

step-variable costs

that follow a step-cost behavior with narrow steps are defined as step-variable costs. If the width of the step is narrow, we usually approximate step-variable costs with a strictly variable-cost assumption.

Step-Fixed Costs In reality, many so-called fixed costs probably are best described by a step-cost function. Many resources acquired in advance of usage, particularly those that involve implicit contracting, follow a step-cost function. Suppose, for example, that a company hires three sustaining engineers; these are engineers responsible for redesigning existing products to meet customer requirements. By hiring the engineers, the company has acquired the ability to perform an activity, engineering redesign. The salaries

Exhibit
Step-Cost Function

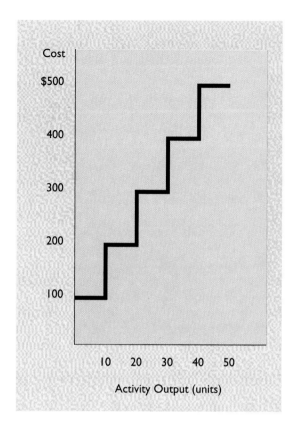

paid the engineers represent the cost of acquiring the engineering redesign capacity, and the number of engineering changes that can be *efficiently* processed by the three engineers is a quantitative measure of that capacity. The number of change orders processed, on the other hand, is a measure of the actual usage. Assume the engineers are each paid an annual salary of $50,000 and that each can process 2,500 engineering change orders per year. The company has acquired the capacity to process 7,500 (3 × 2,500) change orders per year at a total cost of $150,000 (3 × $50,000). The nature of the resource requires that the capacity be acquired in chunks (one engineer hired at a time). The cost function for this example is displayed in Exhibit 3-5. Notice that the width of the steps is 2,500 units, a much wider step than the cost function displayed in Exhibit 3-4. Costs that follow a step-cost behavior with wide steps are defined as step-fixed costs.

step-fixed costs

Step-fixed costs are assigned to the fixed-cost category. Most step-fixed costs are fixed over the normal operating range of a firm. If that range is 5,000 to 7,500 change orders (as shown in Exhibit 3-5), then the firm will spend $150,000 on engineering resources. This is equivalent to spending $20 per change order ($150,000/7,500). The average unit cost, obtained by dividing the resource expenditure by the activity's practical capacity, is the activity rate. The activity rate is used to calculate the cost of resource usage and the cost of unused activity.

activity rate

For example, during the year, the company may not actually process 7,500 orders; that is, all of the available order processing capacity may not be used. Resource usage is the number of change orders *actually* processed. Assume that 6,000 change orders were processed during the year. The cost of resource usage is the activity rate times the actual activity usage: $20 × 6,000 = $120,000. Further, the cost of unused activity is the activity rate times the unused activity: $20 × 1,500 = $30,000. Note that the cost of unused activity occurs because the resource (engineering redesign) must be acquired in lumpy (whole) amounts. Even if the company had anticipated the need for only 6,000 change orders, it would have been difficult to hire the equivalent of 2.4 engineers (6,000/2,500).

cost of resource usage
cost of unused activity

Exhibit
Step-Fixed Costs

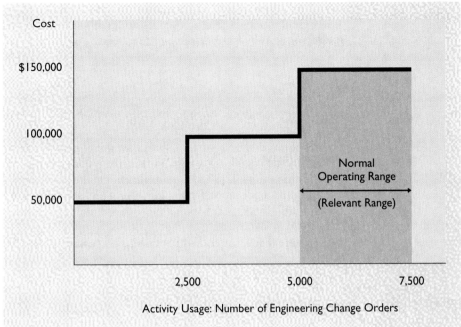

Activity Usage: Number of Engineering Change Orders

The example illustrates that when resources are acquired in advance, there may be a difference between the *resources supplied* and the *resources used (demanded)* to perform activities. This can only occur for activity costs that display a fixed-cost behavior (resources acquired in advance of usage). Typically, the traditional management accounting system provides information only about the cost of the resources supplied. A contemporary management accounting system, on the other hand, tells us how much of the activity is used and the cost of its usage. Furthermore, the relationship between resources supplied and resources used is expressed by either of the following two equations:

$$\text{Activity availability} = \text{Activity usage} + \text{Unused capacity} \qquad (3.1)$$
$$\text{Cost of activity supplied} = \text{Cost of activity used} + \text{Cost of unused activity} \quad (3.2)$$

Equation 3.1 expresses the relationship between supply and demand in physical units while Equation 3.2 expresses it in financial terms.

For the engineering order example, the relationships appear as follows:

Physical units (Equation 3.1):
$$\text{Available orders} = \text{Orders used} + \text{Orders unused}$$
$$7{,}500 \text{ orders} = 6{,}000 \text{ orders} + 1{,}500 \text{ orders}$$

Financial terms (Equation 3.2):
$$\text{Cost of orders supplied} = \text{Cost of orders used} + \text{Cost of unused orders}$$
$$\$150{,}000 = \$120{,}000 + \$30{,}000$$

Activities and Mixed-Cost Behavior

Since it is possible that activities simultaneously may have resources associated with them that are acquired in advance and resources that are acquired as needed, activity costs can display a mixed-cost behavior. Consider, for example, a specific activity within a law firm: copying documents. To enable the activity to be performed, the law firm leases a photocopier. The lease agreement calls for a lease payment of $3,000 paid at the beginning of each year. The firm is responsible for paying for the operating costs, which average $0.02 per copy and cover the cost of toner, paper, and maintenance. The copier is leased for five years and has the capability of producing 600,000 copies. Thus, the

$3,000 represents the cost of resources acquired in advance of usage, and the $0.02 represents the cost of acquiring resources as needed and used. The cost behavior for the copying activity is expressed by the following equation:

$$Y = \$3,000 + \$0.02X$$

where Y = Total cost
    X = Number of copies per year (activity output measure)

   The fixed charge of $3,000 makes the copying capacity available, but use of that capacity also produces a cost. In fact, for every copy produced, the company must pay an additional $0.02. The more copies made, the more the company must pay. If 100,000 copies are made during the year, then the total cost is $5,000 [$3,000 + ($0.02 × 100,000)]. If 150,000 copies are produced, the total cost is $6,000 [$3,000 + ($0.02 × 150,000)]. Total cost increases as the activity increases, but regardless of how many copies are made, the company must pay at least $3,000. Exhibit 3-6 displays the mixed-cost relationship. Notice that at zero units of activity output, there is still a cost. As activity output increases, total cost increases.

What the Accounting Records Reveal Sometimes, as in the photocopier example, it is easy to identify the variable and fixed components of a mixed cost. Many times, however, the only information available is the total cost of an activity and a measure of activity usage (the variables Y and X). For example, the accounting system will usually record both the total cost of the maintenance activity for a given period and the number of maintenance hours provided during that period. How much of the total maintenance cost represents a fixed charge and how much represents a variable charge is not revealed by the accounting records. (In fact, the accounting records may not even reveal the breakdown of costs in the photocopier example.) Often, the total cost is simply recorded with no attempt to segregate the fixed and variable costs.

Exhibit
Mixed-Cost Behavior

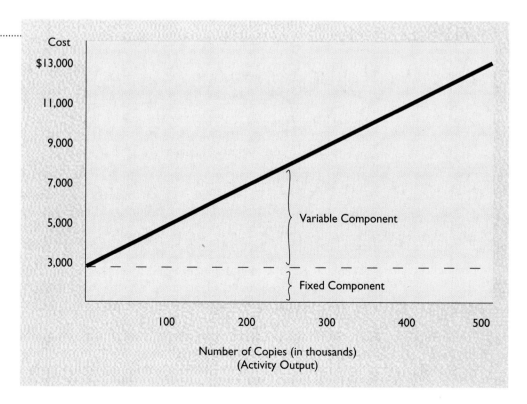

Need for Cost Separation Since accounting records may reveal only the total cost and the associated activity usage of a mixed-cost item, it is necessary to separate the total cost into its fixed and variable components. Only through a formal effort to separate costs can all costs be classified into the appropriate cost behavior categories.

METHODS FOR SEPARATING MIXED COSTS INTO FIXED AND VARIABLE COMPONENTS

Objective 2

Separate mixed costs into their fixed and variable components using the high-low method, the scatterplot method, and the method of least squares.

There are three widely used methods of separating a mixed cost into its fixed and variable components: the high-low method, the scatterplot method, and the method of least squares. Each method requires us to make the simplifying assumption of a linear cost relationship. Therefore, before we examine each of these methods more closely, let's review the expression of cost as an equation for a straight line.

$$Y = F + VX$$

where Y = Total activity cost (the dependent variable)
F = Fixed-cost component (the intercept parameter)
V = Variable cost per unit of activity (the slope parameter)
X = Measure of activity output (the independent variable)

dependent variable

independent variable

intercept parameter
slope parameter

The dependent variable is a variable whose value depends on the value of another variable. In the previous equation, total activity cost is the dependent variable; it is the cost we are trying to predict. The independent variable is a variable that measures activity output and explains changes in the activity cost. It is an activity driver. The choice of an independent variable is related to its economic plausibility. That is, the manager will attempt to find an independent variable that causes or is closely associated with the dependent variable. The intercept parameter corresponds to fixed activity cost. Graphically, the intercept parameter is the point at which the mixed-cost line intercepts the cost (vertical) axis. The slope parameter corresponds to the variable cost per unit of activity. Graphically, this represents the slope of the mixed-cost line.

Since accounting records reveal only X and Y, those values must be used to estimate the parameters F and V. With estimates of F and V, the fixed and variable components can be estimated and the behavior of the mixed cost can be predicted as activity usage changes. Three methods will be described for estimating F and V. These methods are the high-low method, the scatterplot method, and the method of least squares.

The same data will be used with each method so that comparisons among them can be made. The data have been accumulated for the setup activity of Larson Company's Newark, New Jersey, plant. The plant manager believes that setup hours is a good driver for the activity. Assume that the accounting records of the plant disclose the following setup costs and setup hours for the past five quarters:

Month	Setup Cost	Setup Hours
January	$1,000	100
February	1,250	200
March	2,250	300
April	2,500	400
May	3,750	500

The High-Low Method

From basic geometry, we know that two points are needed to determine a line. Once we know two points on a line, then its equation can be determined. Recall that F, the fixed-cost component, is the intercept of the total-cost line, and that V, the variable cost per unit, is the slope of the line. Given two points, the slope and the intercept can be

high-low method   determined. The high-low method preselects the two points that will be used to compute the parameters F and V. Specifically, the method uses the high and low points. The high point is defined as the point with the highest activity level. The low point is defined as the point with the lowest activity level.

Letting (X_1, Y_1) be one point, say the low point, and (X_2, Y_2) be the second point, the high point, the equations for determining the slope and intercept are, respectively:

$$V = \frac{\text{Change in cost}}{\text{Change in activity}}$$
$$= \frac{(Y_2 - Y_1)}{(X_2 - X_1)}$$

and

$$F = \text{Total mixed cost} - \text{Variable cost}$$
$$= Y_2 - VX_2$$

or

$$F = Y_1 - VX_1$$

Notice that the fixed-cost component is computed using the total cost at either (X_1, Y_1) or (X_2, Y_2).

For Larson, the high point is a \$3,750 setup cost when 500 setup hours are used, or (500, \$3,750). The low point is a \$1,000 setup cost when 100 setups are used, or (100, \$1,000). Once the high and low points are defined, the values of F and V can be computed:

$$V = \frac{(Y_2 - Y_1)}{(X_2 - X_1)}$$
$$= \frac{(\$3,750 - \$1,000)}{(500 - 100)}$$
$$= \frac{\$2,750}{400}$$
$$= \$6.875$$

$$F = Y_2 - VX_2$$
$$= \$3,750 - (\$6.875 \times 500)$$
$$= \$312.50$$

The cost formula using the high-low method is

$$Y = \$312.50 + \$6.875X$$

If the number of setup hours for June is expected to be 350, this cost formula will predict a total cost of \$2,718.75, with fixed costs of \$312.50 and variable costs of \$2,406.25.

The high-low method has the advantage of objectivity. That is, any two people using the high-low method on a particular data set will arrive at the same answer. In addition, the high-low method allows a manager to get a quick fix on a cost relationship using only two data points. For example, a manager may have only two years of data. Sometimes this will be enough to get a crude approximation of the cost relationship.

The high-low method is usually not as good as the other methods. Why? First, the high and low points often can be what are known as *outliers*. They may represent atypical cost-activity relationships. If so, the cost formula computed using these two points will not represent what usually takes place. The scatterplot method can help a **scatterplot method** manager avoid this trap by selecting two points that appear to be representative of the general activity cost pattern. Second, even if these points are not outliers, other pairs of points may clearly be more representative. Again, the scatterplot method allows the choice of the more representative points.

The Scatterplot Method

scattergraph

The first step in applying the scatterplot method is to plot the data points so that the relationship between setup costs and activity level can be seen. This plot is referred to as a scattergraph and is shown in Exhibit 3-7. The vertical axis is total activity cost and the horizontal axis is activity output (setup cost and setup hours, respectively, for the example). Inspecting Exhibit 3-7 gives us increased confidence that the assumption of a linear relationship between setup costs and setup hours is reasonable for the indicated range of activity. Thus, one purpose of a scattergraph is to assess the validity of the assumed linear relationship. Additionally, inspecting the scattergraph may reveal several points that do not seem to fit the general pattern of behavior. Upon investigation, it may be discovered that these points (the outliers) were due to some irregular occurrences. This knowledge can provide justification for their elimination and perhaps lead to a better estimate of the underlying cost function.

A scattergraph can help provide insight concerning the relationship between cost and activity usage. In fact, a scattergraph allows one to visually fit a line to the points on the scattergraph. In doing so, the line should be chosen that appears to fit the points the best. In making that choice, a manager or cost analyst is free to use past experience with the behavior of the cost item. Experience may provide a good intuitive sense of how setup costs behave; the scattergraph then becomes a useful tool to quantify this intuition. Fitting a line to the points in this way is how the scatterplot method works. Keep in mind that the scattergraph and the other statistical aids are tools that can help managers improve their judgment. Using the tools does not restrict the manager from using judgment to alter any of the estimates produced by formal methods.

Examine Exhibit 3-7 carefully. Based only on the information contained in the graph, how would you fit a line to the points in it? Suppose that you decide that a line passing through points 1 and 3 provides the best fit. If so, how could this decision be

3-7

Exhibit

Scattergraph for Larson Company

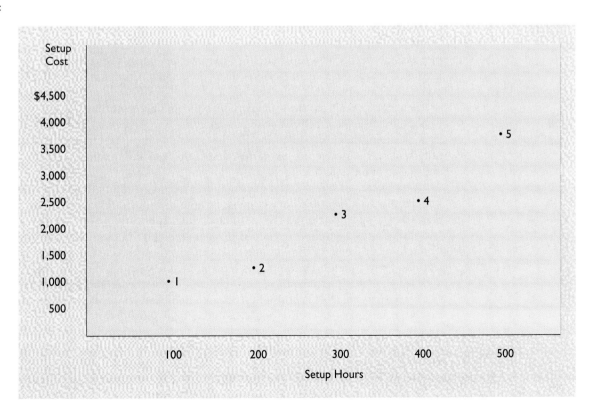

used to compute the parameters F and V so that the fixed- and variable-cost components can be estimated?

Assuming your choice of the best-fitting line is the one passing through points 1 and 3, the variable cost per unit can be computed in the following way. First, let point 1 be designated by $X_1 = 100$, $Y_1 = \$1,000$ and point 3 by $X_2 = 300$, $Y_2 = \$2,250$. (This designation is arbitrary; it really doesn't matter which point is designated (X_1, Y_1) and which one is designated (X_2, Y_2).) Next, use these two points to compute the slope:

$$
\begin{aligned}
V &= \frac{(Y_2 - Y_1)}{(X_2 - X_1)} \\
&= \frac{(\$2,250 - \$1,000)}{(300 - 100)} \\
&= \frac{\$1,250}{200} \\
&= \$6.25
\end{aligned}
$$

Thus, the variable cost per material move is \$6.25. Given the variable cost per unit, the final step is to compute the fixed-cost component using (X_2, Y_2) in the intercept equation:

$$
\begin{aligned}
F &= Y_2 - VX_2 \\
&= \$2,250 - (\$6.25 \times 300) \\
&= \$375
\end{aligned}
$$

Of course, the fixed-cost component can also be computed using (X_1, Y_1), which produces the same result.

$$
\begin{aligned}
F &= Y_1 - VX_1 \\
&= \$1,000 - (\$6.25 \times 100) \\
&= \$375
\end{aligned}
$$

cost formula

The fixed and variable components of setup cost have now been identified. The cost formula for the setup activity can be expressed as:

$$
Y = \$375 + \$6.25X
$$

Using this formula, the total cost of setups for activity output between 100 and 500 can be predicted and then broken down into fixed and variable components. For example, assume that 350 setup hours are planned for June. Using the cost formula, the predicted cost is \$2,562.50 [\$375 + (\$6.25 × 350)]. Of this total cost, \$375 is fixed and \$2,187.50 is variable.

The cost formula for the setup activity was obtained by fitting a line to points 1 and 3 in Exhibit 3-7. Judgment was used to select the line. Whereas one person may decide, by inspection, that the best-fitting line is the one that passes through points 1 and 3, others, using their own judgment, may decide that the line should pass through points 2 and 4—or points 1 and 5.

A significant advantage of the scatterplot method is that it affords a cost analyst the opportunity to inspect the data visually. Exhibit 3-8 illustrates cost behavior situations that are not appropriate for the straightforward application of the high-low method. Graph A shows a nonlinear relationship between activity cost and activity usage. An example of this might be a volume discount given on direct materials or evidence of learning by workers (for example, as more hours are worked, the total cost increases at a decreasing rate due to the increased efficiency of the workers). Graph B indicates that there is an upward shift in cost if more than X_1 units are made. Perhaps this could mean that an additional supervisor must be hired or a second shift run. Graph C shows outliers that are not representative of the overall cost relationship.

The scatterplot method suffers from the lack of any objective criterion for choosing the best-fitting line. The quality of the cost formula depends on the quality of the subjective judgment of the analyst. The high-low method removes the subjectivity in the choice of the line. Regardless of who uses the method, the same line will result.

Exhibit
Cost Behavior Patterns

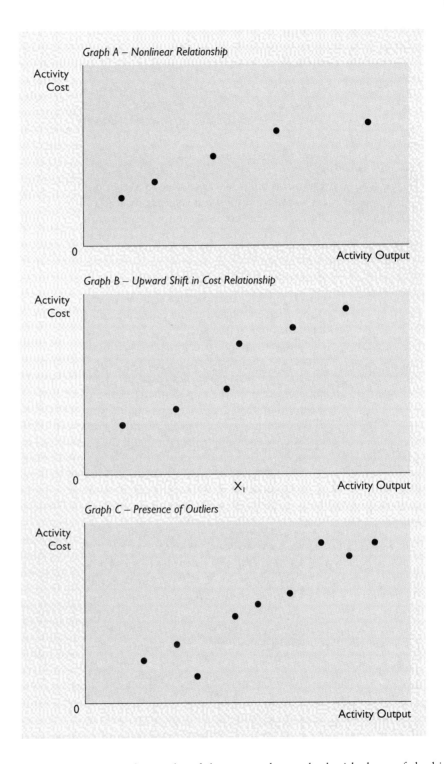

Exhibit 3-9 compares the results of the scatterplot method with those of the high-low method. There is a large difference between the fixed-cost components and the variable rates. The predicted setup cost for 350 setup hours is $2,562.50 according to the scatterplot method and $2,718.75 according to the high-low method. Which is "right"? Since the two methods can produce significantly different cost formulas, the question of which method is the best naturally arises. Ideally, a method that is objective and, at the same time, produces the best-fitting line is needed. The method of least squares defines *best-fitting* and is objective in the sense that using the method for a given set of data will produce the same cost formula.

Exhibit
Comparison of High-Low
and Scatterplot Formulas

	Fixed Cost	Variable Rate	Setup Cost for 350 Hours
High-low	$312.50	$6.875	$2,718.75
Scatterplot	375.00	6.250	2,562.50

The Method of Least Squares

Up to this point, we have alluded to the concept of a line that best fits the points shown on a scattergraph. What is meant by a best-fitting line? Intuitively, it is the line in which the data points are closer to the line than any other line. But what is meant by closer?

Consider Exhibit 3-10. Here an arbitrary line $(Y = F + VX)$ has been drawn. The closeness of each point to the line can be measured by the vertical distance of the point from the line. This vertical distance is the difference between the actual cost and the cost predicted by the line. For point 5, this is $E_5 = Y_5 - (F + VX_5)$, where Y_5 is the actual cost, $F + VX_5$ is the predicted cost, and the deviation is represented by E_5. The **deviation** is the difference between the predicted and actual cost, which is shown by the distance from the point to the line.

The vertical distance measures the closeness of a single point to the line, but we need a measure of closeness of *all* points to the line. One possibility is to add all the single measures to obtain an overall measure. However, this overall measure may be misleading. For example, the sum of small positive deviations could result in an overall measure greater than the sum of large positive deviations and large negative deviations because of the canceling effect of positive and negative numbers. To correct for this problem, we first square each single deviation and then sum these squared deviations as the overall

deviation

Exhibit
Line Deviations

$$*E_5 = Y_5 - (F + VX_5)$$

measure of closeness. Squaring the deviations avoids the cancellation problem caused by a mix of positive and negative numbers.

To illustrate this concept, we calculate a measure of closeness for the cost formula produced by the scatterplot method.

Actual Cost	Predicted Cost[a]	Deviation[b]	Deviation Squared
$1,000	$1,000	$ —	—
1,250	1,625	-375	140,625
2,250	2,250	—	—
2,500	2,875	-375	140,625
3,750	3,500	250	62,500
Total measure of closeness			343,750

[a]Predicted cost = $375 + $6.25X, where X is the actual activity usage associated with the actual activity cost and cost is rounded to the nearest dollar.
[b]Deviation = Actual cost − Predicted cost.

Since the measure of closeness is the sum of the squared deviations of the points from the line, the smaller the measure, the better the line fits the points. For example, the scatterplot method line has a closeness measure of 343,750. A similar calculation produces a closeness measure of 523,438 for the high-low line. Thus, the scatterplot line fits the points better than the high-low line. This outcome supports the earlier claim that the use of judgment in the scatterplot method is superior to the high-low method.

In principle, comparing closeness measures can produce a ranking of all lines from best to worst. The line that fits the points better than any other line is called the best-fitting line. It is the line with the smallest (least) sum of squared deviations. The method of least squares identifies the best-fitting line. We rely on statistical theory to obtain the formulas that produce the best-fitting line. These formulas follow:

best-fitting line

method of least squares

$$V = \frac{[\Sigma XY - \Sigma X \Sigma Y/n]}{[\Sigma X^2 - (\Sigma X)^2/n]} \qquad (3.3)$$

$$F = \frac{\Sigma Y}{n} - v\left(\frac{\Sigma X}{n}\right) \qquad (3.4)$$

Manual Computation In order to compute V and F, five inputs are needed: n, ΣX, ΣY, ΣXY, and ΣX^2. The first input, n, is the easiest to obtain; simply count the number of data points in the data set. For the Larson Company example, there are five data points. The other four inputs are computed as follows:

ΣX	ΣY	ΣXY	ΣX^2
100	$ 1,000	$ 100,000	10,000
200	1,250	250,000	40,000
300	2,250	675,000	90,000
400	2,500	1,000,000	160,000
500	3,750	1,875,000	250,000
1,500	$10,750	$3,900,000	550,000

Substituting these summations (Σ) into Equations 3.3 and 3.4, we obtain:

$$V = \frac{[3,900,000 - (1,500 \times 10,750)/5]}{[550,000 - (1,500)^2/5]}$$
$$= 675,000/100,000$$
$$= \$6.75$$

and

$$F = \frac{\$10,750}{5} - \$6.75\left(\frac{1,500}{5}\right)$$
$$= \$125$$

Thus, the cost formula for the method of least squares can be expressed as follows:

$$Y = \$125 + \$6.75X$$

Since this cost formula is the best-fitting line, it should produce better predictions of setup costs. For 350 setup hours, the setup cost predicted by the least-squares line is $2,487.50 [$125 + ($6.75 × 350)], with a fixed component of $125 plus a variable component of $2,362.50. Using this prediction as a standard, the scatterplot line most closely approximates the least-squares line.

Computer Computation Computing the formula manually is tedious, even with only five data points. As the number of data points increases, manual computation becomes impractical. Fortunately, spreadsheet packages such as Lotus® 1-2-3®, Quattro Pro®, and Microsoft Excel®[4] have regression routines that will perform the computations. All that the user needs to do is input the data points. A computer printout for the Larson example is provided in Exhibit 3-11. The computer printout supplies more than the estimates of the coefficients. It also provides information that can be used to assess the reliability of the cost equation, a feature that is not available for the scatterplot and high-low methods.

RELIABILITY OF COST FORMULAS

Objective 3

Evaluate the reliability of a cost equation.

goodness of fit

The computer output in Exhibit 3-11 provides information that can be used to assess how reliable the estimated cost formula is. This is a feature not provided by either the scatterplot or high-low methods. We will use the printout in Exhibit 3-11 as the point of reference for discussing a statistical assessment of a cost formula's reliability: *goodness of fit*. Although the printout provides other useful information for assessing statistical reliability, we will restrict our attention to goodness of fit. For our setting, goodness of fit measures the degree of association between activity cost and activity output. This measure is important because the method of least squares identifies the best-fitting line, but it does not reveal how good the fit is. The best-fitting line may not be a good-fitting line. It may perform miserably when it comes to predicting costs.

Coefficient of Determination

Initially, we assume that a single activity driver (activity usage variable) explains changes (variability) in activity cost. Our experience with the Larson Company example suggests that setup hours can explain changes in setup costs. The scattergraph shown in Exhibit 3-7 confirms this belief because it reveals that setup cost and activity usage (as measured by setup hours) seem to move together. It is quite likely that a significant percentage of

3-11

Exhibit
Computer Printout:
Larson Example

Parameter	Estimate	t for H_0 Parameter = 0	Pr > t	Std Error of Parameter
Intercept	125	0.398	0.710	313.91
Setup hours	6.75	7.131	0.002	9.76

R Square (R^2) 0.94
Standard Error (S_e) 299
Observations   5

4. Quattro Pro is a registered trademark of Novell, Inc. Excel is a registered trademark of Microsoft Corporation. Any reference to Quattro Pro or Excel refers to this footnote.

the total variability in cost is explained by our activity output variable. We can determine statistically just how much variability is explained by looking at the coefficient of determination. The percentage of variability in the dependent variable explained by an independent variable (in this case, a measure of activity usage) is called the coefficient of determination. This percentage is a goodness-of-fit measure. The higher the percentage of cost variability explained, the better the fit. Since the coefficient is the *percentage* of variability explained, it always has a value between 0 and 1.0. In the printout in Exhibit 3-11, the coefficient of determination is labeled "R Square (R^2)." The value given is 0.94, which means that 94 percent of the variability in setup cost is explained by the setup hours. This result tells us that the least-squares line is a good-fitting line.

coefficient of determination

There is no cutoff point for a good versus a bad coefficient of determination. Clearly, the closer R^2 is to 1, the better. However, is 89 percent good enough? How about 73 percent? Or even 46 percent? The answer is that it depends. If your cost equation yields a coefficient of determination of 75 percent, you know that your independent variable explains three-fourths of the variability in cost. You also know that some other factor or combination of factors explains the remaining one-fourth. Depending on your tolerance for error, you may want to improve the equation by trying different independent variables (for example, setup hours worked rather than setup hours) or by trying multiple regression (which is explained in a succeeding section of this chapter).

Manual Computation

The coefficient of determination (R^2) is computed using the following formula:

$$R^2 = \frac{V[\Sigma XY - \Sigma X \Sigma Y/n]}{[\Sigma Y^2 - (\Sigma Y)^2/n]} \tag{3.5}$$

where V is the slope computed using the method of least squares.

To compute the coefficient of determination (R^2) for the setup cost example, the required inputs are V, n, ΣX, ΣXY, ΣY, and ΣY^2. In our prior computation of V, the same inputs were required except for ΣY^2. The computation of ΣY^2 is as follows:

ΣY^2
$ 1,000,000
1,562,500
5,062,500
6,250,000
14,062,500
$27,937,500

Using these inputs, the coefficient of determination can be calculated:

$$R^2 = \frac{6.75 \, [3,900,000 - (1,500) \times (10,750)/5]}{[27,937,500 - (10,750)^2/5]}$$

$$= \frac{(6.75 \times 675,000)}{4,825,000}$$

$$= 0.94$$

This result tells us that the least-squares line is a good-fitting line.

Coefficient of Correlation

coefficient of correlation

An alternative measure of goodness of fit is the coefficient of correlation, which is the square root of the coefficient of determination. Since square roots can be negative, the value of the coefficient of correlation can range between -1 and $+1$. If the coefficient of correlation is positive, then the two variables (in this example, cost and activity) move together in the *same direction* and positive correlation exists. Perfect positive correlation would yield a value of 1.00 for the coefficient of correlation. If, on the other hand, the coefficient of correlation is negative, then the two variables move in a predictable fashion but in *opposite directions*. Perfect negative correlation would yield a coefficient of correlation of −1.00. A coefficient of correlation value close to zero indicates no correlation. That is, knowledge of the movement of one variable gives us no clue as to the movement of the other variable. Exhibit 3-12 illustrates the concept of correlation.

For the Larson Company example, the coefficient of correlation (r) is computed as follows:

$$r = \sqrt{0.94}$$
$$= 0.97$$

The square root is positive because the correlation between X and Y is positive. In other words, as activity usage (setup hours) increases, the setup cost increases. This positive correlation is reflected by a positive value for V. If cost decreases as activity usage increases, then the coefficient of correlation (and the value of V) is negative. The sign of V reveals the sign of the coefficient of correlation. The very high positive correlation between setup cost and setup hours indicates that setup hours is a good choice for a cost driver.

MULTIPLE REGRESSION

Objective 4

Explain the role of multiple regression in assessing cost behavior.

Sometimes obtaining the best cost equation is more complicated than simply identifying an activity driver and regressing activity cost on this driver. The outcome may not

Exhibit
Correlation Illustrated

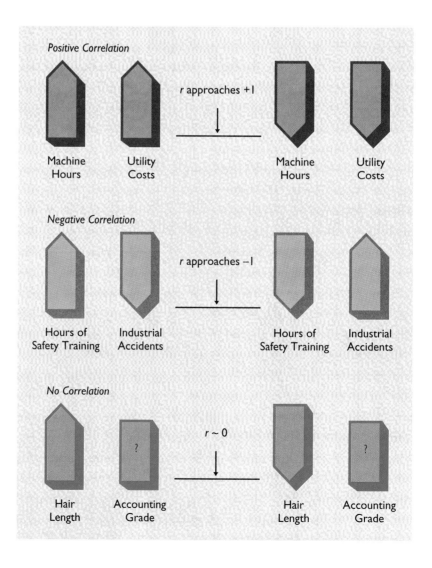

produce a cost equation that is good enough for managerial use. In the Larson Company example, 94 percent of the variability in setup cost was explained by changes in activity output (setup hours). Suppose, however, that only 55 percent of the variability could be explained by this variable. In this case, one possible solution is to search for additional explanatory variables. For example, suppose after further investigation, the company's cost analysts have decided that the number of different parts—a measure of product complexity—might be an additional driver of setup costs. The more complex products require the use of different tools and more skilled labor than the less complex products, thus increasing setup costs (or so argued the production managers). Thus, activity cost is explained by more than one variable and produces a more complex cost equation.

In the case of two explanatory variables (activity drivers), the linear equation is expanded to include the additional variable:

$$Y = F + V_1 X_1 + V_2 X_2$$

where X_1 is setup hours and X_2 is number of parts.

With three variables (Y, X_1, X_2), a minimum of three points is needed to compute the parameters F, V_1, and V_2. Seeing the points becomes difficult because they must be plotted in three dimensions. Using the scatterplot method or the high-low method is not practical.

However, the extension of the method of least squares is straightforward. It is relatively simple to develop a set of equations that provide values for F, V_1, and V_2 that yield the best-fitting equation. Whenever least squares is used to fit an equation involving two or more explanatory variables, the method is called multiple regression. The computational complexity of multiple regression, which increases significantly, is facilitated by the computer. In fact, any practical application of multiple regression requires the use of the computer.

Suppose that the cost analysts for Larson Company have tried several different cost drivers to explain the variability in setup cost. Using 50 different setups as a data source, they run a multiple regression using the setup hours and the number of different parts. The following cost equation is computed:

$$Y = \$200 + \$5X_1 + \$10X_2$$
$$R^2 = 0.92$$

Notice that the R^2 goes from 55 percent (previously assumed) to 92 percent, clearly indicating the value of adding the second driver. As with the cost equation involving a single cost driver, the preceding equation can be used to predict activity cost. For example, suppose that in July, 350 setup hours and 100 different parts are projected. The predicted setup cost for July is as follows:

$$Y = \$200 + \$5(350) + \$10(100)$$
$$= \$2,950$$

Larson can use the information provided by the cost equation to assess the effect of actions that may change the nature of activity output measures. For example, finding ways to reduce setup hours and/or reduce the number of different parts can reduce the overall cost of the setup activity.

MANAGERIAL JUDGMENT

Objective 5

Describe the use of managerial judgment in determining cost behavior.

Managerial judgment is critically important in determining cost behavior, and is by far the most widely used method in practice.[5] Many managers simply use their experience and past observation of cost relationships to determine fixed and variable costs. This method, however, may take a number of forms. Some managers simply assign particular

---

5. Maryanne M. Mowen, *Accounting for Costs as Fixed and Variable* (Montvale, N.J.: National Association of Accountants, 1986), 19–20. This practice of using managerial judgment to assign costs to cost behavior categories has continued to be practiced on the more advanced cost accounting systems.

margin note: multiple regression

activity costs to the fixed category and others to the variable category. They ignore the possibility of mixed costs. Thus, a chemical firm may regard materials and utilities as strictly variable with respect to pounds of chemical produced and all other costs as fixed. Even labor, a traditional and common example of a unit-based variable cost, may be fixed for this firm. The appeal of this method is simplicity. Before opting for this course, management would do well to make sure that each cost is predominantly fixed or variable and that the decisions being made are not highly sensitive to errors in classifying costs. To illustrate the use of judgment in assessing cost behavior, consider Elgin Sweeper Company, a leading manufacturer of motorized street sweepers. Using production volume as the cost driver, Elgin revised its chart of accounts to organize costs into fixed and variable components. Elgin's accountants used their knowledge of the company to assign expenses, using a decision rule that categorized an expense as fixed if it were fixed 75 percent of the time, and variable if it were variable 75 percent of the time.[6]

Management may instead identify mixed costs and divide these costs into fixed and variable components by deciding just what the fixed and variable parts are—that is, using experience to say that a certain amount of a cost is fixed and that, therefore, the rest must be variable. Our photocopier example with the fixed cost of $3,000 per year and the variable rate of $0.02 per copy falls into this category. Then the variable component can be computed using one or more cost/volume data points. This has the advantage of accounting for mixed costs but is subject to a similar type of error as the strict fixed/variable dichotomy. That is, management may be wrong in its assessment.

Finally, management may use experience and judgment to refine statistical estimation results. Perhaps the experienced manager might "eyeball" the data and throw out several points as being highly unusual or might revise results of estimation to take into account projected changes in cost structure or technology. Martin Color-Fi, a recycler, is paying top prices for discarded plastics. Demand for recyclable plastics has mushroomed, and prices have tripled in the space of a year. The reason for the growth in demand? A run-up in the price of cotton due to poor crops in China, Pakistan, and India. The shortage of cotton led Asian mills to substitute polyester and other synthetics. These synthetic fabrics are made from PET (the polyethylene-terephthalate found in recyclable plastic bottles). Companies like Martin must look forward, not back, to predict the impact of demand for substitute products on prices and profits.[7] Statistical techniques are highly accurate in depicting the past; but they cannot foresee the future, which is, of course, what management really wants.

The advantage of using managerial judgment to separate fixed and variable costs is its simplicity. In situations in which the manager has a deep understanding of the firm and its cost patterns, this method can give good results. However, if the manager does not have good judgment, errors will occur. Therefore, it is important to consider the experience of the manager, the potential for error, and the effect that error could have on related decisions.

7. Stephanie Anderson Forrest, "There's Gold in Those Hills of Soda Bottles," *Business Week*, 11 September 1995, 48.
6. John P. Callan, Wesley N. Tredup, Randy S. Wissinger. "Elgin Sweeper Company's Journey Toward Cost Management," *Management Accounting* (July 1991): 24–27.

S UMMARY OF LEARNING OBJECTIVES

1. Define and describe cost behavior and explain the role of the resource usage model in understanding cost behavior.

Cost behavior is the way in which a cost changes in relation to changes in activity usage. The time horizon is important in deter-

mining cost behavior because costs can change from fixed to variable depending on whether the decision takes place over the short run or the long run. Variable costs are those that change in total as activity usage changes. Usually, we assume that variable costs increase in direct proportion to increases in activity usage.

Fixed costs are those that do not change in total as activity usage changes. Mixed costs have both a variable and a fixed component. The resource usage model adds additional understanding of cost behavior. Resources acquired in advance of usage are categorized as committed fixed and discretionary fixed expenses. Resources acquired as used and needed are variable expenses. Some costs, especially discretionary fixed costs, tend to follow a step-cost function. These resources are acquired in lumpy amounts. If the width of the step is sufficiently large, then the costs are viewed as fixed; otherwise they are approximated by a variable cost function.

2. Separate mixed costs into their fixed and variable components using the high-low method, the scatterplot method, and the method of least squares.

There are three formal methods of decomposing mixed costs: the high-low method, the scatterplot method, and the method of least squares. In the high-low method, the two points chosen from the scattergraph are the high and the low points with respect to activity level. These two points are then used to compute the intercept and the slope of the line on which they lie. The high-low method is objective and easy. However, if either the high or low point is not representative of the true cost relationship, the relationship will be misestimated.

The scatterplot method involves inspecting a scattergraph (a plot showing total mixed cost at various activity levels) and selecting two points that seem best to represent the relationship between cost and activity. Since two points determine a line, the two selected points can be used to determine the intercept and the slope of the line on which they lie. The intercept gives an estimate of the fixed-cost component and the slope an estimate of the variable cost per unit of activity. The scatterplot method is a good way to identify nonlinearity, the presence of outliers, and the presence of a shift in the cost relationship. Its disadvantage is that it is subjective.

The method of least squares uses all of the data points (except outliers) on the scattergraph and produces a line that best fits all of the points. The line is best fitting in the sense that it is closest to all the points as measured by the sum of the squared deviations of the points from the line. The method of least squares produces the line that best fits the data points and is, therefore, recommended over the high-low and scatterplot methods.

3. Evaluate the reliability of a cost equation.

The least-squares method has the advantage of offering methods to assess the reliability of cost equations. The coefficient of determination allows an analyst to compute the amount of cost variability explained by a particular cost driver. The correlation coefficient also measures the strength of the association but has the additional advantage of indicating the direction of the relationship.

4. Explain the role of multiple regression in assessing cost behavior.

One driver may not be sufficient in explaining enough of the variability in activity cost behavior. In this case, adding additional variables to the equation may increase its ability to predict activity costs as well as provide insights on how activity cost can be managed.

5. Describe the use of managerial judgment in determining cost behavior.

Managerial judgment can be used alone or in conjunction with the high-low, scatterplot, or least-squares method. Managers use their experience and knowledge of cost and activity-level relationships to identify outliers, understand structural shifts, and adjust parameters due to anticipated changing conditions.

K EY TERMS

Activity capacity *68*
Activity rate *74*
Best-fitting line *83*
Coefficient of correlation *85*
Coefficient of
    determination *85*
Committed fixed expenses
    69
Cost behavior *68*
Cost formula *80*

Cost of resource usage *74*
Cost of unused activity *74*
Dependent variable *77*
Deviation *82*
Discretionary fixed
    expenses *70*
Goodness of fit *84*
High-low method *78*
Independent variable *77*
Intercept parameter *77*

Long run *68*
Method of least squares *83*
Multiple regression *87*
Practical capacity *69*
Resources *69*
Resource spending *69*
Resources supplied as used
    and needed *69*
Resources supplied in
    advance of usage *69*

Resource usage *69*
Scattergraph *79*
Scatterplot method *78*
Short run *68*
Slope parameter *77*
Step-cost function *73*
Step-fixed cost *74*
Step-variable cost *73*
Unused capacity *69*

R EVIEW PROBLEMS

I. Resource Usage and Cost Behavior Kaylin Manufacturing Company has three salaried accounts payable clerks responsible for processing purchase invoices. Each clerk is paid a salary of $30,000 and is capable of processing 5,000 invoices per year (working efficiently). In addition to the salaries, Kaylin spends $9,000 per year for forms, postage, checks, and so on (assuming 15,000 invoices are processed). During the year, 12,500 invoices were processed.

REQUIRED:
1. Calculate the activity rate for the purchase order activity. Break the activity into fixed and variable components.
2. Compute the total activity availability and break this into activity usage and unused activity.
3. Calculate the total cost of resources supplied and break this into activity usage and unused activity.

Solution

1.
$$\text{Activity rate} = \frac{[(3 \times \$30,000) + \$9,000]}{15,000}$$
$$= \$6.60 \text{ per invoice}$$

$$\text{Fixed rate} = \frac{\$90,000}{15,000}$$
$$= \$6.00 \text{ per invoice}$$

$$\text{Variable rate} = \frac{\$9,000}{15,000}$$
$$= \$0.60 \text{ per invoice}$$

2.
$$\text{Activity availability} = \text{Activity usage} + \text{Unused capacity}$$
$$15,000 \text{ invoices} = 12,500 \text{ invoices} + 2,500 \text{ invoices}$$

3.
$$\text{Cost of activity supplied} = \text{Cost of activity used} + \text{Cost of unused activity}$$
$$\$90,000 + (\$0.60 \times 12,500) = (\$6.60 \times 12,500) + (\$6.00 \times 2,500)$$
$$\$97,500 = \$82,500 + \$15,000$$

II. High-Low and Method of Least Squares Kim Wilson, controller for Max Enterprises, has decided to estimate the fixed and variable components associated with the company's shipping activity. She has collected the following data for the past six months:

Packages Shipped	Total Shipping Costs
10	$ 800
20	1,100
15	900
12	900
18	1,050
25	1,250

REQUIRED:

1. Estimate the fixed and variable components for the shipping costs using the high-low method. Using the cost formula, predict the total cost of shipping if 14 packages are shipped.
2. Estimate the fixed and variable components using the method of least squares. Using the cost formula, predict the total cost of shipping if 14 packages are shipped.
3. For the method of least squares, compute the coefficient of determination and the coefficient of correlation.

Solution

1. The estimate of fixed and variable costs using the high-low method, where Y = total cost and X = number of hours, is as follows:

$$V = \frac{(Y_2 - Y_1)}{(X_2 - X_1)}$$
$$= \frac{(1,250 - 800)}{(25 - 10)}$$
$$= \frac{450}{15}$$
$$= \$30 \text{ per package}$$

$$F = Y_2 - VX_2$$
$$= \$1,250 - \$30(25)$$
$$= \$500$$

$$Y = \$500 + \$30X$$
$$= \$500 + \$30(14)$$
$$= \$920$$

2. The calculation using the method of least squares is as follows:

ΣX^2	ΣX	ΣY	ΣXY
100	10	$ 800	$ 8,000
400	20	1,100	22,000
225	15	900	13,500
144	12	900	10,800
324	18	1,050	18,900
625	25	1,250	31,250
1,818	100	$6,000	$104,450

$$V = \frac{[\Sigma XY - \Sigma X \Sigma Y/n]}{[\Sigma X^2 - (\Sigma X)^2/n]}$$

$$= \frac{[104,450 - (100 \times 6,000/6)]}{[1,818 - (100 \times 100/6)]}$$

$$= \frac{4,450}{151.33}$$

$$= \$29.41 \text{ per package}$$

$$F = \frac{\Sigma Y}{n} - V\left(\frac{\Sigma X}{n}\right)$$

$$= \frac{6,000}{6} - 29.41\left(\frac{100}{6}\right)$$

$$= \$509.83$$

$$Y = 509.83 + 29.41X$$
$$= 509.83 + 29.41(14)$$
$$= \$921.57$$

3. The computation of the coefficient of determination (R^2) and the correlation coefficient (r) is as follows:

ΣY^2
$ 640,000
1,210,000
810,000
810,000
1,102,500
1,562,500
$6,135,000

$$R^2 = \frac{[v(\Sigma XY - \Sigma X \Sigma Y/n)]}{[\Sigma Y^2 - (\Sigma Y)^2/n]}$$

$$= \frac{29.41(4,450)}{(6,135,000 - 6,000,000)}$$

$$= 0.969$$

$$r = \sqrt{0.969}$$
$$= 0.984$$

QUESTIONS FOR WRITING AND DISCUSSION

1. Why is knowledge of cost behavior important for managerial decision making? Give an example to illustrate your answer.

2. How does the length of the time horizon affect the classification of cost as fixed or variable? What is the meaning of short run? long run?

3. Explain the difference between resource spending and resource usage.
4. What is the relationship between resources supplied as needed and cost behavior?
5. What is the relationship between resources supplied in advance of usage and cost behavior?
6. Explain the difference between committed and discretionary fixed costs. Give examples of each.
7. Describe the difference between a variable cost and a step-variable cost. When is it reasonable to treat step-variable costs as if they were variable costs?
8. What is the difference between a step-fixed cost and a step-variable cost?
9. What is an activity rate?
10. Why do mixed costs pose a problem when it comes to classifying costs into fixed and variable categories?
11. Why is a scattergraph a good first step in decomposing mixed costs into their fixed and variable components?
12. Describe how the scatterplot method breaks out the fixed and variable costs from a mixed cost. Now describe how the high-low method works. How do the two methods differ?

13. What are the advantages of the scatterplot method over the high-low method? the high-low method over the scatterplot method?
14. Describe the method of least squares. Why is this method better than either the high-low method or the scatterplot method?
15. What is meant by the "best-fitting line"?
16. Is the best-fitting line necessarily a good-fitting line? Explain.
17. Describe what is meant by "goodness of fit." Explain the meaning of the coefficient of determination.
18. What is the difference between the coefficient of determination and the coefficient of correlation? Which of the two measures of goodness of fit do you prefer? Why?
19. When is multiple regression required to explain cost behavior?
20. Some firms assign mixed costs to either the fixed or variable cost categories without using any formal methodology to separate them. Explain how this practice can be defended.

 ARM-UP EXERCISES

This section provides short warm-up exercises based on the examples in the chapter. Each warm-up exercise gives the page number on which the text example can be found. You may want to refer to the text example to see how the exercise can be set up and solved.

W3-1
Resources Acquired in Advance; Step-Cost Function
LO 1
pp. 74–75

Jackson Company has three accounts payable clerks, each capable of processing 5,000 invoices per year. Each clerk receives a salary of $35,000 per year.

REQUIRED:
1. Prepare a graph for the clerical cost function. Identify the relevant operating range. Would you classify this as a variable or fixed cost? Explain.
2. Do the clerks represent a resource acquired as used and needed? If not, how would you classify the resource? Explain.

W3-2
Resource Usage Model
LO 1
p. 75

Refer to W3-1. Suppose that during the year the three clerks processed 12,000 orders.

REQUIRED:
1. Use Equation 3.1 to illustrate the relationship between resources supplied and resources used in physical terms.
2. Use Equation 3.2 to illustrate the relationship between resources supplied and resources used in financial terms.

W3-3
Separation of Mixed Costs
LO 2
pp. 77–78

Suppose that you have the following data:

Inspection Cost	Inspection Hours
$120	10
220	20
320	30
440	40
500	50

REQUIRED: Prepare a cost formula using the high-low method.

W3-4 **Separation of Mixed Costs** LO 2 p. 83–84	Refer to W3-3. REQUIRED: Prepare a cost formula using the method of least squares.
W3-5 **Reliability of Equation** LO 3 p. 85	Refer to W3-3. REQUIRED: Compute the coefficient of determination. Comment on its usefulness to evaluate the reliability of the equation computed in W3-3.

E XERCISES

E3-1
Resource Usage Model and Cost Behavior
LO 1

For the following activities and their associated resources, identify: (1) an activity driver, (2) resources acquired as needed, (3) resources acquired in advance of usage (long-term), and (4) resources acquired in advance of usage (short-term). Also, label each resource as one of the following with respect to the cost driver: (1) variable, (2) committed fixed, or (3) discretionary fixed.

Activity	Resource Description
Maintenance	Equipment, labor, parts
Inspection	Test equipment, inspectors (each inspector can inspect five batches per day), units inspected (process requires destructive sampling)*
Packing	Materials, labor (each packer places five units in a box), conveyor belt
Payable Processing	Clerks, materials, equipment, and facility
Assembly	Conveyor belt, supervision (one supervisor for every three assembly lines), direct labor, materials

*Destructive sampling occurs whenever it is necessary to destroy a unit as inspection occurs.

E3-2
Resource Supply and Usage; Activity Rates; Service Organization
LO 1

Alva Community Hospital has five laboratory technicians who are responsible for doing a series of standard blood tests. Each technician is paid a salary of $30,000 and is capable of processing 4,000 tests per year. The lab facility represents a recent addition to the hospital and cost $300,000. It is expected to last 20 years. Equipment used for the testing cost $10,000 and has a life expectancy of 5 years. Both facility and equipment are depreciated on a straight-line basis. In addition to the salaries, facility, and equipment, Alva expects to spend $200,000 for chemicals, forms, power, and other supplies (assuming 20,000 tests are processed). During the year, 16,000 blood tests were run.

REQUIRED:
1. Classify the resources associated with the blood-testing activity into one of the following: (1) long-term resources supplied in advance, (2) short-term resources supplied in advance, or (3) resources supplied as needed.
2. Calculate the activity rate for the blood-testing activity. Break the activity rate into fixed and variable components.
3. Compute the total activity availability and break this into activity usage and unused activity.
4. Calculate the total cost of resources supplied and break this into the cost of activity used and the cost of unused activity.

E3-3
Step Costs; Relevant Range
LO 1

Harker produces large industrial machinery. Harker has a machining department and a group of direct laborers called machinists. Each machinist is paid $24,000 and can machine up to 250 units per year. Harker also hires supervisors to develop machine specification plans and to oversee production within the machining department. Given the planning and supervisory work, a supervisor can oversee at most three machinists. Harker's accounting and production history reveals the following relationships between units produced and the costs of materials handling and supervision (measured on an annual basis):

Units Produced	Direct Labor	Supervision
0–250	$ 24,000	$ 40,000
250–500	48,000	40,000
500–750	72,000	40,000
750–1,000	96,000	80,000
1,000–1,250	120,000	80,000
1,250–1,500	144,000	80,000
1,500–1,750	168,000	120,000
1,750–2,000	192,000	120,000

REQUIRED:

1. Prepare two graphs, one that illustrates the relationship between direct labor cost and units produced and one that illustrates the relationship between the cost of supervision and units produced. Let cost be the vertical axis and units produced the horizontal axis.
2. How would you classify each cost? Why?
3. Suppose that the normal range of activity is between 1,250 and 1,500 units, and that the exact number of machinists is currently hired to support this level of activity. Further suppose that production for the next year is expected to increase by an additional 500 units. By how much will the cost of direct labor increase (and how will this increase be realized)? supervision?

E3-4
Cost Behavior;
Classification and
Graphing
LO 1

PLW Concrete Company owns 10 ready-mix trucks. Each truck can deliver (on average) 10,000 cubic yards of concrete per year (considering the truck's capacity, weather, and distance to each job). One driver per truck is needed. The labor cost for each driver is $25,000 per year. Depreciation on each truck averages $20,000. Raw materials (cement, gravel, and so on) cost about $25 per cubic yard of concrete.

REQUIRED:

1. Prepare a graph for each of three costs: truck drivers' wages, truck depreciation, and raw materials. Use the vertical axis for cost and the horizontal axis for concrete sold per year. Assume concrete sales can range from 0 to 100,000 cubic yards.
2. How would you classify each of the three types of cost? Why? Assume that the normal operating range for the company is 80,000 to 90,000 cubic yards. Does this change your cost classification? Why?

E3-5
Scatterplot Method;
Service Setting
LO 2

Betty Yeager has been operating a dental practice for the past five years. As part of her practice, she provides a dental hygiene service. She has found that her costs for this service increase with patient load. Costs for this service over the past eight months are as follows:

Month	Patients Served	Total Cost
May	320	$2,000
June	480	2,500
July	600	3,000
August	200	1,900
September	720	4,500
October	560	2,900
November	630	3,400
December	300	2,200

REQUIRED:

1. Prepare a scattergraph based on these data. Use cost for the vertical axis and number of patients for the horizontal. Based on an examination of the scattergraph, does there appear to be a linear relationship between the cost of dental hygiene services and patients served?
2. Upon examining the scattergraph, suppose that a cost analyst decides that the points (560, 2,900) and (300, 2,200) best describe the relationship between costs and activity. Determine

the equation of this line. What points would you have chosen? What is the equation of your line?

3. Assume that 450 patients are expected to receive dental hygiene services in January. Using the equation you found in requirement 2 (based on the analyst's selection), what is the predicted cost of dental hygiene services for that month?

E3-6

High-Low Method

LO 2

Refer to the data in E3-5. (*Note*: Either do E3-5 before this exercise or exclude requirement 3.)

REQUIRED:

1. Compute the cost formula for dental hygiene services using the high-low method.
2. Calculate the predicted cost of dental hygiene services for January for 450 patients using the formula found in requirement 1.
3. Which cost formula—the one you computed using the scatterplot method or the one using the high-low method—do you think is the best? Explain.

E3-7

Method of Least Squares

LO 2, LO 3

Refer to the data in E3-5.

REQUIRED:

1. Compute the cost formula for dental hygiene services using the method of least squares.
2. Using the formula computed in requirement 1, what is the predicted cost of dental hygiene services for January for 450 patients?
3. Compute the coefficient of determination. What does this measure tell you about the cost formula computed in requirement 1?

E3-8

High-Low Method; Cost Formulas

LO 2

During the past year, the high and low levels of resource usage occurred in April and October (for three different resources). The three resources are associated with the machining activity. Machine hours is the activity driver. The total costs of the three resources, and the activity output, as measured by machine hours for the two different levels follow:

Activity	Machine Hours	Total Cost
Machine depreciation		
Low	10,000	$130,000
High	25,000	130,000
Power usage		
Low	10,000	13,000
High	25,000	32,500
Drilling labor		
Low	10,000	22,000
High	25,000	37,000

REQUIRED:

1. Determine the cost behavior of each resource. Use the high-low method to assess the fixed and variable components.
2. Using your knowledge of cost behavior, predict the cost of each item for an activity output level of 15,000 machine-hours.
3. Construct a cost formula that can be used to predict the total cost of the three resources combined. Using this formula, predict the total machining cost if activity usage (output) is 18,000 direct labor hours. In general, when can cost formulas be combined to form a single cost formula?

E3-9

Method of Least Squares; Evaluation of Cost Equation

LO 2, LO 3

The method of least squares was used to develop a cost equation to predict the cost of purchasing goods. Eighty data points were used for the regression. The following computer output was received:

Intercept	$30,500
Slope	10
Coefficient of correlation	0.85
Standard error	$1,500

The driver used was "number of purchase orders."

REQUIRED:
1. What is the cost formula?
2. Using the cost formula, predict the cost of purchasing if 10,000 orders are processed.
3. What percentage of the variability in purchasing cost is explained by number of purchase orders? Do you think the equation will predict well? Why or why not?

E3-10
Multiple Regression
LO 4

Materhorn, a manufacturer of VCRs, is interested in determining the cost of its warranty repair activity. Two cost drivers have been identified that are believed to be important in explaining the cost of this activity: the number of defective products produced and the hours of inspection. To see if the belief is valid, the company's cost analysts gather 100 weeks of data and run a multiple regression analysis. The following printout is obtained:

Parameter	Estimate	t for H_o Parameter $= 0$	$Pr > t$	Std Error of Parameter
Intercept	2,000	80.00	.0001	25.000
Number of defects	60	2.58	.0050	23.256
Inspection hours	−10	−1.96	.0250	5.103

$R^2 = 0.88$
$S_e = 150$
Observations 100

REQUIRED:
1. Write out the cost equation for Materhorn's warranty repair activity.
2. If Materhorn expects to have 100 defects per week and to spend 150 hours on inspection, what are the anticipated warranty repair costs?
3. Is number of defects positively or negatively correlated with warranty repair costs? Are inspection hours positively or negatively correlated with quality control costs?
4. What does R^2 mean in this equation? Overall, what is your evaluation of the cost equation that was developed for the warranty repair activity?

E3-11
Cost Behavior Patterns
LO 1

The graphs on page 97 represent cost behavior patterns that might occur in a company's cost structure. The vertical axis represents total cost and the horizontal axis represents activity output.

REQUIRED: For each of the following situations, choose the graph that best illustrates the cost pattern involved. Also, for each situation identify the driver that measures activity usage.

1. The cost of power when a fixed fee of $500 per month is charged plus an additional charge of $0.12 per kilowatt-hour used.
2. Commissions paid to sales representatives. Commissions are paid at the rate of 5 percent of sales made up to total annual sales of $500,000, and 7 percent of sales above $500,000.
3. A part purchased from an outside supplier costs $12 per part for the first 3,000 parts and $10 per part for all parts purchased in excess of 3,000 units.
4. The cost of surgical gloves purchased in increments of 100 units (gloves come in boxes of 100 pairs).
5. The cost of tuition at a local college that charges $250 per credit hour up to 15 credit hours. Hours taken in excess of 15 are free.
6. The cost of tuition at another college that charges $4,500 per semester for any course load ranging from 12 to 16 credit hours. Students taking fewer than 12 credit hours are charged

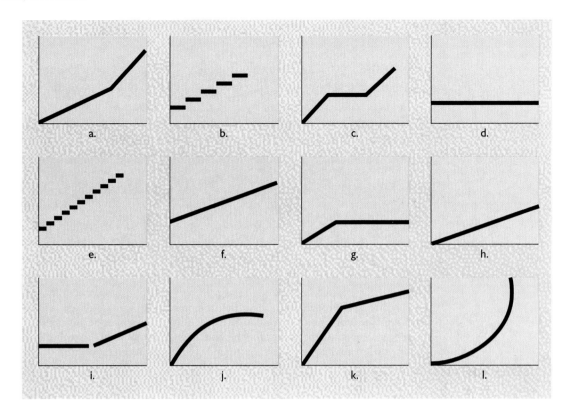

$375 per credit hour. Students taking more than 16 credit hours are charged $4,500 plus $300 per credit hour in excess of 16.

7. A beauty shop's purchase of soaking solution to remove artificial nails. Each jar of solution can soak off approximately 50 nails before losing effectiveness.

8. The purchase of diagnostics equipment by a company for inspection of incoming orders.

9. Use of disposable gowns by patients in a hospital.

10. The cost of labor at a local fast-food restaurant. Three employees are always on duty during working hours; more employees can be called in during periods of heavy demand to work on an "as-needed" basis.

11. A manufacturer found that maintenance cost of its heavy machinery was tied to the age of the equipment. Experience indicated that maintenance cost increased at an increasing rate as the equipment aged.

PROBLEMS

P3-1
Cost Behavior;
Resource Usage
Model
LO 1

Rolertyme Company manufactures roller skates. With the exception of the rollers, all parts of the skates are produced internally. Neeta Booth, president of Rolertyme, has decided to make the rollers instead of buying them from external suppliers. The company needs 100,000 sets per year (currently it pays $1.90 per set of rollers).

The rollers can be produced using an available area within the plant. Equipment, however, for production of the rollers would need to be leased ($30,000 per-year lease payment). Additionally, it would cost $0.50 per machine-hour for power, oil, and other operating expenses. The equipment will provide 60,000 machine-hours per year. Direct material costs will average $0.75 per set of four and direct labor will average $0.25 per set. Since only one type of roller would be produced, there would be no additional demands made on the setup activity. Other overhead activities (besides machining and setups), however, would be affected. The company's cost management system provides the following information about the current status of the overhead activities that would be affected (the supply and demand figures do not include the effect of roller production on these activities). The lumpy quantity indicates how much capacity must be purchased should any expansion of activity supply be needed. The purchase price is the cost of acquiring the capacity represented by the lumpy quantity. This price also represents the cost of current spending on the existing activity supply (for each block of activity).

Activity	Activity Driver	Supply	Usage	Lumpy Quantity	Purchase Price
Purchasing	Orders	25,000	22,000	5,000	$25,000
Inspection	Hours	10,000	9,000	2,000	30,000
Material handling	Moves	4,500	4,300	500	15,000

The demands that production of rollers would place on the overhead activities follow:

Activity	Resource Demands
Machine	50,000 machine hours
Purchasing	2,000 purchase orders (associated with raw materials used to make the rollers)
Inspection	750 inspection hours
Material handling	500 moves

Producing the rollers also means that the purchase of outside rollers will cease. By not purchasing the rollers, purchase orders (associated with the outside acquisition of rollers) will drop by 5,000. Similarly, the moves for the handling of incoming orders will decrease by 200. The company has not inspected the rollers purchased from outside suppliers.

REQUIRED:
1. Classify all resources associated with the production of rollers as resources acquired as needed and resources acquired in advance of usage. For those resources acquired in advance of usage, label them as short-term and long-term commitments. How should we describe the cost behavior of these short-term and long-term resource commitments? Explain.
2. Calculate the total annual resource spending (for all overhead activities except for setups) that the company will incur after production of the rollers begins. Break this cost into fixed and variable activity costs. In calculating these figures, assume that the company will spend no more than necessary. What is the effect on resource spending caused by production of the rollers (include the effect of materials and labor)?
3. Refer to requirement 2. For each activity, break down the cost of activity supplied into the cost of activity usage and the cost of unused activity.
4. Prepare a graph for the cost function associated with each of the following two activities: (a) machining and (b) purchasing.

P3-2

Cost Behavior; High-Low Method; Pricing Decision

LO 1, LO 2

Monson Medical Clinic offers a number of specialized medical services, one of which is cancer care. Because of the reputation the clinic's physicians (oncologists) have developed over the years, demand for these services is strong. As a result, Monson recently added a 100-bed cancer wing to the clinic. The cost of the cancer facility is depreciated on a straight-line basis. All equipment within the facility is leased.

Since the clinic had no experience with inpatient cancer services, it decided to operate the cancer-care center for two months before determining how much to charge per patient day on an ongoing basis. As a temporary measure, the clinic adopted a patient-day charge of $100, an amount equal to the charges made by a hospital specializing in cancer care in a nearby city.

This initial per-day charge was quoted to patients entering the cancer-care center during the first two months with assurances that if the actual operating costs of the new center justified it, the charge could be less. In no case would the charges be more. A temporary policy of billing after 60 days was adopted so that adjustments could be made if necessary.

The cancer-care center opened on January 1. During January, the center had 2,100 patient days of activity. During February, the activity was 2,250 patient days. Costs for these two levels of activity usage are as follows:

	2,100 Patient Days	2,250 Patient Days
Salaries, nurses	$ 6,000	$ 6,000
Aides	1,200	1,200

	2,100 Patient Days	2,250 Patient Days
Laboratory	$110,000	$117,500
Pharmacy	31,000	32,500
Depreciation	11,800	11,800
Laundry	16,800	18,000
Administration	12,000	12,000
Lease (equipment)	30,000	30,000

REQUIRED:
1. Classify each cost as fixed, variable, or mixed, using patient days as the activity driver.
2. Use the high-low method to separate the mixed costs into their fixed and variable components.
3. Karl Johnson, the administrator of the cancer center, has estimated that the center will average 2,000 patient days per month. If the center is to be operated as a nonprofit organization, how much will it need to charge per patient day? How much of this charge is variable? How much is fixed?
4. Suppose the cancer center averages 2,500 patient days per month. How much would need to be charged per patient day for the center to cover its costs? Explain why the per-patient-day charge decreased as the activity output increased.

P3-3
High-Low Method;
Method of Least
Squares; Correlation
LO 2, LO 3, LO 5

Farnsworth Company has gathered data on its overhead activities and associated costs for the past ten months. Tracy Heppler, a member of the controller's department, has convinced management that overhead costs can be better estimated and controlled if the fixed and variable components of each overhead activity are known. Tracy has identified 150 different activities and has grouped them into sets based on her belief that they share a common driver. (This classification process has reduced the number of cost formulas needed from 150 to 25.) For example, she has decided that unloading incoming goods, counting goods, and inspecting goods can be grouped together as a more general receiving activity based on her belief that the costs of the three related activities are all driven by the same driver, number of purchase orders. To confirm her activity classification and driver assignment, she has gathered data for each set of activities. Ten months of data have been gathered for the receiving activity:

Month	Number of Receiving Orders	Receiving Cost
1	1,000	$18,000
2	700	15,000
3	1,500	28,000
4	1,200	17,000
5	1,300	25,000
6	1,100	18,000
7	1,600	30,000
8	1,400	24,000
9	1,700	21,000
10	900	15,000

REQUIRED:
1. Prepare a scattergraph, plotting the receiving costs against the number of receiving orders. Use the vertical axis for costs and the horizontal for orders.
2. Select two points that make the best fit and compute a cost formula for receiving costs.
3. Using the high-low method, prepare a cost formula for the receiving activity.
4. Using the method of least squares, prepare a cost formula for the receiving activity. What is the coefficient of determination?

P3-4
Cost Formulas;
Single and Multiple
Cost Drivers;
Coefficient of
Correlation
LO 1, LO 3, LO 4

Kimball Company has developed the following cost formulas:

Material usage: $Y_m = \$80X$, $r = 0.95$
Labor usage (direct): $Y_l = \$20X$, $r = 0.96$

Overhead activity: $Y_o = \$350,000 + \$100X, r = 0.75$
Selling activity: $Y_s = \$50,000 + \$10X, r = 0.93$

where X = direct labor hours

The company has a policy of producing on demand and keeps very little, if any, finished goods inventory (thus, units produced = units sold).

The president of Kimball Company has recently implemented a policy that any special orders will be accepted if they cover the costs that the orders cause. This policy was implemented because Kimball's industry is in a recession and the company is producing well below capacity (and expects to continue doing so for the coming year). The president is willing to accept orders that at least cover their variable costs so that the company can keep its employees and avoid layoffs. Also, any orders above variable costs will increase overall profitability of the company.

REQUIRED:
1. Compute the total unit variable cost. Suppose that Kimball has an opportunity to accept an order for 20,000 units at $220 per unit. Each unit uses one direct labor hour for production. Should Kimball accept the order? (The order would not displace any of Kimball's regular orders.)
2. Explain the significance of the coefficient of correlation measures for the cost formulas. Did these measures have a bearing on your answer in requirement 1? Should they have a bearing? Why?
3. Suppose that a multiple regression equation is developed for overhead costs: $Y = \$100,000 + \$100X_1 + \$5,000X_2 + \$300X_3$, where X_1 = direct labor hours, X_2 = number of setups, and X_3 = engineering hours. The correlation coefficient for the equation is 0.94. Assume that the order of 20,000 units requires 12 setups and 600 engineering hours. Given this new information, should the company accept the special order referred to in requirement 1? Is there any other information about cost behavior that you would like to have? Explain.

P3-5
Scattergraph; High-Low Method; Method of Least Squares
LO 2, LO 3

The management of Franklin Company has decided to develop cost formulas for its major overhead activities. Franklin uses a highly automated manufacturing process, and power usage is considered a major resource used by the machining activity. Power costs are a significant manufacturing cost. Cost analysts have decided that power costs are mixed; thus, they must be broken into their fixed and variable elements so that the cost behavior of power usage can be properly described. Machine hours have been selected as the driver for power costs. The following data for the past eight quarters have been collected:

Quarter	Machine Hours	Power Cost
1	20,000	$26,000
2	25,000	38,000
3	30,000	42,500
4	22,000	37,000
5	21,000	34,000
6	18,000	29,000
7	24,000	36,000
8	28,000	40,000

REQUIRED:
1. Prepare a scattergraph by plotting power costs against machine hours. Fit a line to the data set; select two points and determine the cost formula for power.
2. Using the high and low points, compute a power cost formula.
3. Use the method of least squares to compute a power cost formula. Also compute the coefficient of determination.
4. Compute the expected cost for 23,000 machine hours using each of the three formulas. Which cost formula would you recommend? Explain.

P3-6
Method of Least Squares
LO 1, LO 2, LO 3

Dotter Company is developing a cost formula for its packing activity. Past experience has convinced management that packing costs and the number of customer orders are highly correlated.

Data for the past 20 months have been gathered and the following expressions have been computed:

$$\Sigma X = 40,000 \qquad \Sigma XY = \$1,200,000,000 \qquad \Sigma X^2 = 120,000,000 \qquad \Sigma Y = \$500,000$$

REQUIRED:
1. Using the method of least squares, determine the packing cost formula.
2. Suppose that $\Sigma Y^2 = 13,600,000,000$. Is the management of Dotter Company justified in assuming that packing costs and customer orders are highly correlated?
3. Predict the total packing cost for 2,000 customer orders. How much of this total cost is a fixed activity cost? How much is variable? Now suppose that the fixed activity cost provides an activity capacity for processing 2,500 orders. What is the cost of the unused activity for a level of 2,000 orders?

P3-7
High-Low Method;
Scatterplot
LO 2, LO 5

Weber Valley Regional Hospital has collected data on all of its activities for the past seven months. Data for cardiac nursing care follow:

Month	Cost	Hours of Nursing Care
September 1997	$69,500	1,700
October 1997	64,250	1,550
November 1997	52,000	1,200
December 1997	66,000	1,600
January 1998	83,000	1,800
February 1998	66,550	1,330
March 1998	79,500	1,700

REQUIRED:
1. Using the high-low method, calculate the variable rate per hour and the fixed cost for the nursing-care activity.
2. Prepare a scatterplot for the nursing-care activity using the given data. (*Hint:* Use one symbol, perhaps an "x," for observations occurring in 1997, and another symbol for observations occurring in 1998.)
3. Upon looking into the events that happened at the end of 1997, you find that the cardiology ward bought a cardiac-monitoring machine for the nursing station. A decision was also made to add a new supervisory position for the evening shift. Monthly depreciation on the monitor and the salary of the new supervisor total $10,000. Now, using the scatterplot from requirement 2, calculate the fixed cost and variable rate applicable to October 1997; calculate the fixed cost and variable rate applicable to March 1998. Discuss your findings. Which cost formula should be used to budget the cost of the cardiac nursing care activity for the remainder of 1998?

P3-8
Comparison of
Regression Equations
LO 1, LO 2, LO 5

Loving Toys Company is attempting to determine cost behavior of its overhead activities for its Kansas City plant. One of the major activities is the setup activity. Two possible drivers have been mentioned: setup hours and number of setups. The plant controller has accumulated the following data for the setup activity:

Month	Setup Costs	Setup Hours	Number of Setups
February	$ 7,700	2,000	70
March	7,650	2,100	50
April	10,052	3,000	50
May	9,400	2,700	60
June	9,584	3,000	20
July	8,480	2,500	40
August	8,550	2,400	60
September	9,735	2,900	50
October	10,500	3,000	90

REQUIRED:

1. Estimate a cost equation with setup hours as the driver and only independent variable. If the Kansas City plant forecasts 2,600 setup hours for the next month, what will the budgeted setup cost be?

2. Estimate an equation with number of setups as the cost driver and only independent variable. If the Kansas City plant forecasts 80 setups for the next month, what will the budgeted setup cost be?

3. Which of the two regression equations do you think does a better job of predicting setup costs? Explain.

4. The multiple regression equation using both setup hours and number of setups as independent variables follows:

$$Y = \$1,493.27 + \$2.61 \text{ (setup hours)} + \$13.71 \text{ (setups)} \quad R^2 = 0.998$$

Calculate the budgeted cost using the multiple regression equation. Would you recommend using the multiple-driver equation over a single-driver equation? Explain.

MANAGERIAL DECISION CASES

C3-1
Simple and Multiple Regression; Evaluating Reliability of Equation
LO 2, LO 3, LO 4

The Lockit Company manufactures doorknobs for residential homes and apartments. Lockit is considering the use of simple (single driver) and multiple regression analysis to forecast annual sales because previous forecasts have been inaccurate. The sales forecast will be used to initiate the budgeting process and to identify better the underlying process that generates sales.

Larry Husky, the controller of Lockit, has considered many possible independent variables and equations to predict sales and has narrowed his choices to four equations. Larry used annual observations from 20 prior years to estimate each of the four equations.

Following is a definition of the variables used in the four equations and a statistical summary of these equations:

$$S_t = \text{Forecasted sales in dollars for Lockit in period } t$$
$$S_{t-1} = \text{Actual sales in dollars for Lockit in period } t-1$$
$$G_t = \text{Forecasted U.S. gross domestic product in period } t$$
$$G_{t-1} = \text{Actual U.S. gross domestic product in period } t-1$$
$$N_{t-1} = \text{Lockit's net income in period } t-1$$

Statistical Summary of Four Equations

Equation	Dependent Variable	Independent Variable(s)	Intercept	Independent Variable (rate)	R Square
1	S_t	S_{t-1}	$ 500,000	$ 1.10	0.94
2	S_t	G_t	1,000,000	0.00001	0.90
3	S_t	G_{t-1}	900,000	0.000012	0.81
4	S_t		600,000		0.96
		N_{t-1}		10.00	
		G_t		0.000002	
		G_{t-1}		0.000003	

REQUIRED:

1. Write equations 2 and 4 in the form $Y = F + VX$.
2. If actual sales are $1,500,000 in 1997, what would be the forecasted sales for Lockit in 1998?
3. Explain why Larry Husky might prefer equation 3 to equation 2.
4. Explain the advantages and disadvantages of using equation 4 to forecast sales. (CMA adapted)

C3-2
Suspicious Acquisition of Data; Ethical Issues

Bill Lewis, manager of the Thomas Electronics Division, called a meeting with his controller, Brindon Peterson, CMA, and his marketing manager, Patty Fritz. The following is a transcript of the conversation that took place during the meeting.

Bill: "Brindon, the variable-costing system that you developed has proved to be a big plus for our division. Our success in winning bids has increased and, as a result, our revenues have increased by 25 percent. However, if we intend to meet this year's profit targets, we are going to need something extra—am I not right, Patty?"

Patty: "Absolutely. While we have been able to win more bids, we still are losing too many, particularly to our major competitor, Kilborn Electronics. If I knew more about their bidding strategy, I imagine we could be more successful competing with them."

Bill: "Would knowing their variable costs help?"

Patty: "Certainly. It would give me their minimum price. With that knowledge, I'm sure we could find a way to beat them on several jobs, particularly for those jobs where we are at least as efficient. It would also help us identify where we are not cost competitive. With this information, we might be able to find ways to increase our efficiency."

Bill: "Well, I have good news. I have some data here in these handouts that reveal bids that Kilborn made on several jobs. I have also been able to obtain the direct labor hours worked for many of these jobs. But that's not all. I have monthly totals for manufacturing costs and direct labor hours for all their jobs for the past ten months. Brindon, with this information, can you estimate what the variable manufacturing cost per hour is? If you can, we can compute the variable costs for each job and the markup that Kilborn is using."

Brindon: "Yes, an analysis of the data you're requesting is possible. I have a question, though, before I do this. How did you manage to acquire these data? I can't imagine that Kilborn would willingly release this information."

Bill: "What does it matter how the data were acquired? The fact is, we have them, and we have an opportunity to gain a tremendous competitive advantage. With that advantage, we can meet our profit targets, and we will all end the year with a big bonus."

After the meeting, in a conversation with Patty, Brindon learned that Bill was dating Jackie Wilson, a cost accountant (and CMA) who happened to work for Kilborn. Patty speculated that Jackie might be the source of the Kilborn data. Upon learning this, Brindon expressed some strong reservations to Patty about analyzing the data.

REQUIRED:
1. Assume that Bill did acquire the data from Jackie Wilson. Comment on Jackie's behavior. Which standards of ethical conduct did she violate? (See Chapter 1 for a listing of the ethical code.)
2. Were Brindon's instincts correct—should he have felt some reservations about analyzing the data? Would it be ethical to analyze the data? Do any of the IMA standards of ethical conduct apply? What would you do if you were Brindon? Explain.

Learning Objectives

After studying Chapter 4, you should be able to:

1. Discuss the importance of unit costs.

2. Define actual and normal costing and explain why normal costing is preferred.

3. Describe traditional costing approaches.

4. Explain why traditional costing approaches may produce distorted costs.

5. Explain how an activity-based cost system can produce more accurate product costs.

6. Provide a detailed description of how activities are identified and classified so that homogeneous cost pools can be formed.

7. Describe the role of activity-based costing in a JIT environment.

CHAPTER

Activity-Based Costing

SCENARIO

Ryan Chesser, president and owner of Sharp Paper, Inc., was reviewing the most recent financial reports. Profits had once again declined. The company had failed to achieve its targeted return for the third consecutive year. The inability of the company to improve its profits frustrated Chesser. After all, Sharp Paper had been a dominant factor in the industry for more than two decades. The company owns three paper mills, which produce coated and uncoated specialty printing papers. Customers have access to a variety of papers differing in finish, color, weight, and packages. More than four hundred individual products were marketed by the company.[1]

To ascertain the reasons for the declining fortunes of the company, Ryan had asked his vice-presidents of production (Jeff Clark) and marketing (Jennifer Woodruff) to do some research on why the competition was winning bids on some major product lines in spite of aggressive pricing by Sharp. Four weeks after making the assignment, he received the following report:

MEMO
To: Ryan Chesser, President
From: Jeff Clark and Jennifer Woodruff
Subject: Competitive Position of Sharp
Date: February 12, 1997

Our investigation has revealed some rather interesting information—information that we believe can benefit our company. We began by contacting some customers who have switched some of their purchases to competitors. We discovered that the switch usually involved our high-volume products. We have been losing bids on these products even when they were aggressively priced. Often the loss of business was to smaller competitors with less diverse product lines. Their prices were significantly lower than ours, and, in fact, seemed unrealistically low.

Our next effort was focused on determining whether competitors were employing a new technology that might provide significant cost advantages. Virtually all of our small competitors use the same manufacturing processes that we use. No evidence of significant differences in efficiency emerged.

Curiously, our low-volume products appear to be the most profitable. In some cases, we are the only company that produces these specialty products. At times, we even receive referrals from some of our competitors. But, some of our operational managers have urged us to drop some of these low-volume products, arguing that they're more bother than they're worth. Yet these products are being reported as highly profitable. Our initial discussions with Jan Booth, our controller, failed to reveal any logical reasons explaining why the profit margins of the low-volume products were so much greater than our high-volume products, which seems counterintuitive given the special processes and handling required for the low-volume products. We were even told that we could increase our margin on the low-volume products by increasing prices. Recent price increases were readily accepted by customers—without any complaints.

Yesterday Jan approached us and indicated that she had given some thought to our questions and concerns. She mentioned the possibility that many of our problems may be rooted in the way we are currently assigning costs to products. She noted that we are using a traditional, labor-based cost system and that it may be causing distortions in product costs. Given the results of our other inquiries, this possibility may be worth further investigation.

1. The setting and the issues in this introductory case are based in part on the following three articles: James P. Borden, "Review of Literature on Activity-Based Costing," *Journal of Cost Management for the Manufacturing Industry*, vol. 4, no. 1 (Spring 1990); John K. Shank and Vijay Govindarajan, "Transaction-Based Costing for the Complex Product Line: A Field Study," *Journal of Cost Management for the Manufacturing Industry*, vol. 2, no. 2 (Summer 1988): 31–38; and Robin Cooper, "Does Your Company Need a New Cost System?" *Journal of Cost Management for the Manufacturing Industry*, vol. 1, no. 1 (Spring 1987): 45–49.

Questions to Think About

1. *What are product costs?*
2. *What role do product costs play in bids?*
3. *If product costing is the root of the bidding difficulties, why are the smaller, less diverse firms having more success?*
4. *Why wasn't the controller's office able to explain the high-profit*

margins on the low-volume products?

5. *What is meant by a traditional, labor-based costing system? Why might it cause distortions in product costs?*
6. *Assuming Sharp's problems are founded in the way costs are assigned to products, what can Sharp do to solve the problem?*

UNIT PRODUCT COSTS

Objective 1

Discuss the importance of unit costs.

Consider first an organization that produces a single product. Conceptually, computing the unit product cost is simple. The unit cost is the total cost associated with the units produced divided by the number of units produced. For example, if a construction company builds 100 subdivision homes of the same size and quality and the total cost for these homes is $6 million, then the cost of each home is $60,000 ($6 million/100 homes). Similarly, for a service firm, if Jiffy-Change, a shop that specializes in changing oil, works on 400 autos per month and total costs are $4,000, then the cost per car serviced is $10. Although the concept is simple, the practical reality of the computation can be somewhat more complex. First, what is meant by "total cost"? Does this consist only of production costs? or production costs plus marketing costs? or all costs of the organization? Second, how do we measure the costs to be assigned? Do we use actual costs incurred or estimated costs? Third, how do we associate costs with the product? When only one product is produced, this question is trivial (because all costs incurred are traceable to the product), but when more than one product is produced, the answer is more complex.

The first question is answered by defining what is meant by "product cost." Recall that the product cost definition depends on the managerial objective being served. For example, product cost is often defined as production costs: direct materials, direct labor, and overhead. This product cost definition is mandated for external financial reporting. But, it is also useful for making certain decisions. For example, it can serve as a critical input for establishing bid prices. Furthermore, this common product cost definition can be used to illustrate the differences between traditional and activity-based approaches for assigning costs. The second and third questions are concerned with how costs are measured and assigned to products. Total manufacturing costs must be measured, and then these costs must be associated with the units produced. **Cost measurement** consists of determining the dollar amounts of direct materials, direct labor, and overhead used in production. The dollar amounts may be the actual amounts expended for the manufacturing inputs, or they may be estimated amounts. Often, estimated amounts are used to ensure timeliness of cost information or to control costs. The process of associating the costs, once measured, with the units produced is called **cost assignment**.

cost measurement

cost assignment

Importance of Unit Costs to Manufacturing Firms

A cost accounting system has the purpose of measuring and assigning costs so that the unit cost of a product can be determined. Unit cost is a critical piece of information for a manufacturer. Unit costs are essential for valuing inventory, determining income, and making a number of important decisions. Disclosing the cost of inventories and determining income are financial reporting requirements that a firm faces at the end of each period. In order to report the cost of its inventories, a firm must know the number of units on hand and the unit manufacturing cost. The cost of goods sold, used to determine income, also requires knowledge of the units sold and their unit cost. Unit costs are also important for making a wide variety of decisions. For example, bidding is a common requirement in the markets for custom homes and industrial buildings. It is virtually impossible to submit a meaningful bid without knowing the costs associated with the units to be produced. Product cost information is vital in a number of other areas as well. Decisions concerning product design and introduction of new products are affected by expected unit costs. Decisions to make or buy a product, accept or reject a special order, or keep or drop a product line require unit cost information.

Whether the unit cost is defined using manufacturing costs or variable costs or manufacturing plus nonmanufacturing costs depends on the setting and the purpose for which the information is going to be used. For financial reporting, manufacturing unit cost information is required. If a firm is operating below its production capacity, however, variable cost information may be much more useful in a decision to accept or reject a special order. For strategic planning and analysis, comprehensive cost information may be demanded. Different costs are needed for different purposes.

Importance of Unit Costs to Service Firms

Service firms also require unit cost information. Conceptually, the way we measure and assign costs is the same whether the firm is a manufacturing firm or not. The service firm must first identify the service "unit" that is being provided. In an auto repair shop, the service unit would be the work performed on an individual customer's car. Because each car is different in terms of the work required (an oil change versus a transmission overhaul, for example), the costs must be assigned individually to each job. A hospital may assign costs to patients, patient day, and type of procedure (for example, X ray, complete blood count test). A governmental agency must also identify the service provided. For example, city government might provide household trash pickup and calculate the cost by truck run or by pickup per house.

Service firms use cost data in much the same way that manufacturing firms do. They use costs to determine profitability, the feasibility of introducing new services, making pricing decisions, and so on. However, because service firms do not produce physical products, they do not need to value finished goods inventories. Nonprofit service firms must track costs to be sure that they provide their services in a cost efficient way. 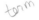 Governmental agencies have a fiduciary responsibility to taxpayers to use funds wisely. This requires accurate accounting for costs.

Production of Unit Cost Information

To produce unit cost information, a product cost definition, cost measurement, and cost assignment are required. Although different product cost definitions are possible, this chapter emphasizes the *production* cost definition: direct materials, direct labor, and overhead. There are also a number of different ways to measure and assign costs. This chapter introduces two measurement systems, actual and normal, and recommends the use of the normal measurement approach. Three assignment systems, two traditional and one contemporary, are also introduced and discussed.

ACTUAL COSTING AND NORMAL COSTING: TWO WAYS TO MEASURE COST

Objective 2

Define actual and normal costing and explain why normal costing is preferred.

There are two commonly used ways to measure the costs associated with production: actual costing and normal costing. *Actual costing* requires the firm to use the actual cost of all resources used in production to determine unit cost. While intuitively reasonable, this method has drawbacks, as we will see. The second method, *normal costing*, requires the firm to apply actual costs of direct materials and direct labor to units produced. However, overhead is applied based on a predetermined estimate. Normal costing is most widely used in practice.

Actual Costing

actual cost system

An actual cost system uses actual costs for direct materials, direct labor, and overhead. These actual costs are then used to determine the unit cost. In practice, strict actual cost systems are rarely used because they cannot provide accurate unit cost information on a *timely* basis. Interestingly, per-unit computation of the direct materials and direct labor costs is not the source of the difficulty. The amount of actual direct materials and direct labor used by a product can be physically observed as the units are produced. Thus, actual prime costs can be assigned using direct tracing and they can be assigned on a timely basis. For these two manufacturing inputs, there are no significant problems with either accuracy or timeliness. The main problem with using actual costs for calculation of unit cost is with manufacturing overhead.

Assigning actual overhead costs creates a conflict between timeliness and accuracy. For example, consider a firm that produces a single product. In this case, we know that all the year's overhead costs belong to the units produced during the year. Thus, if we wait until the end of the year, an accurate cost per unit can be computed simply by dividing the year's overhead costs by the year's production. Unfortunately, waiting until the end of the year to compute an overhead rate is unacceptable. A company needs unit cost information throughout the year. This information is needed on a timely basis both for interim financial statements and to help managers make decisions such as pricing. Most decisions requiring unit cost information cannot wait until the end of the year. Managers must react to day-to-day conditions occurring in the marketplace in order to maintain a sound competitive position.

Some might suggest that more timely overhead cost information can be obtained using the same procedure for a shorter period, say a week or a month (for example, dividing a month's overhead by a month's output). This approach, however, tends to produce unit costs that fluctuate from month to month. This outcome occurs for two major reasons: (1) nonuniform incurrence of overhead and (2) nonuniform production. Many overhead costs are not incurred uniformly throughout the year. Thus, they can differ significantly from one period (month, for example) to the next. Similarly, per-unit overhead costs can fluctuate dramatically because of nonuniform production levels.

To illustrate, consider the following example. Assume a company produces a toy truck made of plastic. Each truck requires 6 ounces of plastic and 15 minutes of direct labor. For the technology used, this input-output relationship is reasonably stable. Thus, the quantity of raw materials and the direct labor used for each toy truck are essentially the same regardless of how many toy trucks are produced or when they are produced. The unit cost of these two inputs can be accurately computed.

If the cost of plastic in January is $0.30 per ounce and the price of labor is $6 per hour, then the cost of plastic per truck is $1.80 ($0.30 × 6 ounces), and the cost of direct labor per truck is $1.50 ($6 × 0.25 hour). The actual prime cost per truck, then, is $1.80 + $1.50, or $3.30. If the prices of materials and labor are reasonably stable, the $3.30 per-unit prime cost is the same regardless of how many trucks are made or when they are produced during the year.

Overhead costs, however, are a different story as the following figures reveal:

	April	August	November
Actual overhead	$20,000	$40,000	$40,000
Actual units produced	40,000	40,000	160,000
Per-unit overhead*	$0.50	$1.00	$0.25

*Actual overhead/Actual production

Notice that the overhead cost per unit is different for each of the three months. April and August have the same production but different monthly overhead costs. The difference in overhead cost could be attributable to higher utility costs due to increased cooling requirements in August. Thus, the toy trucks produced in August have a higher per-unit overhead cost ($1.00 rather than $0.50) just because they happened to be produced when cooling was required. The difference in the per-unit overhead cost is because overhead costs were incurred nonuniformly.

Nonuniform production is the second reason for variability in per-unit overhead costs, as August and November figures show. Both months have the same total monthly overhead costs but different output levels. November's output may be much larger because of anticipation of Christmas sales. Whatever the reason, the higher output in November creates a lower per-unit overhead cost ($0.25 compared to August's $1.00).

Notice that the varying per-unit overhead costs do not signal differences in value, or even in the underlying cost structure. A toy truck produced in April is identical to one produced in August or November. The higher utility costs in August may equal August utility costs of the previous year. The problem of fluctuating per-unit overhead costs can be avoided if the firm waits until the end of the year to assign the overhead costs. For example, if April, August, and November were the only months of operation for the toy truck manufacturer, the total overhead costs for the year are $100,000 ($20,000 + $40,000 + $40,000), and the total production is 240,000 trucks (40,000 + 40,000 + 160,000). The per-unit overhead cost is $100,000/240,000, or $0.417. By waiting until the end of the year, the firm eliminates the problems of nonuniform overhead cost incurrence and nonuniform production. The result is the same overhead cost per unit for every unit produced. But as mentioned, managers cannot wait until the end of the year to know the product cost information.

Normal Costing

Another possible solution is to approximate the end-of-the-year actual overhead rate at the beginning of the year and then use the *predetermined rate* throughout the year to obtain the needed unit cost information. A predetermined overhead rate is calculated using the following formula:

predetermined overhead rate

Overhead rate = Budgeted overhead/Budgeted activity usage

Budgeted overhead is simply the firm's best estimate of the amount of overhead cost to be incurred in the coming year. Thus, the end-of-the-year actual rate can be approximated by estimating the overhead costs for the coming year and dividing these estimated costs by expected production. Suppose, for example, that the toy manufacturer estimates on January 1 that overhead costs for the year will be $90,000 and that expected production is 225,000 units. Using these estimated data, the predetermined overhead rate is $0.40 ($90,000/225,000).

Cost systems that measure overhead costs on a predetermined basis and use actual costs for direct materials and direct labor are called normal costing systems. The principal difficulty with normal costing is that the predetermined rate is likely to differ from the actual rate. Either actual overhead costs differ from the estimated costs or the actual level of production differs from the expected level, or both. If the measurement error is

normal costing systems

small, however, the product cost resulting from normal costing will not differ significantly from the actual product cost determined after the fact. In the preceding example, the predetermined rate was $0.40, and the end-of-the-year actual rate was $0.417. Most would agree that this is not a significant difference.

Virtually all firms assign overhead to production on a predetermined basis. This fact seems to suggest that most firms successfully approximate the end-of-the-year overhead rate. Thus, the measurement problems associated with the use of actual overhead costs are solved by the use of estimated overhead costs. Both traditional and activity-based approaches for assigning costs rely on the use of predetermined rates. How these rates are computed and used defines the differences between traditional and contemporary costing systems. Actually, as will be seen, the traditional system is simply a special case of the more general activity-based system.

TRADITIONAL PRODUCT COSTING

Objective 3

Describe traditional costing approaches.

Traditional product costing assigns only manufacturing costs to products. As mentioned, assigning the cost of direct materials and direct labor to products poses no particular challenge. These costs can be assigned to products using direct tracing or very accurate driver tracing, and most traditional cost systems are designed to ensure this takes place. Overhead costs, on the other hand, pose a different problem. The physically observable input-output relationship that exists between direct labor, direct materials, and products, is simply not available for overhead. Thus, assignment of overhead must rely on driver tracing and allocation.

unit-level activity drivers

In a traditional cost system, only unit-level activity drivers are used to assign costs to products. Unit-level activity drivers are factors that cause changes in cost as the units produced change. The use of only unit-based drivers to assign overhead costs to products assumes that the overhead consumed by products is highly correlated with the number of units produced. These unit-based activity drivers assign overhead to products through the use of either plantwide or departmental rates. Examples of unit-level drivers commonly used to assign overhead include:

1. Units produced
2. Direct labor hours
3. Direct labor dollars
4. Machine-hours
5. Direct materials

Now that we have identified possible unit-level drivers, we still need to predict the level of activity output that the driver measures. Although any reasonable level of activity could be chosen, the two leading candidates are expected actual activity and normal activity. Expected activity level is the activity output the firm expects to attain for the coming year. Normal activity level is the average activity output that a firm experiences in the long term (normal volume is computed over more than one year). Of the two choices, normal activity has the advantage of using the same activity level year after year. As a result, it produces less fluctuation from year to year in the assignment of per-unit overhead cost.

expected activity level

normal activity level

theoretical activity level

practical activity level

Other activity levels used for computing predetermined overhead rates are those corresponding to the theoretical and practical levels. Theoretical activity level is the absolute maximum activity output. It is the output that can be realized if everything operates *perfectly*. Practical activity level is the maximum output that can be realized if everything operates *efficiently*. Efficient operation allows for some imperfections, such as normal breakdowns, some shortages, workers operating at less than peak capability, and so on. Normal and expected actual activities tend to reflect consumer demand while theoretical and practical activities reflect a firm's production capabilities. Exhibit 4-1 illustrates these four measures of activity.

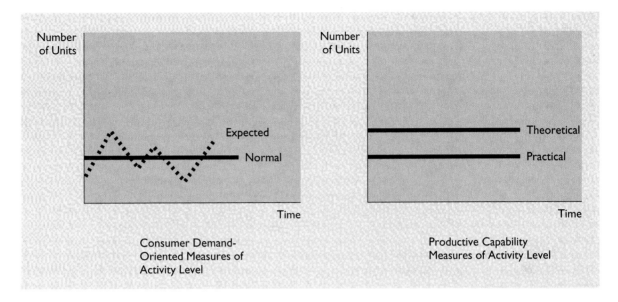

4-1

Exhibit ·Measures of Activity Level

Plantwide Rates

Exhibit 4-2 illustrates how plantwide overhead rates are computed. For plantwide rates, overhead costs are first accumulated in one large plantwide pool (first-stage cost assignment). Overhead costs are assigned to the pool simply by adding all the overhead costs expected to be incurred within the plant for a year. Since all overhead costs belong to the plant, assignment to the pool is done with complete accuracy. In this first stage, the cost object is the plant and direct tracing is used to assign costs to the plantwide pool.

4-2 ·

Exhibit
Traditional Overhead
Assignment Plantwide
Rates

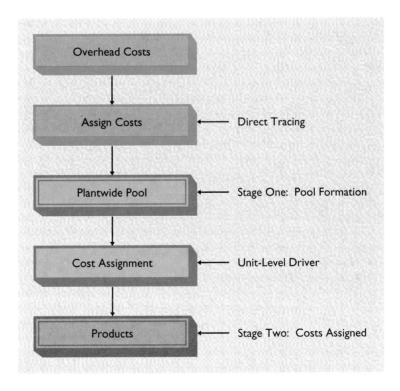

These auto workers are assembling a car at Saturn's Spring Hill, Tennessee, plant. As direct labor, they are an integral part of the manufacturing process.

In a sense, we could argue that the costs are assigned to a very broad macro activity: production. Once costs are accumulated in this pool, we then compute a plantwide rate using a single unit-level driver, which is usually direct labor hours. Products are assumed to consume overhead resources in proportion to the direct labor hours used. Thus, in the second stage, overhead costs are assigned to products, multiplying the rate by the actual total direct labor hours used by each product.

Computation of a Plantwide Rate The computation of a plantwide rate is best illustrated with an example. Belring produces two telephones: a cordless phone and a regular model. The company has the following estimated and actual data for 1998:

Budgeted overhead	$360,000
Expected activity (in direct labor hours)	100,000
Actual activity (in direct labor hours)	100,000
Actual overhead	$380,000

Now assume that the firm bases its predetermined overhead rate on expected production activity measured in direct labor hours (DLH). Thus, for 1998:

$$\text{Predetermined overhead rate} = \frac{\text{Budgeted overhead}}{\text{Expected activity}}$$
$$= \frac{\$360,000}{100,000 \text{ direct labor hours}}$$
$$= \$3.60 \text{ per DLH}$$

applied overhead

Applied Overhead Predetermined overhead rates are used to apply overhead costs to production as the actual production activity unfolds. The total overhead assigned to actual production at any point in time is called applied overhead. Applied overhead is computed using the following formula:

$$\text{Applied overhead} = \text{Overhead rate} \times \text{Actual activity output}$$

Using the overhead rate, applied overhead for 1998 is:

$$\text{Applied overhead} = \text{Overhead rate} \times \text{Actual activity}$$
$$= \$3.60 \times 100{,}000 \text{ DLH}$$
$$= \$360{,}000$$

[handwritten: Predetermined (above "Overhead rate")]

overhead variance

The difference between the actual overhead and the applied overhead is called an overhead variance. For Belring, the overhead variance is $20,000 ($380,000 − $360,000 = $20,000). If the actual overhead is greater than the applied overhead, the variance is called underapplied overhead. For the Belring example, the overhead is $20,000 underapplied. If the actual overhead is less than the applied overhead, the variance is called overapplied overhead. Usually, at the end of the year, underapplied overhead is added to cost of goods sold and overapplied overhead is subtracted from cost of goods sold.

underapplied overhead +

overapplied overhead −

[handwritten: from COGS Sold]

Per-unit Cost Unit manufacturing costs are the sum of prime and overhead costs. Prime costs (direct materials and direct labor) are assigned by direct tracing. In a normal costing system, the predetermined overhead rate is the basis for per-unit overhead cost calculation. To illustrate unit-cost computation, assume the following actual data were collected for each product:

[handwritten: Actual]	Cordless	Regular	
Units produced	10,000	100,000	
Prime costs	$78,000	$738,000	*[handwritten: + average overhead]*
Direct labor hours	10,000	90,000	

The unit cost can be computed by adding the total prime costs for a product to its assigned overhead costs. This total manufacturing cost is then divided by the units produced to yield a unit cost. These calculations are summarized in Exhibit 4-3. Notice the role the predetermined rate of $3.60 per hour plays in calculating the unit manufacturing cost.

Departmental Rates

[handwritten: Plant wide OH costs ÷ & assign. to depts. (→Pools)]
[handwritten: 2 stages]

Exhibit 4-4 illustrates the conceptual framework for departmental overhead rates. As with plantwide rates, there are two stages of cost assignment. In the first stage, the plantwide overhead costs are divided up and assigned to individual production departments, creating departmental overhead cost pools. In this first-stage cost assignment, departments are cost objects and overhead costs are assigned using direct tracing, driver tracing, and allocation. Chapter 7 discusses this first-stage cost assignment in detail and, in particular, describes how to assign costs *external* to the production departments (internal costs are assigned using a direct-tracing rationale). Although an effort is made to assign these external costs using causal factors (driver tracing), some overhead costs are assigned using assumed linkages (allocation). Once costs are assigned to individual production departments, then unit-based drivers such as direct labor hours (for labor-

4-3

Exhibit

[handwritten: Step 2]
[handwritten: Step 1]
[handwritten: Direct labor hrs. (beside the $3.60 lines)]

Unit-Cost Computation: Plantwide Rate		
	Cordless	Regular
Prime costs	$ 78,000	$ 738,000
Overhead costs:		
$3.60 × 10,000	36,000	
$3.60 × 90,000		324,000
Total manufacturing costs	$114,000	$1,062,000
Units of production	10,000	100,000
Unit cost (total costs/units)	$11.40	$10.62

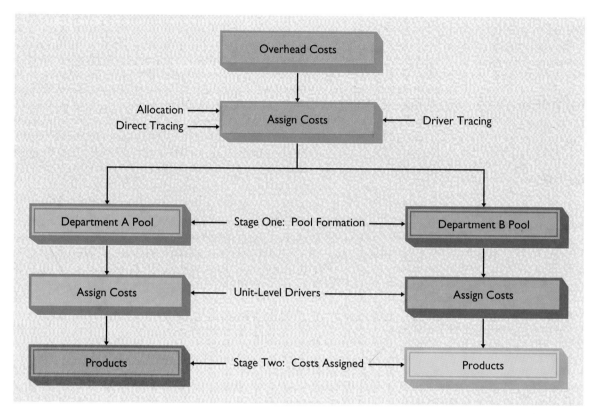

intensive departments) and machine hours (for machine-intensive departments) are used
to compute departmental rates. Products passing through the departments are assumed
to consume overhead resources in proportion to the department's unit-based drivers
(such as machine hours or direct labor hours used). Thus, in the second stage, overhead
is assigned to products by multiplying the departmental rates by the amount of the driver
used in the respective departments. The total overhead assigned to products is simply
the sum of the amounts received in each department.

The rationale for departmental rates is simple. Some producing departments may be
more "overhead-intensive" than other producing departments. Thus, products spending
more time in overhead-intensive departments should be assigned more overhead cost
than those spending less time. Departmental rates pick up these possible effects while
plantwide rates lose them through averaging.

Computation of Departmental Rates Assume that Belring has two production departments: fabrication and assembly. In fabrication, the major electronic component is
made. Other parts are purchased from suppliers and sister divisions. Data relating to the
departments for 1998 are given in Exhibit 4-5. Notice that fabrication is machine-
intensive (compare expected machine hours) while assembly tends to be labor-intensive.
Observing this, Belring bases its departmental overhead rates on machine hours in
fabrication and on direct labor hours in assembly. Two overhead rates are calculated:

$$\text{Fabrication rate} = \frac{\text{Budgeted overhead}}{\text{Expected machine hours}}$$

$$= \frac{\$252,000}{40,000}$$

$$= \$6.30 \text{ per machine hour}$$

4-5

Exhibit
Departmental Data

machine Intense   *Labor Intens*   115

	Fabrication	Assembly
Budgeted overhead	$252,000	$108,000
Expected and actual activity (direct labor hours):		
Cordless	7,000	3,000
Regular	13,000	77,000
	20,000	80,000
Expected and actual activity (machine hours):		
Cordless	4,000	1,000
Regular	36,000	9,000
	40,000	10,000

$$\text{Assembly rate} = \frac{\text{Budgeted overhead}}{\text{Expected direct labor hours}}$$
$$= \frac{\$108,000}{80,000}$$
$$= \$1.35 \text{ per direct labor hour}$$

Applied Overhead Total applied overhead for the year is simply the sum of the amounts applied in each department:

Cost assign based on driver intensity.

$$\text{Applied overhead} = (\$6.30 \times \text{actual machine hours}) + (\$1.35 \times \text{actual direct labor hours})$$
$$= (\$6.30 \times 40,000) + (\$1.35 \times 80,000)$$
$$= \$252,000 + \$108,000$$
$$= \$360,000$$

Notice that the applied overhead equals the budgeted overhead. This happens *only* when the actual activity output measures are the same as the expected activity output measures.

Per-unit Cost Using the departmental rates, the data from Exhibit 4-5, and the earlier information on prime costs and units produced, the computation of the unit cost is shown in Exhibit 4-6.

LIMITATIONS OF TRADITIONAL COST ACCOUNTING SYSTEMS

Objective 4
Explain why traditional costing approaches may produce distorted costs.

advanced manufacturing environment

Plantwide and departmental rates have been used for decades and continue to be used successfully by many organizations. In some settings, however, they do not work well and may actually cause severe product cost distortions. For companies operating in what is called the *advanced manufacturing environment,* product cost distortions can be particularly distressing. The advanced manufacturing environment is characterized by intense competition (usually on a world wide level), continuous improvement, total quality management, total customer satisfaction, and sophisticated technology. As firms operating in this advanced environment adopt new strategies to achieve competitive

4-6

Exhibit

Unit-Cost Computation: Departmental Rates		
	Cordless	Regular
Prime costs	$ 78,000	$ 738,000
Overhead costs:		
($1.35 × 3,000) + ($6.30 × 4,000)	29,250	
($1.35 × 77,000) + ($6.30 × 36,000)		330,750
Total manufacturing costs	$107,250	$1,068,750
Units of production	10,000	100,000
Unit cost (total costs/units)	$10.73	$10.69

excellence, their cost accounting systems often must change to keep pace. Specifically, the need for more accurate product costs has forced many companies to take a serious look at their costing procedures. Cost systems that worked reasonably well in the past may no longer be acceptable.

Often organizations experience certain symptoms indicating that their cost accounting system is outdated. Many of these symptoms were described in the opening scenario involving Sharp Paper Company. For example, if costs are distorted and severe overcosting of a major, high-volume product is the outcome, then bids will be systematically lost, even when the company feels it is pursuing an aggressive bidding strategy. This can be especially puzzling when the company is confident that it is operating as efficiently as its competitors. Thus, one symptom of an outdated cost system is the inability to explain the outcome of bids. On the flip side, if competitors' prices seem unrealistically low, it should cause managers to wonder about the accuracy of their cost system. Similarly, if somehow an organization's cost system is systematically understating the cost of low-volume, specialty products—products that require special processes and handling—then the organization may find it has a seemingly profitable niche all to itself. Yet, it may find operational managers wanting to drop some of these "niche" products. These symptoms of an outdated system along with several others are listed in Exhibit 4-7.[2]

Organizations, such as John Deere Component Works, that have experienced the symptoms listed in Exhibit 4-7, have found that their plantwide or departmental rates are simply no longer capable of accurately assigning overhead costs to individual products. At least two major factors impair the ability of unit-based plantwide and departmental rates to assign overhead costs accurately: (1) the proportion of nonunit-related overhead costs to total overhead costs is large and (2) the degree of product diversity is great.   *Both must be present for rate failure*

Nonunit-related Overhead Costs

The use of either plantwide rates or departmental rates assumes that a product's consumption of overhead resources is related strictly to the units produced. But what if there are overhead activities that are unrelated to the number of units produced? Setup costs, for example, are incurred each time a batch of products is produced. A batch may consist of 1,000 or 10,000 units and the cost of setup is the same. Yet as more setups are done, setup costs increase. The number of setups, not the number of units produced, is the cause of setup costs. Furthermore, product engineering costs may depend on the number of different engineering work orders rather than the units produced of any given product. Both these examples illustrate the existence of nonunit-based drivers. Nonunit-based activity cost drivers are factors, other than the number of units produced, that

nonunit-based activity cost drivers

2. The list of warning signals is based on Robin Cooper, "You Need a New Cost System When . . . ," *Harvard Business Review* (January–February, 1989): 77–82.

4-7

Exhibit
Symptoms of an
Outdated Cost System

1. The outcome of bids is difficult to explain.
2. Competitors' prices appear unrealistically low.
3. Products that are difficult to produce show high profits.
4. Operational managers want to drop products that appear profitable.
5. Profit margins are difficult to explain.
6. The company has a highly profitable niche all to itself.
7. Customers do not complain about price increases.
8. The accounting department spends a lot of time supplying cost data for special projects.
9. Some departments are using their own accounting system.
10. Product costs change because of changes in financial reporting regulations.

measure the demands that cost objects place on activities. Thus, unit-based activity drivers cannot assign these costs accurately to products.

Using only unit-based activity drivers to assign nonunit-related overhead costs can create distorted product costs. The severity of this distortion depends on what proportion of total overhead costs these nonunit-based costs represent. For many companies, this percentage can be significant. Schrader Bellows and John Deere Component Works, for example, experienced nonunit-based overhead cost ratios of about 50 percent and 40 percent, respectively.[3] This suggests that some care should be exercised in assigning nonunit-based overhead costs. If nonunit-based overhead costs are only a small percentage of total overhead costs, the distortion of product costs would be quite small. In such a case, using only unit-based activity drivers to assign overhead costs might be acceptable.

Product Diversity

product diversity

The presence of significant nonunit overhead costs is a necessary but not sufficient condition for plantwide and departmental rate failure. If products consume the nonunit overhead activities in the same proportion as the unit overhead activities, then no product-costing distortion will occur (with the use of traditional overhead assignment methods). The presence of product diversity is also necessary. Product diversity simply means that products consume overhead activities in different proportions. There are several reasons that products might consume overhead in different proportions. For example, differences in product size, product complexity, setup time, and size of batches all can cause products to consume overhead at different rates. Regardless of the nature of the product diversity, product cost will be distorted whenever the quantity of unit-based overhead that a product consumes does not vary in direct proportion to the quantity consumed of nonunit-based overhead. The proportion of each activity consumed by a product is defined as the consumption ratio. How nonunit overhead costs and product diversity can produce distorted product costs is best illustrated with an example.

consumption ratio

An Example Illustrating the Failure of Unit-based Overhead Rates

To illustrate how traditional unit-based overhead rates can distort product costs, we will use the Belring example, this time providing more detailed information about the overhead activities that define their total overhead cost. The detailed data are provided in Exhibit 4-8 (assume that the measures are expected and actual outcomes). Because the quantity of regular phones produced is ten times greater than that of cordless phones, we can label the regular phones a high-volume product and the cordless phones a low-volume product. The phones are produced in batches.

For simplicity, only four types of overhead activities, performed by four distinct support departments, are assumed: setting up the equipment for each batch (different configurations are needed for the electronic components associated with each phone), moving a batch, providing power, and testing. Testing is performed after each department's operations. After fabrication, each component is tested to ensure functionality. After assembly, the entire unit is tested to ensure that it is operational.

Problems with Costing Accuracy The activity usage data in Exhibit 4-8 reveal some serious problems with either plantwide or departmental rates for assigning overhead costs. The accuracy of the overhead cost assignment can be challenged regardless of whether the plantwide or departmental rates are used. The main problem with either procedure is the assumption that machine hours or direct labor hours drive or cause all overhead costs.

3. See Robin Cooper, "Cost Classification in Unit-Based and Activity-Based Manufacturing Cost Systems," *Journal of Cost Management for the Manufacturing Industry* (Fall 1990): 4–14.

Exhibit
Product-Costing Data

Activity Usage Measures			
	Cordless	Regular	Total
Units produced per year	10,000	100,000	—
Prime costs	$78,000	$738,000	$816,000
Direct labor hours	10,000	90,000	100,000
Machine hours	5,000	45,000	50,000
Production runs	20	10	30
Number of moves	60	30	90

Activity Cost Data (overhead activities)	
Activity	Activity Cost
Setup	$120,000
Material handling	60,000
Power	100,000
Testing	80,000
Total	$360,000

From Exhibit 4-8, we know that producing regular phones, the high-volume product, uses nine times as much direct labor hours as producing cordless phones, the low-volume product (90,000 hours versus 10,000 hours). Thus, if a plantwide rate is used, the regular phones will be assigned nine times more overhead cost than the cordless phones. But is this reasonable? Do unit-based activity drivers explain the consumption of all overhead activities? In particular, can we reasonably assume that each product's consumption of overhead increases in direct proportion to the direct labor hours used? Let's look at the four overhead activities and see if unit-based drivers accurately reflect the demands of regular and cordless phone production.

Examination of the data in Exhibit 4-8 suggests that a significant portion of overhead costs is not driven or caused by the units produced (as measured by direct labor hours). For example, each product's demands for setup and material-handling activities are more logically related to the number of production runs and the number of moves, respectively. These nonunit activities represent 50 percent ($180,000/$360,000) of the total overhead costs—a significant percentage. Notice that the low-volume product, cordless phones, uses twice as many runs as the regular phones (20/10) and twice as many moves (60/30). However, use of direct labor hours, a unit-based activity driver, and a plantwide rate assigns *nine* times more setup and material-handling costs to the regular phones than to the cordless. Thus, we have product diversity and we should expect product cost distortion because the quantity of unit-based overhead that each product consumes does not vary in direct proportion to the quantity consumed of nonunit-based overhead.

The consumption ratios for the two products are illustrated in Exhibit 4-9. *Consumption ratios* are simply the proportion of each activity consumed by a product. The consumption ratios suggest that a plantwide rate based on direct labor hours will over-cost the regular phones and undercost the cordless phones.

The problem is only aggravated when departmental rates are used (refer to Exhibit 4-5). In the assembly department, regular phones consume 25.67 times as many direct labor hours as the cordless phones (77,000/3,000). In the fabrication department, regular phones consume nine times as many machine hours as the cordless phones (36,000/ 4,000). Thus, the regular phones receive about 25.67 times more overhead than the cordless phones in the assembly department, and in the fabrication department they receive nine times more overhead. As Exhibit 4-6 shows, with departmental rates, the unit cost of the cordless phones *decreases* to $10.73, and the unit cost of the regular

Overhead Activity	Cordless Phones	Regular Phones	Activity Driver
Setups	0.67[a]	0.33[a]	Production runs
Material handling	0.67[b]	0.33[b]	Number of moves
Power	0.10[c]	0.90[c]	Machine hours
Testing	0.10[d]	0.90[d]	Direct labor hours[e]

(handwritten: grouped set; ")

4-9 Exhibit
Product Diversity:
Consumption Rates

(handwritten: Consump. Ratios)

[a]20/30 (cordless) and 10/30 (regular)
[b]60/90 (cordless) and 30/90 (regular)
[c]5,000/50,000 (cordless) and 45,000/50,000 (regular)
[d]10,000/100,000 (cordless) and 90,000/100,000 (regular)
[e]Because direct labor hours are perfectly correlated with testing hours, direct labor hours are
used as the activity driver for the inspection activity.

phones *increases* to $10.69. This change is in the wrong direction, which emphasizes the failure of unit-based activity drivers to reflect accurately each product's demands for setup and material-handling costs.

ACTIVITY-BASED PRODUCT COSTING: GENERAL DESCRIPTION

(handwritten: Traces costs to activities US Traditional (to dept.))

Objective 5

Explain how an activity-based cost system can produce more accurate product costs.

activity-based cost (ABC) system

In Exhibits 4-1 and 4-2, we saw that traditional overhead assignment involves two stages: first, overhead costs are assigned to an organizational unit (plant or departments), and second, overhead costs are then assigned to products. As Exhibit 4-10 illustrates, an activity-based cost (ABC) system first *traces* costs to activities and then to products. Thus, activity-based costing is also a two-stage process, but in the first stage it traces overhead costs to activities rather than to an organizational unit such as the plant or departments. In both traditional and activity-based costing, the second stage consists of assigning costs to the product. An ABC cost system, however, emphasizes direct tracing and driver tracing (exploiting cause-and-effect relationships) while a traditional cost system tends to be allocation-intensive (largely ignoring cause-and-effect relationships).

Thus, the principal computational difference between the two methods concerns the nature and the number of cost drivers used. Activity-based costing uses both unit-based

4-10 Exhibit
Activity-based Costing:
Two-Stage Cost
Assignment

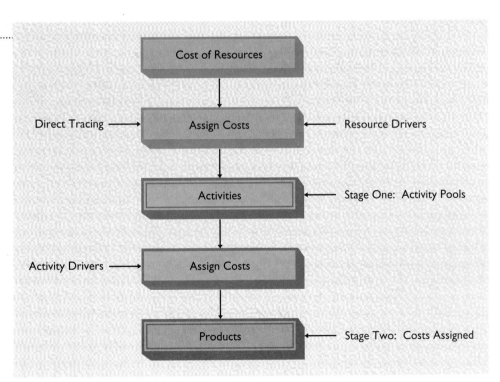

The grocery industry is enthusiastically behind activity-based costing. Wholesale and retail grocers are using ABC in all aspects of their business. For example, King Soopers automated the routing and scheduling process in one of its Denver warehouses. By getting specific information about unloading rates for various product types and information about each store's ordering habits, they are better able to tailor scheduling for the different stores. The resultant reduction and elimination of activities related to picking up, transporting, and unloading have resulted in savings of more than $10,000 per week. Overall, a Spartan Stores Vice President estimates, the use of ABC could reduce the price of goods by 30 percent, as manufacturers and distributors who operate more efficiently can take fees out of their cost structure.

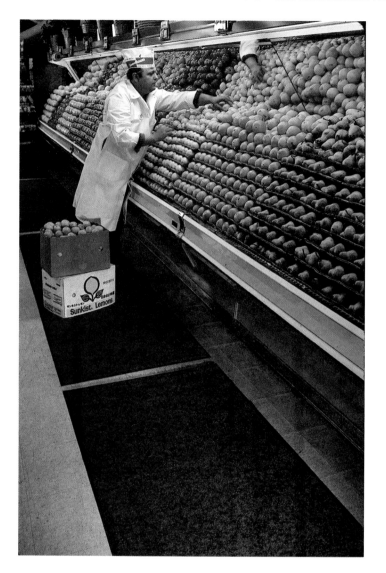

and nonunit-based activity drivers. These drivers must reflect a cause-and-effect relationship. In practical terms, drivers must explain a large percentage of activity cost variability. This criterion can be tested by preparing cost formulas for each activity and using the activity drivers that have high R^2s.[4] Generally, the number of drivers is greater than the number of unit-based drivers commonly used in a traditional system. As a result, the ABC method produces increased product-costing accuracy.

From a managerial perspective, however, an ABC system offers more than just more accurate product cost information. It also provides information about the cost and performance of activities and resources, and can trace costs accurately to cost objects other than products such as customers and channels of distribution. For example, knowing the cost of activities, their importance to the organization, and how efficiently they are performed allows managers to focus on those activities that might offer opportunities for cost savings—provided they are simplified, performed more efficiently, eliminated, and so on. The strategic insights and process improvement capabilities gained from an ABC system are extremely important and are explored in Chapter 10, contemporary control systems. Furthermore, activity-based costing can significantly affect tra-

---

4. See Chapter 3 for a description of how activity cost formulas are estimated. Also, it should be mentioned that practical application of the R^2 criterion may require a firm to first generate data on candidate activity drivers and activity costs. For example, a traditional cost system may not have been producing data on either drivers or activity costs, thereby providing input for a least-squares formula. Once data are available, an organization may need to adjust its cost assignment methods based on statistical evidence.

ditional decision-making models. These effects are explored in Part 3 and are integrated into the various chapters in that section. In this chapter, however, we will focus only on ABC's product-costing dimension, beginning with a general explanation of the first-stage procedure.

First-Stage Procedure

In the first stage of activity-based costing, activities are identified, costs are associated with individual activities, and activities and their associated costs are divided into homogeneous sets. Recall that an *activity* is work performed within an organization. Thus, activity identification requires a listing of all the different kinds of work, such as materials handling, inspections, process engineering, and product enhancement. A firm may have hundreds of different activities. Once an activity is defined, the cost of performing the activity is determined (by using direct tracing and resource drivers). At this point, the firm could determine the activity driver associated with each activity and calculate individual activity overhead rates. For the average setting, this could literally produce hundreds of overhead rates, a cumbersome method of assigning overhead to products.

To reduce the number of overhead rates required and streamline the process, activities are grouped in homogeneous sets based on similar characteristics: (1) they are logically related and (2) they have the same consumption ratios for all products. Costs are associated with each of these homogeneous sets by summing the costs of the individual activities belonging to the set. The collection of overhead costs associated with each set of activities is called a homogeneous cost pool. Since the activities within a homogeneous cost pool have the same consumption ratio, the cost variations for this pool can be explained by a single activity driver. Once a cost pool is defined, the cost per unit of the activity driver is computed by dividing the pool costs by the activity driver's practical capacity. This is called the pool rate. Computation of the pool rate completes the first stage. Thus, the first stage produces five outcomes: (1) activities are identified, (2) costs are assigned to activities, (3) related activities are grouped to form homogeneous sets, (4) the costs of grouped activities are summed to define homogeneous cost pools, and (5) pool (overhead) rates are computed.[5]

To illustrate this process, consider once again the Belring example. Four overhead activities have been identified: setups, material handling, power, and testing. The costs of the individual activities have been assigned and are described in Exhibit 4-8. Logical relationships also exist. Setup activities and material-handling activities are performed each time a batch of products is produced. Thus, these two activities are logically related by the more general batch-level production activity. Similarly, testing and power activities are performed each time a unit of product is produced (recall that each unit is tested). Thus, these two activities are logically related by the more general activity of producing a unit of product. Moreover, from Exhibit 4-9 we know that the setups and material-handling grouping and the power and testing grouping have the same consumption ratios for both products. Thus, we are able to reduce four activities to two sets of activities. These two sets can now be used to form homogeneous cost pools. Let's call the set with setups and material handling the *batch-level pool* and the set with power and testing the *unit-level pool*. The total cost associated with each pool is simply the sum of the related activities. Using the data from Exhibit 4-8, the pool costs follow:

homogeneous cost pool

pool rate

Batch-level Pool		Unit-level Pool	
Setups	$120,000	Power	$100,000
Material handling	60,000	Testing	80,000
Total	$180,000	Total	$180,000

---

5. This definition of the first stage in an activity-based cost system is similar to that found in H. Thomas Johnson and Robert S. Kaplan, *Relevance Lost: The Rise and Fall of Management Accounting* (Boston: Harvard Business Press, 1987), Chapter 10.

Now that we have identified homogeneous cost pools and determined their costs, we can assign the pool costs to each product. To do this, a pool rate must be calculated based on activity drivers. For the batch-level cost pool, the number of production runs or number of moves could be the activity driver. Since the two activity drivers have the same consumption ratios, either driver, number of setups or number of moves, will assign the same amount of overhead to both products. For the unit-level cost pool (power and testing), machine hours or direct labor hours could be selected as the activity driver. Assume for purposes of illustration that the number of production runs and machine hours are the activity drivers chosen.[6] Using data from Exhibit 4-8, the first-stage outcomes are illustrated in Exhibit 4-11.

Second-Stage Procedure

In the second stage, the costs of each overhead pool are traced to products. This is done using the pool rates computed in the first stage and measures of the amount of resources consumed by each product. This measure is simply the quantity of the activity driver used by each product. In our example, that would be the number of production runs and machine hours used by each type of phone. Thus, the overhead assigned from each cost pool to each product is computed as follows:

Applied overhead (to a product) = Pool rate × Driver units consumed by product

To illustrate, consider the assignment of costs from the first overhead pool to regular phones. From Exhibit 4-11, we know that the rate for this pool is $6,000 per production run. We also know from Exhibit 4-8 that the cordless phones use 20 production runs and 5,000 machine hours. Thus, the overhead assigned to cordless phones from the batch-level cost pool is $120,000 ($6,000 × 20 runs) and the amount assigned from the unit-level pool is $18,000 ($3.60 × 5,000 machine hours). Similar overhead cost assignments would be made for the regular phones. The total manufacturing cost for each product is obtained by adding the prime costs to the assigned overhead costs. This total is then divided by the number of units produced. The result is the manufacturing cost per unit. Exhibit 4-12 illustrates the activity-based product cost computation for each product.

---

6. You may want to recalculate pool rates using number of moves and direct labor hours to prove that the choice of cost drivers does not affect the assignment of costs to the individual products.

Exhibit
First-Stage Procedure:
Activity-based Costing

Batch-level Pool:	
Setup costs	$120,000
Material-handling costs	60,000
Total costs	$180,000
Production runs	30
Pool rate (cost per run)	$6,000
Unit-level Pool:	
Power cost	$100,000
Testing cost	80,000
Total costs	$180,000
Machine hours	50,000
Pool rate (cost per machine hour)	$3.60

4-12

Exhibit
Unit Costs: Activity-
based Costing

	Cordless	Regular
Prime costs	$ 78,000	$738,000
Overhead costs:		
Batch-level pool:		
($6,000 × 20)	120,000	
($6,000 × 10)		60,000
Unit-level pool:		
($3.60 × 5,000)	18,000	
($3.60 × 45,000)		162,000
Total manufacturing costs	$216,000	$960,000
Units of production	10,000	100,000
Unit cost (total costs/units)	$21.60	$9.60

Comparison of Traditional and ABC Product Costs

In Exhibit 4-13, the unit cost from activity-based costing is compared with the unit costs produced by traditional costing using either a plantwide or a departmental rate. This comparison clearly illustrates the effects of using only unit-based activity drivers to assign overhead costs. The activity-based cost assignment better reflects the pattern of overhead consumption and is, therefore, the most accurate of the three costs shown in Exhibit 4-13. Activity-based product costing reveals that the traditional method under-costs the cordless phones and overcosts the regular phones. In fact, the ABC assignment almost doubles the cost of the cordless phones and decreases the cost of the regular phones by almost $1.00 per unit.

Using only unit-based activity drivers can lead to one product subsidizing another (as the regular phones are subsidizing the cordless phones). This subsidy could create the appearance that one group of products is highly profitable and can adversely impact the pricing and competitiveness of another group of products. In a highly competitive environment, the more accurate the cost information the better the planning and decision making.

ABC and Service Organizations

Although the discussion of ABC so far has focused on manufacturing, ABC can also be useful to service organizations. All service organizations have activities and output that places demands on these activities. There are, however, some fundamental differences between service and manufacturing organizations. Activities within manufacturing organizations tend to be of the same type and performed in a similar way. The same cannot be said of service organizations. Imagine, for example, how dissimilar activities are for a bank and a hospital! Another basic difference between service and manufacturing organizations is output definition. For manufacturing firms, output is easily defined (the tangible products that are manufactured) but for service organizations output definition

4-13

Exhibit
Comparison of Unit
Costs

	Cordless	Regular	Source
Activity-based cost	$21.60	$ 9.60	Exhibit 4-12
Traditional:			
Plantwide rate	11.40	10.62	Exhibit 4-3
Departmental rate	10.73	10.69	Exhibit 4-6

is more difficult.[7] Output for service organizations is less tangible. Yet output must be defined so that it can be costed.

Consider, for example, a hospital. What is the output of a hospital? The product of a hospital is commonly defined as a patient's stay and treatment. If we accept this definition, then it becomes immediately obvious that a hospital is a multiproduct firm because there are many different kinds of "stays and treatments." During the stay a patient will consume many different services. To the extent that this consumption of services is homogeneous, product groups can be defined. For example, maternity patients without complications would all stay about the same time in the hospital and consume essentially the same services.

To illustrate the potential of activity-based costing, we will focus on one type of service provided to each patient: daily care. Daily care is made up of three activities: occupancy, feeding, and nursing. We will define output as "patient days" (the "stay" part of the output only). Hospitals have traditionally assigned the cost of daily care by using a daily rate (a rate per patient day). There are actually different kinds of daily care, and rates are structured to reflect these differences. For example, a higher daily rate is charged for an intensive care unit than for a maternity care unit. Within units, however, the daily rates are the same for all patients. Under the traditional approach, the daily rate is computed by dividing the annual costs of occupancy, feeding, and nursing of a unit by the unit's capacity expressed in patient days. A single activity driver (patient days) is used to assign the costs of daily care to each patient.

But what if the costs of the three care activities are consumed in different proportions by patients? This would imply product diversity and a possible requirement to use more than one activity driver to assign daily care costs accurately to patients. To illustrate, assume that the demands for nursing care vary within the maternity unit, depending on the severity of a patient's case. Specifically, demand for nursing services per day increases with severity. Assume that within the maternity unit there are three levels of increasing severity: normal patients, cesarean patients, and patients with complications. Now suppose that a hospital has provided the following activity and cost information:

Activity	Annual Cost	Activity Driver	Annual Quantity
Occupancy and feeding	$1,000,000	Patient days	10,000
Nursing care	1,000,000	Hours of nursing care	50,000

The activity pool rates are $100 per patient day and $20 per nursing hour.

To see how activity costing can affect patient charges, assume that the three types of patients have the following annual demands:

Patient Type	Patient Days Demanded	Nursing Hours Demanded
Normal	7,000	17,500
Cesarean	2,000	12,500
Complications	1,000	20,000
Total	10,000	50,000

The traditional approach for charging daily care would produce a rate of $200 per patient day ($2,000,000/10,000)—the total cost of care divided by patient days. Every maternity patient—regardless of type—would pay the daily rate of $200. Using the pool rates for each activity, however, produces a different daily rate for each patient; one that reflects the different demands for nursing services:

---

7. For a more complete discussion on ABC and potential applications to service organizations see John Antos, "Activity-Based Management for Service, Not-for-Profit, and Governmental Organizations," *Journal of Cost Management* (Summer 1992): 13–23 and William Rotch, "Activity-Based Costing in Service Industries," *Journal of Cost Management* (Summer 1990): 4–14. The discussion in this chapter is based on these two articles.

Patient	Daily Rate*
Normal	$150
Cesarean	225
Complications	500

*($100 × 7,000) + ($20 × 17,500)/7,000;
($100 × 2,000) + ($20 × 12,500)/2,000;
($100 × 1,000) + ($20 × 20,000)/1,000

This example illustrates that activity-based costing can produce significant product-costing improvements in service organizations that experience product diversity. Although ABC has not yet had the reception in service organizations compared to manufacturing organizations, it has been adopted by some. Examples of service organizations that have adopted an ABC approach include Union Pacific, Amtrak, and Armistead Insurance Company.[8]

ACTIVITY IDENTIFICATION AND CLASSIFICATION

Objective 6

Provide a detailed description of how activities are identified and classified so that homogeneous cost pools can be formed.

In describing activity-based product costing, the basic features have been described and illustrated using the Belring example and reinforced with an application in a hospital setting. We have learned that activity-based costing is a two-stage process. In the first stage, activities are identified, costs are assigned to activities, related activities are grouped into sets, homogeneous cost pools are formed, and pool rates are computed. In the second stage, each product's demands for the pool's resources are measured and costs are assigned to products using these demands and the respective pool rates. However, to avoid confusing the basic concepts, we avoided any detailed discussion of several steps of the first-stage procedure. We now turn to a more detailed description of the first two steps: (1) activity identification and (2) classification of activities into homogeneous sets. How costs are assigned to activities is discussed in a separate section.

Activity Identification

activity

The focus of activity-based costing is activities. Thus, identifying activities must be the first step in designing an activity-based costing system. Activity implies action taken or work performed. Identifying activities is as simple as asking individual managers and workers the following question: What work do you do? Thus, activity identification entails observing and listing the work performed within an organization—work or actions taken that involve the consumption of resources. Generally, activities are what an organization does to satisfy customer needs. Activities are the building blocks for both product costing and continuous improvement.

activity inventory

Once activities are identified, they are listed in a document called the activity inventory. A sample activity inventory is listed in Exhibit 4-14. Notice that each activity is described by an action verb and an object. Of course, the activity inventory for an actual organization would list more than 12 activities (200 to 300 activities are not uncommon).

activity attributes

Once an inventory of activities exists, then activity attributes are used to further describe and classify the activities. Activity attributes are nonfinancial and financial information items that describe individual activities. What attributes are used depends on the purpose served. If the purpose is improving performance, then quality and efficiency attributes would be used. If the purpose is product costing, then attributes that reflect how products consume activities would be used. The use of activity attributes to improve performance is explored in Chapter 10 (contemporary responsibility accounting). Since product costing is our current concern, we now turn to the identification of activity attributes that facilitate this objective.

8. William Rotch, "Activity-Based Costing in Service Industries."

Exhibit
Sample: Activity Inventory

Activity Inventory
1. Ordering materials
2. Receiving materials
3. Testing products
4. Setting up batches
5. Collecting engineering data
6. Moving materials
7. Welding subassemblies
8. Providing utilities
9. Providing space
10. Packaging goods
11. Shipping goods
12. Paying for materials

Classification of Activities

For product-costing purposes, activity attributes are used to group related activities into sets that form the basis for homogeneous cost pools. Grouping activities reduces the number of overhead rates needed, simplifies the task of product costing, and decreases the overall complexity of the ABC product-costing model. Activities qualify for membership in the same set provided they have two attributes in common: (1) *activity-level attribute,* meaning they are performed at the same general activity level and (2) *driver attribute,* meaning they can use the same activity driver to assign costs to a cost object.[9] The first attribute defines what "logically related" means and the second attribute simply means that activities must have the same consumption ratio. These two attributes define filters that are used for grouping activities into homogeneous cost pools. Essentially, activities are combined to form homogeneous sets provided they have the *same* activity-level classification, and the *same* activity-driver classification. A homogeneous set of activities with its associated costs corresponds to what we have defined as a homogeneous cost pool. To understand this classification process, we need to understand exactly how (and why) each attribute is used to classify activities.

Activity-level Classification In building sets of related activities, activities are classified into one of the following four general activity categories: (1) unit level, (2) batch level, (3) product level, and (4) facility level.[10] Classifying activities into these general categories facilitates product costing because the costs of activities associated with the different levels respond to different types of cost drivers (cost behavior differs by level). The definition of the activities belonging to each general category clearly illustrates this feature. **unit-level activities** Unit-level activities are those performed each time a unit is produced. For example, power and machine hours are used each time a unit is produced. Direct materials and direct labor activities are also unit-level activities, even though they are not overhead costs. The costs of unit-level activities vary with the number of units produced. **batch-level activities** Batch-level activities are those performed each time a batch of goods is produced. The costs of batch-level activities vary with the number of batches but are fixed with respect to the

---

9. Finer classifications can be used by using additional attributes. For example, we could require activities with the same objective or purpose to be classified together. Since processes are collections of activities that are linked by a common objective, this would add a process-classification attribute. While additional attributes may improve the accuracy of product costing, they add little to our basic understanding of activity-based costing. Thus, we will leave the study of process classification to a more advanced course. For readers who wish for more information on the three classification criteria, see Don R. Hansen and Maryanne M. Mowen, *Cost Management: Accounting and Control* (Cincinnati: South-Western Publishing, 1997), Chapter 8; Michael R. Ostrenga and Frank Probst, "Process Value Analysis: The Missing Link in Cost Management," *Journal of Cost Management* (Fall 1992): 4–13; and Peter B. B. Turney and Alan J. Stratton, "Using ABC to Support Continuous Improvement," *Management Accounting* (September 1992): 46–50.

10. This classification and the associated definitions are taken from Robin Cooper, "Cost Classification in Unit-Based and Activity-Based Manufacturing Cost Systems."

product-level (sustaining) activities

number of units in each batch. Setups, inspections (unless each unit is inspected), production scheduling, and material handling are examples of batch-level activities. Product-level (sustaining) activities are those performed as needed to support the various products produced by a company. These activities consume inputs that develop products or allow products to be produced and sold. These activities and their costs tend to increase as the number of different products increases. Engineering changes, development of product-testing procedures, marketing a product, process engineering, and expediting are examples of product-level activities. Facility-level activities are those that sustain a factory's general manufacturing processes. These activities benefit the organization at some level but do not provide a benefit for any specific product. Examples include plant management, landscaping, support of community programs, security, property taxes, and plant depreciation.

facility-level activities

Activity Driver Classification Of the four general levels, the first three, unit level, batch level, and product level, contain product-related activities. For these three levels, it is possible to measure the demands placed on the activities by individual products. Activities within these three levels can be further subdivided on the basis of consumption ratios. Activities with the same consumption ratios can use the same activity driver to assign costs. Thus, in effect, all activities *within* each of the first three levels that have the same activity driver are grouped together. This final grouping creates a homogeneous set of activities: a collection of activities that are at the same level *and* use the same activity driver. Exhibit 4-15 illustrates the activity classification model that creates

4-15 ·································· Activity Classification Model

Exhibit

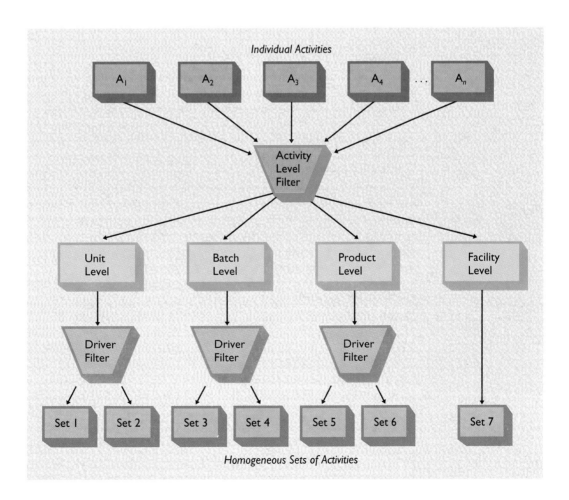

homogeneous sets of activities. Notice that facility-level activities do not undergo the driver classification.

The fourth general category, facility-level activities, poses a problem for the ABC philosophy of tracing costs to products. Tracing activity costs to individual products depends on the ability to identify the amount of each activity consumed by a product (product demands for activities must be measured). Facility-level activities (and their costs) are common to a variety of products, and it is not possible to identify how individual products consume these activities. A pure ABC system, therefore, would not assign these costs to products. They would be treated as period costs. In effect, these costs are fixed costs—costs that are not driven by any of the cost drivers found in any of the first three categories. In practice, companies adopting ABC systems usually implement a full-costing approach and allocate these facility-level costs to individual products.[11] Unit-level, batch-level, or product-level cost drivers are often used for the allocation. As a practical matter, assigning these costs may not significantly distort product costs because they are likely to be small relative to the total costs that are appropriately traced to individual products.[12]

There is, however, a possible exception to this observation about facility-level costs and activity drivers. When a company has organized its production facilities around product lines, then it can be argued that space drivers measure the consumption of facility-level costs. This is because floor space within a plant is dedicated to the production of a single product or subassembly. In this case, square footage occupied can be viewed as a possible activity driver for facility costs. Assigning facility-level costs on the basis of space drivers can also serve to motivate managers to reduce the space needed for production, thus reducing facility-level costs over time. This outcome has been observed for firms that implement just-in-time manufacturing and is described in Chapter 18.

Comparison with Traditional Costing

The hierarchial classification of activities allows us to illustrate the fundamental differences between activity-based and traditional cost systems. In a traditional system, the consumption of overhead by products is assumed to be explained only by unit-based activity drivers. In a sophisticated traditional system, overhead costs are classified as fixed or variable with respect to unit-based drivers. Unit-based cost systems allocate fixed overhead to individual products, using fixed overhead rates, and assign variable overhead using variable overhead rates. From the perspective of activity-based costing, the variable overhead is appropriately traced to individual products (for this category, overhead consumption increases as units produced increases). However, assigning fixed overhead costs using unit-based activity drivers can be arbitrary, and may not reflect the activities actually consumed by the products. Many of the costs assigned in the traditional fixed overhead category are, in reality, batch-level, product-level, and facility-level costs that vary with drivers other than unit-level drivers.

Activity-based cost systems improve product-costing accuracy by recognizing that many of the so-called fixed overhead costs vary in proportion to changes other than production volume. By understanding what causes these costs to increase or decrease, they can be traced to individual products. This cause-and-effect relationship allows managers to improve product-costing accuracy, which can significantly improve decision making. Additionally, this large pool of fixed overhead costs is no longer so mysterious. Knowing the underlying behavior of many of these costs allows managers to exert more control over the activities that cause the costs. It also allows managers to identify

---

11. A study of 31 companies and 51 cost systems revealed that all companies using an ABC system allocated facility-level costs to products. See Robin Cooper, "Cost Classification in Unit-Based and Activity-Based Manufacturing Systems."

12. At least this appears to be the experience of General Motors based on its implementation of an ABC system. See Beaujon and Singhal, "Understanding the Activity Costs in an Activity-Based Cost System," 51–72.

which of the activities add value and which do not. *Value analysis* is the heart of activity-based management and is the basis for continuous improvement. Activity-based management and its relationship to the world of continuous improvement is explored in later chapters that deal with contemporary control systems.

An Illustrative Example

To illustrate the classification approach just described, we will build a homogeneous cost model for Marvel Components, an electronics products manufacturer.[13] In one of its plants, Marvel produces two types of wafers: wafer A and wafer B. A wafer is a thin slice of silicon used as a base for integrated circuits or other electronic components. The dies on each wafer represent a particular configuration designed for use by a particular end product. Marvel produces wafers in batches, where each batch corresponds to a particular type of wafer (A or B). In the wafer inserting and sorting process, dies are inserted and the wafers are tested to ensure that the dies are not defective.

Assume that Marvel has the following activity inventory and costs:

Activity	Budgeted Activity Cost
1. Developing test programs	$300,000
2. Making probe cards	160,000
3. Testing products	275,000
4. Setting up batches	120,000
5. Engineering design	130,000
6. Handling wafer lots	90,000
7. Inserting dies	225,000
8. Purchasing materials	200,000
9. Receiving materials	320,000
10. Paying suppliers	180,000
11. Providing utilities (heat, lighting, and so on)	20,000
12. Providing space	50,000

Activity-level Classification Classification by level is accomplished by asking a series of questions relating to the definitions of activity level. For example, for the inserting and sorting process, we ask the following question: Which activities are performed each time a wafer is produced? Inserting dies and testing dies are done for each wafer, and therefore, are unit-level activities. Next, which activities are performed each time a batch is produced? Setting up and handling the batches are done for each batch, and therefore are batch-level activities. Finally, which activities are performed to enable a product to be produced? Developing test programs, making probe cards, and engineering design are done to enable the wafers to be produced, and therefore, are product-level activities. The performance of these activities increases as the number of products increases. Similar questions are asked for the procurement activities. Assuming materials are ordered each time a batch is scheduled for production, purchasing can be classified as a batch-level activity. If not, then we might argue that it is a product-level activity. A similar classification is argued for the receiving activity. Paying suppliers would not correspond to either a batch-level or unit-level activity (terms and payment policies make it unlikely). Thus, it can be classified as a product-level activity. Assuming that parts are shipped to accommodate batch production, then it can be argued that receiving is a batch activity. Finally, the activities of the sustaining process are facility-level. They are performed to enable production to occur. Exhibit 4-16 illustrates how Marvel's activities are grouped by level.

13. Some facts of the example are taken from a description of National Semiconductor's wafer-sorting process. Certain elements of this model are described in Peter B. B. Turney and Alan J. Stratton, "Using ABC to Support Continuous Improvement."

4-16 ....

Exhibit
Activity-level
Classification: Marvel
Components

Unit Level	Batch Level
Testing products	Purchasing materials
Inserting dies	Receiving materials
	Setting up batches
	Handling wafer lots

Product Level	Facility Level
Developing test programs	Providing utilities
Making probe cards	Providing space
Engineering design	
Paying suppliers	

Activity Driver Classification Once activities have been classified by level, then we must search for those activities that have the same activity driver. Activity drivers measure the demands of products for activity resources; thus, activities that have the same activity drivers are consumed in the same proportions by products. These activities can be grouped (review Exhibit 4-9 and the associated Belring example for the specifics on how this is done). Grouping activities that have common activity drivers finishes the classification effort and homogeneous sets of activities are formed. Driver-grouped activities with their associated costs form a homogeneous cost pool. Exhibit 4-17 illustrates activity driver classification and the formation of homogeneous cost pools. Notice that once homogeneous sets of activities are defined, then homogeneous cost pools are formed by simply adding the costs of individual activities within each homogeneous set.

ABC, JIT, AND PRODUCT COSTING

Objective 7

Describe the role of activity-based costing in a JIT environment.

In an activity-based cost system, product-costing accuracy is improved by creating cost pools and identifying activity drivers that can be used to assign costs to each pool. Because of the large number of overhead activities that are shared by products, the effort and expense of an activity-based cost system can be considerable. Single-product firms and multiple-product firms that choose to dedicate entire facilities to the production of a single product have no problems with costing accuracy. All overhead activities and costs are directly traceable to a single product.

Some of the same product-costing benefits found in a single-product environment are achieved by firms that install a JIT manufacturing system. These benefits are realized because JIT manufacturing adopts a more focused approach than that found in traditional manufacturing. Installing a JIT system affects product costing because it affects the traceability of costs, enhances product-costing accuracy, diminishes the need for allocation of service-center costs, and changes the behavior and relative importance of direct labor costs. To understand and appreciate these effects, we need a fundamental understanding of what JIT manufacturing is and how it differs from traditional manufacturing.

Basic Features of JIT

JIT manufacturing

JIT, or just-in-time manufacturing, is a demand-pull system. The objective of JIT manufacturing is to eliminate waste by producing a product only when it is needed and only in the quantities demanded by customers. Demand pulls products through the manufacturing process. Each operation produces only what is necessary to satisfy the demand of

4-17

Exhibit
Activity Driver
Classification and
Homogeneous Cost
Pools

Activity Level	Activity Driver	Activity Cost
Unit-level Activities		
Pool 1:		
Testing products	Number of dies	$275,000
Inserting dies	Number of dies	225,000
		$500,000
Batch-level Activities		
Pool 2:		
Setting up batches	Number of batches	$120,000
Handling wafer lots	Number of batches	90,000
		$210,000
Pool 3:		
Purchasing materials	Number of purchase orders	$200,000
Receiving materials	Number of receiving orders	320,000
		$520,000
Product-level Activities		
Pool 4:		
Developing test programs	Number of products	$300,000
Making probe cards	Number of products	160,000
		$460,000
Pool 5:		
Engineering design	Number of change orders	$130,000
Pool 6:		
Paying suppliers	Number of parts	$180,000
Facility-level Activities		
Pool 7:		
Providing space	Direct labor hours	$20,000
Providing utilities	Direct labor hours	30,000
		$50,000

(Note: Either driver of pool 3 may be used—they have the same consumption ratio.)

the succeeding operation. No production takes place until a signal from a succeeding process indicates a need to produce. Parts and materials arrive just in time to be used in production. JIT assumes that all costs other than direct materials are driven by time and space drivers. JIT then focuses on eliminating waste by compressing time and space. Successful implementation of JIT has brought about significant improvements such as better quality, increased productivity, reduced lead times, major reductions in inventories, reduced setup times, lower manufacturing costs, and increased production rates. For example, Oregon Cutting Systems (OCS), a manufacturer of cutting chain (for chain saws), timber harvesting equipment, and sporting equipment, within a period of three to five years, reduced defects by 80 percent, waste by 50 percent, setup times from hours to minutes (one punch press had setup time reduced from 3 hours to 4.5 minutes), lead times from 21 days to 3 days, and manufacturing costs by 35 percent.[14] JIT techniques have also been implemented by the following companies:

14. Jack C. Bailes and Ilene K. Kleinsorge, "Cutting Waste with JIT," *Management Accounting* (May 1992): 28–32.

Wal-Mart	General Motors	Toys "R" Us
Ford	General Electric	Black and Decker
Chrysler	Hewlett-Packard	Harley Davidson
Motorola	AT&T	Xerox
Intel	Borg Warner	Westinghouse
John Deere	Mercury Marine	

JIT purchasing

Inventory Effects JIT purchasing requires suppliers to deliver parts and materials just in time to be used in production. Supplier linkages are vital. Supply of parts must be linked to production, which is linked to demand. JIT exploits supplier linkages by negotiating long-term contracts with a few chosen suppliers located as close to the production facility as possible and establishing more extensive supplier involvement. One effect of successful exploitation of these linkages is to reduce all inventories to much lower levels. For example, Mercedes-Benz U.S. International plans to build the company's first mass-marketed sport utility vehicle at a Vance, Alabama plant. The vehicle is to be an application of the new "cost-driven ethic." To save both time and money, the supplier list has been pared to 100 (versus 1,000 for the E-class sedan). Mercedes-Benz has offered suppliers multiyear contracts in exchange for 5 percent price cuts.[15]

Contrast this with the traditional push-through system of manufacturing. In traditional manufacturing, materials are supplied and parts produced and transferred to the succeeding process in an effort to meet customer demand and delivery schedules. However, in a traditional, push-through environment, slow or delayed reaction time is often a problem which, in turn, creates a demand for finished goods inventories (otherwise customers would grow old waiting for the firm to produce and deliver the needed goods). In a push-through environment, finished goods inventories are also needed to serve as a buffer when production, for whatever reason, is less than demand. Usually, the push-through system produces significantly higher levels of finished goods inventory than a JIT system.

Plant Layout The type and efficiency of plant layout is managed differently under JIT manufacturing. In traditional job and batch manufacturing, products are moved from one group of identical machines to another. Typically, machines with identical functions are located together in an area referred to as a *department* or *process*. Workers who specialize in the operation of a specific machine are located in each department. JIT replaces this traditional plant layout with a pattern of *manufacturing cells*. Cell structure is directly related to some of the efficiencies cited earlier for Oregon Cutting Systems, such as reduced lead times and lower manufacturing costs. The cellular manufacturing design can also affect plant size and number of plants because it typically requires less space. Compaq Computer Corp., for example, cut its space requirement by 23 percent and increased output per square foot by 16 percent at its Scotland plant. Space savings like this can reduce the demand to build new plants and will affect the size of new plants when they are needed.

manufacturing cells

Manufacturing cells contain machines that are grouped in families, usually in a semicircle. The machines are arranged so that they can be used to perform a variety of operations in sequence. Each cell is set up to produce a particular product or product family. Products move from one machine to another from start to finish. Workers are assigned to cells and are trained to operate all machines within the cell. Thus, labor in a JIT environment is multiskilled, not specialized. Each manufacturing cell is essentially a minifactory, and cells are often referred to as a *factory within a factory*. Exhibit 4-18 compares JIT's plant layout with the traditional pattern.

Grouping of Employees Another major structural difference between JIT and traditional organizations relates to how employees are grouped. As just indicated, each cell

---

15. David Woodruff and Karen Lowry Miller, "Mercedes' Maverick in Alabama," *Business Week*, 11 September 1995, 64–65.

Traditional Manufacturing Layout

Product A →   Lathes   → A   Abrasive Grinders → A   Welding Equipment → A   Finished Product A

Product B →   → B   → B   → B   Finished Product B

Department 1   Department 2   Department 3

Each product passes through departments that specialize in one process. Departments process multiple products.

JIT Manufacturing Layout

Cell A   Cell B

Grinder   Grinder

Lathe   Welding   Lathe   Welding

Product A   Finished Product   Product B   Finished Product

Notice that each product passes through its own cell. All machines necessary to process each product are placed within the cell. Each cell is dedicated to the production of one product or one subassembly.

is viewed as a minifactory; thus, each cell requires easy and quick access to support services, which means that centralized service departments must be scaled down and their personnel reassigned to work directly with manufacturing cells. For example, with respect to raw materials, JIT calls for multiple stock points, each one near where the material will be used. There is no need for a central store location—in fact, such an arrangement actually hinders efficient production. A purchasing agent can be assigned to each cell to handle material requirements. Similarly, other service personnel, such as manufacturing and quality engineers, can be assigned to cells.

Other support services may be relocated to the cell by training cell workers to perform the services. For example, in addition to direct production work, cell workers may perform setup duties, move partially completed goods from station to station within the cell, perform preventive maintenance and minor repairs, conduct quality inspections, and perform janitorial tasks. This multiple-task capability is directly related to the pull-through production approach. Producing on demand means that *production workers* (formerly direct laborers) may often have "free" time. This nonproduction time can be used to perform some of the other support activities.

Employee Empowerment A major procedural difference between traditional and JIT environments is the degree of participation allowed workers in the management of the organization. According to the JIT view, increasing the degree of participation increases productivity and overall cost efficiency. Workers are allowed a say in how the plant operates. For example, workers are allowed to shut down production to identify and correct problems. Input is sought and used to improve production processes. Workers, as at Saturn and Southwest Airlines, are often involved in interviewing and hiring other employees, sometimes even including prospective bosses. The reason? If the "chemistry is right," then the workforce will be more efficient—and will work together better. Employee empowerment calls for a different style of management: managers in the JIT environment need to act as facilitators more than as supervisors. Their role is to develop people and their skills so that they can make value-adding contributions.

Total Quality Control JIT necessarily carries with it a much stronger emphasis on managing quality. A defective part brings production to a grinding halt. Poor quality simply cannot be tolerated in a manufacturing environment that operates without inventories. Simply put, JIT cannot be implemented without a commitment to total quality control (TQC). TQC is essentially a neverending quest for perfect quality, the striving for a defect-free product design and manufacturing process. This approach to managing quality is diametrically opposed to the traditional doctrine, called acceptable quality level (AQL). AQL permits or allows defects to occur provided they do not exceed a predetermined level.

acceptable quality level (AQL)

The major differences between JIT manufacturing and traditional manufacturing are summarized in Exhibit 4-19. These differences have some fairly direct implications for product costing and for the role of ABC in a JIT environment.

Traceability of Overhead Costs

A cost system uses three methods to assign costs to individual products: direct attribution, driver tracing, and allocation. Of the three methods, the most accurate is direct attribution, and, thus, preferred over the other two methods. In a JIT environment, many overhead costs assigned to products using either driver tracing or allocation are now directly attributable to products. Cellular manufacturing, multiskilled labor, and decentralized service activities are the major features of JIT responsible for this change in traceability.

In a departmental structure, many different products may be subjected to a process located in a single department (for example, grinding). After completion of the process, the products are then transferred to other processes located in different departments (for example, assembly, painting, and so on). Although a different set of processes is usually required for each product, most processes are applicable to more than one product. For example, 30 different products may need grinding. Because more than one product is processed in a department, the costs of that department are common to all products passing through it and, therefore, must be assigned to products using activity drivers or allocation. In a manufacturing-cell structure, however, all processes necessary for the production of each product or major subassembly are collected in one area called a cell. Thus, the costs of operating that cell can be assigned to the cell's product or subassembly using direct attribution. (However, if a family of products uses a cell, then we must resort to drivers and allocation to assign costs.)

4-19

Exhibit
Comparison of JIT Approach with Traditional Manufacturing and Purchasing

JIT	Traditional
1. Pull-through system	1. Push-through system
2. Insignificant inventories	2. Significant inventories
3. Small supplier base	3. Large supplier base
4. Long-term supplier contracts	4. Short-term supplier contracts
5. Cellular structure	5. Departmental structure
6. Multiskilled labor	6. Specialized labor
7. Decentralized services	7. Centralized services
8. High employee involvement	8. Low employee involvement
9. Facilitating management style	9. Supervisory management style
10. Total quality control	10. Acceptable quality level

Equipment formerly located in other departments, for example, is now reassigned to cells, where it may be dedicated to the production of a single product or subassembly. In this case, depreciation is now a directly attributable product cost. Multiskilled workers and decentralized services add to the effect. Workers in the cell are trained to set up the equipment in the cell, maintain it, and operate it. Additionally, cell workers may also be used to move a partially finished part from one machine to the next, perform maintenance, setups, and material handling, support functions previously done by a different set of laborers for all product lines. Additionally, people with specialized skills (for example, industrial engineers and production schedulers) are assigned directly to manufacturing cells. Thus, because of multitask assignments and redeployment of other support personnel, many support costs can now be assigned to a product using direct attribution. Exhibit 4-20 compares the traceability of some selected costs in a traditional manufacturing environment with their traceability in the JIT environment (assuming single-product cells). Comparisons are based on the three cost assignment methods.

Product Costing and ABC

One consequence of increasing directly attributable costs is to increase the accuracy of product costing. Directly attributable costs are physically associated (usually by physical observation) with the product and can safely be said to belong to it. Other costs, however, are common to several products and must be assigned to these products using activity drivers and allocation. Because of cost and convenience, activity drivers that are less than perfectly correlated with the consumption of overhead activities may be chosen. JIT manufacturing reduces the need for this difficult assessment by converting many common costs to directly attributable costs. While activity-based costing offers significant improvement in product-costing accuracy, focusing offers even more potential improvement.

Exhibit 4-20 illustrates that JIT does not convert all costs into directly traceable costs. Even with JIT in place, some overhead activities remain common to the manufacturing cells. These remaining support activities are mostly facility-level activities. In a JIT system, the batch size is one unit of product. Thus, all batch-level activities convert into unit-level activities. Additionally, many of the batch-level activities are reduced or eliminated. For example, material handling may be significantly reduced because of

Exhibit
Product Cost
Assignment: Traditional
versus JIT Manufacturing

Manufacturing Cost	Traditional Environment	JIT Environment
Direct labor	Direct tracing	Direct tracing
Direct materials	Direct tracing	Direct tracing
Material handling	Driver tracing	Direct tracing
Repairs and maintenance	Driver tracing	Direct tracing
Energy	Driver tracing	Direct tracing
Operating supplies	Driver tracing	Direct tracing
Supervision (department)	Allocation	Direct tracing
Insurance and taxes	Allocation	Allocation
Plant depreciation	Allocation	Allocation
Equipment depreciation	Driver tracing	Direct tracing
Custodial services	Allocation	Direct tracing
Cafeteria services	Driver tracing	Driver tracing

reorganizing from a departmental structure to a cellular structure. Similarly, for single-product cells, there is no setup activity. Even for cells that produce a family of products, setup times would be minimal. Furthermore, it is likely that the need to use activity drivers for the cost of product-level activities is significantly diminished because of decentralizing these support activities to the cell level. Is there, then, a role for ABC in a JIT firm?

Although JIT diminishes the value of ABC for tracing manufacturing costs to individual products, an activity-based costing system has much broader application than just tracing manufacturing costs to products. For many strategic and tactical decisions the product cost definition needs to include nonmanufacturing costs. Thus, knowing and understanding general and administrative, research, development, marketing, customer service, and postpurchase activities and their cost drivers is essential for sound cost analysis. Oregon Cutting System, the firm whose JIT experience we described earlier, in 1990 appointed a special multidisciplinary team to explore the possibility of implementing an activity-based cost system. The team was given the charge to identify cost drivers for the organization's service areas (value-line activities other than manufacturing). The objective was to exploit activities and their drivers to achieve efficiency gains comparable to the manufacturing area. Furthermore, we should keep in mind managers are interested in more than just products as cost objects. Thus, although JIT may diminish the importance of ABC for product costing, it may actually provide impetus for using ABC for other applications, such as customer cost analysis.

ABC and Customer-driven Costs

Customers, distribution channels, and markets are also cost objects of fundamental interest. For example, consider customers. It is possible to have customer diversity just as it is possible to have product diversity. Customers can consume customer-driven activities in different proportions. Sources of customer diversity include such things as order frequency, delivery frequency, geographic distance, sales and promotional support, and engineering support requirements. Knowing how much it costs to service different customers can be vital information for such purposes as pricing, determining customer mix, and improving profitability.

Customer Costing versus Product Costing Assigning the costs of customer service to customers is done in the same way that manufacturing costs are assigned to products. Customer-driven activities such as order entry, order picking, shipping, making sales calls, and evaluating a client's credit are identified and listed in an activity inventory. The cost of the resources consumed is assigned to activities and the cost of the activities is assigned to individual customers. The same model and procedures apply to customers that apply to products. Although we will not define them, it is also possible to have different levels of customer-driven activities, such as order level, customer level, and channel level.[16] Thus, in principle, it is possible to build homogeneous customer-driven cost pools using level and driver attributes. A simple example will illustrate the basics of ABC customer costing.

An Example Suppose that Milan Company produces precision parts for eleven major buyers. ABC is used to assign production costs to products. Of the eleven customers, one accounts for 50 percent of the sales, with the ten accounting for the remainder of the sales. The ten smaller customers purchase parts in roughly equal quantities. Orders placed by the smaller customers are about the same size. Data concerning Milan's customer activity follow:

---

16. A detailed discussion of customer-driven costs, including formal definitions of customer-level activities, can be found in Michael C. O'Guin and Stephen A. Rebishke, "Customer-Driven Costs Using Activity-Based Costing," in *Handbook of Cost Management*, ed. Barry Brinker (New York: Warren Gorham Lamont, 1993), B5-1 and B5-29.

	Large Customer	Ten Smaller Customers
Units purchased	500,000	500,000
Orders placed	2	200
Number of sales calls	10	210
Manufacturing cost	$3,000,000	$3,000,000
Order-filling costs allocated*	$202,000	$202,000
Sales-force costs allocated*	$110,000	$110,000

*Allocated based on sales volume

Currently, customer-driven costs are assigned to customers based on units sold, a unit-level driver. ABC improves the assignment by using drivers that better reflect the consumption of the activities by customers: number of orders and number of sales calls. The activity rates are $2,000 per order ($404,000/202 orders) for order filling and $1,000 per call ($220,000/220 calls) for the sales-force activity. Using this information, the customer-driven costs can be assigned to each group of customers as follows:

	Large Customer	Ten Smaller Customers
Order-filling costs	$ 4,000	$400,000
Sales-force costs	$10,000	$210,000

This reveals a much different picture of the cost of servicing each type of customer. The smaller customer is costing more, attributable to smaller, more frequent orders and the evident need of the sales force to engage in more negotiation to make a sale.

What does this tell management that it didn't know before? First, the large customer costs much less to service than the smaller customers and perhaps should be charged less. Second, it raises some significant questions relative to the smaller customers. Is it possible, for example, to encourage larger, less frequent orders? Perhaps offering discounts for larger orders would be appropriate. Why are the smaller customers more difficult to sell? Why are more calls needed? Are they less informed than the larger customer about the products?

This example illustrates the power and value of ABC even for firms that have implemented JIT. It also shows the potential value of ABC in areas other than manufacturing and this value is also available for non-JIT firms.

SUMMARY OF LEARNING OBJECTIVES

1. Discuss the importance of unit costs.

Unit costs are important for inventory valuation, income determination, and providing input to a variety of decisions such as pricing, make or buy, and accept or reject special orders. Because of their importance, their accuracy becomes a critical issue.

2. Define actual and normal costing and explain why normal costing is preferred.

An actual cost system requires the firm to determine the actual cost of direct materials, direct labor, and overhead to calculate unit cost. Normal cost is a mixture of actual costs for direct labor and direct materials and predetermined costs for overhead. Normal costing is preferred because it supplies unit cost information in a timely way. An actual cost system cannot supply the needed cost information on a timely basis.

3. Describe traditional costing approaches.

Traditional costing assigns direct materials and direct labor using direct tracing; overhead is assigned using a two-stage process. In the first stage, overhead costs are collected in pools, either at the plant level or the departmental level. Once the pools are defined, the costs of the overhead pools are assigned to products using unit-level drivers, the most common being direct labor hours.

4. Explain why traditional costing approaches may produce distorted costs.

Overhead costs have increased in significance over time and in many firms represent a much higher percentage of product costs than direct labor. At the same time, many overhead activities are unrelated to the units produced. Traditional cost systems are not able to assign the costs of these nonunit-related overhead activities properly. These overhead activities are consumed by products in different proportions than unit-based overhead activities. Because of this, assigning overhead using only unit-based drivers can distort product costs. This can be a serious matter if the nonunit-based overhead costs are a significant proportion of total overhead costs.

5. Explain how an activity-based cost system can produce more accurate product costs.

Overhead assignments should reflect the amount of overhead demanded (consumed) by each product. Activity-based costing recognizes that not all overhead varies with the number of units produced. By using both unit-based and nonunit-based cost drivers, overhead can be more accurately traced to individual products. This tracing is achieved by implementing the following steps: (1) identifying the major activities, (2) determining the cost of those activities, (3) identifying what causes or drives these activity costs (cost drivers), (4) grouping activities into homogeneous cost pools, (5) calculating a pool rate, (6) measuring the demands placed on activities by each product, and (7) calculating product costs.

6. Provide a detailed description of how activities are identified and classified so that homogeneous cost pools can be formed.

Activities are basic units of work. Homogeneous sets of activities are collections of activities that have the same activity level classi-

fication and the same activity driver classification. Level classification places activitiesinto one of four categories: unit level, batch level, product level, or facility level. Unit-level activities occur each time a unit of product is produced. Batch-level activities occur when batches of products are produced. Product-level activities are incurred to enable production of each different type of product. Facility-level activities sustain a facility's general manufacturing processes. Finally, level-classified activities with the same activity driver are combined to form homogeneous sets. Summing the costs associated with activities within homogeneous sets defines homogeneous cost pools. Activity drivers are then used to compute pool rates and assign costs to individual products.

7. Describe the role of activity-based costing in a JIT environment.

In a JIT environment, more costs become directly traceable to the products being produced. Batch-level activities either convert to unit-level activities or are eliminated. The net effect is to diminish the need for ABC to trace production costs to products. ABC, however, is still very useful in other areas of the company. The need for tracing costs to other objects such as customers still exists. Tracing customer-driven costs to customers, markets, and distribution channels can provide significant information to managers, allowing them to make better pricing decisions, customer-mix decisions, and decisions that improve profitability.

K EY TERMS

Acceptable quality level (AQL) *134*	Batch-level activities *127*	Nonunit-based activity cost drivers *116*	Product diversity *117*
Activity *125*	Consumption ratio *117*	Normal activity level *110*	Product-level (sustaining) activities *127*
Activity attributes *125*	Cost assignment *106*	Normal costing systems *109*	Theoretical activity level *110*
Activity-based cost (ABC) system *119*	Cost measurement *106*	Overapplied overhead *113*	Underapplied overhead *113*
Activity inventory *125*	Expected activity level *110*	Overhead variance *113*	Unit-level activities *127*
Actual cost system *108*	Facility-level activities *127*	Pool rate *121*	Unit-level activity drivers *110*
Advanced manufacturing environment *115*	Homogeneous cost pool *121*	Practical activity level *110*	
Applied overhead *112*	JIT manufacturing *130*	Predetermined overhead rate *109*	
	JIT purchasing *132*		
	Manufacturing cells *132*		

R EVIEW PROBLEM

Inca Pottery Company is noted for a full line of quality vases. The company operates one of its plants in Lima, Peru. That plant produces two types of vases: Indian design and contemporary. Maria Vinueza, the president of the company, recently decided to change from a volume-based costing system to an activity-based cost system. Before making the change companywide, she wanted to assess the effect on the product costs of the Lima plant. This plant was chosen because it produces only two types of vases; most other plants produce at least a dozen.

To assess the effect of the change, the following data have been gathered (for simplicity, costs are expressed in dollars rather than in Peruvian currency).

Vase	Quantity	Prime Costs	Machine Hours	Material Moves	Setups
Indian	200,000	$700,000	50,000	700,000	100
Contemporary	50,000	150,000	12,500	100,000	50
Dollar value	—	$850,000	$250,000*	$300,000	$450,000

*Cost of maintenance

Under the current system, the costs of maintenance, material handling, and setups are assigned to the vases on the basis of machine hours.

REQUIRED:
1. Compute the unit cost of each vase using the current unit-based approach.
2. Compute the unit cost of each vase using an activity-based costing approach.
3. Assume that Maria decides to install JIT manufacturing. Two manufacturing cells are created—one for each vase (the I-cell and the C-cell). The overhead costs traceable to each cell are as follows:

Cell	Maintenance	Material Handling	Setups	Total
I-Cell	$210,000	$260,000	$300,000	$770,000
C-Cell	40,000	40,000	150,000	230,000

Assume the same level of output and prime costs as in the current system. Compute the unit cost for each vase in the JIT system. Is this cost more accurate than the activity-based cost? Explain.

Solution
1. Total overhead is $1,000,000. The plantwide rate is $16 per machine hour ($1,000,000/ 62,500). Overhead is assigned as follows:

Indian vase: $16 × 50,000 = $800,000
Contemporary vase: $16 × 12,500 = $200,000

The unit costs for the two products are as follows:

Indian vase: $\dfrac{\$800,000 + \$700,000}{200,000} = \$7.50$

Contemporary vase: $\dfrac{\$200,000 + \$150,000}{50,000} = \$7.00$

2. In the activity-based approach, the consumption ratios are different for all three overhead activities, so overhead pools are formed for each activity. The overhead rates for each of these pools are as follows:

Maintenance: $\dfrac{\$250,000}{62,500} = \$4/\text{hour}$

Material handling: $\dfrac{\$300,000}{800,000} = \$0.375 \text{ per move}$

Setup: $\dfrac{\$450,000}{150} = \$3,000 \text{ per setup}$

Overhead is assigned as follows:

Indian vases:	
$4 × 50,000	$200,000
$0.375 × 700,000	262,500
$3,000 × 100	300,000
Total	$762,500

Contemporary vases:	
$4 × 12,500	$ 50,000
$0.375 × 100,000	37,500
$3,000 × 50	150,000
Total	$237,500

This produces the following unit costs:

Indian vases:	
Prime costs	$ 700,000
Overhead costs	762,500
Total costs	$1,462,500
Units produced	200,000
Unit cost	$7.3125

Contemporary vases:	
Prime costs	$150,000
Overhead costs	237,500
Total costs	$387,500
Units produced	50,000
Unit cost	$7.75

3. With a JIT manufacturing system, costs would be computed as follows:

Indian vases:	
Prime costs	$ 700,000
Overhead costs	770,000
Total	$1,470,000
Units produced	200,000
Unit cost	$7.35

Contemporary vases:	
Prime costs	$150,000
Overhead costs	230,000
Total	$380,000
Units produced	50,000
Unit cost	$7.60

The unit cost here is the most accurate since all costs are directly traceable to each product. This is because of the focusing effect of JIT.

QUESTIONS FOR WRITING AND DISCUSSION

1. Explain why knowing the unit cost of a product or service is important.
2. What is cost measurement? cost assignment? What is the difference between the two?
3. Explain why an actual overhead rate is rarely used for product costing.
4. Describe the two-stage process associated with plantwide overhead rates.
5. Describe the two-stage process for departmental overhead rates.
6. Explain why departmental rates might be chosen over plantwide rates.
7. Explain how a plantwide overhead rate, using a unit-based cost driver, can produce distorted product costs. In your answer, identify two major factors that impair the ability of plantwide rates to assign cost accurately.
8. Explain how low-volume products can be undercosted and high-volume products overcosted if only unit-based cost drivers are used to assign overhead costs.
9. Explain how undercosting low-volume products and overcosting high-volume products can affect the competitive position of a firm.
10. What are nonunit-related overhead activities? nonunit-based cost drivers? Give some examples.
11. What is meant by "product diversity"?
12. What is an overhead consumption ratio?
13. Explain how departmental overhead rates can produce product costs that are more distorted than those computed using a plantwide rate.
14. Overhead costs are the source of product cost distortions. Do you agree? Explain.
15. What is activity-based product costing?

16. Explain how homogeneous sets of activities are produced. Why are they produced?
17. What is a homogeneous cost pool?
18. What is the first-stage procedure in assigning overhead costs to products when using an activity-based system?
19. What is the second-stage procedure in assigning overhead costs to products when using an activity-based system?
20. What is an activity? a homogeneous set of activities?
21. What are unit-level activities? batch-level activities? product-level activities? facility-level activities?
22. What is JIT manufacturing? List four ways in which JIT manufacturing differs from traditional manufacturing.

23. What are manufacturing cells? Explain how they differ from production departments.
24. Explain why some indirect manufacturing costs in traditional manufacturing become direct costs in JIT manufacturing. Give some examples of costs that change in this way.
25. In JIT manufacturing, direct labor costs are less important and largely fixed in nature. Do you agree? Explain.
26. Without inventories, there is no distinction between product and period costs. Do you agree? Explain.
27. How does JIT manufacturing increase product-costing accuracy?

W ARM-UP EXERCISES

This section provides short warm-up exercises based on the examples in the chapter. Each warm-up exercise gives the page number on which the text example can be found. You may want to refer to the text example to see how the exercise can be set up and solved.

W4-1
Normal versus
Actual Costing
LO 2
p. 109

At the beginning of the year, the controller of Golding Company budgeted overhead costs at $180,000 and production at 200,000 units. Actual overhead costs and actual production for four-month periods follow:

	Period Ending		
	April 30	August 31	December 31
Actual overhead	$40,000	$80,000	$ 60,000
Actual units produced	40,000	40,000	120,000

	Cordless	Regular
Units produced	10,000	100,000
Prime costs	$78,000	$738,000
Direct labor hours	10,000	90,000

REQUIRED:
1. Calculate the actual unit costs for each four-month period.
2. Calculate the actual unit cost for the entire year.
3. What problems with actual costing are revealed by the calculations?
4. What is the cost per unit using a predetermined rate? How does this compare with the answer in requirement 2? Would this be a normal outcome? Explain.

W4-2
Plantwide Rate
LO 1, LO 3
p. 112

Nabors Company produces two types of telephones. For the most recent year, Nabors reports the following data:

Budgeted overhead	$180,000
Expected activity (in direct labor hours)	50,000
Actual activity (in direct labor hours)	51,000
Actual overhead	$200,000

	Cordless	Regular
Units produced	5,000	50,000
Prime costs	$40,000	$300,000
Direct labor hours	5,000	46,000 = 51,000

REQUIRED:
1. Calculate a predetermined overhead rate based on direct labor hours.
2. What is the applied overhead?
3. What is the underapplied or overapplied overhead?
4. Calculate the unit cost of each phone.

W4-3
Departmental Rates
LO 3
p. 113–114

Nabors Company gathers the following departmental data for a second year. Two types of telephones are produced: cordless and regular.

	Departmental Data	
	Fabrication	Assembly
Budgeted overhead	$120,000	$60,000
Expected and actual activity (direct labor hours):		
Cordless	3,000	2,000
Regular	8,000	43,000
	11,000	45,000
Expected and actual activity (machine hours):		
Cordless	2,000	500
Regular	18,000	5,000
	20,000	5,500

In addition to the departmental data, the following information is provided:

	Cordless	Regular
Units produced	5,000	50,000
Prime costs	$40,000	$300,000

REQUIRED:
1. Calculate departmental overhead rates, using machine-hours for fabrication and direct labor hours for assembly.
2. Calculate the applied overhead by department.
3. Calculate the applied overhead by product.
4. Calculate unit costs.

W4-4
Activity Product Costs
LO 5, LO 6
p. 118–122

Nabors Company produces two types of phones. Activity data follow:

	Product-Costing Data		
Activity Usage Measures	Cordless	Regular	Total
Units produced per year	5,000	50,000	—
Prime costs	$39,000	$369,000	$408,000
Direct labor hours	5,000	45,000	50,000
Machine-hours	10,000	90,000	100,000
Production runs	10	5	15
Number of moves	120	60	180

Activity Cost Data (overhead activities)	
Activity	Activity Cost
Setting up equipment	$ 60,000
Material handling	30,000
Using power	50,000
Testing	40,000
Total	$180,000

REQUIRED:
1. Calculate the consumption ratios for each activity.
2. Group activities based on the consumption ratios and activity level.
3. Calculate a rate for each pooled group of activities.
4. Using the pool rates, calculate unit product costs.

XERCISES

E4-1
Normal versus
Actual Costing
LO 1, LO 2

Nublado Company produces ski boots. At the beginning of the year, the cost manager estimated that overhead costs would be $2,910,000 and that the units produced would be 300,000. Actual data concerning production for the past year follow:

	Quarter 1	Quarter 2	Quarter 3	Quarter 4	Total
Units produced	100,000	40,000	20,000	140,000	300,000
Prime costs	$2,000,000	$800,000	$400,000	$2,800,000	$6,000,000
Overhead costs	$800,000	$600,000	$900,000	$700,000	$3,000,000

REQUIRED:
1. Calculate the unit cost for each quarter and for the year using the following costs:
   a. Actual prime costs
   b. Actual overhead costs
   c. Actual total manufacturing costs
2. What do the calculations in requirement 1 tell you about actual costing?
3. Using supporting calculations, describe how normal costing would work.

E4-2
Plantwide Rates;
Overhead Variance
LO 1, LO 2, LO 3

Hite Manufacturing uses a normal costing system. Budgeted overhead for the coming year is $750,000. Expected actual activity is 200,000 direct labor hours. During the year, Hite worked a total of 192,000 direct labor hours and actual overhead totaled $736,000.

REQUIRED:
1. Compute the predetermined overhead rate for Hite Manufacturing.
2. Compute the applied overhead.
3. Compute the overhead variance and label the variance as underapplied or overapplied overhead.
4. Explain why predetermined rates are used.

E4-3
Unit Cost; Plantwide
Overhead Rate;
Applied Overhead
LO 1, LO 2, LO 3

Computer Systems Design develops specialized software for companies, and uses a normal costing system. The following data are available for 1998:

Budgeted	
Overhead	$600,000
Machine hours	24,000
Direct labor hours	75,000
Actual	
Units produced	100,000
Overhead	$603,500
Prime costs	$900,000
Machine hours	25,050
Direct labor hours	75,700

Overhead is applied on the basis of direct labor hours.

REQUIRED:
1. What is the predetermined overhead rate?
2. What is the applied overhead for 1998?

3. Was overhead overapplied or underapplied and by how much?

4. What is the unit cost for the year?

E4-4
Unit Overhead Cost;
Predetermined
Plantwide Overhead
Rate; Applied
Overhead
LO 1, LO 2, LO 3

Using the information from E4-3, suppose Computer Systems Design applied overhead to production on the basis of machine hours instead of direct labor hours.

REQUIRED:

1. What is the predetermined overhead rate?

2. What is the applied overhead for 1998?

3. Is overhead overapplied or underapplied and by how much?

4. What is the unit cost?

5. How can Computer Systems Design decide whether to use direct labor hours or machine hours as the basis for applying factory overhead?

E4-5
Unit Overhead Cost;
Predetermined
Departmental
Overhead Rates;
Overhead Variance
LO 1, LO 2, LO 3

Kildoz Pharmaceutical uses a predetermined overhead rate to apply overhead. Overhead is applied on the basis of direct labor hours in the mixing department and on the basis of machine hours in the encapsulating department. At the beginning of 1998, the following estimates are provided for the coming year:

	Mixing	Encapsulating
Direct labor hours	200,000	40,000
Machine hours	20,000	70,000
Direct labor cost	$900,000	$190,000
Overhead cost	$300,000	$196,000

Actual results reported for 1998 are as follows:

	Mixing	Encapsulating
Direct labor hours	196,000	42,000
Machine hours	22,000	72,000
Direct labor cost	$882,400	$168,000
Overhead cost	$301,000	$206,000

REQUIRED:

1. Compute the predetermined overhead rate for each department.

2. Compute the applied overhead for 1998. What is the underapplied or overapplied overhead for each department? for the firm?

3. Suppose a batch of pills used 1,000 direct labor hours in mixing and 400 machine hours in encapsulating. If the batch size is 10,000 units, what is the overhead cost per pill?

E4-6
Product-Costing
Accuracy and
Overhead Costs
LO 3, LO 5

Gator Company has traditionally produced a handcrafted ladies' purse (sold under the label Gator Elegant). A marketing consultant has recommended that a second purse be produced—using lower-quality materials and automation so that it can be produced in larger quantities. (This purse will be sold under the label Gator Eminent.) Gator decides to produce the second purse and buys the equipment for automated production and installs it in a currently unused part of its plant. Gator discovers that a small part of the operation associated with the handcrafted purse can be automated (using the same equipment just purchased) without compromising its claim that the purse is essentially handcrafted.

The production equipment is expected to last five years, with a capability of supplying a total of 25,000 machine hours. The costs associated with the equipment follow:

Depreciation	$5,000*
Operating costs	4,000

*Depreciation is computed on a straight-line basis; book value at the beginning of the year was $25,000.

The controller has collected the expected annual prime costs for each purse, the machine hours, and the expected production.

	Elegant	Eminent
Direct labor	$9,000	$3,000
Direct materials	$3,000	$3,000
Units	3,000	3,000
Machine hours	500	4,500

REQUIRED:
1. Do you think that the direct labor costs and direct materials costs are accurately traced to each purse? Explain.
2. The controller has suggested that overhead costs be assigned to each product using a plantwide rate based on direct labor costs. Machine costs are overhead costs. Calculate the machine cost per unit for each purse that would be assigned using this approach. Do you think that machine costs are traced accurately to each purse? Explain.
3. Now calculate the machine cost per unit for each purse using an overhead rate based on machine hours. Do you think machine costs are traced accurately to each purse? Explain.
4. Suppose machine hours are used to assign *all* overhead costs of the plant to the two products. Do you think this will produce an accurate cost assignment for each purse? Explain.

E4-7

Multiple versus Single Overhead Rates; Activity Drivers

LO 3, LO 4, LO 5

Assume that a plant has two categories of overhead: moving materials and testing products. The costs expected for these categories for the coming year are as follows:

Moving materials	$200,000
Testing products	600,000

The plant currently applies overhead using machine hours and expected actual capacity. This figure is 80,000 machine hours. Natalie Nabors, the plant manager, has been asked to submit a bid and has assembled the following data on the proposed order:

	Potential Order
Direct materials	$4,000
Direct labor (1,000 hours)	$7,000
Overhead	$?
Number of material moves	12
Number of inspections	5
Machine hours	900

Natalie has been told that many competitors use an activity-based approach to assign overhead to products. Before submitting her bid, she wants to assess the effects of this alternative approach. She estimates that the expected number of material moves for all orders during the year is 1,000; she also expects 5,000 product tests to be performed.

REQUIRED:
1. Compute the total cost of the potential order using machine hours to assign overhead. Assuming that the bid price is full manufacturing cost plus 25 percent, what would Natalie's bid be?
2. Compute the total cost of the potential order using the number of material moves to allocate material-handling costs and the number of inspections to allocate the quality inspection costs. Assuming a bid price of full manufacturing cost plus 25 percent, what is Natalie's bid using this approach?
3. Which approach do you think best reflects the actual cost of the order? Explain.

E4-8
Activity versus Plantwide Overhead Rates: Activity Drivers
LO 4, LO 5

Milan Machining Company has identified the following overhead activities, costs, and activity drivers for the coming year:

Activity	Expected Cost	Activity Driver	Activity Capacity
Setting up	$60,000	Number of setups	300
Inspecting	45,000	Inspection hours	4,500
Grinding	90,000	Machine hours	18,000
Receiving	25,000	Number of parts	50,000

The company produces several different machine subassemblies used by other manufacturers. Information on separate batches for two of these subassemblies follows:

	Subassembly A	Subassembly B
Direct materials	$850	$950
Direct labor	$600	$600
Units completed	100	50
Number of setups	1	1
Inspection hours	4	2
Machine hours	20	30
Parts used	20	40

The company's normal activity is 4,000 direct labor hours. Each batch uses 50 hours of direct labor.

REQUIRED:
1. Determine the unit cost for each product using direct labor hours to apply overhead.
2. Determine the unit cost for each product using the four activity drivers.
3. Which method produces the more accurate cost assignment? Why?

E4-9
Activity-based Costing: Homogeneous Cost Pools; Activity Drivers
LO 5, LO 6

Rico Manufacturing produces two types of battery-operated toy cars: sports and police. The cars are produced using one continuous process. Four activities have been identified: machining, set-ups, receiving, and packing. Resource drivers have been used to assign costs to each activity. The overhead activities, their costs, and the other related data are as follows:

Product	Machine Hours	Setups	Receiving Orders	Packing Orders
Sports	10,000	100	100	800
Police	10,000	50	200	400
Costs	$200,000	$7,500	$4,500	$30,000

REQUIRED:
1. Classify the overhead activities as unit level, batch level, product level, or facility level.
2. Create homogeneous cost pools. Identify the activities that belong to each pool.
3. Identify the activity driver for each pool and compute the pool rate.
4. Assign the overhead costs to each product using the pool rates computed in requirement 3.

E4-10
Conventional Costing; Activity-based Costing; Pricing
LO 5, LO 6

Hammer Company produces a variety of electronic equipment. One of its plants produces two laser printers: the deluxe and the regular. At the beginning of the year, the following data were prepared for this plant:

	Deluxe	Regular
Quantity	100,000	800,000
Selling price	$900.00	$750.00
Unit prime cost	$529.00	$482.75
Unit overhead cost	$47.00	$117.25

Overhead is applied using direct labor hours.

Upon examining the data, the vice-president of marketing was particularly impressed with the per-unit profitability of the deluxe printer and suggested that more emphasis be placed on producing and selling this product. The plant manager objected to this strategy, arguing that the cost of the deluxe printer was understated. He argued that overhead costs could be assigned more accurately by using activity drivers—factors that reflected each product's demands for overhead activities. To convince higher management that overhead rates using activity drivers could produce a significant difference in product costs, he obtained the following projected information from the controller for the production output given:

Pool Name[a]	Activity Driver	Pool Rate[b]	Deluxe	Regular
Setups	Number of setups	$3,000	300	200
Machining	Machine hours	200	100,000	300,000
Engineering	Engineering hours	40	50,000	100,000
Packing	Packing orders	20	100,000	400,000
Providing space	Machine hours	1	200,000	800,000

[a]Pools are named according to the nature of the activities found within each pool. Providing space is a collection of facility-level activities. Packing and setups are collections of batch-level activities. Engineering is a collection of product-level activities, and machining is a collection of unit-level activities.
[b]Cost per unit of activity driver

REQUIRED:
1. Using the projected data based on conventional costing, compute gross profit percentage, gross profit per unit, and total gross profit for each product.
2. Using the pool rates, compute the overhead cost per unit for each product. Using this new unit cost, compute gross profit percentage, gross profit per unit, and total gross profit for each product.
3. In view of the outcome in requirement 2, evaluate the suggestion of the vice-president of marketing to switch the emphasis to the deluxe model.

E4-11
Two-Stage
Procedure;
Activity-based
Costing
LO 5, LO 6

Mendoza Company has recently decided to convert from conventional product costing to an activity-based system. The company produces two types of clocks: small and large. The clocks are produced in batches. Information concerning these two products follows:

	Small Clock	Large Clock
Quantity produced	100,000	200,000
Machine hours	50,000	50,000
Direct labor hours	100,000	100,000
Material handling (number of moves)	2,000	4,000
Engineering (hours)	10,000	5,000
Receiving (number of orders processed)	250	500
Setups	60	20
Maintaining (hours used)	4,000	2,000
Kilowatt-hours	25,000	25,000
Inspecting (number of hours)	3,000	1,000

Additionally, the following overhead costs are reported for the activities associated with the two products:

Material handling	$120,000
Maintaining equipment	80,000
Producing power	30,000
Depreciation (machines)*	60,000
Engineering	100,000

Receiving	$ 30,000
Setups	96,000
Inspecting	60,000

*Depreciation is straight line; book value at the beginning of the year was $600,000. The machine hours reported represent the normal activity level. The remaining life of the machinery is ten years or 1 million machine hours.

REQUIRED:

1. Classify activities by level and then by driver.
2. Group all overhead costs into homogeneous cost pools. Select an activity driver for each cost pool and compute a pool rate.
3. Using the pool rates calculated in requirement 2, assign all overhead costs to the two products and compute the overhead cost per unit for each.

E4-12
Classification of Activities
LO 6

Classify the following activities as unit level, batch level, product level, or facility level. Also identify a potential activity driver for each activity.

1. Setting up equipment
2. Receiving materials
3. Inspecting goods
4. Shipping goods
5. Ordering supplies
6. Ordering production
7. Administering parts
8. Moving materials
9. Processing customer orders
10. Supervising plant
11. Welding subassemblies
12. Assembling components
13. Testing special products
14. Providing heating and air conditioning in the plant
15. Expediting goods
16. Providing plant space

E4-13
Selection of an ABC System
LO 4, LO 5

In 1988, Sterling Company changed its cost system. It went from using a single, plantwide overhead rate based on direct labor hours to a system using departmental overhead rates. The departmental overhead rates used direct labor hours, machine hours, and direct material dollars to assign overhead to products.

In 1998, the president of Sterling, Pamela Jones, was mulling over the possibility of changing to an ABC system. She had heard that the life of a cost system was about ten years and was worried that the current system was no longer serving the needs of the company. She was also convinced, however, that a change to ABC simply because it was a "hot" topic was not the right approach. Any change had to be in the best economic interests of the company.

REQUIRED: As a consultant to Pamela, identify the factors that should be considered in changing to an ABC system. In your discussion, include a definition of an outmoded or obsolete cost system.

E4-14
JIT and Product-Costing Accuracy
LO 7

Prior to installing a JIT system, Rumple Company used machine hours to assign maintenance costs to its three products (small, medium, and large tablecloths). The maintenance costs totaled $280,000 per year. The machine hours used by each product and the quantity of each product produced are as follows:

	Machine Hours	Quantity Produced
Small	30,000	7,500
Medium	30,000	7,500
Large	40,000	10,000

After installing JIT, three manufacturing cells were created, and cell workers were trained to perform maintenance. Maintenance costs for the three cells still totaled $280,000; however, these costs are now traceable to each cell as follows:

Cell, small tablecloths	$ 76,000
Cell, medium tablecloths	84,000
Cell, large tablecloths	120,000

REQUIRED:
1. Compute the pre-JIT maintenance cost per tablecloth for each type.
2. Compute maintenance cost per unit for each type after installing JIT.
3. Explain why the JIT maintenance cost per unit is more accurate than the pre-JIT cost.

E4-15
JIT; Traceability of Costs; Product-Costing Accuracy
LO 7

The manufacturing costs assigned to an electronic component before and after installing JIT follow:

	Before	After
Direct materials	$60,000	$60,000
Direct labor	40,000	50,000
Maintenance	50,000	30,000
Power	10,000	8,000
Depreciation	12,500	10,000
Material handling	8,000	4,000
Engineering	9,600	8,000
Setups	15,000	8,500
Building and grounds	11,800	12,400
Supplies	4,000	3,000
Supervision (plant)	8,200	8,200
Cell supervision	—	30,000
Departmental supervision	18,000	—
Total	$247,100	$232,100

In both the pre- and post-JIT setting, 100,000 units of the component are manufactured. In the JIT setting, manufacturing cells are used to produce each product.

REQUIRED:
1. Compute the unit cost of the product before and after JIT. Explain why the JIT unit cost is more accurate.
2. Identify the costs in the JIT environment that are directly traceable to the electronic component. Classify the remaining costs as those that must be traced using drivers or allocated if truly indirect.

E4-16
Customer-driven Costs
LO 7

Emery Company has two classes of customers: JIT firms and non-JIT firms. The JIT customer category places small, frequent orders, and the non-JIT customer category tends to place larger, less frequent orders. Both types of customer are buying the same product. Emery charges manufacturing cost plus 25 percent for a given order. The 25 percent markup is set large enough to cover nonmanufacturing costs and provide a reasonable return for Emery. Both customer types generated the same sales in units and so Emery's management had assumed that the customer support costs were about the same and priced the goods the same for each customer. Emery recently received some complaints from some of the non-JIT customers. Several of these customers are threatening to take their business to other suppliers who allegedly charge less. For example, one customer said that he could buy the same 5,000 units from a competitor for $3 per unit less than Emery's price. This customer wanted a price concession.

A new cost accountant recently hired suggested that the problem may have to do with unfair cost assignments and suggested that customer costs be assigned to each customer category using activity-based costing. She collected the following information about customer-related activities and costs for the most recent quarter:

	JIT Customers	Non-JIT Customers
Sales orders	200	20
Sales calls	20	20
Service calls	100	50
Average order size	500	5,000
Manufacturing cost/unit	$100	$100
Customer costs:		
Processing sales orders	$ 880,000	
Selling goods	320,000	
Servicing goods	300,000	
Total	$1,500,000	

REQUIRED:
1. Calculate the total revenues per customer category and assign the customer costs to each customer type using revenues as the allocation base.
2. Calculate the customer cost per customer type using activity-based cost assignments. Discuss the merits of offering the non-JIT customers a $3 price decrease.
3. Assume that the JIT customers are simply imposing the frequent orders on Emery. There has been no formal discussion between JIT customers and Emery regarding supply of goods on a just-in-time basis. The sales pattern has simply evolved over time. As an independent consultant, what would you suggest to Emery's management?

PROBLEMS

P4-1
Activity Drivers and Product-Costing Accuracy
LO 3, LO 4, LO 5

Janeiro Company for years produced only one product: backpacks. Recently, the company decided to add a line of duffel bags. With this addition, the need to assign service costs to the producing departments became necessary. Surprisingly, after the addition of the duffel-bag line the costs to produce the backpacks increased and their profitability dropped.

The marketing manager and the production manager both complained about the increase in the production cost of backpacks. The marketing manager was concerned because the increase in unit costs led to pressure to increase the unit price of backpacks. She was resisting this pressure because she was certain that the increase would harm the company's market share. The production manager was receiving pressure to cut costs also, yet he was convinced that nothing different was being done in the way the backpacks were produced. He was also convinced that further efficiency in the manufacture of the backpacks was unlikely. After some discussion, the two managers decided that the problem had to be connected with the addition of the duffel-bag line.

Upon investigation, they were informed that the only real change in product-costing procedures was in the way overhead costs were assigned. A two-stage procedure was now in use. First, the support department costs are assigned to the two producing departments, patterns and finishing. Support costs are assigned to producing departments using a driver that measures the consumption of the service by the producing departments. For example, the costs of the accounting department are assigned to producing departments by calculating a rate per transaction processed and multiplying this rate by the number of transactions caused by each producing department. (In effect, accounting costs are assigned in proportion to the number of transactions processed for each department.) Second, the costs accumulated in the producing departments are assigned to the two products using direct labor hours as a driver. The managers were assured that great care was taken to associate overhead costs with individual products. So that they could construct their own example of cost assignment, the controller made the following information available for one of the company's service departments (the accounting department):

	Department		
	Accounting	Pattern	Finishing
Service cost	$100,000	—	—
Transactions processed	—	40,000	60,000
Total direct labor hours	—	10,000	20,000
Direct labor hours per backpack*	—	0.10	0.20
Direct labor hours per duffel bag*	—	0.40	0.80

*Hours required to produce one unit of each product

The controller remarked that the cost of operating the accounting department had doubled with the addition of the new product line. The increase came because of the need to process additional transactions, which had also doubled in number.

During the first year of producing duffel bags, the company produced and sold 100,000 backpacks and 25,000 duffel bags. The 100,000 backpacks matched the prior year's output for that product.

REQUIRED:

1. Compute the amount of accounting cost assigned to each backpack and duffel bag using the traditional two-stage assignment process described by the controller.
2. Compute the amount of accounting cost assigned to a backpack before the duffel-bag line was added.
3. Suppose that the company decided to assign the accounting costs directly to the product lines using the number of transactions as the activity driver. What is the accounting cost per unit of backpacks? per unit of duffel bags?
4. Which way of assigning overhead does the best job, the traditional two-stage departmental approach or the activity-based approach using transactions processed for each product? Explain. Discuss the benefits of using activity drivers to assign overhead costs directly to individual products.

P4-2

Departmental Rates; Product-Costing Accuracy; Pool Rates

LO 3, LO 4, LO 5

Maxwell Company produces two small engines for model boats (engine A and engine B). Both products pass through two producing departments. Engine B is by far the most popular of the two engines. The following data have been gathered for these two products:

	Product Data	
	Engine A	Engine B
Units produced per year	30,000	300,000
Prime costs	$100,000	$1,000,000
Direct labor hours	40,000	400,000
Machine hours	20,000	200,000
Production runs	40	60
Inspection hours	800	1,200

	Departmental Data	
	Department 1	Department 2
Direct labor hours:		
Engine A	30,000	10,000
Engine B	45,000	355,000
Total	75,000	365,000
Machine hours:		
Engine A	10,000	10,000
Engine B	160,000	40,000
Total	170,000	50,000

	Departmental Data	
	Department 1	Department 2
Overhead costs:		
Setup costs	$ 90,000	$ 90,000
Inspection costs	70,000	70,000
Power	100,000	60,000
Maintenance	80,000	100,000
Total	$340,000	$320,000

REQUIRED:

1. Compute the overhead cost per unit for each product using a plantwide rate based on direct labor hours.
2. Compute the overhead cost per unit for each product using departmental rates. In calculating departmental rates, use machine hours for department 1 and direct labor hours for department 2. Repeat using direct labor hours for department 1 and machine hours for department 2.
3. Compute the overhead cost per unit for each product using activity-based costing.
4. Comment on the ability of departmental rates to improve the accuracy of product costing.

P4-3
Traditional Costing versus Activity-based Costing
LO 4, LO 5, LO 6

Willow Company produces lawn mowers. One of its plants produces two versions of mowers: a basic model and a deluxe model. The deluxe model has a sturdier frame, a higher horsepower engine, a wider blade, and mulching capability. At the beginning of the year, the following data were prepared for this plant:

	Basic Model	Deluxe Model
Expected quantity	20,000	10,000
Selling price	$180	$360
Prime costs	$80	$160
Machine hours	5,000	5,000
Direct labor hours	10,000	10,000
Engineering support (hours)	1,500	4,500
Receiving (orders processed)	250	500
Material handling (number of moves)	2,000	4,000
Purchasing (number of requisitions)	100	200
Maintenance (hours used)	1,000	3,000
Paying suppliers (invoices processed)	250	500
Setting up batches (number of setups)	20	60

Additionally, the following overhead activity costs are reported:

Maintaining equipment	$114,000
Engineering support	120,000
Material handling	120,000
Setting up equipment	96,000
Purchasing materials	60,000
Receiving goods	40,000
Paying suppliers	30,000
Providing space	20,000
Total	$600,000

Facility-level costs are allocated in proportion to machine hours (provides a measure of time the facility is used by each product).

Basic 87.56 per unit
84.40 per unit

REQUIRED:

1. Calculate the cost per unit for each product using direct labor hours to assign all overhead costs.
2. Form homogeneous cost pools and calculate pool rates. Explain why you group activities in pools.
3. Using the pool rates computed in requirement 2, calculate the cost per unit for each product. Compare these costs with those calculated using the traditional method. Which cost is the most accurate? Explain.

P4-4
ABC Costing and Cost Behavior
LO 5, LO 6

Underwood Company produces several different models of a stereo system. The company has recently adopted an ABC system. The unit cost expected for one of the models follows:

Model B	
Unit-level costs (includes materials and labor)	$ 60
Batch-level costs	40
Product-sustaining costs	20
Facility-level costs	10
Total unit cost	$130

The unit cost is based on an expected volume of 10,000 units. These units will be produced in ten equal batches. The product-sustaining costs are all from engineering support. The product-sustaining costs are driven by engineering orders. The $20 cost assignment is based on five orders. Facility-level costs are allocated on the basis of direct labor hours (one hour per unit produced).

REQUIRED:

1. Calculate the total manufacturing cost to produce 10,000 units of model B. Present the total cost for each activity category.
2. Now assume that the company has revised its forecast for model B and expects to produce 15,000 units. A decision was made to handle the increased production by increasing batch size to 1,500 units. The increased production will not require an increase in engineering support. Calculate the total cost to produce the 15,000 units of model B. Present the total cost for each activity category. Explain the outcome.
3. Assume that the revised forecast of 15,000 units is made. Now, however, the decision is made to handle the extra production by increasing the number of batches from 10 to 15. Also, the sales of the extra 5,000 units is possible only if an engineering modification is made. This increases the expected engineering orders from 5 to 6. Explain why the costs changed from those predicted in requirement 2.
4. Discuss the value of classifying and reporting costs by activity category.

P4-5
Activity-based Costing: Service Industry
LO 4, LO 5

Alva Hospital operates an intensive care unit. Currently, patients are charged the same rate per patient day for daily care services. Daily care services are broadly defined as occupancy, feeding, and nursing care. A recent study, however, revealed several interesting outcomes. First, the demands patients place on daily care services vary with the severity of case being treated. Second, the occupancy activity is a combination of two activities: lodging and use of monitoring equipment. Since some patients require more monitoring than others, these activities should be separated. Third, the daily rate should reflect the difference in demands resulting from differences in patient type. To compute a daily rate that reflected the difference in demands, patients were placed in three categories according to illness severity, and the following annual data were collected:

Activity	Cost of Activity	Activity Driver	Quantity
Lodging	$ 900,000	Patient days	6,000
Monitoring	1,200,000	Number of monitoring devices used	10,000
Feeding	100,000	Patient days	6,000
Nursing care	945,000	Nursing hours	63,000
Total	$3,145,000		

The demands associated with patient severity are also provided:

Severity	Patient Days	Monitoring Devices	Nursing Hours
High	2,000	5,000	40,000
Medium	3,000	4,000	18,000
Low	1,000	1,000	5,000

REQUIRED:
1. Suppose that the costs of daily care are assigned using only patient days as the activity driver (which is also the measure of output). Compute the daily rate using this traditional unit-based approach of cost assignment.
2. Compute pool rates using the given activity drivers.
3. Compute the charge per patient day for each patient type using the pool rates from requirement 2 and the demands on each activity.
4. Comment on the value of activity-based costing in service industries.

P4-6
Product-Costing Accuracy; Corporate Strategy; Activity-based Costing
LO 4, LO 5, LO 6

Pearson Manufacturing is engaged in the production of chemicals for industrial use. One plant specializes in the production of chemicals used in the copper industry. Two compounds are produced: compound X-12 and compound S-15. Compound X-12 was originally developed by Pearson's chemists and played a key role in copper extraction from low-grade ore. The patent for X-12 has expired and competition for this market has intensified dramatically. Compound X-12 produced the highest volume of activity and for many years was the only chemical compound produced by the plant. Five years ago, S-15 was added. Compound S-15 was more difficult to manufacture and required special handling and setups. For the first three years after the addition of the new product, profits increased. In the last two years, however, the plant has faced intense competition, and its sales of X-12 have dropped. In fact, the plant showed a small loss in the most recent reporting period. The plant manager is convinced that competing producers have been guilty of selling X-12 below the cost to produce it—perhaps with the objective of expanding market share. The following conversation between Diane Woolridge, plant manager, and Rick Dixon, divisional marketing manager, reflects the concerns of the division about the future of the plant and its products.

Rick: "You know, Diane, the divisional manager is real concerned about the plant's trend. He indicated that in this budgetary environment, we can't afford to carry plants that don't show a profit. We shut one down just last month because it couldn't handle the competition."

Diane: "Rick, our compound X-12 has a reputation for quality and value—we have a very pure product. It has been a mainstay for years. I don't understand what's happening."

Rick: "I just received a call from one of our major customers concerning X-12. He said that a sales representative from another firm had offered the chemical at $10 per kilogram—about $6 less than what we ask. It's hard to compete with a price like that. Perhaps the plant is simply obsolete."

Diane: "No. I don't agree. We have good technology. I think that we are efficient. And it's costing a little more than $10 to produce X-12. I don't see how these companies can afford to sell it so cheaply. I'm not convinced that we should meet the price. Perhaps we should emphasize producing and selling more of S-15. Our margin is high on this product, and we have virtually no competition for it. We just recently raised the price per kilogram and our customers didn't blink an eye."

Rick: "You may be right. I think we can increase the price even more and not lose business. I called a few customers to see how they would react to a 25 percent increase in price, and they all said that they would still purchase the same quantity as before."

Diane: "It sounds promising. However, before we make a major commitment to S-15, I think we had better explore other possible explanations. The market potential is much less than that for X-12. I want to know how our production costs compare to our competitors. Perhaps we could be more efficient and find a way to earn our normal return on X-12. Besides my production people hate producing S-15. It's very difficult to produce."

After meeting with Rick, Diane requested an investigation of the production costs and comparative efficiency. Independent consultants were hired. After a three-month assessment, the consulting group provided the following information on the plant's production activities and costs associated with the two products:

	X-12	S-15
Production (kilograms)	1,000,000	200,000
Selling price	$15.93	$12.00
Overhead per unit*	$6.41	$2.89
Prime cost per kilogram	$4.27	$3.13
Number of production runs	100	200
Receiving orders	400	1,000
Machine hours	125,000	60,000
Direct labor hours	250,000	22,500
Engineering hours	5,000	5,000
Material handling	500	400

*Calculated using a plantwide rate based on direct labor hours, which is the current way of assigning the plant's overhead to its products.

The consulting group recommended switching the overhead assignment to an activity-based approach. They maintained that activity-based cost assignment is more accurate and will provide better information for decision making. To facilitate this recommendation, they grouped the plant's activities into homogeneous sets based on common processes, activity levels, and consumption ratios. The costs of these pooled activities follow:

Overhead Pool:*	
Setup costs	$ 240,000
Machine costs	1,750,000
Receiving costs	2,100,000
Engineering costs	2,000,000
Material-handling costs	900,000
Total	$6,990,000

*The pools are named for the major activities found within them. All overhead costs within each pool can be assigned using a single driver (based on the major activity after which the pool is named).

REQUIRED:
1. Verify the overhead cost per unit reported by the consulting group using direct labor hours to assign overhead. Compute the per-unit gross margin for each product.
2. Recompute the unit cost of each product using activity-based costing. Compute the per-unit gross margin for each product.
3. Should the company switch its emphasis from the high-volume product to the low-volume product? Comment on the validity of the plant manager's concern that competitors are selling below the cost of producing compound X-12.
4. Explain the apparent lack of competition for S-15. Comment also on the willingness of customers to accept a 25 percent increase in price for this compound.
5. Describe what actions you would take based on the information provided by the activity-based unit costs.

P4-7
JIT and Traceability of Costs
LO 7

Assume that a company has just recently switched to JIT manufacturing. Each manufacturing cell produces a single product or major subassembly. Cell workers have been trained to perform a variety of tasks. Additionally, many services have been decentralized. Costs are assigned to products using direct attribution, driver tracing, and allocation. For the costs that follow indicate the most likely product cost assignment method used *before JIT* and *after JIT*. Use three columns:

Cost Item, Before JIT, and After JIT. You may assume that direct tracing is used whenever possible, followed by driver tracing, with allocation being the method of last resort.

a. Inspection costs
b. Power to heat, light, and cool plant
c. Minor repairs on production equipment
d. Salary of production supervisor (department/cell)
e. Oil to lubricate machinery
f. Salary of plant supervisor
g. Costs to set up machinery
h. Salaries of janitors
i. Power to operate production equipment
j. Taxes on plant and equipment
k. Depreciation on production equipment
l. Raw materials
m. Salary of industrial engineer
n. Parts for machinery
o. Pencils and paper clips for production supervisor (department/cell)
p. Insurance on plant and equipment
q. Overtime wages for cell workers
r. Plant depreciation
s. Material handling
t. Preventive maintenance

P4-8
Cost Assignment and JIT
LO 5, LO 7

Lisboa Company produces two types of lamp bases (modern and traditional). Both pass through two producing departments: molding and painting. It also has a maintenance department that services and repairs the equipment used in each producing department. Budgeted data for the three departments follow:

	Maintenance	Molding	Painting
Overhead	$200,000	$330,000	$238,000
Maintenance hours	—	7,500	2,500
Machine hours	—	24,000	2,000
Direct labor hours	—	2,000	12,000

In the molding department, the modern lamp base requires 1 hour of machine time, and the traditional lamp base requires 2 hours. In the painting department, the modern lamp base requires 0.5 hour of direct labor, and the traditional lamp base requires 1 hour. Production of 8,000 modern units and 8,000 traditional units is expected. Before calculating departmental overhead rates, maintenance costs are assigned to molding and painting in proportion to the maintenance hours used. Maintenance costs are added to the direct overhead costs found in each department to form departmental overhead pools. An overhead rate is then calculated for each producing department using machine hours for molding and direct labor hours for painting.

Immediately after preparing the budgeted data, a consultant suggests that two manufacturing cells be created: one for the manufacture of the modern model and the other for the manufacture of the traditional model. Cell workers would be trained to perform maintenance; hence, the maintenance department is decentralized. The total direct overhead costs estimated for each cell are $200,000 for cell M (modern) and $184,000 for cell T (traditional).

REQUIRED:
1. Assign the maintenance costs to each producing department and compute the overhead cost per unit for each lamp base.
2. Compute the overhead cost per unit if manufacturing cells are created. Which unit overhead cost do you think is the more accurate—the one computed with a departmental structure or the one computed using a cell structure? Explain.
3. Note that the total overhead costs under each system are assumed to be the same. Would you expect the overhead costs to remain the same if the JIT manufacturing system is implemented? Explain.

P4-9
ABC and Customer-driven Costs
LO 5

Sorensen Manufacturing produces several types of bolts used in aircrafts. The bolts are produced in batches according to customer order. Although there are a variety of bolts, they can be grouped into three product families. Because the product families are used in different kinds of aircraft, customers also can be grouped into three categories, corresponding to the product family they purchase. The number of units sold to each customer class is the same. The selling prices for the three product families range from $0.50 to $0.80 per unit. Historically, the costs of order entry, processing, and handling costs were expensed and not traced to individual customer groups. These costs are not trivial and totaled $4,500,000 for the most recent year. Furthermore, these costs had been increasing over time. Recently, the company had begun to emphasize a cost reduction strategy; however, any cost reduction decisions had to contribute to the creation of a competitive advantage.

Because of the magnitude and growth of order-filling costs, management decided to explore the causes of these costs. They discovered that order-filling costs were driven by the number of customer orders processed. Further investigation revealed the following cost behavior for the order-filling activity:

Step-fixed cost component: $50,000 per step (2,000 orders define a step)*
Variable cost component: $20 per order

*Sorensen currently has sufficient steps to process 100,000 orders.

The expected customer orders for the year total 100,000. The expected usage of the order-filling activity and the average size of an order by customer category follow:

	Category I	Category II	Category III
Number of orders	50,000	30,000	20,000
Average order size	600	1,000	1,500

As a result of the cost behavior analysis, the marketing manager recommended the imposition of a charge per customer order. The president of the company concurred. The charge was implemented by adding the cost per order to the price of each order (computed using the projected ordering costs and expected orders). This ordering cost was then reduced as the size of the order increased and eliminated as the order size reached 2,000 units (the marketing manager indicated that any penalties imposed for orders greater than this size would lose sales from some of the smaller customers). Within a short period of communicating this new price information to customers, the average order size for all three product families increased to 2,000 units.

REQUIRED:
1. Sorensen traditionally has expensed order-filling costs. What is the most likely reason for this practice?
2. Calculate the cost per order for each customer category.
3. Calculate the reduction in order-filling cost produced by the change in pricing strategy (assume that resource spending is reduced as much as possible and that the total units sold remain unchanged). Explain how exploiting customer activity information produced this cost reduction. Are there any other internal activities that might benefit from this pricing strategy?

 M ANAGERIAL DECISION CASES

C4-1
Activity-based Costing; Consideration of Customer-driven Costs
LO 5, LO 7

Sharp Paper, Inc., has three paper mills, one of which is located in Memphis, Tennessee. The Memphis mill produces 300 different types of coated and uncoated specialty printing papers. This large variety of products was the result of a full-line marketing strategy adopted by Sharp's management. Management was convinced that the value of variety more than offset the extra costs of the increased complexity.

During 1998, the Memphis mill produced 120,000 tons of coated paper and 80,000 tons of uncoated. Of the 200,000 tons produced, 180,000 were sold. Sixty products account for 80 percent of the tons sold. Thus, 240 products are classified as low-volume products.

Lightweight lime hopsack in cartons (LLHC) is one of the low-volume products. LLHC is produced in rolls, converted into sheets of paper, and then sold in cartons. In 1998, the cost to produce and sell one ton of LLHC was as follows:

Raw materials:		
Furnish (3 different pulps)	2,225 pounds	$ 450
Additives (11 different items)	200 pounds	500
Tub size	75 pounds	10
Recycled scrap paper	(296 pounds)	(20)
Total raw materials		$ 940
Direct labor		$ 450
Overhead:		
Paper machine ($100/ton × 2,500 pounds)		$ 125
Finishing machine ($120/ton × 2,500 pounds)		150
Total overhead		$ 275
Shipping and warehousing		$ 30
Total manufacturing and selling cost		$1,695

Overhead is applied using a two-stage process. First, overhead is allocated to the paper and finishing machines using the direct method of allocation with carefully selected cost drivers. Second, the overhead assigned to each machine is divided by the budgeted tons of output. These rates are then multiplied by the number of pounds required to produce one good ton.

In 1998, LLHC sold for $2,400 per ton, making it one of the most profitable products. A similar examination of some of the other low-volume products revealed that they also had very respectable profit margins. Unfortunately, the performance of the high-volume products was less impressive, with many showing losses or very low profit margins. This situation led Ryan Chesser to call a meeting with his marketing vice-president, Jennifer Woodruff, and his controller, Jan Booth.

Ryan: "The above-average profitability of our low-volume specialty products and the poor profit performance of our high-volume products make me believe that we should switch our marketing emphasis to the low-volume line. Perhaps we should drop some of our high-volume products, particularly those showing a loss."

Jennifer: "I'm not convinced that the solution you are proposing is the right one. I know our high-volume products are of high quality, and I am convinced that we are as efficient in our production as other firms. I think that somehow our costs are not being assigned correctly. For example, the shipping and warehousing costs are assigned by dividing these costs by the total tons of paper sold. Yet. . . ."

Jan: "Jennifer, I hate to disagree, but the $30 per ton charge for shipping and warehousing seems reasonable. I know that our method to assign these costs is identical to a number of other paper companies."

Jennifer: "Well, that may be true, but do these other companies have the variety of products that we have? Our low-volume products require special handling and processing, but when we assign shipping and warehousing costs, we average these special costs across our entire product line. Every ton produced in our mill passes through our mill shipping department and is either sent directly to the customer or to our distribution center and then eventually to customers. My records indicate quite clearly that virtually all the high-volume products are sent directly to customers, whereas most of the low-volume products are sent to the distribution center. Now all the products passing through the mill shipping department should receive a share of the $2,000,000 annual shipping costs. I am not convinced, however, that all products should receive a share of the receiving and shipping costs of the distribution center as currently practiced."

Ryan: "Jan, is this true? Does our system allocate our shipping and warehousing costs in this way?"

Jan: "Yes, I'm afraid it does. Jennifer may have a point. Perhaps we need to reevaluate our method to assign these costs to the product lines."

Ryan: "Jennifer, do you have any suggestions concerning how the shipping and warehousing costs ought to be assigned?"

Jennifer: "It seems reasonable to make a distinction between products that spend time in the distribution center and those that do not. We should also distinguish between the receiving and shipping activities at the distribution center. All incoming shipments are packed on pallets and weigh 1 ton each (there are 14 cartons of paper per pallet). In 1998, receiving processed 56,000 tons of paper. Receiving employs 15 people at an annual cost of $600,000. Other receiving costs total about $500,000. I would recommend that these costs be assigned using tons processed.

Shipping, however, is different. There are two activities associated with shipping: picking the order from inventory and loading the paper. We employ 30 people for picking and 10 for loading, at an annual cost of $1,200,000. Other shipping costs total $1,100,000. Picking and loading are more concerned with the number of shipping items than with tonnage. That is, a shipping item may consist of two or three cartons instead of pallets. Accordingly, the shipping costs of the distribution center should be assigned using the number of items shipped. In 1998, for example, we handled 190,000 shipping items."

Ryan: "These suggestions have merit. Jan, I would like to see what effect Jennifer's suggestions have on the per-unit assignment of shipping and warehousing for LLHC. If the effect is significant, then we will expand the analysis to include all products."

Jan: "I'm willing to compute the effect, but I'd like to suggest one additional feature. Currently, we have a policy to carry about 25 tons of LLHC in inventory. Our current cost system totally ignores the cost of carrying this inventory. Since it costs us $1,665 to produce each ton of this product, we are tying up a lot of money in inventory—money that could be invested in other productive opportunities. In fact, the return lost is about 16 percent per year. This cost should also be assigned to the units sold."

Ryan: "Jan, this also sounds good to me. Go ahead and include the carrying cost in your computation."

To help in the analysis, Jan gathered the following data for LLHC for 1998:

Tons sold	10
Average cartons per shipment	2
Average shipments per ton	7

REQUIRED:
1. Identify the flaws associated with the current method of assigning shipping and warehousing costs to Sharp's products.
2. Compute the shipping and warehousing cost per ton of LLHC sold using the new method suggested by Jennifer and Jan.
3. Using the new costs computed in requirement 2, compute the profit per ton of LLHC. Compare this with the profit per ton computed using the old method. Do you think that this same effect would be realized for other low-volume products? Explain.
4. Comment on Ryan's proposal to drop some high-volume products and place more emphasis on low-volume products. Discuss the role of the accounting system in supporting this type of decision making.
5. After receiving the analysis of LLHC, Ryan decided to expand the analysis to all products. He also had Jan reevaluate the way in which mill overhead was assigned to products. After the restructuring was completed, Ryan took the following actions: (a) the prices of most low-volume products were increased, (b) the prices of several high-volume products were decreased, and (c) some low-volume products were dropped. Explain why his strategy changed so dramatically.

C4-2
Activity-based Product Costing and Ethical Behavior

Consider the following conversation between Leonard Bryner, president and manager of a firm engaged in job manufacturing, and Chuck Davis, CMA, the firm's controller.

Leonard: "Chuck, as you know, our firm has been losing market share over the past three years. We have been losing more and more bids, and I don't understand why. At first I thought other firms were undercutting simply to gain business, but after examining some of the public financial reports, I believe that they are making a reasonable rate of return. I am beginning to believe that our costs and costing methods are at fault."

Chuck: "I can't agree with that. We have good control over our costs. Like most firms in our industry, we use a normal job-costing system. I really don't see any significant waste in the plant."

Leonard: "After talking with some other managers at a recent industrial convention, I'm not so sure that waste by itself is the issue. They talked about activity-based management, activity-based costing, and continuous improvement. They mentioned the use of something called activity drivers to assign overhead. They claimed that these new procedures can help produce more efficiency in manufacturing, better control of overhead, and more accurate product costing. A big deal was made of eliminating activities that added no value. Maybe our bids are too high because these other firms have found ways to decrease their overhead costs and to increase the accuracy of their product costing."

Chuck: "I doubt it. For one thing, I don't see how we can increase product-costing accuracy. So many of our costs are indirect costs. Furthermore, everyone uses some measure of production activity to assign overhead costs. I imagine that what they are calling activity drivers is just some new buzzword for measures of production volume. Fads in costing come and go. I wouldn't worry about it. I'll bet that our problems with decreasing sales are temporary. You might recall that we experienced a similar problem about 12 years ago—it was 2 years before it straightened out."

REQUIRED:
1. Do you agree with Chuck Davis and the advice that he gave Leonard Bryner? Explain.
2. Was there anything wrong or unethical in the behavior that Chuck Davis displayed? Explain your reasoning.
3. Do you think that Chuck was well informed—that he was aware of what the accounting implications of activity-based costing were and that he knew what was meant by cost drivers? Should he have been? Review (in Chapter 1) the first category of the standards of ethical conduct for management accountants. Do any of these apply to Chuck's case?

After studying Chapter 5, you should be able to:

CHAPTER

Job-Order Costing

1. Describe the differences between job-order costing and process costing and identify the types of firms that would use each method.

2. Describe the cost flows and prepare the journal entries associated with job-order costing.

3. Identify and set up the source documents used in job-order costing.

SCENARIO

he Applegate Construction Company[1] was established in 1957. For more than thirty years, the company specialized in building subdivisions. The company could be described as a small, successful business with a good reputation for building quality homes. Recently, Walter Applegate, the founder and owner of the company, retired and his son, Jay Applegate, assumed control of the company.

Jay decided that the company needed to expand into custom-built homes and nonresidential construction. As he began to explore these possibilities, he encountered some problems with the company's current accounting system. Accordingly, he requested a meeting with his aunt, Bonnie Barlow, the financial manager. She was responsible for bookkeeping and payroll. A local CPA firm prepared all financial reports and filed the company's tax returns.

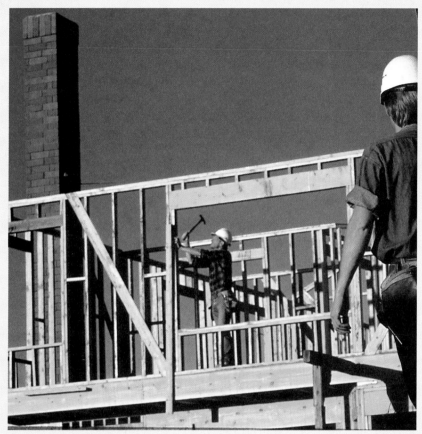

"Bonnie, as you know, I want our company to become one of the largest in this region. To accomplish this, I am convinced that we need to expand our operations to include both custom homes and industrial buildings. I think we can gain business in both of these areas by capitalizing on our reputation for quality. However, I am afraid that as we enter these markets, we are going to have to change our accounting system. I'm going to need your help in making the changes."

"I'm not sure why you want to change our accounting procedures. They are simple, and they've worked well for 30 years."

"In the past, our company has built homes in subdivisions that were basically the same. We've had slight variations in design so that they weren't carbon copies, but each home has required essentially the same work and materials. The cost of each home has been computed by simply accumulating the actual costs incurred over the period of time it took to build all the homes and then dividing this total by the number of units constructed. But, this approach will not work when we enter the market for custom-built homes or industrial units."

"I think I see the problem. Custom-built homes, for example, may require different cement work, different carpentry work, and may use more expensive materials, like a jacuzzi instead of a regular bathtub. They may also differ significantly in size from our standard units. If we simply divide the total construction costs of a period by the number of units produced, we don't get a very accurate representation of what it's costing to build any individual home. Additionally, the cost of our standard units could be distorted. Industrial units would cause even worse problems. It sounds like we do need a different method to accumulate our construction costs."

"I agree. We need some way of tracking the labor, materials, and overhead used by each job. In addition, by moving into custom home building, we'll be working much more closely with the customers and their architects. I know there will be times when the customer doesn't go through with building the house, but we will have spent a considerable amount of time on design. How will we measure the cost of our consulting service?"

"Jay, these costing issues are more complicated than what we are used to dealing with. Let me talk to our CPA and see what advice she can give us. I am sure that she can suggest a cost system that will address these issues."

---

1. This scenario is based on the actual experiences of a mid-sized construction firm. The names of the company and people involved have been changed to preserve confidentiality.

Questions to Think About

1. *Does Applegate Construction Company produce a product or provide a service? Would the buyer of a typical subdivision house answer this question differently than a custom house buyer?*

2. *List some examples of direct materials, direct labor, and overhead for Applegate's typical subdivision home. List some examples of each for custom homes. Is Jay Applegate right—will the accounting system need to change? How?*

UNIT COST IN THE JOB-ORDER ENVIRONMENT

Objective I

Describe the differences between job-order costing and process costing and identify the types of firms that would use each method.

We have seen that companies keep track of total and unit costs for a number of reasons, including the generation of financial statements, the determination of profitability, and the making of decisions (for example, what price to charge). However, we have not yet given much thought to the way that the *kinds* of products or services produced might affect the kind of accounting system to be used.

Manufacturing and service firms can be divided into two major types depending on whether or not their products/services are unique. Consider Applegate Construction Company. At first, the company built houses in subdivisions. These houses were quite similar to one another, and the basic cost of each was the same. Certainly, the houses looked somewhat different—one might have red brick, another multicolored brick, still another white brick. However, these cosmetic differences did not much affect *cost*. Therefore, Applegate could treat each house as an identical unit for accounting purposes. However, as Jay Applegate noted, this accounting system would not work with custom houses. Custom houses vary significantly, and more importantly from our standpoint, their costs vary significantly. The cost of one custom house with 3,000 square feet, three bathrooms, and aluminum-clad windows will be quite different from the cost of another custom house with 4,200 square feet, four bathrooms, three fireplaces, and wood-trimmed windows. As a result, Applegate Construction Company must tailor its accounting system to its production.

Job-Order Production and Costing

Firms operating in job-order industries produce a wide variety of products or jobs that are usually quite distinct from each other. Customized or built-to-order products fit into this category, as do services that vary from customer to customer. Examples of job-order processes include printing, construction, furniture making, automobile repair, and beautician services. In manufacturing, a job may be a single unit such as a house, or it may be a batch of units such as eight tables.

Improved technology is enabling companies to produce even more products to special order. For example, Israeli firm Indigo Ltd. has developed a new printing system that makes it economical to print very small batches of cans, bottles, labels, and so on. Thus, this process would make it feasible to produce 500 soda cans for the year-end party for a campus organization.[2] Job-order systems may be used to produce goods for inventory that are subsequently sold in the general market. Often, however, a job is associated with a particular customer order. The key feature of job-order costing is that the cost of one job differs from that of another job, and must be kept track of separately.

**job-order costing
system**

For job-order production systems, costs are accumulated by job. This approach to assigning costs is called a job-order costing system. In a job-order firm, collecting costs by job provides vital information for management. For example, frequently prices are based on costs in a job-order environment.

Process Production and Costing

Firms in process industries mass-produce large quantities of similar or homogeneous products. Examples of process manufacturers include food, cement, petroleum, and chemical firms. One gallon of paint is the same as another gallon; one bottle of aspirin is the same as another bottle. The important point here is that the cost of one unit of a product is identical to the cost of another. Likewise, service firms can also use a process-costing approach. For example, check-clearing departments of banks incur a uniform cost to clear a check, no matter the size of the check or the name of the person to whom it is written.

2. Peter Coy and Neal Sandler, "A Package for Every Person," *Business Week*, 6 February 1995, 44.

process-costing system

Process firms accumulate production costs by process or by department for a given period of time. The output for the process for that period of time is measured. Unit costs are computed by dividing the process costs for the given period by the output of the period. This approach to cost accumulation is known as a process-costing system. Exhibit 5-1 summarizes and contrasts the characteristics of job-order and process costing.

Calculating Unit Cost with Job-Order Costing

While the variety of product cost definitions discussed in Chapter 2 applies to both job-order and process costing, we will use the traditional product-costing definition to illustrate job-order costing procedures. That is, production costs consist of direct materials, direct labor, and overhead. Overhead can be assigned using an activity-based approach or traditional approaches, depending on the need for product-costing accuracy found within a particular job-order company. It should be understood that the traditional unit-level approaches to assigning overhead are simply special cases of the more general ABC cost system. Unit-level systems can be used effectively whenever one of three conditions is met: (1) the nonunit-level overhead is a small percentage of the total overhead, (2) the products produced in the job environment have the same overhead consumption ratios, or (3) the cost of using both unit-level and nonunit-level drivers exceeds the benefits. It is also important in a job-order environment to use predetermined overhead rates since the completion of a job rarely coincides with the completion of a fiscal year. Therefore, in the remainder of this chapter, we will use normal costing. Recall that normal costing requires us to cost units of production using actual direct materials cost, actual direct labor cost, and overhead applied using one or more predetermined rates.

The unit cost of a job is simply the total cost of materials used on the job, labor worked on the job, and overhead assigned using one or more activity drivers. Although the concept is simple, the practical reality of the computation can be somewhat more complex, especially when there are products that differ from one another. Initially, to illustrate the unit cost computation, we use only a single unit-level driver to assign overhead. Later on, job-order costing procedures are illustrated using the multiple-driver approach of activity-based costing.

Suppose that Stan Johnson forms a new company, Johnson Leathergoods, which specializes in the production of custom leather products. Stan believes that there is a market for one-of-a-kind leather purses, briefcases, and backpacks. In its first month of operation, he obtains two orders: the first is for 20 leather backpacks for a local sporting goods store; the second is for 10 distinctively tooled briefcases for the coaches of a local college. Stan agrees to provide these orders at a price of cost plus 50 percent.

Let's look at the computation of unit cost for Stan's first order. The backpacks will require direct materials (leather, thread, buckles), direct labor (cutting, sewing, assembling), and overhead. Assume that overhead is assigned using a single unit-level driver, direct labor hours (a plantwide rate). Suppose that the materials cost $1,000 and the direct labor costs $600 (120 hours at $5 per hour). If the predetermined overhead rate is $2 per direct labor hour, then the overhead applied to this job is $240 (120 hours at

5-1

Exhibit
Comparison of Job-Order and Process Costing

Job-Order Costing	Process Costing
1. Wide variety of distinct products	1. Homogeneous products
2. Costs accumulated by job	2. Costs accumulated by process or department
3. Unit cost computed by dividing total job costs by units produced on that job	3. Unit cost computed by dividing process costs of the period by the units produced in the period

Custom sewing and tailoring require the use of job-order costing. The materials and time of the seamstress working on this shirt will be recorded on a job order cost sheet, and the total cost will be specific to this item. The overhead can be assigned using a predetermined overhead rate.

$2 per hour). Now we can see that the total cost of the backpacks is $1,840, and the unit cost is $92, computed as follows:

Job order Cost sheet

Direct materials	$1,000
Direct labor	600
Overhead	240
Total	$1,840
÷ 20 units	÷20
Unit cost	$ 92

job-order cost sheet

This example, with the total cost of materials, labor, and overhead for a single job, is the simplest example of a job-order cost sheet. The job-order cost sheet is prepared for every job. It is subsidiary to the work-in-process account and is the primary document for accumulating all costs related to a particular job. Of course, there is much more information that could be presented on a job-order cost sheet, and this will be discussed in a later section of this chapter (p. 175).

Since cost is so closely linked to price in this case, it is easy to see that Stan will charge the sporting goods store $2,760 (cost of $1,840 plus 50 percent of $1,840) or $138 per backpack.

THE FLOW OF COSTS THROUGH THE ACCOUNTS

Objective 2

Describe the cost flows and prepare the journal entries associated with job-order costing.

When we talk about cost flow we are talking about the way we account for costs from the point at which they are incurred to the point at which they are recognized as an expense on the income statement. Of principal interest in a job-order system is the flow of manufacturing costs. Accordingly, we begin with a description of exactly how the three manufacturing cost elements, direct materials, direct labor, and overhead, flow through the the following accounts: Raw Materials, Work in Process, Overhead Control, Finished Goods, and Cost of Goods Sold.

Let's continue to use the simplified job-shop environment provided by our example of Johnson Leathergoods. To start the business, Stan leased a small building and bought the necessary production equipment. Recall that he finalized two orders for January: one for 20 backpacks for a local sporting goods store, and a second for 10 briefcases for the coaches of a local college. Both orders must be delivered January 31 and will be sold for manufacturing cost plus 50 percent. Stan expects to average two orders per month for the first year of operation.

Stan created two job-order cost sheets, one for each order. The first job-order cost sheet is for the backpacks, the second is for the engraved briefcases.

Accounting for Materials

Since the company is just beginning business, it has no beginning inventories. To produce the 30 products in January and have a supply of materials on hand at the beginning of February, Stan purchases, on account, $2,500 of raw materials. This purchase is recorded as follows:

1. Raw Materials   2,500
        Accounts Payable   2,500

Raw Materials is an inventory account. It also is the controlling account for all raw materials. When materials are purchased, the cost of these materials "flows" into the raw materials account through the debit to Raw Materials.

When the production supervisor needs materials for a job, materials are removed from the storeroom. The cost of the materials is removed from the materials account and added to the Work in Process account. Of course, in a job-order environment, the materials moved from the storeroom to work in process must be "tagged" with the appropriate job name. Suppose that Stan needs $1,000 of materials for the backpacks and $500 for the briefcases. Then the following entry would be made:

2. Work in Process   1,500
        Raw Materials   1,500

This second entry captures the notion of raw materials flowing from the storeroom to work in process. All such flows are summarized in the Work in Process account as well as being posted individually to the respective jobs on their job-order cost sheets. Recall that Work in Process is a controlling account, and the job cost sheets are the subsidiary accounts. Therefore, the job-order cost sheet for backpacks would show $1,000 for direct materials, and the job-order cost sheet for the briefcases would show $500 for direct materials. Exhibit 5-2 summarizes the raw materials cost flows.

Accounting for Direct Labor Cost

Since two jobs were in progress during January, Stan must determine not only the total number of direct labor hours worked, but also the time worked on each job. The backpacks required 120 hours at an average wage rate of $5 per hour, for a total direct labor cost of $600. For the briefcases, the total was $250, based on 50 hours at an average

5-2

Exhibit
Summary of Materials
Cost Flows

hourly wage of $5. In addition to the postings to each job's cost sheet, the following summary entry would be made:

3. Work in Process   850
        Wages Payable   850

The summary of the labor cost flows is given in Exhibit 5-3. Notice that the direct labor costs assigned to the two jobs exactly equal the total assigned to Work in Process. Remember that the labor cost flows reflect only direct labor cost. Indirect labor is assigned as part of overhead.

Accounting for Overhead

The use of normal costing means that actual overhead costs are never assigned directly to jobs. Overhead is applied to each individual job using a *predetermined* rate or rates. The more general case, of course, is the application of overhead using activity-based costing. A specialized case of ABC is the use of a single, plantwide overhead rate. Finally, actual overhead costs incurred must be accounted for as well, but on an overall (not job-specific) basis. Thus, first we will describe how to account for applied overhead using ABC; next we will look at the application of overhead using a plantwide rate; and then we will discuss accounting for actual overhead.

5-3

Exhibit
Summary of Direct Labor
Cost Flows

ABC and Job-Order Costing Recall that activity-based costing requires the firm to identify production activities and related activity drivers. Then a rate is computed for each activity (or homogeneous sets of activities). Suppose that Stan estimates annual overhead of $9,600, and that this amount can be broken down into three categories: purchasing (locating vendors, preparing purchase documents, and purchasing materials), machining (power, lubricants, and use of machines), and a pool of unit-level activities called "other." Purchasing cost is driven by the number of purchase orders, machining cost is driven by machine hours, and the unit-level pool costs are assigned using number of direct labor hours. The budgeted cost for each activity pool and the expected demands for each driver are as follows:

Purchasing	$3,000	Purchase orders	100
Machining	$4,200	Machine hours	2,800
Other	$2,400	Direct labor hours	4,800

Activity-based rates would be:

$$\text{Purchasing rate} = \frac{\$3,000}{100} = \$30 \text{ per purchase order}$$

$$\text{Machining rate} = \frac{\$4,200}{2,800} = \$1.50 \text{ per machine-hour}$$

$$\text{Other rate} = \frac{\$2,400}{4,800} = \$0.50 \text{ per direct labor hour}$$

To assign overhead costs to each job, the demands each job places on the three activity drivers must be known. The demands the two jobs place on the three activity groups follow:

	Backpacks	Briefcases
Purchase orders	3	1
Machine hours	60	30
Direct labor hours	120	50

Then overhead assigned to each job is calculated as follows:

	Backpacks	Briefcases
Purchasing (3 × $30); (1 × $30)	$ 90	$ 30
Machining (60 × $1.50); (30 × $1.50)	90	45
Other (120 × $0.50); (50 × $0.50)	60	25
Total overhead applied	$240	$100

Overhead applied using ABC is credited to the overhead account in the amount of $340, $240 for the backpack job and $100 for the briefcase job. The summary entry reflects a total of $340 (assigning all overhead to jobs worked on in January):

4. Work in Process   340
    Overhead Control   340

The credit balance in the Overhead Control account equals the total applied overhead at a given point in time. In normal costing, only applied overhead ever enters the Work in Process account.

Applying Overhead Using Traditional Approaches Overhead costs can also be assigned using plantwide overhead or departmental rates. Typically, direct labor hours is the measure used to calculate a plant overhead rate and departmental rates are based on unit-level drivers such as direct labor hours, machine hours, and direct materials dollars. The use of a plantwide rate has the virtue of being simple and reduces data collection requirements. To illustrate these two features, recall that total estimated overhead costs for Johnson Leathergoods is $9,600. Assume that the budgeted direct labor hours total 4,800 hours. Accordingly, the predetermined overhead rate is:

$$\text{Overhead rate} = \frac{\$9,600}{4,800} = \$2 \text{ per direct labor hour}$$

For the backpacks, with a total of 120 hours worked, the amount of overhead cost posted to the Work in Process account is $240 ($2 × 120). For the briefcases, the overhead cost is $100 ($2 × 50). Compared to the ABC assignments, there are fewer calculations. Note also that assigning overhead to jobs only requires a rate and the direct labor hours used by the job. Since direct labor hours are already being collected to assign direct labor cost to jobs, overhead assignment would not demand any additional data collection.

Unfortunately, use of a plantwide rate may also significantly reduce the accuracy of cost assignment. The use of a single, unit-level driver may not reflect the actual consumption of resources by individual jobs. For example, a third job that requires six purchase orders, 200 machine hours, and 100 direct labor hours would have an overhead assignment of $530 [(6 × $30) + (200 × $1.50) + (100 × $0.50)] using ABC, but only $200 (100 × $2) using a unit-level rate. Clearly, this job would be undercosted using a single rate because the impact of increased machine usage and purchasing is ignored when direct labor hours alone is used as the driver. This increased cost could have a significant effect on product-mix decisions and pricing decisions (among others).

Accounting for Actual Overhead Costs To illustrate how actual overhead costs are recorded, assume that Johnson Leathergoods incurred the following indirect costs for January:

Lease payment	$200
Utilities	50
Equipment depreciation	100
Indirect labor	65
Total overhead costs	$415

Notice that these overhead costs reflect what is spent by account category, not by activity. These resources were used to enable the three activities, purchasing, machining, and other (unit-level activities), to be performed. For an ABC system, determining the actual cost of activities requires that these costs be unbundled and assigned to individual activities. For example, how much of the indirect labor cost belongs to purchasing? When separate support departments exist, activity costs are traced to them and then assigned to products on the basis of usage. This is discussed in Chapter 7. What is important at this point is to understand that the actual overhead costs never enter the Work in Process account. The usual procedure is to record actual overhead costs on the debit side of the Overhead Control account. For example, the actual overhead costs would be recorded as follows:

5.	Overhead Control	415	
	Lease Payable		200
	Utilities Payable		50
	Accumulated Depreciation		100
	Wages Payable		65

The debit balance in the Overhead Control account gives the total actual overhead costs at a given point in time. Since actual overhead costs are on the debit side of this account and applied overhead costs are on the credit side, the balance in the Overhead

Control account is the overhead variance at a given point in time. For Johnson Leathergoods at the end of January, the actual overhead of $415 and applied overhead of $340 produce underapplied overhead of $75 ($415 − $340).

The flow of overhead costs is summarized in Exhibit 5-4. Notice that the total overhead applied from all jobs is entered in the Work in Process account. Therefore, the information in Exhibit 5-4 is pertinent to both ABC and a plantwide overhead rate.

Accounting for Finished Goods

We have already seen what takes place when a job is completed. The direct materials, direct labor, and applied overhead amounts are totaled to yield the manufacturing cost of the job. This job cost sheet is then transferred to a finished goods file. Simultaneously, the costs of the completed job are transferred from the Work in Process account to the Finished Goods account.

For example, assume that the backpacks were completed in January with the completed cost sheet shown in Exhibit 5-5. Since the backpacks are completed, the total manufacturing costs of $1,840 must be transferred from the Work in Process account to the Finished Goods account. This transfer is described by the following entry:

6. Finished Goods   1,840
    Work in Process   1,840

A summary of the cost flows occurring when a job is finished is shown in Exhibit 5-5.

The completion of a job is an important step in the flow of manufacturing costs. The cost of the completed job must be removed from work in process, added to finished goods, and, eventually, added to cost of goods sold expense on the income statement. To ensure accuracy in computing these costs, a cost of goods manufactured statement is prepared. The schedule of the cost of goods manufactured presented in Exhibit 5-6 summarizes the production activity of Johnson Leathergoods for January. It is important to note that applied overhead is used to arrive at the cost of goods manufactured. Both work-in-process and finished goods inventories are carried at normal cost rather than actual cost.

Notice that ending work in process is $850. Where did we obtain this figure? Of the two jobs, the backpacks were finished and transferred to finished goods. The briefcases are still in process, however, and the manufacturing costs assigned thus far are direct materials, $500; direct labor, $250; and overhead applied, $100. The total of these costs gives the cost of ending work in process. You may want to check these figures against the job-order cost sheet for briefcases given in Exhibit 5-4.

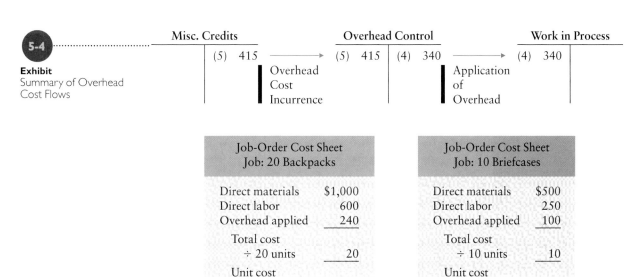

Exhibit 5-4
Summary of Overhead Cost Flows

Misc. Credits	Overhead Control	Work in Process
(5) 415 → Overhead Cost Incurrence	(5) 415 | (4) 340 → Application of Overhead	(4) 340

Job-Order Cost Sheet
Job: 20 Backpacks

Direct materials	$1,000
Direct labor	600
Overhead applied	240
Total cost	
÷ 20 units	20
Unit cost	

Job-Order Cost Sheet
Job: 10 Briefcases

Direct materials	$500
Direct labor	250
Overhead applied	100
Total cost	
÷ 10 units	10
Unit cost	

5-5 ·······························

Exhibit
Summary of Finished
Goods Cost Flows*

Work in Process		Finished Goods	
(6) 1,840		(6) 1,840	

Transfer of
Finished
Goods

Job-Order Cost Sheet
Job: 20 Backpacks

Direct materials	$1,000
Direct labor	600
Overhead applied	240
Total cost	$1,840
÷ 20 units	20
Unit cost	$ 92

*There is no reason to show the job-order cost sheet for the briefcases since they are still in process.

5-6 ·······························

Exhibit

Johnson Leathergoods Company
Schedule of Cost of Goods Manufactured
For the Month Ended January 31, 1998

Direct materials:		
Beginning raw materials inventory	$ 0	
Purchases of raw materials	2,500	
Total raw materials available	$2,500	
Ending raw materials	1,000	
Total raw materials used		$1,500
Direct labor		850
Overhead:		
Lease	$200	
Utilities	50	
Depreciation	100	
Indirect labor	65	
	$415	
Less: Underapplied overhead	(75)	
Overhead applied		340
Current manufacturing costs		$2,690
Add: Beginning work in process		0
Total manufacturing costs		$2,690
Less: Ending work in process		(850)
Cost of goods manufactured		$1,840

Accounting for Cost of Goods Sold

In a job-order firm, units can be produced for a particular customer or they can be produced with the expectation of selling the units later. If a job is produced specially for a customer (as with the backpacks), when the job is shipped to the customer, the cost of the finished job becomes the cost of the goods sold. When the backpacks are completed, the following entries would be made (recall that the selling price is 150 percent of manufacturing cost).

7. Cost of Goods Sold   1,840
       Finished Goods   1,840
8. Accounts Receivable   2,760
       Sales Revenue   2,760

In addition to these entries, a schedule of cost of goods sold usually is prepared at the end of each reporting period (for example, monthly and quarterly). Exhibit 5-7 presents such a schedule for Johnson Leathergoods for January. Typically, the overhead variance is not material and, therefore, is closed to the Cost of Goods Sold account. Cost of goods sold before adjustment for an overhead variance is called normal cost of goods sold. After adjustment for the period's overhead variance takes place, the result is called the adjusted cost of goods sold. It is this latter figure that appears as an expense on the income statement.

> **normal cost of goods sold**
> **adjusted cost of goods sold**

However, closing the overhead variance to the Cost of Goods Sold account is not done until the end of the year. Variances are expected each month because of nonuniform production and nonuniform actual overhead costs. As the year unfolds, these monthly variances should, by and large, offset each other so that the year-end variance is small. Nonetheless, to illustrate how the year-end overhead variance would be treated, we will close out the overhead variance experienced by Johnson Leathergoods in January.

Closing the underapplied overhead to cost of goods sold requires the following entry:

9. Cost of Goods Sold   75
       Overhead Control   75

Notice that debiting Cost of Goods Sold is equivalent to adding the underapplied amount to the normal cost of goods sold figure. If the overhead variance had been overapplied, the entry would reverse and Cost of Goods Sold would be credited.

If the backpacks had not been ordered by a customer but had been produced with the expectation that they could be sold through a subsequent marketing effort, then all 20 units might not be sold at the same time. Assume that on January 31, 15 backpacks were sold. In this case, the cost of goods sold figure is the unit cost times the number of units sold ($92 × 15, or $1,380). The unit cost figure is found on the cost sheet in Exhibit 5-5.

Closing out the overhead variance of Cost of Goods Sold completes the description of manufacturing cost flows. To facilitate a review of these important concepts, Exhibit 5-8 shows a complete summary of the manufacturing cost flows for Johnson Leathergoods. Notice that these entries summarize information from the underlying job-order cost sheets. Although the description in this exhibit is specific to the example, the pattern of cost flows shown would be found in any manufacturing firm that uses a normal job-order cost system.

5-7
Exhibit

Statement of Cost of Goods Sold	
Beginning finished goods inventory	$ 0
Cost of goods manufactured	1,840
Goods available for sale	$1,840
Less: Ending finished goods inventory	(0)
Normal cost of goods sold	$1,840
Add: Underapplied overhead	75
Adjusted cost of goods sold	$1,915

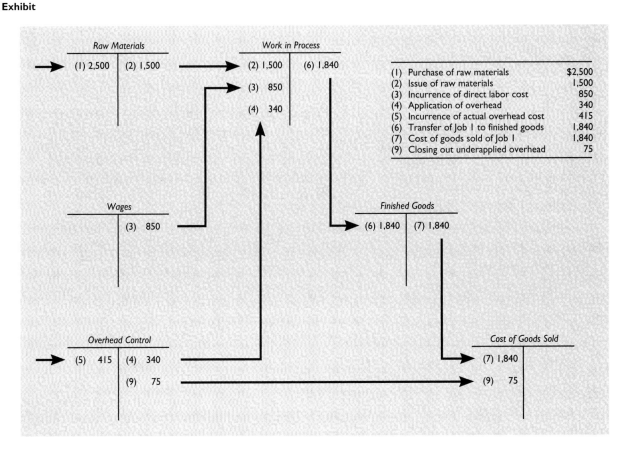

Manufacturing cost flows, however, are not the only cost flows experienced by a firm. Nonmanufacturing costs are also incurred. A description of how we account for these costs follows.

Accounting for Nonmanufacturing Costs

Recall that costs associated with selling and general administrative activities are classified as nonmanufacturing costs. According to the traditional product cost definition, these costs are period costs and are never assigned to the product. They are not part of the manufacturing cost flows. They do not belong to the overhead category and are treated as a totally separate category.

To illustrate how these costs are accounted for, assume Johnson Leathergoods had the following additional transactions in January:

Advertising circulars	$ 75
Sales commission	125
Office salaries	500
Depreciation, office equipment	50

The following compound entry could be used to record these costs:

Selling Expense Control	200	
Administrative Expense Control	550	
Accounts Payable		75
Wages Payable		625
Accumulated Depreciation		50

Controlling accounts accumulate all of the selling and administrative expenses for a period. At the end of the period, all of these costs flow to the period's income statement. An income statement for Johnson Leathergoods is shown in Exhibit 5-9.

With the description of the accounting procedures for selling and administrative expenses completed, the basic essentials of a normal job-order costing system are also complete.

5-9

Exhibit

Johnson Leathergoods Company Income Statement For the Month Ended January 31, 1998		
Sales		$ 2,760
Less: Cost of goods sold		(1,915)
Gross margin		$ 845
Less selling and administrative expenses:		
Selling expense	$200	
Administrative expense	550	(750)
Net income		$ 95

SOURCE DOCUMENTS: KEEPING TRACK OF INDIVIDUAL COSTS

Objective 3

Identify and set up the source documents used in job-order costing.

We have seen how costs for each job flow through the accounts and onto the financial statements. Now let's take a closer look at the accounting for job-order production by focusing on the source documents that support the job-order cost sheet.

Job-Order Cost Sheet

Every time a new job is started, a job-order cost sheet is prepared. As you recall, the job-order cost sheet is subsidiary to the Work in Process account, and contains all information pertinent to a job. For our simple example, the job-order cost sheet was quite brief, containing only the job description (backpacks) and cost of materials, labor, and overhead. However, a real company typically has many more orders and much more information to keep track of.

Johnson Leathergoods had only two jobs in January, and these could be easily identified by calling them "backpacks" and "briefcases." Some companies may find that the customer's name is sufficient to identify a job. For example, Applegate Construction Company may identify its custom houses as the "Smith residence" or the "Malkovich residence." As more and more jobs are produced, a company will usually find it most convenient to number them. Thus, you will see Job 13, Job 22, and Job 44. Perhaps the job number starts with the year, so that the first job of 1998 is 98-1, the second is 98-2, and so on. The key point is that each job is unique and must have a uniquely identifiable name. This name, or job order number, heads the job-order cost sheet.

In a manual accounting system, the job-order cost sheet is a document. In today's world, however, most accounting systems are automated. The cost sheet usually corresponds to a record in a work-in-process master file. The collection of all job cost sheets defines a **work-in-process file.** In a manual system, the file would be located in a filing cabinet, whereas in an automated system it is stored electronically on magnetic tape or disk. In either system, the file of job-order cost sheets serves as a subsidiary work-in-process ledger.

work-in-process file

Both manual and automated systems require the same kind of data in order to accumulate costs and track the progress of a job. A job cost system must have the ability to identify the quantity of direct materials, direct labor, and overhead consumed by each job. In other words, documentation and procedures are needed to associate the manufacturing inputs used by a job with the job itself. This need is satisfied through the use of materials requisitions for direct materials, time tickets for direct labor, and source documents for other activity drivers that might be used in applying overhead.

Materials Requisitions

**materials
   requisition form**

The cost of direct materials is assigned to a job by the use of a source document known as a materials requisition form, illustrated in Exhibit 5-10. Notice that the form asks for the type, quantity, and unit price of the direct materials issued and, most importantly, for the number of the job. Using this form, the cost accounting department can enter the cost of direct materials onto the correct job-order cost sheet.

If the accounting system is automated, this posting may entail directly entering the data at a computer terminal, using the materials requisition forms as source documents. A program enters the cost of direct materials into the record for each job.

In addition to providing essential information for assigning direct materials costs to jobs, the materials requisition form may also have other data items, such as a requisition number, a date, and a signature. These data items are useful for maintaining proper control over a firm's inventory of direct materials. The signature, for example, transfers responsibility for the materials from the storage area to the person receiving the materials, usually a production supervisor.

No attempt is made to trace the cost of other materials, such as supplies, lubricants, and so on, to a particular job. You will recall that these indirect materials are assigned to jobs through the predetermined overhead rate.

Job Time Tickets

time ticket

Direct labor also must be associated with each particular job. The means by which direct labor costs are assigned to individual jobs is the source document known as a time ticket (see Exhibit 5-11). When an employee works on a particular job, he or she fills out a time ticket that identifies his or her name, wage rate, hours worked, and job number. These time tickets are collected daily and transferred to the cost accounting department where the information is used to post the cost of direct labor to individual jobs. Again, in an automated system, posting involves entering the data into the computer.

5-10

Exhibit
Materials Requisition
Form

Date	April 8, 1998		Material Requisition Number 12
Department	Grinding		
Job Number	16		

Description	Quantity	Cost/Unit	Total Cost
Casing	100	$3	$300

Authorized Signature _____ Jim Lawson _____

5-11

Exhibit
Job Time Ticket

				Job Time Ticket Number 68

Employee Number 45

Name Ed Wilson

Date April 12, 1998

Start Time	Stop Time	Total Time	Hourly Rate	Amount	Job Number
8:00	10:00	2	6	$12	16
10:00	11:00	1	6	6	17
11:00	12:00	1	6	6	16
1:00	5:00	4	6	24	16

Approved by *Jim Lawson*
Department Supervisor

Time tickets are used only for direct laborers. Since indirect labor is common to all jobs, these costs belong to overhead and are allocated using one or more predetermined overhead rates.

Other Source Documents

The use of activity-based costing to assign overhead to jobs clearly requires the company to keep track of more than one activity driver. These other bases must be accounted for as well. That is, the actual amount used of the other drivers (for example, machine hours, number of purchase orders, number of setups) must be collected and posted to the job cost sheets. If the amount of the driver is already accounted for (for example, number of purchase orders) no new source document is needed. However, if the driver is not currently being kept track of, a new source document must be developed. For example, a source document that will track the machine hours used by each job can be modeled on job time tickets.

All completed job-order cost sheets of a firm can serve as a subsidiary ledger for the finished goods inventory. In a manual accounting system, the completed sheets would be transferred from the work-in-process files to the finished goods inventory file. In an automated accounting system, an updating run would delete the finished job from the work-in-process master file and add this record to the finished goods master file. In either case, adding the totals of all completed job-order cost sheets gives the cost of finished goods inventory at any point in time. As finished goods are sold and shipped, the cost records would be pulled (or deleted) from the finished goods inventory file. These records then form the basis for calculating a period's cost of goods sold.

SUMMARY OF LEARNING OBJECTIVES

1. Describe the differences between job-order costing and process costing and identify the types of firms that would use each method.
Job-order costing and process costing are two major cost assignment systems. Job-order systems are used for firms that produce a wide variety of heterogeneous (unique) products. Process costing is used by firms that mass-produce a homogeneous product.

2. Describe the cost flows and prepare the journal entries associated with job-order costing.

In job-order costing, materials and direct labor are charged to the Work in Process account (Raw Materials and Payroll are credited, respectively). Overhead costs are assigned to Work in Process using a predetermined rate. The cost of completed units is credited to Work in Process and debited to Finished Goods. When goods are sold, the cost is debited to Cost of Goods Sold and credited to Finished Goods.

3. Identify and set up the source documents used in job-order costing.

In job-order costing, the key document or record for accumulating manufacturing costs is the job-order cost sheet. Materials requisition forms (for direct materials), time tickets (for direct labor), and source documents for manufacturing activities are the source documents needed to assign manufacturing costs to jobs.

K EY TERMS

R EVIEW PROBLEM

Timter Company uses a normal job-order costing system. The company has two departments through which most jobs pass. Selected budgeted and actual data for the past year follow:

	Department A	Department B
Budgeted overhead	$100,000	$500,000
Actual overhead	$110,000	$520,000
Expected activity (direct labor hours)	50,000	10,000
Expected machine hours	10,000	50,000
Actual direct labor hours	51,000	9,000
Actual machine hours	10,500	52,000

During the year, several jobs were completed. Data pertaining to one such job follow:

	Job 10
Direct materials	$20,000
Direct labor cost:	
Department A (5,000 hours @ $6)	$30,000
Department B (1,000 hours @ $6)	$6,000
Machine hours used:	
Department A	100
Department B	1,200
Units produced	10,000

Handwritten note to the right of table:
OH
5,000 × 10 = 50,000
1,000 × 10 = 10,000
56,000 + 60,000 = 116,000
$\frac{116,000}{10,000}$ = 11.10

Timter Company uses a plantwide predetermined overhead rate to assign overhead to jobs. Direct labor hours (DLH) is used to compute the predetermined overhead rate.

REQUIRED:
1. Compute the predetermined overhead rate. *(handwritten: $10 DLH)*
2. Using the predetermined rate, compute the per-unit manufacturing cost for Job 10.
3. Recalculate the unit manufacturing cost for Job 10 using departmental overhead rates. Use direct labor hours for department A and machine hours for department B. Explain why this approach provides a more accurate unit cost.

Solution
1. The predetermined overhead rate is $\frac{\$600,000}{60,000}$ = $10 per DLH. Add the budgeted overhead for the two departments and divide by the total expected direct labor hours (DLH = 50,000 + 10,000).

2.

Direct materials	$ 20,000
Direct labor	36,000
Overhead ($10 × 6,000 DLH)	60,000
Total manufacturing cost	$116,000
Unit cost ($\frac{\$116,000}{10,000}$)	$ 11.60

3. The predetermined rate for department A is $\frac{\$100,000}{50,000}$ = \$2 per DLH. The predetermined rate for department B is $\frac{\$500,000}{50,000}$ = \$10 per machine hour.

Direct materials	\$20,000
Direct labor	36,000
Overhead:	
Department A (\$2 × 5,000)	10,000
Department B (\$10 × 1,200)	12,000
Total manufacturing costs	\$78,000
Unit cost ($\frac{\$78,000}{10,000}$)	\$ 7.80

Overhead assignment using departmental rates is more accurate because there is a higher correlation with the overhead assigned and the overhead consumed. Notice that Job 10 spends most of its time in department A, the least overhead intensive of the two departments. Departmental rates reflect this differential time and consumption better than plantwide rates do.

QUESTIONS FOR WRITING AND DISCUSSION

1. Explain the differences between job-order costing and process costing.
2. Explain the role of cost drivers in assigning overhead costs to jobs.
3. Explain how overhead is assigned to production when a predetermined overhead rate is used.
4. Wilson Company has a predetermined overhead rate of \$5 per direct labor hour. The job-order cost sheet for Job 145 shows 1,000 direct labor hours costing \$10,000 and materials requisitions totaling \$7,500. Job 145 had 500 units completed and transferred to finished goods. What is the cost per unit for Job 145?
5. Why are the accounting requirements for job-order costing more demanding than those for process costing?

6. Give some examples of service firms that might use job-order costing and explain why it is used there.
7. Suppose that you and a friend decide to set up a lawn-mowing service next summer. Describe the source documents that you would need to account for your activities.
8. How is job-order costing related to profitability analysis? to pricing?
9. What are some differences between a manual job-order cost system and an automated job-order cost system?
10. What is the role of materials requisition forms in a job-order cost system? time tickets? predetermined overhead rates?

WARM-UP EXERCISES

This section provides short warm-up exercises based on the examples in the chapter. Each warm-up exercise gives the page number on which the text example can be found. You may want to refer to the text example to see how the exercise can be set up and solved.

W5-1
Unit Cost Calculation
LO 1
p. 166

Carol Taylor, owner of the Sewing Room, does alterations and sews clothing to order. She just completed making 26 dance costumes for a tap class at Encore Dance Studio. The job required materials costing \$234 and 39 direct labor hours at \$10 per hour. Overhead is applied on the basis of direct labor hours at a rate of \$4 per hour.

REQUIRED:
1. What is the total cost of the job? the unit cost?
2. If Carol charges a price that is one-and-one-half times cost, what price is charged to each member of the dance class?

W5-2
Unit Cost Calculation
LO 1
p. 166

Ben Webster, owner of Webster Landscaping, develops landscape plans and puts in plant material for his clients. He just signed a contract with the developer of a new subdivision to landscape the five model houses in the subdivision. This will involve laying sod and planting trees, shrubs, and flowers. Ben figures that the job will require materials costing $950 and 60 direct labor hours at $6 per hour. Overhead is applied on the basis of direct labor hours at a rate of $15 per hour.

REQUIRED:
1. What is the total cost of the job? the unit cost?
2. If Ben charges a price that is 40 percent above cost, what price is charged to the developer for the entire job?

W5-3
Applying Overhead to Jobs Using ABC
LO 2
p. 169

Refer to W5-2, and assume that Ben decides to break down his overhead into various activities. He decides that purchasing, plan development, and general are the most important activities. Purchasing involves locating suppliers, ordering and picking up plant material, and storing plant material. Plan development occurs when a client wants a formal landscape plan; it requires meeting with clients, drawing the plans, and making copies using the blueprint copier. General refers to all other overhead activities. The budgeted cost of each activity pool and the expected demands for each driver are as follows:

Purchasing	$20,000	Purchase orders	1,000	
Plan development	$15,000	Planning hours	500	
General	$40,000	Direct labor hours	5,000	

Suppose that the subdivision job requires five purchase orders and 60 direct labor hours. There are no plan development hours involved since the subdivision developers do not want a formal plan.

REQUIRED:
1. What are the activity rates for purchasing, plan development, and general?
2. How much overhead is applied to the subdivision job using the activity-based rates?
3. What is the total cost of the job? the unit cost?
4. If Ben charges a price that is 40 percent above cost, what price is charged to the subdivision for the entire job?

W5-4
Applying Overhead to Jobs Using ABC
LO 2
p. 169

Refer to W5-3, and assume that Ben has just received a call from Linda Patterson. She and her husband are building a new house and want Ben to landscape it. Upon meeting with the Pattersons, Ben determines that they need a full-scale landscape plan with a variety of unusual plant material, and that they want his company to plant all of it. In developing a price quote for the Pattersons, Ben estimates the following:

Direct materials cost	$3,500
Planning hours	25
Purchase orders	10
Direct labor hours	50
Direct labor rate	$6 per hour

REQUIRED:
1. How much overhead will be applied to the Patterson job using the activity-based rates?
2. What is the total cost of the job?
3. If Ben charges a price that is 40 percent above cost, what price is quoted to the Pattersons?
4. Recall that the plantwide rate given in W5-2 for Ben's business was $15 per direct labor hour. How much would the Patterson job cost using a single plantwide rate? Which method of overhead application (ABC or plantwide) is more accurate?

W5-5
Journal Entries
LO 2
pp. 167–173

The following transactions occurred during the month of April for Kearney Company.

a. Materials costing $3,000 were purchased on account.
b. Materials totaling $1,700 were requisitioned for use in production, $500 for Job 443 and the remainder for Job 444.

c. During the month, direct labor worked 50 hours on Job 443 and 100 hours on Job 444. Direct labor is paid at the rate of $8 per hour.

d. Overhead is applied using a plantwide rate of $7.50 per direct labor hour.

e. Actual overhead for the month was $1,230 and was paid in cash.

f. Job 443 was completed and transferred to Finished Goods.

g. Job 442, which had been completed and transferred to Finished Goods in March, was sold on account for cost ($2,000) plus 25 percent.

REQUIRED:

1. Prepare journal entries for transactions (a) through (e).

2. Prepare job-order cost sheets for Jobs 443 and 444. Prepare journal entries for transactions (f) and (g).

3. Prepare a statement of cost of goods manufactured for April. Assume that the beginning balance in the Raw Materials account was $1,400 and the beginning balance in the Work in Process account was zero.

W5-6
Journal Entries
LO 2
pp. 170–171

Paxton Company incurred the following actual overhead costs for the year:

Equipment lease	$ 5,000
Depreciation on building	20,000
Indirect labor	100,000
Utilities	15,000
Other overhead	45,000

Paxton applied overhead at the rate of $12 per direct labor hour, and 15,400 direct labor hours were worked during the year.

REQUIRED:

1. Prepare the journal entries to record actual overhead, and to apply overhead to production for the year.

2. Is overhead overapplied or underapplied? By how much?

3. Assuming that the normal cost of goods sold for the year is $700,000, what is the adjusted cost of goods sold?

W5-7
Nonmanufacturing Costs and the Income Statement
LO 3
pp. 174–175

Kaylen Company produces and sells snack-sized bags of potato chips. Last year, Kaylen sold 1,000,000 bags of chips at $0.30. Each bag had manufacturing costs of $0.14. Kaylen incurred the following marketing and administrative costs:

Advertising	$30,000
Delivery expense	28,000
Sales commissions	25,000
Office salaries	22,000
Depreciation, office equipment	9,000

REQUIRED:

1. Prepare the journal entry (or entries) to record selling and administrative expenses. (Assume that accounts payable or wages payable would be appropriate credit entries.)

2. Prepare an income statement for Kaylen Company for last year.

E XERCISES

E5-1
Cost Flows
LO 2

For each of the following independent jobs, fill in the missing data. Factory overhead is applied in department 1 at the rate of $6 per direct labor hour (DLH). Factory overhead is applied in department 2 at the rate of $8 per machine hour. Direct labor wages average $10 per hour in each department.

	Job 213	Job 214	Job 217	Job 225
Total sales revenue	$?	$4,375	$5,600	$1,150
Price per unit	12	?	14	5
Material used in production	365	?	488	207
DLH cost, department 1	?	700	2,000	230
Machine hours, department 1	15	35	50	12
DLH cost, department 2	50	100	?	0
Machine hours, department 2	25	50	?	?
Overhead applied, department 1	90	?	1,200	138
Overhead applied, department 2	?	400	160	0
Total manufacturing cost	855	3,073	?	575
Number of units	?	350	400	?
Unit cost	8.55	?	9.87	?

E5-2
Calculating Ending WIP
LO 2

Brandt Company produces unique metal sculptures. On January 1, there were three jobs in process with the following costs:

	Job 35	Job 36	Job 37
Direct materials	$100	$ 340	$ 780
Direct labor	350	700	1,050
Applied overhead	420	840	1,260
Total	$870	$1,880	$3,090

During January, two more jobs were started, Job 38 and Job 39. Materials and direct labor costs incurred by each job in process in January follow:

	Materials	Direct Labor
Job 35	$400	$300
Job 36	150	200
Job 37	260	150
Job 38	800	650
Job 39	760	700

Jobs 37 and 38 were completed and sold by January 31.

REQUIRED:
1. If overhead is applied on the basis of direct labor dollars, what is the overhead rate?
2. Prepare simple job-order cost sheets for each of the five jobs in process during January.
3. What is the ending balance of Work in Process on January 31? What is the Cost of Goods Sold in January?

E5-3
Income Statement in Job-Order Firm
LO 2

Refer to E5-2. Suppose that Brandt Company prices its jobs at cost plus 50 percent. In addition, during January selling and administrative costs of $1,200 were incurred. Prepare an income statement for the month of January.

E5-4
Journal Entries; T-Accounts
LO 2

Parish, Inc. builds custom equipment for manufacturing firms. During May, the following events occurred:

a. Raw Materials were purchased on account for $32,475.

b. Raw Materials totaling $27,000 were requisitioned for use in production, $15,000 for Job 644 and the remainder for Job 648.

c. The direct labor payroll for the month was $26,250 with an average wage of $12.50 per hour. Job 644 required 1,000 direct labor hours; Job 648 required 1,100 direct labor hours.

d. Actual overhead of $19,950 was incurred and paid.

e. Factory overhead is charged to production at the rate of $10 per direct labor hour.

f. Job 644 was completed and transferred to finished goods.

g. Job 648, which was started during May, remained in process at the end of the month.

h. Job 640, which had been completed in March, was sold on account for cost plus 25 percent.

Beginning balances as of May 1 were:

Materials	$ 6,070
Work in Process (for Job 644)	10,000
Finished Goods (for Job 640)	6,240

REQUIRED:

1. Prepare the journal entries for events (a) through (e).
2. Prepare simple job-order cost sheets for Jobs 644 and 648.
3. Prepare the journal entry for events (f) and (h).
4. Calculate the ending balances of:
   a. Materials
   b. Work in Process
   c. Finished Goods

E5-5
Actual and Applied Overhead, Journal Entries, Disposition of Variance
LO 2

Basinger Company uses a predetermined overhead rate to assign overhead to jobs. Because Basinger's production is machine dominated, overhead is applied on the basis of machine hours. The expected overhead for the year was $2.7 million, and the practical level of activity is 60,000 machine hours.

During the year, Basinger worked on 1,920 jobs, which used an average of 25 machine hours each. Basinger incurred actual overhead costs of $2 million, and had the following balances of applied overhead in its accounts:

Work in Process	$ 691,200
Cost of Goods Sold	1,296,000
Finished Goods	172,800

REQUIRED:

1. Compute a predetermined overhead rate for Basinger.
2. Compute the overhead variance and label it as underapplied or overapplied.
3. Assume the overhead variance is immaterial. Prepare the journal entry to dispose of the variance at the end of the year.
4. In accounting for the overhead variance, does it matter whether the jobs are complete or still in process?

E5-6
Multiple versus Single Overhead Rates; Activity Drivers
LO 2

Assume that a plant has two categories of overhead: material handling and quality inspection. The costs expected for these categories for the coming year are as follows:

Material handling	$200,000
Quality inspection	600,000

The plant currently applies overhead using machine hours and expected actual capacity. This figure is 80,000 machine hours. Linda Bixby, the plant manager, has been asked to submit a bid and has assembled the following data on the proposed job:

Direct materials	$3,700
Direct labor (1,000 hours)	$7,000
Overhead	$?
Number of material moves	10
Number of inspections	5
Machine hours	900

Linda has been told that many competitors use an activity-based approach to assign overhead to jobs. Before submitting her bid, she wants to assess the effects of this alternative approach. She estimates that the expected number of material moves for all jobs during the year is 1,000; she also expects 5,000 quality inspections to be performed.

REQUIRED:
1. Compute the total cost of the potential job using machine hours to assign overhead. Assuming that the bid price is full manufacturing cost plus 25 percent, what would Linda's bid be?
2. Compute the total cost of the job using the number of material moves to allocate material-handling costs and the number of inspections to allocate the quality inspection costs. Assuming a bid price of full manufacturing cost plus 25 percent, what is Linda's bid using this approach?
3. Which approach do you think best reflects the actual cost of the job? Explain.

E5-7
Journal Entries;
T-Accounts
LO 2

Dearinger Company uses job-order costing. During January, the following data were reported:

a. Materials purchased: direct materials, $62,000; indirect materials, $8,500
b. Materials issued: direct materials, $62,100; indirect materials, $4,000
c. Labor cost incurred: direct labor, $44,000; indirect labor, $12,250
d. Other manufacturing costs incurred (all payables), $59,000
e. Overhead is applied on the basis of 130 percent of direct labor cost.
f. Work finished and transferred to finished goods cost $150,000.
g. Finished goods costing $140,000 were sold on account for 120 percent of cost.

REQUIRED:
1. Prepare journal entries to record these transactions.
2. Prepare a T-account for Overhead Control. Post all relevant information to this account. What is the ending balance in this account? What does the ending balance represent?
3. Prepare a T-account for Work in Process. Assume a beginning balance of $10,000 and post all relevant information to this account. Did you assign any actual overhead costs to Work in Process? Why or why not?

E5-8
Overhead
Assignment: Actual
and Normal Activity
Compared
LO 2

Reynolds Printing Company specializes in wedding announcements. Reynolds uses an actual job-order cost system. An actual overhead rate is calculated at the end of each month using actual direct labor hours and overhead for the month. Once the actual cost of a job is determined, the customer is billed at actual cost plus 50 percent.

During April, Mrs. Lucky, a good friend of owner Jane Reynolds, ordered three sets of wedding announcements to be delivered May 10, June 10, and July 10, respectively. Reynolds scheduled production for each order on May 7, June 7, and July 7, respectively. The orders were assigned job numbers 115, 116, and 117, respectively.

Reynolds assured Mrs. Lucky that she would attend each of her daughters' weddings. Out of sympathy and friendship, she also offered a lower price. Instead of cost plus 50 percent, she gave her a special price of cost plus 25 percent. Additionally, she agreed to wait until the final wedding to bill for the three jobs.

On August 15, Reynolds asked her accountant to bring the completed job-order cost sheets for Jobs 115, 116, and 117. She also gave instructions to lower the price as had been agreed upon. The cost sheets revealed the following information:

	Job 115	Job 116	Job 117
Cost of direct materials	$250.00	$250.00	$250.00
Cost of direct labor (5 hours)	25.00	25.00	25.00
Cost of overhead	200.00	400.00	400.00
Total cost	$475.00	$675.00	$675.00
Total price	$593.75	$843.75	$843.75
Number of announcements	500	500	500

Reynolds could not understand why the overhead costs assigned to Jobs 116 and 117 were so much higher than those for Job 115. She asked for an overhead cost summary sheet for the months of May, June, and July, which showed that actual overhead costs were $20,000 each month. She also discovered that direct labor hours worked on all jobs were 500 hours in May and 250 hours each in June and July.

REQUIRED:
1. How do you think Mrs. Lucky will feel when she receives the bill for the three sets of wedding announcements?
2. Explain how the overhead costs were assigned to each job.
3. Assume that Reynolds's average activity is 500 hours per month and that the company usually experiences overhead costs of $240,000 each year. Can you recommend a better way to assign overhead costs to jobs? Recompute the cost of each job and its price given your method of overhead cost assignment. Which method do you think is best? Why?

E5-9
Overhead Applied to Jobs; Departmental Overhead Rates
LO 2

Watson Products, Inc. uses a normal job-order cost system. Currently, a plantwide overhead rate based on machine hours is used. Marlon Burke, the plant manager, has heard that departmental overhead rates can offer significantly better cost assignments than a plantwide rate can offer. Watson has the following data for its two departments for the coming year:

	Department A	Department B
Overhead costs (expected)	$50,000	$22,000
Normal activity (machine hours)	20,000	16,000

REQUIRED:
1. Compute a predetermined overhead rate for the plant as a whole based on machine hours.
2. Compute predetermined overhead rates for each department using machine hours. (Carry your calculations out to three decimal places.)
3. Job 73 used 20 machine hours from department A and 50 machine hours from department B. Job 74 used 50 machine hours from department A and 20 from department B. Compute the overhead cost assigned to each job using the plantwide rate computed in requirement 1. Repeat the computation using the departmental rates found in requirement 2. Which of the two approaches gives the fairer assignment? Why?
4. Repeat requirement 3 assuming the expected overhead cost for department B is $40,000. For this company, would you recommend departmental rates over a plantwide rate?

E5-10
Unit Cost; Ending Work in Process; Journal Entries
LO 2

During October, Harrison Company worked on two jobs. Data relating to these two jobs follow:

	Job 34	Job 35
Units in each order	60	100
Units sold	60	—
Materials requisitioned	$640	$530
Direct labor hours	370	550
Direct labor cost	$1,980	$1,480

Overhead is assigned on the basis of direct labor hours at a rate of $5. During October, Job 34 was completed and transferred to finished goods. Job 35 was the only unfinished job at the end of the month.

REQUIRED:
1. Calculate the per-unit cost of Job 34.
2. Compute the ending balance in the Work in Process account.
3. Prepare the journal entries reflecting the completion and sale of Job 34. The selling price is 140 percent of cost.

E5-11
Unit Cost; Journal Entries; Assignment Procedures
LO 2

Hystle Furniture, Inc. received an order for ten specially designed sofas to be delivered by September 30. The order was assigned Job 237 and work began on September 1. During September, the following activities were associated with Job 237:

a. Purchased $2,000 worth of wood, $1,500 worth of fabric, and $200 worth of foam on account
b. Issued into production $2,000 of wood, $1,500 of fabric, and $200 of foam
c. Direct labor cost incurred: $1,360
d. Overhead is assigned using a rate of 125 percent of direct labor cost.
e. Completed units are transferred to the warehouse.
f. Completed units are shipped to the customer; selling price is 135 percent of cost.

REQUIRED:
1. Prepare the journal entries for the activity associated with Job 237.
2. What is the manufacturing cost per sofa?
3. Describe the procedures for identifying the materials issued to Job 237 and for identifying the cost of laborers who worked on the sofas.

E5-12
Predetermined Overhead Rates; Variances; Cost Flows
LO 2

Barrymore Costume Company, located in New York City, sews costumes for plays and musicals. Barrymore considers itself primarily a service firm, as it never produces costumes without a preexisting order, and purchases materials to the specifications of the particular job. Any finished goods ending inventory is temporary and is zeroed out as soon as the show producer pays for the order. Overhead is applied on the basis of direct labor cost. During the first quarter of 1998, the following activity took place in each of the accounts below:

Work in Process		
Bal	17,000	245,000
DL	80,000	
OH	140,000	
DM	40,000	
Bal	32,000	

Finished Goods		
Bal	40,000	210,000
	245,000	
Bal	75,000	

Overhead		
	138,500	140,000
Bal		1,500

Cost of Goods Sold	
210,000	

Job 32 was the only job in process at the end of the first quarter. A total of 1,000 direct labor hours at $10 per hour was charged to Job 32.

REQUIRED:
1. Assuming that overhead is applied on the basis of direct labor cost, what was the overhead rate used during the first quarter of 1998?
2. What was the applied overhead for the first quarter? the actual overhead? the underapplied or overapplied overhead?
3. What was the cost of the goods manufactured for the quarter?
4. Assume that the overhead variance is closed to the Cost of Goods Sold account. Prepare the journal entry to close out the Overhead account. What is the adjusted balance in Cost of Goods Sold?
5. For Job 32, identify the costs incurred for direct materials, direct labor, and overhead.

E5-13
**Activity-based
Costing and
Overhead Rates;
Unit Costs**
LO 2, LO 3

Courtney Company manufactures specialty tools to customer order. Budgeted overhead for the coming year is:

Purchasing	$30,000
Setups	15,000
Other	25,000

Previously, Jennifer Langston, Courtney Company's controller, had applied overhead on the basis of machine hours. Expected machine hours for the coming year are 10,000. Jennifer has been reading about activity-based costing and she wonders whether or not it might offer some advantages to her company. She decided that appropriate drivers for Courtney's overhead activities are purchase orders for purchasing; number of setups for setup cost; and machine hours for other. Budgeted amounts for these drivers are 5,000 purchase orders and 1,000 setups.

Jennifer has been asked to prepare a bid for a potential job with the following information:

Direct materials	$4,500
Direct labor	1,000
Number of setups	2
Number of purchase orders	15
Number of machine hours	200

The typical bid price includes a 30 percent markup over full manufacturing cost.

REQUIRED:
1. Calculate a plantwide rate for Courtney Company based on machine hours. What is the bid price of the job using this rate?
2. Calculate activity rates for the three overhead activities. What is the bid price of the job using these rates?
3. Which bid is more accurate? Why?

E5-14
**Activity-based
Costing and
Overhead Rates;
Unit Costs**
LO 2, LO 3

Mueller Custom Cabinets designs and makes cabinets to customer order. Mark Mueller identified the following budgeted overhead activities and drivers:

Machine operation	$40,000	Machine hours	10,000
Setups	$10,000	Number of setups	2,000
Designing costs	$30,000	Design hours	5,000

Frank and Sally Willis were building a large custom house and wanted "lots of storage." Their job had the following data:

Direct materials	$3,750
Direct labor wages	$5,000
Machine hours	600
Number of setups	100
Design hours	225

Cindy and Ray Gordon were remodeling an older house. They needed some basic cabinets for the kitchen. Mark Mueller suggested a basic design he had built numerous times before. The Gordon job had the following data:

Direct materials	$2,000
Direct labor wages	$1,750
Machine hours	80
Number of setups	1
Design hours	0

REQUIRED:
1. Calculate a unit-based overhead rate based on machine hours. What is the total cost of the Willis job using this rate? What is the total cost of the Gordon job using this rate?
2. Calculate activity rates. What is the cost of the Willis job using the three activity rates? What is the cost of the Gordon job using the three activity rates?

P ROBLEMS

P5-1
Predetermined
Overhead Rates;
Overhead Variances;
Unit Costs
LO 2

Palace Lighting Fixtures, Inc. uses a unit-level predetermined overhead rate to apply overhead. Overhead is applied on the basis of direct labor hours in department 1 and on the basis of machine hours in department 2. At the beginning of 1998, the following estimates are provided for the coming year:

	Department 1	Department 2
Direct labor hours	100,000	20,000
Machine hours	10,000	35,000
Direct labor cost	$900,000	$190,000
Overhead cost	$300,000	$196,000

Actual results reported for all jobs during 1998 are as follows:

	Department 1	Department 2
Direct labor hours	98,000	21,000
Machine hours	11,000	36,000
Direct labor cost	$882,400	$168,000
Overhead cost	$301,000	$200,600

The accounting records of the company show the following data for Job 689:

	Department 1	Department 2
Direct labor hours	125	50
Machine hours	10	205
Direct materials cost	$1,610	$3,000
Direct labor cost	$1,125	$400

REQUIRED:
1. Compute the predetermined overhead rate for each department.
2. Compute the applied overhead for all jobs during 1998. What is the underapplied or overapplied overhead for each department? for the firm?
3. Prepare the journal entry that disposes of the overhead variance, assuming it is not material in amount.
4. Compute the total cost of Job 689. If there are 50 units in Job 689, what is the unit cost?

P5-2
Activity-based
Costing; Accuracy of

Ferguson Equipment, Inc. manufactures custom-designed manufacturing equipment. Ferguson recently received a request to manufacture 40 units of a specialized machine at a price lower than it normally accepts. Marketing manager Emily Dorr indicated that if the order were accepted at

**Unit Costs; Multiple-
Overhead Rates
Using Activity
Drivers versus Single
Overhead Rates;
Pricing Decisions**
LO 2

that price, the company could expect additional orders from the same customer; in fact, if the company could offer this price in the market generally, she believed that sales of this machine would increase by 50 percent.

Cleon Skowsen, president of Ferguson, was skeptical about accepting the order. The company had a policy of not accepting any order that did not provide revenues that at least equaled its full manufacturing cost plus 15 percent. The price offered was $2,100 per unit. However, before a final decision was made, Cleon decided to request information on the estimated cost per unit. He was concerned because the company was experiencing increased competition, and the number of new orders was dropping. Also, the controller's office had recently researched the possibility of using activity-based, multiple-overhead rates instead of the single rate currently in use. The controller had promised more accurate product costing, and Cleon was curious about how this approach would affect the pricing of this particular machine.

Within 24 hours, the controller assembled the following data:

a. The plantwide overhead rate is based on an expected volume of 400,000 direct labor hours and the following budgeted overhead (all figures are yearly):

Depreciation, building	$ 500,000
Depreciation, equipment	300,000
Material handling	800,000
Power (machine usage)	500,000
Rework costs	300,000
Supervision (plantwide)	200,000
Cost of scrapped units	640,000
Other plantwide overhead	460,000
Total	$3,700,000

(handwritten: ÷ 400,000 DLH = 9.25)

b. Expected activity for selected activity drivers (for the year) follows:

Material moves	10,000
Kilowatt-hours	100,000
Units reworked	2,000
Units scrapped	1,000
Machine hours	100,000

c. Estimated data for the potential job (based on the production of 40 units) follow:

Direct labor (4,000 hours)	$20,000
Direct materials	$24,000
Number of material moves	6
Number of kilowatt-hours	1,000
Number of units reworked	2
Number of units scrapped	3
Number of machine hours	1,000

(handwritten: 4,000 @ 9.25 = 37,000 OH)

REQUIRED:

1. Compute the estimated unit cost for the potential job using the current method to assign overhead on a plantwide basis. Given this unit cost, compute the total gross margin earned by the job. Would the job be accepted under normal operating conditions?
2. Classify overhead activities as unit level, batch level, product sustaining, or facility level. Calculate pool rates using the activity drivers in (b). The rate for facility-level overhead is based on direct labor hours.

3. Compute the estimated unit cost for the potential job using the pool rates computed in requirement 2. Report per-unit costs by activity category. Given this cost per unit, compute the total gross margin earned by the job. Should the job be accepted?
4. Which approach—the plantwide rate or the multiple-overhead rate with activity drivers—is the best for the company? Explain.

P5-3
Job Cost Sheets;
Journal Entries;
Inventories
LO 2, LO 3

On July 1, Polk Company had the following balances in its inventory accounts:

Raw Materials	$22,000
Work in Process	7,905
Finished Goods	25,000

Work in Process is made up of three jobs with the following costs:

	Job 17	Job 18	Job 19
Raw materials	$1,100	$910	$1,415
Direct labor	900	850	1,050
Applied overhead	540	510	630

During July, Polk experienced the following transactions:

a. Materials purchased on account, $13,000
b. Materials requisitioned: Job 17, $8,500; Job 18, $7,200; Job 19, $12,300
c. Job tickets collected and summarized: Job 17, 175 hours at $10 per hour; Job 18, 165 hours at $11 per hour; and Job 19, 225 hours at $10 per hour
d. Overhead is applied on the basis of direct labor cost.
e. Actual overhead: $3,500
f. Jobs 17 and 18 were completed and transferred to the finished goods warehouse.
g. Job 18 was shipped; the customer was billed for 160 percent of the cost.

REQUIRED:
1. Prepare job-order cost sheets for Jobs 17, 18, and 19. Post the beginning inventory data and then update the cost sheets for the July activity.
2. Prepare journal entries for the July transactions.
3. Prepare a schedule of inventories on July 31.

P5-4
Job-Order Costing:
Housing
Construction
LO 2, LO 3

Butter, Inc. is a privately held, family-founded corporation that builds single- and multiple-unit housing. Most projects Butter undertakes involve the construction of multiple units. Butter has adopted a job-order cost system for determining the cost of each unit. The costing system is fully computerized. Each project's costs are divided into the following five categories:

a. General conditions, including construction site utilities, project insurance permits and licenses, architect's fees, decorating, field office salaries, and cleanup costs
b. Hard costs, such as subcontractors, direct materials, and direct labor
c. Finance costs, including title and recording fees, inspection fees, and taxes and discounts on mortgages
d. Land costs, which refer to the purchase price of the construction site
e. Marketing costs, such as advertising, sales commissions, and appraisal fees

Recently, Butter purchased land for the purpose of developing 20 new single-family houses. The cost of the land was $250,000. Lot sizes vary from one-quarter to one-half acre. The 20 lots occupy a total of eight acres. General condition costs for the project totaled $120,000. This $120,000 is common to all 20 units that were constructed on the building site.

Job 3, the third house built in the project, occupied a quarter-acre lot and had the following hard costs:

Materials	$ 8,000	
Direct labor	6,000	
Subcontractor	14,000	

For Job 3, finance costs totaled $4,765 and marketing costs, $800. General condition costs are allocated on the basis of units produced. Each unit's selling price is determined by adding 40 percent to the total of all costs.

REQUIRED:

1. Identify all production costs that are directly traceable to Job 3. Are all remaining production costs equivalent to overhead found in a manufacturing firm? Are there nonproduction costs that are directly traceable to the housing unit? Which ones?
2. Develop a job-order cost sheet for Job 3. What is the cost of building this house? Did you include finance and marketing costs in computing the unit cost? Why or why not? How did you determine the cost of land for Job 3?
3. Which of the five cost categories corresponds to overhead? Do you agree with the way in which this cost is allocated to individual housing units? Can you suggest a different allocation method?
4. Calculate the selling price of Job 3. Calculate the profit made on the sale of this unit.

P5-5

Plantwide Overhead Rate; Departmental Rates; Effects on Job Pricing Decisions

LO 2, LO 3

Alden Peterson, marketing manager for Retlief Company, was puzzled by the outcome of two recent bids. The company's policy was to bid 150 percent of the full manufacturing cost. One job (labeled Job SS) had been turned down by a prospective customer who had indicated that the proposed price was $3 per unit higher than the winning bid. A second job (Job TT) had been accepted by a customer who was amazed that Retlief could offer such favorable terms. This customer revealed that Retlief's price was $43 per unit lower than the next lowest bid.

Alden has been informed that the company was more than competitive in terms of cost control. Accordingly, he began to suspect that the problem was related to cost assignment procedures. Upon investigating, Alden was told that the company uses a plantwide overhead rate based on direct labor hours. The rate is computed at the beginning of the year using budgeted data. Selected budgeted data follow:

	Department A	Department B	Total
Overhead	$500,000	$2,000,000	$2,500,000
Direct labor hours	200,000	50,000	250,000
Machine hours	20,000	120,000	140,000

Alden also discovered that the overhead costs in department B were higher than those in department A because B has more equipment, higher maintenance, higher power consumption, higher depreciation, and higher setup costs. In addition to the general procedures for assigning overhead costs, Alden was supplied with the following specific manufacturing data on Job SS and Job TT:

	Job SS		
	Department A	Department B	Total
Direct labor hours	5,000	1,000	6,000
Machine hours	200	500	700
Prime costs	$100,000	$20,000	$120,000
Units produced	14,400	14,400	14,400

	Job TT		
	Department A	Department B	Total
Direct labor hours	400	600	1,000
Machine hours	200	3,000	3,200
Prime costs	$10,000	$40,000	$50,000
Units produced	1,500	1,500	1,500

REQUIRED:
1. Using a plantwide overhead rate based on direct labor hours, develop the bid prices for Job SS and Job TT. (Express the bid prices on a per-unit basis.)
2. Using departmental overhead rates (use direct labor hours for department A and machine hours for department B), develop per-unit bid prices for Job SS and Job TT.
3. Compute the difference in gross margin that would have been earned had the company used departmental rates in its bids instead of the plantwide rate.
4. Explain why the use of departmental rates in this case provides a more accurate product cost.

P5-6
ABC, Departmental Rates, and Pricing Decisions
LO 1, LO 2, LO 3

(A continuation of P5-5 with activity data added.) With some help from the controller, Peterson had the bids recalculated using departmental rates. Alden knew this could improve the accuracy of the cost assignment because one of the two producing departments was labor intensive and the other was machine intensive. Both jobs spent time in each department although Job TT spent most of its time in the machine-intensive department. The unit bid price for the different approaches follow:

	Job SS	Job TT
Plantwide rate:		
Bid price	$18.75	$ 60.00
Departmental rates:		
Bid price	14.67	101.01

Alden had been reading about the increased accuracy of an ABC system and convinced the controller to help in obtaining the following information:

Overhead Activities	Cost	Activity Category	Activity Driver
Maintenance	$500,000	Product sustaining	Machine hours
Power	225,000	Unit level	Kilowatt-hours
Setups	150,000	Batch level	Setup hours
General factory	625,000	Facility level	Machine hours*

*This is an arbitrary allocation. The controller argued that machine hours used by a job would be correlated with square footage occupied by the producing departments.

The expected levels of the activity drivers for the year follow:

Machine hours	140,000
Kilowatt-hours	100,000
Setup hours	20,000

The activity data for each job are also provided.

	Job SS	Job TT
Machine hours	700	3,200
Kilowatt-hours	400	2,500
Setup hours	20	100
Prime costs	$120,000	$50,000
Units	14,400	1,500

REQUIRED:
1. Calculate the cost of each job using activity-based costing. List the costs for each job by activity category.

2. Calculate the bid price for each job using the normal markup. How do the bid prices compare with the bids using plantwide and departmental rates? Does this offer any real improvement? Explain.

3. Suppose that the best competing bid for Job SS was $4.20 lower than the original bid based on a plantwide rate. Also, assume that the bid on Job TT was $25 lower than the next lowest bid. Now compare the ABC bids with the bids based on departmental rates. What does this imply about the value of ABC as price competition intensifies?

4. Discuss the importance of having the facility-level costs listed separately as the job costs are detailed. Should these costs be included in the base for calculating the bid?

P5-7

Overhead Rates; Unit Cost

LO 1, LO 2

Stoney End Recordings produces cassette tapes and compact discs on a job-order basis for individuals and groups who want their music recorded. In some cases, customers want one or two copies for family and friends. In others, several hundred cassettes or CDs are ordered to send to radio stations across the country in hopes of getting air time. In still other cases, several thousand CDs may be ordered by fledgling bands to leave with music stores on a consignment basis.

Stoney End uses a normal costing system with departmental overhead rates for the use of the recording studio (based on direct labor hours), the cassette tape production department (based on machine hours), and the CD production department (based on machine hours).

Budgeted amounts for 1998 were:

Overhead:	
Recording studio	$18,000
Cassette tape production	$ 8,000
CD production	$28,000
Direct labor hours:	
Recording studio	6,000
Cassette tape production	900
CD production	16,000
Machine hours:	
Recording studio	5,000
Cassette tape production	1,000
CD production	8,000
Average wage rates:	
Recording studio	$12/DLH
Cassette tape production	$6/DLH
CD production	$25/DLH

In September, Billy Ryan and the Black Irish (a heavy metal rock band) ordered 300 cassette tapes to distribute to radio stations and music company executives. Stoney End assigned this job the number 98-413. Job 98-413 used 12 direct labor hours of recording studio time; and 1 direct labor hour, and 5 machine hours in the cassette tape production department. Supplies (tape, packaging, and so on) amounted to $453.

REQUIRED:

1. Calculate overhead rates for the recording, cassette tape, and CD departments.
2. Determine the total cost of Job 98-413. What is the unit cost?
3. Is Stoney End a manufacturing firm or a service firm? Does it matter?

P5-8

Predetermined Overhead Rate; Departmental Overhead Rates; Job Cost

LO 1, LO 2

Peregrino Printing provides a variety of photocopying and printing services. On June 5, 1998, Peregrino invested in some computer-aided photography equipment that enables customers to reproduce a picture or illustration, input it digitally into the computer, enter text into the computer, and then print out a four-color, professional-quality brochure. Prior to the purchase of this equipment, Peregrino Printing's overhead averaged $45,000 per year. After the installation of the new equipment, the total overhead increased to $105,000 per year. Peregrino Printing has always costed jobs on the basis of actual materials and labor plus overhead assigned using a predetermined overhead rate based on direct labor hours. Budgeted direct labor hours for 1998 are 5,000, and the wage rate is $6.50 per hour.

REQUIRED:
1. What was the predetermined overhead rate prior to the purchase of the new equipment?
2. What was the predetermined overhead rate after the new equipment was purchased?
3. Suppose Jim Hargrove brought in several items he wanted photocopied. The job required 100 sheets of paper at $0.015 each, and 12 minutes of direct labor time. What was the cost of Jim's job on May 20, 1998? on June 20, 1998?
4. Suppose that Peregrino Printing decides to calculate two overhead rates, one for the photocopying area based on direct labor hours as before, and one for the computer-aided printing area based on machine time. Estimated overhead applicable to the computer-aided printing area is $60,000; forecast usage of the equipment is 2,000 hours. What are the two overhead rates? Which overhead rate system is better—one rate or two?

P5-9
Departmental Overhead Rates; Job Cost
LO 1, LO 2

Zorba Novelties, Inc. produces T-shirts and pottery (mugs, glassware, and so on) to customer order. The T-shirt department takes the design selected by the customer and hot presses it onto each shirt. The shirts are then inspected, folded, and slipped into plastic wrappers. The pottery department affixes a customer-selected decal onto the mug or glass and then boxes each individual item to prevent breakage.

Zorba uses a normal job-order costing system. That is, each job accumulates actual direct materials and labor, and overhead is applied using a predetermined rate.

Zorba determined the following budgeted costs for the year:

	T-Shirt Department	Pottery Department
Overhead	$10,000	$2,100
Direct labor hours	5,000	1,500

Overhead is applied on the basis of direct labor hours.
Actual costs for one of each are as follows:

T-shirt	$3.22
Design transfer	0.46
Mug	2.50
Mug decal (each)	0.25

It takes three minutes of direct labor time to select a T-shirt from inventory, place the selected design transfer on it, place it on the hot press, press the design on it, dispose of the paper transfer backing, and fold and wrap the T-shirt. In the pottery department, five minutes of direct labor time are required to put one decal on a mug and individually box the mug (extra decals can be affixed at the rate of one minute each). Direct labor is paid at the rate of $6.50 per hour.

Ordinarily, Zorba charges cost plus 50 percent. However, the owner gives a quantity discount of 10 percent off the price for 75 or more identical items ordered. He also hates to be rushed and imposes a 25 percent surcharge on orders with less than 72 hours of lead time. (The rush surcharge is calculated on the basis of the price figured after any quantity discounts are subtracted.)

On May 17, Katie Stephens of the Campus Orientation Committee ordered 150 T-shirts to be imprinted with the campus "Welcome Frosh" design. These shirts were to be available August 1— in plenty of time for sophomore volunteers to pick one up to wear during Orientation Week.

On October 31, Leslie Adams, president of Campus Chest, raced into Zorba's to order 50 coffee mugs with the campus logo on one side and the phrase "Campus Chest Sponsor" on the other. Leslie, who was supposed to place the order in September but forgot, wanted it by noon, November 1.

REQUIRED:

1. What are the predetermined overhead rates for the two departments?
2. What is the cost of Katie's T-shirt order? cost per unit? What price did Zorba charge Katie?
3. What is the cost of Leslie's order? cost per unit? What price did Zorba charge Leslie?

P5-10
Activity-based Costing; Job Costs and Prices
LO 2, LO 3

Mountain View Rentals, located in Evergreen, Colorado, rents bikes to tourists for bike hiking in the Rocky Mountains. The rental price is tied to cost, so it is important to know the cost of the bikes, labor, and overhead. The bikes can be categorized into three levels, depending on sophistication and anticipated use. The cost per bike-rental-day for the three levels is as follows:

Level 1	$ 7.50
Level 2	$12.00
Level 3	$20.00

Since each worker performs a number of tasks (for example, answering the phone, renting bikes, cleaning the shop, and maintaining bikes) there is no separate category for direct labor, and labor is included in overhead. Overhead for last year was $50,000, and it was applied to the jobs based on a unit-level rate of $5 per bike-rental-day (the rental of one bike for one day).

The rental rate is calculated by adding a 40 percent markup to total cost.

Recently, Mountain View Rentals added a picnic catering service in which customers call the day before to order a picnic lunch to be taken on the bike hike. As a result, budgeted annual overhead increased to $100,000, while budgeted bike rental days remained at 10,000.

The addition of the picnic catering service rendered the unit-based overhead application method obsolete, so Mountain View Rentals decided to use a modified activity-based costing system. Major overhead activities identified are purchasing (based on number of purchase orders); power (based on number of kilowatt-hours); maintenance (based on number of maintenance hours); and other (based on direct labor hours).

Budgeted activity levels for the coming year are as follows:

Activity		Driver	
Purchasing	$30,000	Purchase orders	10,000
Power	$20,000	Kilowatt-hours	50,000
Maintenance	$ 6,000	Maintenance hours	600
Other	$44,000	Direct labor hours	22,000

Usage by the two different departments of Mountain View Rentals is as follows:

	Bike Rental	Picnic Catering
Purchase orders	7,000	3,000
Kilowatt-hours	5,000	45,000
Maintenance hours	500	100
Direct labor hours	11,000	11,000

Once the overhead is assigned to the bike rental segment, an overhead rate based on bike rental days is computed. Initially for the catering operation, overhead assigned to catering, using activity rates, is totaled and a single rate based on direct labor hours is computed.

REQUIRED:

1. Ignoring the desired shift to an activity-based costing system, calculate a single unit-based rate for last year and this year based on bike rental days. Suppose that the Carson family vacations in Evergreen each year and rents five bikes from Mountain View Rental for a two-day period. Maria and Fred Carson rent level 3 bikes, while the Carson children rent level 2 bikes. What was the cost of the Carson family rental last year? this year? What price was charged last year? this year? How do you suppose that Maria and Fred feel about this?

2. Calculate activity-based rates for the four activities. How much total overhead is assigned to the bike rental operation? to the catering operation?

3. Suppose that the overhead allocated to the bike rental operation is then applied to jobs on the basis of bike rental days, as before. Now what are this year's cost and price of the Carson rental?

4. Carol and Thurman Estes are honeymooning in Evergreen and decide to spend one day biking in the mountains. They rent two level 1 bikes and order a picnic lunch for two. The materials for the picnic cost $12 and it takes one hour to make and pack the picnic. Using the overhead assigned to the catering operation in requirement 2, calculate a catering overhead rate based on direct labor hours. What is the total cost of the Estes job?

5. Mountain View Rentals is considering adding level 4 bikes to their lineup. However, these bikes are high-performance racing bikes and require considerably more maintenance and specialized parts ordering than the level 1 through 3 bikes. How can activity-based costing help Mountain View decide what the cost of the level 4 bikes is and whether or not they should add these bikes to their rental list?

MANAGERIAL DECISION CASES

**C5-1
Assigning Overhead
to Jobs; Ethical Issues**
LO 2, LO 3

Tonya Martin, CMA, and controller of the Parts Division of Gunderson, Inc. was meeting with Doug Adams, manager of the division. The topic of discussion was the assignment of overhead costs to jobs and their impact on the division's pricing decisions. Their conversation follows.

Tonya: "Doug, as you know, about 25 percent of our business is based on government contracts, with the other 75 percent based on jobs from private sources won through bidding. During the last several years, our private business has declined. We have been losing more bids than usual. After some careful investigation, I have concluded that we are overpricing some jobs because of improper assignment of overhead costs. Some jobs are also being underpriced. Unfortunately, the jobs being overpriced are coming from our higher-volume, labor-intensive products; thus, we are losing business."

Doug: "I think I understand. Jobs associated with our high-volume products are being assigned more overhead than they should be receiving. Then, when we add our standard 40 percent markup, we end up with a higher price than our competitors, who assign costs more accurately."

Tonya: "Exactly. We have two producing departments, one labor intensive and the other machine intensive. The labor-intensive department generates much less overhead than the machine-intensive department. Furthermore, virtually all of our high-volume jobs are labor intensive. We have been using a plantwide rate based on direct labor hours to assign overhead to all jobs. As a result, the high-volume, labor-intensive jobs receive a greater share of the machine-intensive department's overhead than they deserve. This problem can be greatly alleviated by switching to departmental overhead rates. For example, an average high-volume job would be assigned $100,000 of overhead using a plantwide rate and only $70,000 using departmental rates. The change would lower our bidding price on high-volume jobs by an average of $42,000 per job. By increasing the accuracy of our product costing, we can make better pricing decisions and win back much of our private-sector business."

Doug: "Sounds good. When can you implement the change in overhead rates?"

Tonya: "It won't take long. I can have the new system working within four to six weeks—certainly by the start of the new fiscal year."

Doug: "Hold it. I just thought of a possible complication. As I recall, most of our government contract work is done in the labor-intensive department. This new overhead assignment scheme will push down the cost on the government jobs, and we will lose revenues. They pay us full cost plus our standard markup. This business is not threatened by our current costing procedures, but we can't switch our rates for only the private business. Government auditors would question the lack of consistency in our costing procedures."

Tonya: "You do have a point. I thought of this issue also. According to my estimates, we will gain more revenues from the private sector than we will lose from our government contracts. Besides, the costs of our government jobs are distorted; in effect, we are overcharging the government."

Doug: "They don't know that and never will unless we switch our overhead assignment procedures. I think I have the solution. Officially, let's keep our plantwide overhead rate. All of the official records will reflect this overhead costing approach for both our private and government business. Unofficially, I want you to develop a separate set of books that can be used to generate the information we need to prepare competitive bids for our private-sector business."

REQUIRED:
1. Do you believe that the solution proposed by Doug Adams is ethical? Explain.
2. Suppose that Tonya Martin decides that Doug's solution is not right. In your opinion, is Tonya supported in this view by the standards of ethical conduct described in Chapter 1? Explain.
3. Suppose that, despite Tonya's objections, Doug insists strongly on implementing the action. What should Tonya Martin do?

C5-2
Job-Order Costing:
Dental Practice
LO 2, LO 3

Dr. Sherry Bird is employed by Dental Associates. Dental Associates recently installed a computerized job-order costing system to help monitor the cost of its services. Each patient is treated as a job and assigned a job number when he or she checks in with the receptionist. The receptionist-bookkeeper notes the time the patient enters the treatment area and when the patient leaves the area. The difference between the entry and exit times is the patient hours used and is the direct labor time assigned to the dental assistant (a dental assistant is constantly with the patient). Fifty percent of the patient hours is the direct labor time assigned to the dentist (the dentist typically splits her time between two patients).

The chart filled out by the dental assistant provides additional data that are entered into the computer. For example, the chart contains service codes that identify the nature of the treatment, such as whether the patient received a crown, a filling, or a root canal. The chart not only identifies the type of service but its level as well. For example, if a patient receives a filling, the dental assistant indicates (by a service-level code) whether the filling was one, two, three, or four surfaces. The service and service-level codes are used to determine the rate to be charged to the patient. The costs of providing different services and their levels also vary.

Costs assignable to a patient consist of materials, labor, and overhead. The type of materials used, and the quantity, are identified by the assistant and entered into the computer by the bookkeeper. Material prices are kept on file and accessed to provide the necessary cost information. Overhead is applied on the basis of patient hours. The rate used by Dental Associates is $20 per patient hour. Direct labor cost is also computed using patient hours and the wage rates of the direct laborers. Dr. Bird is paid an average of $36 per hour for her services. Dental assistants are paid an average of $6 per hour. Given the treatment time, the software program calculates and assigns the labor cost for the dentist and her assistant; overhead cost is also assigned using the treatment time and the overhead rate.

The overhead rate does not include a charge for any X rays. The X-ray department is separate from dental services; X rays are billed and costed separately. The cost of an X ray is $3.50 per film; the patient is charged $5 per film. If cleaning services are required, cleaning labor costs $9 per patient hour.

Glen Johnson, a patient (Job 267), spent 30 minutes in the treatment area and had a two-surface filling. He received two Novocain shots and used three ampules of amalgam. The cost of the shots was $1. The cost of the amalgam was $3. Other direct materials used were insignificant in amount and were included in the overhead rate. The rate charged to the patient for a two-surface filling is $45. One X ray was taken.

REQUIRED:
1. Prepare a job-order cost sheet for Glen Johnson. What is the cost for providing a two-surface filling? What is the gross margin earned? Is the X ray a direct cost of the service? Why are the X rays costed separately from the overhead cost assignment?
2. Suppose that the patient time and associated patient charges are given for the following fillings:

	1 Surface	2 Surfaces	3 Surfaces	4 Surfaces
Time	20 minutes	30 minutes	40 minutes	50 minutes
Charge	$35	$45	$55	$65

Compute the cost for each filling and the gross margin for each type of filling. Assume that the cost of Novocain is $1 for all fillings. Ampules of amalgam start at two and increase by one for each additional surface. Assume also that only one X-ray film is needed for all four cases. Does the increase in billing rate appear to be fair to the patient? Is it fair to the dental corporation?

C5-3
**Job-Order Costing
and Pricing Decisions**
LO 2, LO 3

Nutratask, Inc. is a pharmaceutical manufacturer of amino-acid-chelated minerals and vitamin supplements. The company was founded in 1974 and is capable of performing all manufacturing functions, including packaging and laboratory functions. Currently, the company markets its products in the United States, Canada, Australia, Japan, and Belgium.

Mineral chelation enhances the mineral's availability to the body, making the mineral a more effective supplement. Most of the chelates supplied by Nutratask are in powder form, but the company has the capability to make tablets or capsules.

The production of all chelates follows a similar pattern. Upon receiving an order, the company's chemist prepares a load sheet (a bill of materials that specifies the product, the theoretical yield, and the quantities of raw materials that should be used). Once the load sheet is received by production, the materials are requisitioned and sent to the blending room. The chemicals and minerals are added in the order specified and blended for two to eight hours, depending on the product. After blending, the mix is put on long trays and sent to the drying room, where it is allowed to dry until the moisture content is 7 to 9 percent. Drying time for most products is from one to three days.

After the product is dry, several small samples are taken and sent to a laboratory to be checked for bacterial level and to see whether the product meets customer specifications. If the product is not fit for human consumption or if it fails to meet customer specifications, additional materials are added under the direction of the chemist to bring the product up to standard. Once the product passes inspection, it is ground into a powder of different meshes (particle sizes) according to customer specifications. The powder is then placed in heavy cardboard drums and shipped to the customer (or, if requested, put in tablet or capsule form and then shipped).

Since each order is customized to meet the special needs of its customers, Nutratask uses a job-order costing system. Recently, Nutratask received a request for a 300-kilogram order of potassium aspartate. The customer offered to pay $8.80 per kilogram. Upon receiving the request and the customer's specifications, Lanny Smith, the marketing manager, requested a load sheet from the company's chemist. The load sheet prepared showed the following material requirements:

Material	Amount Required
Aspartic acid	195.00 kg
Citric acid	15.00 kg
K_2CO_3 (50%)	121.50 kg
Rice	30.00 kg

The theoretical yield is 300 kilograms.

Lanny also reviewed past jobs that were similar to the requested order and discovered that the expected direct labor time was 16 hours. The production workers at Nutratask earn an average of $6.50 per hour plus $6 per hour for taxes, insurance, and additional benefits.

Purchasing sent Smith a list of prices for the materials needed for the job.

Material	Price per Kg
Aspartic acid	$5.75
Citric acid	2.02
K_2CO_3	4.64
Rice	0.43

Overhead is applied using a companywide rate based on direct labor costs. The rate for the current period is 110 percent of direct labor costs.

Whenever a customer requests a bid, Nutratask usually estimates the manufacturing costs of the job and then adds a markup of 30 percent. This markup varies depending on the competition and general economic conditions. Currently, the industry is thriving, and Nutratask is operating at capacity.

REQUIRED:
1. Prepare a job cost sheet for the proposed job. What is the expected per-unit cost? Should Nutratask accept the price offered by the prospective customer? Why or why not?

2. Suppose Nutratask and the prospective customer agree on a price of cost plus 30 percent. What is the gross margin that Nutratask expects to earn on the job?

3. Suppose that the actual costs of producing 300 kilograms of potassium aspartate were as follows:

Direct materials:		
Aspartic acid	$1,170	
Citric acid	30	
K_2CO_3	577	
Rice	13	
Total materials cost		$1,790.00
Direct labor		225.00
Overhead		247.50

What is the actual per-unit cost? The bid price is based on expected costs. How much did Nutratask gain (or lose) because of the actual costs differing from the expected costs? Suggest some possible reasons why the actual costs differed from the projected costs. How can management use this information for dealing with future jobs?

4. Assume that the customer had agreed to pay actual manufacturing costs plus 30 percent. Suppose the actual costs are as described in requirement 3 with one addition: an underapplied overhead variance is allocated to Cost of Goods Sold and spread across all jobs sold in proportion to their total cost (unadjusted cost of goods sold). Assume that the underapplied overhead cost added to the job in (3) is $30. Upon seeing the addition of the underapplied overhead in the itemized bill, the customer calls and complains about having to pay for Nutratask's inefficient use of overhead costs. If you were assigned to deal with this customer, what kind of response would you prepare? How would you explain and justify the addition of the underapplied overhead cost to the customer's bill?

C5-4
Research Assignment
LO 1, LO 2, LO 3

Interview an accountant that works for a service organization that uses job-order costing. For a small firm, you may need to talk to an owner or a manager. Examples are a funeral home, insurance firm, repair shop, medical clinic, and dental clinic. Write a paper that describes the job-order cost system used by the firm. Some of the questions that the paper should address are:

a. What service or services does the firm offer?
b. What document or procedure do you use to collect the costs of the services performed for each customer?
c. How do you assign the cost of direct labor to each job?
d. How do you assign overhead to individual jobs?
e. How do you assign the cost of direct materials to each job?
f. How do you determine what to charge each customer?
g. How do you account for a completed job?

As you write the paper, state how the service firm you investigated adapted the job-order accounting procedures described in the chapter to its particular circumstances. Were the differences justified? If so, explain why. Also, offer any suggestions you might have for improving the approach that you observed.

1. Describe the basic characteristics and cost flows associated with process manufacturing.

2. Define *equivalent units* and explain their role in process costing. Explain the differences between the weighted average method and the FIFO method of accounting for process costs.

3. Prepare a departmental production report using the weighted average method.

4. Explain how process costing is affected by nonuniform application of manufacturing inputs and the existence of multiple processing departments.

5. Prepare a departmental production report using the FIFO method. (Appendix)

CHAPTER

Process Costing

SCENARIO

Makenzie Gibson, owner of Healthblend Nutritional Supplements, was reviewing last year's income statement. Net income was up 33 percent over last year's and Makenzie was pleased. The idea for the company was the result of her recovery from some personal health problems. By working with health-care professionals, she had learned to blend a number of different herbs into therapeutic formulas that had brought about an amazing recovery. Hoping to share her discoveries, Makenzie began producing some of these same therapeutic formulas in the basement of her home. Now, ten years later, she was the owner of a multimillion-dollar business housed in a modern facility with more than sixty employees.

Despite her business success, Makenzie was convinced that she could not afford to be complacent. Recently, the owner of a health food store had told her that some other suppliers had dropped competing lines because they were no longer profitable. He asked Makenzie if all of her products were profitable or if she simply offered the full range as a marketing strategy. She had been forced to admit that she did not know whether all of her products were profitable—in fact, she didn't even know the manufacturing cost of each individual product. All she knew was that overall profits were high.

After some reflection, she decided that knowing individual product costs would be useful for decisions regarding production methods, prices, and the mix of products. So, she contacted Judith Manesfield, manager of a regional CPA firm's small business practice section, for help. After several visits by Judith and her staff, Makenzie received the following preliminary report:

Makenzie Gibson
Healthblend Nutritional Supplements
Tucson, Arizona

Dear Ms. Gibson:

As you know, your current accounting system does not collect the necessary data for costing out the various products that you produce. You currently manufacture three major product lines: mineral, herb, and vitamin. Each product, regardless of the type, passes through three processes: picking, encapsulating, and bottling. In picking, the ingredients are measured, sifted, and blended. In encapsulating, the powdered mix from the first process is put into capsules. The capsules are then transferred to the bottling department where they are bottled, and the bottles are labeled and fitted with safety seals and lids.

Each bottle contains 50 capsules, and the capsules are of equal size for all three product lines. The cost of materials among the three product lines differs, but within a product line, the cost of materials for different products is not significantly different. The layout of the plant is structured so that all three product lines are produced simultaneously; thus, there are three different picking departments, one for each major product line.

Based on the nature of the manufacturing processes, our tentative recommendation is to accumulate costs of manufacturing by process for a given period of time and measure the output for that same period. By dividing the costs accumulated for the period by the output for the period, a good measure of individual product cost can be obtained.

The cost system we recommend will require a minimal increase in your bookkeeping activities. With your permission, we will proceed with the development of the cost system. As part of this development, we will conduct several training seminars so that your financial staff can operate the system once it is implemented.

CHARACTERISTICS OF PROCESS MANUFACTURING

Objective 1

Describe the basic
characteristics and cost
flows associated with
process manufacturing.

Makenzie Gibson hired the consultant to help her decide how best to cost out Health-blend's products. The consultant first studied Healthblend's methods of production. This is vital, since the production process helps determine the best way of accounting for costs. The study showed that a large number of similar products pass through an identical set of processes. Since each product within a product line passing through the three processes would receive similar "doses" of materials, labor, and overhead, Judith Manesfield saw no need to accumulate costs by batches (a job-costing system). Instead, she recommended accumulating costs by process.

Process costing works well whenever relatively homogeneous products pass through a series of processes and receive similar amounts of manufacturing costs. Large manufacturing plants, such as chemical, food, and tire manufacturers, use process costing.

Let's consider the Healthblend example in more detail. From the consultant's letter, we know that there are three processes, each centered in a producing department. In the picking department, direct labor selects the appropriate herbs, vitamins, minerals, and inert materials (typically some binder such as cornstarch) for the product to be manufactured. Then the materials are measured and combined in a mixer to blend them thoroughly. When the mix is complete, the resulting mixture is sent to the encapsulation department. In encapsulation, the vitamin, mineral, or herb blend is loaded into a machine that fills one-half of a gelatin capsule. The filled half is matched to another half of the capsule and a safety seal is applied. This process is entirely mechanized. Overhead in this department consists of depreciation on machinery, maintenance of machinery, supervision, fringe benefits, light, and power. The final department is bottling. Filled capsules are transferred to this department, loaded into a hopper, and automatically counted into bottles. Filled bottles are mechanically capped, and direct labor then manually packs the correct number of bottles into boxes to ship to retail outlets.

Now let's look at Healthblend from an accounting perspective. Suppose that Health-blend has only one picking department through which all three major product lines pass. Since the product lines differ significantly in the cost of their material inputs, accumulating material costs by process no longer makes any sense. More accurate product costing can be achieved by accumulating material costs by batch. In this case, labor and overhead could still be accumulated by process, but raw materials would be assigned to batches using the usual job-cost approach. Note, however, that even with this change, process costing could still be used for the encapsulating department and the bottling department. In these two departments, each product receives the same amount of material, labor, and overhead.

This example illustrates that some manufacturing settings may need to use a blend of job and process costing. Using job-order procedures to assign material costs to prod-

operation costing

ucts and a process approach to assign conversion costs is known as operation costing. Other blends are possible as well. The example also shows that it is possible to use more than one form of costing within the same firm. This is the case if Healthblend uses operation costing for the picking department and process costing for the other two departments.

The fundamental point is that the cost accounting system should be designed to fit the nature of operations. Job-order and process-costing systems fit pure job and pure process production environments. There are many settings, however, in which blends of the two costing systems may be suitable. By studying the pure forms of job-order and process costing, we can develop the ability to understand and use any hybrid form.

Types of Process Manufacturing

In a process firm, units typically pass through a series of manufacturing or producing departments; in each department or process is an operation that brings a product one step closer to completion. In each department, materials, labor, and overhead may be needed. Upon completion of a particular process, the partially completed goods are transferred to the next department. After passing through the final department, the goods are completed and transferred to the warehouse.

sequential processing

Production at Healthblend Nutritional Supplements is an example of sequential processing. In a sequential process, units must pass through one process before they can be worked on in later processes. Exhibit 6-1 shows the sequential pattern of the manufacture of Healthblend's minerals, herbs, and vitamins.

parallel processing

Another processing pattern is parallel processing, in which two or more sequential processes are required to produce a finished good. Partially completed units (for example, two subcomponents) can be worked on simultaneously in different processes and then brought together in a final process for completion. Consider, for example, the manufacture of hard disk drives for personal computers. In one series of processes, write-heads and cartridge disk drives are produced, assembled, and tested. In a second series of processes, printed circuit boards are produced and tested. These two major subcomponents then come together for assembly in the final process. Exhibit 6-2 portrays this type of process pattern. Notice that processes 1 and 2 can occur independently of (or parallel to) processes 3 and 4.

Other forms of parallel processes also exist. However, regardless of which processing pattern exists within a firm, all units produced share a common property. Since units are homogeneous and subjected to the same operations for a given process, each unit produced in a period should receive the same unit cost. Understanding how unit costs are computed requires an understanding of the manufacturing cost flows that take place in a process-costing firm.

How Costs Flow Through the Accounts in Process Costing

The manufacturing cost flows for a process cost system are generally the same as those for a job-order system. As raw materials are purchased, the cost of these materials flows into a Raw Materials inventory account. Similarly, raw materials, direct labor, and applied overhead costs flow into a Work in Process account. When goods are completed, the cost of the completed goods is transferred from Work in Process to the Finished Goods account. Finally, as goods are sold, the cost of the finished goods is transferred to the Cost of Goods Sold account. The journal entries generally parallel those described in a job-order costing system.

6-1

Exhibit
Sequential Processing
Illustrated

Picking → Encapsulating → Bottling → Finished Goods

Exhibit
Parallel Processing
Illustrated

Process 1: Production and assembly of write-head and disk drive
Process 2: Testing of write-head and disk drive
Process 3: Production of circuit board
Process 4: Testing of circuit board

Although job-order and process cost flows are generally similar, some differences exist. In process costing, each producing department has its own Work in Process account. As goods are completed in one department, they are transferred to the next department. Exhibit 6-3 illustrates this process for Healthblend. Notice that a product (let's say multivitamins) starts out in the picking department, where the proper amounts of vitamin, mineral, and inert materials are mixed. Picking direct labor and applied overhead are recognized and added to the picking WIP account. When the mixture is properly blended, it is transferred to the encapsulating department, where capsules are filled. The filled capsules are transferred out to the bottling department. In bottling, the capsules are bottled and the bottles are packaged. The important point is that as the product is transferred from one department to another, so are all of the costs attached to the product. By the end of the process, all manufacturing costs end up in the final department (here, bottling) with the final product.

Let's attach some costs to the various departments and follow them through the accounts. For example, suppose that Healthblend decides to produce 2,000 bottles of multivitamins, with the following costs:

	Picking	Encapsulating	Bottling
Direct materials	$1,700	$1,000	$800
Direct labor	50	60	300
Applied overhead	450	500	600

Exhibit
Flow of Manufacturing
Costs Through the
Accounts of a Process-
Costing Firm

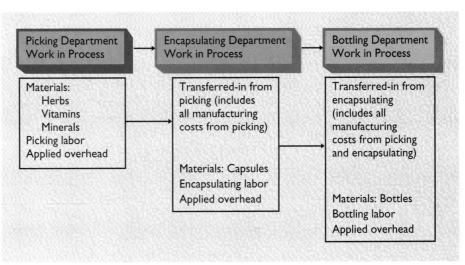

When the multivitamin mixture is transferred to the encapsulating de
picking department, it takes $2,200 of cost along with it ($1,700 + $
$2,200 is *transferred-in cost* to the encapsulating department and is ti
type of direct material cost. (You could think of the encapsulating depɑ
ing" the mixture from the picking department.) Then encapsulating add
from its process and transfers completed capsules plus $3,760 of cosɩ
picking and $1,560 added in encapsulating) to the bottling department. ɪ ɒ...ɪ, bottling
treats the $3,760 of transferred-in cost as a direct materials cost and adds its own cost
of $1,700 ($800 + $300 + $600) to come up with a total cost of $5,460. The completed
bottles of multivitamins are transferred to the finished goods warehouse along with the
$5,460 of manufacturing cost. If there were 2,000 bottles manufactured, each would
have a manufacturing cost of $2.73 ($\frac{\$5,460}{2,000}$).

When the mixture is transferred from picking to encapsulating, the following journal
entry would occur:

Work in Process (Encapsulating)	2,200	
Work in Process (Picking)		2,200

Similarly, the journal entry to record the transferred-in costs from encapsulating to
bottling would be:

Work in Process (Bottling)	3,760	
Work in Process (Encapsulating)		3,760

Finally, when the completed multivitamins leave the bottling department for the finished
goods warehouse, the following entry would be made:

Finished Goods	5,460	
Work in Process (Bottling)		5,460

transferred-in costs

The costs transferred from a prior process to a subsequent process (for example,
from encapsulating to bottling) are referred to as transferred-in costs. These transferred-
in costs are (from the viewpoint of the subsequent process) a type of raw material cost.

Accumulating Costs in the Production Report

production report

In process costing, costs are accumulated by department for a period of time. The
production report is the document that summarizes the manufacturing activity that
takes place in a process department for a given period of time. A production report
contains information on costs transferred-in from prior departments as well as costs
added in the department such as direct materials, direct labor, and overhead; it is subsidiary to the Work in Process account, just as the job-order cost sheet is subsidiary to the
Work in Process account in a job-costing system.

A production report provides information about the physical units processed in a
department and also about the manufacturing costs associated with them. Thus, a production report is divided into a unit information section and a cost information section.
The unit information section has two major subdivisions: (1) units to account for and
(2) units accounted for. Similarly, the cost information section has two major subdivisions: (1) costs to account for and (2) costs accounted for. A production report traces
the flow of units through a department, identifies the costs charged to the department,
shows the computation of unit costs, and reveals the disposition of the department's
costs for the reporting period.

Service and Manufacturing Firms

Any product or service that is basically homogeneous and repetitively produced can take
advantage of a process-costing approach. Let's look at three possibilities: services, manufacturing firms with a JIT orientation, and traditional manufacturing firms.

Check processing in a bank, teeth cleaning by a hygienist, air travel between Dallas
and Los Angeles, sorting mail by zip code, and laundering and pressing shirts are

...ss costing is best
...ed in plants that
manufacture many units
of the same product—
like this bakery. The
manufacturing cost
elements you can identify
include direct materials,
direct labor, and
overhead. It is the
accounting that differs
from job-order costing,
in that the cost of each
individual roll or batch
of rolls need not be
accounted for separately.

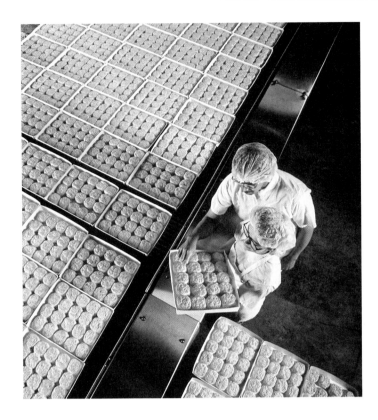

examples of homogeneous services that are repetitively produced. Although services cannot be stored, it is possible for firms engaged in service production to have work-in-process inventories. For example, a batch of tax returns can be partially completed at the end of a period. However, many services are provided so quickly that there are no work-in-process inventories. Tooth cleaning, funerals, surgical operations, sonograms, and carpet cleaning are a few examples where work-in-process inventories would be virtually nonexistent. Therefore, process costing for services is relatively simple. The total costs for the period are divided by the number of services provided to compute unit cost.

Manufacturing firms may also operate without significant work-in-process inventories. Specifically, firms that have adopted a JIT (just in time) approach to manufacturing view the carrying of unnecessary inventories as wasteful. These firms try to reduce work-in-process inventories to very low levels. Furthermore, JIT firms usually structure their manufacturing so that process costing can be used to determine product costs.

In many JIT firms, work cells are created that produce a product or subassembly from start to finish. Costs are collected by cell for a period of time, and output for the cell is measured for the same period. Units costs are computed by dividing the costs of the period by output of the period. There is no ambiguity concerning what costs belong to the period and how output is measured. One of the objectives of JIT manufacturing is simplification. Keep this in mind as you study the process-costing requirements of manufacturing firms that carry work-in-process inventories. The difference between the two settings is impressive and illustrates one of the significant benefits of JIT.

Finally, traditional manufacturing firms may have significant beginning and ending work-in-process inventories. It is the presence of these inventories that leads to much of the complication surrounding process costing. These complications are due to several factors: the presence of beginning and ending work-in-process inventories; different approaches to the treatment of beginning inventory cost; and nonuniform application of manufacturing costs. We will discuss the treatment of these complicating factors in the following sections.

THE IMPACT OF WORK-IN-PROCESS INVENTORIES ON PROCESS COSTING

Objective 2

Define *equivalent units* and explain their role in process costing. Explain the differences between the weighted average method and the FIFO method of accounting for process costs.

The computation of unit cost for the work performed during a period is a key part of the production report. This unit cost is needed both to compute the cost of goods transferred out of a department and to value ending work-in-process inventory.[1] You might think that this is easy—just divide total cost by the number of units produced. However, the presence of work-in-process inventories causes problems. First, defining a unit of production, given that some units produced during a period are complete while those in ending inventory are not, is a problem. This is handled through the concept of equivalent units of production. Second, how should the costs of beginning work in process be treated? Should they be pooled with current period costs or separated and transferred out first? Two methods have been developed to handle this problem: the weighted average method and the FIFO method.

Equivalent Units of Production

By definition, ending work in process is not complete. Thus, a unit completed and transferred out during the period is not identical (or equivalent) to one in ending work-in-process inventory, and the cost attached to the two units should not be the same. In computing the unit cost, the output of the period must be defined. A major problem of process costing is making this definition.

To illustrate the output problem of process costing, assume that department A had the following data for October:

Units, beginning work in process	—
Units completed	1,000
Units, ending work in process (25% complete)	600
Total manufacturing costs	$11,500

What is the output in October for this department? 1,000? 1,600? If we say 1,000 units, we ignore the effort expended on the units in ending work in process. Furthermore, the manufacturing costs incurred in October belong to both the units completed and to the partially completed units in ending work in process. On the other hand, if we say 1,600 units, we ignore the fact that the 600 units in ending work in process are only partially completed. Somehow output must be measured so that it reflects the effort expended on both completed and partially completed units.

equivalent units of output

The solution is to calculate equivalent units of output. Equivalent units of output are the complete units that could have been produced given the total amount of manufacturing effort expended for the period under consideration. Determining equivalent units of output for transferred-out units is easy; a unit would not be transferred out unless it were complete. Thus, every transferred-out unit is an equivalent unit. Units remaining in ending work-in-process inventory, however, are not complete. Thus, someone in production must "eyeball" ending work in process to estimate its degree of completion. In the example, the 600 units in ending work in process are 25 percent complete; this is equivalent to 150 fully completed units (600 × 25%). Therefore, the equivalent units for October would be the 1,000 completed units plus 150 equivalent units in ending work in process, a total of 1,150 units of output. Exhibit 6-4 illustrates the concept of equivalent units of production.

Knowing the output for a period and the manufacturing costs for the department for that period ($11,500 in this example), we can calculate a unit cost, which in this

---

1. While both manufacturing and service firms can use process costing, typically only manufacturing firms encounter the problems connected with the valuation of ending inventories of work in process and finished goods. As a result, much of the material in this chapter concerns process manufacturing.

Exhibit
Equivalent Units of
Production

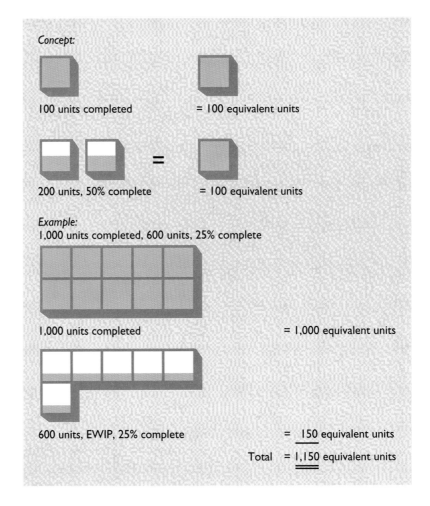

case is \$10 ($\frac{\$11,500}{1,150}$). The unit cost is used to assign a cost of \$10,000 (\$10 × 1,000) to the 1,000 units transferred out and a cost of \$1,500 (\$10 × 150) to the 600 units in ending work in process. This unit cost is \$10 per equivalent unit. Thus, when valuing ending work in process, the \$10 unit cost is multiplied by the equivalent units, not the actual number of partially completed units.

Two Methods of Treating Beginning Work-in-Process Inventory

The presence of beginning work-in-process inventories also complicates the computation of the unit cost. The work done on these partially completed units represents prior-period work, and the costs assigned to them are prior-period costs. In computing a current-period unit cost for a department, two approaches have evolved for dealing with the prior-period output and prior-period costs found in beginning work in process: the weighted average method and the first-in, first-out (FIFO) method. Basically, the weighted average costing method combines beginning inventory costs with current-period costs to compute unit cost. In essence, the costs are pooled and only one average unit cost is computed and applied to both units transferred out and units remaining in ending inventory.

The FIFO costing method, on the other hand, separates units in beginning inventory from those produced during the current period. It is assumed that units from beginning inventory are completed first, and transferred out along with all of the prior-period costs as well as the current-period costs necessary to complete those units. Then current-period production is started and completed (and transferred out with only current costs) or left incomplete as ending work-in-process inventory.

**weighted average
costing method**

**FIFO costing
method**

If product costs do not change from period to period, or if there is no beginning work-in-process inventory, the FIFO and weighted average methods yield the same results. The weighted average method is discussed in more detail in the next section. Further discussion of the FIFO method is found in the Appendix.

WEIGHTED AVERAGE COSTING

Objective 3

Prepare a departmental production report using the weighted average method.

The weighted average costing method treats beginning inventory costs and the accompanying equivalent output as if they belong to the current period. This is done for costs by adding the manufacturing costs in beginning work in process to the manufacturing costs incurred during the current period. The total cost is treated as if it were the current period's total manufacturing cost. Similarly, beginning inventory output and current-period output are merged in the calculation of equivalent units. Under the weighted average method, equivalent units of output are computed by adding units completed to equivalent units in ending work in process. Notice that the equivalent units in beginning work in process are included in the computation. Consequently, these units are counted as part of the current period's equivalent units of output.

Five Steps in Preparing a Production Report (a Subsid. to WIP acct.)

Recall that the production report summarizes cost and manufacturing activity for a producing department for a given period of time. The production report is subsidiary to the work-in-process account for a department. The general pattern is described by the following five steps:

1. Analysis of the flow of physical units   *Remember these are not equivalent units!*
2. Calculation of equivalent units
3. Computation of unit cost
4. Valuation of inventories (goods transferred out and ending work in process)
5. Cost reconciliation

Both the weighted average and FIFO approaches follow the same general pattern for costing out production. In the ensuing discussion, we will follow the five steps previously listed. Doing so gives some structure to the method of accounting for process costs and makes it easier to learn and remember.

Example of the Weighted Average Method

To illustrate the weighted average method, let's use cost and production data for Healthblend's picking department for July (assume that units are measured in gallons):

Production:	
Units in process, July 1 (75% complete)	20,000
Units completed and transferred out	50,000
Units in process, July 31 (25% complete)	10,000
Costs:	
Work in process, July 1 (Begin Costs)	$3,525
Costs added during July	$10,125

Beg. Inv Costs + Current prod costs } / avg. unit cost

Using the data for the picking department, Exhibit 6-5 illustrates the use of the weighted average method to allocate manufacturing costs to units transferred out and to units remaining in ending work in process. Notice that costs from beginning work in process (BWIP) are pooled with costs added to production during July. These total pooled costs ($13,650) are averaged and assigned to units transferred out and to units in ending work in process (EWIP). On the units side, we concentrate on the degree of completion of all units at the end of the period. We do not care about the percentage of completion

6-5 ·······························Weighted Average Method

Exhibit

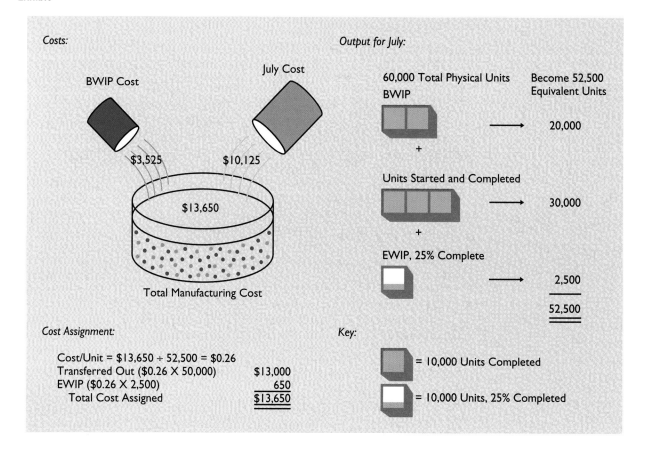

Costs:

BWIP Cost

July Cost

$3,525 $10,125

$13,650

Total Manufacturing Cost

Output for July:

60,000 Total Physical Units   Become 52,500
BWIP   Equivalent Units

                                            20,000
+

Units Started and Completed

                                            30,000
+

EWIP, 25% Complete

                                            2,500
                                   ──────
                                            52,500

Cost Assignment:

Cost/Unit = $13,650 ÷ 52,500 = $0.26
Transferred Out ($0.26 X 50,000) $13,000
EWIP ($0.26 X 2,500)   650
        Total Cost Assigned $13,650

Key:

= 10,000 Units Completed

= 10,000 Units, 25% Completed

of beginning work-in-process inventory. We care only about whether these units are complete or not by the end of July. Thus, equivalent units are computed by pooling manufacturing effort from June and July.

Let's take a closer look at the July production in Healthblend's picking department by focusing on the five steps of the weighted average method.

physical flow schedule

Step 1: Physical Flow Analysis The purpose of step 1 is to trace the physical units of production. Physical units are not equivalent units; they are units that may be in any stage of completion. We can see in Exhibit 6-5 that there are 60,000 physical units.[2] In this example, 20,000 are from beginning inventory. Another 40,000 were started in July. From those 40,000, 10,000 remain in ending inventory, 25 percent complete. The analysis of physical flow of units is usually accomplished by preparing a physical flow schedule like the one shown in Exhibit 6-6. To construct the schedule from the information given in the example, two calculations are needed. First, units started and completed in this period are obtained by subtracting the units in beginning work in process from the total units completed. Next, the units started are obtained by adding the units started and completed to the units in ending work in process. Notice that the "total units to account for" must equal the "total units accounted for." The physical flow schedule in Exhibit 6-6 is important because it contains the information needed to calculate equivalent units (step 2).

2. In Exhibit 6-5, every box represents 10,000 units. The key thing to remember is that a unit may be in any stage of completion. We can see that output for July consists of six boxes: two for BWIP, three for units started and completed, and one for EWIP. Hence, there are 60,000 physical units to account for.

Physical Flow Schedule		
Units to account for:		
Units, beginning work in process (75% complete)		20,000
Units started during the period		40,000
Total units to account for		60,000 ←
Units accounted for:		
Units completed and transferred out:		
Units started and completed	30,000	
Units, beginning work in process	20,000	50,000
Units, ending work in process (25% complete)		10,000
Total units accounted for		60,000 ←

must equal

Step 2: Calculation of Equivalent Units Given the information in the physical flow schedule, the weighted average equivalent units for July can be calculated. This calculation is shown in Exhibit 6-7.

Notice that July's output is measured as 52,500 units, 50,000 units completed and transferred out and 2,500 equivalent units from ending inventory (10,000 × 25%). What about beginning inventory? There were 20,000 units in beginning inventory, 75 percent complete. These units are included in the 50,000 units completed and transferred out during the month. Thus, beginning inventory units are treated as if they were started and completed during the current period.

Step 3: Computation of Unit Cost In addition to July output, July manufacturing costs are needed to compute a unit cost. The weighted average method rolls back and includes the manufacturing costs associated with the units in beginning work in process. Thus, the total manufacturing cost for July is defined as $13,650 ($3,525 + $10,125). The manufacturing costs carried over from the prior period ($3,525) are treated as if they were current-period costs.

Given the manufacturing costs for July and the output for the month, the unit cost can be calculated and used to determine the cost of goods transferred out and the cost of ending work in process. For July, the weighted average method gives the following unit cost:

$$\text{Unit cost} = \frac{\$13,625}{52,500} = \$0.26 \text{ per equivalent unit}$$

Step 4: Valuation of Inventories Using the unit cost of $0.26, the cost of goods transferred to the encapsulating department is $13,000 (50,000 units × $0.26 per unit), and the cost of ending work in process is $650 (2,500 equivalent units × $0.26 per unit). Notice that units completed (from step 1), equivalent units in ending work in process (from step 2), and the unit cost (from step 3) were all needed to value both goods transferred out and ending work in process.

Step 2

includes begin. Inv.

Equivalent Units of Production: Weighted Average Method	
Units completed	50,000
Add: Units, ending work in process × fraction completed	
(10,000 units × 25%)	2,500
Equivalent units of output	52,500

Step 5: Cost Reconciliation The total manufacturing costs assigned to inventories are as follows:

Goods transferred out	$13,000
Goods, ending work in process	650
Total costs accounted for	$13,650

The manufacturing costs to account for are also $13,650.

Beginning work in process	$ 3,525
Incurred during the period	10,125
Total costs to account for	$13,650

cost reconciliation

Thus, the costs to account for are exactly assigned to inventories, and we have the necessary cost reconciliation. Remember, the total costs assigned to goods transferred out and to ending work in process must agree with the total costs in beginning work in process and the manufacturing costs incurred during the current period.

Production Report Steps 1 through 5 provide all of the information needed to prepare a production report for the picking department for July. This report is given in Exhibit 6-8.

Evaluation of the Weighted Average Method

The major benefit of the weighted average method is simplicity. By treating units in beginning work in process as belonging to the current period, all equivalent units belong to the same category when it comes to calculating unit costs. Thus, unit cost computations are simplified. The main disadvantage of this method is reduced accuracy in computing unit costs for current-period output and for units in beginning work in process. If the unit cost in a process is relatively stable from one period to the next, the weighted average method is reasonably accurate. However, if the price of manufacturing inputs increases significantly from one period to the next, the unit cost of current output is understated, and the unit cost of beginning work-in-process units is overstated. If greater accuracy in computing unit costs is desired, a company should use the FIFO method to determine unit costs.

MULTIPLE INPUTS AND MULTIPLE DEPARTMENTS

Objective 4

Explain how process costing is affected by nonuniform application of manufacturing inputs and the existence of multiple processing departments.

Accounting for production under process costing is complicated by nonuniform application of manufacturing inputs and the presence of multiple processing departments. How process-costing methods address these complications will now be discussed.

Nonuniform Application of Manufacturing Inputs

Up to this point, we have assumed that work in process being 60 percent complete meant that 60 percent of materials, labor, and overhead needed to complete the process have been used and that another 40 percent are needed to finish the units. In other words, we have assumed that manufacturing inputs are applied uniformly as the manufacturing process unfolds.

Assuming uniform application of conversion costs (direct labor and overhead) is not unreasonable. Direct labor input is usually needed throughout the process, and overhead is normally assigned on the basis of direct labor hours. Direct materials, on the

6-8

Exhibit

step 1+2

Healthblend Company Picking Department Production Report for July 1998 (Weighted Average Method) **Unit Information**		

Physical Flow

Units to account for:		Units accounted for:	
Units, beginning work in			
process	20,000	Units completed	50,000
Units started	40,000	Units, ending work in process	10,000
Total units to account for	60,000	Total units accounted for	60,000

Equivalent Units

Units completed	50,000
Units, ending work in process	2,500
Total equivalent units	52,500

Cost Information

step 3

Costs to account for:

Beginning work in process	$ 3,525
Incurred during the period	10,125
Total costs to account for	$13,650

Cost per equivalent unit	$ 0.26

step 4

	Transferred Out	Ending Work in Process	Total
Costs accounted for:			
Goods transferred out ($0.26 × 50,000)	$13,000	—	$13,000
Goods, ending work in process			
($0.26 × 2,500)	—	$650	650
Total costs accounted for	$13,000	$650	$13,650

other hand, are not as likely to be applied uniformly. In many instances, materials are added at either the beginning or the end of the process.

For example, look at the differences in Healthblend's three departments. In the picking and encapsulating departments, all materials are added at the beginning of the process. However, in the bottling department, materials are added both at the beginning (filled capsules and bottles) and at the end (bottle caps and boxes).

Work in process in the picking department that is 50 percent complete with respect to conversion inputs would be 100 percent complete with respect to the material inputs. But work in process in bottling that is 50 percent complete with respect to conversion would be 100 percent complete with respect to bottles and transferred-in capsules, but 0 percent complete with respect to bottle caps and boxes.

Different percentage completion figures for manufacturing inputs pose a problem for the calculation of equivalent units. Fortunately, the solution is relatively simple. Equivalent-unit calculations are done for each category of manufacturing input. Thus, there are equivalent units calculated for each category of materials and for conversion cost. The conversion cost category can be broken down into direct labor and overhead, if desired. If direct labor and overhead are applied uniformly, however, this serves no useful purpose.

To illustrate, assume the picking department of Healthblend has the following data for September:

Production:		
Units in process, September 1 (50% complete)*		10,000
Units completed and transferred out		60,000
Units in process, September 30 (40% complete)*		20,000
Costs:		
Work in process, September 1:		
Materials		$1,600
Conversion costs		200
Total		$1,800
Current costs:		
Materials		$12,000
Conversion costs		3,200
Total		$15,200

*With respect to conversion costs

Assuming that Healthblend uses the weighted average method for process costing, the effect of nonuniform application of manufacturing inputs is easily illustrated. Exhibit 6-9 illustrates step 1, creating the physical flow schedule. Accounting for the flow of physical units is not affected by the nonuniform application of manufacturing inputs because physical units may be in any stage of completion.

Nonuniform application of inputs, however, does affect the computation of equivalent units (step 2). Exhibit 6-10 illustrates this computation. Notice that two categories of input are used to calculate equivalent units. Since all materials are added at the beginning of the process, all units are 100 percent complete with respect to materials. Thus, there are 20,000 equivalent units of materials in ending work in process. However, since only 40 percent of the conversion costs have been applied, there are only 8,000 conversion equivalent units in ending work in process.

When different categories of equivalent units exist, a unit cost for each category must be computed. The cost per completed unit (step 3) is the sum of these individual unit costs. The computations for the example are as follows:

$$\text{Unit materials cost} = \frac{(\$1,600 + \$12,000)}{80,000}$$
$$= \$0.17$$

Exhibit

Physical Flow Schedule: Nonuniform Inputs		
Units to account for:		
Units, beginning work in process		10,000
Units started during September		70,000
Total units to account for		80,000
Units accounted for:		
Units completed and transferred out:		
Units started and completed	50,000	
Units, beginning work in process	10,000	60,000
Units, ending work in process (40% complete)		20,000
Total units accounted for		80,000

6-10

Exhibit

Calculation of Equivalent Units: Nonuniform Application	Materials	Conversion
Units completed	60,000	60,000
Add: Units, ending work in process × percentage complete:		
(20,000 × 100%)	20,000	—
(20,000 × 40%)	—	8,000
Equivalent units of output	80,000	68,000

$$\text{Unit conversion cost} = \frac{(\$200 + \$3,200)}{68,000}$$
$$= \$0.05$$

$$\text{Total unit cost} = \text{Unit materials cost} + \text{Unit conversion cost}$$
$$= \$0.17 + \$0.05$$
$$= \$0.22 \text{ per completed unit}$$

Valuation of goods transferred out (step 4) is accomplished by multiplying the unit cost by the number of units completed:

$$\text{Cost of goods transferred out} = \$0.22 \times 60,000$$
$$= \$13,200$$

Costing out ending work in process is done by obtaining the cost of each manufacturing input and then summing these individual input costs. For the example, this requires adding the cost of the materials in ending work in process to the conversion costs in ending work in process.

The cost of materials is the unit material cost multiplied by the material equivalent units in ending work in process. Similarly, the conversion cost in ending work in process is the unit conversion cost times the conversion equivalent units. Thus, the cost of ending work in process is as follows:

Materials: $0.17 × 20,000	$3,400
Conversion: $0.05 × 8,000	400
Total cost	$3,800

Step 5 reconciles the costs to ensure that the computations are correct.

Costs to account for:	
Beginning work in process	$ 1,800
Incurred during the period	15,200
Total costs to account for	$17,000
Costs accounted for:	
Goods transferred out	$13,200
Goods, ending work in process	3,800
Total costs accounted for	$17,000

Using the information generated from the five steps, a production report can be prepared (see Exhibit 6-11). As the example has shown, applying manufacturing inputs at different stages of a process poses no serious problems. However, the effort required to compute the costs has increased.

Exhibit

Healthblend Company			
Picking Department			
Production Report for September 1998			
(Weighted Average Method)			
Unit Information			

Units to account for:		Units accounted for:	
Units, beginning work in process	10,000	Units completed	60,000
Units started	70,000	Units, ending-work-in-process	20,000
Total units to account for	80,000	Total units accounted for	80,000

Equivalent Units

	Materials	Conversion Cost
Units completed	60,000	60,000
Units, ending work in process	20,000	8,000
Total equivalent units	80,000	68,000

Cost Information

	Materials	Conversion Cost	Total
Costs to account for:			
Beginning work in process	$ 1,600	$ 200	$ 1,800
Incurred during the period	12,000	3,200	15,200
Total costs to account for	$13,600	$3,400	$17,000
Cost per equivalent unit	$0.17	$0.05	$0.22

	Transferred Out	Ending Work in Process	Total
Costs accounted for:			
Goods transferred out			
($0.22 × 60,000)	$13,200	—	$13,200
Goods, ending work in process:			
Materials ($0.17 × 20,000)	—	$3,400	3,400
Conversion ($0.05 × 8,000)	—	400	400
Total costs accounted for	$13,200	$3,800	$17,000

Multiple Departments

In process manufacturing, some departments receive partially completed goods from prior departments. The usual approach is to treat transferred-in goods as a separate material category when calculating equivalent units.

In dealing with transferred-in goods, two important points should be remembered. First, the cost of this material is the cost of the goods transferred out as computed in the prior department. Second, the units started in the subsequent department correspond to the units transferred out from the prior department (assuming that there is a one-to-one relationship between the output measures of both departments).

For example, let's consider the month of September for Healthblend and restrict our attention to the transferred-in category. Assume that the encapsulating department had 15,000 units in beginning inventory (with transferred-in costs of $3,000) and completed 70,000 units during the month. Further, the picking department completed and transferred out 60,000 units at a cost of $13,200 in September. In constructing a physical flow schedule for the encapsulating department, its dependence on the picking department must be considered:

Units to account for:	
Units, beginning work in process	15,000
Units transferred in during September	60,000
Total units to account for	75,000
Units accounted for:	
Units completed and transferred out:	
Units started and completed	55,000
Units, beginning work in process	15,000
Units, ending work in process	5,000
Total units accounted for	75,000

Equivalent units for the transferred-in category are calculated as follows (ignoring other input categories):

Transferred in:	
Units completed	70,000
Add: Units, ending work in process × fraction completed (5,000 × 100%)*	5,000
Equivalent units of output	75,000

*Remember that the EWIP is 100% complete with respect to transferred-in costs, not to all costs of the encapsulating department.

To compute the unit cost, we add the cost of the units transferred in from picking in September to the transferred-in costs in beginning work in process and divide by transferred-in equivalent units:

$$\text{Unit cost (transferred-in category)} = \frac{(\$13,200 + \$3,000)}{75,000}$$
$$= \frac{\$16,200}{75,000}$$
$$= \$0.216$$

The only additional complication introduced in the analysis for a subsequent department is the presence of the transferred-in category. As has just been shown, dealing with this category is similar to handling any other category. However, it must be remembered that the current cost of this special type of raw material is the cost of the units transferred in from the prior process and that the units transferred in are the units started.

APPENDIX: PRODUCTION REPORT—FIFO COSTING

Objective 5

Prepare a departmental production report using the FIFO method.

Under the FIFO costing method, the equivalent units and manufacturing costs in beginning work in process are excluded from the current-period unit cost calculation. This method recognizes that the work and costs carried over from the prior period legitimately belong to that period.

If changes occur in the prices of the manufacturing inputs from one period to the next, then FIFO produces a more accurate (that is, more current) unit cost than does the weighted average method. A more accurate unit cost means better cost control, better pricing decisions, and so on. Keep in mind that if the period is as short as a week or a month, however, the unit costs calculated under the two methods are not likely to differ much. In that case, the FIFO method has little, if anything, to offer over the weighted average method. Perhaps for this reason, many firms use the weighted average method.

Since FIFO excludes prior-period work and costs, we need to create two categories of completed units. FIFO assumes that units in beginning work in process are completed first, before any new units are started. Thus, one category of completed units is beginning work-in-process units. The second category is for those units started and completed during the current period.

For example, assume that a department had 20,000 units in beginning work in process and completed and transferred out a total of 50,000 units. Of the 50,000 completed units, 20,000 are the units initially found in work in process. The remaining 30,000 were started and completed during the current period.

These two categories of completed units are needed in the FIFO method so that each category can be costed correctly. For the units started and completed, the unit cost is obtained by dividing total current manufacturing costs by the current-period equivalent output. However, for the beginning work-in-process units, the total associated manufacturing costs are the sum of the prior-period costs plus the costs incurred in the current period to finish the units. As can be seen in Exhibit 6-12, costs from the current period and from beginning inventory are not pooled. Instead, current-period cost is added to beginning inventory cost in order to complete the units on hand at the start of the period.

The computations in Exhibit 6-12 are based on the same Healthblend data used for the weighted average method when we assumed uniform use of manufacturing inputs (see Exhibit 6-5). Using the same data highlights the differences between the two methods. The five steps to cost-out production follow.

Production:	
Units in process, July 1 (75% complete)	20,000
Units completed and transferred out	50,000
Units in process, July 31 (25% complete)	10,000
Costs:	
Work in process, July 1	$3,525
Costs added during July	$10,125

Step 1: Physical Flow Analysis The purpose of step 1 is to trace the physical units of production. As with the weighted average method, in the FIFO method, a physical flow schedule is prepared. This schedule, shown in Exhibit 6-13, is identical for both methods.

Step 2: Calculation of Equivalent Units Exhibit 6-14 (page 220) illustrates the calculation of equivalent units under the FIFO method. From the equivalent-unit computation in Exhibit 6-14, one difference between weighted average and FIFO becomes immediately apparent. Under FIFO, the equivalent units in beginning work in process, work done in the prior period, are not counted as part of the total equivalent work. Only the equivalent work *to be completed* this period is counted. The equivalent work to be completed for the units from the prior period is computed by multiplying the number of units in beginning work in process by the percentage of work remaining. Since in this example the percentage of work done in the prior period is 75 percent, the percentage left to be completed this period is 25 percent, or an equivalent of 5,000 additional units of work.

Costs:

BWIP Cost

Costs to
Complete BWIP

July Cost

$3,525 $10,125

BWIP Units   Current-Period
                            Units

Output for July:

60,000 Total Physical Units   Become 37,500
BWIP   Equivalent Units

→ 5,000

+

Units Started and Completed

→ 30,000

+

EWIP

→ 2,500

37,500

Cost Assignment:

Unit Cost = $10,125 ÷ 37,500 = $0.27
Transferred Out:
   From BWIP $ 3,525
   Complete BWIP ($0.27 X 5,000)   1,350
   Start & Complete in July
   ($0.27 X 30,000)   8,100
      Total Cost Assigned $12,975

Key:

= 10,000 Units, 100% Completed in July

= 10,000 Units, 25% Completed in July

The effect of excluding prior-period effort is to produce the current-period equivalent output. Recall that under the weighted average method, 52,500 equivalent units were computed for this month. Under FIFO, only 37,500 units are calculated for the same month. These 37,500 units represent current-period output. The difference, of course, is explained by the fact that the weighted average method rolls back and counts the 15,000 equivalent units of prior-period work (20,000 units BWIP × 75%) as belonging to this period.

Physical Flow Schedule		
Units to account for:		
Units, beginning work in process (75% complete)		20,000
Units started during the period		40,000
Total units to account for		60,000
Units accounted for:		
Units completed:		
Units started and completed	30,000	
Units, beginning work in process	20,000	50,000
Units, ending work in process (25% complete)		10,000
Total units accounted for		60,000

Equivalent Units of Production: FIFO Method	
Units started and completed	30,000
Add: Units, beginning work in process × fraction to be completed (20,000 × 25%)	5,000
Add: Units, ending work in process × fraction completed (10,000 × 25%)	2,500
Equivalent units of output	37,500

Step 3: Computation of Unit Cost The additional manufacturing costs incurred in the current period are $10,125. Thus, the current-period unit manufacturing cost is $\frac{\$10,125}{37,500}$, or $0.27. Notice that the costs of beginning inventory are excluded from this calculation. Only current-period manufacturing costs are used.

Step 4: Valuation of Inventories Since all equivalent units in ending work in process are current-period units, the cost of ending work in process is simply $0.27 × 2,500, or $675. However, when it comes to valuing goods transferred out, another difference emerges between the weighted average method and FIFO.

Under weighted average, the cost of goods transferred out is simply the unit cost times the units completed. Under FIFO, however, there are two sources of completed units: 20,000 units from beginning inventory and 30,000 units started and completed. The cost of the 30,000 units that were started and completed in the current period and transferred out is $8,100 ($0.27 × 30,000). For these units, the use of the current-period unit cost is entirely appropriate.

However, the cost of the beginning work-in-process units that were transferred out is another matter. These units started the period with $3,525 of manufacturing costs already incurred and 15,000 units of equivalent output already completed. To finish these units, the equivalent of 5,000 units were needed. The cost of finishing the units in beginning work in process is $1,350 ($0.27 × 5,000). Adding this $1,350 to the $3,525 in cost carried over from the prior period gives a total manufacturing cost for these units of $4,875. The unit cost of these 20,000 units, then, is about $0.244 ($\frac{\$4,875}{20,000}$).

Step 5: Cost Reconciliation With the completion of step 5, the production report can be prepared. This report is shown in Exhibit 6-15. The total costs assigned to production are as follows:

Goods transferred out:	
Units, beginning work in process	$ 4,875
Units started and completed	8,100
Goods, ending work in process	675
Total costs accounted for	$13,650

The total manufacturing costs to account for during the period are:

Beginning work in process	$ 3,525
Incurred during the period	10,125
Total costs to account for	$13,650

Often the total costs accounted for do not precisely equal the costs to account for due to rounding error. An easy way to bring the amounts into balance is to adjust the cost of goods transferred out by the amount of the rounding error.

Exhibit 6-15

Healthblend Company Picking Department Production Report for July 1998 (FIFO Method) Unit Information		
Units to account for:		
Units, beginning work in process	20,000	
Units started during the period	40,000	
Total units to account for	60,000	

	Physical Flow	Equivalent Units
Units accounted for:		
Units started and completed	30,000	30,000
Units completed from beginning work in process	20,000	5,000
Units, ending work in process	10,000	2,500
Total units accounted for	60,000	37,500

Cost Information		
Costs to account for:		
Beginning work in process	$ 3,525	
Incurred during the period	10,125	
Total costs to account for	$13,650	
Cost per equivalent unit	$0.27	

	Transferred Out	Ending Work in Process	Total
Costs accounted for:			
Units, beginning work in process:			
From prior period	$ 3,525	—	$ 3,525
From current period ($0.27 × 5,000)	1,350	—	1,350
Units started and completed ($0.27 × 30,000)	8,100	—	8,100
Goods, ending work in process ($0.27 × 2,500)	—	$675	675
Total costs accounted for	$12,975	$675	$13,650

S UMMARY OF LEARNING OBJECTIVES

1. Describe the basic characteristics and cost flows associated with process manufacturing.

Cost flows under process costing are similar to those under job-order costing. Raw materials are purchased and debited to the Materials account. Direct materials used in production, direct labor, and overhead applied are charged to the Work in Process account. In a production process with several processes, there is a Work in Process account for each department or process. Goods completed in one department are transferred out to the next department. When units are completed in the final department

or process, their cost is credited to Work in Process and debited to Finished Goods.

2. Define *equivalent units* and explain their role in process costing. Explain the difference between the weighted method and the FIFO method of accounting for process costs.

Equivalent units of production are the complete units that could have been produced given the total amount of manufacturing effort expended during the period. The number of physical units is multiplied by the percentage of completion to calculate equivalent units. Two approaches have evolved for dealing with beginning work-in-process inventory costs. The weighted average costing method combines beginning inventory costs with current period costs to compute unit costs. The FIFO costing method separates units in beginning inventory from those produced during the current period.

3. Prepare a departmental production report using the weighted average method.

The production report summarizes the manufacturing activity occurring in a department for a given period. It discloses information concerning the physical flow of units, equivalent units, unit costs, and the disposition of the manufacturing costs associated with the period.

4. Explain how process costing is affected by nonuniform application of manufacturing inputs and the existence of multiple processing departments.

Nonuniform application of productive inputs requires the determination of separate percentage of completion figures for each input. This, in turn, requires the computation of separate equivalent units and unit costs. When a company has more than one processing department, the output of one department becomes the raw material of a succeeding department. The usual method is to handle the transferred-in units and costs as another form of material.

5. Prepare a departmental production report using the FIFO method. (Appendix)

A production report prepared according to the FIFO method separates the cost of beginning work in process from the cost of the current period. BWIP is assumed to be completed and transferred out first. Cost from BWIP is not pooled with current-period cost in computing unit cost. Additionally, equivalent units of production exclude work done in the prior period.

K EY TERMS

R EVIEW PROBLEM

Payson Company, which uses the weighted average method, produces a product that passes through two departments: mixing and cooking. In the mixing department, all materials are added at the beginning of the process. All other manufacturing inputs are added uniformly. The following information pertains to the mixing department for February:

a. Beginning work in process (BWIP), February 1: 100,000 pounds, 40 percent complete with respect to conversion costs. The costs assigned to this work are as follows:

Materials	$20,000
Labor	10,000
Overhead	30,000

b. Ending work in process (EWIP), February 28: 50,000 pounds, 60 percent complete with respect to conversion costs.

c. Units completed and transferred out: 370,000 pounds. The following costs were added during the month:

Materials	$211,000
Labor	100,000
Overhead	270,000

REQUIRED:
1. Prepare a physical flow schedule.
2. Prepare a schedule of equivalent units.
3. Compute the cost per equivalent unit.
4. Compute the cost of goods transferred out and the cost of ending work in process.
5. Prepare a cost reconciliation.

Solution

1. Physical flow schedule:

finished – EWIP

Units to account for:		Units accounted for:	
Units, BWIP	100,000	Units completed and transferred out	370,000*
Units started	320,000	Units, EWIP	50,000
Total	420,000	Total	420,000

*270,000 units started and completed plus 100,000 units from BWIP

2. Schedule of equivalent units:

	Materials	Conversion
Units completed	370,000	370,000
Units, EWIP × fraction completed:		
Materials (50,000 × 100%)	50,000	—
Conversion (50,000 × 60%)	—	30,000
Equivalent units of output	420,000	400,000

3. Cost per equivalent unit:

$$\text{Direct materials unit cost} = \frac{(\$20,000 + \$211,000)}{420,000} = \$0.55$$

$$\text{Conversion unit cost} = \frac{(\$40,000 + \$370,000)}{400,000} = \$1.025$$

$$\text{Total unit cost} = \$1.575 \text{ per equivalent unit}$$

4. Cost of goods transferred out and cost of ending work in process:

$$\text{Cost of goods transferred out} = \$1.575 \times 370,000$$
$$= \$582,750$$

$$\text{Cost of EWIP} = (\$0.55 \times 50,000) + (\$1.025 \times 30,000)$$
$$= \$58,250$$

5. Cost reconciliation:

Costs to account for:		Costs accounted for:	
BWIP	$ 60,000	Goods transferred out	$582,750
Costs added	581,000	EWIP	58,250
Total to account for	$641,000	Total costs accounted for	$641,000

QUESTIONS FOR WRITING AND DISCUSSION

1. Distinguish between sequential processing and parallel processing.
2. Describe the differences between process costing and job-order costing.
3. What are equivalent units? Why are they needed in a process cost system?
4. Under the weighted average method, how are prior-period costs and output treated? How are they treated under the FIFO method?
5. Under what conditions will the weighted average and FIFO methods give essentially the same results?
6. How is the equivalent-unit calculation affected when materials are added at the beginning or end of the process rather than uniformly throughout the process?
7. Explain why transferred-in costs are a special type of raw material for the receiving department.
8. What are the similarities in and differences between the manufacturing cost flows for job-order firms and process firms?
9. What journal entry would be made as goods are transferred out from one department to another department? from the final department to the warehouse?

10. Describe the five steps in accounting for the manufacturing activity of a processing department and explain how they interrelate.
11. What is a production report? What purpose does this report serve?
12. In assigning costs to goods transferred out, how do the weighted average and FIFO methods differ?
13. Describe the effect of automation on the process accounting system.
14. How does the adoption of a JIT (just in time) approach to manufacturing affect process costing?
15. How would process costing for services differ from process costing for manufactured goods?

Ⓦ ARM-UP EXERCISES

This section provides short warm-up exercises based on the examples in the chapter. Each warm-up exercise gives the page number on which the text example can be found. You may want to refer to the text example to see how the exercise can be set up and solved.

W6-1
Basic Cost Flows
LO 1
p. 205

Jumpin Jeans produces a variety of styles of jeans in three departments: cutting, sewing, and packaging. During the month the three departments recorded the following costs:

	Cutting	Sewing	Packaging
Direct materials	$1,800	$ 300	$ 75
Direct labor	50	600	300
Applied overhead	250	1,200	300

Three hundred pairs of jeans were completed during the month.

REQUIRED:
1. Prepare a schedule showing, for each department, the cost of direct materials, direct labor, applied overhead, product transferred in from a prior department, and total manufacturing.
2. Prepare the journal entries to transfer costs from the (a) cutting to sewing departments, (b) sewing to packaging departments, (c) packaging department to finished goods.
3. What is the total unit cost of a pair of jeans?

W6-2
Equivalent Units
LO 2
p. 207

Department B had the following data for November:

Units, beginning work in process	—
Units completed	500
Units, ending work in process (30% complete)	300
Total manufacturing cost	$1,652

REQUIRED:
1. Calculate equivalent units of production in ending work-in-process inventory. Calculate total equivalent units of production for department B for November.
2. What is the unit manufacturing cost for department B for November?
3. What is the cost of goods transferred out? What is the cost of ending work-in-process inventory?

W6-3
Steps in Preparing Cost of Production Report
LO 3
pp. 210–212

Palomino Paints, Inc. manufactures a variety of inside and outside paints in three departments: grinding, mixing, and canning. The following are cost and production data for the grinding department for March (assume that units are measured in pounds):

Production:	
Units in process, March 1 (60% complete)	40,000
Units completed and transferred out	100,000
Units in process, March 31 (20% complete)	20,000

Costs:

Work in process, March 1	$187,200
Costs added during March	629,200

REQUIRED:

1. Prepare a physical flow analysis for the grinding department for March.
2. Calculate equivalent units of production for the grinding department for March.
3. Calculate unit cost for the grinding department for March.
4. Calculate the cost of units transferred out and the cost of ending work-in-process inventory.
5. Prepare a cost reconciliation for the grinding department for March.

W6-4

Cost of Production Report

LO 3

p. 213

Refer to W6-3. Prepare a cost of production report for the grinding department for the month of March.

W6-5

Nonuniform Inputs

LO 4

pp. 214–215

Terry Linens, Inc. manufactures bed and bath linens. The bath linens department sews terry cloth into towels of various sizes. All materials are added at the beginning of the process. The following data are for the bath linens department for June:

Production:	
Units in process, June 1 (25% complete)*	10,000
Units completed and transferred out	60,000
Units in process, June 30 (60% complete)*	20,000
Costs:	
Work in process, June 1:	
Materials	$49,000
Conversion costs	2,625
Total	$51,625
Current costs:	
Materials	$351,000
Conversion costs	78,735
Total	$429,735

*With respect to conversion costs

REQUIRED:

1. Prepare a physical flow analysis for the bath linens department for June.
2. Calculate equivalent units of production for the bath linens department for June.
3. Calculate unit cost for materials, for conversion, and in total for the bath linens department for June.
4. Calculate the cost of units transferred out and the cost of ending work-in-process inventory.
5. Prepare a cost reconciliation for the bath linens department for June.

W6-6

Cost of Production Report; Nonuniform Inputs

LO 3, LO 4

p. 216

Refer to W6-5. Prepare a cost of production report for the bath linens department for June.

W6-7

Nonuniform Inputs; Transferred-in Cost

LO 4

p. 217

Drysdale Dairy produces a variety of dairy products. In department 12, cream (transferred in from department 6) and other materials (sugar and flavorings) are mixed and churned to make ice cream. The following data are for department 12 for August:

Production:

Units in process, August 1 (25% complete)*	40,000
Units completed and transferred out	120,000
Units in process, August 31 (60% complete)*	30,000

Costs:

Work in process, August 1:	
Transferred in from department 6	$2,100
Materials	1,500
Conversion costs	3,000
Total	$6,600
Current costs:	
Transferred in from department 6	$30,900
Materials	22,500
Conversion costs	45,300
Total	$98,700

*With respect to conversion costs

REQUIRED:

1. How many units were transferred in during the month?
2. Calculate equivalent units for the following categories: transferred-in, materials, and conversion.
3. Calculate unit costs for the following categories: transferred-in, materials, and conversion. Calculate total unit cost.

W6-8

Appendix Required: FIFO Equivalent Units; Unit Cost

LO 5

pp. 218–220

Halligan Company manufactures a product in four departments. Data for the first department follow:

Production:

Units in process, July 1 (75% complete)	60,000
Units completed and transferred out	150,000
Units in process, July 31 (25% complete)	30,000

Costs:

Work in process, July 1	$193,500
Costs added during the month	500,625

Halligan uses FIFO costing.

REQUIRED:

1. Prepare a physical flow analysis for the first department for July.
2. Calculate equivalent units of production for department 1 for July.
3. Calculate unit cost for materials, for conversion, and in total for the first department for July.
4. Calculate the cost of units transferred out and the cost of ending work-in-process inventory.
5. Prepare a cost reconciliation for the first department for July.

W6-9

Appendix Required: FIFO Cost of Production Report

LO 5

p. 221

Refer to W6-8. Prepare a cost of production report for department 1 of Halligan Company for the month of July.

EXERCISES

E6-1

Physical Flow; Equivalent Units;

Jadlow Company manufactures a product that passes through two processes. The following information was obtained for the first department for May:

Weighted Average Method

LO 1, LO 2, LO 3

a. All materials are added at the beginning of the process.
b. Beginning work in process had 9,000 units, 30 percent complete with respect to conversion costs.
c. Ending work in process had 4,400 units, 20 percent complete with respect to conversion costs.
d. Jadlow started in process 10,000 units.

REQUIRED:
1. Prepare a physical flow schedule.
2. Compute equivalent units.

E6-2
Weighted Average Method; Valuation of Goods Transferred Out and Ending Work in Process

LO 3

Happy Toddler, Inc. manufactures products that pass through two or more processes. Happy Toddler uses the weighted average method to compute unit costs. During April, equivalent units were computed as follows:

	Materials	Conversion Cost
Units completed	5,000	5,000
Units, ending work in process × fraction completed:		
(3,000 × 0%)	—	—
(3,000 × 70%)	—	2,100
Equivalent units of output	5,000	7,100

The unit cost was computed as follows:

Materials	$0.50
Conversion cost	0.25
Total	$0.75

REQUIRED:
1. Determine the cost of ending work in process and the cost of the goods transferred out.
2. If possible, prepare a physical flow schedule.

E6-3
Appendix Required: FIFO Method; Valuation of Goods Transferred Out and Ending Work in Process

LO 5

Bijan Company uses FIFO to account for the costs of production. For the first processing department, the following equivalent-unit schedule has been prepared:

	Materials	Conversion Cost
Units started and completed	45,000	45,000
Units, beginning work in process × fraction to be completed:		
(8,000 × 0%)	—	—
(8,000 × 40%)	—	3,200
Units, ending work in process × fraction completed:		
(16,000 × 100%)	16,000	—
(16,000 × 75%)	—	12,000
Equivalent units of output	61,000	60,200

The cost per equivalent unit for the period was as follows:

Materials	$1.00
Conversion cost	2.50
Total	$3.50

The cost of beginning work in process was materials, $10,000; conversion costs, $18,000.

REQUIRED:
1. Determine the cost of ending work in process and the cost of goods transferred out.
2. If possible, prepare a physical flow schedule.

E6-4
Weighted Average Method; Valuation of Goods Transferred Out and Ending Work in Process
LO 3

Refer to the data in E6-3.

REQUIRED: Compute the cost of ending work in process and the cost of goods transferred out using the weighted average method.

E6-5
Production Report; No Beginning Inventory
LO 3

Banray, Inc. produces nonprescription sunglasses. The sunglasses are produced in two departments. The data for department 1 are as follows:

Work in process, 1/1/98	—
Units started	86,000
Units transferred out	67,000
Raw materials cost	$16,340
Direct labor cost	$16,820
Overhead applied	$37,845

Materials are added at the beginning of the process. Ending inventory is 90 percent complete with respect to labor and overhead.

REQUIRED: Prepare a production report for department 1 for 1998.

E6-6
Physical Flow; Equivalent Units; Unit Costs; Cost Assignment
LO 2, LO 3

Selwick Company manufactures powdered laundry detergent. Department 1 mixes the chemicals required for the detergent. The following data are for 1998:

Beginning work in process	—
Units started	92,500
Raw materials cost	$92,500
Direct labor cost	$9,150
Overhead applied	$13,725
Units, ending work in process	
(100% materials; 80% conversion)	5,000

REQUIRED:
1. Prepare a physical flow schedule.
2. Calculate equivalent units of production for:
   a. Raw materials
   b. Conversion
3. Calculate unit costs for:
   a. Raw materials
   b. Conversion
   c. Total manufacturing
4. What is the total cost of units transferred out? What is the cost assigned to units in ending inventory?

E6-7
Equivalent Units—Weighted Average Method
LO 2, LO 3

The following are data for four independent process-costing departments.

	A	B	C	D
Beginning inventory	3,200	1,000	—	30,000
Percent completed	30%	40%	—	75%
Units started	17,000	23,000	40,000	40,000
Ending inventory	4,000	—	9,000	10,000
Percent completed	25%	—	10%	25%

REQUIRED: Compute the equivalent units of production for each of the four departments using the weighted average method.

E6-8
Appendix Required:
Equivalent Units—
FIFO Method
LO 5

Using the data from E6-7, compute the equivalent units of production for each of the four departments using the FIFO method.

E6-9
Weighted Average Method; Unit Cost; Valuation of Goods Transferred Out and Ending Work in Process
LO 3

Poston Products, Inc. produces a chemical product that passes through three departments. For May, the following equivalent-unit schedule was prepared for the first department:

	Materials	Conversion Cost
Units completed	5,000	5,000
Units, ending work in process × fraction completed:		
(6,000 × 100%)	6,000	—
(6,000 × 50%)	—	3,000
Equivalent units of output	11,000	8,000

Costs assigned to beginning work in process were materials, $30,000; conversion, $5,000. Manufacturing costs incurred during May were materials, $25,000; conversion, $65,000. Poston Products uses the weighted average method.

REQUIRED:
1. Compute the unit cost for May.
2. Determine the cost of ending work in process and the cost of goods transferred out.

E6-10
Appendix Required:
FIFO Method; Unit Cost; Valuation of Goods Transferred Out and Ending Work in Process
LO 5

Tolliver Company is a manufacturer that uses FIFO to account for its production costs. The product Tolliver makes passes through two processes. Tolliver's controller prepared the following equivalent-unit schedule:

	Materials	Conversion Cost
Units started and completed	8,000	8,000
Units, beginning work in process × fraction to be completed:		
(2,000 × 0%)	—	—
(2,000 × 50%)	—	1,000
Units, ending work in process × fraction completed:		
(4,000 × 100%)	4,000	—
(4,000 × 25%)	—	1,000
Equivalent units of output	12,000	10,000

Costs in beginning work in process were materials, $6,000; conversion costs, $24,000. Manufacturing costs incurred during October were materials, $72,000; conversion costs, $96,000.

REQUIRED:
1. Prepare a physical flow schedule for October.
2. Compute the cost per equivalent unit for October.
3. Determine the cost of ending work in process and the cost of goods transferred out.

E6-11

Weighted Average Method; Equivalent Units; Unit Cost; Multiple Departments

LO 2, LO 3, LO 4

Hogarth, Inc. manufactures a product that passes through three processes. During July, the first department transferred 12,000 units to the second department. The cost of the units transferred into the second department was $25,200. Materials are added uniformly in the second process.

The second department had the following physical flow schedule for July:

Units to account for:	
Units, beginning work in process (40% complete)	2,000
Units started	?
Total units to account for	?
Units accounted for:	
Units, ending work in process (50% complete)	4,000
Units completed	?
Total units accounted for	?

Costs in beginning work in process for the second department were materials, $3,200; conversion costs, $3,120; transferred in, $4,000. Costs added during the month were materials, $16,000; conversion costs, $24,960; transferred in, $20,500.

REQUIRED:
1. Assuming the use of the weighted average method, prepare a schedule of equivalent units.
2. Compute the unit cost for the month.

E6-12

Appendix Required: FIFO Method; Equivalent Units; Unit Cost; Multiple Departments

LO 2, LO 4, LO 5

Using the same data found in E6-11, assume the company uses the FIFO method.

REQUIRED: Prepare a schedule of equivalent units and compute the unit cost for July.

E6-13

Weighted Average Method; Unit Costs; Inventory Valuation; Cost Reconciliation

LO 3

Brandy Company prepared the following schedule for the most recent month of operation:

	Beginning Work in Process	Costs Added	Total
Materials	$ 5,000	$15,000	$20,000
Conversion costs	10,000	30,000	40,000
Total	$15,000	$45,000	$60,000

The equivalent units produced are summarized in the following schedule:

	Materials	Conversion Costs
Units completed	3,000	3,000
Units, ending work in process		
× fraction completed:		
(2,000 × 100%)	2,000	—
(2,000 × 50%)	—	1,000
Equivalent units of output	5,000	4,000

REQUIRED:

1. Calculate the unit costs for materials, conversion costs, and the total unit costs.
2. Compute the cost of ending work in process and the cost of goods transferred out.
3. Prepare a cost reconciliation.

E6-14

Journal Entries; Cost of Ending Inventories

LO 1

Naylor Company has two processing departments: assembly and finishing. A predetermined overhead rate of $6 per DLH is used to assign overhead to production. The company experienced the following operating activity for November:

a. Raw materials issued to assembly, $15,200
b. Direct labor cost: assembly, 550 hours at $9.50 per hour; finishing, 400 hours at $8.80 per hour
c. Overhead is applied to production
d. Goods transferred to finishing, $21,340
e. Goods transferred to finished goods warehouse, $25,500
f. Actual overhead incurred, $6,000

REQUIRED:

1. Prepare the required journal entries for these transactions.
2. Assuming assembly and finishing have no beginning work-in-process inventories, determine the cost of each department's ending work-in-process inventories.

E6-15

Process Costing: Food Manufacturing

LO 1, LO 2

Wholesome Bread makes and supplies bread throughout the western United States. Six operations describe the production process.

a. Flour, milk, yeast, salt, butter, and so on are mixed in a large vat.
b. A conveyor belt transfers the dough to a machine that weighs it and shapes it into loaves.
c. The individual loaves are allowed to sit and rise.
d. The dough is moved to a 100-foot-long funnel oven (the dough enters the oven on racks and spends 20 minutes moving slowly through the oven).
e. The bread is removed from the oven, sucked from the pan by a vacuum, and allowed to cool.
f. The bread is sliced and wrapped.

During the week, 4,500 loaves of bread were produced. The total cost of materials (ingredients and wrapping material) was $675. The cost of direct labor and overhead totaled $1,575. There were no beginning or ending work-in-process inventories.

REQUIRED:

1. Compute the unit cost for the 4,500 loaves of bread produced during the week.
2. Would Wholesome Bread ever need to worry about using FIFO or weighted average? Why or why not? What implication does this have for the food industry in general?
3. Assume that Wholesome Bread also produces rolls and buns. Also, assume that the only difference is that the machine is set to shape the dough differently. What adjustments would need to be made to cost out the three different bread products?

E6-16

Process Costing: Automated Operations

LO 2

Sahara Soft Diapers has just opened a new plant for making its popular line of diapers. This plant is experimental in the sense that it has implemented a fully automated production process. Human hands never touch the diaper while it is in production. The production line operates as follows.

First, fluff pulp is shredded from large rolls (mechanically fed into a shredder). Next, diaper wrap is mechanically placed on a conveyor belt. The shredded pulp is sprayed onto the diaper wrap sheet as it passes underneath. As the wrap and pulp move along, another machine covers the pulp with a liner sheet. The three materials are held together by a construction adhesive. The next machine attaches a leg elastic along the sides (the product now has the appearance of a long sausage). A cutting machine then cuts the diapers into the proper length. The final machines attach the waist elastic, outer poly cover, and the release tapes. The diapers are placed in bags and then in boxes (four per box). The boxes move down the conveyor belt to a point where they are picked up by robots and cranes and carried to the finished goods storage area.

REQUIRED:
1. Describe how you would compute the unit cost of a box of diapers. Do you think that the computation of equivalent units will be needed? Explain. Also, discuss the need for predetermined overhead rates.
2. Now assume that there are small, medium, and large diapers produced. Describe how you would compute unit costs for these three products.

E6-17 **Appendix Required:** **FIFO Method;** **Physical Flow;** **Equivalent Units** LO 5	Boyzee, Inc. manufactures a product that is processed through two departments. The following information was obtained from the first department in July: a. All materials are added at the beginning of the process. b. Beginning work in process had 10,000 units, which were 40 percent complete with respect to conversion costs. c. Ending work in process consisted of 2,000 units, 25 percent complete with respect to conversion costs. d. During the month, 13,000 units were started in process. REQUIRED: 1. Prepare a physical flow schedule. 2. Compute equivalent units using the FIFO method.
E6-18 **Weighted Average** **Method; Physical** **Flow; Equivalent** **Units; Unit Costs;** **Cost Assignment** LO 1, LO 2, LO 3	Funnifaces, Inc. manufactures various Halloween masks. Each mask is shaped from a piece of rubber in the molding department. The masks are then transferred to the finishing department where they are painted and have elastic bands attached. In April, the molding department reported the following data: a. In molding, all materials are added at the beginning of the process. b. Beginning work in process consisted of 6,000 units, 20 percent complete with respect to direct labor and overhead. Cost in beginning inventory included direct materials, $1,800; and conversion costs, $552. c. Costs added to production during the month were direct materials, $3,800; and conversion costs, $8,698. d. At the end of the month, 18,000 units were transferred out to finishing. Then 2,000 units remained in ending work in process, 25 percent complete. REQUIRED: 1. Prepare a physical flow schedule. 2. Calculate equivalent units of production for direct materials and conversion cost. 3. Compute unit cost. 4. Calculate the cost of goods transferred to finishing at the end of the month. Calculate the cost of ending inventory.
E6-19 **Appendix Required:** **FIFO Method;** **Physical Flow;** **Equivalent Units;** **Unit Costs; Cost** **Assignment** LO 5	Refer to the data in E6-18. Calculate the following using the FIFO method: REQUIRED: 1. Prepare a physical flow schedule. 2. Calculate equivalent units of production for direct materials and conversion cost. 3. Compute unit cost. 4. Calculate the cost of goods transferred to finishing at the end of the month. Calculate the cost of ending inventory.

E6-20

Weighted Average Method; Equivalent Units; Cost per Unit; Cost of Ending Inventory; Cost of Completed Units

LO 2, LO 3

Cheyenne Walking Tours produces maps of the Colorado Rockies that outline a variety of walking tours through the area. In June, Cheyenne Walking Tours incurred costs of $105 for materials (paper, ink, and so on) and $403.20 for direct labor and overhead. June production consisted of 280 completed maps and 140 maps that were 100 percent complete with respect to materials but only 40 percent complete with respect to conversion cost. There was no work-in-process inventory on June 1.

REQUIRED:

1. How many units were started and completed in June?
2. Compute the cost per equivalent unit for June.
3. Determine the cost of ending work-in-process inventory and the cost of the completed maps.

P ROBLEMS

P6-1

Weighted Average Method; Single Department Analysis; One Cost Category

LO 3

Ellis Company produces a product that passes through two processes: assembly and finishing. All manufacturing costs are added uniformly for both processes. The following information was obtained for the assembly department for December:

a. Work in process, December 1, had 4,000 units (40 percent completed) and the following costs:

Direct materials	$3,282
Direct labor	4,800
Overhead applied	1,200

b. During December, 10,600 units were completed and transferred to the finishing department, and the following costs were added to production:

Direct materials	$23,440
Direct labor	35,160
Overhead applied	8,700

c. On December 31, there were 3,400 partially completed units in process. These units were 70 percent complete.

REQUIRED: Prepare a production report for the assembly department for December using the weighted average method of costing. The report should disclose the physical flow of units, equivalent units, and unit costs and should track the disposition of manufacturing costs.

P6-2

Appendix Required: FIFO Method; Single Department Analysis; One Cost Category

LO 5

Refer to the data in P6-1.

REQUIRED: Prepare a production report for the assembly department for December using the FIFO method of costing. The report should contain the same schedules described in Problem 6-1. (Hint: Carry the unit cost computation to four decimal places.)

P6-3

Weighted Average Method; Single Department Analysis; Three Cost Categories

LO 3

Tristar Chemicals produces an industrial chemical that passes through two processes: blending and drying. The weighted average method is used to account for the costs of production. Two chemicals, A and B, are added at the beginning of the blending process and allowed to cook for 6 to 7 hours. After blending, the resulting product is sent to the drying department, where it is dried under heat lamps for 24 hours. The following information relates to the blending process for August:

a. Work in process, August 1, had 20,000 pounds, 60 percent complete with respect to conversion costs. Costs associated with partially completed units were:

Material A	$1,000
Material B	5,000
Direct labor	500
Overhead applied	1,500

b. Work in process, August 31, had 30,000 pounds, 70 percent complete with respect to conversion costs.
c. Units completed and transferred out totaled 500,000 pounds. Costs added during the month were:

Material A	$ 25,500
Material B	127,500
Direct labor	12,750
Overhead applied	38,250

REQUIRED:
1. Prepare the following: (a) a physical flow schedule and (b) an equivalent-unit schedule with cost categories for material A, material B, and conversion cost.
2. Calculate the unit cost for each cost category.
3. Compute the cost of ending work in process and the cost of goods transferred out.
4. Prepare a cost reconciliation.

P6-4
Weighted Average Method; Single Department Analysis; Two Cost Categories
LO 3

Lamdin, Inc. produces a product that goes through two departments, grinding and polishing. Materials are added at the beginning of the grinding operation; labor and overhead are added uniformly throughout the process. The grinding department had work in process at the beginning and end of 1998 as follows:

	Percentage of Completion	
	Materials	**Conversion Costs**
January 1, 1998 (2,500 units)	100	60
December 31, 1998 (4,000 units)	100	50

The company completed 42,500 units during the year and incurred the following manufacturing costs:

Direct materials	$158,000
Direct labor	98,750
Overhead applied	79,000

The inventory at the beginning of the year was carried at the following costs:

Direct materials	$9,750
Direct labor	6,125
Overhead applied	4,950

REQUIRED: Prepare a production report using the weighted average method.

P6-5

Appendix Required: FIFO Method; Single Department Analysis; Two Cost Categories

LO 5

Refer to the data in P6-4.

REQUIRED: Prepare a production report using the FIFO method.

P6-6

Weighted Average Method; Single Department Analysis; Transferred-in Goods

LO 3, LO 4

Keating Company manufactures a product that passes through three departments. In department C, materials are added at the end of the process. Conversion costs are incurred uniformly throughout the process. During January, department C received 20,000 units from department B. The transferred-in cost of the 20,000 units was $70,350.

Costs added by department C during January included the following:

Direct materials	$40,635
Direct labor	58,500
Overhead applied	29,400

On January 1, department C had 4,000 units in inventory that were 30 percent complete with respect to conversion costs. On January 31, 3,000 units were in inventory, one-third complete with respect to conversion costs. The costs associated with the 4,000 units in beginning inventory were as follows:

Transferred in	$14,970
Direct labor	7,560
Overhead applied	4,200

REQUIRED: Prepare a production report using the weighted average method. Follow the five steps outlined in the chapter in preparing the report.

P6-7

Appendix Required: FIFO Method; Single Department Analysis; Transferred-in Goods

LO 4, LO 5

Merrifield, Inc. manufactures a single product that passes through several processes. During the first quarter of the year, the mixing department received 45,000 gallons of liquid from the cooking department (transferred in at $28,800). Upon receiving the liquid, the mixing department adds a powder and allows blending to take place for 30 minutes. The product is then passed on to the bottling department.

There were 9,000 gallons in process at the beginning of the quarter, 75 percent complete with respect to conversion costs. The costs attached to the beginning inventory were as follows:

Transferred in	$5,700
Powder	804
Conversion costs	1,800

Costs added by the mixing department during the first quarter were:

Powder	$4,200
Conversion costs	9,080

There were 7,875 gallons in ending inventory, 20 percent complete with respect to conversion costs.

REQUIRED: Prepare a production report using the FIFO method. Follow the five steps outlined in the chapter in preparing the report. Carry out unit costs to three decimal places. Round to the nearest dollar in the production report.

P6-8
Weighted Average Method; Transferred-in Goods
LO 3, LO 4

Refer to P6-7.

REQUIRED: Prepare a production report for the mixing department using the weighted average method.

P6-9
Weighted Average Method; Journal Entries
LO 1, LO 3

Seacrest Company uses a process-costing system. The company manufactures a product that is processed in two departments, A and B. In department A, materials are added at the beginning of the process; in department B, additional materials are added at the end of the process. In both departments, conversion costs are incurred uniformly throughout the process. As work is completed, it is transferred out. The following summarizes the production activity and costs for November:

	Department A	Department B
Beginning inventories:		
Physical units	5,000	8,000
Costs:		
Transferred in	—	$45,320
Direct materials	$10,000	—
Conversion costs	$6,900	$16,800
Current production:		
Units started	25,000	?
Units transferred out	28,000	33,000
Costs:		
Transferred in	—	?
Direct materials	$57,800	$37,950
Conversion costs	$95,220	$128,100
Percentage completion:		
Beginning inventory	40	50
Ending inventory	80	50

REQUIRED:
1. Using the weighted average method, prepare the following for department A:
   a. A physical flow schedule
   b. An equivalent-units calculation
   c. Calculation of unit costs
   d. Cost of ending work in process and cost of goods transferred out
   e. A cost reconciliation
2. Prepare journal entries that show the flow of manufacturing costs for department A.
3. Repeat requirements 1 and 2 for department B.

P6-10
Appendix Required: FIFO Method; Two Department Analysis
LO 4, LO 5

Refer to the data in P6-9.

REQUIRED: Repeat the requirements in Problem 6-9 using the FIFO method.

P6-11
Weighted Average Method; Two Department Analysis
LO 3, LO 4

Benson Pharmaceuticals uses a process-costing system to compute the unit costs of the over-the-counter cold remedies that it produces. It has three departments: picking, encapsulating, and bottling. In picking, the ingredients for the cold capsules are measured, sifted, and blended. The mix is transferred out in gallon containers. The encapsulating department takes the powdered mix and places it in capsules. One gallon of powdered mix converts into 1,500 capsules. After the capsules are filled and polished, they are transferred to bottling where they are placed in bottles, which are then affixed with a safety seal and a lid and labeled. Each bottle receives 50 capsules.

During March, the following results are available for the first two departments:

	Picking	Encapsulating
Beginning inventories:		
Physical units	10 gallons	4,000
Costs:		
Materials	$252	$ 32
Labor	$282	$ 20
Overhead applied	$?	$?
Transferred in	$ —	$140
Current production:		
Transferred out	140 gallons	208,000
Ending inventory	20 gallons	6,000
Costs:		
Materials	$3,636	$1,573
Labor	$4,618	$1,944
Overhead applied	$?	$?
Transferred in	$ —	$?
Percentage of completion:		
Beginning inventory	40	50
Ending inventory	50	40

Overhead in both departments is applied as a percentage of direct labor costs. In the picking department, overhead is 200 percent of direct labor. In the encapsulating department, the overhead rate is 150 percent of direct labor.

REQUIRED:
1. Prepare a production report for the picking department using the weighted average method. Follow the five steps outlined in the chapter.
2. Prepare a production report for the encapsulating department. Follow the five steps outlined in the chapter.

P6-12
**Appendix Required:
FIFO Method; Two
Department Analysis**
LO 4, LO 5

Refer to the data in P6-11.

REQUIRED: Prepare a production report for each department using the FIFO method.

P6-13
**Weighted Average
Method; Multiple
Department Analysis**
LO 3, LO 4

Strathmore, Inc. manufactures educational toys using a weighted average process-costing system. Plastic is molded into the appropriate shapes in the molding department. Molded components are transferred to the assembly department where the toys are assembled and additional materials (for example, fasteners, decals) are applied. Completed toys are then transferred to the packaging department where each toy is boxed.

Strathmore showed the following data on toy production for February:

	Molding	Assembly	Packaging
Beginning inventory:			
Units	500	—	150
Costs:			
Prior department	—	—	$1,959
Direct materials	$2,500	—	$ 375
Conversion cost	$1,050	—	$ 225

	Molding	Assembly	Packaging
Started or transferred in:			
Units	1,000	?	?
February costs:			
Prior department	—	$14,950.00	$11,754.00
Direct materials	$5,000	$ 487.60	$ 2,407.50
Conversion cost	$7,660	$ 1,166.00	$ 2,977.50
Ending inventory, units	200	400	—

Beginning and ending work in process for the three departments showed the following degree of completion:

	Molding	Assembly	Packaging
Degree of completion:			
BWIP, direct materials	100%	—	100%
BWIP, conversion costs	30	—	50
EWIP, direct materials	100	40%	—
EWIP, conversion costs	20	40	—

REQUIRED:
1. Prepare a physical flow schedule for February for the:
   a. Molding department
   b. Assembly department
   c. Packaging department
2. Compute equivalent units of production for direct materials and for conversion costs for the:
   a. Molding department
   b. Assembly department
   c. Packaging department
3. Complete the following unit cost chart:

	Molding	Assembly	Packaging
Unit prior department cost*			
Unit direct material cost			
Unit conversion cost	_____	_____	_____
Total unit cost			

*Cost transferred in from prior department

4. Determine the cost of ending work in process and the cost of goods transferred out for each of the three departments.
5. Reconcile the costs for each department.

P6-14
Appendix Required:
FIFO Method;
Multiple Department
Analysis
LO 4, LO 5

Refer to the data in P6-13.

REQUIRED: Repeat requirements 2 through 5 using the FIFO method.

P6-15
Production Report
LO 3

Susan Manners, cost accountant for Lean Jeans, Inc., spent the weekend completing a production report for the inspection department for the month of December. Inspection is the final department in the production of fashion jeans. In that department, each pair of jeans is carefully inspected for quality workmanship. At the end of the inspection process, a slip of paper with "Inspected by #_____" is slipped into a back pocket and the jeans are placed in a bin to be transferred to finished goods.

First thing Monday morning, Susan returned to work and found that someone had accidentally spilled coffee on her report, partially obliterating some of the figures. Susan has only one hour to reconstruct her report.

Production Report for the Inspection Department
For the Month of December
(Weighted Average Method)
Unit Information

Units to account for:	
Beginning inventory	? *700*
Transferred in from assembly	4,000
Total units to account for	4,700

Equivalent Units

	Physical Flow	Prior Department	Materials	Conversion Cost
Units accounted for:				
Units completed	*3,800*	*4,000*	*3,800*	*3,800*
Units, ending WIP	900	?	—	*450*
Total units accounted for	4,700	*4,000*	3,800	4,250

Cost Information

	Prior Department	Materials	Conversion Costs	Total
Costs to account for:				
Beginning WIP	$11,900	?	$ 210	$12,110
Incurred in December	*68,000*	*?57*	4,040	72,097
Total costs to account for	$79,900	$57	$4,250	$84,207
Unit cost	$17.00	?	$1.00	?

	Transferred Out	Ending WIP	Total
Costs accounted for:			
Goods transferred out	?	—	?
Ending inventory:			
Prior department	—	?	?
Materials	—	—	—
Conversion cost	—	?	?
Total costs accounted for	$?	$15,750	$84,207

REQUIRED: Help Susan meet the deadline by filling in the appropriate number for each question mark.

Ⓜ ANAGERIAL DECISION CASES

C6-1
Production Report;
Ethical Behavior
LO 3

Consider the following conversation between Gary Means, manager of a division that produces industrial machinery, and his controller, Donna Simpson, a CMA and CPA:

Gary: "Donna, we have a real problem. Our operating cash is too low, and we are in desperate need of a loan. As you know, our financial position is marginal, and we need to show as much income as possible—and our assets need bolstering as well."

Donna: "I understand the problem, but I don't see what can be done at this point. This is the last week of the fiscal year, and it looks like we'll report income just slightly above breakeven."

Gary: "I know all this. What we need is some creative accounting. I have an idea that might help us, and I wanted to see if you would go along with it. We have 200 partially finished machines in process, about 20 percent complete. That compares with the 1,000 units that we completed and sold during the year. When you computed the per-unit cost, you used 1,040 equivalent units, giving us a manufacturing cost of $1,500 per unit. That per-unit cost gives us cost of goods sold equal to $1.5 million and ending work in process worth $60,000. The presence of the work in process gives us a chance to improve our financial position. If we report the units in work in process as 80 percent complete, this will increase our equivalent units to 1,160. This, in turn, will decrease our unit cost to about $1,345 and cost of goods sold to $1.345 million. The value of our work in process will increase to $215,200. With those financial stats, the loan would be a cinch."

Donna: "Gary, I don't know. What you're suggesting is risky. It wouldn't take much auditing skill to catch this one."

Gary: "You don't have to worry about that. The auditors won't be here for at least six to eight more weeks. By that time, we can have those partially completed units completed and sold. I can bury the labor cost by having some of our more loyal workers work overtime for some bonuses. The overtime will never be reported. And, as you know, bonuses come out of the corporate budget and are assigned to overhead—next year's overhead. Donna, this will work. If we look good and get the loan to boot, corporate headquarters will treat us well. If we don't do this, we could lose our jobs."

REQUIRED:

1. Should Donna agree to Gary's proposal? Why or why not? To assist in deciding, review the standards of ethical conduct for management accountants described in Chapter 1. Do any apply?

2. Assume that Donna refuses to cooperate and that Gary accepts this decision and drops the matter. Does Donna have any obligation to report the divisional manager's behavior to a superior? Explain.

3. Assume that Donna refuses to cooperate; however, Gary insists that the changes be made. Now what should she do? What would *you* do?

4. Suppose that Donna is 63 and that the prospects for employment elsewhere are bleak. Assume again that Gary insists that the changes should be made. Donna also knows that his supervisor, the owner of the company, is his father-in-law. Under these circumstances, would your recommendations for Donna differ? If you were Donna, what would you do?

C6-2
Process Costing versus Alternative Costing Methods; Impact on Resource Allocation Decision
LO 1, LO 3

Golding Manufacturing, a division of Farnsworth Sporting, Inc., produces two different models of bows and eight models of knives. The bow-manufacturing process involves the production of two major subassemblies: the limbs and the handle. The limbs pass through four sequential processes before reaching final assembly: layup, molding, fabricating, and finishing. In the layup department, limbs are created by laminating layers of wood. In molding, the limbs are heat treated, under pressure, to form a strong resilient limb. In the fabricating department, any protruding glue or other processing residue is removed. Finally, in finishing, the limbs are cleaned with acetone, dried, and sprayed with the final finishes.

The handles pass through two processes before reaching final assembly: pattern and finishing. In the pattern department, blocks of wood are fed into a machine that is set to shape the handles. Different patterns are possible, depending on the machine's setting. After coming out of the machine, the handles are cleaned and smoothed. They then pass to the finishing department where they are sprayed with the final finishes. In final assembly, the limbs and handles are assembled into different models using purchased parts such as pulley assemblies, weight adjustment bolts, side plates, and string.

Golding, since its inception, has been using process costing to assign product costs. A predetermined overhead rate is used based on direct labor dollars (80 percent of direct labor dollars). Recently, Golding has hired a new controller, Karen Jenkins. After reviewing the product-costing procedures, Karen requested a meeting with the divisional manager, Aaron Suhr. The following is a transcript of their conversation.

Karen: "Aaron, I have some concerns about our cost accounting system. We make two different models of bows and are treating them as if they were the same product. Now I know that the only real difference between the models is the handle. The processing of the handles is the same, but the handles differ significantly in the amount and quality of wood used. Our current costing does not reflect this difference in material input."

Aaron: "Your predecessor is responsible. He believed that tracking the difference in material cost wasn't worth the effort. He simply didn't believe that it would make much difference in the unit cost of either model."

Karen: "Well, he may have been right, but I have my doubts. If there is a significant difference, it could affect our views of which model is the more important to the company. The additional bookkeeping isn't very stringent. All we have to worry about is the pattern department. The other departments fit what I view as a process-costing pattern."

Aaron: "Why don't you look into it? If there is a significant difference, go ahead and adjust the costing system."

After the meeting, Karen decided to collect cost data on the two models: the Deluxe model and the Econo model. She decided to track the costs for one week. At the end of the week, she had collected the following data from the pattern department:

a. There were a total of 2,500 bows completed: 1,000 Deluxe models and 1,500 Econo models.
b. There was no beginning work in process; however, there were 300 units in ending work in process: 200 Deluxe and 100 Econo models. Both models were 80 percent complete with respect to conversion costs and 100 percent complete with respect to materials.
c. The pattern department experienced the following costs:

| Direct materials | $114,000 |
| Direct labor | 45,667 |

d. On an experimental basis, the requisition forms for materials were modified to identify the dollar value of the materials used by the Econo and Deluxe models:

| Econo model | $30,000 |
| Deluxe model | 84,000 |

REQUIRED:
1. Compute the unit cost for the handles produced by the pattern department assuming that process costing is totally appropriate.
2. Compute the unit cost of each handle using the separate cost information provided on materials.
3. Compare the unit costs computed in requirements 1 and 2. Is Karen justified in her belief that a pure process-costing relationship is not appropriate? Describe the costing system that you would recommend.
4. In the past, the marketing manager has requested more money for advertising the Econo line. Aaron has repeatedly refused to grant any increase in this product's advertising budget because its per-unit profit (selling price less manufacturing cost) is so low. Given the results in requirements 1 through 3, was Aaron justified in his position?

1. Describe the difference between support departments and producing departments.

2. Explain five reasons why support-department costs may be assigned to producing departments.

3. Calculate charging rates and distinguish between single and dual charging rates.

4. Allocate support-center costs to producing departments using the direct, sequential, and reciprocal methods.

5. Calculate departmental overhead rates.

CHAPTER

Support Department Cost Allocation

SCENARIO

Hamilton and Barry, a large regional public accounting firm, consists of three major departments: audit, tax, and management advisory services (MAS). Gary Premark, head of management advisory services, is talking with Jan McAndrews, partner in charge.

Jan: So far, this has been a good year for MAS, Gary. We're very pleased with the way you increased your client base and billing hours. Our only remaining problem is profitability. As you can see, the total costs of your department rose at a faster pace last year than the year before.

Gary: My profitability is just fine—or would be if I weren't forced to use the inefficient services of this firm. Look at my photocopying costs! These are way out of line! I'd be better off using Kopykats a block away.

Jan: Gary, as you know, we went to an in-house photocopying department to provide convenience and security. If it costs a little more, so be it. Besides, the convenience of just walking down the hall to get your reports and bids copied outweighs any small increase in cost allocation.

Gary: Look, Jan, I don't mind paying a little extra for convenience, but this allocation is much more than a little extra. My department's going to boycott photocopying until this problem gets resolved.

Jan: Don't take that step just yet. Carol Morton is in charge of photocopying, let's get some answers from her first.

Two days later Gary, Jan, and Carol Morton, executive assistant in charge of the photocopying service, meet in Jan's office.

Carol: Gary, I understand you have some questions about the way photocopying is run. Let me assure you that we work very hard to keep costs down while providing top-notch service. Your department was charged only for the copies you made.

Gary: Carol, I took my total cost allocation and divided by the number of copies. Do you realize that it comes to $0.12 per page? Why is your department so much higher than outside services?

Carol: Gary, you have to realize that we bought machinery for peak usage. In our firm that's the month of April when tax runs most of their copies. Other months are slower, but I can't trade in the copier on a month-to-month basis. Also, we need at least one person ready to handle your copies or you'll really hit the ceiling.

As a result, the per-page charges are higher.

Gary: I think I'm beginning to see what's happening. Still, I'd like to explore different charging systems.

Jan: If there's a problem here, it is a firmwide problem. I can assign Cynthia Bowles, our firm's new intern from State University, to take this on as a special project.

Questions to Think About

1. Why do you think that the copying department charges amount to $0.12 per page? List the types of costs incurred for photocopying and divide them into fixed and variable categories.

2. Jan mentioned the security and convenience of in-house photocopying. How do you think the firm might weigh these factors in deciding whether or not the cost of in-house copying is "worth it"?

3. Since the firm as a whole has decided to have an in-house copying department, why are copying costs charged to the individual departments? What purpose does the practice of developing support department charging rates serve?

The complexity of many modern firms leads the accountant to allocate costs of support departments to a variety of cost objectives, such as divisions, departments, and individual product lines. *Allocation* is simply a means of dividing a pool of cost and assigning it to various subunits. It is important to realize that allocation does not affect the total cost. Total cost is neither reduced nor increased by allocation. However, the amounts of cost assigned to the subunits can be affected by the allocation procedure chosen. Because cost allocation can affect bid prices, the profitability of individual products, and the behavior of managers, it is an important topic.

AN OVERVIEW OF COST ALLOCATION

Objective 1

Describe the difference between support departments and producing departments.

common costs

Mutually beneficial costs, which occur when the same resource is used in the output of two or more services or products, are common costs. While these common costs may pertain to periods of time, individual responsibilities, sales territories, and classes of customers, this chapter will concentrate on the costs common to departments and to products. For example, the wages paid to security guards at a factory is a common cost of all of the different products manufactured there. The benefits of security are applicable to each product, yet the assignment of security cost to the individual products is an arbitrary process. In other words, while it is clear that the products (or services) require the common resource, and that the resource cost should be assigned to these cost objects, it is often not clear how best to go about assigning the cost. Usually, common cost assignment is made through a series of consistent allocation procedures.

Types of Departments

producing departments

support departments

The first step in cost allocation is to determine just what the cost objects are. Usually, they are departments. There are two categories of departments: producing departments and support departments. Producing departments are directly responsible for creating the products or services sold to customers. In the opening scenario's public accounting firm, examples of producing departments are auditing, tax, and management advisory services. In a manufacturing setting, producing departments are those that work directly on the products being manufactured (for example, grinding and assembly). Support departments provide essential support services for producing departments. These departments are indirectly connected with an organization's services or products. Examples include maintenance, grounds, engineering, housekeeping, personnel, and stores. Of course, the photocopying department of Hamilton and Barry is a support department.

Once the producing and support departments have been identified, the overhead costs incurred by each department can be determined. Note that this involves tracing costs to the departments, not allocating costs, because the costs are directly associated with the individual department. A factory cafeteria, for example, would have food costs, salaries of cooks and servers, depreciation on dishwashers and stoves, and supplies (napkins, plastic forks). Overhead directly associated with a producing department, such as assembly in a furniture-making plant, would include utilities (if measured in that department), supervisory salaries, and depreciation on equipment used in that department. Overhead that cannot be easily assigned to a producing or support department is assigned to a catchall department such as general factory. General factory might include depreciation on the factory building, rental of a Santa Claus suit for the factory Christmas party, the cost of restriping the parking lot, the plant manager's salary, and telephone service. In this way, all costs are assigned to a department.

Exhibit 7-1 shows how a manufacturing firm and a service firm can be divided into producing and support departments. The manufacturing plant, which makes furniture, may be departmentalized into two producing departments (assembly and finishing) and four support departments (materials storeroom, cafeteria, maintenance, and general factory). The service firm, a bank, might be departmentalized into three producing departments (auto loans, commercial lending, and personal banking) and three support

7-1

Exhibit
Examples of
Departmentalization for a
Manufacturing Firm and a
Service Firm

Manufacturing Firm: Furniture Maker	
Producing Departments	**Support Departments**

Assembly
   Supervisory salaries
   Small tools
   Indirect materials
   Depreciation on machinery
 	
Finishing
   Sandpaper
   Depreciation on sanders and buffers
	Materials storeroom
	   Clerk's salary
	   Depreciation on forklift
	
	Cafeteria
	   Food
	   Cooks' salaries
	   Depreciation on stoves
	
	Maintenance
	   Janitors' salaries
	   Cleaning supplies
	   Machine oil and lubricants
	
	General factory
	   Depreciation on building
	   Security and utilities

Service Firm: Bank	
Producing Departments	**Support Departments**

Auto loans
   Loan processors' salaries
   Forms and supplies
 	
Commercial lending
   Lending officers' salaries
   Depreciation on office equipment
   Bankruptcy prediction software
 	
Personal banking
   Supplies and postage for statements
	Drive through
	   Tellers' salaries
	   Depreciation on equipment
	
	Data processing
	   Personnel salaries
	   Software
	   Depreciation on hardware
	
	Bank administration
	   Salary of CEO
	   Receptionist salary
	   Telephone costs
	   Depreciation on bank vault

departments (drive through, data processing, and bank administration). Overhead costs are traced to each department. Note that each kind of factory or service overhead cost must be assigned to one, and only one, department.

Once the company has been departmentalized, and all overhead costs have been traced to the individual departments, support-department costs are assigned to producing departments and overhead rates are developed to cost product. Although support departments do not work directly on the products or services that are sold, the costs of providing these support services are part of the total product costs and must be assigned to the products. This assignment of costs consists of a two-stage allocation: (1) allocation of support-department costs to producing departments and (2) assignment of these allocated costs to individual products. The second-stage allocation, achieved through the use of departmental overhead rates, is necessary because there are multiple products being worked on in each producing department. If there were only one product within a producing department, all the service costs allocated to that department would belong to that product. Recall that a predetermined overhead rate is computed by taking total estimated overhead for a department and dividing it by an estimate of an appropriate base. Now we see that a producing department's overhead consists of two parts: overhead directly associated with a producing department and overhead allocated to the producing department from the support departments. A support department cannot have an overhead rate that assigns overhead costs to units produced because it does not make a salable product. That is, products do not pass through support departments. The nature of support departments is to service producing departments, not the products that pass through the producing departments. For example, maintenance personnel repair and maintain the equipment in the assembly department, not the furniture that is assembled in that department. Exhibit 7-2 summarizes the steps involved.

Types of Allocation Bases

causal factors

Producing departments *cause* services; therefore, the costs of support departments are also caused by the activities of the producing departments. Causal factors are variables or activities within a producing department that provoke the incurrence of service costs. In choosing a basis for allocating support-department costs, every effort should be made to identify appropriate causal factors (cost drivers). Using causal factors results in product costs being more accurate; furthermore, if the causal factors are known, managers are more able to control the consumption of support services.

To illustrate the types of cost drivers that can be used, consider the following three support departments: power, personnel, and materials handling. For power costs, a logical allocation base is kilowatt-hours, which can be measured by separate meters for each department. If separate meters do not exist, perhaps machine hours used by each department would provide a good *proxy*, or means to approximate power usage. For personnel costs, both the number of producing-department employees and the labor turnover (for example, number of new hires) are possible cost drivers. For material handling, the number of material moves, the hours of material handling used, and the quantity of material moved are all possible cost drivers. Exhibit 7-3 lists some possible cost drivers that can be used to allocate support-department costs. When competing cost drivers exist, managers need to assess which provides the most convincing relationship.

While the use of a causal factor to allocate common cost is the best, sometimes an easily measured causal factor cannot be found. In that case, the accountant looks for a good proxy. For example, the common cost of plant depreciation may be allocated to producing departments on the basis of square footage. Square footage does not cause depreciation; however, it can be argued that the number of square feet a department occupies is a good proxy for the services provided to it by the factory building. The choice of a good proxy to guide allocation is dependent upon the company's objectives for allocation.

OBJECTIVES OF ALLOCATION

Objective 2
Explain five reasons why support-department costs may be assigned to producing departments.

A number of important objectives are associated with the allocation of support-department costs to producing departments and ultimately to specific products. The following major objectives have been identified by the IMA:[1]

1. To obtain a mutually agreeable price
2. To compute product-line profitability

1. *Statements of Management Accounting (Statement 4B), Allocation of Service and Administrative Costs* (Montvale, NJ: NAA, 1985). The NAA is now known as the Institute of Management Accountants (IMA).

Exhibit
Steps in Allocating
Support-Department
Costs to Producing
Departments

1. Departmentalize the firm.
2. Classify each department as a support department or a producing department.
3. Trace all overhead costs in the firm to a support or producing department.
4. Allocate support-department costs to the producing departments.
5. Calculate predetermined overhead rates for producing departments.
6. Allocate overhead costs to the units of individual product through the predetermined overhead rates.

Exhibit 7-3

Examples of Possible
Cost Drivers for Support
Departments

Accounting
    Number of transactions

Cafeteria
    Number of employees

Data processing
    Number of lines entered
    Number of hours of service

Engineering
    Number of change orders
    Number of hours

Maintenance
    Machine hours
    Maintenance hours

Materials storeroom
    Number of material moves
    Pounds of material moved
    Number of different parts

Payroll
    Number of employees

Personnel
    Number of employees
    Number of firings or layoffs
    Number of new hires
    Direct labor cost

Power
    Kilowatt-hours
    Machine hours

Purchasing
    Number of orders
    Cost of orders

Shipping
    Number of orders

3. To predict the economic effects of planning and control
4. To value inventory
5. To motivate managers

Competitive pricing requires an understanding of costs. Only by knowing the costs of each service or product can the firm create meaningful bids. If costs are not accurately allocated, the costs of some services could be overstated, resulting in bids that are too high and a loss of potential business. Alternatively, if the costs are understated, bids could be too low, producing losses on these services.

Good estimates of individual product costs also allow a manager to assess the profitability of individual products and services. Multiproduct companies need to be sure that all products are profitable, and that the overall profitability of the firm is not disguising the poor performance of individual products. This meets the profitability objective identified by the IMA.

By assessing the profitability of various services, a manager may evaluate the mix of services offered by the firm. From this evaluation, it may be decided to drop some services, reallocate resources from one service to another, reprice certain services, or exercise greater cost control in some areas. These steps would meet the IMA's planning and control objective. The validity of any evaluation, however, depends to a great extent on the accuracy of the cost assignments made to individual products.

For a service organization such as a hospital, the IMA objective of inventory valuation is not relevant. For manufacturing organizations, however, this objective must be given special attention. Rules of financial reporting (GAAP)[2] require that direct manufacturing costs and all indirect manufacturing costs be assigned to the products produced. The procedure of allocating service costs to producing departments and then reassigning those costs to products going through the producing departments is in keeping with this requirement. Inventories and cost of goods sold must include direct materials, direct labor, and all manufacturing overhead.

Allocations also can be used to motivate managers. If the costs of support departments are not allocated to producing departments, managers may tend to overconsume these services. Consumption of a service may continue until the marginal benefit of the service equals zero. In reality, of course, the marginal cost of a service is greater than zero. By allocating the costs and holding managers of producing departments responsible for the economic performance of their units, the organization ensures that managers will use a service until the marginal benefit of the service equals its marginal cost. Thus, allocating service costs helps each producing department select the correct level of service consumption.

There are other behavioral benefits. Allocating support-department costs to producing departments encourages managers of those departments to monitor the performance of support departments. Since the costs of the support departments affect the economic performance of their own departments, those managers have an incentive to control service costs through means other than simple usage of the service. We can see this happening in the opening scenario as Gary compared the cost of in-house copying with external copy companies. If a support department is not as cost effective as an outside source, perhaps the company should not continue to supply the service internally. For example, many university libraries are moving toward the use of outside contractors for photocopying services. They have found that these contractors are more cost efficient and provide a higher level of service to library users than did the previous method of using professional librarians to make change, keep the copy machines supplied with paper, fix paper jams, and so on. This possibility of comparison should result in a more efficient internal support department. Monitoring by managers of producing departments will also encourage managers of support departments to be more sensitive to the needs of the producing departments.

Clearly, then, there are good reasons for allocating support-department costs. The validity of these reasons, however, depends on the accuracy and fairness of the cost assignments made. Although it may not be possible to identify a single method of allocation that simultaneously satisfies all of these objectives, several guidelines have been developed to assist in determining the best allocation method. These are (1) cause-and-effect, (2) benefits received, (3) fairness, and (4) ability to bear. Another guideline to be used in conjunction with any of the others is (5) cost-benefit. That is, the method used must provide sufficient benefits to justify any effort involved.

Cause-and-effect requires the determination of causal factors to guide allocation. For example, the corporate legal department may track the number of hours spent on legal work for the various divisions (handling patent applications, lawsuits, and so on). The number of hours worked by lawyers and paralegals has a clear cause-and-effect relationship with the overall cost of the legal department and may be used to allocate the cost of the corporate legal department to the various company divisions.

Benefits received associates the cost with perceived benefits. Research and development costs may be allocated on the basis of the sales of each division. The idea would

---

2. Generally accepted accounting principles.

Companies that sell and/or lease musical instruments to students must have maintenance departments to make necessary repairs. These departments support the primary objective of the firm—to rent musical instruments.

be that not all R&D efforts pay off, and that while the successful efforts may happen to benefit one division in one year, all divisions have a stake in corporate R&D and will at some point have increased sales because of it.

Fairness or equity is a guideline often mentioned in government contracting. In the case of cost allocation methods, fairness usually means that the government contract should be costed in a method similar to nongovernmental contracts. For example, an airplane engine manufacturer may allocate a portion of corporate legal department costs to the government contract if these costs are usually allocated to private contracts.

Ability to bear is the least desirable guideline. It tends to "penalize" the most profitable division by allocating to it the largest proportion of a support-department cost—no matter whether the profitable division receives any services from the allocated department or not. As a result, no motivational benefits of allocation are realized.

In determining how to allocate support-department costs, the guideline of cost-benefit must be considered. In other words, the costs of implementing a particular allocation scheme must be compared to the benefits to be derived. As a result, companies try to use easily measured and understood bases for allocation.

ALLOCATING ONE DEPARTMENT'S COSTS TO ANOTHER DEPARTMENT

Objective 3

Calculate charging rates and distinguish between single and dual charging rates.

Frequently, the costs of a support department are allocated to another department through the use of a charging rate. In this case, we focus on the allocation of one department's costs to other departments. For example, a company's data processing department may serve various other departments. The cost of operating the data processing department is then allocated to the user departments. While this seems simple and straightforward, a number of considerations go into determining an appropriate charging rate. The two major factors are the choice of a single or a dual charging rate, and the use of budgeted versus actual support-department costs.

A Single Charging Rate

Some companies prefer to develop a single charging rate. Let's return to the case of Hamilton and Barry, the public accounting firm from the opening scenario. Recall that the firm developed an in-house photocopying department to serve its three producing departments (audit, tax, and management advisory systems or MAS). The costs of the photocopying department include fixed costs of $26,190 per year (salaries and machine rental) and variable costs of $0.023 per page copied (paper and toner). Estimated usage (in pages) by the three producing departments is as follows:

Audit department	94,500
Tax department	67,500
MAS department	108,000
Total	270,000

If a single charging rate is used, the fixed costs of $26,190 will be combined with estimated variable costs of $6,210 (270,000 x $0.023). Total costs of $32,400 are divided by the estimated 270,000 pages to be copied to yield a rate of $0.12 per page.

The amount charged to the producing departments is solely a function of the number of pages copied. Suppose that the actual usage is audit, 92,000 pages; tax, 65,000 pages; and MAS, 115,000 pages. The total photocopying department charges would be as shown.

	Number of Pages	× Charge per Page =	Total Charges
Audit	92,000	$0.12	$11,040
Tax	65,000	0.12	7,800
MAS	115,000	0.12	13,800
Total	272,000		$32,640

Notice that the use of a single rate results in the fixed cost being treated as if it were variable. In fact, to the producing departments, photocopying is strictly variable. Did the photocopying department need $32,640 to copy 272,000 pages? No, it needed only $32,446 [$26,190 + (272,000 × $0.023)]. The extra amount charged is due to the treatment of a fixed cost in a variable manner.[3]

Dual Charging Rates

While the use of a single rate is simple, it ignores the differential impact of changes in usage on costs. The variable costs of a support department increase as the level of service increases. For example, the cost of paper and toner for the photocopying department

---

3. Note that the photocopying department would have charged out less than the cost needed if the number of pages copied had been less than the budgeted number of pages. You might calculate the total cost charged for a total of 268,000 pages ($0.12 × 268,000 =$32,160) and compare it with the cost incurred of $32,354 [$26,190 + ($0.023 × 268,000)].

increases as the number of pages copied increases. Fixed costs, on the other hand, do not vary with the level of service. For example, the rental payment for photocopying machines does not change as the number of pages increases or decreases. We can avoid the treatment of fixed costs as variable by developing two rates: one for fixed costs and one for variable costs. The development of dual charging rates (which are used as the basis for pricing) is particularly important in companies such as public utilities.

Developing a Fixed Rate Fixed service costs can be considered capacity costs; they are incurred to provide the capacity necessary to deliver the service units required by the producing departments. When the support department was established, its delivery capability was designed to serve the long-term needs of the producing departments. Since the original service needs caused the creation of the service capacity, it seems reasonable to allocate fixed service costs based on those needs.

Either the normal or peak activity of the producing departments provides reasonable measures of original service needs. Normal capacity is the average capacity achieved over more than one fiscal period. If service is required uniformly over the time period, normal capacity is a good measure of activity. Peak capacity allows for variation in the need for the support department, and the size of the department is structured to allow for maximum need. In our example, the tax department may need much more photocopying during the first four months of the year, and its usage may be based on that need. The choice of normal or peak capacity in allocating budgeted fixed service costs depends on the needs of the individual firm. Budgeted fixed costs are allocated in this way regardless of whether the purpose is product costing or performance evaluation.

The allocation of fixed costs follows a three-step procedure:

1. *Determination of budgeted fixed service costs.* The fixed service costs that should be incurred for a period need to be identified.
2. *Computation of the allocation ratio.* Using the practical or normal capacity of each producing department, it is necessary to compute an allocation ratio. The allocation ratio simply gives a producing department's share or percentage of the total capacity of all producing departments:

$$\text{Allocation ratio} = \frac{\text{Producing department capacity}}{\text{Total capacity}}$$

3. *Allocation.* The fixed service costs are then allocated in proportion to each producing department's original service needs:

$$\text{Allocation} = \text{Allocation ratio} \times \text{Budgeted fixed service costs}$$

Let's assume that the three departments in our example originally decided that they would need an amount equal to the budgeted number given before:

	Budgeted Original Number of Copies	Percent of Copies	×	Fixed Cost	=	Department Share of Fixed Cost
Audit	94,500	35		$26,190		$ 9,167
Tax	67,500	25		26,190		6,548
MAS	108,000	40		26,190		10,476
Total	270,000	100				$26,191

The fixed costs allocated are then the relevant percentages for each department multiplied by the support department's fixed costs. Notice that in this example, the department shares of fixed cost total $26,191, not $26,190. The difference is due to rounding error.

Developing a Variable Rate The variable rate depends on the costs that change as the cost driver changes. In the photocopying department, the cost driver is the number of pages copied. As the number of pages increases, more paper and toner are used. Since these average $0.023 per page, the variable rate is $0.023. This variable rate is used in conjunction with the fixed amount allocated to determine total charges. In our example, the audit department would be allocated 35 percent of fixed cost plus $0.023 per-page copied. The tax department would be allocated 25 percent of fixed cost plus $0.023 per-page copied. MAS would be allocated 40 percent of fixed cost plus $0.023 per-page copied. Let's see how photocopying costs are allocated under the dual rate method.

	Number of Copies	Fixed Amount	Variable Amount	Total Charge
Audit	92,000	$ 9,167	$2,116	$11,283
Tax	65,000	6,548	1,495	8,043
MAS	115,000	10,476	2,645	13,121
Total	272,000	$26,191	$6,256	$32,447

Under the dual charging rates, the fixed photocopying rates are charged to the departments in accordance with their original capacity needs. Especially in a case like this one, in which fixed costs are such a high proportion of total costs, the additional effort needed to develop the dual rates may be worthwhile. Additionally, the dual rate method has the benefit of sending the correct signal regarding increased usage of the support department. Suppose that the tax department wants to have several research articles on changes in the tax law copied for clients. Should this be done in-house by the photocopying department or sent to a private photocopying firm that charges $0.06 per page? Under the single rate method, the in-house cost charged would be too high because it wrongly assumes that fixed cost will increase as pages copied increases. However, under the dual rate method, the additional cost would be only $0.023 per page, which correctly approximates the additional cost of the job.

Budgeted versus Actual Usage

The second factor to be considered in charging costs from a single support department to other departments is whether actual usage or budgeted usage should be the basis for allocating costs. In truth, this factor only has an impact on allocated costs when fixed costs are involved. As a result, we need to consider it in the case of a single charging rate (which combines fixed with variable costs to generate a rate) and of the fixed portion of the dual charging rate.

When we allocate support-department costs to the producing departments, should we allocate actual or budgeted costs? The answer is budgeted costs. There are two basic reasons for allocating support-department costs. One is to cost units produced. In this case, the budgeted support-department costs are allocated to producing departments as a preliminary step in forming the overhead rate. Recall that the overhead rate is calculated at the beginning of the period, when actual costs are not known. Thus, budgeted costs must be used. The second usage of allocated support-department costs is for performance evaluation. In this case, too, budgeted support-department costs are allocated to producing departments.

Managers of support and producing departments usually are held accountable for the performance of their units. Their ability to control costs is an important factor in their performance evaluation. This ability is usually measured by comparing actual costs with planned or budgeted costs. If actual costs exceed budgeted costs, the department may be operating inefficiently, with the difference between the two costs the measure of that inefficiency. Similarly, if actual costs are less than budgeted costs, the unit may be operating efficiently.

A general principle of performance evaluation is that managers should not be held responsible for costs or activities over which they have no control. Since managers of producing departments have significant input regarding the level of service consumed, they should be held responsible for their share of service costs. This statement, however, has an important qualification: A department's evaluation should not be affected by the degree of efficiency achieved by another department.

This qualifying statement has an important implication for the allocation of support-department costs. *Actual* costs of a support department should not be allocated to producing departments because they include efficiencies or inefficiencies achieved by the support department. Managers of producing departments have no control over the degree of efficiency achieved by a support-department manager. By allocating *budgeted* costs instead of actual costs, no inefficiencies or efficiencies are transferred from one department to another.

Whether budgeted usage or actual usage is used depends on the purpose of the allocation. For *product costing,* the allocation is done at the beginning of the year on the basis of budgeted usage so that a predetermined overhead rate can be computed. If the purpose is *performance evaluation,* however, the allocation is done at the end of the period and is based on actual usage. The use of cost information for performance evaluation is covered in more detail in Chapter 9, "Standard Costing."

Let's return to our photocopying example. Recall that annual budgeted fixed costs were $26,190 and the budgeted variable cost per page was $0.023. The three producing departments, audit, tax, and MAS, estimated usage at 94,500 copies, 67,500 copies and 108,000 copies, respectively. Given these data, the cost allocated to each department at the beginning of the year are shown in Exhibit 7-4. Note that the single rate method produces the same allocation as the dual rate method when budgeted figures are used. This is because budgeted fixed cost is just absorbed by the number of budgeted pages.

When the allocation is done for the purpose of budgeting the producing departments' costs, then of course the budgeted support-department costs are used. The photocopying costs allocated to each department would be added to other producing-department costs, including those directly traceable to each department plus other support-department allocations, to compute each department's anticipated spending. In a manufacturing plant, the allocation of budgeted support-department costs to the producing departments would precede the calculation of the predetermined overhead rate.

During the year, each producing department would also be responsible for actual charges incurred based on the actual number of pages copied. Going back to the actual

7-4

Exhibit
Use of Budgeted Data
for Product Costing:
Comparison of Single and
Dual Rate Methods

	Single Rate Method		
	Number of Copies ×	Total Rate =	Allocated Cost
Audit	94,500	$0.12	$11,340
Tax	67,500	0.12	8,100
MAS	108,000	0.12	12,960
Total			$32,400

	Dual Rate Method			
	Number of Copies ×	Variable Rate +	Fixed Allocation =	Allocated Cost
Audit	94,500	$0.023	$ 9,167	$11,340
Tax	67,500	0.023	6,548	8,100
MAS	108,000	0.023	10,476	12,960
Total				$32,400

usage assumed previously, a second allocation is now made to measure the actual performance of each department against its budget. The actual photocopying costs allocated to each department for performance evaluation purposes are shown in Exhibit 7-5.

Fixed versus Variable Bases: A Note of Caution

Using normal or practical capacity to allocate fixed service costs provides a fixed base. As long as the capacities of the producing departments remain at the level originally anticipated, there is no reason to change the allocation ratios. Thus, each year the audit department receives 35 percent of the budgeted fixed photocopying costs, the tax department 25 percent, and the MAS department 40 percent no matter what their actual usage is. If the capacities of the departments change, the ratios should be recalculated.

In practice, some companies choose to allocate fixed costs in proportion to actual usage or expected actual usage. Since usage may vary from year to year, allocation of fixed costs would then use a variable base. Variable bases, however, have a significant drawback: they allow the actions of one department to affect the amount of cost allocated to another department.

To see how this is so, let's return to Hamilton and Barry's photocopying department and assume that fixed costs are allocated on the basis of anticipated usage for the coming year. The audit and tax departments budget the same number of copies as before. However, the MAS department anticipates much less activity due to a regional recession, which will cut down the number of new clients served; the anticipated number of photocopies for this department falls to 68,000. The adjusted fixed-cost allocation ratios and allocated fixed cost based on the newly budgeted usage are as follows:

	Number of Copies	Percent	Allocated Fixed Cost
Audit	94,500	41.1	$10,764
Tax	67,500	29.3	7,674
MAS	68,000	29.6	7,752
Total	230,000	100.0	$26,190

7-5

Exhibit
Use of Actual Data for Performance Evaluation Purposes: Comparison of Single and Dual Rate Methods

Single Rate Method			
	Number of Copies	× Total Rate	= Allocated Cost
Audit	92,000	$0.12	$11,040
Tax	65,000	0.12	7,800
MAS	115,000	0.12	13,800
Total			$32,640

Dual Rate Method				
	Number of Copies	× Variable Rate	+ Fixed Allocation	= Allocated Cost
Audit	92,000	$0.023	$ 9,167	$11,283
Tax	65,000	0.023	6,548	8,043
MAS	115,000	0.023	10,476	13,121
Total				$32,447

Notice that both the audit and tax departments' allocation of fixed costs increased even though the fixed costs of the photocopying department remained unchanged. This increase is caused by a decrease in the MAS department's use of photocopying. In effect, the audit and tax departments are being penalized because of MAS's decision to reduce the number of pages copied. Imagine the feelings of the first two managers when they realize that their copying charges have increased due to the increase in allocated fixed costs! The penalty occurs because a variable base is used to allocate fixed service costs; it can be avoided by using a fixed base.

CHOOSING A SUPPORT DEPARTMENT COST ALLOCATION METHOD

Objective 4

Allocate support-center costs to producing departments using the direct, sequential, and reciprocal methods.

So far, we have considered cost allocation from a single support department to several producing departments. We used the direct method of support department cost allocation, in which support-department costs are allocated only to producing departments. This was appropriate in the earlier example because no other support departments existed, and there was no possibility of interaction among support departments. Many companies do have multiple support departments, and they frequently interact. For example, in a factory, personnel and cafeteria serve each other and other support departments as well as the producing departments.

Ignoring these interactions and allocating service costs directly to producing departments may produce unfair and inaccurate cost assignments. For example, power, although a support department, may use 30 percent of the services of the maintenance department. The maintenance costs caused by the power department belong to the power department. By not assigning these costs to the power department, its costs are understated. In effect, some of the costs caused by power are "hidden" in the maintenance department because maintenance costs would be lower if the power department did not exist. As a result, a producing department that is a heavy user of power and an average or below-average user of maintenance may then receive, under the direct method, a cost allocation that is understated.

In determining which support department cost allocation method to use, companies must determine the extent of support-department interaction. In addition, they must weigh the costs and benefits associated with three methods of allocating costs. In the next three sections, the direct, sequential, and reciprocal methods are described and illustrated.

Direct Method of Allocation

direct method

When companies allocate support-department costs only to the producing departments, they are using the direct method of allocation. The direct method is the simplest and most straightforward way to allocate support-department costs. Variable service costs are allocated directly to producing departments in proportion to each department's usage of the service. Fixed costs are also allocated directly to the producing department, but in proportion to the producing department's normal or practical capacity.

Exhibit 7-6 illustrates the lack of support-department reciprocity on cost allocation using the direct method. In Exhibit 7-6, we see that using the direct method, support-department cost is allocated to producing departments only. No cost from one support department is allocated to another support department. Thus, no support-department interaction is recognized.

To illustrate the direct method, consider the data in Exhibit 7-7 that show the budgeted activity and budgeted costs of two support departments and two producing departments. Assume that the causal factor for power costs is kilowatt-hours, and the causal factor for maintenance costs is maintenance hours. These causal factors are used as the bases for allocation. In the direct method, only the kilowatt-hours and the maintenance hours in the producing departments are used to compute the allocation ratios. The direct

7-6

Exhibit
·························Allocation of Support-Department Costs to Producing Departments: Direct Method

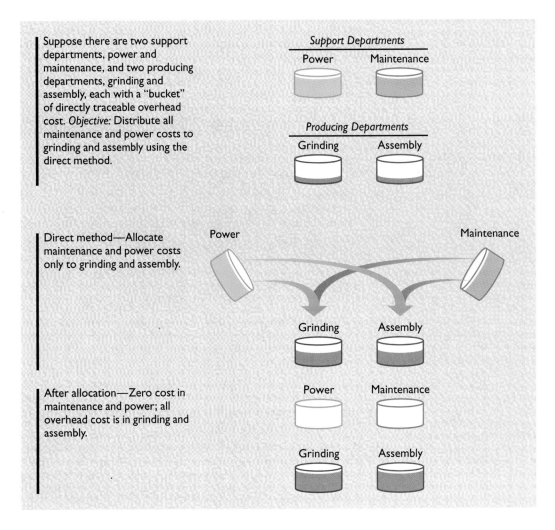

Suppose there are two support departments, power and maintenance, and two producing departments, grinding and assembly, each with a "bucket" of directly traceable overhead cost. *Objective:* Distribute all maintenance and power costs to grinding and assembly using the direct method.

Support Departments
Power   Maintenance

Producing Departments
Grinding   Assembly

Direct method—Allocate maintenance and power costs only to grinding and assembly.

Power   Maintenance

Grinding   Assembly

After allocation—Zero cost in maintenance and power; all overhead cost is in grinding and assembly.

Power   Maintenance

Grinding   Assembly

method allocation ratios and the support department cost allocations based on the data given in Exhibit 7-7 are shown in Exhibit 7-8. (To simplify the illustration, no distinction is made between fixed and variable costs.)

Sequential Method of Allocation

sequential (or step) method

The sequential (or step) method of allocation recognizes that interactions among the support departments occur. However, the sequential method does not fully recognize support-department interaction. Cost allocations are performed in step-down fashion,

7-7

Exhibit
·····················
Data for Illustrating
Allocation Methods

	Support Departments		Producing Departments	
	Power	Maintenance	Grinding	Assembly
Direct costs:*	$250,000	$160,000	$100,000	$60,000
Normal activity:				
Kilowatt-hours	—	200,000	600,000	200,000
Maintenance hours	1,000	—	4,500	4,500

*For a producing department, direct costs refer only to overhead costs that are directly traceable to the department.

7-8 ....

Exhibit
Direct Allocation
Illustrated

Supt. dept. interact
(note - no)

Step 1 Calculate allocation ratios		
	Grinding	Assembly
Power: $\dfrac{600,000}{(600,000 + 200,000)}$	0.75	—
$\dfrac{200,000}{(600,000 + 200,000)}$	—	0.25
Maintenance: $\dfrac{4,500}{(4,500 + 4,500)}$	0.50	—
$\dfrac{4,500}{(4,500 + 4,500)}$	—	0.50

Step 2 Allocate support-department costs using the allocation ratios				
	Support Departments		Producing Departments	
	Power	Maintenance	Grinding	Assembly
Direct costs	$ 250,000	$ 160,000	$100,000	$ 60,000
Power[a]	(250,000)	—	187,500	62,500
Maintenance[b]	—	(160,000)	80,000	80,000
	$ 0	$ 0	$367,500	$202,500

[a]Allocation of power based on allocation ratios from step 1: 0.75 × $250,000; 0.25 × $250,000
[b]Allocation of maintenance based on allocation ratios from step 1: 0.50 × $160,000; 0.50 × $160,000

following a predetermined ranking procedure. Usually, the sequence is defined by ranking the support departments in order of the amount of service rendered, from the greatest to the least. Degree of service is usually measured by the direct costs of each support department; the department with the highest cost is seen as rendering the greatest service.

Exhibit 7-9 illustrates the sequential method. First, the support departments are ranked, usually in accordance with direct costs; here power is first, then maintenance. Then, power costs are allocated to maintenance and the two producing departments. Then, the costs of maintenance are allocated only to producing departments.

The costs of the support department rendering the greatest service are allocated first. They are distributed to all support departments below it in the sequence and to all producing departments. Then the costs of the support department next in sequence are similarly allocated, and so on. In the sequential method, once a support department's costs are allocated, it never receives a subsequent allocation from another support department. In other words, costs of a support department are never allocated to support departments above it in the sequence. Also, note that the costs allocated from a support department are its direct costs *plus* any costs it receives in allocations from other support departments. The direct costs of a department, of course, are those that are directly traceable to the department.

To illustrate the sequential method, consider the data provided in Exhibit 7-7. Using cost as a measure of service, the support department rendering more service is power. Thus, its costs will be allocated first, followed by those for maintenance.

The allocations obtained with the sequential method are shown in Exhibit 7-10 (page 259). The first step is to compute the allocation ratios. Note that the allocation ratios for the maintenance department ignore the usage by the power department since its costs cannot be allocated to a support department above it in the allocation sequence. The second step is to allocate the support-department costs using the allocation ratios computed in the first step. Notice that $50,000 of the power department's costs are

Suppose there are two support
departments, power and
maintenance, and two producing
departments, grinding and
assembly, each with a "bucket"
of directly traceable overhead
cost.
Objective: Distribute all
maintenance and power costs to
grinding and assembly using the
sequential method.

Support Departments

Power   Maintenance

Producing Departments

Grinding   Assembly

Step 1: Rank service
departments—#1 power, #2
maintenance.

Step 2: Distribute power to
maintenance, grinding, and
assembly.

Power

Maintenance   Grinding   Assembly

Then, distribute maintenance to
grinding and assembly.

Maintenance

Grinding   Assembly

After allocation—Zero cost in
maintenance and power; all
overhead cost is in grinding and
assembly.

Power   Maintenance

Grinding   Assembly

allocated to the maintenance department. This reflects the fact that the maintenance department uses 20 percent of the power department's output. As a result, the cost of operating the maintenance department increases from $160,000 to $210,000. Also notice that when the costs of the maintenance department are allocated, no costs are allocated back to the power department, even though it uses 1,000 hours of the output of the maintenance department.

The sequential method is more accurate than the direct method because it recognizes some interactions among the support departments. It does not recognize all interactions, however; no maintenance costs were assigned to the power department even though it used 10 percent of the maintenance department's output. The reciprocal method corrects this deficiency.

Step 1 Calculate allocation ratios			
	Maintenance	Grinding	Assembly
Power: $\dfrac{200{,}000}{(200{,}000 + 600{,}000 + 200{,}000)}$	0.20	—	—
$\dfrac{600{,}000}{(200{,}000 + 600{,}000 + 200{,}000)}$	—	0.60	—
$\dfrac{200{,}000}{(200{,}000 + 600{,}000 + 200{,}000)}$	—	—	0.20
Maintenance: $\dfrac{4{,}500}{(4{,}500 + 4{,}500)}$	—	0.50	—
$\dfrac{4{,}500}{(4{,}500 + 4{,}500)}$	—	—	0.50

Step 2 Allocate support-department costs using the allocation ratios			
	Support Departments		Producing Departments	
	Power	Maintenance	Grinding	Assembly
Direct costs	$ 250,000	$ 160,000	$100,000	$ 60,000
Power[a]	(250,000)	50,000	150,000	50,000
Maintenance[b]	—	(210,000)	105,000	105,000
	$ 0	$ 0	$355,000	$215,000

[a]Allocation of power based on allocation ratios from step 1: 0.20 × $250,000; 0.60 × $250,000; 0.20 × $250,000

[b]Allocation of maintenance costs based on allocation ratios from step 1: 0.50 × $210,000; 0.50 × $210,000

Reciprocal Method of Allocation

reciprocal method

The reciprocal method of allocation recognizes all interactions among support departments. Under the reciprocal method, one support department's use by another figures in determining the total cost of each support department, where the total cost reflects interactions among the support departments. Then, the new total of support-department costs is allocated to the producing departments. This method fully accounts for support-department interaction.

Total Cost of Support Departments To determine the total cost of a support department, so that it reflects interactions with other support departments, a system of simultaneous linear equations must be solved. Each equation, which is a cost equation for a support department, is defined as the sum of the department's direct costs plus the proportion of service received from other support departments:

$$\text{Total cost} = \text{Direct costs} + \text{Allocated costs}$$

The method is best described using an example, employing the same data used to illustrate the direct and sequential methods (see Exhibit 7-11). The allocation ratios needed for the simultaneous equations are interpreted as follows: maintenance receives 20 percent of power's output; power receives 10 percent of maintenance's output. Now let P equal the total cost of the power department and M equal the total cost of the maintenance department. As previously indicated, the total cost of a support department is the sum of its direct costs plus the proportion of service received from other support

7-11

Exhibit
Data for Illustrating
Reciprocal Method

	Support Departments		Producing Departments	
	Power	Maintenance	Grinding	Assembly
Direct costs:*				
Fixed	$200,000	$100,000	$ 80,000	$50,000
Variable	50,000	60,000	20,000	10,000
Total	$250,000	$160,000	$100,000	$60,000
Normal activity:				
Kilowatt-hours	—	200,000	600,000	200,000
Maintenance hours	1,000	—	4,500	4,500

	Proportion of Output Used by Department			
	Power	Maintenance	Grinding	Assembly
Allocation ratios:				
Power	—	0.20	0.60	0.20
Maintenance	0.10	—	0.45	0.45

*For a producing department, direct costs are defined as overhead costs that are directly traceable to the department.

departments. Using the data and allocation ratios from Exhibit 7-11, the cost equation for each support department can be expressed as follows:

$$P = \text{Direct costs} + \text{Share of maintenance's cost} \qquad (7.1)$$
$$= \$250,000 + 0.10M \text{ (power's cost equation)}$$

$$M = \text{Direct costs} + \text{Share of power's costs} \qquad (7.2)$$
$$= \$160,000 + 0.20P \text{ (maintenance's cost equation)}$$

The direct-cost components of each equation are taken from Exhibit 7-11, as are the allocation ratios.

The power cost equation (7.1) and the maintenance cost equation (7.2) can be solved simultaneously to yield the total cost for each support department. Substituting equation 7.1 into equation 7.2 gives the following:

$$M = \$160,000 + 0.20(\$250,000 + 0.10M)$$
$$M = \$160,000 + \$50,000 + 0.02M$$
$$0.98M = \$210,000$$
$$M = \$214,286$$

Substituting this value for M into equation 7.1 yields the total cost for power:

$$P = \$250,000 + 0.10(\$214,286)$$
$$= \$250,000 + \$21,429$$
$$= \$271,429$$

After the equations are solved, the total costs of each support department are known. These total costs, unlike the direct or sequential methods, reflect all interactions between the two support departments.

Allocation to Producing Departments Once the total costs of each support department are known, the allocations to the producing departments can be made. These allocations, based on the proportion of output used by each producing department, are shown in Exhibit 7-12. Notice that the total costs allocated to the producing departments (from power and maintenance) equal $410,000, the total direct costs of the two

7-12·····························Allocate support-department costs using the allocation ratios (Exhibit 7-11) and the total
support-department costs from reciprocal method equations

Exhibit
Reciprocal Allocation
Illustrated

	Support Departments		**Producing Departments**	
	Power	**Maintenance**	**Grinding**	**Assembly**
Direct costs	$ 250,000	$ 160,000	$100,000	$ 60,000
Power[a]	(271,429)	54,286	162,857	54,286
Maintenance[b]	21,429	(214,286)	96,429	96,429
Total	$ 0	$ 0	$359,286	$210,715

[a]Power: 0.20 × $271,429; 0.60 × $271,429; 0.20 × $271,429
[b]Maintenance: 0.10 × $214,286; 0.45 × $214,286; 0.45 × $214,286

support departments ($250,000 + $160,000). (Actually, the total allocated costs equal
$410,001, but the difference is due to a rounding error.)

Comparison of the Three Methods

Exhibit 7-13 gives the cost allocations from the power and maintenance departments to
the grinding and assembly departments using the three support department cost allocation methods. How different are the results; does it really matter which method is used?
Depending on the degree of interaction among the support departments, the three allocation methods can give radically different results. In this particular example, the direct
method allocated $12,500 more to the grinding department (and $12,500 less to the
assembly department). Surely, the manager of the assembly department would prefer
the direct method and the manager of the grinding department would prefer the sequential method. Because allocation methods do affect the cost responsibilities of managers,
it is important for the accountant to understand the consequences of the different methods and to have good reasons for the eventual choice.

It is important to keep a cost-benefit perspective in choosing an allocation method.
The accountant must weigh the advantages of better allocation against the increased
cost using a more theoretically preferred method, such as the reciprocal method. For
example, about twenty years ago, the controller for the IBM Poughkeepsie plant decided
that the reciprocal method of cost allocation would do a better job of allocating support
department costs. He identified more than seven hundred support departments and
solved the system of equations using a computer. Computationally, he had no problems.
However, the producing-department managers did not understand the reciprocal
method. They were sure that extra cost was being allocated to their departments; they
just were not sure how. After months of meetings with the line managers, the controller
threw in the towel and returned to the sequential method—which everyone did understand.

7-13·····························

Exhibit
Comparison of Support
Department Cost
Allocations Using the
Direct, Sequential, and
Reciprocal Methods

	Direct Method		**Sequential Method**		**Reciprocal Method**	
	Grinding	**Assembly**	**Grinding**	**Assembly**	**Grinding**	**Assembly**
Direct costs	$100,000	$ 60,000	$100,000	$ 60,000	$100,000	$ 60,000
Allocated from power	187,500	62,500	150,000	50,000	162,857	54,286
Allocated from maintenance	80,000	80,000	105,000	105,000	96,429	96,429
Total cost	$367,500	$202,500	$355,000	$215,000	$359,286	$210,715

Another factor in allocating support-department cost is the rapid change in technology. Many firms currently find that support department cost allocation is useful for them. However, the move toward activity-based costing and just-in-time manufacturing can virtually eliminate the need for support-department cost allocation. In the case of the JIT factory with manufacturing cells, much of the service (for example, maintenance, material handling, and setups) is performed by cell workers. Allocation is not necessary.

DEPARTMENTAL OVERHEAD RATES AND PRODUCT COSTING

Objective 5

Calculate departmental overhead rates.

Upon allocating all support costs to producing departments, an overhead rate can be computed for each department. This rate is computed by adding the allocated support costs to the overhead costs that are directly traceable to the producing department and dividing this total by some measure of activity, such as direct labor hours or machine hours.

For example, from Exhibit 7-10, the total overhead costs for the grinding department after allocation of support costs are $355,000. Assume that machine hours are the base for assigning overhead costs to products passing through the grinding department and that the normal level of activity is 71,000 machine hours. The overhead rate for the grinding department is computed as follows:

$$\text{Overhead rate} = \frac{\$355,000}{71,000 \text{ machine hours}}$$
$$= \$5 \text{ per machine hour}$$

Similarly, assume that the assembly department uses direct labor hours to assign its overhead. With a normal level of activity of 107,500 direct labor hours, the overhead rate for the assembly department is as follows:

$$\text{Overhead rate} = \frac{\$215,000}{107,500 \text{ direct labor hours}}$$
$$= \$2 \text{ per direct labor hour}$$

Using these rates, the product's unit cost can be determined. To illustrate, suppose a product requires two machine hours of grinding per unit produced and one hour of assembly. The overhead cost assigned to one unit of this product would be $12 [(2 × $5) + (1 × $2)]. If the same product uses $15 of materials and $6 of labor (totaled from grinding and assembly), then its unit cost is $33 ($12 + $15 + $6).

One might wonder, however, just how accurate this $33 cost is. Is this really what it costs to produce the product in question? Since materials and labor are directly traceable to products, the accuracy of product costs depends largely on the accuracy of the assignment of overhead costs. This, in turn, depends on the degree of correlation between the factors used to allocate service costs to departments and the factors used to allocate the department's overhead costs to the products. For example, if power costs are highly correlated with kilowatt-hours and machine hours are highly correlated with a product's consumption of the grinding department's overhead costs, then we can have some confidence that the $5 overhead rate accurately assigns costs to individual products. However, if the allocation of service costs to the grinding department or the use of machine hours is faulty—or both—then product costs will be distorted. The same reasoning can be applied to the assembly department. To ensure accurate product costs, great care should be used in identifying and using causal factors for both stages of overhead assignment.

S UMMARY OF LEARNING OBJECTIVES

I. Describe the difference between support departments and producing departments.

Producing departments create the products or services that the firm is in business to manufacture and sell. Support departments provide support for the producing departments but do not themselves create a salable product. Because support departments exist to support a variety of producing departments, the costs of the support departments are common to all producing departments.

2. Explain five reasons why support-department costs may be assigned to producing departments.

These reasons include inventory valuation, product-line profitability, pricing, and planning and control. Allocation can also be used to encourage favorable managerial behavior.

3. Calculate charging rates and distinguish between single and dual charging rates.

When the costs of one support department are allocated to other departments, a charging rate must be developed. A single rate combines variable and fixed costs of the support department to generate a charging rate. A dual rate separates the fixed and variable costs. Fixed support-department costs are allocated on the basis of original capacity and a variable rate is developed on the basis of budgeted usage.

Budgeted, not actual costs, should be allocated so that the efficiencies or inefficiencies of the support departments themselves are not passed on to the producing departments. Because the causal factors can differ for fixed and variable costs, these types of cost should be allocated separately.

4. Allocate support-center costs to producing departments using the direct, sequential, and reciprocal methods.

Three methods can be used to allocate support costs to producing departments: the direct method, the sequential method, and the reciprocal method. They differ in the degree of support-department interaction considered. By considering support-department interactions, more accurate product costing is achieved. The result can be improved planning, control, and decision making. Two methods of allocation recognize interactions among support departments: the *sequential (or step) method* and the *reciprocal method*. These methods allocate service costs among some (or all) interacting support departments before allocating costs to the producing departments.

5. Calculate departmental overhead rates.

Departmental overhead rates are calculated by adding direct departmental overhead costs to those costs allocated from the support departments and dividing the sum by the budgeted departmental base.

K EY TERMS

R EVIEW PROBLEM

Antioch Manufacturing produces machine parts on a job-order basis. Most business is obtained through bidding. Most firms competing with Antioch bid full cost plus a 20 percent markup. Recently, with the expectation of gaining more sales, Antioch reduced its markup from 25 percent to 20 percent. The company operates two support departments and two producing departments. The budgeted costs and the normal activity levels for each department follow.

	Support Departments		Producing Departments	
	A	**B**	**C**	**D**
Overhead costs	$100,000	$200,000	$100,000	$50,000
Number of employees	8	7	30	30
Maintenance hours	2,000	200	6,400	1,600
Machine hours	—	—	10,000	1,000
Labor hours	—	—	1,000	10,000

The direct costs of department A are allocated on the basis of employees, those of department B on the basis of maintenance hours. Departmental overhead rates are used to assign costs to products. Department C uses machine hours, and department D uses labor hours.

The firm is preparing to bid on a job (Job K) that requires three machine hours per unit produced in department C and no time in department D. The expected prime costs (direct materials and direct labor) per unit are $67.

REQUIRED:
1. Allocate the support costs to the producing departments using the direct method.
2. What will the bid be for Job K if the direct method of allocation is used?
3. Allocate the support costs to the producing departments using the sequential method.
4. What will the bid be for Job K if the sequential method is used?
5. Allocate the support costs to the producing departments using the reciprocal method.
6. What will the bid be for Job K if the reciprocal method is used?

Solution

(handwritten: Ratio A = 36 ea. dept / 60 , 50%)

(handwritten: Ratio B: 6400/8,000 + 1,600/8,000 ; 80% 20%)

1.

	Support Departments		Producing Departments	
	A	**B**	**C**	**D**
Direct costs	$ 100,000	$ 200,000	$100,000	$ 50,000
Department A	(100,000)	—	50,000	50,000
Department B	—	(200,000)	160,000	40,000
Total	$ 0	$ 0	$310,000	$140,000

2. Department C: Overhead rate = $\frac{\$310,000}{10,000}$ = \$31 per machine hour. Product cost and bid price:

(handwritten: Dept. OH (Direct) based on machine hrs.)

Prime costs *(handwritten: expected mach. hrs. per unit)*	$ 67
Overhead (3 × $31)	93
Total unit cost	$160
Bid price ($160 × 1.2)	$192

3.

(handwritten margin: Step 1 allocate B; 3,000/10,000 + 64000/10,000 + 1,600/10,000 × 200,000; 20% 64% 16%; Step 2 alloc. A; 30/60 + 30/60)

	Support Departments		Producing Departments	
	A *(handwritten: #2 based on # emp)*	**B** *(handwritten: #1 (largest!) based on mach hrs)*	**C**	**D**
Direct costs	$ 100,000	$ 200,000	$100,000	$ 50,000
Department B	40,000	(200,000)	128,000	32,000
Department A	(140,000)	—	70,000	70,000
Total	$ 0	$ 0	$298,000	$152,000

4. Department C: Overhead rate = $\frac{\$298,000}{10,000}$ = \$29.80 per machine hour. Product cost and bid price:

(handwritten: Total OH / machine hrs.)

Prime costs	$ 67.00
Overhead (3 × $29.80)	89.40
Total unit cost	$156.40
Bid price ($156.40 × 1.2)	$187.68

5. Allocation ratios:

(handwritten: Dept. A: 7/67 + 30/67 + 30/67 ; Dept B: 2000/10,000 + 6400/10,000 + 1600/10,000)

	Proportion of Output Used by Department			
	A	**B**	**C**	**D**
Department A	—	0.1045	0.4478	0.4478
Department B	0.2000	—	0.6400	0.1600

(handwritten: Formula for Allocation)

$$A = \$100,000 + .2000B$$
$$B = \$200,000 + .1045A$$

$$A = \$100,000 + .2(\$200,000 + .1045A)$$
$$= \$100,000 + \$40,000 + .0209A$$
$$.9791A = \$140,000$$
$$A = \$142,988$$

$$B = \$200,000 + .1045(\$142,988)$$
$$= \$214,942$$

	Support Departments		Producing Departments	
	A	**B**	**C**	**D**
Direct costs	$ 100,000	$ 200,000	$100,000	$ 50,000
Department B	42,988	(214,942)	137,563	34,391
Department A	(142,988)*	14,942	64,030	64,030
Total	$ 0	$ 0	$301,593	$148,421

Note: *The $14 difference is the result of rounding error.

6. Department C: Overhead rate $= \frac{\$301,593}{10,000} = \$30.16$ per machine hour. Product cost and bid price:

Prime costs	$ 67.00
Overhead (3 × $30.16)	90.48
Total unit cost	$157.48
Bid price ($157.48 × 1.2)	$188.98

QUESTIONS FOR WRITING AND DISCUSSION

1. Describe the two-stage allocation process for assigning service costs to products in a traditional manufacturing environment.
2. Explain how allocating service costs can be helpful in pricing decisions.
3. Why must service costs be assigned to products for purposes of inventory valuation?
4. Explain how allocation of service costs is useful for planning and control.
5. Assume that a company has decided not to allocate any service costs to producing departments. Describe the likely behavior of the managers of the producing departments. Would this be good or bad? Explain why allocation would correct this type of behavior.
6. Explain how allocating service costs will encourage support departments to operate more efficiently.
7. Why is it important to identify and use causal factors to allocate service costs?
8. Identify some possible causal factors for the following support departments:
    a. Cafeteria
    b. Custodial services
    c. Laundry
    d. Receiving, shipping, and stores
    e. Maintenance
    f. Personnel
    g. Accounting
9. Explain why it is better to allocate budgeted service costs rather than actual service costs.
10. Why is it desirable to allocate variable costs and fixed costs separately?
11. Explain why either normal or peak capacity of the producing (or user) departments should be used to allocate the fixed costs of support departments.
12. Explain why variable bases should not be used to allocate fixed costs.
13. Why is the dual-rate charging method better than the single rate method? In what circumstance would it not matter whether dual or single rates were used?
14. Explain the difference between the direct method and the sequential method.
15. The reciprocal method of allocation is more accurate than either the direct or sequential methods. Do you agree? Explain.

ARM-UP EXERCISES

This section provides short warm-up exercises based on the examples in the chapter. Each warm-up exercise gives the page number on which the text example can be found. You may want to refer to the text example to see how the exercise can be set up and solved.

W7-1
Single Charging Rate
LO 3
p. 250

Hathaway Electronics recently established a computer support department to handle all computer-related purchasing, installation, troubleshooting, and so on. The costs of the computer support department include fixed costs of $44,100 per year (salaries and computers for the department itself) and variable costs of $3.45 per hour (supplies, small tools, use of software pay-per-use services). Estimated usage in hours by the three producing departments is as follows:

Insertion and kitting	1,750
Assembly	700
Testing	4,550
Total	7,000

By the end of the first year, the actual usage of the computer support department was insertion and kitting, 1,800 hours; assembly, 400 hours; and testing, 4,600 hours.

REQUIRED:
1. Calculate a single charging rate per hour of support-department time.
2. At the end of the year, what were the computer support-department charges for each of the three producing departments? What was the total amount charged by the computer support department to the producing departments?
3. Based on the fixed and variable amounts budgeted, how much should it have cost the computer support department to provide 6,800 actual hours of service? Is this amount different from the amount calculated in requirement 2? Why?

W7-2
Dual Charging Rates
LO 3
p. 251

Now let's assume that the three producing departments from W7-1 originally decided that they would need an amount equal to the budgeted number given in that exercise.

REQUIRED:
1. Calculate the percentage of the total hours of computing service demanded for each of the three producing departments. Calculate the amount of budgeted fixed cost to be allocated to each of the producing departments based on those percentages.
2. Using the fixed amounts calculated in requirement 1, and the variable rate given, what were the computer support-department charges for each of the three producing departments for the year? What was the total amount charged by the computer support department to the producing departments?
3. Based on the fixed and variable amounts budgeted, how much should it have cost the computer support department to provide 6,800 actual hours of service? Is this amount different from the amount calculated in requirement 2? Why or why not?

W7-3
Changes in the Use of the Support Department and the Impact on Fixed-Cost Allocation
LO 3
p. 254

Refer to W7-1. Suppose that the fixed costs of the computer support department are allocated to each producing department based on their anticipated usage each year. Further, suppose that for the second year of operation, the three departments budgeted the following amounts of activity:

Insertion and kitting	1,000
Assembly	700
Testing	4,550
Total	6,250

REQUIRED: How much fixed cost would be allocated to each department based on their second-year anticipated usage?

W7-4
Allocating Support-Department Cost

Quillen Company manufactures a product in a factory that has two producing departments, fabrication and assembly, and two support departments, maintenance and human resources. The

Using the Direct Method
LO 4
p. 257

activity driver for maintenance is machine hours and the activity driver for human resources is number of employees. The following data pertain to Quillen Company:

	Support Departments		Producing Departments	
	Human Resources	**Maintenance**	**Fabrication**	**Assembly**
Direct costs	$200,000	$130,000	$176,000	$94,000
Normal activity:				
Number of employees	—	10	21	49
Maintenance hours	600	—	8,000	2,000

REQUIRED:

1. Calculate the allocation ratios to be used under the direct method for the human resources and maintenance departments. (Each support department will have two allocation ratios—one for fabrication and the other for assembly.)
2. Allocate the support-department costs to the producing departments using the direct method.

W7-5
Allocating Support-Department Cost Using the Sequential Method
LO 4
p. 259

Refer to W7-4. Under the sequential method, the human resource department costs are allocated first.

REQUIRED:

1. Calculate the allocation ratios to be used under the sequential method for the human resources and maintenance departments. Carry your calculations out to four digits. (The human resource department will have three allocation ratios—one each for maintenance, fabrication, and assembly. The maintenance department will have two allocation ratios—one for each producing department.)
2. Allocate the support-department costs to the producing departments using the sequential method.

W7-6
Allocating Support-Department Cost Using the Reciprocal Method
LO 4
pp. 260–261

Refer to W7-4.

REQUIRED:

1. Calculate the allocation ratios to be used under the reciprocal method for the human resources and maintenance departments. Carry your calculations out to four digits. (The human resource department will have three allocation ratios—one each for maintenance, fabrication, and assembly. The maintenance department will have three allocation ratios—one each for human resources, fabrication, and assembly.)
2. Develop a cost equation for each support department and solve for the total support department costs.
3. Based on the calculations in requirement 1, allocate the support-department costs to the producing departments using the reciprocal method.

W7-7
Computing Departmental Overhead Rates and Product Cost
LO 5
p. 262

Yolanda Bakery, Inc. has two producing departments, mixing and baking. At the beginning of the year, the following budgeted information was provided:

	Mixing	Baking
Machine hours	2,000	5,000
Direct labor hours	10,000	500
Total overhead	$250,000	$200,000

Each batch of 1,000 loaves of bread requires two hours in the mixing department and one hour in the baking department. Overhead in the mixing department is based on direct labor hours; overhead in the baking department is based on the number of machine hours. Direct materials cost $170 per batch of 1,000 loaves, and direct labor costs $60 per batch of 1,000 loaves.

REQUIRED:

1. Calculate overhead rates for each producing department.
2. What is the unit cost of one loaf of bread?

EXERCISES

E7-1

Classifying Departments as Producing or Support

LO 1

Classify each of the following departments in a factory as a producing department or a service department:

a. Power
b. Maintenance
c. Finishing
d. Landscaping
e. Payroll
f. Quality control of suppliers
g. Cooking
h. Blending
i. General factory
j. Timekeeping
k. Packaging
l. Data processing
m. Engineering
n. Drilling
o. Cutting

E7-2

Identifying Causal Factors

LO 1

For the following support departments, identify one or more causal factors that might be useful for support-department cost allocation purposes.

a. Supervision
b. Data processing
c. Quality control
d. Purchasing
e. Receiving
f. Shipping
g. Vending (stocking snack machines throughout the plant)
h. Grounds
i. Building depreciation
j. Power and light
k. Employee benefits
l. Housekeeping
m. Equipment repair
n. Heating and cooling

E7-3

Actual versus Budgeted Costs

LO 3, LO 4

McGarvey Tool and Die, Inc. evaluates managers of producing departments on their ability to control costs. In addition to the costs directly traceable to their departments, each production manager is held responsible for a share of the costs of a support department, the maintenance department. The total costs of the maintenance department are allocated on the basis of actual maintenance hours used. The total costs of maintenance and the actual hours used by each producing department follow.

	1997	1998
Maintenance hours used:		
Department A	6,300	8,000
Department B	11,700	8,000
Total hours	18,000	16,000
Actual maintenance cost	$160,000	$155,000
Budgeted maintenance cost	$156,000*	$142,000*

*$7 per maintenance hour plus $30,000

REQUIRED:
1. Allocate the maintenance cost to each producing department for 1997 and 1998 using the direct method with actual maintenance hours and actual maintenance costs.
2. Discuss the following statement: "The costs of maintenance increased by more than 38 percent for department A and decreased by more than 25 percent for department B. Thus, the manager of department B is controlling maintenance costs better than the manager of department A."
3. Can you think of a way to allocate maintenance costs so that a more reasonable and fairer assessment of cost control can be made? Explain.

E7-4
Fixed- and Variable-Cost Allocation
LO 3, LO 4

Refer to the data in E7-3. When the capacity of the maintenance department was originally established, the normal usage expected for each department was 8,000 maintenance hours. This usage is also the amount of activity planned for the two departments in 1997 and 1998.

REQUIRED:
1. Allocate the costs of the maintenance department using the direct method and assuming that the purpose is product costing.
2. Allocate the costs of the maintenance department using the direct method and assuming that the purpose is to evaluate performance.

E7-5
Direct Method and Overhead Rates
LO 4, LO 5

Gordon Company manufactures a product in two producing departments: P1 and P2. Three support departments support the production departments: SA, SB, and SC. Budgeted data on the five departments follow:

	Support Departments			Producing Departments	
	SA	**SB**	**SC**	**P1**	**P2**
Overhead	$130,000	$240,000	$120,000	$60,000	$116,000
Kilowatt-hours	—	13,000	25,000	30,000	70,000
Square feet	2,000	—	6,000	24,000	8,000
Machine hours	—	—	—	4,000	6,000

SA is allocated on the basis of kilowatt-hours, SB is allocated on the basis of square footage, and SC is allocated on the basis of machine hours. The company does not break overhead into fixed and variable components.

REQUIRED:
1. Allocate the overhead costs to the producing departments using the direct method.
2. Using machine hours, compute departmental overhead rates.

E7-6
Sequential Method
LO 4, LO 5

Refer to the data in E7-5. The company has decided to use the sequential method of allocation instead of the direct method.

REQUIRED:
1. Allocate the overhead costs to the producing departments using the sequential method.
2. Using machine hours, compute departmental overhead rates.

E7-7
Reciprocal Method
LO 4, LO 5

Mandelbrot Company produces fractals in two producing departments (generating and coloring) and two support departments (human resources and power). The following budgeted data pertain to these four departments:

	Support Departments		Producing Departments	
	Human Resources	**Power**	**Generating**	**Coloring**
Overhead	$144,000	$130,000	$50,000	$80,000
Payroll	—	$80,000	$160,000	$160,000
Kilowatt-hour	50,000	—	200,000	150,000
Direct labor hours	—	—	20,000	30,000

Costs of the human resources department are allocated on the basis of payroll and costs of the power department are allocated on the basis of kilowatt-hours.

REQUIRED:

1. Allocate the overhead costs of the support departments to the producing departments using the reciprocal method.
2. Using direct labor hours, compute departmental overhead rates (to the nearest penny).

E7-8
Direct Method
LO 4, LO 5

Refer to the data in E7-7. The company has decided to simplify its method of allocating service costs by switching to the direct method.

REQUIRED:

1. Allocate the costs of the support departments to the producing departments using the direct method.
2. Using direct labor hours, compute departmental overhead rates (to the nearest penny). Which rate do you consider more accurate—the one using the reciprocal method or the one using the direct method? Explain.

E7-9
Sequential Method
LO 4, LO 5

Refer to the data in E7-7.

REQUIRED:

1. Allocate the costs of the support departments using the sequential method.
2. Using direct labor hours, compute departmental overhead rates (to the nearest penny). Explain why these rates are generally more accurate than those computed using the direct method.

E7-10
Allocation: Fixed and Variable Costs
LO 3

Toren Computer Services, Inc. has two Nebraska offices, one in Omaha and the other in Lincoln. Jules Toren, the owner of the company, set up a business center in Omaha to handle all billing and accounting. The business center has budgeted fixed costs of $100,000 per year and a variable rate of $1.85 per invoice. After an analysis of expected needs, normal usage was established in the amounts of 10,000 invoices for the Omaha office and 30,000 invoices for the Lincoln office. This corresponds to expected usage for the coming year.

REQUIRED:

1. Determine the amount of business office costs that should be assigned to each office.
2. Since the offices produce services, not tangible products, what purpose is served by allocating the budgeted costs? Should each office compute a predetermined overhead rate? If so, how would you use this rate?

E7-11
Allocation: Budgeted Fixed and Variable Costs
LO 3

Refer to E7-10. Assume that during the year, the business center incurred actual fixed costs of $103,500 and actual variable costs of $79,765; it processed 43,000 invoices, 10,000 for Omaha and 33,000 for Lincoln.

REQUIRED:

1. Determine the amount of the business center's costs that should be allocated to each office. Explain the purposes of this allocation.
2. Did the costs allocated differ from the costs incurred by the business center? If so, explain why.

E7-12
Fixed-Cost Allocation; Variable Base
LO 3

Restum Hotels are located throughout the Southwest. The central office's fixed administrative expenses are allocated to each hotel in proportion to the unit's revenues. In 1997, the total administrative expenses were $3.5 million. In 1998, this total increased to $4 million. The hotel chain had $100 million in revenues in 1997 and 1998. The hotel with the greatest proportion of revenues was located in Phoenix, Arizona. This hotel's revenues were $10 million in 1997 and $15 million in 1998.

REQUIRED:

1. Compute the amount of fixed administrative expenses allocated to the Phoenix hotel in 1997.
2. Compute the amount of fixed administrative expenses allocated to the Phoenix hotel in 1998.
3. Compare the 1997 and 1998 allocations for the Phoenix hotel. Explain why the allocation increased.
4. Assume that you are the manager of the Phoenix hotel and that your annual bonus is a function of net income, the computation of which includes the allocated fixed administrative expenses.

How would you react to Restum's allocation method? Can you recommend a better method of allocation?

E7-13
Reciprocal Method
LO 4

Trinity Medical Clinic has two support departments and two revenue-producing departments. The controller for the clinic has decided to use the reciprocal method to allocate the costs of the support departments (A and B) to the producing departments (C and D). She has prepared the following cost equations for the two support departments. *A* equals the total cost for the first support department, and *B* equals the total cost for the second support department:

$$A = \$35,000 + 0.30B$$
$$B = \$40,000 + 0.20A$$

Before the controller was able to complete the allocation, she had to leave to take care of an emergency. In addition to these equations, she left a hastily scribbled note indicating that department C uses 20 percent of A's output and 40 percent of B's output.

REQUIRED: Allocate the costs of the two support departments to each of the two producing departments using the reciprocal method.

E7-14
Direct Method;
Overhead Rates
LO4, LO 5

Carroll Publishing Company prints religious music. There are two producing departments (printing and binding), and two support departments (cafeteria and general factory). Budgeted data for the four departments are as follows:

	Producing Departments		Support Departments	
	Printing	Binding	Cafeteria	General Factory
Overhead before allocation	$40,000	$60,000	$20,000	$100,000
Employees	10	40	—	10
Square feet	1,500	4,500	2,000	—
DLH	20,000	80,000	10,000	32,000

Cafeteria costs are allocated on the basis of number of employees; general factory costs are allocated on the basis of square feet.

REQUIRED:
1. Allocate overhead costs to producing departments using the direct method.
2. Using direct labor hours, compute departmental overhead rates.

E7-15
Sequential Method;
Overhead Rates
LO 4, LO 5

Refer to the data in E7-14. Assume Carroll Publishing Company decides to use the sequential method.

REQUIRED:
1. Allocate overhead costs to producing departments using the sequential method.
2. Using direct labor hours, compute departmental overhead rates.

E7-16
Reciprocal Method;
Overhead Rates
LO 4, LO 5

Refer to the data in E7-14. Assume Carroll Publishing Company decides to use the reciprocal method.

REQUIRED:
1. Allocate overhead costs to producing departments using the reciprocal method.
2. Using direct labor hours, compute departmental overhead rates.
3. Which of the three methods do you think is best? Why?

E7-17
Allocation: Fixed and
Variable Costs
LO 3

Nielson Company is a medium-sized advertising firm based in Chicago. Nielson has three departments that specialize in advertising and public relations services for different markets: tangible goods, public relations, and nonprofit organizations. Previously, Nielson had subcontracted out necessary printing and graphics work. However, recent technological advances in desktop publishing led to the formation of a new in-house graphics department that could produce brochures, booklets, posters, and so on. The tangible goods and public relations departments immediately began to use the new graphics services. However, Karel James, head of nonprofit organizations, was reluctant to switch her department from its traditional outside supplier. Top management strongly supported the new support department, and had encouraged all departments "to get on board" with graphics. Paul Murphy, the head of graphics, assured Karel James that graphics could serve her departmental needs by spending an additional $2,000 above total 1997 costs. So during 1998, Karel switched her department's graphics work to the in-house department.

Data for the graphics department are as follows:

	1997	1998
Actual costs	$22,000	$24,000
DLH used by:		
Tangible goods	2,000	2,000
Public relations	2,000	2,000
Nonprofit organizations	—	1,000

Actual costs equaled budgeted costs in both 1997 and 1998. Graphics services are charged to user departments on the basis of actual cost per hour of graphics time used.

REQUIRED:
1. What was the graphics rate per hour charged in 1997? in 1998?
2. How much was the nonprofit organizations department charged for graphics services in 1998? How do you think Karel James reacted to the charges?
3. How can you reconcile the difference between the rate charged Karel James during 1998 and the $2,000 incremental cost cited by Paul Murphy?

PROBLEMS

P7-I

Direct Method; Variable versus Fixed Costing and Performance Evaluation

LO 3, LO 4

SunAir is a small airline operating out of Phoenix, Arizona. Its three flights travel to Las Vegas, Reno, and Los Angeles. The owner of the airline wants to assess the full cost of operating each flight. As part of this assessment, the costs of two support departments (baggage and maintenance) must be allocated to the three flights. The two support departments that support all three flights are located in Phoenix (any baggage or maintenance costs at the destination airports are directly traceable to the individual flights). Budgeted and actual data for 1997 are as follows for the support departments and the three flights:

	Support Departments		Flights		
	Maintenance	Baggage	Las Vegas	Reno	Los Angeles
Budgeted data:					
Fixed overhead	$260,000	$175,000	$20,000	$18,000	$30,000
Variable overhead	$32,000	$66,000	$5,000	$10,000	$6,000
Number of passengers*	—	—	10,000	15,000	5,000
Hours of flight time*	—	—	2,000	4,000	2,000
Actual data:					
Fixed overhead	$235,000	$176,000	$22,000	$17,000	$29,500
Variable overhead	$80,000	$53,000	$6,200	$11,000	$5,800
Number of passengers	—	—	6,600	14,400	9,000
Hours of flight time	—	—	1,800	4,200	2,500

*Normal activity levels

REQUIRED:
1. Using the direct method, allocate the service costs to each flight, assuming that the objective is to determine the cost of operating each flight.
2. Using the direct method, allocate the service costs to each flight, assuming that the objective is to evaluate performance.

P7-2

Comparison of Methods of Allocation

LO 4

Powell-Morgan, Inc. is divided into two operating divisions: the Midwest region and the Eastern region. The company allocates personnel and accounting costs to each operating division. Personnel costs are allocated on the basis of employees and accounting costs on the basis of the number of transactions processed. No effort is made to separate fixed and variable costs; however, only budgeted costs are allocated. Allocations for the coming year are based on the following data:

	Support Departments		Operating Divisions	
	Personnel	Accounting	Midwest	Eastern
Overhead costs	$340,000	$260,000	$170,000	$140,000
Number of employees	20	60	60	80
Transactions processed	2,000	200	3,000	5,000

REQUIRED:

1. Allocate the service costs using the direct method.
2. Allocate the service costs using the sequential method.
3. Allocate the service costs using the reciprocal method.

P7-3

Comparison of Methods of Allocation

LO 4, LO 5

Gojar Uniform Company manufactures a variety of uniforms for the armed services. Gojar has two producing departments, cutting and sewing. Usually, the uniforms are ordered in batches of 100.

Two support departments provide support for Gojar's operating units: maintenance and power. Budgeted data for the coming quarter follow. The company does not separate fixed and variable costs.

	Support Departments		Producing Departments	
	Maintenance	Power	Cutting	Sewing
Overhead costs	$240,000	$380,000	$65,000	$87,000
Machine hours	—	30,000	40,000	10,000
Kilowatt-hours	20,000	—	18,000	162,000
Direct labor hours	—	—	5,000	30,000

The predetermined overhead rate for cutting is computed on the basis of machine hours; direct labor hours are used for sewing.

Recently, the U.S. Air Force has requested a bid on a three-year contract that would supply fatigues to soldiers at a nearby fort. Fatigues are uniforms consisting of a long-sleeved shirt and pants made of sturdy olive-drab cotton material. The prime costs for a batch of 100 sets of fatigues total $817.50. It takes two machine hours to produce a batch in the cutting department and 50 direct labor hours to sew the 100 uniforms in the sewing department.

Gojar Uniform Company policy is to bid full manufacturing cost plus 25 percent.

REQUIRED:

1. Prepare bids for Gojar Uniform Company using each of the following allocation methods:
   a. Direct method
   b. Reciprocal method
2. Which method most accurately reflects the cost of producing the uniforms? Why?

P7-4

Comparison of Ranking of Support Departments Using the Sequential Method

LO 4, LO 5

Refer to the data in P7-3.

REQUIRED:

1. Prepare bids for Gojar Uniform Company using each of the following allocation methods:
   a. Sequential method, allocating maintenance first, then power.
   b. Sequential method, allocating power first, then maintenance.
2. Was there a difference in the bids calculated in requirement 1? Why?

P7-5
Predetermined
Rates; Allocation
for Performance
Evaluation
LO 3

Jensen Auto-Rental Company operates three vehicle rental divisions: Personal, Corporate, and Truck. The Personal Division specializes in renting compact and subcompact cars to individuals traveling away from home; the Corporate Division specializes in renting large fleets of cars and vans; and the Truck Division rents pickups and small enclosed trucks for local moving.

Jensen has one support department, which is responsible for the service, maintenance, and cleanup of its fleet of vehicles. The costs of this support department are allocated to each operating unit on the basis of total miles driven. During the first quarter, the support department was expected to spend a total of $85,000. Of this total, $20,000 was viewed as fixed. During the quarter, the support department incurred actual variable costs of $66,719 and actual fixed costs of $20,700. The normal and actual miles logged for each rental unit during the first quarter are as follows:

	Personal	Corporate	Truck
Normal activity	160,000	280,000	60,000
Actual activity	163,000	250,000	74,000

REQUIRED:
1. Compute the predetermined service cost per mile-driven.
2. Compute the costs that would be allocated at the end of the quarter for purposes of performance evaluation.
3. Identify the costs of the support department that were not allocated to the three rental divisions. Why were these costs not allocated to the operating units?

P7-6
Sequential and
Direct Methods
LO 4, LO 5

Lilly Candies has three producing departments, mixing, cooking, and packaging, and five support departments. The following is the basic information on all departments (bases represent practical annual levels):

	Number of Items Processed	Number of Employees	Square Feet Occupied	Machine Hours	Labor Hours
Cafeteria	300	5	5,000	—	—
Personnel	1,000	10	7,000	—	—
Custodial services	200	7	2,000	—	—
Maintenance	2,500	15	16,000	—	—
Cost accounting	—	13	5,000	—	—
Mixing	2,800	20	40,000	4,000	30,000
Cooking	2,700	10	30,000	10,000	20,000
Packaging	3,000	20	20,000	6,000	50,000
Total	12,500	100	125,000	20,000	100,000

The budgeted overhead costs for the department are as follows for the coming year:

	Fixed	Variable	Total
Cafeteria	$ 20,000	$ 40,000	$ 60,000
Personnel	70,000	20,000	90,000
Custodial services	80,000	—	80,000
Maintenance	100,000	100,000	200,000
Cost accounting	130,000	16,500	146,500
Mixing	120,000	20,000	140,000
Cooking	60,000	10,000	70,000
Packaging	25,000	40,000	65,000

REQUIRED:
1. Allocate the service costs to the producing departments using the direct method.

2. Compute a predetermined fixed overhead rate and a predetermined variable overhead rate. Assume that overhead is applied using direct labor hours for mixing and packaging and machine hours for cooking.

3. Allocate the service costs to the producing departments using the sequential method. (*Hint:* Allocate fixed costs in order of descending magnitude of direct fixed costs. Allocate variable costs in order of descending magnitude of direct variable costs.)

4. Compute predetermined fixed and variable overhead rates based on requirement 3. Overhead is applied using direct labor hours for mixing and packaging and machine hours for cooking.

5. Assume that the prime costs for a batch of chocolate bars total $60,000. The batch requires 1,000 direct labor hours in mixing, 1,500 machine hours in cooking, and 5,000 direct labor hours in packaging. Assume that the selling price is equal to full manufacturing cost plus 30 percent. Compute the selling price of the batch assuming that costs are allocated using the direct method. Repeat using the sequential method. Comment on the implications of using different allocation methods, assuming that a markup of 30 percent is typical for the industry. Which allocation method do you think should be used?

P7-7
Reciprocal Method;
Cost of Operating a
Support Department
LO 4

Watterman Company has two producing departments (machining and assembly) and two support departments (power and maintenance). The budgeted costs and normal usage are as follows for the coming year:

	Power	Maintenance	Machining	Assembly
Overhead costs*	$50,000	$40,000	$120,000	$60,000
Kilowatt-hours	—	100,000	300,000	100,000
Machine hours	5,000	—	10,000	5,000

*All overhead costs are variable.

The president of Watterman was approached by a local utility company and offered the opportunity to buy power for $0.11 per kilowatt-hour. The president has asked you to determine the cost of producing the power internally so that a response to the offer can be made.

REQUIRED:

1. Compute the unit cost of kilowatts for overall plant usage. Based on this computation, how would you respond to the offer to buy the kilowatts externally?

2. Now use the reciprocal method to compute the cost of operating the power department. Divide this total cost by the total kilowatts produced by the power department to find a cost per kilowatt-hour. Based on this computation, how would you respond to the offer to buy kilowatts externally?

3. Show that the decision associated with the reciprocal method (requirement 2) is correct by following two steps: (a) computing the savings realized if the power department is eliminated and (b) computing the cost per kilowatt-hour saved by dividing the total savings by the kilowatts needed if the power department is eliminated. (*Hint:* Total savings include the direct costs of the power department plus any costs avoided by the maintenance department since it no longer needs to serve the power department. The total kilowatt-hours consumed by the company need to be adjusted since the power needs of the maintenance department decrease when they decrease the amount of service they offer.)

P7-8
Direct Method;
Sequential Method;
Overhead Rates
LO 4, LO 5

Bright, Inc. has two producing departments and four support departments. It currently uses the direct method of support department cost allocation. Data for the company follow:

	Producing Departments		Support Departments			
	PD1	PD2	SD1	SD2	SD3	SD4
Overhead	$183,000	$212,400	$30,000	$35,000	$40,000	100,000
Square feet	2,000	2,000	400	5,000	600	—
Employees	15	45	—	12	20	3
DLH	30,000	90,000	—	24,000	20,000	6,000
Machine hours	10,000	20,000	—	—	—	—

Original Allocation Base

SD1	Machine hours
SD2	Number of employees
SD3	Direct labor hours
SD4	Square feet

Cara James, controller of Bright, Inc., is considering changing to a more accurate method of support department cost allocation. She has discovered the following:

1. SD1 provides its services only to the producing departments based on machine hours.
2. SD2 provides services to both producing and support departments based on the number of employees.
3. SD3 provides 15 percent of its service to SD1 and the remainder to PD1 and PD2 based on direct labor hours.
4. SD4 provides services to all other departments based on square footage.

Cara has decided to rank the support departments in the following order for purposes of cost allocation: SD4, SD2, SD3, SD1.

REQUIRED:

1. Allocate support-department costs using the direct method and the original allocation bases.
2. Allocate support-department costs using the sequential method as outlined by Cara James.
3. Calculate overhead rates for PD1 (based on machine hours) and PD2 (based on direct labor hours) using total departmental overhead costs as determined by the:
   a. Direct method
   b. Sequential method

P7-9

Fixed- and Variable-Cost Allocation

LO 3

El Greco's is a chain of restaurants serving Mediterranean (Greek, Italian, and Spanish) food in a family-type atmosphere. The chain has grown from one restaurant in 1989 to five restaurants located in California and Arizona. In 1998, the owner of the company decided to set up a centralized purchasing department to purchase food and other supplies, and to coordinate inventory decisions. The purchasing department was opened in January 1998 by renting space adjacent to corporate headquarters in Riverside, California. All restaurants have been supplied with personal computers and modems by which to transfer information to central purchasing on a daily basis.

The purchasing department has budgeted fixed costs of $50,000 per year. Variable costs are budgeted at $16 per hour. Actual costs in 1998 equaled budgeted costs. Further information is as follows:

	Actual Revenues		Actual Hours of Accounting
	1997	1998	Used in 1998
El Gato	$337,500	$390,500	1,475
Northridge	360,000	375,000	938
Riverside	450,000	456,000	400
Sedona	562,500	549,000	375
Yuma	540,000	550,000	562
	2,250,000	2,320,500	3,750

REQUIRED:

1. Suppose the total costs of the purchasing department are allocated on the basis of 1998 sales revenue. How much will be allocated to each restaurant?
2. Suppose that El Greco's views 1997 sales figures as a proxy for budgeted capacity of the restaurants. Thus, fixed purchasing department costs are allocated on the basis of 1997 sales, and variable costs are allocated according to 1998 usage multiplied by the variable rate. How much purchasing department cost will be allocated to each restaurant?
3. Comment on the two allocation schemes. Which is better? Explain.

P7-10

Support Department-Cost Allocation;

Alden Peterson, marketing manager for Retlief Company, had been puzzled by the outcome of two recent bids. The company's policy was to bid 150 percent of the full manufacturing cost. One

Plantwide Overhead
Rate versus
Departmental Rates;
Effects on Pricing
Decisions
LO 4, LO 5
job (labeled Job SS) had been turned down by a prospective customer, who had indicated that the proposed price was $3 per unit higher than the winning bid. A second job (Job TT) had been accepted by a customer, who was amazed that Retlief could offer such favorable terms. This customer revealed that Retlief's price was $43 per unit lower than the next lowest bid.

Alden knew that Retlief Company was more than competitive in terms of cost control. Accordingly, he suspected that the problem was related to cost assignment procedures. Upon investigating, Alden was told that the company used a plantwide overhead rate based on direct labor hours. The rate was computed at the beginning of the year using budgeted data. Selected budgeted data follow:

	Department A	Department B	Total
Overhead	$500,000	$2,000,000	$2,500,000
Direct labor hours	200,000	50,000	250,000
Machine hours	20,000	120,000	140,000

These data led to a plantwide overhead rate of $10 per direct labor hour. In addition, the following specific manufacturing data on Job SS and Job TT were given.

	Job SS		
	Department A	Department B	Total
Direct labor hours	5,000	1,000	6,000
Machine hours	200	500	700
Prime costs	$100,000	$20,000	$120,000
Units produced	14,400	14,400	14,400

	Job TT		
	Department A	Department B	Total
Direct labor hours	400	600	1,000
Machine hours	200	3,000	3,200
Prime costs	$10,000	$40,000	$50,000
Units produced	1,500	1,500	1,500

This information led to the original bid prices of $18.75 per unit for Job SS and $60 per unit for Job TT.

Then Alden discovered that the overhead costs in department B were higher than those of department A because B has more equipment, higher maintenance, higher power consumption, higher depreciation, and higher setup costs. So he tried reworking the two bids by using departmental overhead rates. Department A's overhead rate was $2.50 per direct labor hour; department B's overhead rate was $16.67 per machine hour. These rates resulted in unit prices of $14.67 for Job SS and $101.01 for Job TT.

Alden still was not satisfied, however. He did some reading on overhead allocation methods and learned that proper support department cost allocation can lead to more accurate product costs. He decided to create four support departments and recalculate departmental overhead rates. Information on departmental costs and related items follows:

	Maintenance	Power	Setups	General Factory	Department A	Department B
Overhead	$500,000	$225,000	$150,000	$625,000	$200,000	800,000
Maintenance hours	—	1,500	500	—	1,000	7,000
Kilowatt-hours	4,500	—	500	15,000	10,000	50,000
DLH	10,000	12,000	6,000	8,000	200,000	50,000
Number of setups	—	—	—	—	40	160
Square feet	25,000	40,000	5,000	15,000	35,360	94,640

The following allocation bases (cost drivers) seemed reasonable:

Support Department	Allocation Base
Maintenance	Maintenance hours
Power	Kilowatt-hours
Setups	Number of setups
General factory	Square feet

REQUIRED:

1. Using the direct method, verify the original departmental overhead rates.
2. Using the sequential method, allocate support-department costs to the producing departments. Calculate departmental overhead rates using direct labor hours for department A and machine hours for department B. What would the bids for Job SS and Job TT have been if these overhead rates had been in effect?
3. Which method of overhead cost assignment would you recommend to Alden? Why?
4. Suppose that the best competing bid was $4.10 lower than the original bid price (based on a plantwide rate). Does this affect your recommendation in requirement 3? Explain.

 M ANAGERIAL DECISION CASES

C7-1

Allocation; Pricing; Ethical Behavior

LO 1, LO 2

Emma Hanks, manager of a division that produces valves and castings on a special-order basis, was excited about an order received from a new customer. The customer, a personal friend of Bob Johnson, Emma's supervisor, had placed an order for 10,000 valves. The customer agreed to pay full manufacturing cost plus 25 percent. The order was timely since business was sluggish, and Emma had some concerns about her division's ability to meet its targeted profits. Even with the order, the division would likely fall short in meeting the target by at least $50,000. After examining the cost sheet for the order, however, Emma thought she saw a way to increase the profitability of the job. Accordingly, she called Larry Smith, CMA, the controller of the division.

Emma: "Larry, this cost sheet for the new order reflects an allocation of maintenance costs to the grinding department based on maintenance hours used. Currently, 60 percent of our maintenance costs are allocated to grinding on that basis. Can you tell me what the allocation ratio would be if we used machine hours instead of maintenance hours?"

Larry: "Sure. Based on machine hours, the allocation ratio would increase from 60 percent to 80 percent."

Emma: "Excellent. Now tell me what would happen to the unit cost of this new job if we used machine hours to allocate maintenance costs."

Larry: "Hold on. That'll take a few minutes. . . . The cost would increase by $10 per unit."

Emma: "And with the 25 percent markup, the revenues on that job would jump by $12.50 per unit. That would increase the profitability of the division by $125,000. Larry, I want you to change the allocation base from maintenance hours worked to machine hours."

Larry: "Are you sure? After all, if you recall, we spent some time assessing the causal relationships, and we found that maintenance hours reflect the consumption of maintenance cost much better than machine hours. I'm not sure that would be a fair cost assignment. We've used this base for years now."

Emma: "Listen, Larry, allocations are arbitrary anyway. Changing the allocation base for this new job will increase its profitability and allow us to meet our targeted profit goals for the year. If we meet or beat those goals, we'll be more likely to get the capital we need to acquire some new equipment. Furthermore, by beating the targeted profit, we'll get our share of the bonus pool. Besides, this new customer has a prosperous business and can easily afford to pay somewhat more for this order."

REQUIRED:

1. Evaluate Emma's position. Do you agree with her reasoning? Explain. What should Emma do?
2. If you were the controller, what would you do? Do any of the standards for ethical conduct for management accountants apply to the controller (see Exhibit 1-4 of Chapter 1)? Explain.
3. Suppose Larry refused to change the allocation scheme. Emma then issued the following ultimatum: "Either change the allocation or look for another job!" Larry then made an appoint-

ment with Bob Johnson and disclosed the entire affair. Bob, however, was not sympathetic. He advised Larry to do as Emma had requested, arguing that the request represented good business sense. Now what should Larry do?

4. Refer to requirement 3. Larry decided that he cannot comply with the request to change the allocation scheme. Appeals to higher-level officials have been in vain. Angered, Larry submitted his resignation and called the new customer affected by the cost reassignment. In his phone conversation, Larry revealed Emma's plans to increase the job's costs in order to improve the division's profits. The new customer expressed her gratitude and promptly canceled her order for 10,000 valves. Evaluate Larry's actions. Should he have informed the customer about Emma's intent? Explain.

C7-2

Direct Method; Settlement of a Contract Dispute

LO 4, LO 5

A state government agency contracted with FlyRite Helicopters to provide helicopter services on a requirements contract. After six months, FlyRite discovered that the agency's original estimates of the number of flying hours needed were grossly overstated. FlyRite Helicopters is now making a claim against the state agency for defective specifications. The state has been advised by its legal advisers that its chances in court on this claim would not be strong, and, therefore, an out-of-court settlement is in order. As a result of the legal advice, the state agency has hired a local CPA firm to analyze the claim and prepare a recommendation for an equitable settlement.

The particulars on which the original bid was based follow. The contract was for three different types of helicopters and had a duration of one year. Thus, the data reflect the original annual expectations. Also, the costs and activity pertain only to the contract.

	Aircraft Type		
	Hughes 500D	206B Jet Ranger	206L-1 Long Ranger
Flying hours	1,200	1,600	900
Direct costs:			
Fixed:			
Insurance	$32,245	$28,200	$55,870
Lease payments	31,000	36,000	90,000
Pilot salaries	30,000	30,000	30,000
Variable:			
Fuel	$24,648	$30,336	$22,752
Minor servicing	6,000	8,000	4,500
Lease	—	—	72,000

In addition to the direct costs, the following indirect costs were expected:

	Fixed Costs	Variable Costs
Maintenance	$ 26,000	$246,667
Hangar rent	18,000	—
General administrative	110,000	—

Maintenance costs and general administrative costs are allocated to each helicopter on the basis of flying hours; hangar rent is allocated on the basis of the number of helicopters. The company has one of each type of aircraft.

During the first six months of the contract, the actual flying hours were as follows:

Type	Flying Hours
500D	299
206B	160
206L-1	204

The state agency's revised projection of total hours for the year follows:

Type	Flying Hours
500D	450
206B	600
206L-1	800

REQUIRED:

1. Assume that FlyRite won the contract with a bid of cost plus 15 percent, where cost refers to cost per flying hour. Compute the original bid price per flying hour for each type of helicopter. Next, compute the original expected profit of the contract.

2. Compute the profit (or loss) earned by FlyRite for the first six months of activity. Assume that the planned costs were equal to the actual costs. Also, assume that 50 percent of the fixed costs for the year have been incurred. Compute the profit that FlyRite should have earned during the first six months, assuming that 50 percent of the hours originally projected (for each aircraft type) had been flown.

3. Compute the profit (or loss) that the contract would provide FlyRite assuming the original price per flying hour and using the state agency's revised projection of hours needed.

4. Assume that the state has agreed to pay what is necessary so that FlyRite receives the profit originally expected in the contract. This will be accomplished by revising the price paid per flying hour based on the revised estimates of flying hours. What is the new price per flying hour?

C7-3
Research Assignment

Contact the controller of a local hospital and arrange an interview. Ask the hospital controller the following questions and write up the responses:

a. How many support departments do you have in the hospital? Will you describe several for me?

b. How many different revenue-producing departments are there in the hospital? Will you describe several for me?

c. How do you assign support-department costs to revenue-producing departments?

d. How many different products are there in the hospital?

e. How do you assign the costs of the support departments to individual products?

f. How many different products are costed in your hospital?

g. How do you determine the cost of a particular product?

MANAGEMENT ACCOUNTING
IN ACTION

The purpose of this photo essay is to help you visualize an actual manufacturing process and associate with it the many management accounting terms you have learned. The factory shown here is the Panasonic plant at Troy, Ohio. The Troy plant produces about 2 million television tubes each year, assembling 20", 27", and 31" tubes using two production lines. Both lines run 24 hours a day. The process is highly automated and robots are used extensively. Let's follow the assembly of a TV tube from start to finish.

This is the materials storeroom and receiving area. Raw materials come from numerous sources in the United States and overseas. In the materials storeroom, the incoming parts (glass panels, funnels, screens, electron guns, and special coatings) are inspected and stored. What overhead activities do you think are associated with the receiving and storing of raw materials?

1

The glass panel that is the front of the tube is unpacked and prepared for washing in a special chemical solution. Try to find the direct materials, direct labor and overhead items that are visible in this picture.

2

Funnels that form the sides and back of the TV tubes are unpacked and coated with a dag coating. This coating acts as a conductor that helps direct electrons to the front glass panel.

3

The glass panel undergoes a series of different colored phosphorus coatings (green, blue, and red). After each coating, the panels are exposed with a light table, similar to a process used in photography. The red coating is applied last because it includes gold. Then, if any prior step fails, the costly red phosphor coating will be saved. Phosphor stripes act as a target for the electrons.

4

Here, the interior of the funnel is coated with a special silica coating and matched to a glass panel, creating a "bulb." All of these coatings are designed to provide proper conduction for the electrons streaming from the electron gun (inserted in the neck of the funnel), ensuring that the tubes will provide good color.

Electron guns provide the electron beam to excite the phosphorus materials on the screen. The excited phosphorus material is what we see as the picture and color. At this plant the electron guns are purchased, quality checked, and inserted into the neck of the bulb. A vacuum is drawn on the entire bulb. When the electron gun is sealed into the bulb and the vacuum drawn, the bulb becomes a TV tube.

1

2

3

4

5

Robots are used extensively throughout production. Here, a robot picks up the tube and puts it into a machine that places a rim band around the outside of the tube. This rim band serves two purposes: it helps Panasonic's customers install the tube into the TV cabinet; and it helps ensure implosion protection should a tube break.

6

Once fully assembled, the tubes are cleaned, tested, inspected, and prepared for shipment. After the required number of a particular sized tube is assembled, the line is set up for another size. This changeover necessitates special procedures. For example, Panasonic retests the integrity of the tubes with every changeover. A solid metal projectile, hanging on a string, is driven straight into a newly completed tube. The first strike cracks the glass panel, the second strike properly implodes the tube. This continual testing is part of Panasonic's quality program.

7 (a, b)
The electron guns are inspected and tested.

7a

7b

8

The final product is ready to be shipped to TV assemblers. The primary customer for the Troy plant's output is the Panasonic plant in Tijuana, Mexico. However, these TV tubes are also sold to television assembly plants in Asia and in North and South America.

8

9

While the factory purchases electricity from Dayton Power and Light, it makes its own steam, as well as chilled and deionized water. The boiler room is an important part of the steam production process.

9

10

The basic engineering for Panasonic TV tubes is done in Japan. However, any problems at the factory are solved by its own engineers. Minor adjustments to specific products are handled here as well.

11

An important part of overhead in any manufacturing plant is purchasing. What activities can you associate with purchasing?

10

11

PART

2

Planning and Control

8

Learning Objectives

After studying Chapter 8, you should be able to:

1. Define *budgeting* and discuss its role in planning, control, and decision making.

2. Define and prepare the *master budget,* identify its major components, and explain the interrelationships of its various components.

3. Identify and discuss the key features that a budgetary system should have to encourage managers to engage in goal-congruent behavior.

4. Describe budgets for merchandising and service firms and zero-base budgeting.

CHAPTER

Budgeting for Planning and Control

SCENARIO[1]

By all outward appearances, Dr. Roger Jones was a successful dentist. He owned his office building, which he leased to the professional corporation housing his dental practice. Annual revenues from his practice of more than $250,000 provided him with a salary of $75,000. He and his family lived in a large home in a well-regarded neighborhood.

However, Dr. Jones recently received a registered letter from the IRS threatening to impound his business and sell its assets for failure to pay payroll taxes for the past six months. Furthermore, the professional corporation has had difficulty paying its suppliers. The corporation owed one supplier more than $100,000 and had made arrangements to pay interest on the bill but has missed even those payments. These same kinds of difficulty have been experienced repeatedly for the past five years.

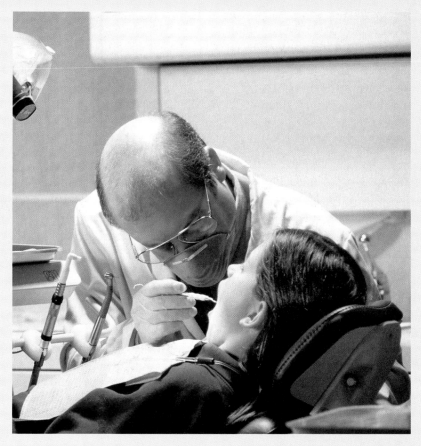

In the past, Dr. Jones had solved similar problems by borrowing money on the equity in either his personal residence or his office building. Sufficient equity still existed in his office building to solve the IRS problem. A visit to a local bank resulted in a refinancing agreement that produced enough money to pay the back taxes and the associated penalties and interest.

This time, however, Dr. Jones was determined to get to the root of his financial difficulties. His latest loan had exhausted his personal financial resources; further difficulties simply couldn't be tolerated. His first action was to dismiss his receptionist-bookkeeper, reasoning that a significant part of the blame was hers for failing to properly manage the financial resources of the corporation. He then called Lawson, Johnson, and Smith, a local CPA firm, and requested that a consultant determine the cause of his recurring financial difficulties.

Jeanette Smith, a partner in the CPA firm, accepted the assignment. After spending a week examining the records of the practice and extensively interviewing Dr. Jones, Jeanette delivered the following report:

Dr. Roger Jones
1091 West Apple Avenue
Reno, Nevada

Dear Dr. Jones:

The cause of your current financial difficulties is the absence of proper planning and control. Currently, many of your expenditure decisions are made in a haphazard and arbitrary manner. Affordability is seldom, if ever, considered. Because of this, resources are often committed beyond the capabilities of the practice. To meet these additional commitments, your bookkeeper has been forced to postpone payments for essential operating expenses such as payroll taxes, supplies, and laboratory services.

The following examples illustrate some of the decisions that have contributed to your financial troubles:

1. *Salary decisions.* You have granted 5 percent increases each year whether or not the business could successfully absorb these increases. Also, your salary is 10 percent higher than dentists with comparable practices.
2. *Withdrawal decisions.* For the past five years, you have withdrawn from cash receipts approximately $500 per month. These withdrawals have been treated as a loan from the corporation to you, the president of the corporation.
3. *Equipment acquisition decisions.* During the past five years, the corporation has acquired a van, a video recorder, a refrigerator, and a micro-computer system. Some of these items were cash acquisitions, and some are being paid for on an installment basis. None of them was essential to the mission of your corporation.

These decisions, and others like them, have adversely affected both your personal financial status and that of your dental practice. The mortgage payments for your home and for your office building have increased by 50 percent over the past five years. Additionally, the liabilities of the corporation have increased by 200 percent for the same period of time.

To solve your financial problems, I recommend the installation of a formal budgetary system. A comprehensive financial plan is needed so that you know where you are going and what you are capable of doing.

My firm would be pleased to assist you in designing and implementing the recommended system. For it to be successful, you and your staff need to be introduced to the elementary principles of budgeting. As a part of implementation, we will offer three 2-hour seminars on budgeting. The first will describe the basic philosophy of budgeting, the second will teach you how to prepare budgets, and the third will explore the use of budgets for planning, control, and performance evaluation.

Sincerely,
Jeanette Day, CPA

1. This scenario is based on the experience of a real company. The names are changed to preserve confidentiality.

Questions to Think About

1. Why did Dr. Jones fire his bookkeeper? Were his financial problems her fault? Why or why not?

2. How would a formal budgeting system help Dr. Jones get out of his financial difficulties?

3. Many small businesses do not budget, reasoning that they are small enough to mentally keep track of all revenues and expenditures. Comment on this idea.

4. Do you budget? Explain why or why not.

DESCRIPTION OF BUDGETING

Objective 1

Define *budgeting* and discuss its role in planning, control, and decision making.

All businesses should prepare budgets; all large businesses do. As the scenario for Dr. Jones shows, budgeting is vital for small businesses, too. Every for-profit and not-for-profit entity can benefit from the planning and control provided by budgets.

Budgeting and Planning and Control

Planning and control are inextricably linked. Planning is looking ahead, determining what actions should be taken to realize particular goals. Control is looking backward, determining what actually happened and comparing it with the previously planned outcomes. This comparison can then be used to adjust the budget, looking forward once more. Exhibit 8-1 illustrates the cycle of planning, results, and control. Let's look further at the planning component of this exhibit.

budgets

A key component of planning, budgets are financial plans for the future; they identify objectives and the actions needed to achieve them. Before a budget is prepared, an organization should develop a strategic plan. The strategic plan identifies strategies for future activities and operations generally covering at least five years. The organization can translate the overall strategy into long-term and short-term objectives. These objectives form the basis of the budget. Notice that there should be a tight linkage between the budget and the strategic plan. In developing this linkage, however, management should ensure that all attention is not focused on the short run. This is important because budgets, as one-period plans, are short run in nature.

strategic plan

To illustrate the process, consider again the case of Dr. Jones. (Refer to Exhibit 8-1 as you read this illustration.) Assume that Dr. Jones's strategic plan is to increase the size and profitability of his business by building a practice that has a reputation for quality and timely service. A key element in achieving this strategy is the addition of a dental

8-1

Exhibit
Planning, Control, and
Budgets

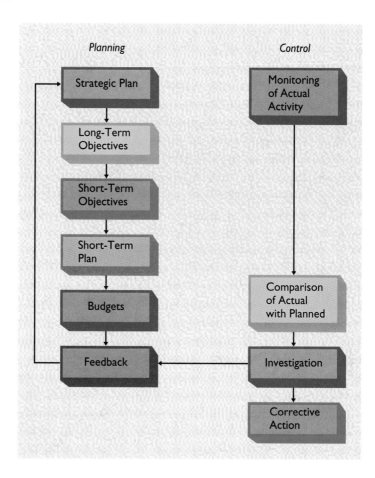

laboratory to his building so that crowns, bridges, and dentures can be made in-house. This is his long-term objective. In order to add the laboratory, he needs additional money. His financial status dictates that the capital must be obtained by increasing revenues. After some careful calculation, Dr. Jones concludes that annual revenues must be increased by 10 percent; this is a short-term objective.

How are these long-term and short-term objectives to be achieved? Suppose that Dr. Jones finds that his fees for fillings and crowns are below the average in his community and decides that the 10 percent increase can be achieved by increasing these fees. He now has a short-term plan. A sales budget would outline the quantity of fillings and crowns expected for the coming year, the new per-unit fee, and the total fees expected. Thus, the sales budget becomes the concrete plan of action needed to achieve the 10 percent increase in revenues. As the year unfolds, Dr. Jones can compare the actual revenues received with the budgeted revenues (monitoring and comparing). If actual revenues are less than planned, he should figure out why (investigation). Then he can act to remedy the shortfall, such as working longer hours or increasing fees for other dental services (corrective action). The reasons for the shortfall may also lead to an alteration of future plans (feedback).

Purposes of Budgeting

A budgetary system gives an organization several advantages.

1. It forces managers to plan.
2. It provides resource information that can be used to improve decision making.
3. It provides a standard for performance evaluation.
4. It improves communication and coordination.

Budgeting forces management to plan for the future. It encourages managers to develop an overall direction for the organization, foresee problems, and develop future policies. If Dr. Jones had spent time planning, he would have known the capabilities of his practice and where the resources of the business should be used.

Budgets improve decision making. For example, if Dr. Jones had known the expected revenues and the costs of supplies, lab fees, utilities, salaries, and so on, he might have lowered the rate of salary increases, avoided borrowing money from the corporation, and limited the purchase of nonessential equipment. These better decisions, in turn, might have prevented the problems that arose and resulted in a better financial status for both the business and Dr. Jones.

control

Budgets also set standards that can control the use of a company's resources and motivate employees. A vital part of the budgetary system, control is achieved by comparing actual results with budgeted results on a periodic basis (for example, monthly). A large difference between actual and planned results is feedback revealing that the system is out of control. Steps should be taken to find out why, and then to correct the situation. For example, if Dr. Jones knows how much amalgam should be used in a filling and what the cost should be, he can evaluate his use of this resource. If more amalgam is being used than expected, Dr. Jones may discover that he is often careless in its use and that extra care will produce savings. The same principle applies to other resources used by the corporation. In total, the savings could be significant.

Budgets also serve to communicate and coordinate. Budgets formally communicate the plans of the organization to each employee. Accordingly, all employees can be aware of their role in achieving those objectives. Since budgets for the various areas and activities of the organization must all work together to achieve organizational objectives, coordination is promoted. Managers can see the needs of other areas and are encouraged to subordinate their individual interests to those of the organization. The role of communication and coordination becomes more significant as an organization increases in size.

Two Dimensions of Budgeting

There are two dimensions to budgeting: (1) how the budget is prepared and (2) how the budget is used to implement the organization's plans. The first dimension concerns the mechanics of budget preparation.

The second involves how individuals within an organization react to a budgetary system. The use of budgets to exercise control, evaluate performance, communicate, and encourage coordination suggests that budgeting is a human activity. As such, budgeting carries a strong behavioral dimension. In fact, the success or failure of budgeting depends on how well management considers its behavioral implications.

The remainder of this chapter is primarily concerned with these two dimensions.

PREPARING THE BUDGET

Objective 2
Define and prepare the *master budget*, identify its major components, and explain the interrelationships of its various components.

continuous budget

Most organizations prepare the budget for the coming year during the last four or five months of the current year. However, some organizations have developed a continuous budgeting philosophy. A continuous budget is a moving 12-month budget. As a month expires in the budget, an additional month in the future is added so that the company always has a 12-month plan on hand. Proponents of continuous budgeting maintain that it forces managers to plan ahead constantly.

Typically, the budget is for a one-year period corresponding to the fiscal year of the company. Yearly budgets are broken down into quarterly budgets, and quarterly budgets are broken down into monthly budgets. The use of smaller time periods allows managers to compare actual data with budgeted data more frequently, so problems may be noticed and solved sooner.

Directing and Coordinating

budget director
budget committee

Someone must be responsible for directing and coordinating an organization's overall budgeting process. This budget director, usually the controller, works under the direction of the budget committee. The budget committee reviews the budget, provides policy guidelines and budgetary goals, resolves differences that arise as the budget is prepared, approves the final budget, and monitors the actual performance of the organization as the year unfolds. The president of the organization appoints the members of the committee, who are usually the president, vice-presidents, and the controller.

The Master Budget

master budget

operating budgets

financial budgets

The master budget is the comprehensive financial plan for the organization as a whole; it is made up of various individual budgets. A master budget can be divided into *operating* and *financial* budgets. Operating budgets describe the income-generating activities of a firm: sales, production, and finished goods inventories. The ultimate outcome of the operating budgets is a pro forma or budgeted income statement. Financial budgets detail the inflows and outflows of cash and the overall financial position. Planned cash inflows and outflows appear in the cash budget. Expected financial position at the end of the budget period is shown in a budgeted, or pro forma, balance sheet. Since many of the financing activities are not known until the operating budgets are known, the operating budget is prepared first.

Preparing the Operating Budget

The operating budget consists of a budgeted income statement accompanied by the following supporting schedules:

1. Sales budget
2. Production budget
3. Direct materials purchases budget
4. Direct labor budget
5. Overhead budget
6. Selling and administrative expenses budget
7. Ending finished goods inventory budget
8. Cost of goods sold budget

The sales forecast is the basis for the sales budget, which, in turn, is the basis for all of the other operating budgets and most of the financial budgets. Accordingly, the accuracy of the sales forecast strongly affects the soundness of the entire master budget.

Creating the sales forecast is usually the responsibility of the marketing department. One approach to forecasting sales is the *bottom-up approach,* which requires individual salespeople to submit sales predictions. These are aggregated to form a total sales forecast. The accuracy of this sales forecast may be improved by considering other factors such as the general economic climate, competition, advertising, pricing policies, and so on. Some companies supplement the bottom-up approach with other, more formal approaches, such as time-series analysis, correlation analysis, and econometric modeling.

An example of the basis of sales forecasting can be found in the globalization of the market for personal computers. That market is exploding globally. Link Resources (a market research firm) predicts that foreign PC sales volume will be nearly double that in the United States by the year 2000.[2] The basis for that prediction can be found in the recent experience of computer manufacturers as well as in certain industry-specific and cultural factors. Examples of increased sales abound. Compaq noted that sales of its

2. The information about global demand for PCs is taken from Jim Carlton, "Foreign Markets Give PC Makers a Hearty Hello," *The Wall Street Journal,* 15 September 1995, B1, B8.

Presario computers outside North America increased from 20 percent to 35 percent of total sales in 1995. Compaq expects foreign sales to account for half of its volume in 1996. Apple Computer, Inc. expects to ship 60 percent more Macintosh computers to Japan in 1995 than it did in 1994. Since just 20 percent of Japanese households own PCs, Apple sees "tremendous pent-up demand." Similarly, AST Research, Inc. (based in Irvine, California) is the number one computer seller in Norway and a contender for number one in Great Britain and China. AST sees real growth potential overseas. Other forecasts have been more modest, but all expect huge growth in the overseas market.

The rosy scenario for future computer sales is fueled to a significant extent by falling prices for hardware and the proliferation of foreign language software. In addition to price and software improvements, cultural factors affect demand. Especially in Third-World countries, home-based work and the importance of education support the continuing upsurge in demand.

sales budget

Sales Budget The sales forecast is merely the initial estimate. The sales budget is the projection approved by the budget committee that describes expected sales in units and dollars.

The sales forecast is presented to the budget committee for consideration. The budget committee may decide that the forecast is too pessimistic or too optimistic and revise it appropriately. For example, if the budget committee decides that the forecast is too pessimistic and not in harmony with the strategic plan of the organization, it may recommend specific actions to increase sales beyond the forecast level, such as increasing promotional activities and hiring additional salespeople.

To illustrate the master-budgeting process, let's look at the activities of CalBlock, Inc., which manufactures concrete blocks and pipes in plants located in several Western cities. Schedule 1 illustrates the sales budget for CalBlock's concrete block line. For simplicity, we assume that CalBlock has only one product: a standard block, measuring $8 \times 8 \times 16$ inches. (For a multiple-product firm, the sales budget reflects sales for each product in units and sales dollars.)

Schedule 1
Calblock, Inc.
Sales Budget (in thousands)
For the Year Ended December 31, 1998

	Quarter				
	1	2	3	4	Year
Units	2,000	6,000	6,000	2,000	16,000
Unit selling price	$\times$ $0.70	$\times$ $0.70	$\times$ $0.80	$\times$ $0.80	$\times$ $0.75
Sales	$1,400	$4,200	$4,800	$1,600	$12,000

Notice that the sales budget reveals that CalBlock's sales fluctuate seasonally. Most sales (75 percent) take place in the spring and summer quarters. Also, note that the budget reflects an expected increase in selling price beginning in the summer quarter (from $0.70 to $0.80). Because of the price change within the year, an average price must be used for the column that describes the total year's activities ($0.75 = \frac{\$12,000}{16,000 \text{ units}}$).

production budget

Production Budget The production budget describes how many units must be produced in order to meet sales needs and satisfy ending inventory requirements. From Schedule 1, we know how many concrete blocks are needed to satisfy sales demand for each quarter and for the year. If there were no beginning or ending inventories, the concrete blocks to be produced would exactly equal the units to be sold. In the JIT firm, for example, units sold equal units produced since a customer order triggers production.

Usually, however, the production budget must consider the existence of beginning and ending inventories since traditional manufacturing firms use inventories as a buffer against uncertainties in demand or production. Assume that company policy requires 100,000 concrete blocks to be available in inventory at the beginning of the first and fourth quarters and 500,000 blocks at the beginning of the second and third quarters. The policy is equivalent to budgeting 100,000 concrete blocks as ending inventory for the third and fourth quarters and 500,000 concrete blocks as ending inventory for the first and second quarters.

To compute the units to be produced, both unit sales and units of beginning and ending finished goods inventory are needed:

$$\text{Units to be produced} = \text{Expected unit sales} + \text{Units, ending inventory} \\ - \text{Units, beginning inventory}$$

The formula is the basis for the production budget in Schedule 2. Let's go through the first column of Schedule 2, the production needs for the first quarter. We see that CalBlock anticipates sales of 2 million concrete blocks. In addition, the company wants 500,000 blocks in ending inventory at the end of the first quarter. Thus, 2.5 million blocks are needed during the first quarter. Where will these 2.5 million blocks come from? Beginning inventory can provide 100,000 blocks, leaving 2.4 million blocks to be produced during the quarter. Notice that the production budget is expressed in terms of units.

Schedule 2
CalBlock, Inc.
Production Budget (in thousands)
For the Year Ended December 31, 1998

	Quarter				
	1	2	3	4	Year
Sales (Schedule 1)	2,000	6,000	6,000	2,000	16,000
Desired ending inventory	500	500	100	100	100
Total needs	2,500	6,500	6,100	2,100	16,100
Less: Beginning inventory	(100)	(500)	(500)	(100)	(100)
Units to be produced	2,400	6,000	5,600	2,000	16,000

Direct Materials Budget After the production schedule is completed, the budgets for direct materials, direct labor, and overhead can be prepared. The direct materials budget is a purchases budget and it depends on the expected use of materials in production and the raw materials inventory needs of the firm.

The amount of direct materials needed for production depends on the number of units to be produced. Suppose that a lightweight concrete block (a single unit of output) requires cement, sand, gravel, shale, pumice, and water. For simplicity, we will treat all raw materials jointly (as if there were only one raw material input) and assume that 26 pounds of raw material are needed per block. Then, if CalBlock wants to produce 2.4 million blocks in the first quarter, it will need 62.4 million pounds of raw material (26 pounds × 2.4 million blocks).

Once expected usage is computed, the purchases (in units) can be computed as follows:

$$\text{Purchases} = \text{Direct materials needed for production} + \text{Desired} \\ \text{direct materials, ending inventory} - \text{Direct} \\ \text{materials, beginning inventory}$$

The quantity of direct materials in inventory is determined by the firm's inventory policy. CalBlock's policy is to have 5 million pounds of raw materials in ending inventory for the third and fourth quarters and 8 million pounds of raw materials in ending inventory for the first and second quarters.

direct materials budget

The direct materials budget for CalBlock is presented in Schedule 3. Notice how similar the direct materials purchases budget is to the production budget. Again, let's go through the first quarter of Schedule 3. The 2.4 million blocks to be produced are multiplied by 26 pounds to yield the total raw material needed for production. Then, the desired ending inventory of 8 million pounds is added. We see that 70.4 million pounds of raw materials are required during the first quarter. Of these total needs, 5 million pounds are provided by beginning inventory, meaning the remaining 65.4 million pounds must be purchased. Multiplying the 65.4 million pounds by the cost of $0.01 gives CalBlock the $654,000 expected cost of raw materials purchases for the first quarter of the year. Of course, there would be a separate direct materials purchases budget for each type of raw material in a firm.

Schedule 3
CalBlock, Inc.
Direct Materials Budget (in thousands)
For the Year Ended December 31, 1998

	Quarter				
	1	2	3	4	Year
Units to be produced (Schedule 2)	2,400	6,000	5,600	2,000	16,000
Direct materials per unit (lb)	× 26	× 26	× 26	× 26	× 26
Production needs (lb)	62,400	156,000	145,600	52,000	416,000
Desired ending inventory (lb)	8,000	8,000	5,000	5,000	5,000
Total needs	70,400	164,000	150,600	57,000	421,000
Less: Beginning inventory*	(5,000)	(8,000)	(8,000)	(5,000)	(5,000)
Direct materials to be purchased (lb)	65,400	156,000	142,600	52,000	416,000
Cost per pound	× $0.01	× $0.01	× $0.01	× $0.01	× $0.01
Total purchase cost	$654	$1,560	$1,426	$520	$4,160

*This follows the inventory policy of having 8 million pounds of raw materials on hand at the end of the first and second quarters and 5 million pounds on hand at the end of the third and fourth quarters.

direct labor budget

Direct Labor Budget The direct labor budget shows the total direct labor hours needed and the associated cost for the number of units in the production budget. As with direct materials, the budgeted hours of direct labor are determined by the relationship between labor and output. For example, if a batch of 100 concrete blocks requires 1.5 direct labor hours, then the direct labor time per block is 0.015 hour.

Given the direct labor used per unit of output and the units to be produced from the production budget, the direct labor budget is computed as shown in Schedule 4. In the

Schedule 4
CalBlock, Inc.
Direct Labor Budget (in thousands)
For the Year Ended December 31, 1998

	Quarter				
	1	2	3	4	Year
Units to be produced (Schedule 2)	2,400	6,000	5,600	2,000	16,000
Direct labor time per unit (hr)	× 0.015	× 0.015	× 0.015	× 0.015	× 0.015
Total hours needed	36	90	84	30	240
Average wage per hour	× $10	× $10	× $10	× $10	× $10
Total direct labor cost	$360	$900	$840	$300	$2,400

direct labor budget, the wage rate ($10 per hour in this example) is the *average* wage paid the direct laborers associated with the production of the concrete blocks. Since it is an average, it allows for the possibility of differing wage rates paid to individual laborers.

overhead budget

Overhead Budget The overhead budget shows the expected cost of all indirect manufacturing items. Unlike direct materials and direct labor, there is no readily identifiable input-output relationship for overhead items. Instead, there are a series of activities and related drivers. Past experience can be used as a guide to determine how these overhead activities vary with their drivers. Individual items that will vary are identified (for example, supplies and utilities), and the amount that is expected to be spent for each item per unit of activity is estimated. Individual rates are then totaled to obtain a variable overhead rate. For our example, let's assume that two overhead cost pools are created, one for overhead activities that vary with direct labor hours, and one for all other activities, which are fixed. The variable overhead rate is $8 per direct labor hour; fixed overhead is budgeted at $1.28 million ($320,000 per quarter). Using this information and the budgeted direct labor hours from the direct labor budget (Schedule 4), the overhead budget in Schedule 5 is prepared.

Schedule 5
CalBlock, Inc.
Overhead Budget (in thousands)
For the Year Ended December 31, 1998

		Quarter			
	1	2	3	4	Year
Budgeted direct labor hours (Schedule 4)	36	90	84	30	240
Variable overhead rate	× $8	× $8	× $8	× $8	× $8
Budgeted variable overhead	$288	$ 720	$672	$240	$1,920
Budgeted fixed overhead*	320	320	320	320	1,280
Total overhead	$608	$1,040	$992	$560	$3,200

*Includes $200,000 of depreciation in each quarter

selling and administrative expenses budget

Selling and Administrative Expenses Budget The next budget to be prepared, the selling and administrative expenses budget, outlines planned expenditures for non-manufacturing activities. As with overhead, selling and administrative expenses can be broken down into fixed and variable components. Such items as sales commissions, freight, and supplies vary with sales activity. The selling and administrative expenses budget is illustrated in Schedule 6.

Schedule 6
CalBlock, Inc.
Selling and Administrative Expenses Budget (in thousands)
For the Year Ended December 31, 1998

		Quarter			
	1	2	3	4	Year
Planned sales in units (Schedule 1)	2,000	6,000	6,000	2,000	16,000
Variable selling and administrative expenses per unit	× $0.05	× $0.05	× $0.05	× $0.05	× $0.05
Total variable expense	$100	$300	$300	$100	$800

Fixed selling and administrative expenses:					
Salaries	$ 35	$ 35	$ 35	$ 35	$ 140
Advertising	10	10	10	10	40
Depreciation	15	15	15	15	60
Insurance	—	—	15	—	15
Travel	5	5	5	5	20
Total fixed expense	$ 65	$ 65	$ 80	$ 65	$ 275
Total selling and administrative expenses	$165	$365	$380	$165	$1,075

ending finished goods inventory budget

Ending Finished Goods Inventory Budget The ending finished goods inventory budget supplies information needed for the balance sheet and also serves as an important input for the preparation of the cost of goods sold budget. To prepare this budget, the unit cost of producing each concrete block must be calculated using information from Schedules 3, 4, and 5. The unit cost of a concrete block and the cost of the planned ending inventory are shown in Schedule 7.

Schedule 7
CalBlock, Inc.
Ending Inventory Budget (in thousands)
For the Year Ended December 31, 1998

Unit-cost computation:
Direct materials (26 lb @ $0.01)	$0.26
Direct labor (0.015 hr @ $10)	0.15
Overhead:	
Variable (0.015 hr @ $8)	0.12
Fixed (0.015 hr @ $5.33*)	0.08
Total unit cost	$0.61

$$*\frac{\text{Budgeted fixed overhead (Schedule 5)}}{\text{Budgeted direct labor hours (Schedule 4)}} = \frac{\$1,280}{240} = \$5.33$$

	Units	Unit Cost	Total
Finished goods: Concrete blocks	100	$0.61	$61

Cost of Goods Sold Budget Assuming that the beginning finished goods inventory is valued at $55,000, the budgeted cost of goods sold schedule can be prepared using Schedules 3, 4, 5, and 7. The cost of goods sold schedule (Schedule 8) is the last schedule needed before the budgeted income statement can be prepared.

Schedule 8
CalBlock, Inc.
Cost of Goods Sold Budget (in thousands)
For the year ended December 31, 1998

Direct materials used (Schedule 3)*	$4,160
Direct labor used (Schedule 4)	2,400
Overhead (Schedule 5)	3,200
Budgeted manufacturing costs	$9,760
Beginning finished goods	55
Goods available for sale	$9,815
Less: Ending finished goods (Schedule 7)	(61)
Budgeted cost of goods sold	$9,754

*Production needs × $0.01 = 416,000 × $0.01

Budgeted Income Statement With the completion of the budgeted cost of goods sold schedule, CalBlock has all the operating budgets needed to prepare an estimate of operating income. This budgeted income statement is shown in Schedule 9. The eight schedules already prepared, along with the budgeted operating income statement, define the operating budget for CalBlock.

Schedule 9 CalBlock, Inc. Budgeted Income Statement (in thousands) For the Year Ended December 31, 1998	
Sales (Schedule 1)	$12,000
Less: Cost of goods sold (Schedule 8)	(9,754)
Gross margin	$ 2,246
Less: Selling and administrative expenses (Schedule 6)	(1,075)
Operating income	$ 1,171
Less: Interest expense (Schedule 10, p. 300)	(54)
Income before taxes	$ 1,117
Less: Income taxes (Schedule 10)	(650)
Net income	$ 467

Operating income is *not* equivalent to the net income of a firm. To yield net income, interest expenses and taxes must be subtracted from operating income. The interest expense deduction is taken from the cash budget shown in Schedule 10 (p. 300). The taxes owed depend on the current tax laws.

Preparing the Financial Budget

The remaining budgets found in the master budget are the financial budgets. The usual financial budgets prepared are

1. The cash budget
2. The budgeted balance sheet
3. The budget for capital expenditures

The master budget also contains a plan for acquiring long-term assets—assets that have a time horizon that extend beyond the one-year operating period. Some of these assets may be purchased during the coming year; plans to purchase others may be detailed for future periods. This part of the master budget is typically referred to as the *capital budget*. Decision making for capital expenditures is considered in Chapter 17. Accordingly, only the cash budget and the budgeted balance sheet will be illustrated here.

cash budget

Cash Budget Knowledge of cash flows is critical to managing a business. Often a business is successful in producing and selling a product but fails because of timing problems associated with cash inflows and outflows. By knowing when cash deficiencies and surpluses are likely to occur, a manager can plan to borrow cash when needed and to repay the loans during periods of excess cash. Bank loan officers use a company's cash budget to document the need for cash, as well as the ability to repay. Because cash flow is the lifeblood of an organization, the cash budget is one of the most important budgets in the master budget. The cash budget is illustrated in Exhibit 8-2.

Cash available consists of the beginning cash balance and the expected cash receipts. Expected cash receipts include all sources of cash for the period being considered. The principal source of cash is from sales. Because a significant proportion of sales is usually on account, a major task of an organization is to determine the pattern of collection for its accounts receivable.

8-2

Exhibit
The Cash Budget

Beginning cash balance
+ Cash receipts
Cash available
− Cash disbursements
− Minimum cash balance
Excess or deficiency of cash
+ Loans, or
− Repayments
+ Minimum cash balance
Ending cash balance

deduct beginning excess/deficit

added back

If a company has been in business for a while, it can use past experience in creating an accounts receivable aging schedule. In other words, the company can determine, on average, what percentages of its accounts receivable are paid in the months following sale. For example, let's say that Patton Hardware Store has the following accounts receivable payment experience:

Percent paid in the month of sale	30%
Percent paid in the month after the sale	60%
Percent paid in the second month after the sale	10%

If Patton sells $100,000 worth of goods on account in the month of May, then it would expect to receive $30,000 cash from May credit sales in the month of May; $60,000 cash from May credit sales in June; and $10,000 from May credit sales in July. (Notice that Patton expects to receive all of its accounts receivable. This is not typical. If a company experiences, let's say, 3 percent uncollectible accounts, then this 3 percent of sales is ignored for the purpose of cash budgeting—it is simply not received.)

The cash disbursements section lists all planned cash outlays for the period. All expenses not resulting in a cash outlay are excluded from the list (depreciation, for example, is never included in the disbursements section). A disbursement that is typically not included in this section is interest on short-term borrowing. This interest expenditure is reserved for the section on loan repayments.

The cash excess or deficiency line compares the cash available with the cash needed. Cash needed is the total cash disbursements plus the minimum cash balance required by company policy. The minimum cash balance is simply the lowest amount of cash on hand that the firm finds acceptable. Consider your own checking account. You probably try to keep at least some cash in the account, perhaps because a minimum balance avoids service charges, or because a minimum balance allows you to make an unplanned purchase. Similarly, companies also require minimum cash balances. The amount varies from firm to firm and is determined by each company's particular needs and policies. If the total cash available is less than the cash needs, a deficiency exists. In such a case, a short-term loan will be needed. On the other hand, with a cash excess (cash available is greater than the firm's cash needs), the firm has the ability to repay loans and perhaps make some temporary investments.

The final section of the cash budget consists of borrowings and repayments. If there is a deficiency, this section shows the necessary amount to be borrowed. When excess cash is available, this section shows planned repayments, including interest expense.

The last line of the cash budget is the planned ending cash balance. Remember that the minimum cash balance was subtracted to find the cash excess or deficiency. However, the minimum cash balance is not a disbursement, so it must be added back to yield the planned ending balance.

To illustrate the cash budget, assume the following for CalBlock:

a. A $100,000 minimum cash balance is required for the end of each quarter.
b. Money can be borrowed and repaid in multiples of $100,000. Interest is 12 percent per year. Interest payments are made only for the amount of the principal being repaid. All borrowing takes place at the beginning of a quarter and all repayment takes place at the end of a quarter.
c. Half of all sales are for cash, 70 percent of credit sales are collected in the quarter of sale, and the remaining 30 percent are collected in the following quarter. The sales for the fourth quarter of 1997 were $2 million.
d. Purchases of raw materials are made on account; 80 percent of purchases are paid for in the quarter of purchase. The remaining 20 percent are paid for in the following quarter. The purchases for the fourth quarter of 1997 were $500,000.
e. Budgeted depreciation is $200,000 per quarter for overhead and $15,000 per quarter for selling and administration (see Schedules 5 and 6).
f. The capital budget for 1998 revealed plans to purchase additional equipment to handle increased demand at a small plant in Nevada. The cash outlay for the equipment, $600,000, will take place in the first quarter. The company plans to finance the acquisition of the equipment with operating cash, supplementing it with short-term loans as necessary.
g. Corporate income taxes are approximately $650,000 and will be paid at the end of the fourth quarter (Schedule 9).
h. Beginning cash balance equals $120,000.

Given this information, the cash budget for CalBlock is shown in Schedule 10 (all figures are rounded to the nearest thousand).

Much of the information needed to prepare the cash budget comes from the operating budgets. In fact, Schedules 1, 3, 4, 5, and 6 contain important input. However, these schedules by themselves do not supply all of the needed information. The collection pattern for revenues and the payment pattern for materials must be known before the cash flow for sales and purchases on credit can be found.

Exhibit 8-3 displays the pattern of cash inflows from both cash and credit sales. Let's look at the cash receipts for the first quarter of 1998. Cash sales during the quarter are budgeted for $700,000 (0.50 × $1,400,000; Schedule 1). Collections on account for the first quarter relate to credit sales made during the last quarter of the previous year and the first quarter of 1998. Quarter 4, 1997, credit sales equaled $1,000,000 (0.50 × $2,000,000) and $300,000 of those sales (0.30 × $1,000,000) remain to be collected in quarter 1, 1998. Quarter 1, 1998, credit sales are budgeted at $700,000 and 70 percent will be collected in that quarter. Therefore, $490,000 will be collected on account for

8-3

Exhibit
Pattern of Cash Receipts
for CalBlock

Source	Quarter 1	Quarter 2	Quarter 3	Quarter 4
Cash sales	$ 700,000	$2,100,000	$2,400,000	$ 800,000
Received on account from sales in:				
Quarter 4, 1997	300,000			
Quarter 1, 1998	490,000	210,000		
Quarter 2, 1998		1,470,000	630,000	
Quarter 3, 1998			1,680,000	720,000
Quarter 4, 1998				560,000
Total cash receipts	$1,490,000	$3,780,000	$4,710,000	$2,080,000

Schedule 10
CalBlock, Inc.
Cash Budget (in thousands)
For the Year Ended December 31, 1998

| | Quarter | | | | | |
	1	2	3	4	Year	Source[a]
Beginning cash balance	$ 120	$ 169	$ 162	$ 986	$ 120	
Collections:						
Cash sales	700	2,100	2,400	800	6,000	c, 1
Credit sales:						
Current quarter	490	1,470	1,680	560	4,200	c, 1
Prior quarter	300	210	630	720	1,860	c, 1
Total cash available	$ 1,610	$ 3,949	$ 4,872	$ 3,066	$ 12,180	
Less disbursements:						
Raw materials:						
Current quarter	$ (523)	$(1,248)	$(1,141)	$ (416)	$ (3,328)	d, 3
Prior quarter	(100)	(131)	(312)	(285)	(828)	d, 3
Direct labor	(360)	(900)	(840)	(300)	(2,400)	4
Overhead	(408)	(840)	(792)	(360)	(2,400)	e, 5
Selling and administrative	(150)	(350)	(365)	(150)	(1,015)	e, 6
Income taxes	—	—	—	(650)	(650)	g, 9
Equipment	(600)	—	—	—	(600)	f
Total disbursements	$(2,141)	$(3,469)	$(3,450)	$(2,161)	$(11,221)	
Minimum cash balance	(100)	(100)	(100)	(100)	(100)	a
Total cash needs	$(2,241)	$(3,569)	$(3,550)	$(2,261)	$(11,321)	
Excess (deficiency) of cash available over needs	$ (631)	$ 380	$ 1,322	$ 805	$ 859	
Financing:						
Borrowings	700	—	—	—	700	
Repayments	—	(300)	(400)	—	(700)	b
Interest[b]	—	(18)	(36)	—	(54)	b
Total financing	700	(318)	(436)	—	(54)	
Ending cash balance[c]	$ 169	$ 162	$ 986	$ 905	$ 905	

[a]Letters refer to the information on page 299. Numbers refer to schedules already developed.
[b]Interest payments are $\frac{6}{12} \times 0.12 \times \$300$ and $\frac{9}{12} \times 0.12 \times \$400$, respectively. Since borrowings occur at the beginning of the quarter and repayments at the end of the quarter, the first principal repayment takes place after six months, and the second principal repayment takes place after nine months.
[c]Total cash available minus total disbursements plus (or minus) total financing.

credit sales made in that quarter. Similar computations are made for the remaining quarters.

Similar computations are done for purchases. In both cases, patterns of collection and payment are needed in addition to the information supplied by the schedules. Additionally, all noncash expenses, such as depreciation, need to be removed from the total amounts reported in the expense budgets. Thus, the budgeted expenses in Schedules 5 and 6 were reduced by the budgeted depreciation for each quarter. Overhead expenses in Schedule 5 were reduced by depreciation of $200,000 per quarter. Selling and administrative expenses were reduced by $15,000 per quarter. The net amounts are what appear in the cash budget.

The cash budget shown in Schedule 10 underscores the importance of breaking down the annual budget into smaller time periods. The cash budget for the year gives the impression that sufficient operating cash will be available to finance the acquisition of the new equipment. Quarterly information, however, shows the need for short-term borrowing ($700,000) because of both the acquisition of the new equipment and the timing of the firm's cash flows. Most firms prepare monthly cash budgets, and some even prepare weekly and daily budgets.

Another significant piece of information emerges from CalBlock's cash budget. By the end of the third quarter, the firm has a considerable amount of cash ($986,000). It is certainly not wise to allow this much cash to sit idly in a bank account. The management of CalBlock should consider paying dividends and making long-term investments. At the very least, the excess cash should be invested in short-term marketable securities. Once plans are finalized for use of the excess cash, the cash budget should be revised to reflect those plans. Budgeting is a dynamic process. As the budget is developed, new information becomes available and better plans can be formulated.

Budgeted Balance Sheet The budgeted balance sheet depends on information contained in the current balance sheet and in the other budgets in the master budget. The balance sheet for the beginning of the year is given in Exhibit 8-4. The budgeted balance sheet for December 31, 1998, is given in Schedule 11. Explanations for the budgeted figures follow the schedule.

As we have described the individual budgets that make up the master budget, the interdependencies of the component budgets have become apparent. A diagram displaying these interrelationships is shown in Exhibit 8-5.

USING BUDGETS FOR PERFORMANCE EVALUATION

Budgets are usefulcontrol measures. To be used in performance evaluation, however, two major considerations must be addressed. The first is to determine how budgeted

8-4

Exhibit

CalBlock, Inc. Balance Sheet (in thousands) December 31, 1997 Assets		
Current assets:		
Cash	$ 120	
Accounts receivable	300	
Raw materials inventory	50	
Finished goods	55	
Total current assets		$ 525
Property, plant, and equipment (PP&E):		
Land	$ 2,500	
Building and equipment	9,000	
Accumulated depreciation	(4,500)	
Total PP&E		7,000
Total assets		$7,525
Liabilities and Stockholders' Equity		
Current liabilities:		
Accounts payable		$ 100
Stockholders' equity:		
Common stock, no par	$ 600	
Retained earnings	6,825	
Total stockholders' equity		7,425
Total liabilities and stockholders' equity		$7,525

Schedule 11
CalBlock, Inc.
Budgeted Balance Sheet (in thousands)
December 31, 1998
Assets

Current assets:		
Cash	$ 905[a]	
Accounts receivable	240[b]	
Raw materials inventory	50[c]	
Finished goods	61[d]	
Total current assets		$1,256
Property, plant, and equipment (PP&E):		
Land	$ 2,500[e]	
Building and equipment	9,600[f]	
Accumulated depreciation	(5,360)[g]	
Total PP&E		6,740
Total assets		$7,996

Liabilities and Stockholders' Equity

Current liabilities:		
Accounts payable		$ 104[h]
Stockholders' equity:		
Common stock, no par	$ 600[i]	
Retained earnings	7,292[j]	
Total stockholders' equity		7,892
Total liabilities and stockholders' equity		$7,996

[a]Ending balance from Schedule 10
[b]30 percent of fourth-quarter credit sales (0.30 × $800,000)—see Schedules 1 and 10
[c]From Schedule 3 (5 million pounds @ $0.01)
[d]From Schedule 8
[e]From the December 31, 1997, balance sheet
[f]December 31, 1997, balance ($9,000,000) plus new equipment acquisition of $600,000 (see the 1997 ending balance sheet and Schedule 10)
[g]From the December 31, 1997, balance sheet, Schedule 5, and Schedule 6 ($4,500,000 + $800,000 + $60,000)
[h]20 percent of fourth-quarter purchases (0.20 × $520,000)—see Schedules 3 and 10
[i]From the December 31, 1997, balance sheet
[j]$6,825,000 + $467,000 (December 31, 1997, balance plus net income from Schedule 9)

Objective 3

Identify and discuss the key features that a budgetary system should have to encourage managers to engage in goal-congruent behavior.

amounts should be compared with actual results. The second consideration involves the impact of budgets on human behavior.

Static Budgets versus Flexible Budgets

Budgets can be used for both planning and control. In planning, companies prepare a master budget based on their best estimate of the level of activity to be achieved in the coming year. However, typically the actual level of activity does not equal the budgeted level. As a result, budgeted amounts cannot be compared with actual results. Therefore, companies may also prepare flexible budgets to be used for performance evaluation.

static budget

Static Budgets The master budget developed for CalBlock is an example of a static budget. A static budget is a budget for a particular level of activity. For CalBlock,

8-5 ································ The Master Budget and Its Interrelationships

Exhibit

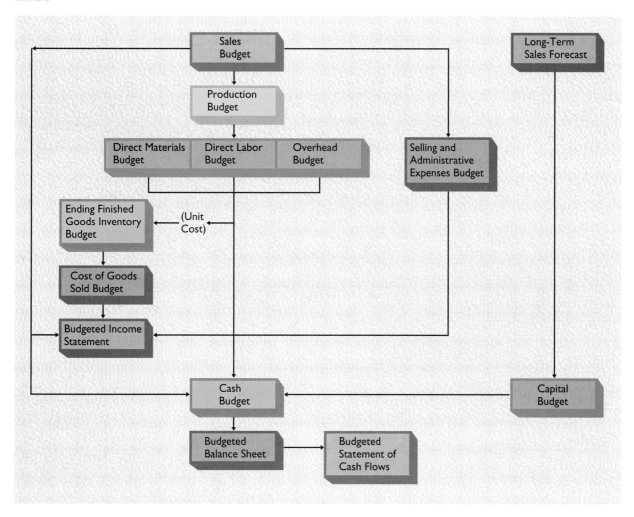

budgets were developed based on expected annual sales of 16 million units. Because static budgets depend on a particular level of activity, they are not very useful when it comes to preparing performance reports.

To illustrate, suppose that CalBlock's first quarter sales were greater than expected; 2.6 million concrete blocks were sold instead of the 2 million budgeted in Schedule 1. Because of increased sales activity, production was increased over the planned level. Instead of producing 2.4 million units (Schedule 2), CalBlock produced 3 million units.

A performance report comparing the actual production costs for the first quarter with the original planned production costs is given in Exhibit 8-6. In contrast to Schedule 5, budgeted amounts for individual overhead items are provided. Thus, the individual budgeted amounts for each overhead item are new information (except for depreciation). Usually, this information would be detailed in an overhead budget.

According to the report, unfavorable variances occurred for direct materials, direct labor, supplies, indirect labor, and rent. However, there is something fundamentally wrong with the report. Actual costs for production of 3 million concrete blocks are being compared with planned costs for production of 2.4 million. Because direct materials, direct labor, and variable overhead are variable costs, we would expect them to be greater at a higher activity level. Thus, even if cost control were perfect for the production

8-6

Exhibit
Performance Report:
Quarterly Production
Costs (in thousands)

	Actual	Budgeted	Variance
Units produced	3,000	2,400	600 Fª
Direct materials cost	$ 927.3	$ 624.0ᵇ	$303.3 Uᶜ
Direct labor cost	450.0	360.0ᵈ	90.0 U
Overhead:ᵉ			
Variable:			
Supplies	80.0	72.0	8.0 U
Indirect labor	220.0	168.0	52.0 U
Power	40.0	48.0	(8.0) F
Fixed:			
Supervision	90.0	100.0	(10.0) F
Depreciation	200.0	200.0	0.0
Rent	30.0	20.0	10.0 U
Total	$2,037.3	$1,592.0	$445.3 U

ªF means the variance is favorable.
ᵇThis is from Schedule 3 (62,400 lb × $0.01).
ᶜU means the variance is unfavorable.
ᵈThis is from Schedule 4.
ᵉSchedule 5 provides the aggregate amount of budgeted overhead (for example, the aggregate variable overhead is 0.015 × 2,400,000 × $8 = $288,000, and the total budgeted fixed overhead is $320,000).

of 3 million units, unfavorable variances would be produced for at least some of the variable costs.

To create a meaningful performance report, actual costs and expected costs must be compared at the *same* level of activity. Since actual output often differs from planned output, some method is needed to compute what the costs should have been for the actual output level.

Flexible Budgets The budget that provides a firm with the capability to compute expected costs for a range of activity is called a flexible budget. Flexible budgeting has three major uses.

flexible budget

1. The flexible budget can be used to prepare the budget before the fact for the expected level of activity.
2. Because flexible budgeting can determine what costs should be at various levels of activity, the budget can be used after the fact to compute what costs should have been for the actual level of activity. Once expected costs are known for the actual level of activity, a performance report that compares those expected costs to actual costs can be prepared.
3. Flexible budgeting can help managers deal with uncertainty by allowing them to see the expected outcomes for a range of activity. It can be used to generate financial results for a number of plausible scenarios.

Flexible budgeting is the key to providing the frequent feedback that managers need to exercise control and effectively carry out the plans of an organization.

To compute the expected cost at different levels of activity, we need to know the cost behavior pattern of each item in the budget. That is, we need to know the variable cost per unit of activity, and the fixed cost per item.

Let's prepare a flexible budget for CalBlock where activity level is measured by the number of concrete blocks produced. From Schedule 7, we know the variable costs for direct materials ($0.26 per unit), direct labor ($0.15 per unit), and variable overhead ($0.12 per unit). To increase the detail of the flexible budget, let's assume these variable costs per unit for supplies ($0.03), indirect labor ($0.07), and power ($0.02). These three individual variable overhead amounts sum to $0.12. From Schedule 5, we also know that fixed overhead is budgeted at $320,000 per quarter. Exhibit 8-7 displays a flexible budget for production costs at three levels of activity.

Notice in Exhibit 8-7 that total budgeted production costs increase as the activity level increases. Budgeted costs change because of variable costs. Because of this, flexible budgets are sometimes referred to as variable budgets.

variable budgets

Flexible budgets are powerful control tools because they allow management to compute what the costs should be for any level of activity. Exhibit 8-7 reveals what the costs should have been for the actual level of activity (3 million units). Now we can provide management with a useful performance report, one that compares actual and budgeted costs for the actual level of activity. This report is given in Exhibit 8-8.

The revised performance report in Exhibit 8-8 paints a much different picture from the one in Exhibit 8-6. By comparing budgeted costs for the actual level of activity with actual costs for the same level, a problem area can be immediately identified—expenditures for direct materials are excessive. (The other unfavorable variances seem relatively small.) With this knowledge, management can search for the causes of the excess expenditures and take action to prevent the same problems from occurring in future quarters.

flexible budget variance

A difference between the actual amount and the flexible budget amount is the flexible budget variance. The flexible budget provides the capability to assess the efficiency of a manager. In addition to measuring the efficiency of a manager, it is often desirable to measure whether a manager accomplishes his or her goals. The static budget is important for this since it represented certain goals that the firm wanted to achieve. A manager is *effective* if the goals described by the static budget are achieved or exceeded. In the CalBlock example, production volume was 600,000 units greater than the original budgeted amount; the manager exceeded the original budgeted goal. Therefore, the effectiveness of the manager is not in question. The main issue is how well the manager controlled costs as revealed by the flexible budget variances.

The Behavioral Dimension of Budgeting

Budgets are often used to judge the actual performance of managers. Bonuses, salary increases, and promotions are all affected by a manager's ability to achieve or beat budgeted goals. Since a manager's financial status and career can be affected, budgets can have a significant behavioral effect. Whether that effect is positive or negative depends to a large extent on how budgets are used.

8-7

Exhibit
Flexible Production
Budget (in thousands)

Production Costs	Variable Cost per Unit	Range of Production (units)		
		2,400	3,000	3,600
Variable:				
Direct materials	$0.26	$ 624	$ 780	$ 936
Direct labor	0.15	360	450	540
Variable overhead:				
Supplies	0.03	72	90	108
Indirect labor	0.07	168	210	252
Power	0.02	48	60	72
Total variable costs	$0.53	$1,272	$1,590	$1,908
Fixed overhead:				
Supervision		$ 100	$ 100	$ 100
Depreciation		200	200	200
Rent		20	20	20
Total fixed costs		$ 320	$ 320	$ 320
Total production costs		$1,592	$1,910	$2,228

Exhibit
Actual versus Flexible
Performance Report:
Quarterly Production
Costs (in thousands)

	Actual	Budget*	Variance
Units produced	3,000	3,000	—
Production costs:			
Direct materials	$ 927.3	$ 780.0	$147.3 U
Direct labor	450.0	450.0	0.0
Variable overhead:			
Supplies	80.0	90.0	(10.0) F
Indirect labor	220.0	210.0	10.0 U
Power	40.0	60.0	(20.0) F
Total variable costs	$1,717.3	$1,590.0	$127.3 U
Fixed overhead:			
Supervision	$ 90.0	$ 100.0	$(10.0) F
Depreciation	200.0	200.0	0.0
Rent	30.0	20.0	10.0 U
Total fixed costs	$ 320.0	$ 320.0	0.0
Total production costs	$2,037.3	$1,910.0	$127.3 U

*From Exhibit 8-7

goal congruence

Positive behavior occurs when the goals of individual managers are aligned with the goals of the organization and the manager has the drive to achieve them. The alignment of managerial and organizational goals is often referred to as goal congruence. In addition to goal congruence, however, a manager must also exert effort to achieve the goals of the organization.

dysfunctional behavior

If the budget is improperly administered, subordinate managers may subvert the organization's goals. Dysfunctional behavior is individual behavior that is in basic conflict with the goals of the organization.

A theme underlying the behavioral dimension of budgeting is ethics. The importance of budgets in performance evaluation and managers' pay raises and promotions leads to the possibility of unethical action. All of the dysfunctional actions that can be taken regarding budgets can have an unethical aspect. For example, a manager who deliberately underestimates sales and overestimates costs for the purpose of making the budget easier to achieve is engaging in unethical behavior. It is the responsibility of the company to create budgetary incentives that do not encourage unethical behavior. It is the responsibility of the manager not to engage in such behavior.

An ideal budgetary system is one that achieves complete goal congruence, and, simultaneously, creates a drive in managers to achieve the organization's goals in an ethical manner. While an ideal budgetary system probably does not exist, research and practice have identified some key features that promote a reasonable degree of positive behavior. These features include: frequent feedback on performance; monetary and nonmonetary incentives; participative budgeting; realistic standards; controllability of costs; and multiple measures of performance.

Frequent Feedback on Performance Managers need to know how they are doing as the year unfolds. Providing them with frequent, timely performance reports allows them to know how successful their efforts have been, to take corrective actions, and to change plans as necessary. Frequent performance reports can reinforce positive behavior and give managers the time and opportunity to adapt to changing conditions.

The use of flexible budgets allows management to see if actual costs and revenues are in accord with budgeted amounts. Selective investigation of significant variances allows managers to focus only on areas that need attention. This process is called *management by exception*.

Monetary and Nonmonetary Incentives A sound budgetary system encourages goal-congruent behavior. The means an organization uses to influence a manager to exert effort to achieve an organization's goal are called incentives. Incentives can be either negative or positive. Negative incentives use fear of punishment to motivate; positive incentives use the expectation of reward. What incentives should be tied into an organization's budgetary system?

incentives

Traditional organizational theory assumes that individuals are primarily motivated by monetary rewards, resist work, and are inefficient and wasteful.[3] Companies accepting this view impose budgets from above and hold managers strictly accountable for each line in the budget. In this way, top management can control a subordinate manager's tendency to shirk and waste resources. Since managers are believed to be primarily motivated by monetary incentives, this control is achieved by relating budgetary performance to salary increases, bonuses, and promotions. The threat of dismissal is the ultimate economic sanction for poor performance.

monetary incentives

This view of human behavior is too simplistic. Individuals are motivated by more than just external rewards. In addition to the economic factors, individuals are motivated by a complex set of intrinsic psychological and social factors. These factors include: the satisfaction of a job well done, recognition, responsibility, self-esteem, and the nature of the work itself. A successful budgetary control system does not ignore the complex forces motivating individuals. Monetary rewards alone are not enough to achieve the desired level of motivation in managers. Nonmonetary incentives, including job enrichment, increased responsibility and autonomy, nonmonetary recognition programs, and so on, can be used to enhance a budgetary control system.

nonmonetary incentives

participative budgeting

Participative Budgeting Rather than imposing budgets on subordinate managers, participative budgeting allows subordinate managers considerable say in how the budgets are established. Typically, overall objectives are communicated to the manager, who helps develop a budget that will accomplish these objectives. In participative budgeting, the emphasis is on the accomplishment of the broad objectives, not on individual budget items.

Participative budgeting communicates a sense of responsibility to subordinate managers and fosters creativity. Since the subordinate manager creates the budget, it is more likely that the budget's goals will become the manager's personal goals, resulting in greater goal congruence. Advocates of participative budgeting claim that the increased responsibility and challenge inherent in the process provide nonmonetary incentives that lead to a higher level of performance. They argue that individuals involved in setting their own standards will work harder to achieve them. In addition to the behavioral benefits, participative budgeting has the advantage of involving individuals whose knowledge of local conditions may enhance the entire planning process.

Participative budgeting has three potential problems:

1. Setting standards that are either too high or too low
2. Building slack into the budget (often referred to as *padding the budget*)
3. Pseudoparticipation

Some managers may tend to set the budget either too loose or too tight. Since budgeted goals tend to become the manager's goals when participation is allowed, making this mistake in setting the budget can result in decreased performance levels. If goals are too easily achieved, a manager may lose interest and performance may actually drop. Challenge is important to aggressive and creative individuals. Similarly, setting the budget too tight ensures failure to achieve the standards and frustrates the manager. This frustration, too, can lead to poorer performance. The trick is to get managers in a participative setting to set high but achievable goals.

3. An excellent discussion of traditional and modern views of organizational theory and their implications for managerial accounting is given by Edwin H. Caplan, *Management Accounting and Behavioral Science* (Reading, MA: Addison-Wesley, 1971).

Ski resorts must forecast many factors in preparing a budget for the coming year. They must consider the weather, the probability of snow, the prices to be charged by competing resorts, and a host of other factors. For example, Colorado ski resorts were concerned that the opening of Denver International Airport with its higher airport taxes would reduce the number of passengers willing to fly into Denver to ski.

budgetary slack

The second problem with participative budgeting is the opportunity for managers to build slack into the budget. Budgetary slack (or *padding the budget*) exists when a manager deliberately underestimates revenues or overestimates costs. Either approach increases the likelihood that the manager will achieve the budget and consequently reduces the risk that the manager faces. Padding the budget also unnecessarily ties up resources that might be used more productively elsewhere.

Slack in budgets can be virtually eliminated by having top management dictate lower expense budgets; however, the benefits to be gained from participation may far exceed the costs associated with padding the budget. Even so, top management should carefully review budgets proposed by subordinate managers and provide input, where needed, in order to decrease the effects of building slack into the budget.

pseudoparticipation

The third problem with participation occurs when top management assumes total control of the budgeting process, seeking only superficial participation from lower-level managers. This practice is termed pseudoparticipation. Top management is simply obtaining formal acceptance of the budget from subordinate managers, not seeking real input. Accordingly, none of the behavioral benefits of participation will be realized.

Realistic Standards Budgeted objectives are used to gauge performance; accordingly, they should be based on realistic conditions and expectations. Budgets should reflect operating realities such as actual levels of activity, seasonal variations, efficiencies, and general economic trends. Flexible budgets, for example, are used to ensure that the budgeted costs provide standards that are compatible with the actual activity level. Another factor that should be considered is seasonality. Some businesses receive revenues and incur costs uniformly throughout the year; thus, spreading the annual revenues and costs evenly over quarters and months is reasonable for interim performance reports. However, for businesses with seasonal variations, this practice would result in distorted performance reports. Nintendo, for example, must gear up production and selling efforts for the Christmas season, when 70 percent of all video game machines are bought.[4]

Such factors as efficiency and general economic conditions are also important. Occasionally, top management makes arbitrary cuts in prior-year budgets with the belief that the cuts will reduce fat or inefficiencies that allegedly exist. In reality, some units may be operating efficiently and others inefficiently. An across-the-board cut without any formal evaluation may impair the ability of some units to carry out their missions. General economic conditions also need to be considered. Budgeting for a significant increase in sales when a recession is projected is not only foolish but potentially dangerous.

controllable costs

Controllability of Costs Conventional thought maintains that managers should be held accountable only for costs over which they have control. Controllable costs are costs whose level a manager can influence. In this view, a manager who has no responsibility for a cost should not be held accountable for it. For example, divisional managers have no power to authorize such corporate-level costs as research and development and salaries of top managers. Therefore, they should not be held accountable for the incurrence of those costs.

Many firms, however, do put noncontrollable costs in the budgets of subordinate managers. Making managers aware of the need to cover all costs is one rationale for this practice. If noncontrollable costs are included in a budget, they should be separated from controllable costs and labeled as *noncontrollable*.

It is important to note that controllable does not mean that managers have complete control over costs. For example, United Airlines budgeted lower costs for 1995 than were realized. Wage increases for flight attendants, the unforeseen added costs of Denver International Airport (a major United hub), and increased food, beverage, and travel-agent commissions led to higher actual costs. While United managers had little say in the costs of Denver International Airport, for example, they were still responsible for the costs incurred by the company.

myopic behavior

ST Benefit
LT harm

Multiple Measures of Performance Often organizations make the mistake of using budgets as their only measure of managerial performance. Overemphasis on this measure can lead to a form of dysfunctional behavior called *milking the firm* or *myopia*. Myopic behavior occurs when a manager takes actions that improve budgetary performance in the short run but bring long-run harm to the firm.

There are numerous examples of myopic behavior. To meet budgeted cost objectives or profits, managers can reduce expenditures for preventive maintenance, for advertising, and for new product development. Managers can also fail to promote promotable employees to keep the cost of labor low and choose to use lower-quality materials to reduce the cost of raw materials. In the short run, these actions will lead to improved budgetary performance, but in the long run, productivity will fall, market share will decline, and capable employees will leave for more attractive opportunities.

Managers who engage in this kind of behavior often have a short tenure. In these cases, managers spend three to five years before being promoted or moving to a new area of responsibility. Their successors are the ones who pay the price for their myopic behavior. The best way to prevent myopic behavior is to measure the performance of managers on several dimensions, including some long-run attributes. Productivity, quality, and personnel development are examples of other areas of performance that could be evaluated. Financial measures of performance are important, but overemphasis on them can be counterproductive.

4. Heidi Dawley and Paul M. Eng, "Killer Instinct for Hire," *Business Week*, 29 May 1995, 91–92.

OTHER TYPES OF BUDGETS

Objective 4

Describe budgets for merchandising and service firms and zero-base budgeting.

While the master and flexible budgets described are widely used for planning and control in manufacturing firms, the special needs of service and merchandising firms deserve mention. Additionally, a different approach to budgeting, called *zero-base budgeting*, can be used for long-term planning.

Operating Budgets for Merchandising and Service Firms

In a merchandising firm, the production budget is replaced with a merchandise purchases budget. This budget identifies the quantity of each item that must be purchased for resale, the unit cost of the item, and the total purchase cost. The format is identical to that of the direct materials budget in a manufacturing firm. The only other difference between the operating budgets of manufacturing and merchandising firms is the absence of direct materials and direct labor budgets in a merchandising firm.

In a for-profit service firm, the sales budget is also the production budget. The sales budget identifies each service and the quantity of it that will be sold. Since finished goods inventories are nonexistent, the services produced will be identical to the services sold.

In a not-for-profit service firm, the sales budget is replaced by a budget that identifies the levels of the various services that will be offered for the coming year and the associated funds that will be assigned to the services. The source of the funds may be tax revenues, contributions, payments by users of the services, or some combination. For example, the board of directors for a local United Way budgets the campaign target (dollars of contributions) for the coming year, and then distributes the total among the qualifying agencies according to three levels—pessimistic, expected, and optimistic.

Both for-profit and not-for-profit service organizations lack finished goods inventory budgets. However, all the remaining operating budgets found in a manufacturing organization have counterparts in service organizations. For a not-for-profit service organization, the income statement is replaced by a statement of sources and uses of funds.

Zero-Base Budgeting

incremental (or baseline) budgeting

The traditional approach to budgeting is the incremental approach. Incremental (or baseline) budgeting starts with last year's budget and adds or subtracts from that budget to reflect changing assumptions for the coming year. For example, if last year's budgeted expenditures for an agency or department were $1.2 million, the agency or department may request a 5 percent increase ($60,000) to provide the same level of service for the coming year. The typical justification for increased expenditures is the increased cost of inputs (labor, materials, and so on). The incremental approach may not entail a careful evaluation of the level of services being offered or of whether they are being offered efficiently.

Under the incremental approach, heads of budgeting units often strive to spend all of the year's budget so that no surplus exists at the end of the year. (This is particularly true for government agencies.) This action is taken to maintain the current level of the budget and enable the head of the unit to request additional funds. For example, at a U.S. Air Force base, a bomber wing was faced with the possibility of a surplus at the end of the fiscal year. The base commander, however, found ways to spend the extra money before the year ended. Missile officers, who normally drove to the missile command site, were flown to the sites in helicopters; several bags of lawn fertilizer were given away to all personnel with houses on base; and new furniture was acquired for the bachelor officer quarters. The waste and inefficiency portrayed in this example is often perpetuated and encouraged by incremental budgeting.

zero-base budgeting

Zero-base budgeting is an alternative approach.[5] Unlike incremental budgeting, the prior year's budgeted level is not taken for granted. Existing operations are analyzed, and continuance of the activity or operation must be justified on the basis of its need or

decision package

usefulness to the organization. The burden of proof is on each manager to justify why any money should be spent at all. In effect, each subunit of a company starts from ground zero and prepares a series of budgets—one for every decision package being considered.

A decision package is a description of services, with associated costs, that a decision unit can or would like to offer. Along with a budget, each package should contain a statement of the unit's goals, programs to achieve these goals, the benefits expected, and the consequences of not approving the package. The best of the alternative packages is chosen and the others are discarded. This process forces managers to take a fresh look at their operations and consider the best way to carry out their objectives.

Zero-base budgeting requires extensive, in-depth analysis. Although this approach has been used successfully in industry and government (for example, Texas Instruments and the state of Georgia), it is time consuming and costly. Advocates of the incremental approach argue that incremental budgeting should also use extensive, in-depth reviews but not as frequently because they are not justified on a cost-benefit basis. A reasonable compromise may be to use zero-base budgeting every three to five years in order to weed out waste and inefficiency. Especially in a period of intense competition and reengineering, zero-base budgeting can force managers to "break set" and see their units in a different perspective.

5. Zero-base budgeting was developed by Peter Pyhrr of Texas Instruments. For a detailed discussion of the approach, see Peter Pyhrr, *Zero-Base Budgeting* (New York: Wiley, 1973).

SUMMARY OF LEARNING OBJECTIVES

1. Define *budgeting* and discuss its role in planning, control, and decision making.
Budgeting is the creation of a plan of action expressed in financial terms. Budgeting plays a key role in planning, control, and decision making. Budgets also serve to improve communication and coordination, a role that becomes increasingly important as organizations grow in size.

2. Define and prepare the *master budget,* identify its major components, and explain the interrelationships of its various components.
The master budget, the comprehensive financial plan of an organization, is made up of the operating and financial budgets. The operating budget is the budgeted income statement and all supporting schedules. The sales budget (Schedule 1) consists of the anticipated quantity and price of all products to be sold. The production budget (Schedule 2) gives the expected production in units to meet forecast sales and desired ending inventory goals; expected production is supplemented by beginning inventory. The direct materials purchases budget (Schedule 3) gives the necessary purchases during the year for every type of raw material to meet production and desired ending inventory goals. The direct labor budget (Schedule 4) and overhead budget (Schedule 5) give the amounts of these resources necessary for the coming year's production. The overhead budget may be broken down into fixed and variable components to facilitate preparation of the budget. The selling and administrative expenses budget (Schedule 6) gives the forecast costs for these functions. The finished goods inventory budget (Schedule 7) and the cost of goods sold budget (Schedule 8) detail production costs for the expected ending inventory and the units sold, respectively. The budgeted income

statement (Schedule 9) outlines the net income to be realized if budgeted plans come to fruition.

The financial budget includes the cash budget, the capital expenditures budget, and the budgeted balance sheet. The cash budget (Schedule 10) is simply the beginning balance in the cash account, plus anticipated receipts, minus anticipated disbursements, plus or minus any necessary borrowing. The budgeted (or pro forma) balance sheet (Schedule 11) gives the anticipated ending balances of the asset, liability, and equity accounts if budgeted plans hold.

3. Identify and discuss the key features that a budgetary system should have to encourage managers to engage in goal-congruent behavior.
The success of a budgetary system depends on how seriously human factors are considered. To discourage dysfunctional behavior, organizations should avoid overemphasizing budgets as a control mechanism. Other areas of performance should be evaluated in addition to budgets. Budgets can be improved as performance measures by using participative budgeting and other nonmonetary incentives, providing frequent feedback on performance, using flexible budgeting, ensuring that the budgetary objectives reflect reality, and holding managers accountable for only controllable costs.

4. Describe budgets for merchandising and service firms and zero-base budgeting.
Budgets for merchandising and service firms are similar to those prepared for manufacturing firms except that a purchases budget replaces the production budget and direct materials and labor budgets are not needed. Zero-base budgeting does not take the prior year's budgeted levels for granted. Existing operations are analyzed, and continuance of the activity must be justified on the basis of its usefulness to the organization.

KEY TERMS

REVIEW PROBLEM

Young Products produces coatracks. The projected sales for the first quarter of the coming year and the beginning and ending inventory data are as follows:

Unit sales	100,000
Unit price	$15
Units, beginning inventory	8,000
Units, targeted ending inventory	12,000

The coatracks are molded and then painted. Each rack requires 4 pounds of metal, which costs $2.50 per pound. The beginning inventory of raw materials is 4,000 pounds. Young Products wants to have 6,000 pounds of metal in inventory at the end of the quarter. Each rack produced requires 30 minutes of direct labor time, which is billed at $9 per hour.

REQUIRED:
1. Prepare a sales budget for the first quarter.
2. Prepare a production budget for the first quarter.
3. Prepare a direct materials purchases budget for the first quarter.
4. Prepare a direct labor budget for the first quarter.

Solution

1.

Young Products
Sales Budget
For the First Quarter

Units	100,000
Unit price	× $15
Sales	$1,500,000

2.

Young Products
Production Budget
For the First Quarter

Sales (in units)	100,000
Desired ending inventory	12,000
Total needs	112,000
Less: Beginning inventory	8,000
Units to be produced	104,000

3.

Young Products
Direct Materials Budget
For the First Quarter

Units to be produced		104,000
Direct materials per unit (lb)	×	4
Production needs (lb)		416,000
Desired ending inventory (lb)		6,000
Total needs (lb)		422,000
Less: Beginning inventory (lb)		(4,000)
Materials to be purchased (lb)		418,000
Cost per pound	×	$2.50
Total purchase cost		$1,045,000

4.

Young Products
Direct Labor Budget
For the First Quarter

Units to be produced		104,000
Labor: Time per unit	×	0.5
Total hours needed		52,000
Cost per hour	×	$9
Total direct labor cost		$468,000

QUESTIONS FOR WRITING AND DISCUSSION

1. Define the term *budget*. How are budgets used in planning?
2. Define *control*. How are budgets used to control?
3. Explain how both small and large organizations can benefit from budgeting.
4. Discuss some of the reasons for budgeting.
5. What is a master budget? an operating budget? a financial budget?
6. Explain the role of a sales forecast in budgeting. What is the difference between a sales forecast and a sales budget?
7. All budgets depend on the sales budget. Is this true? Explain.
8. Discuss the differences between static and flexible budgets. Why are flexible budgets superior to static budgets for performance reporting?
9. Explain why mixed costs must be broken down into their fixed and variable components before a flexible budget can be developed.
10. Why is goal congruence important?
11. Why is it important for a manager to receive frequent feedback on his or her performance?
12. Discuss the roles of monetary and nonmonetary incentives. Do you believe that nonmonetary incentives are needed? Why?

13. What is participative budgeting? Discuss some of its advantages.
14. A budget too easily achieved will lead to diminished performance. Do you agree? Explain.
15. What is the role of top management in participative budgeting?
16. Explain why a manager has an incentive to build slack into the budget.
17. Explain how a manager can *milk the firm* to improve budgetary performance.
18. Identify performance measures other than budgets that can be used to discourage myopic behavior. Discuss how you would use these measures.
19. How important are the behavioral aspects of a budgetary control system? Explain.
20. How do the master budgets differ among manufacturing, merchandising, and service organizations?
21. Explain the difference between incremental budgeting and zero-base budgeting.
22. Advocates of zero-base budgeting maintain that padding the budget is easier under an incremental system than under a zero-base system. Explain why padding is less likely for a zero-base budgeting system.
23. In an era of budgetary cuts, across-the-board cuts harm good programs more than bad programs. Do you agree? What approach would you recommend? Why?

W ARM-UP EXERCISES

This section provides short warm-up exercises based on the examples in the chapter. Each warm-up exercise gives the page number on which the text example can be found. You may want to refer to the text example to see how the exercise can be set up and solved.

W8-1
Sales Budget
LO 2
p. 292

Carrigan Company produces two laundry products: detergent, and a powdered presoak. Both products are sold in 32-ounce boxes. Detergent sells for $3.50 per box and presoak sells for $3.00 per box. Projected sales (in boxes) for the coming four quarters follow.

	Detergent	Presoak
First quarter	40,000	50,000
Second quarter	55,000	50,000
Third quarter	62,000	60,000
Fourth quarter	70,000	70,000

The president of the company believes that the projected sales are realistic and can be achieved by the company.

REQUIRED:
1. Prepare a sales budget for each quarter and for the year in total for detergent.
2. Prepare a sales budget for each quarter and for the year in total for presoak.
3. Prepare a sales budget for the two products as a whole by quarter and for the year.

W8-2
Production Budget
LO 2
p. 293

Refer to W8-1. For detergent, Carrigan Company requires that 6,000 boxes be available in beginning inventory for the first and second quarters of the year, and that 10,000 boxes be available in beginning inventory for the third and fourth quarters of the year, as well as for the first quarter of the year after next.

REQUIRED: Prepare a production budget for detergent for each quarter of the coming year, and for the year in total.

W8-3
Direct Materials
Budget
LO 2
p. 294

Carebear, Inc. manufactures a variety of crib blankets. On average, each blanket requires $\frac{3}{4}$ yard of fabric and 3 yards of satin binding. Anticipated production for the coming year is as follows:

Quarter 1	5,000
Quarter 2	4,000
Quarter 3	6,000
Quarter 4	8,000

Carebear's inventory policy for fabric is to have 750 yards in ending inventory for quarter 1, 1,000 yards in ending inventory for quarters 2 and 3, and 500 yards in ending inventory for quarter 4. The policy for satin binding is to have 10 percent of the next quarter's production needs in ending inventory.

REQUIRED:
1. Prepare a direct materials budget for fabric for quarters 1 and 2 of the coming year. Assume that fabric costs $3.10 per yard.
2. Prepare a direct materials budget for satin binding for quarters 1 and 2 of the coming year. Assume that satin binding costs $1.25 per yard.

W8-4
Direct Labor Budget
and Overhead
Budget
LO 2
p. 294

Refer to W8-3. Each crib blanket requires 0.2 direct labor hour at $9.50 per hour. Variable overhead is applied at the rate of $4 per direct labor hour and fixed overhead averages $8,500 per quarter.

REQUIRED:
1. Prepare a direct labor budget for quarters 1 and 2.
2. Prepare an overhead budget for quarters 1 and 2.

W8-5
Cash Receipts Budget
LO 2
pp. 299–300

Adams and Company has the following accounts receivable payment experience:

Percent paid in the month of sale	40%
Percent paid in the month after the sale	35%
Percent paid in the second month after the sale	20%

Adams and Company sold $230,000 worth of goods on account in May, $250,000 in June, and $200,000 in July.

REQUIRED: How much cash will Adams and Company receive on account in July?

W8-6
Cash Budget
LO 2
pp. 299–300

Rogier, Inc. expects to receive cash from sales of $45,000 in March. In addition, Rogier expects to sell property worth $3,500. Payments for materials and supplies are expected to total $10,000; direct labor payroll will be $12,500, and other expenditures are budgeted at $14,900. On March 1, the cash account balance is $1,230.

REQUIRED:
1. Prepare a cash budget for Rogier, Inc. for the month of March.
2. Assume that Rogier, Inc. wanted a minimum cash balance of $15,000 and that it could borrow from the bank in multiples of $1,000 at an interest rate of 12 percent per year. What would Rogier's adjusting ending balance for March be? How much interest would Rogier owe in April, assuming that the entire amount borrowed in March would be paid back?

W8-7
Flexible Budget
LO 3
p. 305

Cosmetico, Inc. developed a new perfume called "Moonswept." At the beginning of the year, Cosmetico budgeted the following manufacturing costs based on production of 100,000 bottles of Moonswept:

Direct materials	$ 400,000
Direct labor	230,000
Variable overhead	310,000
Fixed overhead	440,000
Total manufacturing costs	$1,380,000

Demand for Moonswept was disappointing, and by the end of the year production had been scaled back to 75,000 bottles. Actual costs were as follows:

Direct materials	$ 315,000
Direct labor	176,250
Variable overhead	255,000
Fixed overhead	400,000
Total manufacturing costs	$1,146,250

REQUIRED:
1. Prepare a performance report comparing actual costs with the flexible budget amounts for actual production of 75,000 bottles. Include a column for variances.
2. Prepare a flexible budget for the following levels of activity: 50,000, 100,000, and 150,000 bottles of Moonswept.

EXERCISES

E8-1
Sales Budget
LO 1, LO 2

Benton Sporting Goods sells a variety of sporting goods and clothing, including custom screen-printed T-shirts. Benton produces one of the T-shirts for a popular singing group. (The group goes on tour and sells various T-shirts and merchandise imprinted with its name and the name of the tour). In the coming summer, the group plans an 18-city tour and will require screen-printed T-shirts in the following quantities:

June	20,000
July	15,000
August	10,000

Benton sells each shirt for $13.50.

REQUIRED:
1. Prepare a sales budget for June, July, and August.
2. How will Benton use this sales budget?

E8-2
Production Budget
LO 2

Refer to E8-1. To meet its sales commitment for the T-shirts, Benton plans to begin production during the last half of May. At that time, there will be no T-shirts in beginning inventory. Benton requires that ending inventory for one month be equal to 50 percent of sales for the next month (this requirement was met on June 1). However, desired ending inventory for August is zero since once the concerts are over, demand for the T-shirts will be minimal.

REQUIRED: Prepare a production budget for May, June, July, and August. Show the number of units that should be produced each month as well as for the four-month period in total.

E8-3
Direct Materials
Purchases Budget
LO 2

Refer to E8-2. Suppose that each T-shirt requires, on average, 1.4 ounces of a special ink that costs $0.83 per ounce. The ending inventory policy for ink is that there must be a sufficient amount on hand to meet 20 percent of the next month's production requirement. The ending inventory of ink for August is zero. The beginning inventory of ink May 1 is 3,000 ounces.

REQUIRED: Prepare a direct materials purchases budget for May, June, July, and August.

E8-4
Production Budget
LO 2

Medsupply, Inc. produces a variety of supplies for hospitals and clinics. Among them is a 200-yard roll of gauze. The sales budget for the first four months of the year follows.

	Unit Sales	Dollar Sales
January	100,000	$50,000
February	120,000	60,000
March	110,000	55,000
April	100,000	50,000

Company policy requires that ending inventories for each month be 15 percent of next month's sales. At the beginning of January, the inventory of gauze is 9,000 rolls.

REQUIRED: Prepare a production budget for the first quarter of the year. Show the number of units that should be produced each month as well as for the quarter in total.

E8-5
Direct Materials
Purchases Budget
LO 2

Lester Company produces a variety of labels, including iron-on name labels which are sold to parents of camp-bound children. (The camps require campers to have their name on every article of clothing.) The labels are sold in a roll of 1,000 which requires about 25 yards of paper strip.

Each yard of paper strip costs $0.17. Lester has budgeted production of the label rolls for the next four months as follows:

	Units
March	5,000
April	25,000
May	35,000
June	6,000

Inventory policy requires that sufficient paper strip be in ending monthly inventory to satisfy 20 percent of the following month's production needs. Inventory of paper strip at the beginning of March equals exactly the amount needed to satisfy the inventory policy.

REQUIRED: Prepare a direct materials purchases budget for March, April, and May showing purchases in units and in dollars for each month and in total.

E8-6
Direct Labor Budget
LO 2

Refer to the production budget in E8-5. Each roll of labels produced requires (on average) 0.03 direct labor hour. The average cost of direct labor is $8 per hour.

REQUIRED: Prepare a direct labor budget for March, April, and May showing the hours needed and the direct labor cost for each month and in total.

E8-7
Sales Budget
LO 2

Garland, Inc. manufactures six models of molded plastic waste containers. Garland's budgeting team is finalizing the sales budget for the coming year. Sales in units and dollars for last year follow:

Model	Number Sold	Price	Revenue
W-1	16,800	$9	$151,200
W-2	18,000	15	270,000
W-3	25,200	13	327,600
W-4	16,200	10	162,000
W-5	2,400	22	52,800
W-6	1,000	26	26,000
Total			$989,600

In looking over the previous year's sales figures, Garland's sales budgeting team recalled the following:

a. Model W-1 costs were rising faster than price could rise. Preparatory to phasing out this model, Garland, Inc. planned to slash advertising for this model and raise its price by 50 percent. The number of units of model W-1 to be sold were forecast at 20 percent of the previous year's units.

b. Models W-5 and W-6 were introduced on November 1 last year. They are brightly colored, heavy-duty, wheeled garbage containers designed for household use. Garland estimates that demand for both models will continue at the previous year's rate.

c. A competitor has announced plans to introduce an improved version of model W-3. Garland believes that the model W-3 price must be cut 20 percent to maintain unit sales at the previous year's level.

d. It was assumed that unit sales of all other models would increase by 10 percent, prices remaining constant.

REQUIRED: Prepare a sales budget by product and in total for Garland, Inc. for the coming year.

E8-8
Purchases Budget
LO 2

Barron's Furniture Warehouse carries beds and mattresses, including a popular style of bunk bed. The sales budget for bunk beds for the first six months of the year follows.

	Unit Sales	Dollar Sales
January	160	$23,200
February	180	26,100
March	120	17,400
April	80	11,600
May	200	29,000
June	260	37,700

Barron's believes that ending inventories should be sufficient to cover 20 percent of the next month's projected sales. On January 1, 24 bunk beds were in inventory.

REQUIRED:
1. Prepare a purchases budget in units of bunk beds for as many months as you can.
2. If bunk beds are priced at 50 percent above cost, what is the dollar cost of purchases for each month of your purchases budget? (Round off the cost per bunk bed to the nearest dollar.)

E8-9
Cash Receipts
Budget
LO 2

Andrea's Shop sells china, silverware, and kitchenware. A popular feature is her wedding registry service, which includes free gift wrapping and delivery of gifts to local brides. Andrea accepts cash, checks, and Visa, MasterCard, and American Express charges. These methods of payment have the following characteristics:

Cash	Payment is immediate; no fee is charged.
Check	Payment is immediate; the bank charges $0.25 per check; 1 percent of check revenue is from "bad" checks that Andrea cannot collect.
Visa/MasterCard	Andrea accumulates these credit card receipts throughout the month and submits them in one bundle for payment on the last day of the month. The money is credited to Andrea's account by the fifth day of the following month. A fee of 1.5 percent is charged by the credit card company.
American Express	Andrea accumulates these receipts throughout the month and mails them in for payment on the last day of the month. American Express credits Andrea's account by the sixth day of the following month. A fee of 3.5 percent is charged by American Express.

During a typical month, Andrea has sales of $24,000, broken down as follows:

American Express	20%	
Visa/MasterCard	50%	
Check	5%	(checks average $37.50 each)
Cash	25%	

REQUIRED: If Andrea estimates sales of $30,000 in April and $60,000 in May, what are her planned net cash receipts for May?

E8-10
Production Budget;
Direct Materials
Purchases Budget
LO 2

Jenna Mitchell, owner of Jenna's Jams and Jellies, produces homemade-style jellies using fruits indigenous to her local area. Jenna has estimated the following sales of 16-ounce jars of fruit jelly for the rest of the year and January of next year.

September	100
October	150
November	170
December	225
January	100

Jenna likes to have 20 percent of the next month's sales needs on hand at the end of each month. This requirement was met on August 31.

Materials needed for each jar of fruit jelly are as follows:

Fruit	1 lb
Sugar	1 lb
Pectin	3 oz
Jar sets	1

The materials inventory policy is to have 5 percent of the next month's fruit needs on hand as well as 50 percent of the next month's production needs for all other materials. (The relatively low inventory amount for fruit is designed to prevent spoilage.) Materials inventory on September 1 met this company policy.

REQUIRED:
1. Prepare a production budget for September, October, November, and December for fruit jelly.
2. Prepare a purchases budget for all materials used in the production of fruit jelly for the months of September, October, and November. (Round all answers to the nearest whole unit.)
3. Why can't you prepare a purchases budget for December?

E8-11
Overhead Budget;
Flexible Budget
LO 2, LO 3

Armstrong, Inc. manufactures drill bits in its Guthrie plant. Armstrong has developed the following flexible budget for overhead for the coming year. Activity level is measured in direct labor hours.

	Variable Cost Formula	Activity Level (hours)		
		10,000	15,000	20,000
Variable costs:				
Maintenance	$1.00	$10,000	$15,000	$ 20,000
Supplies	0.50	5,000	7,500	10,000
Power	0.10	1,000	1,500	2,000
Total variable costs	$1.60	$16,000	$24,000	$ 32,000
Fixed costs:				
Depreciation		$ 7,200	$ 7,200	$ 7,200
Salaries		64,800	64,800	64,800
Total fixed costs		$72,000	$72,000	$ 72,000
Total overhead costs		$88,000	$96,000	$104,000

The Guthrie plant produces two different types of drill bits. The production budget for October is 24,000 units for bit-type 301 and 12,000 units for bit-type 414. Type 301 requires three minutes of direct labor time and type 414 requires two minutes. Fixed overhead costs are incurred uniformly throughout the year.

REQUIRED: Prepare an overhead budget for October.

E8-12
Cash Budget
LO 2

The owner of a small mining supply company has requested a cash budget for June. After examining the records of the company, you find the following:

a. Cash balance on June 1 is $345.
b. Actual sales for April and May are:

	April	May
Cash sales	$10,000	$15,000
Credit sales	25,000	35,000
Total sales	$35,000	$50,000

c. Credit sales are collected over a three-month period: 50 percent in the month of sale, 30 percent in the second month, and 15 percent in the third month. The sales collected in the third month are subject to a $1\frac{1}{2}$ percent late fee, but only half of the affected customers pay the late fee, and the owner does not think it is worth his while to try to collect from the other half. The remaining sales are uncollectible.

d. Inventory purchases average 60 percent of a month's total sales. Of those purchases, 40 percent are paid for in the month of purchase. The remaining 60 percent are paid for in the following month.

e. Salaries and wages total $8,700 a month, including a $4,500 salary paid to the owner.

f. Rent is $1,200 per month.

g. Taxes to be paid in June are $5,500.

The owner also tells you that he expects cash sales of $20,000 and credit sales of $40,000 for June. There is no minimum cash balance required. The owner of the company does not have access to short-term loans.

REQUIRED:

1. Prepare a cash budget for June. Include supporting schedules for cash collections and cash payments.

2. Did the business show a negative cash balance for June? Assuming that the owner has no hope of establishing a line of credit for the business, what recommendations would you give the owner for dealing with a negative cash balance?

E8-13
Overhead Budget;
Flexible Budget
LO 2, LO 3

Regina Johnson, controller for Pet-Care Company, has been instructed to develop a flexible budget for overhead costs. The company produces two types of dog food. One, Basicdiet, is a standard mixture for healthy dogs. The second, Specdiet, is a reduced protein formulation for older dogs with health problems. The two dog foods use common raw materials in different proportions. The company expects to produce 100,000 fifty-pound bags of each product during the coming year. Basicdiet requires 0.25 direct labor hour per bag and Specdiet requires 0.30. Regina has developed the following fixed and variable costs for each of the four overhead items:

Overhead Item	Fixed Cost	Variable Rate per DLH
Maintenance	$17,000	$0.40
Power		0.50
Indirect labor	26,500	1.60
Rent	18,000	

REQUIRED:

1. Prepare an overhead budget for the expected activity level for the coming year.

2. Prepare an overhead budget that reflects production that is 10 percent higher than expected (for both products) and one for production that is 20 percent lower than expected.

E8-14
Performance Report
LO 3

Refer to the information given in E8-13. Assume that Pet-Care actually produced 120,000 bags of Basicdiet and 100,000 of Specdiet. The actual overhead costs incurred were:

Maintenance	$ 40,500
Power	31,700
Indirect labor	119,000
Rent	18,000

REQUIRED:

1. Prepare a performance report for the period.

2. Based on the report, would you judge any of the variances to be significant? Can you think of some possible reasons for the variances?

E8-15
Budgeted Cash Collections; Budgeted Cash Payments
LO 2

Information pertaining to Noskey Corporation's sales revenue follows:

	November 1997 (Actual)	December 1997 (Budgeted)	January 1998 (Budgeted)
Cash sales	$ 80,000	$100,000	$ 60,000
Credit sales	240,000	360,000	180,000
Total sales	$320,000	$460,000	$240,000

Management estimates that 5 percent of credit sales are uncollectible. Of the credit sales that are collectible, 60 percent are collected in the month of sale and the remainder in the month following the sale. Purchases of inventory each month are 70 percent of the next month's projected total sales. All purchases of inventory are on account; 25 percent are paid in the month of purchase, and the remainder are paid in the month following the purchase.

REQUIRED:
1. What are Noskey's budgeted cash collections in December 1997 from November 1997 credit sales?
2. What are total budgeted cash receipts in January 1998?
3. What is Noskey budgeting for total cash payments in December 1997 for inventory purchases? (CMA adapted)

E8-16
Zero-Base Budgeting
LO 4

Zero-base budgeting promises much but often delivers little. Some organizations have experienced the following difficulties:

1. Lack of agreement on what needs to be accomplished
2. Lack of credibility in the process itself
3. Resistance of middle managers (too much paperwork and perceived threat to their units)
4. Inability of top management to make tough decisions

REQUIRED: Suppose you are a consultant retained by an organization to implement zero-base budgeting. What actions would you take to avoid some of these problems?

E8-17
Participative versus Imposed Budgeting
LO 3

An effective budget converts the goals and objectives of an organization into data. The budget serves as a blueprint for management's plans. The budget is also the basis for control. Management performance can be evaluated by comparing actual results with the budget.

Thus, creating the budget is essential for the successful operation of an organization. Finding the resources to implement the budget—that is, getting from a starting point to the ultimate goal—requires the extensive use of human resources. How managers perceive their roles in the process of budgeting is important to the successful use of the budget as an effective tool for planning, communicating, and controlling.

REQUIRED:
1. Discuss the behavioral implications of planning and control when a company's management employs
   a. An imposed budgetary approach
   b. A participative budgetary approach
2. Communications plays an important role in the budgetary process whether a participative or imposed budgetary approach is used.
   a. Discuss the differences between communication flows in these two budgetary approaches.
   b. Discuss the behavioral implications associated with the communication process for each of the budgetary approaches. (CMA adapted)

E8-18
Flexible Budgeting
LO 3

Budgeted overhead costs for two different levels of activity follow.

	Direct Labor Hours	
	1,000	2,000
Maintenance	$10,000	$16,000
Depreciation	5,000	5,000
Supervision	15,000	15,000
Supplies	1,400	2,800
Power	750	1,500
Other	8,100	8,200

REQUIRED: Prepare a flexible budget for an activity level of 1,650 direct labor hours.

E8-19
Cash Receipts
Budget
LO 2

Barrett's Department Store has found from past experience that 30 percent of its sales are for cash. The remaining 70 percent are on credit. An aging schedule for accounts receivable reveals the following pattern:

10% of credit sales are paid in the month of sale
70% of credit sales are paid in the month following the sale
17% of credit sales are paid in the second month following the sale
3% of credit sales are never collected

Credit sales that have not been paid until the second month following the sale are considered overdue and are subject to a 2 percent late charge.

Barrett Department Store has developed the following sales forecast:

May	$ 76,000
June	85,000
July	68,000
August	80,000
September	100,000

REQUIRED: Prepare a schedule of cash receipts for August and September.

E8-20
Cash Payments
Schedule
LO 2

Barrett's Department Store purchases a wide variety of merchandise. Purchases are made evenly throughout the month and all are on account. On the first of every month, Barrett's accounts payable clerk pays for all of the previous month's purchases. Terms are 2/10, n/30 (that is, a 2 percent discount can be taken if the bill is paid within 10 days; otherwise the entire amount is due within 30 days).

The forecast purchases for the months of May through September are as follows:

May	$40,000
June	50,000
July	42,000
August	60,000
September	66,000

REQUIRED:
1. Prepare a cash payments schedule for inventory for the months of August and September.
2. Now suppose that the store manager wants to see what difference it would make to have the accounts payable clerk pay for any purchases that have been made three times per month, on the 1st, the 11th, and the 21st. Prepare a cash payments schedule for the months of August and September assuming this new payment schedule.

3. Suppose that Barrett's accounts payable clerk does not have time to make payments on two extra days per month and that a temporary employee is hired on the 11th and 21st at $22 per hour, for four hours each of those two days. Is this a good decision? Explain.

P ROBLEMS

P8-1
Operating Budget;
Comprehensive
Analysis
LO 2

The Morgan Division of Smith Manufacturing produces a handle assembly used in the production of bows. The assembly is sold to various bow manufacturers throughout the United States. Projected sales for the coming four months follow.

January	20,000
February	25,000
March	30,000
April	30,000

The following data pertain to production policies and manufacturing specifications followed by the Morgan Division:

a. Finished goods inventory on January 1 is 16,000 units. The desired ending inventory for each month is 80 percent of the next month's sales.

b. The data on materials used are as follows:

Direct Material	Per-Unit Usage	Unit Cost
Number 325	5	$8
Number 326	3	2

Inventory policy dictates that sufficient materials be on hand at the beginning of the month to produce 50 percent of that month's estimated sales. This is exactly the amount of material on hand on January 1.

c. The direct labor used per unit of output is two hours. The average direct labor cost per hour is $9.25.

d. Overhead each month is estimated using a flexible budget formula. (Activity is measured in direct labor hours.)

	Fixed-Cost Component	Variable-Cost Component
Supplies	—	$1.00
Power	—	0.50
Maintenance	$ 15,000	0.40
Supervision	8,000	—
Depreciation	100,000	—
Taxes	6,000	—
Other	40,000	1.50

e. Monthly selling and administrative expenses are also estimated using a flexible budgeting formula. (Activity is measured in units sold.)

	Fixed Costs	Variable Costs
Salaries	$25,000	—
Commissions	—	$1.00
Depreciation	20,000	—
Shipping	—	0.50
Other	10,000	0.30

f. The unit selling price of the handle assembly is $90.

g. All sales and purchases are for cash. The cash balance on January 1 equals $200,000. If the firm develops a cash shortage by the end of the month, sufficient cash is borrowed to cover the shortage. Any cash borrowed is repaid one month later, as is the interest due. The interest rate is 12 percent per annum.

REQUIRED: Prepare a monthly operating budget for the first quarter with the following schedules:

1. Sales budget
2. Production budget
3. Direct materials purchases budget
4. Direct labor budget
5. Overhead budget
6. Selling and administrative expenses budget
7. Ending finished goods inventory budget
8. Cost of goods sold budget
9. Budgeted income statement
10. Cash budget

P8-2
Cash Budget; Pro
Forma Balance Sheet
LO 2

Ryan Richards, controller for Grange Retailers, has assembled the following data to assist in the preparation of a cash budget for the third quarter of 1998:

a. Sales:

May (actual)	$100,000
June (actual)	120,000
July (estimated)	90,000
August (estimated)	100,000
September (estimated)	135,000
October (estimated)	110,000

b. Each month, 30 percent of sales are for cash and 70 percent are on credit. The collection pattern for credit sales is 20 percent in the month of sale, 50 percent in the following month, and 30 percent in the second month following the sale.

c. Each month the ending inventory exactly equals 50 percent of the cost of next month's sales. The markup on goods is 25 percent of cost.

d. Inventory purchases are paid for in the month following the purchase.

e. Recurring monthly expenses are as follows:

Salaries and wages	$10,000
Depreciation on plant and equipment	4,000
Utilities	1,000
Other	1,700

f. Property taxes of $15,000 are due and payable on July 15, 1998.

g. Advertising fees of $6,000 must be paid on August 20, 1998.

h. A lease on a new storage facility is scheduled to begin on September 2. Monthly payments are $5,000.

i. The company has a policy to maintain a minimum cash balance of $10,000. If necessary, it will borrow to meet its short-term needs. All borrowing is done at the beginning of the month. All payments on principal and interest are made at the end of a month. The annual interest rate is 9 percent. The company must borrow in multiples of $1,000.

j. A partially completed balance sheet as of June 30, 1998, follows. (Accounts payable is for inventory purchases only.)

Cash	$?		
Accounts receivable	?		
Inventory	?		
Plant and equipment	425,000		
Accounts payable		$?	
Common stock		210,000	
Retained earnings		268,750	
Total	$?	$?	

REQUIRED:

1. Complete the balance sheet given in (j).
2. Prepare a cash budget for each month in the third quarter and for the quarter in total (the third quarter begins on July 1). Provide a supporting schedule of cash collections.
3. Prepare a pro forma balance sheet as of September 30, 1998.

P8-3
Participative Budgeting; Not-for-Profit Setting
LO 3

Scott Weidner, the controller in the division of social services for the state, recognizes the importance of the budgetary process for planning, control, and motivation. He believes that a properly implemented process of participative budgeting and management by exception will motivate his subordinates to improve productivity within their particular departments. Based upon this philosophy, Scott has implemented the following budgetary procedures:

1. An appropriation target figure is given to each department manager. This amount represents the maximum funding that each department can expect to receive in the next fiscal year.
2. Department managers develop their individual budgets within the following spending constraints as directed by the controller's staff:
   a. Requests for spending cannot exceed the appropriated target.
   b. All fixed expenditures should be included in the budget. Fixed expenditures include such items as contracts and salaries at current levels.
   c. All government projects directed by higher authority should be included in the budget in their entirety.
3. The controller's staff consolidates the requests from the various departments into one budget for the entire division.
4. Upon final budget approval by the legislature, the controller's staff allocates the appropriation to the various departments on instructions from the division manager. However, a specified percentage of each department's appropriation is held back in anticipation of potential budget cuts and special funding needs. The amount and use of this contingency fund is left to the discretion of the division manager.
5. Each department is allowed to adjust its budget when necessary to operate within the reduced appropriation level. However, as stated in the original directive, specific projects authorized by higher authority must remain intact.
6. The final budget is used as the basis of control for a management-by-exception form of reporting. Excessive expenditures by account for each department are highlighted on a monthly basis. Department managers are expected to account for all expenditures over budget. Fiscal responsibility is an important factor in the overall performance evaluation of department managers. Scott believes his policy of allowing the department managers to participate in the budget process and then holding them accountable for the final budget is essential, especially in times of limited resources. He further believes that the department managers will be motivated to increase the efficiency and effectiveness of their departments because they have provided input into the initial budgetary process and are required to justify any unfavorable performances.

REQUIRED:

1. Discuss the advantages and limitations of participative budgeting.
2. Identify deficiencies in Scott Weidner's outline for a budgetary process. Recommend how each deficiency identified can be corrected. (CMA adapted)

P8-4
Cash Budget
LO 2

The controller of Weller Company is gathering data to prepare the cash budget for April 1998. He plans to develop the budget from the following information:

a. Of all sales, 30 percent are cash sales.
b. Of credit sales, 60 percent are collected within the month of sale. Half of the credit sales collected within the month receive a 2 percent cash discount (for accounts paid within ten days). Twenty percent of credit sales are collected in the following month; remaining credit sales are collected the month thereafter. There are virtually no bad debts.
c. Sales for the first six months of the year follow. (The first three months are actual sales and the last three months are estimated sales.)

	Sales
January	$230,000
February	300,000
March	500,000
April	570,000
May	600,000
June	567,000

d. The company sells all that it produces each month. The cost of raw materials equals 24 percent of each sales dollar. The company requires a monthly ending inventory equal to the coming month's production requirements. Of raw materials purchases, 50 percent are paid for in the month of purchase. The remaining 50 percent is paid for in the following month.
e. Wages total $55,000 each month and are paid in the month incurred.
f. Budgeted monthly operating expenses total $168,000, of which $25,000 is depreciation and $3,000 is expiration of prepaid insurance (the annual premium of $36,000 is paid on January 1).
g. Dividends of $70,000, declared on March 31, will be paid on April 15.
h. Old equipment will be sold for $12,600 on April 4.
i. On April 13, new equipment will be purchased for $84,000.
j. The company maintains a minimum cash balance of $10,000.
k. The cash balance on April 1 is $13,500.

REQUIRED: Prepare a cash budget for April. Give a supporting schedule that details the cash collections from sales.

P8-5
Revision of Operating Budget; Pro Forma Statements for Income and Cost of Goods Sold
LO 2

Mary Dalid founded Molid Company three years ago. The company produces a modem for use with minicomputers and microcomputers. Business has expanded rapidly since the company's inception. Bob Wells, the company's general accountant, prepared a budget for the fiscal year ending August 31, 1998. The budget was based on the prior year's sales and production activity because Mary believed that the sales growth experienced during the prior year would not continue at the same pace. The pro forma statements of income and cost of goods sold that were prepared as part of the budgetary process follow:

Molid Company Pro Forma Statement of Income (in thousands) For the Year Ending August 31, 1998	
Net sales	$ 31,248
Less: Cost of goods sold	(20,765)
Gross margin	$ 10,483
Less: Operating expenses	(5,400)
Income before taxes	$ 5,083

Molid Company
Pro Forma Statement of Cost of Goods Sold (in thousands)
For the Year Ending August 31, 1998

Direct materials:		
Materials inventory, September 1, 1997	$ 1,360	
Materials purchased	14,476	
Available for use	15,836	
Less: Materials inventory, August 31, 1998	(1,628)	
Direct materials used		$14,208
Direct labor		1,134
Overhead:		
Indirect materials	$1,421	
General	3,240	4,661
Cost of goods manufactured		$20,003
Finished goods, September 1, 1997		1,169
Total goods available		$21,172
Less: Finished goods, August 31, 1998		(407)
Cost of goods sold		$20,765

On December 10, 1997, Mary and Bob met to discuss the first quarter operating results. Bob believed that several changes should be made to the budget assumptions that had been used to prepare the pro forma statements. He prepared the following notes that summarized the changes, which had not become known until the first quarter results were compiled. He submitted the following data to Mary:

a. Actual first quarter production was 35,000 units. The estimated production for the fiscal year should be increased from 162,000 to 170,000, with the balance of production being scheduled in equal segments over the last nine months of the fiscal year.

b. The planned ending inventory for finished goods of 3,300 units at the end of the fiscal year remains unchanged. The finished goods inventory of 9,300 units as of September 1, 1997, had dropped to 9,000 units by November 30, 1998. The finished goods inventory at the end of the fiscal year will be valued at the average manufacturing costs for the year.

c. Direct materials sufficient to produce 16,000 units were on hand at the beginning of the fiscal year. The plan to have the equivalent of 18,500 units of production in direct materials inventory at the end of the fiscal year remains unchanged. Direct materials inventory is valued on a LIFO basis. Direct materials equivalent to 37,500 units of output were purchased for $3.3 million during the first quarter of the fiscal year. Molid's suppliers have informed the company that direct materials prices will increase 5 percent on March 1, 1998. Direct materials needed for the rest of the fiscal year will be purchased evenly through the last nine months.

d. On the basis of historical data, indirect material cost is projected at 10 percent of the cost of direct materials consumed.

e. One-half of general factory overhead and all selling and general and administrative expenses are considered fixed.

REQUIRED: Based on the revised data presented by Bob Wells, prepare new pro forma statements for income and cost of goods sold for the year ending August 31, 1998. (CMA adapted)

P8-6

Performance
Reporting;
Behavioral
Considerations
LO 1, LO 3

Berwin, Inc. is a manufacturer of small industrial tools with annual sales of approximately $3.5 million. Sales growth has been steady during the year, and there is no evidence of cyclical demand. Production has increased gradually during the year and has been evenly distributed throughout each month. The company has a sequential processing system. The four manufacturing departments—casting, machining, finishing, and packaging—are all located in the same building. Fixed overhead is assigned using a plantwide rate.

Berwin has always been able to compete with other manufacturers of small tools. However, its market has expanded only in response to product innovation. Thus, research and development is very important and has helped Berwin to expand as well as maintain demand.

Carla Viller, controller, has designed and implemented a new budget system in response to concerns voiced by George Berwin, president. Carla prepared an annual budget that has been divided into 12 equal segments; this budget can be used to assist in the timely evaluation of monthly performance. George was visibly upset upon receiving the May performance report for the machining department. George exclaimed, "How can they be efficient enough to produce nine extra units every working day and still miss the budget by $300 per day?" Gene Jordan, supervisor of the machining department, could not understand "all the red ink" when he knew that the department had operated more efficiently in May than it had in months. Gene stated, "I was expecting a pat on the back and instead the boss tore me apart. What's more, I don't even know why!"

Berwin, Inc.
Machining Department Performance Report
For the Month Ended May 31, 1998

	Budgeted	Actual	Variance
Volume in units	3,000	3,185	185 F
Variable manufacturing costs:			
Direct materials	$24,000	$24,843	$ 843 U
Direct labor	27,750	29,302	1,552 U
Variable overhead	33,300	35,035	1,735 U
Total variable costs	$85,050	$89,180	$4,130 U
Fixed manufacturing costs:			
Indirect labor	$3,300	$3,334	$ 34 U
Depreciation	1,500	1,500	—
Taxes	300	300	—
Insurance	240	240	—
Other	930	1,027	97 U
Total fixed costs	$6,270	$6,401	$ 131 U
Corporate costs:			
Research and development	$2,400	$3,728	$1,328 U
Selling and administrative	3,600	4,075	475 U
Total corporate costs	$6,000	$7,803	$1,803 U
Total costs	$97,320	$103,384	$6,064 U

REQUIRED:
1. Review the May performance report. Use the information given in the report and elsewhere.
   a. Discuss the strengths and weaknesses of the new budgetary system.
   b. Identify the weaknesses of the performance report and explain how it should be revised to eliminate each weakness.
2. Prepare a revised report for the machining department using the May data.
3. What other changes would you make to improve Berwin's budgetary system? (CMA adapted)

P8-7
Master Budget;
Comprehensive
Review
LO 2

Optima Company is a high-technology organization that produces a mass-storage system. The design of Optima's system is unique and represents a breakthrough in the industry. The units Optima produces combine positive features of both floppy and hard disks. The company is completing its fifth year of operations and is preparing to build its master budget for the coming year (1998). The budget will detail each quarter's activity and the activity for the year in total. The master budget will be based on the following information:

a. Fourth quarter sales for 1997 are 55,000 units.
b. Unit sales by quarter (for 1998) are projected as follows:

First quarter	65,000
Second quarter	70,000
Third quarter	75,000
Fourth quarter	90,000

The selling price is $400 per unit. All sales are credit sales. Optima collects 85 percent of all sales within the quarter in which they are realized; the other 15 percent are collected in the following quarter. There are no bad debts.

c. There is no beginning inventory of finished goods. Optima is planning the following ending finished goods inventories for each quarter:

First quarter	13,000 units
Second quarter	15,000 units
Third quarter	20,000 units
Fourth quarter	10,000 units

d. Each mass-storage unit uses five hours of direct labor and three units of direct materials. Laborers are paid $10 per hour, and one unit of materials costs $80.

e. There are 65,700 units of direct materials in beginning inventory as of January 1, 1998. At the end of each quarter, Optima plans to have 30 percent of the raw materials needed for next quarter's unit sales. Optima will end the year with the same level of raw materials found in this year's beginning inventory.

f. Optima buys raw materials on account. Half of the purchases are paid for in the quarter of acquisition and the remaining half are paid for in the following quarter. Wages and salaries are paid on the 15th and 30th of each month.

g. Fixed overhead totals $1 million each quarter. Of this total, $350,000 represents depreciation. All other fixed expenses are paid for in cash in the quarter incurred. The fixed overhead rate is computed by dividing the year's total fixed overhead by the year's expected actual units produced.

h. Variable overhead is budgeted at $6 per direct labor hour. All variable overhead expenses are paid for in the quarter incurred.

i. Fixed selling and administrative expenses total $250,000 per quarter, including $50,000 depreciation.

j. Variable selling and administrative expenses are budgeted at $10 per unit sold. All selling and administrative expenses are paid for in the quarter incurred.

k. The balance sheet as of December 31, 1997, is as follows:

Assets	
Cash	$ 250,000
Inventory	5,256,000
Accounts receivable	3,300,000
Plant and equipment	33,500,000
Total assets	$42,306,000

Liabilities and Stockholders' Equity	
Accounts payable	$ 7,248,000*
Capital stock	27,000,000
Retained earnings	8,058,000
Total liabilities and stockholders' equity	$42,306,000

*For purchase of materials only

l. Optima will pay quarterly dividends of $300,000. At the end of the fourth quarter, $2 million of equipment will be purchased.

REQUIRED: Prepare a master budget for Optima Company for each quarter of 1998 and for the year in total. The following component budgets must be included:

a. Sales budget
b. Production budget

    c. Direct materials purchases budget
    d. Direct labor budget
    e. Overhead budget
    f. Selling and administrative expenses budget
    g. Ending finished goods inventory budget
    h. Cost of goods sold budget
    i. Cash budget
    j. Pro forma income statement (using absorption costing)
    k. Pro forma balance sheet

P8-8

Flexible Budgeting

LO 2, LO 3

Jay Besoin, controller of Dunvacans, Inc., prepared the following budget for manufacturing costs at two levels of activity for 1998:

	Direct Labor Hours	
	100,000	**120,000**
Supervision	$ 177,000	$ 177,000
Utilities	18,000	21,000
Depeciation	34,000	34,000
Supplies	24,000	28,800
Direct labor	980,000	1,176,000
Direct materials	220,000	264,000
Maintenance	239,000	283,000
Rent	15,000	15,000
Other	60,000	70,000
Total manufacturing cost	$1,767,000	$2,068,800

During the year, the company worked a total of 112,000 direct labor hours and incurred the following actual costs:

Supervision	$183,000
Utilities	20,500
Depreciation	34,000
Supplies	24,640
Direct labor	963,200
Direct materials	248,000
Maintenance	237,000
Rent	15,000
Other	60,500

Dunvacans applies overhead on the basis of direct labor hours. Normal volume of 120,000 direct labor hours is the activity level to compute the predetermined overhead rate.

REQUIRED:
1. Prepare a performance report for Dunvacans' manufacturing costs in the year 1998. Should any cost item be given special attention? Explain.
2. Assume that the product produced by Dunvacans uses two direct labor hours. Calculate the normal unit manufacturing cost.
3. Compute the total applied overhead for 1998. Compute the overhead variance for the year.

P8-9

Budgeting and Behavioral Consequences

LO 1, LO 3

Denny Daniels is production manager of the Alumalloy Division of WRT, Inc. Alumalloy has limited contact with outside customers and no sales staff. Most of its customers are handled by other corporate divisions. Therefore, Alumalloy's performance is evaluated on the basis of cost control.

    Denny perceives the accounting department as the unit that generates historical numbers but provides little useful information. The accounting department creates the budgets at the beginning of the year and then gathers the actual costs incurred by production. Denny wonders whether the accountants even understand the nature of the production process itself. It seems all they are concerned with are numbers—whether they mean anything or not. In his opinion, the whole accounting process is a negative motivational device that does not reflect how hard or efficiently he has worked as a production manager.

Denny tried to discuss these perceptions and concerns with John Scott, the controller for Alumalloy, telling him, "I know I've had better production over a number of operating periods, but the cost report still says I have excessive costs. Look, I'm not an accountant, I'm a production manager. I know how to get a good quality product out. Over a number of years, I've even cut the raw materials used to do it. But the cost report doesn't show any of this. It's always negative no matter what I do. There is no way you can win with accounting or those people at corporate who use those reports."

John gave Denny little consolation, telling him that the accounting system and the cost reports generated by headquarters are just part of the corporate game and almost impossible for an individual to change. "Although these reports are the basis for evaluating the efficiency of your division and the means for corporate to determine whether you have done the job it wants, you shouldn't worry too much. You haven't been fired yet! Besides, these cost reports have been used by WRT for the last 25 years."

From talking to the production manager of the Zinc Division, Denny perceived that most of what John said was true. However, some minor cost reporting changes for Zinc had been agreed to by corporate headquarters. He also knew from the trade grapevine that the turnover of production managers was considered high at WRT, even though relatively few managers were fired. Most seemed to end up quitting, usually in disgust, out of the belief that they were not being evaluated fairly.

A recent copy of the cost report prepared by corporate headquarters for Alumalloy follows. Because of an unexpected increase in demand for the final product, Alumalloy produced 10,000 units more than the 40,000 originally budgeted. Denny does not like this report because he believes that it fails to reflect the division's operations properly, thereby resulting in an unfair evaluation of performance.

| | Alumalloy Division Cost Report (in thousands) For the Month of April 1998 | | |
	Master Budget	Actual Cost	Variance
Aluminum	$ 400	$ 477	$ 77 U
Labor	560	675	115 U
Overhead	100	110	10 U
Total	$1,060	$1,262	$202 U

REQUIRED:
1. Comment on Denny's perception of:
   a. John Scott, the controller
   b. Corporate headquarters
   c. The cost report
   d. Himself as a production manager
2. Discuss how his perception of these items affects his performance as a production manager of WRT.
3. List the deficiencies of WRT's budgetary system. Prepare a list of recommendations to improve the system so that the process and the reports produced are more useful and less threatening to the production managers. (CMA adapted)

P8-10
Purchases Budget;
Direct Labor Budget;
Cash Budget;
Flexible Budget
LO 2, LO 3

SubStop is a hole-in-the-wall sandwich shop just off the State University campus. Customers enter off the street into a small counter area to order one of ten varieties of sandwich and a soft drink. All orders must be taken out because there is no space for dining.

The owner of SubStop, Arlen Lector, is attempting to construct a series of budgets. He has accumulated the following information:

a. The average sandwich (which sells for $4.50) requires 1 roll, 4 ounces of meat, 2 ounces of cheese, 0.05 head of lettuce, 0.25 of a tomato, and a healthy squirt (1 ounce) of secret sauce.
b. Each customer typically orders one soft drink (average price $1) consisting of a cup and 12 ounces of soda.
c. Use of paper supplies (napkins, bag, sandwich wrap, cup) varies from customer to customer but averages $400 per month.
d. SubStop is open for two 8-hour shifts. The noon shift on Monday through Friday requires five workers earning $6.50 per hour (this includes fringe benefits). The evening shift is only on Friday, Saturday, and Sunday nights; the three evening shift employees earn $7 per hour. There are 4.3 weeks in a month.
e. Rent is $75 per month. Other monthly cash expenses average $465.
f. Food costs are:

Meat	$5.00/lb
Cheese	$3.50/lb
Rolls	$24/gross
Lettuce	$12/box (contains 24 heads)
Tomatoes	$1.50/box (contains approximately 20 tomatoes)
Special sauce	$6/gal
Soda (syrup and carbonated water)	$2/gal

In a normal month when school is in session, Arlen sells 6,000 sandwiches. In October, State University holds its homecoming celebration. Therefore, Arlen figures that if he adds a noon shift on Saturday and Sunday of homecoming weekend, October sales will be 30 percent higher than normal.

REQUIRED: Prepare flexible budgets for a normal school month and for the month of October.

P8-11
Flexible Budgeting
LO 3

Patterson Company employs flexible budgeting techniques to evaluate the performance of several of its activities. The selling expense flexible budgets for three representative monthly activity levels follow.

Representative Monthly Flexible Budgets for Selling Expenses			
Activity measures:			
Unit sales volume	400,000	425,000	450,000
Dollar sales volume	$10,000,000	$10,625,000	$11,250,000
Number of orders	4,000	4,250	4,500
Number of salespersons	72	72	72
Monthly expenses:			
Advertising and promotion	$ 1,200,000	$ 1,200,000	$ 1,200,000
Administrative salaries	57,000	57,000	57,000
Sales salaries	75,600	75,600	75,600
Sales commissions	300,000	318,750	337,500
Salesperson travel	170,000	175,000	180,000
Sales office expense	490,000	498,750	507,500
Shipping expense	675,000	712,500	750,000
Total	$ 2,967,600	$ 3,037,600	$ 3,107,600

The following assumptions were used to develop the selling expense flexible budgets:

a. The average size of Patterson's sales force during the year was planned to be 72 people.
b. Salespersons are paid a monthly salary plus commission on gross dollar sales.
c. The travel costs are best characterized as a step-variable cost. The fixed portion is related to the number of salespersons; the variable portion tends to fluctuate with gross dollar sales.

d. Sales office expense is a mixed cost with the variable portion related to the number of orders processed.
e. Shipping expense is a mixed cost with the variable portion related to the number of units sold.

A sales force of 80 persons generated a total of 4,300 orders resulting in a sales volume of 420,000 units during November. The gross dollar sales amounted to $10.9 million. The selling expenses incurred for November were as follows:

Advertising and promotion	$1,350,000
Administrative salaries	57,000
Sales salaries	84,000
Sales commissions	327,000
Salesperson travel	185,000
Sales office expense	497,200
Shipping expense	730,000
Total	$3,230,200

REQUIRED:
1. Explain why the selling expense flexible budgets presented would not be appropriate for evaluating Patterson Company's November selling expenses; indicate how the flexible budget would have to be revised.
2. Prepare a selling expense report for November that Patterson Company can use to evaluate its control over selling expenses. The report should have a line for each selling expense item showing the appropriate budgeted amount, the actual selling expense, and the monthly dollar variation. (CMA adapted)

P8-12

Importance of Cash Budget; Cash Budget
LO 1, LO 2

CrossMan Corporation, a rapidly expanding crossbow distributor to retail outlets, is in the process of formulating plans for 1998. Joan Caldwell, director of marketing, has completed her 1998 forecast and is confident that sales estimates will be met or exceeded. The following sales figures show the growth expected and will provide the planning basis for other corporate departments.

Month	Forecasted Sales
January	$1,800,000
February	2,000,000
March	1,800,000
April	2,200,000
May	2,500,000
June	2,800,000
July	3,000,000
August	3,000,000
September	3,200,000
October	3,200,000
November	3,000,000
December	3,400,000

George Brownell, assistant controller, has been given the responsibility for formulating the cash flow projection, a critical element during a period of rapid expansion. The following information will be used in preparing the cash analysis.

CrossMan has experienced an excellent record in accounts receivable collection and expects this trend to continue. Sixty percent of billings are collected in the month after the sale and 40 percent in the second month after the sale. Uncollectible accounts are nominal and will not be considered in the analysis.

The purchase of the crossbows is CrossMan's largest expenditure; the cost of these items equals 50 percent of sales. Sixty percent of the crossbows are received one month prior to sale and 40 percent are received during the month of sale.

Prior experience shows that 80 percent of accounts payable are paid by CrossMan one month after receipt of the purchased crossbows, and the remaining 20 percent are paid the second month after receipt.

Hourly wages, including fringe benefits, are a factor of sales volume and are equal to 20 percent of the current month's sales. These wages are paid in the month incurred.

General and administrative expenses are projected to be $2,640,000 for 1998. The composition of the expenses follows. All of these expenses are incurred uniformly throughout the year except the property taxes, which are paid in four equal installments in the last month of each quarter.

Salaries	$ 480,000
Promotion	660,000
Property taxes	240,000
Insurance	360,000
Utilities	300,000
Depreciation	600,000
Total	$2,640,000

Income tax payments are made by CrossMan in the first month of each quarter based on the income for the prior quarter. CrossMan's income tax rate is 40 percent. CrossMan's net income for the first quarter of 1998 is projected to be $612,000.

CrossMan has a corporate policy of maintaining an end-of-month cash balance of $100,000. Cash is invested or borrowed monthly, as necessary, to maintain this balance.

CrossMan uses a calendar year reporting period.

REQUIRED:

1. Prepare a pro forma schedule of cash receipts and disbursements for CrossMan Corporation, by month, for the second quarter of 1998. Be sure that all receipts, disbursements, and borrowing and investing amounts are presented on a monthly basis. Ignore the interest expense and/or interest income associated with the borrowing and investing activities.

2. Discuss why cash budgeting is particularly important for a rapidly expanding company such as CrossMan Corporation. (CMA adapted)

 ANAGERIAL DECISION CASES

C8-1
Budgetary Performance; Rewards; Ethical Behavior
LO 3

Linda Ellis, division manager, is evaluated and rewarded on the basis of budgetary performance. She, her assistants, and the plant managers are all eligible to receive a bonus if actual divisional profits are between budgeted profits and 120 percent of budgeted profits. The bonuses are based on a fixed percentage of actual profits. Profits above 120 percent of budgeted profits earn a bonus at the 120 percent level (in other words, there is an upper limit on possible bonus payments). If the actual profits are less than budgeted profits, no bonuses are awarded. Now consider the following actions taken by Linda:

a. Linda tends to overestimate expenses and underestimate revenues. This approach facilitates the ability of the division to attain budgeted profits. Linda believes the action is justified because it increases the likelihood of receiving bonuses and helps keep the morale of the managers high.

b. Suppose that toward the end of the fiscal year, Linda saw that the division would not achieve budgeted profits. Accordingly, she instructed the sales department to defer the closing of a number of sales agreements to the following fiscal year. She also decided to write off some inventory that was nearly worthless. Deferring revenues to next year and writing off the inventory in a no-bonus year increased the chances of a bonus for next year.

c. Assume that toward the end of the year, Linda saw that actual profits would likely exceed the 120 percent limit. She took actions similar to those described in (b).

REQUIRED:

1. Comment on the ethics of Linda's behavior. Are her actions right or wrong? What role does the company play in encouraging her actions?

2. Suppose that you are the marketing manager for the division and you receive instructions to defer the closing of sales until the next fiscal year. What would you do?

3. Suppose that you are a plant manager and you know that your budget has been padded by the division manager. Further suppose that the padding is common knowledge among the plant managers, who support it because it increases the ability to achieve the budget and receive a bonus. What would you do?

4. Suppose that you are the division controller and you receive instructions from the division manager to accelerate the recognition of some expenses that legitimately belong to a future period. What would you do?

C8-2

Cash Budget

LO 2

According to the analysis of a local consultant, the financial difficulties facing Dr. Roger Jones have been caused by the absence of proper planning and control.[6] Budgetary control is sorely needed. To assist you in preparing a plan of action that will help his dental practice regain financial stability, Dr. Jones has made available the following financial information that describes a typical month:

Revenues

	Average Fee	Quantity
Fillings	$ 50	90
Crowns	300	19
Root canals	170	8
Bridges	500	7
Extractions	45	30
Cleaning	25	108
X rays	15	150

Costs

Salaries:		
Two dental assistants	$1,900	
Receptionist/bookkeeper	1,500	
Hygienist	1,800	
Public relations (Mrs. Jones)	1,000	
Personal salary	6,500	
Total salaries		$12,700
Benefits		1,344
Building lease		1,500
Dental supplies		1,200
Janitorial		300
Utilities		400
Phone		150
Office supplies		100
Lab fees		5,000
Loan payments		570
Interest payments		500
Miscellaneous		500
Depreciation		700
Total costs		$24,964

Benefits include Dr. Jones's share of social security and a health insurance premium for all employees. Although all revenues billed in a month are not collected, the cash flowing into the business is approximately equal to the month's billings because of collections from prior months.

6. Review the introduction to the chapter for a description of the financial difficulties that Dr. Jones faces on a recurring basis.

The dental office is open Monday through Thursday from 8:30 A.M. to 4:00 P.M. and on Friday from 8:30 A.M. to 12:30 P.M. A total of 32 hours are worked each week. Additional hours could be worked, but Dr. Jones is reluctant to do so because of other personal endeavors that he enjoys.

Dr. Jones has noted that the two dental assistants and the receptionist are not fully utilized. He estimates that they are busy about 65 to 70 percent of the time. Dr. Jones's wife spends about five hours each week on a monthly newsletter that is sent to all patients; she also maintains a birthday list and sends cards to the patients on their birthdays.

Dr. Jones spends about $2,400 yearly on informational seminars. These seminars, targeted especially for dentists, teach them how to increase their revenues. It is from one of these seminars that Dr. Jones decided to invest in promotion and public relations (the newsletter and the birthday list).

REQUIRED:
1. Prepare a monthly cash budget for Dr. Jones. Does Dr. Jones have a significant cash flow problem? How would you use the budget to show Dr. Jones why he is having financial difficulties?
2. Using the cash budget prepared in requirement 1 and the information given in the case, recommend actions to solve Dr. Jones's financial problems. Prepare a cash budget that reflects these recommendations and demonstrates to Dr. Jones that the problems can be corrected. Do you think that Dr. Jones will accept your recommendations? Do any of the behavioral principles discussed in the chapter have a role in this type of setting? Explain.

C8-3
Participative
Budgeting
LO 3

Five years ago, Jack Cadence and two colleagues left their positions with a large industrial firm to start Advanced Technologies Company (ATC), a software design company. Cadence, the major owner, obtained venture capital, and ATC commenced work on the design of a unique software package to make the use and integration of PCs easier. Since the completion of this package, there has been good market acceptance, and Cadence has been able to raise the additional capital necessary to operate during the initial marketing stages. Cadence has concentrated on managing the company while the other two minority owners focused on design and development activities. ATC has now started on the development of new software to permit the ready usage of the underapplied power of the advanced microprocessors that have entered the marketplace.

With the continued sales growth of the initial software and the ongoing development of new programming products, Cadence has hired several seasoned marketing, sales, and production managers, as well as Jeff Cross, a senior accountant with a budgeting background.

ATC currently employs 70 people in the design and development, marketing, sales, accounting, and legal departments. Recently, Cadence decided that, with the expansion of ATC, a formalized planning and control process should be established. Cadence asked Cross to work with him in developing the initial budget for ATC.

As several of the senior managers were new to the company, Cadence forecast the sales revenue based on his projections for both the market growth for the initial software and the successful completion of new product developments. Cadence further prepared production and expense projections. Cross used this information to construct departmental budgets and the overall company budget. Cadence and Cross reviewed and revised these budgets on several occasions.

When Cadence and Cross were satisfied, the various budgets were distributed with a cover letter, which advised that ATC was adopting a formalized planning procedure. The letter further requested everyone's assistance in working together to achieve the budget objectives in order to continue the company's successful and growing operations.

Several of the department managers, particularly the newly hired seasoned personnel, were displeased with how the planning process was undertaken. In discussing the situation among themselves, they felt that some of the budget projections were overly optimistic and not realistically attainable.

REQUIRED:
1. The planning process that Jack Cadence and Jeff Cross utilized is referred to as a *top-down* budgeting process.
   a. Explain why this is a top-down budgeting process, and compare it to a participative budgeting process.
   b. Describe the advantages associated with a top-down budgeting process.
2. a. Describe the personal behavioral issues faced by Jack Cadence, as the founder of ATC in initiating a formalized budgeting process.

b. Describe the behavioral problems for the remainder of the employees at ATC that may result from a top-down budgeting process.

3. a. Outline specific recommendations that Cadence and Cross could have employed to initiate a participative budgeting process.

b. Describe the advantages associated with a participative budgeting process. (CMA adapted)

C8-4
Research Assignment

A formal master budgeting process is important to many companies. Locate a manufacturing plant in your community that has headquarters elsewhere. Interview the controller for the plant regarding the master-budgeting process. Ask when the process starts each year, what schedules and budgets are prepared at the plant level, how the controller forecasts the amounts, and how those schedules and budgets fit in with the overall corporate budget.

Learning Objectives

After studying Chapter 9, you should be able to:

1. Explain how unit standards are set and why standard cost systems are adopted.

2. Explain the purpose of a standard cost sheet.

3. Describe the basic concepts underlying variance analysis and explain when variances should be investigated.

4. Compute the materials and labor variances and explain how they are used for control.

5. Compute the variable and fixed overhead variances and explain their meanings.

6. Prepare journal entries for materials and labor variances and describe the accounting for overhead variances. (Appendix)

CHAPTER

Standard Costing: A Managerial Control Tool

SCENARIO

illie Anderson, manager of Honley Medical's IV Products Division, was more than satisfied with the performance of her division last year. At the beginning of the year, the division had introduced a new line of polyurethane catheters, replacing the old teflon catheters, and sales had more than tripled. The reaction of the market to the new catheter represented a virtual replay of the company's history. Once again, Honley Medical was establishing a dominant position in the IV market.

Nearly thirty years ago, Lindell Honley, the founder of Honley Medical, had perceived the need for something other than a metal needle for long-term insertion into veins. Metal needles were irritating and could damage the vein. Based on this observation, Honley had developed a

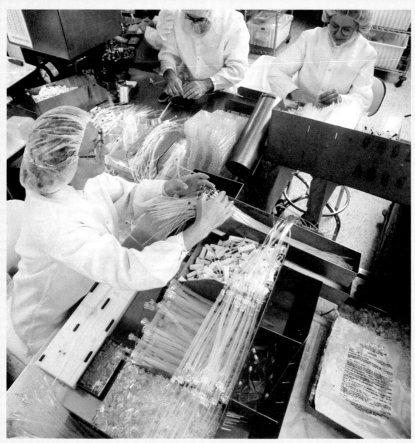

catheter using teflon since it was a lubricated plastic and easy to insert into the vein. The new development was well received by the medical community and produced a new and successful company, one that had expanded its activities into a variety of medical products.

For years, the new technology allowed Honley to dominate the market. Eventually, however, the patent expired and other companies entered the market with their own teflon catheters, making competition exceptionally keen. Prices had been driven down, and profit margins were eroding.

The eroding profit margins had prompted Millie and other high-level managers to examine the continued viability of the teflon catheters. After many years, the medical profession had noted that after 24 hours of use, an infection tended to develop

around the point of insertion. Researchers at Honley Medical had discovered that the problem was one of incompatibility of the blood and tissue with the teflon. Further studies showed that different plastics produced different reactions. Research began immediately on finding a material that was more biocompatible than teflon. The outcome was polyurethane catheters. The new catheter could be left in for 72 hours, compared to the 24 hours for teflon catheters.

Millie also knew that history would repeat itself in the later stages—the time would come when other firms would produce catheters with the same degree of biocompatibility. In fact, Honley's research scientists estimated that competitors would have a competing catheter on the market within three years. This time, however, Millie was determined

to protect the division's market share. Since most patients had little need for a catheter beyond 72 hours, further improvements in biocompatibility were not likely to yield the same market benefits as in the past. Price competition would become more important. Competing on price meant that cost control would become more critical. In the past, because of its dominant position, the division had not been too concerned with control of manufacturing costs. By implementing cost control measures now, she believed that the division would be better able to compete on price when the competition resurfaced within a few years. Her conversation with Reed McCourt, division controller, reflects this decision.

Millie: "Reed, as I see it, the only attempt we make to control manufacturing costs is our budgetary system. Is that right?"

Reed: "Yes. But it really isn't a very good effort. Budgets are based on last year's costs plus some allowance for inflation. At this point, we have never tried to identify what the costs ought to be. Nor have we really held managers responsible for cost control. Our profitability has always been good—resources have always been plentiful. My guess is that we are spending much more than necessary simply because we have been so successful."

Millie: "Well, resources wouldn't be so plentiful now if we hadn't developed the polyurethane catheter. And I'm afraid that resources won't be plentiful in the future unless we take actions now to control our manufacturing costs. Besides, if we can be more profitable now by using better cost control, we ought to use it. I want better cost control, and I want my plant and production managers to recognize their responsibilities in this area. What suggestions do you have?"

Reed: "We need to inject more formality into the budgetary system. First, budgets should reflect what costs should be, not what they have been. Second, we can encourage managers to be cost conscious by allowing them to help identify efficient levels of cost on which the budget will be based and tying their bonuses and promotions into the system as well. However, I think we can gain the cost control by going one step further and establishing a standard cost system."

Millie: "Doesn't that entail the specification of unit price and quantity standards for materials and labor?"

Reed: "That's essentially correct. Using the unit price and quantity standards, budgeted costs for labor, materials, and overhead are established for each unit produced. The standards are based on efficiency expectations and will demand less resource usage than our traditional incremental budgetary approach. The unit price and quantity standards are used to develop budgets and, once actual costs are in, to break down the budgetary variances into a price variance and an efficiency variance. A standard cost system provides more detailed control information than a budgetary system using normal costing. We can hold our managers responsible for meeting the standards that are established."

Millie: "I think our division needs this type of system. It's about time that our managers become cost conscious. Reed, prepare a report that provides more detail on what a standard cost system is all about."

Questions to Think About

1. What was motivating Millie to implement a more formal cost control system?

2. Why does a standard cost system provide more detailed control information?

3. What type of control is being exercised with the use of standards?

4. How can standards be used to control costs?

5. What kind of behavior will standards encourage?

UNIT STANDARDS

Objective 1

Explain how unit standards are set and why standard cost systems are adopted.

Millie and Reed both recognized the need to encourage operating managers to control costs. Cost control often means the difference between success and failure or between above-average profits and lesser profits. Millie was convinced that cost control meant that her managers had to be cost conscious and they had to assume responsibility for this important objective. Reed suggested that the way to control costs and involve managers is through the use of a formal budgetary system.

In Chapter 8, we learned that budgets set standards that are used to control and evaluate managerial performance. However, budgets are aggregate measures of performance; they identify the revenues and costs in total that an organization should experience if plans are executed as expected. By comparing the actual costs and actual revenues with the corresponding budgeted amounts at the same level of activity, a measure of managerial efficiency emerges.

Although the process just described provides significant information for control, control can be enhanced by developing standards for unit amounts as well as for total amounts. In fact, the groundwork for unit standards already exists within the framework of flexible budgeting. For flexible budgeting to work, the budgeted variable cost per unit of input for each unit of output must be known for every item in the budget. The budgeted variable input cost per unit of output is a unit standard. Unit standards are the basis or foundation on which a flexible budget is built.

To determine the unit standard cost for a particular input, two decisions must be made: (1) how much of the input should be used per unit of output (the quantity decision) and (2) how much should be paid for the quantity of the input to be used (the pricing decision). The quantity decision produces quantity standards, and the pricing decision produces price standards. The unit standard cost can be computed by multiplying these two standards: quantity standard × price standard.

For example, a soft-drink bottling company may decide that 5 ounces of fructose should be used for every 16-ounce bottle of cola (the quantity standard), and the price of the fructose should be $0.05 per ounce (the price standard). The standard cost of the fructose per bottle of cola is then $0.25 (5 × $0.05). The standard cost per unit of fructose can be used to predict what the total cost of fructose should be as the activity level varies; it thus becomes a flexible budget formula. Thus, if 10,000 bottles of cola are produced, the total expected cost of fructose is $2,500 ($0.25 × 10,000); if 15,000 bottles are produced, the total expected cost of fructose is $3,750 ($0.25 × 15,000).

How Standards Are Developed

Historical experience, engineering studies, and input from operating personnel are three potential sources of quantitative standards. Although historical experience may provide an initial guideline for setting standards, it should not be used without caution. Often, processes are operating inefficiently; adopting input-output relationships from the past thus perpetuates these inefficiencies. The IV Division of Honley Medical, for example, had never emphasized cost control and had operated in a resource-rich environment. Both the division manager and controller were convinced that significant inefficiencies existed. Engineering studies can determine the most efficient way to operate and can provide very rigorous guidelines; however, engineered standards are often too rigorous. They may not be achievable by operating personnel. Since operating personnel are accountable for meeting the standards, they should have significant input in setting standards. The same principles pertaining to participative budgeting pertain to setting unit standards.

Price standards are the joint responsibility of operations, purchasing, personnel, and accounting. Operations determines the quality of the inputs required; personnel and purchasing have the responsibility of acquiring the input quality requested at the lowest price. Market forces, trade unions, and other external forces limit the range of choices for price standards. In setting price standards, purchasing must consider discounts, freight, and quality; personnel, on the other hand, must consider payroll taxes, fringe benefits, and qualifications. Accounting is responsible for recording the price standards and preparing reports that compare actual performance to the standard.

Types of Standards

Standards are generally classified as either *ideal* or *currently attainable*. Ideal standards demand maximum efficiency and can be achieved only if everything operates perfectly. No machine breakdowns, slack, or lack of skill (even momentarily) are allowed. Currently attainable standards can be achieved under efficient operating conditions. Allowance is made for normal breakdowns, interruptions, less than perfect skill, and so on. These standards are demanding but achievable.

Of the two types, currently attainable standards offer the most behavioral benefits. If standards are too tight and never achievable, workers become frustrated and performance levels decline. However, challenging but achievable standards tend to extract higher performance levels—particularly when the individuals subject to the standards have participated in their creation.

quantity standards
price standards

ideal standards

currently attainable standards

Why Standard Cost Systems Are Adopted

Two reasons for adopting a standard cost system are frequently mentioned: to improve planning and control and to facilitate product costing.

Planning and Control Standard costing systems enhance planning and control and improve performance measurement. Unit standards are a fundamental requirement for a flexible budgeting system, which is a key feature of a meaningful planning and control system. Budgetary control systems compare actual costs with budgeted costs by computing variances, the difference between the actual and planned costs for the actual level of activity. By developing unit price and quantity standards, an overall variance can be decomposed into a price variance and a usage or efficiency variance.

By performing this decomposition, a manager has more information. If the variance is unfavorable, a manager can tell whether it is attributable to discrepancies between planned prices and actual prices, to discrepancies between planned usage and actual usage, or to both. Since managers have more control over the usage of inputs than over their prices, efficiency variances provide specific signals regarding the need for corrective action and where that action should be focused. Thus, in principle, the use of efficiency variances enhances operational control. Additionally, by breaking out the price variance, over which managers potentially have less control, the system provides an improved measure of managerial efficiency.

The benefits of operational control, however, may not extend to the advanced manufacturing environment. The use of a standard cost system for operational control in an advanced manufacturing environment can produce dysfunctional behavior. For example, materials price variance reporting may encourage the purchasing department to buy in large quantities, to take advantage of discounts. Yet this may lead to holding significant inventories, something not desired by JIT firms. Thus, the detailed computation of variances—at least at the operational level—is discouraged in this new environment. Nonetheless, standards in the advanced manufacturing environment are still useful for planning, for example, in the creation of bids. Also, variances may still be computed and presented in reports to higher-level managers so that the financial dimension can be monitored.

Finally, it should be mentioned that there are many firms operating with conventional manufacturing systems. Standard cost systems are widely used. In a recent survey, 87 percent of the firms responding used a standard cost system.[1] Furthermore, the survey revealed that significant numbers of the respondents were calculating variances at the operational level. For example, about 40 percent of the firms using a standard costing system reported labor variances for small work crews or individual workers.

Product Costing In a standard cost system, costs are assigned to products using quantity and price standards for all three manufacturing costs: direct materials, direct labor, and overhead. In contrast, a normal cost system predetermines overhead costs for the purpose of product costing but assigns direct materials and direct labor to products by using actual costs. Overhead is assigned using a budgeted rate and actual activity. At the other end of the cost assignment spectrum, an actual cost system assigns the actual costs of all three manufacturing inputs to products. Exhibit 9-1 summarizes these three cost assignment approaches. Standard product costing has several advantages over normal costing and actual costing. One, of course, is the greater capacity for control. Standard cost systems also provide readily available unit cost information that can be used for pricing decisions. This is particularly helpful for companies that do a significant amount of bidding and those paid on a cost-plus basis.[2]

1. Bruce R. Gaumnitz and Felix P. Kollaritsch, "Manufacturing Variances: Current Practice and Trends," *Journal of Cost Management* (Spring 1991), 58–64.
2. For example, CalBlock, Inc., the concrete and pipe company in Chapter 8, conducts the vast majority of its business through bidding. This company recently adopted a standard cost system primarily to facilitate the bidding process.

Exhibit
Cost Assignment
Approaches

	Manufacturing Costs		
	Direct Materials	Direct Labor	Overhead
Actual cost system	Actual	Actual	Actual
Normal cost system	Actual	Actual	Budgeted
Standard cost system	Standard	Standard	Standard

Other simplifications are also possible. For example, if a process-costing system uses standard costing to assign product costs, there is no need to compute a unit cost for each equivalent-unit cost category. A standard unit cost would exist for each category.[3] Additionally, there is no need to distinguish between the FIFO and weighted-average methods of accounting for beginning inventory costs. Usually, a standard process costing system will follow the equivalent unit calculation of the FIFO approach. That is, current equivalent units of work are calculated. By calculating current equivalent work, current actual production costs can be compared with standard costs for control purposes.

STANDARD PRODUCT COSTS

Objective 2

Explain the purpose of a standard cost sheet.

Standard costs can also be used in service organizations. The IRS, for example, could set standard processing times for different categories of returns. If the standard processing time is 3 minutes for a 1040EZ, and the standard price of labor is $9 per hour, then the standard cost of processing a 1040EZ is $0.45 ($9 x $\frac{3}{60}$). Other examples exist. The federal government is using a standard-costing system for reimbursing Medicare costs. Based on several studies, illnesses have been classified into diagnostic related groups (DRGs), and the hospital costs that should be incurred for an average case identified. (The costs include patient days, food, medicine, supplies, use of equipment, and so on.) The government pays the hospital the standard cost for the DRG. If the cost of the patient's treatment is greater than the DRG allows, the hospital suffers a loss. If the cost of the patient's treatment is less than the DRG reimbursement, the hospital gains. On average, the hospital supposedly breaks even. Although service organizations can and do make use of standard costing, applications are more common in manufacturing organizations. Furthermore, the concepts are more easily illustrated in manufacturing settings.

standard cost per unit
standard cost sheet

In manufacturing firms, standard costs are developed for materials, labor, and overhead. Using these costs, the standard cost per unit is computed. The standard cost sheet provides the detail underlying the standard unit cost. To illustrate, let's develop a standard cost sheet for a 16-ounce bag of corn chips produced by Crunchy Chips, Inc. The production of corn chips begins by steaming and soaking corn kernels overnight in a lime solution. This process softens the kernels so that they can be shaped into a sheet of dough. The dough is then cut into small triangular chips. Next, the chips are toasted in an oven and dropped into a deep fryer. After cooking, the chips pass under a salting device and are inspected for quality. Substandard chips are sorted and discarded; the chips passing inspection are bagged by a packaging machine. The bagged chips are manually packed into boxes for shipping.

Four materials are used to process corn chips: yellow corn, cooking oil, salt, and lime. The package in which the chips are placed is also classified as a direct material. Crunchy Chips has two types of direct laborers: machine operators and inspectors (or sorters). Variable overhead is made up of three costs: gas, electricity, and water. Both

---

3. If you have not read the chapter on process costing, the example illustrating the simplifications made possible by standard costing will not be as meaningful. However, the point is still relevant. Standard costing can bring useful computational savings.

variable and fixed overhead are applied using direct labor hours. The standard cost sheet is given in Exhibit 9-2. Note that it should cost $0.56 to produce a 16-ounce package of corn chips. Also, notice that the company uses 18 ounces of corn to produce a 16-ounce package of chips. There are two reasons. First, some chips are discarded during the inspection process. The company plans on a normal amount of waste. Second, the company wants to have more than 16 ounces in each package to increase customer satisfaction with its product and avoid any problems with fair packaging laws.

Exhibit 9-2 also reveals other important insights. The standard usage for variable and fixed overhead is tied to the direct labor standards. For variable overhead, the rate is $3.85 per direct labor hour. Since one package of corn chips uses 0.0078 direct labor hour, the variable overhead cost assigned to a package of corn chips is $0.03 ($3.85 × 0.0078). For fixed overhead, the rate is $32.05 per direct labor hour, making the fixed overhead cost per package of corn chips $0.25 ($32.05 × 0.0078). Nearly half of the cost of production is fixed, indicating a capital-intensive production effort. Indeed, much of the operation is mechanized.

The standard cost sheet also reveals the quantity of each input that should be used to produce one unit of output. The unit quantity standards can be used to compute the total amount of inputs allowed for the actual output. This computation is an essential component in computing efficiency variances. A manager should be able to compute the **standard quantity of materials allowed** (SQ) and the **standard hours allowed** (SH) for the actual output. This computation must be done for every class of direct material and every class of direct labor. Assume, for example, that 100,000 packages of corn chips are produced during the first week of March. How much yellow corn should have been used for the actual output of 100,000 packages? The unit quantity standard is 18 ounces of yellow corn per package (see Exhibit 9-2). For 100,000 packages, the standard quantity of yellow corn allowed is computed as follows:

$$SQ = \text{Unit quantity standard} \times \text{Actual output}$$
$$= 18 \times 100,000$$
$$= 1,800,000 \text{ ounces}$$

The computation of standard direct labor hours allowed can be illustrated using machine operators. From Exhibit 9-2, we see that the unit quantity standard is 0.0008

margin: standard quantity of materials allowed / standard hours allowed

9-2 Exhibit

Standard Cost Sheet for Corn Chips				
Description	Standard Price	Standard Usage	Standard Cost*	Subtotal
Direct materials:				
Yellow corn	$ 0.006	18 oz	$0.108	
Cooking oil	0.031	2 oz	0.062	
Salt	0.005	1 oz	0.005	
Lime	0.400	0.01 oz	0.004	
Bags	0.044	1 bag	0.044	
Total direct materials				$0.223
Direct labor:				
Inspection	7.00	0.0070 hr	$0.049	
Machine operators	10.00	0.0008 hr	0.008	
Total direct labor				0.057
Overhead:				
Variable overhead	3.85	0.0078 hr	$0.030	
Fixed overhead	32.05	0.0078 hr	0.250	
Total overhead				0.280
Total standard unit cost				$0.560

*Calculated by multiplying price times usage

hour per package produced. Thus, if 100,000 packages are produced, the standard hours allowed is as follows:

$$SH = \text{Unit labor standard} \times \text{Actual output}$$
$$= 0.0008 \times 100,000$$
$$= 80 \text{ direct labor hours}$$

VARIANCE ANALYSIS: GENERAL DESCRIPTION

Objective 3

Describe the basic concepts underlying variance analysis and explain when variances should be investigated.

A flexible budget can be used to identify the costs that should have been incurred for the actual level of activity. This figure is obtained by multiplying the amount of input allowed for the actual output by the standard unit price. Letting SP be the standard unit price of an input and SQ the standard quantity of inputs allowed for the actual output, the planned or budgeted input cost is $SP \times SQ$. The actual input cost is $AP \times AQ$, where AP is the actual price per unit of the input and AQ is the actual quantity of input used.

Price and Efficiency Variances

total budget variance

The total budget variance is simply the difference between the actual cost of the input and its planned cost. For simplicity, we will refer to the total budget variance as the total variance:

$$\text{Total variance} = (AP \times AQ) - (SP \times SQ)$$

price (rate) variance
usage (efficiency) variance

In a standard cost system, the total variance is broken down into price and usage variances. Price (rate) variance is the difference between the actual and standard unit price of an input multiplied by the number of inputs used: $(AP - SP)AQ$. Usage (efficiency) variance is the difference between the actual and standard quantity of inputs multiplied by the standard unit price of the input: $(AQ - SQ)SP$. It is easy to show that the total variance is the sum of price and usage variances:

$$\text{Total variance} = \text{Price variance} + \text{Usage variance}$$
$$= (AP - SP)AQ + (AQ - SQ)SP$$
$$= [(AP \times AQ) - (SP \times AQ)] + [(SP \times AQ) - (SP \times SQ)]$$
$$= (AP \times AQ) - (SP \times AQ) + (SP \times AQ) - (SP \times SQ)$$
$$= (AP \times AQ) - (SP \times SQ)$$

Exhibit 9-3 presents a three-pronged diagram that describes this process. Usually, the total variance is divided into price and efficiency components for direct materials and direct labor. The treatment of overhead is discussed later in the chapter.

unfavorable (U) variances
favorable (F) variances

Unfavorable (U) variances occur whenever actual prices or usage of inputs is greater than standard prices or usage. When the opposite occurs, favorable (F) variances are obtained. Favorable and unfavorable variances are not equivalent to good and bad variances. The terms merely indicate the relationship of the actual prices or quantities to the standard prices and quantities. Whether or not the variances are good or bad depends on *why* they occurred. Determining why requires managers to do some investigation.

The Decision to Investigate

Rarely will actual performance exactly meet the established standards, and management does not expect it to. Random variations around the standard are expected. Because of this, management should have in mind an acceptable range of performance. When variances are within this range, they are assumed to be caused by random factors. When a variance falls outside this range, the deviation is likely to be caused by nonrandom factors, either factors that managers can control or factors they cannot control. In the noncontrollable case, managers need to revise the standard.

Exhibit
Variance Analysis:
General Description

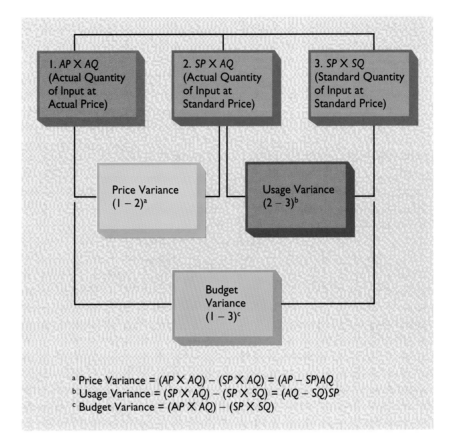

An example from the pharmaceutical industry may drive home the importance of variance investigation.[4] Drugs must contain a certain amount of the active ingredient, plus or minus a small percent (for example, aspirin claiming to have 5 grains per tablet must really have somewhere between 90 and 110 percent of the specified amount). The FDA is responsible for ensuring the safety and efficacy of drugs manufactured at home and abroad. In 1991, an anonymous letter alerted the FDA to manufacturing problems with an antibiotic produced by a Canadian firm, Novopharm Ltd. Basically, the drug was too strong, and could possibly destroy beneficial bacteria along with the harmful bacteria. Upon investigation, the FDA found the blending process to be "out of control." The result was that the firm stopped shipping that drug until the process could be corrected. Another FDA investigation centered on Haimen Pharmaceutical Factory in China. There, the FDA found the samples of an antileukemia drug to be too weak. Again, large variances from standard triggered an investigation. Interestingly, the question of what to do about the company and the drug was not clear-cut. The FDA did not withdraw its approval because the drug was in short supply. FDA investigations into the manufacturing processes of the company continue.

Now that we understand why variance investigation is important, we need to understand *when* to investigate. Investigating the cause of variances and taking corrective action, like all activities, have a cost associated with them. As a general principle, an investigation should be undertaken only if the anticipated benefits are greater than the expected costs. Assessing the costs and benefits of a variance investigation is not an easy task, however. A manager must consider whether a variance will recur. If so, the process may be permanently out of control, meaning that periodic savings may be achieved if corrective action is taken. But how can we tell if the variance is going to recur unless an

---

4. The examples given here are taken from an article by Christopher Drew, "Medicines from Afar Raise Safety Concerns," *The New York Times*, 29 October 1995, A1 and A16.

investigation is conducted? And how do we know the cost of corrective action unless the cause of the variance is known?

Because it is difficult to assess the costs and benefits of variance analysis on a case-by-case basis, many firms adopt the general guideline of investigating variances only if they fall outside an acceptable range. They are not investigated unless they are large enough to be of concern. They must be large enough to be caused by something other than random factors and large enough (on average) to justify the costs of investigating and taking corrective action.

How do managers determine whether variances are significant? How is the acceptable range established? The acceptable range is the standard plus or minus an allowable deviation. The top and bottom measures of the allowable range are called the control limits. The upper control limit is the standard plus the allowable deviation, and the lower control limit is the standard minus the allowable deviation. Current practice sets the control limits subjectively: based on past experience, intuition, and judgment, management determines the allowable deviation from standard.[5] Exhibit 9-4 graphically illustrates the concept of control limits. The assumed standard is $100,000 and the allowable deviation is plus or minus $10,000. The upper limit is $110,000 and the lower limit is $90,000. Investigation occurs whenever an observation falls outside of these limits (as would be the case for the sixth observation). Trends can also be important.

The control limits are often expressed both as a percentage of the standard and as an absolute dollar amount. For example, the allowable deviation may be expressed as the lesser of 10 percent of the standard amount, or $10,000. In other words, management will not accept a deviation of more than $10,000 even if that deviation is less than 10 percent of the standard. Alternatively, even if the dollar amount is less than $10,000,

control limits

5. Gaumnitz and Kollaritsch, "Manufacturing Variances: Current Practice and Trends," report that about 45 to 47 percent of the firms use dollar or percentage control limits. Most of the remaining use judgment rather than any formal identification of limits.

9-4 ···························· Control Chart

Exhibit

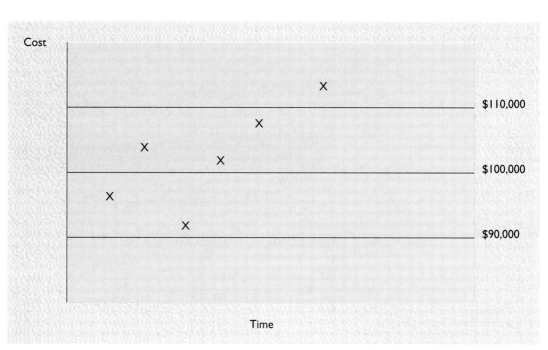

an investigation is required if the deviation is more than 10 percent of the standard amount.

Formal statistical procedures can also be used to set the control limits. In this way, less subjectivity is involved and a manager can assess the likelihood of the variance being caused by random factors. At this time, the use of such formal procedures has gained little acceptance.[6]

VARIANCE ANALYSIS: MATERIALS AND LABOR

Objective 4

Compute the materials and labor variances and explain how they are used for control.

The total variance measures the difference between the actual cost of materials and labor and their budgeted costs for the actual level of activity. To illustrate, consider these selected data for Crunchy Chips from the first week of March:[7]

Actual production	48,500 bags of corn chips
Actual cost of corn	780,000 ounces at $0.0069 = $5,382
Actual cost of inspection labor	360 hours at $7.35 = $2,646

Using these actual data and the unit standards from Exhibit 9-2, a performance report for the first week of March can be developed (see Exhibit 9-5). As has been mentioned, the total variance can be divided into price and usage variances, providing more information to the manager. We will do so in the following sections.

Direct Materials Variances

The three-pronged (columnar) or formula approaches may be used to calculate materials price and usage variances.

The Columnar Approach The columnar approach illustrated in Exhibit 9-3 can be used to calculate the materials price and usage variances. This calculation for the Crunchy Chips example is illustrated in Exhibit 9-6. Only the price and usage variances for corn are shown. Many find this graphical approach easier than the use of variance formulas.

6. According to Gaumnitz and Kollaritsch, only about 1 percent of the responding firms used formal statistical procedures.
7. To keep the example simple, only one material (corn) and one type of labor (inspection) are illustrated. A complete analysis for the company would include all types of materials and labor categories.

9-5

Exhibit
Performance Report:
Total Variances

	Actual Costs	Budgeted Costs*	Total Variance
Corn	$5,382.00	$5,238.00	$144.00 U
Inspection labor	2,646.00	2,376.50	269.50 U

*The standard quantities for materials and labor are computed as unit quantity standards from Exhibit 9-2:

Corn: 18 × 48,500 = 873,000 ounces
Labor: 0.007 × 48,500 = 339.5 hours

Multiplying these standard quantities by the unit standard prices given in Exhibit 9-2 produces the budgeted amounts appearing in this column:

Corn: $0.006 × 873,000 = $5,238
Labor: $7.00 × 339.5 = $2,376.50

Exhibit
Material Variances:
Columnar Approach

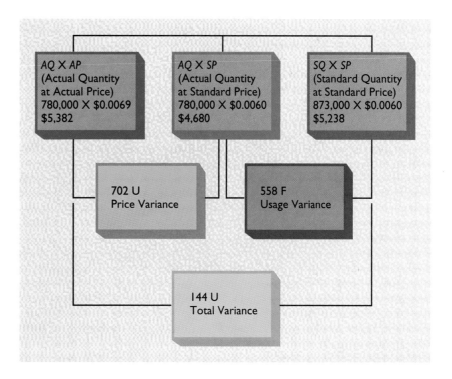

Materials Price Variance: Formula Approach The materials price variance can be calculated separately. The materials price variance (*MPV*) measures the difference between what should have been paid for raw materials and what was actually paid. The formula for computing this variance is:

$$MPV = (AP \times AQ) - (SP \times AQ)$$

or, factoring, we have:

$$MPV = (AP - SP)AQ$$

where

$$AP = \text{The actual price per unit}$$
$$SP = \text{The standard price per unit}$$
$$AQ = \text{The actual quantity of material used}$$

Computation of the Materials Price Variance Crunchy Chips purchased and used 780,000 ounces of yellow corn for the first week of March. The purchase price was $0.0069 per ounce. Thus, *AP* is $0.0069, *AQ* is 780,000 ounces, and *SP* (from Exhibit 9-2) is $0.0060. Using this information, the materials price variance is computed as follows:

$$
\begin{aligned}
MPV &= (AP - SP)AQ \\
&= (\$0.0069 - \$0.0060)780,000 \\
&= \$0.0009 \times 780,000 \\
&= \$702 \text{ U}
\end{aligned}
$$

$$\text{Percent of } SP \times AQ = \frac{\$702}{\$4,680} = 15\%$$

Responsibility for the Materials Price Variance The responsibility for controlling the materials price variance is usually the purchasing agent's. Admittedly, the price of materials is largely beyond his or her control; however, the price variance can be influenced

Many manufacturing plants set precise standards for the type and amount of materials as well as the type and amount of direct labor to be used in making each unit. The amount of time this worker actually spends in welding will be compared with the standard time allowed to see if labor time is being used efficiently.

by such factors as quality, quantity discounts, distance of the source from the plant, and so on. These factors are often under the control of the agent.

Using the price variance to evaluate the performance of purchasing has some limitations. Emphasis on meeting or beating the standard can produce some undesirable outcomes. For example, if the purchasing agent feels pressured to produce favorable variances, materials of lower quality than desired may be purchased or too much inventory may be acquired to take advantage of quantity discounts.

Analysis of the Materials Price Variance The first step in variance analysis is deciding whether the variance is significant or not. If it is judged insignificant, no further steps are needed. Assume that an unfavorable materials price variance of $702 is judged significant (15% of the standard cost). The next step is to find out why it occurred.

For the Crunchy Chips example, the investigation revealed that a higher-quality corn was purchased because of a shortage of the usual grade in the market. Once the reason is known, corrective action can be taken if necessary—and if possible. In this case, no corrective action is needed. The firm has no control over the supply shortage; it will simply have to wait until market conditions improve.

Timing of the Price Variance Computation The materials price variance can be computed at one of two points: (1) when the raw materials are issued for use in production or (2) when they are purchased. Computing the price variance at the point of purchase is preferable. It is better to have information on variances earlier than later. The more timely the information, the more likely proper managerial action can be taken. Old information is often useless information.

Materials may sit in inventory for weeks or months before they are needed in production. By the time the materials price variance is computed, signaling a problem, it may be too late to take corrective action. Or, even if corrective action is still possible, the delay may cost the company thousands of dollars. For example, suppose a new purchasing agent is unaware of the availability of a quantity discount on a raw material. If the materials price variance that ignores the discount is computed when a new purchase is made, the resulting unfavorable signal would lead to quick corrective action. (In this case, the action would be to use the discount for future purchases.) If the materials price variance is not computed until the material is issued to production, it may be several weeks or even months before the problem is discovered.

If the materials price variance is computed at the point of purchase, AQ needs to be redefined as the actual quantity of materials purchased, rather than actual materials used. Since the materials purchased may differ from the materials used, the overall materials budget variance is not necessarily the sum of the materials price variance and the materials usage variance. When the materials purchased are all used in production for the period in which the variances are calculated, the two variances will equal the total variance.

Recognizing the price variance for materials at the point of purchase also means that the raw materials inventory is carried at standard cost. The journal entry associated with the purchase of raw materials for a standard cost system is illustrated in the Appendix to this chapter.

materials usage variance (MUV)

Direct Materials Usage Variance: Formula Approach The materials usage variance (MUV) measures the difference between the direct materials actually used and the direct materials that should have been used for the actual output. The formula for computing this variance is:

$$MUV = (SP \times AQ) - (SP \times SQ)$$

or, factoring:

$$MUV = (AQ - SQ)SP$$

where

AQ = The actual quantity of materials used
SQ = The standard quantity of materials allowed for the actual output
SP = The standard price per unit

Computation of the Materials Usage Variance Crunchy Chips used 780,000 ounces of yellow corn to produce 48,500 bags of corn chips. Therefore, AQ is 780,000. From Exhibit 9-2, we see that SP is $0.006 per ounce of yellow corn. Although standard materials allowed (SQ) has already been computed in Exhibit 9-5, the details underlying the computation need to be reviewed. Recall that SQ is the product of the unit quantity standard and the actual units produced. From Exhibit 9-2, the unit standard is 18 ounces of yellow corn for every bag of corn chips. Thus, SQ is $18 \times 48,500$, or 873,000 ounces. Thus, the materials usage variance is computed as follows:

$$
\begin{aligned}
MUV &= (AQ - SQ)SP \\
&= (780,000 - 873,000)(\$0.006) \\
&= \$558 \text{ F}
\end{aligned}
$$

$$\text{Percent of } SQ \times SP = \frac{\$558}{\$5,238} = 10.7\%$$

When materials are issued, the materials usage variance can be calculated. Accounting for the issuance of materials in a standard cost system is illustrated in the Appendix to this chapter.

Responsibility for the Materials Usage Variance The production manager is generally responsible for materials usage. Minimizing scrap, waste, and rework are all ways in which the manager can ensure that the standard is met. However, at times the cause of the variance is attributable to others outside the production area, as the next section shows.

As with the price variance, using the usage variance to evaluate performance can lead to undesirable behavior. For example, a production manager feeling pressure to produce a favorable variance might allow a defective unit to be transferred to finished goods. While this avoids the problem of wasted materials, it may create customer-relations problems.

Analysis of the Materials Usage Variance Investigation revealed that the favorable materials usage variance is the result of the higher-quality corn acquired by the purchasing department. In this case, the favorable variance is essentially assignable to purchasing. Since the materials usage variance is favorable—but smaller than the unfavorable price variance—the overall result of the change in purchasing is unfavorable. In the future, management should try to resume purchasing of the normal-quality corn.

If the overall variance had been favorable, a different response would be expected. If the favorable variance were expected to persist, the higher-quality corn should be purchased regularly and the price and quantity standards revised to reflect it. As this possibility reveals, standards are not static. As improvements in production take place and conditions change, standards may need to be revised to reflect the new operating environment.

Direct Labor Variances

The rate (price) and efficiency (usage) variances for labor can be calculated using either the columnar approach of Exhibit 9-3 or a formula approach.

Columnar Approach The three-pronged calculation for inspection labor at the Crunchy Chips plant is illustrated in Exhibit 9-7. The calculation using formulas is discussed next.

labor rate variance (LRV)

Labor Rate Variance: Formula Approach The labor rate variance (*LRV*) computes the difference between what was paid to direct laborers and what should have been paid:

$$LRV = (AR \times AH) - (SR \times AH)$$

or, factoring:

$$LRV = (AR - SR)AH$$

Exhibit
Labor Variances:
Columnar Approach

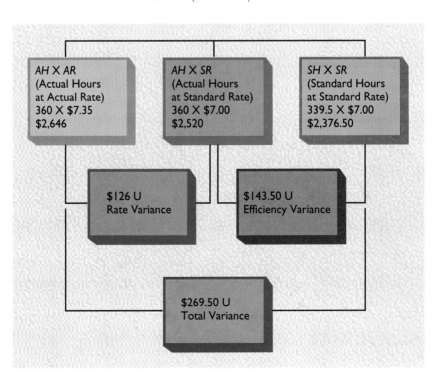

| AH × AR (Actual Hours at Actual Rate) 360 × $7.35 $2,646 | AH × SR (Actual Hours at Standard Rate) 360 × $7.00 $2,520 | SH × SR (Standard Hours at Standard Rate) 339.5 × $7.00 $2,376.50 |

$126 U
Rate Variance

$143.50 U
Efficiency Variance

$269.50 U
Total Variance

where

$$AR = \text{The actual hourly wage rate}$$
$$SR = \text{The standard hourly wage rate}$$
$$AH = \text{The actual direct labor hours used}$$

Computation of the Labor Rate Variance Direct labor activity for Crunchy Chips' inspectors will be used to illustrate the computation of the labor rate variance. We know that 360 hours were used for inspection during the first week in March. The actual hourly wage paid for inspection was $7.35. From Exhibit 9-2, the standard wage rate is $7.00. Thus, AH is 360, AR is $7.35, and SR is $7.00. The labor rate variance is computed as follows:

$$\begin{aligned} LRV &= (AR - SR)AH \\ &= (\$7.35 - \$7.00)360 \\ &= \$0.35 \times 360 \\ &= \$126 \text{ U} \end{aligned}$$

$$\text{Percent of } SR \times AH = \frac{\$126}{\$2,520} = 5\%$$

Responsibility for the Labor Rate Variance Labor rates are largely determined by such external forces as labor markets and union contracts. The actual wage rate rarely departs from the standard rate. When labor rate variances do occur, they usually do so because an average wage rate is used for the rate standard and because more skilled and more highly paid laborers are used for less skilled tasks. Unexpected overtime can also be the cause of a labor rate variance.

Wage rates for a particular labor activity often differ among workers because of differing levels of seniority. Rather than selecting labor rate standards reflecting those different levels, an average wage rate is often chosen. As the seniority mix changes, the average rate changes. This will give rise to a labor rate variance; it also calls for a new standard to reflect the new seniority mix. Controllability is not assignable for this cause of a labor rate variance.

However, the use of labor is controllable by the production manager. The use of more skilled workers to perform less skilled tasks (or vice versa) is a decision that a production manager consciously makes. For this reason, responsibility for the labor rate variance is generally assigned to the individuals who decide how labor will be used.

Analysis of the Labor Rate Variance Although a 5 percent variance is not likely to be judged significant, for illustrative purposes assume that an investigation is conducted. The cause of the variance is found to be the use of more highly paid and skilled machine operators as inspectors, which occurred because two inspectors quit without formal notice. The corrective action is to hire and train two new inspectors.

labor efficiency variance (LEV)

Labor Efficiency Variance: Formula Approach The labor efficiency variance (*LEV*) measures the difference between the labor hours that were actually used and the labor hours that should have been used:

$$LEV = (AH \times SR) - (SH \times SR)$$

or, factoring:

$$LEV = (AH - SH)SR$$

where

$$AH = \text{The actual direct labor hours used}$$
$$SH = \text{The standard direct labor hours that should have been used}$$
$$SR = \text{The standard hourly wage rate}$$

Computation of the Labor Efficiency Variance Crunchy Chips used 360 direct labor hours for inspection while producing 48,500 bags of corn chips. From Exhibit 9-2, 0.007 hour per bag of chips at a cost of $7 per hour should have been used. The standard hours allowed for inspection or sorting are 339.5 (0.007 × 48,500). Thus, *AH* is 360, *SH* is 339.5, and *SR* is $7. The labor efficiency variance is computed as follows:

$$LEV = (AH - SH)SR$$
$$= (360 - 339.5)\$7$$
$$= 20.5 \times \$7$$
$$= \$143.50 \text{ U}$$

$$\text{Percent of } SH \times SR = \frac{\$143.50}{\$2,376.50} = 6\%$$

Responsibility for the Labor Efficiency Variance Generally speaking, production managers are responsible for the productive use of direct labor. However, as is true of all variances, once the cause is discovered, responsibility may be assigned elsewhere. For example, frequent breakdowns of machinery may cause interruptions and nonproductive use of labor. But the responsibility for these breakdowns may be faulty maintenance. If so, the maintenance manager should be charged with the unfavorable labor efficiency variance.

Production managers may be tempted to engage in dysfunctional behavior if too much emphasis is placed on the labor efficiency variance. For example, to avoid losing hours and avoid using additional hours because of possible rework, a production manager could deliberately transfer defective units to finished goods.

Analysis of the Labor Efficiency Variance Assume that the $143.50 unfavorable variance was judged significant and its cause was investigated. The investigation revealed that more shutdowns of the process occurred because the duties of the machine operators were split between machine operations and inspection. (Recall that this reassignment was necessary because two inspectors quit unexpectedly.) This resulted in more idle time for inspection. Also, the machine operators were unable to meet the standard output per hour for inspection because of their lack of experience with the sorting process. The corrective action needed to solve the problem is the same as that recommended for the unfavorable rate variance—hire and train two new inspectors.

Sum of *LRV* and *LEV* From Exhibit 9-7, we know that the total labor variance is $269.50 unfavorable. This total variance is the sum of the unfavorable labor rate variance and the unfavorable labor efficiency variance ($126.00 + $143.50).

VARIANCE ANALYSIS: OVERHEAD COSTS

Objective 5

Compute the variable and fixed overhead variances and explain their meanings.

For direct materials and direct labor, total variances are broken down into price and efficiency variances. The total overhead variance, the difference between applied and actual overhead, is also broken down into component variances. How many component variances are computed depends on the method of variance analysis used. We will focus on one method only. First, we will divide overhead into categories: fixed and variable. Next, we will look at component variances for each category. The total variable overhead variance is divided into two components: the variable overhead spending variance and the variable overhead efficiency variance. Similarly, the total fixed overhead variance is divided into two components: the fixed overhead spending variance and the fixed overhead volume variance.

Variable Overhead Variances

To illustrate the variable overhead variances, we will examine one week of activity for Crunchy Chips (for the first week in March). The following data were gathered for this time period:

Variable overhead rate (standard)	$3.85/DLH
Actual variable overhead costs	$1,600
Actual hours worked	400
Bags of chips produced	48,500
Hours allowed for production	378.3[a]
Applied variable overhead	$1,456[b]

[a]$0.0078 \times 48,500$
[b]3.85×378.3 (rounded to nearest dollar; overhead is applied using hours allowed in a standard cost system)

Total Variable Overhead Variance The total variable overhead variance is the difference between the actual and the applied variable overhead. For our example, the total variable overhead variance is computed as follows:

$$\text{Total variance} = \$1,600 - \$1,456$$
$$= \$144\ \text{U}$$

This total variance can be divided into spending and efficiency variances. This computation is illustrated using a three-pronged approach in Exhibit 9-8.

variable overhead spending variance

Variable Overhead Spending Variance The variable overhead spending variance measures the aggregate effect of differences between the actual variable overhead rate (*AVOR*) and the standard variable overhead rate (*SVOR*). The actual variable overhead rate is simply actual variable overhead divided by actual hours. For our example, this rate is $4 per hour ($\frac{\$1,600}{400\ \text{hours}}$). The formula for computing the variable overhead spending variance is:

$$\text{Variable overhead spending variance} = (AVOR \times AH) - (SVOR \times AH)$$
$$= (AVOR - SVOR)AH$$
$$= (\$4 - \$3.85)400$$
$$= \$60\ \text{U}$$

Comparison to the Price Variances of Materials and Labor The variable overhead spending variance is similar but not identical to the price variances of materials and labor; there are some conceptual differences. Variable overhead is not a homogeneous

9-8

Exhibit
Variable Overhead
Variances: Columnar
Approach

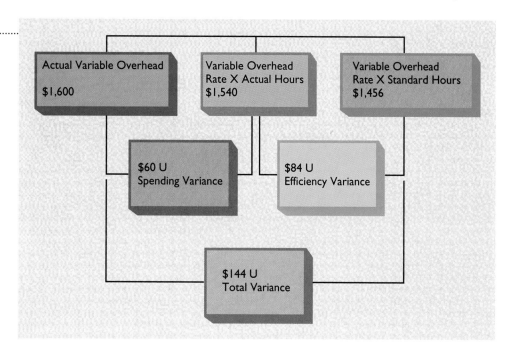

input—it is made up of a large number of individual items such as indirect materials, indirect labor, electricity, maintenance, and so on. The standard variable overhead rate represents the weighted cost per direct labor hour that should be incurred for all variable overhead items. The difference between what should have been spent per hour and what actually was spent per hour is a type of price variance.

A variable overhead spending variance can arise because prices for individual variable overhead items have increased or decreased. Assume, for the moment, that the price changes of individual overhead items are the only cause of the spending variance. If the spending variance is unfavorable, price increases for individual variable overhead items are the cause; if the spending variance is favorable, price decreases are dominating.

If the only source of the variable overhead spending variance was price changes, then it would be completely analogous to the price variances of materials and labor. Unfortunately, the spending variance also is affected by how efficiently overhead is used. Waste or inefficiency in the use of variable overhead increases the actual variable overhead cost. This increased cost, in turn, is reflected in an increased actual variable overhead rate. Thus, even if the actual prices of the individual overhead items were equal to the budgeted or standard prices, an unfavorable variable overhead spending variance could still take place. For example, more kilowatt-hours of power may be used than should be—yet, this is not captured by any change in direct labor hours but the effect is reflected by an increase in the total cost of power and, thus, the total cost of variable overhead. Similarly, efficiency can decrease the actual variable overhead cost and decrease the actual variable overhead rate. Efficient use of variable overhead items contributes to a favorable spending variance. If the waste effect dominates, the net contribution will be unfavorable; if efficiency dominates, the net contribution is favorable. Thus, the variable overhead spending variance is the result of both price and efficiency.

Responsibility for the Variable Overhead Spending Variance Many variable overhead items are affected by several responsibility centers. For example, utilities are a joint cost.[8] To the extent that consumption of variable overhead can be traced to a responsibility center, responsibility can be assigned. Consumption of indirect materials is an example of a traceable variable overhead cost.

Controllability is a prerequisite for assigning responsibility. Price changes of variable overhead items are essentially beyond the control of supervisors. If price changes are small (as they often are), the spending variance is primarily a matter of the efficient use of overhead in production, which is controllable by production supervisors. Accordingly, responsibility for the variable overhead spending variance is generally assigned to production departments.

Analysis of the Variable Overhead Spending Variance The $60 unfavorable variance simply reveals that, in the aggregate, Crunchy Chips spent more on variable overhead than expected. Even if the variance were insignificant, it reveals nothing about how well costs of individual variable overhead items were controlled. Control of variable overhead requires line-by-line analysis for each individual item. Exhibit 9-9 presents a performance report that supplies the line-by-line information essential for proper control of variable overhead. Assume that the numbers come from Crunchy's accounting records.

From Exhibit 9-9, it is clear that two of the three items present no control problems for the firm. Electricity is the only item showing an unfavorable variance; in fact, it is the cause of the overall variable overhead spending variance. If the variance is significant, an investigation may be warranted. This investigation may reveal that the power

---

8. If a company installs meters to measure consumption of utilities for each responsibility center, responsibility can be assigned. However, the cost of assigning responsibility can sometimes exceed any potential benefit. The alternative is allocation. Unfortunately, allocations can be arbitrary, and it is often difficult to identify accurately the amount actually consumed.

9-9

Exhibit

Crunchy Chips, Inc. Flexible Budget Performance Report For the Week Ended March 8, 1998				
	Cost Formula[a]	Actual Costs	Budget[b]	Spending Variance
Gas	$3.00	$1,190	$1,200	$10 F
Electricity	0.78	385	312	73 U
Water	0.07	25	28	3 F
Total cost	$3.85	$1,600	$1,540	$60 U

[a]Per direct labor hour
[b]Computed using the cost formula and an activity level of 400 actual direct labor hours

company raised the price of electricity. If so, the cause of the variance is beyond the control of the company. The correct response is to revise the budget formula to reflect the increased cost of electricity. However, if the price of electricity has remained unchanged, the usage of electricity is greater than expected. For example, the company may find that there were more startups and shutdowns of machinery than normal, causing an increased consumption of electricity.

variable overhead efficiency variance

Variable Overhead Efficiency Variance Variable overhead is assumed to vary as the production volume changes. Thus, variable overhead changes in proportion to changes in the direct labor hours used. The variable overhead efficiency variance measures the change in variable overhead consumption that occurs because of efficient (or inefficient) use of direct labor. The efficiency variance is computed using the following formula:

$$\text{Variable overhead efficiency variance} = (AH - SH)SVOR$$
$$= (400 - 378.3)\$3.85$$
$$= \$84 \text{ U (rounded)}$$

Responsibility for the Variable Overhead Efficiency Variance The variable overhead efficiency variance is directly related to the direct labor efficiency or usage variance. If variable overhead is truly proportional to direct labor consumption, then like the labor usage variance, the variable overhead efficiency variance is caused by efficient or inefficient use of direct labor. If more (or fewer) direct labor hours are used than the standard calls for, the total variable overhead cost will increase (or decrease). The validity of the measure depends on the validity of the relationship between variable overhead costs and direct labor hours. In other words, do variable overhead costs really change in proportion to changes in direct labor hours? If so, responsibility for the variable overhead efficiency variance should be assigned to the individual who has responsibility for the use of direct labor: the production manager.

Analysis of the Variable Overhead Efficiency Variance The reasons for the unfavorable variable overhead efficiency variance are the same as those offered for the unfavorable labor usage variance. More hours were used than the standard called for because of excessive idle time for inspectors and because the machine operators used as substitute inspectors were inexperienced in sorting.

More information concerning the effect of labor usage on variable overhead is available in a line-by-line analysis of individual variable overhead items. This can be accomplished by comparing the budget allowance for the actual hours used with the budget allowance for the standard hours allowed for each item. A performance report that makes this comparison for all variable overhead costs is shown in Exhibit 9-10.

Cost	Cost Formula[a]	Budget for Actual Costs	Actual Hours	Spending Variance[b]	Budget for Standard Hours[c]	Efficiency Variance[d]
Gas	$3.00	$1,190	$1,200	$10 F	$1,135	$65 U
Electricity	0.78	385	312	73 U	295	17 U
Water	0.07	25	28	3 F	26	2 U
Total	$3.85	$1,600	$1,540	$60 U	$1,456	$84 U

Crunchy Chips, Inc.
Performance Report
For the Week Ended March 8, 1998

[a]Per direct labor hour
[b]Spending variance = Actual costs − Budget for actual hours
[c]Computed using the cost formula and an activity level of 378.3 standard hours. Rounded to the nearest dollar
[d]Efficiency variance = Budget for actual hours − Budget for standard hours

From Exhibit 9-10, we can see that the cost of gas is affected most by inefficient use of labor. This can be explained by the need to keep the cooking oil hot (assuming gas is used for cooking) even though the cooking process is slowed down by the subsequent sorting process.

The column labeled "Budget for Standard Hours" gives the amount that should have been spent on variable overhead for the actual output. The total of all items in this column is the applied variable overhead, the amount assigned to production in a standard cost system. Note that in a standard cost system, variable overhead is applied using the hours allowed for the actual output (*SH*), while in normal costing, variable overhead is applied using actual hours (see Chapter 3). Although not shown in Exhibit 9-10, the difference between actual costs and this column is the total variable overhead variance (underapplied by $143.55). Thus, the underapplied variable overhead variance is the sum of the spending and efficiency variances.

Fixed Overhead Variances

We will again use the Crunchy Chips example to illustrate the computation of the fixed overhead variances. The yearly data needed for the example follow.

Budgeted or Planned Items	
Budgeted fixed overhead	$749,970
Expected activity	23,400 direct labor hours[a]
Standard fixed overhead rate	$32.05[b]

[a]Hours allowed to produce 3,000,000 bags of chips: 0.0078 × 3,000,000
[b]$\dfrac{\$749,970}{23,400}$

Actual Results	
Actual production	2,750,000 bags of chips
Actual fixed overhead cost	$749,000
Standard hours allowed for actual production	21,450*

*0.0078 × 2,750,000

Total Fixed Overhead Variance The total fixed overhead variance is the difference between actual fixed overhead and applied fixed overhead, when applied fixed overhead is obtained by multiplying the standard fixed overhead rate times the standard hours allowed for the actual output. Thus, the applied fixed overhead is:

$$\text{Applied fixed overhead} = \text{Standard fixed overhead rate} \times \text{Standard hours}$$
$$= \$32.05 \times 21{,}450$$
$$= \$687{,}473 \text{ (rounded)}$$

The total fixed overhead variance is the difference between the actual fixed overhead and the applied fixed overhead:

$$\text{Total fixed overhead variance} = \$749{,}000 - \$687{,}473$$
$$= \$61{,}527 \text{ underapplied}$$

To help managers understand why fixed overhead was underapplied by $61,527, the total variance can be broken into two variances: the fixed overhead spending variance and the fixed overhead volume variance. The calculation of the two variances is illustrated in Exhibit 9-11.

fixed overhead spending variance

Fixed Overhead Spending Variance The fixed overhead spending variance is defined as the difference between the actual fixed overhead and the budgeted fixed overhead. The spending variance is favorable because less was spent on fixed overhead items than was budgeted.

Responsibility for the Fixed Overhead Spending Variance Fixed overhead is made up of a number of individual items such as salaries, depreciation, taxes, and insurance. Many fixed overhead items—long-run investments, for instance—are not subject to change in the short run; consequently, fixed overhead costs are often beyond the immediate control of management. Since many fixed overhead costs are affected primarily by long-run decisions, not by changes in production levels, the budget variance is usually small. For example, depreciation, salaries, taxes, and insurance costs are not likely to be much different from planned.

Analysis of the Fixed Overhead Spending Variance Because fixed overhead is made up of many individual items, a line-by-line comparison of budgeted costs with actual costs provides more information concerning the causes of the spending variance. Exhibit 9-12 provides such a report. The report reveals that the fixed overhead spending

Exhibit
Fixed Overhead
Variances

Crunchy Chips, Inc. Performance Report For the Year Ended 1998			
Fixed Overhead Items	Actual Cost	Budgeted Cost	Variance
Depreciation	$530,000	$530,000	$ —
Salaries	159,370	159,970	600 F
Taxes	50,500	50,000	500 U
Insurance	9,130	10,000	870 F
Total fixed overhead	$749,000	$749,970	$970 F

variance is essentially in line with expectations. The fixed overhead spending variances, both on a line-item basis and in the aggregate, are relatively small.

fixed overhead volume variance

Fixed Overhead Volume Variance The fixed overhead volume variance is the difference between budgeted fixed overhead and applied fixed overhead. The volume variance measures the effect of the actual output departing from the output used at the beginning of the year to compute the predetermined standard fixed overhead rate. To see this, let $SH(D)$ represent the standard hours allowed for the denominator volume (the volume used at the beginning of the year to compute the predetermined fixed overhead rate). The standard fixed overhead rate is computed in the following way:

$$\text{Standard fixed overhead rate} = \frac{\text{Budgeted fixed overhead}}{SH(D)}$$

From this equation, we know that the budgeted fixed overhead can be computed by multiplying the standard fixed overhead rate by the denominator hours:

$$\text{Budgeted fixed overhead} = \text{Standard fixed overhead rate} \times SH(D)$$

From Exhibit 9-11, we know that the volume variance can be computed as follows:

$$
\begin{aligned}
\text{Volume variance} &= \text{Budgeted fixed overhead} - \text{Applied fixed overhead} \\
&= \text{Standard fixed overhead rate} \times SH(D) - \text{Standard} \\
&\quad \text{fixed overhead rate} \times SH \\
&= \text{Standard fixed overhead rate} \times (SH(D) - SH) \\
&= \$32.05(23{,}400 - 21{,}450) \\
&= \$62{,}497 \text{ U (rounded down)}
\end{aligned}
$$

Thus, for a volume variance to occur, the denominator hours, $SH(D)$, must differ from the standard hours allowed for the actual volume, SH. At the beginning of the year, Crunchy Chips expected to produce 3,000,000 bags of chips, using 23,400 direct labor hours. The actual outcome was 2,750,000 bags produced, using 21,450 standard hours. Thus, less was produced than expected and an unfavorable volume variance arises.

But what is the meaning of this variance? The variance occurs because the actual output differs from the predicted output volume. At the beginning of the year, if management had used 2.75 million bags of corn chips as the denominator volume, the volume variance would not have existed. In this view, the volume variance is seen as prediction error—a measure of the inability of management to select the correct volume over which to spread fixed overhead.

If, however, the denominator volume represented the amount that management believed could be produced and sold, the volume variance conveys more significant information. If the actual volume is less than the denominator volume, the volume variance signals management that a loss has occurred. That loss is not equivalent, however, to the dollar value of the volume variance. The loss is equal to the lost contribution margin on the units that were not produced and sold. However, the volume variance is positively correlated with the loss. For example, suppose that the contribution margin per standard direct labor hour is $40. By producing only 2.75 million bags of chips instead of 3 million bags, the company lost sales of 250,000 bags. This is equivalent to 1,950 hours (0.0078 × 250,000). At $40 per hour, the loss is $78,000. The unfavorable volume variance of $62,497 signals this loss but understates it. In this sense, the volume variance is a measure of utilization of capacity.

Responsibility for the Fixed Overhead Volume Variance Assuming that volume variance measures capacity utilization implies that the general responsibility for this variance should be assigned to the production department. At times, however, investigation into the reasons for a significant volume variance may reveal the cause to be factors beyond the control of production. In this instance, specific responsibility may be assigned elsewhere. For example, if purchasing acquires a raw material of lower quality than usual, significant rework time may result, causing lower production and an unfavorable volume variance. In this case, responsibility for the variance rests with purchasing, not production.

APPENDIX: ACCOUNTING FOR VARIANCES

Objective 6

Prepare journal entries for materials and labor variances and describe the accounting for overhead variances.

To illustrate recording variances, we will assume that the materials price variance is computed at the time materials are purchased. With this assumption, we can state a general rule for a firm's inventory accounts: all inventories are carried at standard cost. Actual costs are never entered into an inventory account. In recording variances, unfavorable variances are always debits and favorable variances are always credits.

Entries for Direct Materials Variances

Materials Price Variance The entry to record the purchase of materials follows (assuming an unfavorable MPV and that AQ is materials purchased):

Materials	$SP \times AQ$	
Materials Price Variance	$(AP - SP)AQ$	
Accounts Payable		$AP \times AQ$

For example, if AP is $0.0069 per ounce of corn, SP is $0.0060 per ounce, and 780,000 ounces of corn are purchased, the entry would be:

Materials	4,680	
Materials Price Variance	702	
Accounts Payable		5,382

Notice that the raw materials are carried in the inventory account at standard cost.

Materials Usage Variance The general form for the entry to record the issuance and usage of materials, assuming a favorable MUV, is as follows:

Work in Process	$SQ \times SP$	
Materials Usage Variance		$(AQ - SQ)SP$
Materials		$AQ \times SP$

Here AQ is the materials issued and used, not necessarily equal to the materials purchased. Notice that only standard quantities and standard prices are used to assign costs to Work in Process; no actual costs enter this account.

    For example, if AQ is 780,000 ounces of corn, SQ is 873,000 ounces, and SP is $0.006, then the entry would be:

Work in Process	5,238	
Materials Usage Variance		558
Materials		4,680

Notice that the favorable usage variance appears as a credit entry.

Entries for Direct Labor Variances

Unlike the materials variances, the entry to record both types of labor variances is made simultaneously. The general form of this entry follows (assuming a favorable labor rate variance and an unfavorable labor efficiency variance).

Work in Process	$SH \times SR$	
Labor Efficiency Variance	$(AH - SH)SR$	
Labor Rate Variance		$(AR - SR)AH$
Accrued Payroll		$AH \times AR$

Again, notice that only standard hours and standard rates are used to assign costs to Work in Process. Actual prices or quantities are not used.

To give a specific example, assume that AH is 360 hours of inspection, SH is 339.5 hours, AR is \$7.35 per hour, and SR is \$7.00 per hour. The following journal entry would be made:

Work in Process	2,376.50	
Labor Efficiency Variance	143.50	
Labor Rate Variance	126.00	
Accrued Payroll		2,646

Disposition of Material and Labor Variances

At the end of the year, the variances for materials and labor are usually closed to Cost of Goods Sold. (This practice is acceptable provided that variances are not material in amount.) Using the previous data, the entries would take the following form:

Cost of Goods Sold	971.50	
Materials Price Variance		702.00
Labor Efficiency Variance		143.50
Labor Rate Variance		126.00
Materials Usage Variance	558.00	
Cost of Goods Sold		558.00

If the variances are material, they must be prorated among various accounts. For the materials price variance, it is prorated among Materials Inventory, Materials Usage Variance, Work in Process, Finished Goods, and Cost of Goods Sold. The remaining materials and labor variances are prorated among Work in Process, Finished Goods, and Cost of Goods Sold. Typically, materials variances are prorated on the basis of the materials balances in each of these accounts and the labor variances on the basis of the labor balances in the accounts.

Overhead Variances

Although overhead variances can be recorded following a pattern similar to that described for labor and materials, these variances are more generally treated as part of a periodic overhead analysis. Applied overhead is accumulated in the applied accounts, and actual overhead is accumulated in the control accounts. Periodically (for example, monthly), performance reports that provide overhead variance information are prepared. At the end of the year, the applied accounts and control accounts are closed out and the variances isolated. The overhead variances are then disposed of by closing them to Cost of Goods Sold if they are not material, or by prorating them among Work in Process, Finished Goods, and Cost of Goods Sold if they are material.

S UMMARY OF LEARNING OBJECTIVES

1. Explain how unit standards are set and why standard cost systems are adopted.

A standard cost system budgets quantities and costs on a unit basis. These unit budgets are for labor, material, and overhead. Standard costs, therefore, are the amount that should be expended to produce a product or service. Standards are set using historical experience, engineering studies, and input from operating personnel, marketing, and accounting. Currently attainable standards are those that can be achieved under efficient operating conditions. Ideal standards are those achievable under maximum efficiency, or ideal operating conditions. Standard cost systems are adopted to improve planning and control and to facilitate product costing. By comparing actual outcomes with standards, and breaking the variance into price and quantity components, detailed feedback is provided to managers. This information allows managers to exercise a greater degree of cost control than that found in a normal or actual cost system. Decisions such as bidding are also made easier when a standard cost system is in place.

2. Explain the purpose of a standard cost sheet.

The standard cost sheet provides the detail for the computation of the standard cost per unit. It shows the standard costs for materials, labor, and variable and fixed overhead. It also reveals the quantity of each input that should be used to produce one unit of output. Using these unit quantity standards, the standard quantity of materials allowed and the standard hours allowed can be computed for the actual output. These computations play an important role in variance analysis.

3. Describe the basic concepts underlying variance analysis and explain when variances should be investigated.

The budget variance is the difference between actual costs and planned costs. In a standard cost system, the budget variance is broken down into price and usage variances. By breaking the budget variances into price and usage variances, managers have more ability to analyze and control the total variance. Variances should be investigated if they are material and if the benefits of corrective action are greater than the costs of investigation. Because of the difficulty of assessing cost and benefits on a case-by-case basis, many firms set up formal control limits—either a dollar amount, a percentage, or both. Others use judgment to assess the need to investigate.

4. Compute the materials and labor variances and explain how they are used for control.

The materials price and usage variances are computed using either a three-pronged approach or formulas. The three-pronged approach for materials is illustrated in Exhibit 9-6. The materials price variance is the difference between what should have been paid for materials and what was paid (generally associated with the purchasing activity). The materials usage variance is the difference between the cost of the materials that should have been used and the amount that was used (generally associated with the production activity). When a significant variance is signaled, an investigation occurs to find the cause. Corrective action is taken, if possible, to put the system back in control.

The labor variances are computed using either a three-pronged approach or formulas. The three-pronged approach for labor is illustrated in Exhibit 9-7. The labor rate variance is caused by the actual wage rate differing from the standard wage rate. It is the difference between the wages that were paid and those that should have been paid. The labor efficiency variance is the difference between the cost of the labor that was used and the cost of the labor that should have been used. When a significant variance is signaled, investigation is called for and corrective action should be taken, if possible, to put the system back in control.

5. Compute the variable and fixed overhead variances and explain their meanings.

The variable overhead spending variance is the difference between the actual variable overhead cost and the budgeted variable overhead cost for actual hours worked. It therefore is a budget variance, resulting from price changes and efficient or inefficient use of variable overhead inputs. The variable efficiency variance is the difference between budgeted variable overhead at actual hours and applied variable overhead. It is strictly attributable to the efficiency of labor usage and assumes that the variable overhead items are all driven by direct labor hours.

The fixed overhead spending variance is the difference between the actual fixed overhead costs and the budgeted fixed overhead costs. Therefore, it is simply a budget variance. The volume variance is the difference between the budgeted fixed overhead and the applied fixed overhead. It occurs whenever the actual production volume is different from the expected production volume and, thus, is a measure of capacity utilization.

6. Prepare journal entries for materials and labor variances and describe the accounting for overhead variances. (Appendix)

Assuming that the materials price variance is computed at the point of purchase, all inventories are carried at standard cost. Actual costs are never entered into an inventory account. Accounts are created for materials price and usage variances and for labor rate and efficiency variances. Unfavorable variances are always debits; favorable variances are always credits. Overhead variances are generally not journalized. Instead, periodic overhead reports are prepared that provide overhead variance information.

K EY TERMS

Control limits *347*
Currently attainable
  standards *341*
Favorable (F) variances *345*
Fixed overhead spending
  variance *359*

Fixed overhead volume
  variance *360*
Ideal standards *341*
Labor efficiency variance
  (*LEV*) *353*

Labor rate variance (*LRV*)
  352
Materials price variance
  (*MPV*) *349*
Materials usage variance
  (*MUV*) *351*

Price standards *341*
Price (rate) variance *345*
Quantity standards *341*
Standard cost per unit *343*
Standard cost sheet *343*
Standard hours allowed *344*

REVIEW PROBLEM

Wangsgard Manufacturing has the following standard cost sheet for one of its products:

Direct materials (2 ft @ $5)	$10
Direct labor (0.5 hr @ $10)	5
Fixed overhead (0.5 hr @ $2)*	1
Variable overhead (0.5 hr @ $4)	2
Standard unit cost	$18

*Rate based on expected activity of 2,500 hours

During the most recent year, the following actual results were recorded:

Production	6,000 units
Direct materials (11,750 ft purchased and used)	$61,100
Direct labor (2,900 hr)	29,580
Fixed overhead	6,000
Variable overhead	10,500

REQUIRED: Compute the following variances:

1. Materials price and usage variances
2. Labor rate and efficiency variances
3. Fixed overhead spending and volume variances
4. Variable overhead spending and efficiency variances

Solution

1. Material variances:

| Actual Quantity at Actual Price[a] 11,750 × $5.20 $61,100 | Actual Quantity at Standard Price 11,750 × $5.00 $58,750 | Standard Quantity[b] at Standard Price 12,000 × $5.00 $60,000 |

$2,350 U
Price

$1,250 F
Usage

[a] $61,100/11,750 = $5.20 = Actual Price
[b] 2 × 6,000 = 12,000 = Standard Quantity

Or, using formulas:

$$MPV = (AP - SP)AQ$$
$$= (\$5.20 - \$5.00)11{,}750$$
$$= \$2{,}350 \text{ U}$$

$$MUV = (AQ - SQ)SP$$
$$= (11{,}750 - 12{,}000)\$5.00$$
$$= \$1{,}250 \text{ F}$$

2. Labor variances:

Or, using formulas:

$$LRV = (AR - SR)AH$$
$$= (\$10.20 - \$10.00)2{,}900$$
$$= \$580 \text{ U}$$

$$LEV = (AH - SH)SR$$
$$= (2{,}900 - 3{,}000)\$10.00$$
$$= \$1{,}000 \text{ F}$$

3. Fixed overhead variances:

4. Variable overhead variances:

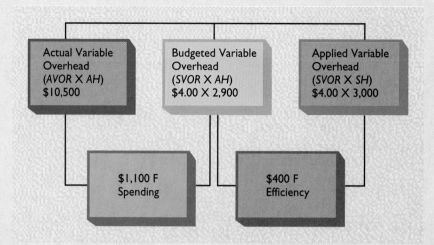

UESTIONS FOR WRITING AND DISCUSSION

1. Discuss the difference between budgets and standard costs.
2. Describe the relationship that unit standards have with flexible budgeting.
3. What is the *quantity decision*? the *pricing decision*?
4. Why is historical experience often a poor basis for establishing standards?
5. Should standards be set by engineering studies? Why or why not?
6. What are ideal standards? currently attainable standards? Of the two, which is usually adopted? Why?
7. Explain why standard cost systems are adopted.
8. How does standard costing improve the control function?
9. Discuss the differences among actual costing, normal costing, and standard costing.
10. What is the purpose of a standard cost sheet?
11. The budget variance for variable production costs is broken down into quantity and price variances. Explain why the quantity variance is more useful for control purposes than the price variance.
12. When should a standard cost variance be investigated?
13. What are control limits and how are they set?

14. Explain why the materials price variance is often computed at the point of purchase rather than at the point of issuance.
15. The materials usage variance is always the responsibility of the production supervisor. Do you agree or disagree? Why?
16. The labor rate variance is never controllable. Do you agree or disagree? Why?
17. Suggest some possible causes of an unfavorable labor efficiency variance.
18. Explain why the variable overhead spending variance is not a pure price variance.
19. The variable overhead efficiency variance has nothing to do with efficient use of variable overhead. Do you agree or disagree? Why?
20. Explain why the fixed overhead spending variance is usually very small.
21. What is the cause of an unfavorable volume variance? Does the volume variance convey any meaningful information to managers?
22. Which do you think is more important for control of fixed overhead costs: the spending variance or the volume variance? Explain.

W ARM-UP EXERCISES

This section provides short warm-up exercises based on the examples in the chapter. Each warm-up exercise gives the page number on which the text example can be found. You may want to refer to the text example to see how the exercise can be set up and solved.

W9-1
Standard Quantities
LO 2
pp. 344–345

Crunchy Chips supplied the following information from its standard cost sheet for packages of corn chips:

Cooking oil (2 oz @ $0.031)	$0.062
Machine operators (0.0008 hr @ $10)	0.008

During a week, 50,000 bags of corn chips are produced.

REQUIRED:
1. Compute the standard quantity of cooking oil allowed for the 50,000 bags.
2. Compute the standard hours allowed for the 50,000 bags.

W9-2
Performance Report
LO 3
p. 348

See W9-1. During a week, 50,000 bags of corn chips are produced. The following actual costs are incurred:

Cooking oil (102,000 oz @ $0.03)	$3,060
Machine operators (45 hr @ $9.80)	441

REQUIRED: Prepare a performance report comparing actual costs with standard costs.

W9-3
Materials and Labor Variances
LO 4
pp. 349, 352

See W9-2.

REQUIRED:
1. Compute the materials price and usage variances. Assume that there are no beginning or ending inventories of cooking oil.
2. Compute the labor rate and efficiency variances.

W9-4
Variable Overhead Variances
LO 5
pp. 355–356

Crunchy Chips provided the following information for one week of operation:

Variable overhead rate (standard)	$3.85 per direct labor hour
Actual variable overhead costs	$2,000
Actual hours worked	400
Bags of chips produced	50,000
Hours allowed for production	390[a]
Applied variable overhead	$1,502[b]

[a]0.0078 × 50,000
[b]$3.85 × 390 (rounded to nearest dollar; overhead is applied using hours allowed in a standard cost system)

REQUIRED:
1. Calculate the total variable overhead variance.
2. Break the total variable overhead variance into spending and efficiency variances.

W9-5
Fixed Overhead Variances
LO 5
p. 359

Crunchy Chips provided the following information for the most recent year:

Budgeted or Planned Items	
Budgeted fixed overhead	$819,000
Expected activity	27,300 direct labor hours[a]
Standard fixed overhead rate	$30[b]

[a]Hours allowed to produce 3,500,000 bags of chips: 0.0078 × 3,500,000
[b]$819,000 / 27,300

Actual Results

Actual production	3,250,000 bags of chips
Actual fixed overhead cost	$800,000
Standard hours allowed for actual production	25,350*

*0.0078 × 3,250,000

REQUIRED: Compute the fixed spending and volume variances.

EXERCISES

E9-1
Setting Standards and Assigning Responsibility
LO 1

Associated Media Graphics (AMG) is a rapidly expanding company involved in the mass reproduction of instructional materials. Ralph Boston, owner and manager of AMG, has made a concerted effort to provide a quality product at a fair price with delivery on the promised due date. Expanding sales have been attributed to this philosophy. As the business grows, however, Ralph is finding it increasingly difficult to personally supervise the operations of AMG. As a result, he is beginning to institute an organizational structure that would facilitate management control.

One recent change was to designate the operating departments as cost centers, with control over departmental operations transferred from Ralph to each departmental manager. However, quality control still reports directly to Ralph, as do the finance and accounting functions. A materials manager was hired to purchase all raw materials and oversee inventory handling (receiving, storage, and so on) and record keeping. The materials manager is also responsible for maintaining an adequate inventory based upon planned production levels.

The loss of personal control over the operations of AMG caused Ralph to look for a method to evaluate performance efficiently. Dave Cress, a new cost accountant, proposed the use of a standard cost system. Variances for material, labor, and overhead could then be calculated and reported directly to Ralph.

REQUIRED:
1. Assume that AMG is going to implement a standard cost system and establish standards for materials, labor, and overhead.
   a. Who should be involved in setting the standards for each cost component?
   b. What factors should be considered in establishing the standards for each cost component?
2. Describe the basis for assignment of responsibility under a standard cost system. (CMA adapted)

E9-2
Computation of Inputs Allowed; Materials and Labor
LO 2

During the year, Mangos Company produced 60,000 electrical components for a television manufacturer. Mangos' material and labor standards are:

Direct materials (3 circuits @ $0.80)	$2.40
Direct labor (0.6 hr @ $12.00)	7.20

REQUIRED:
1. Compute the standard hours allowed for the production of 60,000 units.
2. Compute the standard number of circuits allowed for the production of 60,000 units.

E9-3
Materials and Labor Variances
LO 4

Sumo Company produces fruit juices, sold in gallons. Recently, the company adopted the following standards for one gallon of its apple juice:

Direct materials (128 oz @ $0.025)	$3.20
Direct labor (0.06 hr @ $7.00)	0.42
Standard prime cost	$3.62

During the first week of operation, the company experienced the following actual results:

a. Gallon units produced: 10,000
b. Ounces of materials purchased: 1,284,000 ounces at $0.02
c. No beginning or ending inventories of raw materials
d. Direct labor: 500 hours at $7.50

REQUIRED:
1. Compute price and usage variances for direct materials.
2. Compute the rate variance and the efficiency variance for direct labor.

E9-4
Overhead Variances
LO 5

Young, Inc. has gathered the following data on last year's operations:

a. Units produced: 28,000
b. Direct labor: 20,000 hours at $9
c. Actual fixed overhead: $280,000
d. Actual variable overhead: $92,000

Young employs a standard cost system. During the year, the following rates were used: standard fixed overhead rate, $12 per hour; standard variable overhead rate, $4.05 per hour. The labor standard requires 0.75 hour per unit produced. (These rates were based on a standard normal volume of 22,500 direct labor hours.)

REQUIRED:
1. Compute the fixed overhead spending and volume variances.
2. Compute the variable overhead spending and efficiency variances.

E9-5
Decomposition of Budget Variances; Materials and Labor
LO 4

Logo Corporation produces high-quality leather belts. The company uses a standard cost system and has set the following standards for materials and labor:

Leather (4 strips @ $8)	$32
Direct labor (1 hr @ $12)	12
Total prime cost	$44

During the year, Logo produced 5,000 leather belts. Actual leather purchased was 20,500 strips at $7.96 per strip. There were no beginning or ending inventories of leather. Actual direct labor was 5,200 hours at $12.50.

REQUIRED:
1. Compute the costs of leather and direct labor that should have been incurred for the production of 5,000 leather belts.
2. Compute the total budget variances for material and labor.
3. Break down the total variance for materials into a price variance and a usage variance.
4. Break down the total variance for labor into a rate variance and an efficiency variance.

E9-6
Appendix Required: Materials and Labor Variances; Journal Entries
LO 4, LO 6

Escrevem Products produces instructional aids. Among the company's products are "white boards," which use colored markers instead of chalk. They are particularly popular for conference rooms in educational institutions and executive offices of large corporations. The standard cost of materials and labor for this product follows.

Direct materials	12 lb @ $8.25
Direct labor	4 hr @ $9.65

During the first month of the year, 3,200 boards were produced. Information concerning actual costs and usage of materials and labor follows.

Materials purchased	38,000 lb @ $8.35
Material used	37,500 lb
Direct labor	12,520 hr; total cost: $122,696

REQUIRED:

1. Compute the materials price and usage variances.
2. Compute the labor rate and efficiency variances.
3. Prepare journal entries for all activity relating to materials and labor for the month.

E9-7
Overhead
Application;
Overhead Variances
LO 5

Hermentas Company is planning to produce 600,000 sets of socket wrenches for the coming year. Each set requires two standard hours of labor for completion. The company uses direct labor hours to assign overhead to products. The total overhead budgeted for the coming year is $2,700,000, and the standard fixed overhead rate is $2.20 per unit produced. Actual results for the year follow.

Actual production (units)	590,000
Actual direct labor hours	1,190,000
Actual variable overhead	$1,410,000
Actual fixed overhead	$1,260,000

REQUIRED:

1. Compute the applied fixed overhead.
2. Compute the fixed overhead spending and volume variances.
3. Compute the applied variable overhead.
4. Compute the variable overhead spending and efficiency variances.

E9-8
Investigation of
Variances
LO 3

Underwood Company uses the following rule to determine whether material usage variances ought to be investigated. A materials usage variance will be investigated anytime the amount exceeds the lesser of $8,000 or 10 percent of the standard cost. Reports for the past five weeks provided the following information:

Week	MUV	Standard Materials Cost
1	$7,000 F	$80,000
2	7,800 U	75,000
3	6,000 F	80,000
4	9,000 U	85,000
5	7,000 U	69,000

REQUIRED:

1. Using the rule provided, identify the cases that will be investigated.
2. Suppose that investigation reveals that the cause of an unfavorable materials usage variance is the use of lower-quality materials than are usually used. Who is responsible? What corrective action would likely be taken?
3. Suppose that investigation reveals that the cause of a significant unfavorable materials usage variance is attributable to a new approach to manufacturing that takes less labor time but causes more material waste. Upon examining the labor efficiency variance, it is discovered that it is favorable and is larger than the unfavorable materials usage variance. Who is responsible? What action should be taken?

E9-9
Appendix Required:

Tavera Company uses a standard cost system. The direct labor standard indicates that 4 direct labor hours should be used for every unit produced. Tavera produces one product. The normal

Overhead Application; Overhead Variances; Journal Entries

LO 5, LO 6

production volume is 120,000 units of this product. The budgeted overhead for the coming year (1998) follows.

Fixed overhead	$1,440,000
Variable overhead	960,000*

*At normal volume

Tavera applies overhead on the basis of direct labor hours.

During 1998, Tavera produced 119,000 units, worked 487,900 direct labor hours, and incurred actual fixed overhead costs of $1.5 million and actual variable overhead costs of $950,000.

REQUIRED:

1. Calculate the standard fixed overhead rate and the standard variable overhead rate.
2. Compute the applied fixed overhead and the applied variable overhead. What is the total fixed overhead variance? total variable overhead variance?
3. Break down the total fixed overhead variance into a spending variance and a volume variance. Discuss the significance of each.
4. Compute the variable overhead spending and efficiency variances. Discuss the significance of each.
5. Prepare the journal entries that would be related to fixed and variable overhead at the end of the year. Assume variances are closed to Cost of Goods Sold.

E9-10

Materials, Labor, and Overhead Variances

LO 4, LO 5

At the beginning of 1998, Maximoa Company had the following standard cost sheet for one of its products:

Direct materials (5 lb @ 1.60)	$ 8.00
Direct labor (2.0 hr @ $9.00)	18.00
Fixed overhead (1.5 hr @ $2.00)	3.00
Variable overhead (1.5 hr @ $1.50)	2.25
Standard cost per unit	$31.25

Maximoa computes its overhead rates using practical volume, which is 72,000 units. The actual results for 1998 are:

a. Units produced: 70,000
b. Materials purchased: 372,000 pounds at $1.65
c. Materials used: 370,000 pounds
d. Direct labor: 145,000 hours at $9.05
e. Fixed overhead: $242,000
f. Variable overhead: $218,000

REQUIRED:

1. Compute price and usage variances for materials.
2. Compute the labor rate and labor efficiency variances.
3. Compute the fixed overhead spending and volume variances.
4. Compute the variable overhead spending and efficiency variances.

E9-11

Appendix Required: Journal Entries

LO 6

Refer to the data in E9-10. Prepare journal entries for the following:

1. The purchase of raw materials
2. The issuance of raw materials to production (Work in Process)
3. The addition of labor to Work in Process
4. The addition of overhead to Work in Process
5. Closing out of material and labor variances to Cost of Goods Sold

E9-12
Variances,
Evaluation, and
Behavior
LO 1

Jackie Iverson was furious. She was about ready to fire Tom Rich, her purchasing agent. Just a month ago, she had given him a salary increase and a bonus for his performance. She had been especially pleased with his ability to meet or beat the price standards. But now she had found out that it was because of a huge purchase of raw materials. It would take months to use that inventory and there was hardly space to store it. In the meantime, where could the other materials supplies that would be ordered and processed on a regular basis be put? Additionally, it was a lot of capital to tie up in inventory—money that could have been used to help finance the cash needs of the new product just coming on line.

Her interview with Tom had been frustrating. He was defensive, arguing that he thought that she wanted those standards met and that the means were not that important. He also pointed out that quantity purchases were the only way to meet the price standards. Otherwise, an unfavorable variance would have been realized.

REQUIRED:
1. Why did Tom Rich purchase the large quantity of raw materials? Do you think that this behavior was the objective of the price standard? If not, what is the objective(s)?
2. Suppose that Tom is right and that the only way to meet the price standards is through the use of quantity discounts. Also, assume that using quantity discounts is not a desirable practice for this company. What would you do to solve this dilemma?
3. Should Tom be fired? Explain.

E9-13
Straightforward
Computation of
Variances; Materials
and Labor
LO 4

Basura Company produces plastic garbage cans. The following standards for producing one unit have been established:

Direct materials (5 lb @ $0.90)	$ 4.50
Direct labor (1.5 hr @ $7.00)	10.50
Standard prime cost	$15.00

During December, 53,000 pounds of material were purchased and used in production. There were 10,000 cans produced, with the following actual prime costs:

Direct materials	$ 42,000
Direct labor	$102,000 (for 14,900 hr)

REQUIRED: Compute the materials and labor variances, labeling each variance as favorable or unfavorable.

E9-14
Appendix Required:
Journal Entries
LO 6

Refer to E9-13. Prepare journal entries for the following:

1. The purchase of raw materials
2. The issuance of raw materials
3. The addition of labor to Work in Process
4. Closing of variances to Cost of Goods Sold

E9-15
Incomplete Data
LO 2, LO 4, LO 5

Layner Company uses a standard cost system. During the past quarter, the following variances were computed:

Variable overhead efficiency variance	$ 8,000 U
Labor efficiency variance	$20,000 U
Labor rate variance	$ 6,000 U

Layner applies variable overhead using a standard rate of $2 per direct labor hour allowed. Four direct labor hours are allowed per unit produced (only one type of product is manufactured). During the quarter, Layner used 20 percent more direct labor hours than should have been used.

REQUIRED:

1. What were the actual direct labor hours worked? the total hours allowed?
2. What is the standard hourly rate for direct labor? the actual hourly rate?
3. How many actual units were produced?

PROBLEMS

P9-1
Basics of Variance Analysis: Variable Inputs
LO 3, LO 4

Lukma Company manufactures plastic baseball helmets. The following standards have been established for the helmet's variable inputs:

	Standard Quantity	Standard Price (Rate)	Standard Cost
Direct materials	1.20 lb	$ 1.50	$1.80
Direct labor	0.16 hr	10.00	1.60
Variable overhead	0.16 hr	2.50	0.40
Total			$3.80

During the first week of July, the company had the following actual results:

Units produced	40,000
Actual labor costs	$70,000
Actual labor hours	6,600
Materials purchased and used	46,000 lb @ $1.55
Actual variable overhead costs	$26,500

Other information: The purchasing agent located a new source of slightly higher-quality plastic, and this material was used during the first week in July. Also, a new manufacturing layout was implemented on a trial basis. The new layout required a slightly higher level of skilled labor. The higher-quality material has no effect on labor utilization. Similarly, the new manufacturing approach has no effect on material usage.

REQUIRED:

1. Compute the materials price and usage variances. Assuming that the material variances are essentially attributable to the higher-quality material, would you recommend that the purchasing agent continue to buy this quality? Or should the usual quality be purchased? Assume that the quality of the end product is not affected significantly.
2. Compute the labor rate and efficiency variances. Assuming that the labor variances are attributable to the new manufacturing layout, should it be continued or discontinued? Explain.
3. Refer to requirement 2. Suppose that the industrial engineer argued that the new layout should not be evaluated after only one week. His reasoning was that it would take at least a week for the workers to become efficient with the new approach. Suppose that the production is the same the second week and that the actual labor hours were 6,000 and the labor cost was $62,000. Should the new layout be adopted? Assume the variances are attributable to the new layout. If so, what would be the projected annual savings?

P9-2
Setting Standards; Material and Labor Variances
LO 1, LO 2, LO 4

Osgood Company is a small manufacturer of wooden household items. Ellen Rivkin, the controller, plans to implement a standard cost system for Osgood. She has the information needed to develop standards for Osgood's products.

One of Osgood's products is a wooden cutting board. Each cutting board requires 1.25 board feet of lumber and 12 minutes of direct labor time to prepare and cut the lumber. The cutting boards are inspected after they are cut. Because the cutting boards are made of a natural material that has imperfections, one board is normally rejected for each five that are accepted (the rejected boards are totally scrapped). Four rubber foot pads are attached to each good cutting board. A total of 15 minutes of direct labor time is required to attach all four foot pads and finish each cutting board. The lumber for the cutting boards costs $3 per board foot, and each foot pad costs $0.05. Direct labor is paid at the rate of $8 per hour.

REQUIRED:

1. Develop the standard costs for the direct-cost components of the cutting board. The standard cost should identify the standard quantity, standard rate, and standard cost per unit for each direct-cost component of the cutting board.
2. Identify the advantages of implementing a standard cost system.
3. Explain the role of each of the following persons in developing standards:
   a. Purchasing manager
   b. Industrial engineer
   c. Cost accountant
4. Assume that the standards have been set and that the following actual results occur during the first month under the new standard cost system:
   a. Actual good units produced: 10,000
   b. Lumber purchased: 16,000 board feet at $3.10
   c. Lumber used: 16,000 board feet
   d. Rubber foot pads purchased (and used): 51,000 at $0.048
   e. Direct labor cost: 5,550 hours at $8.05
   Compute the price and usage variances for materials and the rate and efficiency variances for labor. (CMA adapted)

P9-3

Setting a Direct Labor Standard; Learning Effects

LO 1, LO 2

Norris Company produces customized parts for industrial equipment. Although the parts are custom-made, most follow a fairly standard pattern. Recently, a potential new customer has approached the company and requested a new part, one significantly different from the usual parts manufactured by Norris. New equipment and some new labor skills will be needed to manufacture the part. The customer is placing an initial order of 15,000 units and has indicated that if the part is satisfactory, several additional orders of the same size will be placed over the next two to three years.

Norris uses a standard cost system and wants to develop a set of standards for the new part. The usage standard for direct materials is four pounds per part; the materials price standard is $3 per pound. Management has also decided on standard rates for labor and overhead: the standard labor rate is $11 per hour, the standard variable overhead rate is $6 per hour, and the standard fixed overhead rate is $2 per hour. The only remaining decision is the standard for labor usage. To assist in developing this standard, the production engineering department has estimated the following relationship between units produced and average direct labor hours used:

Cumulative Average	
Units Produced	Time per Unit
20	1.00 hr
40	0.80 hr
80	0.64 hr
160	0.512 hr
320	0.448 hr

As the workers learn more about the production process, they become more efficient in manufacturing the part, and the average time needed to produce one unit declines. Engineering estimates that all of the learning effects will be achieved by the time 160 units are produced. No further improvement will be realized past this level.

REQUIRED:

1. If no further improvement in labor time per unit is possible past 160 units, explain why the cumulative average time per unit at 320 is lower than the time at 160 units.
2. What standard would you set for the per-unit usage of direct labor? Explain.

3. Using the standard you set in requirement 2, prepare a standard cost sheet that details the standard cost per unit for the new part.
4. Given the standard you set in requirement 2, would you expect favorable or unfavorable labor and variable overhead efficiency variances for production of the first 160 units? Explain.

P9-4

Appendix Required: Basic Variance Analysis; Revision of Standards; Journal Entries

LO 3, LO 4, LO 5, LO 6

The El Paso plant of Moss Company's Kitchen Appliance Division produces toaster ovens. The plant uses a standard cost system for production costing and control. The standard cost sheet for a toaster oven follows.

Direct materials (3.0 lb @ $5.00)	$15.00
Direct labor (0.8 hr @ $12.00)	9.60
Variable overhead (0.8 hr @ $5.00)	4.00
Fixed overhead (0.8 hr @ $3.00)	2.40
Standard unit cost	$31.00

During the year, the El Paso plant had the following actual production activity:

a. Production of toaster ovens totaled 50,000 units.
b. A total of 130,000 pounds of raw materials was purchased at $4.70 per pound.
c. There were 30,000 pounds of raw materials in beginning inventory (carried at $5 per pound). There was no ending inventory.
d. The company used 41,000 direct labor hours at a total cost of $533,000.
e. Actual fixed overhead totaled $99,000.
f. Actual variable overhead totaled $215,000.

The El Paso plant's normal activity is 45,000 units per year. Standard overhead rates are computed based on normal activity measured in standard direct labor hours.

REQUIRED:
1. Compute the materials price and usage variances.
2. Compute the labor rate and efficiency variances.
3. Compute the variable overhead spending and efficiency variances.
4. Compute the fixed overhead spending and volume variances.
5. Assume that the purchasing agent for the toaster oven plant purchased a lower-quality raw material from a new supplier. Would you recommend that the El Paso plant continue to use this cheaper raw material? If so, what standards would likely need revision to reflect this decision? Assume that the end product's quality is not significantly affected.
6. Prepare all possible journal entries.

P9-5

Appendix Required: Unit Costs; Multiple Products; Variance Analysis; Journal Entries

LO 2, LO 4, LO 5, LO 6

Koolkare Company manufactures two types of ice makers, small and regular. The standard quantities of labor and materials per unit for 1998 are:

	Small	Regular
Direct materials (oz)	12	20
Direct labor (hr)	0.2	0.3

The standard price paid per pound of direct materials is $1.60. The standard rate for labor is $8. Overhead is applied on the basis of direct labor hours. A plantwide rate is used. Budgeted overhead for the year follows.

Budgeted fixed overhead	$720,000
Budgeted variable overhead	960,000

The company expects to work 24,000 direct labor hours in 1998; standard overhead rates are computed using this activity level. For every small ice maker produced, the company produces two regular ice makers.

Actual operating data for 1998 are:

a. Units produced: small ice makers, 35,000; regular ice makers, 70,000
b. Direct materials purchased and used: 112,000 pounds at $1.55—26,000 for the small ice maker and 86,000 for the regular ice maker; no beginning or ending raw materials inventories
c. Direct labor: 29,600 hours—7,200 hours for the small ice maker, and 22,400 hours for the regular; total cost of labor, $229,400
d. Variable overhead: $1,215,000
e. Fixed overhead: $700,000

REQUIRED:
1. Prepare a standard cost sheet showing the unit cost for each product.
2. Compute the materials price and usage variances for each product. Prepare journal entries to record materials activity.
3. Compute the labor rate and efficiency variances. Prepare journal entries to record labor activity.
4. Compute the variances for variable and fixed overhead. Prepare journal entries to record overhead activity. All variances are closed to Cost of Goods Sold.
5. Assume that you know only the total direct materials used for both products and the total direct labor hours used for both products. Can you compute the total materials usage and labor efficiency variances? Explain.

P9-6
Incomplete Data;
Overhead Analysis
LO 2, LO 4, LO 5

Compton Company produces extension cords. To help control costs, Compton employs a standard cost system and uses a flexible budget to predict overhead costs at various levels of activity. For the most recent year, Compton used a standard overhead rate of $18 per direct labor hour. The rate was computed using normal activity. Budgeted overhead costs are $296,000 for 18,000 direct labor hours and $440,000 for 30,000 direct labor hours. During the past year, Compton generated the following data:

a. Actual production: 100,000 units
b. Fixed overhead volume variance: $20,000 U
c. Variable overhead efficiency variance: $18,000 F
d. Actual fixed overhead costs: $90,000
e. Actual variable overhead costs: $110,000

REQUIRED:
1. Determine the fixed overhead spending variance.
2. Determine the variable overhead spending variance.
3. Determine the standard hours allowed per unit of product.
4. If the standard labor rate is $9.50 per hour, compute the labor efficiency variance.

P9-7
Control Limits;
Variance
Investigation
LO 3, LO 4, LO 5

Demismell Company produces a well-known cologne. The standard manufacturing cost of the cologne is described by the following standard cost sheet:

Direct materials:	
Liquids (4.2 oz @ $0.25)	$1.05
Bottles (1 @ $0.05)	0.05
Direct labor (0.2 hr @ $12.50)	2.50
Variable overhead (0.2 hr @ $4.70)	0.94
Fixed overhead (0.2 hr @ $1.00)	0.20
Standard cost per unit	$4.74

Management has decided to investigate only those variances that exceed the lesser of 10 percent of the standard cost for each category or $20,000.

During the past quarter, 250,000 four-ounce bottles of cologne were produced. Descriptions of actual activity for the quarter follow.

a. A total of 1.15 million ounces of liquids were purchased, mixed, and processed. Evaporation was higher than expected (no inventories of liquids are maintained). The price paid per ounce averaged $0.27.
b. Exactly 250,000 bottles were used. The price paid for each bottle was $0.048.
c. Direct labor hours totaled 48,250 with a total cost of $622,425.
d. Variable overhead costs totaled $239,000.
e. Fixed overhead costs were $50,500.

Normal production volume for Demismell is 250,000 bottles per quarter. The standard overhead rates are computed using normal volume. All overhead costs are incurred uniformly throughout the year.

REQUIRED:
1. Calculate the upper and lower control limits for each manufacturing cost category.
2. Compute the total materials variance and then break it into price and usage variances. Would these variances be investigated?
3. Compute the total labor variance and break it into rate and efficiency variances. Would these variances be investigated?
4. Compute all overhead variances. Would any of them be investigated? Would you recommend a different approach to deal with overhead? Explain.

P9-8

Appendix Required:
Flexible Budget;
Standard Cost
Variances;
T-Accounts
LO 3, LO 4, LO 5, LO 6

Shumaker Company manufactures a line of high-top basketball shoes. At the beginning of the year, the following plans for production and costs were revealed:

Pairs of shoes to be produced and sold	55,000
Standard cost per unit:	
Direct materials	$15
Direct labor	12
Variable overhead	6
Fixed overhead	3
Total unit cost	$36

During the year, 50,000 units were produced and sold. The following actual costs were incurred:

Direct materials	$775,000
Direct labor	590,000
Variable overhead	310,000
Fixed overhead	180,000

There were no beginning or ending inventories of raw materials. The materials price variance was $5,000 unfavorable. In producing the 50,000 units, 63,000 hours were worked, 5 percent more hours than the standard allowed for the actual output. Overhead costs are applied to production using direct labor hours.

REQUIRED:
1. Using a flexible budget, prepare a performance report comparing expected costs for the actual production with actual costs.
2. Determine the following:
   a. Materials usage variance
   b. Labor rate variance
   c. Labor efficiency variance
   d. Fixed overhead spending and volume variances
   e. Variable overhead spending and efficiency variances
3. Use T-accounts to show the flow of costs through the system.

P9-9
Control Limits;
Variance
Investigation
LO 3, LO 4

The management of Golding Company has determined that the cost to investigate a variance produced by its standard cost system ranges from $2,000 to $3,000. If a problem is discovered, the average benefit from taking corrective action usually outweighs the cost of investigation. Past experience from the investigation of variances has revealed that corrective action is rarely needed for deviations within 8 percent of the standard cost. Golding produces a single product, which has the following standards for materials and labor:

Direct materials (8 lb @ $0.25)	$2
Direct labor (0.4 hr @ $7.50)	3

Actual production for the past three months with the associated actual usage and costs for materials and labor follow. There were no beginning or ending raw material inventories.

	April	May	June
Production (units)	90,000	100,000	110,000
Direct materials:			
Cost	$189,000	$218,000	$230,000
Usage (lb)	723,000	870,000	885,000
Direct labor:			
Cost	$270,000	$323,000	$360,000
Usage (hr)	36,000	44,000	46,000

REQUIRED:
1. What upper and lower control limits would you use for materials variances? For labor variances?
2. Compute the materials and labor variances for April, May, and June. Identify those that would require investigation.
3. Let the horizontal axis be time and the vertical axis be variances measured as a percentage deviation from standard. Draw horizontal lines that identify upper and lower control limits. Plot the labor and material variances for April, May, and June. Prepare a separate graph for each type of variance. Explain how you would use these graphs (called *control charts*) to assist your analysis of variances.

P9-10
Standard Costing;
Planned Variances
LO 2, LO 4

As part of its cost control program, Hepler Company uses a standard cost system for all manufactured items. The standard cost for each item is established at the beginning of the fiscal year, and the standards are not revised until the beginning of the next fiscal year. Changes in costs, caused during the year by changes in material or labor inputs or by changes in the manufacturing process, are recognized as they occur by the inclusion of planned variances in Hepler's monthly operating budgets.

Following is the labor standard that was established for one of Hepler's products effective June 1, 1998, the beginning of the fiscal year:

Assembler A labor (5 hr @ $10)	$ 50
Assembler B labor (3 hr @ $11)	33
Machinist labor (2 hr @ $15)	30
Standard cost per 100 units	$113

The standard was based on the labor being performed by a team consisting of five persons with assembler A skills, three persons with assembler B skills, and two persons with machinist skills; this team represents the most efficient use of the company's skilled employees. The standard also assumed that the quality of materials that had been used in prior years would be available for the coming year.

For the first seven months of the fiscal year, actual manufacturing costs at Hepler have been within the standards established. However, the company has received a significant increase in orders, and there is an insufficient number of skilled workers to meet the increased production. Therefore, beginning in January, the production teams will consist of eight persons with assembler A skills, one person with assembler B skills, and one person with machinist skills. The reorganized teams will work more slowly than the normal teams; and, as a result, only 80 units will be produced in the same time period in which 100 units would normally be produced. Faulty work has never been a cause for units to be rejected in the final inspection process, and it is not expected to be a cause for rejection with the reorganized teams.

Furthermore, Hepler has been notified by its material supplier that lower-quality materials will be supplied beginning January 1. Normally, one unit of raw materials is required for each good unit produced, and no units are lost due to defective material. Hepler estimates that 10 percent of the units manufactured after January 1 will be rejected in the final inspection process due to defective material.

REQUIRED:

1. Determine the number of units of lower-quality material that Hepler Company must enter into production in order to produce 54,000 good finished units.
2. How many hours of each class of labor must be used to manufacture 54,000 good finished units?
3. Determine the amount that should be included in Hepler's January operating budget for the planned labor variance caused by the reorganization of the labor teams and the lower-quality material. (CMA adapted)

P9-11

Standard Cost Sheet; Incomplete Data; Variance Analysis

LO 2, LO 4, LO 5

Emerson Company had recently acquired Madera, Inc., a small manufacturing firm located in the Midwest. Unfortunately, Madera had very poor internal controls and a master disk with some fundamental cost data for the past year was accidentally erased. No backup existed. Kathy Shorts, an internal auditor for Emerson, was assigned to Madera and given the task of reconstructing some of the cost records. At first, she was discouraged with the assignment, but became excited when she discovered part of a computer printout that contained some information about last year's operations. The information, pertaining to Madera's cost accounting system, follows.

Selected Actual Results

Direct materials: 5,000 pounds purchased and used, costing $25,500
Production: 10,000 units
Labor cost: 2,200 hours totaling $17,160
Fixed overhead cost: $11,500
Variable overhead cost: $23,000

Variances

MPV	$ 500 U
MUV	5,000 F
LEV	1,500 U
Variable overhead efficiency	2,000 F
Variable overhead spending	1,000 U
Underapplied fixed overhead	1,500 U
Volume variance	2,000 U

Kathy also interviewed Madera's controller and discovered that overhead rates are based on expected actual activity. Madera calculates two variances for variable overhead and two for fixed overhead. However, before Kathy could analyze the information she had gathered, she had to take emergency leave because of a family crisis. You have been given the task of performing the analysis described by the following requirements.

REQUIRED:

1. Prepare a standard cost sheet in good form. Show fixed and variable overhead as separate items.
2. Compute the fixed overhead spending variance.

3. Compute the labor rate variance.
4. Determine the expected actual activity used to compute the predetermined fixed overhead rate.

 M ANAGERIAL DECISION CASES

C9-1
Standard Costing
LO 1, LO 2, LO 3

Mark Wright, Inc. (MWI) is a specialty frozen-food processor located in the midwestern states. Since its founding in 1982, MWI has enjoyed a loyal clientele that is willing to pay premium prices for the high-quality frozen food it prepares from specialized recipes. In the last two years, the company has experienced rapid sales growth in its operating region and has had many inquiries about supplying its products on a national basis. To meet this growth, MWI expanded its processing capabilities, which resulted in increased production and distribution costs. Furthermore, MWI has been encountering pricing pressure from competitors outside its normal marketing region.

Because MWI desires to continue its expansion, Jim Condon, CEO, has engaged a consulting firm to assist MWI in determining its best course of action. The consulting firm recommended instituting a standard cost system that would also facilitate a flexible budgeting system to better accommodate the changes in demand that can be expected when serving an expanding market area.

Condon met with his management team and explained the consulting firm's recommendations. Condon then assigned the task of establishing standard costs to his management team. After discussing the situation with the respective staffs, the management team met to review the matter.

Jane Morgan, purchasing manager, advised that meeting expanded production would necessitate obtaining basic food supplies from other than MWI's traditional sources. This would entail increased raw material and shipping costs and might result in lower-quality supplies. Consequently, these increased costs would need to be made up by the processing department if current costs are to be maintained or reduced.

Stan Walters, processing manager, countered that the need to accelerate processing cycles to increase production, coupled with the possibility of receiving lower-grade supplies, could be expected to result in a slip in quality and a greater product rejection rate. Under these circumstances, per-unit labor utilization could not be maintained or reduced, and forecasting future unit labor content would become very difficult.

Tom Lopez, production engineer, advised that if the equipment is not properly maintained and thoroughly cleaned at prescribed daily intervals, the quality and unique taste of the frozen-food products would probably be affected. Jack Reid, vice-president of sales, stated that if quality could not be maintained, MWI could not expect to increase sales to the levels projected.

When Condon was apprised of the problems encountered by his management team, he advised them that if agreement could not be reached on the appropriate standards, he would arrange to have them set by the consulting firm and everyone would have to live with the results.

REQUIRED:
1. List the major advantages of using a standard cost system.
2. List disadvantages that can result from the use of a standard cost system.
3. Identify those who should participate in setting standards and describe the benefits of their participation in the standard setting process.
4. What characteristics of a standard cost system make it an effective tool for cost control?
5. What could be the consequences if Jim Condon, CEO, has the standards set by the outside consulting firm? (CMA adapted)

C9-2
Establishment of Standards; Variance Analysis
LO 1, LO 2, LO 4

Crunchy Chips was established in 1938 by Paul Golding and his wife Nancy (Nancy sold her piano to help raise capital to start the business). Paul assumed responsibility for buying potatoes and selling chips to local grocers; Nancy assumed responsibility for production. Since Nancy was already known for her delicious, thin potato chips, the business prospered.

Over the past 60 years, the company has established distribution channels in 11 western states, with production facilities in Utah, New Mexico, and Colorado. In 1980, Paul Golding died, and his son, Edward, took control of the business. By 1998, the company was facing stiff competition from national snack-food companies. Edward was advised that the company's plants needed to gain better control over production costs. To assist in achieving this objective, he hired a consultant to install a standard cost system. To help the consultant in establishing the necessary standards, Edward sent her the following memo:

To: Diana Craig, CMA
From: Edward Golding, President, Crunchy Chips
Subject: Description and Data Relating to the Production of Our Plain Potato Chips
Date: September 28, 1998

The manufacturing process for potato chips begins when the potatoes are placed into a large vat in which they are automatically washed. After washing, the potatoes flow directly to an automatic peeler. The peeled potatoes then pass by inspectors who manually cut out deep eyes or other blemishes. After inspection, the potatoes are automatically sliced and dropped into the cooking oil. The frying process is closely monitored by an employee. After they are cooked, the chips pass under a salting device and then pass by more inspectors, who sort out the unacceptable finished chips (those that are discolored or too small). The chips then continue on the conveyor belt to a bagging machine that bags them in one-pound bags. After bagging, the bags are placed in a box and shipped. The box holds 15 bags.

The raw potato pieces (eyes and blemishes), peelings, and rejected finished chips are sold to animal feed producers for $0.16 per pound. The company uses this revenue to reduce the cost of potatoes; we would like this reflected in the price standard relating to potatoes.

Crunchy Chips purchases high-quality potatoes at a cost of $0.245 per pound. Each potato averages 4.25 ounces. Under efficient operating conditions, it takes four potatoes to produce one 16-ounce bag of plain chips. Although we label bags as containing 16 ounces, we actually place 16.3 ounces in each bag. We plan to continue this policy to ensure customer satisfaction. In addition to potatoes, other raw materials are the cooking oil, salt, bags, and boxes. Cooking oil costs $0.04 per ounce, and we use 3.3 ounces of oil per bag of chips. The cost of salt is so small that we add it to overhead. Bags cost $0.11 each, and boxes $0.52.

Our plant produces 8.8 million bags of chips per year. A recent engineering study revealed that we would need the following direct labor hours to produce this quantity if our plant operates at peak efficiency:

Raw potato inspection	3,200
Finished chip inspection	12,000
Frying monitor	6,300
Boxing	16,600
Machine operators	6,300

I'm not sure that we can achieve the level of efficiency advocated by the study. In my opinion, the plant is operating efficiently for the level of output indicated if the hours allowed are about 10 percent higher.

The hourly labor rates agreed upon with the union are:

Raw potato inspectors	$7.60
Finished chip inspectors	5.15
Frying monitor	7.00
Boxing	5.50
Machine operators	6.50

Overhead is applied on the basis of direct labor dollars. We have found that variable overhead averages about 116 percent of our direct labor cost. Our fixed overhead is budgeted at $1,135,216 for the coming year.

REQUIRED:
1. Discuss the benefits of a standard cost system for Crunchy Chips.
2. Discuss the president's concern about using the result of the engineering study to set the labor standards. What standard would you recommend?
3. Develop a standard cost sheet for Crunchy Chips' plain potato chips.
4. Suppose that the level of production was 8.8 million bags of potato chips for the year as planned. If 9.5 million pounds of potatoes were used, compute the materials usage variance for potatoes.

C9-3
Standard Costing and Ethical Behavior

Pat James, the purchasing agent for a local plant of the Oakden Electronics Division, was considering the possible purchase of a component from a new supplier. The component's purchase price, $0.90, compared favorably with the standard price of $1.10. Given the quantity that would be purchased, Pat knew that the favorable price variance would help offset an unfavorable variance for another component. By offsetting the unfavorable variance, his overall performance report would be impressive and good enough to help him qualify for the annual bonus. More importantly, a good performance rating this year would help him secure a position at division headquarters at a significant salary increase.

Purchase of the part, however, presented Pat with a dilemma. Consistent with his past behavior, Pat made inquiries regarding the reliability of the new supplier and the part's quality. Reports were basically negative. The supplier had a reputation for making the first two or three deliveries on schedule but being unreliable from then on. Worse, the part itself was of questionable quality. The number of defective units was only slightly higher than that for other suppliers, but the life of the component was 25 percent less than what normal sources provided.

If the part were purchased, no problems with deliveries would surface for several months. The problem of shorter life would cause eventual customer dissatisfaction and perhaps some loss of sales, but the part would last at least eighteen months after the final product began to be used. If all went well, Pat expected to be at headquarters within six months. He saw very little personal risk associated with a decision to purchase the part from the new supplier. By the time any problems surfaced, they would belong to his successor. With this rationalization, Pat decided to purchase the component from the new supplier.

REQUIRED:
1. Do you agree with Pat's decision? Why or why not? How important do you think Pat's assessment of his personal risk was in the decision? Should it be a factor?
2. Do you think that the use of standards and the practice of holding individuals accountable for their achievement played major roles in Pat's decision?
3. Review the ethical standards for management accountants in Exhibit 1-4 of Chapter 1. Even though Pat is not a management accountant, identify the standards that might apply to his situation. Should every company adopt a set of ethical standards that apply to their employees, regardless of their specialty?

C9-4
Research Assignment

The usefulness of standard costing has been challenged in recent years. Some claim that its use is an impediment to the objective of continuous improvement (an objective that many feel is vital in today's competitive environment). Write a short paper that analyzes the role and value of standard costing in today's manufacturing environment. Address the following questions:

1. What are the major criticisms of standard costing?
2. Will standard costing disappear, or is there still a role for it in the new manufacturing environment? If so, what is the role?
3. Given the criticisms, can you explain why its use continues to be so prevalent? Will this use eventually change?
4. If standard costing is no longer completely suitable for some manufacturing environments, what control approaches are being used to supplement (replace?) the traditional control model?

In preparing your paper, the following references may be useful; however, do not restrict your literature search to these references. They are simply to help you get started.

1. Robin Cooper and Robert S. Kaplan, "Activity-Based Systems: Measuring the Costs of Resource Usage," *Accounting Horizons* (September 1992): 1–13.
2. Forrest B. Green and Felix E. Amenkhienan, "Accounting Innovations: A Cross-Sectional Survey of Manufacturing Firms," *Journal of Cost Management* (Spring 1992): 58–64.
3. Bruce R. Gaumnitz and Felix P. Kollaritsch, "Manufacturing Variances: Current Practice and Trends," *Journal of Cost Management* (Spring 1991): 58–64.

4. Robert S. Kaplan, "Limitations of Cost Accounting in Advanced Manufacturing Environments," in *Measures for Manufacturing Excellence*, ed. Robert S. Kaplan (Boston: Harvard Business School Press, 1990).

5. George Foster and Charles Horngren, "JIT: Cost Accounting and Cost Management Issues," *Management Accounting* (June 1987): 19–25.

CHAPTER

Activity-based Management

SCENARIO

ichelle Anderson, president and owner of Anderson Parts, Inc., was looking forward to her meeting with Henry Jensen, a consultant from a national public accounting firm. Anderson Parts was in desperate need to improve its competitive position. About six months ago, Michelle had approved the implementation of a JIT purchasing and manufacturing system. Early results were respectable but well below Michelle's expectations. Inventories had been reduced, but they were still well above desired levels. Furthermore, although lead times had been reduced, they, too, were still higher than projected. Significant problems with quality, delivery, excessive scrap, and machine performance were persisting. Before she became too concerned, however, she wanted to hear what Henry had to say. He had to understand that activity-based management is a totally different way of looking at things. You need to know what activities you are performing, why you are doing them, and how well you are performing them. Good evaluation and control are critical for the success of activity-based management."

"Henry, we do have a good system for evaluating and controlling our operations. We have a standard costing system and budgetary control of all our major responsibility centers. We also have good incentive pay schemes in place to encourage both labor and managerial productivity."

"Michelle, measuring and controlling performance is fundamental—but performance measurement must be compatible with the concept of continuous improvement. Otherwise, the measures used can actually limit the efficiency made possible by JIT and activity-based management. Unfortunately, some of the traditional control measures you mentioned are no longer suitable for your new environment."

"Explain. I don't see why our performance measures are so bad. They've worked well for years."

"The traditional approach concerns managing costs, but costs can't be managed—only the activities that cause the costs can be. The typical accounting report produces variances and these variances are supposed to signal problems, if any exist. This approach encourages reactive decision making and is essentially backward-looking management. After all, the events that caused the costs are past, and we can't change those events."

come to provide a progress report and additional recommendations for changes. In particular, he had mentioned to her that Anderson needed to consider the possibility of implementing what he had called activity-based management.

"Glad to see you again, Henry. I'm anxious to hear what you have to say about this activity-based management system and what can be done to continue improving our efficiency. It appears that we still haven't realized many of the benefits from JIT that my manufacturing engineers had predicted six months ago."

"Well, that's certainly true. Change does take time, but actually your company is making the transition from traditional manufacturing to JIT much more easily than other firms I've had as

clients. You've already shown some significant improvement—more so than usual for this stage of development."

"That's encouraging. How much longer will it take to realize the full benefits? What else do we need to do?"

"The levels of improvement that I predicted should be achieved within a year. After that, I would expect to see additional improvement each year. You should focus your efforts to improve on more than just manufacturing activities. Improving your overall competitive position means focusing your attention on processes. Process improvement and process innovation are fundamental to your objective of continuous improvement. Since processes are defined by activities, activity management is needed. But you need

Questions to Think About	3. Why are process innovation and improvement key to continuous improvement?	5. Why is activity-based management compatible with continuous improvement?
1. What is meant by continuous improvement?	4. How can we measure activity performance?	6. What role, if any, do cost reports play in the advanced manufacturing environment?
2. Why are traditional evaluation and control measures not suitable for the advanced manufacturing environment?		

RESPONSIBILITY ACCOUNTING

Objective 1

Compare and contrast traditional responsibility accounting with contemporary responsibility accounting.

The type of environment in which a firm operates can have a significant effect on the type of control system chosen and implemented. Consider, for example, a firm that produces concrete pipes and blocks. The products and production processes are well defined and relatively stable. Competition tends to be local or regional as opposed to national or international. A successful firm operating in this type of environment would tend to emphasize maintaining the status quo: preservation of market share, stable growth, and continuation of efficient production. On the other hand, a firm like Hewlett-Packard, involved in producing computers and computer-related products, operates in an environment where change is rapid. Products and processes are constantly being redesigned and improved and stiff national and international competition are always present. Organizations operating in a dynamic, rapidly changing environment are finding that adaptation and change are essential to survival. To find ways to improve performance, Hewlett-Packard and other firms in this kind of environment are forced to reevaluate how they do things. Improving performance translates into constantly searching for ways to eliminate waste—a process known as *continuous improvement*. Waste reduction, the theme of continuous improvement, is made possible through the use of various waste reduction tools such as JIT purchasing and manufacturing, reengineering, total quality management, employee empowerment, and computer-aided manufacturing. These tools, or methods, attempt to eliminate waste, which appears in the form of such things as inventories, unnecessary activities, defective products, rework, setup time, and underutilization of employee talents and skills.

What is measured, monitored, and rewarded can have an important effect on an organization's efforts to achieve its objectives. The adages, "You get what you measure and reward," and "If you don't measure it, it won't improve, and if you don't monitor it, it will get worse," are both relevant issues when designing and selecting a control system. Consider, for example, the unemployment agency that wanted to increase the number of applicants placed in the workplace. To encourage achievement of this objective, management selected "number of persons interviewed" as the performance measure and rewarded their employees based on this measure. What the agency got was an increase in the number of interviews and fewer placements. When they changed the measure to "number of applicants placed," instead of number interviewed, behavior and results changed. This anecdotal example suggests that the control system for firms operating in a stable environment ought to be different from those operating in a dynamic environment. After all, maintaining status quo is a very different objective from that of continuous improvement. In other words, the control system selected is contingent on the environment in which the firm operates.

The accounting system plays a key role in measuring actions and outcomes and in defining the rewards to be received by individuals. This role is referred to as *responsibility accounting* and is a fundamental tool of managerial control. The responsibility control model is defined by four essential elements: (1) assigning responsibility, (2) establishing performance measures or benchmarks, (3) evaluating performance, and (4) assigning rewards.

Traditional versus Contemporary Responsibility Accounting

traditional responsibility accounting contemporary responsibility accounting

The responsibility accounting system for a stable environment is referred to as traditional responsibility accounting. The traditional system was developed when most firms were operating in relatively stable environments. Contemporary responsibility accounting, on the other hand, is the responsibility accounting system that is emerging for those firms operating in dynamic environments. Exhibits 10-1 and 10-2 illustrate the four responsibility elements for each of the two approaches. An element-by-element comparison of these two approaches provides some key insights into the differences between the two environments.

Assigning Responsibility Exhibit 10-1 reveals that traditional responsibility accounting focuses on organizational units and individuals. First, a responsibility center is identified. This center is typically an organizational unit such as a department or production line, or a work team. Whatever the unit is, responsibility is assigned to the individual in charge. Responsibility is defined in financial terms (for example, costs). Exhibit 10-2 reveals that in a contemporary responsibility system, the control point changes from units and individuals to processes and teams. The reasons for the change in focus are simple. In a dynamic environment, continuous improvement is the governing principle.

Exhibit
Elements of a Traditional Responsibility Accounting System

Exhibit
Elements of a
Contemporary
Responsibility Accounting
System

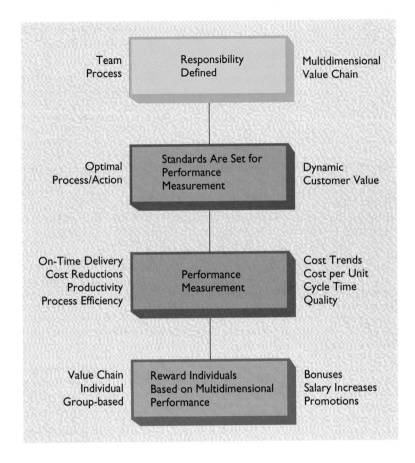

Constant change and constant learning are needed for continuous improvement to work. Processes are chosen because they are the units of change. *Processes* are activities linked by a common objective, and describe the way things are done in an organization. Processes have inputs and create an output that is of value to a customer. The customer can be internal or external to the organization. Procurement, product development, customer acquisition, and customer service are examples of processes.

Since processes are the way things are done, changing the way things are done means changing processes. There are two methods of changing the way things are done: *process improvement* and *process innovation*. Process improvement refers to incremental and constant increases in the efficiency of an existing process. Process innovation (business reengineering) refers to the performance of a process in a radically new way with the objective of achieving dramatic improvements in response time, quality, and efficiency. IBM Credit, for example, radically redesigned its credit approval process and reduced its time for preparing a quote for leasing or buying a computer from 7 days to 1; similarly, Federal-Mogul, a parts manufacturer, used process innovation to reduce development time for part prototypes from 20 weeks to 20 days.[1]

Many processes cut across functional boundaries. This facilitates an integrated approach that emphasizes the firm's value-chain activities. It also means that cross-functional skills are needed for effective process management. Teams are the natural outcome of this process management requirement. Teams also improve the quality of work life by fostering friendships and a sense of belonging. Process improvement and innovation require significant group activity (and support) and cannot be carried out effectively by individuals. General Electric, Xerox, Martin Marietta, and Aetna Life Insurance have all begun to use teams as their basic work unit.[2]

process improvement
process innovation (business reengineering)

1. Thomas H. Davenport. *Process Innovation* (Boston: Harvard Business School Press, 1993), 2.
2. Davenport, *Process Innovation*, 97.

Establishing Performance Measures Standards are set to serve as benchmarks for performance measurement. According to Exhibit 10-1, budgeting and standard costing are the cornerstones of the benchmark activity for a traditional framework. Standards tend to remain fairly stable over time. Furthermore, they tend to support a currently attainable norm. Exhibit 10-2 shows some striking differences for firms operating in a dynamic environment. First, standards are process oriented. They relate to process efficiency and process output. Standards also are structured to support change. Thus, optimal or ideal standards are set and effort exerted to reach the ideal levels. Furthermore, standards are dynamic in nature. They need to change to reflect new conditions and new goals and to help maintain any progress that has been realized. For example, standards can be set that reflect some desired level of improvement for a process. Once the desired level is achieved, the standard is changed to encourage an additional increment of improvement. In an environment where constant improvement is sought, standards cannot be static. Standards also should support the objective of increasing customer value.

Evaluating Performance In a traditional framework (see Exhibit 10-1) performance is measured by comparing actual outcomes with budgeted outcomes. In principle, individuals are held accountable only for those items over which they have control. Cost performance is strongly emphasized. In the contemporary framework, time, quality, and efficiency are all critical dimensions of performance (see Exhibit 10-2). Decreasing the time a process takes to deliver its output to customers is viewed as basic. Thus, measures such as cycle time and on-time deliveries become important. Performance measures relating to quality and efficiency are also vital. Productivity and cost measures are emphasized for assessing changes in efficiency. Improving a process should translate into better financial results. Thus, measures of cost reductions achieved, trends in cost, and cost per unit of output are all useful indicators of whether a process has improved. Progress toward achieving optimal standards and interim standards needs to be measured. One approach is to measure the trends of actual costs (or other actual operational measures) against optimal standards. The objective is to provide low-cost, high-quality products, delivered on a timely basis. Thus, performance measures are a blend of operational and financial factors, all of which relate to process performance.

Assigning Rewards In both systems, individuals are rewarded or penalized according to the policies and discretion of higher management. Of course, as Exhibit 10-1 reveals, the traditional reward system is designed to encourage individuals to manage costs—to achieve or beat budgetary standards. For the contemporary system illustrated in Exhibit 10-2, rewarding individuals is more complicated than in the traditional setting. Individuals simultaneously have accountability for team and individual performance. Since the emphasis is on process improvement, and improvement is mostly achieved through team efforts, group-based rewards are more suitable than individual rewards. In one company (a producer of electronic components), for example, optimal standards have been set for unit costs, on-time delivery, quality, inventory turns, scrap, and cycle time.[3] Bonuses are awarded to the team whenever performance is maintained on all measures and improves on at least one measure. Notice the multidimensional nature of this measurement and reward system.

The differences between the two approaches are significant. Yet, a logical question to ask is why the traditional responsibility system is not suitable for a firm operating in a dynamic environment. The emphasis of the traditional responsibility accounting system is on managing costs, maintaining the status quo, and organizational stability. However, in a dynamic environment, firms are competing on the basis of time, quality, and efficiency—in response to customer demands. Customers are demanding that the

3. C. J. McNair, "Responsibility Accounting and Controllability Networks," *Handbook of Cost Management* (Boston: Warren Gorham Lamont, 1993), E4-1–E4-33.

products they want be delivered on time and defect free, and have short lead times, low prices, and low postpurchase costs. Customers want greater value: more realization and less sacrifice. To provide this greater value, firms must do more with less; they must find ways of being more productive. Firms that advocate continuous improvement usually alter the role of standard costing and budgeting as managerial control tools. The reason is simple. Traditional performance measures provide incentives that actually may serve as impediments to continuous improvement. Traditional performance measures are limited in their ability to support the objective of continuous improvement and the use of its associated tools such as just-in-time, total quality management, and advanced technology. To fully understand this reasoning, some specific limitations need to be listed and described.

Limitations of Traditional Responsibility Accounting

Traditional responsibility accounting places too much emphasis on standards and variance computations (for a dynamic environment). Standards tend to be static and sometimes dated and may not reflect the changes that are taking place within the organization (or environment). Rather than supporting change, they encourage the status quo and organizational stability. Standards also typically allow for given levels of inefficiency, accepting some downtime, some waste, some lack of skill, and so on. Furthermore, the variances computed are the *result* of management action and organizational performance and not the *cause* of it. Understanding what causes performance is fundamental to improving performance. To quote one manager, "Using financial measures to improve performance is like concentrating on the scoreboard in a football game. While the scoreboard tells you whether you are winning or losing, it doesn't provide much guidance about the plays that should be called."[4]

For a dynamic environment, a number of specific limitations can be listed and described—limitations that clearly suggest the need for the type of responsibility accounting model described in Exhibit 10-2.

Internal Focus Standards, budgets, and variances tend to be internally focused. Standards are usually based on internal expectations. Variances, then, are comparisons of internal expectations with actual outcomes. Yet as one executive remarked, "A revenue increase of 15% over last year and 5% ahead of budget is not such good news when the market grew 30% and our leading competitor increased its sales by 40%."[5] An external focus is also needed.

Overemphasis on Labor In the traditional setting, many companies emphasize control of labor costs over the cost of any other input. But, for companies that have automated, the direct labor content in products is greatly decreased. Furthermore, for companies that have implemented JIT, the distinction between labor and indirect labor is largely artificial. Cell workers do much more than work on products. According to one source, labor content in some manufacturing is less than 2 percent, making labor standards much less meaningful.[6] Hewlett-Packard, for example, no longer tracks labor separately but includes it as a component of overhead.

In the advanced manufacturing environment, there is more emphasis on *process* efficiency than on labor efficiency. A manager of a plant using a JIT approach made this observation, "The system converts materials into product, not people at workstations.

4. Robert G. Eccle and Phillip J. Pyburn, "Creating a Comprehensive System to Measure Performance," *Management Accounting* (October 1992): 41–44.

5. Ibid., 41–42.

6. F. B. Green, Felix Amenkhienan, and George F. Johnson, "Performance Measures and JIT," *Management Accounting* (February 1991): 50–53.

Therefore, process efficiency is more important than labor efficiency. As well, the process may be improved by using direct labor to perform indirect tasks, . . ."[7]

Ignores Nonvalue-added Costs The traditional responsibility accounting system does not classify and report costs that are targeted for elimination. In a continuous improvement environment, certain costs called *nonvalue-added costs* are identified and isolated so they can eventually be eliminated. As we will see in more detail later on (pp. 394–396), these costs are targeted for elimination because they are unnecessary and provide no value to the customer or organization. This targeting is basic to a continuous improvement program. Nonvalue-added costs must be tracked and reported, otherwise there is no promise of change: "Costs not reported are invisible and are all but ignored in the management process."[8]

Perverse Incentives Standard costing encourages those responsible for the achievement of standards to produce favorable variances. But the pressure to meet standards may create dysfunctional behavior. For example, purchasing agents may acquire materials of low quality or in large lots in order to produce a favorable materials price variance. As a consequence, scrap, the number of defective units, and the amount of rework activity may increase, or raw materials inventories may be excessive. These outcomes run contrary to the advanced environment's objectives of total quality control and zero inventories.

As indicated, in the advanced manufacturing environment, labor efficiency reporting receives considerably less emphasis—but this decrease in emphasis is attributable to incentive problems as well as the reduction in labor content (some firms may still have significant labor content). Labor efficiency variances computed at the cell level may encourage workers to produce more than needed to achieve targeted efficiency levels or to avoid an unfavorable volume variance. For example, including setup labor as part of the labor standard (as is often done) encourages large production runs and, thus, excess production; by using fewer setup hours, the actual hours reported move closer to standard. But producing more product than needed is diametrically opposed to the goal of zero inventories. In a JIT environment, idle workers (in the short run) are not necessarily viewed as bad; keeping workers active by overproducing can be much more costly than the labor services lost.

The computation of materials usage variances can also pose problems for the advanced manufacturing environment. Workers may pass on poor-quality components to avoid an unfavorable materials usage variance. Unfortunately, defective parts disrupt production in a JIT environment. Because there are no inventories to buffer interruptions in production, incentives that encourage defective components are not desirable. Thus, the traditional approach, to control operations through efficiency reporting and variance analysis, is not compatible with the advanced manufacturing environment.

Emphasis on individual overhead variances can also be detrimental. Avoiding preventive maintenance to ensure a favorable budget variance may result in equipment being unavailable for production. This behavior, however, runs counter to the JIT objective of total preventive maintenance and creates an incentive for buffer inventories.

The concept of currently attainable standards is also opposed to the objective of continuous improvement. Currently attainable standards allow for a certain level of inefficiency. All too often, in a standard costing system, those who achieve the standard believe that they have arrived and that no further efforts are needed to improve efficiency. Of course, this is possible because the standard allows for inefficiency and is viewed as somewhat static. But JIT and this new business process demand that efforts be continually exerted to improve quality, to improve efficiency, to find better ways to do the same task. Innovation and simplicity are encouraged and rewarded. A dynamic

---

7. McNair, "Responsibility Accounting," E4-17.
8. McNair, E4-7.

view of efficiency, not a static one, is needed for an environment in which continuous improvement is stressed.

Overemphasis on Financial Measures Traditional responsibility accounting emphasizes financial control; yet many gains are nonfinancial. Response time, for example, is not measured in dollars, yet this has emerged as one of the key competitive dimensions. This suggests that a contemporary responsibility accounting system must incorporate both financial and nonfinancial measures of performance. Exhibit 10-3 summarizes the limitations of a traditional responsibility accounting system.

Activity-based Management

Identifying the limitations helps us understand why the contemporary responsibility accounting model shown in Exhibit 10-2 is needed. Although Exhibit 10-2 offers a general overview of a contemporary responsibility accounting system, it does not offer operational details. The emergence of activity accounting is the key to operationalizing the concepts presented in Exhibit 10-2. Processes are the focus of responsibility and control. Processes are made up of activities that are linked to perform a specific objective. Improving processes means improving the way activities are performed. Thus, management of activities, not costs, is the key to successful control for firms operating in dynamic environments. The realization that activities are crucial to both improved product costing and effective control has led to a new view of business processes called *activity-based management.*

activity-based management (ABM)

Activity-based management (ABM) is a systemwide, integrated approach that focuses management's attention on activities with the objective of improving customer value and the profit achieved by providing this value. Activity-based management encompasses both product costing and process value analysis. Thus, the activity-based management model has two dimensions: a *cost dimension* and a *process dimension.* This two-dimensional model was first introduced in Chapter 2 (Exhibit 2-14) and for convenience is updated in Exhibit 10-4. The cost dimension provides cost information about resources, activities, products, and customers (and other cost objects that may be of interest). As the model suggests, the cost of resources is traced to activities, and then the cost of activities is assigned to products and customers. This activity-based costing dimension is useful for product costing, strategic cost management, and tactical analysis. The second dimension, the process dimension, provides information about what activities are performed, why they are performed, and how well they are done. It is this dimension that provides the ability to engage in and measure continuous improvement. To understand how the process view connects with the world of continuous improvement, we need to have a more explicit understanding of process value analysis.

10-3

Exhibit
Limitations of Traditional Responsibility Accounting

1. Overreliance on standards and variances
2. Standards tend to be static
3. Standards support the status quo and organizational stability
4. Standards allow for given levels of inefficiency
5. Variances are lagged indicators, revealing results—not the cause
6. Focus is internal not external
7. Overemphasizes direct labor
8. Ignores nonvalue-added costs

9. Traditional variances and performance reports provide perverse incentives (inappropriate measures of performance):
   a. Encourages overproduction and unneeded inventories
   b. Works against zero defects and total quality control
   c. May work against machine availability (especially bad for bottlenecks)
10. Overemphasizes financial measures

Exhibit
The Two-Dimensional
ABM Model

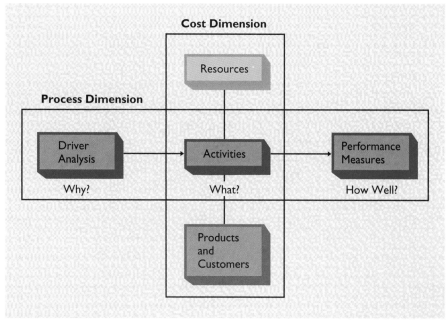

PROCESS VALUE ANALYSIS

Objective 2

Explain process value analysis.

process value analysis

Process value analysis defines activity-based responsibility accounting, focuses on accountability for activities rather than costs, and emphasizes the maximization of system-wide performance instead of individual performance. Process value analysis allows the concepts of contemporary responsibility accounting to become operational. As the model in Exhibit 10-4 illustrates, process value analysis is concerned with (1) *driver analysis*, (2) *activity analysis*, and (3) *performance measurement*.

Driver Analysis: The Search for Root Causes

activity inputs
activity output

activity output measure

driver analysis

Managing activities requires an understanding of what causes activity costs. We know from Chapter 2 that every activity has inputs and outputs. Recall that activity inputs are the resources consumed by the activity in producing its output. Activity output is the result or product of an activity. For example, if the activity is writing a computer program, the inputs would be such things as a programmer, a computer, a printer, computer paper, and disks. The output would be a computer program. An activity output measure is the number of times the activity is performed. It is the quantifiable measure of the output. For example, the number of programs is a possible output measure for writing programs.

The output measure effectively is a measure of the demands placed on an activity and is what we have been calling an *activity driver*. As the demands for an activity change, the cost of the activity can change. For example, as the number of programs written increases, the activity of writing programs may need to consume more inputs (labor, disks, paper, and so on). However, output measures, such as the number of programs, may not and usually do not correspond to the root causes of activity costs; rather they are the consequences of the activity being performed. The purpose of *driver analysis* is to reveal the root causes. Thus, driver analysis is the effort expended to identify those factors that are the root causes of activity costs. For example, an analysis may reveal that the root cause of the cost of moving materials is plant layout. Once the root cause is known, then action can be taken to improve the activity. The cost of moving materials can be reduced by reorganizing plant layout.

Often the root cause of the cost of an activity is also the root cause of other related activities. For example, the costs of inspecting purchased parts (output measure = number of inspection hours) and reordering (output measure = number of reorders) may both be caused by poor supplier quality. By implementing total quality management and a supplier evaluation program, both activities and the procurement process itself may be improved. Quality management approach and degree of employee involvement are examples of other possible root drivers of activities within an organization.

Activity Analysis: Identifying and Assessing Value Content

activity analysis

The heart of process value analysis is *activity analysis*. Activity analysis is the process of identifying, describing, and evaluating the activities an organization performs. Activity analysis should produce four outcomes: (1) what activities are done, (2) how many people perform the activities, (3) the time and resources required to perform the activities, and (4) an assessment of the value of the activities to the organization, including a recommendation to select and keep only those that add value. Step 4, determining the value-added content of activities, may be the most important step in activity analysis. Activities can be classified as *value-added* or *nonvalue-added*.

value-added activities
required activities

Value-added Activities Value-added activities are those necessary to remain in business. Some activities, required activities, are necessary to comply with legal mandates. Activities needed to comply with the reporting requirements of the SEC and the filing requirements of the IRS are examples. These activities are value-added by mandate. The remaining activities in the firm are discretionary. A *discretionary activity* is classified as value-added provided it simultaneously satisfies three conditions: (1) the activity produces a change of state, (2) the change of state was not achievable by preceding activities, and (3) the activity enables other activities to be performed.

For example, consider the production of rods used in hydraulic cylinders. The first activity, cutting rods, cuts long rods into the correct lengths for the cylinders. Next, the cut rods are welded to cut plates. The cutting rod activity is value-added because it (1) causes a change of state—uncut rods become cut rods, (2) no prior activity was supposed to create this change of state, and (3) it enables the welding activity to be performed. The value-added properties are easy to see for an operational activity like cutting rods, but what about a more general activity like supervising production workers? A managerial activity is specifically designed to manage other value-added activities—to ensure that they are performed in an efficient and timely manner. Supervision certainly satisfies the enabling condition. Is there a change in state? There are two ways of answering in the affirmative. First, supervising can be viewed as an enabling resource that is consumed by the operational activities that do produce a change of state. Thus, supervising is an input that is needed to help bring about the change of state expected for value-added operational activities. Second, it could be argued that the supervision brings order by changing the state from uncoordinated activities to coordinated activities. Once value-added activities are identified, we can define value-added costs. Value-added costs are the costs to perform value-added activities with perfect efficiency.

value-added costs

nonvalue-added activities

Nonvalue-added Activities Nonvalue-added activities are unnecessary; that is, all activities other than those that are absolutely essential to remain in business. A nonvalue-added activity can be identified by its failure to satisfy any one of the three previous defining conditions. Violation of the first two is the usual case for nonvalue-added activities. Inspecting cut rods (for correct length), for example, is a nonvalue-added activity. Inspection is a state-detection activity, not a state-changing activity (it tells us the state of the cut rod—whether it is the right length or not). Thus, it fails the first condition. Consider the activity of reworking goods or subassemblies. Rework is designed to bring a good from a nonconforming state to a conforming state. Thus, a change of state occurs. Yet the activity is nonvalue-added because it repeats work; it is doing something that should have been done by preceding activities (condition 2 is violated). Nonvalue-added costs are costs that are caused either by nonvalue-added activities or the inefficient performance of valued-added activities. Because of increased

nonvalue-added costs

In this picture, a worker at the Cooper Tire plant inspects a tire. Is quality control a value-added or nonvalue-added activity? How would you categorize it?

competition, many firms are attempting to eliminate nonvalue-added activities because they add unnecessary cost and impede performance; firms are also striving to optimize value-added activities. Thus, activity analysis attempts to identify and eventually eliminate all unnecessary activities and, simultaneously, increase the efficiency of necessary activities.

The theme of activity analysis is waste elimination. As waste is eliminated, costs are reduced. The cost reduction *follows* the elimination of waste. Note the value of managing the *causes* of the costs rather than the costs themselves. Managing costs may increase the efficiency of an activity—but if the activity is unnecessary, what does it matter if it's performed efficiently? An unnecessary activity is wasteful and should be eliminated. For example, moving raw materials and partially finished goods is often cited as a nonvalue-added activity. Installing an automated material-handling system may increase the efficiency of this activity, but changing to cellular manufacturing with on-site, just-in-time delivery of raw materials could virtually eliminate the activity. It's easy to see which is preferable.

Examples of Nonvalue-added Activities Reordering parts, expediting production, and rework because of defective parts are examples of nonvalue-added activities. Other examples include warranty work, handling customer complaints, and reporting defects. Nonvalue-added activities can exist anywhere in the organization. In the manufacturing operation, five major activities are often cited as wasteful and unnecessary:

1. *Scheduling* An activity that uses time and resources to determine when different products have access to processes (or when and how many setups must be done) and how much will be produced.
2. *Moving* An activity that uses time and resources to move raw materials, work in process, and finished goods from one department to another.
3. *Waiting* An activity in which raw materials or work in process use time and resources by waiting on the next process.
4. *Inspecting* An activity in which time and resources are spent ensuring that the product meets specifications.
5. *Storing* An activity that uses time and resources while a good or raw material is held in inventory.

None of these activities adds any value for the customer. (Note that inspection would not be necessary if the product is produced correctly the first time, and thus adds no value for the customer.) The challenge of activity analysis is to find ways to produce the good without using any of these activities.

Cost Reduction Continuous improvement carries with it the objective of cost reduction. Competitive conditions dictate that companies must deliver products the customers want, on time, and at the lowest possible cost. This means that an organization must continually strive for cost improvement. Activity analysis is the key to achieving cost reduction objectives. Activity analysis can reduce costs in four ways:[9]

1. Activity elimination
2. Activity selection
3. Activity reduction
4. Activity sharing

activity elimination

Activity elimination focuses on nonvalue-added activities. Once activities that fail to add value are identified, measures must be taken to rid the organization of these activities. For example, the activity of inspecting incoming parts seems necessary to ensure that the product using the parts functions according to specifications. Use of a bad part can produce a bad final product. Yet this activity is necessary only because of the poor-quality performance of the supplying firms. Selecting suppliers that are able to supply high-quality parts or who are willing to improve their quality performance to achieve this objective eventually will allow the elimination of incoming inspection. Cost reduction then follows.

activity selection

Activity selection involves choosing among different sets of activities that are caused by competing strategies. Different strategies cause different activities. Different product design strategies, for example, can require significantly different activities. Activities, in turn, cause costs. Each product design strategy has its own set of activities and associated costs. All other things equal, the lowest-cost design strategy should be chosen. Thus, activity selection can have a significant effect on cost reduction.

activity reduction

Activity reduction decreases the time and resources required by an activity. This approach to cost reduction should be primarily aimed at improving the efficiency of necessary activities or a short-term strategy for improving nonvalue-added activities until they can be eliminated. Setup activity is a necessary activity that is often cited as an example for which less time and fewer resources need to be used.

activity sharing

Activity sharing increases the efficiency of necessary activities by using economies of scale. Specifically, the quantity of the cost driver is increased without increasing the total cost of the activity itself. This lowers the per-unit cost of the cost driver and the amount of cost traceable to the products that consume the activity. For example, a new product can be designed to use components already being used by other products. By using existing components, the activities associated with these components already exist and the company avoids the creation of a whole new set of activities.

Activity Performance Measurement

Assessing how well activities (and processes) are performed is fundamental to management's efforts to improve profitability. Activity performance measures exist in both financial and nonfinancial forms. These measures are designed to assess how well an activity was performed and the results achieved. They are also designed to reveal if constant improvement is being realized. Measures of activity performance center on three major dimensions: (1) efficiency, (2) quality, and (3) time.

---

9. This classification and its discussion are based on Peter B. B. Turney, "How Activity-Based Costing Helps Reduce Cost," *Journal of Cost Management* (Winter 1991): 29–35.

Efficiency focuses on the relationship of activity inputs to activity outputs. For example, one way to improve activity efficiency is to produce the same activity output with lower cost for the inputs used. *Quality* is concerned with doing the activity right the first time it is performed. If the activity output is defective, then the activity may need to be repeated, causing unnecessary cost and reduction in efficiency. The *time* required to perform an activity is also critical. Longer times usually mean more resource consumption and less ability to respond to customer demands. Time measures of performance tend to be nonfinancial, whereas efficiency and quality measures are both financial and nonfinancial.

Financial measures of activity efficiency include (1) value- and nonvalue-added activity cost reports, (2) trends in activity cost reports, (3) benchmarking, (4) activity flexible budgeting, and (5) life-cycle budgeting. These measures are treated in the following section. Nonfinancial measures relating to the efficiency, quality, and time dimensions are also discussed in this chapter, in the final section. Additional financial measures pertaining to quality and efficiency are discussed in Chapter 11.

FINANCIAL MEASURES OF ACTIVITY PERFORMANCE

Objective 3

Describe the role of financial measures of activity performance.

Knowing how well we are currently performing an activity should disclose the potential for doing better. Financial measures of performance should also provide specific information about the dollar effects of activity performance changes. Thus, financial measures should indicate both potential and actual savings.

Value- and Nonvalue-added Cost Reporting

Reducing nonvalue-added costs is one way to increase activity efficiency. A company's accounting system should distinguish between value-added costs and nonvalue-added costs because improving activity performance requires eliminating nonvalue-added activities and optimizing value-added activities. Thus, a firm should identify and formally report the value-added and nonvalue-added costs of each activity. Highlighting nonvalue-added costs reveals the magnitude of the waste the company is currently experiencing, thus providing some information about the potential for improvement. This encourages managers to place more emphasis on controlling nonvalue-added activities. Progress can then be assessed by preparing trend and cost reduction reports. Tracking these costs over time permits managers to assess the effectiveness of their activity-management programs.

Knowing the amount of costs saved is important for strategic purposes. For example, if an activity is eliminated, then the costs saved should be traceable to individual products. These savings can produce price reductions for customers, making the firm more competitive. Changing the pricing strategy, however, requires knowledge of the cost reductions created by activity analysis. A cost-reporting system, therefore, is an important ingredient in an activity-based responsibility accounting system.

Value-added costs are the only costs that an organization should incur. The value-added standard calls for the complete elimination of nonvalue-added activities; for these activities the optimal output is zero with zero cost. The value-added standard also calls for the complete elimination of the inefficiency of activities that are necessary but inefficiently carried out. Thus, value-added activities also have an optimal output level. A **value-added standard** value-added standard, therefore, identifies the optimal activity output. Identifying the optimal activity output requires activity output measurement.

Setting value-added standards does not mean that they will be (or should be) achieved immediately. The idea of continuous improvement is to move toward the ideal, not to achieve it immediately. Workers (teams) can be rewarded for improvement. Moreover, nonfinancial operational performance measures can be used to supplement and support the goal of eliminating nonvalue-added costs (these are discussed later in the chapter). Finally, measuring the efficiency of individual workers and supervisors is not the way to eliminate nonvalue-added activities. Remember, activities cut across departmental boundaries and are part of processes. Focusing on activities and providing incentives to improve processes is a more productive approach. Improving the process should lead to improved results.

By comparing actual activity costs with value-added activity costs, management can assess the level of nonproductive activity (activity inefficiency) and assess the potential for improvement. Fundamental to identifying and calculating value- and nonvalue-added costs is the identification of output measures for each activity. Once output measures are identified, then value-added standard quantities (SQ) for each activity can be defined. Value-added costs can be computed by multiplying the value-added standard quantities by the price standard (SP). Nonvalue-added costs can be calculated as the difference between the actual level of the activity's output (AQ) and the value-added level, multiplied by the unit standard cost. These formulas are presented in Exhibit 10-5. Some further explanation is needed. For resources acquired as needed, AQ is the actual quantity of activity used.

For resources acquired in advance of usage, AQ represents the actual quantity of activity capacity acquired, as measured by the activity's practical capacity. This definition of AQ allows the computation of nonvalue-added costs for both variable and fixed activity costs. For fixed activity costs, SP is the budgeted activity costs divided by AQ, where AQ is practical activity capacity.

To illustrate the power of these concepts, let's focus on the following four production activities for a JIT firm: material usage, rework of defective products, setups, and incoming inspections. Of the four activities, two are viewed as necessary—material usage and setups; inspection and rework are unnecessary. Furthermore, assume that the first three activities acquire resources as needed; the last, incoming inspecting capacity, is acquired in advance of usage (salaries are budgeted at $60,000 for two inspectors). The following data pertain to the four activities:

Activity	Activity Driver	SQ	AQ	SP
Material usage	Pounds	40,000	44,000	$40.00
Rework	Labor hours	0	10,000	9.00
Setups	Setup time	0	6,000	60.00
Inspection	Inspection hours	0	4,000	15.00

Notice that the value-added standards (SQ) for rework and inspection call for their elimination; the value-added standard for setups calls for a zero setup time. Ideally, there should be no defective products; by improving quality, changing production processes, and so on, inspection can eventually be eliminated. Setups are necessary, but in a JIT environment, efforts are made to drive setup times to zero.

Exhibit 10-6 classifies the costs for the four activities as value-added or nonvalue-added. For simplicity, and to show the relationship to actual costs, the actual price per unit of the cost driver is assumed to be equal to the standard price. In this case, the

Exhibit
Computational Formulas for Value- and Nonvalue-added Costs

Value-added costs = $SQ \times SP$
Nonvalue-added costs = $(AQ - SQ)SP$

where SQ = The value-added output level for an activity
           SP = The standard price per unit of activity output measure
           AQ = The actual quantity of activity output used (if resources are supplied as needed)
or AQ = The actual quantity of activity capacity acquired (if resources are supplied in advance of usage)

Exhibit
Value- and Nonvalue-
added Cost Report For
the Year Ended
December 31, 1998

Activity	Costs		
	Value Added	Nonvalue Added	Actual
Material usage	$1,600,000	$160,000	$1,760,000
Rework	0	90,000	90,000
Setups	0	360,000	360,000
Inspection	0	60,000	60,000
Total	$1,600,000	$670,000	$2,270,000

value-added cost plus the nonvalue-added cost equals actual cost. Normally, it might be necessary to add a price variance column. This possibility is illustrated later in this section when flexible budgeting is discussed (pp. 401–406).

The cost report in Exhibit 10-6 allows managers to see the nonvalue-added costs; as a consequence, it emphasizes the opportunity for improvement. By decreasing scrap and waste, management can reduce its material cost. By training cell workers, and improving labor skill, management can reduce rework. Reducing setup time and implementing a supplier evaluation program are actions that can be taken to improve performance for the setup and inspection activities.

Thus, reporting value- and nonvalue-added costs at a point in time may trigger actions to manage activities more effectively. Seeing the amount of waste may induce managers to search for ways to reduce, select, share, and eliminate activities to bring about cost reductions. Reporting these costs may also help managers improve planning, budgeting, and pricing decisions. For example, lowering the selling price to meet a competitor's price may be seen as possible if a manager can see the potential for reducing nonvalue-added costs to absorb the effect of the price reduction.

Drivers and Behavioral Effects Activity output measures are needed to compute and track nonvalue-added costs. Reducing nonvalue-added activity should produce a reduction in the demand for the activity and, therefore, a reduction in the activity output measures. If a team's performance is affected by their ability to reduce nonvalue-added costs, then the selection of activity drivers (as output measures), and how they are used, can affect behavior. For example, if the output measure for setup costs is chosen as setup time, an incentive is created for workers to reduce setup time. Since the value-added standard for setup costs calls for their complete elimination, then the incentive to drive setup time to zero is compatible with the company's objectives, and the induced behavior is beneficial.

Suppose, however, that the objective is to reduce the number of unique parts a company processes, thus simplifying activities such as incoming inspection, preparation of bills of materials, and vendor selection.[10] If the costs of these activities are assigned to products based on the number of parts, the incentive created is to reduce the number of parts in a product. While this behavior may be desirable to a point, it can also have negative consequences. Design teams may actually reduce the marketability of the product by reducing the number of parts too greatly and adversely affecting its functionality.

This type of behavior can be discouraged by the proper use of standards. First, if the number of parts truly drives the costs of incoming inspection, preparation of bills of materials, and vendor selection, then a budgeted cost per unit of activity driver can be computed (that is, a standard price per unit). Next, the value-added standard number of parts for each product should be identified (the standard quantity). The value-added costs are then simply the product of the standard price and standard quantity

---

10. This example is based on the discussion concerning behavioral effects of cost drivers found in Robin Cooper, "The Rise of Activity-Based Costing—Part Three: How Many Cost Drivers Do You Need, and How Do You Select Them?" *Journal of Cost Management for the Manufacturing Industry* (Winter 1989): 34–46.

$(SP \times SQ)$. As before, nonvalue-added costs are the difference between the actual parts used and the standard parts allowed, multiplied by the standard price $[(AQ - SQ)SP]$.

Designers should be encouraged to reduce the nonvalue-added costs by designing to reach the value-added standard number of parts, SQ. The absence of any standard can lead designers to reduce parts in order to reduce costs, without any sense of direction or purpose. However, by identifying, before the fact, the number of parts each product should have, using the number of parts as an activity driver can encourage reduction of only nonvalue-added costs. The standard has provided a concrete objective and defined the kind of behavior that the incentive allows.

Trend Reporting

As managers take actions to reduce, eliminate, select, and share activities, do the cost reductions follow as expected? One way to answer this question is to compare the costs for each activity over time. The goal is activity improvement as measured by cost reduction, and so we should see a decline in nonvalue-added costs from one period to the next—provided the activity analysis is effective. Assume, for example, that at the beginning of 1998, four major activity-management decisions were implemented: the use of statistical process control, product redesign, a labor training program for a new assembly process, and a supplier evaluation program. How effective were these decisions? Did a cost reduction occur as expected? Exhibit 10-7 provides a cost report that compares the nonvalue-added costs of 1998 with those that occurred in 1997. The 1998 costs are assumed but would be computed the same way as shown for 1997. We assume that SQ is the same for both years. Comparing 1998 nonvalue-added costs directly with those in 1997 requires SQ to be the same for both years. If SQ changes, prior-year nonvalue-added costs are adjusted by simply assuming the same percentage deviation from standard in the current year as was realized in the prior year.

The trend report reveals that cost reductions followed, as expected. More than half of the nonvalue-added costs have been eliminated. There is still ample room for improvement, but activity improvement so far has been successful. As a note of interest, comparison of the actual costs of the two periods would have revealed the same reduction. Reporting nonvalue-added costs, however, not only reveals the reduction but also provides managers with information on how much potential for cost reduction remains. There is an important qualification, however. Value-added standards, like other standards, are not cast in stone. New technology, new designs, and other innovations can change the nature of activities performed. Value-added activities can be converted to nonvalue-added activities and value-added levels can change as well. Thus, as new ways for improvement surface, value-added standards can change. Managers should not become content but should continually seek higher levels of efficiency.

The Role of Interim (Currently Attainable) Standards If a company is emphasizing the reduction of nonvalue-added costs, interim standards that identify the amount of improvement planned for the coming year can be set. The planned improvement is

10-7 ....

Exhibit
Trend Report: Nonvalue-added Costs

Activity	Nonvalue-added Costs		
	1997	1998	Change
Material usage	$160,000	$100,000	$ 60,000 F
Rework	90,000	50,000	40,000 F
Setups	360,000	160,000	200,000 F
Inspection*	60,000	30,000	30,000 F
Total	$670,000	$340,000	$330,000 F

*During the year, the supplier evaluation program decreased the number of defective parts to the point where one inspector was reassigned to an open position in the assembly department.

assumed to be attainable, and thus defines a form of currently attainable standards. Comparing actual costs with the currently attainable standards provides a measure of how well the current year's goals for improvement have been met.

For example, assume that a medical products division inspects every unit produced of a particular surgical instrument. The unit-level, value-added standard for this product calls for zero inspection hours per unit and a value-added inspection cost of $0 per unit. Assume that in the prior year, the company used 15 minutes to inspect each instrument at a cost of $15 per inspection hour. Thus, the actual inspection cost per unit is $3.75 ($15 × $\frac{1}{4}$ hr). This is also the nonvalue-added cost. For the coming year, the company is installing a new production process that is expected to increase the precision with which the instrument is produced. These changes are expected to reduce the inspection time from 15 minutes to 10 minutes. Thus, the planned cost reduction is $1.25 per unit. The interim or currently attainable standard is defined as 10 minutes per unit. The currently attainable standard cost of inspection per unit is $2.50, the actual prior year cost less the targeted reduction ($3.75 − $1.25). For the following year, additional improvements would be sought and a new currently attainable standard defined. For example, the company is planning on installing a statistical process control system that will increase the reliability of the process even more so that inspection time can be further reduced. This will then produce a different standard from the one for the current year. Changing the standard from year to year to reflect new improvement targets is the key difference between this type of currently attainable standard and the type described in Chapter 9, "Standard Costing."

Benchmarking

benchmarking

Another approach to standard setting that is used to help identify opportunities for activity improvement is called *benchmarking*. Benchmarking uses best practices as the standard for evaluating activity performance. Within an organization, different units (for example, different plant sites) that perform the same activities are compared. The unit with the best performance for a given activity sets the standard. Other units then have a target to meet or exceed. Furthermore, the best practices unit can share information with other units on how they have achieved their superior results. For this process to work, it is necessary to ensure that activity definitions and activity output measures are consistent across units. Such things as activity rates, the cost per unit of activity output, or the amount of activity output per unit of process output can be used to rank activity performance and identify the best performer.

For example, assume the output of the purchasing activity is measured by the number of purchase orders. Suppose further that the cost of the purchasing activity for one plant is $90,000 and activity output is 4,500 purchase orders. Dividing the cost of the purchasing activity by the number of purchase orders prepared gives a unit cost of $20 per order. Now if the best unit cost is $15 per purchase order, then the plant with the $20 per-unit cost knows it has the ability to improve activity efficiency by at least $5 per unit. By studying the purchasing practices of the best plant, activity efficiency should increase.

The objective of this approach is to become the best at performing activities and processes. Ideally, benchmarking should involve comparisons with competitors or other industries. However, it is often difficult to obtain the necessary data for external benchmarking to work. In some cases, it may be possible to study best practices of noncompetitors. There are certain activities and processes that are common to all organizations. If superior external best practices can be identified, then they can be used as standards to motivate internal improvements.

Activity Flexible Budgeting

activity flexible budgeting

The ability to identify changes in activity costs as the activity output measure changes allows managers to more carefully plan and monitor activity improvements. Activity flexible budgeting allows the prediction of what activity costs will be as activity usage changes. Variance analysis within this activity framework allows managers to break activity costs into value-added and nonvalue-added components, distinguish between price effects and volume effects, and report the cost of used and unused activity capacity. Also, the ability to compute costs for different activity usage levels makes it possible to compute the expected cost for interim activity standards. Finally, traditional budgetary performance reporting can be markedly improved through the use of activity flexible budgets.

In a traditional setting, budgeted costs for the actual level of activity are obtained by assuming that all costs are driven by a single unit-based driver (usually direct labor hours). A cost formula is developed for each cost item as a function of direct labor hours. This formula is then used to predict what the costs ought to be for any level of activity. Exhibit 10-8 illustrates a traditional flexible budget. If, however, costs vary with respect to more than one driver, and the drivers are not highly correlated with direct labor hours, then the predicted activity costs can be misleading.

The solution, of course, is to build flexible budget formulas for more than one driver. To simplify the presentation of a multiple-driver flexible budget, homogeneous activities are grouped together and budgets are developed for each homogeneous set using a single driver. Cost estimation procedures (high-low method, the method of least squares, and so on) can be used to estimate the cost formulas for each activity. In principle, the variable-cost component for each activity should correspond to resources acquired as needed and the fixed-cost component should correspond to resources acquired in advance of usage. This multiple-formula approach allows managers to predict more accurately what costs ought to be for different levels of activity usage, as measured by the activity output measure. These costs can then be compared with the actual costs to help assess budgetary performance. Exhibit 10-9 illustrates an activity flexible budget. Notice that the budgeted amounts for materials, labor, and supplies are the same as those reported in Exhibit 10-8; they use the same activity output measure. The budgeted amounts for the other items differ significantly from the traditional amounts because the activity output measures differ.

Assume that the first level of drivers for Exhibit 10-9 corresponds to the actual activity usage levels. Exhibit 10-10 compares the budgeted costs for the actual activity usage levels with the actual costs. One item is on target, and the other seven items are mixed. The net outcome is a favorable variance of $18,000.

The performance report in Exhibit 10-10 compares total budgeted costs for the actual level of activity with the total actual costs for each activity. It is also possible to compare the actual fixed activity costs with the budgeted fixed activity costs and the actual variable activity costs with the budgeted variable costs. For example, assume that the actual fixed inspection costs are $82,000 (due to a midyear salary adjustment, reflecting a more favorable union agreement than anticipated) and that the actual vari-

<table>
<tr><th rowspan="2"></th><th colspan="2">Formula</th><th colspan="2">Direct Labor Hours</th></tr>
<tr><th>Fixed</th><th>Variable</th><th>10,000</th><th>20,000</th></tr>
<tr><td>Direct materials</td><td>—</td><td>$10</td><td>$100,000</td><td>$200,000</td></tr>
<tr><td>Direct labor</td><td>—</td><td>8</td><td>80,000</td><td>160,000</td></tr>
<tr><td>Supplies</td><td>—</td><td>2</td><td>20,000</td><td>40,000</td></tr>
<tr><td>Maintenance</td><td>$ 20,000</td><td>3</td><td>50,000</td><td>80,000</td></tr>
<tr><td>Power</td><td>15,000</td><td>1</td><td>25,000</td><td>35,000</td></tr>
<tr><td>Inspections</td><td>120,000</td><td>—</td><td>120,000</td><td>120,000</td></tr>
<tr><td>Setups</td><td>16,000</td><td>—</td><td>16,000</td><td>16,000</td></tr>
<tr><td>Receiving</td><td>22,000</td><td>—</td><td>22,000</td><td>22,000</td></tr>
<tr><td>Total</td><td>$193,000</td><td>$24</td><td>$433,000</td><td>$673,000</td></tr>
</table>

10-8

Exhibit
Traditional Flexible Budget

10-9

Exhibit
Activity Flexible Budget

	Formula		Level of Activity	
	Fixed	**Variable**	**Driver: Direct Labor Hours**	
			10,000	**20,000**
Direct materials	$ —	$10	$100,000	$200,000
Direct labor	—	8	80,000	160,000
Supplies	—	2	20,000	40,000
Subtotal	$ 0	$20	$200,000	$400,000

	Fixed	**Variable**	**Driver: Machine Hours**	
			8,000	**16,000**
Maintenance	$20,000	$5.50	$64,000	$108,000
Power	15,000	2.00	31,000	47,000
Subtotal	$35,000	$7.50	$95,000	$155,000

	Fixed	**Variable**	**Driver: Number of Setups**	
			25	**30**
Setups	—	$ 800	$ 20,000	$ 24,000
Inspections	$80,000	2,100	132,500	143,000
Subtotal	$80,000	$2,900	$152,500	$167,000

	Fixed	**Variable**	**Driver: Number of Orders**	
			120	**150**
Receiving	$6,000	$200	$ 30,000	$ 36,000
Total			$477,500	$758,000

able inspection costs are $43,500. The variable and fixed budget variances for the inspection activity are computed as follows:

Activity	Actual Cost	Budgeted Cost	Variance
Inspection			
Fixed	$ 82,000	$ 80,000	$2,000 U
Variable	43,500	52,500	9,000 F
Total	$125,500	$132,500	$7,000 F

10-10

Exhibit
Activity-based
Performance Report*

	Actual Costs	**Budgeted Costs**	**Budget Variance**
Direct materials	$101,000	$100,000	$ 1,000 U
Direct labor	80,000	80,000	—
Supplies	23,500	20,000	3,500 U
Maintenance	55,000	64,000	9,000 F
Power	29,000	31,000	2,000 F
Setups	21,500	20,000	1,500 U
Inspections	125,500	132,500	7,000 F
Receiving	24,000	30,000	6,000 F
Total	$459,500	$477,500	$18,000 F

*Actual levels of cost drivers: 10,000 direct labor hours, 8,000 machine hours, 25 setups, 120 receiving orders

Breaking each variance into fixed and variable components provides more insight into the source of the variation in planned and actual expenditures.

These total variances, however, do not tell the whole story. Comparing budgeted activity costs for the actual level of activity with actual activity costs may have some value, but it does not reveal opportunities for improvement. Nor does it reveal what improvement has occurred. Managers need to know where money is being wasted and where opportunities for improvement exist. If activity flexible budgeting is to be a useful tool in the advanced manufacturing environment, then there must be a connection to the objective of continuous improvement.[11] The connection is made by classifying activities within the budget as value-added and nonvalue-added and by identifying the standard quantities of cost driver associated with each activity. Given this information, more detailed analyses can be made that provide managers with valuable information for planning and control.

To illustrate how fixed activity variance analysis can be expanded, we will continue to focus on inspection cost. Similar analyses would be carried out for the fixed costs of the other activities in the budget. Assume the $80,000 of budgeted fixed inspection costs represents the salaries of two inspectors, where each is paid $40,000. Thus, the $80,000 is the expected cost of resources *acquired in advance of usage* for the inspection activity. Suppose that each inspector is capable of efficiently carrying out inspections of 20 batches. The *practical activity capacity* is 40 batches and the *fixed activity rate* (SP) is $2,000 per batch ($\frac{\$80,000}{40}$).[12]

Spending and Volume Variances   Exhibit 10-11, Part A, illustrates how the total flexible fixed budget variance is broken down using two levels of activity: the actual activity level acquired (practical capacity, AQ) and the value-added standard quantity of activity that should be used (SQ). We assume that inspection is a nonvalue-added activity that can be eliminated eventually; thus, SQ = 0 is the value-added standard. The volume variance in this framework has a useful economic interpretation: it is the *nonvalue-added cost* of the inspection activity. The spending variance is a *price* variance.

Unused Capacity Variance   The volume variance measures the amount of improvement that is possible through analysis and management of activities. However, since the supply of the activity in question (inspections) must be acquired in blocks (one inspector at a time), it is also important to measure the demand for the activity (actual usage). When supply exceeds demand by a large enough quantity, management can take action to reduce the quantity of the activity performed. Thus, the *unused capacity variance*, the difference between activity availability and activity usage, is important information that should be provided to management. The calculation of this variance is illustrated in Exhibit 10-11, Part B. Notice that the unused capacity is 15 batches valued at $30,000. Assume that this unused capacity exists because management has been engaged in a quality-improvement program that has reduced the need to inspect certain batches of products. This difference between the supply of the inspection resources and their usage should impact future spending plans (reduction of a nonvalue-added activity is labeled as favorable).

For example, we know that the supply of inspection resources is greater than its usage. Furthermore, because of the quality-improvement program, we can expect this difference to persist and even become greater (with the ultimate goal of reducing the

---

11. Much of the material in this section is based on the following two papers: (1) Y. T. Mak and Melvin L. Roush, "Flexible Budgeting and Variance Analysis in an ABC Environment," *Accounting Horizons* (June 1994): 93–103. This paper argues that the basic flexible budgeting and variance analysis frameworks remain useful for cost control and performance evaluation in an ABC setting. (2) Robin C. Cooper and Robert Kaplan, "Activity-Based Systems: Measuring the Costs of Resource Usage," *Accounting Horizons* (September 1992): 1–13. This paper argues that flexible budgeting in an ABC setting for nonunit-level activities is unnecessary. Our approach basically agrees with the Mak and Roush position; however, we must also confess that our fixed activity cost variance analysis reflects the insights provided by the Cooper and Kaplan paper. These insights mesh very well with the activity-based flexible budgeting framework.

12. We assume that each batch requires a setup; therefore, the number of setups equals the number of batches.

Exhibit
Variance Analysis of Fixed
Activity Costs

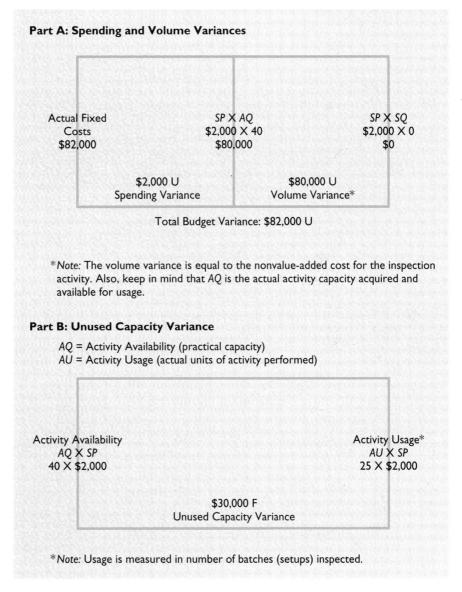

Part A: Spending and Volume Variances

Actual Fixed	SP X AQ	SP X SQ
Costs	$2,000 X 40	$2,000 X 0
$82,000	$80,000	$0

$2,000 U
Spending Variance

$80,000 U
Volume Variance*

Total Budget Variance: $82,000 U

*Note: The volume variance is equal to the nonvalue-added cost for the inspection activity. Also, keep in mind that AQ is the actual activity capacity acquired and available for usage.

Part B: Unused Capacity Variance

AQ = Activity Availability (practical capacity)
AU = Activity Usage (actual units of activity performed)

Activity Availability	Activity Usage*
AQ X SP	AU X SP
40 X $2,000	25 X $2,000

$30,000 F
Unused Capacity Variance

*Note: Usage is measured in number of batches (setups) inspected.

cost of inspection activity to zero). Management now must be willing to exploit the unused capacity they have created. Essentially, activity availability can be reduced and, thus, the spending on inspection can be decreased. There are several options that a manager can use to achieve this outcome. When inspection demand is reduced by five more batches, the company will need only one full-time inspector. The extra inspector could be permanently reassigned to an activity where resources are in short supply. (Even now 75 percent of the inspector's time could be reassigned to other activities that are short in resources.) If reassignment is not feasible, the company should lay off the extra inspector.

This example illustrates an important feature of activity improvement. Activity improvement can create unused capacity, but managers must be willing and able to make the tough decisions to reduce resource spending on the redundant activities to gain the potential profit increase. Profits can be increased by reducing resource spending or by transferring the resources to other activities that will generate more revenues.

Variable Activity Variances: Detailed Analysis We continue using the inspection activity to analyze the variable activity variances. Assume that the budgeted $52,500 represents the cost of a chemical that must be used in the inspection process. This resource is acquired as needed, and, therefore, is a variable activity cost. The budget of $52,500 is for 25 actual setups; thus, the *variable activity rate* is $\frac{\$52,500}{25 \text{ setups}} = \$2,100$ per setup (the rate is also given in Exhibit 10-9). The actual rate (AP) is the actual cost divided by the number of setups: $\frac{\$43,500}{25 \text{ setups}} = \$1,740$ per setup.

The variable activity budget variance can be decomposed into two variances: the variable spending variance and the variable efficiency variance. The variable spending variance is a *price* variance—it can only occur if the amount paid for each unit of resource is greater than the expected price. The variable efficiency variance is the *non-value-added cost* of performing the inspection activity. Exhibit 10-12 illustrates the computation of the two variances.

There is no unused capacity variance for a variable activity cost. Since the resource is acquired as needed, the actual usage always equals the actual amount of the activity acquired. This makes the analysis simpler for variable activity costs.

Life-Cycle Cost Budgeting

product life cycle
life-cycle costs

The product design stage can have a significant effect on costs. In fact, 90 percent or more of the costs associated with a product are committed during the development stage of the product's life cycle.[13] Product life cycle is simply the time a product exists, from conception to abandonment. Life-cycle costs are all the costs associated with the product for its entire life cycle. They include development (planning, design, and testing), production (conversion activities), and logistics support (advertising, distribution, warranty, and so on). The product life cycle and the associated cost commitment curve are illustrated in Exhibit 10-13.[14]

whole-life cost

Because total customer satisfaction has become a vital issue in the new business setting, whole-life cost has emerged as the central focus of life-cycle cost management. Whole-life cost is the life-cycle cost of a product plus postpurchase costs that consumers

---

13. John P. Campi, "Corporate Mindset: Strategic Advantage or Fatal Vision," *Journal of Cost Management* (Spring 1991): 53–57; Callie Berliner and James A. Brimson (eds.), *Cost Management for Today's Advanced Manufacturing* (Boston: Harvard Business School Press, 1988). The section on life-cycle costing is based on these two sources, with particular emphasis on the second source.

14. Life cycle can be viewed from a production or marketing perspective. We have adopted a production perspective, with stages of the life cycle defined by changes in the types of activities performed: development, production, and logistical. The marketing perspective, on the other hand, focuses on sales demand and has the following four stages: start-up, growth, maturity, and decline.

10-12

Exhibit
Variance Analysis for
Variable Activity Costs

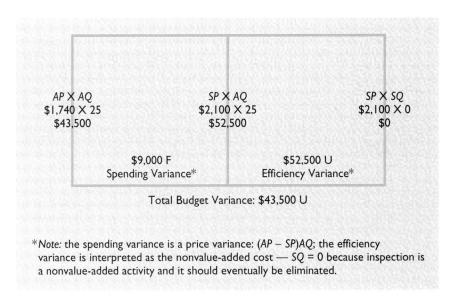

AP X AQ	SP X AQ	SP X SQ
$1,740 X 25	$2,100 X 25	$2,100 X 0
$43,500	$52,500	$0

$9,000 F
Spending Variance*

$52,500 U
Efficiency Variance*

Total Budget Variance: $43,500 U

*Note: the spending variance is a price variance: (AP − SP)AQ; the efficiency
variance is interpreted as the nonvalue-added cost — SQ = 0 because inspection is
a nonvalue-added activity and it should eventually be eliminated.

Exhibit

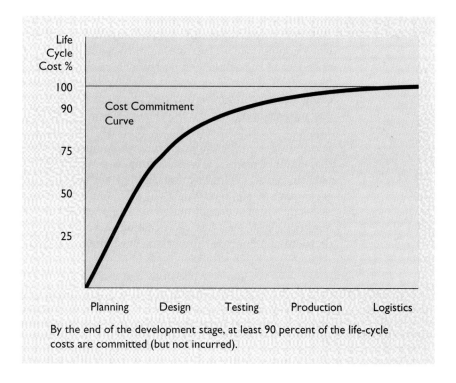

By the end of the development stage, at least 90 percent of the life-cycle costs are committed (but not incurred).

incur, including operation, support, maintenance, and disposal.[15] Since the costs a purchaser incurs after buying a product can be a significant percentage of whole-life costs and, thus, an important consideration in the purchase decision, managing activities so that whole-life costs are reduced can provide an important competitive advantage. Notice that cost reduction not cost control is the emphasis. Moreover, cost reduction is achieved by judicious analysis and management of activities. Whole-life costing emphasizes management of the entire value chain. The value chain is the set of activities required to design, develop, produce, market, and service a product (or service). Thus, **life-cycle cost management** focuses on managing value-chain activities so that a long-term competitive advantage is created. To achieve this goal, managers must balance a product's whole-life cost, method of delivery, innovativeness, and various product attributes including performance, features offered, reliability, conformance, durability, aesthetics, and perceived quality.

life-cycle cost management

Cost Reduction Since 90 percent or more of a product's costs are committed during the development stage, it makes sense to emphasize management of activities during this phase of a product's existence. Studies have shown that every dollar spent on premanufacturing activities saves $8 to $10 on manufacturing and postmanufacturing activities.[16] The real opportunities for cost reduction occur before manufacturing begins! Managers need to invest more in premanufacturing assets and dedicate more resources to activities in the early phases of the product life cycle so that overall whole-life costs can be reduced.

Yet, in spite of this observation, the traditional emphasis has been on controlling costs during the production stage (when much less can be done to influence them).

15. It can be argued that whole-life cost is an alternative definition of life-cycle cost—one that includes the customer's perspective as well as the production point of view. For an excellent treatment of life-cycle costing, see Michael D. Shields and S. Mark Young, "Managing Product Life Cycle Costs: An Organizational Model," *Journal of Cost Management* (Fall 1991): 39–52. Many of the concepts presented in this section are based on this article.
16. Mark D. Shields and S. Mark Young, "Managing Product Life Cycle Costs: An Organizational Model"; R. L. Engwall, "Cost Management Systems for Defense Contractors," *Cost Accounting for the 90s, Responding to Technological Change* (Montvale, N.J., National Association of Accountants, 1988).

Furthermore, product cost has been narrowly defined as production costs; development and logistics costs have been treated as period costs and have been virtually ignored when computing product profitability. Additionally, little attention has been given to the effect of the customer's postpurchase costs. While this practice may be acceptable for external reporting, it is not acceptable for managerial product costing. In the highly competitive environment of today, world-class competitors need comprehensive product cost information.

Whole-Life Product Cost From a whole-life point of view, product cost is made up of four major elements: (1) nonrecurring costs (planning, designing, and testing), (2) manufacturing costs, (3) logistic costs, and (4) the customer's postpurchase costs. Measuring, accumulating, and reporting all of a product's whole-life costs allow managers to better assess the effectiveness of life-cycle planning and build more effective and sophisticated marketing strategies. Life-cycle costing also increases their ability to make good pricing decisions and improve the assessment of product profitability.

target cost

Role of Target Costing Life-cycle cost management emphasizes cost reduction, not cost control. Thus, target costing becomes a particularly useful tool for establishing cost reduction goals. A target cost is the difference between the sales price needed to capture a predetermined market share and the desired per-unit profit. If the target cost is less than what is currently achievable, then management budgets cost reductions that move the actual cost toward the target cost. Progress is measured by comparing actual costs with target costs.

For example, suppose that the current sales price of a product is $10 and that the market share is 12 percent. The marketing manager indicates that reducing the sales price to $8.50 will increase market share from 12 percent to 20 percent. The president of the company indicates that the desired per-unit profit is $2. The target cost is computed as follows:

$$\text{Target cost} = \$8.50 - \$2.00 = \$6.50$$

Suppose that it currently costs $7.75 per unit to produce the product. Thus, the cost reduction needed to achieve the target cost and desired profit is $1.25 ($7.75 − $6.50). To realize the target cost, management must build in cost reductions by judicious activity analysis and management. The idea is to achieve the reduction needed over time. Variances are computed periodically by comparing actual costs with targeted costs.

Target costs are a type of currently attainable standard. But they are conceptually different from the modified standards discussed earlier. What makes them different is the motivating force. The initial modified definition of currently attainable standards was motivated by the objective of moving toward a value-added standard generated internally by industrial engineers and production managers. Target costs, on the other hand, are externally driven, generated by an analysis of markets and competitors. Toyota, for example, calculates the lifetime target profit for a new car model by multiplying a target profit ratio times the target sales. They then calculate the estimated profit by subtracting the estimated costs from target sales. Usually, (at this point), target profit is greater than estimated profit. The cost reduction goal is defined by the difference between the target profit and the estimated profit. Toyota then searches for cost reduction opportunities through better design of the new model. Toyota's management recognizes that more opportunities exist for cost reduction during product planning than in actual development and production.[17]

Short Life Cycles Although life-cycle cost management is important for all manufacturing firms, it is particularly important for firms that have products with short life

---

17. For a complete description of Toyota's approach, see Takao Tanaka, "Target Costing at Toyota," *Journal of Cost Management* (Spring 1993): 4–11.

cycles. Products must recover all life-cycle costs and provide an acceptable profit. If a firm's products have long life cycles, profit performance can be increased by such actions as redesigning, changing prices, cost reduction, and altering the product mix. In contrast, firms that have products with short life cycles usually do not have time to react in this way and so their approach must be proactive. Thus, for short life cycles, good life-cycle planning is critical and prices must be set properly to recover all the life-cycle costs and provide a good return. Activity-based costing can be used to encourage good life-cycle planning. By careful selection of cost drivers, design engineers can be motivated to choose cost-minimizing designs.[18] (This is a proactive strategy—how this can be done was discussed in the "Drivers and Behavioral Effects" section.)

Life-Cycle Costing: An Example Murphy Company produces electronic products that typically have about a 27-month life cycle. At the beginning of the last quarter of 1996, a new component was proposed. Design engineering believed that the product would be ready to produce by the beginning of 1997. To produce this and other similar products, resistors had to be inserted into a circuit board. Management had discovered that the cost of the circuit board was driven by the number of insertions. Knowing this, design engineering produced the new component using fewer insertions than the products in the past had employed.

The budgeted costs and profits for the product over its two-year life cycle are illustrated in Exhibit 10-14. Notice that the life-cycle unit cost is $10 compared with the conventional definition of $6 (which includes only the production costs) and the whole-life cost of $12. To be viable, of course, the product must cover all of its life-cycle costs and produce an acceptable profit. The $15 price was set with this objective in mind.

18. Robin Cooper and Peter B. B. Turney, "Internally Focused Activity-Based Cost Systems," in *Measures for Manufacturing Excellence*, ed. Robert S. Kaplan (Boston: Harvard Business School Press, 1990), 291–305.

10-14

Exhibit
Life-Cycle Costing:
Budgeted Costs and
Income

Unit Cost and Price Information	
Unit production cost	$ 6
Unit life-cycle cost	10
Unit whole-life cost	12
Budgeted unit selling price	15

| Item | Budgeted Costs | | | |
	1996	1997	1998	Item Total
Development costs	$200,000	—	—	$ 200,000
Production costs	—	$240,000	$360,000	600,000
Logistics costs	—	80,000	120,000	200,000
Annual subtotal	$200,000	$320,000	$480,000	$1,000,000
Postpurchase costs*	—	80,000	120,000	200,000
Annual total	$200,000	$400,000	$600,000	$1,200,000
Units produced		40,000	60,000	

| Budgeted Product Income Statements | | | | |
Year	Revenues	Costs	Annual Income	Cumulative Income
1996	—	$(200,000)	$(200,000)	$(200,000)
1997	$600,000	(320,000)	280,000	80,000
1998	900,000	(480,000)	420,000	500,000

*Note: the postpurchase costs are costs incurred by the customer and so would not be included in the budgeted income statements.

Focusing only on the $6 cost could have led to a suboptimal pricing decision. Changing the focus requires managers to move away from the traditional, financially driven definition of product cost. Conventional cost systems do not directly identify development costs with the product being developed. The whole-life cost provides even more information—information that could prove vital for the company's life-cycle strategy. For example, if competitors sell a similar product for the same price but with postpurchase costs of only $1 per unit, the company could be at a competitive disadvantage. Given this information, actions can be considered that can eliminate the disadvantage (for example, redesigning the product to lower the postpurchase costs).

Feedback on the effectiveness of life-cycle planning is also helpful. This information can help future new product planning as well as be useful for assessing how design decisions affect operational and support costs. Comparing actual costs with the budgeted costs can provide useful insights. Exhibit 10-15 illustrates a simple life-cycle cost performance report. As can be seen, production costs were greater than expected. Investigation revealed that costs are driven by total number of insertions, not just insertions of resistors. Further analysis also revealed that by reducing the total number of insertions, postpurchase costs could be reduced. Thus, future design work on similar products can benefit by the assessment.

NONFINANCIAL MEASURES OF ACTIVITY PERFORMANCE

Objective 4

Discuss the role of nonfinancial measures of performance.

Nonfinancial measures of performance play a key role in a contemporary responsibility accounting system. In the advanced environment, operational control becomes more before the fact than after the fact. In a traditional environment, actual results are periodically compared with standards. While the comparison may be made as often as weekly or monthly, there is often a delay from the time actual performance is achieved and when it is reported to managers. Continuous improvement requires more timely evaluation. To achieve this change in orientation, worker involvement in the evaluation of activity performance must increase.

operational measures

Operational measures are the key to increasing worker involvement. Operational measures concern physical measures of activity performance. Workers relate more readily to operational measures, and operational results can be reported on a real-time, rather than a delayed, basis. Immediate feedback allows a quicker reaction time and increases in efficiency. Operational measures should relate to the factors considered essential to successful competition. The measures should also motivate and support the overall objective of continuous improvement. Furthermore, the use of the measures should translate into improved financial results. Finally, operational measures should relate to the three activity performance dimensions: (1) efficiency, (2) quality, and (3) time.

Efficiency Measures

Productivity measures how efficiently inputs are used in producing output. This topic is covered thoroughly in Chapter 11, where both operational and financial measures of

10-15

Exhibit
Performance Report:
Life-Cycle Costs*

Year	Item	Actual Costs	Budgeted Costs	Variance
1996	Development	$190,000	$200,000	$10,000 F
1997	Production	300,000	240,000	60,000 U
	Logistics	75,000	80,000	5,000 F
1998	Production	435,000	360,000	75,000 U
	Logistics	110,000	120,000	10,000 F

*Analysis: Production costs were higher than expected because insertions of diodes and integrated circuits also drive costs (both production and postpurchase costs). Conclusion: The design of future products should try to minimize total insertions.

productivity are developed and presented. Specifically, the operational measures of productivity are linked with financial measures. Nonetheless, a brief overview of operational productivity measures is offered here. Operational measures of activity (or process productivity) include *output/materials, output/labor hours, output/kilowatt-hours*, and *output/persons employed*. Output for the manufacturing process is measured in units of product. Measures used depend on the activity. The output for the inspection activity, for example, can be measured by inspection hours. The objective is to improve the productivity of the inspection activity. This can be achieved, for example, by using fewer inputs to produce the same output (same inspection hours) or to produce more output (more inspection hours) with the same inputs.

Machining Other efficiency measures are also possible. For example, the efficiency of a machining activity could be measured by machine utilization, the percentage of the machine capacity being used, or by machine availability: the percentage of time a machine is available when needed. In a JIT environment, machine performance receives increased attention. Equipment can be placed into one of two categories: *nonbottleneck equipment* and *bottleneck equipment*. Bottleneck equipment is critical for production, and the demand for its services is the greatest (often more than it can handle, thus the label *bottleneck*). When equipment in this category is down, it usually means an interruption in production. For a JIT firm, this downtime can be costly since there are no inventories to buffer interruptions in production. Thus, great efforts are made to ensure that machinery in this category is available and utilized. When available, one would expect bottleneck equipment to be utilized 100 percent of the time.

For nonbottleneck equipment, machine availability is the relevant performance measure, not machine utilization. This equipment is not needed all the time and thus should not be used constantly. Using machine utilization as the measure encourages unnecessary production and, thus, the buildup of inventories. However, when needed, the equipment should be available; thus, availability is important for all equipment.

Carrying Inventory Control of work-in-process and finished goods inventories also presents a firm with exceptional opportunities for savings. These savings and how they can be achieved are discussed in Chapter 18. Carrying inventory is viewed as a non-value-added activity and the goal is to reduce the output of the activity (output can be defined as units on hand). The key to controlling these inventories is the use of JIT manufacturing and purchasing. Operational measures such as *inventory turnover rates, days of inventory*, and *number of inventoried items* can be used to assess how successfully the firm is reducing inventories to reasonable levels. For example, trends in days of inventory can be assessed; if the number of days of inventory is decreasing, the trend is favorable.

Quality

Control of quality costs is discussed extensively in Chapter 11. The importance of control of quality cannot be overemphasized. Significant savings are available to firms if they increase the quality of their activity output. Operational measures of quality depend on the activity or process and its output. For manufacturing activities or processes, with products or components as output, operational measures of quality would include *defects per unit, number of defective units/total units produced, percentage of external failures*, and *pounds of scrap divided by total pounds of material issued*. For other activities, like purchasing, the measures would need to be adjusted appropriately. First, activity output needs to be defined. For purchasing, output could be defined as purchase orders. Two possible operational measures for purchasing are *number of orders in error/total number of orders* and *number of errors per order*. The overall objective of total quality control is zero defects: flawless performance of activities. Thus, the objective of operational measures is to assess the firm's progress and to motivate workers to continue looking for ways to improve. Tracking these operational measures over time is particularly useful. Some firms display graphical reports posted on bulletin boards in operational areas. These operational measures, as well as the costs of quality, are reported and used for control purposes.

Time

Every activity has a customer. The output of an activity is used by others—often to perform other activities. There are two important performance characteristics related to time: *reliability* and *responsiveness*. Reliability means that activity output is delivered on time. For final products, this translates into the ability to meet promised delivery dates. Responsiveness measures the lead time required to produce the needed output. The objective is to increase responsiveness by decreasing lead time. Operational measures relating to both characteristics are needed.

Reliability To illustrate a reliability measure, let's focus on the activity of delivering finished goods to customers. *On-time delivery* is a commonly used operational measure of reliability. To measure on-time delivery, a firm sets delivery dates, then finds on-time delivery performance by dividing the orders delivered on time by the total number of orders delivered. The goal, of course, is to achieve a ratio of 100 percent. Some, however, have found that this measure used by itself may produce undesirable behavioral consequences.[19] Specifically, plant managers were giving priority to filling orders *not yet late* over orders that were already late. The performance measure was encouraging managers to have one very late shipment rather than several moderately late shipments! A chart measuring the age of late deliveries could help mitigate this problem.

Responsiveness Although reliability is important, responsiveness may even be more critical. For the order-filling activity, responsiveness reflects the ability of a company to respond to a customer's request. *Cycle time* and *velocity* are two operational measures of responsiveness. Cycle time is the length of time it takes to produce a unit of activity output. For manufacturing, cycle time is the time required to manufacture a product (time divided by units produced). Velocity is the number of units of activity output that can be produced in a given period of time.

Velocity and cycle time have become important operational measures of performance because of the increased emphasis on time-based capabilities. In fact, time-based capabilities may be one of the more critical competitive dimensions for firms in the 1990s. If this is true, then these time-based measures and others may receive increased attention.

Incentives can be used to encourage operational managers to reduce manufacturing cycle time or to increase velocity, thus improving delivery performance. A natural way to accomplish this objective is to tie product costs to cycle time and reward operational managers for reducing product costs. For example, cell conversion costs can be assigned to products on the basis of the time that it takes a product to move through the cell. Using the theoretical productive time available for a period (in minutes), a value-added standard cost per minute can be computed.

$$\text{Standard cost per minute} = \frac{\text{Cell conversion costs}}{\text{Minutes available}}$$

To obtain the conversion cost per unit, this standard cost per minute is multiplied by the actual cycle time used to produce the units during the period. By comparing the unit cost computed using the actual cycle time with the unit cost possible using the theoretical or optimal cycle time, a manager can assess the potential for improvement. Note that the more time it takes a product to move through the cell, the greater the unit

cycle time

velocity

---

19. Joseph Fisher, "Nonfinancial Performance Measures," *Journal of Cost Management*, Spring, 1992, pp. 31–38.

product cost. With incentives to reduce product cost, this approach to product costing encourages operational managers and cell workers to find ways to decrease cycle time or increase velocity.

An example will illustrate the concepts. Assume that a company has the following data for one of its manufacturing cells:

Theoretical velocity: 12 units per hour
Productive minutes available (per year): 400,000
Annual conversion costs: $1,600,000
Actual velocity: 10 units per hour

The actual and theoretical conversion costs per unit are shown in Exhibit 10-16. Notice from Exhibit 10-16 that the per-unit conversion cost can be reduced from $24 to $20 by decreasing cycle time from six minutes per unit to five minutes per unit (or increasing velocity from ten units per hour to twelve units per hour). At the same time, the objective of improving delivery performance is achieved.

Manufacturing Cycle Efficiency Another time-based operational measure calculates manufacturing cycle efficiency (MCE) as follows:

$$\text{MCE} = \frac{\text{Processing time}}{\text{Processing time} + \text{Move time} + \text{Inspection time} + \text{Waiting time}}$$

where *processing time* is the time it takes to convert raw materials into a finished good. The other activities have been defined earlier in the chapter (p. 395) and were identified as nonvalue-added activities. Processing, on the other hand, is a value-added activity. Thus, the ideal is to eliminate the nonvalue-added activities by reducing to zero the time spent on them. If this is accomplished, the value of MCE would be 1.0. As MCE improves (moves toward 1.0), cycle time decreases. Furthermore, since the only way MCE can improve is by decreasing the nonvalue-added activities, cost reduction must also follow.[20]

To illustrate MCE, let's use the data from Exhibit 10-16. The actual cycle time is 6.0 minutes and the theoretical cycle time is 5.0 minutes. Thus, the time attributable to nonvalue-added activities is 1.0 minute (6.0 − 5.0), and MCE is computed as follows:

20. Berliner and Brimson, *Cost Management for Today's Advanced Manufacturing.*

10-16

Exhibit
Conversion Cost
Computations

Actual Conversion Cost per Unit		
Standard cost per minute	=	$\dfrac{\$1,600,000}{400,000}$
	=	$4 per minute
Actual cycle time	=	$\dfrac{60 \text{ minutes}}{10 \text{ units}}$
	=	6 minutes per unit
Actual conversion cost	=	$4 × 6
	=	$24 per unit
Theoretical (Ideal) Conversion Cost per Unit		
Theoretical cycle time	=	$\dfrac{60 \text{ minutes}}{12 \text{ units}}$
	=	5 minutes per unit
Ideal conversion cost	=	$4 × 5
	=	$20 per unit

$$\text{MCE} = \frac{5.0}{6.0}$$
$$= 0.83$$

Actually, this is a fairly efficient process, as measured by MCE. Many manufacturing companies have MCEs less than 0.10.[21]

Operational Measures: A Qualification

Operational measures can be of tremendous value. They can be produced quickly and can be expressed in terms that operational personnel can readily understand. However, if used in isolation, these measures can be detrimental to the firm's overall objectives. Operational measures may actually conflict—for instance, increasing material productivity may cause a decline in labor productivity. Yet encouraging this outcome may be much better than increasing both operational measures. It depends on the value of the trade-offs. For operational measures to work, there must be a tight linkage between the operational control system and the overall objectives of the business.[22] Since the overall success of the firm is defined in financial terms, there must be a linkage between operational performance and financial performance. The profit-linked productivity measure described in Chapter 11 is an example of how these linkages ought to exist. By knowing the linkages, operational measures can be used to foster the achievement of the firm's strategic objectives.

For convenience, the operational measures are summarized in Exhibit 10-17. You should realize that this listing is simply a sample of possible measures and is not exhaustive by any means.

21. Berliner and Brimson, 4.
22. Kelvin Cross and Richard Lynch, "Accounting for Competitive Performance," *Journal of Cost Management* (Spring 1989): 20–28.

10-17

Exhibit
Summary of Operational Measures

Efficiency	
Productivity	*Machine Performance*
Output/pounds of material	Machine availability
Output/hours of labor	Machine utilization
Output/kilowatt-hours	*Carrying Inventory*
Output/person employed	Inventory turnover
	Days of inventory
	Number of inventoried items
	Trends in days of inventory

Quality
Defects/units
Number of defective units/total units
Percentage of external failures
Pounds of scrap/Pounds of materials issued
Purchase orders in error/Total purchase orders
Number of errors per purchase order

Time Based
On-time deliveries/Total deliveries
Cycle time
Velocity
MCE

SUMMARY OF LEARNING OBJECTIVES

1. Compare and contrast traditional responsibility accounting with contemporary responsibility accounting.
The control procedures used in traditional manufacturing environments are not directly transferable to an advanced environment. Detailed variance analysis, based on currently attainable standards, can provide incentives that are not compatible with the operating objectives found in an advanced environment. Using materials price variances as a measure, for example, can encourage purchase of lots larger than desirable in order to take advantage of quantity discounts or lesser quality. This behavior encourages inventories of raw materials and low-quality materials, both of which are in opposition to the objectives of zero inventories and total quality control.

Contemporary responsibility accounting focuses on managing activities rather than the costs. It recognizes that activities cause costs and that management of activities will produce more efficient outcomes. Two dimensions define activity-based management: the cost dimension and the process view dimension. The cost dimension is concerned with accurate assignment of activity costs to cost objects—particularly products. The second dimension, process value analysis, provides information about why work is done and how well it is done.

2. Explain process value analysis.
Process value analysis provides information about why work is done and how well it is done. It involves cost driver analysis, activity analysis, and performance measurement. It is this dimension that connects it to the concept of continuous improvement. A key

element of activity-based control is activity analysis—the process of identifying and describing a firm's activities, assessing their value to the organization, and selecting only those that are of value. Cost reduction is realized by decreasing, eliminating, selecting, and sharing activities. Emphasis is placed on identifying nonvalue-added costs and eliminating them. These costs are the result of unnecessary activities and inefficiencies found in necessary activities.

3. Describe the role of financial measures of activity performance.
Activity performance is evaluated on three dimensions: efficiency, quality, and time. Financial measures of efficiency allow managers to identify the dollar values for potential improvement and for improvements achieved. Value- and nonvalue-added cost reports, trends in costs, benchmarking, activity flexible budgeting, and life-cycle budgeting are examples of financial measures of activity efficiency.

4. Discuss the role of nonfinancial measures of performance.
Operational measures are increasing in importance in the advanced manufacturing environment. At this level, there is an increased emphasis on real-time feedback and the use of operational measures. More worker involvement in the day-to-day control process is being encouraged. Efforts are being made to improve activity efficiency, quality, and cycle time. Operational measures are a key part of the efforts to make these improvements.

KEY TERMS

Activity analysis *394*
Activity-based management (ABM) *392*
Activity elimination *396*
Activity flexible budgeting *401*
Activity inputs *393*
Activity output *393*
Activity output measure *393*
Activity reduction *396*

Activity selection *396*
Activity sharing *396*
Benchmarking *401*
Contemporary responsibility accounting *387*
Cycle time *412*
Driver analysis *393*
Life-cycle cost management *407*

Life-cycle costs *406*
Nonvalue-added activities *394*
Nonvalue-added costs *394*
Operational measures *410*
Process improvement *388*
Process innovation (business reengineering) *388*
Process value analysis *393*

Product life cycle *406*
Required activities *394*
Target cost *408*
Traditional responsibility accounting *387*
Value-added activities *394*
Value-added costs *394*
Value-added standard *397*
Velocity *412*
Whole-life cost *406*

REVIEW PROBLEMS

I. Traditional Responsibility versus Contemporary Responsibility The labor standard for a company is 2.0 hours per unit produced, which includes setup time. At the beginning of the last quarter, 20,000 units had been produced and 44,000 hours used. The production manager was concerned about the prospect of reporting an unfavorable labor efficiency variance at the end of the year. Any unfavorable variance over 9 to 10 percent of the standard usually meant a negative performance rating. Bonuses were adversely affected by negative ratings. Accordingly, for the last quarter, the production manager decided to reduce the number of setups and use longer production runs. He knew that his production workers usually were within 5 percent of the standard. The real problem was with setup times. By reducing the setups, the actual hours used would be within 7 to 8 percent of the standard hours allowed.

REQUIRED:
1. Explain why the behavior of the production manager is unacceptable for an advanced manufacturing environment.

2. Explain how a contemporary responsibility accounting approach would discourage the kind of behavior described.

Solution

1. In an advanced manufacturing environment, efforts are made to reduce inventories and eliminate nonvalue-added costs. The production manager is focusing on meeting the labor usage standard and is ignoring the impact on inventories that longer production runs may have.
2. Contemporary responsibility accounting focuses on activities and activity performance. For the setup activity, the value-added standard would be zero setup time and zero setup costs. Thus, avoiding setups would not save labor time and it would not affect the labor variance. Of course, labor variances themselves would not be computed—at least not at the operational level.

II. Value- and Nonvalue-added Cost Reports; Currently Attainable (Interim) Standards

Pollard Manufacturing has developed value-added standards for material usage, purchasing, and inspecting. The value-added output levels for each of the activities, their actual levels achieved, and the standard prices are as follows:

Activity	Activity Driver	SQ	AQ	SP
Material usage	Board feet	24,000	30,000	$10
Purchasing	Purchase orders	800	1,000	50
Inspection	Inspection hours	0	4,000	12

Assume that material usage and purchasing represent resources acquired as needed and inspection is acquired in blocks or steps of 2,000 hours. The actual prices paid for the inputs equal the standard prices.

REQUIRED:

1. Prepare a cost report that details value- and nonvalue-added costs.
2. Suppose that the company wants to reduce nonvalue-added costs by 30 percent in the coming year. Prepare interim standards that can be used to evaluate the company's progress toward this goal. How much will this save in resource spending?

Solution

1.

	Costs		
	Value Added	Nonvalue Added	Total
Material usage	$240,000	$ 60,000	$300,000
Purchasing	40,000	10,000	50,000
Inspection	0	48,000	48,000
Total	$280,000	$118,000	$398,000

2.

	Interim Standards	
	Quantity	Cost
Material usage	28,200	$282,000
Purchasing	940	47,000
Inspection	2,800	33,600

If the standards are met, then the savings are as follows:

Material usage: $10 × 1,800 =	$18,000
Purchasing: $50 × 60 =	3,000
Total	$21,000

There is no reduction in resource spending for inspections because it must be purchased in steps of 2,000 and only 1,200 hours were saved—another 800 hours must be reduced before any reduction in resource spending is possible.

Q UESTIONS FOR WRITING AND DISCUSSION

1. Describe a traditional responsibility accounting system.
2. Describe a contemporary responsibility accounting system. How does it differ from traditional responsibility accounting?
3. Explain how materials price variances can work against the JIT objectives of zero inventories and total quality control.
4. Explain how materials usage variances can impede JIT manufacturing.
5. Traditional currently attainable standards are not compatible with the objective of continuous improvement. Do you agree? Explain your reasoning.
6. What are the two dimensions of the activity-based management model? How do they differ?
7. What is driver analysis? What role does it play in process value analysis?
8. What is meant by "activity inputs"? "activity output"? Explain what is meant by "activity output measurement."
9. What is activity analysis? Why is this approach compatible with the goal of continuous improvement?
10. What are value-added activities? value-added costs?
11. What are nonvalue-added activities? nonvalue-added costs? Give an example of each.
12. Identify and define four different ways to manage activities so that costs can be reduced.
13. Explain how value-added standards are used to identify value-added and nonvalue-added costs.
14. What is the standard cost allowed for nonvalue-added activities that are unnecessary? Explain why.
15. Explain how trend reports of nonvalue-added cost can be used.

16. Explain how benchmarking can be used to improve activity performance.
17. In controlling nonvalue-added costs, explain how activity output measures (activity drivers) can induce behavior that is either beneficial or harmful. How can value-added standards be used to reduce the possibility of dysfunctional behavior?
18. Explain how the use of multiple cost drivers can improve performance reports that compare actual costs with budgeted costs.
19. What is the meaning of the fixed activity volume variance? Explain how the unused capacity variance is useful to managers.
20. Describe the benefits of life-cycle cost budgeting.
21. Why are nonfinancial measures of performance used more at the operating level?
22. In a non-JIT company, price reductions for raw materials are often obtained through the use of quantity discounts. In a JIT company, how are price reductions obtained?
23. Identify two operational measures of machine performance.
24. Machine performance is more important in a JIT environment than in a non-JIT environment. Do you agree? Explain.
25. Explain why time-based performance measures are becoming more important.
26. Identify and define two operational measures of delivery performance.
27. What is cycle time? velocity?
28. What is manufacturing cycle efficiency?

W ARM-UP EXERCISES

This section provides short warm-up exercises based on the examples in the chapter. Each warm-up exercise gives the page number on which the text example can be found. You may want to refer to the text example to see how the exercise can be set up and solved.

W10-1
Value- and Nonvalue-added Cost Report
LO 2
pp. 398–399.

Durham Company has assembled the following information about four activities:

Activity	Activity Driver	SQ	AQ	SP
Material usage	Pounds	80,000	88,000	$50.00
Rework	Labor hours	0	20,000	9.00
Setups	Setup time	0	12,000	25.00
Inspection	Inspection hours	0	8,000	8.00

REQUIRED: Prepare a value- and nonvalue-added cost report.

W10-2
Activity Flexible
Budgeting and
Variance Analysis
LO 3
pp. 404–405

Rummer, Inc. is investigating the cost of expediting. The following actual and budgeted data are given:

Activity	Actual Cost	Budgeted Cost	Variance
Expediting			
Fixed	$63,000	$60,000	$3,000 U
Variable	24,000	20,000	4,000 U
Total	$87,000	$80,000	$7,000 U

The $60,000 of budgeted fixed inspection costs represent the salaries of two expeditors, where each is paid $30,000. Each expeditor is capable of efficiently expediting 200 orders per year. During the year, 350 orders were expedited.

REQUIRED:
1. Calculate the fixed activity rate.
2. Calculate the spending and volume variances and interpret them.
3. Calculate the unused capacity variance.

W10-3
MCE; Cycle Time
LO 4
pp. 412–413

Marzo Company has provided the following data for one of its manufacturing cells:

Theoretical velocity: 24 units per hour
Productive minutes available (per year): 800,000
Annual conversion costs: $1,600,000
Actual velocity: 20 units per hour

REQUIRED:
1. Calculate the conversion cost per unit, assuming conversion cost is applied using cycle time.
2. Calculate the theoretical conversion cost per unit.
3. Calculate MCE.

EXERCISES

E10-1
Labor Efficiency
Variance; Ethical
Issues; Incentives
LO 1

David Christensen, plant manager, was given the charge to produce 120,000 bolts used in the manufacture of small twin engine aircraft. Directed by his divisional manager to give the bolt production priority over other jobs, he had two weeks to produce the units. Meeting the delivery date was crucial for renewal of a major contract with a large airplane manufacturer. Each bolt requires 20 minutes of direct labor and 5 ounces of metal. After producing a batch of bolts, each bolt is subjected to a stress test. Those that pass are placed in a carton, which is stamped "Inspected by inspector no. _____" (the inspector's identification number is inserted). Defective units are discarded, having no salvage value. Because of the nature of the process, rework is not possible.

At the end of the first week, the plant had produced 60,000 acceptable units and used 24,000 direct labor hours, 4,000 hours more than the standard allowed. Furthermore, 65,000 total bolts had been produced and 5,000 had been rejected, creating an unfavorable materials usage variance of 25,000 ounces. David knew that a performance report would be prepared when the 120,000 bolts were completed. This report would compare the labor and materials used with that allowed. Any variance in excess of 5 percent of standard would be investigated. David expected the same or worse performance for the coming week and was worried about a poor performance rating for himself. Accordingly, at the beginning of the second week, David moved his inspectors to the production line (all inspectors had production experience). However, for reporting purposes the production hours provided by inspectors would not be counted as part of direct labor. They would still appear as a separate budget item on the performance report. Additionally, David instructed the inspectors to pack the completed bolts in the cartons and stamp them as inspected. One inspector objected; David reassigned the inspector temporarily to material handling and gave an inspection stamp with a fabricated identification number to a line worker who was willing to stamp the cartons of bolts as inspected.

REQUIRED:

1. Explain why David stopped inspections on the bolts and reassigned inspectors to production and material handling. Discuss the ethical ramifications of this decision.
2. What features in the traditional responsibility accounting system provided the incentive(s) for David to take the actions described? Would a contemporary responsibility system have provided incentives that discourage this kind of behavior? Explain.
3. What likely effect would David's actions have on the quality of the bolts? Was the decision justified by the need to obtain renewal of the contract, particularly if the plant returns to a normal inspection routine after the rush order is completed? Do you have any suggestions about the quality approach taken by this company?

E10-2

Limitations of Traditional Control Measures

LO 1

Assume that a company is operating in a dynamic environment with rapidly changing product designs, high-quality emphasis, and intense cost competition. Suppose that a firm operating in this environment continues to use a traditional responsibility accounting system. For each of the following actions, describe: (1) what feature or features of a traditional responsibility accounting system motivated the action, and (2) the weaknesses or limitations of the control feature, including a brief discussion of the consequences of the action.

1. Defective subassemblies were not reworked but passed on to the next operation.
2. Five top salespeople were laid off in order for the division to meet budget.
3. A large lot of raw materials is purchased to take advantage of a quantity discount.
4. Preventive maintenance was delayed to the next budgetary period.
5. Production is increased so that idle time for direct laborers is minimized.
6. Nonbottleneck equipment was operated at 100 percent utilization rates.
7. The plant manager refuses to accept recommendations for reengineering key manufacturing processes. Reason? All material and labor efficiency variances have been favorable for the past three years. No improvement is really needed—we are already operating efficiently.

E10-3

Traditional versus Contemporary Responsibility Accounting

LO 1

Consider the following three quotes taken from within the chapter:

Quote 1 *"A revenue increase of 15% over last year and 5% ahead of budget is not such good news when the market grew 30% and our leading competitor increased its sales by 40%."*

Quote 2 *"The system converts materials into product, not people at work stations. Therefore, process efficiency is more important than labor efficiency. . . ."*

Quote 3 *"Costs not reported are invisible and are all but ignored in the management process."*

REQUIRED: Discuss how these comments can be viewed as criticisms of traditional responsibility accounting, and then describe the features of a contemporary responsibility accounting system that address the criticisms.

E10-4

Contemporary versus Traditional Responsibility Accounting

LO 1

For each of the following situations, identify which characteristic is descriptive of contemporary responsibility accounting and which is descriptive of traditional responsibility accounting. Provide a brief commentary on the differences between the two systems for each situation, addressing the advantages of the contemporary view over the traditional view. Characteristics of each situation are labeled *A* and *B*.

Situation 1
A: Control point focuses on processes and teams
B: Control point focuses on organizational units and individuals

Situation 2
A: Rewards group-based and criteria use multidimensional performance
B: Individuals rewarded based on budgetary performance

Situation 3
A: Assumes that activities can be collected into independent subgroups
B: Assumes that activities are linked

Situation 4
A: Focus is the organization
B: Focus is individuals

Situation 5
A: Performance measured by comparing actual financial outcomes with budgeted financial outcomes
B: A blend of financial and nonfinancial factors, all of which relate to process performance characteristics such as time, quality, cost, and efficiency, measures performance

Situation 6
A: Control emphasis is costs
B: Control emphasis is activities

Situation 7
A: Standards are engineered and tend to be static
B: Standards are optimal, dynamic, and process-oriented

Situation 8
A: Focus is both internal and external
B: Focus is mostly internal

E10-5
Driver Analysis;
Activity Analysis
LO 2

For each of the following situations, provide the following information:

a. An estimate of the nonvalue-added cost caused by each activity
b. The root causes of the activity cost (such as plant layout, process design, and product design)
c. The cost reduction measure: activity elimination, activity reduction, activity sharing, or activity selection

1. It takes 45 minutes and 6 pounds of material to produce a product using a traditional manufacturing process. A process reengineering study provided a new manufacturing process design (using existing technology) that would take 15 minutes and 4 pounds of material. The cost per labor hour is $12 and the cost per pound of materials is $8.
2. With its original design, a product requires 15 hours of setup time. Redesigning the product could reduce the setup time to an absolute minimum of 30 minutes. The cost per hour of setup time is $200.
3. A product currently requires eight moves. By redesigning the manufacturing layout, the number of moves can be reduced from eight to zero. The cost per move is $10.
4. Inspection time for a plant is 8,000 hours per year. The cost of inspection consists of salaries of four inspectors, totaling $120,000. Inspection also uses supplies costing $2 per inspection hour. A supplier evaluation program, product redesign, and process redesign reduced the need for inspection by creating a zero-defect environment.
5. Each unit of a product requires 5 components. The average number of components is 5.3 due to component failure, requiring rework and extra components. By developing relations with the right suppliers and increasing the quality of the purchased component, the average number of components can be reduced to 5 components per unit. The cost per component is $600.
6. A plant produces 100 different electronic products. Each product requires an average of eight components that are purchased externally. The components are different for each part. By redesigning the products, it is possible to produce the 100 products so that they all have four components in common. This will reduce the demand for purchasing, receiving, and paying bills. Estimated savings from the reduced demand are $900,000 per year.

E10-6
Calculation of
Value-added and
Nonvalue-added
Costs; Unused
Capacity
LO 2, LO 3

Maurice Entertainment Products produces a variety of plastic toys. The company uses a conventional, departmental structure. After a careful study, the company decided that the number of purchase orders was a good cost driver for purchasing costs. During the last year, the company incurred fixed purchasing costs of $104,000 (salaries of four employees), and also spent an average of $3 per purchase order for variable purchasing costs. Management decided that the value-added standard number of purchase orders is 8,000. The fixed costs provide a capacity of processing 16,000 orders (4,000 per employee at practical capacity). Assume that the actual orders processed were 14,000.

REQUIRED:
1. Calculate the cost of unused capacity for purchasing.
2. Calculate the value-added and nonvalue-added costs for purchasing.
3. Prepare a report that presents value-added, nonvalue-added, and actual costs. Explain why highlighting the nonvalue-added costs is important.
4. Explain why purchasing would be viewed as a value-added activity. List all possible reasons.

E10-7
Cost Report; Value-added and Nonvalue-added Costs
LO 2, LO 3

Lemmons Company has developed value-added standards for four activities: purchasing parts, assembling parts, administering parts, and inspecting parts. The activities, the activity driver, the standard and actual quantities, and the price standards follow for 1997:

Activities	Activity Driver	SQ	AQ	SP
Purchasing parts	Orders	500	700	$300
Assembling parts	Labor hours	60,000	66,500	12
Administering parts	Number of parts	6,000	8,600	110
Inspecting parts	Inspection hours	0	25,000	15

The actual prices paid per unit of each activity driver were equal to the standard prices.

REQUIRED:
1. Prepare a cost report that lists the value-added costs, nonvalue-added costs, and actual costs for each activity.
2. Which activities are nonvalue-added? Explain why. Explain why value-added activities can have nonvalue-added costs.

E10-8
Trend Report: Nonvalue-added Costs
LO 2, LO 3

Refer to E10-7. Suppose that Lemmons Company used an activity analysis program during 1998 in an effort to reduce nonvalue-added costs. The value-added standards, actual quantities, and prices for 1998 follow:

Activities	Activity Driver	SQ	AQ	SP
Purchasing parts	Orders	500	600	$300
Assembling parts	Labor hours	60,000	62,000	12
Administering parts	Number of parts	6,000	8,000	110
Inspecting parts	Inspection hours	0	15,000	15

REQUIRED:
1. Prepare a report that compares the nonvalue-added costs for 1997 with those of 1998.
2. Comment on the value of a trend report.

E10-9
Activity Analysis, Activity Drivers, Driver Analysis, and Behavioral Effects
LO 3

Kenzie Sorensen, controller of Riqueza Company, has been helping an outside consulting group install a contemporary cost management system. This new accounting system is designed to support the company's efforts to become more competitive (by creating a competitive advantage). For the past two weeks, she has been identifying activities, associating workers with activities, and assessing the time and resources consumed by individual activities. Now she and the consulting group have entered into the fourth phase of activity analysis: assessing value content. At this stage, Kenzie and the consultants also plan to identify drivers for assigning costs to cost objects. Furthermore, as a preliminary step to improving activity efficiency, they decided to identify potential root causes of activity costs. Kenzie's assignment for today is to assess the value content of five activities, choose a suitable activity driver, and identify the possible root causes of the activities. Following are the five activities she is investigating along with possible activity drivers:

Activity	Possible Activity Drivers
Setting up equipment	Setup time, Number of setups
Creating scrap*	Pounds of scrap, Number of defective units
Welding subassemblies	Welding hours, Subassemblies welded
Material handling	Number of moves, Distance moved
Inspecting parts	Hours of inspection, Number of defective parts

*Scrap is defined as a bad product or subassembly that cannot be reworked and so must be discarded.

Kenzie ran a regression analysis for each potential activity driver, using the method of least squares to estimate the variable- and fixed-cost components. In all five cases, costs were highly correlated with the potential drivers. Thus, all drivers appeared to be good candidates for assigning costs to products. The company plans to reward production managers for reducing product costs.

REQUIRED:
1. For each activity, assess the value content and classify each activity as value-added or nonvalue-added (justify the classification). Identify some possible root causes of each activity and describe how this knowledge can be used to improve activity management. For purposes of discussion, assume that the value-added activities are not performed with perfect efficiency.
2. Describe the behavior that each activity driver will encourage and evaluate the suitability of that behavior for the company's objective of creating a sustainable competitive advantage.

E10-10
Cycle Time and Conversion Cost per Unit
LO 4

The theoretical cycle time for a product is 20 minutes per unit. The budgeted conversion costs for the manufacturing cell are $1,800,000 per year. The total labor minutes available are 400,000. During the year, the cell was able to produce two units of the product per hour. Suppose also that production incentives exist to minimize unit product costs.

REQUIRED:
1. Compute the theoretical conversion cost per unit.
2. Compute the applied conversion cost per minute (the amount of conversion cost actually assigned to the product).
3. Discuss how this approach to assigning conversion cost can improve delivery time performance.

E10-11
Cycle Time and Velocity; MCE
LO 4

A manufacturing cell has the theoretical capability to produce 30,000 stereo speakers per quarter. The conversion cost per quarter is $60,000. There are 5,000 production hours available within the cell per quarter.

REQUIRED:
1. Compute the theoretical velocity (per hour) and the theoretical cycle time (minutes per unit produced).
2. Compute the ideal amount of conversion cost that will be assigned per speaker.
3. Suppose the actual time required to produce a speaker is 15 minutes. Compute the amount of conversion cost actually assigned to each speaker. Now calculate MCE.
4. Based on your analysis in requirements 2 and 3, how much nonvalue-added time is being used? How much is it costing per speaker?

P R O B L E M S

P10-1
Continuous Improvement; Performance Measurement
LO 1, LO 4

At the beginning of 1996, Wilson Company installed a JIT purchasing and manufacturing system as part of its efforts to improve its competitive position. At the same time, Wilson implemented a total quality management program. Now, after two years of operation, the president of Wilson wants some assessment of the system's achievements. To help provide this assessment, the following information on one product has been gathered:

	1996	1998
Theoretical annual capacity[a]	96,000	96,000
Actual production[b]	76,000	88,000
Production hours available	4,000	4,000
On-time deliveries	7,200	8,160
Total deliveries	10,000	9,600
Scrap (pounds)	10,000	8,000
Materials used (pounds)	100,000	100,000
Actual cost per unit	$125	$110
Days of inventory	6	3
Number of defective units	4,500	6,000

[a]Amount that could be produced given the available production hours
[b]Amount that was produced given the available production hours

REQUIRED:

1. Compute the following measures for 1996 and 1998:
   a. Theoretical velocity and cycle time
   b. Actual velocity and cycle time
   c. On-time delivery percentage
   d. Scrap as a percentage of total material issued
   e. Percentage change in actual product cost
   f. Percentage change in days of inventory
   g. Defective units as a percentage of total units produced
2. Based on your computations in requirement 1, evaluate the progress that Wilson Company is making with its JIT and quality systems. As part of this evaluation, indicate the ultimate goals that the company is striving for and how each performance measure helps achieve these goals.

P10-2

Activity-based Management; Nonvalue-added Costs; Target Costs

LO 2, LO 3

Danna Martin, president of Mays Electronics, was concerned about the end-of-the year marketing report that she had just received. According to Larry Savage, marketing manager, a price decrease for the coming year was again needed to maintain the company's annual sales volume of integrated circuit boards (CBs). This would make a bad situation worse. The current selling price of $18 per unit was producing a $2 per-unit profit—half the customary $4 per-unit profit. Foreign competitors kept reducing their prices. To match the latest reduction would reduce the price from $18 to $14. This would put the price below the cost to produce and sell it. How could these firms sell for such a low price?

Determined to find out if there were problems with the company's operations, Danna decided to hire a consultant to evaluate the way in which the CBs were produced and sold. After two weeks, the consultant had identified the following activities and costs:

Batch-level activities:	
Setting up equipment	$ 125,000
Material handling	180,000
Inspecting products	122,000
Product-sustaining activities:	
Engineering support	120,000
Handling customer complaints	100,000
Filling warranties	170,000
Storing goods	80,000
Expediting goods	75,000
Unit-level activities:	
Using materials	500,000
Using power	48,000
Manual insertion labor[a]	250,000
Other direct labor	150,000
Total costs	$1,920,000[b]

[a]Diodes, resistors, and integrated circuits are inserted manually into the circuit board.
[b]This total cost produces a unit cost of $16 for last year's sales volume.

The consultant indicated that some preliminary activity analysis shows that per-unit costs can be reduced by at least $7. Since the marketing manager had indicated that the market share (sales volume) for the boards could be increased by 50 percent if the price could be reduced to $12, Danna became quite excited.

REQUIRED:

1. What is activity-based management? What phases of activity analysis were provided by the consultant? What else remains to be done?
2. Identify as many nonvalue-added costs as possible. Compute the cost savings per unit that would be realized if these costs were eliminated. Was the consultant correct in his preliminary

cost reduction assessment? Discuss actions that the company can take to reduce or eliminate the nonvalue-added activities.

3. Compute the target cost required to maintain current market share, while earning a profit of $4 per unit. Now compute the target cost required to expand sales by 50 percent. How much cost reduction would be required to achieve each target?

4. Assume that further activity analysis revealed the following: switching to automated insertion would save $60,000 of engineering support and $90,000 of direct labor. Now what is the total potential cost reduction per unit available from activity analysis? With these additional reductions, can Mays achieve the target cost to maintain current sales? to increase it by 50 percent? What form of activity analysis is this: reduction, sharing, elimination, or selection?

5. Calculate income based on current sales, prices, and costs. Now calculate the income using a $14 price and a $12 price, assuming that the maximum cost reduction possible is achieved (including requirement 4's reduction). What price should be selected?

P10-3

Value-added and Interim Standards; Nonvalue-added Costs; Volume Variance; Unused Capacity

LO 3

Clement Mallett, vice-president of Suegros Company (a producer of a variety of plastic products), has been supervising the implementation of a contemporary cost management system. One of Clement's objectives is to improve process efficiency by improving the activities that define the processes. To illustrate the potential of the new system to the president, Clement has decided to focus on two processes: production and customer service.

Within each process, one activity will be selected for improvement: material usage for production and sustaining engineering for customer service (sustaining engineers are responsible for redesigning products based on customer needs and feedback). Value-added standards are identified for each activity. For material usage, the value-added standard calls for 6 pounds per unit of output (although the plastic products differ in shape and function, their size, as measured by weight, is uniform). The value-added standard is based on the elimination of all waste due to defective molds. The standard price of materials is $5 per pound. For sustaining engineering, the standard is 50 percent of current practical activity capacity. This standard is based on the fact that about half of the complaints have to do with design features that could have been avoided or anticipated by the company.

Current practical capacity (at the end of 1997) is defined by the following requirements: 3,000 engineering hours for each product group that has been on the market or in development for five years or less, and 1,200 hours per product group of more than five years. Four product groups have fewer than five years' experience and ten product groups have more. There are 12 engineers, each paid a salary of $50,000. Each engineer can provide 2,000 hours of service per year. There are no other significant costs for the engineering activity.

Actual material usage for 1997 was 20 percent above the level called for by the value-added standard; engineering usage was 23,000 hours. There were 40,000 units of output produced. Clement and the operational managers have selected some improvement measures that promise to reduce nonvalue-added activity usage by 30 percent in 1998. Selected actual results achieved for 1998 are as follows:

Units produced	40,000
Materials used	292,400
Engineering hours	17,700

The actual prices paid for materials and engineering hours are identical to the standard or budgeted prices.

REQUIRED:

1. For 1997, calculate the nonvalue-added usage and costs for material usage and sustaining engineering. Also, calculate the cost of unused capacity for the engineering activity.

2. Using the targeted reduction, establish interim standards for materials and engineering (for 1998).

3. Using the interim standards prepared in requirement 2, compute the 1998 usage variances, expressed in both physical and financial measures, for materials and engineering (for engineering compare actual resource usage with the interim (current) standard (why?)). Comment on

the company's ability to achieve its targeted reductions. In particular, discuss what measures the company must take to capture any realized reductions in resource usage.

P10-4
Benchmarking and Nonvalue-added Costs
LO 3, LO 4

Arequipa Products has two plants that manufacture a line of recliners. One is located in Denver and the other in Fresno. Each plant is set up as a profit center. During the past year, both plants sold the regular model for $450. Sales volume averages 20,000 units per year in each plant. Recently, the Fresno plant reduced the price of the regular model to $400. Discussion with the Fresno manager revealed that the price reduction was possible because the plant had reduced its manufacturing and selling costs by reducing what was called "nonvalue-added costs." The Fresno plant manufacturing and selling costs for the regular chair were $350 per unit. The Fresno manager offered to loan the Denver plant his cost accounting manager to help them achieve similar results. The Denver plant manager readily agreed knowing that his plant must keep pace—not only with the Fresno plant but also with competitors. A local competitor had also reduced its price on a similar model and Denver's marketing manager had indicated that the price must be matched or sales would drop dramatically. In fact, the marketing manager suggested that if the price were dropped to $390 by the end of the year, the plant could expand its share of the market by 20 percent. The plant manager agreed but insisted that the current profit per unit must be maintained and wants to know if the plant can at least match the $350 per-unit cost of the Fresno plant. He also wants to know if the plant can achieve the cost reduction using the approach of the Fresno plant.

The plant controller and the Fresno cost accounting manager have assembled the following data for the most recent year. The actual cost of inputs, their value-added (ideal) quantity levels, and the actual quantity levels are provided (for production of 20,000 units). Assume there is no difference between actual prices of activity units and standard prices.

	SQ	AQ	Actual Cost
Materials (lb)	237,500	250,000	$5,250,000
Labor (hr)	57,000	60,000	750,000
Setups (hr)	—	4,000	300,000
Material handling (moves)	—	10,000	700,000
Warranties (no. repaired)	—	10,000	1,000,000
Total			$8,000,000

REQUIRED:
1. Calculate the target cost for expanding the Denver market share by 20 percent, assuming that the per-unit profitability is maintained as requested by the plant manager.
2. Calculate the nonvalue-added cost per unit. Assuming that nonvalue-added costs can be reduced to zero, can the Denver plant match the Fresno plant's per-unit cost? Can the target cost for expanding market share be achieved? What actions would you take if you were the plant manager?
3. Describe the role benchmarking played in the effort of the Denver plant to protect and improve its competitive position.

P10-5
Flexible Budgeting; Single Cost Driver versus Multiple Cost Drivers
LO 3

Amy Bunker, production manager, was upset with the latest performance report, which indicated that she was $100,000 over budget. Given the efforts that she and her workers had made, she was confident that they had met or beat the budget. Now she was not only upset but also genuinely puzzled over the results. Three items—supplies, power, and setups—were over budget. The actual costs for these three items follow:

	Actual Costs
Supplies	$210,000
Power	135,000
Setups	140,000
Total	$485,000

Amy knew that her operation had produced more units than originally had been budgeted, so that more power and supplies had naturally been used. She also knew that the uncertainty in scheduling had led to more setups than planned. When she pointed this out to Gary Grant, the controller, he assured her that the budgeted costs had been adjusted for the increase in productive activity. Curious, Amy questioned Gary about the methods used to make the adjustment.

Gary: If the actual level of activity differs from the original planned level, we adjust the budget by using budget formulas—formulas that allow us to predict what the costs will be for different levels of activity.

Amy: The approach sounds reasonable. However, I'm sure something is wrong here. Tell me exactly how you adjusted the costs of supplies, power, and setups.

Gary: First, we obtain formulas for the individual items in the budget by using the method of least squares. We assume that cost variations can be explained by variations in productive activity where activity is measured by direct labor hours. Here is a list of the cost formulas for the three items you mentioned. The variable X is the number of direct labor hours:

Supplies cost = $5X
Power cost = $5,000 + $2X
Setup cost = $100,000

Amy: I think I see the problem. Power costs don't have a lot to do with direct labor hours. They have more to do with machine hours. As production increases, machine hours increase more rapidly than direct labor hours. Also, . . .

Gary: You know, you have a point. The coefficient of determination for power cost is only about 50 percent. That leaves a lot of unexplained cost variation. The coefficient for supplies, however, is much better—it explains about 96 percent of the cost variation. Setup costs, of course, are fixed.

Amy: Well, as I was about to say, setup costs also have very little to do with direct labor hours. And I might add that they certainly are not fixed—at least not all of them. We had to do more setups than our original plan called for because of the scheduling changes. And we have to pay our people when they work extra hours. It seems like we are always paying overtime. I wonder if we simply do not have enough people for the setup activity. Also, there are supplies that are used for each setup and these are not cheap. Did you build these extra costs of increased setup activity into your budget?

Gary: No, we assumed that setup costs were fixed. I see now that some of them could vary as the number of setups increases. Amy, let me see if I can develop some cost formulas based on better explanatory variables. I'll get back with you in a few days.

Assume that after a few days work, Gary developed the following cost formulas, all with a coefficient of determination greater than 90 percent:

Supplies cost = $5X, where X = Direct labor hours
Power cost = $68,000 + 0.9Y, where Y = Machine hours
Setup cost = $98,000 + $400Z, where Z = Number of setups

The actual measures of each of the cost drivers are as follows:

Direct labor hours	40,000
Machine hours	90,000
Number of setups	110

REQUIRED:
1. Prepare a performance report for supplies, power, and setups using the direct-labor-based formulas.
2. Prepare a performance report for supplies, power, and setups using the multiple cost driver formulas that Gary developed.
3. Of the two approaches, which provides the most accurate picture of Amy's performance? Why?

P10-6
Life-Cycle Cost
Management
LO 3

Boyce Products manufactures products with life cycles that average three years. The first year involves product development, and the remaining two years emphasize production and sales. A budgeted life-cycle income statement developed for two proposed products follows. Each product will sell 200,000 units. The price has been set to yield a 50 percent gross margin ratio.

	Product A	Product B	Total
Sales	$4,000,000	$5,000,000	$9,000,000
Cost of goods sold	(2,000,000)	(2,500,000)	(4,500,000)
Gross margin	$2,000,000	$2,500,000	$4,500,000
Period expenses:			
Research and development			(2,000,000)
Marketing			(1,150,000)
Life-cycle income			$1,350,000

Upon seeing the budget, Rick Moss, president of Boyce Products, called in LeeAnn Gordon, marketing manager, and Art Cummings, design engineer.

Rick: These two products are earning only a 15 percent return on sales. We need 20 percent to earn an acceptable return on our investment. Can't we raise prices?

LeeAnn: I doubt the market would bear any increase in prices. However, I will do some additional research and see what's possible. The gross-profit ratio is already high. The problem appears to be with R & D. Those expenses seem higher than normal.

Art: These products are more complex than usual and we need to have the extra resources—at least if you want to have a product that functions as we are claiming it will. Also, we are charting some new waters with the features these products are offering. Specifically, our design is intended to reduce the postpurchase costs that consumers incur, including operation, support, maintenance, and disposal. LeeAnn, if you recall, you mentioned to us a year ago that our competitors were providing products that had lower postpurchase costs. This new design was intended to make us market leaders in this area. At any rate, in the future, we can probably get by on less—after we gain some experience. But it wouldn't be much less, perhaps $50,000.

Art: That would still allow us to earn only about 15.6 percent—even after you get more proficient. Maybe we ought to stay with our more standard features.

LeeAnn: Before we abandon these new lines, perhaps we ought to look at each product individually. Maybe one could be retained. These new features will give us an edge in the market. Also, I'll bet that if he knew what was driving those costs Art could redesign the product so that production costs could be lowered. I'm concerned that our competitors will exploit their postpurchase cost advantage. We really need to be leaders in this postpurchase area—our reputation is at stake. If we're not careful, we could begin losing market share.

REQUIRED:
1. What specific improvements would you suggest to Rick to improve Boyce's life-cycle cost management system?
2. Assume that the "period" expenses are traceable to each product. Product A is responsible for 60 percent of R&D costs and 50 percent of marketing costs. Prepare a revised income statement for each product. Based on this analysis, should either product be produced?
3. Based on the revised income statements (of requirement 2), how much must production costs be reduced to make each product acceptable? Discuss how activity analysis can help achieve this outcome. Explain why this should occur now, not after the products are in production.
4. According to Art, the motivation for the new design was to reduce the postpurchase costs of the new products. Explain why whole-life cost should be the focus of life-cycle cost management.

P10-7
Cycle Time and
Velocity; Conversion

A manufacturing cell has the theoretical capability to produce 60,000 space heaters per quarter. The conversion cost per quarter is $600,000. There are 20,000 production hours available within the cell per quarter.

Cost per Unit; MCE
LO 4

REQUIRED:

1. Compute the theoretical velocity (per hour) and the theoretical cycle time (minutes per unit produced).
2. Compute the ideal amount of conversion cost that will be assigned per heater.
3. Suppose the actual time required to produce a heater is 30 minutes. Compute the amount of conversion cost actually assigned to each heater. Discuss how this approach to assigning conversion cost can improve delivery time.
4. Calculate MCE. How much nonvalue-added time is being used? How much is it costing per heater?
5. Cycle time, velocity, MCE, conversion cost per unit (theoretical conversion rate $\times$ actual conversion time), and nonvalue-added costs are all measures of performance for the cell process. Discuss the incentives provided by these measures.

P10-8
MCE
LO 2, LO 4

A company makes a product that experiences the following activities (and times):

	Hours
Scheduling	2
Processing (two departments)	15
Moving (three moves)	4
Inspecting	1
Waiting (for the second process)	13
Storage (before delivery to customer)	15

REQUIRED:

1. Compute the MCE for this product.
2. Discuss how process value analysis can help improve this efficiency measure.

P10-9
Traditional versus Contemporary Responsibility Accounting
LO 1

Continuous improvement is the governing principle of a contemporary responsibility accounting system. Following are several performance measures. Some of these measures would be associated with a traditional responsibility accounting system and some would be associated with a contemporary system.

a. Materials price variances
b. Cycle time
c. Comparison of actual product costs with target costs
d. Materials quantity or efficiency variances
e. Comparison of actual product costs over time (trend reports)
f. Comparison of actual overhead costs, item by item, with the corresponding budgeted costs
g. Comparison of product costs with competitors' product costs
h. Percentage of on-time deliveries
i. Quality reports
j. Reports of value-added and nonvalue-added costs
k. Labor efficiency variances
l. Machine utilization rates
m. Days of inventory
n. Downtime
o. Manufacturing cycle efficiency (MCE)
p. Unused activity capacity variance
q. Labor rate variance
r. Using a sister plant's best practices as a performance standard

REQUIRED:

1. Classify each measure as traditional or contemporary. If traditional, discuss the measure's limitations for a contemporary environment. If contemporary, describe how the measure supports the objectives of a contemporary environment.
2. Classify the measures into operational and financial categories. Explain why operational measures are better for control at the shop level (production floor) than financial measures. Should any financial measures be used at the operational level?

P10-10
Flexible Budgeting; Multiple Cost Drivers; Variance Analysis
LO 3

Billy Adams, controller for Westcott, Inc., prepared the following budget for manufacturing costs at two different levels of activity for 1998:

Direct Labor Hours

	Level of Activity	
	50,000	100,000
Direct materials	$ 300,000	$ 600,000
Direct labor	200,000	400,000
Depreciation	100,000	100,000
Subtotal	$ 600,000	$1,100,000

Machine Hours

	Level of Activity	
	200,000	300,000
Maintenance	$ 360,000	$ 510,000
Power	112,000	162,000
Subtotal	$ 472,000	$ 672,000

Material Moves

	Level of Activity	
	20,000	40,000
Material handling	$ 120,000	$ 120,000

Number of Batches Inspected

	Level of Activity	
	100	200
Inspections	$ 125,000	$ 225,000
Total	$1,317,000	$2,117,000

During 1998, Westcott worked a total of 80,000 direct labor hours, used 250,000 machine hours, made 32,000 moves, and performed 120 batch inspections. The following actual costs were incurred:

Direct materials	$440,000
Direct labor	355,000
Depreciation	100,000
Maintenance	425,000
Power	142,000
Material handling	132,500
Inspections	160,000

Westcott applies overhead using pool rates based on direct labor hours, machine hours, number of moves, and number of batches. The second level of activity (the right column in the preceding table) is the practical level of activity (the available activity for resources acquired in advance of usage) and is used to compute predetermined overhead pool rates.

REQUIRED:
1. Prepare a performance report for Westcott's manufacturing costs in 1998.

2. Assume that one of the products produced by Westcott used 10,000 direct labor hours, 15,000 machine hours, and 500 moves and was produced in five batches. A total of 10,000 units was produced during the year. Calculate the unit manufacturing cost.

3. Assume that the value-added quantity for material handling is zero ($SQ = 0$). Also, assume that the material-handling activity must be purchased in blocks (whole units) of 2,000 moves. Calculate spending, volume, and unused capacity variances and discuss their meaning.

4. Assume that $SQ = 0$ is the value-added quantity of batch inspections. Calculate the variable spending and efficiency variances for inspections and explain their meaning. Assume that actual variable inspections costs are $135,000.

P10-11
Cycle Time; Velocity; Product Costing
LO 4

Silverman Company has a JIT system in place. Each manufacturing cell is dedicated to the production of a single product or major subassembly. One cell, dedicated to the production of guns, has four operations: machining, finishing, assembly, and qualifying (testing). The machining process is automated, using computers. In this process, the gun's frame, slide, and barrel are constructed. In finishing, sandblasting, buffing, and bluing are done. In assembly, the three parts of the gun are assembled along with the grip, the sight, the label, the magazine, and the clip. Finally, each firearm is tested using 20 rounds of ammunition.

For the coming year, the firearm cell has the following budgeted costs and cell time (both at theoretical capacity):

Budgeted conversion costs	$2,500,000
Budgeted raw materials	$3,000,000
Cell time	4,000 hours
Theoretical output	30,000 guns

During the year, the following actual results were obtained:

Actual conversion costs	$2,500,000
Actual materials	$2,600,000
Actual cell time	4,000 hours
Actual output	25,000 guns

REQUIRED:

1. Compute the velocity (number of guns per hour) that the cell can theoretically achieve. Now compute the theoretical cycle time (number of hours or minutes per gun) that it takes to produce one gun.

2. Compute the actual velocity and the actual cycle time.

3. Compute MCE. Comment on the efficiency of the operation.

4. Compute the budgeted conversion cost per minute. Using this rate, compute the conversion cost per gun if theoretical output is achieved. Using this measure, compute the conversion cost per gun for actual output. Does this product-costing approach provide an incentive for the cell manager to reduce cycle time? Explain.

Ⓜ ANAGERIAL DECISION CASES

C10-1
Ethical Considerations

Tim Ireland, controller of Roberts Electronics Division, was having lunch with Jimmy Jones, chief design engineer. Tim and Jimmy were good friends, having belonged to the same fraternity during their college days. The luncheon, however, was more business than pleasure.

Jimmy: Well, Tim, you indicated this morning that you have something important to tell me. I hope this isn't too serious. I don't want my weekend ruined.

Tim: Well, the matter is important. You know that at the beginning of this year, I was given the charge to estimate postpurchase costs for new products. This is not an easy task.

Jimmy: Yeah. I know. That's why I had our department supply you engineering specs on the new products—stuff like expected component life.

Tim: This new product you've been developing has a problem. According to your reports, there are two components that will wear out within about 14 months. According to your test runs, the product starts producing subpar performance during the 13th month.

Jimmy: Long enough to get us past the 12-month warranty. So why worry? There are no warranty costs for us to deal with.

Tim: Yes, but the customer then must incur substantial repair costs. And the product will have to be repaired once again before its useful life is ended. The estimated repair costs, when added to the normal life-cycle costs, puts the whole-life cost above the target cost. According to the new guidelines, we are going to have to scrap this new product—at least using its current design. Perhaps you can find a new design that avoids the use of these two components—or find ways that they won't be so stressed so that they last much longer.

Jimmy: Listen, Tim. I don't have the time or the budget to redesign this product. I have to come under budget and I have to meet the targeted production date or I'll have the divisional manager down my throat. Besides, you know that I'm up for the engineering management position at headquarters. If this project goes well, then it'll give me what I need to edge out Thompson Division's chief engineer. If I do the redesign, my opportunity for the job is gone. Help me out on this. You know how much this opportunity means to me.

Tim: I don't know what I can do. I have to file the whole-life cost report and I'm required to supply supporting documentation from marketing and engineering.

Jimmy: Well, that's easy to solve. Linda, the engineer who ran the tests on this product, owes me a favor. I'll get her to redo the tests so that the data produce a 24-month reliability period for the components. That should cut your estimated repair costs in half. Would that be enough to meet the targeted whole-life costs?
Tim: Yes, but. . . .

Jimmy: Hey, don't worry. If I tell Linda that I'll push her for chief divisional engineer, she'll cooperate. No sweat. This is a one-time thing. How about it? Are you a player?

REQUIRED:
1. Assume you are Tim. What pressures does he have to comply with Jimmy's request? Do you think he should comply? Would you, if you were Tim? If not, how would you handle the situation?
2. Assume that Tim cooperates with Jimmy and covers up the design deficiency. What standards of ethical conduct for management accountants were violated? (See the IMA code described in Chapter 1.)
3. Suppose that Tim refuses to cooperate. Jimmy then gets Linda to rerun the tests anyway, with the new, more optimistic results. He then approaches Tim with the tests and indicates that he is sending a copy of the latest results to the divisional manager. Jimmy indicates that he will challenge any redesign recommendations that Tim recommends. What should Tim do?

C10-2
Research Assignment

You are a newly employed accountant working for a medium-sized manufacturing firm. This firm is facing intense competition from foreign and domestic competitors. You have been asked by your supervisor, Kathy Bumstead, to research the use of nonfinancial performance measures. Use your library resources and pay particular attention to articles appearing in the following journals: *Management Accounting*, *Journal of Cost Management*, and *Harvard Business Review*. Once you have collected what you can on the topic, write a memo to Kathy that addresses the following issues:

1. What has brought about the rise of nonfinancial measures?
2. What are the deficiencies of the traditional accounting performance measures?
3. What nonfinancial measures should be used and why? In particular, what is the firm trying to measure?
4. How can control be achieved through the use of nonfinancial measures?
5. What problems or limitations are associated with nonfinancial measures?
6. What is your recommendation concerning the use of nonfinancial measures?

Kathy also wants you to list the sources for the views that you articulate in your memo. She also is willing for you to address any other substantive issues that you encounter in your research. However, the memo must be no longer than two pages.

Learning Objectives

After studying Chapter 11, you should be able to:

1. Identify and describe the four types of quality costs.

2. Prepare a quality cost report and explain the difference between the conventional view of acceptable quality level and the view espoused by total quality control.

3. Explain why quality cost information is needed and how it is used.

4. Explain what productivity is and calculate the impact of productivity changes on profits.

CHAPTER

Quality Costs and Productivity: Measurement, Reporting, and Control

SCENARIO

R ussell Walsh, president of Ladd Lighting Corporation, had just returned from a productivity seminar, excited and encouraged by what he had heard. He immediately called a meeting with Sarah Burke, the company's quality manager, and Dennis Schmitt, the company's controller and financial vice-president.

Russell: "I am convinced that we can become more competitive by increasing productivity and improving quality. Something needs to be done given the direction our profits have been heading over the past several years."

Sarah: "I agree that we need to do something. Improving quality will cost and I am not sure that spending more on quality will help much. After all, right now we spend a lot on quality-related activities. Pouring more money into quality may not be the answer."

Russell: "I don't intend to spend more on quality—just the opposite. At the seminar, a representative of Tennant Company, a manufacturer of industrial floor maintenance products, related an interesting experience—one that provides an important message for our own company.[1] Tennant decided to focus on productivity to remain competitive in the world market.

"At the same time that the plans for productivity improvement were unfolding, Tennant had a delivery of one of its most popular sweepers rejected by a customer. The sweeper was rejected as defective because it leaked hydraulic fluid. The problem of leaking fluid was known to Tennant, but other customers had never made a fuss over it. This was the first such reaction. The experience created a managerial awareness of the importance of quality. As a result, the company hired a consultant, Phil Crosby, and embarked on a major quality-improvement program."[2]

Sarah: "I think I know where you're headed now. Crosby advocates improving quality so that the costs of quality can be reduced. It costs us when we do things wrong, in terms of rework, scrap, repairs, and so on. By controlling quality costs, profitability can be improved, and we become more competitive."

Russell: "Exactly. Tennant's quality-improvement efforts have been remarkable. The sweeper that was rejected averaged 1.5 hydraulic leaks per machine. Within five or six years, they reduced the average to only 0.1 leak per machine. Other improvements were made as well. Within the first year, errors in inventory transactions were reduced from 41 per month to 12 per month. Within three years, machines damaged in shipping dropped from 5 percent to less than 1 percent. Furthermore, since more than 65 percent of Tennant's product costs consisted of materials and parts provided by suppliers, much of the failure and rejects could be attributed to poor components purchased externally. Consequently, Tennant concentrated on working with key suppliers to improve the specifications and quality of those components. Reaction from suppliers was strongly positive; one supplier reduced its level of defects from 6.4 percent to 0.8 percent.

"The most exciting thing about Tennant's experience, however, is the effect of the improved quality on its profitability. When the quality-improvement program began, Tennant estimated that its cost of doing things wrong was as high as 17 percent of sales. Within a six-year period, this cost had dropped to 8 percent of sales. Based on annual sales of $136 million, savings from improved quality totaled $12.24 million."

Dennis: "I'm impressed by the potential savings through improved quality. I'm not sure, however, what role you envision for me, other than being aware of the importance of a quality-improvement program. Sarah's department has been responsible for quality cost reporting."

Russell: "I envision your role as being much more extensive than simple awareness. We need a solid, reliable quality cost reporting system, and I expect you to assume responsibility for its development and operation. Our company needs quality information to help our managers make quality-improvement decisions. We also need to monitor and control the programs that we implement. Sarah, do you have any problem with this arrangement?"

Sarah: "None at all. It seems sensible that the controller's office is responsible for collecting and reporting quality costs. I know that other companies have this arrangement. The quality department should be responsible for analyzing and controlling these costs. Besides, I have a feeling that given the increased emphasis on

quality, my department will have plenty to do without worrying about a cost-reporting system."[3]

1. The facts in the Tennant example are based largely on a talk given by Tim K. Shenert at the Eleventh Annual Productivity Seminar at Utah State University (April 23–24, 1986). The talk focused on the actual experiences of Tennant Company with a quality-improvement program.
2. Crosby, former quality manager for ITT, is the author of *Quality Is Free* (New York: New American Library, 1980). While he served as quality manager for ITT, the company reduced its manufacturing cost of quality by 5 percent of sales. The savings in 1976 alone were estimated at $530 million. His book provides an excellent account of the 14-step quality program he developed and Tennant Company followed.
3. North American Philips Consumer Electronics Corporation, ITT, and Xerox are examples of companies that have assigned responsibility for quality cost

reporting to the accounting or financial departments. See Chapters 6 and 9 in Wayne J. Morse, Harold P. Roth, and Kay M. Poston, *Measuring, Planning, and Controlling Quality Costs* (Montvale, N.J.: National Association of Accountants, 1987).

Questions to Think About

1. Why has measurement of productivity and quality become so important?
2. What are quality costs?
3. How can improving quality reduce quality costs?
4. What kind of quality cost reports should be prepared by the accounting department?
5. What is meant by "productivity"?
6. How is productivity measured?

MEASURING THE COSTS OF QUALITY

Objective 1

Identify and describe the four types of quality costs.

By attending a productivity seminar, Russell Walsh discovered that paying more attention to quality can increase profitability. Quality improvement can increase profitability in two ways: (1) by increasing customer demand, and (2) by decreasing costs. In a tightly competitive market, increased demand and cost savings can mean the difference between surviving and thriving. The U.S. government has recognized the importance of quality in today's economy. One indication is the creation in 1987 of the Malcolm Baldridge National Quality Award.[4] The Baldridge award was created to recognize U.S. companies that excel in quality management and achievement. The award categories include: manufacturing, small business, service, educational, and health entities. Since no more than two awards are given per category, they are difficult to achieve and highly sought after. Past winners include: Motorola, Inc., Federal Express, General Motors' Cadillac Division, Zytec, Globe Metallurgical, Inc., Texas Instruments, Inc., and the Ritz-Carlton Hotel Company.

The costs of quality can be substantial and a source of significant savings. Studies indicate that costs of quality for American companies are typically 20 to 30 percent of sales.[5] Yet quality experts maintain that the optimal quality level should be about 2 to 4 percent of sales. This difference between actual and optimal figures represents a veritable gold mine of opportunity. Improving quality can produce significant improvements in profitability. Xerox, for example, over a four-year period saved over $200 million by improving quality.[6]

4. The Malcolm Baldridge Quality Award was created by Public Law 100-107 in 1987. The first awards were given in 1988.
5. Michael R. Ostrenga, "Return on Investment Through the Cost of Quality," *Journal of Cost Management* (Summer 1991): 37–44.
6. Lawrence P. Carr, "How Xerox Sustains the Cost of Quality," *Management Accounting* (August 1995): 26–32.

In the last two decades, quality has become an important competitive dimension for both service and manufacturing organizations. Quality is an integrating theme for all organizations. Foreign firms' ability to sell higher-quality products at lower prices, has cost many U.S. firms market share. In an effort to combat this stiff competition, U.S. firms have increasingly paid more attention to quality and productivity, especially given the potential to reduce costs and improve product quality simultaneously. The senior management of IBM, for example, identified poor quality as the root cause of problems it was having. In an effort to solve some of these problems the company implemented a quality program called "Market Driven Quality." According to former IBM chairman John Akers, quality improvement is a survival issue for today's businesses.[7] Other American companies are following suit and are striving to meet consumer quality expectations. Some are even calling this push for increased quality a "second industrial revolution."[8]

As these companies implement quality-improvement programs, a need arises to monitor and report on the progress of these programs. Managers need to know what quality costs are and how they are changing over time. Reporting and measuring quality performance is absolutely essential to the success of an ongoing quality-improvement program. A fundamental prerequisite for this reporting is measuring the costs of quality. But to measure those costs, an operational definition of *quality* is needed.

Quality Defined

The typical dictionary definition of *quality* refers to the "degree or grade of excellence"; in this sense, quality is a relative measure of goodness. Defining quality as goodness is so general that it offers no operational content. How do we build an operational definition? The answer is, "Adopt a customer focus." Operationally, a **quality product or service** is one that meets or exceeds customer expectations. In effect, quality is customer satisfaction. But what is meant by "customer expectations"? Customer expectations can be described by quality attributes or what are often referred to as "dimensions of quality."[9] Thus, a quality product or service is one that meets or exceeds customer expectations on the following eight dimensions:

(margin term) **quality product or service**

1. Performance
2. Aesthetics
3. Serviceability
4 Features
5. Reliability
6. Durability
7. Quality of conformance
8. Fitness for use

(margin term) **performance**

The first four dimensions describe important quality attributes, but are difficult to measure. Performance refers to how consistently and well a product functions. For services, the inseparability principle means that the service is performed in the presence of the customer. Thus, the performance dimension for services can be further defined by the attributes of responsiveness, assurance, and empathy. *Responsiveness* is simply the willingness to help customers and provide prompt, consistent service. *Assurance* refers to the knowledge and courtesy of employees and their ability to convey trust and confidence. *Empathy* means providing caring, individualized attention to customers. Aesthetics is concerned with the appearance of tangible products (for example, style and

(margin term) **aesthetics**

---

7. Lawrence Carr and Thomas Tyson, "Planning Quality Cost Expenditures," *Management Accounting* (October 1992), pp. 52–56.
8. James B. Simpson and David L. Muthler, "Quality Costs: Facilitating the Quality Initiative," *Journal of Cost Management* (Spring 1987): 25–34.
9. These dimensions are based on Edwin S. Schecter, *Managing for World Class Quality* (Milwaukee: ASQC Quality Press, 1992) and Leonard L. Berry and A. Parasurman, *Marketing Services: Competing Through Quality* (New York: The Free Press, Macmillan, 1991), 16.

serviceability

features (quality of design)

beauty) as well as the appearance of the facilities, equipment, personnel, and communication materials associated with services. Serviceability measures the ease of maintaining and or repairing the product. Features (quality of design) refer to characteristics of a product that differentiate functionally similar products. For example, the function of automobiles is to provide transportation. Yet one auto may have a four-cylinder engine, a manual transmission, vinyl seats, room to seat four passengers comfortably, and front disk brakes; another may have a six-cylinder engine, an automatic transmission, leather seats, room to seat six passengers comfortably, and antilock brakes. Similarly, first-class air travel and economy air travel reflect different design qualities. First-class air travel, for example, offers more legroom, better meals, and more luxurious seats. Obviously, in both cases the product features are different. Higher design quality is usually reflected in higher manufacturing costs and in higher selling prices. Quality of design helps a company determine its market. There is a market for both the four-cylinder and the six-cylinder cars as well as economy air travel and first-class air travel.

reliability

durability

quality of conformance

fitness of use

Reliability is the probability that the product or service will perform its intended function for a specified length of time. Durability is defined as the length of time a product functions. Quality of conformance is a measure of how a product meets its specifications. For example, the specifications for a machined part may be a drilled hole that is 3 inches in diameter plus or minus $\frac{1}{8}$ inch. Parts falling within this range are defined as conforming parts. Fitness of use is the suitability of the product for carrying out its advertised functions. If there is a fundamental design flaw, the product may fail in the field even if it conforms to its specifications. Product recalls are frequently the result of fitness-of-use failures.

Improving quality, then, means improving one or more of the eight quality dimensions while maintaining performance on the remaining dimensions. Providing a higher-quality product than a competitor means outperforming the competitor on at least one dimension while matching performance on the remaining dimensions. Although all eight dimensions are important and can affect customer satisfaction, the quality attributes that are measurable tend to receive more emphasis. Conformance, in particular, is strongly emphasized. In fact, many quality experts believe that "quality is conformance" is the best operational definition. There is some logic to this position. Product specifications should explicitly consider such things as reliability, durability, fitness for use, and performance. Implicitly, a conforming product is reliable, durable, fit for use, and performs well. The product should be produced as the design specifies it; specifications should be met. Conformance is the basis for defining what is meant by a nonconforming, or *defective*, product.

defective product

zero defects

A defective product is one that does not conform to specifications. Zero defects means that all products conform to specifications. But what is meant by "conforming to specifications"? The *traditional view* of conformance assumes that there is an acceptable range of values for each specification or quality characteristic. A target value is defined and upper and lower limits are set that describe acceptable product variation for a given quality characteristic. Any unit that falls within the limits is deemed nondefective. For example, losing or gaining zero minutes per month may be the target value for a watch and any watch that keeps time correctly within plus or minus two minutes per month is judged acceptable. On the other hand, the *robust quality view* of conformance emphasizes fitness of use. *Robustness* means hitting the target value every time. There is no range in which variation is acceptable. A nondefective watch in the robust setting would be one that does not gain or lose any minutes during the month. Since evidence exists that product variation can be costly, the robust quality definition of conformance is superior to the traditional definition.

Costs of Quality Defined

Quality-linked activities are those activities performed because poor quality may or does exist. The costs of performing these activities are referred to as *costs of quality*. Thus,

costs of quality

control activities

control costs
failure activities

failure costs

prevention costs

appraisal costs

**internal failure
    costs**

**external failure
    costs**

the costs of quality are the costs that exist because poor quality may or does exist.[10] This definition implies that quality costs are associated with two subcategories of quality-related activities: *control activities* and *failure activities*. Control activities are performed by an organization to prevent or detect poor quality (because poor quality *may* exist). Thus, control activities are made up of prevention and appraisal activities. Control costs are the costs of performing control activities. Failure activities are performed by an organization or its customers in response to poor quality (poor quality *does* exist). If the response to poor quality occurs before delivery of a bad (nonconforming, unreliable, not durable, and so on) product to a customer, the activities are classified as internal failure activities; otherwise, they are classified as external failure activities. Failure costs are the costs incurred by an organization because failure activities are performed. Notice that the definitions of failure activities and failure costs imply that customer response to poor quality can impose costs on an organization. The definitions of quality-related activities also imply four categories of quality costs: (1) prevention costs, (2) appraisal costs, (3) internal failure costs, and (4) external failure costs.

Prevention costs are incurred to prevent poor quality in the products or services being produced. As prevention costs increase, we would expect the costs of failure to decrease. Examples of prevention costs are quality engineering, quality training programs, quality planning, quality reporting, supplier evaluation and selection, quality audits, quality circles, field trials, and design reviews.

Appraisal costs are incurred to determine whether products and services are conforming to their requirements or customer needs. Examples include inspecting and testing raw materials, packaging inspection, supervising appraisal activities, product acceptance, process acceptance, measurement (inspection and test) equipment, and outside endorsements. Two of these terms require further explanation.

Product acceptance involves sampling from batches of finished goods to determine whether they meet an acceptable quality level; if so, the goods are accepted. *Process acceptance* involves sampling goods while in process to see if the process is in control and producing nondefective goods; if not, the process is shut down until corrective action can be taken. The main objective of the appraisal function is to prevent nonconforming goods from being shipped to customers.

Internal failure costs are incurred because products and services do not conform to specifications or customer needs. This nonconformance is detected prior to being shipped or delivered to outside parties. These are the failures detected by appraisal activities. Examples of internal failure costs are scrap, rework, downtime (due to defects), reinspection, retesting, and design changes. These costs disappear if no defects exist.

External failure costs are incurred because products and services fail to conform to requirements or satisfy customer needs after being delivered to customers. Of all the costs of quality, this category can be the most devastating. Costs of recalls, for example, can run into the hundreds of millions. Other examples include lost sales because of poor product performance, returns and allowances because of poor quality, warranties, repair, product liability, customer dissatisfaction, lost market share, and complaint adjustment. External failure costs, like internal failure costs, disappear if no defects exist.

Measuring Quality Costs

**observable quality
    costs**
**hidden quality
    costs**

Quality costs can also be classified as *observable* or *hidden*. Observable quality costs are those that are available from an organization's accounting records. Hidden quality costs are opportunity costs resulting from poor quality (opportunity costs are not usually recognized in accounting records). Consider, for example, all the examples of quality costs listed in the prior section. With the exception of lost sales, customer dissatisfaction, and lost market share, all the quality costs are observable and should be available from

10. This is the definition in Morse, Roth, and Poston, *Measuring, Planning, and Controlling*, 19.

the accounting records. Note also that the hidden costs are all in the external failure category. These hidden quality costs can be significant and should be estimated. Although estimating hidden quality costs is not easy, three methods have been suggested: (1) the multiplier method, (2) the market research method, and (3) the Taguchi quality loss function.

The Multiplier Method The multiplier method assumes that the total failure cost is simply some multiple of measured failure costs:

$$\text{Total external failure cost} = k(\text{Measured external failure costs})$$

where k is the multiplier effect. The value of k is based on experience. For example, Westinghouse Electric reports a value of k between 3 and 4.[11] Thus, if the measured external failure costs are $2 million, the actual external failure costs are between $6 million and $8 million. Including hidden costs in assessing the amount of external failure costs allows management to more accurately determine the level of resource spending for prevention and appraisal activities. Specifically, with an increase in failure costs, we would expect management to increase its investment in control costs.

The Market Research Method Formal market research methods are used to assess the effect of poor quality on sales and market share. Customer surveys and interviews with members of a company's sales force can provide significant insights into the magnitude of a company's hidden costs. Market research results can be used to project future profit losses attributable to poor quality.

The Taguchi Quality Loss Function The traditional zero defects definition assumes that hidden quality costs exist only for units that fall outside the upper and lower specification limits. The Taguchi loss function assumes any variation from the target value of a quality characteristic causes hidden quality costs. Furthermore, the hidden quality costs increase quadratically as the actual value deviates from the target value. The Taguchi quality loss function, illustrated in Exhibit 11-1, can be described by the following equation:

$$L(y) = k(y - T)^2 \qquad\qquad \textbf{(11.1)}$$

where

k = *A proportionality constant dependent upon the organization's external failure cost structure*
y = *Actual value of quality characteristic*
T = *Target value of quality characteristic*
L = *Quality loss*

Exhibit 11-1 demonstrates that the quality cost is zero at the target value and increases symmetrically, at an increasing rate, as the actual value varies from the target value. Assume, for example, that k = $400 and T = 10 inches in diameter. Exhibit 11-2 illustrates the computation of the quality loss for four units. Notice that the cost quadruples when the deviation from the target doubles (from units 2 to 3). Notice also the average deviation squared and the average loss per unit can be computed. These averages can be used to compute the total expected hidden quality costs for a product. If, for example, the total units produced are 2,000 and the average squared deviation is 0.025, then the expected cost per unit is $10 (0.025 × $400) and the total expected loss for the 2,000 units would be $20,000 ($10 × 2,000).

11. T. L. Albright and P. R. Roth, "The Measurement of Quality Costs: An Alternative Paradigm," *Accounting Horizons* (June 1992): 15–27. This article also describes the three approaches to measuring hidden quality costs.

Taguchi loss
function

Exhibit
The Taguchi Quality Loss
Function

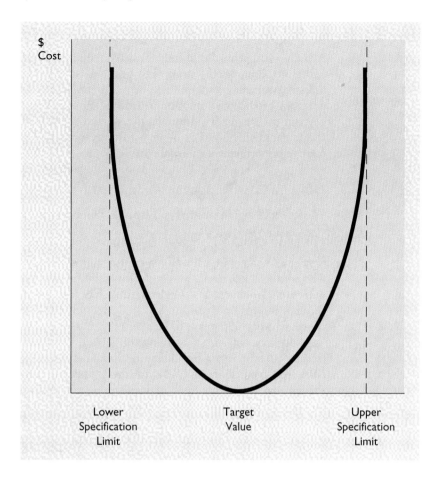

To apply the Taguchi loss function, k must be estimated. The value for k is computed by dividing the estimated cost at one of the specification limits by the squared deviation of the limit from the target value:

$$k = c/d^2$$

where

$c = $ *Loss at the lower or upper specification limit*
$d = $ *Distance of limit from target value*

This means that we still must estimate the loss for a given deviation from the target value. The first two methods, the multiplier method or the market research method, may be used to help in this estimation (a one-time assessment need). Once k is known, the hidden quality costs can be estimated for any level of variation from the target value.

Exhibit
Quality-Loss
Computation Illustrated

Unit	Actual Diameter (y)	$y - T$	$(y - T)^2$	$k(y - T)^2$
1	9.9	−0.10	0.010	$ 4.00
2	10.1	0.10	0.010	4.00
3	10.2	0.20	0.040	16.00
4	9.8	−0.20	0.040	16.00
Total			0.100	$40.00
Average			0.025	$10.00

REPORTING QUALITY COST INFORMATION

Objective 2

Prepare a quality cost report and explain the difference between the conventional view of acceptable quality level and the view espoused by total quality control.

A quality cost reporting system is essential if an organization is serious about improving and controlling quality costs. The first and simplest step in creating such a system is assessing current actual quality costs. A detailed listing of actual quality costs by category can provide two important insights. First, it reveals the magnitude of the quality costs in each category, allowing managers to assess their financial impact. Second, it shows the distribution of quality costs by category, allowing managers to assess the relative importance of each category.

Quality Cost Reports

The financial significance of quality costs can be assessed more easily by expressing these costs as a percentage of actual sales. Exhibit 11-3, for example, reports the quality costs of Jensen Products for fiscal 1998.[12] According to the report, quality costs represent almost 12 percent of sales. Given the rule of thumb that quality costs should be no more than about 2.5 percent, Jensen Products has ample opportunity to improve profits by decreasing quality costs. Understand, however, that reduction in costs should come through improvement of quality. Reduction of quality costs without any effort to improve quality could prove to be a disastrous strategy.

Additional insight concerning the relative distribution of quality costs can be realized by constructing a pie chart. Exhibit 11-4 provides such a chart, using the quality costs reported in Exhibit 11-3. Managers, of course, have the responsibility of assessing the optimal level of quality and determining the relative amount that should be spent in each category. There are two views concerning optimal quality costs: the traditional

12. The quality cost report given in Exhibit 11-3 parallels the format used by ITT except for several minor differences. First, the ITT report combines the internal and external categories into one failure category. Second, the ITT report has a third column allowing the reporting unit to express quality costs as a percentage of a measure other than sales. For more detail, see Morse, Roth, and Poston, *Measuring, Planning, and Controlling*, 78–81.

11-3

Exhibit

		Jensen Products Quality Cost Report For the Year Ended March 31, 1998	
		Quality Costs	**Percentage (%) of Sales**[a]
Prevention costs:			
Quality training	$35,000		
Reliability engineering	80,000	$115,000	4.11
Appraisal costs:			
Materials inspection	$20,000		
Product acceptance	10,000		
Process acceptance	38,000	68,000	2.43
Internal failure costs:			
Scrap	$50,000		
Rework	35,000	85,000	3.04
External failure costs:			
Customer complaints	$25,000		
Warranty	25,000		
Repair	15,000	65,000	2.32
Total quality costs		$333,000	11.90[b]

[a]Actual sales of $2,800,000

[b]$\frac{\$333,000}{\$2,800,000} = 11.89$ percent; difference is rounding error

Morse, Roth, and Poston, *Measuring, Planning, and Controlling*, 78–81.

Exhibit
Relative Distribution of
Quality Costs

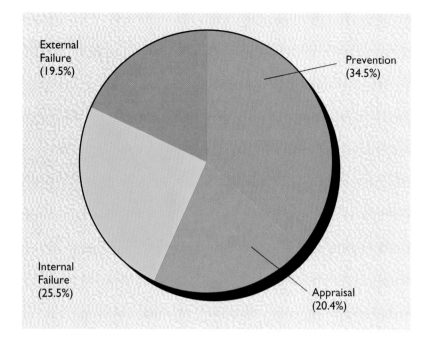

view, calling for an *acceptable quality level*, and the contemporary view referred to as *total quality control*. Each view offers managers insights about how quality costs ought to be managed.

Quality Cost Function: Traditional View

The traditional view assumes that there is a trade-off between control costs and failure costs. As control costs increase, failure costs should decrease. As long as the decrease in failure costs is greater than the corresponding increase in control costs, a company should continue increasing its efforts to prevent or detect nonconforming units. Eventually, a point is reached at which any additional increase in this effort costs more than the corresponding reduction in failure costs. This point represents the minimum level of total quality costs. It is the optimal balance between control costs and failure costs and **acceptable quality** defines what is known as the acceptable quality level (AQL). This theoretical relation- **level (AQL)** ship is illustrated in Exhibit 11-5.

In Exhibit 11-5, two cost functions are assumed: one for control costs and one for failure costs. It is also assumed that the percentage of defective units increases as the amount spent on prevention and appraisal activities decreases; failure costs, on the other hand, increase as the number of defective units increases. From the total quality cost function, we see that total quality costs decrease as quality improves up to a point. After that, no further improvement is possible. An optimal level of defective units is identified and the company works to achieve this level. This level of allowable defective units is the *acceptable quality level*.

Quality Cost Function: Contemporary View

The AQL viewpoint is based on a traditional defective product definition. In the classic sense, a product is defective if it falls outside the tolerance limits for a quality characteristic. Under this view, failure costs are incurred only if the product fails to conform to specifications and an optimal trade-off exists between failure and control costs. The AQL view permitted and, in fact, encouraged the production of a given number of defective units. This model prevailed in the quality control world until the late 1970s, when the AQL model was challenged by the *zero-defects* model. Essentially, the zero-defects model made the claim that it was cost-beneficial to reduce nonconforming units

Exhibit
Traditional Quality Cost
Graph

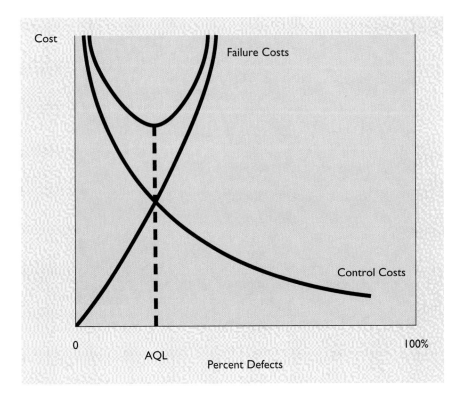

to zero. Firms producing increasingly fewer nonconforming units became more competitive relative to firms that continued the traditional AQL model. In the mid-1980s, the zero-defects model was taken one step further by the *robust quality* model, which challenged the definition of a defective unit. According to the robust view, a loss is experienced from producing products that vary from a target value, and the greater the distance from the target value the greater the loss. Furthermore, the loss is incurred even if the deviation is within the specification limits. In other words, variation from the ideal is costly and specification limits serve no useful purpose, and, in fact, may be deceptive. The zero-defects model understates the quality costs and thus the potential for savings from even greater efforts to improve quality (remember the multiplication factor of Westinghouse Electric). Thus, the robust quality model tightened the definition of a defective unit, refined our view of quality costs and intensified the quality race.

For firms operating in an intensely competitive environment, quality can offer an important competitive advantage. If the robust quality view is correct, then firms can capitalize on it, decreasing the number of defective units (robustly defined) while simultaneously decreasing their total quality costs. This is what appears to be happening for those firms that are striving to achieve a robust zero-defect state for their products (a robust zero-defect state is one with zero tolerance). The optimal level for quality costs is where products are produced that meet their target values. The quest to find ways to achieve the target value creates a dynamic quality world as opposed to the static quality world of AQL.

Dynamic Nature of Quality Costs The discovery that trade-offs among quality cost categories can be managed differently from what is implied by the relationships portrayed in Exhibit 11-5 is analogous to the discovery that inventory cost trade-offs can be managed differently from what the traditional inventory model (EOQ) implied. Essentially, what happens is that as firms increase their prevention and appraisal costs and reduce their failure costs, they discover that they can then cut back on the prevention and appraisal costs. What initially appears to be a trade-off turns out to be a permanent reduction in costs for all quality cost categories. Exhibit 11-6 displays the changes in

Exhibit
Contemporary Quality
Cost Graph

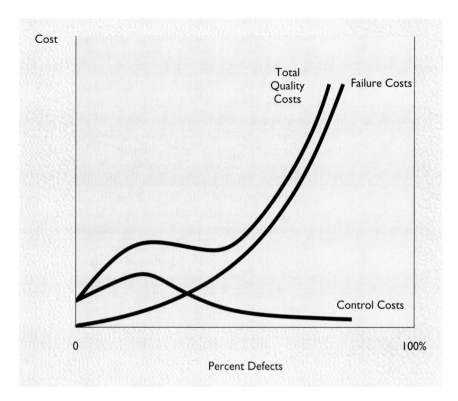

quality cost relationships; it shows a total quality cost function consistent with the quality cost relationships described. There are some key differences. First, control costs do not increase without limit as a robust zero-defect state is approached. Second, control costs may increase and then decrease as the robust state is approached. Third, failure costs can be driven to zero.

Suppose, for example, that a firm has decided to improve the quality of its raw material inputs through the implementation of a supplier selection program. The objective is to identify and use suppliers who are willing to meet certain quality standards. As the firm works to implement this program, additional costs may be incurred (for example, review of suppliers, communication with suppliers, contract negotiations, and so on). And, initially, other prevention and appraisal costs may continue at their current levels. However, once the program is fully implemented and evidence is surfacing that the failure costs are being reduced (for example, less rework, fewer customer complaints, and fewer repairs), then the company may decide to cut back on inspections of incoming raw materials, reduce the level of product acceptance activities, and so on. The net effect is a reduction in all quality cost categories. And quality has increased!

This example is consistent with the strategy to reduce quality costs recommended by the American Society for Quality Control:

The strategy for reducing quality costs is quite simple: (1) take direct attack on failure costs in an attempt to drive them to zero; (2) invest in the "right" prevention activities to bring about improvement; (3) reduce appraisal costs according to results achieved; and, (4) continuously evaluate and redirect prevention efforts to gain further improvement.

This strategy is based on the premise that:

- *For each failure there is a* root cause.
- *Causes are* preventable.
- *Prevention is always* cheaper.[13]

13. Jack Campanella, ed., *Principles of Quality Costs* (Milwaukee: ASQC Quality Press, 1990), 12.

This ability to reduce total quality costs dramatically in all categories is borne out by real-world experiences. Tennant, for example, reduced its costs of quality from 17 percent of sales in 1980 to 2.5 percent of sales in 1988, and, at the same time, significantly altered the relative distribution of the quality cost categories. In 1980, failure costs accounted for 50 percent of the total costs of quality (8.5 percent of sales) and control costs 50 percent (8.5 percent of sales). In 1988, failure costs accounted for only 15 percent of the total costs of quality (0.375 percent of sales) and control costs had increased to 85 percent of the total (2.125 percent of sales). Tennant increased quality, reduced quality costs in every category and in total, and shifted the distribution of quality costs to the control categories, with the greatest emphasis on prevention. This outcome argues strongly against the traditional quality cost model portrayed in Exhibit 11-5. According to this model, total quality costs can be decreased only by trading off control and failure costs (increasing one while decreasing the other). Further support for the total quality control model is provided by Westinghouse Electric. Similar to Tennant, Westinghouse Electric found that their profits continued to improve until their control costs accounted for about 70 percent to 80 percent of total quality costs.[14] Based on these two companies' experiences, we know that it is possible to reduce total quality costs significantly—in all categories—and that the process radically alters the relative distribution of the quality cost categories.

Activity-based Management and Optimal Quality Costs Activity-based management classifies activities as value-added and nonvalue-added and keeps only those that add value. This principle can be applied to quality-related activities. Internal and external failure activities and their associated costs are nonvalue-added and should be eliminated. Prevention activities—performed efficiently—can be classified as value-added and should be retained. Initially, however, prevention activities may not be performed efficiently and activity reduction and activity selection (and perhaps even activity sharing) can be used to achieve the desired value-added state. Appraisal activities are more difficult to assess. The initial reaction may be to classify all appraisal activities as nonvalue-added. However, in reality, some of these activities may be needed at some level to prevent backsliding. Statistical process control, for example, may serve a value-added objective. Similarly, it seems unrealistic to totally eliminate supplier verification. Conditions change, and without any monitoring, suppliers may also backslide.[15]

Once the activities are identified for each category, resource drivers can be used to improve cost assignments to the individual activities. Root (cost) drivers can also be identified, especially for failure activities, and used to help managers understand what is causing the costs of the activities. This information can then be used to select ways of reducing quality costs to the level demonstrated in Exhibit 11-6. In effect, activity-based management supports the robust zero-defect view of quality costs. There is no optimal trade-off between control and failure costs; the latter are nonvalue-added costs and should be reduced to zero. Some control activities are nonvalue-added and should be eliminated. Other control activities are value-added but may be performed inefficiently and the costs caused by the inefficiency are nonvalue-added. Thus, costs for these categories may also be reduced to lower levels.

Trend Analysis

Quality cost reports reveal the magnitude of quality costs and their distribution among the four categories, thus revealing opportunities for improvement. Once quality-improvement measures are undertaken, it is important to determine whether quality

---

14. These factual observations are based on those reported by Lawrence P. Carr and Thomas Tyson, "Planning Quality Cost Expenditures."

15. In Michael Ostrega, "Return on Investment Through the Cost of Quality," it is suggested that activity-based costing can be used to help managers understand the nature of quality costs. In this article, failure and appraisal activities are labeled as nonvalue-added. Only prevention activities are classified as value-added.

costs are being reduced as planned. Quality cost reports will not reveal whether improvement has occurred or not. It would be useful to have a picture of how the quality-improvement program has been doing since its inception. Is the multiple-period trend—the overall change in quality costs—moving in the right direction? Are significant quality gains being made each period? Answers to these questions can be given by providing a trend chart or graph that tracks the change in quality costs through time. Such a graph is called a multiple-period quality trend report. By plotting quality costs as a percentage of sales against time, the overall trend in the quality program can be assessed. The first year plotted is the year prior to the implementation of the quality improvement program. Assume that a company has experienced the following:

multiple-period quality trend report

	Quality Costs	Actual Sales	Costs as a Percentage (%) of Sales
1994	$440,000	$2,200,000	20.0
1995	423,000	2,350,000	18.0
1996	412,500	2,750,000	15.0
1997	392,000	2,800,000	14.0
1998	280,000	2,800,000	10.0

Letting 1994 be year 0, 1995 be year 1, and so on, the trend graph is shown in Exhibit 11-7. Periods of time are plotted on the horizontal axis and percentages of sales on the vertical. The ultimate quality cost objective of 3 percent, the target percentage, is represented as a horizontal line on the graph.

The graph reveals that there has been a steady downward trend in quality costs expressed as a percentage of sales. The graph also reveals that there is still ample room for improvement toward the long-run target percentage.

Exhibit
Multiple-Period Trend Graph: Total Quality Costs

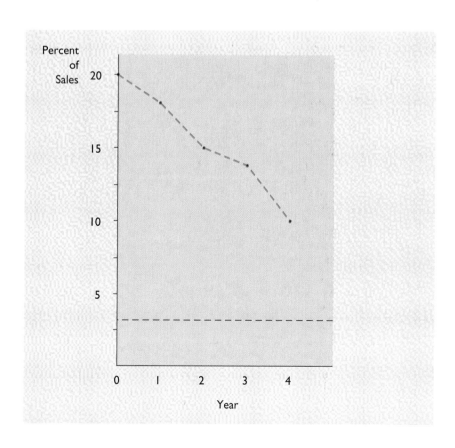

Additional insight can be provided by plotting the trend for each individual quality category. Assume that each category is expressed as a percentage of sales for the same period of time.

	Prevention	Appraisal	Internal Failure	External Failure
1994	2.0%	2.0%	6.0%	10.0%
1995	3.0	2.4	4.0	8.6
1996	3.0	3.0	3.0	6.0
1997	4.0	3.0	2.5	4.5
1998	4.1	2.4	2.0	1.5

The graph showing the trend for each category is displayed in Exhibit 11-8. From Exhibit 11-8, we can see that the company has had dramatic success in reducing external and internal failures. More money is being spent on prevention (the amount has doubled as a percentage). Appraisal costs have increased and then decreased. Note also that the relative distribution of costs has changed. In 1994, failure costs were 80 percent of the total quality costs ($\frac{16\%}{20\%}$). In 1998, they are 35 percent of the total ($\frac{3.5\%}{10\%}$). The potential to reduce quality costs also affects the way decisions are made. The usefulness of quality cost information for decision making and planning should not be underestimated.

USING QUALITY COST INFORMATION

Objective 3

Explain why quality cost information is needed and how it is used.

The principal objective of reporting quality costs is to improve and facilitate managerial planning, control, and decision making. For example, to decide to implement a supplier selection program to improve the quality of material inputs, a manager will need an assessment of current quality costs by item and by category, an assessment of the addi-

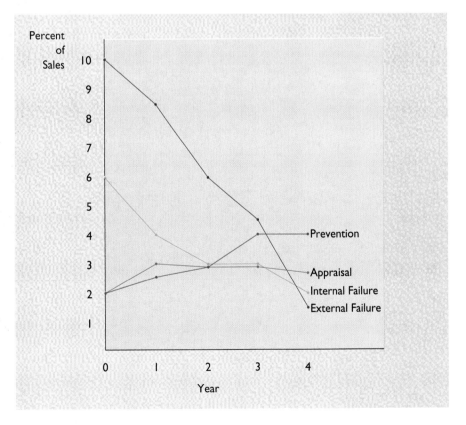

11-8

Exhibit
Multiple-Period Trend Graph: Individual Quality Cost Categories

tional costs associated with the program, and an assessment of the projected savings by item and by category. When the costs and savings will occur must also be projected. Once these cash effects are projected, then a capital budgeting analysis can be done to assess the merits of the proposed program. If the outcome is favorable and the program is initiated, then it becomes important to monitor the program through fairly standard performance reporting.

Using quality cost information for quality program implementation decisions and for evaluating the effectiveness of these programs, once implemented, is only one potential use of a quality cost system. Other important uses can also be identified. The following scenarios illustrate the utility of quality cost information for a strategic pricing decision and profitability analysis of a new product design.

Scenario A: Strategic Pricing

Leola Wise, marketing manager, muttered to herself as she reviewed the latest market share data for the company's low-priced electronic measurement instruments. Once again the share had dropped! The Japanese firms were continuing to put pressure on this product line. Anticipating this outcome, Leola had begun preparing a brief to support a significant price decrease for this line of products. A price decrease of $3 was needed to recapture the lost market share. The new price less the desired profit per unit produced a target cost that was less than the current actual cost of producing and selling the lower-end instruments. To continue producing this line, cost reductions would need to be made. A cost reduction strategy was needed to reestablish its competitive position.

In the last executive meeting, the discussion focused on how to achieve cost reductions. Ben Blackburn, the chief engineer, indicated that process redesign could offer about half the needed cost reduction. Leola suggested that the company should adopt a total quality control position and work to reduce the cost of the lower-level instruments by decreasing quality costs. To determine the potential magnitude of the cost reductions, she asked Earl Simpson, the controller, what the quality costs were for the lower-level instruments. Earl admitted that the costs were not tracked separately. For example, the cost of scrap was buried in the Work in Process account. He did promise, however, to have some estimates of the costs—perhaps not complete—by the end of the month. The report for the lower-level instruments (in the form of a memo from Earl Simpson), which arrived a week ago, follows.

MEMO

To: Leola Wise
From: Earl Simpson
Subject: Quality Costs

Lee, I have assembled some data that may be useful to you. As requested, I have provided some estimates of the quality costs associated with this line. I have not included any costs of lost sales due to nonconforming products. You are probably in a better position to assess this effect.

Quality costs (estimated):	
Inspection of raw materials	*$ 200,000*
Scrap	*800,000*
Rejects	*500,000*
Rework	*400,000*
Product inspection	*300,000*
Warranty work	*1,000,000*
Total estimate	*$3,200,000*

Upon receiving the memo, Leola had immediately called the quality control department and arranged a meeting with the manager, Art Smith. Art indicated that implementing total quality initiatives would reduce quality costs by 50 percent within 18 months. He had already begun planning the implementation of a new quality program. With this information, Leola calculated that a 50 percent reduction in the quality costs associated with the low-quality instruments would reduce costs by about $1.60 per unit $(\frac{\$1,600,000}{1,000,000})$. This would make up slightly more than half of the $3 reduction in selling price that would be needed (the reduction is 15 percent of $20). Based on this outcome, Leola decided to implement the price reduction in three phases: a $1 reduction immediately, a $1 reduction in 6 months, and the final reduction of $1 in 12 months. This phased reduction would likely prevent any further erosion of market share and would start increasing it sometime into the second phase. By phasing in the price reductions, it would give the quality department time to reduce costs so that any big losses could be avoided.

Scenario A illustrates that both quality cost information and the implementation of a total quality control program contributed to a significant strategic decision. It also illustrates that improving quality is not a panacea. The reductions are not large enough to bear the full price reduction. Other productivity gains such as those promised by engineering will be needed to ensure the long-range viability of the product line.

Scenario B: New Product Analysis

Tara Anderson, the marketing manager, and Britany Fox, the design engineer, were both unhappy. They had been certain that a proposal for the new product was going to be approved. Instead, they received the following report from the controller's office.

Report: New Product Analysis, Project #675

Estimated product life cycle: 2 years
Projected sales potential: 50,000 units (life cycle)
Projected life-cycle income statement:

Sales (50,000 @ $60)	$3,000,000
Cost of inputs:	
Materials	800,000
Labor	400,000
Scrap	150,000
Inspection	350,000
Repair work	200,000
Product development	500,000
Selling	300,000
Life-cycle income	$ 300,000

Decision: Reject
Reason(s): Life-cycle income is less than the company required 18 percent return on sales.

"You know," Tara remarked, "I can't quite believe this report. Why don't we ask Bob how he came up with these figures?"

"I agree," responded Britany. "I'll arrange a meeting for tomorrow. I'll ask him to provide more detail than just the aggregate figures shown on the report."

The next day, the following conversation was recorded. Tara and Britany had just completed a review of the detailed cost projections supplied by Bob Brown, the assistant controller.

Britany: Bob, I would like to know why there is a $3 per-unit scrap cost. And the inspection costs—they seem high. Can you explain these costs?

Bob: Sure. It's based on the scrap cost that we track for existing, similar products. Also, as you know, we have a 10 percent destructive-sampling requirement for these type of products.

Britany: Well, I think you have overlooked the new design features of this new product. Its design virtually eliminates any waste—especially when you consider that the product will be made on a numerically controlled machine.

Tara: Also, this $2 per-unit charge for repair work should be eliminated. The new design that Britany is proposing solves the failure problems we have had with related products. It also means that the $100,000 of fixed costs associated with the repair activity can be eliminated. Furthermore, because of the new design, destructive sampling is not required and we need one less inspector than you have budgeted.

Bob: Britany, how certain are you that this new design will eliminate some of these quality problems?

Britany: I'm absolutely positive. The early prototypes did exactly as we expected. The results of those tests are included in the proposal. You must not have read the prototype results.

Bob: Right. I didn't. Eliminating scrap reduces the unit-level variable cost by $3 per unit. I also see where the repair and inspection activities are overcosted. We only need one inspector costing $50,000. And eliminating the repair activity saves $200,000. That means the projected life-cycle profits are $650,000 more than I have projected. That means that the return on sales is more than 30 percent.

   Scenario B illustrates the importance of further classifying quality costs by behavior. The scenario also reinforces the importance of identifying and reporting quality costs separately. The new product was designed to reduce its quality costs and only by knowing the quality costs assigned could Britany and Tara have discovered the error in the cost-volume-profit analysis.

   Reporting quality costs so that they can be used for decision making is only one objective of a good quality-costing system. Another objective is controlling quality costs—a factor critical in helping expected outcomes of decisions come to fruition. The pricing decision of scenario A, for example, depended on the plan to reduce quality costs.

PRODUCTIVITY: MEASUREMENT AND CONTROL

Objective 4

Explain what productivity is and calculate the impact of productivity changes on profits.

productivity
total productive efficiency
technical efficiency

input trade-off efficiency

Productivity is concerned with producing output efficiently and specifically addresses the relationship of output and the inputs used to produce the output. Usually, different combinations or mixes of inputs can be used to produce a given level of output. Total productive efficiency is the point at which two conditions are satisfied: (1) for any mix of inputs that will produce a given output, no more of any one input is used than necessary to produce the output and (2) given the mixes that satisfy the first condition, the least costly mix is chosen. The first condition is driven by technical relationships and, therefore, is referred to as technical efficiency. Viewing activities as inputs, the first condition requires the elimination of all nonvalue-added activities and that value-added activities be performed with the minimal quantities needed to produce the given output. The second condition is driven by relative input price relationships and, therefore, is referred to as input trade-off efficiency. Input prices determine the *relative proportions* that should be used of each input. Deviation from these fixed proportions creates input trade-off inefficiency.

   Productivity improvement programs attempt to move toward a state of total productive efficiency. Technical improvements in productivity can be achieved by using fewer inputs to produce the same output or by producing more output using the same inputs or more output with relatively fewer inputs. For example, in 1987, Birmingham Steel produced 167,000 tons of steel with 184 workers—an average of 912 tons of steel per

Investments in technology can lead to increased productivity. Here, a supermarket scanner records the price of a bag of sugar. The scanner simultaneously adds the price to the customer's bill and updates the store's inventory records. This decreases the amount of labor necessary to track inventory and increases productivity.

worker. By 1992, the output had increased to 276,000 tons of steel using 207 workers—an average of 1,335 tons per worker.[16] By 1987 productivity standards, about 303 workers would have been needed to produce 276,000 tons. Thus, output increased and fewer workers were needed.

Exhibit 11-9 illustrates the three ways to achieve an improvement in technical efficiency. The output is tons of steel and the inputs are labor (number of workers) and capital (dollars invested in automated equipment). Notice that the relative proportions of the inputs are held constant so that all productivity improvement is attributable to improving technical efficiency.

Productivity improvement can also be achieved by trading off more costly inputs for less costly inputs. Exhibit 11-10 (page 452) illustrates the possibility of improving productivity by increasing input trade-off efficiency. Although improving technical efficiency is what most think of when improving productivity is mentioned, input trade-off efficiency can offer significant opportunities for increasing overall economic efficiency. Choosing the right combination of inputs can be as critical as choosing the right quantity of inputs. Notice in Exhibit 11-10 that input combination I produces the same output as input combination II—but that the cost is $5 million less. Total measures of productivity are usually a combination of changes in technical and input trade-off efficiency.

Partial Productivity Measurement

productivity measurement

Productivity measurement is simply a quantitative assessment of productivity changes. The objective is to assess whether productive efficiency has increased or decreased. Productivity measurement can be actual or prospective. *Actual* productivity measurement allows managers to assess, monitor, and control changes. *Prospective* measurement is forward looking and it serves as input for strategic decision making. Specifically, prospective measurement allows managers to compare relative benefits of different input combinations, choosing the inputs and input mix that provide the greatest benefit.

16. Steven Rattner, "If Productivity's Rising, Why Are Jobs Paying Less?" *New York Times Magazine* 19 September 1993, pp. 54, 96–97.

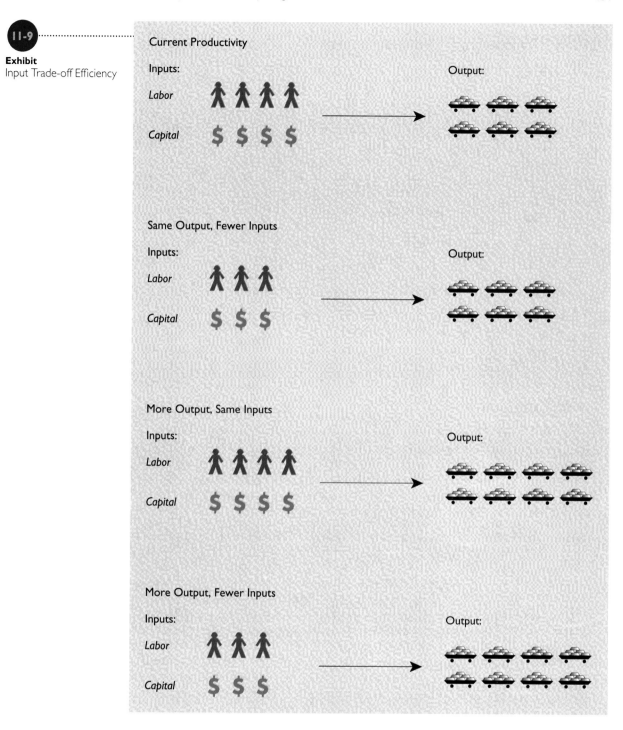

11-9

Exhibit
Input Trade-off Efficiency

Productivity measures can be developed for each input separately or for all inputs jointly. Measuring productivity for one input at a time is called partial productivity measurement.

partial productivity measurement

Partial Productivity Measurement Defined Productivity of a single input is typically measured by calculating the ratio of the output to the input:

$$\text{Productivity ratio} = \frac{\text{Output}}{\text{Input}}$$

Because the productivity of only one input is being measured, the measure is called a *partial productivity measure*. If both output and input are measured in physical quantities,

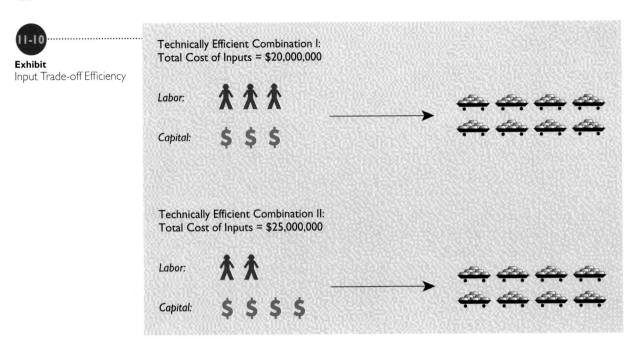

Exhibit 11-10
Input Trade-off Efficiency

operational productivity measure
financial productivity measure

then we have an operational productivity measure. If output or input is expressed in dollars, then we have a financial productivity measure.

Assume, for example, that in 1997, Kankul Company produced 120,000 motors for small window air-conditioning units and used 40,000 hours of labor. The labor productivity ratio is three motors per hour ($\frac{120,000}{40,000}$). This is an operational measure since the units are expressed in physical terms. If the selling price of each motor is $50 and the cost of labor is $12 per hour, then output and input can be expressed in dollars. The labor productivity ratio, expressed in financial terms, is $12.50 of revenue per dollar of labor cost ($\frac{\$6,000,000}{\$480,000}$).

Partial Measures and Measuring Changes in Productive Efficiency The labor productivity ratio of three motors per hour measures the 1997 productivity experience of Kankul. By itself the ratio conveys little information about productive efficiency or whether the company has improving or declining productivity. It is possible, however, to make a statement about increasing or decreasing productivity efficiency by measuring changes in productivity. To do so, the actual current productivity measure is compared with the productivity measure of a prior period. This prior period is referred to as the

base period

base period and sets the benchmark or standard for measuring changes in productive efficiency. The prior period can be any period desired. It could, for example, be the preceding year, the preceding week, or even the period during which the last batch of products was produced. For strategic evaluations, the base period is usually chosen as an earlier year. For operational control, the base period tends to be close to the current period—such as the preceding batch of products or the preceding week.

To illustrate, assume that 1997 is the base period and the labor productivity standard, therefore, is three motors per hour. Further assume that late in 1997, Kankul decided to try a new procedure for producing and assembling the motors with the expectation that the new procedure would use less labor. In 1998, 150,000 motors were produced, using 37,500 hours of labor. The labor productivity ratio for 1998 is four motors per hour ($\frac{150,000}{37,500}$). The *change* in productivity is a one-unit per hour *increase* in productivity (from three units per hour in 1997 to four units per hour in 1998). The change is a significant improvement in labor productivity and provides evidence supporting the efficacy of the new process.

Advantages of Partial Measures Partial measures allow managers to focus on the use of a particular input. Operating partial measures have the advantage of being easily interpreted by all within the organization, so they are easy to use for assessing productivity performance of operating personnel. Laborers, for instance, can relate to units produced per hour or units produced per pound of material. Thus, partial operational measures provide feedback that operating personnel can relate to and understand—measures that deal with the specific inputs over which they have control. This increases the likelihood that they will be accepted by operating personnel. Furthermore, for operational control, the standards for performance are often very short term. For example, standards can be the productivity ratios of prior batches of goods. Using this standard, productivity trends within the year can be tracked.

Disadvantages of Partial Measures Partial measures, used in isolation, can be misleading. A decline in the productivity of one input may be necessary to increase the productivity of another. Such a trade-off is desirable if overall costs decline, but the effect would be missed by using either partial measure. For example, changing a process so that direct laborers take less time to assemble a product may increase scrap and waste while leaving total output unchanged. Labor productivity has increased but productive use of materials has declined. If the increase in the cost of waste and scrap outweighs the savings of the decreased labor, overall productivity has declined.

Two important conclusions can be drawn from this example. First, the possible existence of trade-offs mandates a total measure of productivity for assessing the merits of productivity decisions. Only by looking at the total productivity effect of all inputs can managers accurately draw any conclusions about overall productivity performance. Second, because of the possibility of trade-offs, a total measure of productivity must assess the aggregate financial consequences, and, therefore, should be a financial measure.

Total Productivity Measurement

total productivity measurement

Measuring productivity for all inputs at once is called total productivity measurement. In practice, it may not be necessary to measure the effect of all inputs. Many firms measure the productivity of only those factors that are thought to be relevant indicators of organizational performance and success. Thus, in practical terms, total productivity measurement can be defined as focusing on a limited number of inputs, which, in total, indicate organizational success. In either case, total productivity measurement requires the development of a multifactor measurement approach. A common multifactor approach suggested in the productivity literature (but found rarely in practice) is the use of aggregate productivity indices. Aggregate indices are complex and difficult to interpret and have not been generally accepted. Two approaches that have gained some acceptance are *profile measurement* and *profit-linked productivity measurement*.

profile measurement

Profile Productivity Measurement Producing a product involves numerous critical inputs such as labor, materials, capital, and energy. Profile measurement provides a series or a vector of separate and distinct partial operational measures. Profiles can be compared over time to provide information about productivity changes. To illustrate the profile approach, we will use only two inputs: labor and materials. Let's return to the Kankul Company example. As before, Kankul implements a new production and assembly process in 1998. Only now let's assume that the new process affects both labor and materials. Initially, let's look at the case for which the productivity of both inputs moves in the same direction. The following data for 1997 and 1998 are available:

	1997	1998
Number of motors produced	120,000	150,000
Labor hours used	40,000	37,500
Materials used (lb)	1,200,000	1,428,571

Exhibit 11-11 provides productivity ratio profiles for each year. The 1997 profile is (3, 0.100) and the 1998 profile is (4, 0.105). Comparing profiles for the two years, we can see that productivity increased for both labor and materials (from 3 to 4 for labor and from 0.100 to 0.105 for materials). The profile comparison provides enough information so that a manager can conclude that the new assembly process has definitely improved overall productivity. The *value* of this improvement, however, is not revealed by the ratios.

As just shown, profile analysis can provide managers with useful insights about changes in productivity. However, comparing productivity profiles will not always reveal the nature of the overall change in productive efficiency. In some cases, profile analysis will not provide any clear indication of whether a productivity change is good or bad.

To illustrate this, let's revise the Kankul data to allow for trade-offs among the two inputs. Assume that all the data are the same except for materials used in 1998. Let the materials used in 1998 be 1,700,000 pounds. Using this revised number, the productivity profiles for 1997 and 1998 are presented in Exhibit 11-12. The productivity profile for 1997 is still (3, 0.100) but the profile for 1998 has changed to (4, 0.088). Comparing productivity profiles now provides a mixed signal. Productivity for labor has increased from 3 to 4, but productivity for materials has decreased from 0.100 to 0.088. The new process has caused a trade-off in the productivity in the two measures. Furthermore, while a profile analysis reveals that the trade-off exists, it does not reveal whether it is good or bad. If the economic effect of the productivity changes is positive, then the trade-off is good; otherwise, it must be viewed as bad. Valuing the trade-offs would allow us to assess the economic effect of the decision to change the assembly process. Furthermore, by valuing the productivity change, we obtain a total measure of productivity.

profit-linked
productivity
measurement

Profit-linked Productivity Measurement Assessing the effects of productivity changes on current profits is one way to value productivity changes. Profits change from the base period to the current period. Some of that profit change is attributable to productivity changes. Measuring the amount of profit change attributable to productivity change is defined as profit-linked productivity measurement.[17]

Assessing the effect of productivity changes on current-period profits will help managers understand the economic importance of productivity changes. Linking productivity changes to profits is described by the following rule:

17. Several profit-linked productivity measures have been developed and used by firms. The American Productivity Center has developed a profit-linked measure described in J. G. Belcher Jr., *The Productivity Management Process* (Houston: The American Productivity Center, 1984). D. M. Miller developed and used a profit-linked measure while working for Ethyl Corporation. It is described in D. M. Miller, "Profitability = Productivity + Price Recovery," *Harvard Business Review* (May–June 1984): 145–153. A third profit-linked measure is described in R. D. Banker, S. M. Datar, and R. S. Kaplan, "Productivity Measurement and Management Accounting," *Journal of Accounting, Auditing, and Finance* (1989). The profit-linked measure described in this text is essentially a modification of these three measures. The modification increases the accuracy of profit-linked measurement and allows a connection to the operational and partial measures of productivity. It also establishes an equivalency among the three measures. See Don R. Hansen, Maryanne Mowen, and Lawrence Hammer, "Profit-Linked Productivity Measurement," *Journal of Management Accounting Research* (Fall 1992): 79–98.

11-11 ....

Exhibit
Productivity
Measurement: Profile
Analysis, No Trade-offs

Partial Operational Productivity Ratios		
	1997 Profile[a]	1998 Profile[b]
Labor productivity ratio	3.000	4.000
Material productivity ratio	0.100	0.105

[a]Labor: $\frac{120,000}{40,000}$; materials: $\frac{120,000}{1,200,000}$
[b]Labor: $\frac{150,000}{37,500}$; materials: $\frac{150,000}{1,428,571}$

Exhibit
Productivity
Measurement: Profile
Analysis with Trade-offs

	Partial Operational Productivity Ratios	
	1997 Profile[a]	1998 Profile[b]
Labor productivity ratio	3.000	4.000
Material productivity ratio	0.100	0.088

[a]Labor: $\frac{120,000}{40,000}$; materials: $\frac{120,000}{1,200,000}$

[b]Labor: $\frac{150,000}{37,500}$; materials: $\frac{150,000}{1,700,000}$

Profit-linkage Rule

For the current period, calculate the cost of the inputs that would have been used in the absence of any productivity change and compare this cost with the cost of the inputs actually used. The difference in costs is the amount by which profits changed because of productivity changes.

To apply the linkage rule, the inputs that would have been used for the current period in the absence of a productivity change must be calculated. Let PQ represent this productivity-neutral quantity of input. To determine PQ for a particular input, divide the current-period output by the input's base-period productivity ratio:

$$PQ = \frac{\text{Current output}}{\text{Base-period productivity ratio}}$$

To illustrate the application of the profit-linked rule, let's return to the Kankul example with input trade-offs. To the data, we must add some cost information. The expanded Kankul data follow:

	1997	1998
Number of motors produced	120,000	150,000
Labor hours used	40,000	37,500
Materials used (lb)	1,200,000	1,700,000
Unit selling price (motors)	$50	$48
Wages per labor hour	$11	$12
Cost per pound of material	$2	$3

Current output (1998) is 150,000 motors. From Exhibit 11-12, we know that the base-period productivity ratios are 3 and 0.10 for labor and materials respectively. Using this information, the productivity-neutral quantity for each input is computed as follows:

$$PQ \text{ (labor)} = \frac{150,000}{3} = 50,000 \text{ hrs}$$

$$PQ \text{ (materials)} = \frac{150,000}{0.10} = 1,500,000 \text{ lbs}$$

For our example, PQ gives labor and material inputs that *would have been used* in 1998, assuming no productivity change. What the cost would have been is computed by multiplying each individual input quantity (PQ) by its current price (P) and adding:[18]

Cost of labor: $PQ \times P = 50,000 \times \$12$	$= \$\ \ \ 600,000$
Cost of materials: $PQ \times P = 1,500,000 \times \$3 =$	$4,500,000$
Total PQ cost	$\$5,100,000$

18. Base-period input prices are frequently used to value productivity changes. It has been shown, however, that current input prices should be used for accurate profit-linked productivity measurement. See Hansen, Mowen, and Hammer, "Profit-Linked Productivity Measurement."

The actual cost of inputs is obtained by multiplying the actual quantity (AQ) by current input price (P) for each input and adding:

$$
\begin{array}{ll}
\text{Cost of labor: } AQ \times P = 37{,}500 \times \$12 & = \$\ \ 450{,}000 \\
\text{Cost of materials: } AQ \times P = 1{,}700{,}000 \times \$3 & = \underline{\ \ 5{,}100{,}000} \\
\text{Total current cost} & \$5{,}550{,}000
\end{array}
$$

Finally, the productivity effect on profits is computed by subtracting the total current cost from the total PQ cost.

$$
\begin{aligned}
\text{Profit-linked effect} &= \text{Total } PQ \text{ cost} - \text{Total current cost} \\
&= \$5{,}100{,}000 - \$5{,}550{,}000 \\
&= \$450{,}000 \text{ decrease in profits}
\end{aligned}
$$

The calculation of the profit-linked effect is summarized in Exhibit 11-13.

The summary in Exhibit 11-13 reveals that the net effect of the process change was unfavorable. Profits declined by $450,000 because of the productivity changes. Notice also that profit-linked productivity effects can be assigned to individual inputs. The increase in labor productivity creates a $150,000 increase in profits; however, the drop in materials productivity caused a $600,000 decrease in profits. Most of the profit decrease came from an increase in materials usage—apparently waste, scrap, and spoiled units are much greater with the new process. Thus, the profit-linked measure provides partial measurement effects as well as a total measurement effect. The total profit-linked productivity measure is the sum of the individual partial measures. This property makes the profit-linked measure ideal for assessing trade-offs. A much clearer picture of the effects of the changes in productivity emerges. Unless waste and scrap can be brought under better control, the company ought to return to the old assembly process. Of course, it is possible that the learning effects of the new process are not yet fully captured and further improvements in labor productivity might be observed. As labor becomes more proficient at the new process, it is possible that the material usage could also decrease.

Price-Recovery Component

The profit-linked measure computes the amount of profit change from the base period to the current period attributable to productivity changes. This generally will not be equal to the total profit change between the two periods. The difference between the total profit change and the profit-linked productivity change is called the price-recovery component. This component is the change in revenue less a change in the cost of inputs, *assuming no productivity changes*. It therefore measures the ability of revenue changes to cover changes in the cost of inputs, assuming no productivity change.

	(1)	(2)	(3)	(4)	(2) − (4)
Input	PQ*	$PQ \times P$	AQ	$AQ \times P$	$PQ \times P - AQ \times P$
Labor	50,000	$ 600,000	37,500	$ 450,000	$ 150,000
Materials	1,500,000	4,500,000	1,700,000	5,100,000	(600,000)
Total		$5,100,000		$5,550,000	$(450,000)

*Labor: $\frac{150{,}000}{3}$; materials: $\frac{150{,}000}{0.10}$

11-13

Exhibit
Profit-linked Productivity
Measurement

**price-recovery
component**

To calculate the price-recovery component, we first need to compute the change in profits for each period:

	1998	1997	Difference
Revenues[a]	$7,200,000	$6,000,000	$1,200,000
Cost of inputs[b]	5,550,000	2,840,000	2,710,000
Profit	$1,650,000	$3,160,000	$(1,510,000)

[a]$48 × 150,000; $50 × 120,000
[b]($12 × 37,500) + ($3 × 1,700,000); ($11 × 40,000) + ($2 × 1,200,000)

$$\text{Price recovery} = \text{Profit change} - \text{Profit-linked productivity change}$$
$$= \$(1,510,000) - \$(450,000)$$
$$= \$(1,060,000)$$

The increase in revenues would not have been sufficient to recover the increase in the cost of the inputs. The decrease in productivity simply aggravated the price-recovery problem. Note, however, that increases in productivity can be used to offset price-recovery losses.

Quality and Productivity

Improving quality may improve productivity and vice versa. For example, if rework is reduced by producing fewer defective units, less labor and fewer materials are used to produce the same output. Reducing the number of defective units improves quality; reducing the amount of inputs used improves productivity.

Since most quality improvements reduce the amount of resources used to produce and sell an organization's output, most quality improvements will improve productivity. Thus, quality improvements generally will be reflected in productivity measures. However, there are other ways to improve productivity. A firm may produce a good with little or no defects but still have an inefficient process.

For example, consider a good that passes through two 5-minute processes. (Assume the good is produced free of defects.) One unit, then, requires 10 minutes to pass through both processes. Currently, units are produced in batches of 1,200. Process 1 produces 1,200 units; then the batch is conveyed by forklift to another location, where the units pass through process 2. Thus, for each process, a total of 6,000 minutes, or 100 hours, are needed to produce a batch. The 1,200 finished units, then, require a total of 200 hours (100 hours for each process) plus conveyance time; assume that to be 15 minutes.

By redesigning the manufacturing process, efficiency can be improved. Suppose that the second process is located close enough to the first process so that as soon as a unit is completed by the first process, it is passed to the second process. In this way, the first and second processes can be working at the same time. The second process no longer has to wait for the production of 1,200 units plus conveyance time before it can begin operation. The total time to produce 1,200 units now is 6,000 minutes plus the waiting time for the first unit (5 minutes). Thus, production of 1,200 units has been reduced from 200 hours, 15 minutes to 100 hours, 5 minutes. More output can be produced with fewer inputs (time).

S UMMARY OF LEARNING OBJECTIVES

1. Identify and describe the four types of quality costs.

To understand quality costs, it is first necessary to understand what is meant by *quality*. There are two types of quality: quality of design and quality of conformance. Quality of design concerns quality differences that arise for products with the same function but different specifications. Quality of conformance, on the other hand, concerns meeting the specifications required by the product. Quality costs are incurred because products may or do fail to meet design specifications (and are, therefore, associated with quality of conformance). There are four categories of quality costs: prevention, appraisal, internal failure, and external failure. Prevention costs are those incurred to prevent poor quality. Appraisal costs are those incurred to detect poor quality. Internal failure costs are those incurred because products fail to conform to requirements and this lack of conformity is discovered before an external sale. External failure costs are those incurred because products fail to conform to requirements after an external sale is made.

2. Prepare a quality cost report and explain the difference between the conventional view of acceptable quality level and the view espoused by total quality control.

A quality cost report is prepared by listing costs for each item within each of the four major quality cost categories. See Exhibit 11-3. There are two views concerning the optimal distribution of quality costs: the traditional view and the contemporary view. The traditional view holds that there is a trade-off between costs of failure and prevention and appraisal costs. This trade-off produces an optimal level of performance called the *acceptable quality level.* AQL is the level at which the number of defects allowed minimizes total quality costs. The contemporary view, on the other hand, espouses total quality control. Total quality control maintains that the conflict between failure and appraisal and prevention costs is more conjecture than real. The actual optimal level of defects is the zero-defect level; companies should be striving to achieve

this level of quality. Although quality costs do not vanish at this level, they are much lower than the optimal envisioned by the traditional view.

3. Explain why quality cost information is needed and how it is used.

Quality cost information is needed to help managers control quality performance and to serve as input for decision making. It can be used to evaluate the overall performance of quality improvement programs. It can also be used to help improve a variety of managerial decisions, for example, strategic pricing and new product analysis. Perhaps the most important observation is that quality cost information is fundamental to a company's pursuit of continual improvement. Quality is one of the major competitive dimensions for world-class competitors.

4. Explain what productivity is and calculate the impact of productivity changes on profits.

Productivity concerns how efficiently inputs are used to produce the output. Partial measures of productivity evaluate the efficient use of single inputs. Total measures of productivity assess efficiency for all inputs. Profit-linked productivity effects are calculated by using the linkage rule. Essentially, the profit effect is computed by taking the difference between the cost of the inputs that would have been used without any productivity change and the cost of the actual inputs used. Because of the possibility of input trade-offs, it is essential to value productivity changes. Only in this way can the effect of productivity changes be properly assessed.

K EY TERMS

Acceptable quality level (AQL) *441*
Aesthetics *435*
Appraisal costs *437*
Base period *452*
Control activities *437*
Control costs *437*
Costs of quality *437*
Defective product *436*
Durability *436*
External failure costs *437*
Failure activities *437*
Failure costs *437*

Features (quality of design) *436*
Financial productivity measure *452*
Fitness of use *436*
Hidden quality costs *437*
Input trade-off efficiency *449*
Internal failure costs *437*
Multiple-period quality trend report *445*
Observable quality costs *437*

Operational productivity measure *452*
Partial productivity measurement *451*
Performance *435*
Prevention costs *437*
Price-recovery component *456*
Productivity *449*
Productivity measurement *450*
Profile measurement *453*
Profit-linked productivity measurement *454*

Quality of conformance *436*
Quality product or service *435*
Reliability *436*
Serviceability *436*
Taguchi loss function *438*
Technical efficiency *449*
Total productive efficiency *449*
Total productivity measurement *453*
Zero defects *436*

R EVIEW PROBLEMS

1. Quality At the beginning of 1998, Kare Company initiated a quality-improvement program. Considerable effort was expended to reduce the number of defective units produced. By the end of the year, reports from the production manager revealed that scrap and rework had both decreased. The president of the company was pleased to hear of the success but wanted some assessment of the financial impact of the improvements. To make this assessment, the following financial data were collected for the preceding and current years:

	1997	1998
Sales	$10,000,000	$10,000,000
Scrap	400,000	300,000
Rework	600,000	400,000

	1997	1998
Product inspection	100,000	125,000
Product warranty	800,000	600,000
Quality training	40,000	80,000
Materials inspection	60,000	40,000

REQUIRED:

1. Classify the costs as prevention, appraisal, internal failure, and external failure.
2. Compute quality cost as a percentage of sales for each of the two years. By how much has profit increased because of quality improvements? Assuming that quality costs can be reduced to 2.5 percent of sales, how much additional profit is available through quality improvements (assume that sales revenues will remain the same)?
3. Prepare a quality cost report for 1998.

Solution

1. Appraisal costs: product inspection and materials inspection; prevention costs: quality training; internal failure costs: scrap and rework; external failure costs: warranty.
2. For 1997—total quality costs: $2,000,000; percentage of sales: 20 percent ($\frac{\$2,000,000}{\$10,000,000}$). For 1998—total quality costs: $1,545,000; percentage of sales: 15.45 percent ($\frac{\$1,545,000}{\$10,000,000}$). Profit has increased by $455,000. If quality costs drop to 2.5 percent of sales, another $1,295,000 of profit improvement is possible ($1,545,000 − $250,000).

3.

Kare Company Quality Cost Report For the Year Ended 1998	
Prevention costs:	
Quality training	$ 80,000
Appraisal costs:	
Product inspection	$ 125,000
Materials inspection	40,000
Total control costs	$ 165,000
Internal failure costs:	
Scrap	$ 300,000
Rework	400,000
Total internal failure	$ 700,000
External failure costs:	
Product warranty	$ 600,000
Total quality costs	$1,545,000
Percentage of sales	15.45%

II. Productivity Bearing Company made some changes at the end of 1997 that it hoped would favorably affect the efficiency of the input usage. Now, at the end of 1998, the president of the company wants an assessment of the changes on the company's productivity. The data needed for the assessment follow:

	1997	1998
Output	5,000	6,000
Output prices	$10	$10
Materials (lb)	4,000	4,200
Materials unit price	$3	$4
Labor (hr)	2,500	2,400
Labor rate per hour	$8	$8
Power (kwh)	1,000	1,500
Price per kwh	$2	$3

REQUIRED:
1. Compute the partial operational measures for each input for both 1997 and 1998. What can be said about productivity improvement?
2. Prepare an income statement for each year and calculate the total change in profits.
3. Calculate the profit-linked productivity measure for 1998. What can be said about the productivity program?
4. Calculate the price-recovery component. What does this tell you?

Solution

1. Partial measures:

	1997	1998
Material	$\dfrac{5{,}000}{4{,}000} = 1.25$	$\dfrac{6{,}000}{4{,}200} = 1.43$
Labor	$\dfrac{5{,}000}{2{,}500} = 2.00$	$\dfrac{6{,}000}{2{,}400} = 2.50$
Power	$\dfrac{5{,}000}{1{,}000} = 5.00$	$\dfrac{6{,}000}{1{,}500} = 4.00$

Productive efficiency has increased for materials and labor and decreased for power. The outcome is mixed and no statement about overall productivity improvement can be made without valuing the trade-off.

2. Income statements:

	1997	1998
Sales	$50,000	$60,000
Cost of inputs	34,000	40,500
Income	$16,000	$19,500

Total change in profits: $19,500 − $16,000 = $3,500 increase

3. Profit-linked measurement:

	(1)	(2)	(3)	(4)	(2) − (4)
Input	PQ^*	$PQ \times P$	AQ	$AQ \times P$	$PQ \times P - AQ \times P$
Materials	4,800	$19,200	4,200	$16,800	$2,400
Labor	3,000	24,000	2,400	19,200	4,800
Power	1,200	3,600	1,500	4,500	(900)
		$46,800		$40,500	$6,300

*Materials: $\frac{6{,}000}{1.25}$; Labor: $\frac{6{,}000}{2}$; Power: $\frac{6{,}000}{5}$

The value of the increases in efficiency for materials and labor more than offsets the increased usage of power. Thus, the productivity program should be labeled successful.

4. Price recovery:

Price-recovery component = Total profit change − Profit-linked productivity change
Price-recovery component = $3,500 − $6,300
= $(2,800)

This says that without the productivity improvement, profits would have declined by $2,800. The $10,000 increase in revenues would not have offset the increase in the cost of inputs. From the solution to requirement 3, the cost of inputs without a productivity increase would have been $46,800 (column (2)). The increase in the input cost without productivity would have been $46,800 − $34,000 = $12,800. This is $2,800 more than the increase in revenues. Only because of the productivity increase did the firm show an increase in profitability.

QUESTIONS FOR WRITING AND DISCUSSION

1. Explain what is meant by "quality."
2. What is reliability? durability?
3. What is quality of conformance?
4. Explain the difference between the traditional view of conformance and the robust view.
5. Why are quality costs the costs of doing things wrong?
6. Identify and discuss the four kinds of quality costs.
7. Explain why external failure costs can be more devastating to a firm than internal failure costs.
8. What are hidden quality costs? Provide an example.
9. What are the three methods for estimating hidden quality costs?
10. Discuss the value of a quality cost report.
11. What is the difference between the AQL model and the zero-defects model?
12. What is the difference between the zero-defects model and the robust quality model?
13. Explain the purpose of multiple-period trend analysis for quality costs.
14. Define *total productive efficiency*.
15. Explain the difference between partial and total measures of productivity.
16. Discuss the advantages and disadvantages of partial measures of productivity.
17. How can a manager measure productivity improvement?
18. What is profit-linked productivity measurement?
19. Explain why profit-linked productivity measurement is important.
20. What is the price-recovery component?
21. Can productivity improvements be achieved without improving quality? Explain.
22. Why is it important for managers to be concerned with both productivity and quality?
23. What are the differences between quality and productivity? similarities?

WARM-UP EXERCISES

This section provides short warm-up exercises based on the examples in the chapter. Each warm-up exercise gives the page number on which the text example can be found. You may want to refer to the text example to see how the exercise can be set up and solved.

W11-1
Hidden Quality Costs
LO 1
pp. 437–439

Thames Company has decided to estimate its hidden external failure costs using the Taguchi loss function. After some study, it was determined that $k = \$200$ and $T = 15$ inches in diameter. A sample of four units produced the following values:

Unit	Actual Diameter (y)
1	14.9
2	15.1
3	15.2
4	14.8

REQUIRED:
1. Calculate the average loss per unit.
2. Assuming that 5,000 units were produced, what is the total hidden cost?

W11-2
Quality Cost Report
LO 2
pp. 440–441

At the end of 1998, Barton Company listed the following quality costs:

Design review	$75,000
Recalls	25,000
Reinspection	40,000
Materials inspection	30,000
Quality training	40,000
Process acceptance	28,000
Scrap	45,000
Lost sales	30,000
Product acceptance	10,000
Returned goods	10,000

REQUIRED: Prepare a quality cost report with costs listed by category. Are there any hidden costs listed in the report? Explain.

W11-3
Productivity Analysis
LO 4
pp. 453–456

Langosta Company reported the following data for 1997 and 1998:

	1997	1998
Number of motors produced	60,000	75,000
Labor hours used	20,000	18,750
Materials used (lb)	600,000	850,000
Unit selling price (motors)	$50	$45
Wages per labor hour	$10	$11
Cost per pound of material	$2	$4

REQUIRED:
1. Calculate a productivity profile for 1997 and 1998. Has productivity improved?
2. Calculate the profit-linked productivity measure for 1998. Has productivity improved?

EXERCISES

E11-1
Quality Cost Classification
LO 1

Classify the following quality costs as prevention costs, appraisal costs, internal failure costs, or external failure costs:

1. Downgrading because of defects
2. Receiving inspection
3. Scrap
4. Product recalls
5. Product liability suits
6. Design verification and review to evaluate the quality of new products
7. Training program for new personnel
8. Work stoppage to correct process malfunction (discovered using statistical process control procedures)
9. Settlement of a product liability suit
10. Reinspection of rework
11. Lost sales because of incorrect product labeling
12. Internal audit
13. Engineering design changes
14. Purchase order changes
15. Replacement of defective product
16. Test labor
17. Field service personnel
18. Software correction
19. Supplier evaluations
20. In-process inspection
21. Consumer complaint department
22. Prototype inspection and testing
23. Retest work

E11-2
Quality Improvement and Profitability
LO 2, LO 4

Carnie Company reported the following sales and quality costs for the past four years. Assume that all quality costs are variable with sales and that all changes in the quality cost ratios are due to a quality-improvement program.

Year	Sales Revenues	Quality Costs as Percent of Revenues
1	$20,000,000	0.25
2	22,000,000	0.20
3	23,000,000	0.18
4	25,000,000	0.12

REQUIRED:

1. Compute the quality costs for all four years. By how much did net income increase from year 1 to year 2 because of quality improvements? from year 2 to year 3? from year 3 to year 4?
2. The management of Carnie Company believes it is possible to reduce quality costs to 2.5 percent of sales. Assuming sales will continue at the year 4 level, calculate the additional profit potential facing Carnie. Is the expectation of improving quality and reducing costs to 2.5 percent of sales realistic? Explain.
3. Assume that Carnie produces one type of product, which is sold on a bid basis. In years 1 and 2, the average bid was $200. In year 1, total variable costs were $125 per unit. In year 3, competition forced the bid to drop to $190. Compute the total contribution margin in year 3 assuming the same quality costs as in year 1. Now compute the total contribution margin in year 3 using the actual quality costs for year 3. What is the increase in profitability resulting from the quality improvements made from year 1 to year 3?

E11-3

Quality Costs: Profit Improvement and Distribution across Categories

LO 2, LO 3

Perez Company had sales of $20 million in 1991. In 1998, sales had increased to $25 million. A quality-improvement program was implemented in 1991. Overall conformance quality was targeted for improvement. The quality costs for 1991 and 1998 follow. Assume any changes in quality costs are attributable to improvements in quality.

	1991	1998
Internal failure costs	$1,500,000	$ 75,000
External failure costs	2,000,000	50,000
Appraisal costs	900,000	187,500
Prevention costs	600,000	312,500
Total quality costs	$5,000,000	$625,000

REQUIRED:

1. Compute the quality cost/sales ratio for each year. Is this type of improvement possible?
2. Calculate the relative distribution of quality costs by category for 1991. What do you think of the way costs are distributed? How do you think they will be distributed as the company approaches a zero-defects state?
3. Calculate the relative distribution of costs by category for 1998. What do you think of the level and distribution of quality costs? Do you think further reductions are possible?
4. A newly hired quality engineer indicated that the external failure costs reported are only the measured costs. He argued that the 1998 external costs were much higher than those reported and that additional investment ought to be made in control costs. Discuss the validity of his viewpoint.

E11-4

Trade-offs among Quality Cost Categories; Total Quality Control

LO 2

Cooper Company has sales of $2 million and quality costs of $400,000. The company is embarking on a major quality-improvement program. During the next three years, Cooper intends to increase its appraisal and prevention costs in order to reduce failure costs. The increase in control costs will result from adding five specific activities: sorting, process control, quality training, supplier evaluation, and engineering redesign of two major products. Current quality costs and the costs of these five activities are given in the following table. Each activity is added sequentially so that its effect on the cost categories can be assessed. For example, after sorting is added, the control costs increase to $150,000 and the failure costs drop to $164,000. Even though the activities are presented sequentially, they are totally independent of each other.

	Control Costs	Failure Costs
Current quality costs	$ 40,000	$360,000
Quality training	80,000	260,000
Process control	130,000	180,000
Sorting	150,000	164,000
Supplier evaluation	180,000	50,000
Engineering redesign	240,000	30,000

Upon seeing the effect of the quality-improvement program, the president of Cooper was pleased—especially with the fact that total failure costs would be reduced to only $30,000 after all five activities are implemented. Even so, the president was concerned about whether all five activities should be implemented or some subset of the five. He wanted to be sure that the most profitable outcome was achieved.

REQUIRED:
1. Identify the control activities that should be implemented and calculate the total quality costs associated with this selection.
2. Given the activities selected in requirement 1, calculate the following: (a) the reduction in total quality costs, and (b) the percentage distribution for control and failure costs.
3. What does the outcome in requirements 1 and 2 suggest about the relationship between the two failure categories and appraisal and prevention? Do you think that quality costs can be reduced more? Discuss the role of activity management in this process.

E11-5
Quality Cost Report; Taguchi Loss Function
LO 1, LO 2

At the end of 1998, Minot Metal Works began to focus on its quality costs. As a first step, they identified the following costs in their accounting records as quality related:

	1998
Sales (50,000 units @ $20)	$1,000,000
Scrap	30,000
Rework	40,000
Training program	12,000
Consumer complaints	20,000
Warranty	40,000
Test labor	30,000
Inspection labor	25,000
Supplier evaluation	3,000

REQUIRED:
1. Prepare a quality cost report by quality cost category.
2. Calculate the relative distribution percentages for each quality cost category. Comment on the distribution.
3. Using the Taguchi loss function, an average loss per unit is computed at $3. What are the hidden costs of external failure? How does this affect the relative distribution? What effect will the hidden-cost information have on a quality-improvement program?

E11-6
Taguchi Loss Function
LO 1

Nestten Company manufactures a product that has a target value of 20 ounces. Specification limits are 20 ounces plus or minus 0.50 ounce. Products produced at the lower specification limit of 19.50 ounces lose $80. A sample of five units produced the following measures:

Unit	Measured Weight
1	20.20
2	20.50
3	20.30
4	19.50
5	19.25

During April, 12,500 units were produced.

REQUIRED:
1. Calculate the loss for each unit. Calculate the average loss for the sample of five.
2. Using the average loss, calculate the hidden quality costs for April.

E11-7
Multiple-Year Trend Reports
LO 2

The controller of Golden Company has computed quality costs as a percentage of sales for the past five years (1994 was the first year the company implemented a quality-improvement program). This information follows:

	Prevention	Appraisal	Internal	External	Total
1994	2%	3%	8%	12%	25%
1995	3	4	8	10	25
1996	4	4	5	7	20
1997	5	3	3	5	16
1998	6	4	1	2	13

REQUIRED:

1. Prepare a trend graph for total quality costs. Comment on what the graph has to say about the success of the quality-improvement program.
2. Prepare a graph that shows the trend for each quality cost category. What does the graph have to say about the success of the quality-improvement program? Does this graph supply more insight than the total cost trend graph? What does the graph have to say about the distribution of quality costs in 1994? in 1998?

E11-8
Productivity Measurement; Partial Measures
LO 4

Peralta Company produces a product that uses two inputs, materials and labor. During the past month, 20 units of the product were produced, requiring 16 pounds of material and 64 hours of labor. An engineering study revealed that Peralta can produce the same output of 20 units using either of the following two combinations of inputs:

	Materials	Labor
Combination A	10	40
Combination B	16	25

The cost of materials is $6 per pound; the cost of labor is $10 per hour.

REQUIRED:

1. Compute the output/input ratio for each input of combination A. Does this represent a productivity improvement over the current use of inputs? What is the total dollar value of the improvement? Classify this as technical or price efficiency improvement.
2. Calculate output/input ratios for each input of combination B. Does this represent a productivity improvement over the current use of inputs? Now compare these ratios to those of combination A. What has happened?
3. Compute the cost of producing the 20 units of output using combination B. Compare this to the cost using combination A. Does moving from combination A to combination B represent a productivity improvement? Explain.

E11-9
Interperiod Measurement of Productivity; Basic Computations
LO 4

The following data pertain to the last two years of operation of Chelsey, Inc.:

	1997	1998
Output	16,000	20,000
Power (quantity used)	2,000	2,000
Materials (quantity used)	4,000	4,500
Unit price (power)	$1.00	$2.00
Unit price (materials)	$4.00	$5.00
Unit selling price	$2.00	$2.50

REQUIRED:

1. Compute the partial operational productivity ratios for each year. Did productivity improve? Explain.
2. Compute the profit-linked productivity measure. By how much did profits increase due to productivity?
3. Calculate the price-recovery component for 1998. Explain its meaning.

E11-10
Productivity
Measurement:
Trade-offs
LO 4

Manson Company decided to install an automated manufacturing system. The decision to automate was made because of the promise to reduce the use of material and labor inputs. After one year of operation, management wants to evaluate the productivity change. The president is particularly interested in knowing whether the trade-off between capital, labor, and materials was favorable. Data concerning output, labor, materials, and capital are provided for the year before implementation and the year after.

	Year Before	Year After
Output	200,000	240,000
Input quantities:		
Materials (lb)	50,000	40,000
Labor (hr)	10,000	4,000
Capital	$10,000	$600,000
Input prices:		
Materials	$2	$2
Labor	$5	$5
Capital	15%	15%

REQUIRED:
1. Compute the partial measures for materials, labor, and capital for each year. What caused the change in labor and materials productivity?
2. Calculate the change in profits attributable to the change in productivity of the three inputs. Assuming that these are the only three inputs, evaluate the decision to automate.

E11-11
Productivity
Measurement:
Technical and Price
Efficiency Illustrated
LO 4

The manager of Dowson Company was reviewing two competing proposals for the machining department. The fiscal year was coming to a close and the manager wanted to make a decision concerning the proposed process changes so that they could be used, if beneficial, during the coming year. The process changes would affect the department's input usage. For the year just ended, the accounting department provided the following information about the inputs used to produce 50,000 units of output:

	Quantity	Unit Prices
Materials	90,000 lb	$ 8
Labor	40,000 hr	10
Energy	20,000 kwh	2

Each proposal offers a process design different from the one currently used. Neither proposal would cost anything to implement. Both proposals project input usage for producing 60,000 units (the expected output for the coming year).

	Proposal A	Proposal B
Materials	90,000 lb	100,000 lb
Labor	40,000 hr	30,000 hr
Energy	20,000 kwh	20,000 kwh

Input prices are expected to remain the same for the coming year.

REQUIRED:
1. Compute the operational partial productivity measures for the most recently completed year and each proposal. Does either proposal improve technical efficiency? Explain. Can you make a recommendation about either proposal using only the physical measures?
2. Calculate the profit-linked productivity measure for each proposal. Which proposal offers the best outcome for the company? How does this relate to the concept of price efficiency? Explain.

E11-12
Productivity and Quality
LO 4

Rington Company is considering the acquisition of an automated system that would decrease the number of units scrapped because of poor quality. (This proposal is part of an ongoing effort to improve quality.) The production manager is pushing for the acquisition because he believes that productivity will be greatly enhanced—particularly when it comes to labor and material inputs. Output and input data follow. The after-acquisition data are projections.

	Current	After Acquisition
Output (units)	10,000	10,000
Output selling price	$40	$40
Input quantities:		
Materials (lb)	40,000	35,000
Labor (hr)	20,000	15,000
Capital	$20,000	$100,000
Energy (kwh)	10,000	25,000
Input prices:		
Materials	$4.00	$4.00
Labor	$9.00	$9.00
Capital	10.00%	10.00%
Energy	$2.00	$2.50

REQUIRED:

1. Compute the partial operational ratios for materials and labor under each alternative. Is the production manager right in thinking that materials and labor productivity increases with the automated system?
2. Compute the partial ratios for all four inputs. Does the system improve productivity?
3. Determine the amount by which profits will change if the system is adopted. Are the trade-offs among the inputs favorable? Comment on the system's ability to improve productivity.

E11-13
Basics of Productivity Measurement
LO 4

Lau Company gathered the following data for the past two years:

	Base Year	Current Year
Output	150,000	180,000
Output prices	$20	$20
Input quantities:		
Materials (lb)	200,000	180,000
Labor (hr)	50,000	90,000
Input prices:		
Materials	$5	$6
Labor	$8	$8

REQUIRED:

1. Calculate the partial operational measures for each year.
2. Prepare income statements for each year. Calculate the total change in income.
3. Calculate the change in profits attributable to productivity changes.
4. Calculate the price-recovery component. Explain its meaning.

PROBLEMS

P11-1
Classification of Quality Costs
LO 1

Classify the following quality costs as prevention, appraisal, internal failure, or external failure.

1. Quality design review
2. Reinspection of reworked product
3. Returned repaired goods
4. Scrap
5. Data reentered because of keyboarding errors

6. Maintenance of inspection equipment
7. Quality planning
8. Design and development of quality equipment
9. Quality training
10. Rework
11. Product liability
12. Internal audit assessing the effectiveness of the quality system
13. Disposal of defective product
14. Downtime attributable to quality problems
15. Quality reporting
16. Proofreading
17. Correction of typing errors
18. Setup for testing
19. Supplier evaluations
20. Pilot studies
21. Returns and allowances because of quality problems
22. Supervision of in-process inspection
23. Component inspection and testing
24. Customer service
25. Outside laboratory endorsements

P11-2
Quality Cost
Summary
LO 2

Mary Bush, the president of Wayne Company, has recently returned from a conference on quality and productivity. At the conference she was told that many American firms have quality costs totaling 20 percent to 30 percent of sales. She, however, was skeptical about this statistic. But even if the quality gurus were right, she was sure that her company's quality costs were much lower—probably less than 5 percent. On the other hand, if she was wrong, she would be passing up an opportunity to improve profits significantly and simultaneously strengthen her competitive position. The possibility was at least worth exploring. She knew that her company produced most of the information needed for quality cost reporting—but there never had been a need to bother with any formal quality data gathering and analysis.

This conference, however, had convinced her that a firm's profitability can increase significantly by improving quality—provided the potential for improvement exists. Thus, before committing the company to a quality-improvement program, Mary requested a preliminary estimate of the total quality costs currently being incurred. She also indicated that the costs should be classified into four categories: prevention, appraisal, internal failure, and external failure costs. She has asked you to prepare a summary of quality costs and to compare the total costs to sales and profits. To assist you in this task, the following information has been prepared from the past year, 1998:

a. Sales revenue is $10,000,000; net income is $1,000,000.
b. During the year, customers returned 30,000 units needing repair. Repair cost averages $7 per unit.
c. Six inspectors are employed, each earning an annual salary of $25,000. These six inspectors are involved only with final inspection (product acceptance).
d. Total scrap is 30,000 units. All scrap is quality related. The cost of scrap is about $15 per unit.
e. Each year, approximately 150,000 units are rejected in final inspection. Of these units, 80 percent can be recovered through rework. The cost of rework is $3.00 per unit.
f. A customer canceled an order that would have increased profits by $250,000. The customer's reason for cancellation was poor product performance. The accounting and marketing departments agree the company loses at least this much each year for the same reason.
g. The company employs five full-time employees in its complaint department. Each earns $20,000 a year.
h. The company gave sales allowances totaling $130,000 due to substandard products being sent to the customer.
i. The company requires all new employees to take its three-hour quality training program. The estimated annual cost of the program is $80,000.
j. Inspection of the final product requires testing equipment. The annual cost of operating and maintaining this equipment is $120,000.

REQUIRED:

1. Prepare a simple quality cost report classifying costs by category. Comment on the quality cost/sales ratio.
2. Discuss the distribution of quality costs among the four categories. Are they properly distributed? Explain.
3. Discuss how the company can improve its overall quality and at the same time reduce total quality costs. Consider specifically the strategy advocated by the American Society for Quality Control (p. 443).
4. Suppose Wayne Company decides a six-year program will reduce quality costs to 2.5 percent of sales and that control costs will be 80 percent of total quality costs. Calculate the income increase that will occur if sales remain at $10,000,000. Also, calculate the total amount spent on control and failure costs.
5. For Mary's company, hidden quality costs are estimated by using a multiplier of 3. What are the actual external failure costs? What methods are available for estimating hidden quality costs? What effect does this estimation have on a quality-improvement strategy?

P11-3
Quality Costs;
Pricing Decisions;
Market Share
LO 3

Tannert Company manufactures furniture. One of its product lines is an economy-line kitchen table. During the last year, Tannert produced and sold 100,000 units for $100 per unit. Sales of the table are on a bid basis, but Tannert has always been able to win sufficient bids using the $100 price. This year, however, Tannert was losing more than its share of bids. Concerned, Larry Franklin, owner and president of the company, called a meeting of his executive committee (Megan Johnson, marketing manager; Fred Davis, quality manager; Kevin Jones, production manager; and Helen Jackson, controller).

Larry: I don't understand why we're losing bids. Megan, do you have an explanation?

Megan: Yes, as a matter of fact. Two competitors have lowered their price to $92 per unit. That's too big a difference for most of our buyers to ignore. If we want to keep selling our 100,000 units per year, we will need to lower our price to $92. Otherwise, our sales will drop to about 20,000 to 25,000 per year.

Helen: The unit contribution margin on the table is $10. Lowering the price to $92 will cost us $8 per unit. Based on a sales volume of 100,000, we'd make $200,000 in contribution margin. If we keep the price at $100, our contribution margin would be $200,000 to $250,000. If we have to lose, let's just take the lower market share. It's better than lowering our prices.

Megan: Perhaps. But the same thing could happen to some of our other product lines. My sources tell me that these two companies are on the tail end of a major quality-improvement program—one that allows them significant savings. We need to rethink our whole competitive strategy—at least if we want to stay in business. Ideally, we should match the price reduction and work to reduce the costs to recapture the lost contribution margin.

Fred: I think I have something to offer. We are about to embark on a new quality-improvement program of our own. I have brought the following estimates of the current quality costs for this economy line. As you can see on the overhead, these costs run about 16 percent of current sales. That's excessive, and we believe that they can be reduced to about 4 percent of sales over time.

Scrap	$ 700,000
Rework	300,000
Rejects (sold as seconds to discount houses)	250,000
Returns (due to poor workmanship)	350,000
	$1,600,000

Larry: This sounds good. Fred, how long will it take you to achieve this reduction?

Fred: All these costs vary with sales level, so I'll express their reduction rate in those terms. Our best guess is that we can reduce these costs by about 1 percent of sales per quarter. So it should take about 12 quarters, or three years, to achieve the full benefit. Keep in mind that this is with an improvement in quality.

Megan: This offers us some hope. If we meet the price immediately, we can maintain our market share. Furthermore, if we can ever reach the point of reducing the price beyond the $92 level, then we can increase our market share. I estimate that we can increase sales by about 10,000 units for every $1 of price reduction beyond the $92 level. Kevin, how much extra capacity for this line do we have?

Kevin: We can handle an extra 30,000 or 40,000 tables per year.

REQUIRED:
1. Assume that Tannert immediately reduces the bid price to $92. How long will it be before the unit contribution margin is restored to $10, assuming that quality costs are reduced as expected and that sales are maintained at 100,000 units per year (25,000 per quarter)?
2. Assume that Tannert holds the price at $92 until the 4 percent target is achieved. At this new level of quality costs, should the price be reduced? If so, by how much should price be reduced and what is the increase in contribution margin? Assume that price can be reduced only in $1 increments.
3. Assume that Tannert immediately reduces the price to $92 and begins the quality-improvement program. Now suppose that Tannert does not wait until the end of the three-year period before reducing prices. Instead, prices will be reduced when profitable to do so. Assume that prices can be reduced only by $1 increments. Identify when the first future price change should occur (if any).
4. Discuss the differences in viewpoints concerning the decision to decrease prices and the short-run contribution margin analysis done by Helen, the controller. Did quality cost information play an important role in the strategic decision making illustrated by the problem?

P11-4
Quality Costs;
Profitability Analysis
LO 2, LO 3

At the end of 1995, Leigh Company, a large electronics firm, hired Gary Cooper to manage one of its troubled divisions. Gary had the reputation of turning around businesses that were having difficulty. In 1996, the division had sales of $50 million, a variable cost ratio of 0.8, and total fixed costs of $12 million. The division produced only one product and sales were all to external customers. Seeking to solve the division's problems, Gary asked for a report on quality costs for 1996, and received the following report:

	Fixed	Variable
Prevention	$ 400,000	—
Appraisal	600,000	$ 2,000,000
Internal failure	1,000,000	4,000,000
External failure	2,000,000	10,000,000
Total	$4,000,000	$16,000,000

Gary was astounded at the level of expenditure on quality costs. Although he had heard of companies with quality costs that had reached as high as 60 percent of sales, he had never personally seen any greater than 20 percent to 30 percent of sales. This division's level of 40 percent was clearly excessive. He immediately implemented a program to improve conformance quality. By the end of 1997, the following quality costs were reported:

	Fixed	Variable (unit-level)
Prevention	$2,000,000	—
Appraisal	2,000,000	$ 2,000,000
Internal failure	1,000,000	2,000,000
External failure	2,000,000	7,000,000
Total	$7,000,000	$11,000,000

Revenues and other costs were unchanged for 1997.

Gary projects that by 2001 the defective rate will be 0.1 percent, compared to the AQL rate of 2 percent for 1996. He also projects that quality costs will be reduced to $1 million distributed as follows:

	Fixed	Variable (unit-level)
Prevention	$400,000	—
Appraisal	400,000	—
Internal failure	—	$ 40,000
External failure	—	160,000
Total	$800,000	$200,000

REQUIRED:

1. Calculate the break-even point in revenues for 1996. How much was the division losing?
2. Calculate the break-even point in 1997. Explain the change.
3. Calculate the break-even point in 2001, assuming that revenues and other costs have remained the same. Is it possible to reduce quality costs as dramatically as portrayed?
4. Assume that from 1996 to 2001, the division was forced to cut selling prices so that total revenues dropped to $30 million. Calculate the income (loss) that would be reported under a 1996 cost structure. Now calculate the income (loss) that would be reported under the 2001 quality cost structure (assuming all other costs remain unchanged). Discuss the strategic significance of quality cost management.

P11-5
Quality Cost Report; Quality Cost Categories
LO 1, LO 2

In September 1997, Olson Company received a report from an external consulting group on its quality costs. The consultants reported that the company's quality costs total about 25 percent of its sales revenues. Somewhat shocked by the magnitude of the costs, Frank Roosevelt, president of Olson Company, decided to launch a major quality-improvement program. This program was scheduled for implementation in January 1998. The program's goal was to reduce quality costs to 2.5 percent by the end of the year 2000 by improving overall quality.

In 1998, it was decided to reduce quality costs to 22 percent of sales revenues. Management felt that the amount of reduction was reasonable, and that the goal could be realized. To improve the monitoring of the quality-improvement program, Frank directed Pamela Golding, the controller, to prepare quarterly performance reports comparing budgeted and actual quality costs. He told Pamela that improving quality should reduce quality costs by 1 percent of sales for each of the first three quarters and 2 percent in the last quarter. Sales are projected at $5 million per quarter. Based on the consulting report and the targeted reductions, Pamela prepared the budgets for the first two quarters of the year:

	Quarter 1	Quarter 2
Sales	$5,000,000	$5,000,000
Quality costs:		
Warranty	$ 300,000	$ 250,000
Scrap	150,000	125,000
Incoming materials inspection	25,000	50,000
Product acceptance	125,000	150,000
Quality planning	40,000	60,000
Field inspection	30,000	0
Retesting	50,000	40,000
Allowances	65,000	50,000
New product review	10,000	10,000
Rework	130,000	100,000
Complaint adjustment	60,000	20,000
Downtime (defective parts)	50,000	40,000
Repairs	50,000	35,000
Product liability	85,000	60,000
Quality training	30,000	70,000
Quality engineering	0	40,000
Design verification	0	20,000
Process control measurement	0	30,000
Total budgeted costs	$1,200,000	$1,150,000
Quality costs/sales ratio	24%	23%

REQUIRED:

1. Assume that Olson Company reduces quality costs as indicated. What will quality costs be as a percent of sales for the entire year? for the end of the fourth quarter? Will the company achieve its goal of reducing quality costs to 22 percent of sales?

2. Reorganize the quarterly budgets so that quality costs are grouped in one of four categories: prevention, appraisal, internal failure, or external failure (effectively, prepare a budgeted cost of quality report). Also, identify each cost as variable or fixed. (Assume that none are mixed costs.)

3. Compare the two quarterly budgets. What do they reveal about the quality improvement plans of Olson Company?

P11-6
Distribution of
Quality Costs
LO 2

Paper Products Division produces paper diapers, napkins, and paper towels. The divisional manager has decided that quality costs can be minimized by distributing quality costs evenly among the four quality categories and reducing them to no more than 5 percent of sales. He has just received the following quality cost report:

Paper Products Division
Quality Cost Report
For the Year Ended December 31, 1998

	Diapers	Napkins	Towels	Total
Prevention:				
Quality training	$ 3,000	$ 2,500	$ 2,000	$ 7,500
Quality engineering	3,500	1,000	2,500	7,000
Quality audits	—	500	1,000	1,500
Quality reporting	2,500	2,000	1,000	5,500
Total	$ 9,000	$ 6,000	$ 6,500	$ 21,500
Appraisal:				
Inspection, materials	$ 2,000	$ 3,000	$ 3,000	$ 8,000
Process acceptance	4,000	2,800	1,200	8,000
Product acceptance	2,000	1,200	2,300	5,500
Total	$ 8,000	$ 7,000	$ 6,500	$ 21,500
Internal failure:				
Scrap	$10,000	$ 3,000	$ 2,500	$ 15,500
Disposal costs	7,000	2,000	1,500	10,500
Downtime	1,000	1,500	2,500	5,000
Total	$18,000	$ 6,500	$ 6,500	$ 31,000
External failure:				
Allowances	$10,000	$ 3,000	$ 2,750	$ 15,750
Customer complaints	4,000	1,500	3,750	9,250
Product liability	1,000	—	—	1,000
Total	$15,000	$ 4,500	$ 6,500	$ 26,000
Total quality costs	$50,000	$24,000	$26,000	$100,000

Assume that all prevention costs are fixed and that the remaining quality costs are variable.

REQUIRED:

1. Assume that the sales revenue for the year totaled $2 million, with sales for each product as follows: diapers, $1 million; napkins, $600,000; towels, $400,000. Evaluate the distribution of costs for the division as a whole and for each product line. What recommendations do you have for the divisional manager?

2. Now assume that total sales of $1 million have this breakdown: diapers, $500,000; napkins, $300,000; towels, $200,000. Evaluate the distribution of costs for the division as a whole and for each product line in this case. Do you think it is possible to reduce the quality costs to 5

percent of sales for each product line and for the division as a whole and, simultaneously, achieve an equal distribution of the quality costs? What recommendations do you have?

3. Assume total sales of $1 million with this breakdown: diapers, $500,000; napkins, $180,000; towels, $320,000. Evaluate the distribution of quality costs. What recommendations for the divisional manager do you have?

4. Discuss the value of having quality costs reported by segment.

P11-7
Trend Analysis;
Quality Costs
LO 2

In 1994, Jack Donaldson, president of Thayn Electronics, received a report indicating that quality costs were 21 percent of sales. Faced with increasing pressures from imported goods, Jack resolved to take measures to improve the overall quality of the company's products. After hiring a consultant, the company began, in 1995, an aggressive program of total quality control. At the end of 1998, Jack requested an analysis of the progress the company had made in reducing and controlling quality costs. The accounting department assembled the following data:

	Sales	Prevention	Appraisal	Internal Failure	External Failure
1994	$500,000	$ 5,000	$10,000	$40,000	$50,000
1995	600,000	20,000	20,000	50,000	60,000
1996	700,000	30,000	25,000	30,000	40,000
1997	600,000	35,000	35,000	20,000	25,000
1998	500,000	35,000	15,000	8,000	12,000

REQUIRED:

1. Compute the quality costs as a percentage of sales by category and in total for each year.

2. Explain why quality costs increased in total and as a percentage of sales in 1995, the first year of the quality-improvement program.

3. Prepare a multiple-year trend graph for quality costs, both by total costs and by category. Using the graph, assess the progress made in reducing and controlling quality costs. Does the graph provide evidence that quality has improved? Explain.

P11-8
Productivity
Measurement; Basics
LO 4

Mays Company produces handcrafted leather belts. Virtually all the manufacturing cost consists of materials and labor. Over the past several years profits have been declining because the cost of the two major inputs has been increasing. John Mays, the president of the company, has indicated that the price of the belts cannot be increased; thus, the only way to improve or at least stabilize profits is by increasing overall productivity. At the beginning of 1998, John implemented a new productivity program. John now wants to know how much profits have increased from the prior year because of the program. In order to provide this information to the president, the following data have been gathered:

	1997	1998
Unit selling price	$16	$16
Output produced and sold	9,000	12,000
Materials used	18,000	20,000
Labor used	4,500	5,000
Unit price of materials	$4	$4.50
Unit price of labor	$9	$10.00

REQUIRED:

1. Compute the partial productivity ratios for each year. Comment on the effectiveness of the productivity improvement program.

2. Compute the increase in profits attributable to increased productivity.

3. Calculate the price-recovery component and comment on its meaning.

P11-9
Productivity
Measurement
LO 4

In 1997, Brindon Products, Inc. used the following input combination to produce 2,000 units of output:

Materials	2,200 lb
Labor	2,000 hr

The following combination is optimal for an output of 2,000 units (but unknown to Brindon Products):

Materials	1,000 lb
Labor	4,000 hr

The cost of materials is $40 per pound, and the cost of labor is $10 per hour. These input prices hold for 1997 and 1998. In 1998, Brindon Products again produced 2,000 units, with the following input combination:

Materials	1,200 lb
Labor	5,000 hr

REQUIRED:
1. Compute the partial productivity ratios for each of the following:
   a. The actual inputs used in 1997
   b. The actual inputs used in 1998
   c. The optimal input combination
   Did productivity increase in 1998—as measured by the partial ratios?
2. Compute the cost of 1997's productive inefficiency relative to the optimal input combination.
3. By how much did profits increase because of improvements in productive efficiency from 1997 to 1998?
4. How much additional improvement in profits is possible after 1998 (assuming input costs remain the same and that output doesn't change)?

P11-10
Productivity Measurement: Partial and Total Measures; Price Recovery
LO 4

The battery division of Chalmur Company has recently been engaged in a vigorous effort to increase productivity. Over the past several years, competition had become very intense, and the divisional manager knew that a significant price decrease for Chalmur's batteries was in order. Otherwise, the division would lose at least 50 percent of its market share.

To maintain its market share, Chalmur had to decrease its per-unit price by $2.50 by the end of 1998. Decreasing the price by $2.50, however, absolutely required a similar increase in cost efficiency. If divisional profits dropped by $2.50 per unit, the division's continued existence would be in question. To assess the outcome of the productivity improvement program the following data were gathered:

	1997	1998
Output	400,000	500,000
Input quantities:		
Materials (lb)	100,000	100,000
Labor (hr)	400,000	200,000
Capital	$4,000,000	$10,000,000
Energy (kwh)	100,000	300,000
Input prices:		
Materials	$2.00	$ 3.00
Labor	8.00	10.00
Capital	15%	10%
Energy	2.00	2.00

REQUIRED:
1. Calculate the partial productivity ratios for each year. Can you say that productivity has improved? Explain.

2. Calculate the profit change attributable to productivity changes.

3. Calculate the cost per unit for 1997 and 1998. Was the division able to decrease its per-unit cost by at least $2.50? Comment on the relationship between competitive advantage and productive efficiency.

P11-11
Quality and Productivity; Interaction; Use of Operational Measures
LO 4

Andy Confer, production-line manager, had arranged a visit with Will Keating, plant manager. He had some questions about the new operational measures that were being used.

Andy: Will, my questions are more to satisfy my curiosity than anything else. At the beginning of the year, we began some new procedures that require us to work toward increasing our output per pound of material and decreasing our output per labor hour. As instructed, I've been tracking these operational measures for each batch we've produced so far this year. Here's a copy of a trend report for the first five batches of the year. Each batch had 10,000 units in it.

Batches	Materials Usage (lb)	Ratio	Labor Usage (hr)	Ratio
1	4,000	2.50	2,000	5.00
2	3,900	2.56	2,020	4.95
3	3,750	2.67	2,150	4.65
4	3,700	2.70	2,200	4.55
5	3,600	2.78	2,250	4.44

Will: Andy, this report is very encouraging. The trend is exactly what we hoped for. I'll bet we meet our goal of getting the batch productivity measures. Let's see, those goals were 3.00 units per pound for materials and 4.00 units per hour for labor. Last year's figures were 2.50 for materials and 5.00 for labor. Things are looking good. I guess tying bonuses and raises to improving these productivity stats was a good idea.

Andy: Maybe so, but I don't understand why you want to make these trade-offs between materials and labor. The materials cost only $5 per pound and labor costs $10 per hour. It seems like you're simply increasing the cost of making this product.

Will: Actually, it may seem that way, but it's not so. There are other factors to consider. You know we've been talking quality improvement. Well, the new procedures you are implementing are producing products that conform to the product's specification. More labor time is needed to achieve this and, as we take more time, we do waste fewer materials. But the real benefit is the reduction in our external failure costs. Every defect in a batch of 10,000 units costs us $1,000— warranty work, lost sales, a customer service department, and so on. If we can reach the materials and labor productivity goals, our defects will drop from 20 per batch to 5 per batch.

REQUIRED:

1. Discuss the advantages of using only operational measures of productivity for controlling shop-level activities.

2. Assume that the batch productivity statistics are met by the end of the year. Calculate the change in a batch's profits from the beginning of the year to the end attributable to changes in materials and labor productivity.

3. Now assume that three inputs are to be evaluated: materials, labor, and quality. Quality is measured by the number of defects per batch. Calculate the change in a batch's profits from the beginning of the year to the end attributable to changes in productivity of all three inputs. Do you agree that quality is an input? Explain.

P11-12
Productivity; Trade-offs; Price Recovery
LO 4

Connie Baker, president of Fleming Chemicals, had just concluded a meeting with two of her plant managers. She had told each that their product was going to have a 50 percent increase in demand next year over this year's output (which is expected to be 10,000 gallons). A major foreign source of the raw material had been shut down because of civil war. It would be years before the source would be available again. The result was twofold. First, the price of the raw material was expected to quadruple. Second, many of the less efficient competitors would leave the business, creating more demand and higher output prices—in fact, output prices would double.

In discussing the situation with her plant managers, she had reminded them that the automated process now allowed them to increase the productivity of the raw material. By using more machine hours, evaporation could be decreased significantly (this was a recent development and would be operational by the beginning of the new fiscal year). There were, however, only two other feasible settings beyond the current setting. The current usage of inputs for the 10,000 gallon output (current setting) and the input usage for the other two settings follow. The input usage for the remaining two settings is for an output of 15,000 gallons. Inputs are measured in gallons for the material and in machine hours for the equipment.

	Current	Setting A	Setting B
Input quantities:			
Materials	25,000	15,000	30,000
Equipment	6,000	15,000	7,500

The current prices for this year's inputs are $3 per gallon for materials and $12 per machine hour for the equipment. The materials price will change for next year as explained, but the $12 rate for machine hours will remain the same. The chemical is currently selling for $20 per gallon. Based on separate productivity analyses, one plant manager chose setting A and the other chose setting B.

The manager who chose setting B justified his decision by noting that it was the only setting that clearly signaled an increase in both partial measures of productivity. The other manager agreed that setting B was an improvement but that setting A was even better.

REQUIRED:
1. Calculate the partial measures of productivity for the current year and for the two settings. Which of the two settings signals an increase in productivity for both inputs?
2. Calculate the profits that will be realized under each setting for the coming year. Which setting provides the greatest profit increase?
3. Calculate the profit change for each setting attributable to productivity changes. Which setting offers the greatest productivity improvement? By how much? Explain why this happened. (*Hint:* Look at trade-offs.)

M ANAGERIAL DECISION CASES

C11-1
Quality Cost
Performance Reports
LO 2

Nickles Company, a large printing company, is in its fourth year of a five-year, quality-improvement program. The program began in 1994 with an internal study that revealed the quality costs being incurred. In that year, a five-year plan was developed to lower quality costs to 10 percent of sales by the end of 1998. Sales and quality costs for each year are as follows:

	Sales Revenues	Quality Costs
1994	$10,000,000	$2,000,000
1995	10,000,000	1,800,000
1996	11,000,000	1,815,000
1997	12,000,000	1,680,000
1998*	12,000,000	1,320,000

*Budgeted figures

Quality costs by category are expressed as a percentage of sales as follows:

	Prevention	Appraisal	Internal Failure	External Failure
1994	1.0%	3.0%	7.0%	9.0%
1995	2.0	4.0	6.0	6.0
1996	2.5	4.0	5.0	5.0
1997	3.0	3.5	4.5	3.0
1998	3.5	3.5	2.0	2.0

The detail of the 1998 budget for quality costs is also provided.

Prevention costs:	
Quality planning	$ 150,000
Quality training	20,000
Quality improvement (special project)	80,000
Quality reporting	10,000
Appraisal costs:	
Proofreading	$ 500,000
Other inspection	50,000
Failure costs:	
Correction of typos	$ 150,000
Rework (because of customer complaints)	75,000
Plate revisions	55,000
Press downtime	100,000
Waste (because of poor work)	130,000
Total quality costs	$1,320,000

All prevention costs are fixed; all other quality costs are variable.

During 1998, the company had $12 million in sales. Actual quality costs for 1997 and 1998 are as follows:

	1997	1998
Quality planning	$140,000	$150,000
Quality training	20,000	20,000
Special project	120,000	100,000
Quality reporting	12,000	12,000
Proofreading	580,000	520,000
Other inspection	80,000	60,000
Correction of typos	200,000	165,000
Rework	131,000	76,000
Plate revisions	83,000	58,000
Press downtime	123,000	102,000
Waste	191,000	136,000

REQUIRED:
1. Prepare a quality cost performance report for 1998 that compares actual 1998 quality costs with budgeted quality costs. Comment on the firm's ability to achieve its quality goals for the year.
2. Prepare a one-period quality performance report for 1998 that compares the actual costs of 1997 with the actual costs of 1998. How much did profits change because of improved quality?
3. Prepare a graph that shows the trend in total quality costs as a percentage of sales since the inception of the quality-improvement program.
4. Prepare a graph that shows the trend for all four quality cost categories for 1994 through 1998. How does this graph help management know that the reduction in total quality costs is attributable to quality improvements?

. . . .

C11-2
Quality Performance and Ethical Behavior

Reece Manufacturing rewards its plant managers for their ability to meet budgeted quality cost reductions. The bonus is increased if the productivity goal is met or exceeded. The productivity goal is computed by multiplying the units produced by the prevailing market price and dividing this measure of output by the total cost of the inputs used. Additionally, if the plant as a whole met the budgeted targets, the production supervisors and workers receive salary and wage increases. Matt Rasmussen, the manager of a plant in Nebraska, felt obligated to do everything he could to provide this increase to his employees. Accordingly, he has decided to take the following actions during the last quarter of the year to meet the plant's budgeted targets and increase the productivity ratio:

a. Decrease inspections of the process and final product by 50 percent and transfer inspectors temporarily to quality training programs. Matt believes this move will increase the inspectors' awareness of the importance of quality; also, decreasing inspection will produce significantly less downtime and less rework. By increasing the output and decreasing the costs of internal failure, the plant can meet the budgeted reductions for internal failure costs and, simultaneously, increase its productivity measure. Also, by showing an increase in the costs of quality training, the budgeted level for prevention costs can be met.

b. Delay replacing and repairing defective products until the beginning of the following year. While this may increase customer dissatisfaction somewhat, Matt believes that most customers expect some inconvenience. Besides, the policy of promptly dealing with dissatisfied customers could be reinstated in three months. In the meantime, the action would significantly reduce the costs of external failure, allowing the plant to meet its budgeted target.

REQUIRED:

1. Evaluate Matt's ethical behavior. In this evaluation, consider his concern for his employees. Was he justified in taking the actions described in the problem? If not, what should he have done?

2. Assume that the company views Matt's behavior as undesirable. What can it do to discourage it?

3. Assume that Matt is a CMA and a member of the NAA (National Association of Accountants). Refer to the ethical code for management accountants in Chapter 1. Are any of these ethical standards violated?

C11-3
Research Assignment

Listed below are articles that describe some of the quality improvement efforts of five companies:

Corning Incorporated:

Hammonds, Keith H. "Corning's Class Act: How Jamie Houghton Reinvented the Company," *Business Week*, May 13, 1991: 68–73.

Federal Express:

American Management Association. Blueprint for Service Quality: The Federal Express Approach. American Management Association, 1991.

Motorola:

Bhote, Keki R. "Motorola's Long March to the Malcolm Baldridge National Quality Award," *National Productivity Review*, VIII, 4 (Autumn, 1989): 365–375.

Solectron:

"What Drives Quality?," *Internal Auditor Magazine*, (April 1992): 39–45.

Southern Pacific:

Welty, Gus, "Southern Pacific's Quality Comeback," *Railway Age*, (November 1992): 30–34.

REQUIRED: Write a three–five page paper that compares and contrasts the experiences of any three of the five companies where at least one of the three is a service company. Include in your discussion the ways in which the companies defined quality. Also describe how quality was measured, if at all. Were the financial effects measured? Was there any mention of quality costs? Finally, conduct a library search to see if there is anything written that describes how any one of the companies is doing now and determine if the quality achievements have been maintained or not. You might even try writing the corporate relation or quality control departments of one or more of the companies. For example, the address for Federal Express is: Federal Express Corporate Relations Department, 2005 Corporate Avenue, Memphis, TN 38132.

1. Define responsibility accounting and describe four types of responsibility centers.

2. Explain why firms choose to decentralize.

3. Compute and explain return on investment (ROI) and residual income (RI).

4. Discuss methods of evaluating and rewarding managerial performance.

5. Explain the role of transfer pricing in a decentralized firm.

CHAPTER

Decentralization: Responsibility Accounting, Performance Evaluation, and Transfer Pricing

SCENARIO

Ted Munsen was worried. He had founded Technoco in the mid-1980s to manufacture a scrubbing device that cleaned airborne contaminants from industrial smokestacks. Back then, the company consisted of Ted and a few other young engineers who were excited by the potential for the device. They routinely worked 16-hour days, seven days a week to see their vision turn into reality. The hard work paid off; the scrubbing device was efficient and effective. Profits at Technoco soared. Over time, Ted and his associates had purchased several other loosely related companies in the pollution cleanup field, and had gone public with the conglomerate just a few years ago. Now, as CEO of an established company, Ted faced new problems. He met with Steve Scully, head of U.S. operations, to discuss them.

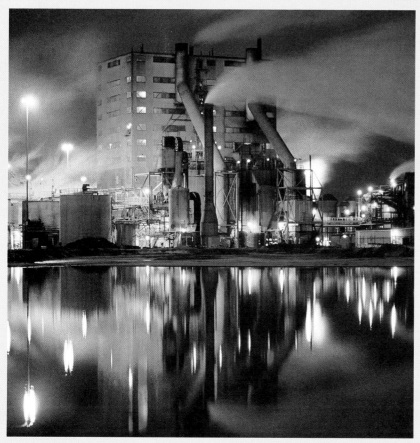

"Steve, look at these projected financial statements. Our net income has increased at a barely noticeable rate. Our return on investment has actually declined from last year. Divisional managers are squabbling over transfer prices when they should be cooperating. What's happening here? I remember when working at this company meant something. We shared a vision. We were working not just for ourselves, but for a better world. It may sound corny, but that vision sure kept me going through some pretty dark days."

Steve chuckled, "Don't forget the dark nights! Look, Ted, we're older now, larger, it's harder to keep that culture going when you're a multidivisional company. I hardly know some of our newer managers, much less feel sure that we share the same values. What can you do? We

just have to accept the inevitable, cut costs or something. I don't know. What would GM or IBM do?"

"I don't care what those companies would do—they have problems enough of their own. I also don't want to throw in the towel just yet. Surely, we can structure an incentive program to get our managers moving in the same direction again, and have some fun doing it. I want you to do some research on management incentive plans. See what's out there, maybe some other company has faced this problem and solved it. Let's meet again on this matter in two weeks."

Two weeks later.

"Ted, I may have a solution to our problems. I spoke to a friend of mine at Thermo Electro. They make high-tech devices, such as very sensitive bomb and drug detectors, and

remediation facilities for cleaning gasoline-contaminated soil. They're a lot like us, a great small company that grew like crazy. They were having problems keeping their entrepreneurial spirit alive, so they handed out stock options to motivate their managers—but it didn't seem to work. Their R&D expenditures were crucial to their long-term success, but were dragging down earnings. Anyway, they experimented with splitting up the company. In 1983, they sold 16 percent of one of their divisions, Thermedics. The managers of Thermedics got 3 percent of the shares; it really turned them into entrepreneurs. It also raised more than $5 million."[1]

"So far, so good. But what happened to return on investment? And what about the other divisions? Did they resent the special deal Thermedics got?"

"No, the other managers have the same chance. The other Thermo Electro divisions compete to become the new spin-off. But they're not considered until the business shows the potential to grow 30 percent per year. Thermo Electro has an average annual ROI of about 20 percent in its spin-offs."

"Sounds good! Let's go through these divisional financial statements, and see what we've got. Maybe we can apply some of Thermo Electro's lessons to our own situation."

1. Jennifer Reese, "How to Grow Big by Staying Small," *Fortune,* 28 December 1992, 50, 54.

Questions to Think About

1. *What problems does Ted face as the CEO of a large, divisionalized company that he did not face as the head of a small company?*

2. What values did Steve and Ted share in the early days of the company? What values do you suppose that the division

managers hold now? Are these values the same? Different?

3. How do managerial values affect profit? Should they?

4. What is a management incentive plan? Can you think of a plan or plans that would help Ted and Steve to move their managers in the directions they want?

RESPONSIBILITY ACCOUNTING

Objective I

Define responsibility accounting and describe four types of responsibility centers.

In general, a company is organized along the lines of responsibility. The traditional organizational chart, with its pyramid shape, illustrates the lines of responsibility flowing from the CEO down through the vice-presidents to middle- and lower-level managers. As the opening scenario indicates, when organizations increase in size, these lines of responsibility become longer and more numerous. The structure becomes cumbersome. Contemporary practice is moving toward a flattened hierarchy. This structure, emphasizing teams, is consistent with decentralization. South-Western College Publishing, for example, eliminated much of its previous departmental organization and developed cross-functional teams. As a result, South-Western reduced its levels of hierarchy from five to three.

There is a strong link between the structure of an organization and its responsibility accounting system. Ideally, the responsibility accounting system mirrors and supports the structure of an organization.

Types of Responsibility Centers

As a firm grows, top management typically creates areas of responsibility, known as *responsibility centers*, and assigns subordinate managers to those areas. A responsibility center is a segment of the business whose manager is accountable for specified sets of activities. Responsibility accounting is a system that measures the results of each responsibility center according to the information managers need to operate their center. There are four major types of responsibility centers:

responsibility center
responsibility accounting

cost center
1. Cost center   A responsibility center in which a manager is responsible only for costs.

revenue center
2. Revenue center   A responsibility center in which a manager is responsible only for sales.

profit center
3. Profit center   A responsibility center in which a manager is responsible for both revenues and costs.

investment center
4. Investment center   A responsibility center in which a manager is responsible for revenues, costs, and investments.

Exhibit 12-1 displays these centers along with the type of information they need to manage their operations.

A production department within the factory, such as assembly or finishing, is an example of a cost center. The supervisor of a production department controls manufacturing costs, but does not set price or make marketing decisions. Therefore, the producing-department supervisor is evaluated on the basis of how well costs are controlled.

The marketing department manager sets price and projected sales. Therefore, the marketing department may be evaluated as a revenue center. Direct costs of the marketing department and overall sales are the responsibility of the sales manager.

12-1

Exhibit
Types of Responsibility
Centers and Accounting
Information Used to
Measure Performance

	Accounting Information Used to Measure Performance			
	Cost	Sales	Capital Investment	Other
Cost center	X			
Revenue center	Direct cost only	X		
Profit center	X	X		
Investment center	X	X	X	X

In some companies, plant managers are given the responsibility for manufacturing and marketing their products. These plant managers control both costs and revenues, putting them in control of a profit center. Operating income would be an important performance measure for profit center managers.

Finally, divisions are often cited as examples of investment centers. In addition to having control over cost and pricing decisions, divisional managers have the power to make investment decisions, such as plant closings and openings, and decisions to keep or drop a product line. As a result, both operating income and some type of return on investment are important performance measures for investment center managers.

It is important to realize that while the responsibility center manager has responsibility for only the activities of that center, decisions made by that manager can affect other responsibility centers. Suppose the sales force at a floor care products firm routinely offers customers price discounts at the end of the month. Sales increase dramatically, and the factory is forced to institute overtime shifts to keep up with demand.

The Role of Information and Accountability

Information is the key to appropriately holding managers responsible for outcomes. For example, a production department manager is held responsible for departmental costs but not for sales. This is because the production department manager not only controls some of these costs, but knows and understands them. Any deviation between actual and expected costs can best be explained at this level. Sales are the responsibility of the sales manager, again because this manager can best explain what is happening regarding price and quantity sold.

Responsibility also entails *accountability*. Accountability implies performance measurement, which means that actual outcomes are compared with expected or budgeted outcomes. This system of responsibility, accountability, and performance evaluation is often referred to as *responsibility accounting* because of the key role that accounting measures and reports play in the process. A key distinction must be made between responsibility and blame. For example, in 1991, Anne Busquet was the general manager of the Optima Card unit at American Express when the company discovered that 5 of her 2,000 employees had deliberately hidden $24 million in losses on the Optima Card accounts. Busquet was held responsible and accountable (she lost her Optima job) despite the fact that she, personally, was not to blame. Basically, as manager, she was expected to be aware of what was going on in her shop. On a happier note, Busquet accepted the challenge of turning around American Express' merchandise services unit. She is now executive vice-president for consumer-card marketing at American Express.[2]

DECENTRALIZATION

Objective 2

Explain why firms choose
to decentralize.

**centralized
  decision making**

Firms with multiple responsibility centers usually choose one of two decision-making approaches to manage their diverse and complex activities: *centralized* or *decentralized*. In centralized decision making, decisions are made at the very top level, and lower-level managers are charged with implementing these decisions. On the other hand,

2. Patricia Sellers, "So You Fail. Now Bounce Back!" *Fortune*, 1 May 1995, 48–66.

Large companies are generally decentralized. KFC is owned by Pepsico, but has wide latitude in decision making. Similarly, this KFC outlet has local authority in determining the appropriate mix of food offerings for its Chinese clientele.

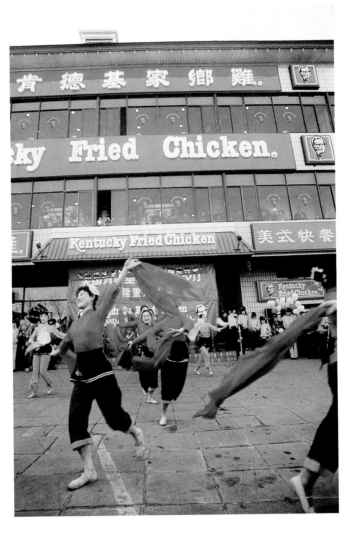

**decentralized
decision making
decentralization**

decentralized decision making allows managers at lower levels to make and implement key decisions pertaining to their areas of responsibility. Decentralization is the practice of delegating decision-making authority to the lower levels.

Organizations range from highly centralized to strongly decentralized. Most firms fall somewhere in between, with the majority tending toward decentralization. The reasons for the popularity of decentralization and the ways in which a company may choose to decentralize are discussed next.

Reasons for Decentralization

There are many reasons to explain firms' decision to decentralize including: (1) ease of gathering and using local information; (2) focusing of central management; (3) training and motivating segment managers; and (4) enhanced competition, exposing segments to market forces.

Gathering and Using Local Information The quality of decisions is affected by the quality of information available. As a firm grows in size and operates in different markets and regions, central management may not understand local conditions. Lower-level managers, however, who are in contact with immediate operating conditions (such as the strength and nature of local competition, the nature of the local labor force, and so on) have access to this information. As a result, local managers are often in a position to make better decisions. For example, Kmart practices micromarketing by allowing individual store managers to decide what goods to stock. The result is that each Kmart store can differentiate to meet the needs of its local market. Thus, two stores only five miles apart can stock very different items. This advantage of decentralization is particularly applicable to multinational corporations, where far-flung divisions may be operating in a number of different countries, subject to various legal systems and customs. (International issues in management accounting are discussed in Chapter 13.)

A second problem is information overload. In an organization that operates in diverse markets with hundreds or thousands of different products, no one person has all of the expertise and training needed to process and use the information. Individuals with specialized skills would still be needed. Rather than having different individuals at headquarters for every specialized area, why not let these individuals have direct responsibility in the field? For example, a manager with an engineering background may head a factory while another manager with specialized skills in data analysis may be in charge of the computer center.

In a centralized setting, time is needed to transmit the local information to headquarters and to transmit the decision back to the local unit. Furthermore, the two transmissions increase the probability that the manager responsible for implementing the decision might misinterpret the instructions. This decreases the effectiveness of the response. In a decentralized organization, where the local manager both makes and implements the decision, this problem does not arise.

Focusing of Central Management By decentralizing the operating decisions, central management is free to engage in strategic planning and decision making. The long-run survival of the organization should be of more importance to central management than day-to-day operations.

Training and Motivating Managers Organizations always need well-trained managers to replace higher-level managers who leave to take advantage of other opportunities. What better way to prepare a future generation of higher-level managers than by providing them the opportunity to make significant decisions? These opportunities also enable top managers to evaluate local managers' capabilities. Those who make the best decisions are the ones who can be promoted.

Greater responsibility can produce more job satisfaction and motivate the local manager to exert greater effort. More initiative and more creativity may result. Of course, the extent to which the behavioral benefits can be realized depends to a large degree on how managers are evaluated and rewarded for their performance.

Enhanced Competition In a highly centralized company, overall profit margins can mask inefficiencies within the various subdivisions. Large companies now find that they cannot afford to keep a noncompetitive division. "In many cases, the best way to improve performance of a division or factory—indeed, just to measure it—is to expose it more fully to market forces."[3] That is happening at IBM, where in 1992, 14 semiautonomous business units were formed. Each unit keeps its own books and is evaluated on the basis of its contribution to profits. Noncompetitive units are released.

The Units of Decentralization

Decentralization is usually achieved by creating units called *divisions*. One way in which divisions are differentiated is by the types of goods or services produced. For example, divisions of PepsiCo include the Snack Ventures Europe division (a joint venture with General Mills), Frito-Lay, Inc., and Pizza Hut, as well as its flagship soft drink division. These divisions are organized on the basis of product lines. Notice that some divisions depend on other divisions. At Pizza Hut, for example, the cola you drink will be Pepsi—

3. John W. Verity, "Deconstructing the Computer Industry," *Business Week*, 23 November 1992, 92.

not Coke. In a decentralized setting, some interdependencies usually exist; otherwise, a company would merely be a collection of totally separate entities.

Divisions may also be created along geographic lines. For example, Northwest Airlines, Inc. has three regional divisions: the Pacific Division; the Atlantic Division; and the Domestic Division. The presence of divisions spanning one or more regions creates the need for performance evaluation that can take into account differences in divisional environments.

A third way divisions differ is by the type of responsibility given to the divisional manager. Recall the four major types of responsibility centers: cost centers, revenue centers, profit centers, and investment centers. Investment centers represent the greatest degree of decentralization (followed by profit centers and finally by cost and revenue centers) because their managers have the freedom to make the greatest variety of decisions.

Organizing divisions as responsibility centers creates the opportunity to control the divisions through the use of responsibility accounting. Control of cost or revenue centers is achieved by evaluating the efficiency and the effectiveness of divisional managers based on control of costs or sales. Profit centers are evaluated on the basis of income. Since performance reports and contribution income statements have been discussed elsewhere, this chapter will not go into the evaluation of managers of cost centers, revenue centers, or profit centers. The focus will be on the evaluation of managers of investment centers.

MEASURING THE PERFORMANCE OF INVESTMENT CENTERS

Objective 3

Compute and explain return on investment (ROI) and residual income (RI).

We need to make a distinction between the evaluation of investment centers and the evaluation of the managers who run them. The distinction is sometimes subtle, and often lost. Still, it is clear that a division can do well or poorly irrespective of the efforts of its manager. For this reason, a company tries to separate the evaluations. The evaluation of the segment is examined in this section, the evaluation of the manager is reserved for the section on measuring and rewarding the performance of managers.

Return on Investment

Divisions that are investment centers will have an income statement and a balance sheet. So, could we simply rank the divisions on the basis of net income? Suppose, for example, that a company has two divisions—Alpha and Beta. Alpha's net income is $100,000 and Beta's is $200,000. Did Beta perform better than Alpha? What if Alpha used an investment of $500,000 to produce the contribution of $100,000 while Beta used an investment of $2 million to produce the $200,000 contribution? Does your response change? Clearly, relating the reported operating profits to the assets used to produce them is a more meaningful measure of performance.

One way to relate operating profits to assets employed is to compute the profit earned per dollar of investment. Return on investment (ROI) is the most common measure of performance for an investment center. It can be defined as follows:

return on investment (ROI)

$$\text{ROI} = \frac{\text{Operating income}}{\text{Average operating assets}}$$

operating income
operating assets

First let's define terms. Operating income refers to earnings before interest and taxes. Operating assets are all assets acquired to generate operating income, including cash, receivables, inventories, land, buildings, and equipment. The figure for average operating assets is computed as follows:

$$\text{Average operating assets} = \frac{\text{Beginning net book value} + \text{Ending net book value}}{2}$$

Opinions vary regarding how long-term assets (plant and equipment) should be valued (for example, gross book value versus net book value or historical cost versus current cost). Most firms use historical cost, net book value.[4]

Going back to our example, Alpha's ROI is 0.20 ($\frac{\$100,000}{\$500,000}$), while Beta's ROI was only 0.10 ($\frac{\$200,000}{\$2,000,000}$).

The formula for ROI is quick and easy to use. However, the decomposition of ROI into margin and turnover ratios gives additional information. Let's look at this possibility in more detail.

Margin and Turnover

A second formula for ROI is simply margin times turnover. Thus, the formula for ROI can also be expressed as follows:

$$\#2 \quad \text{ROI} = \text{Margin} \times \text{Turnover}$$
$$= \frac{\text{Operating income}}{\text{Sales}} \times \frac{\text{Sales}}{\text{Average operating assets}}$$

Suppose, for example, that Alpha had sales of $400,000. Then margin would be 0.25 ($\frac{\$100,000}{\$400,000}$) and turnover would be 0.80 ($\frac{\$400,000}{\$500,000}$). Alpha's ROI would still be 0.20 (0.25 × 0.80).

margin
turnover

Margin is simply the ratio of operating income to sales. It expresses the portion of sales that is available for interest, taxes, and profit. Turnover is a different measure; it is found by dividing sales by average operating assets. The result shows how productively assets are being used to generate sales.

While both approaches yield the same ROI, the calculation of margin and turnover gives a manager valuable information. To illustrate this additional information, consider the data presented in Exhibit 12-2. The Electronics Division improved its ROI from 18 percent to 20 percent from 1996 to 1997. The Medical Supplies Division's ROI, however, dropped from 18 percent to 15 percent. A better picture of what caused the change in rates is revealed by computing the margin and turnover ratios for each division. These ratios are also presented in Exhibit 12-2.

Notice that the margins for both divisions dropped from 1996 to 1997. In fact, the divisions experienced the *same* percentage of decline (16.67 percent). A declining margin could be explained by increasing expenses, by competitive pressures (forcing a decrease in selling prices), or both.

In spite of the declining margin, the Electronics Division was able to increase its rate of return. The reason is that the increase in turnover more than compensated for the decline in margin. One explanation for the increased turnover could be a deliberate policy to reduce inventories. (Notice that the average assets employed remained the same for the Electronics Division even though sales increased by $10 million.)

The experience of the other division was less favorable. Because its turnover rate remained unchanged, its ROI dropped. This division, unlike the other one, could not overcome the decline in margin.

Advantages of ROI

At least three positive results stem from the use of ROI:

1. It encourages managers to focus on the relationship among sales, expenses, and investment, as should be the case for a manager of an investment center.
2. It encourages managers to focus on cost efficiency.
3. It encourages managers to focus on operating asset efficiency.

4. For a discussion of the relative merits of gross book value, see James S. Reese and William R. Cool, "Measuring Investment Center Performance," *Harvard Business Review* (May–June 1978): 28–46, 174–176.

Comparison of ROI	Electronics Division	Medical Supplies Division
1996:		
Sales	$30,000,000	$117,000,000
Operating income	1,800,000	3,510,000
Average operating assets	10,000,000	19,500,000
ROI[a]	18%	18%
1997:		
Sales	$40,000,000	$117,000,000
Operating income	2,000,000	2,925,000
Average operating assets	10,000,000	19,500,000
ROI[a]	20%	15%

Margin and Turnover Comparisons	Electronics Division		Medical Supplies Division	
	1996	**1997**	**1996**	**1997**
Margin[b]	6.0%	5.0%	3.0%	2.5%
Turnover[c]	× 3.0	× 4.0	× 6.0	× 6.0
ROI[a]	18.0%	20.0%	18.0%	15.0%

[a]Operating income divided by average operating assets
[b]Operating income divided by sales
[c]Sales divided by average operating assets

These advantages are illustrated by the following three scenarios.

Focus on ROI Relationships Della Barnes, manager of the Plastics Division, is mulling over a suggestion from her marketing vice-president to increase the advertising budget by $100,000. The marketing vice-president is confident that this increase will boost sales by $200,000 and raise the contribution margin by $110,000. Della realizes that an additional $50,000 of operating assets will be needed to support this large an increase in sales. Currently, the division has sales of $2 million, net operating income of $150,000, and operating assets of $1 million.

If advertising increases by $100,000 and the contribution margin by $110,000, operating income would go up by $10,000 ($110,000 − $100,000). The ROI without the additional advertising is 15 percent ($\frac{\$150,000}{\$1,000,000}$). With the additional advertising and $50,000 investment in assets, the ROI is 15.24 percent ($\frac{\$160,000}{\$1,050,000}$). Since ROI is increased by the proposal, Della decides to authorize the increased advertising.

Focus on Cost Efficiency Kyle Chugg, manager of Turner's Battery Division, groaned as he reviewed the projections for the last half of the current fiscal year. The recession was hurting his division's performance. Adding the projected operating income of $200,000 to the actual operating income of the first half produced expected annual earnings of $425,000. Kyle then divided the expected operating income by the division's average operating assets to obtain an expected ROI of 12.15 percent. "This is awful," muttered Kyle. "Last year our ROI was 16 percent. And I'm looking at a couple more bad years before business returns to normal. Something has to be done to improve our performance."

Kyle directed all operating managers to cut costs by specified amounts without impairing the company's ability to maintain expected sales. Lower-level managers found ways to reduce costs by $150,000 for the remaining half of the year. This reduction increased the annual operating income from $425,000 to $575,000, increasing ROI from 12.15 percent to 16.43 percent as a result. Interestingly, Kyle found that some of the reductions could be maintained after business returned to normal.

Focus on Operating Asset Efficiency The Electronic Storage Division prospered during its early years. In the beginning, the division developed a new technology for mass storage of data; sales and return on investment were extraordinarily high. However, during the past several years, competitors had developed competing technology, and the division's ROI had plunged from 30 percent to 15 percent. Cost cutting had helped initially, but the fat had all been removed, and further improvements from cost reductions were not possible. Moreover, any increase in sales was unlikely—competition was too stiff. The divisional manager searched for some way to increase the ROI by at least 3 to 5 percent. Only by raising the ROI so that it compared favorably to that of the other divisions could the division expect to receive additional capital for research and development.

The divisional manager initiated an intensive program to reduce operating assets. Most of the gains were made in the area of inventory reductions; however, one plant was closed because of a long-term reduction in market share. By installing a just-in-time purchasing and manufacturing system, the division was able to reduce its asset base without threatening its remaining market share. Finally, the reduction in operating assets meant that operating costs could be decreased still further. The end result was a 50 percent increase in the division's ROI, from 15 percent to more than 22 percent.

Disadvantages of the ROI Measure

Overemphasis on ROI can produce myopic behavior. Two negative aspects associated with ROI are frequently mentioned.

1. It can produce a narrow focus on divisional profitability at the expense of profitability for the overall firm.
2. It encourages managers to focus on the short run at the expense of the long run.

These disadvantages are illustrated by the following two scenarios.

Narrow Focus on Divisional Profitability A cleaning products division has the opportunity to invest in two projects for the coming year. The outlay required for each investment, the dollar returns, and the ROI are as follows:

	Project I	Project II
Investment	$10,000,000	$4,000,000
Operating income	1,300,000	640,000
ROI	13%	16%

The division currently earns ROI of 15 percent, with operating assets of $50 million, and operating income on current investment of $7.5 million. The division has approval to request up to $15 million in new investment capital. Corporate headquarters requires that all investments earn at least 10 percent (this rate represents the corporation's cost of acquiring the capital). Any capital not used by a division is invested by headquarters and it earns exactly 10 percent.

The divisional manager has four alternatives: invest in Project I; invest in Project II; invest in both Projects I and II; and invest in neither project. The divisional ROI was computed for each alternative.

	Alternatives		
	Select Project I	Select Project II	Select Both Project
Operating income	$ 8,800,000	$ 8,140,000	$ 9,440,00
Operating assets	60,000,000	54,000,000	64,000,00
ROI	14.67%	15.07%	14.7

The divisional manager chose to invest only in Project II since it would boost ROI from 15.00 percent to 15.07 percent.

While the manager's choice maximized divisional ROI, it actually cost the company profit. If Project I had been selected, the company would have earned $1.3 million. By not selecting Project I, the $10 million in capital is invested at 10 percent, earning only $1 million ($0.10 \times \$10,000,000$). The single-minded focus on divisional ROI, then, cost the company $300,000 in profits ($\$1,300,000 - \$1,000,000$).

Encourages Short-Run Optimization Ruth Lunsford, manager of a small tools division, was displeased with her division's performance during the first three quarters. Given the expected income for the fourth quarter, the ROI for the year would be 13 percent, at least two percentage points below where she had hoped to be. Such an ROI might not be strong enough to justify the early promotion she wanted. With only three months left, drastic action was needed. Increasing sales for the last quarter was unlikely. Most sales were booked at least two to three months in advance. Emphasizing extra sales activity would benefit next year's performance. What was needed were some ways to improve this year's performance.

After careful thought, Ruth decided to take the following actions:

1. Lay off five of the highest paid salespeople.
2. Cut the advertising budget for the fourth quarter by 50 percent.
3. Delay all promotions within the division for three months.
4. Reduce the preventive maintenance budget by 75 percent.
5. Use cheaper raw materials for fourth-quarter production.

In the aggregate, these steps would reduce expenses, increase income, and raise the ROI to about 15.2 percent.

While Ruth's actions increase the profits and ROI in the short run, they have some long-run negative consequences. Laying off the highest paid (and possibly the best) salespeople may harm the division's future sales-generating capabilities. Future sales could also be hurt by cutting back on advertising and using cheaper raw materials. Delaying promotions could hurt employee morale, which could, in turn, lower productivity and future sales. Finally, reducing preventive maintenance will likely increase downtime and decrease the life of the productive equipment.

Residual Income

residual income

To compensate for the tendency of ROI to discourage investments that are profitable for the company but that lower a division's ROI, some companies have adopted an alternative performance measure known as *residual income*. Residual income is the difference between operating income and the minimum dollar return required on a company's operating assets:

Residual income = Operating income − (Minimum rate of return × Operating assets)

Advantage of Residual Income Let's reconsider the case of the cleaning products division. Recall that the divisional manager rejected Project I because it would have reduced divisional ROI; however, that decision cost the company $300,000 in profits. The use of residual income as the performance measure would have prevented this loss. The residual income for each project is computed next.

Project I
Residual income = Operating income − (Minimum rate of return × Operating assets)
         = $1,300,000 − (0.10 × $10,000,000)
         = $1,300,000 − $1,000,000
         = $300,000

Project II

$$Residual\ income = \$640,000 - (0.10 \times \$4,000,000)$$
$$= \$640,000 - \$400,000$$
$$= \$240,000$$

Notice that both projects have positive residual income. For comparative purposes, the divisional residual income for each of the four alternatives identified follows:

	Alternatives			
	Select Project I	Select Project II	Select Both Projects	Select Neither Project
Operating assets	$60,000,000	$54,000,000	$64,000,000	$50,000,000
Operating income	$ 8,800,000	$ 8,140,000	$ 9,440,000	$ 7,500,000
Minimum return*	6,000,000	5,400,000	6,400,000	5,000,000
Residual income	$ 2,800,000	$ 2,740,000	$ 3,040,000	$ 2,500,000

*0.10 × Operating assets

The table shows that selecting both projects produces the greatest increase in residual income. The use of residual income encourages managers to accept any project that earns above the minimum rate.

Disadvantages of Residual Income Residual income, like ROI, can encourage a short-run orientation. If Ruth Lunsford were being evaluated on the basis of residual income, she could have taken the same actions.

Another problem with residual income is that it, unlike ROI, is an absolute measure of profitability. Thus, direct comparisons of the performance of two different investment centers become difficult, since the level of investment may differ. For example, consider the residual income computations for division A and division B, where the minimum required rate of return is 8 percent.

	Division A	Division B
Average operating assets	$15,000,000	$2,500,000
Operating income	$ 1,500,000	$ 300,000
Minimum return[a]	1,200,000	200,000
Residual income	$ 300,000	$ 100,000
Residual return[b]	2%	4%

[a]0.08 × Operating assets
[b]Residual income divided by operating assets

It is tempting to claim that division A is outperforming division B since its residual income is three times higher. Notice, however, that division A used six times as many assets to produce this difference. If anything, division B is more efficient.

One possible way to correct this disadvantage is to compute a residual return on investment by dividing residual income by average operating assets. This measure indicates that division B earned 4 percent while division A earned only 2 percent. Another possibility is to compute both return on investment and residual income and use both measures for performance evaluation. ROI could then be used for interdivisional comparisons.[5]

5. In their study, Reese and Cool found that only 2 percent of the companies surveyed used residual income by itself, whereas 28 percent used both residual income and return on investment. See Reese and Cool, "Measuring Investment Center Performance."

Multiple Measures of Performance

Residual income and ROI are important measures of managerial performance. However, they are both short-run measures. As such, the temptation exists for managers to trade off short-run benefits at the expense of the long-run well-being of the company. One way to discourage this myopic behavior is to use additional measures of performance that relate more closely to the long-run health of the division. For example, in addition to ROI and residual income, top management could look at such factors as market share, customer complaints, personnel turnover ratios, and personnel development. By letting lower-level managers know that attention to long-run factors is also vital, the tendency to overemphasize ROI or residual income should diminish.

Managers in an advanced manufacturing environment are especially likely to use multiple measures of performance, and to include nonfinancial as well as financial measures. For example, the Saturn plant measures absenteeism (it averages 2.5 percent versus the 10 to 14 percent experienced by other General Motors plants).[6] Hewlett-Packard has found that the sooner a new product reaches the market, the higher the product's profitability. Thus, in the design phase of a new product, strict conformance to schedule is one of Hewlett-Packard's key performance measures.[7]

MEASURING AND REWARDING THE PERFORMANCE OF MANAGERS

Objective 4

Discuss methods of evaluating and rewarding managerial performance.

While some companies consider the performance of the division to be equivalent to the performance of the manager, there is a compelling reason to separate the two. Often, the performance of the division is subject to factors beyond the manager's control. It is particularly important, then, to link managerial compensation to factors under the manager's control.

Incentive Pay for Managers

The subjects of managerial evaluation and incentive pay would be of little concern if all managers were equally likely to perform up to the best of their abilities, and if those abilities were known in advance. In the case of a small company, owned and managed by the same person, there is no problem. The owner puts in as much effort as he or she wishes, and receives all of the income from the firm as a reward for performance. However, in most companies, the owner hires managers to operate the company on a day-to-day basis and delegates decision-making authority to them. For example, the stockholders of a company hire the CEO through the board of directors. Similarly, divisional managers are hired by the CEO to operate their divisions on behalf of the owners. Then the owners must ensure that the managers are providing good service.

Why would managers not provide good service? There are three reasons: (1) they may have low ability, (2) they may prefer to work less hard than needed, and (3) they may prefer to spend company resources on *perquisites*. The first reason requires owners to discover information about the manager before hiring him or her. Think back to the reasons for decentralization; one was that it provided training for future managers. This is true, and it also provides signals to higher management about the managerial ability of divisional managers. The second and third reasons require the owner to monitor the manager, or to arrange an incentive scheme that will more closely ally the manager's goals with those of the owner. In general, it is thought that managers may prefer not to do hard or routine work. Thus, it is necessary to compensate them for this. Closely

perquisites

related is the tendency of some managers to overuse perquisites. Perquisites are a type of fringe benefit received over and above salary. Some examples are a nice office, use of a company car or jet, expense accounts, and company-paid country club memberships. While some perquisites are legitimate uses of company resources, they can be abused. A

---

6. David Woodruff, "Where Employees Are Management," *Business Week*, Reinventing America 1992, 66.
7. Robert D. Hof, "From Dinosaur to Gazelle," *Business Week*, Reinventing America 1992, 65.

well-structured incentive pay plan can help to encourage goal congruence between managers and owners.

Management Compensation: Encouraging Goal Congruence

Management compensation frequently includes incentives tied to performance. The objective is to encourage goal congruence, so that managers will act in the best interests of the firm. As the opening scenario reveals, arranging managerial compensation to encourage managers to adopt the same goals as the overall firm is an important issue. Managerial rewards include salary increases, bonuses based on reported income, stock options, and noncash compensation.

Cash Compensation   Cash compensation includes salaries and bonuses. A company may reward good managerial performance by granting periodic raises. However, once the raise takes effect it is usually permanent. Bonuses give a company more flexibility. Many companies use a combination of salary and bonus to reward performance by keeping salaries fairly level and allowing bonuses to fluctuate with reported income. A manager may find the bonus tied to divisional net income, or to targeted increases in net income. For example, a divisional manager may receive an annual salary of $75,000 and a yearly bonus of 5 percent of the increase in reported net income. If net income does not rise, the manager's bonus is zero. This incentive pay scheme makes increasing net income, an objective of the owner, important to the manager as well.

Of course, income-based compensation can encourage dysfunctional behavior. The manager may engage in unethical practices, such as postponing needed maintenance. If the bonus is capped at a certain amount (say the bonus is equal to 1 percent of net income, but cannot exceed $50,000), managers may postpone revenue recognition at the end of the year in which the maximum bonus has already been achieved to the next year. Those who structure the reward systems need to understand both the positive incentives built into the system as well as the potential for negative behavior.

stock option

Stock Options   Companies frequently offer stock options to managers. A stock option is the right to buy a certain number of shares of the company's stock, at a particular price, and after a set length of time. Stock is a share in the company, and theoretically it should increase in value as the company does well and decrease in value as the company does poorly. Issuing stock to managers makes them part owners of the company and should encourage goal congruence. The objective of awarding stock options is to encourage managers to focus on the longer term. The price of the option shares is usually set approximately at market price at the time of issue. Then, if the stock price rises in the future, the manager may exercise the option, thus purchasing stock at a below market price and realizing an immediate gain.

For example, suppose Jane Reynolds, head of the Toiletries Division of Gilpal, Inc., was granted an option to purchase 100,000 shares of Gilpal stock at the current market price of $20 per share. The option was granted in August 1997, and could be exercised after two years. If, by August 1999, Gilpal stock has risen to $23 per share, Jane can purchase all 100,000 shares for $2,000,000 ($20 × 100,000 option price) and immediately sell them for $2,300,000 ($23 × 100,000). She will realize a profit of $300,000. Of course, if Gilpal drops below $20, Jane will not exercise the option. Typically, however, a stock's price rises along with the market and Jane can safely bet on a future profit as long as Gilpal does not perform worse than the market.

Companies are becoming more aware of the opportunity for windfall profits based on the sale of stock purchased with low-cost options, profits that appear to be more closely related to the overall rise in the stock market and less related to outstanding performance by top management. As a result, many companies are starting to attach strong performance requirements to the exercise of stock options. For example, fertilizer maker Terra Industries, Inc., granted options on 300,000 shares to its chairman and chief executive Burton Joyce. However, Joyce cannot exercise all of the options until the share price rises from 50 percent to 100 percent above its $5 market price (at the time of the September 1992 grant). Similarly, in January 1993, Colgate-Palmolive granted its CEO options to purchase up to one million shares. However, the exercise price ranges from $61 to $100 per share, while the market price at the time of issue was about $55.[8] These packages are designed to firmly ally the CEOs' interests with those of the stockholders of the two firms.

Typically, there are constraints on the exercise of the options. For example, the stock purchased with options may not be sold for a certain period of time. A disadvantage of stock options is that the price of the stock is based on many factors not completely within the manager's control.

Issues in Structuring Income-based Compensation Single measures of performance, which are often the basis of bonuses, often encourage gaming behavior. That is, managers may increase short-term measures at the expense of the long-term health of the firm. For example, a manager may keep net income up by refusing to invest in more modern and efficient equipment. Depreciation expense remains low, but so do productivity and quality. Clearly, the manager has an incentive to understand the computation of the accounting numbers used in performance evaluation. An accounting change from FIFO to LIFO or in the method of depreciation, for example, will change net income even though sales and costs remain unchanged. Frequently, we see that a new CEO of a troubled corporation will take a number of losses (for example, inventory write-downs) all at once. This is referred to as the "big bath" and usually results in very low (or negative) net income in that year. Then, the books are cleared for a good increase in net income, and a correspondingly large bonus, for the next year.

Both cash bonuses and stock options can encourage a short-term orientation. To encourage a longer-term orientation, some companies are requiring top executives to purchase and hold a certain amount of company stock to retain employment. Eastman Kodak, Xerox, CSX, Gerber Products, Union Carbide, and Hershey Foods all have stock ownership guidelines for their top management. A survey of companies in which top executives own relatively large amounts of company stock shows that they tend to perform better in terms of share price than low-ownership companies.[9]

Another issue in structuring management compensation plans is that frequently owners and managers are affected differently by risk. When managers have so much of their own capital—both financial and human—invested in the company, they may be less apt to take risks. Owners, because of their ability to diversify away some of the risk, may prefer a more risk-taking attitude. As a result, managers must be somewhat insulated from catastrophic downside risk in order to encourage them to make entrepreneurial decisions.

Noncash Compensation Noncash compensation is also important. We see this at work for managers, as they may trade-off increased salary for improvements in title, office location and trappings, use of expense accounts, and so on. Autonomy in the conduct of their daily business is also an important perquisite. Each of these perquisites signals upper management's approval of lower managers' performance. Use of perquisites is an important feature of management compensation. They can be used well to make the manager more efficient. For example, a busy manager may be able to effectively employ several assistants, and may find that use of a corporate jet allows him or her to more efficiently schedule travel in overseeing far-flung divisions. However, perquisites may be abused as well. For instance, one wonders how the shareholders of RJR Nabisco bene-

---

8. Joann S. Lublin, "Higher Profits Fatten CEO Bonuses," *The Wall Street Journal*, 21 April 1993, pp. R1–R2. Interestingly, by June 14, 1995, the stock of both companies had moved up sufficiently to make the exercise of the options possible. Terra Industries closing price on that day was $10\frac{7}{8}$; Colgate-Palmolive's closing price was $75\frac{3}{4}$.
9. Joann S. Lublin, "Buy or Bye," *The Wall Street Journal*, 21 April 1993, p. R9.

fited from former CEO F. Ross Johnson's use of corporate jets to fly friends around the country.[10]

TRANSFER PRICING

Objective 5

Explain the role of transfer pricing in a decentralized firm.

transfer price

In many decentralized organizations, the output of one division is used as the input of another. This raises an accounting issue. How do we value the transferred good? When divisions are treated as responsibility centers, they are evaluated on the basis of operating income and return on investment. As a result, the value of the transferred good is revenue to the selling division and cost to the buying division. This value, or internal price, is called the transfer price. Transfer pricing is a complex issue. We will examine the impact of transfer prices on divisions and the company as a whole, as well as methods of setting transfer prices, in the following sections.

Impact on Performance Measures

Transfer pricing affects both transferring divisions and the firm as a whole. It does this through its impact on: (1) divisional performance measures, (2) firmwide profits, and (3) divisional autonomy.

Impact on Divisional Performance Measures The price charged for the transferred good affects the costs of the buying division and the revenues of the selling division. Thus, the profits of both divisions are affected by the transfer price. Since profit-based performance measures of the two divisions are affected (for example, ROI and residual income), transfer pricing can often be a very emotionally charged issue. Exhibit 12-3 illustrates the effect of the transfer price on two divisions of ABC, Inc. Division A produces a component and sells it to another division of the same company, division C. The $30 transfer price is revenue to division A; clearly division A wants the price to be as high as possible. Conversely, the $30 transfer price is cost to division C, just like the cost of any raw materials. Division C prefers a lower transfer price.

Impact on Firmwide Profits While the actual transfer price nets out for the company as a whole, transfer pricing can affect the level of profits earned by the company in two ways: if it affects divisional behavior, and if it affects income taxes. Divisions, acting independently, may set transfer prices that maximize divisional profits but adversely affect firmwide profits. For example, the buying division may decide to purchase the good from an outside party because the outside price is lower than the transfer price, when, in reality, the cost of producing the good internally is much lower than the transfer price. Suppose that division A in Exhibit 12-3 sets a transfer price of $30 for a

10. Bryan Burrough and John Helyar, *Barbarians at the Gate: The Fall of RJR Nabisco* (New York: Harper and Row, 1990), 95.

Exhibit

Impact of Transfer Price on Transferring Divisions and the Company as a Whole

ABC, Inc.	
Division A	**Division C**
Produces component and transfers it to C for transfer price of $30 per unit	Purchases component from A at transfer price of $30 per unit and uses it in production of final product
Transfer price = $30 per unit	Transfer price = $30 per unit
Revenue to A	Cost to C
Increases net income	Decreases net income
Increases ROI	Decreases ROI

Transfer price revenue = Transfer price cost
Zero impact on ABC, Inc.

component that costs $24 to produce. If division C can obtain the component from an outside supplier for $28, it will refuse to buy from division A. Division C will realize a savings of $2 per component ($30 internal transfer price − $28 external price). However, assuming that division A cannot replace the internal sales with external sales, the company as a whole will be worse off by $4 per component ($28 external cost − $24 internal cost). This outcome would increase the total cost to the firm.

Transfer pricing can affect overall corporate income taxes. This is particularly true for multinational corporations. As a general rule, however, the corporation may try to set the transfer price so that more revenue is assigned to divisions in low-tax countries and more cost is assigned to divisions in high-tax countries. The international transfer pricing situation is examined in detail in Chapter 13.

Impact on Autonomy Because transfer pricing decisions can affect firmwide profitability, top management is often tempted to intervene and dictate desirable transfer prices. If such intervention becomes a frequent practice, however, the organization has effectively abandoned decentralization and all of its advantages. Organizations decentralize because the benefits are greater than the associated costs. One of these costs is occasional suboptimal behavior by divisional managers. Thus, intervention by central management to reduce this cost may actually prove to be more expensive in the long run than nonintervention.

The Transfer Pricing Problem

transfer pricing problem

A transfer pricing system should satisfy three objectives: accurate performance evaluation, goal congruence, and preservation of divisional autonomy.[11] *Accurate performance evaluation* means that no one divisional manager should benefit at the expense of another (in the sense that one division is made better off while the other is made worse off). *Goal congruence* means that divisional managers select actions that maximize firmwide profits. *Autonomy* means that central management should not interfere with the decision-making freedom of divisional managers. The transfer pricing problem concerns finding a system that simultaneously satisfies all three objectives.

Although direct intervention by central management to set specific transfer prices may not be advisable, the development of some general guidelines may be appropriate. One such guideline, called the *opportunity cost approach*, can be used to describe a wide variety of transfer pricing practices. Under certain conditions, this approach is compatible with the objectives of performance evaluation, goal congruence, and autonomy.

The Opportunity Cost Approach as a Guide for Transfer Pricing

opportunity cost approach

In establishing a transfer pricing policy, the views of both the selling division and the buying division must be considered. The opportunity cost approach achieves this goal by identifying the minimum price that a selling division would be willing to accept and the maximum price that the buying division would be willing to pay. These minimum and maximum prices correspond to the opportunity costs of transferring internally. They are defined for each division as follows:

minimum transfer price

1. The minimum transfer price is the transfer price that would leave the selling division no worse off if the good were sold to an internal division than if the good were sold to an external party.

maximum transfer price

2. The maximum transfer price is the transfer price that would leave the buying division no worse off if an input were purchased from an internal division than if the same good were purchased externally.

The opportunity cost approach guides divisions in determining when internal transfers should occur. Specifically, the good should be transferred internally whenever the

11. Joshua Ronen and George McKinney, "Transfer Pricing for Divisional Autonomy," *Journal of Accounting Research* (Spring 1970): 100–101.

opportunity cost (minimum price) of the selling division is less than the opportunity cost (maximum price) of the buying division. By its very definition, this approach ensures that *neither* divisional manager is worse off by transferring internally. But what is meant by indifferent or no worse off? In practical terms, this means that total divisional profits are not decreased by the internal transfer.

Market Price

If there is a perfectly competitive outside market for the transferred product, the correct transfer price is the market price.[12] In such a case, divisional managers' actions will simultaneously optimize divisional profits and firmwide profits. Furthermore, no division can benefit at the expense of another. In this setting, central management will not be tempted to intervene.

The opportunity cost approach also signals that the correct transfer price is the market price. Since the selling division can sell all that it produces at the market price, transferring internally at a lower price would make the division worse off. Similarly, the buying division can always acquire the good at the market price, so it would be unwilling to pay more for an internally transferred good. Since the minimum transfer price for the selling division is the market price and the maximum price for the buying division is also the market price, the only possible transfer price is the market price.

In fact, moving away from the market price will decrease the overall profitability of the firm. This principle can be used to resolve divisional conflicts that may occur, as the following example illustrates.

Tyson Manufacturers is a large, privately held corporation that produces small appliances. The company has adopted a decentralized organizational structure. The Small Parts Division, managed by Ned Kimberly, produces parts that are used by the Small Motor Division managed by Andrea Ferguson. The parts can also be sold to other manufacturers and to wholesalers. For all practical purposes, the market for the parts is perfectly competitive. Frank Johnston, a vice-president at corporate headquarters and the immediate supervisor of Ned and Andrea, just received the following memo from Andrea.

MEMORANDUM

To: Frank Johnston, Vice-President
From: Andrea Ferguson
Subject: Transfer Price of Component No. 14
Date: October 15, 1997

Frank, as you know, our division is operating at 70 percent capacity. Last week we received a request for 100,000 units of Model 1267 at a price of $30. Detailed below are the costs we incur to produce that particular motor (because of the special arrangements, we avoid any costs of distribution). The full cost includes the component that we usually buy from Ned's division.

Direct materials	*$10*
Transferred-in component	*8*
Direct labor	*2*
Variable overhead	*1*
Fixed overhead	*10*
Total cost	*$31*

---

12. A perfectly competitive market for the intermediate product requires four conditions: (1) the division producing the intermediate product is small relative to the market as a whole and cannot influence the price of the product; (2) the intermediate product is indistinguishable from the same product of other sellers; (3) firms can easily enter and exit the market; and (4) consumers, producers, and resource owners have perfect knowledge of the market.

As you can see, if we accept the order we will lose $1 per unit. The purpose of this memo is to register a complaint about the Small Parts Division. I must confess that I am somewhat irritated with Ned. I know the full cost of the component supplied by his division is $5. Well, I asked for a more favorable transfer price—$6.50 instead of the $8 we normally pay. He absolutely refused and seemed somewhat put out by my request. I believe the concession was needed so that I could accept the order and show a small profit. The benefits of this order are appealing. My capacity utilization jumps to 85 percent and I avoid the need to lay off some skilled workers. Avoiding the layoff will save the company at least $50,000 in training costs next year. Also, the special order may open up some new markets for the company within a year.

Can't you persuade Ned to make this small concession for the good of the company? In my opinion, more teamwork is needed. After all, I have been a faithful customer of Ned's for several years.

If you were Frank Johnston, how would you react to the memo? Should Frank intervene and dictate a lower transfer price? Is the market price guideline for transfer pricing invalid for this particular case? To answer these questions, let's turn to the opportunity cost approach. Since Ned can sell all he produces, the minimum transfer price for his division is the market price of $8. Any lower price would make his division worse off. For Andrea's division, identifying the maximum transfer price that can be paid so that her division is no worse off requires more analysis.

Since the Small Motor Division is under capacity, the $10 of fixed overhead allocated to Model 1267 is not relevant. The relevant costs are those additional costs that will be incurred only if the order is accepted. These costs, excluding for the moment the cost of the transferred-in component, are as follows:

Direct materials	$10
Direct labor	2
Variable overhead	1
Total	$13

Thus, the contribution to profits before considering the cost of the transferred-in component is $17 ($30 − $13). The division could actually pay $17 for the component and still break even on the special order; however, since the component can always be purchased from an outside supplier for $8, the maximum price that the division should pay internally is $8. If the buying division pays $8, the selling division is no worse off. Furthermore, relative to the status quo, the buying division is better off by $9 ($17 − $8). Thus, the transfer price of $8 should be paid and the special order accepted.

There is no reason for central management to intervene; market price is the correct transfer price. The vice-president could point out the benefits of the special order to Andrea. The need to do so, however, raises some questions about Andrea's managerial abilities or her training in the use of accounting information.

Negotiated Transfer Prices

In reality, perfectly competitive markets seldom exist. In many cases, buyers or sellers can influence price to some degree (for example, through large size, or by selling closely related but differentiated products, or by selling a unique product). When imperfections exist in the market for the intermediate product, market price may no longer be suitable. In this case, negotiated transfer prices may be a practical alternative. Opportunity costs can be used to define the boundaries of the negotiation set.

Example I: Avoidable Distribution Costs To illustrate, assume that a division produces a circuit board that can be sold in the outside market for $22. The division can sell all that it produces at $22. Currently, the division is selling 1,000 units per day, with a variable manufacturing cost of $12 per unit, and a variable distribution cost of $2 per unit. Alternatively, the board can be sold internally to the company's Electronic Games Division. The $2 distribution cost is avoided if the board is sold internally.

The Electronic Games Division is also at capacity, producing and selling 350 games per day. Each game is priced at $45 and has variable manufacturing cost of $32. Variable selling expenses of $3 per unit are also incurred. Sales and production data for each division are summarized in Exhibit 12-4.

Since the Electronic Games Division was acquired very recently, no transfers between the two divisions have yet taken place. Susan Swift, the manager of the Circuit Board Division, requested a meeting with Randy Schrude, manager of the Electronic Games Division, to discuss the possibility of internal transfers. The following is their conversation:

Susan: Randy, I'm excited about the possibility of supplying your division with circuit boards. What is your current demand for the type of board we produce? And how much are you paying for the boards?

Randy: We would use one in each of our video games, and our production is about 350 games per day. We pay $22 for each board.

Susan: We can supply that amount simply by displacing external sales. Furthermore, we would be willing to sell them at the same price we charge outside customers. We can at least meet your price; that way you are no worse off.

Randy: Actually, I was hoping for a better price than $22. The circuit board is by far our most expensive input. By transferring internally, you can avoid some selling, transportation, and collection expenses. I called corporate headquarters, which estimated these costs at approximately $2 per unit. I'd be willing to pay $20 each for your units. You'd be no worse off, and, with a less expensive component, I can make about $700 per day more profit. This deal would make the company $182,000 more during the coming year.

Susan: Your information about avoiding $2 per unit is accurate. I also understand how the cheaper component can allow you to increase your profits. However, if you were to purchase the board at $22, I could increase my division's profits, and the corporation's for that matter, by $700 per day—just by selling you the 350 units and saving the $2 per unit I must spend to sell externally. You would be no worse off, and my division and the corporation would be better off by the $182,000 per year that you mentioned. It seems to me that most of the benefits to the corporation come from avoiding the distribution costs incurred when we sell externally. Nonetheless, I'll sweeten the deal. Since we're both members of the same family, I'll let you have the 350 boards for $21.50 each. That price allows you to increase your profits by $175 per day and reflects the fact that most of the savings are generated by my division.

Exhibit
Summary of Sales and
Production Data

	Board Division	Games Division
Units sold:		
Per day	1,000	350
Per year*	260,000	91,000
Unit data:		
Selling price	$22	$45
Variable costs		
Manufacturing	$12	$32
Selling	$2	$3
Annual fixed costs	$1,480,000	$610,000

*There are 260 selling days in a year.

Randy: I don't agree that most of the savings are generated by your division. You can't achieve those savings unless I buy from you. I'm willing to buy internally, but only if there is a fair sharing of the joint benefits. I think a reasonable arrangement is to split the benefits equally; however, I will grant a small concession. I'll buy 350 units at $21.10 each—that will increase your divisional profits by $385 per day and mine by $315 per day. Deal?

Susan: Sounds reasonable. Let's have a contract drawn up.

This dialogue illustrates how the minimum transfer price ($20) and the maximum transfer price ($22) set the limits of the negotiation set. The example also demonstrates how negotiation can lead to improved profitability for each division and for the firm as a whole. Exhibit 12-5 provides income statements for each division before and after the agreement. Notice how total profits of the firm increase by $182,000 as claimed; notice, too, how that profit increase is split between the two divisions.

Example 2: Excess Capacity In a perfectly competitive market, the selling division can sell all that it wishes at the prevailing market price. In a less ideal setting, a selling division may not be able to sell all that it produces, leading to excess capacity.[13]

To illustrate the role of transfer pricing and negotiation in this setting, consider the dialogue between Sharon Bunker, manager of a plastics division, and Carlos Rivera, manager of a pharmaceutical division:

Carlos: Sharon, my division has shown a loss for the past three years. When I took over the division at the beginning of the year, I set a goal with headquarters to break even. At

---

13. Output can be increased by decreasing selling price. Of course, decreasing selling price to increase sales volume may not increase profits—in fact, profits could easily decline. We assume in this example that the divisional manager has chosen the most advantageous selling price and that the division is still left with excess capacity.

12-5

Exhibit
Comparative Income
Statements

	Before Negotiation: All Sales External		
	Board Division	Games Division	Total
Sales	$5,720,000	$4,095,000	$9,815,000
Less variable expenses:			
Cost of goods sold	(3,120,000)	(2,912,000)	(6,032,000)
Variable selling	(520,000)	(273,000)	(793,000)
Contribution margin	$2,080,000	$ 910,000	$2,990,000
Less: Fixed expenses	(1,480,000)	(610,000)	(2,090,000)
Net income	$ 600,000	$ 300,000	$ 900,000

	After Negotiation: Internal Transfers @ $21.10		
	Board Division	Games Division	Total
Sales	$5,638,100	$4,095,000	$9,733,100
Less variable expenses:			
Cost of goods sold	(3,120,000)	(2,830,100)	(5,950,100)
Variable selling	(338,000)	(273,000)	(611,000)
Contribution margin	$2,180,100	$ 991,900	$3,172,000
Less: Fixed expenses	(1,480,000)	(610,000)	(2,090,000)
Net income	$ 700,100	$ 381,900	$1,082,000
Change in net income	$ 100,100	$ 81,900	$ 182,000

this point, projections show a loss of $5,000—but I think I have a way to reach my goal, if I can get your cooperation.

Sharon: If I can help, I certainly will. What do you have in mind?

Carlos: I need a special deal on your plastic bottle Model 3. I have the opportunity to place our aspirin with a large retail chain on the West Coast—a totally new market for our product. But we have to give it a real break on price. The chain has offered to pay $0.85 per bottle for an order of 250,000 bottles. My variable cost per unit is $0.60, not including the cost of the plastic bottle. I normally pay $0.40 for your bottle, but if I do that the order will lose me $37,500. I cannot afford that kind of loss. I know that you have excess capacity. I'll place an order for 250,000 bottles, and I'll pay your variable cost per unit, provided it is no more than $0.25. Are you interested? Do you have sufficient excess capacity to handle a special order of 250,000 bottles?

Sharon: I have enough excess capacity to handle the order easily. The variable cost per bottle is $0.15. Transferring at that price would make me no worse off; my fixed costs will be there whether I make the bottles or not. However, I would like to have some contribution from an order like this. I'll tell you what I'll do. I'll let you have the order for $0.20. That way we both make $0.05 contribution per bottle, for a total contribution of $12,500. That'll put you in the black and help me get closer to my budgeted profit goal.

Carlos: Great. This is better than I expected. If this West Coast chain provides more orders in the future—as I expect it will—and at better prices, I'll make sure you get our business.

Notice the role that opportunity costs play in the negotiation. In this case, the minimum transfer price is the plastic division's variable cost ($0.15), representing the incremental outlay if the order is accepted. Since plastics has excess capacity, only variable costs are relevant to the decision. For the buying division, the maximum transfer price is the purchase price that would allow the division to cover its incremental costs on the special order ($0.25). Adding the $0.25 to the other costs of processing ($0.60), the total incremental costs incurred are $0.85 per unit; since the selling price is also $0.85 per unit, the division is made no worse off. Both divisions, however, can be better off if the transfer price is between the minimum price of $0.15 and the maximum price of $0.25.

Comparative statements showing the contribution margin earned by each division and the firm as a whole are shown in Exhibit 12-6 for each of the four transfer prices discussed. These statements show that the firm earns the same profit for all four transfer prices; however, different prices do affect the individual divisions' profits differently. Because of the autonomy of each division, however, there is no guarantee that the firm will earn the maximum profit. For example, if Sharon had insisted on maintaining the price of $0.40, no transfer would have taken place, and the $25,000 increase in profits would have been lost.

Disadvantages of Negotiated Transfer Prices Three disadvantages of negotiated transfer prices are commonly mentioned.

1. A divisional manager who has private information may take advantage of another divisional manager.
2. Performance measures may be distorted by the negotiating skills of managers.
3. Negotiation can consume considerable time and resources.

It is interesting to observe that Carlos, the manager of the pharmaceutical division, did not know the variable cost of producing the plastic bottle. Yet that cost was a key to the negotiation. This lack of knowledge gave Sharon, the plastics divisional manager, the opportunity to exploit the situation. For example, she could have claimed that the variable cost was $0.27 and offered to sell for $0.25 per unit as a favor to Carlos, saying

Exhibit
Comparative Statements

	Transfer Price of $0.40		
	Pharmaceuticals	Plastics	Total
Sales	$212,500	$100,000	$312,500
Less: Variable expenses	(250,000)	(37,500)	(287,500)
Contribution margin	$ (37,500)	$ 62,500	$ 25,000

	Transfer Price of $0.25		
Sales	$212,500	$ 62,500	$275,000
Less: Variable expenses	(212,500)	(37,500)	(250,000)
Contribution margin	$ 0	$ 25,000	$ 25,000

	Transfer Price of $0.20		
Sales	$212,500	$ 50,000	$262,500
Less: Variable expenses	(200,000)	(37,500)	(237,500)
Contribution margin	$ 12,500	$ 12,500	$ 25,000

	Transfer Price of $0.15		
Sales	$212,500	$ 37,500	$250,000
Less: Variable expenses	(187,500)	(37,500)	(225,000)
Contribution margin	$ 25,000	$ 0	$ 25,000

that she would be willing to absorb a $5,000 loss in exchange for a promise of future business. In this case, she would capture the full $25,000 benefit of the transfer. Alternatively, she could have misrepresented the figure and used it to turn down the request, thus preventing Carlos from achieving his budgetary goal; after all, she is in competition with Carlos for promotions, bonuses, salary increases, and so on.

Fortunately, Sharon displayed sound judgment and acted with integrity. For negotiation to work, managers must be willing to share relevant information. How can this requirement be satisfied? The answer lies in the use of good internal control procedures. Perhaps the best internal control procedure is to hire managers with integrity. Another possibility would be for top management to give divisional managers access to relevant accounting information of other divisions. This step would minimize the possibility of exploitive behavior because of differences in information.

The second disadvantage of negotiated transfer prices is that divisional profitability may be affected too strongly by the negotiating skills of managers, masking the actual management of resources entrusted to each manager. Although this argument may have some merit, it ignores the fact that negotiating skill is itself a desirable managerial skill. Perhaps divisional profitability should reflect differences in negotiating skills.

The third criticism of this technique is that negotiating can be very time consuming. The time spent in negotiation by divisional managers could be spent managing other activities, which may have a greater bearing on the success of the division. Occasionally, negotiations may reach an impasse, forcing top management to spend time mediating the process.[14] Although the use of managerial time may be costly, it may prove to be far more costly if this interaction is not allowed to take place. A mutually satisfactory

14. The involvement of top management may be very cursory, however. In the case of a very large oil company that negotiates virtually all transfer prices, two divisional managers could not come to an agreement after several weeks of effort and appealed to their superior. His response: "Either come to an agreement within twenty-four hours, or you are both fired." Needless to say, an agreement was reached within the allotted time.

negotiated outcome can produce increased profits for the firm that easily exceed the cost of the managerial time involved. Furthermore, negotiation does not have to be repeated each time for similar transactions.

Advantages of Negotiated Transfer Prices Despite the disadvantages, negotiated transfer prices offer some hope of complying with the three criteria of goal congruence, autonomy, and accurate performance evaluation. In addition, negotiated transfer prices have been identified as a means by which goal congruence throughout the entire firm can be achieved.[15] If negotiation helps ensure goal congruence, there is no need for top management to intervene in divisional affairs. Finally, if negotiating skills of divisional managers are comparable, or if the firm views these skills as an important managerial skill, concerns about motivation and accurate performance measures are avoided.

Cost-based Transfer Prices

Companies that use cost-based transfer pricing require that all transfers take place at some form of cost. Three forms of cost-based transfer pricing will be considered: (1) full cost, (2) full cost plus markup, and (3) variable cost plus fixed fee. In all three cases, to avoid passing on the inefficiencies of one division to another, standard costs should be used to determine the transfer price. For example, the Micro Products Division of Tandem Computers, Inc., uses a corporate materials overhead rate, rather than the division-specific rate, to facilitate cost-based transfers between divisions.[16] A more important issue, however, is the propriety of cost-based transfer prices. Should they be used? If so, under what circumstances?

Full-Cost Transfer Pricing Full cost includes the cost of direct materials, direct labor, variable overhead, and a portion of fixed overhead. Possibly the least desirable transfer-pricing approach, its only real virtue is simplicity. Its disadvantages are considerable. Full-cost transfer pricing can provide perverse incentives and distort performance measures. As we have seen, the opportunity costs of both the buying and selling division are essential for determining the propriety of internal transfers; at the same time, they provide useful reference points for determining a mutually satisfactory transfer price. Only rarely will full cost provide accurate information about opportunity costs.

A full-cost transfer price would have shut down the negotiated prices described in the examples. In the first example, the selling division manager would never have considered transferring internally if the price had to be full cost. Yet by transferring at selling price less some distribution expenses, both divisions—and the firm as a whole—were better off. In the second example, the manager of the pharmaceutical division could never have accepted the special order with the West Coast chain. Both divisions and the company would have been worse off, both in the short run and in the long run.

Full Cost Plus Markup Full cost plus markup suffers from the same problems as full cost. It is somewhat less perverse, however, if the markup can be negotiated. For example, a full cost plus markup formula could have been used to represent the negotiated transfer price of the first example. In some cases, a full cost plus markup formula may be the outcome of negotiation; if so, it is simply another example of negotiated transfer pricing. In these cases, the use of this method is justified. Using full cost plus markup to represent all negotiated prices, however, is not possible (for example, it could not be used to represent the negotiated price of the second example). The superior approach is negotiation since more cases can be handled and opportunity costs can be considered.

15. For an excellent discussion of the role of negotiated transfer prices in a decentralized organization, see David Watson and John Baumler, "Transfer Pricing: A Behavioral Context," *The Accounting Review* (July 1975): 466–474.

16. Earl D. Bennett, Sarah A. Reed, and Ted Simmonds, "Learning from a CIM Experience," *Management Accounting* (July 1991): 28–33.

Variable Cost Plus Fixed Fee Like full cost plus markup, variable cost plus fixed fee can be a useful transfer pricing approach provided that the fixed fee is negotiable. This method has one advantage over full cost plus markup: if the selling division is operating below capacity, variable cost is its opportunity cost. Assuming that the fixed fee is negotiable, the variable-cost approach can be equivalent to negotiated transfer pricing. Negotiation with full consideration of opportunity costs is preferred.

Propriety of Use In spite of the disadvantages of cost-based transfer prices, companies actively use these methods, especially full cost and full cost plus markup.[17] There must be some compelling reasons for their use—reasons that outweigh the benefits associated with negotiated transfer prices and the disadvantages of these methods. The methods do have the virtue of being simple and objective. These qualities, by themselves, cannot justify their use, however. Some possible explanations for the use of these methods can be given.

In many cases, transfers between divisions have a small impact on the profitability of either division. For this situation, it may be cost beneficial to use an easy-to-identify, cost-based formula rather than spending valuable time and resources on negotiation.

In other cases, the use of full cost plus markup may simply be the formula agreed upon in negotiations. That is, the full cost plus markup formula is the outcome of negotiation, but the transfer pricing method being used is reported as full cost plus markup. Once established, this formula could be used until the original conditions change to the point where renegotiation is necessary. In this way, the time and resources of negotiation can be minimized. For example, the goods transferred may be custom-made, and the managers may have little ability to identify an outside market price. In this case, reimbursement of full costs plus a reasonable rate of return may be a good surrogate for the transferring division's opportunity costs.

A final note regarding corporate use of transfer prices is that many corporations are moving toward the use of benchmarking and outsourcing. Both of these reduce the need for internal pricing by tying divisional behavior to the outside market. Benchmarking involves tracking the most effective and efficient provider of a particular activity. For example, USAA, an insurance company, is widely considered to be a world leader in the use of technology to respond to customers; L.L. Bean, Inc. (the Maine catalog company) is a world leader in fast and accurate order filling. Other companies routinely visit these companies to learn how they do it. The result for transfer pricing is that the company is less interested in setting a transfer price and more interested in getting the cost/price as low as possible. With outsourcing, the internally provided good or service is provided by an external company. Now, the price is a true market price.

17. In a survey of profit centers, Umapathy found that 42 percent used full cost and full cost plus markup. Over 50 percent used either market price or negotiated prices. See Srinivasan Umapathy, "Transfers Between Profit Centers," in *Decentralization: Managerial Ambiguity by Design*, ed. Richard F. Vancil (Homewood, Ill.: Dow Jones-Irwin, 1978).

S UMMARY OF LEARNING OBJECTIVES

1. Define responsibility accounting and describe four types of responsibility centers.
Responsibility accounting is a system that measures the results of responsibility centers and compares those results with expected outcomes. The four types of responsibility centers are cost center, revenue center, profit center, and investment center.

2. Explain why firms choose to decentralize.
To increase overall efficiency, many companies choose to decentralize. The essence of decentralization is decision-making freedom. In a decentralized organization, lower-level managers make and implement decisions, whereas in a centralized organization, lower-level managers are responsible only for implementing decisions.

Reasons for decentralization are numerous. Companies decentralize because local managers can make better decisions using local information. Local managers can also provide a more timely response to changing conditions. Additionally, decentralization for large, diversified companies is necessary because of cognitive limitations—it is impossible for any one central manager to be fully knowledgeable about all products and markets. Other reasons include training and motivating local managers and freeing top management from day-to-day operating conditions so that they can spend time on more long-range activities, such as strategic planning.

3. Compute and explain return on investment (ROI) and residual income (RI).

ROI is the ratio of operating income to average operating assets. This ratio can be broken down into two components: margin (the ratio of operating income to sales) and turnover (the ratio of sales to average operating assets). Residual income is the difference between operating income and the minimum required dollar return on a company's operating assets.

Return on investment is the most common measure of performance for managers of decentralized units. Return on investment encourages managers to focus on improving their divisions' profitability by improving sales, controlling costs, and using assets efficiently. Unfortunately, the measure can also encourage managers to increase ROI by sacrificing the long-run for short-run benefits (for example, encouraging managers to forego investments that are profitable for the firm but that would lower the divisional ROI).

Residual income is an alternative performance measure that overcomes managers' tendency to pass up investments that are profitable for the company as a whole. Unfortunately, residual income also can encourage myopic behavior. Because it is a measure expressed in absolute terms, residual income is difficult to use for interdivisional comparisons.

4. Discuss methods of evaluating and rewarding managerial performance.

Decentralized firms may encourage goal congruence by constructing management compensation programs that reward managers for taking actions that benefit the firm. Possible reward systems include cash compensation, stock options, and noncash benefits.

5. Explain the role of transfer pricing in a decentralized firm.

When one division of a company produces a product that can be used in production by another division, transfer pricing exists. The transfer price is revenue to the selling division and cost to the buying division, thus the price charged for the intermediate good affects the operating income of both divisions. Since both divisions are evaluated on their profitability, the price charged for the intermediate good can be a point of serious contention.

The transfer pricing problem involves finding a mutually satisfactory transfer price that is compatible with the company's goals of accurate performance evaluation, divisional autonomy, and goal congruence.

Three methods generally are used for setting transfer prices; they are market based, negotiated, and cost based. If a perfectly competitive market exists for the intermediate product, market price is the best transfer price. In this case, the market price reflects the opportunity costs of both the buying and selling divisions. If no perfectly competitive market exists, a negotiated transfer price is preferred. In this case, opportunity costs for the buying and selling divisions differ and they form the upper and lower boundaries for the transfer price. The use of cost-based transfer prices is not generally recommended; however, if the transfers have little effect on either division's profitability, such an approach is acceptable. Additionally, cost-based pricing formulas may be appropriate if they are set through the process of negotiation.

K EY TERMS

Centralized decision making 483	Margin 487	Opportunity cost approach 496	Return on investment (ROI) 486
Cost center 482	Maximum transfer price 496	Perquisites 492	Revenue center 482
Decentralization 484	Minimum transfer price 496	Profit center 482	Stock option 493
Decentralized decision making 484	Operating assets 486	Residual income 490	Transfer price 495
Investment center 482	Operating income 486	Responsibility accounting 482	Transfer pricing problem 496
		Responsibility center 482	Turnover 487

R EVIEW PROBLEM

The Components Division produces a part that is used by the Goods Division. The cost of manufacturing the part follows:

Direct materials	$10
Direct labor	2
Variable overhead	3
Fixed overhead[a]	5
Total cost	$20

[a]Based on a practical volume of 200,000 parts

Other costs incurred by the Components Division are as follows:

| Fixed selling and administrative | $500,000 |
| Variable selling (per unit) | $1 |

The part usually sells for between $28 and $30 in the external market. Currently, the Components Division is selling it to external customers for $29. The division is capable of producing 200,000 units of the part per year; however, because of a weak economy, only 150,000 parts are expected to be sold during the coming year. The variable selling expenses are avoidable if the part is sold internally.

The Goods Division has been buying the same part from an external supplier for $28. It expects to use 50,000 units of the part during the coming year. The manager of the Goods Division has offered to buy 50,000 units from the Components Division for $18 per unit.

REQUIRED:
1. Determine the minimum transfer price that the Components Division would accept.
2. Determine the maximum transfer price that the manager of the Goods Division would pay.
3. Should an internal transfer take place? Why? If you were the manager of the Components Division, would you sell the 50,000 components for $18 each? Explain.
4. Suppose that the average operating assets of the Components Division total $10 million. Compute the ROI for the coming year, assuming that the 50,000 units are transferred to the Goods Division for $21 each.

Solution

1. The minimum transfer price is $15. The Components Division has idle capacity and so must cover only its incremental costs, which are the variable manufacturing costs. (Fixed costs are the same whether or not the internal transfer occurs; the variable selling expenses are avoidable.)
2. The maximum transfer price is $28. The Goods Division would not pay more for the part than it has to pay an external supplier.
3. Yes, an internal transfer ought to occur; the opportunity cost of the selling division is less than the opportunity cost of the buying division. The Components Division would earn an additional $150,000 profit ($3 × 50,000). The total joint benefit, however, is $650,000 ($13 × 50,000). The manager of the Components Division should attempt to negotiate a more favorable outcome for that division.
4. Income statement:

Sales [($29 × 150,000) + (21 × 50,000)]	$5,400,000
Less: Variable cost of goods sold ($15 × 200,000)	(3,000,000)
Less: Variable selling expenses ($1 × 150,000)	(150,000)
Contribution margin	$2,250,000
Less: Fixed overhead ($5 × 200,000)	(1,000,000)
Less: Fixed selling and administration	(500,000)
Operating income	$ 750,000

$$\text{ROI} = \frac{\text{Operating income}}{\text{Average operating assets}}$$
$$= \frac{\$750,000}{\$10,000,000}$$
$$= 0.075$$

QUESTIONS FOR WRITING AND DISCUSSION

1. Discuss the differences between centralized and decentralized decision making.
2. What is decentralization?
3. Explain why firms choose to decentralize.
4. Explain how access to local information can improve decision making.

5. One division had operating profits of $500,000, and a second division had operating profits of $3 million. Which divisional manager did the best job? Explain.
6. Assume that a division earned operating profits of $500,000 on average operating assets of $2 million. What is the division's return on investment? Suppose

that a second division had operating profits of $3 million and average operating assets of $30 million. Compute this division's ROI. Which division did the better job? Explain.

7. What are *margin* and *turnover*? Explain how these concepts can improve the evaluation of an investment center.

8. What are the three benefits of ROI? Explain how each can lead to improved profitability.

9. What are two disadvantages of ROI? Explain how each can lead to decreased profitability.

10. What is residual income? Explain how residual income overcomes one of ROI's disadvantages.

11. What disadvantage is shared by ROI and residual income? What can be done to overcome this problem?

12. What problems do owners face in encouraging goal congruence of managers?

13. What is a stock option? How can it encourage goal congruence?

14. What is a transfer price?

15. Explain how transfer prices can impact performance measures, firmwide profits, and the decision to decentralize decision making.

16. What is the transfer pricing problem?

17. Explain the opportunity cost approach to transfer pricing.

18. If the minimum transfer price of the selling division is less than the maximum transfer price of the buying division, the intermediate product should be transferred internally. Do you agree? Why?

19. If an outside, perfectly competitive market exists for the intermediate product, what should the transfer price be? Why?

20. Suppose that a selling division can sell all that it produces for $50 per unit. Of that $50, however, $3 represents the costs of distribution (commissions, freight, collections, and so on). Assuming the distribution costs are avoidable if the product is sold internally, what is the minimum transfer price? the maximum transfer price?

21. Discuss the advantages of negotiated transfer prices.

22. Discuss the disadvantages of negotiated transfer prices.

23. Identify three cost-based transfer prices. What are the disadvantages of cost-based transfer prices? When might it be appropriate to use cost-based transfer prices?

24. The performance of the divisional manager is equivalent to the performance of a division. Do you agree? Explain.

(W) ARM-UP EXERCISES

This section provides short warm-up exercises based on the examples in the chapter. Each warm-up exercise gives the page number on which the text example can be found. You may want to refer to the text example to see how the exercise can be set up and solved.

W12-1
Unit-Cost
Calculation
LO 3
pp. 486–487

Norton Logistics, Inc. has two divisions, the Western Division and the Southern Division. Last year, the Western Division earned $360,000 using average operating assets of $1,440,000. The Southern Division earned $560,000 on average operating assets of $2,800,000. Sales for the Western Division were $3,600,000; sales for the Southern Division were $7,000,000.

REQUIRED:
1. What is the ROI for the Western Division? for the Southern Division?
2. Calculate the margin and turnover for the Western Division. Calculate the margin and turnover for the Southern Division.

W12-2
ROI of Individual
Projects
LO 3
pp. 489–490

An electronics division has the opportunity to invest in two projects for the coming year, a digital telephone answering machine and a portable video game player. The outlay required for each investment, the dollar returns, and the ROI follow:

	Answering Machine	Video Game Player
Investment	$10,000,000	$4,000,000
Operating income	1,300,000	640,000
ROI	13%	16%

The division is currently earning an ROI of 18 percent, using operating assets of $75 million; operating income on current investment is $13.5 million. The division has approval to request up to $15 million in new investment capital. Corporate headquarters requires that all investments earn at least 12 percent (this rate represents the amount the corporation must earn to cover the cost of acquiring the capital). Any capital not used by a division is invested by headquarters and it earns exactly 12 percent.

REQUIRED:

1. Calculate the ROI for the division for each of the following scenarios: invest in the answering machine; invest in the video game player; invest in both; or invest in neither. Which option would the divisional manager choose?
2. Did the divisional manager's choice cost the company any profit? If so, how much?

W12-3
Rate of Return on Residual Income
LO 3
pp. 490–491

Refer to W12-2.

REQUIRED:

1. Calculate the residual income for the answering machine.
2. Calculate the residual income for the video game player.
3. Calculate the residual income for the division if neither investment is made. If the manager is evaluated on the basis of residual income, what choice of investments (answering machine, video game player, neither, or both) will be made? Why?

W12-4
Stock Options
LO 4
p. 493

Daniel Burns, head of the Medical Services Division of TechMed, Inc., was granted an option to purchase 10,000 shares of TechMed stock at the current market price of $14 per share. The option was granted in March 1996, and could be exercised after two years. On April 12, 1998, TechMed stock is priced at $17.50.

REQUIRED:

1. Suppose that Daniel wants to buy a house and needs money for the down payment. If he chooses to exercise the option and purchase 10,000 shares of TechMed stock, what will be his gain on the sale?
2. Suppose the price of TechMed is less than $14 on April 12, 1998. Will Daniel choose to exercise the option? Why or why not?

W12-5
Transfer Pricing
LO 5
p. 498

Padgett, Inc. has a number of divisions, including a mattress division and a furniture division. The furniture division manufactures a line of sofa beds, which use a mattress purchased from an outside supplier for $90. Jim Jackson, manager of the mattress division, has approached Cynthia Tucker, manager of the furniture division, about selling mattresses to the furniture division for the sofa beds. Jim has researched the mattress costs, and determined the following costs:

Direct materials	$20
Direct labor	18
Variable overhead	17
Fixed overhead	30
Total manufacturing cost	$85

Currently, the mattress division has capacity to produce 100,000 mattresses but is only producing 50,000. The furniture division needs 30,000 mattresses per year.

REQUIRED:

1. What is the maximum transfer price? the minimum transfer price? Should the transfer occur?
2. Suppose that Jim and Cynthia agree on a transfer price of $75. What is the benefit to each division? What is the benefit to the company as a whole?
3. Suppose that the mattress division were operating at capacity. What would be the maximum transfer price? the minimum transfer price? Should the transfer take place in this case? Why or why not?

EXERCISES

E12-1
ROI; Margin;

The following data have been collected for the past two years for the Cypress Division of Forester Company:

Turnover

LO 3

	1996	1997
Sales	$40,000,000	$40,000,000
Net operating income	2,880,000	2,800,000
Average operating assets	16,000,000	16,000,000

REQUIRED:

1. Compute the ROI for each year.
2. Compute the margin and turnover ratios for each year.
3. Explain why the division experienced decreased ROI from 1996 to 1997.

E12-2
ROI; Margin;
Turnover
LO 3

Data follow for the Birch Division of Forester Company (see E12-1).

	1996	1997
Sales	$25,000,000	$25,000,000
Net operating income	1,800,000	1,750,000
Average operating assets	10,000,000	9,470,000

REQUIRED:

1. Compute the ROI for the Birch Division for each year.
2. Compute the margin and turnover ratios for each year.
3. How does the performance of the Birch Division compare with that of the Cypress Division?

E12-3
ROI and Investment
Decisions
LO 3

The manager of a division that produces hair care and personal appliances is faced with the opportunity to invest in two independent projects. The first will provide the capability to produce a travel-size hair dryer; the second will provide the opportunity to produce a jumbo curling iron, a product the division does not currently offer. Without the investments, the division will have average assets for the coming year of $15 million and expected operating income of $2.55 million. The outlay required for each investment and the expected operating incomes are as follows:

	Hair Dryer	Curling Iron
Outlay	$975,000	$600,000
Operating income	136,500	78,000

Corporate headquarters has made available $2 million of capital for the Camping Goods division. Any funds not invested by the division will be retained by headquarters and invested to earn the company's minimum required rate, 10 percent.

REQUIRED:

1. Compute the ROI for each investment.
2. Compute the divisional ROI for each of the following four alternatives:
   a. No investment is made.
   b. The hair dryer investment is made.
   c. The curling iron investment is made.
   d. Both investments are made.
   Assuming that divisional managers are evaluated and rewarded on the basis of ROI performance, which alternative do you think the divisional manager will choose?
3. Compute the profit gained or lost for the company as a whole, based on your answer to requirement 2. Was the correct decision made?

E12-4
Residual Income and
Investment Decisions
LO 3

Refer to the data given in E12-3.

REQUIRED:

1. Compute the residual income for each of the opportunities.

2. Compute the divisional residual income for each of the four alternatives. Assuming that divisional managers are evaluated and rewarded on the basis of residual income, which alternative do you think the divisional manager will choose?

3. Based on your answer to requirement 2, compute the gain or loss from the divisional manager's investment decision. Was the correct decision made?

E12-5
Transfer Pricing; Outside Market with Full Capacity
LO 5

Delbert Company's Can Division produces a variety of cans that are used for food processing. Delbert's Nut Division buys nuts; deshells, roasts, and salts them; and places them in cans. It sells the cans of roasted nuts to various retailers. The most frequently used can is the 12-ounce size. In the past, the Nut Division has purchased these cans from external suppliers for $0.65 each. The manager of the Nut Division has approached the manager of the Can Division and has offered to buy 200,000 12-ounce cans each year. The Can Division currently is producing at capacity and produces and sells 300,000 12-ounce cans to outside customers for $0.65 each.

REQUIRED:

1. What is the minimum transfer price for the Can Division? What is the maximum transfer price for the Nut Division? Is it important that transfers take place internally? If transfers do take place, what should the transfer price be?

2. Now assume that the Can Division incurs selling costs of $0.04 per can that could be avoided if the cans are sold internally. Identify the minimum transfer price for the Can Division and the maximum transfer price for the Nut Division. Should internal transfers take place? If so, what is the benefit to the firm as a whole?

3. Suppose you are the manager of the Can Division. Selling costs of $0.04 per can are avoidable if the cans are sold internally. Would you accept an offer of $0.63 from the manager of the other division? How much better off (or worse off) would your division be if this price is accepted?

E12-6
Transfer Pricing; Idle Capacity
LO 5

The Film Division of Photolife, Inc. produces 35mm film that can be sold externally or internally to Photolife's School Photography Division. Sales and cost data per roll of 35mm film follow:

Unit selling price	$2.95
Unit variable cost	1.40
Unit product fixed cost*	1.20
Practical capacity	500,000 units

*$\frac{\$600,000}{500,000}$

During the coming year, the Film Division expects to sell 350,000 rolls of this film. The School Photography Division currently plans to buy 150,000 rolls of the film on the outside market for $2.95 each. Andrea Harper, manager of the Film Division, has approached Karel Padgett, manager of the School Photography Division, and offered to sell the 150,000 rolls for $2.94 each. Andrea explained to Karel that she can avoid selling costs of $0.02 per film roll and that she would split the savings by offering a $0.01 discount on the usual price.

REQUIRED:

1. What is the minimum transfer price that the Film Division would be willing to accept? What is the maximum transfer price that the School Photography Division would be willing to pay? Should an internal transfer take place? What would be the benefit (or loss) to the firm as a whole if the internal transfer takes place?

2. Suppose Karel knows that the Film Division has idle capacity. Do you think that she would agree to the transfer price of $2.94? Suppose she counters with an offer to pay $2.85. If you were Andrea, would you be interested in this price? Explain with supporting computations.

3. Suppose that Photolife, Inc. policy is that all internal transfers take place at full manufacturing cost. What would the transfer price be? Would the transfer take place?

E12-7
ROI; Margin;

Ready Electronics is facing stiff competition from imported goods. Its operating income margin has been declining steadily for the past several years; the company has been forced to lower prices

Turnover

LO 3

so that it can maintain its market share. The operating results for the past three years are as follows:

	1995	1996	1997
Sales	$10,000,000	$ 9,500,000	$ 9,000,000
Net operating income	1,200,000	1,045,000	945,000
Average assets	15,000,000	15,000,000	15,000,000

For the coming year, Ready's president plans to install a JIT purchasing and manufacturing system. She estimates that inventories will be reduced by 70 percent during the first year of operations, producing a 20 percent reduction in the average operating assets of the company, which would remain unchanged without the JIT system. She also estimates that sales and operating income will be restored to the 1995 level because of simultaneous reductions in operating expenses and selling prices. Lower selling prices will allow Ready to expand its market share.

REQUIRED:
1. Compute the ROI, margin, and turnover for 1995, 1996, and 1997.
2. Suppose that in 1998 the sales and operating income were achieved as expected but inventories remained at the same level as in 1997. Compute the expected ROI, margin, and turnover. Explain why the ROI increased over the 1997 level.
3. Suppose that the sales and net operating income for 1998 remained the same as in 1997 but inventory reductions were achieved as projected. Compute the ROI, margin, and turnover. Explain why the ROI exceeded the 1997 level.
4. Assume that all expectations for 1998 were realized. Compute the expected ROI, margin, and turnover. Explain why the ROI increased over the 1997 level.

E12-8
ROI and Residual Income

LO 3

Consider the following data for two divisions of the same company:

	North Woods	Midwest
Sales	$3,000,000	$10,000,000
Average operating assets	1,000,000	3,000,000
Net operating income	140,000	330,000
Minimum required return	8%	8%

REQUIRED:
1. Compute residual income for each division. By comparing residual income, is it possible to make a useful comparison of divisional performance? Explain.
2. Compute the residual rate of return by dividing the residual income by the average operating assets. Is it possible now to say that one division outperformed the other? Explain.
3. Compute the return on investment for each division. Can we make meaningful comparisons of divisional performance? Explain.
4. Add the residual rate of return computed in requirement 2 to the required rate of return. Compare these rates with the ROI computed in requirement 3. Will this relationship always be the same?

E12-9
Transfer Pricing and Autonomy

LO 5

The Parts Division supplies Part 678 to the Medical Products Division, which uses it in manufacturing a heart monitor. The Medical Products Division is currently operating below capacity (by 10,000 units), while the Parts Division is operating at capacity. Part 678 sells externally for $50. The cost of producing the heart monitor follows:

Part 678	$ 50
Direct materials	100
Direct labor	20
Variable overhead	30
Fixed overhead	40
Total unit cost	$240

The Medical Products Division has received an order for 1,000 heart monitors from a wholesaler, with an offering price of $230. Since company policy prohibits selling any product below full cost, the divisional manager requested a price concession from the Parts Division. When that manager refused the request, the manager of the Medical Products Division filed an appeal with higher-level management, arguing that a transfer price of full cost should be used so that pricing decisions in his division would not be distorted.

REQUIRED:
1. Assume that the full cost of Part 678 is $30. Will the firm as a whole benefit if the part is transferred at $30? Should top management intervene?
2. Is anything wrong with the company policy that a division's selling price cannot be below full cost?
3. Compute the minimum and maximum transfer prices. Is an internal transfer indicated? If a transfer were to take place, what should the transfer price be?

E12-10
Margin; Turnover; ROI
LO 3

Calculate the missing data for each of these four independent companies:

	A	B	C	D
Revenue	$10,000	$45,000	$200,000	—
Expenses	7,800	—	188,000	—
Net income	2,200	18,000	—	—
Assets	20,000	—	100,000	9,600
Margin	— %	40%	— %	6.25%
Turnover	—	0.3125	—	2.00
ROI	—	—	—	—

E12-11
Residual Income
LO 3

Refer to E12-10. Assume that the cost of capital is 12 percent for each of the four firms.

REQUIRED: Compute the residual income for each of the four firms.

E12-12
Transfer Pricing
LO 5

Adler Industries is a vertically integrated firm with several divisions that operate as decentralized profit centers. Adler's Systems Division manufactures scientific instruments and uses the products of two of Adler's other divisions. The Board Division manufactures printed circuit boards (PCBs). One PCB model is made exclusively for the Systems Division using proprietary designs, while less complex models are sold in outside markets. The products of the Transistor Division are sold in a well-developed competitive market; however, one transistor model is also used by the Systems Division. The costs per unit of the products used by the Systems Division follow:

	PCB	Transistor
Direct material	$2.50	$0.80
Direct labor	4.50	1.00
Variable overhead	2.00	0.50
Fixed overhead	0.80	0.75
Total cost	$9.80	$3.05
	12.25	3.70

The Board Division sells its commercial product at full cost plus a 25 percent markup and believes the proprietary board made for the Systems Division would sell for $12.25 per unit on the open market. The market price of the transistor used by the Systems Division is $3.70 per unit.

REQUIRED:
1. What is the minimum transfer price for the Transistor Division? What is the maximum transfer price of the transistor for the Systems Division?

2. Assume the Systems Division is able to purchase a large quantity of transistors from an outside source at $2.90 per unit. Further assume that the Transistor Division has excess capacity. Can the Transistor Division meet this price?

3. The Board and Systems divisions have negotiated a transfer price of $11 per printed circuit board. Discuss the impact this transfer price will have on each division. (CMA adapted)

E12-13
Stock Options
LO 4

Spang, Inc. has acquired two new companies, one in consumer products and the other in financial services. Spang's top management believes that the executives of the two newly acquired companies can be most quickly assimilated into the parent company if they own shares of Spang stock. Accordingly, on February 1, Spang approved a stock option plan whereby the top four executives of each company could purchase up to 10,000 shares of Spang stock at $45 per share. The option will expire in five years.

REQUIRED:

1. If Spang stock rises to $67 per share by December 1, what is the value of the option to each executive?

2. Discuss some of the advantages and disadvantages of the Spang stock option plan.

E12-14
Bonuses and Stock Options
LO 4

Jill Fredericks graduated from State University with a major in accounting five years ago. She obtained a position with a well-known public accounting firm upon graduation and has become one of their outstanding performers. In the course of her work, she has developed numerous contacts with business firms in the area. One of them, Posner, Inc., recently offered her a position as head of their Financial Services Division. The offer includes a salary of $40,000 per year, annual bonuses of 1 percent of divisional net income, and a stock option for 5,000 shares of Posner stock to be exercised at $10 per share in two years. Last year the Financial Services Division earned $1,110,000. This year it is budgeted to earn $1,600,000. Posner's stock has increased in value at the rate of 20 percent per year over the past five years. Jill currently earns $55,000.

REQUIRED: Advise Jill on the relative merits of the Posner offer.

E12-15
ROI; Residual Income; Evaluating Performance
LO 3, LO 4

Raddington Industries produces tool and die machinery for manufacturers. The company expanded vertically in 1984 by acquiring one of its suppliers of alloy steel plates, Reigis Steel Company. To manage the two separate businesses, the operations of Reigis are reported separately as an investment center.

Raddington monitors its divisions on the basis of both unit contribution and return on average investment (ROI), with investment defined as average operating assets employed. Management bonuses are determined on ROI. All investments in operating assets are expected to earn a minimum return of 11 percent before income taxes.

Reigis's cost of goods sold is considered to be entirely variable while the division's administrative expenses are not dependent on volume. Selling expenses are a mixed cost with 40 percent attributed to sales volume. Reigis contemplated a capital acquisition with an estimated ROI of 11.5 percent; however, divisional management decided against the investment because it believed that the investment would decrease Reigis's overall ROI.

The 1998 operating statement for Reigis follows. The division's operating assets employed were $15,750,000 at November 30, 1998, a 5 percent increase over the 1997 year-end balance.

Reigis Steel Division Operating Statement (in thousands) For the Year Ended November 30, 1998		
Sales revenue		$25,000
Less expenses:		
Cost of goods sold	$16,500	
Administrative expenses	3,955	
Selling expenses	2,700	23,155
Income from operations before income taxes		$ 1,845

REQUIRED:

1. Calculate the unit contribution for Reigis Steel Division if 1,484,000 units were produced and sold during the year ended November 30, 1998.
2. Calculate the following performance measures for 1998 for the Reigis Steel Division:
   a. Pre-tax return on average investment in operating assets employed (ROI)
   b. Residual income calculated on the basis of average operating assets employed
3. Explain why the management of the Reigis Steel Division would have been more likely to accept the contemplated capital acquisition if residual income rather than ROI had been used as a performance measure.
4. The Reigis Steel Division is a separate investment center within Raddington Industries. Identify several items that Reigis should control if it is to be evaluated fairly by either the ROI or residual income performance measures. (CMA adapted)

 ROBLEMS

P12-1

Setting Transfer Prices—Market Price versus Full Cost

LO 5

Videodays, Inc. manufactures stereo receivers, televisions, and VCRs in its four divisions: Receiver, TV, VCR, and Components. The Components Division produces electronic components that can be used by the other three. All the components this division produces can be sold to outside customers; however, from the beginning, about 70 percent of its output has been used internally. The current policy requires that all internal transfers of components be transferred at full cost.

Recently, Will Ferguson, the new chief executive officer of Videodays, decided to investigate the transfer pricing policy. He was concerned that the current method of pricing internal transfers might force decisions by divisional managers that would be suboptimal for the firm. As part of his inquiry, he gathered some information concerning Component 12F, used by the Receiver Division in its production of a clock radio, Model 357K.

The Receiver Division sells 100,000 units of Model 357K each year at a unit price of $21. Given current market conditions, this is the maximum price that the division can charge for Model 357K. The cost of manufacturing the radio follows:

Component 12F	$ 6.50
Direct materials	5.50
Direct labor	4.00
Variable overhead	1.00
Fixed overhead	2.00
Total unit cost	$19.00

The radio is produced efficiently and no further reduction in manufacturing costs is possible.

The manager of the Components Division indicated that she could sell 100,000 units (the division's capacity for this part) of Component 12F to outside buyers at $12 per unit. The Receiver Division could also buy the part for $12 from external suppliers. She supplied the following detail on the manufacturing cost of the component:

Direct materials	$2.50
Direct labor	0.50
Variable overhead	1.50
Fixed overhead	2.00
Total unit cost	$6.50

REQUIRED:

1. Compute the firmwide contribution margin associated with Component 12F and Model 357K. Also, compute the contribution margin earned by each division.

2. Suppose that Will Ferguson abolishes the current transfer pricing policy and gives divisions autonomy in setting transfer prices. Can you predict what transfer price the manager of the Components Division will set? What should the minimum transfer price for this part be? the maximum?

3. Given the new transfer pricing policy, predict how this will affect the production decision for Model 357K of the Receiver Division manager. How many units of Component 12F will the manager of the Receiver Division purchase, either internally or externally?

4. Given the new transfer price set by the Components Division and your answer to requirement 3, how many units of 12F will be sold externally?

5. Given your answers to requirements 3 and 4, compute the firmwide contribution margin. What has happened? Was Will's decision to grant additional decentralization good or bad?

P12-2
ROI; Transfer Pricing with Idle Capacity
LO 3, LO 5

Wildcat, Inc. is an oil production services firm. It has three divisions: the Western Division, the Southern Division, and the Offshore Division. The Southern Division produces a variety of drill bits that are sold both externally and internally. Company policy permits each manager to decide whether to buy or sell internally. Each divisional manager is evaluated on the basis of return on investment and residual income.

Recently, an outside supplier has offered to sell the drill bit to the Western Division for $67. Since the current price paid to the Southern Division is $70, Carla Fuller, the manager of the Western Division, was interested in the offer. However, before making the decision to switch to the outside supplier, Carla decided to approach Esteban Delorio, manager of the Southern Division, to see if he wanted to offer an even better price. If not, then Carla would buy from the outside supplier.

Upon receiving the information from Carla about the outside offer, Esteban gathered the following information about the drill bit:

Direct materials	$20
Direct labor	10
Variable overhead	10
Fixed overhead*	10
Total unit cost	$50
Selling price	$70
Production capacity	20,000
Internal sales	10,000

*Fixed overhead is based on $\frac{\$200,000}{20,000}$ units.

REQUIRED:

1. Suppose that the Southern Division is producing at capacity and can sell all that it produces to outside customers. How should Esteban respond to Carla's request for a lower transfer price? What will be the effect on firmwide profits? Compute the effect of this response on each division's profits.

2. Now assume that the Southern Division is currently selling 18,000 units. If no units are sold internally, the total sales of the drill bit will drop to 15,000 units. Suppose that Esteban refuses to lower the transfer price from $70. Compute the effect on firmwide profits and on each division's profits.

3. Refer to requirement 2. What are the minimum and maximum transfer prices? Suppose that the transfer price is the maximum price less $1. Compute the effect on the firm's profits and on each division's profits. Who has benefited from the outside bid?

4. Refer to requirement 2. Suppose that the Southern Division has operating assets of $2,000,000. What is divisional ROI based on the current situation? Now refer to requirement 3. What will divisional ROI be if the transfer price of the maximum price less $1 is

implemented? How will the change in ROI affect Esteban? What information has he gained as a result of the transfer pricing negotiations?

P12-3
ROI Calculations with Varying Assumptions
LO 3

Knitpix Products is a division of Parker Textiles, Inc. During the coming year, it expects to earn a net operating income of $310,000 based on sales of $3.45 million; without any new investments, the division will have average net operating assets of $3 million. The division is considering a capital investment project—adding knitting machines to produce gaiters—that requires an additional investment of $600,000 and increases net operating income by $57,500 (sales would increase by $575,000). If made, the investment would increase beginning net operating assets by $600,000 and ending net operating assets by $400,000. Assume that the minimum rate of return required by the company is 7 percent.

REQUIRED:

1. Compute the ROI for the division without the investment.
2. Compute the margin and turnover ratios without the investment. Show that the product of the margin and turnover ratios equals the ROI computed in requirement 1.
3. Compute the ROI for the division with the new investment. Do you think the divisional manager will approve the investment?
4. Compute the margin and turnover ratios for the division with the new investment. Compare these with the old ratios.
5. Assume that a JIT purchasing and manufacturing system is installed, reducing average operating assets by $800,000. Compute the ROI with and without the investment under this new scenario. Now do you think the divisional manager will accept the new investment? Should he accept it? Explain your answer.
6. Refer to requirement 5. Compute the margin and turnover ratios without the investment. Use these ratios to explain why the ROI increases.

P12-4
Market Price versus Full Cost Plus
LO 2, LO 3, LO 4, LO 5

Nashmen Manufacturing Corporation produces lawn mowers, snowblowers, and tillers. The company has six divisions, each set up as investment centers. Managers of the divisions are evaluated and rewarded on the basis of return on investment and residual income. Company policy dictates that internal transfers must take place whenever possible and that the transfer price will be full cost plus 10 percent. Ken Booth, vice-president of operations, is reevaluating the company's current internal transfer policy in light of a recent memo received from Dana Lemmons, manager of the Parts Division. The memo follows.

MEMORANDUM

To: Ken Booth, Vice-President of Operations
From: Dana Lemmons, Manager of Parts Division
Subject: Transfer Pricing Policy

Ken, I must register serious concern about our current transfer pricing policy of full cost plus 10 percent. First, I believe this policy creates a significant understatement of my division's ROI. Second, it creates a disincentive for my division to decrease our costs of manufacturing.

For example, consider our production of Part 34 (small carburetors). Currently, we are capable of producing 300,000 of these units each year. Of these 300,000 carburetors, 200,000 are transferred to the Small Motor Division at a price of $16.50 per unit; 100,000 are sold to external customers at $20 each. I know that we can sell every carburetor we make to external customers. By forcing us to transfer internally, we are losing income and showing a much smaller ROI than we could otherwise.

But the problem is even greater. My engineers have created a new design that will allow us to decrease our fixed manufacturing costs for carburetors by $5 per unit. However, if we implement this design, our transfer price will drop to $11, and the revenues we receive from internal sales will drop significantly. All the savings and more are transferred to the buying division.

In my opinion, all of these problems can be resolved by allowing each divisional manager to set transfer prices and allowing each of us to buy or sell our products as we see fit.

After reading the memo, Ken gathered production information.

Manufacturing cost of carburetor:	
Direct materials	$ 6.00
Direct labor	1.25
Variable overhead	1.50
Fixed overhead	6.25
Total cost	$15.00

Manufacturing cost of small motor:	
Carburetor	$16.50
Direct materials	23.50
Direct labor	8.75
Variable overhead	3.25
Fixed overhead	8.40
Total cost	$60.40

Production and sales of small motor:	
Production	200,000
Sales	200,000
Unit price	$75

REQUIRED:

1. Assume that the Parts Division implements the new design change. Assume also that the internal demand for the carburetors remains constant. Compute the change in profits for the firm as a whole from this decision. Now compute the change in profits for the Parts Division and the Small Motor Division. Was Dana's concern valid? Were all the benefits of the improved design captured by the Small Motor Division?
2. Refer to requirement 1. Now assume that the reduced cost of the carburetor increases the internal demand from 200,000 to 300,000 units. Evaluate the impact on firmwide profits and on each division's profits. If Dana anticipated this effect, do you think she would implement the cost-reducing design?
3. Refer to the original data. Ken Booth wants to know the effect of decentralizing the internal pricing decisions. Assuming that the Small Motor Division can buy carburetors of equal quality for $20 from outside suppliers, provide Dana with a complete assessment of the effect. In your assessment, include the change in firmwide and divisional profits. Also, comment on the incentives that Dana would have for implementing the cost-reducing design.

P12-5
Full Cost Plus Pricing and Negotiation
LO 5

Technovia, Inc. has two divisions: Auxiliary Components and Audio Systems. Divisional managers are encouraged to maximize return on investment and residual income. Managers are essentially free to determine whether goods will be transferred internally and what internal transfer prices will be. Headquarters has directed that all internal prices be expressed on a full cost plus basis. The markup in the full-cost pricing arrangement, however, is left to the discretion of the divisional managers. Recently, the two divisional managers met to discuss a pricing agreement for a subwoofer that would be sold with a personal computer system. Production of the subwoofers is at capacity. Subwoofers can be sold for $31 to outside customers. The Audio Systems Division can also buy the subwoofer from external sources for the same price; however, the manager of this division is hoping to obtain a price concession by buying internally. The full cost of manufacturing the subwoofer is $20. If the manager of the Auxiliary Components Division sells the subwoofer internally, $5 of selling and distribution costs can be avoided. The volume of business would be 250,000 units per year, well within the capacity of the producing division.

After some discussion, the two managers agreed on a full cost-plus pricing scheme that would be reviewed annually. Any increase in the outside selling price would be added to the transfer price by simply increasing the markup by an appropriate amount. Any major changes in the factors that led to the agreement could initiate a new round of negotiation; otherwise, the full cost-plus arrangement would continue in force for subsequent years.

REQUIRED:

1. Calculate the minimum and maximum transfer prices.

2. Assume that the transfer price agreed upon between the two managers is halfway between the minimum and maximum transfer prices. Calculate the full cost plus transfer price that would represent this transfer price.
3. Refer to requirement 2. Assume that in the following year the outside price of subwoofers increases to $32. What is the new full cost plus transfer price?
4. Assume that two years after the initial agreement, the market for subwoofers has softened considerably, causing excess capacity for the Auxiliary Components Division. Would you expect a renegotiation of the full cost-plus pricing arrangement for the coming year? Explain.

P12-6
Transfer Pricing;
Various
Computations
LO 5

Courtland Company has a decentralized organization with a divisional structure. Each divisional manager is evaluated on the basis of ROI.

The Plastics Division produces a plastic container that the Chemical Division can use. Plastics can produce up to 100,000 of these containers per year. The variable costs of manufacturing the plastic containers are $4.50. The Chemical Division labels the plastic containers and uses them to store an important industrial chemical, which is sold to outside customers for $50 per container. The division's capacity is 20,000 units. The variable costs of processing the chemical (in addition to the cost of the container itself) are $26.

REQUIRED:
1. (Assume each requirement is independent, unless otherwise indicated.) Assume that all of the plastic containers produced can be sold to external customers for $12 each. The Chemical Division wants to buy 20,000 containers per year. What should the transfer price be?
2. Refer to requirement 1. Assume $2 of avoidable distribution costs. Identify the maximum and minimum transfer prices. Identify the actual transfer price, assuming that negotiation splits the difference.
3. Assume that the Plastics Division is operating at 75 percent of capacity. The Chemical Division is currently buying 20,000 containers from an outside supplier for $9.50 each. Assume that any joint benefit will be split evenly between the two divisions. What is the expected transfer price? How much will the profits of the firm increase under this arrangement? How much will the profits of the Plastics Division increase, assuming that it sells the extra 20,000 containers internally?
4. Assume that both divisions have excess capacity. Currently, 15,000 containers are being transferred between divisions at a price of $8. The Chemical Division has an opportunity to take a special order for 5,000 containers of chemical at a price of $33.75 per container. The manager of the Chemical Division approached the manager of the Plastics Division and offered to buy an additional 5,000 plastic containers for $5 each. Assuming that the Plastics Division has excess capacity totaling at least 5,000 units, should the manager take the offer? What is the minimum transfer price? the maximum? Assume that the Plastics Division manager counters with a price of $5.50. Would the Chemical Division manager be interested?

P12-7
Transfer Pricing;
Custom-made
Subassembly
LO 3, LO 5

The Industrial Machine Division has requested a specially designed subassembly from the Metal Fabricating Division. Because the subassembly is specially designed, there is no outside market price that can serve as a reference point for establishing an internal transfer price. The estimated cost of manufacturing the subassembly follows:

Direct materials	$100
Direct labor	25
Variable overhead	50
Fixed overhead*	30
Total unit cost	$205

*Representing an allocation of existing fixed overhead. The total fixed overhead is the same regardless of whether the Metal Fabricating Division produces the subassembly.

The Industrial Machine Division will use 10,000 of the subassemblies per year.

REQUIRED:

1. Assume that producing the special subassembly displaces other potential jobs. How should the manager of the Metal Fabricating Division set the transfer price for the custom-made subassembly?

2. Assume that two potential jobs will be displaced by the special subassembly. The expected revenues and the total expected costs of these jobs are as follows:

	Job 1	Job 2
Revenues	$2,600,000	$1,500,000
Variable manufacturing	1,950,000	1,050,000
Fixed overhead	200,000	300,000

Compute the minimum price the Metal Fabricating Division should charge.

3. Now assume that the Metal Fabricating Division can produce the special subassembly without displacing any work for outside customers. What is the minimum transfer price that should be charged for the subassembly?

4. Refer to requirement 3. The manager of the Metal Fabricating Division has offered to supply the subassembly for full cost plus the division's average markup. Assuming that average markup is 35 percent, compute the offered transfer price. What do you think of the pricing scheme suggested by the manager of the selling division?

5. Refer to requirement 4. The manager of the Industrial Machine Division refuses to pay the average markup. He indicates that an outside supplier has offered to produce the subassembly for $200 per unit. He offers to pay variable costs plus a lump sum of $125,000 to help cover fixed costs and provide some profit. Do you think the manager of the Metal Fabricating Division should accept this last offer? Would she be tempted to do so? Explain.

P12-8
Transfer Pricing and ROI; Various Computations
LO 3, LO 5

Stamwell Company has two divisions: the Milk Division and the Dairy Products Division. Divisional managers are evaluated on the basis of return on investment. The Milk Division has the capability to produce 500,000 gallons of milk per year. The Dairy Products Division uses milk to produce ice cream, cheese, and cottage cheese. The following data are available for the Milk Division:

Selling price per gallon	$2.25
Variable production cost	0.50
Fixed production cost*	1.00

*Based on 500,000 gallons of output

The Dairy Products Division uses 600,000 gallons of milk per year when it is operating at capacity.

REQUIRED:

1. (Unless otherwise indicated, assume that the requirements are independent of each other.) Assume that the Milk Division can sell all that it produces. The Dairy Products Division is operating at 90 percent of capacity. It can buy all the milk that it needs for $2.35 per gallon from outside suppliers. What are the minimum and maximum transfer prices? What transfer price would you recommend? How many gallons of milk will the Dairy Products Division buy internally, assuming that it is operating at 90 percent of capacity?

2. Refer to requirement 1. How would your answers differ if the Milk Division can avoid distribution costs of $0.15 per gallon if the milk is sold internally?

3. The manager of the Milk Division realizes that excess capacity will exist for the last six months of the current year. He is reluctant to sell any of the milk cows to reduce production because he expects the market to rebound in the coming year. Accordingly, the cows will continue to be milked, creating excess production of 40,000 gallons. Unless a market for the excess milk can be found, it will simply be dumped. Discouraged with the possibility of finding any new outside customers, the manager of the Milk Division approaches the manager of the Dairy

Products Division to see if a deal for internal sales can be arranged. The Dairy Products Division has been buying all of its milk from outside suppliers at $2 per gallon. Assume that production of milk is spread evenly over the year and that milk sold externally is sold for the normal price. Under these conditions, identify the minimum and maximum transfer prices. Assume that the managers split the difference between the two prices. How many gallons will be transferred internally? By how much will the profits of the firm and each division increase?

4. Refer to requirement 3. Now assume that the Milk Division has an offer to sell the 40,000 gallons of extra milk to a government agency for conversion into powdered milk. The offering price is $1 per gallon. How does this change your answers to requirement 3?

P12-9
Transfer Pricing
LO 5

PortCo Products is a divisionalized furniture manufacturer. The divisions are autonomous segments with each responsible for its own sales, costs of operations, working capital management, and equipment acquisition. Each division serves a different market in the furniture industry. Because the markets and products of the divisions are so different, there have never been any transfers between divisions.

The Commercial Division manufactures equipment and furniture that is purchased by the restaurant industry. The division plans to introduce a new line of counter and chair units that feature a cushioned seat for the counter chairs. John Kline, the divisional manager, has discussed the manufacture of the cushioned seat with Russ Fiegel of the Office Division. They both believe a cushioned seat currently made by the Office Division for use on its deluxe office stool could be modified for use on the new counter chair. Consequently, Kline has asked Russ Fiegel for a price for 100 unit lots of the cushioned seat. The following conversation took place about the price to be charged for the cushioned seats.

Russ: John, we can make the necessary modifications to the cushioned seat easily. The raw materials used in your seat are slightly different and should cost about 10 percent more than those used in our deluxe office stool. However, the labor time (0.5 DLH) should be the same because the seat fabrication operation basically is the same. I would price the seat at our regular rate—full cost plus 30 percent markup.

John: That's higher than I expected, Russ. I was thinking that a good price would be your variable manufacturing costs. After all, your capacity costs will be incurred regardless of this job.

Russ: John, I'm at capacity. By making the cushion seats for you, I'll have to cut my production of deluxe office stools. Of course, I can increase my production of economy office stools. The labor time freed by not having to fabricate the frame or assemble the deluxe stool can be shifted to the frame fabrication and assembly of the economy office stool. Fortunately, I can switch my labor force between these two models of stools without any loss of efficiency. As you know, overtime is not a feasible alternative in our community. I'd like to sell it to you at variable cost, but I have excess demand for both products. I don't mind changing my product mix to the economy model if I get a good return on the seats I make for you. Here are my standard costs for the two stools and a schedule of my manufacturing overhead.

Office Division Standard Costs and Prices		
	Deluxe Office Stool	Economy Office Stool
Raw materials (framing)	$ 8.15	$ 9.76
Cushioned seat (padding)	2.40	—
Vinyl	4.00	—
Molded seat (purchased)	—	6.00
Direct labor		
1.5 DLH @ $7.50	11.25	
0.8 DLH @ $7.50		6.00
Manufacturing overhead		
1.5 DLH @ $12.80	19.20	
0.8 DLH @ $12.80		10.24
Total standard cost	$45.00	$32.00
Selling price (30% markup)	$58.50	$41.60

Office Division
Manufacturing Overhead Budget

Overhead Item	Nature	Amount
Supplies	Variable (at current market prices)	$ 420,000
Indirect labor	Variable	375,000
Supervision	Nonvariable	250,000
Power	Use varies with activity; rates are fixed	180,000
Heat and light	Nonvariable (light is fixed regardless of production while heat/air conditioning varies with fuel charges)	140,000
Property insurance	Nonvariable (any change in amounts/rates is independent of production)	200,000
Depreciation	Fixed dollar total	1,700,000
Employee benefits	20% of supervision, direct and indirect labor	575,000
Total overhead		$3,840,000
Capacity in DLH		300,000
Overhead rate/DLH		$12.80

John: I guess I see your point, Russ, but I don't want to price myself out of the market. Maybe we should talk to corporate to see if it can give us any guidance.

REQUIRED:
1. John Kline and Russ Fiegel did ask PortCo corporate management for guidance on an appropriate transfer price. Corporate management suggested they consider using a transfer price based upon variable manufacturing cost plus opportunity cost. Calculate a transfer price for the cushioned seat based upon variable manufacturing cost plus opportunity cost.
2. Which alternative transfer price system—full cost, variable manufacturing cost, or variable manufacturing cost plus opportunity cost—would be better as the underlying concept for an intracompany transfer price policy? Explain your answer. (CMA adapted)

P12-10

Managerial Performance Evaluation

LO 3, LO 4

Greg Peterson has recently been appointed vice-president of operations for Webster Corporation. Greg has a manufacturing background and previously served as operations manager of Webster's Tractor Division. The business segments of Webster include the manufacture of heavy equipment, food processing, and financial services.

In a recent conversation with Carol Andrews, Webster's chief financial officer, Greg suggested that segment managers be evaluated on the basis of the segment data appearing in Webster's annual financial report. This report presents revenues, earnings, identifiable assets, and depreciation for each segment for a five-year period. Greg believes that evaluating segment managers by criteria similar to that used to evaluate the company's top management would be appropriate. Carol expressed her reservations about using segment information from the annual financial report for this purpose and suggested that Greg consider other ways to evaluate the performance of segment managers.

REQUIRED:
1. Explain why the segment information prepared for public reporting purposes may not be appropriate for the evaluation of segment management performance.
2. Describe the possible behavioral impact of Webster Corporation's segment managers if their performance is evaluated on the basis of the information in the annual financial report.
3. Identify and describe several types of financial information that would be more appropriate for Greg Peterson to review when evaluating the performance of segment managers. (CMA adapted)

P12-11

Management Compensation

LO 4

Renslen, Inc., a truck manufacturing conglomerate, has recently purchased two divisions, Meyers Service Company and Wellington Products, Inc. Meyers provides maintenance service on large truck cabs for 12-wheeler trucks, and Wellington produces air brakes for the 12-wheeler trucks.

The employees at Meyers take pride in their work, as Meyers is proclaimed to offer the best maintenance service in the trucking industry. The management of Meyers, as a group, has received additional compensation from a 10 percent bonus pool based on income before taxes and bonus; Renslen plans to continue to compensate the Meyers management team on this basis as it is the same incentive plan used for all other Renslen divisions.

Wellington offers a high-quality product to the trucking industry and is the premium choice even when compared to foreign competition. The management team at Wellington strives for zero defects and minimal scrap costs; current scrap levels are at 2 percent. The incentive compensation plan for Wellington management has been a 1 percent bonus based on gross profit margin; Renslen plans to continue to compensate the Wellington management team on this basis.

Following are the condensed income statements for both divisions for the fiscal year ended May 31, 1998.

Renslen, Inc.
Divisional Income Statements
For the Year Ended May 31, 1998

	Meyers Service Company	Wellington Products, Inc.
Revenues	$4,000,000	$10,000,000
Cost of product	75,000	4,950,000
Salaries*	2,200,000	2,150,000
Fixed selling expenses	1,000,000	2,500,000
Interest expense	30,000	65,000
Other operating expense	278,000	134,000
Total expense	3,583,000	9,799,000
Income before taxes and bonus	$ 417,000	$ 201,000

*Each division has $1,000,000 of management salary expense that is eligible for the bonus pool.

Renslen has invited the management teams of all its divisions to an off-site management workshop in July where the bonus checks will be presented. Renslen is concerned that the different bonus plans at the two divisions may cause some heated discussion.

REQUIRED:
1. Determine the 1998 bonus pool available for the management team at
   a. Meyers Service Company
   b. Wellington Products, Inc.
2. Identify at least two advantages and at least two disadvantages to Renslen, Inc. of the bonus pool incentive plan at
   a. Meyers Service Company
   b. Wellington Products, Inc.
3. Having two different types of incentive plans for two operating divisions of the same corporation can create problems.
   a. Discuss the behavioral problems that could arise within management for Meyers Service Company and Wellington Products, Inc. by having different types of incentive plans.
   b. Present arguments that Renslen, Inc. can give to the management teams of both Meyers and Wellington to justify having two different incentive plans.

 ANAGERIAL DECISION CASES

C12-1
ROI and Residual Income; Ethical Considerations
LO 3

Grate Care Company specializes in producing products for personal grooming. The company operates six divisions, including the Hair Products Division. Each division is treated as an investment center. Managers are evaluated and rewarded on the basis of ROI performance. Only those managers who produce the best ROIs are selected to receive bonuses and to fill higher-level managerial positions. Fred Olsen, manager of the Hair Products Division, has always been one of the top performers. For the past two years, Fred's division has produced the largest ROI; last year, the division earned a net operating income of $2.56 million and employed average operating assets valued at $16 million. Fred was pleased with his division's performance and had been told that if the division does well this year, he would be in line for a headquarters position.

For the coming year, Fred's division has been promised new capital totaling $1.5 million. Any of the capital not invested by the division will be invested to earn the company's required rate of return (9 percent). After some careful investigation, the marketing and engineering staff recommended that the division invest in equipment that could be used to produce a crimping and waving iron, a product currently not produced by the division. The cost of the equipment was estimated at $1.2 million. The division's marketing manager estimated operating earnings from the new line at $156,000 per year.

After receiving the proposal and reviewing the potential effects, Fred turned it down. He then wrote a memo to corporate headquarters, indicating that his division would not be able to employ the capital in any new projects within the next eight to ten months. He did note, however, that he was confident that his marketing and engineering staff would have a project ready by the end of the year. At that time, he would like to have access to the capital.

REQUIRED:

1. Explain why Fred Olsen turned down the proposal to add the capability of producing a crimping and waving iron. Provide computations to support your reasoning.
2. Compute the effect that the new product line would have on the profitability of the firm as a whole. Should the division have produced the crimping and waving iron?
3. Suppose that the firm used residual income as a measure of divisional performance. Do you think Fred's decision might have been different? Why?
4. Explain why a firm like Grate Care might decide to use both residual income and return on investment as measures of performance.
5. Did Fred display ethical behavior when he turned down the investment? In discussing this issue, consider why he refused to allow the investment.

C12-2

Transfer Pricing; Behavioral Considerations

LO 5

Lynsar Corporation started as a single plant that produced the major components of electric motors, the company's main product, and then assembled them. Lynsar later expanded by developing outside markets for some of the components used in its motors. Eventually, Lynsar reorganized into four manufacturing divisions: Bearing, Casing, Switch, and Motor. Each of the four manufacturing divisions operates as an autonomous unit, and divisional performance is the basis for year-end bonuses.

Lynsar's transfer pricing policy permits the manufacturing divisions to sell externally to outside customers as well as internally to the other divisions. The price for goods transferred between divisions is to be negotiated between the buying and selling divisions without any interference from top management.

Lynsar's profits have dropped for the current year even though sales have increased, and the drop in profits can be traced almost entirely to the Motor Division. Jere Feldon, Lynsar's chief financial officer, has determined that the Motor Division has purchased switches for its motors from an outside supplier during the current year rather than buying them from the Switch Division. The Switch Division is at capacity and has refused to sell the switches to the Motor Division because it can sell them to outside customers at a price higher than the actual full (absorption) manufacturing cost that has always been negotiated in the past with the Motor Division. When the Motor Division refused to meet the price the Switch Division was receiving from its outside buyer, the Motor Division had to purchase the switches from an outside supplier at an even higher price.

Jere is reviewing Lynsar's transfer pricing policy because he believes that suboptimization has occurred. While the Switch Division made the correct decision to maximize its divisional profit by not transferring the switches at actual full manufacturing cost, this decision was not necessarily in the best interest of Lynsar. The Motor Division paid more for the switches than the selling price the Switch Division charged its outside customer. The Motor Division has always been Lynsar's largest division and has tended to dominate the smaller divisions. Jere has learned that the Casing and Bearing divisions are also resisting the Motor Division's desires to continue using actual full manufacturing cost as the negotiated price.

Jere has requested that the corporate accounting department study alternative transfer pricing methods that would promote overall goal congruence, motivate divisional management performance, and optimize overall company performance. Three of the transfer pricing methods being considered follow. If one of these methods is selected, it will be applied uniformly across all divisions:

a. Standard full manufacturing costs plus markup
b. Market selling price of the products being transferred
c. Outlay (out-of-pocket) costs incurred to the point of transfer plus opportunity cost per unit

REQUIRED:

1. Discuss both the positive and negative behavioral implications that can arise from employing a negotiated transfer price system for goods that are exchanged between divisions. Explain the behavioral problems that can arise from using actual full (absorption) manufacturing costs as a transfer price.

2. Discuss the behavioral problems that could arise if Lynsar Corporation decides to change from its current policy covering the transfer of goods between divisions to a revised transfer pricing policy that would apply uniformly to all divisions.

3. Discuss the likely behavior of both "buying" and "selling" divisional managers for each of the three transfer pricing methods being considered by Lynsar Corporation.
    a. Standard full manufacturing costs plus markup.
    b. Market selling price of the products being transferred.
    c. Outlay (out-of-pocket) costs incurred to the point of transfer plus opportunity cost per unit.
        (CMA adapted)

C12-3
Research Assignment
LO 4

Every year *Fortune* and *Business Week* review current trends in executive compensation. Research this issue in the library, using these two magazines as a starting point, and write a three- to five-page paper on executive compensation. Be sure to give specific examples of the ways in which companies reward executives, and the ways in which compensation is tied to performance.

CHAPTER

International Issues in Management Accounting

SCENARIO[1]

Paterson Company is a U.S.-based company that manufactures and sells electronic components worldwide. Virtually all of the manufacturing takes place in the United States. The company has marketing divisions located throughout Europe, including one in France. Debbie Kishimoto is manager of this division; she was hired away from a competitor three years ago. Debbie, recently informed of a price increase in one of the major product lines, had requested a meeting with Jeff Phillips, the marketing vice-president.

"Jeff, I simply don't understand why the price of our main product has increased from $5 to $5.50 per unit. We negotiated an agreement earlier in the year with our manufacturing division in Philadelphia for a

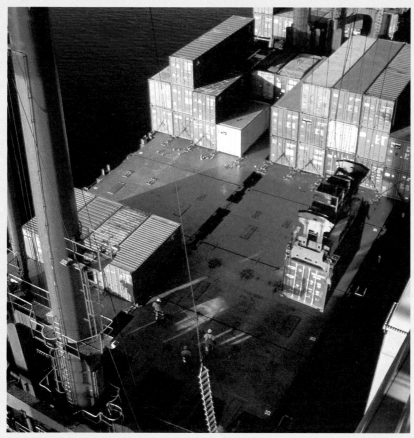

example—we increase revenues and profits in the United States. By decreasing your profits we avoid paying taxes in France; with losses on other U.S. operations to offset the corresponding increase in domestic profits, we avoid paying taxes in the United States as well. The net effect is a much-needed increase in our cash flow. Besides, you know how difficult it is in some of these European countries to transfer out capital. This is a clean way of doing it."

"I'm not so sure that it's clean. It doesn't seem right to me. I can't imagine the tax laws permitting this type of scheme. There is another problem as well. You know that the company's bonus plans are tied to a division's profitability. This plan could cost all the European managers a lot of money."

"Debbie, you have no reason to worry about the effect on your bonus—or on our evaluation of your performance, for that matter. Corporate management has already taken steps to ensure no loss of compensation. The plan is to compute what income would have been if the old price had prevailed and base bonuses on that figure. I plan to meet with the other divisional managers and explain the situation to them as well."

"The bonus adjustment seems fair, although I wonder if the reasons for the drop in profits will be remembered in a couple of years when I'm being considered for promotion. Anyway, I still have some strong concerns about the propriety of all this. How does this scheme relate to the tax laws?"

"We will be in technical compliance with the tax laws. In the

price of $5 for the entire year. I called the manager of that division, and he indicated that the original price was still acceptable—he said that the increase was a directive from headquarters. That's why I requested a meeting with you. I need some explanations. When I was hired, I was told that pricing decisions were made at the divisional level—that divisions were given a lot of decision-making latitude. This directive not only interferes with this decentralized philosophy but also will lower my division's profits. Given current market conditions, there is no way that we can pass on the cost increase. Profits for my division will drop at least $600,000 if this price is maintained. I think a midyear increase of this magnitude is unfair to my division."

"Debbie, under normal operating conditions, headquarters will not interfere with divisional decisions. As a company, however, we are having some problems. What you just told me is exactly why the price of your product has been increased. We want the profits of all of our European marketing divisions to drop."

"Wait a minute. What do you mean that you want the profits to drop? That doesn't make any sense. Aren't we in business to make money?"

"Debbie, what you lack is corporate perspective. We are in business to make money, and that's why we want European profits to decrease. Let me explain. Our divisions in the United States are not doing well this year. Projections show significant losses. At the same time, projections for European operations show good profitability. By increasing the cost of key products transferred to Europe—to your division, for

United States, Section 482 of the Internal Revenue Code governs this type of transaction. The key to this law, as well as most European laws, is evidence of an arm's-length price. Since you're a distributor, we can use the resale price method to determine such a price. Essentially, the arm's-length price for the transferred good is backed into by starting with the price at which you sell the product and then adjusting that price for the markup and other legitimate differences, such as tariffs and transportation."

"If I were a French tax auditor, I would wonder why the markup dropped from last year to this year. I also wonder if we are being good citizens and meeting the fiscal responsibilities imposed on us by each country in which we operate."

"Well, a French tax auditor might wonder about the drop in markup. The markup, however, is

still within reason, and we can make a good argument for increased costs. In fact, we have already instructed the managers of our manufacturing divisions to find as many costs as they can that can be legitimately reassigned to the European product lines affected by this increase. So far they have been very successful. I think our records will support the increase that you are receiving. Debbie, you really do not need to be concerned with the tax authorities. Our tax department assures me that this has been carefully researched and planned—it's unlikely that a tax audit will create any difficulties. It'll all be legal and aboveboard. We've done this several times in the past with total success. We have some good people in that department."

1. This scenario is based on the experiences of an actual firm. Names have been changed to preserve confidentiality.

Questions to Think About

1. Do you think that the transfer pricing scheme interferes with decentralization? How much autonomy should central headquarters grant to the divisions?
2. What does Jeff mean by "corporate perspective"?
3. Discuss Debbie's concerns regarding her bonus and promotion opportunities. To what extent should she be concerned?
4. Jeff says that everything is "legal and aboveboard." Do you agree? Is it ethical? (Note: Case 13-1 addresses this question in more detail.)

MANAGEMENT ACCOUNTING IN THE INTERNATIONAL ENVIRONMENT

Objective 1

Explain the role of the management accountant in the international environment.

Doing business in a global environment requires management to shift perspective. While many aspects of business remain the same, others are quite different. From her conversation with Jeff Phillips, we can see that Debbie Kishimoto is struggling with one of these differences, the income tax implications of transfer pricing. The company doing business in both its home country and other countries may find that practices that work well in the home country work imperfectly or not at all in another country. Much of the difference can be related to the business environment—that is, the cultural, legal, political, and economic environments of the various countries. Just as a fish supposedly is not aware of water, we in the United States take our business environment for granted. We have grown accustomed to a market economy and to the concept of private property. We are also accustomed to a legal system that enforces contracts. Our sense of ethics grew in tandem with the underlying environment. When the environment changes, ethical problems may arise. Of course, the scenario raises the question of the ethics of the tax-avoidance scheme. While this question is not necessarily common to all divisional structures, evaluating the ethical content of divisional decisions is common.

Where does the management accountant fit into the global business environment? Business looks to the management accountant for financial and business expertise. Good training, education, and staying abreast of changes in one's field are important to any accountant. However, the job of the management accountant in the international firm is made more challenging by the ambiguous and ever-changing nature of global business. Since much of the management accountant's job is to provide relevant information to management, staying up-to-date requires reading books and articles in a variety of business areas including information systems, marketing, management, politics, and economics. In addition, the management accountant must be familiar with the financial accounting rules of the countries in which the firm operates.

The remainder of this chapter will touch on various issues facing the multinational firm. Our focus is on the management accountant and how he or she must deal with those issues.

LEVELS OF INVOLVEMENT IN INTERNATIONAL TRADE

Objective 2

Discuss the varying levels of involvement that firms can undertake in international trade.

multinational corporation (MNC)

A multinational corporation (MNC) is one that "does business in more than one country in such a volume that its well-being and growth rest in more than one country."[2] From this definition we can see that the involvement of the MNC in international trade may take many forms. On a fairly simple level, the MNC may import raw materials and/or export finished products. On a more complex level, the MNC may be a large firm consisting of a parent company and a number of divisions in various countries.

In the international environment, the choice of company structure goes beyond the issue of centralized versus decentralized firm structures described in Chapter 12. While multinational companies are very often decentralized, with the subsidiaries being wholly owned by the parent firm, the many legal systems under which the firm must operate require careful consideration of company structure. Some of the choices are importing and exporting, wholly owned subsidiaries, and joint ventures.

Importing and Exporting

A relatively simple form of multinational involvement is importing and exporting. A company may import parts for production. Similarly, a company may export finished products to foreign countries. Even such simple transactions as importing and exporting can present new risks and opportunities for companies.

tariff

Importing A company may import raw materials for use in production. While this transaction may look identical to the purchase of materials from domestic suppliers, U.S. tariffs add complexity and cost. In accounting for materials, freight-in is a materials cost. An imported part may have a tariff (or duty) in addition to freight-in cost. A tariff is a tax on imports levied by the federal government. This tax is also a cost of materials. Companies look hard for ways to decrease tariffs. They may restrict the amount of imported materials, alter the materials by adding U.S. resources (to increase the domestic content and gain more favorable tariff status), or utilize foreign trade zones.

foreign trade zones

Foreign Trade Zones The U.S. government has set up foreign trade zones, areas near a customs port of entry which are physically on U.S. soil but considered to be outside U.S. commerce. San Antonio, New Orleans, and the Port of Catoosa, Oklahoma, are examples of cities with foreign trade zones. Some U.S. companies have set up manufacturing plants within the foreign trade zones. Goods imported into a foreign trade zone are

2. Yair Aharoni, "On the Definition of a Multinational Corporation," in *The Multinational Enterprise in Transition*, eds. A. Kapoor and Phillip D. Grub (Princeton, N.J.: Darwin Press, 1972), 4.

duty-free until they leave the zone. This has important implications for manufacturing firms that import raw materials. Since tariffs are not paid until the imported materials leave the zone, as part of a finished product, the company can postpone payment of duty and the associated loss of working capital. Additionally, the company does not pay duty on defective materials, or inventory that has not yet been included in finished product.

An example may help to illustrate the cost advantages of operating a plant in a foreign trade zone. Suppose that Roadrunner, Inc. operates a petrochemical plant located in a foreign trade zone. The plant imports volatile materials (for example, chemicals that experience substantial evaporation loss during processing) for use in production. Wilycoyote, Inc. operates an identical plant just outside the foreign trade zone. Consider the impact on duty and related expenditures for the two plants for the purchase of $400,000 of crude oil imported from Venezuela. Both Roadrunner and Wilycoyote use the oil in chemical production. Each purchases the oil about three months before use in production, and the finished chemicals remain in inventory about five months before sale and shipment to the customer. About 30 percent of the oil is lost through evaporation during production. Duty is assessed at 6 percent of cost. Each company faces 12 percent carrying cost.

Wilycoyote pays duty, at the point of purchase, of $24,000 (.06 × $400,000). In addition, Wilycoyote has carrying cost associated with the duty payment of 12 percent per year times the portion of the year that the oil is in raw materials or finished goods inventory. In this case, the months in inventory equal 8 (3 + 5). Total duty-related carrying cost is $1,920 (.12 × $\frac{8}{12}$ × $24,000). Total duty and duty-related carrying cost is $25,920. Roadrunner, on the other hand, pays duty at the time of sale because it is in a foreign trade zone, and imported goods do not incur duty until (unless) they are moved out of the zone. Since 70 percent of the original imported oil remains in the final product, duty equals $16,800 (.7 × $400,000 × .06). There is no carrying cost associated with the duty. A summary of the duty-related costs for the two companies follows:

	Roadrunner	Wilycoyote
Duty paid at purchase	$ 0	$24,000
Carrying cost of duty	0	1,920
Duty paid at sale	16,800	0
Total duty and related cost	$16,800	$25,920

Clearly, Roadrunner has saved $9,120 ($25,920 − $16,800) on just one purchase of imported raw materials by locating in the foreign trade zone.

Foreign trade zones provide additional advantages. For example, goods that do not meet U.S. health, safety, and pollution control regulations are subject to fines. Foreign goods can be imported into foreign trade zones and modified to comply with the law without being subject to the fines. Another example of the efficient use of foreign trade zones is the assembly of high-tariff component parts into a lower-tariff finished product. In this case, the addition of domestic labor raises the domestic content of the finished product and makes the embedded foreign parts eligible for more favorable tariff treatment.[3]

The management accountant must be aware of the costs of importing materials. He or she should also be able to evaluate the potential benefits of the foreign trade zone in considering the location of satellite plants.

Exporting Exporting is the sale of a company's products in foreign countries. It is not necessary to have a production facility in the foreign country; finished products can

---

3. These examples are taken from James E. Groff and John P. McCray, "Foreign-Trade Zones: Opportunity for Strategic Development in the Southwest," *Journal of Business Strategies* (Spring 1992): 14–26.

simply be transported to the buyer. However, exporting is usually more complex than the sale of finished goods within the home country. Foreign countries have a variety of import and tariff regulations. The job of complying with the foreign rules and regulations often falls to the controller's office, just as compliance with U.S. tax regulations is an accounting function. Alternatively, a U.S. company may choose to work with an experienced distributor, familiar with the legal complexities of the other countries. In some cases the distributor is wholly owned (as is the one headed by Debbie Kishimoto); in other cases the distributor is a separate company.

Treaties and Tariffs Trade treaties between countries affect the tariffs charged. For example, the North American Free Trade Agreement (NAFTA) allows importers in the United States, Mexico, and Canada to pay reduced tariffs on goods produced in the three countries. However, strict adherence to regulations is required. U.S. Customs has stepped up enforcement of NAFTA regulations by checking for valid certificates of origin on imported goods. A *certificate of origin* is a document summarizing the information enabling companies to qualify for reduced NAFTA duties. The penalties for noncompliance are steep—ranging from twice the revenue lost (in tariffs) to the domestic value of the goods. Management accountants must be aware of the customs regulations and ensure that adequate record keeping and internal control mechanisms exist.[4]

Wholly Owned Subsidiaries

A company may choose to purchase an existing foreign company, making the purchased company a wholly owned subsidiary of the parent. This strategy has the virtue of simplicity. The foreign company has established an outlet for the product, and has the production and distribution facilities already set up. For example, in 1989, Whirlpool expanded into the European market by purchasing the appliance business of Philips N.V., Europe's third largest appliance manufacturer. This purchase gave Whirlpool immediate access to production and distribution facilities, as well as an established brand name. Even so, the approach is not inexpensive. The first three years were spent blending company cultures, before the European operation could be streamlined to cut costs. Finally, more investment was necessary in marketing, to replace the Philips name with Whirlpool's, and to develop a marketing plan for all of Europe as opposed to the more fragmented country-by-country approach used previously.[5]

If the laws of the country permit, an MNC can simply set up a wholly owned subsidiary or branch office in the country. In Ireland, for example, U.S. insurance and software companies have set up branch offices. Quarterdeck Office Systems, a California-based software company, routes customer calls to its second phone-answering operation in Dublin. Scores of multilingual workers take calls from all over Europe, and from the United States. When it is 5:00 A.M. in California, Irish workers are well into their working day and can answer calls from customers in the U.S. eastern standard time zone. The Irish Development Authority provides generous tax and other incentives worth about a year's pay for each job created.[6]

outsourcing   Outsourcing of technical and professional jobs is becoming an important issue for cost-conscious U.S. firms. Outsourcing is the payment by a company for a business function formerly done in-house. For example, some domestic companies outsource their legal needs to outside law firms rather than hiring corporate attorneys. In the context of the MNC, outsourcing refers to the move of a business function to another country. For example, Texas Instruments set up an impressive software programming operation in Bangalore, in southern India. The availability of underemployed college graduates in India meant the combination of low wage rates and high productivity. However, the underdeveloped Indian infrastructure required considerable capital

---

4. "NAFTA and U.S. Customs—The Honeymoon Is Over," *Deloitte & Touche Review* (May 15, 1995): 4–5.
5. Barry Rehfeld, "Where Whirlpool Flies, and Maytag Sputters," *New York Times*, 3 January 1993, p. 5.
6. "Your New Global Work Force," *Fortune*, 14 December 1992, 52–66.

investment—"Even though (Texas Instruments) had to install its own electrical generators and satellite dishes to operate efficiently, wages are low enough that work still gets
done for half what it costs in the U.S."[7]

Outsourcing is done by foreign firms, as well. Toyota Motor outsourced its design
needs for the Previa to California. Benefits to Toyota included the greater familiarity
California designers have with the U.S. minivan market as well as the political advantage
of having part of the Previa's development in the United States.

The management accountant must be aware of numerous costs and benefits of outsourcing that would not be available in the United States. The varying tax structures and
incentives of local authorities, as well as the overall educational level of the country,
and the infrastructure all play a role in the management accountant's assessment of costs
and benefits.

Joint Ventures

joint venture

Sometimes companies with the expertise needed by MNCs do not exist or are not for
sale; in this case, a joint venture may work. A joint venture is a type of partnership in
which investors co-own the enterprise. IBM spent much time and money on plasma
display technology for portable computers until it realized that the technology was
impractical because of excessive power use. Liquid-crystal displays (LCDs) provided
a possible solution, so IBM formed a joint venture with Toshiba to marry its own
expertise in materials with Toshiba's superior manufacturing. IBM, Toshiba, and
Siemens have also united in manufacturing memory chips.[8] More joint ventures include:
Hewlett-Packard and Hitachi, Boeing and Mitsubishi, and Apple Computer and Sharp
Electronics.

Sometimes a joint venture is required because of restrictive laws. In China, for example, MNCs are not allowed to purchase companies or set up their own subsidiaries.
Joint ventures with Chinese firms are required. Similarly, India and Thailand demand
local ownership. Loctite, maker of Super Glue™, runs joint ventures in both India and
Thailand for that reason.

maquiladoras

A special case of joint venture cooperation is the *maquiladora*. Maquiladoras are
manufacturing plants located in Mexico, which process imported materials and reexport them to the United States. Originally designed to encourage U.S. firms to invest in
Mexico, the program has now expanded to include other foreign firms, such as Nissan
Motor and Sony. Basically, the maquiladora enjoys special status in both Mexico, which
grants operators an exemption from Mexican laws governing foreign ownership, and
the United States, which grants exemptions from or reductions in custom duties levied
on reexported goods. Most maquiladoras are located in cities bordering the United
States to take advantage of ready access to U.S. transportation and communication
facilities. The Mexican advantage is low-cost, high-quality labor. The structure of the
maquiladora is flexible. Mexico permits different levels of involvement. The minimal
level combines low risk with low cost savings. In this case, the U.S. firm transfers materials to an existing Mexican firm and imports them back in finished form. All hiring and
operating of the Mexican plant is handled by the Mexican owners. The highest level of
involvement offers both high risk and high cost savings. At this level, the U.S. firm owns
the Mexican subsidiary and oversees all the operations.[9]

Maquiladoras are an example of a government program to increase production that
has worked well. Foreign investment has moved well beyond the border cities to a broad
band of northern Mexico. Improvements in the Mexican infrastructure (for example,
roads, communications) have enticed companies further into the interior, lowering non-

7. "Your New Global Work Force," 64.
8. John Carey, Neil Gross, Mark Maremont, and Guy McWilliams, "Moving the Lab Closer to the Marketplace,"
   Business Week, Reinventing America 1992, 164–171.
9. James E. Groff and John P. McCray, "Maquiladoras: The Mexico Option Can Reduce Your Manufacturing Cost."
   Management Accounting (January 1991): 43–46.

labor costs. While U.S. companies were originally drawn to the maquiladoras for the cheap labor (wage rates of approximately $1.50 per hour versus $17.50 per hour for U.S. assemblers), other reasons keep them. For example, Ford's plant in Chihuahua was built to satisfy export requirements for doing business in Mexico. Now, it supports Ford's sales to Mexico, establishing a marketing reason for the plant's presence.

No matter which structure the MNC takes, it faces issues of foreign trade. An important issue is foreign currency exchange. This is addressed in the next section.

FOREIGN CURRENCY EXCHANGE

Objective 3

Explain the ways management accountants can manage foreign currency risk.

exchange rates

When a company operates only in its home country, only one currency is used and exchange issues never arise. However, when a company begins to operate in the international arena, it must use foreign currencies. These foreign currencies can be exchanged for the domestic currency using exchange rates. If the exchange rates never changed, problems would not occur. Exchange rates do change, however, often on a daily basis. Thus, a dollar which could be traded for 350 yen one day may be worth only 325 yen on another day. Currency rate fluctuations add considerably to the uncertainty of operating in the international arena.

currency risk management
transaction risk
economic risk
translation (or accounting) risk

The management accountant plays an important role in managing the company's exposure to currency risk. Currency risk management refers to the company's management of its transaction, economic, and translation exposure due to exchange rate fluctuations. Transaction risk refers to the possibility that future cash transactions will be affected by changing exchange rates. Economic risk refers to the possibility that a firm's present value of future cash flows will be affected by exchange fluctuations. Translation (or accounting) risk is the degree to which a firm's financial statements are exposed to exchange rate fluctuation. Let's look more closely at these three components of currency risk and ways in which the accountant can manage the company's exposure to them.

Managing Transaction Risk

spot rate

Today's MNC deals in many different currencies. These currencies may be traded for one another, depending on the exchange rate in effect at the time of the trade. The spot rate is the exchange rate of one currency for another for immediate delivery (that is, today). Exhibit 13-1 lists a number of widely used currencies and their spot rates as of December 19, 1995. While the spot rates are surely different now, as you read this book, you can gain an idea of relative values. Changes in the spot rates can affect the value of a company's future cash transactions, posing transaction risk. Let's first get a feel for currency appreciation and depreciation, before we go on to exchange gains and losses and hedging.

currency appreciation
currency depreciation

Currency Appreciation and Depreciation When one country's currency strengthens relative to another country's currency, currency appreciation occurs, and one unit of the first country's currency can buy more units of the second country's currency. Conversely, currency depreciation means that one country's currency has become relatively weaker and buys fewer units of another currency. For example, in mid-1985 the U.S. dollar was worth 240 yen. (Yen is the unit of Japanese currency and is symbolized by ¥.) By mid-1986, the dollar had weakened to only 156 yen. This had an impact on trade between the two countries. Fujinon Optical Company sold rubber-coated marine binoculars for ¥93,600. In mid-1985 this meant a price of $390 ($\frac{93,600}{240}$) to U.S. importers. By mid-1986, however, the same binoculars, priced at the same ¥93,600, would cost U.S. importers $600 ($\frac{93,600}{156}$). Of course, while the dollar weakened, the yen strengthened.

Exchange Gains and Losses Let's examine the impact of changes in exchange rates on the sale of goods to other countries. Suppose that SuperTubs, Inc., based in Oklahoma, sells its line of whirlpool tubs at home and to foreign distributors. On January 15,

Exhibit
Spot Rates as of
December 19, 1995

Country	Currency Name	Exchange Rate for $1 (12/19/95)
Australia	Australian dollar	1.3485
Canada	Canadian dollar	1.3744
China	Renminbi	8.3176
France	Franc	4.9565
Germany	Deutsche mark	1.4410
Great Britain	Pound	0.6484
Hong Kong	Hong Kong dollar	7.7344
India	Rupee	34.970
Indonesia	Rupiah	2,287.00
Israel	Shekel	3.1332
Italy	Lira	1,594.75
Japan	Yen	102.00
Mexico	Peso	7.6750
Netherlands	Guilder	1.6140
Peru	New Sol	2.3155
Russia	Ruble	4,639.00
Saudi Arabia	Riyal	3.7504
Singapore	Singapore dollar	1.4146
South Korea	Won	771.45
Sweden	Krona	6.6395
Switzerland	Swiss franc	1.1565
Taiwan	Taiwan dollar	27.331
Thailand	Baht	25.160
Venezuela	Bolivar	289.62

Bonbain, a French distributor of luxury plumbing fixtures, orders 100 tubs at a price of $1,000 per tub, to be delivered immediately, and to be paid in French francs on March 15. Has SuperTubs just made a sale of $100,000 (100 × $1,000)? The payment is to be in francs, not dollars, so we must look at the exchange rate for francs. If the exchange rate on January 15 is 5 francs per dollar, then Bonbain is really promising to pay 500,000 francs (5 × $100,000) on March 15. If the exchange rate remains at 5 francs per dollar on March 15, SuperTubs would receive 500,000 francs convertible to $100,000. But suppose that the exchange rate on March 15 is 5.1 francs per dollar. Bonbain still pays 500,000 francs, but SuperTubs can convert that amount into only $98,039 $(\frac{500,000}{5.1})$, not the $100,000 it anticipated back in January when the sale was made. The difference between the two amounts, $1,961, is the loss on currency exchange. The impact of transaction risk on this example can be summarized as follows:

Receivable in dollars on 1/15	$100,000
Received in dollars on 3/15	98,039
Exchange loss	$ 1,961

exchange loss

An exchange loss, then, is a loss on the exchange of one currency for another due to depreciation of the home currency.

Of course, if the franc had strengthened against the dollar, say an exchange rate of 4.9 francs per dollar, an exchange gain would occur. An exchange gain is the gain on the exchange of one currency for another due to appreciation of the home currency. In our example Bonbain again pays 500,000 francs, which SuperTubs is able to convert into $102,041 $(\frac{500,000}{4.9})$. In that case, the impact of transaction risk would result in a gain:

exchange gain

Receivable in dollars on 1/15	$100,000
Received in dollars on 3/15	102,041
Exchange gain	$ 2,041

Transaction risk also affects the purchase of commodities from foreign companies. Suppose that on February 20, Americo, Inc. (based in Big Timber, Montana) purchases computers from NEC for $50,000, payable in yen on May 20. Assume the spot rate for yen is 130 per dollar on February 20. It is easy to see that Americo's true payable is for ¥6,500,000 (50,000 × 130). If the spot rate for yen is 135 on May 20, it will only cost Americo $48,148 ($\frac{6,500,000}{135}$) to get enough yen to pay NEC:

Liability in dollars, 2/20	$50,000
Liability in dollars, 5/20	48,148
Exchange gain	$ 1,852

As we can see, the more favorable May 20 spot rate has resulted in an exchange gain. Clearly, transaction risk caused by the movement of foreign currency against the dollar must be taken into account by managers as it affects the prices paid and received for goods. Suppose management does not want to be involved in gambling on exchange rates? What then? The following section on hedging explains how the accountant can manage a company's exposure to exchange gains and losses.

hedging
forward contract

Hedging One way of insuring against gains and losses on foreign currency exchanges is hedging. Typically, a forward exchange contract is used as a hedge. The forward contract requires the buyer to exchange a specified amount of a currency at a specified rate (the forward rate) on a specified future date.

Let's return to our example of SuperTubs' sale of $100,000 worth of tubs to the French company. The spot rate on January 15 was 5 francs per dollar. SuperTubs' problem is that they do not know what the exchange rate will be on March 15. If it is more than 5 francs, SuperTubs will receive less than the $100,000 anticipated in accounts receivable. Of course, if the rate is less, SuperTubs will receive more. But the difficulty is in predicting short-term exchange rate movements. SuperTubs may well decide it is in the business of manufacturing and selling tubs, not in the business of betting on exchange rate fluctuations. Therefore, it will forgo the opportunity for exchange rate gains by hedging against exchange rate losses. Here is how it might work using forward contracts.

On January 15, SuperTubs purchases a contract to exchange 500,000 francs into dollars on March 15 at a forward rate of 5.02 francs. SuperTubs has agreed to sell francs for dollars. At this point, SuperTubs has locked in the exchange rate. The .02 difference between the spot rate of 5 and the forward rate of 5.02 is the premium SuperTubs pays the exchange dealer on the transaction. Think of it as an insurance premium.

On March 15, the following transactions will occur. Bonbain pays SuperTubs 500,000 francs, SuperTubs pays the exchange dealer 500,000 francs, and the exchange dealer pays SuperTubs $99,602 ($\frac{500,000}{5.02}$). The difference between the $100,000 original account receivable and the $99,602 cash paid is charged to an exchange premium expense account. Remember that in our original example, the exchange rate on March 15 is 5.1 francs per dollar. Had SuperTubs not hedged, they would have received only $98,039. Therefore, the exchange premium expense of $398 saved SuperTubs a loss of $1,961; this is a net savings of $1,563:

Receivable in dollars 1/15	$100,000
Received in dollars 3/15	99,602
Premium expense	$ 398

Of course, the hedging can also be done by agreeing to exchange dollars for a foreign currency at a future date. Recall the previous example of Americo's purchase of ¥6,500,000 worth of computer equipment. At a spot rate of 130, Americo expects to pay $50,000 to satisfy its liability. Americo may fear that the rate will decline, say to ¥125. If it does, Americo will have to pay $52,000 ($\frac{6,500,000}{125}$) for the same 6,500,000. A hedging transaction would resolve Americo's uncertainty. Perhaps the forward rate is ¥128.7 per dollar. Then Americo would purchase a forward contract to purchase ¥6,500,000 on May 20 for $50,505 ($\frac{6,500,000}{128.7}$):

Liability in dollars, 2/20	$ 50,000
Payment in dollars, 5/20	(50,505)
Premium expense	$ 505

Hedging transactions can become much more complex than the foregoing examples. Companies with significant transaction exposure may choose to hedge all or part of their exposure. Hedging may also be used as a tool to manage economic risk. That use will be addressed in the following section.

Managing Economic Risk

Dealing in different currencies can introduce an economic dimension into currency exchange transactions. Recall that economic risk was defined as the impact of exchange rate fluctuations on the present value of a firm's future cash flows. The risk can affect the relative competitiveness of the firm, even if it never participates directly in international trade. Take a simple example based on the market for heavy equipment between 1981 and 1985.

Suppose that U.S. consumers can choose to purchase heavy equipment from either Caterpillar (based in the United States) or from Komatsu (based in Japan). Assume the price of one type of equipment is $80,000 from both makers. However, while Caterpillar truly means $80,000, Komatsu really is interested in 10,400,000 yen, its own currency. At an exchange rate of $1 equals 130 yen, the price of $80,000 is set. Now suppose that the value of the dollar strengthens against the yen and the exchange rate becomes $1 equals 140 yen. To get the same 10,400,000 yen, Komatsu requires a price of only $74,286. The cost structures of the two firms have not changed, neither has customer demand, but because of currency fluctuations, the Japanese firm has become more "competitive." Of course, as the dollar weakens, the position is reversed and U.S. exports become relatively cheaper to foreign customers.

How does the accountant manage the company's exposure to economic risk? Most importantly, he or she must be aware of it, by understanding the position of the firm in the global economy. As we can see in the Caterpillar–Komatsu example, the two firms were competitors and were linked through their customers' participation in the global marketplace. The accountant provides financial structure and communication for the firm. In preparing the master budget, for example, budgeted sales must take into account potential strengthening or weakening of the currencies of competitors' countries. Often, the controller's office is responsible for forecasting foreign exchange movements.

Hedging can provide another means of managing economic risk. For example, the Toronto Blue Jays baseball team receives its revenues in Canadian dollars but pays most of its expenses in U.S. dollars. In 1985 the team anticipated a loss due to unfavorable exchange rate fluctuations. To prevent this, in 1984 the team purchased forward contracts of U.S. dollars at $.75 per Canadian dollar. The exchange rate at the end of 1984 was $.7568 per Canadian dollar; the exchange rate dropped steadily throughout 1985, to $.7156 by the end of the fourth quarter of 1985. The depreciation of Canada's currency, carefully hedged against through the purchase of forward contracts, resulted in a profit to the team.[10]

Managing Translation Risk

Often the parent company restates all subsidiaries' income into the home currency. This restatement can result in gain and loss opportunities on the revaluation of foreign currencies and can impact a subsidiary's financial statements and the related ROI and residual income computations.

Suppose you are a divisional manager based in Mexico. Your division earned 320,000 pesos this year, up from 200,000 pesos the year before, a hefty 60 percent increase. Now suppose that your income is translated into dollars. If the exchange rate last year was 1.5 pesos per dollar and the exchange rate this year is 3 pesos per dollar, your net income figures translate into $133,333 net income last year and $106,667 net income this year. Suddenly, there is a 20 percent decrease in net income. Similar unpleasant surprises await ROI and net worth computations. The potential for gain or loss on currency revaluation is particularly relevant for countries whose currencies are volatile—and depreciating relative to the home company's currency.

Foreign currency fluctuations also cause difficulties in evaluating the local manager's adherence to company policy. Monsanto faced this problem in the early 1980s. The company noticed declining sales in some of its foreign markets. The local managers were instructed to increase promotional expenditures. However, dollar-denominated reports showed no increases. Top management continued to press local managers to carry out instructions. Local managers were frustrated by their inability to convince higher management that they had increased expenditures, since the reports showed fewer dollars being spent. Eventually, local currency statements were placed alongside dollar-denominated reports. These comparative statements clearly showed that increased expenditures had taken place.

A simple numerical example based on Monsanto's experience (but not using their figures) may illustrate the problem. Assume that Multinational, Inc. has a foreign division, FD, which has been experiencing eroding sales. Multinational directs FD managers to increase marketing expenditures. FD managers do increase marketing expenditures over the following four quarters as follows:

Quarter	Expenditures in Local Currency
1	LC 10,000
2	LC 11,000
3	LC 12,100
4	LC 13,310

As we can see, marketing expenditures have grown by 10 percent in each quarter. However, multinational managers do not see this table; instead, they see dollar-denominated reports. In order to translate local currency figures into dollars, we need the exchange rates for each quarter. Suppose the dollar has strengthened against the local currency and the quarterly exchange rates of $1 for units of local currency are 1.00, 1.20, 1.35, and 1.50, respectively. Then FD's marketing expenditures in dollars would be as follows:

10. Paul V. Mannino and Ken Milani, "Budgeting for an International Business," *Management Accounting* (February 1992): 36–41.

Quarter	Expenditures in Dollars
1	$10,000
2	9,167
3	8,963
4	8,873

What a difference! Not only have local managers not increased expenditures, it looks like they have actually decreased expenditures. Only by comparing the dollar-denominated figures with those denominated in local currency can Multinational see the two effects of an increase in marketing expenditures and the strengthening of the dollar. In this case, FD's increase was hidden in currency translation.

The objective of dollar-denominated internal reports is to measure all figures on the same basis. While this strategy may work at any one point in time, it may mislead managers when comparisons are made over time. The management accountant must be aware of this source of translation risk.

DECENTRALIZATION

Objective 4

Explain why multinational firms choose to decentralize.

In the opening scenario, Debbie Kishimoto complained about corporate headquarters interfering with a pricing arrangement she had negotiated with the manager of the manufacturing division. She complained because Paterson Company had been espousing decentralization. This was her first experience with any interference by headquarters. This is not an unusual complaint. Frequently, firms that are decentralized in the home country may exercise tighter control over foreign divisions, at least until they gain more experience with their overseas operations. Just as decentralization offers advantages for home country divisions, it also offers advantages for foreign divisions. Let's review some of those advantages.

Advantages of Decentralization in the MNC

The quality of information is better at the local level, and that can improve the quality of decisions. This is particularly true in MNCs, where far-flung divisions may be operating in a number of different countries, subject to various legal systems and customs. As a result, local managers are often in a position to make better decisions. Decentralization allows an organization to take advantage of this specialized knowledge. For example, Loctite has local managers run their own divisions; in particular, marketing and pricing are under local control. Language is not a problem as local managers are in control. Similarly, local managers are conversant with their own laws and customs.

Local managers in the MNC are capable of a more timely response in decision making. They are able to respond quickly to customer discount demands, local government demands, and changes in the political climate.

In Chapter 12, we discussed the need for centralized managers to transmit instructions, and the chance that the manager responsible for implementing the decision might misinterpret the instructions. The different languages native to managers of divisions in the MNC make this an even greater problem. MNCs address this problem in two ways. First, a decentralized structure pushes decision making down to the local manager level, eliminating the need to interpret instructions from above. Second, MNCs are learning to incorporate technology that overrides the language barrier and eases cross-border data transfer. Technology is of great help in smoothing communication difficulties between parent and subsidiary and between one subsidiary and another. Loctite's plant in Ireland uses computerized labeling on adhesives bound for Great Britain or Israel. Bar code technology "reads" the labels, eliminating the need for foreign language translation.

Just as decentralization gives the lower-level managers in the home country a chance to develop managerial skills, foreign subsidiary managers also gain valuable experience.

Across the street and around the world, U.S. companies establish a manufacturing and service presence. Coca-Cola's distinctive red lettering is familiar in a number of languages; the company accounts for nearly half the soda consumed worldwide. While the Coke formula is not changed from country to country, Coca-Cola does offer a variety of different carbonated drinks to appeal to indigenous tastes. For example, strawberry, pineapple, and banana-flavored beverages were supplied in Indonesia in an effort to accustom Indonesians to carbonated drinks.

Just as important, home country managers gain broader experience by interacting with managers of foreign divisions. The chance for learning from each other is much greater in a decentralized MNC. Off and on throughout the latter half of the twentieth century, a tour of duty at a foreign subsidiary has been a part of the manager's climb to the top. Now, foreign subsidiary managers may expect to spend some time at headquarters in the home office, as well.

Creation of Divisions

The MNC has great flexibility in creating types of divisions. Divisions are often created along geographic lines. IBM, for example, has divisional boundaries that organize production and sales for Asia and the Far East (AFE), North America, Latin and South America, and Europe and Africa.

Product lines may afford a rationale for the creation of divisions. Many MNCs are diversified, manufacturing and selling a number of different products. The MNC may decide that the major difference is the type of product sold, not the country in which it is sold. An oil company, for example, may have an exploration division, a refining division, and a chemicals division. Each of these divisions may include plants or operations in a number of different countries.

Divisions may follow functional management lines. In the early 1970s, Avon Products created three regional marketing and planning centers, in New York, London, and Australia. These worked reasonably well for a while and achieved the objective of sharing expertise and training divisional managers. However, national needs and differences caused conflict. So by the late 1980s, Avon had disbanded the regional centers and decentralized to the individual country level.[11]

The presence of divisions in more than one country creates the need for performance evaluation that can take into account differences in divisional environments. The next section examines performance evaluation in the MNC.

11. Louis V. Consiglio, "Global Competitive Advantage: Lessons from Avon," Working paper no. 1, July 1992, Center for Applied Research, Lubin School of Business, Pace University.

MEASURING PERFORMANCE IN THE MULTINATIONAL FIRM

Objective 5

Explain how environmental factors can affect performance evaluation in the multinational firm.

It is important for the MNC to separate the evaluation of the *manager* of a division from the evaluation of the *division*. The manager's evaluation should not include factors over which he or she exercises no control, such as currency fluctuations, taxes, and so on. Instead, managers should be evaluated on the basis of revenues and costs incurred. Once a manager is evaluated, the subsidiary financial statements can be restated to the home currency and uncontrollable costs can be allocated.[12]

It is particularly difficult to compare the performance of a manager of a division (or subsidiary) in one country with the performance of a manager of a division in another country. Even divisions that appear to be similar in terms of production may face very different economic, social, or political forces. International environmental conditions may be very different from, and more complex than, domestic conditions.[13] Environmental variables facing local managers of divisions include economic, legal, political, social, and educational factors. Some important economic variables are inflation, foreign exchange rates, taxes, and transfer prices. Legal and political actions also have differing impacts. For example, a country may not allow cash outflows, forcing the corporation to find ways to trade for the host country's output.[14] Educational variables vary from country to country as does the sophistication of the accounting system. Sociological and cultural variables affect how the multinational firm is treated by the subsidiary's country.

The existence of differing environmental factors makes interdivisional comparison of ROI potentially misleading. Suppose a U.S.-based MNC has three divisions located in Brazil, Canada, and Spain with the following information given in millions of dollars:

	Assets	Revenues	Net Income	Margin	Turnover	ROI*
Brazil	$10	$ 6	$ 3	0.50	0.60	0.30
Canada	18	13	10	0.77	0.72	0.55
Spain	15	10	6	0.60	0.67	0.40

*Rounded to two decimal places

On the basis of ROI, it appears that the manager of the Canadian subsidiary did the best job while the manager of the Brazilian subsidiary did the worst job. But is this a fair comparison? Brazil and Canada face very different legal, political, educational, and economic conditions. Inflation has been very high in South America compared with that in North America. Many South American firms have responded by adjusting reported financial amounts for inflation. Suppose in our example that the Canadian firm reports its assets at historical cost and the Brazilian firm adjusts its assets for inflation. If inflation during the period the assets have been held has averaged 100 percent (not an unreasonable assumption in a country that has faced monthly double-digit inflation rates for years), then the historical cost of the Brazilian assets would be $5 million. The calculation is as follows:

$$x + (100\%)x = \$10$$
$$x + 1.00x = \$10$$
$$2x = \$10$$
$$x = \$5$$

12. Gerhard G. Mueller, Helen Gernon, and Gary Meek, *Accounting: An International Perspective* (Homewood, Ill.: Richard D. Irwin, 1987).

13. Wagdy M. Abdallah, "Change the Environment or Change the System," *Management Accounting* (October 1986): 33–36.

14. One MNC faced with Philippine prohibitions on taking cash out of the country decided to hold its annual meeting in Manila. All corporate costs of the meeting (for example, hotel, meals) could then be paid in pesos earned by the MNC's Philippine subsidiary. Example taken from Jeff Madura, *International Financial Management*, 2d ed. (St. Paul, Minn.: West Publishing Company, 1989), 382.

If we restate the Brazilian subsidiary's assets to historical cost, then the ROI would be 60 percent ($\frac{3}{5} = .6$). If this computation is used, the Brazilian subsidiary appears to be the most successful, not the least. It should be noted that accounting for inflationary effects on income and assets is very complicated, and that the simple restatement just shown is not a comprehensive approach. Additionally, top management is typically aware of the existence of differential inflation rates. Still, the lack of consistency in internal reporting may obscure interdivisional comparisons, and the management accountant must be aware of this problem.

Other environmental factors can differ between countries. A minimum wage law in one country will restrict the manager's ability to affect labor costs. Another country may prevent the export of cash. Still others may have a well-educated workforce but poor infrastructure (transportation and communication facilities). All of these differing environmental factors must be taken into account when assessing managerial performance. Exhibit 13-2 lists some environmental factors that may make interdivisional comparisons misleading.

Political and Legal Factors Affecting Performance Evaluation

On June 3, 1989, the Chinese military opened fire on students in Beijing's Tiananmen Square. The world was stunned, glued to CNN and other media for news of the uprising. Would the Chinese government fall? Would an already repressive regime clamp down even more tightly? Half a world away, the controller of a manufacturer of custom oil field equipment weighed the Chinese events in making a business decision. Should he accept a Chinese letter of credit? His company's product was loaded on a ship in Houston, set to sail for China within the week. The sale was booked, and it was an important one, $3 million (the company's total annual sales revenue was $15 million). But was the letter of credit still good? Ordinarily, the Foreign Credit Insurance Association

13-2································

Exhibit
Environmental Factors
Affecting Performance
Evaluation in the
Multinational Firm*

Economic factors:
  Organization of central banking system
  Economic stability
  Existence of capital markets
  Currency restrictions

Political and legal factors:
  Quality, efficiency, and effectiveness of legal structure
  Effect of defense policy
  Impact of foreign policy
  Level of political unrest
  Degree of governmental control of business

Educational factors:
  Literacy rate
  Extent and degree of formal education and training systems
  Extent and degree of technical training
  Extent and quality of management development programs

Sociological factors:
  Social attitude toward industry and business
  Cultural attitude toward authority and persons in subordinate positions
  Cultural attitude toward productivity and achievement (work ethic)
  Social attitude toward material gain
  Cultural and racial diversity

*Adapted from Wagdy M. Abdallah, "Change the Environment or Change the System," *Management Accounting* (October 1986): 33–36. Used with the permission of the Institute of Management Accountants.

(underwriting insurance through the World Bank) guarantees letters of credit drawn on banks in approved countries. After the Tiananmen Square massacre, China was suspended from the approved countries list. If the Bank of China refused to pay, there would be no insurance, leaving the controller's company holding $3 million of worthless paper. The controller waited three days, evaluating the constantly changing situation, before canceling the shipment.[15]

The management accountant in the MNC must be aware of more than business and finance. Political and legal systems have important implications for the company. Sometimes the political system changes quickly, throwing the company into crisis mode, as it did for the controller in the Chinese letter of credit dilemma. Other times, the situation evolves more slowly. The shift in Spain's political system, from Franco's dictatorship to a democracy, is a case in point.

Management accounting has gained increased importance in Spain since the early 1980s. Part of the increased importance is due to the increase in competitive pressures. The profitability of many Spanish firms has eroded and firms see the need for more formal mechanisms of control, such as budgeting and standard costing. A second reason is the shift from a sheltered economy and political dictatorship to a democratic society. The previous dictatorship favored external methods of control, reinforcing a coercive political and social structure. The system was isolated from the rest of Europe, with a highly regulated economy. The shift to a more democratic society and a loosening of the regulatory environment has allowed Spanish firms more freedom of action in business, and has led to the need for management accounting control.[16]

Multiple Measures of Performance

Both residual income and ROI are important measures of managerial performance. However, they are both short-term measures. As such, the temptation exists for managers to trade off short-term benefits at the expense of the long-term well-being of the company. One way to discourage this myopic behavior is to use additional measures of performance that relate more closely to the long-term health of the division. For example, in addition to ROI and residual income, top management could look at such factors as market share, customer complaints, personnel turnover ratios, and personnel development. By letting lower-level managers know that attention to long-term factors is also vital, the tendency to overemphasize ROI or residual income should diminish.

Additionally, the use of ROI and RI in the evaluation of managerial performance in divisions of an MNC is subject to problems beyond those faced by a decentralized company that operates in only one country. It is particularly important, then, to take a responsibility accounting approach. That is, managers should be evaluated on the basis of factors under their control. This can be facilitated by using multiple measures of performance.

TRANSFER PRICING AND THE MULTINATIONAL FIRM

Objective 6

Discuss the role of transfer pricing in the multinational firm.

For the multinational firm, transfer pricing must accomplish two objectives: performance evaluation and optimal determination of income taxes.

Performance Evaluation

Divisions are frequently evaluated on the basis of net income and return on investment.[17] As is the case for any transfer price, the selling division wants a high transfer price that

15. Several months later, when China had been reinstated on the approved countries list, the company did make the sale.
16. Joan M. Amat Salas, "Management Accounting Systems in Spanish Firms," in the proceedings of the Second European Management Control Symposium, volume 1.
17. A study of 70 multinationals revealed that 80 percent used these measures. See Helen Gernon Morsicato, *Currency Translation and Performance Evaluation in Multinationals* (Ann Arbor: UMI Research Press, 1982).

will raise its net income, and the buying division wants a low transfer price that will raise its net income. But transfer prices in MNCs are frequently set by the parent company (as in the opening scenario), making the use of ROI and net income suspect. Because they are not under the control of divisional managers, in this case they can no longer serve as indicators of management performance.

Income Taxes and Transfer Pricing

If all countries had the same tax structure, then transfer prices would be set independently of taxes. However, as the opening scenario illustrated, this does not happen. Instead, there are high-tax countries (like the United States) and low-tax countries (such as the Cayman Islands). As a result, MNCs may use transfer pricing to shift costs to high-tax countries and shift revenues to low-tax countries.

Exhibit 13-3 illustrates this concept, as two transfer prices are set. The first transfer price is $100 as title for the goods passes from the Belgian subsidiary to the reinvoicing center in Puerto Rico. Because the first transfer price is equal to full cost, profit is zero and taxes on zero profit also equal zero. The second transfer price is set at $200 by the reinvoicing center in Puerto Rico. The transfer from Puerto Rico to the United States does result in profit, but this profit does not result in any tax because Puerto Rico has no corporate income taxes. Finally, the U.S. subsidiary sells the product to an external party at the $200 transfer price. Again, price equals cost so there is no profit on which to pay income taxes.

Consider what would have happened without the reinvoicing center. The goods would have gone directly from Belgium to the United States. If the transfer price was set at $200, the profit in Belgium would have been $100, subject to the 42 percent tax rate. Alternatively, if the transfer price set was $100, no Belgian tax would have been paid, but the U.S. subsidiary would have realized a profit of $100 and that would have been subject to the U.S. corporate income tax rate of 35 percent.

U.S.-based multinationals are subject to Internal Revenue Code Section 482 on the pricing of intercompany transactions. This section gives the IRS the authority to reallocate income and deductions among divisions if it believes that such reallocation will reduce potential tax evasion. Basically, Section 482 requires that sales be made at "arm's length." That is, the transfer price set should match the price that would be set if the transfer were being made by unrelated parties, adjusted for differences that have a measurable effect on the price. Differences include landing costs and marketing costs. Landing costs (freight, insurance, customs duties, and special taxes) can increase the allowable transfer price. Marketing costs are usually avoided for internal transfers and reduce the transfer price. The IRS allows three pricing methods that approximate

13-3

Exhibit
Use of Transfer Pricing to
Affect Taxes Paid

Action	Tax Impact
Belgian subsidiary of parent company produces a component at a cost of $100 per unit. Title to the component is transferred to a reinvoicing center* in Puerto Rico at a transfer price of $100 per unit.	42% tax rate $100 revenue − $100 cost = $0 Taxes paid = $0
Reinvoicing center in Puerto Rico, also a subsidiary of parent company, transfers title of component to U.S. subsidiary of parent company at a transfer price of $200 per unit.	0% tax rate $200 revenue − $100 cost = $100 Taxes paid = $0
U.S. subsidiary sells component to external company at $200 each.	35% tax rate $200 revenue − $200 cost = $0 Taxes paid = $0

*A reinvoicing center takes title to the goods but does not physically receive them. The primary objective of a reinvoicing center is to shift profits to divisions in low-tax countries.

arm's-length pricing. In order of preference, these are the *comparable uncontrolled price method*, the *resale price method*, and the *cost-plus method*.

comparable uncontrolled price method

The comparable uncontrolled price method essentially uses the market price. Suppose that the Belgian division of the company transfers a component to the U.S. division. If the component has a market price of $50 and shipping costs are $4, then the transfer price would be $54. If any costs are avoided as a result of internal transfer (for example, sales commissions of $5), these costs would be subtracted from the market price. In this case, the eventual transfer price would be calculated as follows:

Market price	$50
Add: Shipping	4
Less: Commissions	5
Transfer price	$49

resale price method

The resale price method is equal to the sales price received by the reseller less an appropriate markup. That is, the subsidiary purchasing a good for resale sets a transfer price equal to the resale price less a gross profit percentage. Suppose our U.S. division receives a product from the French division that can be resold in the United States for $60. The U.S. division typically receives a markup of 50 percent on cost. The transfer price would be $40 ($60 = cost + .5 cost; so, cost is $40).

cost-plus method

The cost-plus method is simply the cost-based transfer price. The manufacturing cost of the product is adjusted for any other expenses, such as shipping and duty. Suppose that the U.S. division produces a product that costs $25 to manufacture. It ships the product to the Brazilian division at a cost of $3. The transfer price is $28. This price can be adjusted for a markup on goods.

The determination of an arm's-length price is a difficult one. Many times, the transfer pricing situation facing a company does not "fit" any of the three preferred methods outlined. Then the IRS will permit a fourth method—a transfer price negotiated between the company and the IRS. The IRS, taxpayers, and the tax court have struggled with negotiated transfer prices for years. However, this type of negotiation occurs after the fact—after income tax returns have been submitted and the company is being audited. Recently, the IRS has authorized the issuance of advance pricing agreements

advance pricing agreements

(APAs) to assist taxpaying firms in determining whether or not a proposed transfer price is acceptable to the IRS in advance of tax filing. "An APA is an agreement between the IRS and a taxpayer on the pricing method to be applied in an international transaction. It can cover transfers of intangibles (such as royalties on licenses), sales of property, provision of services and other items. An APA is binding on both the IRS and the taxpayer for the years specified in the APA and is not made public."[18] Since the APA procedure is so new, neither the IRS nor the firms are sure of the informational requirements. Currently, the IRS may limit its advance rulings on transactions between U.S.-based companies and divisions in treaty countries, such as Australia, Canada, Japan, and the United Kingdom. For example, Apple Computer obtained an advance pricing agreement from the IRS on transfers of Apple products to its Australian subsidiary.[19]

Transfer-pricing abuses are illegal—if they can be proved to be abuses. Many examples of both foreign and U.S. firms charging unusual transfer prices exist. The IRS successfully showed that Toyota had been overcharging its U.S. subsidiary for cars, trucks, and parts sold in the United States. The effect was to lower Toyota's reported

18. "New Intercompany Pricing Rulings Create and Eliminate Tax Uncertainty," *Deloitte & Touche Review* (March 25, 1991): 6.
19. Roger Y. W. Tang, "Transfer Pricing in the 1990s," *Management Accounting* (February 1992): 22–26.

income substantially in the United States and increase income reported in Japan. The settlement reportedly approached $1 billion.[20]

The superroyalty provision of Section 482 was added in 1986 to require companies to value their intangibles more fairly. The IRS suspected that U.S. companies were transferring their intangibles (patents, copyrights, customer lists, and so on) to foreign subsidiaries at less than fair market value. For example, a U.S. pharmaceutical firm would develop a new drug and license its Puerto Rican subsidiary to produce it. The drug would then be purchased by the parent company for sale in the United States and a royalty would be charged to the Puerto Rican subsidiary. The royalty rate, taxable income to the parent, was low, but was similar to other third-party transactions. Thus, the IRS could not challenge it. The superroyalty provision changed this situation by linking the transfer price of the intangible to the income attributable to the intangible. "A Study on Intercompany Pricing," issued in 1990, requires much stricter documentation for the pricing of intangibles.[21]

The IRS also regulates the transfer pricing of foreign companies with U.S. subsidiaries. A U.S. company that is at least 25 percent foreign owned must keep extensive documentation of arm's-length transfer pricing.

Of course, MNCs are also subject to taxation by other countries as well as the United States. Since income taxes are virtually universal, consideration of income tax effects pervades management decision making. Canada, Japan, the European Community, and South Korea have all issued transfer pricing regulations within the past ten years.[22] This increased emphasis on transfer price justification may account for the increased use of market prices as the transfer price by MNCs. A survey of transfer pricing methods used by Fortune 500 companies in 1977 and 1990 shows that MNCs have reduced their reliance on cost-based transfer prices in favor of market-based transfer prices over the 13-year period.[23] Additionally, the most important environmental variable considered by MNCs in setting a transfer pricing policy is overall profit to the company—with overall profit including the income tax impact of intracompany transfers.

Managers may legally avoid taxes; they may not evade them. The distinction is important. Unfortunately, the difference between avoidance and evasion is less a line than a blurry gray area. While the situation depicted in Exhibit 13-3 is clearly abusive, other tax-motivated actions are not. For example, an MNC may legally decide to establish a needed research and development center within an existing subsidiary in a high-tax country since the costs are deductible. MNCs may also use tax-planning information systems that attempt to accomplish global tax minimization. This is not an easy task.

ETHICS IN THE INTERNATIONAL ENVIRONMENT

Objective 7

Discuss ethical issues that affect firms operating in the international environment.

Business ethics pose difficulties in a single-country context, but they pose far more problems in a global context. Richard J. Mahoney, former CEO of Monsanto, wrote, "As Monsanto becomes a global enterprise, we continually face the problem of different cultures and different cultural expectations. A service fee in one country is a bribe in another. Environmental laws can be extraordinarily strict in a country but not be enforced—and your industrial neighbors laugh at you for obeying the laws."[24] Given these difficulties, how does the modern corporation conduct business in an ethical manner? Is each country different? Is there a baseline? Some research indicates that human societies do share an ethical basis. However, there are some prerequisites for the establishment of an ethical business environment. These include: basic societal stability; legitimacy and accountability of government; legitimacy of private ownership and personal

20. "The Corporate Shell Game," *Newsweek*, 15 April 1991, 48–49.
21. Alfred M. King, "The IRS's New Neutron Bomb," *Management Accounting* (December 1992): 35–38.
22. Tang, "Transfer Pricing in the 1990s."
23. Tang.
24. Richard J. Mahoney, "Ethics: Doing the Right Thing at Monsanto," *Management Accounting* (June 1991): 24.

wealth; confidence in one's own and society's future; confidence in the ability to provide for one's family; and knowledge of how the system works and how to participate.[25]

For example, the Russian equivalent of insider trading or conflict of interest is *blat*. Blat is "an informal system of acquiring goods and services based on influence and back-door favors between acquaintances."[26] Blat is a natural extension of a culture that emphasized personal relationships over impersonal monetary transactions. Legal contracts are still in a rudimentary phase because enforcement is weak. As a result, personal relationships, which characterize blat, are a stronger basis for business dealings.

A strong underlying system is important for enforcing contracts, and provides the basis for confidence in ethical dealings. For some countries (for example, the United States and Western European countries) that system is legal with deviations punishable by law. For others (for example, Japan and countries in the Middle East), it is cultural and deviations are punished at least as severely by loss of honor. The importance of a strong underlying social code of conduct is clearly evident in illegal business dealings. For obvious reasons, you would be loathe to contact the police or district attorney about your purchase of low-quality marijuana. Similarly in India, where foreign currency exchange is tightly controlled, the black market in currency exchange is rife with unethical conduct. If you would like to exchange dollars for rupees, you can get a markedly better rate from the black market. However, the method of exchange requires you to first hand the black marketeer your rupees and then wait a minute or two while he goes to a back room to get the dollars. Sometimes, he returns with the requisite number of dollars, sometimes not. As an Indian friend of ours said, "Then what? You can hardly go to the police!" Indians do not face this risky situation in a bank.

Other ethical problems with bribes and differing business laws exist. U.S. companies that contract with overseas firms may find themselves the target of unfavorable publicity on use of child labor. They find themselves in a quandary. Do they tell foreign companies what age worker they can hire? Our own history includes immigrant children of ten and twelve at work in the steel mills of Bethlehem, Pennsylvania. What about bribes to government officials? The stories of rampant bribery of Middle Eastern officials are legendary. In some countries, these bribes are a necessary part of doing business. Similarly, insider trading is not illegal in Europe, but is definitely illegal in the United States.

To go back to our original question, what is a company to do when faced with conflicting sets of ethics? What if an action is legally permissible? Early in Monsanto's history, it faced the possibility of bankruptcy. John Queeny, the company's founder, was advised to "close down the plant, lay off all the workers, and then open up with new people at lower wages. 'Since when,' Mr. Queeny asked, 'do we lie to our employees?'" As a result, Monsanto holds that doing the right thing is nonnegotiable.[27] Perhaps the answer is to ask, is the action right legally? And then, is the action right morally?

25. Cynthia Scharf, "The Wild, Wild East: Everyone's a Capitalist in Russia Today, and Nobody Knows the Rules," *Business Ethics* (November/December 1992): 23.
26. Scharf, 22.
27. Scharf, 24.

SUMMARY OF LEARNING OBJECTIVES

1. Explain the role of the management accountant in the international environment.

The management accountant provides financial and business expertise. The job of the management accountant in the international firm is made more challenging by the ambiguous and ever-changing nature of global business. He or she must stay up-to-date in a variety of business areas ranging from information systems, to marketing, to management, to politics, and economics. In addition, the management accountant must be familiar with the fi-

nancial accounting rules of the countries in which his or her firm operates.

2. Discuss the varying levels of involvement that firms can undertake in international trade.

Companies involved in international business may structure their activities in three major ways. They may engage in import and export activities. They may purchase wholly owned subsidiaries. They may participate in joint ventures.

3. Explain the ways management accountants can manage foreign currency risk.

Management accountants must be aware of the potential exposure of their firms to transaction risk, economic risk, and translation risk. They may hedge to limit exposure to these risks.

4. Explain why multinational firms choose to decentralize.

MNCs choose to decentralize for much the same reasons domestic companies choose to decentralize. The reasons are numerous. Companies decentralize because local managers can make better decisions using local information. Local managers can also provide a more timely response to changing conditions. For large, diversified companies, decentralization is necessary because it is impossible for any one central manager to be fully knowledgeable about all products and markets. Other reasons include training and motivating local managers and freeing up top management from day-to-day operating conditions so that they can spend time on more long-range activities, such as strategic planning.

5. Explain how environmental factors can affect performance evaluation in the multinational firm.

Environmental factors are those social, economic, political, legal, and cultural factors that differ from country to country and that managers cannot affect. These factors, however, do affect profits and ROI. Therefore, evaluation of the divisional manager should be separated from evaluation of the subsidiary.

6. Discuss the role of transfer pricing in the multinational firm.

When one division of a company produces a product that can be used in production by another division, transfer pricing exists. The transfer price is revenue to the selling division and cost to the buying division. As is the case with domestic companies, MNCs may use transfer prices in performance evaluation. MNCs with subsidiaries in both high-tax and low-tax countries may use transfer pricing to shift costs to the high-tax countries (where their deductibility will lower tax payments) and to shift revenues to low-tax countries.

7. Discuss ethical issues that affect firms operating in the international environment.

MNCs face ethical issues that do not arise for domestic companies. Other countries have business customs and laws that differ from those of the home country. The firm must determine whether a particular custom is merely a different way of doing business, or is a violation of its own code of ethics.

K EY TERMS

Advance pricing agreements 544	Currency risk management 533	Hedging 535	Resale price method 544
Comparable uncontrolled price method 544	Economic risk 533	Joint venture 532	Spot rate 533
Cost-plus method 544	Exchange gain 534	Maquiladoras 532	Tariff 529
Currency appreciation 533	Exchange loss 534	Multinational corporation (MNC) 529	Transaction risk 533
Currency depreciation 533	Exchange rates 533	Outsourcing 531	Translation (or accounting) risk 533
	Foreign trade zones 529		
	Forward contract 535		

R EVIEW PROBLEM

Golo, Inc. has two manufacturing plants, one in Singapore and the other in San Antonio. The San Antonio plant is located in a foreign trade zone. On March 1, Golo received a large order from a Japanese customer. The order is for ¥10,000,000 to be paid on receipt of the goods, scheduled for June 1. Golo assigned this order to the San Antonio plant; however, one necessary component for the order is to be manufactured by the Singapore plant. The component will be transferred to San Antonio on April 1 using a cost-plus transfer price of $10,000 (U.S. dollars). Typically, 2 percent of the Singapore parts are defective. The U.S. tariff on the component parts is 30 percent. The carrying cost for Golo is 15 percent per year.

The following spot rates for $1 U.S. are as follows:

	Exchange Rates for $1	
	Yen	Singapore Dollars
March 1	107.00	1.60
April 1	107.50	1.55
June 1	107.60	1.50

REQUIRED:

1. What is the total cost of the imported parts from Singapore to the San Antonio plant in U.S. dollars?
2. Suppose the San Antonio plant were not located in a foreign trade zone, what would be the total cost of the imported parts from Singapore?

3. How much does Golo expect to receive from the Japanese customer in U.S. dollars using the spot rate at the time of the order?
4. How much does Golo expect to receive from the Japanese customer in U.S. dollars using the spot rate at the time of payment?
5. Suppose that on March 1, the forward rate for June 1 delivery of $1 for yen is 107.20. If Golo's policy is to hedge foreign currency transactions, what is the amount Golo expects to receive on June 1 in dollars?

Solution

1.

Transfer price	$10,000
Tariff ($9,800 × .3)	2,940
Total cost	$12,940

The transfer price was set in U.S. dollars, so there is no currency exchange involved for the San Antonio plant.

The San Antonio plant is in a foreign trade zone, so the 30 percent tariff is paid only on the good parts, costing $9,800 ($10,000 × .98).

2. If the San Antonio plant were located outside the foreign trade zone, the cost of the imported parts would be as follows:

Transfer price	$10,000
Tariff ($10,000 × .3)	3,000
Carrying cost of tariff*	75
Total cost	$13,075

*$3,000 × $\frac{2}{12}$ × .15 = $75

3. On March 1, Golo expects to receive $93,458 $(\frac{¥10,000,000}{107})$.
4. On June 1, Golo expects to receive $92,937 $(\frac{¥10,000,000}{107.60})$.
5. If Golo hedges, the forward rate is used, and the amount to be received on June 1 is $93,284 $(\frac{¥10,000,000}{107.20})$.

QUESTIONS FOR WRITING AND DISCUSSION

1. How do international issues affect the role of the management accountant?
2. What is a foreign trade zone and what advantages does it offer U.S. companies?
3. Define *outsourcing* and discuss why companies may outsource various functions.
4. What are joint ventures and why do companies engage in them?
5. What are maquiladoras? Why have so many U.S. firms joined forces with maquiladoras?
6. What is an exchange rate for currency? What is the difference between a spot rate and future rate?
7. What is transaction risk? economic risk? translation risk?
8. Define *currency appreciation*. What impact does currency appreciation have on a company's ability to import goods?
9. What impact does currency appreciation have on a company's ability to export its goods?
10. Mexico is considering devaluing the peso versus the dollar. You are the controller for a company considering production in Mexico through the maquiladora program. How does this news affect the decision? Now suppose you are a local labor union leader, how do you take the news?
11. What is hedging? If a company imports raw materials, payable in full in 90 days in the foreign currency, why might the company want to hedge?
12. The performance of the subsidiary manager is equivalent to the performance of a subsidiary. Do you agree? Explain.
13. What environmental factors can affect divisional performance in a multinational firm?
14. What is the purpose of Internal Revenue Code Section 482? What four methods of transfer pricing are acceptable under this section?

WARM-UP EXERCISES

This section provides short warm-up exercises based on the examples in the chapter. Each warm-up exercise gives the page number on which the text example can be found. You may want to refer to the text example to see how the exercise can be set up and solved.

W13-1
Payment of Duty and Duty-related Carrying Cost
LO 2
p. 530

Taylor Manufacturing and Distribution owns a factory located close to, but not inside, a foreign trade zone. The plant imports volatile chemicals that are used in the manufacture of chemical reagents for laboratories. Each year, Taylor imports about $850,000 of chemicals subject to a 10 percent tariff when shipped into the United States. About 25 percent of the imported chemicals are lost through evaporation during the manufacturing process. In addition, Taylor has a carrying cost of 12 percent per year associated with the duty payment. On average, the chemicals are held in inventory for six months.

REQUIRED:
1. How much duty is paid annually by Taylor?
2. What is the carrying cost associated with the payment of duty?

W13-2
Foreign Trade Zone Cost Savings
LO 2
p. 530

Refer to W13-1. Suppose that Taylor is considering building a new plant inside a foreign trade zone to replace their chemical manufacturing plant.

REQUIRED:
1. How much duty will be paid per year by the factory located inside the foreign trade zone?
2. How much in duty and duty-related carrying costs will be saved by relocating inside the foreign trade zone?

W13-3
Exchange Gains and Losses
LO 3
pp. 534–535

On March 1, Scherson Import-Export Company purchased merchandise from a Mexican firm costing 6,000 pesos. Payment was due, in pesos, on June 1. The exchange rates of pesos for $1 were as follows:

March 1	$1 = 6 pesos
June 1	$1 = 6.4 pesos

REQUIRED:
1. What is the liability in dollars on March 1?
2. What is the liability in dollars on June 1?
3. If Scherson pays on June 1, is there an exchange gain or loss? How much is it?

W13-4
Hedging
LO 3
pp. 534–536

Refer to W13-3. Suppose that Scherson also sells to Mexican firms under the same terms—payment is made in pesos three months after purchase. Scherson sells merchandise to Javier, SA, on March 1, for 60,000 pesos. Payment will be made in pesos on June 1. Scherson can purchase a contract to exchange 60,000 pesos into dollars on June 1 at a forward rate of 6.03 pesos.

REQUIRED:
1. What is the value of the receivable in dollars on March 1?
2. What is the dollar value of the amount Javier pays Scherson on June 1?
3. What is the exchange loss for Scherson if no hedging occurs?
4. If Scherson purchases the hedging contract on March 1, what is the premium expense?
5. What is the net savings to Scherson by hedging?

W13-5
Transfer Pricing
LO 6
p. 543

Global, Inc. transfers a product between its U.S. division and its Canadian division. The product sells for $30 in the United States. The cost of shipping to Canada is $2 and Canadian duty is $3. The U.S. division pays approximately $.50 per unit for advertising and related selling expenses.

REQUIRED: Using the comparable uncontrolled price method, calculate the transfer price.

W13-6
Transfer Pricing
LO 6
p. 543

The U.S. division of Global, Inc. purchases a product from the Canadian division, which sells for $45 per unit in the United States. The U.S. division typically has a 40 percent markup on goods. Calculate the transfer price under the resale price method.

E XERCISES

E13-1
Preparation for Becoming a Management Accountant in an MNC
LO 1

A close friend of yours is majoring in accounting and would like to work for a multinational corporation upon graduation. Your friend is unsure just what courses would help prepare for that goal and wants your advice.

REQUIRED: Advise your friend on the kind of courses that might prepare him or her for this goal.

E13-2
Foreign Trade Zones
LO 2

Kauffman Import-Export, Inc. is considering opening a new warehouse to serve the Midwest region. Darla Jones, controller for Kauffman Import-Export, has been reading about the advantages of foreign trade zones. She wonders if locating in one would be of benefit to her company, which imports about 90 percent of its merchandise. Darla estimates that the new warehouse will store imported merchandise costing about $1,200,000 per year. Inventory shrinkage at the warehouse (due to breakage and mishandling) is about 6 percent of the total. The average tariff rate on these imports is 15 percent.

REQUIRED: Will locating the warehouse in a foreign trade zone save Kauffman Import-Export money? How much?

E13-3
Currency Exchange
LO 3

Merz Distributors, Inc., based in Kokomo, Indiana, is an export-import firm. On June 1, Merz purchased goods from a British company costing £80,000. Payment is due in pounds on September 1. The spot rate on June 1 was 1.60 dollars per pound, and on September 1 it was 1.54 dollars per pound.

REQUIRED:
1. Did the dollar strengthen or weaken against the pound during the three-month period?
2. How much would Merz have to pay for the purchase (in dollars) if it paid on June 1? How much would Merz have to pay for the purchase (in dollars) if it paid on September 1?

E13-4
Exchange Gains and Losses
LO 3

Refer to E13-3. If Merz paid for the purchase using the September 1 spot rate, what was the exchange gain or loss?

E13-5
Hedging
LO 3

Lau Company engages in many foreign currency transactions. Company policy is to hedge exposure to exchange gains and losses using forward contracts. On July 1, Lau sold merchandise to a German company for 100,000 deutsche marks (DM), payable on September 30. Exchange rates of $1 for DM were as follows:

Spot rate July 1	1.40
Forward rate September 30	1.36
Spot rate September 30	1.39

REQUIRED:
1. Did Lau Company buy or sell marks for future delivery?
2. According to company policy, how many dollars did Lau receive for this sale?

E13-6
Currency Exchange Rates
LO 3

Suppose you are in the market for a BMW and are considering going to Germany to purchase it, drive it around Europe for a couple of weeks, and then ship it home. The car of your choice costs

DM 65,000. When you first looked into the possibility of buying a car in Germany, the rate of exchange was DM 1.4 to $1; now the exchange rate is DM 1.6 to $1.

REQUIRED: Has the dollar appreciated or depreciated against the German mark? Would this news about the exchange rate change please or displease you? Why?

**E13-7
Divisional
Performance
Evaluation in the
MNC**
LO 5

Bianca Phillips, vice-president of Electronics for Consolidated, Inc., was reviewing the latest results for two divisions. The first, located in Baja California, Mexico, had posted net income of $150,000 on assets of $1,500,000. The second, in Punt-on-Thames, England, showed net income of $230,000 on assets of $2,000,000.

REQUIRED:
1. Calculate the ROI for each division.
2. Can a meaningful comparison be made of the British division's ROI with the Mexican division's ROI? Explain.

**E13-8
Transfer Pricing in
the MNC**
LO 6

Carnover, Inc. manufactures a broad line of industrial and consumer products. One of its plants is located in Madrid, Spain, and another in Singapore. The Madrid plant is operating at 85 percent capacity. Softness in the market for its main product, electric motors, has led to predictions of further softening of the market, leading perhaps to production at 65 percent capacity. If that happens, workers will have to be laid off and one wing of the factory closed. The Singapore plant manufactures heavy-duty industrial mixers that use the motors manufactured by the Madrid plant as an integral component. Demand for the mixers is strong. Price and cost information for the mixers is as follows:

Price	$2,200
Direct materials	630
Direct labor	125
Variable overhead	250
Fixed overhead	100

Fixed overhead is based on an annual budgeted amount of $3,500,000 and budgeted production of 35,000 mixers. The direct materials cost includes the cost of the motor at $200 (market price). The Madrid plant capacity is 20,000 motors per year. Cost data are as follows:

Direct materials	$ 75
Direct labor	60
Variable overhead	60
Fixed overhead	100

Fixed overhead is based on budgeted fixed overhead of $2,000,000.

REQUIRED:
1. What is the maximum transfer price the Singapore plant would accept?
2. What is the minimum transfer price the Madrid plant would accept?
3. Consider the following environmental factors:

Madrid Plant	Singapore Plant
Full employment is very important	Cheap labor is plentiful.
The local government prohibits layoffs without permission (which is rarely granted).	Accounting practices are based on the British-American model, oriented toward decision-making needs of creditors and
Accounting practices are legalistic and conservative, designed to ensure compliance with government objectives.	investors.

How might these environmental factors impact the transfer pricing decision?

E13-9
Transfer Pricing
LO 6

Avery Company has a division in the United States that produces wheels for automobiles. These wheels are transferred to an automobile division in Sweden. The wheels can be (and are) sold externally in the United States for $28 each. It costs $3 per wheel for shipping and $4 per wheel for import duties. When the wheels are sold externally, Avery spends $2 per wheel for commissions and an average of $.50 per wheel for advertising.

REQUIRED:
1. Which Section 482 method should be used to calculate the allowable transfer price?
2. Using the appropriate Section 482 method, calculate the transfer price.

PROBLEMS

P13-1
Decentralization in the MNC
LO 4

Latest Styles Inc. (LSI) supplies a limited range of garments to several boutiques in New York. LSI produces these garments in a small factory owned and operated in Nuevo Laredo, Mexico. LSI has been more responsive to the boutiques' needs for delivery of changing styles than Asian garment producers, whose shipments take 30 days. As a result, several other boutiques have approached LSI as a potential supplier. Victoria Johnson, president of LSI, has decided that expansion will be required to meet the needs of these additional boutiques.

After discussing the situation with her colleagues, Frank Corrigan, the controller, and Tom Conway, the production and shipping manager, it is agreed that the expansion should be undertaken. Since Victoria makes most of the decisions that involve day-to-day operations and does the majority of the designing, Frank and Tom are concerned about her managing the expansion at the same time. They expressed this concern in a meeting with Victoria, who agreed that the additional workload resulting from the planned expansion would be too great for her to handle. Accordingly, she has decided to delegate some of these increased functions to Frank and Tom.

During these discussions, Victoria added that, in view of the Mexican–American negotiations to establish a North American free-trade zone, she is considering even further expansion to increase the range of garments produced and also to supply boutiques in Philadelphia and Boston. Consequently, she is considering further decentralization of the business, as expanded operations in Mexico, increased product lines, and supplying two new geographical areas will require hands-on, operational management at these locations to keep up with inventory needs and differing local fashion trends. Both Frank and Tom are capable of handling these operational duties although they will need to hire new managers to assist them in the expansion and decentralization.

REQUIRED:
1. Decentralization is the extent to which power and authority are systematically delegated throughout an organization.
   a. Discuss the factors that generally determine the degree of decentralization in an organization.
   b. Describe several benefits to an organization that can generally be derived from decentralization.
   c. Discuss several disadvantages to an organization from decentralization.
2. How does NAFTA affect Victoria Johnson's decision? (CMA Adapted)

P13-2
Exporting;
Maquiladoras;
Foreign Trade Zones
LO 2

Paladin Company manufactures plain paper fax machines in a small factory in Minnesota. Sales have increased by 50 percent in each of the past three years, as Paladin has expanded its market from the United States to Canada and Mexico. As a result, the Minnesota factory is at capacity. Beryl Adams, president of Paladin, has examined the situation and developed the following alternatives:

1. Add a permanent second shift at the plant. However, the semiskilled workers who assemble the fax machines are in short supply, and the wage rate of $15 per hour would probably have to be increased across the board to $18 per hour in order to attract sufficient workers from out of town. The total wage increase (including fringe benefits) would amount to $125,000. The heavier use of plant facilities would lead to increased plant maintenance and small tool cost.
2. Open a new plant and locate it in Mexico. Wages (including fringe benefits) would average $3.50 per hour. Investment in plant and equipment would amount to $300,000.

3. Open a new plant and locate it in a foreign trade zone, possibly in Dallas. Wages would be somewhat lower than in Minnesota, but higher than in Mexico. The advantages of postponing tariff payments on imported parts could amount to $50,000 per year.

REQUIRED: Advise Beryl of the advantages and disadvantages of each of her alternatives.

P13-3
Foreign Currency
Exchange; Hedging
LO 3

Storage Lo-Tech, Inc. manufactures custom wooden cabinets for garages and storage sheds on a job-order basis. SLT has invested heavily in precision woodworking equipment. As a result, the company has a reputation for producing excellent quality interior cabinets. Sales are made in all 50 states. On July 1, SLT received orders from contractors in France and Japan. Lee Burke, president and co-owner of SLT, was delighted. The French order is for cabinets priced at $30,000. The order is due in Marseilles on September 1, with payment due in full on October 1. The Japanese order is for cabinets priced at $45,000. It is due in Tokyo on August 1, with payment due in full on October 1. Both orders are to be paid in the customer's currency. The French customer has a reputation in the industry for late payment, and it could take as long as six months. Lee has never received payment in foreign currency before. He had his accountant prepare the following table of exchange rates:

	Exchange Rate for $1	
	French Franc	Yen
Spot Rate	5.4235	107.60
30 Day Forward	5.4456	107.61
90 Day Forward	5.4825	107.60
180 Day Forward	5.5300	107.55

REQUIRED:
1. If the price of the cabinets is set using the spot rate as of July 1, how many francs does Lee expect to be paid on October 1? How many yen does he expect on October 1?
2. Using the number of francs and yen calculated in requirement 1, how many dollars does Lee expect to receive on October 1? Will he receive that much? What is the value of hedging in this situation?

P13-4
Transfer Pricing
LO 6

The U.S. division of MegaBig, Inc. has excess capacity. MegaBig's European division, located in Lisbon, has offered to buy a component that would increase the U.S. division's utilization of capacity from 70 to 80 percent. The component has an outside market in the United States with a unit selling price of $12. The variable costs of production for the component are $6. Landing costs total $2 per unit, and an internal transfer avoids $1.25 per unit of variable marketing costs. The European and U.S. divisions agree on a transfer price of $9. The European division can purchase the component locally for $12.

REQUIRED: Suppose you have scheduled a meeting with an IRS representative. What arguments would you make for an advance pricing agreement that would permit the use of the $9 price?

P13-5
Transfer Pricing
LO 6

Audio-tech, Inc. manufactures stereos and boom boxes at plants in Idaho, Minnesota, and Alabama. It also has distribution centers in Brussels, Belgium and Montreal, Canada. The market price of the Model 655 cd+ stereo is $425. The unit costs are as follows:

Variable product costs	$135
Fixed factory overhead	70
Landing costs (Canada)	20
Landing costs (Belgium)	25
Avoidable marketing costs	35

Audio-tech has set a transfer price of $425 to both the Canadian and Belgian divisions.

REQUIRED:

1. Calculate the transfer price under the comparable uncontrolled price method for both the Canadian and Belgian transfers.
2. Will the IRS be concerned about the transfer price actually set by Audio-tech?

P13-6
Involvement in
International Trade
LO 2

Makenzie Gibson is the owner of Healthblend Nutritional Supplements. (We first met her in the scenario to Chapter 6.) Makenzie feels that the time is ripe for expansion; she would like to begin selling in Europe, Canada, and Mexico. Her major problem right now is to determine how best to do that.

REQUIRED: Advise Makenzie of the ways in which she could become involved in international trade.

 ANAGERIAL DECISION CASES

C13-1
Transfer Pricing and
Ethical Issues
LO 6, LO 7

Reread the scenario at the beginning of the chapter.

REQUIRED:

1. Do you think that the tax minimization scheme described to Debbie Kishimoto is in harmony with the ethical behavior that should be displayed by top corporate executives? Why or why not? What would you do if you were Debbie?
2. Apparently, the tax department of Paterson Company has been strongly involved in developing the tax-minimization scheme. Assume that the accountants responsible for the decision are CMAs and members of the IMA, subject to the IMA standards of ethical conduct. Review the IMA standards for ethical conduct in Chapter 1. Are any of these standards being violated by the accountants in Paterson's tax department? If so, identify them. What should these tax accountants do if requested to develop a questionable tax-minimization scheme?

C13-2
Transfer Pricing;
International Setting;
Tax Implications
LO 6

Valley Electronics Corporation is a large multinational firm involved in the manufacture and marketing of various electronic components. Recently, Rhonda Cooper, president of Valley Electronics, received some complaints from divisional managers about the company's international transfer pricing practices. Essentially, the managers believed that they had less control over how prices were set than they wished. After reviewing some of the practices, Rhonda found that three different methods were being used: (1) the comparable uncontrolled price method, (2) the resale price method, and (3) the cost-plus method. Unable to determine why there were three methods and exactly how each worked, Rhonda requested a meeting with Wayne Sill, vice-president of finance.

Rhonda: "Wayne, I need to respond to our divisional managers' concerns about the transfer pricing policies that we apply to goods shipped internationally. It appears that three methods are being used and that they differ across divisions."

Wayne: "The three methods used are the ones allowed by Section 482 of the Internal Revenue Code. Which method is applicable depends on the operating circumstances surrounding the transfer of a particular component."

Rhonda: "So the way we price these internal transfers is driven to some degree, at least, by tax laws. Interesting. Perhaps you can describe for me how each method works and what conditions dictate that we use that method."

Wayne: "The basic concept underlying any transfer price we use is the notion of an arm's-length price. Ideally, an arm's-length price is the price that an unrelated party would pay for the good being transferred. The IRS allows four methods to determine the arm's-length price. We use three of those methods. The comparable uncontrolled method is based on market price. If the good being transferred has an external market, then the transfer price should be the price paid by an unrelated party, adjusted for differences that have a measurable effect on the price."

Rhonda: "What kind of differences? Give me some examples."

Wayne: "Well, the market price can be adjusted for differences such as landing costs (freight, insurance, customs duties, and special taxes) and marketing costs (commissions and advertising can be avoided with internal transfers). Adding landing costs and subtracting avoidable marketing costs are allowable adjustments to the market price."

Rhonda: "I see. What happens if we sell the product to a related buyer who then resells it without any further processing? Or if the transferred good has no outside market at all?"

Wayne: "For the resale scenario, we use the resale price method. We take the resale price realized by our marketing divisions and adjust that price for the markup percentage and any differences like the ones we mentioned for the comparable uncontrolled method. We work back from the third-party selling price to obtain an allowable transfer price."

Rhonda: "How is the markup determined?"

Wayne: "It corresponds to the percentage of gross profit earned by the reseller or the gross profit percentage earned by other parties who buy and resell similar products."

Rhonda: "I'm beginning to understand why we have three different methods. We have divisions that fit both of the first two types. We also have some transfers that have no outside market, nor do they have any potential for resale. These goods are simply used as components of other products that are sold. Is this where cost-plus pricing is used?"

Wayne: "Absolutely. In this case, the transfer price is defined as the costs of production plus an appropriate gross profit percentage, with adjustments for differences such as landing costs."

Rhonda: "How do we define the appropriate gross profit percentage?"

Wayne: "Well, it could be the gross profit percentage earned by the seller on the sale of the final product. Or if we can obtain the information, it could be the gross profit percentage earned by another party on a similar product."

Rhonda: "Seems to me that the cost-plus method could be used for all three settings. Why don't we do that so that we have some uniformity in the way we compute transfer prices?"

Wayne: "There is a problem. If the requirements are met for any one of the methods, then it must be used—unless we can show that another method is more appropriate. The burden of proof is on us. I doubt that uniformity would be an acceptable justification. If the IRS audits us and determines that the transfer price does not fairly reflect profits recognized in the United States, it can reallocate corporate income for purposes of taxation."

REQUIRED:

1. Assume that Valley Electronics transfers a component from a U.S. division to a German division for $11.70. The landing costs are $2.50 per unit and the avoidable commissions and advertising total $0.50 per unit. The component has a market price within the United States of $10. Is the company complying with the comparable uncontrolled price method? Would the IRS be concerned if the transfer price is greater than the market price after adjustments? Why or why not?

2. Assume that a manufacturing division in the United States transfers a component to a marketing division for resale. The resale price is $8, the gross profit percentage (gross profit divided by sales) is 25 percent, and landing costs total $1.20 per unit. Suppose that the actual transfer price (excluding landing costs) is $4.50. Should the company continue transferring at $4.50?

3. Suppose that a U.S. division has excess capacity. A European division has offered to buy a component that would increase the U.S. division's utilization of its capacity. The component has an outside market in the United States with a unit selling price of $12. The variable costs of production for the component are $6. Landing costs total $2 per unit, and an internal transfer avoids $1.25 per unit of marketing costs. The European division can purchase the component locally for $12. Ignoring income taxes, what is the minimum price that the European division should pay for the component (including landing costs)? the maximum price? Assuming that the joint benefit is split equally, what is the transfer price? Now discuss the impact of the Section 482 regulations on this decision. (*Hint:* Consider Wayne's closing statement.) (CMA Adapted)

C13-3
Research Assignment

Use the library to research the development of the North American Free Trade Agreement (NAFTA). What are the implications of its passage for companies located in the United States? in Mexico? in Canada?

PART 3

Managerial Decision Making

Learning Objectives

After studying Chapter 14, you should be able to:

1. Explain the differences between variable and absorption costing.

2. Explain how variable costing is useful in evaluating the performance of managers.

3. Prepare a segmented income statement based on a variable-costing approach and explain how this format can be used with activity-based costing to assess customer profitability.

4. Explain how variable costing can be used in planning and control.

CHAPTER

Variable Costing and Segmental Reporting: Traditional and ABC Approaches

SCENARIO

K athy Wise had been the manager of the Medical Supplies Division for three years. In the first year, the net income for the division had shown a substantial increase over the prior year. Her second year saw an even greater increase. Kathy's boss, the vice-president for operations, was extremely pleased and promised her a $5,000 bonus if the division showed a similar increase in profits for the upcoming year. Kathy was elated. She was completely confident that the goal could be met. Sales contracts were already well ahead of last year's performance, and she knew that there would be no increases in costs.

At the end of the third year, Kathy received the data regarding operations for the first three years. Upon examining the operating data, Kathy was pleased. Sales had

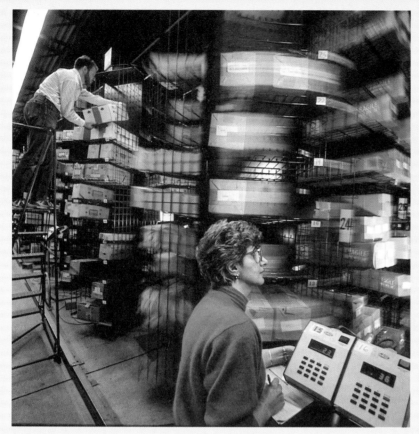

increased by 20 percent over the previous year, and costs had been kept stable. However, when she saw the yearly income statements, she was dismayed and perplexed. Instead of seeing a significant increase in income for the third year, she saw a small decrease. Surely, the accounting department had made an error.

Freda Mathews, controller for the Medical Supplies Division, met with Kathy to explain the anomalous results.

"Kathy, there's been no mistake here. Net income is lower this year than in the past two years. It's easily explained by looking at the changes in inventory."

"Inventory? What's that got to do with income? We did a terrific job managing inventory this year. It had built up in the past two years, and I got sales up and inventory down. That's good, not bad!"

"Sure, Kathy, from an operating perspective. But you have to realize that inventory carries cost with it. That cost doesn't appear on the income statement until the stuff is sold. Then it flows through income and reduces it."

"That's crazy! Do you mean that I'm going to lose my bonus even though we sold off our inventory and met cost and revenue projections?"

"Well, Kathy, I'm sorry about your bonus, but the income figures are solid. I'd be happy to spend a little time with you explaining how we account for income. We use absorption costing; it's required by GAAP. There is another possibility, variable costing, and it sounds to me like you are implicitly using that method."

"There are two ways to figure income? Does it make a difference?"

"Oh yes. Variable costing doesn't permit inventory changes to affect income. So your income this year would be higher under variable costing. However, your income the past couple of years would have been lower. So over the long run, it evens out."

"Hmmm. I wonder if I could get the VP to take a look at variable costing?"

Questions to Think About

1. Why do firms calculate income? What information does it provide?
2. What costs go into inventory? How can they affect income?
3. What is GAAP and how does it affect the income statement of the Medical Supplies Division?
4. Why doesn't Kathy understand accounting? Should she?
5. What do you suppose Kathy's chances are for getting the vice-president to consider evaluating her performance on the basis of variable, instead of absorption, costing?

VARIABLE COSTING AND ABSORPTION COSTING: AN ANALYSIS AND COMPARISON

Objective I

Explain the differences between variable and absorption costing.

In the introductory scenario, two methods of computing income are identified, one based on variable costing and the other based on full or absorption costing. These are costing methods because they refer to the way in which product costs are determined. Recall that *product costs* are inventoried; *period costs* are expensed in the period incurred. The difference between variable and absorption costing hinges on the treatment of one particular cost: fixed factory overhead.

Variable costing stresses the difference between fixed and variable manufacturing costs. Variable costing assigns only variable manufacturing costs to the product; these costs include direct materials, direct labor, and variable overhead. Fixed overhead is treated as a period expense and is excluded from the product cost. The rationale for this is that fixed overhead is a cost of capacity, or staying in business. Once the period is over, any benefits provided by capacity have expired and should not be inventoried. Under variable costing, fixed overhead of a period is seen as expiring that period and is charged in total against the revenues of the period.[1]

variable costing

absorption costing

Absorption costing assigns *all* manufacturing costs to the product. Direct materials, direct labor, variable overhead, and fixed overhead define the cost of a product. Thus, under absorption costing, fixed overhead is viewed as a product cost, not a period cost. Under this method, fixed overhead is assigned to the product through the use of a predetermined fixed overhead rate and is not expensed until the product is sold. In other words, fixed overhead is an inventoriable cost. Exhibit 14-1 illustrates the classification of costs as product or period costs under absorption and variable costing.

Currently, absorption costing is required for external reporting. The FASB, the IRS, and other regulatory bodies do not accept variable costing as a product-costing method for external reporting. Yet, as the dialogue between Kathy and Freda suggests, variable costing can supply vital cost information for decision making and control, information not supplied by absorption costing. For *internal* application, variable costing is an invaluable managerial tool. Let's take a closer look at the way the two costing methods affect inventory valuation and income determination.

Inventory Valuation

Of course, different product-costing methods will affect the value of goods stored in inventory. An example will make the inventory valuations of absorption and variable costing more concrete. During the most recent year, Fairchild Company had the following data associated with the product it makes:

1. Variable costing is more commonly known as *direct costing*. Direct costing, however, is a misnomer. Not all variable manufacturing costs are direct product costs. For example, variable overhead, by definition, consists of *indirect* manufacturing costs. Clearly, the more descriptive name for this method is *variable costing*, which is the term that will be used in this text.

14-1

Exhibit
Classification of Costs as Product or Period Costs under Absorption and Variable Costing

	Absorption Costing	Variable Costing
Product Costs	Direct materials	Direct materials
	Direct labor	Direct labor
	Variable overhead	Variable overhead
	Fixed overhead	
Period Costs		Fixed overhead
	Selling expense	Selling expense
	Administrative expense	Administrative expense

Units, beginning inventory	—
Units produced	10,000
Units sold ($300 per unit)	8,000
Normal volume	10,000
Variable costs per unit:	
Direct materials	$ 50
Direct labor	100
Variable overhead*	50
Variable selling and administrative	10
Fixed costs:	
Fixed overhead*	$250,000
Fixed selling and administrative	100,000

*Estimated and actual overhead are equal.

Recall that the unit product cost obtained under each method differs. Variable costing inventories only variable manufacturing costs, so each unit of product for Fairchild costs $200. Absorption costing includes all manufacturing costs and each unit of product costs $225. The computations follow:

	Variable Costing	Absorption Costing
Direct labor	$100	$100
Direct materials	50	50
Variable overhead	50	50
Fixed overhead ($250,000/10,000)	—	25
Total per unit cost	$200	$225

Of course, the difference in unit costs affects the amount shown on the balance sheet. Fairchild had no beginning inventory and produced 2,000 units more than it sold. Therefore, ending inventory is 2,000 units (10,000 − 8,000). Under variable costing, the value of ending inventory is $400,000 ($200 × 2,000). Under absorption costing, the value of ending inventory is $450,000 ($225 × 2,000).

Exhibit 14-2 illustrates the treatment of manufacturing costs on the balance sheet under variable costing and absorption costing. Note that the only difference between the two approaches is the treatment of fixed factory overhead. Thus, the unit product cost under absorption costing is always greater than the unit product cost under variable costing.

Income Statements: Analysis and Reconciliation

Because unit product costs are the basis for cost of goods sold, the variable- and absorption-costing methods can lead to different net income figures. The difference arises because of the amount of fixed overhead recognized as an expense under the two methods. Let's see how this affects the Fairchild example.

Income statements appear in Exhibits 14-3 and 14-4. These income statements reveal that absorption-costing income is $50,000 higher than variable-costing income. As the following analysis shows, this difference is due to some of the period's fixed overhead flowing into inventory when absorption costing is used.

For variable costing (Exhibit 14-3), the variable cost of goods sold is $1.6 million ($200 × 8,000 units sold). The fixed overhead deducted as an expense is $250,000. Thus, the total manufacturing expenses deducted are $1.85 million. The total selling and administrative expenses deducted are $180,000 ($80,000 variable + $100,000 fixed).

14-2
Exhibit
·····························Balance Sheet Treatment of Costs Under Variable and Absorption Costing

Variable Costing

DM
DL
VOH

= 1,000 Units, Variable Product Cost

Absorption Costing

DM
DL
VOH
FOH

= 1,000 Units, Variable and Fixed Product Cost

Cost Appearing on Balance Sheet:

Ending Inventory

DM
DL
VOH

DM
DL
VOH

Cost Appearing on Balance Sheet:

Ending Inventory

DM
DL
VOH
FOH

DM
DL
VOH
FOH

14-3
Exhibit
·····························

Fairchild Company		
Variable-Costing Income Statement		
Sales		$ 2,400,000
Less variable expenses:		
Variable cost of goods sold	$1,600,000	
Variable selling and administrative	80,000	(1,680,000)
Contribution margin		$ 720,000
Less fixed expenses:		
Fixed overhead	$ 250,000	
Fixed selling and administrative	100,000	(350,000)
Net income		$ 370,000

Exhibit

Fairchild Company Absorption-Costing Income Statement	
Sales	$ 2,400,000
Less: Cost of goods sold	(1,800,000)
Gross margin	$ 600,000
Less: Selling and administrative expenses	(180,000)
Net income	$ 420,000

For absorption costing, the cost of goods sold is $1.8 million ($225 × 8,000 units sold). Of this amount, $200,000 ($25 × 8,000) represents the fixed overhead that was recognized as an expense. The total selling and administrative expenses deducted are $180,000 ($80,000 variable and $100,000 fixed).

Now let's examine Exhibits 14-3 and 14-4 again to see what is the same. Sales, marketing expense, and administrative expense are always the same. Variable cost of goods sold is always the same. However, fixed factory overhead expensed differs. Thus, income determined with variable costing is $50,000 less than income determined with absorption costing. For absorption costing, where did the other $50,000 of fixed overhead go?

Under absorption costing, each unit produced was assigned fixed overhead of $25. Recall that of the 10,000 units produced, 2,000 units were not sold. These 2,000 units went into inventory and carried with them $50,000 ($25 × 2,000) of the period's fixed overhead. Only when these 2,000 units are sold will that $50,000 of fixed overhead be recognized as an expense. Thus, under absorption costing, $50,000 of the period's fixed overhead flows into inventory, and its recognition as an expense is deferred to a future period.

Notice that none of the selling and administrative costs, either variable or fixed, are assigned to the product under either method. Both methods treat these costs as period costs. Therefore, marketing and administrative costs are never inventoried and never appear on the balance sheet.[2]

Production, Sales, and Income Relationships

The relationship between variable-costing income and absorption-costing income changes as the relationship between production and sales changes. If more is sold than was produced, variable-costing income is greater than absorption-costing income. The reason is just the opposite of that for the Fairchild example. Selling more than was produced means that inventory is being used. Under absorption costing, units coming out of inventory have attached to them fixed overhead from a prior period. In addition, units produced and sold have all of the current period's fixed overhead attached. Thus, the amount of fixed overhead expensed by absorption costing is greater than the current period's fixed overhead by the amount of fixed overhead flowing out of inventory. Accordingly, variable-costing income is greater than absorption-costing income by the amount of fixed overhead flowing out of beginning inventory.

If production and sales are equal, of course, no difference exists between the two reported incomes. Since the units produced are all sold, absorption costing, like variable costing, will recognize the total fixed overhead of the period as an expense. No fixed overhead flows into or out of inventory.

The relationships between production, sales, and the two reported incomes are summarized in Exhibit 14-5. Note that if production is greater than sales, then inventory

---

2. What is Fairchild's variable cost per unit? $210. What is Fairchild's variable *product* cost per unit? $200. Note the difference; variable product cost does not include the $10 of variable selling and administrative expense. Total variable cost per unit does include the selling and administrative expenses.

If	Then
1. Production > Sales	Absorption net income > Variable net income
2. Production < Sales	Absorption net income < Variable net income
3. Production = Sales	Absorption net income = Variable net income

has increased. If production is less than sales, inventory must have decreased. If production is equal to sales, beginning inventory is equal to ending inventory.

To illustrate these relationships, consider the following example based on the operating data of Belnip, Inc. in the years 1996, 1997, and 1998.

Variable costs per unit:	
Direct materials	$4.00
Direct labor	1.50
Variable overhead (estimated and actual)	0.50
Variable selling and administrative	0.25

Estimated fixed overhead was $150,000 each year. Actual fixed overhead also was $150,000. Normal production volume is 150,000 units per year. The sales price each year was $10 per unit. Fixed selling and administrative expenses were $50,000 per year. Other operating data were as follows:

	1996	1997	1998
Beginning inventory	—	—	50,000
Production	150,000	150,000	150,000
Sales	150,000	100,000	200,000
Ending inventory	—	50,000	—

Income statements prepared under variable costing are shown in Exhibit 14-6. Exhibit 14-7 gives the income statements for absorption costing.

Exhibit

Variable-Costing Income Statements (in thousands of dollars)			
	1996	1997	1998
Sales	$1,500.0	$1,000	$ 2,000
Less variable expenses:			
Variable cost of goods sold[a]	(900.0)	(600)	(1,200)
Variable selling and administrative[b]	(37.5)	(25)	(50)
Contribution margin	$ 562.5	$ 375	$ 750
Less fixed expenses:			
Fixed overhead	(150.0)	(150)	(150)
Fixed selling and administrative	(50.0)	(50)	(50)
Net income	$ 362.5	$ 175	$ 550

[a]Beginning inventory	—	—	$ 300
Variable cost of goods manufactured	$900	$900	900
Goods available for sale	$900	$900	$1,200
Less: Ending inventory	—	(300)	—
Variable cost of goods sold	$900	$600	$1,200

[b]$0.25 per unit × Units sold

Absorption-Costing Income Statement (in thousands of dollars)			
	1996	1997	1998
Sales	$ 1,500.0	$1,000	$ 2,000
Less: Cost of goods sold*	(1,050.0)	(700)	(1,400)
Gross margin	$ 450.0	$ 300	$ 600
Less: Selling and administrative expenses	(87.5)	(75)	(100)
Net income	$ 362.5	$ 225	$ 500
*Beginning inventory	—	—	$ 350
Cost of goods manufactured	$1,050	$1,050	1,050
Goods available for sale	$1,050	$1,050	$1,400
Less: Ending inventory	—	(350)	—
Cost of goods sold	$1,050	$ 700	$1,400

In 1996, the net incomes for each method are identical. We must conclude that both methods expensed the same amount of fixed overhead. Under variable costing, we know that the period's total fixed overhead of $150,000 was expensed. Under absorption costing, the fixed overhead is unitized and becomes part of the product cost. Estimated fixed overhead was $150,000 each year. The fixed overhead rate is $1 per unit ($\frac{\$150,000}{150,000 \text{ units produced}}$) for all three years. The applied fixed overhead is $150,000 ($1 × 150,000) for all three years. Since the actual fixed overhead in every year is also $150,000, there is no fixed overhead variance in any year. Thus, the fixed overhead expensed for any year is simply the overhead rate times the number of units sold. For 1996, the total fixed overhead expensed under absorption costing is $150,000 ($1 × 150,000 units sold). Both methods did indeed recognize the same amount of fixed overhead expense.

In 1997, however, the story is different. From Exhibits 14-6 and 14-7, we see that the absorption-costing income is $50,000 greater than the variable-costing income ($225,000 − $175,000). The difference between the two incomes exists because there is $50,000 less fixed overhead expensed under the absorption-costing method.

Under absorption costing, each unit produced is assigned $1 of fixed overhead. Since 150,000 units were produced but only 100,000 units were sold, 50,000 units were placed in inventory. These 50,000 units carried with them $1 of fixed overhead each, for a total of $50,000. This $50,000 of the current period's fixed overhead will not be recognized as an expense until the units in inventory are sold. Thus, under absorption costing, the period's $150,000 of fixed overhead can be broken down into two categories: $100,000 is expensed and $50,000 is inventoried.

Under variable costing, however, the total fixed overhead of $150,000 is expensed since it is viewed as a period cost. Because variable costing recognizes $150,000 of fixed overhead expense and absorption costing recognizes only $100,000 of fixed overhead expense, the income reported by absorption costing is $50,000 more.

In 1998, the relationship between the two incomes reverses. The difference is now $50,000 in favor of variable costing. The favorable difference occurs because absorption costing not only recognizes $150,000 of fixed overhead expense for units produced and sold in this period but also recognizes the $50,000 of fixed overhead attached to the units in inventory that were produced in 1997 but sold in 1998. Thus, the total fixed overhead recognized as an expense is $200,000 under absorption costing versus only $150,000 under variable costing.

The key to explaining the difference between the two incomes is an analysis of the flow of fixed overhead. Variable costing always recognizes the period's total fixed overhead as an expense. Absorption costing, on the other hand, recognizes only the fixed overhead *attached* to the units *sold*. If production is different from sales, fixed overhead will either flow into or out of inventory. If the amount of fixed overhead in inventory increases, then absorption-costing income is greater than variable-costing income by the amount of the net increase. If the fixed overhead in inventory decreases, then variable-costing income is greater than absorption-costing income by the amount of the net decrease.

The change in fixed overhead in inventory is exactly equal to the difference between the two incomes. This change can be computed by multiplying the fixed overhead rate times the change in total units in the beginning and ending inventories (which is the difference between production and sales). The difference between absorption-costing net income and variable-costing net income can be expressed as:

$$\text{Absorption-costing income} - \text{Variable-costing income} =$$
$$\text{Fixed overhead rate} \times (\text{Units produced} - \text{Units sold})$$

Exhibit 14-8 shows how this shortcut approach can be used to explain the differences.

The Treatment of Fixed Factory Overhead in Absorption Costing

The difference between absorption and variable costing centers on the recognition of expense associated with fixed factory overhead. Under absorption costing fixed factory overhead must be assigned to units produced. This presents two problems that we have not explicitly considered. First, how do we convert factory overhead applied on the basis of direct labor hours or machine hours into factory overhead applied to units produced? Second, what is done when actual factory overhead does not equal applied factory overhead?

The first problem is solved relatively easily. Suppose that factory overhead is applied on the basis of direct labor hours. Further suppose that it takes 0.25 direct labor hour to produce one unit. If the fixed factory overhead rate is $12 per direct labor hour, then the fixed factory overhead per unit is $3 ($0.25 \times 12).

The solution to the second problem requires more thought. First, we must calculate the applied fixed factory overhead and assign it to units produced. Then, the total applied amount is compared to actual fixed factory overhead. If the over- or underapplied amount is immaterial, it is closed to Cost of Goods Sold. Any units going into ending inventory take with them the applied fixed factory overhead. Variable factory overhead (which can also be over- or underapplied) is treated in the same fashion. Review Problem II at the end of this chapter illustrates the handling of over- and underapplied fixed and variable factory overhead.

If the over- or underapplied amount is material, then it is allocated among ending Work in Process, Finished Goods, and Cost of Goods Sold. This complication is beyond the scope of this text.

14-8

Exhibit
Reconciliation of Variable
and Absorption Costing
(in thousands of dollars)

	1996	1997	1998
Net income:			
Absorption costing	$362.5	$225	$500
Variable costing	362.5	175	550
Difference	$ 0	$ 50	$ (50)
Explanation:			
Units produced	150	150	150
Units sold	(150)	(100)	(200)
Change in inventory	0	50	(50)
Fixed overhead rate	× $1	× $1	× $1
Difference explained*	$ 0	$ 50	$ (50)

*In 1996, absorption costing recognized only the period's fixed overhead as an expense. No fixed overhead flowed into or out of inventory. In 1997, $50,000 of fixed overhead flowed into inventory, and its recognition as an expense is deferred to a future period. In 1998, $50,000 of fixed overhead flowed out of inventory and was recognized as an expense.

VARIABLE COSTING AND PERFORMANCE EVALUATION OF MANAGERS

Objective 2

Explain how variable costing is useful in evaluating the performance of managers.

The evaluation of managers is often tied to the profitability of the units they control. How income changes from one period to the next and how actual income compares to planned income are frequently used as signals of managerial ability. To be meaningful signals, however, income should reflect managerial effort. For example, if a manager has worked hard and increased sales while holding costs in check, income should increase over the prior period, signaling success. In general terms, if income performance is expected to reflect managerial performance, then managers have the right to expect the following:

1. As sales revenue increases from one period to the next, all other things being equal, income should increase.
2. As sales revenue decreases from one period to the next, all other things being equal, income should decrease.
3. As sales revenue remains unchanged from one period to the next, all other things being equal, income should remain unchanged.

Interestingly, income under variable costing always follows this expected association between sales and income; under absorption costing, at times, it does not. To illustrate, assume that a division of Myers, Inc. has the following operating data for its first two years. (For simplicity, we assume no selling and administrative costs.)

	1997	1998
Variable manufacturing costs per unit	$10	$10
Production (expected and actual units)	10,000	5,000
Units sold ($25 per unit)	5,000	10,000
Fixed overhead (estimated and actual)	$100,000	$100,000

The product cost under variable costing is $10 per unit for both years. Assuming that expected actual volume is used to compute a predetermined fixed overhead rate, the product cost under absorption costing is $20 per unit in 1997 and $30 per unit in 1998 ($10 + \frac{$100,000}{10,000}$ for 1997; $10 + \frac{$100,000}{5,000}$ for 1998).

The variable-costing and absorption-costing income statements are shown in Exhibit 14-9. Sales increased from 5,000 to 10,000 units. Total fixed costs, the variable manufacturing cost per unit, and the unit sales price are the same for both periods. Thus, the doubling of sales represents the only change from one period to the next. Under variable costing, income increased by $75,000 from 1997 to 1998 (from a loss of $25,000 to a profit of $50,000). However, under absorption costing, despite the increase in sales, net income decreased by $25,000 (from a profit of $25,000 to a profit of $0)!

The firm improved its sales performance from 1997 to 1998 (twice as many units were sold), fixed costs remained the same, and the unit variable cost was the same; yet absorption costing fails to reveal this improved performance. Variable costing, on the other hand, produces an increase in income corresponding to the improved sales performance. If you were the manager, which income approach would you prefer?

VARIABLE COSTING AND SEGMENTED REPORTING

Objective 3

Prepare a segmented income statement based on a variable-costing approach and explain how this format can be used with activity-based costing to assess customer profitability.

The usefulness of variable costing for performance evaluation extends beyond evaluating managers. Managers need to be able to evaluate the activities over which they have responsibility. For example, managers must continually evaluate the profit contributions of plants, product lines, and sales territories.

The separation of fixed and variable costs basic to variable costing is critical for making accurate evaluations. Implicit in an evaluation is an associated decision— whether to continue to operate a plant or not, or whether to keep or drop a product line. Without a distinction between fixed and variable costs, the evaluation of profit-making activities and the resulting decision may both be erroneous.

Exhibit
Variable- and Absorption-
Costing Income
Statements

Variable-Costing Income	1997	1998
Sales	$ 125,000	$ 250,000
Less variable expenses:		
Variable cost of goods sold[a]	(50,000)	(100,000)
Contribution margin	$ 75,000	$ 150,000
Less fixed expenses:		
Fixed overhead	(100,000)	(100,000)
Net income (loss)	$ (25,000)	$ 50,000

Absorption-Costing Income	1997	1998
Sales	$ 125,000	$ 250,000
Less cost of goods sold[b]	(100,000)	(250,000)
Net income (loss)	$ 25,000	$ 0

[a]$10 × 5,000 in 1997 and $10 × 10,000 in 1998

[b]Beginning inventory	$ —	$100,000
Cost of goods manufactured	200,000	150,000
Goods available for sale	$ 200,000	$250,000
Less: Ending inventory	(100,000)	(—)
Cost of goods sold	$ 100,000	$250,000

**segmented
reporting**

    Reporting the profit contributions of activities or other units within an organization is called segmented reporting. Segmented reports prepared on a variable-costing basis produce better evaluations and decisions than those prepared on an absorption-costing basis. Let's take a closer look at segmented reporting and see why this is true.

    To evaluate many different activities within a firm, a manager needs more than the summary information that appears in a firm's income statement. For example, in a company with several divisions operating in different markets, the manager would certainly want to know how profitable each division has been. This knowledge may lead to greater overall profit by eliminating unprofitable divisions, giving special attention to problem divisions, allocating additional funds to the more profitable divisions, and so on.

    Divisional income statements, however, are not all that a good managerial accounting system should supply. Even finer segmentation is needed for managers to carry out their responsibilities properly. Divisions are made up of different plants. Plants produce products, and information on product profitability is critical. Some products may be profitable; some may not be. Similarly, profit information on sales territories, special projects, individual salespersons, and so on, is important.

segment

    Managers need to know the profitability of various segments within a firm to be able to make evaluations and decisions concerning each segment's continued existence, level of funding, and so on. A segment is any profit-making entity within the organization. A segment report can provide valuable information on costs controllable by the segment manager. Controllable costs are those whose level can be influenced by a manager. Thus, a manager who has no responsibility for a cost should not be held accountable for that cost. For example, divisional managers have no power to authorize corporate-level costs such as research and development and salaries of top managers. Therefore, divisional managers should not be held accountable for the incurrence of those costs. If noncontrollable costs are included in a segment report, they should be separated from controllable costs and labeled as noncontrollable. For example, fixed costs common to two or more plants within a division would not be allocated to each plant but instead would be shown as a common cost for the division.

Segmented Reporting: Absorption-Costing Basis

Should segmented reporting be on a variable-costing basis or an absorption-costing basis? To answer this question, let's consider Elcom, Inc., a firm that manufactures stereos and video recorders in a single plant and uses absorption costing for both external and internal reporting. Exhibit 14-10 gives the absorption-costing income statements by product line and in total for 1997.

Upon seeing the product-line performance, the president of Elcom, Devon Lauffer, decided to stop producing video recorders, reasoning that profits would increase by $30,000. A year later, however, the result was quite different. As the income statement for 1998 in Exhibit 14-11 shows, income actually decreased by $55,000. Why was the outcome so different from what Devon anticipated?

Devon relied on cost information collected by the external financial reporting system. However, the information needed for internal purposes often differs significantly from that required for external reporting. Cost behavior and the traceability of costs may not be critical concerns for reporting results to external parties, but they are vital to managers attempting to make strategic decisions.

Devon discovered that many fixed costs that had been allocated to the video recorders were not eliminated when that product line was dropped. Since both stereos and video recorders were produced in the same plant, much of the fixed factory overhead was common to the two products. This includes depreciation on the plant, taxes, insurance, and the plant manager's salary, among other items. When the video recorders were dropped, all these common fixed overhead costs were loaded entirely on the stereo product line. Similarly, some fixed selling and administrative costs previously assigned to the video recorder line were then fully assigned to the stereo line.

Segmented Reporting: Variable-Costing Basis

A segmented income statement using variable costing, with a slight modification, provides the essential cost information for assessing the role of the video recorder line. Exhibit 14-12 gives the segmented income statement using variable costing for 1997.

Segmented income statements using variable costing have one feature in addition to the variable-costing income statements already shown. Fixed expenses are broken down into two categories: *direct fixed expenses* and *common fixed expenses*. This additional subdivision highlights controllable versus noncontrollable costs and enhances the manager's ability to evaluate each segment's contribution to overall firm performance.

direct fixed expenses   Direct fixed expenses are fixed expenses that are directly traceable to a segment (a product line in this example). These are sometimes referred to as *avoidable fixed expenses* or *traceable fixed expenses* because they vanish if the segment is eliminated. These fixed expenses are caused by the existence of the segment itself. In the Elcom example, depreciation on equipment used in producing video recorders and the salary of the production supervisor of the video recorder production line are examples of direct fixed expenses.

14-10

Exhibit

Elcom, Inc. Segmented Income Statement, 1997 Absorption-Costing Basis			
	Stereos	Video Recorders	Total
Sales	$ 400,000	$ 290,000	$ 690,000
Less: Cost of goods sold	(350,000)	(300,000)	(650,000)
Gross margin	$ 50,000	$ (10,000)	$ 40,000
Less: Selling and administrative expenses	(30,000)	(20,000)	(50,000)
Net income (loss)	$ 20,000	$ (30,000)	$ (10,000)

Elcom, Inc.	
Income Statement, 1998	
Absorption-Costing Basis	
Sales	$ 400,000
Less: Cost of goods sold	(430,000)
Gross margin	$ (30,000)
Less: Selling and administrative expenses	(35,000)
Net income (loss)	$ (65,000)

common fixed expenses

Common fixed expenses are jointly caused by two or more segments. These expenses persist even if one of the segments to which they are common is eliminated. In the Elcom example, plant depreciation and the salary of the plant supervisor are common fixed expenses. Elimination of the video recorder line did not eliminate the plant and its associated depreciation. Similarly, the plant supervisor still was needed to oversee the production of the stereo product line.

Fixed costs that are direct for one segment may be indirect, or common, for another. For example, suppose that the stereo product line is segmented into two sales territories. In that case, the depreciation on the equipment used to produce stereos is common to both territories but directly traceable to the product segment itself.

Now let's examine Exhibit 14-12 to see whether this form of segmented income statement is more useful than the absorption-costing format. Notice that both stereos and video recorders have large positive contribution margins ($95,000 for stereos and $80,000 for video recorders). Both products are providing revenue above variable costs that can be used to help cover the firm's fixed costs. However, some of the firm's fixed costs are caused by the segments themselves. Thus, the real measure of the profit contribution of each segment is what is left over after these direct fixed costs are covered.

segment margin

The profit contribution each segment makes toward covering a firm's common fixed costs is called the segment margin. A segment should at least be able to cover both its

Elcom, Inc. Segmented Income Statement, 1997 Variable-Costing Basis			
	Stereos	Video Recorders	Total
Sales	$ 400,000	$ 290,000	$ 690,000
Less variable expenses:			
Variable cost of goods sold	(300,000)	(200,000)	(500,000)
Variable selling and administrative	(5,000)	(10,000)	(15,000)
Contribution margin	$ 95,000	$ 80,000	$ 175,000
Less direct fixed expenses:			
Direct fixed overhead	(30,000)	(20,000)	(50,000)
Direct selling and administrative	(10,000)	(5,000)	(15,000)
Segment margin*	$ 55,000	$ 55,000	$ 110,000
Less common fixed expenses:			
Common fixed overhead			(100,000)
Common selling and administrative			(20,000)
Net income (loss)			$ (10,000)

*Segments are defined as product lines.

own variable costs and direct fixed costs. A negative segment margin drags down the firm's total profit, making it time to consider dropping the product. Ignoring any effect a segment may have on the sales of other segments, the segment margin measures the change in a firm's profits that would occur if the segment were eliminated.

From Exhibit 14-12, we see that the video recorder line contributes $55,000 toward covering Elcom's common fixed costs. If the line is dropped, total profit decreases by $55,000—exactly what happened, as shown in Exhibit 14-11. Dropping the video recorder line was a disastrous decision, and now we know why.

The correct decision is to retain both product lines. Both are making equal contributions to the firm's profitability. Dropping either product simply aggravates the problem, unless it is replaced by a product with a higher segment margin. Since both products have large, positive contribution margins, other solutions to the net loss are needed. Accounting can help by focusing on a more detailed analysis of costs using activity-based costing.

Segmented Reporting: Activity-based Costing Approach

An activity-based costing approach, with its insight into unit-, batch-, product-, and facility-level costs may give management a more accurate feel for profits attributable to different product lines and for the existence of nonvalue-added costs. Let's look more closely at Elcom's overhead cost by determining activities and drivers.

Suppose that the common fixed overhead includes materials handling and maintenance. Direct fixed overhead includes setups. Elcom figures that the annual cost of each activity is as follows:

Materials handling	$20,000
Maintenance costs	8,000
Setups	18,000

Now Elcom has some idea of where to focus attention. Materials handling is a nonvalue-added activity. Setups, while value-added, can be performed more efficiently. Any reduction in these can go directly to the bottom line. Perhaps a reconfiguration of the plant will lead to lower materials-handling costs, or perhaps a new agreement with suppliers can lead to materials delivered directly to the line. Similarly, a change in the configuration of the assembly process might lead to quicker, cheaper setups. Finally, noticing that maintenance costs $8,000 might lead to a reexamination of the way in which maintenance is done. A JIT approach to manufacturing could lead to maintenance being done by line workers during downtimes.

An activity-based approach shows the complexity of the manufacturing operation and reminds managers that a decrease in power costs can only be achieved with a decrease in machine usage (perhaps by the use of more efficient machinery). Similarly, a decrease in setup cost can only come about through the streamlining or elimination of setup activity. Reducing activities reduces actual costs and leads to increased profits.

Customer Profitability

While customers are clearly important to profit, some are more profitable than others. Companies that assess the profitability of various customer groups can more accurately target their markets and increase profits. The first step in determining customer profitability is to identify the customer. The second step is to determine which customers add value to the company.

The identification of a company's customer may seem obvious. Grocery stores and automobile repair shops can easily identify their customers, and may even know them by name. However, frequently the company is part of a complex chain of customer

Commercial airlines target two very different market segments, one based on convenience (e.g., business travellers) and the other based on price (e.g., vacation travellers). The differing needs of these segments lead to radically different cost structures that impact on profitability. Southwest Airlines has targeted the price-based segment and avoids the costs of: seat assignment, baggage handling to other airlines, and in-flight meals. As a result, Southwest has one of the lowest operating cost structures of the major air carriers, and is consistently profitable.

relationships. For example, Weldcraft Products, Inc. produces welding torches, which are sold to: distributors, retail stores, and, eventually, companies and individuals that use the torches to weld. Weldcraft determined that its main customer is distributors and redistributed its activities so that Weldcraft salespeople now spend much of their time with distributors.[3]

Once customer groups have been identified, the second step is to determine which customer groups are most profitable, eliminate the unprofitable customers, and retain and add to the base of profitable customers.

Some customers are so unprofitable that they should not be kept. Rice Lake Products, Inc. manufactures movable owl and geese decoys. The company sold to both specialty stores and to Wal-Mart. However, the Wal-Mart sales, at $19 each, infuriated the specialty stores that charged $20. Even worse from Rice Lake Products' point of view was that the profit on a Wal-Mart sale averaged just $.50 while the profit on a specialty store sale amounted to $4. The reason for the difference was that Wal-Mart required special packaging and promotion, and returned product that did not sell. The company chose to concentrate on sales to specialty stores.[4]

Sometimes the company may need to add an initially unprofitable customer group, and increase efficiency to make the group profitable. The highly competitive personal computer industry is finding that out. Gateway 2000, Inc. was initially very successful selling personal computing systems to technically inclined customers. These customers know the difference between RAM and ROM and can easily assemble their own components into a working computer. However, the company's explosive growth has meant that less technically inclined customers have become a large proportion of the customer base. This new type of customer causes Gateway to incur additional costs. The early computer-savvy customer required relatively little technical support. The new customer base knows how to operate a computer, but wants the hardware preselected and configured in a package, wants the software installed by the company, and wants one-on-one help in troubleshooting problems. An important part of keeping these customers happy—so that they will continue to upgrade within the Gateway line—is good technical support.

---

3. Ellen Graham, "Meat and Potatoes: Sometimes the Most Successful Courses Are the Most Basic," *The Wall Street Journal*, 10 September 1993, p. R5.
4. Christie Brown, "A Great Way to Retire," *Forbes*, 9 October 1995, 96–97.

Consequently, Gateway has had to greatly increase the number of technical support personnel who work with buyers on their 800 number.[5] Just as important in keeping the profits up in this environment is finding ways to keep the costs down, by improving quality control and simplifying the written instructions that accompany the new computer.

It is generally more costly to win a customer than to keep a customer. Originating a customer may require advertising, sales calls, the drafting of proposals, and the generation of prospective customer lists. All of these activities are costly. Keeping existing customers happy also requires effort. For example, many stores provide free gift wrapping as a service to the customer who has already made a purchase. Firms must have profitability data to understand the profit contribution of customer relationships, to match the costs of increased service with the benefits. Many companies are now taking a customer life-cycle approach, by recognizing that a loyal customer will yield significant revenue over the years. For example, the lifetime revenue stream of a pizza eater can be $8,000. For more expensive products, like a Cadillac, the amount approaches $332,000.[6]

Relational databases and improved accounting systems can greatly assist the effort to track customer profitability. Profitability analysis of various customer classes requires information on product, marketing, and administrative activities used to serve each class. Let's analyze Barton, Inc., a manufacturer of highly realistic model horses sold to three classes of customer: large discount chains, small independent toy stores, and hobbyists. Each model is made of high-density plastic, from a detailed mold. A team of designers ensures that the design is accurate for the breed depicted. Color pigments are deep and rich. While Barton produces many designs, they all incur roughly the same manufacturing costs. Exhibit 14-13 provides manufacturing and marketing data.

Each class of customer places different demands on Barton. The large toy chains purchase 63 percent of the output. They receive price discounts averaging $1.25 per unit, and are linked to Barton through electronic data interchange (EDI). As a result, when supplies at the chains run low, an order is transmitted electronically to Barton's factory and another shipment of models dispatched. No commissions are paid on chain store sales. However, Barton must pay each chain store outlet $1,500 per year for shelf space (this ensures premium shelf position within the stores). There are 75 outlets. Barton pays shipping costs. The chain stores are not particular about which models are shipped; therefore, Barton typically sends whatever is in stock at the time. There is no special packaging involved.

The independent toy stores are smaller and typically stock upscale toys with a heavily educational flavor. About 35 percent of Barton's production is sold to them. No price

---

5. Lois Therrien, "Why Gateway Is Racing to Answer on the First Ring," *Business Week*, 13 September 1993, 92–94.
6. James L. Heskett, Thomas O. Jones, Gary W. Loveman, W. Early Sasser, Jr., and Leonard A. Schlesinger, "Putting the Service-Profit Chain to Work," *Harvard Business Review* (March/April 1994): 164–174.

Exhibit
Cost Information for
Barton, Inc.

Manufacturing expenses:	
Units produced	500,000
Average price per model	$15
Direct materials per unit	$5
Direct labor cost	$3
Overhead per unit	$1
Marketing expenses:	
Commissions (per model sold)	$.75
Special packaging per unit	$.20
EDI costs per year	$100,000
Fair expense	$75,000
Shipping	$157,500
Shelf space charges	$112,500

discounts are given to these stores and no shelf space is paid. However, a sales commission of $.75 per-unit sold is paid to independent wholesale jobbers who sell to the stores. The stores pay any shipping cost from Barton's factory. The independent toy stores prefer models with a story attached. For example, a series of models of Indian war horses with accompanying explanatory booklets and special packaging are quite popular. Therefore, Barton attempts to ship all models with special packaging to the independents.

The final 2 percent of Barton's sales take place at the summer fairs. Each summer Barton stages five model fairs around the United States. Fun and colorful, the fairs are designed to display the Barton models, to provide a meeting opportunity for model horse hobbyists, and to generate interest in the Barton product. Barton reserves meeting rooms at a hotel for two days, invites local area hobbyists to put on shows and demonstrations, and sets up a series of trading booths for model horse fanciers. Several of Barton's staff (designers, the president, the vice-president of marketing) attend to chat with customers, answer questions, and display (and sell) the latest models. To generate additional interest in the fairs, a special model available only at that summer's fairs is designed and produced. The special model requires 150 hours of design time (at $14 per hour), and one setup (costing $1,000).

Given this information, we can analyze profitability by customer class. Exhibit 14-14 provides profit statements for each class of customer. The chain stores yield the most revenue, but it must be adjusted for discounts. Expenses directly attributable to the chain store outlets include: shelf space payments, shipping charges, and the cost of the electronic data interchange equipment and personnel. The independent toy stores receive no price discount, but do require the payment of commissions and special packaging. The fairs have the lowest revenue, and expenses consisting of fair expense, special design, and setup.

Clearly, the chain stores are the most profitable, followed by the independent toy stores. The fairs are unprofitable. An activity-based analysis can give Barton's management a better idea of which activities to emphasize and where cost cutting might occur. For example, the fairs are money losers on the basis of sales. Perhaps management might consider them promotional activity and not a customer class at all. In fact, the major objective of the fairs is to stimulate interest in the entire Barton line, not merely to sell 10,000 models. Thus, the entire cost of the fairs could be added to overall marketing expense.

These activity-based data can also give management a good idea of the cost of expanding into one area and away from another. For example, should Barton sell to one more chain outlet if it is at capacity? Each chain outlet averages sales of 4,200 models ($\frac{315,000}{75\,\text{outlets}}$). These 4,200 models would not be sold to the independent toy stores. The analysis is as follows:

Profit from Adding One More Chain Outlet:

Revenue from additional outlet	$63,000
Less: discount	(5,250)
Net additional revenue	$57,750
Less:	
COGS	(37,800)
Shipping	(2,100)
Shelf space	(1,500)
Profit from added outlet	$16,350

Profit from Selling 4,200 Models to Independent Toy Stores:

Revenue	$63,000
Less:	
COGS	(37,800)
Special packaging	(840)
Commission	(3,150)
Profit from independents	$21,210

14-14··································

Exhibit
Customer Analysis for
Barton, Inc.

	Profit for Chain Stores	
Sales		$4,725,000
Less: Discounts		(393,750)
Net sales		$4,331,250
Less: COGS		2,520,000
Gross Profit		$1,811,250
Less:		
Shelf space		(112,500)
Shipping		(157,500)
EDI		(100,000)
Profit		$1,441,250

	Profit for Independent Toy Stores	
Sales		$2,625,000
Less: COGS		1,400,000
Gross Profit		$1,225,000
Less:		
Commissions		(131,250)
Special packaging		(35,000)
Profit		$1,058,750

	Profit for Fairs	
Sales		$150,000
Less: COGS		(80,000)
Gross Profit		$ 70,000
Less:		
Fair expense		(75,000)
Design time		(2,100)
Setup		(1,000)
Loss		$ (8,100)

Barton should continue to sell to the independent toy stores as the outlet chains are less profitable.

Activity-based accounting can provide data on these marketing activities, which are important in customer profitability analysis. However, it is important to remember that activities alone do not cause costs. Other factors such as time, business volumes, and earlier decisions may lead to efficiencies or inefficiencies.

VARIABLE COSTING FOR PLANNING AND CONTROL

Objective 4

Explain how variable costing can be used in planning and control.

Financial planning requires managers to estimate future sales, future production levels, future costs, and so on. Because sales forecasts, the basis of the budget, are not certain, management may wish to look at several different levels of sales to assess the range of possibilities facing the firm. Knowledge of cost behavior is fundamental to achieving this outcome. Fixed costs do not vary with volume changes, so distinguishing between fixed and variable costs is essential to making an accurate cost assessment at the different possible sales and production volumes.

Once management has chosen one expected sales and production level for the coming year, the costs that should occur can also be determined. The financial plan, then, consists of the expected activity levels and the associated expected costs. This plan can be used to monitor the actual performance as it unfolds.

If actual performance is different from what was expected, corrective action may be necessary. By comparing actual outcomes with the expected outcomes and taking corrective action when necessary, managers exercise control. For the control process to work, though, cost behavior must be known.

Suppose the financial plan called for 12,000 units to be produced for the year, and the utility cost planned for the year is $18,000. At the end of the first month, the company produced 3,000 units and spent $4,500 on utilities. Are utility costs being incurred as planned?

Under an absorption-costing approach, the planned utility cost per-unit produced is $1.50 ($\frac{\$18,000}{12,000}$). Therefore, for 3,000 units, we should spend $4,500 ($1.50 × 3,000). Since the expected utility cost for 3,000 units is $4,500, and the actual cost was $4,500, the plan appears to be unfolding as expected. Unfortunately, this calculation ignores *cost behavior*. It assumes that all costs are variable. In reality, the utility cost is a flat fee of $1,000 per month plus $0.50 per kilowatt-hour. If it takes 1 kilowatt-hour to produce one unit of output, the expected cost for the 3,000 units produced in one month is $2,500 ($1,000 + $0.50 × 3,000 units). The company should have spent $2,500 on utilities to produce 3,000 units, but it spent $4,500. The plan is not unfolding as it should.

The correct signal about the planned utility cost is given when cost behavior is considered. Once again, we see the importance of the distinction between fixed and variable costs. Since this distinction is basic to variable costing, we must conclude that variable costing is superior to absorption costing for internal purposes. Evidence from three different managerial applications supports this conclusion.

S UMMARY OF LEARNING OBJECTIVES

1. Explain the differences between variable and absorption costing.

Variable and absorption costing differ in their treatment of fixed factory overhead. Variable costing treats fixed factory overhead as a period expense. Thus, unit production cost under variable costing consists of direct materials, direct labor, and variable factory overhead. Absorption costing treats fixed factory overhead as a product cost. Thus, unit production cost under absorption costing consists of direct materials, direct labor, variable factory overhead, and a share of fixed factory overhead.

A variable-costing income statement divides expenses according to *cost behavior*. First, variable expenses of manufacturing, marketing, and administration are subtracted from sales to yield the contribution margin. Then all fixed expenses are subtracted from the contribution margin to yield variable-costing net income. An absorption-costing income statement divides expenses according to *function*. First, the cost of goods sold is subtracted from sales to yield gross profit (or gross margin). Then marketing and administrative expenses are subtracted from gross profit to yield absorption-costing net income.

2. Explain how variable costing is useful in evaluating the performance of managers.

By separating costs according to behavior, variable costing enhances traceability and controllability of costs. Variable costing preserves the correspondence between effort and outcome necessary for good evaluation of management performance.

3. Prepare a segmented income statement based on a variable-costing approach and explain how this format can be used with activity-based costing to assess customer profitability.

A segmented income statement takes the following form:

	Segment X	Segment Y	Company
Sales	XXX	YYY	CCC
Less variable expenses	(XX)	(YY)	(CC)
Contribution margin	XXX	YYY	CCC
Less direct fixed expenses	(XX)	(YY)	(CC)
Product margin	XX	YY	CC
Less common fixed expenses			(CC)
Net income (loss)			CC

The use of variable costing emphasizes the cost of behavior of each segment so that management can properly evaluate each segment's contribution to overall firm performance.

Activity-based costing can be used with the segmented income statement to provide more insight into unit-level, batch-level, and product-level costs. Customer profitability can be assessed by treating each customer group as a segment and determining the activities associated with each group.

4. Explain how variable costing can be used in planning and control.

Variable costing requires management to distinguish between fixed and variable costs. This distinction is important in determining budgeted costs.

KEY TERMS

Absorption costing 560   Direct fixed expenses 569   Segmented reporting 568   Variable costing 560
Common fixed expenses 570   Segment 568   Segment margin 570

REVIEW PROBLEMS

I. Absorption and Variable Costing; Segmented Income Statements Fine Leathers Company produces a lady's wallet and a man's wallet. Selected data for the past year follow:

	Lady's Wallet	Man's Wallet
Production (units)	100,000	200,000
Sales (units)	90,000	210,000
Selling price	$5.50	$4.50
Direct labor hours	50,000	80,000
Manufacturing costs:		
Direct materials	$ 75,000	$100,000
Direct labor	250,000	400,000
Variable overhead	20,000	24,000
Fixed overhead:		
Direct	50,000	40,000
Common[a]	20,000	20,000
Nonmanufacturing costs:		
Variable selling	$ 30,000	$ 60,000
Direct fixed selling	35,000	40,000
Common fixed selling[b]	25,000	25,000

[a]Common overhead totals $40,000 and is divided equally between the two products.
[b]Common fixed selling cost totals $50,000 and is divided equally between the two products.

Budgeted fixed overhead for the year, $130,000, equaled the actual fixed overhead. Fixed overhead is assigned to products using a plantwide rate based on expected direct labor hours, which were 130,000. The company had 10,000 man's wallets in inventory at the beginning of the year. These wallets had the same unit cost as the man's wallets produced during the year.

REQUIRED:

1. Compute the unit cost for the lady's and man's wallets using the variable-costing method. Compute the unit cost using absorption costing.
2. Prepare an income statement using absorption costing.
3. Prepare an income statement using variable costing.
4. Reconcile the difference between the two income statements.
5. Prepare a segmented income statement using products as segments.

Solution

1. The unit cost for the lady's wallet is as follows:

Direct materials ($75,000/100,000)	$0.75
Direct labor ($250,000/100,000)	2.50
Variable overhead ($20,000/100,000)	0.20
Variable cost per unit	$3.45
Fixed overhead [(50,000 × $1.00)/100,000]	0.50
Absorption cost per unit	$3.95

The unit cost for the man's wallet is as follows:

Direct materials ($100,000/200,000)	$0.50
Direct labor ($400,000/200,000)	2.00
Variable overhead ($24,000/200,000)	0.12
Variable cost per unit	$2.62
Fixed overhead [(80,000 × $1.00)/200,000]	0.40
Absorption cost per unit	$3.02

Notice that the only difference between the two unit costs is the assignment of the fixed overhead cost. Notice also that the fixed overhead unit cost is assigned using the predetermined fixed overhead rate ($\frac{\$130,000}{130,000 \text{ hours}}$ = $1 per hour). For example, the lady's wallets used 50,000 direct labor hours and so receive $1 × 50,000, or $50,000, of fixed overhead. This total, when divided by the units produced, gives the $0.50 per-unit fixed overhead cost. Finally, observe that variable nonmanufacturing costs are not part of the unit cost under variable costing. For both approaches, only manufacturing costs are used to compute the unit costs.

2. The income statement under absorption costing is as follows:

Sales [($5.50 × 90,000) + ($4.50 × 210,000)]	$1,440,000
Less: Cost of goods sold:	
[($3.95 × 90,000) + ($3.02 × 210,000)]	(989,700)
Gross margin	$ 450,300
Less: Selling expenses*	(215,000)
Net income	$ 235,300

*This is the sum of selling expenses for both products.

3. The income statement under variable costing is as follows:

Sales [($5.50 × 90,000) + ($4.50 × 210,000)]	$1,440,000
Less variable expenses:	
Variable cost of goods sold	
[($3.45 × 90,000) + ($2.62 × 210,000)	(860,700)
Variable selling expenses	(90,000)
Contribution margin	$ 489,300
Less fixed expenses:	
Fixed overhead	(130,000)
Fixed selling	(125,000)
Net income	$ 234,300

4. Reconciliation is as follows:

$$I_A - I_V = \$235,300 - \$234,300 = \$1,000$$

Thus, variable-costing income is $1,000 less than absorption-costing income. This difference can be explained by the net change in fixed overhead found in inventory under absorption costing.

Lady's wallets:	
Units produced	100,000
Units sold	90,000
Increase in inventory	10,000
Unit fixed overhead	× $ 0.50
Increase in fixed overhead	$5,000

Man's wallets:

Units produced	200,000
Units sold	210,000
Decrease in inventory	(10,000)
Unit fixed overhead	×$ 0.40
Decrease in fixed overhead	$(4,000)

The net change is a $1,000 ($5,000 − $4,000) increase in fixed overhead in inventories. Thus, under absorption costing, there is a net flow of $1,000 of the current period's fixed overhead into inventory. Since variable costing recognized all of the current period's fixed overhead as an expense, variable-costing income should be $1,000 lower than absorption costing, as it is.

5. Segmented income statement:

	Lady's Wallets	Man's Wallets	Total
Sales	$495,000	$945,000	$1,440,000
Less variable expenses:			
Variable cost of goods sold	(310,500)	(550,200)	(860,700)
Variable selling expenses	(30,000)	(60,000)	(90,000)
Contribution margin	$154,500	$334,800	$ 489,300
Less direct fixed expenses:			
Direct fixed overhead	(50,000)	(40,000)	(90,000)
Direct selling expenses	(35,000)	(40,000)	(75,000)
Product margin	$ 69,500	$254,800	$ 324,300
Less common fixed expenses:			
Common fixed overhead			(40,000)
Common selling expenses			(50,000)
Net income			$ 234,300

II. Absorption and Variable Costing with Over- and Underapplied Overhead Bellingham, Inc. has just completed its first year of operations. The unit costs on a normal-costing basis are as follows:

Manufacturing costs (per unit):	
Direct materials (2 lb @ $2)	$ 4.00
Direct labor (1.5 hr @ $9)	13.50
Variable overhead (1.5 hr @ $2)	3.00
Fixed overhead (1.5 hr @ $3)	4.50
Total	$25.00
Selling and administrative costs:	
Variable	$5/unit
Fixed	$190,000

During the year, the company had the following activity:

Units produced	24,000
Units sold	21,500
Unit selling price	$42
Direct labor hours worked	36,000

Actual fixed overhead was $12,000 less than budgeted fixed overhead. Budgeted variable overhead was $5,000 less than the actual variable overhead. The company used an expected actual activity level of 36,000 direct labor hours to compute the predetermined overhead rates. Any overhead variances are closed to Cost of Goods Sold.

REQUIRED:
1. Compute the unit cost using (a) absorption costing and (b) variable costing.
2. Prepare an absorption-costing income statement.
3. Prepare a variable-costing income statement.
4. Reconcile the difference between the two income statements.

Solution

1.

Absorption Unit Cost		**Variable Unit Cost**	
Direct materials	$ 4.00	Direct materials	$ 4.00
Direct labor	13.50	Direct labor	13.50
Variable overhead	3.00	Variable overhead	3.00
Fixed overhead	4.50	Total	$20.50
Total	$25.00		

2.

Bellingham, Inc.
Absorption-Costing Income Statement

Sales (21,500 @ $42)		$903,000
Cost of goods sold (21,500 @ $25.00)	$537,500	
Less: Overapplied overhead*	(7,000)	530,500
Gross margin		$372,500
Less: Selling and administrative expenses		(297,500)
Net income		$ 75,000

*The budgeted fixed overhead rate of $3 per direct labor hour was computed based on 36,000 direct labor hours. Therefore, budgeted fixed overhead must have been $108,000. Since actual fixed overhead was $12,000 less than budgeted, actual fixed overhead must be $96,000. Similarly, the variable overhead rate of $2 per direct labor hour implies budgeted variable overhead of $72,000 ($2 × 36,000 direct labor hours). Since actual variable overhead was $5,000 higher than budgeted overhead, actual variable overhead must be $77,000.

Both variable and fixed overhead were applied on the basis of direct labor hours. Since 36,000 hours were worked, total applied overhead amounts to $180,000. Actual overhead was $173,000 (actual fixed cost of $96,000 plus actual variable cost of $77,000).

Applied overhead	$180,000
Actual overhead	(173,000)
Overapplied overhead	$ 7,000

3.

Bellingham, Inc.
Variable-Costing Income Statement

Sales (21,500 @ $42)		$903,000
Variable cost of goods sold (21,500 @ $20.50)	$440,750	
Add: Underapplied variable overhead	5,000	(445,750)
Variable selling expense (21,500 @ $5)		(107,500)
Contribution margin		$349,750
Less:		
Fixed factory overhead	$ 96,000	
Selling and administrative expenses	190,000	(286,000)
Net income		$ 63,750

Note that the underapplied variable overhead is simply the actual variable overhead of $77,000 minus the applied variable overhead of $72,000 ($2 × 36,000 direct labor hours).

Note also that actual fixed factory overhead is charged on the income statement, not applied fixed factory overhead.

4.
$$I_A - I_V = \text{Fixed overhead rate(Production} - \text{Sales)}$$
$$\$75,000 - \$63,750 = 4.50(24,000 - 21,500)$$
$$\$11,250 = \$4.50(2,500)$$
$$\$11,250 = \$11,250$$

QUESTIONS FOR WRITING AND DISCUSSION

1. What is the only difference between the way costs are assigned under variable and absorption costing?
2. The variable manufacturing costs of a company are $10 per unit, variable selling expenses are $2 per unit, and the fixed overhead rate is $5 per unit. What is the per-unit inventory cost of the product under absorption costing? under variable costing?
3. Why is *variable costing* a more descriptive term for the product-costing method popularly known as *direct costing?*
4. If production is greater than sales, why is absorption-costing income greater than variable-costing income?
5. If sales are greater than production, why is variable-costing income greater than absorption-costing income?
6. Assume that a company has a fixed overhead rate of $8 per-unit produced. During the year, the company produced 10,000 units and sold 8,000. What is the difference in income generated according to absorption costing and to variable costing?
7. The fixed overhead expense recognized on an income statement was $100,000. The fixed overhead for the period was $80,000. Was the income statement pre-pared using absorption costing or variable costing? Explain.
8. Why is variable costing better than absorption costing for the evaluation of managerial performance?
9. Why is variable costing better than absorption costing for the evaluation of segment performance?
10. Why is variable costing better than absorption costing for planning and controlling costs?
11. What is the difference between a direct fixed cost and a common fixed cost? Why is this difference important?
12. What is the difference between segment margin and contribution margin?
13. Explain how income under absorption costing can increase from one period to the next even though selling prices and costs have remained the same.
14. How would a segment be identified within a firm?
15. How is activity-based costing applied to segmented reporting?
16. Explain how the treatment of customer groups as segments can be useful to a firm.
17. What is a direct fixed expense? Why is it useful for segment performance evaluation?

WARM-UP EXERCISES

This section provides short warm-up exercises based on the examples in the chapter. Each warm-up exercise gives the page number on which the text example can be found. You may want to refer to the text example to see how the exercise can be set up and solved.

W14-1
Inventory Valuation under Absorption and Variable Costing
LO 1
p. 561

Quester Company has the following data associated with the product it makes:

Units, beginning inventory	—
Units produced	6,000
Units sold ($18 per unit)	5,000
Normal volume	6,000
Variable costs per unit:	
Direct materials	$5
Direct labor	3
Variable overhead*	1
Variable selling and administrative	2
Fixed costs:	
Fixed overhead	$24,000
Fixed selling and administrative	9,000

*Estimated and actual overhead are equal.

REQUIRED:
1. What is the unit cost under absorption costing? What is the value of ending inventory under absorption costing?
2. What is the unit cost under variable costing? What is the value of ending inventory under variable costing?

W14-2
Income Statements Prepared According to Absorption and Variable Costing
LO 1
p. 563

Refer to W14-1 for Quester Company.

REQUIRED:
1. Prepare a variable-costing income statement for Quester Company.
2. Prepare an absorption-costing income statement for Quester Company.

W14-3
Reconciling the Difference Between Absorption-Costing Income and Variable-Costing Income
LO 1
p. 566

Refer to W14-2 for Quester Company.

REQUIRED: Reconcile (explain) the difference between absorption-costing income and variable-costing income.

W14-4
Segmented Reporting
LO 3
p. 570

Kelly Company manufactures two products, casino-type game machines and handheld video game players. Information about the two products is as follows:

	Casino Machines	Video Game Players
Unit sales	10,000	100,000
Price	$500	$40
Variable manufacturing cost	$250	$22
Variable selling cost	$50	$5
Direct fixed expense	$900,000	$350,000

Kelly's common fixed expense amounts to $2,000,000.

REQUIRED:
1. Prepare a segmented income statement using variable costing.
2. By how much would Kelly's net income change if the casino machine line were dropped?

W14-5
Customer Profitability
LO 3
p. 575

Woolywear, Inc. manufactures knitted gloves, hats, and scarves. For several years, Woolywear sold its products to small specialty shops. Recently, the company landed a large contract with Giga-Mart (amounting to half of its output). Cost information for Woolywear is as follows:

Manufacturing expenses:	
Units produced	100,000
Average price per unit	$9.00
Direct material cost per unit	1.75
Direct labor cost per unit	1.50
Overhead per unit	3.00
Marketing expenses:	
Commissions (per unit)	$ .90
Special design (per unit)	2.00
Delivery expense	80,000
Shipping expense	20,000
Return penalties	3,000

The specialty stores require special designs, forcing Woolywear to incur additional setup and materials costs. These amount to about $2 per unit. The shipping expense is for shipment to the specialty stores, as are the commissions. Giga-Mart orders do not incur any commissions; however, the discount giant does require a $1 discount on the unit price and just-in-time deliveries. The delivery expense averages $80,000 per year. Also, Giga-Mart levies return penalties if any order does meet its specifications. These penalties are incurred on about 15 percent of the orders and amount to 5 percent of sales price.

REQUIRED: Compute the profit earned by Woolywear for the specialty shops and for Giga-Mart.

E XERCISES

E14-1
Unit Costs; Inventory Valuation; Variable and Absorption Costing
LO 1

Garfield Company produced 40,000 units during its first year of operations and sold 36,000 at $18 per unit. The company chose practical activity—at 40,000 units—to compute its predetermined overhead rate. Manufacturing costs are as follows:

Expected and actual fixed overhead	$140,000
Expected and actual variable overhead	48,000
Direct labor	320,000
Direct materials	120,000

REQUIRED:
1. Calculate the unit cost and the cost of finished goods inventory under absorption costing.
2. Calculate the unit cost and the cost of finished goods inventory under variable costing.
3. What is the dollar amount that would be used to report the cost of finished goods inventory to external parties. Why?

E14-2
Income Statements; Variable and Absorption Costing
LO 1

The following information pertains to Medina, Inc. for 1997:

Beginning inventory, units	—
Units produced	10,000
Units sold	8,000
Ending inventory, units	2,000
Variable costs per unit:	
Direct materials	$9.00
Direct labor	4.00
Variable overhead	1.50
Variable selling expenses	3.50
Fixed costs per year:	
Fixed overhead	$38,000
Fixed selling and administrative	22,000

There are no work-in-process inventories. Normal activity is 10,000 units. Expected and actual overhead costs are the same.

REQUIRED:
1. Without preparing an income statement, indicate what the difference will be between variable-costing income and absorption-costing income.
2. Assume the selling price per unit is $29. Prepare an income statement (a) using variable costing and (b) using absorption costing.

E14-3
**Income Statements
and Firm
Performance:
Variable and
Absorption Costing**
LO 1, LO 2

Ballenger Company had the following operating data for its first two years of operations:

Variable cost per unit:	
Direct materials	$5
Direct labor	3
Variable overhead	2
Fixed costs per year:	
Overhead	$120,000
Selling and administrative	20,000

Ballenger produced 20,000 units in the first year and sold 16,000. In the second year, it produced 16,000 units and sold 20,000 units. The selling price per unit each year was $24. Ballenger uses an actual cost system for product costing.

REQUIRED:
1. Prepare income statements for both years using absorption costing. Has firm performance, as measured by income, improved or declined from year 1 to year 2?
2. Prepare income statements for both years using variable costing. Has firm performance, as measured by income, improved or declined from year 1 to year 2?

E14-4
**Absorption Costing;
Variable Costing;
Reconciliation with
Fixed Overhead
Variance**
LO 1

Jordan Company uses a predetermined overhead rate based on normal capacity expressed in units of output. Normal capacity is 60,000 units and the expected fixed overhead cost for the year is $120,000.

During the year, Jordan produced 54,000 units and sold 51,000. There was no beginning finished goods inventory. The variable-costing income statement for the year follows:

Sales (51,000 units @ $20)	$1,020,000
Less variable costs:	
Variable cost of goods sold	(510,000)
Variable selling expenses	(255,000)
Contribution margin	$ 255,000
Less fixed costs:	
Fixed overhead	(125,000)
Fixed selling and administrative	(75,000)
Net income	$ 55,000

Any under- or overapplied overhead is closed to Cost of Goods Sold. Variable cost of goods sold is already adjusted for any variable overhead variance.

REQUIRED:
1. Jordan Company needs an income statement based on absorption costing for external reporting. Using the provided information prepare this statement.
2. Explain the difference between the income reported by variable costing and by absorption costing.

E14-5
**Segmented Income
Statements;
Product-Line
Analysis**
LO 3, LO 4

Cocino Company produces blenders and coffee makers. During the past year, 100,000 blenders and 25,000 coffee makers were produced and sold. Fixed costs for Cocino totaled $250,000, of which $90,000 can be avoided if the blenders are not produced and $45,000 can be avoided if the coffee makers are not produced. Revenue and variable cost information follow:

	Blenders	Coffee Makers
Variable expenses per appliance	$20	$43
Selling price per appliance	22	45

REQUIRED:
1. Prepare product-line income statements. Segregate direct and common fixed costs.
2. What would the effect be on Cocino's profit if the coffee-maker line is dropped? the blender line?
3. What would be the effect on firm profits if an additional 10,000 blenders could be produced (using existing capacity) and sold for $20.50 on a special-order basis? Existing sales would be unaffected by the special order.

E14-6
Product Line Analysis with Complementary Effects
LO 3, LO 4

FunTime Company produces three lines of greeting cards: scented, musical, and regular. Segmented income statements for the past year are as follows:

	Scented	Musical	Regular	Total
Sales	$10,000	$15,000	$25,000	$50,000
Less: Variable expenses	(7,000)	(12,000)	(12,500)	(31,500)
Contribution margin	$ 3,000	$ 3,000	$12,500	$18,500
Less: Direct fixed expenses	(4,000)	(5,000)	(3,000)	(12,000)
Segment margin	$ (1,000)	$ (2,000)	$ 9,500	$ 6,500
Common fixed expenses				(7,500)
Net loss				$ (1,000)

Kathy Bunker, president of FunTime, is concerned about the financial performance of her firm and is seriously considering dropping both the scented and musical product lines. However, before making a final decision, she consults Jim Dorn, FunTime's vice-president of marketing.

REQUIRED:
1. Jim believes that by increasing advertising by $1,000 ($250 for the scented line and $750 for the musical line), sales of those two lines would increase by 30 percent. If you were Kathy, how would you react to this information?
2. Jim warns Kathy that eliminating the scented and musical lines would lower the sales of the regular line by 20 percent. Given this information, would it be profitable to eliminate the scented and musical lines?
3. Suppose that eliminating either line reduces sales of the regular cards by 10 percent. Would a combination of increased advertising (the option described in requirement 1) and eliminating one of the lines be beneficial? Identify the best combination for the firm.

E14-7
Absorption Costing;
Variable Costing;
Income Statements;
Inventory Valuations;
Income
Reconciliation
LO 1

Ritter Company produces and sells soccer balls. The operating costs for the past year were as follows:

Variable costs per unit:	
Direct materials	$1.30
Direct labor	0.50
Variable overhead	0.25
Variable selling	0.55
Fixed costs per year:	
Fixed overhead	$180,000
Selling and administrative	60,000

During the year, Ritter produced 200,000 soccer balls and sold 225,000 at $5.50 each. Ritter had 30,000 balls in beginning finished goods inventory; costs have not changed from last year to this year. An actual cost system is used for product costing.

REQUIRED:
1. What is the per-unit inventory cost that will be reported on Ritter's balance sheet at the end of the year? What will be the reported income?
2. What would the per-unit inventory cost be under variable costing? Does this differ from the unit cost computed in requirement 1? Why? What would income be using variable costing?
3. Reconcile the difference between the variable-costing and the absorption-costing income figures.

E14-8
Variable Costing;
Absorption Costing;
Income Statements;
Inventory Valuation;
Underapplied Fixed
Overhead
LO 1

During its first year of operations, Sugarsmooth, Inc., produced 55,000 jars of hand cream based on a formula containing 10 percent glycolic acid. Unit sales were 53,500 jars. Fixed overhead was applied at $0.50 per-unit produced. Fixed overhead was underapplied by $10,000. This fixed overhead variance was closed to Cost of Goods Sold. There was no variable overhead variance. The results of the year's operations are as follows (on an absorption-costing basis):

Sales (53,500 units @ $8.50)	$454,750
Less: Cost of goods sold	(170,500)
Gross margin	$284,250
Less: Selling and administrative (all fixed)	(120,000)
Net income	$164,250

REQUIRED:

1. Give the cost of the firm's ending inventory under absorption costing. What is the cost of the ending inventory under variable costing?
2. Prepare a variable-costing income statement. Reconcile the difference between the two income figures.

E14-9
Customer
Profitability
LO 3

Refer to E14-8. At the end of the first year of operations, Sugarsmooth is considering expanding its customer base. In its first year, it sold to small drugstores and supermarkets. Now, Sugarsmooth wants to add large discount stores and small beauty shops. Working together, the company controller and marketing manager have accumulated the following information:

a. Anticipated sales to discount stores would be 20,000 units at a discounted price of $6.75. Higher costs of shipping and return penalties would be incurred. Shipping would amount to $45,000 per year and return penalties would average 1 percent of sales. In addition, a clerk would need to be hired solely to handle the discount stores' accounts. The clerk's salary and benefits would be $30,000 per year.

b. Anticipated sales to beauty shops would be 10,000 units, at a price of $9. A commission of 10 percent of sales would be paid to independent jobbers who sell to the shops. In addition, an extra packing expense of $.50 per unit would be incurred because the shops require fewer bottles per carton.

c. The fixed overhead and selling and administrative expenses would remain unchanged and are treated as common costs.

REQUIRED:

1. Prepare a segmented variable-costing income statement for next year. The segments correspond to customer groups: drugstores and supermarkets, discount stores, and beauty shops.
2. Are all three customer groups profitable? Should Sugarsmooth expand its marketing base?

E14-10
Segmented Income
Statements;
Absorption Costing;
Variable Costing;
Regional Analysis
LO 3, LO 4

Wilson Company sells its products in the Southwest and Midwest. Major plants are located in each region. Based on a recent quarterly income statement, the president of the company expressed some concern regarding performance in the Southwest. The income statement (prepared on an absorption-costing basis) follows:

Wilson Company
Income Statement (in thousands)

	Midwest	Southwest	Total
Sales	$10,000	$12,000	$22,000
Less: Cost of goods sold	(7,000)	(10,000)	(17,000)
Gross margin	$ 3,000	$ 2,000	$ 5,000
Less: Selling and administrative	(2,000)	(2,500)	(4,500)
Net income (loss)	$ 1,000	$ (500)	$ 500

Wilson sold all of the units produced during the quarter. There were no beginning or ending finished goods inventories. Twenty percent of the cost of goods sold represents fixed costs. Of total fixed production costs, 30 percent are directly traceable to the Midwest and 20 percent to the Southwest. The remaining fixed production costs, common to both regions, are equally allocated between them. Selling and administrative costs are all fixed. Of the total, $2 million representing common costs are equally divided between the two regions. Of the remaining selling and administrative fixed costs, 40 percent are directly traceable to the Midwest and 60 percent to the Southwest.

REQUIRED:
1. Prepare a variable-costing segmented income statement for the quarter ended. Should the company consider eliminating its Southwest regional activity?
2. Express the contribution margin and the segment margin computed in requirement 1 as a percentage of sales. Now assume that each region increases its sales activity in the next quarter by 10 percent. Assuming the same cost relationships, prepare a new variable-costing segmented income statement. Recompute the contribution margin and segment margin ratios. What happened? Explain.

E14-11
Unit Cost; Inventory Valuation; Absorption and Variable Costing; Contribution Margin
LO 1, LO 4

Wetzel Company manufactures yo-yos. In January 1997, Wetzel began producing neon-colored yo-yos. During the month of January, 6,000 were produced and 4,500 were sold at $5.50 each. The following costs were incurred:

Materials (plastic, string, axles)	$4,500
Direct labor	5,400
Variable factory overhead	2,400
Fixed factory overhead	7,500

A selling commission of 10 percent of sales price was paid. Administrative expenses, all fixed, amounted to $2,000.

REQUIRED:
1. Calculate the unit cost and cost of ending inventory under absorption costing.
2. Calculate the unit cost and cost of ending inventory under variable costing.
3. What is the contribution margin per unit?
4. Wetzel believes that neon-colored yo-yos will really take off after one year of sales. They think January 1998 sales should be twice as high as January 1997 sales. Costs are estimated to remain unchanged. What is the planned net income for Wetzel for January 1998? Did you use variable or absorption costing to determine it?

E14-12
Net Income; Absorption and Variable Costing
LO 1

Refer to E14-11.

REQUIRED:
1. Prepare an absorption-costing income statement for Wetzel Company for January 1998.
2. Prepare a variable-costing income statement for Wetzel Company for January 1998.
3. Reconcile the difference between the two net incomes.

E14-13
Inventory Valuation under Absorption and Variable Costing; Variable-Costing Net Income
LO 1

Frost Company manufactured 12,000 units during the year and sold 13,000. Frost's accountant prepared the following income statement:

Sales (13,000 @ $26)		$338,000
Cost of goods sold (13,000 @ $18)		234,000
Gross profit		$104,000
Marketing expenses	$26,000	
Administrative expenses	15,000	(41,000)
Net income		$ 63,000

Marketing expense is strictly variable. Administrative expense is entirely fixed. The fixed factory overhead rate is $3 per unit. Beginning inventory was 3,000 units, and there were no price changes from one year to the next.

REQUIRED:
1. Prepare a variable-costing income statement for Frost Company.
2. What was the value of ending inventory under absorption costing?
3. What was the value of ending inventory under variable costing?

E14-14
Calculating Unit and Total Costs under Absorption Costing
LO 1

Each of the following independent companies, A, B, and C, uses absorption costing. There are no overhead variances. Prices have stayed constant for all relevant time periods.

	A	B	C
Unit information:			
Price	$22	?	?
Direct materials	4	2	6
Direct labor	3	4	1
Variable overhead	1	1	1
Fixed overhead	?	3	1
Contribution margin	$ 14	?	?
Gross profit	$ 9	?	?
Units sold	2,000	7,600	?
Units produced	2,000	8,000	?
Beginning inventory, units	500	0	3,000
Total information:			
Sales	?	$114,000	$136,000
Cost of goods sold	?	?	72,000
Gross profit	?	38,000	?
Variable marketing	?	9,500	24,000
Fixed marketing	5,000	8,000	?
Fixed administrative	3,000	?	8,300
Net income	?	500	16,700
Value of ending inventory	6,500	?	9,000

REQUIRED: Replace each question mark with the correct amount.

E14-15
Inventory Valuation and Net Income under Variable Costing
LO 1

Refer to E14-14.

REQUIRED:
1. What are the net incomes for companies A, B, and C using variable costing?
2. What are the values of ending inventory for companies A, B, and C using variable costing?

E14-16
Variable and Absorption Costing
LO 1

Camrareddy Company manufactures 35mm cameras. The cameras are sold for $25 each. The cost of goods sold is $18; of that amount, $5 is for direct materials. Variable overhead is applied at twice the rate of direct labor. Total fixed overhead is $48,000. Production was 12,000 units for this year due to the need to increase inventory by 2,000 units. Selling and administrative costs, all fixed, amounted to $37,000.

REQUIRED:
1. What was absorption-costing net income for Camrareddy Company for the year? What was variable-costing net income?
2. If beginning inventory was zero, what was the value of ending inventory under absorption costing?
3. What is the contribution margin per unit for Camrareddy Company?

P ROBLEMS

P14-1
Variable- and Absorption-Costing

Vance Company manufactures heavy-duty motors. Sales for last year totaled $957,000. The cost of goods sold amounted to 40 percent of sales; of the total, 20 percent represented fixed manufac-

Income Statements
LO 1

turing expenses. Selling expenses were equally split between fixed and variable components. Administrative expenses, all fixed, totaled $77,000. Net income for last year was $323,400. Vance produced and sold 47,850 motors last year.

REQUIRED:

1. Prepare an absorption-costing income statement for Vance Company for last year.
2. Prepare a variable-costing income statement for Vance Company for last year.
3. What is the variable cost per motor? What is the variable production cost per motor?

P14-2
Variable Costing and
Break-even Analysis
LO 1, LO 4

Gordon Inc. manufactures medical equipment. Gordon's income statement is as follows:

Sales	$1,152,000
Variable cost of goods sold	(460,800)
Variable selling expense	(57,600)
Contribution margin	$ 633,600
Fixed overhead	(300,000)
Fixed selling and administrative	(139,000)
Net income	$ 194,600

Gordon believes it can increase the average price of its products by 9 percent next year. No change in quantity of products sold is forecast. Advertising will increase by $45,000, and administrative expenses will increase by $14,000. Production costs will remain constant.

REQUIRED:

1. Prepare a budgeted variable-costing income statement for next year.
2. Suppose that Gordon's controller believes that a more conservative estimate of the coming year's activity is an 8 percent increase in prices, an increased advertising budget of $50,000, and an increase in administrative expenses of $15,000. Prepare the budgeted variable-costing income statement based on the more conservative figures.

P14-3
Variable Costing;
Targeted Net Income
LO 4

Madengrad Company manufactures a single electronic product called Precisionmix. This unit is a batch-density monitoring device attached to large industrial mixing machines used in flour, rubber, petroleum, and chemical manufacturing. Precisionmix sells for $900 per unit. The following variable costs are incurred to produce each Precisionmix device:

Direct labor	$180
Direct materials	240
Factory overhead	105
Variable product cost	$525
Marketing cost	75
Total variable cost	$600

Madengrad's annual fixed costs are $6,600,000. Except for an operating loss incurred in the year of incorporation, the firm has been profitable over the last five years. Madengrad is forecasting sales of 21,500 units for next year and has budgeted production at that level.

REQUIRED:

1. Prepare a pro forma variable-costing income statement for Madengrad Company for next year.
2. Madengrad has just learned of a significant change in production technology that will cause a 10 percent increase in total annual fixed costs and a 20 percent unit labor cost increase as a result of higher skilled direct labor. However, this change permits the replacement of a costly imported component with a domestic component. The effect is to reduce unit material costs and variable overhead costs by 25 percent. No change in selling price is forecast. Prepare a variable-costing income statement for Madengrad Company for next year assuming it invests in the new production technology. (CMA adapted)

P14-4
Segment Analysis;
Addition of a New
Product
LO 3

Sandia Company currently produces two products, A and B. The company has sufficient floor space to manufacture an additional product, with two (C and D) currently under consideration. Only one of the two products can be chosen. The expected annual sales and associated costs for each product are as follows:

	Product C	Product D
Sales	$100,000	$125,000
Variable costs as a percentage of sales:		
Production	54%	65%
Selling and administrative	12%	5%
Direct fixed expenses	$15,000	$11,250

The common fixed costs of the company are allocated to each product line on the basis of sales revenues.

The following income statement for last year's operations is also available:

	Product A	Product B	Total
Sales	$250,000	$375,000	$625,000
Less variable expenses:			
Cost of goods sold	(100,000)	(250,000)	(350,000)
Selling and administrative	(20,000)	(65,000)	(85,000)
Contribution margin	$130,000	$ 60,000	$190,000
Less: Direct fixed expenses	(10,000)	(55,000)	(65,000)
Segment margin	$120,000	$ 5,000	$125,000
Less: Common fixed expenses			(75,000)
Net income			$ 50,000

REQUIRED:
1. Prepare an income statement that reflects the impact on the firm's profits of adding product C. Repeat for product D. Which of the two would you recommend adding?
2. Suppose that both products C and D could be added if either A or B is dropped. Would you drop one of the current products to add both C and D? If so, which would you drop? Why?

P14-5
Income Statements;
Variable Costing;
Absorption Costing
LO 1

The following information pertains to the first year of operation for Aladdin Company:

Units produced	88,000
Expected actual production	100,000
Units sold	85,000
Unit selling price	$10
Costs:	
Budgeted (and actual) fixed overhead	$200,000
Budgeted (and actual) variable overhead	150,000
Total cost of direct materials used	220,000
Total cost of direct labor	184,800
Variable selling and administrative	42,500
Fixed selling and administrative	100,000

Any under- or overapplied overhead is closed to Cost of Goods Sold.

REQUIRED:
1. Without preparing formal income statements, compute the difference that will exist between absorption-costing and variable-costing income.

2. Prepare absorption-costing and variable-costing income statements.
3. Reconcile the difference between the two income figures. (Have you already done this in answering requirement 1?)

P14-6

Sales; Income Behavior; Variable Costing; Absorption Costing

LO 1

Blades Products Division was organized as a new division of Amalgamated Stuff, Inc. to produce rollerblades. With the continuing popularity of physical fitness, Blades' divisional manager expected a good response to the product. In the first year of operations, Blades reported the following net income to its stockholders:

Blades Products
Income Statement
For the Year Ended December 31, 1996

Sales (@ $85)	$42,500,000
Less: Cost of goods sold (@ $65)[a]	(32,500,000)
Gross margin	$10,000,000
Less: Selling and administrative[b]	(5,125,000)
Net income	$ 4,875,000

[a]Direct materials	$24
Direct labor	12
Variable overhead	15
Fixed overhead	14
Total	$65

[b]$6.25 per-unit variable; $2,000,000 fixed

In 1996, Blades produced 100,000 units more than it sold because sales were less than expected. The divisional manager believed the sales slump was due to a soft economy and was confident that sales for the second year would be 20 percent higher. Overhead is applied on the basis of units produced using expected actual activity. Any under- or overapplied overhead is closed to Cost of Goods Sold. For the first year, there was no under- or overapplied overhead.

For 1997, fixed costs and unit variable costs remained the same; the selling price also remained unchanged. Budgeted fixed costs equaled actual fixed costs. In 1997, Blades produced 500,000 units and sold 600,000. Production was 100,000 less than expected because of unexpected equipment problems; however, the divisional manager was not displeased because the 20 percent sales increase had been achieved, and production costs were completely in line with plans.

REQUIRED:
1. Prepare the 1997 income statement required for stockholders. Did income increase or decrease? What do you think the reaction of the parent company, Amalgamated Stuff, Inc. would be to this income statement? What would the divisional manager's reaction be?
2. Prepare variable-costing income statements for 1996 and 1997. How do you suppose Amalgamated Stuff, Inc. would react now?
3. Reconcile and explain the differences between variable-costing and absorption-costing income figures for 1996 and 1997.
4. Which type of income statement (variable or absorption costing) do you think the divisional manager would prefer? Why?

P14-7

Variable Costing; Absorption Costing; Income Statements; Inventory Valuations

LO 1

Beldar Company produces and sells a single product. Cost data for the product follow:

Unit variable costs:	
Direct materials	$4
Direct labor	2
Variable overhead	2
Variable selling	1
Total	$9

Fixed costs per year:	
Overhead	$ 960,000
Selling and administrative	300,000
Total	$1,260,000

*Fixed costs are incurred uniformly throughout the year.

During the first three months, the company produced and sold the following units:

	Units Produced	Units Sold
Month 1	50,000	40,000
Month 2	40,000	40,000
Month 3	40,000	30,000

The company uses an actual cost system to assign the costs of production. The selling price of the product is $14 per unit. A LIFO inventory system is used.

REQUIRED:
1. What is the unit cost for each month under absorption costing? under variable costing?
2. Without preparing income statements, determine the difference between absorption-costing and variable-costing income for each of the three months.
3. Prepare income statements for absorption costing and variable costing for each of the three months. Reconcile the net income figures.

P14-8
Segmented Income Statements; Analysis of Proposals to Improve Profits
LO 2, LO 3

Harris, Inc. has two divisions. One produces and sells paper diapers; the other produces and sells paper napkins and towels. A segmented income statement for the most recent quarter follows:

	Diaper Division	Napkin and Towel Division	Total
Sales	$500,000	$750,000	$1,250,000
Less: Variable expenses	(425,000)	(460,000)	(885,000)
Contribution margin	$ 75,000	$290,000	$ 365,000
Less: Direct fixed expenses	(85,000)	(110,000)	(195,000)
Segment margin	$ (10,000)	$180,000	$ 170,000
Less: Common fixed expenses			(130,000)
Net income			$ 40,000

On seeing the quarterly statement, Karen Norris, president of Harris, Inc., was distressed. "The Diaper Division is killing us," she complained. "It's not even covering its own fixed costs. I'm beginning to believe that we should shut down that division. This is the seventh consecutive quarter it has failed to provide a positive segment margin. I was certain that Fran Simmons could turn it around. But this is her third quarter, and she hasn't done much better than the previous divisional manager."

"Well, before you get too excited about the situation, perhaps you should evaluate Fran's most recent proposals," remarked Tom Ferguson, the company's vice-president of finance. "She wants to lease some new production equipment and at the same time increase the advertising budget by $25,000 per quarter. She made some improvements in the design of the diaper and wants to let the public know about them. According to her marketing people, sales should increase by 10 percent if the right advertising is done—and done quickly. The new production machinery will increase the rate of production, lower labor costs, and result in less waste of materials. Fran claims that variable costs will be reduced by 30 percent. The cost of the lease is $105,000 per quarter."

Upon hearing this news, Karen calmed considerably, and, in fact, was somewhat pleased. After all, she was the one who had selected Fran and had a great deal of confidence in Fran's judgment and abilities.

REQUIRED:
1. Assuming that Fran's proposals are sound, should Karen Norris be pleased with the prospects for the Diaper Division? Prepare a segmented income statement for the next quarter that reflects the implementation of Fran's proposals. Assume that the Napkin and Towel Division's sales increase by 5 percent for the next quarter and that the same cost relationships hold.
2. Suppose that everything materializes as Fran projected except for the 10 percent increase in sales—no change in sales revenues took place. Are the proposals still sound? What if the variable costs are reduced by 40 percent instead of 30 percent with no change in sales?

P14-9
Performance Evaluation; Absorption Costing Compared with Variable Costing
LO 1, LO 2

Reread the opening scenario for this chapter. The following represent the three years of operating data and income statements that Kathy received.

	Year 1	Year 2	Year 3
Production	10,000	11,000	9,000
Sales (in units)	8,000	10,000	12,000
Unit selling price	$10	$10	$10
Unit costs:			
Fixed overhead*	$2.90	$3.00	$3.00
Variable overhead	1.00	1.00	1.00
Direct materials	1.90	2.00	2.00
Direct labor	1.00	1.00	1.00
Variable selling	0.40	0.50	0.50
Actual fixed overhead	$29,000	$30,000	$30,000
Other fixed costs	$9,000	$10,000	$10,000

*The predetermined fixed overhead rate is based on expected actual units of production and expected fixed overhead. Expected production each year was 10,000 units. Any under- or overapplied fixed overhead is closed to Cost of Goods Sold.

Yearly Income Statements

	Year 1	Year 2	Year 3
Sales revenue	$80,000	$100,000	$120,000
Less: Cost of goods sold*	54,400	67,000	86,600
Gross margin	$25,600	$ 33,000	$ 33,400
Less: Selling and administrative	12,200	15,000	16,000
Net income	$13,400	$ 18,000	$ 17,400

*This assumes a LIFO inventory flow.

Recall that Kathy was pleased with the operating data, but she was dismayed and perplexed by the income statements. Instead of seeing a significant increase in income for the third year, she saw a small decrease. Kathy's initial reaction was that the accounting department had made an error.

REQUIRED:
1. Explain to Kathy why she lost her $5,000 bonus.
2. Prepare variable-costing income statements for each of the three years. Reconcile the differences between the absorption-costing and variable-costing incomes.
3. If you were the vice-president of Kathy's company, which income statement (variable costing or absorption costing) would you prefer to use for evaluating Kathy's performance? Why?

P14-10
Absorption Costing and Performance Evaluation
LO 2

Wilmont Company's executive committee was meeting to select a new vice-president of operations. The leading candidate was Howard Kimball, manager of Wilmont's largest division. Howard had been divisional manager for three years. The president of Wilmont, Larry Olsen, was impressed with the significant improvements in the division's profits since Howard had assumed command. In the first year of operations, divisional profits had increased by 20 percent. They had shown significant improvements for the following two years as well. To bolster support for Howard, the company's president circulated the following divisional income statements (dollars in thousands):

	1995	1996	1997
Sales	$30,000	$32,000	$34,000
Less: Cost of goods sold[a]	(26,250)	(26,400)	(27,200)
Gross margin	$ 3,750	$ 5,600	$ 6,800
Less: Selling and administrative[b]	(3,000)	(3,600)	(3,800)
Net income	$ 750	$ 2,000	$ 3,000

[a]This assumes a LIFO inventory flow.
[b]All costs are fixed.

"As you can see," Larry observed at a meeting, "Howard has increased profits by a factor of four since 1995. That's by far the most impressive performance of any divisional manager. We could certainly use someone with that kind of drive. I definitely believe that Howard should be the new vice-president."

"I'm not quite as convinced that Howard's performance is as impressive as it appears," responded Bill Peters, the vice-president of finance. "I could hardly believe that Howard's division could show the magnitude of improvement revealed by the income statements, so I asked the divisional controller to supply some additional information. As the data suggest, the profits realized by Howard's division may be attributable to a concerted effort to produce for inventory. In fact, I believe it can be shown that the division is actually showing a loss each year and that real profits have declined by as much as 15 percent since 1995." Peters then showed the following information:

	1995	1996	1997
Sales (units)	150,000	160,000	170,000
Production*	200,000	250,000	300,000
Actual (and budgeted) fixed overhead	$15,000,000	$15,000,000	$15,000,000
Fixed overhead rate	$75	$60	$50
Unit variable production costs	$100	$105	$110

*This represents both expected and actual production. Fixed overhead rates are computed using expected actual production.

REQUIRED:

1. Explain what Bill Peters meant by "producing for inventory."
2. Recast the income statements in a variable-costing format. Now how does the performance of the division appear?
3. Reconcile the differences in the income figures using the two methods for each of the three years.
4. If you were a shareholder, how could you detect income increases that are caused mainly by production for inventory?

P14-11
Comparison of Variable and

Jackson, Inc. has just completed its first year of operations. The unit costs on a normal-costing basis are as follows:

**Absorption Costing;
Predetermined
Overhead Rates**
LO 1

Manufacturing costs (per unit):	
Direct materials (2 lb @ $2)	$ 4.00
Direct labor (1.5 hr @ $7)	10.50
Variable overhead (1.5 hr @ $2)	3.00
Fixed overhead (1.5 hr @ $3)	4.50
Total	$22.00

Nonmanufacturing costs:	
Variable	10% of sales
Fixed	$200,000

During the year, the company had the following activity:

Units produced	25,000
Units sold	20,000
Unit selling price	$40
Direct labor hours worked	37,500

Actual fixed overhead was $10,000 greater than budgeted fixed overhead. Actual variable overhead was $5,000 greater than budgeted variable overhead. The company used an expected actual activity level of 37,500 direct labor hours to compute the predetermined overhead rates. Any overhead variances are closed to Cost of Goods Sold.

REQUIRED:
1. Compute the unit cost using (a) absorption costing and (b) variable costing.
2. Prepare an absorption-costing income statement.
3. Prepare a variable-costing income statement.
4. Reconcile the difference between the two income statements.

**P14-12
Segmented Income
Statements; Adding
and Dropping
Product Lines**
LO 2, LO 3

Nancy Henderson has just been appointed manager of Palmroy's Glass Products Division. She has two years to make the division profitable. If the division is still showing a loss after two years, it will be eliminated, and Nancy will be reassigned as an assistant divisional manager in another division. The divisional income statement for the most recent year follows:

Sales	$5,350,000
Less: Variable expenses	(4,750,000)
Contribution margin	$ 600,000
Less: Direct fixed expenses	(750,000)
Divisional margin	$ (150,000)
Less: Common fixed expenses (allocated)	(200,000)
Divisional profit (loss)	$ (350,000)

Upon arriving at the division, Nancy requested the following data on the division's three products:

	Product A	Product B	Product C
Sales (units)	10,000	20,000	15,000
Unit selling price	$150.00	$140.00	$ 70.00
Unit variable cost	$100.00	$110.00	$103.33
Direct fixed costs	$100,000.00	$500,000.00	$150,000.00

She also gathered data on a proposed new product (D). If this product is added, it would displace one of the current products; the quantity that could be produced and sold would equal the quantity sold of the product it displaces. Demand limits the maximum quantity that could be sold to 20,000 units. Because of specialized production equipment, it is not possible for the new product to displace part of the production of a second product. The information on product D is as follows:

Unit selling price	$ 70
Unit variable cost	30
Direct fixed costs	640,000

REQUIRED:
1. Prepare segmented income statements for products A, B, and C.
2. Determine the products that Nancy should produce for the coming year. Prepare segmented income statements that prove your combination is the best for the division. By how much will profits improve given the combination that you selected? (*Hint:* Your combination may include one, two, or three products.)

....

P14-13
Comprehensive Review Problem: Variable Costing, Absorption Costing, Segmented Reporting
LO 1, LO 3

The Clock Division of Thurmond Company produces both wall clocks and table clocks. The clocks are sold in two regions, the West and the Southwest. The following table gives the sales of the Clock Division during 1997 (in units).

	West	Southwest	Total
Wall clocks	100,000	250,000	350,000
Table clocks	250,000	520,000	770,000

Production data for 1997 are as follows (there were no beginning or ending work-in-process inventories):

	Wall Clocks	**Table Clocks**
Production	300,000	800,000
Direct labor hours	30,000	40,000
Manufacturing costs:		
Direct materials	$450,000	$720,000
Direct labor	210,000	200,000
Variable overhead	60,000	90,000
Fixed overhead*	360,000	540,000

*Common fixed overhead of $280,000 has been allocated to the two products on the basis of actual direct labor hours and is included in each total.

The selling prices are $4.50 for wall clocks and $3 for table clocks. Variable nonmanufacturing costs are 20 percent of the selling price for wall clocks and 30 percent of the selling price for table clocks. Total fixed nonmanufacturing costs are $300,000: one-third common to both products, and one-third directly traceable to each product. Of the fixed costs (both manufacturing and nonmanufacturing), 20 percent are common to both sales regions, 40 percent are directly traceable to the West, and 40 percent are directly traceable to the Southwest.

Overhead is applied on the basis of direct labor hours. Normal volume is 75,000 hours (300,000 wall clocks, 900,000 table clocks), and the preceding actual overhead figures correspond to the budgeted figures used to compute the predetermined overhead rate. Any under- or overapplied overhead is closed to Cost of Goods Sold. Assume that any beginning finished goods inventory has the same unit costs as current production. The company uses LIFO to value inventories.

REQUIRED:

1. Compute the unit costs for each product using (a) absorption costing and (b) variable costing.
2. Prepare absorption-costing and variable-costing income statements for 1997. Reconcile the difference between the two income figures.
3. Prepare a segmented income statement on a variable-costing basis where segments are defined as products.
4. Prepare a segmented income statement on a variable-costing basis where segments are defined as sales regions.

 ANAGERIAL DECISION CASES

C14-1
Ethical Issues;
Absorption Costing;
Performance
Measurement
LO 1, LO 2

Ruth Swazey, divisional controller and CMA, was upset by a recent memo she received from the divisional manager, Paul Chesser. Ruth was scheduled to present the division's financial performance at headquarters in one week. In the memo, Paul had given Ruth some instructions for this upcoming report. In particular, she had been told to emphasize the significant improvement in the division's profits over last year. Ruth, however, didn't believe that there was any real underlying improvement in the division's performance and was reluctant to say otherwise. She knew that the increase in profits was because of Paul's conscious decision to produce for inventory.

In an earlier meeting, Paul had convinced his plant managers to produce more than they knew they could sell. He argued that by deferring some of this period's fixed costs, reported profits would jump. He pointed out two significant benefits. First, by increasing profits, the division could exceed the minimum level needed so that all the managers would qualify for the annual bonus. Second, by meeting the budgeted profit level, the division would be better able to compete for much-needed capital. Ruth had objected but had been overruled. The most persuasive counterargument was that the increase in inventory could be liquidated in the coming year as the economy improved. Ruth, however, considered this event unlikely. From past experience, she knew that it would take at least two years of improved market demand before the productive capacity of the division was exceeded.

REQUIRED:

1. Discuss the behavior of Paul Chesser, the divisional manager. Was the decision to produce for inventory an ethical one?
2. What should Ruth Swazey do? Should she comply with the directive to emphasize the increase in profits? If not, what options does she have?
3. In Exhibit 1-4 in Chapter 1, ethical standards for management accountants were listed. Identify any standards that apply in this situation.

C14-2
Variable Costing
versus Absorption
Costing
LO 1, LO 2, LO 3, LO 4

Norma Richardson, manager of a division specializing in concrete pipe and concrete blocks, had just been rebuffed by Eric Hipple, president of the company. Eric had called a meeting of all divisional managers to discuss the downturn in business the company had been experiencing during the past two years. Eric had come down hard on the managers, pointing out that their jobs would be on the line if some immediate improvements were not forthcoming.

Norma, acting as spokesperson for the divisional managers, had tried to explain to Eric why revenues and profits were declining. In the divisional managers' view, business was suffering because residential and commercial construction was down. With the slump in the construction business, competition had intensified. Norma indicated that her division had lost several bids to competitors who were bidding below the full cost of the product. Since company policy prohibited divisional managers from accepting any jobs below full cost, these bids were lost. Norma, on behalf of the managers, requested a change in company policy concerning bids. She proposed that the floor for bids be changed to variable cost rather than full cost. In times of economic distress, bids that cover at least their variable costs would make a positive contribution toward covering fixed costs and would help maintain the divisions' profits.

Norma also proposed that divisional income statements be changed to a variable-costing basis so that a better picture of divisional performance would be available. Additionally, income statements for individual products, organized on a variable-costing basis, would provide better information concerning product performance and would facilitate bidding.

Upon hearing the request, Eric Hipple flatly turned it down. Eric was convinced that all costs must be covered or the company would go under. "It's impossible to sell a product for less than what it costs and stay in business. Those companies that do so will be the first ones to go bankrupt.

Also, I want to see the income produced by your divisions when all costs are considered—not just variable costs. I don't believe in variable costing. If any of you can prove to me that variable costing is a better approach, then I would consider changing."

Upon returning home, Norma decided to prepare more formal arguments to convince Eric of the value of variable costing. To help in building her case, she had the divisional controller supply the following information concerning the concrete block line (8" × 8" × 16" blocks):

Last quarter's production (and sales)	100,000
Productive capacity	140,000
Unit manufacturing cost:	
Direct materials	$0.22
Direct labor	0.14
Variable overhead	0.09
Fixed overhead*	0.10
Total	$0.55

*Based on the productive capacity of 140,000 units

Nonmanufacturing costs:	
Selling costs:	
Fixed	$10,000
Variable	5% of sales
Administrative (all fixed)	$20,000

Total fixed overhead costs were $14,000 (budgeted and actual). Variable overhead was incurred as expected. Overhead variances are closed to Cost of Goods Sold. The average selling price for the 100,000 units sold was $0.90.

REQUIRED:
1. Prepare absorption-costing and variable-costing income statements for the last quarter's results. Will this information help Norma in building her case?
2. Suppose that Norma consults her marketing manager and finds that the division could have produced and sold 30,000 more concrete blocks with a unit selling price of $0.54. Compute the gross margin on the sale of these additional 30,000 blocks, assuming a price of $0.54. Now compute the total contribution margin on the 30,000 blocks. Discuss why the two figures differ.
3. Prepare absorption-costing and variable-costing income statements that reflect the sale of the additional 30,000 units at $0.54. Which figure in requirement 2, gross margin or contribution margin, gave the best indication of the impact of the 30,000 additional units on the division's profits? Explain.
4. What approach would you take to convince Eric that variable costing is a useful managerial tool? Does he have any basis for his contention that a company must cover its full costs and that income statements should reflect all costs, not just variable costs? Explain.

1. Determine the number of units that must be sold to break even or to earn a targeted profit.

2. Determine the amount of revenue required to break even or to earn a targeted profit.

3. Apply cost-volume-profit analysis in a multiple-product setting.

4. Prepare a profit-volume graph and a cost-volume-profit graph and explain the meaning of each.

5. Explain the impact of risk, uncertainty, and changing variables on cost-volume-profit analysis.

6. Discuss the impact of activity-based costing on cost-volume-profit analysis.

CHAPTER

Cost-Volume-Profit Analysis: A Managerial Planning Tool

SCENARIO

For years, Janet McFarland's friends and family raved about her homemade jellies and salsas. Janet traditionally canned several gallons of salsa, ladled it into decorative pint jars, wrapped them, and sent them as gifts. Her friends said, "You ought to sell this stuff— you'd make a fortune!" So, Janet decided to give it a try.

First, she decided to concentrate on one product, a green cactus salsa that had gotten rave reviews. She scouted sources of jars, lids, and labels. In addition, Janet got in touch with her local agricultural extension office and learned a considerable amount about laws regulating food sales. One source of surprise was that she was required to obtain an expert confirmation of the ingredients in her salsa. Usually, Janet added a little of this and a little of that until

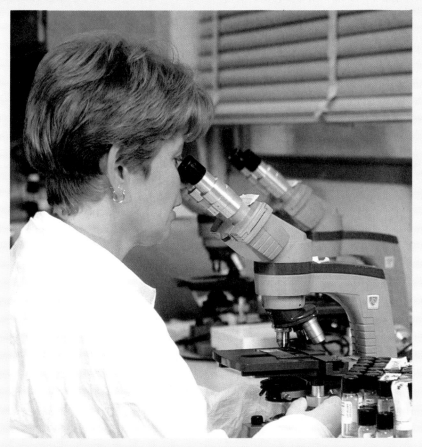

it tasted right. She found out that this off-the-cuff approach would not work. Foods were required to be labeled with the name of each ingredient, in order of amount. Suddenly, it mattered whether ancho or poblano chilis were used, and in what proportion. Janet needed a standardized recipe. She located a professional food chemist to analyze the recipe and certify the proportion of ingredients.

Janet traveled to a number of grocery stores and gift shops in the area. Several were willing to stock her product on consignment, placing a few jars by the cash register; others guaranteed shelf space but required a shelf charge for it. She figured that traveling to the stores, checking on sales and stock, and visiting prospective customers would take about one day a week.

Before starting production, Janet consulted with her family accountant, Bob Ryan.

Janet: Bob, I'm really excited about this opportunity, it all seems to be falling into place.

Bob: I'm happy for you, too, Janet. But first let's do some planning. I need to take a look at the costs and selling price you anticipate.

Janet: I think I can charge $3.50 per jar. It's a new product and I want to build a market for it. The costs I've come up with are on this sheet. They aren't as high as they could be since I'm going to start slowly and cook small batches at a time in our kitchen.

Bob: (After a couple of minutes of figuring) Janet, do you realize that at a price of $3.50, and with the variable costs that you described, you'll lose money! You can't do that.

Janet: What if I sell more jars? Will that help?

Bob: No, that will just make it worse. Let's go back to the drawing board and see if there's a way to decrease those variable costs and/or increase the price. Otherwise, you would be better off never getting involved with this business.

Questions to Think About

1. What kinds of variable and fixed costs do you think Janet will incur?
2. Given Bob's initial assessment that the variable costs are higher than the price, what is wrong with Janet's thought that selling more is the way to go?
3. How important is break-even analysis to a firm? Do you suppose that large companies do break-even analysis as well as small companies?
4. Why is the concept of breaking even important? Doesn't Janet want to make a profit?
5. Janet doesn't know what price to charge. How could she get a better idea?

Cost-volume-profit analysis (CVP analysis) is a powerful tool for planning and decision making. Because CVP analysis emphasizes the interrelationships of costs, quantity sold, and price, it brings together all of the financial information of the firm. CVP analysis can be a valuable tool to identify the extent and magnitude of the economic trouble a division is facing and to help pinpoint the necessary solution. For example, SAAB was on the brink of collapse in 1990 when General Motors bought a 50 percent share in the company. Over the last few years, SAAB has cut costs dramatically and lowered its break-even point from 130,000 cars to 80,000 cars.[1]

CVP analysis can address many other issues as well, such as: the number of units that must be sold to break even; the impact of a given reduction in fixed costs on the break-even point; and the impact of an increase in price on profit. Additionally, CVP analysis allows managers to do sensitivity analysis by examining the impact of various price or cost levels on profit.

While this chapter deals with the mechanics and terminology of CVP analysis, you should keep in mind that CVP analysis is an integral part of financial planning and decision making. Every accountant and manager should be thoroughly conversant with its concepts, not just the mechanics.

BREAK-EVEN POINT IN UNITS

Objective I

Determine the number of units that must be sold to break even or to earn a targeted profit.

break-even point

Since we are interested in how revenues, expenses, and profits behave as volume changes, it is natural to begin by finding the firm's break-even point in units sold. The break-even point is the point where total revenue equals total cost, the point of zero profit. To find the break-even point in units we focus on operating income. We will first discuss the way to find the break-even point, and then see how our approach can be expanded to determine the number of units that must be sold to earn a targeted profit.

The firm's initial decision in implementing a units-sold approach to CVP analysis is the determination of just what a unit is. For manufacturing firms, the answer is obvious. Procter & Gamble may define a unit as a bar of Ivory soap. Service firms face a more difficult choice. Delta Airlines may define a unit as a passenger mile, or as a one-way trip. The Jacksonville Naval Supply Center, which provides naval, industrial, and general supplies to U.S. Navy ships stationed in northeastern Florida and the Caribbean, defines "productive units" to measure the activities involved in delivering services. In this way, more complicated services are assigned more productive units than less complicated services, thereby standardizing service effort.[2]

A second decision centers on the separation of costs into fixed and variable components. CVP analysis focuses on the factors that effect a *change* in the components of profit. Because we are looking at CVP analysis in terms of units sold, we need to determine the fixed and variable components of cost and revenue with respect to units. (This assumption will be relaxed when we incorporate activity-based costing into CVP analysis.) It is important to realize that we are focusing on the firm as a whole. Therefore, the costs we are talking about are *all* costs of the company—manufacturing, marketing, and administrative. Thus, when we say variable cost, we mean all costs that increase as more units are sold, including: direct materials, direct labor, variable overhead, and variable selling and administrative costs. Similarly, fixed cost includes fixed overhead and fixed selling and administrative expenses.

Using Operating Income in CVP Analysis

The income statement is a useful tool for organizing the firm's costs into fixed and variable categories. The income statement can be expressed as a narrative equation:

Operating income = Sales revenues − Variable expenses − Fixed expenses

1. James Bennet, "Eurocars: On the Road Again," *New York Times*, 20 August 1995, sec. 3, pp. 1, 10.
2. David J. Harr, "How Activity Accounting Works in Government," *Management Accounting*, September 1990, pp. 36–40.

operating income

Note that we are using the term operating income to denote income or profit *before* income taxes. Operating income includes only revenues and expenses from the firm's normal operations. We will use the term net income to mean operating income minus income taxes.

net income

Once we have a measure of units sold, we can expand the operating-income equation by expressing sales revenues and variable expenses in terms of unit dollar amounts and number of units. Specifically, sales revenue is expressed as the unit selling price times the number of units sold, and total variable costs are the unit variable cost times the number of units sold. With these expressions, the operating-income equation becomes:

$$\text{Operating income} = (\text{Price} \times \text{Number of units}) - (\text{Variable cost per unit} \times \text{Number of units}) - \text{Total fixed cost}$$

Suppose you were asked how many units must be sold in order to break even, or earn a zero profit. You could answer that question by setting operating income to zero and then solving the operating-income equation for the number of units.

Let's use the following example to solve for the break-even point in units. Assume that Whittier Company manufactures a mulching lawn mower. For the coming year, the controller has prepared the following projected income statement:

Sales (1,000 units @ $400)	$ 400,000
Less: Variable expenses	(325,000)
Contribution margin	$ 75,000
Less: Fixed expenses	(45,000)
Profit before taxes	$ 30,000

We see that for Whittier Company, the price is $400 per unit and the variable cost is $325 ($\frac{\$325,000}{1,000 \text{ units}}$). Fixed cost is $45,000. At the break-even point, then, the operating-income equation would take the following form:

$$0 = (\$400 \times \text{Units}) - (\$325 \times \text{Units}) - \$45,000$$
$$0 = \$75 \times \text{Units} - \$45,000$$
$$\$75 \times \text{Units} = \$45,000$$
$$\text{Units} = 600$$

Therefore, Whittier must sell 600 lawn mowers to just cover all fixed and variable expenses. A good way to check this answer is to formulate an income statement based on 600 units sold.

Sales (600 units @ $400)	$ 240,000
Less: Variable expenses	(195,000)
Contribution margin	$ 45,000
Less: Fixed expenses	(45,000)
Operating income	$ 0

Indeed, selling 600 units does yield a zero profit.

An important advantage of the operating-income approach is that all further CVP equations are derived from the variable-costing income statement. As a result, you can solve any CVP problem by using this approach.

Shortcut to Calculating Break-even Units

We can more quickly calculate break-even units by focusing on the contribution margin. The contribution margin is sales revenue minus total variable cost. At breakeven, the

contribution margin

contribution margin equals the fixed expenses. If we substitute the unit contribution margin for price minus unit variable cost in the operating-income equation and solve for the number of units, we obtain the following fundamental break-even equation:

$$\text{Number of units} = \frac{\text{Fixed cost}}{\text{Unit contribution margin}}$$

Using Whittier Company as an example, we can see that the contribution margin per unit can be computed in one of two ways. One way is to divide the total contribution margin by the units sold for a result of $75 per unit ($\frac{\$75,000}{1,000}$). A second way is to compute price minus variable cost per unit. Doing so yields the same result, $75 per unit ($400 − $325). To calculate the break-even number of units for Whittier Company, use the fundamental break-even equation as follows:

$$\text{Number of units} = \frac{\$45,000}{\$400 - \$325}$$
$$= \frac{\$45,000}{\$75 \text{ per unit}}$$
$$= 600 \text{ units}$$

Of course, the answer is identical to that computed using the income statement.

Unit Sales Needed to Achieve Targeted Profit

While the break-even point is useful information, most firms would like to earn operating income greater than zero. CVP analysis gives us a way to determine how many units must be sold to earn a particular targeted income. Targeted operating income can be expressed as a dollar amount (for example, $20,000) or as a percentage of sales revenue (for example, 15 percent of revenue). Both the operating-income approach and the contribution margin approach can be easily adjusted to allow for targeted income.

Targeted Income as a Dollar Amount Assume that Whittier Company wants to earn operating income of $60,000. How many mulching mowers must be sold to achieve this result? Let's use the income statement to find out:

$$\$60,000 = (\$400 \times \text{Units}) - (\$325 \times \text{Units}) - \$45,000$$
$$\$105,000 = \$75 \times \text{Units}$$
$$= 1,400 \text{ Units}$$

If instead we use the fundamental break-even equation, we simply add targeted profit of $60,000 to the fixed cost and solve for the number of units.

$$\text{Units} = \frac{\$45,000 + \$60,000}{\$400 - \$325}$$

$$\text{Units} = \frac{\$105,000}{\$75}$$

$$\text{Units} = 1,400$$

Whittier must sell 1,400 lawn mowers to earn a before-tax profit of $60,000. The following income statement verifies this outcome:

Sales (1,400 units @ $400)	$ 560,000
Less: Variable expenses	(455,000)
Contribution margin	$ 105,000
Less: Fixed expenses	(45,000)
Profit before taxes	$ 60,000

Another way to check this number of units is to use the break-even point. As just shown, Whittier must sell 1,400 lawn mowers, or 800 more than the break-even volume of 600 units, to earn a profit of $60,000. The contribution margin per lawn mower is $75. Multiplying $75 by the 800 lawn mowers *above* breakeven produces the profit of $60,000 ($75 × 800). This outcome demonstrates that contribution margin per unit for each unit above breakeven is equivalent to profit per unit. Since the break-even point had already been computed, the number of lawn mowers to be sold to yield a $60,000 operating income could have been calculated by dividing the unit contribution margin into the target profit and adding the resulting amount to the break-even volume.

In general, assuming that fixed costs remain the same, the impact on a firm's profits resulting from a change in the number of units sold can be assessed by multiplying the unit contribution margin by the change in units sold. For example, if 1,500 lawn mowers instead of 1,400 are sold, how much more profit will be earned? The change in units sold is an increase of 100 lawn mowers, and the unit contribution margin is $75. Thus, profits will increase by $7,500 ($75 × 100).

Targeted Income as a Percent of Sales Revenue Assume that Whittier Company wants to know the number of lawn mowers that must be sold in order to earn a profit equal to 15 percent of sales revenue. Sales revenue is price multiplied by the quantity sold. Thus, the targeted operating income is 15 percent of price times quantity. Using the income statement (which is simpler in this case), we have the following:

$$.15(\$400)(\text{Units}) = (\$400 \times \text{Units}) - (\$325 \times \text{Units}) - \$45,000$$
$$\$60 \times \text{Units} = (\$400 \times \text{Units}) - (\$325 \times \text{Units}) - \$45,000$$
$$\$60 \times \text{Units} = (\$75 \times \text{Units}) - \$45,000$$
$$\$15 \times \text{Units} = \$45,000$$
$$\text{Units} = 3,000$$

Does a volume of 3,000 lawn mowers achieve a profit equal to 15 percent of sales revenue? For 3,000 lawn mowers, the total revenue is $1.2 million ($400 × 3,000). The profit can be computed without preparing a formal income statement. Remember that above breakeven, the contribution margin per unit is the profit per unit. The break-even volume is 600 lawn mowers. If 3,000 lawn mowers are sold, then 2,400 (3,000 − 600) lawn mowers above the break-even point are sold. The before-tax profit, therefore, is $180,000 ($75 × 2,400), which is 15 percent of sales ($\frac{\$180,000}{\$1,200,000}$).

After-Tax Profit Targets

When calculating the break-even point, income taxes play no role. This is because the taxes paid on zero income are zero. However, when the company needs to know how many units to sell to earn a particular net income, some additional consideration is needed. Recall that net income is operating income after income taxes, and that our targeted income figure was expressed in before-tax terms. As a result, when the income target is expressed as net income, we must add back the income taxes to get operating income.

In general, taxes are computed as a percentage of income. The after-tax profit is computed by subtracting the tax from the operating income (or before-tax profit).

$$\begin{aligned}\text{Net income} &= \text{Operating income} - \text{Taxes}\\ &= \text{Operating income} - (\text{Tax rate} \times \text{Operating income})\\ &= \text{Operating income}(1 - \text{Tax rate})\end{aligned}$$

or

$$\text{Operating income} = \frac{\text{Net income}}{1 - \text{Tax rate}}$$

Thus, to convert the after-tax profit to before-tax profit, simply divide the after-tax profit by (1 − Tax rate).

Suppose that Whittier Company wants to achieve net income of $48,750 and its tax rate is 35 percent. To convert the after-tax profit target into a before-tax profit target, complete the following steps:

$$\$48,750 = \text{Operating income} - (0.35 \times \text{Operating income})$$
$$\$48,750 = 0.65 \,(\text{Operating income})$$
$$\$75,000 = \text{Operating income}$$

In other words, with a tax rate of 35 percent, Whittier Company must earn $75,000 before taxes to have $48,750 after taxes.[3] With this conversion, we can now calculate the number of units that must be sold:

$$\text{Units} = \frac{\$45,000 + \$75,000}{\$75}$$

$$\text{Units} = \frac{\$120,000}{\$75}$$

$$\text{Units} = 1,600$$

Let's check this answer by preparing an income statement based on sales of 1,600 lawn mowers.

Sales (1,600 @ $400)	$ 640,000
Less: Variable expenses	(520,000)
Contribution margin	$ 120,000
Less: Fixed expenses	(45,000)
Profit before taxes	$ 75,000
Less: Taxes (35% tax rate)	(26,250)
Profit after taxes	$ 48,750

BREAK-EVEN POINT IN SALES DOLLARS

Objective 2

Determine the amount of revenue required to break even or to earn a targeted profit.

In some cases when using CVP analysis, managers may prefer to use sales revenues as the measure of sales activity instead of units sold. A units-sold measure can be converted to a sales revenue measure simply by multiplying the unit selling price by the units sold. For example, the break-even point for Whittier Company was computed at 600 mulching mowers. Since the selling price for each lawn mower is $400, the break-even volume in sales revenue is $240,000 ($400 × 600).

Any answer expressed in units sold can be easily converted to one expressed in sales revenues, but the answer can be computed more directly by developing a separate formula for the sales revenue case. In this case, the important variable is sales dollars so both the revenue and the variable costs must be expressed in dollars instead of units. Since sales revenue is always expressed in dollars, measuring that variable is no problem. Let's look more closely at variable costs and see how they can be expressed in terms of sales dollars.

To calculate the break-even point in sales dollars, variable costs are defined as a percentage of sales rather than as an amount per-unit sold. Exhibit 15-1 illustrates the division of sales revenue into variable cost and contribution margin. In this exhibit, price is $10 and variable cost is $6. Of course, the remainder is contribution margin of $4 ($10 − $6). If ten units are sold, total variable costs are $60 ($6 × 10 units). Alternatively, since each unit sold earns $10 of revenue and has $6 of variable cost, we

3. To practice the after-tax to before-tax conversion, calculate how much before-tax income Whittier would need to have $48,750 after-tax income if the tax rate were 40 percent. [Answer: $81,250]

Exhibit
Relationships among
Revenue, Variable Cost,
Contribution Margin, and
Fixed Cost

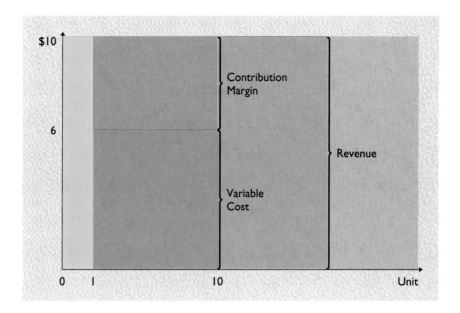

could say that 60 percent of each dollar of revenue earned is attributable to variable cost ($\frac{\$6}{\$10}$). Thus, focusing on sales revenue, we would expect total variable costs of $60 for revenues of $100 (0.60 × $100).

variable cost ratio

This 60 percent is the variable cost ratio. It is simply the proportion of each sales dollar that must be used to cover variable costs. The variable cost ratio can be computed by using either total data or unit data. Of course, the percentage of sales dollars remaining after variable costs are covered is the contribution margin ratio. The contribution

**contribution
   margin ratio**

margin ratio is the proportion of each sales dollar available to cover fixed costs and provide for profit. In Exhibit 15-1, if the variable cost ratio is 60 percent of sales, then contribution margin must be the remaining 40 percent of sales. It makes sense that the complement of the variable cost ratio is the contribution margin ratio. After all, the proportion of the sales dollar left after variable costs are covered should be the contribution margin component.

Just as the variable cost ratio can be computed using total or unit figures, the contribution margin ratio, 40 percent in our exhibit, can also be computed in these two ways. That is, one can divide the total contribution margin by total sales ($\frac{\$40}{\$100}$), or one can use the unit contribution margin divided by price ($\frac{\$4}{\$10}$). Naturally, if the variable cost ratio is known, it can be subtracted from 1 to yield the contribution margin ratio (1 − .60 = .40).

Where do fixed costs fit into this? Since the contribution margin is revenue remaining after variable costs are covered, it must be the revenue available to cover fixed costs and contribute to profit. Exhibit 15-2 uses the same price and variable cost data from Exhibit 15-1 to show the impact of fixed cost on profit. There are three possibilities: fixed cost can equal contribution margin; fixed cost can be less than contribution margin; or fixed cost can be greater than contribution margin. Panel A of Exhibit 15-2 shows fixed cost equal to contribution margin. Of course, profit is zero (the company is at breakeven). Panel B shows fixed cost less than contribution margin. In this case, the company earns a profit. Finally, panel C shows fixed cost greater than contribution margin. Here, the company faces an operating loss.

Now let's turn to a couple of examples based on Whittier Company to illustrate the sales revenue approach. We restate Whittier Company's variable-costing income statement for 1,000 lawn mowers:

Exhibit
Relationships among
Contribution Margin,
Fixed Cost, and Profit

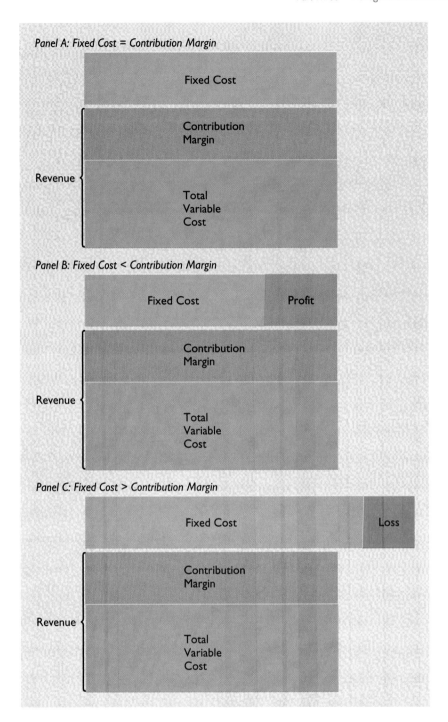

	Dollars	Percent of Sales
Sales	$400,000	100.00
Less: Variable expenses	(325,000)	81.25
Contribution margin	$ 75,000	18.75
Less: Fixed expenses	(45,000)	
Operating income	$ 30,000	

Notice that sales revenue, variable costs, and contribution margin have been expressed in the form of percent of sales. The variable cost ratio is 0.8125 ($\frac{\$325,000}{\$400,000}$); the contribution margin ratio is 0.1875 (computed either as $1 - 0.8125$, or $\frac{\$75,000}{\$400,000}$). Fixed costs are \$45,000. Given the information in this income statement, how much sales revenue must Whittier earn to break even?

$$\text{Operating income} = \text{Sales} - \text{Variable cost} - \text{Fixed cost}$$
$$0 = \text{Sales} - (\text{Variable cost ratio} \times \text{Sales}) - \text{Fixed cost}$$
$$0 = \text{Sales} (1 - \text{Variable cost ratio}) - \text{Fixed costs}$$
$$0 = \text{Sales} (1 - .8125) - \$45,000$$
$$\text{Sales} (.1875) = \$45,000$$
$$\text{Sales} = \$240,000$$

Thus, Whittier must earn revenues totaling \$240,000 in order to break even. (You might want to check this answer by preparing an income statement based on revenue of \$240,000 and verifying that it yields zero profit.) Note that $(1 - .8125)$ is the contribution margin ratio. We can skip a couple of steps by recognizing that *Sales − (Variable cost ratio × Sales)* is equal to *Sales × Contribution margin ratio*.

What about the fundamental break-even equation used to determine the break-even point in units? We can use that approach here as well. Recall that the formula for the break-even point in units is:

$$\text{Break-even units} = \frac{\text{Fixed cost}}{\text{Price} - \text{Unit variable cost}}$$

If we multiply both sides of this equation by price, the left-hand side will equal sales revenue at breakeven:

$$\text{Break-even units} \times \text{Price} = \text{Price} \times \frac{\text{Fixed cost}}{\text{Price} - \text{Unit variable cost}}$$

$$\text{Break-even sales} = \text{Fixed cost} \times \frac{\text{Price}}{\text{Price} - \text{Unit variable cost}}$$

$$\text{Break-even sales} = \text{Fixed cost} \times \frac{\text{Price}}{\text{Contribution margin}}$$

$$\text{Break-even sales} = \frac{\text{Fixed cost}}{\text{Contribution margin ratio}}$$

Again using Whittier Company data, the break-even sales dollars would be computed as $(\frac{\$45,000}{.1875})$ or \$240,000. Same answer, just a slightly different approach.

Profit Targets and Sales Revenue

Consider the following question: How much sales revenue must Whittier generate to earn a before-tax profit of \$60,000? (This question is similar to the one we asked earlier in terms of units, but phrases the question directly in terms of sales revenue.) To answer the question, add the targeted operating income of \$60,000 to the \$45,000 of fixed cost and divide by the contribution margin ratio:

$$\text{Sales} = \frac{\$45,000 + \$60,000}{0.1875}$$
$$= \frac{\$105,000}{0.1875}$$
$$= \$560,000$$

Whittier must earn revenues equal to \$560,000 to achieve a profit target of \$60,000. Since breakeven is \$240,000, additional sales of \$320,000 (\$560,000 − \$240,000) must be earned above breakeven. Notice that multiplying the contribution margin ratio by revenues above breakeven yields the profit of \$60,000 (0.1875 × \$320,000). Above breakeven, the contribution margin ratio is a profit ratio; therefore, it represents the proportion of each sales dollar assignable to profit. For this example, every sales dollar earned above breakeven increases profits by \$0.1875.

In general, assuming that fixed costs remain unchanged, the contribution margin ratio can be used to find the profit impact of a change in sales revenue. To obtain the total change in profits from a change in revenues, simply multiply the contribution margin ratio times the change in sales. For example, if sales revenues are $540,000 instead of $560,000, how will the expected profits be affected? A decrease in sales revenues of $20,000 will cause a decrease in profits of $3,750 ($0.1875 \times \$20,000$).

Comparison of the Two Approaches

For a single-product setting, converting the break-even point in units to breakeven in sales revenue is simply a matter of multiplying the unit sales price by the units sold. Then why bother with a separate formula for the sales revenue approach? There are two reasons. First, the formula for the sales revenue allows us to directly solve for revenue if that is what is desired. Second, the sales revenue approach is much simpler to use in a multiple-product setting, as we will see in the next section.

MULTIPLE-PRODUCT ANALYSIS

Objective 3

Apply cost-volume-profit analysis in a multiple-product setting

Cost-volume-profit analysis is fairly simple in the single-product setting. However, most firms produce and sell a number of products or services. Even though the conceptual complexity of CVP analysis does increase with multiple products, the operation is reasonably straightforward. Let's see how we can adapt the formulas used in a single-product setting to the multiple-product setting by expanding the Whittier Company example.

Whittier Company has decided to offer two models of lawn mowers: a mulching mower to sell for $400 and a riding mower to sell for $800. The marketing department is convinced that 1,200 mulching mowers and 800 riding mowers can be sold during the coming year. The controller has prepared the following projected income statement based on the sales forecast:

	Mulching Mower	Riding Mower	Total
Sales	$ 480,000	$ 640,000	$1,120,000
Less: Variable expenses	(390,000)	(480,000)	(870,000)
Contribution margin	$ 90,000	$ 160,000	$ 250,000
Less: Direct fixed expenses	(30,000)	(40,000)	(70,000)
Product margin	$ 60,000	$ 120,000	$ 180,000
Less: Common fixed expenses			(26,250)
Profit before taxes			$ 153,750

direct fixed expenses

Note that the controller has separated direct fixed expenses from common fixed expenses. The direct fixed expenses are those fixed costs that can be traced to each segment, and would be avoided if the segment did not exist. The common fixed expenses are the fixed costs that are not traceable to the segments, and would remain even if one of the segments was eliminated.

Break-even Point in Units

The owner of Whittier is somewhat apprehensive about adding a new product line and wants to know how many of each model must be sold to break even. If you were given the responsibility of answering this question, how would you respond?

One possible response is to use the equation we developed earlier in which fixed costs were divided by the contribution margin. This equation presents some immediate problems, however. It was developed for a single-product analysis. For two products,

The increasing global competition in the market for luxury automobiles has made manufacturers like Mercedes, Volvo, and BMW very aware of their break-even points. Now product engineers are routinely required to meet target costs and to think about cost in relation to the price that will be paid. For example, at BMW engineers have made numerous changes to the BMW 7-series, allowing costs to increase for options strongly desired by customers. The result is to align cost more closely with revenue, and to drive down the break-even point.

there are two unit contribution margins. The mulching mower has a contribution margin per unit of $75 ($400 − $325), and the riding mower has one of $200 ($800 − $600).[4]

One possible solution is to apply the analysis separately to each product line. It is possible to obtain individual break-even points when income is defined as product margin. Breakeven for the mulching mower is as follows:

$$\text{Mulching mower break-even units} = \frac{\text{Fixed cost}}{\text{Price} - \text{Unit variable cost}}$$

$$= \frac{\$30,000}{\$75}$$

$$= 400 \text{ units}$$

Breakeven for the riding mower can be computed as well:

$$\text{Riding mower break-even units} = \frac{\text{Fixed cost}}{\text{Price} - \text{Unit variable cost}}$$

$$= \frac{\$40,000}{\$200}$$

$$= 200 \text{ units}$$

Thus, 400 mulching mowers and 200 riding mowers must be sold to achieve a break-even product margin. But a break-even product margin covers only direct fixed costs; the common fixed costs remain to be covered. Selling these numbers of lawn mowers would result in a loss equal to the common fixed costs. No break-even point for the firm as a whole has yet been identified. Somehow the common fixed costs must be factored into the analysis.

Allocating the common fixed costs to each product line before computing a break-even point may resolve this difficulty. The problem with this approach is that allocation of the common fixed costs is arbitrary. Thus, no meaningful break-even volume is readily apparent.

Another possible solution is to convert the multiple-product problem into a single-product problem. If this can be done, then all of the single-product CVP methodology

4. The variable cost per unit is derived from the income statement. For the riding mower, total variable costs are $480,000 based on sales of 800 units. This yields a per-unit variable cost of $600 ($\frac{\$480,000}{800}$). A similar computation produces the per-unit variable cost for the mulching mower.

sales mix

can be applied directly. The key to this conversion is to identify the expected *sales mix*, in units, of the products being marketed. Sales mix is the relative combination of products being sold by a firm.

Determining the Sales Mix The sales mix can be measured in units sold or in proportion of revenue. For example, if Whittier plans on selling 1,200 mulching mowers and 800 riding mowers, then the sales mix in units is 1,200:800. Usually, the sales mix is reduced to the smallest possible whole numbers. Thus, the relative mix 1,200:800 can be reduced to 12:8 and further to 3:2. That is, for every three mulching mowers sold, two riding mowers are sold.

Alternatively, the sales mix can be represented by the percent of total revenue contributed by each product. In that case, the mulching mower revenue is $480,000 ($400 × 1,200) and the riding mower revenue is $640,000 ($800 × 800). The mulching mower accounts for 42.86 percent of total revenue and the riding mower accounts for the remaining 57.14 percent. It may seem as though the two sales mixes are different. The sales mix in units is 3:2; that is, of every five mowers sold, 60 percent are mulching mowers and 40 percent are riding mowers. However, the revenue-based sales mix is 42.86 percent for the mulching mowers. What is the difference? The sales mix in revenue takes the sales mix in units and weights it by price. Therefore, even though the underlying proportion of mowers sold remains 3:2, the lower-priced mulching mowers are weighted less heavily when price is factored in. For CVP analysis, we must use the sales mix expressed in units.

A number of different sales mixes can be used to define the break-even volume. For example, a sales mix of 2:1 will define a break-even point of 550 mulching mowers and 275 riding mowers. The total contribution margin produced by this mix is $96,250 [($75 × 550) + ($200 × 275)]. Similarly, if 350 mulching mowers and 350 riding mowers are sold (corresponding to a 1:1 sales mix), the total contribution margin is also $96,250 [($75 × 350) + ($200 × 350)]. Since total fixed costs are $96,250, both sales mixes define break-even points. Fortunately, every sales mix need not be considered. Can Whittier really expect a sales mix of 2:1 or 1:1? For every two mulching mowers sold, does Whittier expect to sell a riding mower? Or for every mulching mower, can Whittier really sell one riding mower?

According to Whittier's marketing study, a sales mix of 3:2 can be expected. That is the ratio that should be used; others can be ignored. The sales mix that is expected to prevail should be used for CVP analysis.

Sales Mix and CVP Analysis Defining a particular sales mix allows us to convert a multiple-product problem into a single-product CVP format. Since Whittier expects to sell three mulching mowers for every two riding mowers, it can define the single product it sells as a *package* containing three mulching mowers and two riding mowers. By defining the product as a package, the multiple-product problem is converted into a single-product one. To use the break-even-point-in-units approach, the package selling price and variable cost per package must be known. To compute these package values, the sales mix, the individual product prices, and the individual variable costs are needed. Given the individual product data found in the projected income statement, the package values can be computed as follows:

Product	Price	Unit Variable Cost	Unit Contribution Margin	Sales Mix	Package Unit Contribution Margin
Mulching	$400	$325	$ 75	3	$225[a]
Riding	$800	$600	200	2	400[b]
Package total					$625

[a]This is found by multiplying the number of units in the package (3) by the unit contribution margin ($75).
[b]This is found by multiplying the number of units in the package (2) by the unit contribution margin ($200).

Given the package contribution margin, the fundamental break-even equation can be used to determine the number of packages that need to be sold to break even. From Whittier's projected income statement, we know that the total fixed costs for the company are $96,250. Thus, the break-even point is:

$$\text{Break-even packages} = \frac{\text{Fixed cost}}{\text{Package contribution margin}}$$

$$= \frac{\$96,250}{\$625}$$

$$= 154 \text{ packages}$$

Whittier must sell 462 mulching mowers (3 × 154) and 308 riding mowers (2 × 154) to break even. An income statement verifying this solution is presented in Exhibit 15-3.

For a given sales mix, CVP analysis can be used as if the firm were selling a single product. However, actions that change the prices of individual products can affect the sales mix because consumers may buy relatively more or less of the product. Accordingly, pricing decisions may involve a new sales mix and must reflect this possibility. Keep in mind that a new sales mix will affect the units of each product that need to be sold in order to achieve a desired profit target. If the sales mix for the coming period is uncertain, it may be necessary to look at several different mixes. In this way, a manager can gain some insight into the possible outcomes facing the firm.

The complexity of the break-even-point-in-units approach increases dramatically as the number of products increases. Imagine performing this analysis for a firm with several hundred products. This observation seems more overwhelming than it actually is. Computers can easily handle a problem with so much data. Furthermore, many firms simplify the problem by analyzing product groups rather than individual products. Another way to handle the increased complexity is to switch from the units-sold to the sales revenue approach. This approach can accomplish a multiple-product CVP analysis using only the summary data found in an organization's income statement. The computational requirements are much simpler.

Sales Dollars Approach

To illustrate the break-even point in sales dollars, the same examples will be used. However, the only information needed is the projected income statement for Whittier Company as a whole.

Sales	$1,120,000
Less: Variable expenses	(870,000)
Contribution margin	$ 250,000
Less: Total fixed expenses	(96,250)
Profit before taxes	$ 153,750

15-3

Exhibit
Income Statement:
Break-even Solution

	Mulching Mower	Riding Mower	Total
Sales	$ 184,800	$ 246,400	$ 431,200
Less: Variable expenses	(150,150)	(184,800)	(334,950)
Contribution margin	$ 34,650	$ 61,600	$ 96,250
Less: Direct fixed expenses	(30,000)	(40,000)	(70,000)
Segment margin	$ 4,650	$ 21,600	$ 26,250
Less: Common fixed expenses			(26,250)
Profit before taxes			$ 0

Notice that this income statement corresponds to the total column of the more detailed income statement examined previously. The projected income statement rests on the assumption that 1,200 mulching mowers and 800 riding mowers will be sold (a 3:2 sales mix). The break-even point in sales revenue also rests on the expected sales mix. (As with the units-sold approach, a different sales mix will produce different results.)

With the income statement, the usual CVP questions can be addressed. For example, how much sales revenue must be earned to break even? To answer this question, we divide the total fixed cost of $96,250 by the contribution margin ratio of 0.2232 $(\frac{\$250,000}{\$1,120,000})$:[5]

$$\text{Break-even sales} = \frac{\text{Fixed cost}}{\text{Contribution margin ratio}}$$

$$= \frac{\$96,250}{0.2232}$$

$$= \$431,228$$

The break-even point in sales dollars implicitly uses the assumed sales mix but avoids the requirement of building a package contribution margin. No knowledge of individual product data is needed. The computational effort is similar to that used in the single-product setting. Moreover, the answer is still expressed in sales revenue. Unlike the break-even point in units, the answer to CVP questions using sales dollars is still expressed in a single summary measure. The sales revenue approach, however, does sacrifice information concerning individual product performance.

GRAPHICAL REPRESENTATION OF CVP RELATIONSHIPS

Objective 4

Prepare a profit-volume graph and a cost-volume-profit graph and explain the meaning of each.

It may further our understanding of CVP relationships to see them portrayed visually. A graphical representation can help managers see the difference between variable cost and revenue. It may also help them understand quickly what impact an increase or decrease in sales will have on the break-even point. Two basic graphs, the *profit-volume graph* and the *cost-volume-profit graph*, are presented here.

The Profit-Volume Graph

profit-volume graph

A profit-volume graph visually portrays the relationship between profits and sales volume. The profit-volume graph is the graph of the operating income equation [Operating income = (Price × Units) − (Unit variable cost × Units) − Fixed cost]. In this graph, operating income is the dependent variable and units is the independent variable. Usually, values of the independent variable are measured along the horizontal axis and values of the dependent variable along the vertical.

To make this discussion more concrete, a simple set of data will be used. Assume that Tyson Company produces a single product with the following cost and price data:

Total fixed costs	$100
Variable costs per unit	5
Selling price per unit	10

Using these data, operating income can be expressed as

---

5. Because of rounding error in the contribution margin ratio, the sales volume is slightly overstated. The correct answer is $431,200 (obtained by multiplying the package selling price by the packages needed to break even: ($2,800 × 154).

$$\text{Operating income} = (\$10 \times \text{Units}) - (\$5 \times \text{Units}) - \$100$$
$$= (\$5 \times \text{Units}) - \$100$$

We can graph this relationship by plotting units along the horizontal axis and operating income (or loss) along the vertical axis. Two points are needed to graph a linear equation. While any two points will do, the two points often chosen are those that correspond to zero sales volume and zero profits. When units sold are zero, Tyson experiences an operating loss of $100 (or a profit of -$100). The point corresponding to zero sales volume, therefore, is (0, -$100). In other words, when no sales take place, the company suffers a loss equal to its total fixed costs. When operating income is zero, the units sold are equal to 20. The point corresponding to zero profits (breakeven) is (20, $0). These two points, plotted in Exhibit 15-4, define the profit graph shown there.

The graph in Exhibit 15-4 can be used to assess Tyson's profit (or loss) at any level of sales activity. For example, the profit associated with the sale of 40 units can be read from the graph by (1) drawing a vertical line from the horizontal axis to the profit line, and (2) drawing a horizontal line from the profit line to the vertical axis. As illustrated in Exhibit 15-4, the profit associated with sales of 40 units is $100. The profit-volume graph, while easy to interpret, fails to reveal how costs change as sales volume changes. An alternative approach to graphing can provide this detail.

The Cost-Volume-Profit Graph

cost-volume-profit graph

The cost-volume-profit graph depicts the relationships among cost, volume, and profits. To obtain the more detailed relationships, it is necessary to graph two separate lines: the

Exhibit
Profit-Volume Graph

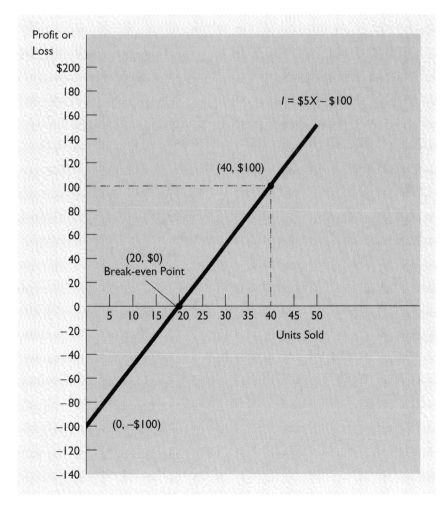

total revenue line and the total cost line. These two lines are represented, respectively, by the following two equations:

$$\text{Revenue} = \text{Price} \times \text{Units}$$
$$\text{Total cost} = \text{Unit variable cost} \times \text{Units} + \text{Fixed cost}$$

Using the Tyson Company example, the revenue and cost equations are

$$\text{Revenue} = \$10 \times \text{Units}$$
$$\text{Total cost} = (\$5 \times \text{Units}) + \$100$$

To portray both equations in the same graph, the vertical axis is measured in dollars and the horizontal axis in units sold.

Two points are needed to graph each equation. We will use the same *x*-coordinates as in the profit-volume graph. For the revenue equation, setting number of units equal to 0 results in revenue of $0; setting number of units equal to 20 results in revenue of $200. Therefore, the two points for the revenue equation are (0, $0) and (20, $200). For the cost equation, units sold of 0 and units sold of 20 produce the points (0, $100) and (20, $200). The graph of each equation appears in Exhibit 15-5.

Notice that the total revenue line begins at the origin and rises with a slope equal to the selling price per unit (a slope of 10). The total cost line intercepts the vertical axis at a point equal to total fixed costs and rises with a slope equal to the variable cost per unit (a slope of 5). When the total revenue line lies below the total cost line, a loss region is defined. Similarly, when the total revenue line lies above the total cost line, a profit region is defined. The point where the total revenue line and the total cost line intersect is the break-even point. To break even, Tyson Company must sell 20 units and thus receive $200 total revenues.

Now let's compare the information available from the CVP graph with that available from the profit-volume graph. To do so, consider the sale of 40 units. Recall that the profit-volume graph revealed that this produced profits of $100. Examine Exhibit 15-5 again. The CVP graph also shows profits of $100, but it reveals more as well. The CVP graph discloses that total revenues of $400 and total costs of $300 are associated with the sale of 40 units. Furthermore, the total costs can be broken down into fixed costs of $100 and variable costs of $200. The CVP graph provides revenue and cost information

Exhibit
Cost-Volume-Profit
Graph

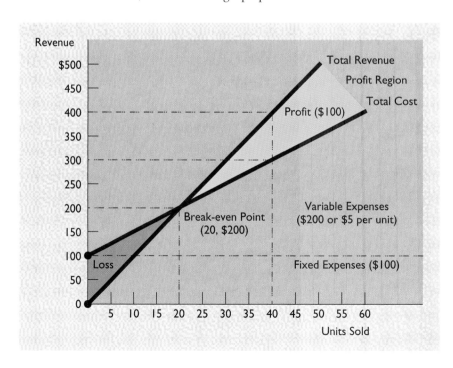

not provided by the profit-volume graph. Unlike the profit-volume graph, some computation is needed to determine the profit associated with a given sales volume. Nonetheless, because of the greater information content, managers are likely to find the CVP graph a more useful tool.

Assumptions of Cost-Volume-Profit Analysis

The profit-volume and cost-volume-profit graphs just illustrated rely on some important assumptions. Some of these assumptions are as follows:

1. The analysis assumes a linear revenue function and a linear cost function.
2. The analysis assumes that price, total fixed costs, and unit variable costs can be accurately identified, and remain constant over the relevant range.
3. The analysis assumes that what is produced is sold.
4. For multiple-product analysis, the sales mix is assumed to be known.
5. The selling prices and costs are assumed to be known with certainty.

Linear Functions The first assumption, linear cost and revenue functions, deserves additional consideration. Let's take a look at the underlying revenue and total cost functions identified in economics. In Exhibit 15-6, panel A portrays the curvilinear revenue and cost functions. We see that as quantity sold increases, revenue also increases, but eventually begins to rise less steeply than before. This is explained quite simply by the need to decrease price as many more units are sold. The total cost function is more complicated, rising steeply at first, then leveling off somewhat (as increasing returns to scale develop), and then rising steeply again (as decreasing returns to scale develop). How can we deal with these complicated relationships?

Relevant Range Fortunately, we do not need to consider all possible ranges of production and sales for a firm. Remember that CVP analysis is a short-run decision-making tool. (We know that it is short run in orientation because some costs are fixed.) It is only necessary for us to determine the current operating range, or relevant range, for which the linear cost and revenue relationships are valid. In Exhibit 15-6, panel B illustrates a relevant range from 5,000 to 15,000 units. Note that the cost and revenue relationships are roughly linear in this range, allowing us to use our linear CVP equations. Of course, if the relevant range changes, different fixed and variable costs, and different prices must be used.

relevant range

The second assumption is linked to the definition of relevant range. Once a relevant range has been identified, then the cost and price relationships are assumed to be known and constant.

Production Equal to Sales The third assumption is that what is produced is sold. There is no change in inventory over the period. That inventory has no impact on break-even analysis makes sense. Break-even analysis is a short-run decision-making technique so we are looking to cover all costs of a particular period of time. Inventory embodies costs of a previous period and is not considered.

Constant Sales Mix In single-product analysis, the sales mix is obviously constant — 100 percent of sales is the one product. Multiple-product break-even analysis requires a constant sales mix. However, it is virtually impossible to predict with certainty the sales mix. Typically, this constraint is handled in practice through sensitivity analysis. By using the capabilities of spreadsheet analysis, the sensitivity of variables to a variety of sales mixes can be readily assessed.

Prices and Costs Known with Certainty In actuality, firms seldom know prices, variable costs, and fixed costs with certainty. A change in one variable usually affects the value of others. Often there is a probability distribution to contend with. Furthermore,

Exhibit
The Relevant Range

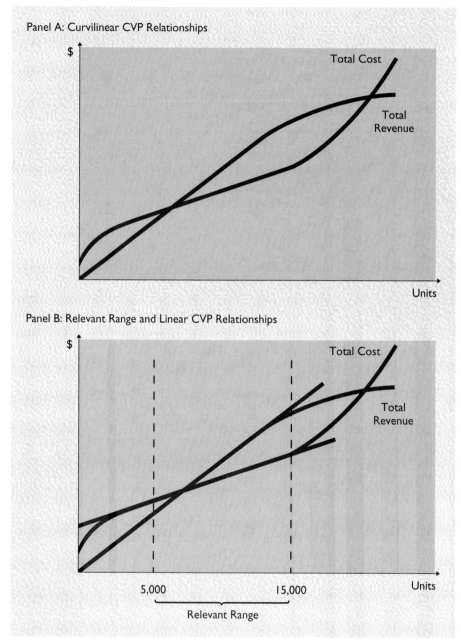

there are formal ways of explicitly building uncertainty into the CVP model. Exploration of these issues is introduced in the next section.

CHANGES IN THE CVP VARIABLES

Objective 5

Explain the impact of risk, uncertainty, and changing variables on cost-volume-profit analysis.

Because firms operate in a dynamic world, they must be aware of changes in prices, variable costs, and fixed costs. They must also account for the effect of risk and uncertainty. We will take a look at the effect of changes in price, unit contribution margin, and fixed cost on the break-even point. We will also look at ways managers can handle risk and uncertainty within the CVP framework.

Suppose that Whittier Company recently conducted a market study that revealed three different alternatives.

- *Alternative 1:* If advertising expenditures increase by $8,000, sales will increase from 1,600 units to 1,725 units.
- *Alternative 2:* A price decrease from $400 to $375 per lawn mower will increase sales from 1,600 units to 1,900 units.
- *Alternative 3:* Decreasing prices to $375 and increasing advertising expenditures by $8,000 will increase sales from 1,600 units to 2,600 units.

Should Whittier maintain its current price and advertising policies, or should it select one of the three alternatives described by the marketing study?

Consider the first alternative. What is the effect on profits if advertising costs increase by $8,000 and sales increase by 125 units? This question can be answered without using the equations but by employing the contribution margin per unit. We know that the unit contribution margin is $75. Since units sold increase by 125, the incremental increase in total contribution margin is $9,375 ($75 × 125 units). However, since fixed costs increase by $8,000, the incremental increase in profits is only $1,375 ($9,375 − $8,000). Exhibit 15-7 summarizes the effects of the first alternative. Notice that we need to look only at the incremental increase in total contribution margin and fixed expenses to compute the increase in total profits.

For the second alternative, fixed expenses do not increase. Thus, it is possible to answer the question by looking only at the effect on total contribution margin. For the current price of $400, the contribution margin per unit is $75. If 1,600 units are sold, the total contribution margin is $120,000 ($75 × 1,600). If the price is dropped to $375, then the contribution margin drops to $50 per unit ($375 − $325). If 1,900 units are sold at the new price, then the new total contribution margin is $95,000 ($50 × 1,900). Dropping the price results in a profit decline of $25,000 ($120,000 − $95,000). The effects of the second alternative are summarized in Exhibit 15-8.

The third alternative calls for a decrease in the unit selling price and an increase in advertising costs. Like the first alternative, the profit impact can be assessed by looking at the incremental effects on contribution margin and fixed expenses. The incremental profit change can be found by (1) computing the incremental change in total contribution margin, (2) computing the incremental change in fixed expenses, and (3) adding the two results.

As shown, the current total contribution margin (for 1,600 units sold) is $120,000. Since the new unit contribution margin is $50, the new total contribution margin is $130,000 ($50 × 2,600 units). Thus, the incremental increase in total contribution

15-7
....

Exhibit
Summary of the Effects
of Alternative 1

	Before the Increased Advertising	With the Increased Advertising
Units sold	1,600	1,725
Unit contribution margin	× $75	× $75
Total contribution margin	$120,000	$129,375
Less: Fixed expenses	(45,000)	(53,000)
Profit	$ 75,000	$ 76,375

	Difference in Profit
Change in sales volume	125
Unit contribution margin	× $75
Change in contribution margin	$ 9,375
Less: Increase in fixed expenses	(8,000)
Increase in profit	$ 1,375

Exhibit
Summary of the Effects
of Alternative 2

	Before the Proposed Price Change	With the Proposed Price Decrease
Units sold	1,600	1,900
Unit contribution margin	× $75	× $50
Total contribution margin	$120,000	$ 95,000
Less: Fixed expenses	(45,000)	(45,000)
Profit	$ 75,000	$ 50,000

	Difference in Profit
Change in contribution margin ($95,000 − $120,000)	$(25,000)
Less: Change in fixed expenses	—
Decrease in profit	$(25,000)

margin is $10,000 ($130,000 − $120,000). However, to achieve this incremental increase in contribution margin, an incremental increase of $8,000 in fixed costs is needed. The net effect is an incremental increase in profits of $2,000. The effects of the third alternative are summarized in Exhibit 15-9.

Of the three alternatives identified by the marketing study, the one that promises the most benefit is the third. It increases total profits by $2,000. The first alternative increases profits by only $1,375, and the second actually decreases profits by $25,000.

These examples are all based on a units-sold approach. However, we could just as easily have applied a sales revenue approach. The answers would be the same.

Introducing Risk and Uncertainty

An important assumption of CVP analysis is that prices and costs are known with certainty. This is seldom the case. Risk and uncertainty are a part of business decision making and must be dealt with somehow. Formally, risk differs from uncertainty in that

Exhibit
Summary of the Effects
of Alternative 3

	Before the Proposed Price and Advertising Change	With the Proposed Price Decrease and Advertising Increase
Units sold	1,600	2,600
Unit contribution margin	× $75	× $50
Total contribution margin	$120,000	$130,000
Less: Fixed expenses	(45,000)	(53,000)
Profit	$ 75,000	$ 77,000

	Difference in Profit
Change in contribution margin ($130,000 − $120,000)	$10,000
Less: Change in fixed expenses ($53,000 − $45,000)	(8,000)
Increase in profit	$ 2,000

under risk the probability distributions of the variables are known; under uncertainty, they are not known. For our purposes, however, the terms will be used interchangeably.

How do managers deal with risk and uncertainty? There are a variety of methods. First, of course, is that management must realize the uncertain nature of future prices, costs, and quantities. Next, managers move from consideration of a break-even point to what might be called a "break-even band." In other words, given the uncertain nature of the data, perhaps a firm might break even when 1,800 to 2,000 units are sold instead of the point estimate of 1,900 units. Further, managers may engage in sensitivity or what-if analysis. In this, a computer spreadsheet is helpful, as managers set up the break-even (or targeted profit) relationships and then check to see the impact that varying costs and prices have on quantity sold. Two concepts useful to management are *margin of safety* and *operating leverage*. Both of these may be considered measures of risk. Each requires knowledge of fixed and variable costs.

margin of safety

Margin of Safety The margin of safety is the units sold or expected to be sold or the revenue earned or expected to be earned above the break-even volume. For example, if the break-even volume for a company is 200 units and the company is currently selling 500 units, the margin of safety is 300 units (500 − 200). The margin of safety can be expressed in sales revenue as well. If the break-even volume is $200,000 and current revenues are $350,000, then the margin of safety is $150,000.

The margin of safety can be viewed as a crude measure of risk. There are always events, unknown when plans are made, that can lower sales below the original expected level. If a firm's margin of safety is large given the expected sales for the coming year, the risk of suffering losses should sales take a downward turn is less than if the margin of safety is small. Managers who face a low margin of safety may wish to consider actions to increase sales or decrease costs. These steps will increase the margin of safety and lower the risk of incurring losses.

Operating Leverage In physics, a lever is a simple machine used to multiply force. Basically, the lever multiplies the effort applied, to create more work. The larger the load moved by a given amount of effort, the greater is the mechanical advantage. In financial terms, operating leverage is concerned with the relative mix of fixed costs and variable costs in an organization. It is sometimes possible to trade off fixed costs for variable costs. As variable costs decrease, the unit contribution margin increases, making the contribution of each unit sold that much greater. In such a case, the effect of fluctuations in sales on profitability increases. Thus, firms that have bought lower variable costs by increasing the proportion of fixed costs will benefit with greater increases in profits as sales increase than will firms with a lower proportion of fixed costs. Fixed costs are being used as leverage to increase profits. Unfortunately, it is also true that firms with a higher operating leverage will also experience greater reductions in profits as sales de-

operating leverage

crease. Therefore, operating leverage is the use of fixed costs to extract higher percentage changes in profits as sales activity changes.

The greater the degree of operating leverage, the more that changes in sales activity will affect profits. Because of this phenomenon, the mix of costs that an organization chooses can have a considerable influence on its operating risk and profit level.

degree of operating leverage (DOL)

The degree of operating leverage (DOL) can be measured for a given level of sales by taking the ratio of contribution margin to profit, as follows:

$$\text{Degree of operating leverage} = \frac{\text{Contribution margin}}{\text{Profit}}$$

If fixed costs are used to lower variable costs such that contribution margin increases and profit decreases, then the degree of operating leverage increases—signaling an increase in risk.

To illustrate the utility of these concepts, consider a firm that is planning to add a new product line. In adding the line, the firm can choose to rely heavily on automation or on labor. If the firm chooses to emphasize automation rather than labor, fixed costs will be higher and unit variable costs will be lower. Relevant data for a sales level of 10,000 units follow:

	Automated System	Manual System
Sales	$1,000,000	$1,000,000
Less: Variable expenses	(500,000)	(800,000)
Contribution margin	$ 500,000	$ 200,000
Less: Fixed expenses	(375,000)	(100,000)
Profit before taxes	$ 125,000	$ 100,000
Unit selling price	$100	$100
Unit variable expense	50	80
Unit contribution margin	50	20

The degree of operating leverage for the automated system is 4.0 $(\frac{\$500,000}{\$125,000})$. The degree of operating leverage for the manual system is 2.0 $(\frac{\$200,000}{\$100,000})$. What happens to profit in each system if sales increase by 40 percent? We can generate the following income statements to see:

	Automated System	Manual System
Sales	$1,400,000	$ 1,400,000
Less: Variable expenses	(700,000)	(1,120,000)
Contribution margin	$ 700,000	$ 280,000
Less: Fixed expenses	(375,000)	(100,000)
Profit before taxes	$ 325,000	$ 180,000

Profits for the automated system would increase by $200,000 ($325,000 − $125,000) for a 160 percent increase. In the manual system, profits increase by only $80,000 ($180,000 − $100,000) for an 80 percent increase. The automated system has a greater percentage increase because it has a higher degree of operating leverage.

In choosing between the two systems, the effect of operating leverage is a valuable piece of information. As the 40 percent increase in sales illustrates, this effect can bring a significant benefit to the firm. However, the effect is a two-edged sword. As sales decrease, the automated system will also show much higher percentage decreases. Moreover, the increased operating leverage is available under the automated system because of the presence of increased fixed costs. The break-even point for the automated system is 7,500 units $(\frac{\$375,000}{\$50})$, whereas the break-even point for the manual system is 5,000 units $(\frac{\$100,000}{\$20})$. Thus, the automated system has greater operating risk. The increased risk, of course, provides a potentially higher profit level (as long as units sold exceed 9,167).[6]

In choosing between the automated and the manual systems, the manager must assess the likelihood that sales will exceed 9,167 units. If, after careful study, there is a strong belief that sales will easily exceed this level, the choice is obvious: the automated system. On the other hand, if sales are unlikely to exceed 9,167 units, the manual system is preferable. Exhibit 15-10 summarizes the relative difference between the manual and the automated systems in terms of some of the CVP concepts.

---

6. This benchmark is computed by setting the profit equations of the two systems equal and solving for x: $50x − 375,000 = 20x − 100,000$; $x = 9,167$.

Exhibit
Difference Between
Manual and Automated
Systems

	Manual System	Automated System
Price	Same	Same
Variable cost	Relatively higher	Relatively lower
Fixed cost	Relatively lower	Relatively higher
Contribution margin	Relatively lower	Relatively higher
Break-even point	Relatively lower	Relatively higher
Margin of safety	Relatively higher	Relatively lower
Degree of operating leverage	Relatively lower	Relatively higher
Downside risk	Relatively lower	Relatively higher
Upside potential	Relatively lower	Relatively higher

Sensitivity Analysis and CVP

sensitivity analysis

The pervasiveness of personal computers and spreadsheets has placed *sensitivity analysis* within reach of most managers. An important tool, sensitivity analysis is a "what if" technique that examines the impact of changes in underlying assumptions on an answer. It is relatively simple to input data on prices, variable costs, fixed costs, and sales mix and to set up formulas to calculate break-even points and expected profits. Then the data can be varied as desired to see what impact changes have on the expected profit.

In the preceding example on operating leverage, a company analyzed the impact on profit of using an automated versus a manual system. The computations were essentially done by hand, and too much variation is cumbersome. Using the power of a computer, it would be an easy matter to change the sales price in $1 increments between $75 and $125, with related assumptions about quantity sold. At the same time, variable and fixed costs could be adjusted. For example, suppose that the automated system has fixed costs of $375,000, but that those costs could easily range up to twice as much in the first year, and come back down in the second and third year as bugs are worked out of the system and workers learn to use it. Again, the spreadsheet can effortlessly handle the many computations.

Finally, we must note that the spreadsheet, while wonderful for cranking out numerical answers, cannot do the most difficult job in CVP analysis. That job is determining the data to be entered in the first place. The accountant must be cognizant of the cost and price distributions of the firm, as well as of the impact of changing economic conditions on these variables. The fact that variables are seldom known with certainty is no excuse for ignoring the impact of uncertainty on CVP analysis. Fortunately, sensitivity analysis can also give managers a feel for the degree to which a poorly forecast variable will affect an answer. That is also an advantage.

CVP ANALYSIS AND ACTIVITY-BASED COSTING

Objective 6

Discuss the impact of activity-based costing on cost-volume-profit analysis.

Conventional CVP analysis assumes that all costs of the firm can be divided into two categories: those that vary with sales volume (variable costs), and those that do not (fixed costs). Further, costs are assumed to be a linear function of sales volume. However, many companies now realize that this fixed versus variable distinction is too simplistic. For example, do you think that the cost of life rafts on airplanes is a fixed or a variable cost? In terms of passenger miles, the raft costs ($5,400 each, carried in sets of three or four—enough to handle all the passengers on a jet) are fixed. In terms of the number of jets, the rafts are a variable cost. And finally, fuel consumption is determined by weight as well as miles flown. The rafts weigh 300 to 400 pounds each, and add approximately $19,000 per plane in annual fuel costs. As a result, a number of airlines have cut back on the number of planes that carry life rafts, among them are Delta, Continental, Northwest, and American Airlines.[7]

7. James S. Hirsch, "To Save Fuel, Some Airlines Ditch Life Rafts," *The Wall Street Journal*, 5 January 1995, p. B1.

In an activity-based costing system, costs are divided into unit- and nonunit-based categories. Activity-based costing admits that some costs vary with units produced and some costs do not. However, while activity-based costing acknowledges that nonunit-based costs are fixed with respect to production volume changes, it also argues that many nonunit-based costs vary with respect to other activity drivers.

The use of activity-based costing does not mean that CVP analysis is less useful. In fact, it becomes more useful since it provides more accurate insights concerning cost behavior. These insights produce better decisions. CVP analysis within an activity-based framework, however, must be modified. To illustrate, assume that a company's costs can be explained by three variables: a unit-level activity driver, units sold; a batch-level activity driver, number of setups; and a product-level activity driver, engineering hours. The ABC cost equation can then be expressed as follows:

$$\text{Total cost} = \text{Fixed cost} + (\text{Unit variable cost} \times \text{Number of units})$$
$$+ (\text{Setup cost} \times \text{Number of setups})$$
$$+ (\text{Engineering cost} \times \text{Number of engineering hours})$$

Operating income, as before, is total revenue minus total cost. This is expressed as:

$$\text{Operating income} = \text{Total revenue} - [\text{Fixed cost} + (\text{Unit variable cost}$$
$$\times \text{Number of units}) + (\text{Setup cost} \times \text{Number of setups})$$
$$+ (\text{Engineering cost} \times \text{Number of engineering hours})]$$

Let's use the contribution margin approach to calculate the break-even point in units. At breakeven, operating income is zero, and the number of units that must be sold to achieve breakeven is as follows:

$$\text{Break-even units} = \frac{\text{Fixed cost} + (\text{Setup cost} \times \text{Number of setups}) + (\text{Engineering cost} \times \text{Number of engineering hours})}{\text{Price} - \text{Unit variable cost}}$$

A comparison of the ABC break-even point with the conventional break-even point reveals two significant differences. First, the fixed costs differ. Some costs previously identified as being fixed may actually vary with nonunit cost drivers, in this case setups and engineering hours. Second, the numerator of the ABC break-even equation has two nonunit-variable cost terms: one for batch-related activities and one for product-sustaining activities.

Example Comparing Conventional and ABC Analysis

To make this discussion more concrete, a comparison of conventional cost-volume-profit analysis with activity-based costing is useful. Let's assume that a company wants to compute the units that must be sold to earn a before-tax income of $20,000. The analysis is based on the following data:

Activity Driver	Unit Variable Cost	Level of Activity Driver
Data about variables:		
Units sold	$ 10	—
Setups	1,000	20
Engineering hours	30	1,000
Other data:		
Total fixed costs (conventional)	$100,000	
Total fixed costs (ABC)	50,000	
Unit selling price	20	

Using CVP analysis, the units that must be sold to earn a before-tax profit of $20,000 are computed as follows:

$$\text{Number of units} = \frac{\text{Targeted income} + \text{Fixed cost}}{\text{Price} - \text{Unit variable cost}}$$

$$= \frac{\$20,000 + \$100,000}{\$20 - \$10}$$

$$= \frac{\$120,000}{\$10}$$

$$= 12,000 \text{ units}$$

Using the ABC equation, the units that must be sold to earn an operating income of $20,000 are computed as follows:

$$\text{Number of units} = \frac{\$20,000 + \$50,000 + (\$1,000 \times 20) + (\$30 \times 1,000)}{\$20 - \$10}$$

$$= 12,000 \text{ units}$$

The number of units that must be sold is identical under both approaches. The reason is simple. The total fixed cost pool under conventional costing consists of non-unit-based variable costs plus costs that are fixed regardless of the activity driver. ABC breaks out the nonunit-based variable costs. These costs are associated with certain levels of each activity driver. For the batch-level activity driver, the level is 20 setups and for the product-level variable, the level is 1,000 engineering hours. As long as the levels of activity for the nonunit-based cost drivers remain the same, then the results for the conventional and ABC computations will be the same. But these levels can change and because of this, the information provided by the two approaches can be significantly different. The ABC equation for CVP analysis is a richer representation of the underlying cost behavior and can provide important strategic insights. To see this, let's use the same data and look at a different application.

Strategic Implications: Conventional CVP Analysis versus ABC Analysis

Suppose that after the conventional CVP analysis, marketing indicates that selling 12,000 units is not possible. In fact, only 10,000 units can be sold. The president of the company then directs the product design engineers to find a way to reduce the cost of making the product. The engineers also have been told that the conventional cost equation, with fixed costs of $100,000 and unit variable cost of $10, holds. The variable cost of $10 per unit consists of the following: direct labor, $4; direct materials, $5; and variable overhead, $1. To comply with the request to reduce the break-even point, engineering produces a new design that requires less labor. The new design reduces the direct labor cost by $2 per unit. The design would not affect materials or variable overhead. Thus, the new variable cost is $8 per unit, and the break-even point is:

$$\text{Number of units} = \frac{\text{Fixed cost}}{\text{Price} - \text{Unit variable cost}}$$

$$= \frac{\$100,000}{\$20 - \$8}$$

$$= 8,333 \text{ units}$$

And the projected income if 10,000 units are sold is:

Sales ($20 × 10,000)	$ 200,000
Less: Variable expenses ($8 × 10,000)	(80,000)
Contribution margin	$ 120,000
Less: Fixed expenses	(100,000)
Income	$ 20,000

Excited, the president approves the new design. A year later, the president discovers that the expected increase in income did not materialize. In fact, a loss is realized. Why? The answer is provided by an ABC approach to CVP analysis.

The original ABC cost relationship for the example follows:

Total cost = $50,000 + ($10 × Units) + ($1,000 × Setups) + ($30 × Engineering hours)

Suppose that the new design requires a more complex setup, increasing the cost per setup from $1,000 to $1,600. Also suppose that the new design, because of increased technical content, requires a 40 percent increase in engineering support (from 1,000 hours to 1,400 hours). The new cost equation, including the reduction in unit-level variable costs, follows:

Total cost = $50,000 + ($8 × Units) + ($1,600 × Setups) + ($30 × Engineering hours)

The break-even point, setting operating income equal to zero, and using the ABC equation, is calculated as follows (assume that 20 setups are still performed):

$$\text{Number of units} = \frac{\$50,000 + (\$1,600 \times 20) + (\$30 \times 1,400)}{\$20 - \$8}$$

$$= \frac{\$124,000}{\$12}$$

$$= 10,333 \text{ units}$$

And the income for 10,000 units is (recall that a maximum of 10,000 can be sold):

Sales ($20 × 10,000)		$200,000
Less: Unit-based variable expenses ($8 × 10,000)		(80,000)
Contribution margin		$120,000
Less: Nonunit-based variable expenses:		
Setups ($1,600 × 20)	$32,000	
Engineering support ($30 × 1,400)	42,000	(74,000)
Traceable margin		$ 46,000
Less: Fixed expenses		(50,000)
Income (loss)		$ (4,000)

How could the engineers have been off by so much? Didn't they know that the new design would increase setup cost and engineering support? Yes and no. They were probably aware of the increases in these two variables, but the conventional cost equation diverted attention from figuring out just how much impact changes in those variables would have. The information conveyed by the conventional equation to the engineers gave the impression that any reduction in labor cost—not affecting materials or variable overhead—would reduce total costs since changes in the level of labor activity would not affect the fixed costs. The ABC equation, however, indicates that a reduction in labor input that adversely affects setup activity or engineering support might be undesirable. By providing more insight, better design decisions can be made. Providing ABC cost information to the design engineers would probably have led them down a different path—one that would have been more advantageous to the company.

CVP Analysis and JIT

If a firm has adopted JIT, the variable cost per-unit sold is reduced and fixed costs are increased. Direct labor, for example, is now viewed as fixed instead of variable. Direct materials, on the other hand, is still a unit-based variable cost. In fact, the emphasis on total quality and long-term purchasing makes the assumption that direct materials cost is strictly proportional to units produced even more true (because waste, scrap, and quantity discounts are eliminated). Other unit-based variable costs such as power and sales commissions also persist. Additionally, the batch-level variable is gone (in JIT the batch is one unit). Thus, the cost equation for JIT can be expressed as follows:

$$\text{Total cost} = \text{Fixed cost} + (\text{Unit variable cost} \times \text{Number of units})$$
$$+ (\text{Engineering cost} \times \text{Number of engineering hours})$$

Since its application is a special case of the ABC equation, no example will be given.

SUMMARY OF LEARNING OBJECTIVES

1. Determine the number of units that must be sold to break even or to earn a targeted profit.

In a single-product setting, the break-even point can be computed in units by dividing the total fixed costs by the contribution margin per unit. In essence, sufficient units must be sold to just cover all fixed and variable costs of the firm.

2. Determine the amount of revenue required to break even or to earn a targeted profit.

Break-even revenue is computed by dividing the total fixed costs by the contribution margin ratio. Targeted profit is added to fixed costs in determining the amount of revenue needed to yield the targeted profit.

3. Apply cost-volume-profit analysis in a multiple-product setting.

Multiple-product analysis requires that an assumption be made concerning the expected sales mix. Given a particular sales mix, a multiple-product problem can be converted into a single-product analysis. However, it should be remembered that the answers change as the sales mix changes. If the sales mix changes in a multiple-product firm, the break-even point will also change. In general, increases in the sales of high contribution margin products will decrease the break-even point, while increases in the sales of low contribution margin products will increase the break-even point.

4. Prepare a profit-volume graph and a cost-volume-profit graph and explain the meaning of each.

CVP is based on several assumptions that must be considered in applying it to business problems. The analysis assumes linear revenue and cost functions, no finished goods ending inventories, and a constant sales mix. CVP analysis also assumes that selling prices and fixed and variable costs are known with certainty. These assumptions form the basis for simple graphical analysis using the profit-volume graph and the cost-volume-profit graph.

5. Explain the impact of risk, uncertainty, and changing variables on cost-volume-profit analysis.

Measures of risk and uncertainty, such as the margin of safety and operating leverage, can be used to give managers more insight into CVP answers. Sensitivity analysis gives still more insight into the effect of changes in underlying variables on CVP relationships.

6. Discuss the impact of activity-based costing on cost-volume-profit analysis.

CVP can be used with activity-based costing but the analysis must be modified. In effect, under ABC a type of sensitivity analysis is used. Fixed costs are separated from a variety of costs that vary with particular cost drivers. At this stage, it is easiest to organize variable costs as unit-level, batch-level, and product-level. Then the impact of decisions on batches and products can be examined within the CVP framework.

The subject of cost-volume-profit analysis naturally lends itself to the use of numerous equations. Some of the more common equations used in this chapter are summarized in Exhibit 15-11.

KEY TERMS

Break-even point *602*
Contribution margin *603*
Contribution margin ratio *607*
Cost-volume-profit graph *615*

Degree of operating
  leverage (DOL) *621*
Direct fixed expenses *610*
Margin of safety *621*

Net income *603*
Operating income *603*
Operating leverage *621*
Profit-volume graph *614*

Relevant range *617*
Sales mix *612*
Sensitivity analysis *623*
Variable cost ratio *607*

15-11

Exhibit
Summary of Important
Equations

1. Sales revenue = Price × Units
2. Operating income = (Price × Units) − (Unit variable cost × Units) − Fixed cost
3. Break-even point in units = $\dfrac{\text{Fixed cost}}{\text{Price} - \text{Unit variable cost}}$
4. Contribution margin ratio = $\dfrac{\text{Contribution margin}}{\text{Sales}}$

   or

   $= \dfrac{\text{Price} - \text{Unit variable cost}}{\text{Price}}$

5. Variable cost ratio $= \dfrac{\text{Total variable cost}}{\text{Sales}}$

     or

     $= \dfrac{\text{Unit variable cost}}{\text{Price}}$

6. Break-even point in sales dollars $= \dfrac{\text{Fixed cost}}{\text{Contribution margin ratio}}$

                                    $= \dfrac{\text{Fixed cost}}{1 - \text{Variable cost ratio}}$

7. Margin of safety $=$ Sales $-$ Break-even sales

8. Degree of operating leverage $= \dfrac{\text{Total contribution margin}}{\text{Profit}}$

9. Percentage change in profits $=$ Degree of operating leverage $\times$ (%) change in sales

10. Income taxes $=$ Tax rate $\times$ Operating income

11. After-tax income $=$ Operating income $-$ (Tax rate $\times$ Operating income)

12. Before-tax income $= \dfrac{\text{After-tax income}}{1 - \text{Tax rate}}$

13. ABC total cost $=$ Fixed cost $+$ (Unit variable cost $\times$ Number of units) $+$ (Batch-level cost $\times$ Batch driver) $+$ (Product-level cost $\times$ Product driver)

14. ABC break-even units $= \dfrac{\text{Fixed cost} + (\text{Batch-level cost} \times \text{Batch driver}) + (\text{Product-level cost} \times \text{Product driver})}{\text{Price} - \text{Unit variable cost}}$

R EVIEW PROBLEMS

I. Cutlass Company's projected profit for the coming year is as follows:

	Total	Per Unit
Sales	$ 200,000	$ 20
Less: Variable expenses	(120,000)	(12)
Contribution margin	$ 80,000	$ 8
Less: Fixed expenses	(64,000)	
Net income	$ 16,000	

REQUIRED:

1. Compute the break-even point in units.
2. How many units must be sold to earn a profit of $30,000?
3. Compute the contribution margin ratio. Using that ratio, compute the additional profit that Cutlass would earn if sales were $25,000 more than expected.
4. Suppose Cutlass would like to earn operating income equal to 20 percent of sales revenue. How many units must be sold for this goal to be realized? Prepare an income statement to prove your answer.
5. For the projected level of sales, compute the margin of safety.

Solution

1. The break-even point is:

$$\text{Units} = \dfrac{\text{Fixed cost}}{\text{Price} - \text{Unit variable cost}}$$

$$= \dfrac{\$64,000}{\$20 - \$12}$$

$$= \frac{\$64,000}{\$8}$$

$$= 8,000$$

2. The number of units that must be sold to earn a profit of $30,000 is:

$$\text{Units} = \frac{\$64,000 + \$30,000}{\$8}$$

$$= \frac{\$94,000}{\$8}$$

$$= 11,750$$

3. The contribution margin ratio is $\frac{\$8}{\$20} = 0.40$. With additional sales of $25,000, the additional profit would be $0.40 \times \$25,000 = \$10,000$.

4. To find the number of units sold for a profit equal to 20 percent of sales, let target income equal $(0.20)(\text{Price} \times \text{Units})$ and solve for units:

$$\text{Operating income} = (\text{Price} \times \text{Units}) - (\text{Units variable cost} \times \text{Units}) - \text{Fixed cost}$$

$$(.2)(\$20) \times \text{Units} = \$20 \times \text{Units} - \$12 \times \text{Units} - \$64,000$$
$$\$4 \times \text{Units} = \$64,000$$
$$\text{Units} = 16,000$$

The income statement is as follows:

Sales (16,000 × $20)	$ 320,000
Less: Variable expenses (16,000 × $12)	(192,000)
Contribution margin	$ 128,000
Less: Fixed expenses	(64,000)
Net income	$ 64,000

5. The margin of safety is $10,000 - 8,000 = 2,000$ units, or $40,000 in sales revenues.

II. Dory Manufacturing Company produces T-shirts screen-printed with the logos of various sports teams. Each shirt is priced at $10. Costs are as follows:

Cost Driver	Unit Variable Cost	Level of Cost Driver
Units sold	$ 5	—
Setups	450	80
Engineering hours	20	500

Other data:

Total fixed costs (conventional)	$96,000
Total fixed costs (ABC)	50,000

REQUIRED:
1. Compute the break-even point in units using conventional analysis.
2. Compute the break-even point in units using activity-based analysis.
3. Suppose that Dory could reduce the setup cost by $150 per setup and the number of engineering hours needed to 425. How many units must be sold to break even in this case?

Solution

1. $\text{Break-even units} = \dfrac{\text{Fixed cost}}{\text{Price} - \text{Unit variable cost}}$

$$= \frac{\$96,000}{\$10 - \$5}$$

$$= 19,200 \text{ units}$$

2. $\text{Break-even units} = \dfrac{\text{Fixed cost} + (\text{Setups} \times \text{Setup cost}) + (\text{Engineering hours} \times \text{Engineering cost})}{\text{Price} - \text{Unit variable cost}}$

$$= \frac{\$50,000 + (\$450 \times 80) + (\$20 \times 500)}{\$10 - \$5}$$

$$= 19{,}200 \text{ units}$$

3. Break-even units $= \dfrac{\$50,000 + (\$300 \times 80) + (\$20 \times 425)}{\$10 - \$5}$

$$= \frac{\$82,500}{\$5}$$

$$= 16{,}500 \text{ units}$$

QUESTIONS FOR WRITING AND DISCUSSION

1. Explain how CVP analysis can be used for managerial planning.
2. Describe the difference between the units-sold approach to CVP analysis and the sales revenue approach.
3. Define the term *break-even point*.
4. Explain why contribution margin per unit becomes profit per unit above the break-even point.
5. If the contribution margin per unit is $7 and the break-even point is 10,000 units, how much profit will a firm make if 15,000 units are sold?
6. What is the variable cost ratio? the contribution margin ratio? How are the two ratios related?
7. Suppose a firm has fixed costs of $20,000 and a contribution margin ratio of 0.4. How much sales revenue must the firm have in order to break even?
8. Suppose a firm with a contribution margin ratio of 0.3 increased its advertising expenses by $10,000 and found that sales increased by $30,000. Was it a good decision to increase advertising expenses?
9. Define the term *sales mix* and give an example to support your definition.
10. Explain how CVP analysis developed for single products can be used in a multiple-product setting.
11. Assume that a firm has two products—A and B. Last year 2,000 units of A and 1,000 units of B were sold. The same sales mix is expected for the coming year. Total fixed expenses are $30,000, and the unit contribution margins are $10 for A and $5 for B. How many units of A and how many units of B must be sold to break even?
12. Wilson Company has a contribution margin ratio of 0.6. The break-even point is $100,000. During the year, Wilson earned total revenues of $200,000. What was Wilson's profit?
13. Explain how a change in sales mix can change a company's break-even point.
14. Define the term *margin of safety*. Explain how it can be used as a crude measure of operating risk.
15. Explain what is meant by the term *operating leverage*. What impact does increased leverage have on risk?
16. How can sensitivity analysis be used in conjunction with CVP analysis?
17. Why does the activity-based costing approach to CVP analysis offer more insight than the conventional approach?
18. How does JIT affect the firm's cost equation? CVP analysis?

WARM-UP EXERCISES

This section provides short warm-up exercises based on the examples in the chapter. Each warm-up exercise gives the page number on which the text example can be found. You may want to refer to the text example to see how the exercise can be set up and solved.

W15-1
Breakeven in Units
LO 1
pp. 603–605

The controller of Dorian Company prepared the following projected income statement:

Sales (2,000 units @ $25)	$ 50,000
Less: Variable expenses	(30,000)
Contribution margin	$ 20,000
Less: Fixed expenses	(18,000)
Profit before taxes	$ 2,000

REQUIRED:
1. Using the income statement format, calculate the break-even number of units.
2. Using the fundamental break-even equation, calculate the break-even number of units.

3. How many units must Dorian sell to earn income equal to $15,000?
4. How many units must Dorian sell to earn income equal to 20 percent of revenue?
5. Assuming an income-tax rate of 40 percent, how many units must Dorian sell to earn after-tax income equal to $15,000?

W15-2
Contribution Margin Ratio; Variable Cost Ratio; Breakeven in Sales Revenue
LO 2
pp. 607–609

Refer to W15-1 for data.

REQUIRED:
1. What is the contribution margin per unit for Dorian Company? What is the contribution margin ratio?
2. What is the variable cost ratio for Dorian Company?
3. Using the income statement format, calculate the break-even revenue.
4. Using the fundamental break-even equation, calculate the break-even revenue.
5. How much revenue must Dorian make to earn income equal to $15,000?

W15-3
Multiple-Product Breakeven
LO 3
pp. 612–613

Lacy Company manufactures two products. In the coming year, Lacy expects to sell 1,000 units of product A and 3,000 units of product B. A budgeted income statement for next year follows:

	Product A	Product B	Total
Sales	$10,000	$ 36,000	$ 46,000
Less: Variable expenses	(6,000)	(27,000)	(33,000)
Contribution margin	$ 4,000	$ 9,000	$ 13,000
Less: Direct fixed expenses	(1,500)	(3,200)	(4,700)
Product margin	$ 2,500	$ 5,800	$ 8,300
Less: Common fixed expenses			(3,100)
Profit before taxes			$ 5,200

REQUIRED:
1. What is the sales mix for Lacy Company?
2. Calculate the number of units of product A and of product B that Lacy must sell to break even.
3. Without forming a package, calculate the break-even revenue for Lacy Company.

W15-4
Margin of Safety and Degree of Operating Leverage
LO 5
p. 621

Halligan Company has prepared the following income statement for the year:

Sales ($50 × 8,000 units)	$400,000
Less: Variable expenses	(140,000)
Contribution margin	$260,000
Less: Fixed expenses	(119,925)
Operating income	$140,075

REQUIRED:
1. What is the margin of safety in sales dollars? in units?
2. What is the degree of operating leverage for Halligan Company?

W15-5
CVP and Activity-based Costing
LO 6
p. 624

The controller of Fremont Company collected the following data for one of Fremont's plants:

Activity Driver	Unit Variable Cost	Level of Activity Driver
Units sold	$ 10	—
Setups	600	50
Engineering hours	60	500

Other data:
Total fixed costs (conventional) $100,000
Total fixed costs (ABC)   40,000
Unit selling price   20

REQUIRED:
1. Calculate the break-even point in units using the traditional approach.
2. Calculate the break-even point in units using the ABC approach.
3. If Fremont's engineers can reduce the variable cost of a setup by $100, what will the new
   break-even point in units be under the ABC approach? under the traditional approach?

E XERCISES

E15-1
**Units Sold; After-Tax
Profit; Margin of
Safety**
LO 1, LO 2, LO 5

Henderson Bottling Company produces and sells generic cola to retailers. The cola is bottled in
2-liter plastic bottles and sold to retailers for $1.00 per bottle. The variable costs per bottle are as
follows:

Ingredients	$0.45
Bottle and cap	0.10
Selling	0.17

Fixed manufacturing costs total $22,000 per year. Administrative costs (all fixed) total $6,000.

REQUIRED:
1. Compute the number of bottles of cola that must be sold for Henderson to break even.
2. How many bottles of cola must be sold for Henderson to earn a before-tax profit of
   $12,600?
3. Assuming a tax rate of 40 percent, how many bottles of cola must be sold to earn an after-tax
   profit of $25,200?
4. Suppose that Henderson expects to sell 115,000 bottles of cola. What is the margin of safety
   in bottles? What is the margin of safety in dollars?

E15-2
**Contribution Margin;
Unit Amounts**
LO 1, LO 2

Information on four independent companies follows. Calculate the correct amount for each question mark.

	A	B	C	D
Sales	$ 5,000	$?	$?	$9,000
Total variable expenses	(4,000)	(11,700)	(9,750)	?
Contribution margin	1,000	3,900	?	?
Total fixed expenses	?	(4,000)	?	(750)
Net income	500	?	400	2,850
Units sold	?	1,300	125	90
Price	$5	?	$130	?
Variable cost/Unit	?	$9	?	?
Contribution margin/Unit	?	$3	?	?
Contribution margin ratio	?	?	60%	?
Breakeven in units	?	?	?	?

E15-3
**CVP; Margin of
Safety**
LO 2, LO 5

Garner Company had revenues of $340,000 last year, with total variable costs of $238,000 and
fixed costs of $45,000.

REQUIRED:
1. What is the contribution margin ratio for Garner based on last year's data? What is the break-
   even point in sales revenue?

2. What was the margin of safety for Garner last year?
3. Garner is considering starting a multimedia advertising campaign that is supposed to increase sales by $15,000 per year. The campaign will cost $5,000. Is the advertising campaign a good idea? Explain.

E15-4
CVP
LO 1, LO 2

James Company's break-even point is 1,500 units. Variable cost per unit is $300; total fixed costs are $120,000 per year.

REQUIRED: What price does James charge?

E15-5
Contribution Margin;
CVP; Net Income;
Margin of Safety
LO 1, LO 2, LO 5

Candyland, Inc. produces a particularly rich praline fudge. Each 10-ounce box sells for $5.60. Variable unit costs are as follows:

Pecans	$0.70
Sugar	0.35
Butter	1.85
Other ingredients	0.34
Box, packing material	0.76
Selling commission	0.20

Fixed overhead cost is $32,300 per year. Fixed selling and administrative costs are $12,500 per year. Candyland sold 35,000 boxes last year.

REQUIRED:
1. What is the contribution margin per unit for a box of praline fudge? What is the contribution margin ratio?
2. How many boxes must be sold to break even? What is the break-even sales revenue?
3. What was Candyland's net income last year?
4. What was the margin of safety?
5. Suppose that Candyland, Inc., raises the price to $6.20 per box but that anticipated sales drop to 31,500 boxes. What will the new break-even point in units be? Should Candyland raise the price? Explain.

E15-6
Sales Revenue
Approach; Variable
Cost Ratio;
Contribution Margin
Ratio; Margin of
Safety
LO 2, LO 5

Wilman produces and sells specialty glass for the automobile industry. The budgeted income statement for the coming year is as follows:

Sales	$ 450,000
Less: Variable expenses	(202,500)
Contribution margin	$ 247,500
Less: Fixed expenses	(90,000)
Profit before taxes	$ 157,500
Less: Taxes	(47,250)
Profit after taxes	$ 110,250

REQUIRED:
1. What is Wilman's variable cost ratio? What is its contribution margin ratio?
2. Suppose Wilman's actual revenues are $50,000 more than budgeted. By how much will before-tax profits increase? Give the answer without preparing a new income statement.
3. How much sales revenue must Wilman earn to break even? What is the expected margin of safety?
4. How much sales revenue must Wilman generate to earn a before-tax profit of $75,000?
5. How much sales revenue must Wilman generate to earn an after-tax profit of $63,000? Prepare a contribution income statement to verify the accuracy of your answer.

E15-7
CVP Analysis with Target Profits
LO 2

Tom Flannery has developed a new recipe for fried chicken and plans to open a take-out restaurant in Oklahoma City. His father-in-law has agreed to invest $500,000 in the operation provided Tom can convince him that profits will be at least 20 percent of sales revenues. Tom estimated that total fixed expenses would be $24,000 per year and that variable expenses would be approximately 40 percent of sales revenues.

REQUIRED:
1. How much sales revenue must be earned to produce profits equal to 20 percent of sales revenue? Prepare a contribution income statement to verify your answer.
2. If Tom plans on selling 12-piece buckets of chicken for $10 each, how many buckets must he sell to earn a profit equal to 20 percent of sales? 25 percent of sales? Prepare a contribution income statement to verify the second answer.
3. Suppose Tom's father-in-law meant that the after-tax profit had to be 20 percent of sales revenue. Under this assumption, how much sales revenue must be generated by Tom's chicken business? (Assume that the tax rate is 40 percent.)

E15-8
Operating Leverage
LO 5

Income statements for two different companies in the same industry are as follows:

	Company A	Company B
Sales	$ 500,000	$ 500,000
Less: Variable expenses	(400,000)	(200,000)
Contribution margin	$ 100,000	$ 300,000
Less: Fixed expenses	(50,000)	(250,000)
Net income	$ 50,000	$ 50,000

REQUIRED:
1. Compute the degree of operating leverage for each company.
2. Compute the break-even point for each company. Explain why the break-even point for company B is higher.
3. Suppose that both companies experience a 50 percent increase in revenues. Compute the percentage change in profits for each company. Explain why the percentage increase in company B's profits is so much larger than that of company A.

E15-9
CVP Analysis with Multiple Products
LO 3

Gernon Company produces scientific and business calculators. For the coming year, Gernon expects to sell 20,000 scientific calculators and 100,000 business calculators. A segmented income statement for the two products follows:

	Scientific	Business	Total
Sales	$ 500,000	$2,000,000	$ 2,500,000
Less: Variable expenses	(240,000)	(900,000)	(1,140,000)
Contribution margin	$ 260,000	$1,100,000	$ 1,360,000
Less: Direct fixed expenses	(120,000)	(960,000)	(1,080,000)
Segment margin	$ 140,000	$ 140,000	$ 280,000
Less: Common fixed expenses			(145,000)
Net income			$ 135,000

REQUIRED:
1. Compute the number of scientific calculators and the number of business calculators that must be sold to break even.

2. Using information from only the "Total" column of the income statement, compute the sales revenue that must be generated for the company to break even.

E15-10
Contribution Analysis
LO 1, LO 2

Fox Company produces a deluxe pen-and-pencil set. The selling price of the set is $50. The variable cost per set is $30. Total fixed costs are $2.5 million. Expected sales for the coming year are 150,000 sets. Management is unhappy with the expected profits and is trying to find ways to increase overall performance. The marketing manager has proposed two alternatives: (1) increase advertising by $100,000, which should produce additional sales of 10,000 units, or (2) decrease the selling price to $45 per set, which should boost sales from 150,000 sets to 165,000 sets.

REQUIRED:
1. Prepare an income statement that reflects expected sales for the coming year. Ignore the proposals by the marketing manager.
2. Without preparing income statements, assess the impact on profits of each of the marketing manager's proposals. Which would you recommend?
3. Prepare income statements for the two proposals to verify your analysis in requirement 2.

E15-11
Changes in Break-even Points with Changes in Unit Prices
LO 1, LO 2

The income statement for Childress, Inc. is as follows:

Sales	$ 600,000
Less: Variable expenses	(228,000)
Contribution margin	$ 372,000
Less: Fixed expenses	(295,000)
Net income	$ 77,000

Childress produces and sells a single product. The income statement is based on sales of 100,000 units.

REQUIRED:
1. Compute the break-even point in units and in revenues.
2. Suppose that the selling price increases by 10 percent. Will the break-even point increase or decrease? Recompute it.
3. Ignoring requirement 2, suppose that the variable cost per unit increases by $0.35. Will the break-even point increase or decrease? Recompute it.
4. Can you predict whether the break-even point increases or decreases if both the selling price and the unit variable cost increase? Recompute the break-even point incorporating both of the changes in requirements 2 and 3.
5. Assume that total fixed costs increase by $50,000. (Assume no other changes from the original data.) Will the break-even point increase or decrease? Recompute it.

E15-12
CVP and Profit-Volume Graphs
LO 4

Lotts Company produces and sells one product. The selling price is $10, and the unit variable cost is $6. Total fixed costs are $10,000.

REQUIRED:
1. Prepare a CVP graph with "units sold" as the horizontal axis and "dollars" as the vertical axis. Label the break-even point on the horizontal axis.
2. Prepare CVP graphs for each of the following independent scenarios:
   a. Fixed costs increase by $5,000.
   b. Unit variable cost increases to $7.
   c. Unit selling price increases to $12.
   d. Assume fixed costs increase by $5,000 and unit variable cost is $7.
3. Prepare a profit-volume graph using the original data. Repeat, following the scenarios in requirement 2.
4. Which of the two graphs do you think provides the most information? Why?

E15-13
Basic CVP Concepts
LO 1, LO 2

Berry Company produces a single product. The projected income statement for the coming year is as follows:

Sales (50,000 units @ $45)	$ 2,250,000
Less: Variable expenses	(1,305,000)
Contribution margin	$ 945,000
Less: Fixed expenses	(812,700)
Net income	$ 132,300

REQUIRED:

1. Compute the unit contribution margin and the units that must be sold to break even. Suppose that 30,000 units are sold above breakeven. What is the profit?
2. Compute the contribution margin ratio and the break-even point in dollars. Suppose that revenues are $200,000 more than expected. What would the total profit be?
3. Compute the margin of safety.
4. Compute the operating leverage. Compute the new profit level if sales are 20 percent higher than expected.
5. How many units must be sold to earn a profit equal to 10 percent of sales?
6. Assume that the tax rate is 40 percent. How many units must be sold to earn an after-tax profit of $180,000?

E15-14
CVP; Before- and
After-Tax Targeted
Net Income
LO 1, LO 2

Yancan Company produces a line of specialty jellies. Currently, Yancan charges a price of $4.50 per jar. Variable costs are $1.80 per jar and fixed costs are $60,000. The tax rate is 35 percent. Last year, 32,400 jars were sold.

REQUIRED:

1. What is Yancan's net income after taxes for last year?
2. What is Yancan's break-even revenue?
3. Suppose Yancan wants to earn a before-tax profit of $20,000. How many units must be sold?
4. Suppose Yancan wants to earn after-tax net income of $20,000. How many units must be sold?

E15-15
Multiproduct
Breakeven
LO 3

Parker Pottery produces a line of vases and a line of ceramic figurines. Each line uses the same equipment and labor; hence, there are no traceable fixed costs. Common fixed costs equal $30,000. Parker's accountant has begun to assess the profitability of the two lines and has gathered the following data for last year:

	Vases	Figurines
Price	$ 40	$ 70
Variable cost	(30)	(42)
Contribution margin	10	28
Number of units	1,000	500

REQUIRED:

1. Compute the number of vases and the number of figurines that must be sold for the company to break even.
2. Parker Pottery is considering undertaking an advertising campaign to highlight the quality of its ceramic figurines. The campaign will cost $5,000 and if it is successful, the projected sales of vases will remain at 1,000 while figurine sales will increase to 1,000 units. What is the new break-even point in units for each of the products?

P15-1
Basic CVP Concepts
LO 1, LO 2, LO 5

Fisper Company produces a variety of industrial products. One division makes solvents. The division's projected income statement for the coming year is as follows:

Sales (137,000 units @ $50)	$ 6,850,000
Less: Variable expenses	(3,425,000)
Contribution margin	$ 3,425,000
Less: Fixed expenses	(3,000,000)
Operating income	$ 425,000

REQUIRED:
1. Compute the contribution margin per unit and calculate the break-even point in units. Repeat using the contribution margin ratio.
2. The divisional manager has decided to increase the advertising budget by $100,000 and cut the selling price to $45. These actions will increase sales revenues by $1 million. Will the division be better off?
3. Suppose sales revenues exceed the estimated amount on the income statement by $540,000. Without preparing a new income statement, by how much are profits underestimated?
4. Refer to the original data. How many units must be sold to earn an after-tax profit of $400,000? Assume a tax rate of 40 percent. Repeat the analysis assuming that the after-tax profit target is 10 percent of sales revenues.
5. Compute the margin of safety based on the original income statement.
6. Compute the operating leverage based on the original income statement. If sales revenues are 20 percent greater than expected, what is the percentage increase in profits?

P15-2
Multiple-Product Analysis; Changes in Sales Mix
LO 3

Unicorn Enterprises produces two strategy games, Mystical Wars and Magical Dragons. The projected income for the coming year, segmented by product line, follows:

	Wars	Dragons	Total
Sales	$ 500,000	$ 800,000	$1,300,000
Less: Variable expenses	(230,000)	(460,000)	(690,000)
Contribution margin	$ 270,000	$ 340,000	$ 610,000
Less: Direct fixed expenses	(120,000)	(180,000)	(300,000)
Product margin	$ 150,000	$ 160,000	$ 310,000
Less: Common fixed expenses			(210,000)
Operating income			$ 100,000

The selling prices are $10 for Mystical Wars and $20 for Magical Dragons.

REQUIRED:
1. Compute the number of games of each kind that must be sold for Unicorn Enterprises to break even.
2. Compute the revenue that must be earned to produce a net income of 10 percent of sales revenues.
3. Assume that the marketing manager changes the sales mix of the two games so that the ratio is seven Mystical War games to three Magical Dragon games. Repeat requirements 1 and 2. Will the owner of Unicorn Enterprises be pleased with the anticipated change in sales mix?
4. Refer to the original data. Suppose that Unicorn can increase the sales of Magical Dragons with increased advertising. The extra advertising would cost an additional $100,000, and some of the potential purchasers of Mystical Wars would switch to Magical Dragons. In total, sales of Magical Dragons would increase by 15,000 units and sales of Mystical Wars would decrease by 5,000 units. Would Unicorn be better off with this strategy? Prepare income statements for each product line to verify your analysis. Do you have any additional recommendations?

P15-3
CVP Equation; Basic

Azucar Company produces a chocolate almond bar. Each bar sells for $0.40. The variable costs for each bar (sugar, chocolate, almonds, wrapper, labor, and so on) total $0.25. The total fixed costs are $60,000. During the most recent year, 1 million bars were sold. The president of Azucar, not fully satisfied with the profit performance of the chocolate bar, was considering the following options to increase the bar's profitability: (1) increase advertising; (2) increase the quality of the ingredients and, simultaneously, increase the selling price; (3) increase the selling price; (4) combinations of the three.

REQUIRED:

1. The sales manager is confident that an advertising campaign could double sales volume. If the company president's goal is to increase this year's profits by 50 percent over last year's, what is the maximum amount that can be spent on advertising?
2. Assume that the company increases the quality of its ingredients, thus increasing variable costs to $0.30. Answer the following questions:
   a. How much must the selling price be increased to maintain the same break-even point?
   b. What will the new price be if the company wants to increase the old contribution margin ratio by 50 percent?
3. The company has decided to increase its selling price to $0.50. The sales volume drops from 1 million to 800,000 bars. Was the decision to increase the price a good one? Compute the sales volume that would be needed at the new price for the company to earn the same profit as last year.
4. The sales manager is convinced that by increasing the quality of the ingredients (increasing variable costs to $0.30) and by advertising the increased quality (advertising dollars would be increased by $100,000), sales volume could be doubled. He has also indicated that a price increase would not affect the ability to double sales volume as long as the price increase is not more than 20 percent of the current selling price. Compute the selling price that would be needed to achieve the goal of increasing profits by 50 percent. Is the sales manager's plan feasible? What selling price would you choose? Why?

....

We-Care Lawn Service is a lawn-care company operating in a northern metropolitan area. We-Care offers chemical fertilization, insect control, and weed and crabgrass control for a customer's lawn and foundation. Four chemical applications are given per growing period, which lasts from April through October. Four chemicals are used in the applications: dacthal for crabgrass control, Roundup™ weed control, urea fertilizer, and Dursban insecticide. In the first application, dacthal accounts for 75 percent of the chemical cost followed by 10 percent Roundup™, 10 percent urea, and 5 percent Dursban; in the remaining three applications, dacthal is not used—it is ineffective after May 31.

We-Care offers two services: residential and commercial. The price charged per residential application is $13.50. The average residential area is 0.1 acre. Commercial applications are for any area larger than an acre and are priced at $40 per acre per application.

We-Care's variable costs consist of chemicals, direct labor, operating expenses for its truck, and operating supplies. For the first application, the cost of chemicals is $40 per acre; for the remaining applications, chemicals cost $10 per application per acre. We-Care has one employee who is classified as direct labor. He is paid $6 per hour. Residential lawns should be sprayed at a rate of three lawns per hour (including travel time). Commercial applications are sprayed at a rate of 45 minutes per acre. Operating expenses for the truck average $13.78 per acre per residential lawn application and $5 per acre per commercial application. Operating supplies average $4.13 per acre per application, regardless of the type of service. Fixed costs for the year follow:

Truck lease	$12,337
Depreciation, equipment	1,747
Truck insurance	1,339
Telephone	1,200
Tax and license	1,085
Advertising	10,000
Salary of supervisor	12,000
Total	$39,708

Based on last year's experience, We-Care services two acres of residential property for every acre of commercial property. The owner expects the same sales mix for the coming year.

REQUIRED:

1. Assume that every customer receives all four applications. Compute the acres of residential applications and the acres of commercial applications that must be serviced for We-Care to break even. Given the acres of residential servicing, compute the average number of residential customers.
2. Given the break-even point computed in requirement 1, determine the labor hours needed to service the break-even volume. Is one employee sufficient? Assume that the employee works eight hours per day and a total of 140 days during the seven-month growing season. What volume is needed before a second employee is hired? Discuss the effect on CVP analysis if additional employees are needed.
3. Assume that 60 percent of all residential customers receive only the first application, with the remaining 40 percent receiving all four. All commercial customers receive all four applications. Redo the break-even analysis. (*Hint:* There are now two types of residential customers, producing a mix of three services.)

P15-5
Basics of the Sales Revenue Approach
LO 2, LO 5

Kiltop Company produces a toy dart gun. The projected income statement for the coming year follows:

Sales	$ 480,000
Less: Variable costs	(249,600)
Contribution margin	$ 230,400
Less: Fixed costs	(180,000)
Net income	$ 50,400

REQUIRED:

1. Compute the contribution margin ratio for the toy gun.
2. How much revenue must Kiltop earn in order to break even?
3. What volume of sales must be earned if Kiltop wants to earn an after-tax income equal to 8 percent of sales? Assume that the tax rate is 34 percent.
4. What is the effect on the contribution margin ratio if the unit selling price and unit variable cost each increase by 10 percent?
5. Suppose that management has decided to give a 3 percent commission on all sales. The projected income statement does not reflect this commission. Recompute the contribution margin ratio assuming that the commission will be paid. What effect does this have on the break-even point?
6. If the commission is paid as described in requirement 5, management expects sales revenues to increase by $80,000. Is it a sound decision to implement the commission? Support your answer with appropriate computations.

P15-6
CVP Analysis: Sales Revenue Approach; Pricing; After-Tax Profit Target
LO 2

Kline Consulting is a service organization that specializes in the design, installation, and servicing of mechanical, hydraulic, and pneumatic systems. For example, some manufacturing firms, with machinery that cannot be turned off for servicing, need some type of system to lubricate the machinery during use. To deal with this type of problem for a client, Kline designed a central lubricating system that pumps lubricants intermittently to bearings and other moving parts.

The operating results for the firm last year are as follows:

Sales	$ 802,429
Less: Variable expenses	(430,000)
Contribution margin	$ 372,429
Less: Fixed expenses	(154,750)
Net income	$ 217,679

Next year, Kline expects variable costs to increase by 5 percent and fixed costs by 4 percent.

REQUIRED:
1. What is the contribution margin ratio for last year?
2. Compute Kline's break-even point for last year in dollars.
3. Suppose that Kline would like to see a 6 percent increase in net income next year. What percent (on average) must Kline raise its bids to cover the expected cost increases and obtain the desired net income? Assume that Kline expects the same mix and volume of services in each year.
4. Next year, how much revenue must be earned for Kline to earn an after-tax profit of $175,000? Assume a tax rate of 34 percent.

P15-7
CVP with Multiple Products; Sales Mix Changes; Changes in Fixed and Variable Costs
LO 3

Artistic Woodcrafting, Inc. began in 1984 as a one-person cabinetmaking operation. Business soon expanded and employees were added. By 1995, sales volume totaled $850,000. Volume for the first five months of 1998 totaled $600,000, and sales were expected to be $1.6 million for the entire year. Unfortunately, the cabinet business in the region where Artistic Woodcrafting is located is highly competitive. More than two hundred cabinet shops are all competing for the same business.

Artistic currently offers two different quality grades of cabinets: grade I and grade II, with grade I being the higher quality. The average unit selling prices, unit variable costs, and direct fixed costs are as follows:

	Unit Price	Unit Variable Cost	Direct Fixed Costs
Grade I	$3,400	$2,686	$95,000
Grade II	1,600	1,328	95,000

Common fixed costs (fixed costs not traceable to either cabinet) are $35,000. Currently, for every three grade I cabinets sold, seven grade II cabinets are sold.

REQUIRED:
1. Calculate the grade I and grade II cabinets that are expected to be sold during 1998.
2. Calculate the number of grade I and grade II cabinets that must be sold for the company to break even.
3. Artistic Woodcrafting can buy computer-controlled machines that will make doors, drawers, and frames. If the machines are purchased, the variable costs for each type of cabinet will decrease by 9 percent, but common fixed costs will increase by $44,000. Compute the effect on net income in 1998 and also calculate the new break-even point. Assume the machines are purchased at the beginning of the sixth month. Fixed costs for the company are incurred uniformly throughout the year.
4. Refer to the original data. Artistic Woodcrafting is considering adding a retail outlet. This will increase common fixed costs by $70,000 per year. As a result of adding the retail outlet, the additional publicity and emphasis on quality will allow the firm to change the sales mix to 1:1. The retail outlet is also expected to increase sales by 30 percent. Assume that the outlet is opened at the beginning of the sixth month. Calculate the effect on the company's expected profits for 1998 and calculate the new break-even point. Assume that fixed costs are incurred uniformly throughout the year.

P15-8
Multiple Products; Break-even Analysis; Operating Leverage
LO 3, LO 5

Carlyle Lighting Products produces two different types of lamps, a floor lamp and a desk lamp. Floor lamps sell for $30, desk lamps for $20. The projected income statement for the coming year follows:

Sales	$ 600,000
Less: Variable expenses	(400,000)
Contribution margin	$ 200,000
Less: Fixed expenses	(150,000)
Net income	$ 50,000

The owner of Carlyle estimates that 60 percent of the sales revenues will be produced by floor lamps with the remaining 40 percent by desk lamps. Floor lamps are also responsible for 60 percent of the variable expenses. Of the fixed expenses, one-third are common to both products, and one-half are directly traceable to the floor lamp product line.

REQUIRED:

1. Compute the sales revenue that must be earned for Carlyle to break even.
2. Compute the number of floor lamps and desk lamps that must be sold for Carlyle to break even.
3. Compute the degree of operating leverage for Carlyle Lighting Products. Now assume that the actual revenues will be 40 percent higher than the projected revenues. By what percentage will profits increase with this change in sales volume?

P15-9
Multiproduct
Breakeven
LO 3

Polaris, Inc. manufactures two types of metal stampings for the automobile industry: door handles and trim kits. Fixed costs equal $146,000. Each door handle sells for $12 and has variable costs of $9; each trim kit sells for $8 and has variable costs of $5.

REQUIRED:

1. What are the contribution margin per unit and the contribution margin ratio for door handles and for trim kits?
2. If Polaris sells 20,000 door handles and 40,000 trim kits, what is the net income?
3. How many door handles and how many trim kits must be sold for Polaris to break even?
4. Assume that Polaris has the opportunity to rearrange its plant to produce only trim kits. If this is done, fixed costs will decrease by $35,000 and 70,000 trim kits can be produced and sold. Is this a good idea? Explain.

P15-10
CVP; Margin of
Safety
LO 2, LO 5

Victoria Company produces a single product. Last year's income statement is as follows:

Sales (29,000 units)	$1,218,000
Less: Variable expenses	(812,000)
Contribution margin	$ 406,000
Less: Fixed expenses	(300,000)
Net income	$ 106,000

REQUIRED:

1. Compute the break-even point in units and sales dollars.
2. What was the margin of safety for Victoria Company last year?
3. Suppose that Victoria Company is considering an investment in new technology that will increase fixed costs by $250,000 per year but will lower variable costs to 45 percent of sales. Units sold will remain unchanged. Prepare a budgeted income statement assuming that Victoria makes this investment. What is the new break-even point in units and sales dollars, assuming that the investment is made?

P15-11
Multiplant Breakeven
LO 2, LO 3

The PTO Division of the Galva Manufacturing Company produces power take-off units for the farm equipment business. The PTO Division, headquartered in Peoria, has a newly renovated plant in Peoria and an older, less automated plant in Moline. Both plants produce the same power take-off units for farm tractors that are sold to most domestic and foreign tractor manufacturers.

The PTO Division expects to produce and sell 192,000 power take-off units during the coming year. The divisional production manager has the following data available regarding the unit costs, unit prices, and production capacities for the two plants.

		Peoria		Moline
Selling price		$150.00		$150.00
Variable manufacturing cost	$72.00		$88.00	
Fixed manufacturing cost	30.00		15.00	
Commission (5%)	7.50		7.50	
General and administrative expenses	25.50		21.00	
Total unit cost		135.00		131.50
Unit profit		$ 15.00		$ 18.50
Production rate per day	400 units		320 units	

All fixed costs are based on a normal year of 240 working days. When the number of working days exceeds 240, variable manufacturing costs increase by $3 per unit in Peoria and $8 per unit in Moline. Capacity for each plant is 300 working days.

Galva Manufacturing charges each of its plants a per-unit fee for administrative services such as payroll, general accounting, and purchasing because Galva considers these services to be a function of the work performed at the plants. For each of the plants, a fee of $6.50 represents the variable portion of the general and administrative expenses.

Wishing to maximize the higher unit profit at Moline, PTO's production manager has decided to manufacture 96,000 units at each plant. This production plan results in Moline's operating at capacity and Peoria's operating at its normal volume. Galva's corporate controller is not happy with this plan; he wonders if it might be better to produce relatively more at the automated plant in Peoria.

REQUIRED:
1. Determine the annual break-even units for each of PTO's plants.
2. Calculate the operating income that would result from the divisional production manager's plan to produce 96,000 units at each plant.
3. Calculate the operating income that would result from sales of 192,000 power take-off units if 120,000 of them were produced at the Peoria plant and the remainder at the Moline plant. (CMA adapted)

P15-12
CVP Analysis and Assumptions
LO 2, LO 6

Marston Corporation manufactures pharmaceutical products that are sold through a network of sales agents located in the United States and Canada. The agents are currently paid an 18 percent commission on sales; this percentage was used when Marston prepared the following pro forma income statement for the fiscal year ended June 30, 1998.

Marston Corporation
Pro Forma Income Statement (in thousands)
For the Year Ended June 30, 1998

Sales		$26,000
Cost of goods sold:		
Variable	$11,700	
Fixed	2,870	14,570
Gross profit		$11,430
Selling and administrative costs:		
Commissions	$4,680	
Fixed advertising cost	750	
Fixed administrative cost	1,850	7,280
Operating income		$ 4,150
Fixed interest cost		650
Income before income taxes		$ 3,500
Income taxes (40%)		1,400
Net income		$ 2,100

Since the completion of this statement, Marston has learned that its agents are requiring an increase in the commission rate to 23 percent for the upcoming year. As a result, Marston's president has decided to investigate the possibility of hiring its own sales staff in place of the network of sales agents and has asked Tom Ross, Marston's controller, to gather information on the costs associated with this change.

Tom estimates that Marston will have to hire eight salespeople to cover the current market area, and the annual payroll cost of each of these employees will average $80,000, including fringe benefit expenses. Travel and entertainment expenses are expected to total $600,000 for the year, and the annual cost of hiring a sales manager and sales secretary will be $150,000. In addition to their salaries, the eight salespeople will each earn commissions at the rate of 10 percent on the first $2 million in sales and 15 percent on all sales over $2 million. For planning purposes, Tom expects that all eight salespeople will exceed the $2 million mark and that sales will be at the level previously projected. Tom believes that Marston should also increase its advertising budget by $500,000.

REQUIRED:

1. Calculate Marston Corporation's break-even point in sales dollars for the fiscal year ended June 30, 1998 if the company hires its own sales force and increases its advertising costs.
2. If Marston Corporation continues to sell through its network of sales agents and pays the higher commission rate, determine the estimated volume in sales dollars for the fiscal year ended June 30, 1998 that would be required to generate the same net income as that projected in the pro forma income statement presented.
3. Describe the general assumptions underlying break-even analysis that might limit its usefulness in this case. (CMA adapted)

 MANAGERIAL DECISION CASES

C15-1
Ethics and a CVP Application
LO 1

Danna Lumus, the marketing manager for a division that produces a variety of paper products, was considering the divisional manager's request for a sales forecast for a new line of paper napkins. The divisional manager was gathering data so that he could choose between two different production processes. The first process would have a variable cost of $10 per-case produced and fixed costs of $100,000. The second process would have a variable cost of $6 per case and fixed costs of $200,000. The selling price would be $30 per case. Danna had just completed a marketing analysis that projected annual sales of 30,000 cases.

Danna was reluctant to report the 30,000 forecast to the divisional manager. She knew that the first process was labor intensive, whereas the second was largely automated with little labor and no requirement for an additional production supervisor. If the first process were chosen, Jerry Johnson, a good friend, would be appointed as the line supervisor. If the second process were chosen, Jerry and an entire line of laborers would be laid off. After some consideration, Danna revised the projected sales downward to 22,000 cases.

She believed that the revision downward was justified. Since it would lead the divisional manager to choose the manual system, it showed a sensitivity to the needs of current employees—a sensitivity that she was afraid her divisional manager did not possess. He was too focused on quantitative factors in his decision making and usually ignored the qualitative aspects.

REQUIRED:

1. Compute the break-even point for each process.
2. Compute the sales volume for which the two processes are equally profitable. Identify the range of sales for which the manual process is more profitable than the automated process. Identify the range of sales for which the automated process is more profitable than the manual process. Why did the divisional manager want the sales forecast?
3. Discuss Danna's decision to alter the sales forecast. Do you agree with it? Did she act ethically? Was her decision justified since it helped a number of employees retain their employment? Should the impact on employees be factored into decisions? In fact, is it unethical not to consider the impact of decisions on employees?
4. Even though Danna is not a management accountant, do any of the ethical standards for management accountants listed in Exhibit 1-4 in Chapter 1 apply? Explain.

C15-2
Service Organization; Multiple Products; Breakeven; Pricing and Scheduling Decisions
LO 1, LO 2, LO 3

Utah Metropolitan Ballet is located in Salt Lake City. The company is housed in the Capitol Theater, one of three buildings that make up the Bicentennial Arts Center in downtown Salt Lake City. The ballet company features five different ballets per year. For the upcoming season, the five ballets to be performed are *The Dream, Petrushka, The Nutcracker, Sleeping Beauty,* and *Bugaku.*

The president and general manager has tentatively scheduled the following number of performances for each ballet for the coming season:

Dream	5
Petrushka	5
Nutcracker	20
Sleeping Beauty	10
Bugaku	5

To produce each ballet, costs must be incurred for costumes, props, rehearsals, royalties, guest artist fees, choreography, salaries of production staff, music, and wardrobe. These costs are fixed for a particular ballet regardless of the number of performances. These direct fixed costs follow for each ballet.

	Dream	Petrushka	Nutcracker	Sleeping Beauty	Bugaku
	$275,500	$145,500	$70,500	$345,000	$155,500

Other fixed costs are incurred as follows:

Advertising	$ 80,000
Insurance	15,000
Administrative salaries	222,000
Office rental, phone, and so on	84,000
Total	$401,000

For each performance of each ballet, the following costs are also incurred:

Utah symphony	$3,800
Auditorium rental	700
Dancers' payroll	4,000
Total	$8,500

The auditorium in which the ballet is presented has 1,854 seats, which are classified as A, B, and C. The best viewing ranges from A seats to C seats. Information concerning the different types of seat follows:

	A Seats	B Seats	C Seats
Quantity	114	756	984
Price	$35	$25	$15
Percentage sold for each performance*			
Nutcracker	100	100	100
All others	100	80	75

*Based on past experience, the same percentages are expected for the coming season.

REQUIRED:
1. Compute the expected revenues from the performances that have been tentatively scheduled. Prepare a variable-costing income statement for each ballet.
2. Calculate the number of performances of each ballet required to produce the revenues needed to cover each ballet's direct fixed expenses.
3. Calculate the number of performances of each ballet required for the company as a whole to break even. If you were the president and general manager, how would you alter the tentative schedule of performances?
4. Suppose that it is possible to offer a matinee of the popular *Nutcracker*. Seats would sell for $5 less than in the evening, and the rental of the auditorium would be $200 less. The president and general manager believes that five matinee performances are feasible and that 80 percent of each type of seat can be sold. What effect will the matinee have on the company's profitability? on the overall break-even point?

5. Suppose that no additional evening performances can be offered beyond those tentatively scheduled. Assume that the company will offer five matinee performances of *The Nutcracker*. Also, the company expects to receive $60,000 in government grants and contributions from supporters of the fine arts. Will the company break even? If not, what actions would you take to bring revenues in line with costs? Assume that no additional performances of *The Nutcracker* are feasible.

CHAPTER

Tactical Decision Making: Relevant Costing, the Activity Resource Usage Model, and Pricing

SCENARIO[1]

Tidwell Products, Inc. manufactures potentiometers, devices that adjust electrical resistance. Potentiometers are used in switches and knobs, for example, to control the volume on a radio or to raise or lower the lights using a dimmer switch. Currently, all parts necessary for the assembly of the products are produced internally. The firm, in operation for five years, has a single plant located in Wichita, Kansas. The facilities for the manufacture of potentiometers are leased, with five years remaining on the lease. All equipment is owned by the company. Because of increases in demand, production has been expanded significantly over the five years of operation, straining the capacity of the leased facilities. Currently, the company needs more warehousing and office space, as well

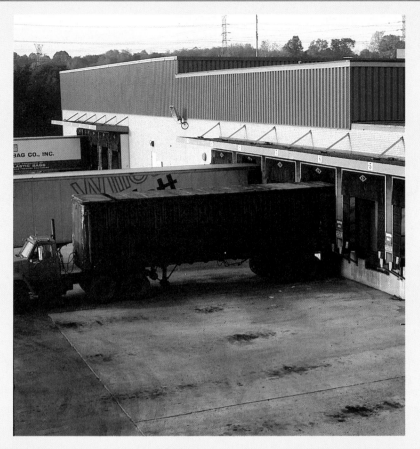

as more space for the production of plastic moldings. The current output of these moldings, used to make potentiometers, needs to be expanded to accommodate the increased demand for the main product.

Leo Tidwell, owner and president of Tidwell Products, has asked his vice-president of marketing, John Tidwell, and his vice-president of finance, Linda Thayn, to meet and discuss the problem of limited capacity. This is the second meeting the three have had concerning the problem. In the first meeting, Leo rejected Linda's proposal to build the company's own plant. He believed it was too risky to invest the capital necessary to build a plant at this stage of the company's development. The combination of leasing a larger facility and subleasing the current plant was also considered but was

rejected; subleasing would be difficult, if not impossible. At the end of the first meeting, Leo asked John to explore the possibility of leasing another facility comparable to the current one. He also assigned Linda the task of identifying other possible solutions. As the second meeting began, Leo asked John to give a report on the leasing alternative.

"After some careful research," John responded, "I'm afraid that the idea of leasing an additional plant is not a very good one. Although we have some space problems, our current level of production doesn't justify another plant. In fact, I expect it will be at least five years before we need to be concerned about expanding into another facility like the one we have now. My market studies reveal a modest growth in sales over the next five years. All this growth can be absorbed by our

current production capacity. The large increases in demand that we experienced the past five years are not likely to be repeated. Leasing another plant would be an overkill solution."

"Even modest growth will aggravate our current space problems," Leo observed. "As you both know, we are already operating three production shifts. But, John, you are right—except for plastic moldings, we could expand production, particularly during the graveyard shift. Linda, I hope that you have been successful in identifying some other possible solutions. Some fairly quick action is needed."

"Fortunately," Linda replied, "I believe that I have two feasible alternatives. One is to rent an additional building to be used for warehousing. By transferring our warehousing needs to the new building, we will free up internal space for offices and for expanding the production of plastic moldings. I have located a building within two miles of our plant that we could use. It has the capacity to handle our current needs and the modest growth that John mentioned. The second alternative may be even more attractive. We currently produce all the parts that we use to manufacture potentiometers, including shafts and bushings. In the last several months, the market has been flooded with these two parts. Prices have tumbled as a result. It might be better to buy shafts and bushings instead of making them. If we stop internal production of shafts and bushings, this would free up the space we need. Well, Leo, what do you think? Are these alternatives feasible? Or should I continue my search for additional solutions?"

"I like both alternatives," responded Leo. "In fact, they are exactly the types of solutions we are looking for. All we have to do now is choose the one best for our company. A key factor that must be examined is the cost of each alternative. Linda, you're the financial chief—prepare a report that details the costs that impact this decision."

1. This scenario is based on the experiences of a real company. The names have been changed to preserve confidentiality.

Questions to Think About

1. Describe the decision to be made by Tidwell; is it a strategic or tactical decision?

2. What costs do you think Leo is referring to in the last paragraph of the scenario? Give examples.

3. Assume Tidwell Products accepts Linda's first alternative. Are there any noncost factors that should be considered? What about her second alternative?

One of the major roles of the management information system is supplying cost and revenue data that serve as the basis for user actions. Although a variety of user actions are possible, one of the more important actions that can be taken by users is tactical decision making. How cost and revenue data can be used to make tactical decisions is the focus of this chapter.

TACTICAL DECISION MAKING

Objective 1
Describe and explain the tactical decision-making model.

tactical decision making

strategic decision making

Tactical decision making consists of choosing among alternatives with an immediate or limited end in view. Accepting a special order for less than the normal selling price to utilize idle capacity and increase this year's profits is an example. Thus, some tactical decisions tend to be *short-run* in nature; however, it should be emphasized that short-run decisions often have long-run consequences. Consider a second example. Suppose that a company is considering producing a component instead of buying it from suppliers. The immediate objective may be to lower the cost of making the main product. Yet this tactical decision may be a small part of the overall strategy of establishing a cost leadership position for the firm. Thus, tactical decisions are often *small-scale actions* that serve a larger purpose.

The overall objective of strategic decision making is to select among alternative strategies so that a long-term competitive advantage is established. Tactical decision making should support this overall objective, even if the immediate objective is short-run (accepting a one-time order to increase profits) or small-scale (making instead of buying a component). Thus, *sound* tactical decision making means that the decisions made achieve not only the limited objective but also serve a larger purpose. In fact, no tactical decision should be made that does not serve the overall strategic goals of an organization. A good example of a company that has made tactical decisions that are in accordance with its strategic goals is Hyatt Hotels Corporation.[2] In the early 1990s, steep costs jeopardized a number of Hyatt's management contracts. It was necessary to reduce the cost structure fast. However, Hyatt attacked only the costs that guests did not particularly care about (for example, turndown service, in which the bedcovers are turned down at night and a mint is left on the pillow). Services that were important to business travelers, whom Hyatt courted, were expanded (for example, in-room fax machines).

2. Richard A. Melcher, "Why Hyatt Is Toning Down the Glitz," *Business Week* (27 February 1995): 92, 94.

Model for Making Tactical Decisions

How does a company go about making good tactical decisions? We can describe a general approach to making tactical decisions. The six[3] steps describing the recommended decision-making process are as follows:

1. Recognize and define the problem.
2. Identify alternatives as possible solutions to the problem; eliminate alternatives that are clearly not feasible.
3. Identify the costs and benefits associated with each feasible alternative. Classify costs and benefits as relevant or irrelevant and eliminate irrelevant ones from consideration.
4. Total the relevant costs and benefits for each alternative.
5. Assess qualitative factors.
6. Select the alternative with the greatest overall benefit.

decision model

These six steps define a simple decision model. A decision model is a set of procedures that, if followed, will lead to a decision. Exhibit 16-1 depicts the sequence of steps to be followed.

Step 1: Define the Problem The first step is to recognize and define a specific problem. For example, the members of Tidwell's management team all recognized the need for additional space for warehousing, offices, and the production of plastic moldings. The amount of space needed, the reasons for the need, and how the additional space would

---

3. The decision-making model described here has six steps. There is nothing special about this particular listing. You may find it more useful to break down the steps into eight or ten segments. Alternatively, you may find it useful to aggregate them into a shorter list. For example, you could use a three-step model: (1) identify the decision; (2) identify alternatives and their associated relevant costs; and (3) make the decision. The key point is to find a comfortable way for you to remember the important steps in the decision-making model.

16-1

Exhibit
Tactical Decision-making
Model for Tidwell
Products' Space Problem

Step 1	Define the problem.	Increase capacity for warehousing and production
Step 2	Identify the alternatives.	1. Build new facility 2. Lease larger facility; sublease current facility 3. Lease additional facility 4. Lease warehouse space 5. Buy shafts and bushings; free up needed space

Step 3	Identify the costs and benefits associated with each feasible alternative.	Alternative 4:
		  Variable production costs $345,000
		  Warehouse lease 135,000
		Alternative 5:
		  Purchase price $460,000

Step 4	Total the relevant costs and benefits for each feasible alternative.	Alternative 4 $480,000 Alternative 5 460,000 Differential cost $ 20,000
Step 5	Assess the qualitative factors.	1. Quality of external supplier 2. Reliability of external supplier 3. Price stability 4. Labor relations and community image
Step 6	Make the decision.	Continue to produce shafts and bushings internally; lease warehouse

be used are all important dimensions of the problem. However, the central question is *how* to acquire the additional space.

Step 2: Identify the Alternatives Step 2 is to list and consider possible solutions. Tidwell Products identified the following possible solutions:

1. Build its own facility with sufficient capacity to handle current and immediately foreseeable needs.
2. Lease a larger facility and sublease its current facility.
3. Lease an additional, similar facility.
4. Lease an additional building that would be used for warehousing only, thereby freeing up space for expanded production.
5. Buy shafts and bushings externally and use the space made available (previously used for producing these parts) to solve the space problem.

As part of this step, Tidwell must eliminate alternatives that are not feasible. The first alternative was eliminated because it carried too much risk for the company. The second alternative was rejected because subleasing was not a viable option. The third was eliminated because it went too far in solving the space problem, and, presumably, was too expensive. The fourth and fifth alternatives were feasible; they were within the cost and risk constraints and solved the space needs of the company. Notice that Leo linked the tactical decision (find more space) to the company's overall growth strategy by rejecting alternatives that involved too much risk at this stage of the company's development.

Step 3: Identify the Costs and Benefits Associated with Each Feasible Alternative In step 3, the costs and benefits associated with each feasible alternative are identified. At this point, clearly irrelevant costs can be eliminated from consideration.[4] The management accountant is responsible for gathering necessary data.

Assume that Tidwell Products determines that the costs of making the shafts and bushings include the following:

Direct materials	$130,000
Direct labor	150,000
Variable overhead	65,000
Total variable production cost	$345,000

In addition, a warehouse must be leased to solve the space problem if Tidwell continues to manufacture the shafts and bushings internally. An appropriate warehouse has been located for $135,000 per year. The second alternative is to purchase the shafts and bushings externally and use the freed-up production space. An outside supplier has offered to supply sufficient product for $460,000 per year.

It should be mentioned that when the cash flow patterns become complicated for competing alternatives, it becomes difficult to produce a stream of equal cash flows for each alternative. In such a case, more sophisticated procedures can and should be used for the analysis. These procedures are discussed in the next chapter, which deals with the long-run investment decisions referred to as *capital expenditure decisions*.

Step 4: Total the Relevant Costs and Benefits for Each Feasible Alternative We now see that alternative 4, continue producing internally and lease more space, costs

---

4. It is fine to include irrelevant costs and benefits in the analysis as long as they are included for *all* alternatives. The reason we usually do not is that focusing only on the relevant costs and benefits reduces the amount of data to be collected.

$480,000 while alternative 5, purchase outside and use internal space, costs $460,000. The comparison follows:

Alternative 4		Alternative 5	
Variable cost of production	$345,000	Purchase price	$460,000
Warehouse lease	135,000		
Total	$480,000		

The differential cost is $20,000 in favor of alternative 5.

Step 5: Assess the Qualitative Factors While the costs and revenues associated with the alternatives are important, they do not tell the whole story. Qualitative factors can significantly affect the manager's decision. Qualitative factors are simply those factors that are hard to put a number on. For example, in the make-or-buy decision facing Tidwell Products, Leo Tidwell likely would be concerned with such qualitative considerations as the quality of the shafts and bushings purchased externally, the reliability of supply sources, the expected stability of prices over the next several years, labor relations, community image, and so on. To illustrate the possible impact of qualitative factors on the make-or-buy decision, consider the first two factors, quality and reliability of supply.

If the quality of shafts and bushings is significantly less if purchased externally than what is available internally, the quantitative advantage from purchasing may be more fictitious than real. Settling for lower-quality materials may reduce the quality of the potentiometers, thus harming sales. Because of this, Tidwell Products may choose to continue to produce the parts internally.

Similarly, if supply sources are not reliable, production schedules could be interrupted, and customer orders could arrive late. These factors can increase labor costs and overhead and hurt sales. Again, depending on the perceived trade-offs, Tidwell Products may decide that producing the parts internally is better than purchasing them, even if relevant cost analysis gives the initial advantage to purchasing.

How should qualitative factors be handled in the decision-making process? First, they must be identified. Secondly, the decision maker should try to quantify them. Often, qualitative factors are simply more difficult to quantify—not impossible. For example, possible unreliability of the outside supplier might be quantified as the probable number of days late multiplied by the labor cost of downtime in Tidwell's plant. Finally, truly qualitative factors, such as the impact of late orders on customer relations, must be taken into consideration in the final step of the decision-making model—the selection of the alternative with the greatest overall benefit.

Step 6: Make the Decision Once all relevant costs and benefits for each alternative have been assessed, and the qualitative factors weighed, a decision can be made. What did Leo decide for Tidwell Products? Given the relatively small difference in costs of the two alternatives, and the weight Tidwell Products assigns to ensuring quality and full employment, the decision was made to make the shafts and bushings internally and lease the warehouse.

Relevant Costs Defined

relevant costs

The tactical decision-making approach just described emphasized the importance of identifying and using relevant costs. But how do we identify and define the costs that affect the decision? Relevant costs are future costs that differ across alternatives. All decisions relate to the future; accordingly, only future costs can be relevant to decisions. However, to be relevant, a cost must not only be a future cost, but must also differ from one alternative to another. If a future cost is the same for more than one alternative, it has no effect on the decision. Such a cost is an *irrelevant* cost. The ability to identify relevant and irrelevant costs is an important decision-making skill.

Relevant Costs Illustrated To illustrate the concept of relevant costs, consider Tidwell's make-or-buy alternatives. We saw that the cost of direct labor used to produce shafts and bushings is $150,000 per year (based on normal volume). Should this cost be a factor in the decision? Is the direct labor cost a future cost that differs across the two alternatives? It is certainly a future cost. To produce the shafts and bushings for another year requires the services of direct laborers, who must be paid. But does it differ across the two alternatives? If shafts and bushings are purchased from an external supplier, no internal production is needed. The services of the direct laborers can be eliminated, reducing the direct labor cost for shafts and bushings under this alternative to zero. Thus, the cost of direct labor differs across alternatives ($150,000 for the make alternative and $0 for the buy alternative). It is, therefore, a relevant cost.

Implicit in this analysis is the use of a past cost to estimate a future cost. The most recent cost of direct labor for normal activity was $150,000. This past cost was used as the estimate of next year's cost. Although past costs are never relevant, they are often used to predict what future costs will be.

Illustration of an Irrelevant Past Cost Tidwell Products uses machinery to manufacture shafts and bushings. This machinery was purchased five years ago and is being depreciated at an annual rate of $125,000. Is this $125,000 a relevant cost? In other words, is depreciation a future cost that differs across the two alternatives?

sunk cost

Depreciation represents an allocation of a cost already incurred. It is a sunk cost, a cost that cannot be affected by any future action. Although we allocate this sunk cost to future periods and call that allocation *depreciation*, none of the original cost is avoidable. Sunk costs are past costs. They are always the same across alternatives and are, therefore, always irrelevant.

In choosing between the two alternatives, the original cost of the machinery used to produce shafts and bushings and its associated depreciation are not factors. However, it should be noted that salvage value of the machinery (what Tidwell could receive for selling the machinery now) would be relevant and would be included as a benefit of purchasing from outside suppliers. To simplify our example, we are assuming that the salvage value of the machinery is zero.

Illustration of an Irrelevant Future Cost Assume that the cost to lease the entire factory, $340,000, is allocated to different production departments, including the department that produces shafts and bushings, which receives $12,000 of the cost. Is this $12,000 cost relevant to the make-or-buy decision facing Tidwell?

The lease payment is a future cost since it must be paid during each of the next five years. But does the cost differ across the make-and-buy alternatives? Whatever option Tidwell chooses, the factory lease payment must be made—it is the same across both alternatives. The amount of the payment allocated to the remaining departments may change if production of shafts and bushings is stopped, but the level of the total payment is unaffected by the decision. It is therefore an irrelevant cost.

The example illustrates the importance of identifying allocations of common fixed costs. Allocations of common fixed costs can be safely classified as irrelevant since any choice usually does not affect the level of cost. The only effect may be a reallocation of those common fixed costs to fewer cost objects or segments.

We can now look at all three cost examples for the production of shafts and bushings to see which are relevant in deciding whether or not to continue production. Of the three, only direct labor cost is relevant since it is the only one that occurs if production continues but stops if production stops.

	Cost to Make	− Cost Not to Make	= Differential Cost
Direct labor	$150,000	—	$150,000
Depreciation	125,000	$125,000	—
Allocated lease	12,000	12,000	—
Total	$287,000	$137,000	$150,000

The same concepts apply to benefits. One alternative may produce an amount of future benefits different from another alternative (for example, differences in future revenues). If future benefits differ across alternatives, then they are relevant and should be included in the analysis.

Ethics in Tactical Decision Making

In tactical decision making, ethical concerns revolve around the way in which decisions are implemented, and the possible sacrifice of long-run objectives for short-run gain. Relevant costs are used in making tactical decisions—decisions that have an immediate view or limited objective in mind. However, decision makers should always maintain an ethical framework. Reaching objectives is important but how you get there is perhaps more important. Unfortunately, many managers have the opposite view. Part of the reason for the problem is the extreme pressure to perform that many managers feel. Often the individual who is not a top performer may be laid off or demoted. Under such conditions, the temptation is often great to engage in questionable behavior today and let the future take care of itself.

For example, laying off employees to increase profits in the short run could loosely qualify as a tactical decision. However, if the only benefit is an increase in short-run profits and there is no evidence that the decision supports the longer-term strategic objectives of the firm, then the decision can be questioned. In fact, the workload may not decrease at all but the number of people available to carry out the work has decreased. Pressure then may be exerted by managers on the remaining employees to work unreasonable amounts of overtime. Is this right?

There should be a consistent message throughout the company on its mission and goals. For example, if marketing enthusiastically touts the product's high quality and reliability, while engineering and production are busily reducing the quality of the materials and reliability of the design, problems are sure to surface. Customers will see this inconsistency as an ethical lapse.

There can be endless debates about what is right and what is wrong. As was pointed out in Chapter 1, ethical standards have been developed to provide guidance for individuals. Additionally, many companies are hiring full-time ethics officers. Often these officers set up hotlines so that employees can call and register complaints or ask about the propriety of certain actions. However, some ethical problems can be avoided simply by using common sense and not focusing solely on the short term at the expense of the long term. Consider two examples of cost cutting at Ford Motor Company. Recently, Ford decided to delete the rubber molding on the side of the Sable, saving about $100 per car. Years earlier, Ford saved approximately $7 per car by installing thin-walled gas tanks on the Pinto. Which decision do you think has ethical ramifications?

RELEVANCY, COST BEHAVIOR, AND THE ACTIVITY RESOURCE USAGE MODEL

Objective 2

Explain how the activity resource usage model is used in assessing relevancy.

Tidwell Products' space problem was a very simple example of tactical decision making. Most tactical decisions require more complicated analysis—in particular, they require more extensive consideration of cost behavior. Earlier work on relevant costing emphasized the importance of variable versus fixed costs. Usually, variable costs were relevant and fixed costs were not. For example, the variable costs of production were relevant to the Tidwell Products make-or-buy decision. The depreciation expense and factory lease were not relevant. However, activity-based costing allows us to go further as we consider variable costs with respect to both unit-based and nonunit-based cost drivers.

The key point is that changes in supply and demand for activity resources must be considered when assessing relevance. If changes in demand and supply for resources across alternatives brings about changes in resource spending, then the changes in resource spending are the relevant costs that should be used in assessing the relative desirability of the two alternatives.

The activity resource usage model has three resource categories: (1) resources acquired as used and needed, (2) resources acquired in advance of usage (single period or short term), and (3) resources acquired in advance (multiperiod service capability). Each of these categories can be used to help identify relevant costs and, thus, facilitate relevant cost analysis.

Resources Acquired as Used and Needed

Some resources can be easily purchased in the amount needed and at the time of use. For example, electricity used to run stoves that boil fruit in the production of jelly is a resource acquired as used and needed. Thus, for this resource category, *if the demand for an activity changes across alternatives*, then resource spending will change and the cost of the activity is relevant to the decision. This type of resource spending is typically referred to as a variable cost. The key point is that the amount of resource demanded by the firm equals the amount of resource supplied.

Now suppose that the jelly producer is asked by a customer to produce a special order of jelly for promotional purposes. The jelly producer must consider the following two alternatives: (1) accept a special, one-time order, and (2) reject the special order. If accepting the order increases the demand for kilowatt-hours (electricity's cost driver), then the cost of electricity will differ across alternatives. Thus, electricity is relevant to the decision.

Resources Acquired in Advance (Short Term)

Resources acquired in advance of usage through implicit contracting are usually acquired in lumpy amounts. (Graphically, we usually think of this cost as step-variable or step-fixed.) This category often represents resource spending associated with an organization's salaried and hourly employees. The implicit understanding is that the organization will maintain employment levels even though there may be temporary downturns in the quantity of an activity used. This means that an activity may have unused capacity available. Thus, an increase in demand for an activity across alternatives may not mean that the activity cost will increase (because all the increased demand is absorbed by the unused activity capacity). For example, assume a company has five manufacturing engineers that supply a capacity of 10,000 engineering hours (2,000 hours each). The cost of this activity capacity is $250,000 or $25 per hour. Suppose that this year the company only expects to use 9,000 engineering hours for its normal business. This means that the engineering activity has 1,000 hours of unused capacity. In deciding to reject or accept a special order that requires 500 engineering hours, the cost of engineering would be irrelevant. The order can be filled using unused engineering capacity and the resource spending is the same for each alternative ($250,000 will be spent whether the order is accepted or not).

However, *if a change in demand across activities produces a change in resource supply*, then the activity cost will change, and, thus be relevant to the decision. A change in resource supply means a change in resource spending, and, consequently, a change in activity cost. A change in resource spending can occur in one of two ways: (1) the demand for the resource exceeds the supply (increasing resource spending), and (2) the demand for the resource drops permanently and supply exceeds demand enough so that activity capacity can be reduced (decreases resource spending).

Many retail stores are aware of the need to consider the cost of the various services provided, and to price them accordingly. For example, at Mathis Brothers, one of the nation's largest furniture stores, delivery service is costed and priced separately from the furniture itself.

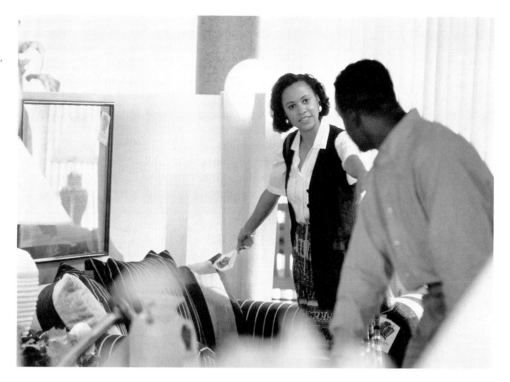

To illustrate the first change, consider once again the engineering activity and the special-order decision. Suppose that the special order requires 1,500 engineering hours. This exceeds the resource supply. To meet the demand, the organization would need to hire a sixth engineer or perhaps use a consulting engineer. Either way, resource spending increases if the order is accepted; thus, the cost of engineering is now a relevant cost.

To illustrate the second type of change, suppose that the company's manager is considering purchasing a component used for production instead of making it. Assume the same facts about engineering capacity: 10,000 hours available and 9,000 used. If the component is purchased, then the demand for engineering hours will drop from 9,000 to 7,000. This is a permanent reduction because engineering support will no longer be needed for manufacturing the component. Unused capacity is now 3,000 hours, 2,000 permanent and 1,000 temporary. Furthermore, since engineering capacity is acquired in chunks of 2,000, this means that the company can reduce activity capacity and resource spending by laying off one engineer or reassigning the engineer to another plant where the services are in demand. Either way, the resource supply is reduced to 8,000 hours. If an engineer's salary is $50,000, then engineering cost would differ by $50,000 across the make-or-buy alternatives. This cost is then relevant to the decision. However, if the demand for the engineering activity drops by less than 2,000 hours, the increase in unused capacity is not enough to reduce resource supply and resource spending; in this case, the cost of the engineering activity would not be relevant.

Resources Acquired in Advance (Multiperiod Service Capacity)

Often resources are acquired in advance for multiple periods, before the resource demands are known. Leasing or buying a building are examples. Buying multiperiod activity capacity is often done by paying cash up front. In this case, an annual expense may be recognized but no additional resource spending is needed. Up-front resource spending is a sunk cost and, thus, never relevant. Periodic resource spending, such as leasing, is essentially independent of resource usage. Even if a permanent reduction of activity usage is experienced, it is difficult to reduce resource spending because of formal contractual commitments.

For example, assume a company leases a plant for $100,000 per year for ten years. The plant is capable of producing 20,000 units of a product—the level expected when the plant was leased. After five years, suppose that the demand for the product drops and the plant needs to produce only 15,000 units each year. The lease payment of $100,000 still must be paid each year even though production activity has decreased. Now suppose that demand increases beyond the 20,000-unit capability. In this case, the company may consider acquiring or leasing an additional plant. Here resource spending could change across alternatives. The decision, however, to acquire long-term activity capacity is not in the realm of tactical decision making. This is not a short-term or small-scale decision. Decisions involving multiperiod capabilities are called *capital investment decisions* and are discussed in Chapter 17.

Thus, for the multiperiod resource category, changes in activity demands across alternatives rarely affect resource spending, and are therefore not usually relevant for tactical decision making. When resource spending does change, it means assessing the prospect of a multiperiod commitment, which is properly treated using capital investment decision models. A good example of the rising importance of resources requiring multiperiod commitments is the technology required for design. Black & Decker Corporation's design budget in North America reached $1 million in 1995 (up from $300,000 in 1990). Companies are trying to turn this expense back into the category of a resource acquired in advance (short term) by outsourcing much of the design work.[5] Exhibit 16-2 summarizes the activity resource usage model's role in assessing relevancy.

ILLUSTRATIVE EXAMPLES OF RELEVANT COST APPLICATIONS

Objective 3

Apply the tactical decision-making concepts in a variety of business situations.

Relevant costing is of value in solving many different types of problems. Traditionally, these applications include decisions to: make or buy a component; keep or drop a segment or product line; accept a special order at less than the usual price; and process a joint product further or sell it at the split-off point. Of course, this is not an exhaustive list. However, many of the same decision-making principles apply to a variety of problems.

Make-or-Buy Decisions

Managers are often faced with the decision of whether to make or buy components used in manufacturing. Indeed, management periodically should evaluate past decisions

5. Bruce Nussbaum, "Is In-House Design on the Way Out?" *Business Week* (25 September 1995): 130.

16-2

Exhibit
Activity Resource Usage Model and Assessing Relevancy

Resource Category	Demand and Supply Relationships	Relevancy
Acquired as needed	Supply = Demand	
	1. Demand changes	1. Relevant
	2. Demand constant	2. Not relevant
Acquired in advance (short term)	Supply − Demand = Unused capacity	
	1. Demand increase < Unused capacity	1. Not relevant
	2. Demand increase > Unused capacity	2. Relevant
	3. Demand decrease (permanent)	
	a. Activity capacity reduced	a. Relevant
	b. Activity capacity unchanged	b. Not relevant
Acquired in advance (multiperiod capacity)	Supply − Demand = Unused capacity	
	1. Demand increase < Unused capacity	1. Not relevant
	2. Demand decrease (permanent)	2. Not relevant
	3. Demand increase > Unused capacity	3. Capital decision

concerning production. Conditions upon which prior decisions were based may have changed and, as a result, a different approach may be required. Periodic evaluations, of course, are not the only source of these make-or-buy decisions. Frequently, as with Tidwell Products, the decision is motivated by an indirectly related, underlying problem.

To illustrate more fully the cost analysis of a make-or-buy problem, assume that Swasey Manufacturing currently produces an electronic component used in one of its printers. In one year, Swasey will switch production to another type of printer and the electronic component will not be used. However, for the coming year, Swasey must produce 10,000 of these parts to support the production requirements for the old printer.

Swasey has been approached by a potential supplier of the component. The supplier will build the electronic component to Swasey's specifications for $4.75 per unit. The offer sounds very attractive since the full manufacturing cost per unit is $8.20. Should Swasey Manufacturing make or buy the component?

The problem and the feasible alternatives are both readily identifiable. Since the horizon for the decision is only one period, there is no need to be concerned about periodically recurring costs. Relevant costing is particularly useful for short-run analysis. We simply need to identify the relevant costs, total them, and make a choice (assuming no overriding qualitative concerns).

First, let's look at the costs associated with the production of these 10,000 parts. The full absorption cost is computed as follows:

	Total Cost	Unit Cost
Rental of equipment	$12,000	$1.20
Equipment depreciation	2,000	0.20
Direct materials	10,000	1.00
Direct labor	20,000	2.00
Variable overhead	8,000	0.80
General fixed overhead	30,000	3.00
Total	$82,000	$8.20

Most of the equipment is rented. However, one specialized piece of machinery had to be custom-made and was purchased. Rental equipment can be returned at any time without penalty; the company is charged only for the time the equipment is held. The specialized machinery will not be fully depreciated at the end of the year; however, the company plans to scrap it since it cannot be sold. The company recently purchased sufficient materials for 5,000 components. There is no alternative use for the materials. Variable overhead is applied to the electronic component at $0.40 per direct labor dollar. General fixed overhead for the plant totals $1 million. General fixed overhead is assigned to products based on the space occupied by each product. The manufacturing facilities for the component under consideration occupy 6,000 of the plant's 200,000 square feet. Thus, $30,000 of the general fixed overhead is allocated to the electronic component (0.03 x $1,000,000).

Of these cost items, depreciation can be eliminated; it is a sunk cost. Since the direct materials already purchased have no alternative use, half of the cost of total direct materials is also a sunk cost. General overhead is not relevant either. The $30,000 is an allocation of a common fixed cost that will continue even if the component is purchased externally.

All other costs are relevant. The cost of renting the equipment is relevant since it will not be needed if the part is bought externally. Similarly, direct labor, the remaining 5,000 units of direct materials, and variable overhead are all relevant; they would not be incurred if the component is bought externally.

Now let's focus on the purchase of the component. Of course, the purchase cost is relevant. If the component is made, this cost would not be incurred. Are there any other costs associated with an outside purchase? A check with the receiving dock elicited the information that the receiving and inspecting crew was at capacity. An additional purchase of this magnitude would require hiring an additional half-time employee for the year at a cost of $8,500. The purchasing department had sufficient excess capacity to handle the purchase of the component, so no additional cost would be incurred there.

A listing of the total relevant costs for each alternative follows:

	Alternatives		Differential Cost to Make
	Make	Buy	
Rental of equipment	$12,000	—	$12,000
Direct materials	5,000	—	5,000
Variable overhead	8,000	—	8,000
Direct labor	20,000	—	20,000
Purchase cost	—	$47,500	(47,500)
Half-time employee	—	8,500	(8,500)
Total relevant cost	$45,000	$56,000	$(11,000)

The analysis shows that making the product is $11,000 cheaper than buying it. The offer of the supplier should be rejected.

The same analysis can be done on a unit-cost basis. Once the relevant costs are identified, relevant unit costs can be compared. For this example, these costs are $4.50 $\left(\frac{\$45,000}{10,000}\right)$ for the make alternative and $5.60 $\left(\frac{\$56,000}{10,000}\right)$ for the buy alternative.

Keep-or-Drop Decisions

Often a manager needs to determine whether or not a segment, such as a product line, should be kept or dropped. Segmented reports prepared on a variable-costing basis provide valuable information for these keep-or-drop decisions. Both the segment's contribution margin and its segment margin are useful in evaluating the performance of segments. However, while segmented reports provide useful information for keep-or-drop decisions, relevant costing describes how the information should be used to arrive at a decision.

To illustrate, consider Norton Materials, Inc., which produces concrete blocks, bricks, and roofing tile. The controller has prepared the following estimated income statement for 1998 (in thousands of dollars):

	Blocks	Bricks	Tile	Total
Sales revenue	$ 500	$ 800	$ 150	$1,450
Less: Variable expenses	(250)	(480)	(140)	(870)
Contribution margin	$ 250	$ 320	$ 10	$ 580
Less direct fixed expenses:				
Salaries	$ (37)	$ (40)	$ (35)	$ (112)
Advertising	(10)	(10)	(10)	(30)
Depreciation	(53)	(40)	(10)	(103)
Total	$(100)	$ (90)	$ (55)	$ (245)
Segment margin	$ 150	$ 230	$ (45)	$ 335
Less: Common fixed expenses				(125)
Net income				$ 210

The projected performance of the roofing tile line shows a negative segment margin. This would represent the third consecutive year of poor performance for that line. The

keep-or-drop decisions

president of Norton Materials, Tom Blackburn, concerned about this poor performance, is trying to decide whether to drop or keep the roofing tile line.

His first reaction is to take steps to increase the sales revenue of roofing tiles. He is considering an aggressive sales promotion coupled with an increase in the selling price. The marketing manager thinks that this approach would be fruitless, however; the market is saturated and the level of competition too keen to hold out any hope for increasing the firm's market share. An increase in the selling price would almost certainly result in a decrease in sales revenue.

Increasing the product line's profitability through cost cutting is not feasible either. Costs were cut the past two years to reduce the loss to its present anticipated level. Any further reductions would lower the quality of the product and adversely affect sales.

With no hope for improving the profit performance of the line beyond its projected level, Tom has decided to drop it. He reasons that the firm will lose a total of $10,000 in contribution margin but save $45,000 by dismissing the line's supervisor and eliminating its advertising budget. (The depreciation cost of $10,000 is not relevant since it represents an allocation of a sunk cost.) Thus, dropping the product line has a $35,000 advantage over keeping it. Before finalizing the decision, Tom decided to notify the marketing manager and the production supervisor. The following memo was sent to both individuals:

MEMO

TO: Karen Golding, Marketing, and Larry Olsen, Production
FROM: Tom Blackburn, President
SUBJECT: Tentative Decision Concerning the Production of Roofing Tiles
DATE: March 14, 1998

Since there is no realistic expectation of improving the profitability of the roofing tile line, I have reluctantly decided to discontinue its production. I realize that this decision will have a negative impact on the community since our workforce will need to be reduced. I am also sympathetic to the disruption this may cause in the personal lives of many employees.

However, we must be prepared to take actions that are in the best interests of the firm. By eliminating the roofing tile line, we can improve the firm's cash position by $35,000 per year. To support this decision, I am including the following analysis (focusing only on the tile segment):

	Keep	*Drop*	*Differential Amount to Keep*
Sales	*$150*	*—*	*$150*
Less: Variable expenses	*(140)*	*—*	*(140)*
Contribution margin	*$ 10*	*—*	*$ 10*
Less: Advertising	*(10)*	*—*	*(10)*
Less: Cost of supervision	*(35)*	*—*	*(35)*
Total relevant benefit (loss)	*$ (35)*	*$0*	*$ (35)*

I have included only future costs and benefits that differ across the two alternatives. Depreciation on the tile equipment is not relevant since it is simply an allocation of a sunk cost. Also, the level of common fixed costs is unchanged regardless of whether we keep or drop the tile line.

At this point, I view the decision as tentative and welcome any response. Perhaps I am overlooking something that would affect the decision. Please respond as soon as possible.

Keep or Drop with Complementary Effects In response to the memo, the marketing manager wrote that dropping the roofing tile line would lower sales of blocks by 10 percent and of bricks by 8 percent. She explained that many customers buy roofing tile at the same time they purchase blocks or bricks. Some will go elsewhere if they cannot buy both products at the same location.

Shortly after receiving this response, Tom Blackburn decided to repeat the analysis, factoring in the effect that dropping the tile line would have on the sales of the other two lines. He decided to use total firm sales and total costs for each alternative. As before, depreciation and common fixed costs were excluded from the analysis on the basis of irrelevancy.

Dropping the product line reduces total sales by $264,000: $50,000 (0.10 × $500,000) for blocks, $64,000 (0.08 × $800,000) for the bricks, and $150,000 for roofing tiles. Similarly, total variable expenses are reduced by $203,400: $25,000 (0.10 × $250,000) for blocks, $38,400 (0.08 × $480,000) for bricks, and $140,000 for tile. Thus, total contribution margin is reduced by $60,600 ($264,000 − $203,400). Since dropping the tile line saves only $45,000 in supervision costs and advertising, the net effect is a disadvantage of $15,600 ($45,000 − $60,600). The following is a summary of the analysis using the new information (in thousands):

	Keep	Drop	Differential Amount to Keep
Sales	$1,450	$1,186.0	$264.0
Less: Variable expenses	(870)	(666.6)	(203.4)
Contribution margin	$ 580	$ 519.4	$ 60.6
Less: Advertising	(30)	(20.0)	(10.0)
Less: Cost of supervision	(112)	(77.0)	(35.0)
Total	$ 438	$ 422.4	$ 15.6

Tom was pleased to find the outcome favoring production of the roofing tile. The unpleasant task of dismissing some of his workforce was no longer necessary. However, just as he was preparing to write a second memo announcing his new decision, he received Larry Olsen's written response to his first memo.

Keep or Drop with Alternative Use of Facilities The production supervisor's response was somewhat different. He agreed that roofing tile should be eliminated but suggested that it be replaced with the production of floor tile. He gave assurances that existing machinery could be converted to produce this new product with little or no cost. He had also contacted the marketing manager about the marketability of floor tile and included this assessment in his response.

The marketing manager saw the market for floor tile as stronger and less competitive than for roofing tile. However, the other two lines would still lose sales at the same rate; producing floor tile would not change that result. The following estimated financial statement for floor tile was also submitted (in thousands of dollars):

Sales	$100
Less: Variable expenses	(40)
Contribution margin	$ 60
Less: Direct fixed expenses	(55)
Segment margin	$ 5

Tom Blackburn was now faced with a third alternative: replacing the roofing tile with floor tile. Should the roofing tile line be kept or should it be dropped and replaced with the floor tile?

From his prior analysis, Tom knows that dropping the roofing tile decreases the firm's contribution margin by $60,600. Producing the floor tile will generate $60,000 more in contribution margin according to the estimate. Dropping the roofing tile line and replacing it with floor tile, then, will cause a $600 net decrease in total contribution margin ($60,600 − $60,000). The same outcome can be developed by directly comparing the relevant benefits and costs of the two alternatives (dollars expressed in thousands).

	Keep	Drop and Replace	Differential Amount to Keep
Sales	$1,450	$1,286.0[a]	$164.0
Variable expenses	(870)	(706.6)[b]	(163.4)
Contribution margin	$ 580	$ 579.4	$ (0.6)

[a]($1,450 − $150 − $50 − $64) + $100
[b]($870 − $140 − $25 − $38.4) + $40

The Norton Materials example again illustrates the tactical decision-making process. First, a problem was identified and defined (the poor performance of the roofing tile product line). Next, possible solutions were listed and those that were not feasible were eliminated. For example, increasing sales or further decreasing costs were both rejected as feasible solutions. Three feasible solutions were examined: (1) keeping the product line, (2) dropping it, and (3) dropping the product line and replacing it with another product. An analysis of the costs and benefits of the feasible alternatives led to the selection of the preferred alternative (keeping the product line).

The example provides some insights beyond the simple application of the decision model. The initial analysis, which focused on two feasible alternatives, led to a tentative decision to drop the product line. Additional information provided by the marketing manager led to a reversal of the first decision. Before that decision could be implemented, the manager was made aware of a third feasible alternative, which required additional analysis.

Often managers do not have all the information necessary to make the best decision. They also may not be able to identify all feasible solutions. Managers benefit from gathering all the information available before finalizing a decision. They should attempt to identify as many feasible solutions as possible. As the example clearly illustrates, limited information can result in poor decisions. If the set of feasible solutions is too narrow, the best solution may never be selected simply because the manager has not thought of it. Managers can benefit from obtaining input from others who are familiar with the problem. By so doing, both the set of information and the set of feasible solutions can be expanded. The result is improved decision making.

Special-Order Decisions

Price discrimination laws require that firms sell identical products at the same price to competing customers in the same market. These restrictions do not apply to competitive bids or to noncompeting customers. Bid prices can vary to customers in the same market, and firms often have the opportunity to consider special orders from potential

special-order decisions

customers in markets not ordinarily served. Special-order decisions focus on whether a specially priced order should be accepted or rejected. These orders often can be attractive, especially when the firm is operating below its maximum productive capacity.

Suppose, for example, that an ice-cream company is operating at 80 percent of its productive capacity. The company has a capacity of 20 million half-gallon units. The company produces only premium ice cream. The total costs associated with producing and selling 16 million units are as follows (in thousands of dollars):

	Total	Unit Cost
Variable costs:		
Dairy ingredients	$11,200	$0.70
Sugar	1,600	0.10
Flavoring	2,400	0.15
Direct labor	4,000	0.25
Packaging	3,200	0.20
Commissions	320	0.02
Distribution	480	0.03
Other	800	0.05
Total variable costs	$24,000	$1.50
Fixed costs:		
Salaries	$ 960	$0.060
Depreciation	320	0.020
Utilities	80	0.005
Taxes	32	0.002
Other	160	0.010
Total fixed costs	$ 1,552	$0.097
Total costs	$25,552	$1.597
Wholesale selling price	$32,000	$2.000

An ice-cream distributor from a geographic region not normally served by the company has offered to buy 2 million units at $1.55 per unit, provided its own label can be attached to the product. The distributor has also agreed to pay the transportation costs. Since the distributor approached the company directly, there is no sales commission. As the manager of the ice-cream company, would you accept this order or reject it?

The offer of $1.55 is well below the normal selling price of $2.00; in fact, it is even below the total unit cost. Even so, accepting the order may be profitable. The company does have idle capacity, and the order will not displace other units being produced to sell at the normal price. Additionally, many of the costs are not relevant; fixed costs will continue regardless of whether the order is accepted or rejected.

If the order is accepted, a benefit of $1.55 per unit will be realized that otherwise wouldn't be. However, all of the variable costs except for distribution ($0.03) and commissions ($0.02) also will be incurred, producing a cost of $1.45 per unit. The net benefit is $0.10 ($1.55 − $1.45) per unit. The relevant cost analysis can be summarized as follows:

	Accept	Reject	Differential Benefit to Accept
Revenues	$3,100,000	—	$3,100,000
Dairy ingredients	(1,400,000)	—	(1,400,000)
Sugar	(200,000)	—	(200,000)
Flavorings	(300,000)	—	(300,000)
Direct labor	(500,000)	—	(500,000)
Packaging	(400,000)	—	(400,000)
Other	(100,000)	—	(100,000)
Total	$ 200,000	$0	$ 200,000

We see that for this company, accepting the special order will increase profits by $200,000 ($0.10 × 2,000,000).

Decisions to Sell or Process Further

joint products

Joint products have common processes and costs of production up to a split-off point. At that point, they become distinguishable. For example, certain minerals such as copper

split-off point

**sell or process
further**

and gold may both be found in a given ore. The ore must be mined, crushed, and treated before the copper and gold are separated. The point of separation is called the split-off point. The costs of mining, crushing, and treatment are common to both products.

Often joint products are sold at the split-off point. Sometimes it is more profitable to process a joint product further, beyond the split-off point, prior to selling it. Determining whether to sell or process further is an important decision that a manager must make.

To illustrate, consider Appletime Corporation. Appletime is a large corporate farm that specializes in growing apples. Each plot produces approximately one ton of apples. The trees in each plot must be sprayed, fertilized, watered, and pruned. When the apples are ripened, workers are hired to pick them. The apples are then transported to a warehouse, where they are washed and sorted. The approximate cost of all these activities (including processing) is $300 per ton per year.

Apples are sorted into three grades (A, B, and C) determined by size and blemishes. Large apples without blemishes (bruises, cuts, wormholes, and so on) are sorted into one bin and classified as grade A. Small apples without blemishes are sorted into a second bin and classified as grade B. All remaining apples are placed in a third bin and classified as grade C. Every ton of apples produces 800 pounds of grade A, 600 pounds of grade B, and 600 pounds of grade C.

Grade A apples are sold to large supermarkets for $0.40 per pound. Grade B apples are packaged in 5-pound bags and sold to supermarkets for $1.30 per bag. (The cost of each bag is $0.05.) Grade C apples are processed further and made into applesauce. The sauce is sold in 16-ounce cans for $0.75 each. The cost of processing is $0.10 per pound of apples. The final output is 500 sixteen-ounce cans. Exhibit 16-3 summarizes the process.

A large supermarket chain recently requested that Appletime supply 16-ounce cans of apple pie filling for which the chain was willing to pay $0.90 per can. Appletime determined that the grade B apples would be suitable for this purpose and estimated that it would cost $0.20 per pound to process the apples into pie filling. The output would be 500 sixteen-ounce cans.

In deciding whether to sell grade B apples at split-off or to process them further and sell them as pie filling, the common costs of spraying, pruning, and so on, are not relevant. The company must pay the $300 per ton for these activities regardless of

Exhibit
Appletime's Joint Process

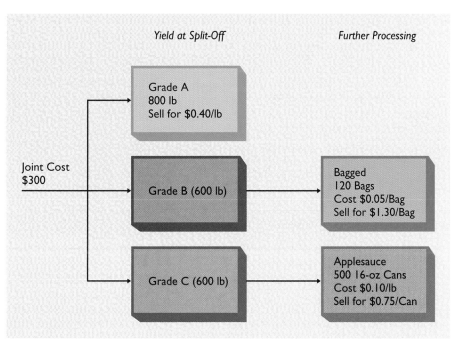

whether it sells at split-off or processes further. However, the revenues earned at split-off are likely to differ from the revenues that would be received if the grade B apples are sold as pie filling. Therefore revenues are a relevant consideration. Similarly, the processing costs occur only if further processing takes place. Hence, processing costs are relevant.

Since there are 600 pounds of grade B apples at split-off, Appletime sells 120 five-pound bags at a net per-unit price of $1.25 ($1.30 − $0.05). Thus, the total net revenues at split-off are $150 ($1.25 × 120). If the apples are processed into pie filling, then the total revenues are $450 ($0.90 × 500). Therefore, the incremental revenues from processing further are $300 ($450 − $150). The incremental costs of processing are $120 ($0.20 × 600 pounds). Since revenues increase by $300 and costs by only $120, the net benefit of processing further is $180. Thus, Appletime should process the grade B apples into pie filling. The analysis is summarized as follows:

	Sell	Process Further	Differential Amount to Process Further
Revenues	$150	$450	$300
Processing cost	—	(120)	(120)
Total	$150	$330	$180

PRODUCT MIX DECISIONS

Objective 4

Choose the optimal product mix when faced with one constrained resource.

In the preceding example, of every 2,000 pounds of apples harvested, 800 were grade A, 600 were grade B, and 600 were grade C. Although the relative amounts of each type of apple can be influenced to some extent by the procedures followed in spraying, watering, fertilizing, and so on, the mix of apples is largely beyond Appletime's control. However, many organizations have total discretion in choosing their product mix. Moreover, decisions about product mix can have a significant impact on an organization's profitability.

Each mix represents an alternative that carries with it an associated profit level. A manager should choose the alternative that maximizes total profits. Since fixed costs do not vary with activity level, the total fixed costs of a firm would be the same for all possible mixes and, therefore, are not relevant to the decision. Thus, a manager needs to choose the alternative that maximizes total contribution margin.

Assume, for example, that Jorgenson Company produces two types of gears: X and Y, with unit contribution margins of $25 and $10, respectively. If the firm possesses unlimited resources and the demand for each product is unlimited, then the product mix decision is simple—produce an infinite number of each product. Unfortunately, every firm faces limited resources and limited demand for each product. These limitations are called constraints. A manager must choose the optimal mix given the constraints found within the firm.

constraints

Assuming that Jorgenson can sell all that is produced, some may argue that only gear X should be produced and sold—it has the larger contribution margin. However, this solution is not necessarily the best. The selection of the optimal mix can be significantly affected by the relationships of the constrained resources to the individual products. These relationships affect the quantity of each product that can be produced and, consequently, the total contribution margin that can be earned. This point is most vividly illustrated when faced with one resource constraint.

One Constrained Resource

Assume that each gear must be notched by a special machine. The firm owns eight machines that together provide 40,000 hours of machine time per year. Gear X requires 2 hours of machine time, and gear Y requires 0.5 hour of machine time. Assuming no other constraints, what is the optimal mix of gears? Since each unit of gear X requires 2 hours of machine time, 20,000 units can be produced per year ($\frac{40,000}{2}$). At $25 per unit, Jorgenson can earn a total contribution margin of $500,000. On the other hand, gear Y requires only 0.5 hour of machine time per unit; therefore, 80,000 ($\frac{40,000}{0.5}$) gears can be produced. At $10 per unit, the total contribution margin is $800,000. Producing only gear Y yields a higher profit level than producing only gear X—even though the unit contribution margin for X is 2.5 times larger than that for Y.

The contribution margin per unit of each product is not the critical concern. The contribution margin per unit of scarce resource is the deciding factor. The product yielding the highest contribution margin per machine hour should be selected. Gear X earns $12.50 per machine hour ($\frac{\$25}{2}$), but gear Y earns $20 per machine hour ($\frac{\$10}{0.5}$). Thus, the optimal mix is 80,000 units of gear Y and none of gear X.

Multiple Constrained Resources

The presence of only one constrained resource is unrealistic. All organizations face multiple constraints: limitations of raw materials, limitations of labor inputs, limited demand for each product, and so on. The solution of the product mix problem in the presence of multiple constraints is considerably more complicated and requires the use of a specialized mathematical technique known as *linear programming*, which is defined and illustrated in the Appendix to this chapter.

PRICING

Objective 5

Explain the impact of cost on pricing decisions.

One of the more difficult decisions faced by a company is pricing. This section examines the impact of cost on price and the role of the accountant in gathering the needed information.

Cost-based Pricing

Demand is one side of the pricing equation, supply is the other side. Since revenue must cover cost for the firm to make a profit, many companies start with cost to determine price. That is, they calculate product cost and add the desired profit. The mechanics of this approach are straightforward. Usually, there is some cost base and a markup. The markup is a percentage applied to the base cost; it includes desired profit and any costs not included in the base cost. Companies that bid for jobs routinely base bid price on cost.

markup

Consider Elvin Company, owned and operated by Clare Elvin, which assembles and installs computers to customer specifications. Costs of the components and other direct materials are easy to trace. Direct labor cost is similarly easy to trace to each job. Assemblers receive, on average, $12 per hour and the company pays benefits of approximately 25 percent of that wage. Last year, Elvin Company worked on 650 jobs, which averaged 5 hours each. Overhead, consisting of utilities, small tools, building space, and so on, amounted to $80,000. Elvin Company's income statement for last year is as follows:

Revenues		$856,500
Cost of goods sold:		
Direct materials	$585,000	
Direct labor	48,750	
Overhead	80,000	713,750
Gross profit		$142,750
Selling & administrative expenses		25,000
Operating income		$117,750

Suppose that Clare wants to earn about the same amount of profit on each job as was earned last year. She could calculate a markup on cost of goods sold by summing selling and administrative expenses and operating income, then dividing by cost of goods sold:

$$\text{Markup on COGS} = \frac{\text{Selling and administrative expenses} + \text{Operating income}}{\text{COGS}}$$

$$= \frac{\$25,000 + \$117,750}{\$713,750}$$

$$= .20$$

The markup on cost of goods sold is 20 percent. Notice that the 20 percent markup covers both profit and selling and administrative costs. The markup is not pure profit.

The markup can be calculated using a variety of bases. Clearly for Elvin Company, the cost of purchased materials is the largest component. Last year, the markup on materials amounted to 46.4 percent of all other costs and profit:

$$\text{Markup on materials} = \frac{\begin{array}{c}\text{Direct labor} + \text{Overhead} + \\ \text{Selling and administrative expenses} + \text{Operating income}\end{array}}{\text{Materials}}$$

$$= \frac{\$48,750 + 80,000 + 25,000 + 117,750}{\$585,000}$$

$$= .464$$

A markup percentage of 46.4 percent of direct materials cost would also yield the same amount of profit, assuming the level of operations and other expenses remained stable. The choice of base and markup percentage generally rests on convenience. If Clare finds that the labor varies in rough proportion to the cost of materials (for example, more expensive components take more time to set up) and that the cost of materials is easier to track than the cost of goods sold, then materials might be the better base.

To see how the markup can be used in bidding, suppose that Clare has the opportunity to bid on a job for a local insurance company. The job requires Elvin Company to assemble 100 computers according to certain specifications. She estimates the following costs:

Direct materials (computer components, software, cables)	$100,000
Direct labor (100 × 6 hours × $15)	9,000
Overhead (@ 60 percent of direct labor cost)	5,400
Estimated cost of goods sold	$114,400
Plus 20 percent markup on COGS	22,880
Bid price	$137,280

Thus, Elvin Company's initial bid price is $137,280. Note that this is the first pass at a bid. Clare can adjust the bid based on her knowledge of competition for the job and other factors. The markup is a guideline, not an absolute rule.

If Elvin Company bids every job at cost plus 20 percent, is it guaranteed a profit? No, not at all. If very few jobs are won, the entire markup will go toward selling and administrative expenses, the costs not explicitly included in the bidding calculations.

Markup pricing is often used by retail stores, and their typical markup is 100 percent of cost. Thus, if a sweater is purchased by Graham Department Store for $24, the retail price marked is $48 [$24 + (1.00)($24)]. Of course, the 100 percent markup is not pure profit, it goes toward the salaries of the clerks, payment for space and equipment (cash registers and so on), utilities, advertising, and so on. A major advantage of markup pricing is that standard markups are easy to apply. Consider the difficulty of setting a price for every piece of merchandise in a hardware or department store. It is much simpler to apply a uniform markup to cost and then adjust prices as needed if less is demanded than anticipated.

Target Costing and Pricing

target costing

We just examined the way in which companies use cost to determine price. Now let's work backward and see how price can determine cost. Target costing is a method of determining the cost of a product or service based on the price (target price) that customers are willing to pay. This is also referred to as *price-driven costing.*

Most American companies, and nearly all European firms, set the price of a new product as the sum of the costs and the desired profit. The rationale is that the company must earn sufficient revenues to cover all costs and yield a profit. Peter Drucker writes, "This is true but irrelevant: Customers do not see it as their job to ensure manufacturers a profit. The only sound way to price is to start out with what the market is willing to pay."[6]

Target costing is a method of working backward from price to find cost. The marketing department determines what characteristics and price for a product are most acceptable to consumers, then it is the job of the company's engineers to design and develop the product such that cost and profit can be covered by that price. Japanese firms have been doing this for years; American companies are beginning to use target costing. For example, Borland International, Inc. used target pricing in developing its 1993 version of Quattro Pro for Windows spreadsheet software. Priced at $49 (compared with $495 for Lotus and Microsoft versions), it was designed to appeal to new spreadsheet users. "When we were developing the product, we anticipated the pricing and the people it would attract. We thought of features for that audience."[7] The features referred to included clear instructions, preformatted spreadsheets for 50 common tasks, and interactive on-screen tutorials. Soothing first-time users wasn't the only reason for Quattro Pro's inclusion of built-in help. At $49, the company could not afford numerous calls for technical advice.

Let's return to the Elvin Company example. Suppose that Clare finds that the insurance company will not consider any bid over $100,000. Her cost-based bid was $137,280. Is she out of the running? No, not if she can tailor her bid to the customer's desired price. Recall that the original bid called for $100,000 of direct materials and $9,000 of direct labor. Clearly, adjusting the materials will yield the greatest savings. Working with the customer specifications, Clare must determine whether or not a less expensive set of components will achieve the insurance company objectives. Suppose that the insurance company has specified sufficient hard-disk space on each drive to accommodate particular software, and that the minimum required is 800 megabytes. Clare's original bid specified 3 GB hard drives. If she reduces the hard-disk space to 1.5 GBs and uses a marginally slower drive, she could save $25,000. Substituting a slightly more expensive monitor (a $20 increase) which does not require the installation of screen-saver software would result in saving $30 per computer on software and 15 minutes of direct labor time (at $15 per hour) to install it. The net reduction is $13.75 [($30 + $3.75) − $20] for each of the 100 computers. So far, Clare has developed the following costs:

Direct materials ($100,000 − $25,000)	$75,000
Direct labor (100 × 5.75 hours × $15)	8,625
Total prime cost	$83,625

6. Peter Drucker, "The Five Deadly Business Sins," *The Wall Street Journal* (21 October 1993): A22.

7. Quotation by Joe Ammirato, group manager of the spreadsheet business unit at Borland, as reported by Lawrence M. Fisher, "Using 'Usability' to Sell Spreadsheets to the Masses," *New York Times* (6 February 1994): 12F.

Recall that Elvin Company applies overhead at the rate of 60 percent of direct labor cost. However, Clare must think carefully about this job. Perhaps somewhat less overhead will be incurred because purchasing is reduced (no need to purchase screen-saver software) and testing is reduced (the smaller hard drives require fewer hours of testing). Perhaps overhead for this job will amount to $4,313 (50 percent of direct labor). That would make the cost of the job $87,938 ($4,313 + $83,625).

Still, not all costs have been covered. There is the administrative cost and desired profit. If the standard markup of 20 percent is applied, the bid would be $105,526. This is still too high. Now Clare must determine if further cuts are possible, or if she wants to decrease desired profit and administrative expenses. As you can see, target costing is an iterative process. Clare will go through the cycle until she either achieves the target cost or determines that she cannot. Note, however, that given the customer's price ceiling, Clare now has a chance of winning the bid.

A further issue might cause concern. Is there anything ethically wrong with changing the components from the initial bid to the target costed bid? No, the new components meet customer specifications and are clearly described in the bid. In fact, Clare's initial bid was overspecified. If the customer wants a Chevrolet the bidder need not provide a Rolls-Royce, especially at Chevrolet prices. However, if in Clare's professional opinion the insurance company should upgrade its specifications, she could point that out. For example, if she knows that the insurance company's word-processing program is due for an upgrade that will take more hard-disk space, she could inform the company of that and encourage an increase in specified disk space.

Target costing involves much more up-front work than cost-based pricing. However, let's not forget the additional work that must be done if the cost-based price turns out to be higher than what customers will accept. Then the arduous task of bringing costs into line to support a lower price, or the opportunity cost of missing the market altogether, begins. For example, the U.S. consumer electronics market is virtually nonexistent because cost-based pricing led to increasingly higher prices. Japanese (and later Korean) firms practicing target costing offered lower prices and won the market.

Target costing can be used most effectively in the design and development stage of the product life cycle. At that point, the features of the product as well as its costs are still fairly easy to adjust.

Legal Aspects of Pricing

Customers and costs are important economic determinants of price. The U.S. government also has an important impact on pricing. The basic principle behind much pricing regulation is that competition is good and should be encouraged. Therefore, collusion by companies to set prices and the deliberate attempt to drive competitors out of business are prohibited. In general, cost is an important justification for price.

predatory pricing

Predatory pricing The practice of setting prices below cost for the purpose of injuring competitors and eliminating competition is called predatory pricing. It is important to note that pricing below cost is not necessarily predatory pricing. Companies frequently price an item below cost—loss leaders or weekly specials in a grocery store, for example. State laws on predatory pricing create a patchwork of legal definitions. Twenty-two states have laws against predatory pricing, each state differing somewhat in definition and rules. Oklahoma, for example, requires retailers to sell products at a price at least 6.75 percent above cost, unless the store is having a sale or matching a competitor's price. A 1937 Arkansas law forbids companies from selling or advertising "any article or product . . . at less than the cost thereof to the vendor . . . for the purpose of injuring competitors and destroying competition."

An example of the application of state predatory pricing laws is the lawsuit filed by three Conway, Arkansas, drugstores against Wal-Mart.[8] The druggists contended that

8. Wal-Mart lost the suit in October 1993 and won the case on appeal.

Wal-Mart engaged in predatory pricing by selling more than one hundred products below cost. One difficulty is showing exactly what cost is. Wal-Mart has low overhead and phenomenal buying power. Suppliers are regularly required to shave prices to win Wal-Mart's business. Smaller concerns cannot win such price breaks. Thus, the fact that Wal-Mart prices products below competitors' costs does not necessarily mean that those products are priced below Wal-Mart's cost. (Although in this case, the CEO of Wal-Mart did concede that Wal-Mart on occasion prices products below its own cost.)

A key legal point is that the below-cost price must be for the purpose of driving out competitors. Usually, this is a difficult point to prove. In general, states follow federal law in predatory pricing cases, and the federal law makes it difficult to prove predatory pricing since price competition is so highly valued.

dumping

Predatory pricing on the international market is called dumping, and occurs when companies sell below cost in other countries. For years, U.S. automobile manufacturers have accused Japanese companies of dumping. Companies found guilty of dumping products in the United States are subject to trade restrictions and stiff tariffs—which act to increase the price of the good. The defense against a charge of dumping is demonstrating that the price is indeed above or equal to cost.

price
discrimination

Price Discrimination Perhaps the most potent weapon against price discrimination in the United States is the 1936 Robinson-Patman Act.[9] Price discrimination refers to the charging of different prices to different customers for essentially the same product. Note that services and intangibles are not covered by this act. The Robinson-Patman Act states that it is unlawful "to discriminate in price between purchasers of commodities of like grade and quality ... where the effect of such discrimination may be substantially to lessen competition, to tend to create a monopoly in any line of commerce, or to injure, destroy, or prevent competition with any person who either grants or knowingly receives the benefit of such discrimination, or with customers of either of them." A key feature is that only manufacturers or suppliers are covered by the act. Importantly, the Robinson-Patman Act does allow price discrimination under certain specified conditions: (1) if the competitive situation demands it, and (2) if costs can justify the lower price. Clearly, this second condition is important for the accountant, as a lower price offered to one customer must be justified by identifiable cost savings. Additionally, the amount of the discount must be at least equaled by the amount of cost saved.

What about quantity discounts—are they permissible under Robinson-Patman? Consider quantity discounts offered by Morton Salt (now Morton International, Inc.) during the 1940s. Less-than-carload shipments were priced at $1.60 per-case delivered. Carload shipments were priced at $1.50 per case, and extra discounts of $.10 and an additional $.05 were given for purchases of 5,000 cases and 50,000 cases respectively, if purchased within a 12-month period. The Supreme Court, in a 1948 decision, found that Morton Salt had violated the Robinson-Patman Act because so few buyers qualified for the quantity discount; at the time only five large chain stores had purchases high enough to qualify for the lowest price of $1.35 per case. While Morton Salt argued that the discounts were available to all purchasers, the Court noted that for all practical purposes, small wholesalers and retail grocers could not qualify for the discounts. A key point here is that so few purchasers were eligible for the discount that competition was lessened. So while the act states that quantity discounts can be given, they must not appreciably lessen competition.

Freight is considered part of price for purposes of the Robinson-Patman Act. If a company requires the customer to pay freight charges then there is no problem. However, price discrimination may occur if the price charged includes delivery. Suppose the firm charges a uniform delivered price. Then customers located next to the firm pay the

9. This section relies on two sources: William A. Rutter, *Antitrust*, 3d ed. (Gardena, Calif.: Gilbert Law Summaries, 1972): 57–64; and William A. Baldwin, *Market Power, Competition, and Antitrust Policy* (Homewood, Ill.: Richard D. Irwin, Inc., 1987): 430–435.

same price as customers located 1,000 miles away. Because the cost of delivering to nearby customers is much less than delivering to far-off customers, the nearby customers are paying "phantom freight."

The burden of proof for firms accused of violating the Robinson-Patman Act is on the firms. The cost justification argument must be buttressed by substantial cost data. Proving a cost justification is an absolute defense, however; the expense of preparing evidence and the FTC's restrictive interpretations of the defense have made it a seldom-used choice in the past. Now, the availability of large databases, the development of activity-based costing, and powerful computing make it a more palatable alternative. Still problems remain. Cost allocations make such determinations particularly thorny. In justifying quantity discounts to larger companies, a company might keep track of sales calls, differences in time and labor required to make small and large deliveries, and so on.

In computing a cost differential, the company must create classes of customers based on the average costs of selling to those customers, and then charge all customers in each group a cost-justifiable price.

Fairness and Pricing

Community standards of fairness have an important effect on prices. For example, should toy stores raise the price of sleds the morning after a heavy snowfall? They could, but generally they do not. Their customers believe that a price increase at such a time would be taking unfair advantage. Whether we characterize the store's reluctance to raise prices in this situation as fairness or as an act in the long-term best interests of the company, the result is the same.

price gouging   Price gouging is said to occur when firms with market power price products "too high." How high is too high? Surely cost is a consideration. Any time price just covers cost, gouging does not occur. This is why so many firms go to considerable trouble to explain their cost structure and point out costs consumers may not realize exist. Pharmaceutical companies, for example, emphasize the research and development costs associated with new drugs. When a high price is clearly not supported by cost, buyers take offense. For example, after Hurricane Andrew in 1992, some companies and individuals sold ice for very high prices. Floridians faced by those prices were outraged that some suppliers would take advantage of the disaster to profiteer.

It is easy to see that cost as a justification for price underlies community standards of fairness. Ethics are founded on a sense of fairness. So unethical behavior in pricing is related to taking unfair advantage of customers. Cost-related price increases are the best defense against customer rebellion.

APPENDIX: LINEAR PROGRAMMING

Objective 6

Use linear programming to find the optimal solution to a problem of multiple constrained resources.

linear programming

Linear programming is a method that searches among possible solutions until it finds the optimal solution. The theory of linear programming permits many solutions to be ignored. In fact, all but a finite number of solutions are eliminated by the theory, with the search then limited to the resulting finite set.

To illustrate how linear programming can be used to solve a problem of multiple constrained resources, we will use the earlier example of the product mix for Jorgenson Company. Assume that there are demand constraints for both gear X and gear Y. For gear X, no more than 15,000 units can be sold and for gear Y no more than 40,000 units. As before, the objective is to maximize Jorgenson's total contribution margin subject to the constraints the company faces.

The objective can be expressed mathematically. Let X and Y be the number of units produced and sold of gear X and gear Y, respectively. Since the unit contribution margins are $25 and $10 for X and Y, respectively, the total contribution margin (Z) can be expressed as:

$$Z = \$25X + \$10Y \tag{10.1}$$

objective function

Equation 10.1 is called the objective function.

Jorgenson also has three constraints. One is the limited machine hours available for production, and the other two reflect the demand limitations for each product. Consider the machine-hour constraint first. Two machine hours are used for each unit of gear X, and 0.5 machine hour is used for each unit of gear Y. Thus, the total machine hours used can be expressed as $2X + 0.5Y$. The maximum of 40,000 machine hours available can be expressed mathematically as follows:

$$2X + 0.5Y \leqslant 40,000 \tag{10.2}$$

The two demand constraint limitations can also be expressed mathematically:

$$X \leqslant 15,000 \tag{10.3}$$
$$Y \leqslant 40,000 \tag{10.4}$$

Jorgenson's problem is to select the number of units of X and Y that maximize total contribution margin subject to the constraints in equations 10.2, 10.3, and 10.4. This problem can be expressed in the following way, which is the standard formulation for a linear programming problem (often referred to as a *linear programming model*):

$$\text{Max } Z = \$25X + \$10Y$$

subject to

$$2X + 0.5Y \leqslant 40,000$$
$$X \leqslant 15,000$$
$$Y \leqslant 40,000$$
$$X \geqslant 0$$
$$Y \geqslant 0$$

constraint set
feasible solution
feasible set of solutions

The last two constraints are called *nonnegativity constraints* and simply reflect the reality that negative quantities of a product cannot be produced. All constraints, taken together, are referred to as the constraint set.

A feasible solution is a solution that satisfies the constraints in the linear programming model. The collection of all feasible solutions is called the feasible set of solutions. For example, producing and selling 10,000 units of gear X and 20,000 units of gear Y would be a feasible solution and a member of the feasible set. This product mix uses 30,000 machine hours [(2 × 10,000) + (0.5 × 20,000)], which is under the limit for machine hours. Additionally, the company can sell the indicated amounts since they do not exceed the demand constraints for each product. If this mix is selected, the company would earn a contribution margin totaling $450,000 [($25 × 10,000) + ($10 × 20,000)].

However, the mix of 10,000 units of X and 20,000 units of Y is not the best mix. One better solution would be to produce and sell 12,000 units of X and 30,000 units of Y. This mix uses 39,000 machine hours [(2 × 12,000) + (0.5 × 30,000)] and produces a total contribution margin of $600,000 [($25 × 12,000) + ($10 × 30,000)]. This feasible solution is better than the first because it produces $150,000 more in profits. There are, however, even better feasible solutions. The objective is to identify the best. The best feasible solution—the one that maximizes the total contribution margin—is called the optimal solution.

optimal solution

When there are only two products, the optimal solution can be identified by graphing. Since solving the problem by graphing provides considerable insight into the way linear programming problems are solved, the Jorgenson problem will be solved in this way.

Four steps are followed in solving the problem graphically.

1. Graph each constraint.
2. Identify the feasible set of solutions.
3. Identify all corner-point values in the feasible set.
4. Select the corner point that yields the largest value for the objective function.

The graph of each constraint for the Jorgenson problem is shown in Exhibit 16-4. The nonnegativity constraints put the graph in the first quadrant. The other constraints are graphed by assuming that equality holds. Since each constraint is a linear equation, the graph is obtained by identifying two points on the line, plotting those points, and connecting them.

A feasible area for each constraint (except for the nonnegativity constraints) is determined by everything that lies below (or to the left) of the resulting line. The *feasible set* or *region* is the intersection of each constraint's feasible area. The feasible set is shown by the figure *ABCDE*; it includes the boundary of the figure.

There are five corner points: *A*, *B*, *C*, *D*, and *E*. Their values, obtained directly from the graph, are (0,0) for *A*, (15,0) for *B*, (15,20) for *C*, (10,40) for *D*, and (0,40) for *E*. The impact of these values on the objective function is as follows (expressed in thousands):

Corner Point	X	Y	Z = \$25X + \$10Y
A	0	0	0
B	15	0	375
C	15	20	575
D	10	40	650*
E	0	40	400

*This is the optimal solution.

The optimal solution calls for producing and selling 10,000 units of gear X and 40,000 units of gear Y. No other feasible solution will produce a larger contribution margin. It has been shown in the literature on linear programming that the optimal solution will always be one of the corner points. Thus, once the graph is drawn and the corner points identified, finding the solution is simply a matter of computing the value of each corner point and selecting the one with the greatest value.

simplex method   Graphical solutions are not practical with more than two or three products. Fortunately, an algorithm called the simplex method can be used to solve larger linear programming problems. This algorithm has been coded and is available for use on computers to solve these larger problems.

16-4 ....

Exhibit
Graphical Solution
(coordinates represent
thousands)

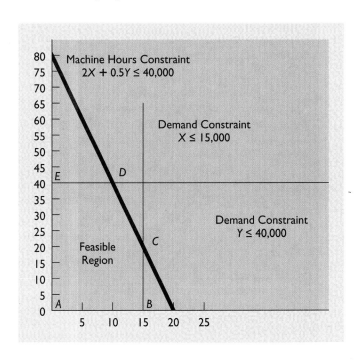

The linear programming model is an important tool for making product mix decisions, though it requires very little independent managerial decision making. The mix decision is made by the linear programming model itself. Assuming that the linear programming model is a reasonable representation of reality, the main role for management is to ensure that accurate data are used as input to the model. This includes the ability to recognize the irrelevancy of fixed costs and the ability to assess the accounting and technological inputs accurately (for example, the unit selling prices, the unit costs, and the amount of resource consumed by each product as it is produced).

SUMMARY OF LEARNING OBJECTIVES

1. Describe and explain the tactical decision-making model.

The decision-making model described in this chapter consists of six steps: recognizing and defining the problem, identifying alternatives, determining the costs and benefits of each alternative, comparing relevant costs and benefits for each alternative, assessing qualitative factors, and making the decision. In using cost analysis to choose among alternatives, managers should take steps to ensure that all important feasible alternatives are being considered.

2. Explain how the activity resource usage model is used in assessing relevancy.

The activity resource usage model breaks costs into three groups: resources acquired as used and needed, resources acquired in advance of use (short term); and resources acquired in advance (multiperiod service capability). For resources acquired as used and needed, supply equals demand. If demand changes, the cost is relevant. For resources acquired in advance (short term), there may be unused capacity. The cost may or may not be relevant. Resources acquired in advance (multiperiod service capability) are not relevant. Changes in these resources involve capital decisions.

3. Apply the tactical decision-making concepts in a variety of business situations.

Several examples illustrating the application of the relevant-costing model were given within the chapter. Applications were illustrated for make-or-buy decisions, keep-or-drop decisions, special-order decisions, and sell-or-process-further decisions. Product mix decisions were also discussed. The list of applications is by no means exhaustive but was given to illustrate the scope and power of relevant-costing analysis.

4. Choose the optimal product mix when faced with one constrained resource.

In dealing with a resource constraint, it is important to phrase the product contribution margin in terms of contribution margin per unit of constrained resource.

5. Explain the impact of cost on pricing decisions.

Costs are important inputs into the pricing decision. Cost-based pricing uses a markup based on a subset of costs. Target pricing works backward from a price acceptable to consumers to find the cost necessary to manufacture the product. The Robinson-Patman Act permits cost data to be used as an absolute defense in price discrimination cases.

6. Use linear programming to find the optimal solution to a problem of multiple constrained resources.

Linear programming is a method that locates the optimal solution in a set of feasible solutions. The graphical method may be used with two products. When more than two products are involved, the simplex method is used. (Appendix)

KEY TERMS

REVIEW PROBLEM

Rianne Company produces a light fixture with the following unit cost:

Direct materials	$2
Direct labor	1
Variable overhead	3
Fixed overhead	2
Unit cost	$8

The production capacity is 300,000 units per year. Because of a depressed housing market, the company expects to produce only 180,000 fixtures for the coming year. The company also has fixed selling costs totaling $500,000 per year and variable selling costs of $1 per-unit sold. The fixtures normally sell for $12 each.

At the beginning of the year, a customer from a geographic region outside the area normally served by the company offered to buy 100,000 fixtures for $7 each. The customer also offered to pay all transportation expenses. Since there would be no sales commissions involved, this order would not have any variable selling expenses.

REQUIRED: Should the company accept the order? Provide both qualitative and quantitative justification for your decision. Assume that no other orders are expected beyond the regular business and the special order.

Solution

The company is faced with a problem of idle capacity. Accepting the special order would bring production up to near capacity. There are two options: accept or reject the order. If the order is accepted, then the company could avoid laying off employees and would enhance and maintain its community image. However, the order is considerably below the normal selling price of $12. Because the price is so low, the company needs to assess the potential impact of the sale on its regular customers and on the profitability of the firm. Considering the fact that the customer is located in a region not usually served by the company, the likelihood of an adverse impact on regular business is not high. Thus, the qualitative factors seem to favor acceptance.

The only remaining consideration is the profitability of the special order. To assess profitability, the firm should identify the relevant costs and benefits of each alternative. This analysis is as follows:

	Accept	Reject
Revenues	$700,000	—
Direct materials	(200,000)	—
Direct labor	(100,000)	—
Variable overhead	(300,000)	—
Total benefits	$100,000	$0

Accepting the order would increase profits by $100,000 (the fixed overhead and selling expenses are all irrelevant since they are the same across both alternatives). Conclusion: The order should be accepted since both qualitative and quantitative factors favor it.

QUESTIONS FOR WRITING AND DISCUSSION

1. What is the difference between tactical and strategic decisions?
2. Explain why depreciation on an existing asset is always irrelevant.
3. Give an example of a future cost that is not relevant.
4. Explain why relevant costs need to be expressed on a periodically recurring basis.
5. Relevant costs always determine which alternative should be chosen. Do you agree? Explain.
6. Give an example of a fixed cost that is relevant.
7. What is the difference, if any, between a relevant cost and a differential cost?
8. When, if ever, is depreciation a relevant cost?
9. What role do past costs play in relevant-costing decisions?
10. Can direct materials ever be irrelevant in a make-or-buy decision? Explain.

11. Discuss the importance of complementary effects in a keep-or-drop decision.
12. What are some ways a manager can expand his or her knowledge of the feasible set of alternatives?
13. Should joint costs be considered in a sell-or-process-further decision? Explain.
14. Suppose that a product can be sold at split-off for $5,000 or processed further at a cost of $1,000 and then sold for $6,400. Should the product be processed further?
15. Why are fixed costs never relevant in a product mix decision?
16. Suppose that a firm produces two products. Should the firm always place the most emphasis on the product with the largest contribution margin per unit? Explain.
17. Why would a firm ever offer a price on a product that is below its full cost?

18. When can a firm legally offer different prices for the same product?
19. Discuss the purpose of linear programming.
20. What is an objective function? a constraint? a constraint set?

21. What is a feasible solution? a feasible set of solutions?
22. Explain the procedures for graphically solving a linear programming problem. What solution method is usually used when the problem includes more than two or three products?

Ⓦ ARM-UP EXERCISES

This section provides short warm-up exercises based on the examples in the chapter. Each warm-up exercise gives the page number on which the text example can be found. You may want to refer to the text example to see how the exercise can be set up and solved.

W16-1
Make-or-Buy Decision
LO 3
pp. 657–658

Cecil's Manufacturing had always made its components in-house. However, Waylo Products had recently offered to supply one component, CZ-43, at a price of $5 each. Cecil uses 2,000 units of part CZ-43 each year. The absorption cost per unit of this component is as follows:

Direct materials	$1.30
Direct labor	.50
Variable overhead	2.50
Fixed overhead	3.00
Total	$7.30

The fixed overhead is an allocated expense, none of it would be eliminated if production of component CZ-43 stopped.

REQUIRED:
1. What are the alternatives facing Cecil Manufacturing with respect to production of component CZ-43?
2. List the relevant costs for each alternative. Which alternative is better?

W16-2
Keep-or-Drop Decision
LO 3
pp. 658, 660

Supralyn Company produces three products: A, B, and C. A segmented income statement, with amounts given in thousands, follows:

	A	B	C	Total
Sales revenue	$700	$1,800	$200	$2,700
Less: Variable expenses	(350)	(1,000)	(140)	(1,490)
Contribution margin	$350	$ 800	$ 60	$1,210
Less: Direct fixed expenses	(100)	(300)	(70)	(470)
Segment margin	$250	$ 500	$ (10)	$ 740
Less: Common fixed expenses				(340)
Operating income				$ 400

Direct fixed expenses include depreciation on equipment dedicated to the product lines of $20,000 for A, $120,000 for B, and $30,000 for C. None of the equipment can be sold.

REQUIRED:
1. What impact on profit would result from dropping product C?
2. Now suppose that 10 percent of the customers for product B choose to buy from Supralyn because it offers a full range of products, including product C. If C were no longer available from Supralyn, these customers would go elsewhere to purchase B. Now what is the impact on profit if product C is dropped?

W16-3
Special-Order Decision
LO 3
p. 662

Mallard Company has been approached by a new customer with an offer to purchase 1,000 units of Mallard's product at a price of $3 each. The new customer is geographically separated from Mallard's other customers, and there would be no effect on existing sales. Mallard normally produces 10,000 units but only plans to produce and sell 8,000 in the coming year. The normal sales price is $5 per unit. Unit cost information is as follows:

Direct materials	$0.50
Direct labor	1.00
Variable overhead	.40
Fixed overhead	2.00
Total	$3.90

REQUIRED: Should Mallard accept the special order? By how much will profit increase or decrease if the order is accepted?

W16-4
Sell at Split-off or Process Further Decision
LO 3
pp. 663–664

Colby Company produces two products from a joint process. Joint costs are $50,000 for one batch, which yields 1,000 gallons of product K-1 and 4,000 gallons of product K-2. K-1 can be sold at the split-off point for $26 or can be processed further at a cost of $4,300 (for the 1,000 gallons) and sold for $30 per gallon.

REQUIRED: Should K-1 be sold at the split-off point or processed further?

W16-5
Product Mix Decision with One Constrained Resource
LO 4
p. 665

O'Connor Company produces two models of machine housings that require the use of a special lathe. The six lathes owned by the firm provide a total of 12,000 hours per year. Model 14-D requires 4 hours of machine time and model 33-P requires 2 hours of machine time. Model 14-D has a contribution margin of $15 per unit and model 33-P has a contribution margin of $10.

REQUIRED:
1. Calculate the optimal number of units of each model that should be produced, assuming that an unlimited number of each model can be sold.
2. Calculate the optimal number of units of each model that should be produced, assuming that no more than 5,000 units of each model can be sold.

W16-6
Cost-based Pricing Decision
LO 5
p. 666

Bob Peters, owner of Peters, Inc., is preparing a bid on a job that requires $1,200 of direct materials, $600 of direct labor, and $250 of overhead. Bob normally applies a standard markup based on cost of goods sold to arrive at an initial bid price. He then adjusts the price as necessary in light of other factors (for example, competitive pressure). Last year's income statement is as follows:

Sales	$100,000
Cost of goods sold	45,000
Gross margin	$ 55,000
Selling and administrative expenses	24,500
Net income	$ 30,500

REQUIRED:
1. Calculate the markup Bob will use.
2. What is Bob's initial bid price?

W16-7
Linear Programming Decision
LO 6
pp. 671–672

Refer to W16-5. Assume that no more than 2,000 units of model 14-D can be sold, and that no more than 5,000 units of model 33-P can be sold.

REQUIRED:

1. Formulate the linear programming problem faced by O'Connor Company. To do so, you must derive mathematical expressions for the objective function and for the lathe constraints.
2. Solve the linear programming problem using the graphical approach.
3. Compute the total contribution margin produced by the optimal mix developed in requirement 2.

 XERCISES

E16-1
Lease Decision;
Relevance of Book
Value
LO 1, LO 2, LO 3

Kim Borden, plant manager, is trying to decide whether to lease a new stamping machine or continue using the one already owned. With careful maintenance, the old stamping machine will last another five years. The lease on the new stamping machine is also for five years, at the end of which it will be returned to the lessor. Information on the stamping machine owned by the company follows:

Original cost	$20,000
Accumulated depreciation	10,000
Annual depreciation	4,000
Annual operating costs	3,250
Annual maintenance	1,100

Cost information for the new stamping machine is as follows:

Annual lease payment	$4,500
Annual operating costs	1,000
Annual maintenance	—

If the decision is to lease, the old stamping machine will be sold for an amount just sufficient to pay off a five-year note that requires annual payments of $1,320.

REQUIRED:

1. What are the alternatives being considered by the plant manager?
2. Identify the relevant costs and benefits of each alternative. Should the plant manager lease the new stamping machine?
3. What is the most that the plant manager would be willing to pay per year for a leased stamping machine?

E16-2
Keep or Buy; Sunk
Costs
LO 1, LO 2, LO 3

Joseph Morris purchased a 1996 Grand Am in 1998 for $8,900. Since purchasing the car, he has spent the following amounts on parts and labor:

New stereo system	$1,200
Trick paint	400
New wide racing tires	800
Total	$2,400

Unfortunately, the new stereo doesn't completely drown out the sounds of a grinding transmission. Apparently, the Grand Am needs a considerable amount of work to make it reliable transportation. Joseph estimates that the needed repairs include the following:

Transmission overhaul	$2,000
Water pump	400
Master cylinder work	1,100
Total	$3,500

In a visit to a used car dealer, Joseph has found a one-year-old Neon in mint condition for $9,400. Joseph has advertised and found that he can sell the Grand Am for only $6,400. If he buys the Neon, Joseph will pay cash, but he would need to sell the Grand Am.

REQUIRED:
1. In trying to decide whether to restore the Grand Am or buy the Neon, Joseph is distressed because he already has spent $11,300 on the Grand Am. The investment seems too much to give up. How would you react to Joseph's concern?
2. Assuming that Joseph would be equally happy with the Grand Am or the Neon, should he buy the Neon or should he restore the Grand Am?

E16-3
Make or Buy
LO 1, LO 2, LO 3

Mason Company is currently manufacturing part 34Z, producing 8,000 units annually. The part is used in the production of several products made by Mason. The cost per unit for 34Z is as follows:

Direct materials	$ 6.00
Direct labor	3.00
Variable overhead	2.00
Fixed overhead	2.50
Total	$13.50

Of the total fixed overhead assigned to 34Z, $4,800 is direct fixed overhead and the remainder is common fixed overhead. An outside supplier has offered to sell the part to Mason for $12. There is no alternative use for the facilities currently used to produce the part.

REQUIRED:
1. Should Mason Company make or buy part 34Z?
2. What is the most Mason would be willing to pay an outside supplier?

E16-4
Keep or Drop;
Product Substitutes
LO 1, LO 2, LO 3

Ernest Golding, president of Golding Corporation, had just received the following variable-costing income statement:

	Product A	Product B
Sales	$100,000	$250,000
Less: Variable expenses	(50,000)	(145,000)
Contribution margin	$ 50,000	$105,000
Less: Fixed expenses	(80,000)	(110,000)
Net income (loss)	$ (30,000)	$ (5,000)

Golding was distressed since this was the fifth consecutive quarter that both products had shown a loss. Upon careful review, Golding discovered that $70,000 of the total fixed costs were common to both products; the common fixed costs are allocated to the individual products on the basis of sales revenues. Golding also was told that the products were substitutes for each other. If either product is dropped, the sales of the other product will increase; product A's by 50 percent if B is dropped and B's by 10 percent if A is dropped.

REQUIRED:
1. Prepare a segmented income statement in proper form for the past quarter.
2. Assume that Golding will choose among one of the following alternatives:
    a. Keep both products
    b. Drop both products
    c. Drop product A
    d. Drop product B

Which is the best alternative? Provide computational support.

E16-5
Special-Order
Decision; Qualitative
Aspects
LO 1, LO 2, LO 3

Randy Stone, the manager of Specialty Paper Products Company, was agonizing over an offer for an order requesting 5,000 calendars. Specialty Paper Products was operating at 70 percent of its capacity and could use the extra business; unfortunately, the order's offering price of $4.20 per box was below the cost to produce the calendars. The controller was opposed to taking a loss on the deal. However, the personnel manager argued in favor of accepting the order even though a loss would be incurred; it would avoid the problem of layoffs and would help maintain the community image of the company. The full cost to produce a calendar follows:

Direct materials	$1.15
Direct labor	1.50
Variable overhead	.60
Fixed overhead	2.00
Total	$5.25

The order is from a customer in a region not ordinarily serviced by the company. No variable selling or administrative expenses would be associated with the order.

REQUIRED:
1. Assume that the company would accept the order only if it increases total profits. Should the company accept or reject the order? Provide supporting computations.
2. Consider the personnel manager's concerns. Discuss the merits of accepting the order even if it decreases total profits.

E16-6
Sell or Process
Further; Basic
Analysis
LO 1, LO 2, LO 3

Lassiter, Inc. produces three products from a common input. The joint costs for a typical quarter follow:

Direct materials	$45,000
Direct labor	55,000
Overhead	60,000

The revenues from each product are as follows: product A, $75,000; product B, $80,000; and product C, $30,000.

Management is considering processing product A beyond the split-off point, which would increase the sales value of A to $116,000. However, to process A further means that the company must rent some special equipment costing $17,500 per quarter. Additional materials and labor also needed would cost $12,650 per quarter.

REQUIRED:
1. What is the gross profit earned by the three products for one quarter?
2. Should the division process product A further or sell it at split-off? What is the effect of the decision on quarterly gross profit?

E16-7
Product Mix
Decision; Single
Constraint
LO 4

Zanbrow Company produces two products that use the same material input. Product A uses 2 pounds of the material for every unit produced; and product B uses 5 pounds. Currently, Zanbrow has 6,000 pounds of the material in inventory. All of the material is imported. For the coming year, Zanbrow plans to import 6,000 pounds to produce 1,000 units of A and 2,000 units of B. The detail of each product's unit contribution margin follows:

	Product A	Product B
Selling price	$81	$139
Less variable expenses:		
Direct materials	(20)	(50)
Direct labor	(21)	(14)
Variable overhead	(10)	(15)
Contribution margin	$30	$ 60

Zanbrow Company has received word that the source of the material has been shut down by embargo. Consequently, the company will not be able to import the 6,000 pounds it planned to use in the coming year's production. There is no other source of the material.

REQUIRED:
1. Compute the total contribution margin that the company would earn if it could import the 6,000 pounds of the material.
2. Determine the optimal usage of the company's inventory of 6,000 pounds of the material. Compute the total contribution margin for the product mix that you recommend.

E16-8
Appendix Required:
Product Mix; Multiple
Constraints
LO 5, LO 6

Refer to the data in E16-7. Assume that product A uses 3 direct labor hours for every unit produced and that product B uses 2 hours. A total of 6,000 direct labor hours are available for the coming year.

REQUIRED:
1. Formulate the linear programming problem faced by Zanbrow Company. To do so, you must derive mathematical expressions for the objective function and for the material and labor constraints.
2. Solve the linear programming problem using the graphical approach.
3. Compute the total contribution margin produced by the optimal mix developed in requirement 2.

E16-9
Buy or Keep;
Identification of
Relevant Costs and
Benefits
LO 2, LO 3

Foster Company is currently using manufacturing machinery that some company officers believe is outdated. They are urging the president to acquire the latest computerized equipment, maintaining that output will increase and operating costs decrease. The company president has commissioned a report that compares costs and revenues of the existing equipment with that of the new equipment. The report is as follows:

	Old	New
Cost of acquisition	$280,000	$540,000
Accumulated depreciation[a]	100,000	—
Annual operating cost	63,000	50,000
Annual maintenance	8,500	4,000
Salvage value[b]	—	—
Output	100,000	120,000
Output selling price	100	100

[a]This is computed using the straight-line method. The expected life for both machines is six years.
[b]This will be the value at the end of the coming six years. Currently, the old machinery does have market value, and if it is sold now a six-year note will be paid off, saving the company annual payments of $16,500.

REQUIRED: Identify all costs and benefits relevant to the decision to keep or buy. Ignore taxes.

E16-10
Keep or Drop;
Complementary
Effects
LO 2, LO 3

Janzen Company manufactures running shoes and tennis shoes. The projected income statements for the two products are as follows:

	Running Shoes	Tennis Shoes
Sales	$450,000	$750,000
Less: Variable expenses	(270,000)	(300,000)
Contribution margin	$180,000	$450,000
Less: Direct fixed expenses	(200,000)	(220,000)
Segment margin	$ (20,000)	$230,000
Less: Common fixed expenses (allocated)	(50,000)	(75,000)
Net income (loss)	$ (70,000)	$155,000

The president of the company is considering dropping the running shoes line. However, if the line is dropped, sales of tennis shoes will drop by 5 percent.

REQUIRED:
1. Should the company drop or keep the line of running shoes? Provide supporting computations.
2. Assume that increasing the advertising budget by $10,000 will increase sales of running shoes by 5 percent and tennis shoes by 3 percent. Prepare a segmented income statement that reflects the effect of increased advertising. Should advertising be increased?

E16-11
Special Order
LO 2, LO 3

The Killian Company manufactures two skin-care lotions, Liquid Skin and Silken Skin, out of a joint process. The joint (common) costs incurred are $420,000 for a standard production run that generates 180,000 gallons of Liquid Skin and 120,000 gallons of Silken Skin. Additional processing costs beyond the split-off point are $1.40 per gallon for Liquid Skin and $0.90 per gallon for Silken Skin. Liquid Skin sells for $2.40 per gallon while Silken Skin sells for $3.90 per gallon.

The Overnight Hotel Chain has asked the Killian Company to supply it with 240,000 gallons of Silken Skin at a price of $3.65 per gallon. Overnight plans to have the Silken Skin bottled in 1.5-ounce personal-use containers that are supplied in each of its hotel rooms as part of the complimentary personal products for guest use.

If Killian accepts the order, it will save $0.05 per gallon in packaging of Silken Skin. There is sufficient excess capacity for the order. However, the market for Liquid Skin is saturated, and any additional sales of Liquid Skin would take place at a price of $1.60 per gallon.

REQUIRED:
1. What is the profit normally earned on one production run of Liquid Skin and Silken Skin?
2. Should Killian accept the special order? Explain. (CMA adapted)

E16-12
Product Mix
Decision; Single
Constraint
LO 4

Sealing Company manufactures three types of floppy disk storage units. Each of the three types requires the use of a special machine that has total operating capacity of 15,000 hours per year. Information on the three types of storage units is as follows:

	Basic	Standard	Deluxe
Selling price	$9.00	$30.00	$35.00
Variable cost	6.00	20.00	10.00
Machine hours required	0.10	0.50	0.75

Sealing Company's marketing director has assessed demand for the three types of storage units and believes that the firm can sell as many units as it can produce.

REQUIRED:
1. How many of each type of unit should be produced and sold to maximize the company's contribution margin? What is the total contribution margin for your selection?
2. Now suppose that Sealing Company believes that it can sell no more than 12,000 of the deluxe model but up to 50,000 each of the basic and standard models at the prices estimated. What product mix would you recommend and what would be the total contribution margin?

E16-13
Effect of Opportunity
Cost on Pricing
Decision
LO 1, LO 2

King Petroleum Company refines crude oil into a number of products (for example, gasoline, kerosene, naphtha) using a joint production process. A by-product of the refining process is sludge. Sludge is trucked to King's asphalt plants, where it is mixed with water and other chemicals to produce an asphalt emulsion used to repair roads. One asphalt manufacturing plant is located at Hutchinson, Kansas. The Hutchinson plant faces seasonal production; two-thirds of its asphalt emulsion sales take place in the months of May through August, and the plant operates at capacity during those months.

King's Hutchinson plant has provided the following data on the emulsion:

Average price per gallon	$0.550
Materials	0.287
Conversion cost	0.070

The average price per gallon is figured as the average accepted bid price on all jobs for the previous year. Materials are direct materials. Conversion cost is a semivariable cost; it is approximately 30 percent variable.

In October 1998, the Hutchinson School District requested bids for resurfacing several school parking lots. The resurfacing job should require 2,400 gallons of asphalt emulsion.

REQUIRED:
1. What is the lowest price per gallon of asphalt emulsion that the Hutchinson plant could bid on the school district job?
2. Suppose the school district wanted to wait until school was out in June to resurface the parking lots. What price per gallon should King's Hutchinson plant bid then?
3. How much will the school district save by resurfacing the parking lots in November instead of June?

E16-14
Make or Buy
LO 2, LO 3

Peterman Company produces automatic coffeemakers. Peterman manufactures all parts necessary for the assembly of the coffeemakers, including the tempered glass pots. Recently, Peterman has received a proposal from Harris Glass Works to produce the tempered glass pots and to sell them for $6 each. Peterman requires 30,000 pots per year, and Harris Glass Works has promised to supply that level of demand.

Internal data on the manufacture of glass pots are as follows:

Direct materials	$3.60
Direct labor	1.20
Factory overhead (25% variable)	4.00
Full manufacturing cost	$8.80

REQUIRED:
1. Should Peterman accept Harris Glass Works' offer? Explain.
2. Independent of your answer to requirement 1, give two qualitative reasons that Peterman might reject the offer. Give two qualitative reasons that Peterman might accept it.

E16-15
Comparison of Alternatives
LO 1, LO 2, LO 3

Alice Knapp is the director of the Newkirk Drug Counseling Center. She and her staff design programs to assist clients in becoming and staying drug free. Most clients are referred to the center through their probation officers. The center is funded through a combination of state and federal grants. Alice anticipates that funding will last for another two to three years. After that, in all probability the center will cease to exist.

The center has just been informed that it will lose the lease on its office in two months. Alice is considering three other sites. Information on the sites is as follows:

- *Site 1*: This site is a 1,600-square-foot office in downtown Newkirk. Other lessees include an attorney, a bail bond agency, and two insurance agencies. Monthly rent is $475. The office has no interior walls, and permanent partitions cannot be installed. However, private meetings between caseworker and client are crucial. Therefore, Alice believes that she must rent moveable partitions to surround each caseworker's desk for $85 per month.
- *Site 2*: This site is a 2,400-square-foot office in a strip mall in a suburban area of Newkirk. It is close to caseworkers' homes but relatively farther from clients' homes. The monthly rent is $500. The office has been subdivided into three smaller offices. One will be suitable for the reception area, one would serve as Alice's office, and the third would accommodate the caseworkers. Permanent partitions could be installed in the caseworkers' office at a cost of $1,500.
- *Site 3*: A former client's parents have heard about the center's need for space. They have offered to donate a house that they previously used as a rental home. This site is an older house in Newkirk that is located in a rapidly commercializing district. The house provides plenty of space and privacy for all caseworkers. However, the plumbing and electrical work are not up to standard and must be repaired before the center can move in. Additionally, federal regulations on handicapped access must be followed, so ramps and handrails must be built. Alice has received estimates on the work needed and figures the total cost will be $15,000.

REQUIRED:

1. Determine the relevant costs associated with each site. Does it matter whether the center will exist for two or three years? Explain.
2. Write a memo to Alice summarizing the qualitative and quantitative aspects of each site.

E16-16
Special Order
LO 2, LO 3

Rimbaud Enterprises has developed DyeMonster!, a popular children's toy in which disappearing dye is shot from a plastic gun. Rimbaud currently sells DyeMonster! to small toy stores throughout the country. Because Rimbaud is too small to have its own sales force, it uses independent brokers and manufacturers' representatives who charge a 10 percent commission on sales. DyeMonster! is priced at $15 each. Manufacturing costs consist of the following:

Direct materials	$ 2.50
Direct labor	1.10
Variable overhead	1.50
Fixed overhead	5.00
Full manufacturing cost	$10.10

Productive capacity is 200,000 units; currently, Rimbaud produces and sells 75,000 DyeMonster!s. Toyland, a national chain of discount toy stores, wants to buy 100,000 DyeMonster!s at $8 each. Toyland wants to have its own logo imprinted on each one. Rimbaud believes this will add $.38 to direct materials cost and will require the purchase of a special imprinting machine costing $50,000. The imprinting machine would be used only for this order and would be scrapped (with zero salvage value) afterward. No sales commission would be paid.

REQUIRED:

1. By how much will Rimbaud Enterprises' net income change if the order is accepted?
2. Discuss three qualitative factors that might be considered in making the decision to accept or reject the special order.

E16-17
Relevant Costs
LO 1, LO 2, LO 3

Corleone Manufacturing Company produced 2,300 units in the third quarter of the year that did not meet specifications. Corleone could rework the units and sell them for their original price of $30 each. If the rework is done, additional costs will be incurred: direct materials of $3.50, direct labor of 1.25 hours at $10 per hour; and variable overhead applied at the rate of $4 per direct labor hour. Alternatively, Corleone could sell the units "as is" for $14.65 each.

Corleone lists the following original manufacturing costs for the 2,300 units:

Direct materials	$ 8
Direct labor	10
Variable overhead	4
Fixed overhead	6
Full manufacturing cost	$28

REQUIRED:

1. What are the relevant costs and revenues for each alternative?
2. Which alternative should Corleone choose and why?

P ROBLEMS

P16-1
Make or Buy;
Qualitative
Considerations
LO 1, LO 2, LO 3

Powell Dentistry Services is part of an HMO that operates in a large metropolitan area. Currently, Powell has its own dental laboratory to produce porcelain and gold crowns. The unit costs to produce the crowns are as follows:

	Porcelain	Gold
Raw materials	$ 55	$ 94
Direct labor	22	22
Variable overhead	5	5
Fixed overhead	22	22
Total	$104	$143

Fixed overhead is detailed as follows:

Salary (supervisor)	$24,000
Depreciation	5,000
Rent (lab facility)	26,000

Overhead is applied on the basis of direct labor hours. These rates were computed using 5,500 direct labor hours.

A local dental laboratory has offered to supply Powell all the crowns it needs. Its price is $100 for porcelain crowns and $132 for gold crowns; however, the offer is conditional on supplying both types of crowns—it will not supply just one type for the price indicated. If the offer is accepted, the equipment used by Powell's laboratory would be scrapped (it is old and has no market value), and the lab facility would be closed. Powell uses 1,500 porcelain crowns and 1,000 gold crowns per year.

REQUIRED:
1. Should Powell continue to make its own crowns or should they be purchased from the external supplier? What is the dollar effect of purchasing?
2. What qualitative factors should Powell consider in making this decision?
3. Suppose that the lab facility is owned rather than rented and that the $26,000 is depreciation rather than rent. What effect does this have on the analysis in requirement 1?
4. Refer to the original data. Assume that the volume of crowns used is 3,000 porcelain and 2,000 gold. Should Powell make or buy the crowns? Explain the outcome.

P16-2
Sell or Process Further
LO 1, LO 2, LO 3

Rudolph Drug Corporation buys three chemicals that are processed to produce two types of analgesics used as ingredients for popular over-the-counter drugs. The purchased chemicals are blended for two to three hours and then heated for 15 minutes. The results of the process are two separate analgesics, tyl and nup, which are sent to a drying room until their moisture content is reduced to 6 to 8 percent. For every 1,100 pounds of chemicals used, 500 pounds of tyl and 500 pounds of nup are produced. After drying, tyl and nup are sold to companies that process them into their final form. The selling prices are $10 per pound for tyl and $25 per pound for nup. The costs to produce 500 pounds of each analgesic are as follows:

Chemicals	$5,500
Direct labor	4,500
Overhead	3,500

The analgesics are packaged in 25-pound bags and shipped. The cost of each bag is $0.75. Shipping costs $0.10 per pound.

Rudolph could process tyl further by grinding it into a fine powder and then molding the powder into tablets. The tablets could then be sold directly to retail drugstores as a generic brand. If this route is taken, the revenue received per bottle of tablets would be $3.00, with five bottles produced by every pound of tyl. The costs of grinding and tableting total $2.50 per pound of tyl. Bottles cost $0.20 each. Bottles are shipped in boxes that hold 25 at a shipping cost of $1.23 per box.

REQUIRED:
1. Should Rudolph sell tyl at split-off or should tyl be processed and sold as tablets?

2. If Rudolph normally sells 265,000 pounds of tyl per year, what will be the difference in profits if tyl is processed further?

P16-3
Keep or Drop
LO 1, LO 2, LO 3

AudioMart is a retailer of radios, stereos, and televisions. The store carries two portable sound systems that have radios, tape players, and speakers. System A, of slightly higher quality than system B, costs $20 more. With rare exceptions, the store also sells a headset when a system is sold. The headset can be used with either system. Variable-costing income statements for the three products follow:

	System A	System B	Headset
Sales	$ 45,000	$ 32,500	$ 8,000
Less: Variable expenses	(20,000)	(25,500)	(3,200)
Contribution margin	$ 25,000	$ 7,000	$ 4,800
Less: Fixed expenses*	(10,000)	(18,000)	(2,700)
Net income	$ 15,000	$(11,000)	$ 2,100

*This includes common fixed costs totaling $18,000, allocated to each product in proportion to its revenues.

The owner of the store is concerned about the profit performance of system B and is considering dropping it. If the product is dropped, sales of system A will increase by 30 percent and sales of headsets will drop by 25 percent.

REQUIRED:
1. Prepare segmented income statements for the three products using a better format.
2. Prepare segmented income statements for system A and the headsets assuming that system B is dropped. Should B be dropped?
3. Suppose that a third system, system C, with a similar quality to system B, could be acquired. Assume that with C the sales of A would remain unchanged; however, C would produce only 80 percent of the revenues of B and sales of the headsets would drop by 10 percent. The contribution margin ratio of C is 50 percent, and its direct fixed costs would be identical to those of B. Should system B be dropped and replaced with system C?

P16-4
Accept or Reject a Special Order
LO 2, LO 3

Kevin McBride, manager of an electronics division, was considering an offer by Ellen Antle, manager of a sister division. Ellen's division was operating below capacity and had just been given an opportunity to produce 10,000 units of one of its products for a customer in a market not normally served. The opportunity involves a product that uses an electrical component produced by Kevin's division. Each unit that Ellen's department produces requires two of the components. However, the price the customer is willing to pay is well below the price usually charged; to make a reasonable profit on the order, Ellen needs a price concession from Kevin's division. Ellen had offered to pay full manufacturing cost for the parts. So that Kevin would know that everything was aboveboard, Ellen had supplied the following unit-cost and price information concerning the special order, excluding the cost of the electrical component:

Selling price	$32
Less costs:	
Direct materials	17
Direct labor	7
Variable overhead	2
Fixed overhead	3
Gross profit	$ 3

The normal selling price of the electrical component is $1.60 per unit. Its full manufacturing cost is $1.25 ($1.05 variable and $0.20 fixed). Ellen had argued that paying $1.60 per component would wipe out the gross profit and result in her division showing a loss. Kevin was interested in the offer because his division was also operating below capacity (the order would not use all the excess capacity).

REQUIRED:

1. Should Kevin accept the order at a selling price of $1.25 per unit? By how much will his division's profits be changed if the order is accepted? By how much will the profits of Ellen's division change if Kevin agrees to supply the part at full cost?
2. Suppose that Kevin offers to supply the component at $1.40. In offering the price, Kevin says that it is a firm offer not subject to negotiation. Should Ellen accept this price and produce the special order? If Ellen accepts the price, what is the change in profits for Kevin's division?
3. Assume that Kevin's division is operating at full capacity and that Kevin refuses to supply the part for less than the full price. Should Ellen still accept the special order? Explain.

P16-5
Keep or Drop a Division
LO 2, LO 3

Jan Shumard, president and general manager of Danbury Company, was concerned about the future of one of the company's largest divisions. The division's most recent quarterly income statement follows:

Sales	$3,751,500
Less: Cost of goods sold	(2,722,400)
Gross profit	$1,029,100
Less: Selling and administrative	(1,100,000)
Net profit (loss)	$ (70,900)

Jan is giving serious consideration to shutting down the division since this is the ninth consecutive quarter that it has shown a loss. To help him in his decision, the following additional information has been gathered:

- The division produces one product at a selling price of $100 to outside parties.
- The division sells 50 percent of its output to another division within the company for $83 per unit (full manufacturing cost plus 25 percent). The internal price is set by company policy. If the division is shut down, the user division would buy the part externally for $100 per unit.
- The fixed overhead assigned per unit is $20.
- There is no alternative use for the facilities if shut down. The facilities and equipment would be sold and the proceeds invested to produce an annuity of $100,000 per year.
- Of the fixed selling and administrative expenses, 30 percent represent allocated expenses from corporate headquarters.
- Variable selling expenses are $5 per-unit sold for units sold externally. These expenses are avoided for internal sales. There are no variable administrative expenses.

REQUIRED:

1. Prepare an income statement that more accurately reflects the division's profit performance.
2. Should the president shut down the division? What would be the effect on the company's profits if the division were closed?

P16-6
Plant Shutdown or Continue to Operate; Qualitative Considerations
LO 2, LO 3

GianAuto Corporation manufactures automobiles, vans, and trucks. Among the various Gian-Auto plants around the United States is the Denver Cover plant, where vinyl covers and upholstery fabric are sewn. These are used to cover interior seating and other surfaces of GianAuto products.

Pam Vosilo is the plant manager for Denver Cover. The plant was the first GianAuto plant in the region. As other area plants were opened, Pam, in recognition of her management ability, was given the responsibility of managing them. She functions as a regional manager although the budget for her and her staff is charged to the Denver plant.

Pam has just received a report indicating that GianAuto could purchase the entire annual output of Denver Cover from outside suppliers for $30 million. Pam is astonished at the low outside price because the budget for Denver Cover's operating costs was set at $52 million. She believes that Denver Cover will have to close down operations in order to realize the $22 million in annual cost savings.

The budget (in thousands) for Denver Cover's operating costs for the coming year follows:

Materials		$12,000
Labor:		
Direct	$13,000	
Supervision	3,000	
Indirect plant	4,000	20,000
Overhead:		
Depreciation (equipment)	$ 5,000	
Depreciation (building)	3,000	
Pension expenses	4,000	
Plant manager and staff	2,000	
Corporate allocation	6,000	20,000
Total budgeted costs		$52,000

Additional facts regarding the plant's operations are as follows:

- Due to Denver Cover's commitment to use high-quality fabrics in all its products, the purchasing department was instructed to place blanket orders with major suppliers to ensure the receipt of sufficient materials for the coming year. If these orders are canceled as a consequence of the plant closing, termination charges would amount to 15 percent of the cost of direct materials.
- Approximately 700 plant employees will lose their jobs if the plant is closed. This includes all direct laborers and supervisors as well as the plumbers, electricians, and other skilled workers classified as indirect plant workers. Some would be able to find new jobs, but many others would have difficulty. All employees would have difficulty matching Denver Cover's base pay of $9.40 per hour, the highest in the area. A clause in Denver Cover's contract with the union may help some employees; the company must provide employment assistance to its former employees for 12 months after a plant closing. The estimated cost to administer this service would be $1 million for the year.
- Some employees would probably elect early retirement because Denver Cover has an excellent pension plan. In fact, $3 million of next year's pension expense would continue whether Denver Cover is open or not.
- Pam and her staff would not be affected by the closing of Denver Cover. They would still be responsible for administering three other area plants.
- Denver Cover considers equipment depreciation to be a variable cost and uses the units-of-production method to depreciate its equipment; Denver Cover is the only GianAuto plant to use this depreciation method. However, Denver Cover uses the customary straight-line method to depreciate its building.

REQUIRED:
1. Prepare a quantitative analysis to help in deciding whether or not to close the Denver Cover plant. Explain how you treated the nonrecurring relevant costs.
2. Consider the analysis in requirement 1 and add to it the qualitative factors that you believe are important to the decision. What is your decision? Would you close the plant? Explain. (CMA adapted)

P16-7

Appendix Required: Product Mix Decision; Single and Multiple Constraints; Basics of Linear Programming

LO 4, LO 6

Paper Products, Inc. produces facial tissues and table napkins. The manufacturing process is highly mechanized; both products are produced by the same machinery by using different settings. For the coming period, 200,000 machine hours are available. Management is trying to decide on the quantities of each product to produce. The following data are available (for napkins, one unit is one package of napkins; for facial tissue, one unit is one box of tissue):

	Napkins	Tissue
Machine hours per unit	1.00	0.50
Unit selling price	$2.50	$3.00
Unit variable cost	$1.50	$2.25

REQUIRED:

1. Determine the units of each product that should be produced in order to maximize profits.
2. Because of market conditions, the company can sell no more than 150,000 packages of napkins and 300,000 boxes of paper tissue. Do the following:
   a. Formulate the problem as a linear programming problem.
   b. Determine the optimal mix using a graph.
   c. Compute the maximum profits given the optimal mix.

P16-8

Keep or Drop;
Product Mix

LO 2, LO 3

Olat Corporation produces three gauges. These gauges measure density, permeability, and thickness and are known as *D-gauges*, *P-gauges*, and *T-gauges*. For many years, the company has been profitable and has operated at capacity (which is 82,000 direct labor hours). In the last two years, however, prices on all gauges were reduced and selling expenses increased to meet competition and keep the plant operating at full capacity. Third-quarter results (in thousands), which follow, are representative of recent experience:

	D-gauge	P-gauge	T-gauge	Total
Sales	$900	$1,600	$ 900	$3,400
Less: Cost of goods sold	(770)	(1,048)	(950)	(2,768)
Gross profit	$130	$ 552	$ (50)	$ 632
Less: Selling and administrative expenses	(185)	(370)	(135)	(690)
Net income (loss)	$ (55)	$ 182	$(185)	$ (58)

Mel Carlo, president of Olat, is concerned about the results of the pricing, selling, and production policies. After reviewing the third-quarter results, he asked his management staff to consider the following three-point course of action:

1. Discontinue production of the T-gauge. T-gauges would not be returned to the line of products unless the problems with the gauge could be identified and resolved.
2. Increase quarterly sales promotion by $100,000 on the P-gauge to increase sales volume by 25 percent.
3. To accommodate the increased demand of P-gauges, cut production of the D-gauge by 50 percent and reduce traceable advertising and promotion costs for this line by $20,000 each quarter.

George Spears, controller, suggested that a more careful study of the financial relationships be made to determine the possible effects on the company's operating results as a consequence of these proposed actions. The president agreed, and JoAnn Brower, assistant controller, was given the assignment. She gathered the following information:

- All three gauges are manufactured with common equipment and facilities.
- The quarterly general selling and administrative expenses are allocated to the three product lines in proportion to their dollar sales volumes.
- Special selling expenses (advertising and shipping) are incurred on each gauge as follows:

	Advertising[a]	Shipping[b]
D-gauge	$100,000	$ 4
P-gauge	210,000	10
T-gauge	40,000	10

[a]Per quarter
[b]Per unit

• The unit manufacturing costs for the three products are as follows:

	D-gauge	P-gauge	T-gauge
Raw materials	$17	$ 31	$ 50
Direct labor*	20	40	60
Variable overhead	30	45	60
Fixed overhead	10	15	20
Total	$77	$131	$190

*The wage rate averages $10 per hour.

• The unit sales prices for the three products are $90 for the D-gauge, $200 for the P-gauge, and $180 for the T-gauge.
• The company is manufacturing at capacity and selling all that it produces.

REQUIRED:
1. Prepare a variable-costing segmented income statement for the three product lines. Make sure that you separate direct fixed expenses from common fixed expenses.
2. Should the T-gauge line be dropped as the president suggests? Explain.
3. Evaluate the remaining two suggestions of the president (combined with the first). Was he correct in promoting the P-gauge rather than the D-gauge? Explain. (CMA adapted)

P16-9
Appendix Required:
Product Mix
Decisions
LO 4, LO 6

Calen Company manufactures and sells three products in a factory of three departments. Both labor and machine time are applied to the products as they pass through each department. The nature of the machine processing and of the labor skills required in each department is such that neither machines nor labor can be switched from one department to another.

Calen's management is attempting to plan its production schedule for the next several months. The planning is complicated by the fact that labor shortages exist in the community and some machines will be down several months for repairs.

Following is information regarding available machine and labor time by department and the machine hours and direct labor hours required per unit of product. These data should be valid for at least the next six months:

	Monthly Capacity by Department		
	1	2	3
Machine hours available	3,000	3,100	2,700
Labor hours available	3,700	4,500	2,750

Product	Input per-Unit Produced			
401	Labor hours	2	3	3
	Machine hours	1	1	2
402	Labor hours	1	2	—
	Machine hours	1	1	—
403	Labor hours	2	2	2
	Machine hours	2	2	1

Sales believes that the monthly demand for the next six months will be as follows:

Product	Units Sold
401	500
402	400
403	1,000

Inventory levels will not be increased or decreased during the next six months. The unit cost and price data for each product are as follows:

	Product		
	401	402	403
Unit costs:			
Direct material	$ 7	$13	$17
Direct labor	66	38	51
Variable overhead	27	20	25
Fixed overhead	15	10	32
Variable selling	3	2	4
Total unit cost	$118	$83	$129
Unit selling price	$196	$123	$167

REQUIRED:

1. Calculate the monthly requirement for machine hours and direct labor hours for producing products 401, 402, and 403 to determine whether the factory can meet the monthly sales demand.
2. Determine the quantities of 401, 402, and 403 that should be produced monthly to maximize profits. Prepare a schedule that shows the contribution to profits of your product mix.
3. Assume that the machine hours available in department 3 are 1,500 instead of 2,700. Calculate the optimal monthly product mix using the graphing approach to linear programming. Prepare a schedule that shows the contribution to profits from this optimal mix. (CMA adapted)

P16-10
Make or Buy
LO 2, LO 3

Henderson Company produces two products, A and B. The segmented income statement for a typical quarter follows:

	Product A	Product B	Total
Sales	$150,000	$80,000	$230,000
Less: Variable expenses	(80,000)	(46,000)	(126,000)
Contribution margin	$ 70,000	$34,000	$104,000
Less: Direct fixed expenses*	(20,000)	(38,000)	(58,000)
Segment margin	$ 50,000	$ (4,000)	$ 46,000
Less: Common fixed expenses			(30,000)
Net income			$ 16,000

*This includes depreciation.

Product A uses a subassembly that is purchased from an external supplier for $25 per unit. Each quarter, 2,000 subassemblies are purchased. All units produced are sold, and there are no ending inventories of subassemblies. Henderson is considering making the subassembly rather than buying it. Unit variable manufacturing costs are as follows:

Direct materials	$2
Direct labor	3
Variable overhead	2

Two alternatives exist to supply the productive capacity:

1. Lease the needed space and equipment at a cost of $27,000 per quarter for the space and $10,000 per quarter for a supervisor. There are no other fixed expenses.
2. Drop product B. The equipment could be adapted with virtually no cost and the existing space utilized to produce the subassembly. The direct fixed expenses, including supervision, would

be $38,000, $8,000 of which is depreciation on equipment. If product B is dropped, there will be no effect on the sales of product A.

REQUIRED:

1. Should Henderson Company make or buy the subassembly? If it makes the subassembly, which alternative should be chosen? Explain and provide supporting computations.
2. Suppose that dropping B will decrease sales of A by 6 percent. What effect does this have on the decision?
3. Assume that dropping B decreases sales of A by 6 percent and that 2,800 subassemblies are required per quarter. As before, assume that there are no ending inventories of subassemblies and that all units produced are sold. Assume also that the per-unit sales price and variable costs are the same as in requirement 1. Include the leasing alternative in your consideration. Now what is the correct decision?

P16-11
Make or Buy
LO 1, LO 2, LO 3

Sportway, Inc. is a wholesale distributor supplying a wide range of moderately priced sporting equipment to large chain stores. About 60 percent of Sportway's products are purchased from other companies while the remainder of the products are manufactured by Sportway. The company's plastics department is currently manufacturing molded fishing tackle boxes. Sportway is able to manufacture and sell 8,000 tackle boxes annually, making full use of its direct labor capacity at available workstations. Following are the selling price and costs associated with Sportway's tackle boxes.

Selling price per box		$86.00
Costs per box:		
Molded plastic	$ 8.00	
Hinges, latches, handle	9.00	
Direct labor ($15/hour)	18.75	
Manufacturing overhead	12.50	
Selling and administrative expenses	17.00	65.25
Profit per box		$20.75

Because Sportway believes it could sell 12,000 tackle boxes if it had sufficient manufacturing capacity, the company has looked into the possibility of purchasing the tackle boxes for distribution. Maple Products, a steady supplier of quality products, would be able to provide up to 9,000 tackle boxes per year at a price of $68 per box delivered to Sportway's facility.

Bart Johnson, Sportway's product manager, has suggested that the company could make better use of its plastics department by manufacturing skateboards. To support his position, Bart has a market study that indicates an expanding market for skateboards and a need for additional suppliers. He believes that Sportway could expect to sell 17,500 skateboards annually at a price of $45 per skateboard. Bart's estimate of the costs to manufacture the skateboards follows:

Selling price per skateboard		$45.00
Costs per skateboard:		
Molded plastic	$5.50	
Wheels, hardware	7.00	
Direct labor ($15/hour)	7.50	
Manufacturing overhead	5.00	
Selling and administrative costs	9.00	34.00
Profit per skateboard		$11.00

In the plastics department, Sportway uses direct labor hours as the application base for manufacturing overhead. Included in the manufacturing overhead for the current year is $50,000 of factorywide, fixed manufacturing overhead that has been allocated to the plastics department. For each unit of product that Sportway sells, regardless of whether the product has been purchased or is manufactured by Sportway, an allocated $6 fixed overhead cost per unit for distribution is included in the selling and administrative costs for all products. Total selling and administrative costs for the purchased tackle boxes would be $10 per unit.

REQUIRED:
1. In order to maximize the company's profitability, prepare an analysis based on the data presented that will show which product or products Sportway, Inc. should manufacture and/or purchase. It should also show the associated financial impact. Support your answer with appropriate calculations.
2. Discuss some qualitative factors that might impact on Sportway's decision. (CMA adapted)

P16-12
Make or Buy
LO 1, LO 2, LO 3

Sarbec Company needs a total of 125 tons of sheet steel, 50 tons of 2-inch width and 75 tons of 4-inch width, for a customer's job. Sarbec can purchase the sheet steel in these widths directly from Jensteel Corporation, a steel manufacturer, or it can purchase sheet steel from Jensteel that is 24 inches wide and have it slit into the desired widths by Precut, Inc. Both vendors are local and have previously supplied materials to Sarbec.

Precut specializes in slitting sheet steel that is provided by a customer into any desired width. When negotiating a contract, Precut tells its customers that there is a scrap loss in the slitting operation but that this loss has never exceeded 2.5 percent of input tons. Precut recommends that if a customer has a specific tonnage requirement, it should supply an adequate amount of steel to yield the desired quantity. Precut's charges for steel slitting are based on good output, not input handled.

The 24-inch-wide sheet steel is a regular stock item of Jensteel and can be shipped to Precut within 5 days after receipt of Sarbec's purchase order. If Jensteel is to do the slitting, shipment to Sarbec would be scheduled for 15 days after receipt of the order. Precut has quoted delivery at 10 days after receipt of the sheet steel. In prior dealings, Sarbec has found both Jensteel and Precut to be reliable vendors with high-quality products.

Sarbec has received the following price quotations from Jensteel and Precut:

Jensteel Rates

Size	Gauge	Quantity	Cost per Ton
2"	14	50 tons	$210
4"	14	75 tons	200
24"	14	125 tons	180

Precut Rates

Size	Gauge	Quantity	Price per Ton of Output
2"	14	50 tons	$18
4"	14	75 tons	15

Freight and Handling Charges

Destination	Cost per Ton
Jensteel to Sarbec	$10.00
Jensteel to Precut	5.00
Precut to Sarbec	7.50

In addition to this information, Precut has informed Sarbec that if it purchases 100 output tons of each width, the per-ton slitting rates would be reduced 12 percent. Sarbec knows that the same customer will be placing a new order in the near future for the same material and estimates it would have to store the additional tonnage for an average of two months at a carrying cost of $1.50 per month for each ton. There would be no change in Jensteel's prices for additional tons delivered to Precut.

REQUIRED:
1. Prepare an analysis that will show whether Sarbec Company should:
   a. Purchase the required slit steel directly from Jensteel Corporation.

b. Purchase the 24-inch-wide sheet steel from Jensteel and have it slit by Precut, Inc. into 50 output tons, 2 inches wide and 75 output tons, 4 inches wide.

c. Take advantage of Precut's reduced slitting rates by purchasing 100 output tons of each width.

2. Ignoring your answer to requirement 1, present three qualitative reasons why Sarbec Company may favor the purchase of the slit steel directly from Jensteel Corporation. (CMA adapted)

Ⓜ ANAGERIAL DECISION CASES

C16-1

Make or Buy: Ethical Considerations

LO 1, LO 2, LO 3, LO 6

Pamela McDonald, CMA and controller for Murray Manufacturing, Inc., was having lunch with Roger Branch, manager of the company's power department. Over the past six months, Pamela and Roger had developed a romantic relationship and were making plans for marriage. To keep company gossip at a minimum, Pamela and Roger had kept the relationship very quiet, and no one in the company was aware of it. The topic of the luncheon conversation centered on a decision concerning the company's power department that Larry Johnson, president of the company, was about to make.

Pamela: Roger, in our last executive meeting, we were told that a local utility company offered to supply power and quoted a price per kilowatt-hour that they said would hold for the next three years. They even offered to enter into a contractual agreement with us.

Roger: This is news to me. Is the bid price a threat to my area? Can they sell us power cheaper than we make it? And why wasn't I informed about this matter? I should have some input. This burns me. I think I should give Larry a call this afternoon and lodge a strong complaint.

Pamela: Calm down, Roger. The last thing I want you to do is call Larry. Larry made us all promise to keep this whole deal quiet until a decision had been made. He did not want you involved because he wanted to make an unbiased decision. You know that the company is struggling somewhat, and they are looking for ways to save money.

Roger: Yeah, but at my expense? And at the expense of my department's workers? At my age, I doubt that I could find a job that pays as well and has the same benefits. How much of a threat is this offer?

Pamela: Jack Lacy, my assistant controller, prepared an analysis while I was on vacation. It showed that internal production is cheaper than buying, but not by much. Larry asked me to review the findings and submit a final recommendation for next Wednesday's meeting. I've reviewed Jack's analysis and it's faulty. He overlooked the interactions of your department with other service departments. When these are considered, the analysis is overwhelmingly in favor of purchasing the power. The savings are about $300,000 per year.

Roger: If Larry hears that, my department's gone. Pam, you can't let this happen. I'm three years away from having a vested retirement. And my workers—they have home mortgages, kids in college, families to support. No, it's not right. Pam, just tell him that your assistant's analysis is on target. He'll never know the difference.

Pamela: Roger, what you're suggesting doesn't sound right either. Would it be ethical for me to fail to disclose this information?

Roger: Ethical? Do you think it's right to lay off employees that have been loyal, faithful workers simply to fatten the pockets of the owners of this company? The Murrays already are so rich that they don't know what to do with their money. I think that it's even more unethical to penalize me and my workers. Why should we have to bear the consequences of some bad marketing decisions? Anyway, the effects of those decisions are about gone, and the company should be back to normal within a year or so.

Pamela: You may be right. Perhaps the well-being of you and your workers is more important than saving $300,000 for the Murrays.

REQUIRED:

1. Should Pamela have told Roger about the impending decision concerning the power department? In revealing this information, did Pamela violate any of the ethical standards described in Exhibit 1-4 of Chapter 1?

2. Should Pamela provide Larry with the correct data concerning the power department? Or should she protect its workers? What would you do if you were Pamela?

C16-2
Centralize versus
Decentralize
LO 1, LO 2, LO 3

Central University, a midwestern university with approximately 13,000 students, was in the middle of a budget crisis. For the third consecutive year, state appropriations for higher education remained essentially unchanged (the university is currently in its 1997-98 academic year). Yet utilities, social security benefits, insurance, and other operating expenses have increased. Moreover, the faculty were becoming restless, and some members had begun to leave for other, higher-paying opportunities.

The president and the academic vice-president had announced their intention to eliminate some academic programs and to reduce others. The savings that result would be used to cover the increase in operating expenses and for raises for the remaining faculty. Needless to say, the possible dismissal of tenured faculty aroused a great deal of concern throughout the university.

With this background, the president and academic vice-president called a meeting of all department heads and deans to discuss the budget for the coming year. As the budget was presented, the academic vice-president noted that Continuing Education, a separate, centralized unit, had accumulated a deficit of $504,000 over the past several years, which must be eliminated during the coming fiscal year. The vice-president noted that allocating the deficit equally among the seven colleges would create a hardship on some of the colleges, wiping out all of their operating budget except for salaries.

After some discussion of alternative ways to allocate the deficit, the head of the accounting department suggested an alternative solution: decentralize Continuing Education, allowing each college to assume responsibility for its own continuing education programs. In this way, the overhead of a centralized continuing education program could be avoided.

The academic vice-president responded that the suggestion would be considered, but it was received with little enthusiasm. The vice-president observed that Continuing Education was now generating more revenues than costs—and that the trend was favorable.

A week later, at a meeting of the deans' council, the vice-president reviewed the role of Continuing Education. He pointed out that only the dean of Continuing Education held tenure. If Continuing Education were decentralized, her salary ($50,000) would continue; however, she would return to her academic department, and the university would save $20,000 of instructional wages since fewer temporary faculty would be needed in her department. All other employees in the unit were classified as staff. Continuing Education had responsibility for all noncredit offerings. Additionally, it had nominal responsibility for credit courses offered in the evening on campus and for credit courses offered off-campus. However, all scheduling and staffing of these evening and off-campus courses were done by the heads of the academic departments. What courses were offered and who staffed them had to be approved by the head of each department. According to the vice-president, one of the main contributions of the Continuing Education Department to the evening and off-campus programs is advertising. He estimated that $30,000 per year is being spent.

After reviewing this information, the vice-president made available the following information pertaining to the department's performance for the past several years (the 1997-98 data were projections). He once again defended keeping a centralized department, emphasizing the favorable trend revealed by the accounting data. (All numbers are expressed in thousands.)

	1994-95	1995-96	1996-97	1997-98
Tuition revenues:				
Off-campus	$ 300	$ 400	$ 400	$ 410
Evening	—ᵃ	525	907	1,000
Noncredit	135	305	338	375
Total	$ 435	$ 1,230	$ 1,645	$ 1,785

	1994-95	1995-96	1996-97	1997-98
Operating costs:				
Administration	$(132)	$ (160)	$ (112)	$ (112)
Off-campus:				
Direct[b]	(230)	(270)	(270)	(260)
Indirect	(350)	(410)	(525)	(440)
Evening	(—)[a]	(220)	(420)	(525)
Noncredit	(135)	(305)	(338)	(375)
Total	$(847)	$(1,365)	$(1,665)	$(1,712)
Income (loss)	$(412)	$ (135)	$ (20)	$ 73

[a]In 1994-95, the department had no responsibility for evening courses. Beginning in 1995, it was given the responsibility of paying for any costs of instruction incurred when temporary or adjunct faculty were hired to teach evening courses. Tuition revenues earned by evening courses also began to be assigned to the department at the same time.

[b]These are instructional wages.

The dean of the College of Business was unimpressed by the favorable trend identified by the academic vice-president. The dean maintained that decentralization still would be in the best interests of the university. He argued that although decentralization would not fully solve the deficit, it would provide a sizable contribution each year to the operating budgets for each of the seven colleges.

The academic vice-president disagreed vehemently. He was convinced that Continuing Education was now earning its own way and would continue to produce additional resources for the university.

REQUIRED: You have been asked by the president of Central University to assess which alternative, centralization or decentralization, is in the best interest of the school. The president is willing to decentralize provided that significant savings can be produced and the mission of Continuing Education will still be carried out. Prepare a memo to the president that details your analysis and reasoning and recommends one of the two alternatives. Provide both qualitative and quantitative reasoning in the memo.

C16-3
Research Assignment

"Dumping" is an accusation that is often made against foreign companies. Japanese automobile companies, for example, have been accused of this practice.

REQUIRED: Go to the library and find out the following:

1. What is *dumping*?
2. Why do international trade agreements usually prohibit dumping? Do you agree that its prohibition is good for the American consumer? Explain.
3. Explain how the relevant-costing principles learned in this chapter relate to dumping.
4. Provide several examples of companies accused of dumping. See if you can determine the outcome of an accusation made against some company. Why do you suppose that international companies pursue dumping, even though it's prohibited? What are the ethical implications?

1. Explain what a capital investment decision is and distinguish between independent and mutually exclusive capital investment decisions.

2. Compute the payback period and accounting rate of return for a proposed investment and explain their roles in capital investment decisions.

3. Use net present value analysis for capital investment decisions involving independent projects.

4. Use the internal rate of return to assess the acceptability of independent projects.

5. Explain the role and value of postaudits.

6. Explain why NPV is better than IRR for capital investment decisions involving mutually exclusive projects.

7. Convert gross cash flows to after-tax cash flows.

8. Describe capital investment in the advanced manufacturing environment.

CHAPTER

17

Capital Investment Decisions

SCENARIO

TastyFood Corporation, a large food-store chain, is considering investing in an automated deposit processing system for all of its stores.[1] An investment of $2 million would provide the system for all 150 existing stores as well as for the 30 stores to be opened by the beginning of the following year. The president of TastyFood assigned the responsibility of assessing the investment to a special capital acquisitions committee. The first act of the committee was to design a pilot study to test such a system in 7 stores for a period of nine months.

At the end of the nine months, Maryanne Wise, chair of the capital acquisitions committee and vice-president of finance, scheduled a

2. Productivity gains. *Automation of the system reduces the amount of additional payroll required during the busy season.*

3. Forms cost reduction. *Automation of the system eliminates nearly 3 million documents used per year to process deposits manually.*

Near-term Benefits

Reduction of cash shortages. *Once the system is connected to the store computer, a cash variance analysis can be provided the next day. Currently, this analysis is performed manually at headquarters and is several weeks old by the time it arrives in the store. The ability to respond more quickly to cash shortages should reduce annual losses.*

Indirect Benefits

1. Greater data integrity. *By reducing manual calculations, greater data integrity will result. This will decrease time spent on making corrections to incorrect deposit information.*

2. Lower training costs. *Since the system is simpler and has fewer forms, new cashiers and new store openings should require less training time.*

Potential for Future Benefits

Interfacing abilities. *By processing data through the store computer to the host computer at headquarters, an interface program at the host can provide savings in time to both the sales audit and cash/banking calculations by eliminating manual entries and expediting bank reconciliations.*

"After seeing these benefits, I'm convinced that automatic deposits are a good idea," observed Ron Thomas. "In fact,

committee meeting to evaluate the outcome of the pilot study. Besides Maryanne, the committee included Stan Miller, controller; Ron Thomas, vice-president of operations; and Paula Summers, area supervisor for the seven stores where the pilot study was conducted.

"As you recall," Maryanne remarked, "we met more than nine months ago and agreed to implement a pilot study before committing ourselves to an automated deposit system. Because of her close scrutiny of the project, Paula has agreed to give us a summary of the benefits observed in the pilot study."

"I'm extremely pleased with the results of the pilot study," Paula replied, "as I think you will be. To quantify the financial impact of this project, I have classified the benefits into four categories: immediate, near term, indirect, and potential for

future. Immediate benefits are those that are available in a store as soon as the equipment is operational. Near-term benefits are those that will be realized only after the local system is connected to the store computer. Indirect benefits are those that accrue from the project but are more difficult to quantify. Potential future benefits can result from the ability of the system to interface directly with the accounting system. Here is a handout that describes some of the specific benefits found in each category."

SPECIFIC BENEFITS BY CATEGORY

Immediate Benefits

1. Bank charge reduction. *An automated deposit processing system reduces the charges for processing checks since it encodes the dollar amount on all checks prior to depositing them.*

I wonder why we weren't smart enough to do this years ago. Since I'm also convinced that committees are notorious for wasting time and resources, I move that we attach Paula's handout to a recommendation to implement the automated system for the entire company. Then we can get back to more pressing matters."

"Wait a minute!" interjected Stan. "While the description of the benefits of the automated system is impressive, we shouldn't be too hasty in our decisions. After all, we are talking about investing $2 million. We need to be certain that this is a sound investment."

"But that's the whole point, Stan. The benefits make it clear that the investment is sound. Why waste any more time deliberating over an obvious conclusion? We could spend hours discussing a matter that is already clearly

decided. What do you say, Maryanne? Can we vote on this matter and adjourn?"

"Well, Ron, we can—if you will first answer the following questions. How much will this investment increase the profits of the firm? What effect will it have on our overall value? Will the investment earn at least the return required by company policy? How long will it take for us to recover the investment through the savings alluded to in Paula's handout? Only when we know the answers to some of those questions can we accurately assess the soundness of the investment. The pilot study provides us with the fundamental information we need to estimate the future cash savings associated with automation. Once we have these estimates, we can use some financial models to assess the merits of the proposed investment. Stan, for our next

meeting, please bring estimates of the cash flows over the life of the proposed system. I will come prepared to discuss some of the financial models that will help us assess the financial merits of the investment."

1. The facts of this case are based on an actual food-store chain; however, the name of the chain has been changed.

Questions to Think About

1. What role should qualitative factors play in capital budgeting decisions?
2. How do we measure the financial benefits of long-term investments?
3. Why are cash flows important for assessing the financial merits of an investment?
4. What role do taxes play in assessing cash flows? What role does inflation play?
5. Should the cash flows of intangible factors be estimated?

Organizations are often faced with the opportunity (or need) to invest in assets or projects that represent long-term commitments. New production systems, new plants, new equipment, and new product development are examples of assets and projects that fit this category. Usually, many alternatives are available. For example, an organization may be faced with the decision whether to invest or not invest in a new plant, or whether to invest in a flexible manufacturing system or continue with an existing traditional manufacturing system. These long-range decisions are examples of *capital investment decisions*. The acquisition of long-term assets usually involves a significant outlay of funds, often referred to as *capital outlays*. Estimating a project's cash flows and using them to assess the project's soundness are critical steps in a capital investment decision. How cash flows can be used to evaluate the merits of a proposed project is the focus of this chapter. We will study four financial models that are useful in capital investment analysis: the payback period, the accounting rate of return, the net present value, and the internal rate of return.

TYPES OF CAPITAL INVESTMENT DECISIONS

Objective 1

Explain what a capital investment decision is and distinguish between independent and mutually exclusive capital investment decisions.

capital investment decisions

Capital investment decisions are concerned with the process of planning, setting goals and priorities, arranging financing, and using certain criteria to select long-term assets. Because capital investment decisions place large amounts of resources at risk for long periods of time and simultaneously affect the future development of the firm, they are among the most important decisions managers make. Every organization has limited resources, which should be used to maintain or enhance its long-run profitability. Poor capital investment decisions can be disastrous. For example, a failure to invest in automated manufacturing when other competitors do so may result in significant losses in market share because of the inability to compete on the basis of quality, cost, and delivery time. Competitors with more modern facilities may produce more output at lower cost and higher quality. Thus, making the right capital investment decisions is absolutely essential for long-term survival.

capital budgeting

independent projects

The process of making capital investment decisions is often referred to as capital budgeting. Two types of capital budgeting projects will be considered. Independent projects are projects that, if accepted or rejected, do not affect the cash flows of other projects. Suppose that the managers of the marketing and the research and development departments jointly propose the addition of a new product line that would entail making significant outlays for working capital and equipment. General Motor's decision to build a new plant for the production of the Saturn line, and Toyota's decision to build a new plant in Georgetown, Kentucky, are examples of independent capital investment decisions.

mutually exclusive projects

The second type of capital budgeting project requires a firm to choose among competing alternatives that provide the same basic service. Acceptance of one option precludes the acceptance of another. Thus, mutually exclusive projects are those projects that, if accepted, preclude the acceptance of all other competing projects. For example, in 1985 Monsanto's Fibers Division decided to automate its Pensacola, Florida, plant. At some point in time, Monsanto was faced with the choice of continuing with its existing manual production operation or replacing it with an automated system. In all likelihood, part of the company's deliberation concerned different types of automated systems. If three different automated systems were being considered, this would produce four alternatives—the current system plus the three potential new systems. Once one system is chosen, the other three are excluded; they are mutually exclusive.

Notice that one of the competing alternatives in the example is that of maintaining the status quo (the manual system). This emphasizes the fact that new investments that replace existing investments must prove to be economically superior. Of course, at times replacement of the old system is mandatory and not discretionary if the firm wishes to remain in business (for example, equipment in the old system may be worn out, making the old system not a viable alternative). In such a situation, going out of business could be a viable alternative, especially if none of the new investment alternatives is profitable.

Capital investment decisions often are concerned with investments in long-term capital assets. With the exception of land, these assets depreciate over their lives, and the original investment is used up as the assets are employed. In general terms, a sound capital investment will earn back its original capital outlay over its life and, at the same time, provide a reasonable return on the original investment. Thus, one task of a manager is to decide whether or not a capital investment will earn back its original outlay and provide a reasonable return. By making this assessment, a manager can decide on the acceptability of independent projects and compare competing projects on the basis of their economic merits.

But what is meant by reasonable return? It is generally agreed that any new project must cover the opportunity cost of the funds invested. For example, if a company takes money from a money market fund that is earning 6 percent and invests it in a new project, then the project must provide at least a 6 percent return (the return that could have been earned had the money been left in the money market fund). Of course, in reality, funds for investment often come from different sources—each representing a different opportunity cost. The return that must be earned is a blend of the opportunity costs of the different sources. Thus, if a company uses two sources of funds, one with an opportunity cost of 4 percent and the other with an opportunity cost of 6 percent, then the return that must be earned is somewhere between 4 percent and 6 percent, depending on the relative amounts used from each source. Furthermore, it is usually assumed that managers should select projects that promise to maximize the wealth of the owners of the firm.

To make a capital investment decision, a manager must estimate the quantity and timing of cash flows, assess the risk of the investment, and consider the impact of the project on the firm's profits. One of the most difficult tasks is to estimate the cash flows. Projections must be made years into the future, and forecasting is far from a perfect science. Obviously, as the accuracy of cash-flow forecasts increases, the reliability of the decision improves. In making projections, managers must identify and quantify the benefits associated with the proposed project(s). For example, an automated cash deposit system can produce the following benefits (relative to a manual system): bank charge reductions, productivity gains, forms cost reduction, greater data integrity, lower training costs, and savings in time required to audit and do bank/cash reconciliations. The dollar value of these benefits must be assessed. Although forecasting future cash flows is a critical part of the capital investment process, forecasting methods will not be considered here. Consequently, cash flows are assumed to be known; the focus will be on making capital investment decisions *given* these cash flows.

Managers must set goals and priorities for capital investments. They also must identify some basic criteria for the acceptance or rejection of proposed investments. In this chapter, we will study four basic methods to guide managers in accepting or rejecting potential investments. The methods include both nondiscounting and discounting decision approaches (two methods are discussed for each approach). The discounting methods are applied to investment decisions involving both independent and mutually exclusive projects.

NONDISCOUNTING MODELS

Objective 2

Compute the payback period and accounting rate of return for a proposed investment and explain their roles in capital investment decisions.

nondiscounting models
discounting models

The basic capital investment decision models can be classified into two major categories: nondiscounting models and discounting models. Nondiscounting models ignore the time value of money, whereas discounting models explicitly consider it. Although many accounting theorists disparage the nondiscounting models because they ignore the time value of money, many firms continue to use these models in making capital investment decisions. However, the use of discounting models has increased over the years, and few firms use only one model—indeed, firms seem to use both types.[2] This suggests that both categories supply useful information to managers as they struggle to make a capital investment decision.

Payback Period

payback period

One type of nondiscounting model is the payback period. The payback period is the time required for a firm to recover its original investment. For example, assume that a

---

2. In the mid-1950s, Robichek and McDonald reported that only 9 percent of large firms were using discounting models; by 1975, Petry reported that 66 percent of large firms were using these techniques. Also in 1975, Petty, Scott, and Bird surveyed Fortune 500 firms and found that 63.4 percent of the respondents used discounting models as their primary evaluation techniques, with most of the remaining firms using them as secondary techniques. The same study also found that more than half of the firms used nondiscounting models as either a primary or a secondary evaluation technique. By 1988, Klammer, Koch, and Wilner reported that discounting models were used by over 80 percent of the firms as the primary evaluation technique for expansion decisions. For additional detail, see A. A. Robichek and J. G. McDonald, "Financial Planning in Transition, Long Range Planning Service," Report no. 268 (Menlo Park, Calif.: Stanford Research Institute, January 1966); G. H. Petry, "Effective Use of Capital Budgeting Tools," *Business Horizons*, vol. 18, no. 5 (October 1975): 57–65; J. W. Petty, D. F. Scott, and M. M. Bird, "The Capital Budgeting Decision Making Process of Large Corporations," *The Engineering Economist*, vol. 20, no. 3 (Spring 1975): 159–186; T. Klammer, B. Koch, and N. Wilner, "Capital Budgeting Practices—A Survey of Corporate Use," working paper, University of North Texas.

dentist invests in a new set of drilling equipment costing $80,000. The cash flow (cash inflows less cash outflows) generated by the equipment is $40,000 per year. Thus, the payback period is two years ($\frac{\$80,000}{\$40,000}$). When the cash flows of a project are assumed to be even, the following formula can be used to compute its payback period:

$$\text{Payback period} = \frac{\text{Original investment}}{\text{Annual cash flow}}$$

If, however, the cash flows are uneven, the payback period is computed by adding the annual cash flows until such time as the original investment is recovered. If a fraction of a year is needed, it is assumed that cash flows occur evenly within each year. For example, suppose that a new car wash facility requires an investment of $100,000 and has a life of five years with the following expected annual cash flows: $30,000, $40,000, $50,000, $60,000, and $70,000. The payback period for the project is 2.6 years, computed as follows: $30,000 (1 year) + $40,000 (1 year) + $30,000 (0.6 year). In the third year, when only $30,000 is needed and $50,000 is available, the amount of time required to earn the $30,000 is found by dividing the amount needed by the annual cash flow ($\frac{\$30,000}{\$50,000}$). Exhibit 17-1 summarizes this analysis.

One way to use the payback period is to set a maximum payback period for all projects and to reject any project that exceeds this level. Why would a firm use the payback period in this way? Some analysts suggest that the payback period can be used as a rough measure of risk, with the notion that the longer it takes for a project to pay for itself, the riskier it is. Also, firms with riskier cash flows could require a shorter payback period than normal. Additionally, firms with liquidity problems would be more interested in projects with quick paybacks. Another critical concern is obsolescence. In some industries, the risk of obsolescence is high; firms within these industries would be interested in recovering funds rapidly.

Another reason, less beneficial to the firm, may also be at work. Many managers in a position to make capital investment decisions may choose investments with quick payback periods out of self-interest. If a manager's performance is measured using such short-run criteria as annual net income, he or she may choose projects with quick paybacks to show improved net income as quickly as possible. Consider that divisional managers often are responsible for making capital investment decisions and are evaluated on divisional profit. The tenure of divisional managers, however, is typically short—three to five years would be average. Consequently, the incentive is for such managers to shy away from investments that promise healthy long-run returns but relatively meager returns in the short run. These problems can be eliminated by corporate budgeting policies and a budget review committee.

The payback period can be used to choose among competing alternatives. Under this approach, the investment with the shortest payback period is preferred over investments with longer payback periods. However, this use of the payback period is less defensible because this measure suffers from two major deficiencies: (1) it ignores the performance of the investments beyond the payback period and (2) it ignores the time value of money.

17-1

Exhibit
Payback Analysis: Uneven Cash Flows

Year	Unrecovered Investment (beginning of year)	Annual Cash Flow
1	$100,000	$30,000
2	70,000	40,000
3	30,000*	50,000
4	—	60,000
5	—	70,000

*At the beginning of year 3, $30,000 is needed to recover the investment. Since a net cash inflow of $50,000 is expected, only 0.6 year ($\frac{\$30,000}{\$50,000}$) is needed to recover the $30,000. Thus, the payback is 2.6 years (2 + 0.6).

These two significant deficiencies are easily illustrated. Assume that an engineering firm is considering two different types of CAD systems—CAD-A and CAD-B. Each system requires an initial outlay of $150,000, has a five-year life, and displays the following annual cash flows:

Investment	Year 1	Year 2	Year 3	Year 4	Year 5
CAD-A	$90,000	$ 60,000	$50,000	$50,000	$50,000
CAD-B	40,000	110,000	25,000	25,000	25,000

Both investments have payback periods of two years. Thus, if a manager uses the payback period to choose among competing investments, the two investments would be equally desirable. In reality, however, the CAD-A system should be preferred over the CAD-B system B for two reasons. First, the CAD-A system provides a much larger dollar return for the years beyond the payback period ($150,000 versus $75,000). Second, the CAD-A system returns $90,000 in the first year while B returns only $40,000. The extra $50,000 that the CAD-A system provides in the first year could be put to productive use, such as investing it in another project. It is better to have a dollar now than one year from now because the dollar on hand can be invested to provide a return one year from now.

In summary, the payback period provides to managers information that can be used as follows:

1. To help control the risks associated with the uncertainty of future cash flows
2. To help minimize the impact of an investment on a firm's liquidity problems
3. To help control the risk of obsolescence
4. To help control the effect of the investment on performance measures

However, the method suffers significant deficiencies: it ignores a project's total profitability and the time value of money. While the computation of the payback period may be useful to a manager, to rely on it solely for a capital investment decision would be foolish.

Accounting Rate of Return

accounting rate of return

The accounting rate of return is the second commonly used nondiscounting model. The accounting rate of return measures the return on a project in terms of income, as opposed to using a project's cash flow. The accounting rate of return is computed by the following formula:

$$\text{Accounting rate of return} = \frac{\text{Average income}}{\text{Original investment or average investment}}$$

(handwritten annotations: Ignores time-value of money discounted proj. profitability)

(handwritten annotation right: = Total net income for x # yrs / Total yrs)

Income is not equivalent to cash flows because of accruals and deferrals used in its computation. The average income of a project is obtained by adding the net income for each year of the project and then dividing this total by the number of years. Average net income for a project can be approximated by subtracting average depreciation from average cash flow. Assuming that all revenues earned in a period are collected and that depreciation is the only noncash expense, the approximation is exact.

Investment can be defined as the original investment or as the average investment. Letting I equal original investment, S equal salvage value, and assuming that investment is uniformly consumed, average investment is defined as follows:[3]

$$\text{Average investment} = \frac{I + S}{2}$$

(handwritten annotations: avg. net Income = Avg Cash flow − avg. Deprec ; Investment + Salvage Value)

To illustrate the computation of the accounting rate of return, assume that an investment requires an initial outlay of $100,000. The life of the investment is five years with the following cash flows: $30,000, $30,000, $40,000, $30,000, $50,000. Assume that the asset has no salvage value after the five years and that all revenues earned within a year are collected in that year. The total cash flow for the five years is $180,000, making the average cash flow $36,000 ($\frac{\$180,000}{5}$). Average depreciation is $20,000 ($\frac{\$100,000}{5}$). The average net income is the difference between these two figures: $16,000 ($36,000 − $20,000). Using the average net income and original investment, the accounting rate of return is 16 percent ($\frac{\$16,000}{\$100,000}$). If average investment is used instead of original investment, then the accounting rate of return would be 32 percent ($\frac{\$16,000}{\$50,000}$).

Often debt contracts require that a firm maintain certain financial accounting ratios, which can be affected by the income reported and by the level of long-term assets. Accordingly, the accounting rate of return may be used as a screening measure to ensure that any new investment will not adversely affect these ratios. Additionally, because bonuses to managers are often based on accounting income or return on assets, they may have a personal interest in seeing that any new investment contributes significantly to net income. A manager seeking to maximize personal income will select investments that return the highest net income per dollar invested.

Unlike the payback period, the accounting rate of return does consider a project's profitability; like the payback period, it ignores the time value of money. Ignoring the time value of money is a critical deficiency in this method as well; it can lead a manager to choose investments that do not maximize profits. It is because the payback period and the accounting rate of return ignore the time value of money that they are referred to as *nondiscounting models*. Discounting models use discounted cash flows, which are future cash flows expressed in terms of their present value. The use of discounting models requires an understanding of the present value concepts. Present value concepts are reviewed in Appendix A. You should review these concepts and make sure that you understand them before studying capital investment discount models. Present value tables (Exhibits 17B-1 and 17B-2) are presented in Appendix B at the end of this chapter. These tables are referred to and used throughout the rest of the chapter.

discounted cash flows

---

3. The average investment formula is computed using the definition of the average value of a function and requires the use of calculus.

DISCOUNTING MODELS: THE NET PRESENT VALUE METHOD

Objective 3

Use net present value analysis for capital investment decisions involving independent projects.

Discounting models explicitly consider the time value of money and, therefore, incorporate the concept of discounting cash inflows and outflows. Two discounting models will be considered: *net present value* (NPV) and *internal rate of return* (IRR). The net present value method will be discussed first; the internal rate of return method is discussed in the following section.

NPV Defined

net present value

Net present value is the difference between the present value of the cash inflows and outflows associated with a project:

$$NPV = \left[\frac{\Sigma CF_t}{(1+i)^t}\right] - I$$

$$= [\Sigma(CF_t)(df_t)] - I$$

$$= P - I$$

(17.1)

where I = The present value of the project's cost (usually the initial outlay)

　　CF_t = The cash inflow to be received in period t, with $t = 1 \ldots n$.

　　n = The useful life of the project

　　i = The required rate of return

　　t = The time period

　　P = The present value of the project's future cash inflows

　　$df_t = \frac{1}{(1+i)^t}$, the discount factor

Net present value (NPV) measures the profitability of an investment. If the NPV is positive, it measures the increase in wealth. For a firm, this means that the size of a positive NPV measures the increase in the value of the firm resulting from an investment. To use the NPV method, a required rate of return must be defined. The required rate of

required rate of return

return is the minimum acceptable rate of return. It is also referred to as the *discount rate*, the *hurdle rate*, and the *cost of capital*.

If the net present value is positive, it signals that (1) the initial investment has been recovered, (2) the required rate of return has been recovered, and (3) a return in excess of (1) and (2) has been received. Thus, if NPV is greater than zero, the investment is profitable and therefore is acceptable. If NPV equals zero, the decision maker will find acceptance or rejection of the investment equal. Finally, if NPV is less than zero, the investment should be rejected. In this case, it is earning less than the required rate of return.

An Example Illustrating Net Present Value

Brannon Company has developed new earphones for portable CD and tape players that it believes is superior to anything on the market. The marketing manager is excited about the new product's prospects after completing a detailed market study that revealed expected annual revenues of $300,000. The earphones have a projected product life cycle of five years. Equipment to produce the earphones would cost $320,000. After five years, that equipment can be sold for $40,000. In addition to equipment, working capital is expected to increase by $40,000 because of increases in inventories and receivables. The firm expects to recover the investment in working capital at the end of the project's life. Annual cash operating expenses are estimated at $180,000. Assuming that the required rate of return is 12 percent, should the company manufacture the new earphones?

In order to answer the question, two steps must be taken: (1) the cash flows for each year must be identified and (2) the NPV must be computed using the cash flows from step 1. The solution to the problem is given in Exhibit 17-2. Notice that step 2 offers two approaches for computing NPV. Step 2A computes NPV by using discount factors

17-2

Exhibit
Cash Flows and NPV
Analysis

Step 1. Cash-Flow Identification		
Year	Item	Cash Flow
0	Equipment	$(320,000)
	Working capital	(40,000)
	Total	$(360,000)
1–4	Revenues	$ 300,000
	Operating expenses	(180,000)
	Total	$ 120,000
5	Revenues	$ 300,000
	Operating expenses	(180,000)
	Salvage	40,000
	Recovery of working capital	40,000
	Total	$ 200,000

Step 2A. NPV Analysis			
Year	Cash Flow[a]	Discount Factor[b]	Present Value
0	$(360,000)	1.000	$(360,000)
1	$120,000	0.893	107,160
2	120,000	0.797	95,640
3	120,000	0.712	85,440
4	120,000	0.636	76,320
5	200,000	0.567	113,400
Net present value			$ 117,960

Step 2B. NPV Analysis			
Year	Cash Flow	Discount Factor	Present Value
0	$(360,000)	1.000	$(360,000)
1–4	120,000	3.037	364,440
5	200,000	0.567	113,400
Net present value			$ 117,840[c]

[a]From step 1
[b]From Exhibit 17B-1
[c]This differs from the computation in step 2A because of rounding.

from Exhibit 17B-1. Step 2B simplifies the computation by using a single discount factor from Exhibit 17B-2, for the even cash flows occurring in years 1 through 4.

INTERNAL RATE OF RETURN   *most widely used*

Objective 4
Use the internal rate of return to assess the acceptability of independent projects.
internal rate of return

Another discounting model is the internal rate of return (IRR) method. The internal rate of return is defined as the interest rate that sets the present value of a project's cash inflows equal to the present value of the project's cost. In other words, it is the interest rate that sets the project's NPV at zero. The following equation can be used to determine a project's IRR:

$$I = \frac{\Sigma CF_t}{(1 + i)^t} \qquad (17.2)$$

where $t = 1 \ldots n$

The right-hand side of equation 17.2 is the present value of future cash flows and the left-hand side is the investment. I, CF_t, and t are known. Thus, the IRR (the interest rate, i, in the equation) can be found using trial and error. Once the IRR for a project is computed, it is compared with the firm's required rate of return. If the IRR is greater than the required rate, the project is deemed acceptable; if the IRR is equal to the required rate of return, acceptance or rejection of the investment is equal; if the IRR is less than the required rate of return, the project is rejected.

The internal rate of return is the most widely used of the capital investment techniques. One reason for its popularity may be that it is a rate of return, a concept that managers are comfortable with using. Another possibility is that managers may believe (in most cases, incorrectly) that the IRR is the true or actual compounded rate of return being earned by the initial investment. Whatever the reasons for its popularity, a basic understanding of the IRR is necessary.

Example: Multiple-Period Setting with Uniform Cash Flows

To illustrate the computation of the IRR in a multiple-period setting, assume that a hospital has the opportunity to invest $120,000 in a new ultrasound system that will produce net cash inflows of $49,950 at the end of each year for the next three years. The IRR is the interest rate that equates the present value of the three equal receipts of $49,950 to the investment of $120,000. Since the series of cash flows is uniform, a single discount factor from Exhibit 17B-2 can be used to compute the present value of the annuity. Letting df be this discount factor and CF be the annual cash flow, equation 17.2 assumes the following form:

$$I = CF(df)$$

Solving for df, we obtain:

$$df = \frac{I}{CF}$$

$$= \frac{\text{Investment}}{\text{Annual cash flow}}$$

Once the discount factor is computed, go to Exhibit 17B-2 and find the row corresponding to the life of the project, then move across that row until the computed discount factor is found. The interest rate corresponding to this discount factor is the IRR.

For example, the discount factor for the hospital's investment is 2.402 $\left(\frac{\$120,000}{\$49,950}\right)$. Since the life of the investment is three years, we must find the third row in Exhibit 17B-2 and then move across this row until we encounter 2.402. The interest rate corresponding to 2.402 is 12 percent, which is the IRR.

Exhibit 17B-2 does not provide discount factors for every possible interest rate. To illustrate, assume that the annual cash inflows expected by the hospital are $51,000 instead of $49,950. The new discount factor is 2.353 $\left(\frac{\$120,000}{\$51,000}\right)$. Going once again to the third row in Exhibit 17B-2, we find that the discount factor—and thus the IRR—lies between 12 and 14 percent. It is possible to approximate the IRR by interpolation (interpolation approximates the actual IRR by assuming that the IRR is the same proportionate distance between 12 percent and 14 percent as the actual discount factor of 2.353 is between the tabled discount factors); however, for our purposes, we will simply identify the range for the IRR as indicated by the tabled values.

Multiple-Period Setting: Uneven Cash Flows

If the cash flows are not uniform, then equation 17.2 must be used. For a multiple-period setting, equation 17.2 can be solved by trial and error or by using a business calculator or a software package like Lotus 1-2-3. To illustrate solution by trial and error, assume that a $10,000 investment in a PC system produces clerical savings of

$6,000 and $7,200 for each of two years. The IRR is the interest rate that sets the present value of these two cash inflows equal to $10,000:

$$P = \left[\frac{\$6,000}{(1 + i)}\right] + \left[\frac{\$7,200}{(1 + i)^2}\right]$$
$$= \$10,000$$

To solve this equation by trial and error, start by selecting a possible value for i. Given this first guess, the present value of the future cash flows is computed and then compared with the initial investment. If the present value is greater than the initial investment, the interest rate is too low; if the present value is less than the initial investment, the interest rate is too high. The next guess is adjusted accordingly.

Assume the first guess is 18 percent. Using i equal to 0.18, Exhibit 17B-1 yields the following discount factors: 0.847 and 0.718. These discount factors produce the following present value for the two cash inflows:

$$P = (0.847 \times \$6,000) + (0.718 \times \$7,200)$$
$$= \$10,252$$

Since P is greater than $10,000, the interest rate selected is too low. A higher guess is needed. If the next guess is 20 percent, we obtain the following:

$$P = (0.833 \times \$6,000) + (0.694 \times \$7,200)$$
$$= \$9,995$$

Since this value is reasonably close to $10,000, we can say that the IRR is 20 percent. (The IRR is, in fact, exactly 20 percent; the present value is slightly less than the investment because of rounding error in the discount factors found in Exhibit 17B-1.)

POSTAUDIT OF CAPITAL PROJECTS

Objective 5
Explain the role and value of postaudits.
postaudit

A key element in the capital investment process is a follow-up analysis of a capital project once it is implemented. This analysis is called a *postaudit*. A postaudit compares the actual benefits with the estimated benefits and actual operating costs with estimated operating costs; it evaluates the overall outcome of the investment and proposes corrective action if any is needed. The following real-world case illustrates the usefulness of a postaudit activity.

Honley Medical Company: An Illustrative Application

Allen Manesfield and Jenny Winters were discussing a persistent and irritating problem present in the process of producing intravenous needles (IVs). Both Allen and Jenny are employed by Honley Medical, which specializes in the production of medical products and has three divisions: the IV Products Division, the Critical Care Monitoring Division, and the Specialty Products Division. Allen and Jenny both are associated with the IV Products Division—Allen as the senior production engineer and Jenny as the marketing manager.

The IV Products Division produces needles of five different sizes. During one stage of the manufacturing process, the needle itself is inserted into a plastic hub and bonded using epoxy glue. According to Jenny the use of epoxy to bond the needles was causing the division all kinds of problems. In many cases, the epoxy wasn't bonding correctly. The rejects were high, and the division was receiving a large number of complaints from its customers. Corrective action was needed to avoid losing sales. After some discussion and analysis, a recommendation was made to use induction welding in lieu of epoxy bonding. In induction welding, the needles are inserted into the plastic hub, and an RF generator is used to heat the needles. The RF generator works on the same principle as a microwave oven. As the needles get hot, the plastic melts and the needles are bonded.

Switching to induction welding required an investment in RF generators and the associated tooling; the investment was justified by the IV Division based on the savings associated with the new system. Induction welding promised to reduce the cost of direct materials, eliminating the need to buy and use epoxy. Savings of direct labor costs were also predicted because the welding process is much more automated. Adding to these savings were the avoidance of daily clean-up costs and the reduction in rejects. Allen presented a formal NPV analysis showing that the welding system was superior to the epoxy system. Its purchase was approved by headquarters.

One Year Later

"Allen," said Jenny Winters, "I'm quite pleased with induction welding for bonding needles. In the year since the new process was implemented, we've had virtually no complaints from our customers. The needles are firmly bonded."

"I wish that positive experience were true for all other areas as well. Unfortunately, implementing the process has uncovered some rather sticky and expensive problems that I simply didn't anticipate. The Internal Audit Department recently completed a postaudit of the project, and now my feet are being held to the fire."

"That's too bad," Jenny sympathized. "What's the problem?"

"You mean problems. Let me list a few for you. One is that the RF generators interfered with the operation of other equipment. To eliminate this interference, we had to install filtering equipment. But that's not all. We also discovered that the average maintenance person doesn't know how to maintain the new equipment. Now we are faced with the need to initiate a training program to upgrade the skills of our maintenance people. Upgrading skills also implies higher wages. Although the RF bonding process is less messy, it is also more complex. The manufacturing people complained to the internal auditors about that. They maintain that a simple process, even if messy, is to be preferred—especially now that demand for the product is increasing by leaps and bounds."

"What did the internal auditors conclude?"

"They observed that many of the predicted savings did take place, but that some significant costs were not foreseen. Because of some of the unforeseen problems, they have recommended that I look carefully at the possibility of moving back to using epoxy. They indicated that NPV analysis using actual data appears to favor that process. With production expanding, the acquisition of additional RF generators and filtering equipment plus the necessary training is simply not as attractive as returning to epoxy bonding. This conclusion is reinforced by the fact that the epoxy process is simpler and by the auditors' conclusion that the mixing of the epoxy can be automated, avoiding the quality problem we had in the first place."

"Well, Allen," Jenny observed, "you can't really blame yourself. You had a real problem and took action to solve it. It's difficult to foresee all the problems and hidden costs of a new process."

"Unfortunately, the internal auditors don't totally agree. In fact, neither do I. I probably jumped too quickly. In the future, I intend to think through new projects more carefully."

Benefits of a Postaudit

In the case of the RF bonding decision, some of the estimated capital investment benefits did materialize: complaints from customers decreased, rejects were fewer, and direct labor and materials costs decreased. However, the investment was greater than expected because filtering equipment was needed, and actual operating costs were much higher because of the increased maintenance cost and the increased complexity of the process. Overall, the internal auditors concluded that the investment was a poor decision. The corrective action they recommended was to abandon the new process and return to epoxy bonding.[4]

Firms that perform postaudits of capital projects experience a number of benefits. First, by evaluating profitability, postaudits ensure that resources are used wisely. If the project is doing well, it may call for additional funds and additional attention. If the project is not doing well, corrective action may be needed to improve performance or abandon the project.

A second benefit of the postaudit is its impact on the behavior of managers. If managers are held accountable for the results of a capital investment decision, they are more likely to make such decisions in the best interests of the firm. Additionally, postaudits supply feedback to managers that should help improve future decision making. Consider Allen's reaction to the postaudit of the RF bonding process. Certainly, we would expect him to be more careful and more thorough in making future investment recommendations. In the future, Allen will probably consider more than one alternative, such as automating the mixing of the epoxy. Also, for those alternatives being considered, he will probably be especially alert to the possibility of hidden costs, such as increased training requirements for a new process.

The case also reveals that the postaudit was performed by the internal audit staff. Generally, more objective results are obtainable if the postaudit is done by an independent party. Since considerable effort is expended to ensure as much independence as possible for the internal audit staff, that group is usually the best choice for this task.

Postaudits, however, are costly. Moreover, even though they may provide significant benefits, they have other limitations. Most obvious is the fact that the assumptions driving the original analysis may often be invalidated by changes in the actual operating environment. Accountability must be qualified to some extent by the impossibility of foreseeing every possible eventuality.

MUTUALLY EXCLUSIVE PROJECTS

Objective 6

Explain why NPV is better than IRR for capital investment decisions involving mutually exclusive projects.

Up to this point, we have focused on independent projects. Many capital investment decisions deal with mutually exclusive projects. How NPV analysis and IRR are used to choose among competing projects is an interesting question. An even more interesting question to consider is whether NPV and IRR differ in their ability to help managers make wealth-maximizing decisions in the presence of competing alternatives. For example, we already know that the nondiscounting models can produce erroneous choices because they ignore the time value of money. Because of this deficiency, the discounting models are judged superior. Similarly, it can be shown that the NPV model is generally preferred to the IRR model when choosing among mutually exclusive alternatives.

NPV Compared with IRR

NPV and IRR both yield the same decision for independent projects; for example, if the NPV is greater than zero, then the IRR is also greater than the required rate of return; both models signal the correct decision. However, for competing projects, the two methods can produce different results. Intuitively, we believe that, for mutually exclusive projects, the project with the highest NPV or the highest IRR should be chosen. Since it is possible for the two methods to produce different rankings of mutually exclusive projects, the method that consistently reveals the wealth-maximizing project is preferred.

NPV differs from IRR in two major ways. First, NPV assumes that each cash inflow received is reinvested at the required rate of return, whereas the IRR method assumes

---

4. The firm whose experience is described in the case did abandon inductive welding and return to epoxy bonding, which was improved by automating the mixing. The simplicity of the epoxy process was a major qualitative factor in deciding to return to the old, but improved, process.

that each cash inflow is reinvested at the computed IRR. Reinvesting at the required rate of return is more realistic and produces more reliable results when comparing mutually exclusive projects. Second, the NPV method measures profitability in absolute terms, whereas the IRR method measures it in relative terms. NPV measures the amount by which the value of the firm changes.

Since NPV measures the impact competing projects have on the value of the firm, choosing the project with the largest NPV is consistent with maximizing the wealth of shareholders. On the other hand, IRR does not consistently result in choices that maximize wealth. IRR, as a relative measure of profitability, has the virtue of measuring accurately the rate of return of funds that remain internally invested. However, maximizing IRR will not necessarily maximize the wealth of firm owners because it cannot, by nature, consider the absolute dollar contributions of projects. In the final analysis, what counts are the total dollars earned—the absolute profits—not the relative profits. Accordingly, NPV, not IRR, should be used for choosing among competing, mutually exclusive projects, or competing projects when capital funds are limited.

An independent project is acceptable if its NPV is positive. For mutually exclusive projects, the project with the largest NPV is chosen. There are three steps in selecting the best project from several competing projects: (1) assessing the cash-flow pattern for each project, (2) computing the NPV for each project, and (3) identifying the project with the greatest NPV. To illustrate NPV analysis for competing projects, an example is provided.

Example: Mutually Exclusive Projects

Hintley Games Corporation has decided to market a game that will allow players to display and develop their knowledge of the geography of the United States. Given the recent interest in trivia games, the company is certain that the product will prove successful. The marketing department has selected *Travel USA* as the name of the game. Two different board designs are being considered. Design B is more elaborate than design A and will require a heavier investment and greater annual operating costs; however, it will also generate greater annual revenues. The projected annual revenues, annual costs, capital outlays, and project life for each design (in after-tax cash flows) follow:

	Design A	Design B
Annual revenues	$179,460	$239,280
Annual operating costs	119,460	169,280
Equipment (purchased before year 1)	180,000	210,000
Project life	5 years	5 years

The firm must decide which design to choose. Assume that the cost of capital for the company is 12 percent.

Design A requires an initial outlay of $180,000 and has a net annual cash inflow of $60,000 (revenues of $179,460 minus costs of $119,460). Design B, with an initial outlay of $210,000, has a net annual cash inflow of $70,000 ($239,280 − $169,280). With this information, the cash-flow pattern for each project can be described and the NPV computed. These are shown in Exhibit 17-3. Based on NPV analysis, design B is more profitable; it has the larger NPV. Accordingly, the company should select design B over design A.

Interestingly, designs A and B have identical internal rates of return. As Exhibit 17-3 illustrates, both designs have a discount factor of 3.000. From Exhibit 17B-2, it is easily seen that a discount factor of 3.000 and a life of five years yields an IRR of about 20 percent. Even though both projects have an IRR of 20 percent, the firm should not consider the two designs equally desirable. The analysis demonstrates that design B produces a larger NPV and, therefore, will increase the value of the firm more than

Exhibit
Cash-Flow Pattern and
NPV Analysis: Designs
A and B

Cash-Flow Pattern		
Year	Design A	Design B
0	$(180,000)	$(210,000)
1	60,000	70,000
2	60,000	70,000
3	60,000	70,000
4	60,000	70,000
5	60,000	70,000

Design A: NPV Analysis			
Year	Cash Flow	Discount Factor*	Present Value
0	$(180,000)	1.000	$(180,000)
1–5	60,000	3.605	216,300
	Net present value		$ 36,300

IRR Analysis

$$\text{Discount factor} = \frac{\text{Initial investment}}{\text{Annual cash flow}}$$

$$= \frac{\$180,000}{60,000}$$

$$= 3.000$$

From Exhibit 17B-2, df = 3.000 for five years implies that IRR = 20%

Design B: NPV Analysis			
Year	Cash Flow	Discount Factor*	Present Value
0	$(210,000)	1.000	$(210,000)
1–5	70,000	3.605	252,350
	Net present value		$ 42,350

IRR Analysis

$$\text{Discount factor} = \frac{\text{Initial investment}}{\text{Annual cash flow}}$$

$$= \frac{\$210,000}{70,000}$$

$$= 3.000$$

From Exhibit 17B-2, df = 3.000 for five years implies that IRR = 20%

*From Exhibit 17B-2

design A. Design B should be chosen. This illustrates the conceptual superiority of NPV over IRR for analysis of competing projects.

Capital Investment and Ethical Issues

Capital investment decisions often offer great temptations for misrepresentations. Divisional managers often must compete for scarce capital resources. With this competition comes the temptation to engage in deceptive behavior. Examples of such behavior are numerous. Managers have been guilty of deliberately overestimating cash inflows and underestimating cash outlays so that a pet project might have the NPV or IRR necessary to be approved. This is particularly tempting when the early cash flows are expected to be good, followed by poor cash flows. Adjusting the estimates of the poor cash flows upward may produce an approved project that has good performance in the early years and poor performance in later years. Other possibilities also exist. For example, a manager may need approval for any capital expenditure above a certain level. To obtain this approval, evidence must exist that the project will produce a positive NPV or an acceptable IRR. In one of a series of IMA ethical cases, an example is given where a local manager acquired a computerized system by purchasing it in pieces, where the cost of each piece was less than the capital expenditure approval limit. Was this right?

Managers need to realize that how objectives are reached is almost as important (maybe more so) than reaching the objectives. Furthermore, the performance evaluation systems of companies should be structured so that the reward system does not provide strong incentives for unethical behavior. As observed in an article on ethics, "No code of ethics and no amount of cajolery by the chief executive will have much effect if promotions go regularly to the people who pile up big numbers by cutting corners."[5] In the same article, another interesting observation was made—one that is particularly appropriate for the capital expenditure framework. A positive net present value means that the value of the firm should increase. According to the article, James Burke, CEO for Johnson & Johnson, identified a group of firms that paid a lot of attention to ethical standards. From 1950 to 1990 the market value of this group of firms grew at 11.3 percent annually compared with the 6.2 percent growth rate of the Dow Jones industrials. Perhaps ethical behavior pays off on the bottom line!

COMPUTATION AND ADJUSTMENT OF CASH FLOWS

Objective 7

Convert gross cash flows to after-tax cash flows.

An important step in capital investment analysis is determining the cash-flow pattern for each project being considered. In fact, the computation of cash flows may be the most critical step in the capital investment process. Erroneous estimates may result in erroneous decisions, regardless of the sophistication of the decision models being used. Two steps are needed to compute cash flows: (1) forecasting revenues, expenses, and capital outlays; and (2) adjusting these gross cash flows for inflation and tax effects. Of the two steps, the more challenging is the first. Forecasting cash flows is technically demanding and its methodology is typically studied in marketing research, management science, and statistics courses. Once gross cash flows are estimated, they should be adjusted for significant inflationary effects. Finally, straightforward applications of tax law can then be used to compute the after-tax flows. At this level of study, we assume that gross cash forecasts are available and focus on adjusting forecasted cash flows to improve their accuracy and utility in capital expenditure analysis.

Adjusting Forecasts for Inflation

In the United States, inflation has been relatively modest and the need to adjust cash flows may not be as critical. For firms, however, that operate in the international environment, inflation can be very high in certain countries and the effect on capital investment decisions can be dramatic. Brazil, for example, has experienced monthly double-digit inflation rates for years. Thus, it is important to know how to adjust the capital budgeting models for inflationary effects—particularly given the fact that many U.S. firms make capital investment decisions within many different national environments.

In an inflationary environment, financial markets react by increasing the *cost of capital* to reflect inflation. Thus, the cost of capital is composed of two elements:

cost of capital

1. the real rate
2. the inflationary element (investors demand a premium to compensate for the loss in general purchasing power of the dollar or local currency).

5. Kenneth Labich, "The New Crisis in Business Ethics," *Fortune* (20 April 1992): 167–176.

Since the required rate of return (which should be the cost of capital) used in capital investment analysis reflects an inflationary component at the time NPV analysis is performed, inflation must also be considered in predicting the operating cash flows. If the operating cash flows are not adjusted to account for inflation, an erroneous decision may result. In adjusting predicted cash flows, specific price change indexes should be used if possible. If that is not possible, a general price index can be used.

Note, however, that the cash inflows due to the tax effects of depreciation need *not* be adjusted for inflation as long as the national tax law requires that depreciation be based on the *original* dollar investment. In this case, depreciation deductions should not be increased for inflation.

To illustrate, assume that a subsidiary of a U.S. firm operating in Peru is considering a project that requires an investment of 5,000,000 soles and is expected to produce annual cash inflows of 2,900,000 soles for the coming two years. The required rate of return is 20 percent, which includes an inflationary component. The general inflation rate in Peru is expected to average 15 percent for the next two years. Net present value analysis with and without the adjustment of predicted cash flows for inflation is given in Exhibit 17-4. As the analysis shows, *not* adjusting predicted cash flows for inflation leads to a decision to reject the project, whereas adjusting for inflation leads to a decision to accept it. Thus, failure to adjust the predicted cash flows for inflationary effects can lead to an incorrect conclusion.

Conversion of Gross Cash Flows to After-Tax Cash Flows

Assuming that inflation-adjusted gross cash flows are predicted with the desired degree of accuracy, the analyst must adjust these cash flows for taxes. To analyze tax effects, cash flows are usually broken into two categories: (1) the initial cash outflows needed to acquire the assets of the project, and (2) the cash inflows produced over the life of the project. Cash outflows and cash inflows adjusted for tax effects are called net cash outflows and inflows. Net cash flows include provisions for revenues, operating expenses, depreciation, and relevant tax implications. They are the proper inputs for capital investment decisions.

After-Tax Cash Flows: Year 0 The net cash outflow in year 0 (the initial out-of-pocket outlay) is simply the difference between the initial cost of the project and any cash inflows directly associated with it. The gross cost of the project includes such things as

Exhibit
The Effects of Inflation on
Capital Investment

Note: All cash flows are
expressed in soles

Without Inflationary Adjustment			
Year	Cash Flow	Discount Factor[a]	Present Value
0	(5,000,000)	1.000	(5,000,000)
1–2	2,900,000	1.528	4,431,200
Net present value			(568,800)

With Inflationary Adjustment			
Year	Cash Flow[b]	Discount Factor[c]	Present Value
0	(5,000,000)	1.000	(5,000,000)
1	3,335,000	0.833	2,778,055
2	3,835,250	0.694	2,661,664
Net present value			439,719

[a]From Exhibit 17B-2
[b]3,335,000 soles = 1.15 × 2,900,000 soles (adjustment for one year of inflation); 3,835,250 soles = 1.15 × 1.15 × 2,900,000 soles (adjustment for two years of inflation)
[c]From Exhibit 17B-1

the cost of land, the cost of equipment (including transportation and installation), taxes on gains from the sale of assets, and increases in working capital. Cash inflows occurring at the time of acquisition include tax savings from the sale of assets, cash from the sale of assets, and other tax benefits such as tax credits.

Under current tax law, all costs relating to the acquisition of assets other than land must be capitalized and written off over the useful life of the assets (the write-off is achieved through depreciation). Depreciation is deducted from revenues in computing taxable income during each year of the asset's life; however, at the point of acquisition, no depreciation expense is computed. Thus, depreciation is not relevant at year 0. The principal tax implications at the point of acquisition are related to recognition of gains and losses on the sale of existing assets and to the recognition of any investment tax credits.

Gains on the sale of assets produce additional taxes and, accordingly, reduce the cash proceeds received from the sale of old assets. Losses, on the other hand, are noncash expenses that reduce taxable income, producing tax savings; consequently, the cash proceeds from the sale of an old asset are increased by the amount of the tax savings.

Adjusting cash inflows and outflows for tax effects requires knowledge of current corporate tax rates. Currently, most corporations face a federal tax rate of 35 percent. State corporate tax rates vary by state. For purposes of analysis, we will assume that 40 percent is the combined rate for state and federal taxes.

Let's look at an example. Currently, Champy Company uses two types of numerically controlled machines (CNC-11 and CNC-12) to produce one of its products. Recent technological advances have created a single CNC machine that can replace them. Management wants to know the net investment needed to acquire the new machine. If the new machine is acquired, the old equipment will be sold.

Disposition of Old Machines

Model	Book Value	Sale Price
CNC-11	$200,000	$260,000
CNC-12	500,000	400,000

Acquisition of New CNC

Purchase cost	$2,500,000
Freight	20,000
Installation	200,000
Additional working capital	180,000
Total	$2,900,000

The net investment can be determined by computing the net proceeds from the sale of the old machines and subtracting those proceeds from the cost of the new machine. The net proceeds are determined by computing the tax consequences of the sale and adjusting the gross receipts accordingly.

The tax consequences can be assessed by subtracting the book value from the selling price. If the difference is positive, the firm has experienced a gain and will owe taxes. Money received from the sale will be reduced by the amount of taxes owed. On the other hand, if the difference is negative, a loss is experienced—a noncash loss. However, this noncash loss does have cash implications. It can be deducted from revenues and, as a consequence, can shield revenues from being taxed; accordingly, taxes will be saved. Thus, a loss produces a cash inflow equal to the taxes saved.

To illustrate, consider the tax effects of selling CNC-11 and CNC-12 illustrated in Exhibit 17-5. By selling the two machines, the company receives the following net proceeds:

Exhibit
Tax Effects of the Sale of
CNC-11 and CNC-12

Asset	Gain (Loss)
CNC-11[a]	$ 60,000
CNC-12[b]	(100,000)
Net gain (loss)	$(40,000)
Tax rate	0.40
Tax savings	$ 16,000

[a]The sale price minus book value is
$260,000 − $200,000.
[b]The sale price minus book value is
$400,000 − $500,000.

Sale price, CNC-11	$260,000
Sale price, CNC-12	400,000
Tax savings	16,000
Net proceeds	$676,000

Given these net proceeds, the net investment can be computed as follows:

Total cost of new machine	$2,900,000
Less: Net proceeds of old machines	(676,000)
Net investment (cash outflow)	$2,224,000

After-Tax Cash Flows: Life of the Project In addition to determining the initial out-of-pocket outlay, managers must also estimate the annual after-tax cash flows expected over the life of the project. If the project generates revenue, the principal source of cash flows is from operations. Operating cash inflows can be assessed from the project's income statement. The annual after-tax cash flows are the sum of the project's after-tax profits and its noncash expenses. In terms of a simple formula, this computation can be represented as follows:

$$\text{After-tax cash flow} = \text{After-tax net income} + \text{Noncash expense}$$
$$CF = NI + NC$$

where CF = After-tax cash flow
NI = After-tax net income
NC = Noncash expenses

The most prominent examples of noncash expenses are depreciation and losses. At first glance, it may seem odd that after-tax cash flows are computed using noncash expenses. Noncash expenses are not cash flows but they do generate cash flows by reducing taxes. By shielding revenues from taxation, actual cash savings are created. The use of the income statement to determine after-tax cash flows is illustrated in the following example. The example is also used to show how noncash expenses can increase cash inflows by saving taxes.

Assume that a company plans to make a new product that requires new equipment costing $800,000. The new product is expected to increase the firm's annual revenues by $600,000. Materials, labor, and other cash operating expenses will be $250,000 per year. The equipment has a life of four years and will be depreciated on a straight-line basis. The machine will have no salvage value at the end of four years. The income statement for the project follows:

Revenues	$600,000
Less:	
Cash operating expenses	(250,000)
Depreciation	(200,000)
Income before taxes	$150,000
Less: Taxes (@ 40%)	(60,000)
Net income	$ 90,000

Cash flow from the income statement is computed as follows:

$$CF = NI + NC$$
$$= \$90,000 + \$200,000$$
$$= \$290,000$$

The income approach to determine operating cash flows can be decomposed to assess the after-tax cash-flow effects of each individual category on the income statement. The decomposition approach calculates the operating cash flows by computing the after-tax cash flows for each item of the income statement:

$$CF = (1 - \text{Tax rate}) \times \text{Revenues} - (1 - \text{Tax rate}) \times \text{Cash expenses}$$
$$+ (\text{Tax rate}) \times \text{Noncash expenses}$$

The first term, $(1 - \text{Tax rate}) \times \text{Revenues}$, gives the after-tax cash inflows from cash revenues. For our example, the cash revenue is projected to be $600,000. The firm, therefore, can expect to keep $360,000 of the revenues received: $(1 - \text{Tax rate}) \times \text{Revenues} = 0.60 \times \$600,000 = \$360,000$. The after-tax revenue is the actual amount of after-tax cash available from the sales activity of the firm.

The second term, $- (1 - \text{Tax rate}) \times \text{Cash expenses}$, is the after-tax cash outflows from cash operating expenses. Because cash expenses can be deducted from revenues to arrive at taxable income, the effect is to shield revenues from taxation. The consequence of this shielding is to save taxes and to reduce the actual cash outflow associated with a given expenditure. In our example, the firm has cash operating expenses of $250,000. The actual cash outflow is not $250,000 but $150,000 ($0.60 \times \$250,000$). The cash outlay for operating expenses is reduced by $100,000 because of tax savings. To see this, assume that operating expense is the only expense and that the firm has revenues of $600,000. If operating expense is not tax deductible, then the tax owed is $240,000 ($0.40 \times \$600,000$). If the operating expense is deductible for tax purposes, then the taxable income is $350,000 ($600,000 - \$250,000$), and the tax owed is $140,000 ($0.40 \times \$350,000$). Because the deductibility of operating expenses saves $100,000 in taxes, the actual outlay for that expenditure is reduced by $100,000.

The third term, $(\text{Tax rate}) \times \text{Noncash expenses}$, is the cash inflow from the tax savings produced by the noncash expenses. Noncash expenses, such as depreciation, also shield revenues from taxation. The depreciation *shields* $200,000 of revenues from being taxed and thus saves $80,000 ($0.40 \times \$200,000$) in taxes.

The sum of the three items follows:

After-tax revenues	$ 360,000
After-tax cash expenses	(150,000)
Depreciation tax shield	80,000
Operating cash flow	$ 290,000

The decomposition approach yields the same outcome as the income approach. For convenience, the three decomposition terms are summarized in Exhibit 17-6.

One feature of decomposition is the ability to compute after-tax cash flows in a spreadsheet format. This format highlights the cash-flow effects of individual items and

Exhibit
Computation of
Operating Cash Flows:
Decomposition Terms

After-tax cash revenues = $(1 - \text{Tax rate}) \times$ Cash revenues

After-tax cash expenses = $-(1 - \text{Tax rate}) \times$ Cash expenses

Tax savings, noncash expenses = Tax rate $\times$ Noncash expenses

facilitates the use of spreadsheet software packages. The spreadsheet format is achieved by creating four columns, one for each of the three cash-flow categories and one for the total after-tax cash flow, which is the sum of the first three. This format is illustrated in Exhibit 17-7 for our example. Recall that cash revenues were $600,000 per year for three years, annual cash expenses were $250,000, and annual depreciation was $200,000.

A second feature of decomposition is the ability to compute the after-tax cash effects on an item-by-item basis. For example, suppose that a firm is considering a project and is uncertain as to which method of depreciation should be used. By computing the tax savings produced under each depreciation method, a firm can quickly assess which method is most desirable.

For tax purposes, all depreciable business assets other than real estate are referred to as *personal property*, which is classified into one of six classes. Each class specifies the life of the assets that must be used for figuring depreciation. This life must be used even if the actual expected life is different from the class life; the class lives are set for purposes of recognizing depreciation and usually will be shorter than the actual life. Most equipment, machinery, and office furniture are classified as *seven-year assets*. Light trucks, automobiles, and computer equipment are classified as *five-year assets*. Most small tools are classified as *three-year assets*. Because the majority of personal property can be put into one of these categories, we will restrict our attention to them.

**modified
accelerated cost
recovery system
(MACRS)**

**half-year
convention**

The taxpayer can use either the straight-line method or the modified accelerated cost recovery system (MACRS) to compute annual depreciation. Current law defines MACRS as the double-declining-balance method.[6] In computing depreciation, no consideration of salvage value is required. However, under either method, a half-year convention applies.[7] This convention assumes that a newly acquired asset is in service for one-half of its first taxable year of service, regardless of the date that use of it actually began. When the asset reaches the end of its life, the other half year of depreciation can be claimed in the following year. If an asset is disposed of before the end of its class life, the half-year convention allows half the depreciation for that year.

For example, assume that an automobile is purchased on March 1, 1997. The automobile costs $20,000, and the firm elects the straight-line method. Automobiles are five-year assets (for tax purposes). The annual depreciation is $4,000 for a five-year period ($\frac{\$20,000}{5}$). However, using the half-year convention, the firm can deduct only

6. The tax law also allows the 150 percent declining balance method; however, we will focus on only the straight-line method and the double-declining version of MACRS.

7. The tax law requires a mid-quarter convention if more than 40 percent of personal property is placed in service during the last three months of the year. We will not illustrate this possible scenario.

17-7

Exhibit
Illustration of the
Spreadsheet Approach

Year	$(1 - t)R^a$	$-(1 - t)C^b$	tNC^c	CF
1	$360,000	$(150,000)	$80,000	$290,000
2	360,000	(150,000)	80,000	290,000
3	360,000	(150,000)	80,000	290,000
4	360,000	(150,000)	80,000	290,000

[a]R = Revenues; t = tax rate; $(1 - t)R = (1 - 0.40)\$600,000 =$ $360,000
[b]C = Cash expenses; $-(1 - t)C = -(1 - 0.40)\$250,000 = \$(150,000)$
[c]NC = Noncash expenses; $tNC = 0.40(\$200,000) = \$80,000$

$2,000 for 1997, half of the straight-line amount (0.5 × $4,000). The remaining half is deducted in the sixth year (or the year of disposal, if earlier):

Year	Depreciation Deduction
1997	$2,000 (half-year amount)
1998	4,000
1999	4,000
2000	4,000
2001	4,000
2002	2,000 (half-year amount)

Assume that the asset is disposed of in April 1999. In this case, only $2,000 of depreciation can be claimed for 1999 (early disposal rule).

If the double-declining-balance method is selected, the amount of depreciation claimed in the first year is twice that of the straight-line method. Under this method, the amount of depreciation claimed becomes progressively smaller until eventually it is exceeded by that claimed under the straight-line method. When this happens, the straight-line method is used to finish depreciating the asset. Exhibit 17-8 provides a table of depreciation rates for the double-declining-balance method for assets belonging to the three-year, five-year, and seven-year classes. The rates shown in this table incorporate the half-year convention, and therefore are the MACRS depreciation rates.

Both the straight-line method and the double-declining-balance method yield the same total amount of depreciation over the life of the asset. Both methods also produce the same total tax savings (assuming the same tax rate over the life of the asset). However, since the depreciation claimed in the early years of a project is greater using the double-declining-balance method, the tax savings are also greater during those years. Considering the time value of money, it is preferable to have the tax savings earlier than later. Thus, firms should prefer the MACRS method of depreciation over the straight-line method. This conclusion is illustrated by the following example.

A firm is considering the purchase of computer equipment for $20,000. The tax guidelines require that the cost of the equipment be depreciated over five years. However, tax guidelines also permit the depreciation to be computed using either method. Of course, the firm should choose the double-declining-balance method because it brings the greater benefit.

From decomposition, we know that the cash inflows caused by shielding can be computed by multiplying the tax rate times the amount depreciated ($t \times NC$). The cash flows produced by each depreciation method and their present value, assuming a discount rate of 10 percent, are given in Exhibit 17-9. As can be seen, the present value of the tax savings from using MACRS is greater than that using straight-line depreciation.

CAPITAL INVESTMENT: THE ADVANCED MANUFACTURING ENVIRONMENT

In the advanced manufacturing environment, long-term investments are generally concerned with the automation of manufacturing. Before any commitment to automation

Exhibit
MACRS Depreciation
Rates

Year	Three-Year Assets	Five-Year Assets	Seven-Year Assets
1	33.33%	20.00%	14.29%
2	44.45	32.00	24.49
3	14.81	19.20	17.49
4	7.41	11.52	12.49
5		11.52	8.93
6		5.76	8.92
7	—	—	8.93
8	—	—	4.46

17-9

Exhibit
Value of Accelerated
Methods Illustrated

		Straight-line Method			
Year	Depreciation	Tax Rate	Tax Savings	Discount Factor	Present Value
1	$2,000	0.40	$ 800.00	0.909	$ 727.20
2	4,000	0.40	1,600.00	0.826	1,321.60
3	4,000	0.40	1,600.00	0.751	1,201.60
4	4,000	0.40	1,600.00	0.683	1,092.80
5	4,000	0.40	1,600.00	0.621	993.60
6	2,000	0.40	800.00	0.564	451.20
Net present value					$5,788.00

		MACRS Method			
Year	Depreciation*	Tax Rate	Tax Savings	Discount Factor	Present Value
1	$4,000	0.40	$1,600.00	0.909	$1,454.40
2	6,400	0.40	2,560.00	0.826	2,114.56
3	3,840	0.40	1,536.00	0.751	1,153.54
4	2,304	0.40	921.60	0.683	629.45
5	2,304	0.40	921.60	0.621	572.31
6	1,152	0.40	460.80	0.564	259.89
Net present value					$6,184.15

*This is computed by multiplying the five-year rates in Exhibit 17-8 by $20,000. For example, depreciation for year 1 is 0.20 × $20,000.

Objective 8

Describe capital
investment in the
advanced manufacturing
environment.

is made, however, a company should first make the most efficient use of existing technology. Many benefits can be realized by redesigning and simplifying the current manufacturing process. An example often given to support this thesis is automation of material handling. Automation of this operation can cost millions—and it is usually unnecessary because greater efficiency can be achieved by eliminating inventories and simplifying material transfers through the implementation of a JIT system.

Once the benefits from redesign and simplification are achieved, however, it becomes apparent where automation can generate additional benefits. Many companies can improve their competitive positions by adding such features as robotics, flexible manufacturing systems, and completely integrated manufacturing systems. The ultimate commitment to automation is the construction of greenfield factories. *Greenfield factories* are new factories designed and built from scratch; they represent a strategic decision by a company to change completely the way it manufactures.

Although discounted cash-flow analysis (using net present value and internal rate of return) remains preeminent in capital investment decisions, the new manufacturing environment demands that more attention be paid to the inputs used in discounted cash-flow models. How investment is defined, how operating cash flows are estimated, how salvage value is treated, and how the discount rate is chosen are all different in nature from the traditional approach.[8]

There is also another important dimension. Contemporary investment management involves both *financial* and *nonfinancial* criteria. It is critical that the investment management process be linked with the company's strategies. Analysis in advanced manufacturing technology should consider the contributions made to support such

8. Much of the information on investment in the new manufacturing environment is based on the following sources: Robert A. Howell and Stephen R. Soucy, "Capital Investment in the New Manufacturing Environment," *Management Accounting* (November1987): 26–32; Callie Berliner and James A. Brimson, eds., *Cost Management for Today's Advanced Manufacturing* (Boston: Harvard Business School Press, 1988); Thomas Klammer, "Improving Investment Decisions," *Management Accounting* (July 1993): 35–43; and David Sinason, "A Dynamic Model for Present Value Analysis," *Journal of Cost Management* (Spring 1991): 40–45.

strategies as product enhancement, diversification, and risk reduction. For example, advanced technology may contribute to product enhancement by allowing a firm more flexibility in responding to fluctuating demands. Improving quality is also a product enhancement feature. Some of these product enhancement features may be possible to quantify. For example, it may be possible to estimate the cost savings attributable to improved quality. Other factors may be more difficult to quantify. Assessing the cost savings or increased revenues from increased flexibility may be quite difficult. Yet the increased flexibility may be as critical for the company as the improved quality. Thus, consideration of nonfinancial factors is also important to the investment management process. Nonetheless, every possible effort should be made to quantify the factors affecting the investment decision.

How Investment Differs

Investment in automated manufacturing processes is much more complex than investment in the standard manufacturing equipment of the past. For standard equipment, the direct costs of acquisition represent virtually the entire investment. For automated manufacturing, the direct costs can represent as little as 50 or 60 percent of the total investment; software, engineering, training, and implementation are a significant percentage of the total costs. Thus, great care must be exercised to assess the actual cost of an automated system. It is easy to overlook the peripheral costs, which can be substantial.

How Estimates of Operating Cash Flows Differ

Estimates of operating cash flows from investments in standard equipment have typically relied on directly identifiable tangible benefits, such as direct savings from labor, power, and scrap. Monsanto's Fibers Division, for example, used direct labor savings as the main justification for automating its Pensacola, Florida, plant.[9] Intangible benefits and indirect savings were ignored as they often are in traditional capital investment analysis.

In the new manufacturing environment, however, the intangible and indirect benefits can be material and critical to the viability of the project. Greater quality, more reliability, reduced lead time, improved customer satisfaction, and an enhanced ability to maintain market share are all important intangible benefits of an advanced manufacturing system. Reduction of labor in support areas such as production scheduling and stores are indirect benefits. More effort is needed to measure these intangible and indirect benefits in order to assess more accurately the potential value of investments. Monsanto discovered, for example, that the new automated system in its Pensacola plant produced large savings in terms of reduced waste, lower inventories, increased quality, and reduced indirect labor. Productivity increased by 50 percent. What if the direct labor savings had not been sufficient to justify the investment? Consider the lost returns that Monsanto would have experienced by what would have been a faulty decision. Monsanto's experience also illustrates the importance of a postaudit, discussed earlier. For Monsanto, the postaudit revealed the importance of intangible and indirect benefits. In future investment decisions, these factors are more likely to be considered.

An example can be used to illustrate the importance of considering intangible and indirect benefits. Consider a company that is evaluating a potential investment in a flexible manufacturing system (FMS). The choice facing the company is to continue producing with its traditional equipment, expected to last ten years, or to switch to the new system, which is also expected to have a useful life of ten years. The company's discount rate is 12 percent. The data pertaining to the investment are presented in Exhibit 17-10. Using these data, the net present value of the proposed system can be computed as follows:

9. The following article provides a good description of Monsanto's experience: Raymond C. Cole and H. Lee Hales, "How Monsanto Justified Automation," *Management Accounting* (January 1992): 39–43.

Present value ($4,000,000 × 5.65*)	$ 22,600,000
Investment	(18,000,000)
Net present value	$ 4,600,000

*This is the discount factor for an interest rate of 12 percent and
a life of ten years (see Exhibit 17B-2).

The net present value is positive and large in magnitude, and it clearly signals the acceptability of the FMS. This outcome, however, is strongly dependent on explicit recognition of both intangible and indirect benefits. If those benefits are eliminated, then the direct savings total $2.2 million, and the NPV is negative:

Present value ($2,200,000 × 5.65)	$ 12,430,000
Investment	(18,000,000)
Net present value	$ (5,570,000)

The rise of activity-based costing has made identifying indirect benefits easier with the use of cost drivers. Once they are identified, they can be included in the analysis if they are material.

Examination of Exhibit 17-10 reveals the importance of intangible benefits. One of the most important intangible benefits is maintaining or improving a firm's competitive position. A key question is what will happen to the cash flows of the firm if the investment is not made. That is, if the company chooses to forgo an investment in technologically advanced equipment, will it be able to continue to compete with other firms on the basis of quality, delivery, and cost? (The question becomes especially relevant if competitors

17-10

Exhibit
Investment Data: Direct,
Intangible, and Indirect
Benefits

	FMS	Status Quo
Investment (current outlay):		
Direct costs	$10,000,000	—
Software, engineering	8,000,000	—
Total current outlay	$18,000,000	$ 0
Net after-tax cash flow	$ 5,000,000	$1,000,000
Less: After-tax cash flow for status quo	(1,000,000)	n/a
Incremental benefit	$ 4,000,000	n/a
Incremental Benefit Explained		
Direct benefits:		
Direct labor	$1,500,000	
Scrap reduction	500,000	
Setups	200,000	$2,200,000
Intangible benefits (quality savings):		
Rework	$ 200,000	
Warranties	400,000	
Maintenance of competitive position	1,000,000	1,600,000
Indirect benefits:		
Production scheduling	$ 110,000	
Payroll	90,000	200,000
Total		$4,000,000

choose to invest in advanced equipment.) If the competitive position deteriorates, the company's current cash flows will decrease.

If cash flows will decrease if the investment is not made, this decrease should show up as an incremental benefit for the advanced technology. In Exhibit 17-10, the company estimates this competitive benefit as $1,000,000. Estimating this benefit requires some serious strategic planning and analysis, but its effect can be critical. If this benefit had been ignored or overlooked, then the net present value would have been negative, and the investment alternative rejected:

Present value ($3,000,000 × 5.65)	$ 16,950,000
Investment	(18,000,000)
Net present value	$ (1,050,000)

Salvage Value

Terminal or salvage value has often been ignored in investment decisions. The usual reason offered is the difficulty of estimating it. Because of this uncertainty, the effect of salvage value has often been ignored or heavily discounted. This approach may be unwise, however, because salvage value could make the difference between investing or not investing. Given the highly competitive environment, companies cannot afford to make incorrect decisions.

sensitivity analysis

what-if analysis

A much better approach to deal with uncertainty is to use sensitivity analysis. Sensitivity analysis changes the assumptions on which the capital investment analysis relies and assesses the effect on the cash-flow pattern. Sensitivity analysis is often referred to as what-if analysis. For example, this approach is used to address such questions as what is the effect on the decision to invest in a project *if* the cash receipts are 5 percent less than projected? 5 percent more? Although sensitivity analysis is computationally demanding if done manually, it can be done rapidly and easily using computers and spreadsheet software packages such as Lotus, Excel, and Quattro. In fact, these packages can also be used to carry out the NPV and IRR computations that have been illustrated manually throughout the chapter. They have built-in NPV and IRR functions that greatly facilitate the computational requirements.

To illustrate the potential effect of terminal value, assume that the after-tax annual operating cash flow of the project shown in Exhibit 17-10 is $3.1 million instead of $4 million. The net present value without salvage value is as follows:

Present value ($3,100,000 × 5.65)	$ 17,515,000
Investment	(18,000,000)
Net present value	$ (485,000)

Without the terminal value, the project would be rejected. The net present value with salvage value of $2 million, however, is a positive result, meaning that the investment should be made:

Present value ($3,100,000 × 5.65)	$ 17,515,000
Present value ($2,000,000 × 0.322*)	644,000
Investment	(18,000,000)
Net present value	$ 159,000

*This is the discount factor, assuming 12 percent and ten years (Exhibit 17B-1).

But what if the salvage value is less than expected? Suppose that the worst possible outcome is a salvage value of $1,600,000? What is the effect on the decision? The NPV can be recomputed under this new scenario:

Present value ($3,100,000 × 5.65)	$ 17,515,000
Present value ($1,600,000 × 0.322)	515,200
Investment	(18,000,000)
Net present value	$ 30,200

Thus, under a pessimistic scenario the NPV is still positive. This illustrates how sensitivity analysis can be used to deal with the uncertainty surrounding salvage value. It can also be used for other cash-flow variables.

Discount Rates

Being overly conservative with discount rates can prove even more damaging. In theory, if future cash flows are known with certainty, the correct discount rate is a firm's cost of capital. In practice, future cash flows are uncertain, and managers often choose a discount rate higher than the cost of capital to deal with that uncertainty. If the rate chosen is excessively high, it will bias the selection process toward short-term investments.

To illustrate the effect of an excessive discount rate, consider the project in Exhibit 17-10 once again. Assume that the correct discount rate is 12 percent but that the firm uses 18 percent. The net present value using an 18 percent discount rate is calculated as follows:

Present value ($4,000,000 × 4.494*)	$ 17,976,000
Investment	(18,000,000)
Net present value	$ (24,000)

*This is the discount rate for 18 percent and ten years (Exhibit 17B-2).

The project would be rejected. With a higher discount rate, the discount factor decreases in magnitude much more rapidly than the discount factor for a lower rate (compare the discount factor for 12 percent, 5.65, with the factor for 18 percent, 4.494). The effect of a higher discount factor is to place more weight on earlier cash flows and less weight on later cash flows, which favors short-term over long-term investments. This outcome makes it more difficult for automated manufacturing systems to appear as viable projects since the cash returns required to justify the investment are received over a longer period of time.

APPENDIX A: PRESENT VALUE CONCEPTS

An important feature of money is that it can be invested and can earn interest. A dollar today is not the same as a dollar tomorrow. This fundamental principle is the backbone of discounting methods. Discounting methods rely on the relationships between current and future dollars. Thus, to use discounting methods, we must understand these relationships.

Future Value

Suppose a bank advertises a 4 percent annual interest rate. If a customer invests $100, he or she would receive, after one year, the original $100 plus $4 interest [+ $100 +

(0.04)($100) = (1 + 0.04)$100 = (1.04)($100) = $104]. This result can be expressed by the following equation, where F is the future amount, P is the initial or current outlay, and i is the interest rate:

$$F = P(1 + i) \qquad (17A.1)$$

For the example, $F = \$100(1 + 0.04) = \$100(1.04) = \$104$.

Now suppose that the same bank offers a 5 percent rate if the customer leaves the original deposit, plus any interest, on deposit for a total of two years. How much will the customer receive at the end of two years? Again assume that a customer invests $100. Using equation 17A.1, the customer will earn $105 at the end of year 1 [$F = \$100 (1 + 0.05) = (\$100)(1.05) = \$105$]. If this amount is left in the account for a second year, equation 17A.1 is used again with P now assumed to be $105. At the end of the second year, then, the total is $110.25 [$F = \$105(1 + 0.05) = (\$105)(1.05) = \$110.25$]. In the second year, interest is earned on both the original deposit and the interest earned in the first year. The earning of interest on interest is referred to as compounding of interest. The value that will accumulate by the end of an investment's life, assuming a specified compound return, is the future value. The future value of the $100 deposit in the second example is $110.25.

A more direct way to compute the future value is possible. Since the first application of equation 17A.1 can be expressed as $F = \$105 = \$100(1.05)$, the second application can be expressed as $F = \$105(1.05) = \$100(1.05)(1.05) = \$100(1.05)^2 = P(1 + i)^2$. This suggests the following formula for computing amounts for n periods into the future:

$$F = P(1 + i)^n \qquad (17A.2)$$

Present Value (Discounting)

Often a manager needs to compute not the future value but the amount that must be invested *now* in order to earn some given future value. The amount that must be invested now to produce the future value is known as the present value of the future amount. For example, how much must be invested now in order to earn $363 two years from now, assuming that the interest rate is 10 percent? Or put another way, what is the present value of $363 to be received two years from now?

In this example, the future value, the years, and the interest rate are all known; we want to know the current outlay that will produce that future amount. In equation 17A.2, the variable representing the current outlay (the present value of F) is P. Thus, to compute the present value of a future outlay, all we need to do is solve equation 17A.2 for P:

$$P = \frac{F}{(1 + i)^n} \qquad (17A.3)$$

Using equation 17A.3, we can compute the present value of $363:

$$P = \frac{\$363}{(1 + 0.1)^2}$$

$$= \frac{\$363}{1.21}$$

$$= \$300$$

The present value, $300, is what the future amount of $363 is worth today. All other things being equal, having $300 today is the same as having $363 two years from now. Put another way, if a firm requires a 10 percent rate of return, the most the firm would be willing to pay today is $300 for any investment that yields $363 two years from now.

compounding of interest

future value

present value

discounting

discount rate
discount factor

The process of computing the present value of future cash flows is often referred to as discounting; thus, we say that we have discounted the future value of $363 to its present value of $300. The interest rate used to discount the future cash flow is the discount rate. The expression $\frac{1}{(1 + i)^n}$ in equation 17A.3 is the discount factor. By letting the discount factor, called *df*, equal $\frac{1}{(1 + i)^n}$, equation 17A.3 can be expressed as $P = F(df)$. To simplify the computation of present value, a table of discount factors is given for various combinations of *i* and *n* (see Exhibit 17B-1 in Appendix B). For example, the discount factor for $i = 10$ percent and $n = 2$ is 0.826 (simply go to the 10 percent column of the table and move down to the second row). With the discount factor, the present value of $363 is computed as follows:

$$P = F(df)$$
$$= \$363 \times 0.826$$
$$= \$300 \text{ (rounded)}$$

annuity

Present Value of an Uneven Series of Cash Flows Exhibit 17B-1 can be used to compute the present value of any future cash flow or series of future cash flows. A series of future cash flows is called an annuity. The present value of an annuity is found by computing the present value of each future cash flow and then summing these values. For example, suppose that an investment is expected to produce the following annual cash flows: $110, $121, and $133.10. Assuming a discount rate of 10 percent, the present value of this series of cash flows is computed in Exhibit 17A-1.

Present Value of a Uniform Series of Cash Flows If the series of cash flows is even, the computation of the annuity's present value is simplified. Assume, for example, that an investment is expected to return $100 per year for three years. Using Exhibit 17B-1 and assuming a discount rate of 10 percent, the present value of the annuity is computed in Exhibit 17A-2.

As with the uneven series of cash flows, the present value in Exhibit 17A-2 was computed by calculating the present value of each cash flow separately and then summing them. However, in the case of an annuity displaying uniform cash flows, the computations can be reduced from three to one as described in the footnote to the exhibit. The sum of the individual discount factors can be thought of as a discount factor for an annuity of uniform cash flows. A table of discount factors that can be used for an annuity of uniform cash flows is available in Exhibit 17B-2.

17A-1

Exhibit
Present Value of an
Uneven Series of Cash
Flows

Year	Cash Receipt	Discount Factor	Present Value*
1	$110.00	0.909	$100.00
2	121.00	0.826	100.00
3	133.10	0.751	100.00
			$300.00

*Rounded

17A-2

Exhibit
Present Value of Uniform
Series of Cash Flows

Year	Cash Receipt*	Discount Factor	Present Value
1	$100	0.909	$ 90.90
2	100	0.826	82.60
3	100	0.751	75.10
		2.486	$248.60

*The annual cash flow of $100 can be multiplied by the sum of the discount factors (2.486) to obtain the present value of the uniform series ($248.60).

APPENDIX B: PRESENT VALUE TABLES

 17B-1 ········· Present Value of $1*

Exhibit

Periods	2%	4%	6%	8%	10%	12%	14%	16%	18%	20%	22%	24%	26%	28%	30%	32%	40%
1	0.980	0.962	0.943	0.926	0.909	0.893	0.877	0.862	0.847	0.833	0.820	0.806	0.794	0.781	0.769	0.758	0.714
2	0.961	0.925	0.890	0.857	0.826	0.797	0.769	0.743	0.718	0.694	0.672	0.650	0.630	0.610	0.592	0.574	0.510
3	0.942	0.889	0.840	0.794	0.751	0.712	0.675	0.641	0.609	0.579	0.551	0.524	0.500	0.477	0.455	0.435	0.364
4	0.924	0.855	0.792	0.735	0.683	0.636	0.592	0.552	0.516	0.482	0.451	0.423	0.397	0.373	0.350	0.329	0.260
5	0.906	0.822	0.747	0.681	0.621	0.567	0.519	0.476	0.437	0.402	0.370	0.341	0.315	0.291	0.269	0.250	0.186
6	0.888	0.790	0.705	0.630	0.564	0.507	0.456	0.410	0.370	0.335	0.303	0.275	0.250	0.227	0.207	0.189	0.133
7	0.871	0.760	0.665	0.583	0.513	0.452	0.400	0.354	0.314	0.279	0.249	0.222	0.198	0.178	0.159	0.143	0.095
8	0.853	0.731	0.627	0.540	0.467	0.404	0.351	0.305	0.266	0.233	0.204	0.179	0.157	0.139	0.123	0.108	0.068
9	0.837	0.703	0.592	0.500	0.424	0.361	0.308	0.263	0.225	0.194	0.167	0.144	0.125	0.108	0.094	0.082	0.048
10	0.820	0.676	0.558	0.463	0.386	0.322	0.270	0.227	0.191	0.162	0.137	0.116	0.099	0.085	0.073	0.062	0.035
11	0.804	0.650	0.527	0.429	0.350	0.287	0.237	0.195	0.162	0.135	0.112	0.094	0.079	0.066	0.056	0.047	0.025
12	0.788	0.625	0.497	0.397	0.319	0.257	0.208	0.168	0.137	0.112	0.092	0.076	0.062	0.052	0.043	0.036	0.018
13	0.773	0.601	0.469	0.368	0.290	0.229	0.182	0.145	0.116	0.093	0.075	0.061	0.050	0.040	0.033	0.027	0.013
14	0.758	0.577	0.442	0.340	0.263	0.205	0.160	0.125	0.099	0.078	0.062	0.049	0.039	0.032	0.025	0.021	0.009
15	0.743	0.555	0.417	0.315	0.239	0.183	0.140	0.108	0.084	0.065	0.051	0.040	0.031	0.025	0.020	0.016	0.006
16	0.728	0.534	0.394	0.292	0.218	0.163	0.123	0.093	0.071	0.054	0.042	0.032	0.025	0.019	0.015	0.012	0.005
17	0.714	0.513	0.371	0.270	0.198	0.146	0.108	0.080	0.060	0.045	0.034	0.026	0.020	0.015	0.012	0.009	0.003
18	0.700	0.494	0.350	0.250	0.180	0.130	0.095	0.069	0.051	0.038	0.028	0.021	0.016	0.012	0.009	0.007	0.002
19	0.686	0.475	0.331	0.232	0.164	0.116	0.083	0.060	0.043	0.031	0.023	0.017	0.012	0.009	0.007	0.005	0.002
20	0.673	0.456	0.312	0.215	0.149	0.104	0.073	0.051	0.037	0.026	0.019	0.014	0.010	0.007	0.005	0.004	0.001
21	0.660	0.439	0.294	0.199	0.135	0.093	0.064	0.044	0.031	0.022	0.015	0.011	0.008	0.006	0.004	0.003	0.001
22	0.647	0.422	0.278	0.184	0.123	0.083	0.056	0.038	0.026	0.018	0.013	0.009	0.006	0.004	0.003	0.002	0.001
23	0.634	0.406	0.262	0.170	0.112	0.074	0.049	0.033	0.022	0.015	0.010	0.007	0.005	0.003	0.002	0.002	0.000
24	0.622	0.390	0.247	0.158	0.102	0.066	0.043	0.028	0.019	0.013	0.008	0.006	0.004	0.003	0.002	0.001	0.000
25	0.610	0.375	0.233	0.146	0.092	0.059	0.038	0.024	0.016	0.010	0.007	0.005	0.003	0.002	0.001	0.001	0.000
26	0.598	0.361	0.220	0.135	0.084	0.053	0.033	0.021	0.014	0.009	0.006	0.004	0.002	0.002	0.001	0.001	0.000
27	0.586	0.347	0.207	0.125	0.076	0.047	0.029	0.018	0.011	0.007	0.005	0.003	0.002	0.001	0.001	0.001	0.000
28	0.574	0.333	0.196	0.116	0.069	0.042	0.026	0.016	0.010	0.006	0.004	0.002	0.002	0.001	0.001	0.000	0.000
29	0.563	0.321	0.185	0.107	0.063	0.037	0.022	0.014	0.008	0.005	0.003	0.002	0.001	0.001	0.000	0.000	0.000
30	0.552	0.308	0.174	0.099	0.057	0.033	0.020	0.012	0.007	0.004	0.003	0.002	0.001	0.001	0.000	0.000	0.000

$$*P_n = \frac{A}{(1+i)^n}$$

17B-2 ······· Present Value of an Annuity of $1 in Arrears

Exhibit

Periods	2%	4%	6%	8%	10%	12%	14%	16%	18%	20%	22%	24%	26%	28%	30%	32%	40%
1	0.980	0.962	0.943	0.926	0.909	0.893	0.877	0.862	0.847	0.833	0.820	0.806	0.794	0.781	0.769	0.758	0.714
2	1.942	1.886	1.833	1.783	1.736	1.690	1.647	1.605	1.566	1.528	1.492	1.457	1.424	1.392	1.361	1.331	1.224
3	2.884	2.775	2.673	2.577	2.487	2.402	2.322	2.246	2.174	2.106	2.042	1.981	1.923	1.868	1.816	1.766	1.589
4	3.808	3.630	3.465	3.312	3.170	3.037	2.914	2.798	2.690	2.589	2.494	2.404	2.320	2.241	2.166	2.096	1.849
5	4.713	4.452	4.212	3.993	3.791	3.605	3.433	3.274	3.127	2.991	2.864	2.745	2.635	2.532	2.436	2.345	2.035
6	5.601	5.242	4.917	4.623	4.355	4.111	3.889	3.685	3.498	3.326	3.167	3.020	2.885	2.759	2.643	2.534	2.168
7	6.472	6.002	5.582	5.206	4.868	4.564	4.288	4.039	3.812	3.605	3.416	3.242	3.083	2.937	2.802	2.677	2.263
8	7.325	6.733	6.210	5.747	5.335	4.968	4.639	4.344	4.078	3.837	3.619	3.421	3.241	3.076	2.925	2.786	2.331
9	8.162	7.435	6.802	6.247	5.759	5.328	4.946	4.607	4.303	4.031	3.786	3.566	3.366	3.184	3.019	2.868	2.379
10	8.983	8.111	7.360	6.710	6.145	5.650	5.216	4.833	4.494	4.192	3.923	3.682	3.465	3.269	3.092	2.930	2.414
11	9.787	8.760	7.887	7.139	6.495	5.938	5.453	5.029	4.656	4.327	4.035	3.776	3.543	3.335	3.147	2.978	2.438
12	10.575	9.385	8.384	7.536	6.814	6.194	5.660	5.197	4.793	4.439	4.127	3.851	3.606	3.387	3.190	3.013	2.456
13	11.348	9.986	8.853	7.904	7.103	6.424	5.842	5.342	4.910	4.533	4.203	3.912	3.656	3.427	3.223	3.040	2.469
14	12.106	10.563	9.295	8.244	7.367	6.628	6.002	5.468	5.008	4.611	4.265	3.962	3.695	3.459	3.249	3.061	2.478
15	12.849	11.118	9.712	8.559	7.606	6.811	6.142	5.575	5.092	4.675	4.315	4.001	3.726	3.483	3.268	3.076	2.484
16	13.578	11.652	10.106	8.851	7.824	6.974	6.265	5.668	5.162	4.730	4.357	4.033	3.751	3.503	3.283	3.088	2.489
17	14.292	12.166	10.477	9.122	8.022	7.120	6.373	5.749	5.222	4.775	4.391	4.059	3.771	3.518	3.295	3.097	2.492
18	14.992	12.659	10.828	9.372	8.201	7.250	6.467	5.818	5.273	4.812	4.419	4.080	3.786	3.529	3.304	3.104	2.494
19	15.678	13.134	11.158	9.604	8.365	7.366	6.550	5.877	5.316	4.843	4.442	4.097	3.799	3.539	3.311	3.109	2.496
20	16.351	13.590	11.470	9.818	8.514	7.469	6.623	5.929	5.353	4.870	4.460	4.110	3.808	3.546	3.316	3.113	2.497
21	17.011	14.029	11.764	10.017	8.649	7.562	6.687	5.973	5.384	4.891	4.476	4.121	3.816	3.551	3.320	3.116	2.498
22	17.658	14.451	12.042	10.201	8.772	7.645	6.743	6.011	5.410	4.909	4.488	4.130	3.822	3.556	3.323	3.118	2.498
23	18.292	14.857	12.303	10.371	8.883	7.718	6.792	6.044	5.432	4.925	4.499	4.137	3.827	3.559	3.325	3.120	2.499
24	18.914	15.247	12.550	10.529	8.985	7.784	6.835	6.073	5.451	4.937	4.507	4.143	3.831	3.562	3.327	3.121	2.499
25	19.523	15.622	12.783	10.675	9.077	7.843	6.873	6.097	5.467	4.948	4.514	4.147	3.834	3.564	3.329	3.122	2.499
26	20.121	15.983	13.003	10.810	9.161	7.896	6.906	6.118	5.480	4.956	4.520	4.151	3.837	3.566	3.330	3.123	2.500
27	20.707	16.330	13.211	10.935	9.237	7.943	6.935	6.136	5.492	4.964	4.524	4.154	3.839	3.567	3.331	3.123	2.500
28	21.281	16.663	13.406	11.051	9.307	7.984	6.961	6.152	5.502	4.970	4.528	4.157	3.840	3.568	3.331	3.124	2.500
29	21.844	16.984	13.591	11.158	9.370	8.022	6.983	6.166	5.510	4.975	4.531	4.159	3.841	3.569	3.332	3.124	2.500
30	22.396	17.292	13.765	11.258	9.427	8.055	7.003	6.177	5.517	4.979	4.534	4.160	3.842	3.569	3.332	3.124	2.500

$$ *P_n = \left(\frac{1}{i}\right)\left[\frac{1}{i} - \frac{1}{i(1+i)^n}\right] $$

S UMMARY OF LEARNING OBJECTIVES

1. Explain what a capital investment decision is and distinguish between independent and mutually exclusive capital investment decisions.

Capital investment decisions are concerned with the acquisition of long-term assets and usually involve a significant outlay of funds. There are two types of capital investment projects: independent and mutually exclusive. Independent projects are projects that, if accepted or rejected, do not affect the cash flows of other projects. Mutually exclusive projects are those projects that, if accepted, preclude the acceptance of all other competing projects.

2. Compute the payback period and accounting rate of return for a proposed investment and explain their roles in capital investment decisions.

Managers make capital investment decisions by using formal models to decide whether to accept or reject proposed projects. These decision models are classified as nondiscounting and discounting, depending on whether they address the question of the time value of money. There are two nondiscounting models: the payback period and the accounting rate of return.

The payback period is the time required for a firm to recover its initial investment. For even cash flows, it is calculated by dividing the investment by the annual cash flow. For uneven cash flows, the cash flows are summed until the investment is recovered. If only a fraction of a year is needed, then it is assumed that the cash flows occur evenly within each year. The payback period ignores the time value of money and the profitability of projects because it does not consider the cash inflows available beyond the payback period. However, it does supply some useful information. The payback period is useful in assessing and controlling risk, minimizing the impact of an investment on a firm's liquidity, and controlling the risk of obsolescence.

The accounting rate of return is computed by dividing the average income expected from an investment by either the original or average investment. Unlike the payback period, it does consider the profitability of a project; however, it ignores the time value of money. The payback period may be useful to managers for screening new investments to ensure that certain accounting ratios are not adversely affected (specifically accounting ratios that may be monitored to ensure compliance with debt covenants).

3. Use net present value analysis for capital investment decisions involving independent projects.

NPV is the difference between the present value of future cash flows and the initial investment outlay. To use the model, a required rate of return must be identified (usually the cost of capital). The NPV method uses the required rate of return to compute the present value of a project's cash inflows and outflows. If the present value of the inflows is greater than the present value of the outflows, the net present value is greater than zero, and the project is profitable; if the NPV is less than zero, the project is not profitable and should be rejected.

4. Use the internal rate of return to assess the acceptability of independent projects.

The IRR is computed by finding the interest rate that equates the present value of a project's cash inflows with the present value of its cash outflows. If the IRR is greater than the required rate of return (cost of capital), the project is acceptable; if the IRR is less than the required rate of return, the project should be rejected.

5. Explain the role and value of postaudits.

Postauditing of capital projects is an important step in capital investment. Postaudits evaluate the actual performance of a project in relation to its expected performance. A postaudit may lead to corrective action to improve the performance of the project or to abandon it. Postaudits also serve as an incentive for managers to make capital investment decisions prudently.

6. Explain why NPV is better than IRR for capital investment decisions involving mutually exclusive projects.

In evaluating mutually exclusive or competing projects, managers have a choice of using NPV or IRR. When choosing among competing projects, the NPV model correctly identifies the best investment alternative. IRR, at times, may choose an inferior project. Thus, since NPV always provides the correct signal, it should be used.

7. Convert gross cash flows to after-tax cash flows.

Accurate and reliable cash-flow forecasts are absolutely critical for capital budgeting analyses. Managers should assume responsibility for the accuracy of cash-flow projections. All cash flows in a capital investment analysis should be after-tax cash flows. There are two different, but equivalent, ways to compute after-tax cash flows: the income method and the decomposition method. Although depreciation is not a cash flow, it does have cash-flow implications because tax laws allow depreciation to be deducted in computing taxable income. Straight-line and double-declining-balance depreciation both produce the same total depreciation deductions over the life of the depreciated asset. Because the latter method accelerates depreciation, however, it would be preferred.

8. Describe capital investment in the advanced manufacturing environment.

Capital investment in the advanced manufacturing environment is affected by the way in which inputs are determined. Much greater attention must be paid to the investment outlays because peripheral items can require substantial resources. Furthermore, in assessing benefits, intangible items such as quality and maintaining competitive position can be deciding factors. Choice of the required rate of return is also critical. The tendency of firms to use required rates of return that are much greater than the cost of capital should be discontinued. Also, since the salvage value of an automated system can be considerable, it should be estimated and included in the analysis.

K EY TERMS

Accounting rate of return *703*	Annuity *725* Capital budgeting *699*	Capital investment decisions *699*	Compounding of interest *724*

R EVIEW PROBLEMS

I. Basics of Capital Investment (Ignore taxes for this exercise.) Kenn Day, manager of Day Laboratory, is investigating the possibility of acquiring some new test equipment. To acquire the equipment requires an initial outlay of $300,000. To raise the capital, Kenn will sell stock valued at $200,000 (the stock pays dividends of $24,000 per year) and borrow $100,000. The loan for $100,000 would carry an interest rate of 6 percent. Kenn figures that his weighted cost of capital is 10 percent [$(\frac{2}{3} \times .12) + (\frac{1}{3} \times .06)$]. This weighted cost of capital is the discount rate that will be used for capital investment decisions.

Kenn estimates that the new test equipment will produce a cash inflow of $50,000 per year. Kenn expects the equipment to last for 20 years.

REQUIRED:

1. Compute the payback period.
2. Assuming that depreciation is $14,000 per year, compute the accounting rate of return (on total investment).
3. Compute the NPV of the franchise.
4. Compute the IRR of the franchise.
5. Should Kenn buy the equipment?

Solution

1. The payback period is $\frac{\$300,000}{\$50,000}$, or six years.
2. The accounting rate of return is $\frac{(\$50,000 - \$14,000)}{\$300,000}$, or 12 percent.
3. From Exhibit 17B-2, the discount factor for an annuity with i at 10 percent and n at 20 years is 8.514. Thus, the NPV is (8.514 × $50,000) − $300,000, or $125,700.
4. The discount factor associated with the IRR is 6.00 ($\frac{\$300,000}{\$50,000}$). From Exhibit 17B-2, the IRR is between 14 and 16 percent (using the row corresponding to period 20).
5. Since the NPV is positive and the IRR is greater than Kenn's cost of capital, the test equipment is a sound investment. This, of course, assumes that the cash flow projections are accurate.

II. Capital Investment with Competing Projects (with tax effects) Weins Postal Service (WPS) has decided to acquire a new delivery truck. The choice has been narrowed to two models. The following information has been gathered for each model:

	Custom	Deluxe
Acquisition cost	$20,000	$25,000
Annual operating costs	$3,500	$2,000
Depreciation method	MACRS	MACRS
Expected salvage value	$5,000	$8,000

WPS's cost of capital is 14 percent. The company plans to use the truck for five years and then sell it for its salvage value. Assume the combined state and federal tax rate is 40 percent.

REQUIRED:

1. Compute the after-tax operating cash flows for each model.
2. Compute the NPV for each model and make a recommendation.

Solution

1. For light trucks, MACRS guidelines allow a five-year life. Using the rates from Exhibit 17-8, depreciation is calculated for each model:

Year	Custom	Deluxe
1	$ 4,000	$ 5,000
2	6,400	8,000
3	3,840	4,800
4	2,304	2,880
5	1,152*	1,440*
Total	$17,696	$22,120

*Only half the depreciation is allowed in the year of disposal.

The after-tax operating cash flows are computed using the spreadsheet format:

Custom

Year	$(1-t)R$	$-(1-t)C$	tNC	Other	CF
1	n/a	$(2,100)	$1,600		$ (500)
2	n/a	(2,100)	2,560		460
3	n/a	(2,100)	1,536		(564)
4	n/a	(2,100)	922		(1,178)
5	1,618[a]	(2,100)	461	$2,304[b]	2,283

[a]Salvage value ($5,000) − Book value ($20,000 − $17,696 = $2,304) = $2,696; 0.60 × $2,696 = $1,618
[b]Recovery of capital = Book value = $2,304. Capital recovered is not taxed—only the gain on sale of the asset. Footnote (a) illustrates how the gain is treated. The nontaxable item requires an additional column for the spreadsheet analysis.

Deluxe

Year	$(1-t)R$	$-(1-t)C$	tNC	Other	CF
1	n/a	$(1,200)	$2,000		$ 800
2	n/a	(1,200)	3,200		2,000
3	n/a	(1,200)	1,920		720
4	n/a	(1,200)	1,152		(48)
5	$3,072[a]	(1,200)	576	$2,880[b]	5,328

[a]Salvage value ($8,000) − Book value ($25,000 − $22,120 = $2,880) = $5,120; 0.60 × $5,120 = $3,072
[b]Recovery of capital = Book value = $2,880. Capital recovered is not taxed—only the gain on sale of the asset. Footnote (a) illustrates how the gain is treated. The nontaxable item requires an additional column for the spreadsheet analysis.

2. NPV computation:

Custom

Year	Cash Flow	Discount Factor	Present Value
0	$(20,000)	1.000	$(20,000)
1	(500)	0.877	(439)
2	460	0.769	354
3	(564)	0.675	(381)
4	(1,178)	0.592	(697)
5	2,283	0.519	1,185
Net present value			$(19,978)

		Deluxe	
Year	Cash Flow	Discount Factor	Present Value
0	$(25,000)	1.000	$(25,000)
1	800	0.877	702
2	2,000	0.769	1,538
3	720	0.675	486
4	(48)	0.592	(28)
5	5,328	0.519	2,765
	Net present value		$(19,537)

The deluxe model should be chosen since it has the largest NPV, indicating that it is the least costly of the two cars. Note also that the net present values are negative and that we are choosing the least costly investment.

QUESTIONS FOR WRITING AND DISCUSSION

1. Explain the difference between independent projects and mutually exclusive projects.
2. Explain why the timing and quantity of cash flows are important in capital investment decisions.
3. The time value of money is ignored by the payback period and the accounting rate of return. Explain why this is a major deficiency in these two models.
4. What is the payback period? Compute the payback period for an investment requiring an initial outlay of $80,000 with expected annual cash inflows of $30,000.
5. Name and discuss three possible reasons that the payback period is used to help make capital investment decisions.
6. What is the accounting rate of return? Compute the accounting rate of return for an investment that requires an initial outlay of $300,000 and promises an average net income of $100,000.
7. The net present value is the same as the profit of a project expressed in present dollars. Do you agree? Explain.
8. Explain the relationship between NPV and a firm's value.
9. What is the cost of capital? What role does it play in capital investment decisions?
10. What is the role that the required rate of return plays in the NPV model? in the IRR model?
11. Explain how the NPV is used to determine whether a project should be accepted or rejected.
12. The IRR is the true or actual rate of return being earned by the project. Do you agree or disagree? Discuss.

13. Explain what a postaudit is and how it can provide useful input for future capital investment decisions, especially those involving advanced technology.
14. Explain why NPV is generally preferred over IRR when choosing among competing or mutually exclusive projects. Why would managers continue to use IRR to choose among mutually exclusive projects?
15. Suppose that a firm must choose between two mutually exclusive projects, both of which have negative NPVs. Explain how a firm can legitimately choose among two such projects.
16. Why is it important to have accurate projections of cash flows for potential capital investments?
17. Describe why it is important for a manager to conduct a careful review of the assumptions and methods used in forecasting cash flows.
18. What are the principal tax implications that should be considered in year 0?
19. Explain why the MACRS method of recognizing depreciation is better than the straight-line method.
20. What is the half-year convention? What is the effect of this convention on the length of time it actually takes to write off the cost of a depreciable asset?
21. Explain the important factors to consider for capital investment in the advanced manufacturing environment.
22. Explain what sensitivity analysis is. How can it help in capital budgeting decisions?

WARM-UP EXERCISES

This section provides short warm-up exercises based on the examples in the chapter. Each warm-up exercise gives the page number on which the text example can be found. You may want to refer to the text example to see how the exercise can be set up and solved.

W17-1
Payback Period; APR
LO 2
pp. 701–703

A new laundromat facility costs $200,000 and has a life of five years with no salvage value. The facility will generate the following annual cash flows:

Year 1	$ 60,000
2	80,000
3	100,000
4	120,000
5	140,000

REQUIRED:
1. Compute the payback period.
2. Compute the accounting rate of return using original investment.

W17-2
NPV
LO 3
pp. 704–705

A new product is being considered. The product is expected to produce annual revenues of $500,000. The product has a life cycle of five years. Equipment to produce the product will cost $550,000. After five years the equipment can be sold for $80,000. Working capital will increase by $60,000 because inventories and receivables will increase. Annual cash operating expenses are estimated at $380,000. The required rate of return is 12 percent. There are no income taxes.

REQUIRED:
1. Compute the annual cash flows.
2. Calculate the NPV for the project.

W17-3
IRR; Even Cash Flows
LO 4
p. 706

A proposed project requires an investment of $300,000 and will produce annual after-tax cash flows of $124,875. The project life is three years.

REQUIRED: Compute the IRR.

W17-4
Mutually Exclusive Projects
LO 6
pp. 710–711

A firm is considering two different product designs: design A and design B. The after-tax cash flows for each design follow:

	Design A	Design B
Annual revenues	$300,000	$400,000
Operating cash	$210,000	$295,000
Investment	$269,190	$314,055
Product life	5 years	5 years

The required rate of return is 12 percent.

REQUIRED:
1. Compute the NPV for each project.
2. Compute the IRR for each project.
3. Which design should be chosen? Explain.

W17-5
After-Tax Cash Flows
LO 7
pp. 715–717

A company has annual revenues of $900,000, cash expenses of $500,000, and annual depreciation of $100,000. The tax rate is 40 percent.

REQUIRED:
1. Compute the annual after-tax cash flow using an income-statement approach.
2. Compute the annual after-tax cash flow for each item of the income statement.

EXERCISES

E17-1
Basic Concepts
LO 1, LO 2, LO 3, LO 4

Each of the following parts is independent. Assume all cash flows are after-tax cash flows.

1. Linda Wheeler has just invested $100,000 in a clothing store. She expects to receive an income of $30,000 per year from the investment. What is the payback period for Linda?

2. Sam Kelly placed $20,000 in a three-year savings plan. The plan pays 10 percent, and he cannot withdraw the money early without a penalty. Assuming that Sam leaves the money in the plan for the full three years, how much money will he have?

3. Lions Company is considering the purchase of an automated purchasing system. The cash benefits will be $120,000 per year. The system costs $680,000 and will last ten years. Compute the NPV assuming a discount rate of 12 percent. Should the company buy the automated purchasing system?

4. Jane Hommer has just invested $50,000 in a company. She expects to receive $8,050 per year for the next eight years. Her cost of capital is 6 percent. Compute the internal rate of return. Did Jane make a good decision?

E17-2
Payback; Accounting Rate of Return; NPV; IRR
LO 1, LO 2, LO 3, LO 4

Henderson Company is considering an investment in equipment that will be used to produce a new product line. The outlay required is $500,000. The equipment is expected to last five years and will have no salvage value. The expected after-tax cash flows associated with the project follow:

Year	Cash Revenues	Cash Expenses
1	$650,000	$500,000
2	650,000	500,000
3	650,000	500,000
4	650,000	500,000
5	650,000	500,000

REQUIRED:

1. Compute the project's payback period.
2. Compute the project's accounting rate of return (a) on initial investment and (b) on average investment.
3. Compute the project's net present value, assuming a required rate of return of 10 percent.
4. Compute the project's internal rate of return.

E17-3
Payback; Accounting Rate of Return; Present Value; NPV; IRR
LO 1, LO 2, LO 3, LO 4

The first two parts are related; the last three are independent of all other parts. Assume all cash flows are after-tax cash flows.

1. Randy Willis is considering investing in one of the two following projects. Either project will require an investment of $10,000. The expected cash flows for the two projects follow. Assume each project is depreciable:

Year	Project A	Project B
1	$ 3,000	$3,000
2	4,000	4,000
3	5,000	6,000
4	10,000	3,000
5	10,000	3,000

What is the payback period for each project? If rapid payback is important, which project should be chosen? Which would you choose?

2. Calculate the accounting rate of return for each project in requirement 1. Which project should be chosen based on the accounting rate of return?

3. Wilma Golding is retiring and has the option to take her retirement as a lump sum of $225,000 or to receive $24,000 per year for 20 years. Wilma's required rate of return is 8 percent. Assuming she will live for another 20 years, should she take the lump sum or the annuity?

4. David Booth is interested in investing in some tools and equipment so that he can do independent dry walling. The cost of the tools and equipment is $20,000. He estimates that the return from owning his own equipment will be $6,000 per year. The tools and equipment will last six years. Assuming a required rate of return of 8 percent, calculate the NPV of the investment. Should he invest?

5. Patsy Folson is evaluating what appears to be an attractive opportunity. She is currently the owner of a small manufacturing company and has the opportunity to acquire another small company's equipment that would provide production of a part currently purchased externally. She estimates that the savings from internal production would be $25,000 per year. She estimates that the equipment would last ten years. The owner is asking $130,400 for the equipment. Her company's cost of capital is 10 percent. Calculate the project's internal rate of return. Should she acquire the equipment?

E17-4
NPV; Accounting Rate of Return; Payback
LO 1, LO 2, LO 3

Kildon Rental Agency is considering the purchase of two new rental items: loading equipment and packaging equipment. The after-tax cash inflows for the two independent investment projects are as follows:

Year	Loading	Packaging
1	$60,000	$10,000
2	30,000	10,000
3	40,000	60,000
4	20,000	80,000
5	10,000	90,000

Both projects require an investment in equipment totaling $100,000. The equipment has a life of five years with no salvage value.

REQUIRED:
1. Assuming a discount rate of 12 percent, compute the net present value of each rental item.
2. Compute the payback period for each item. Assume that the manager of the company accepts only projects with a payback period of three years or less. Offer some reasons why this may be a rational strategy even though the NPV computed in requirement 1 may indicate otherwise.
3. Compute the accounting rate of return for each project using (a) initial investment and (b) average investment.

E17-5
NPV: Basic Concepts
LO 3

A company is considering an investment that requires an outlay of $100,000 and promises an after-tax cash inflow one year from now of $115,500. The company's cost of capital is 10 percent.

REQUIRED:
1. Break the $115,500 future cash inflow into three components: (a) the return of the original investment, (b) the cost of capital, and (c) the profit earned on the investment. Now compute the present value of the profit earned on the investment.
2. Compute the NPV of the investment. Compare this with the present value of the profit computed in requirement 1. What does this tell you about the meaning of NPV?

E17-6
NPV; Cost of Capital; Basic Concepts
LO 3

Real Company has an opportunity to invest in a new product line that will have a two-year life cycle. The investment requires a current $50,000 outlay. The capital will be raised by borrowing $10,000 and by raising $40,000 through the issue of new stock. The $10,000 loan will have net interest payments of $500 at the end of each of the two years, with the principal being repaid at the end of year 2 (thus, the net cost of debt is 5 percent). The stock issue carries with it an expectation of a 10 percent return, expressed in the form of dividends at the end of each year ($4,000 in dividends will be paid each of the next two years). The sources of capital for this investment represent the same proportion and costs that the company typically has. Finally, the project will produce after-tax cash inflows of $30,000 per year for the next two years.

REQUIRED:
1. Compute the cost of capital for the project.
2. Compute the NPV for the project. Explain why it is not necessary to subtract the interest payments and the dividend payments from the annual inflow of $30,000 in carrying out this computation.

E17-7
Solving for Unknowns
LO 3, LO 4

Solve each of the following independent cases (assume all cash flows are after-tax cash flows).

1. Thomas Company is investing $120,000 in a project that will yield a uniform series of cash inflows over the next four years. If the internal rate of return is 14 percent, how much cash inflow per year can be expected?
2. Video Repair has decided to invest in some new electronic equipment. The equipment will have a three-year life and will produce a uniform series of cash savings. The net present value of the equipment is $1,750, using a discount rate of 8 percent. The internal rate of return is 12 percent. Determine the investment and the amount of cash savings realized each year.
3. A new lathe costing $60,096 will produce savings of $12,000 per year. How many years must the lathe last if an IRR of 18 percent is realized?
4. The NPV of a project is $3,927. The project has a life of four years and produces the following cash flows:

Year 1	$10,000
Year 2	12,000
Year 3	15,000
Year 4	?

The cost of the project is two times the cash flow produced in year 4. The discount rate is 10 percent. Find the cost of the project and the cash flow for year 4.

E17-8
NPV versus IRR
LO 6

A company is considering two different modifications to its current manufacturing process. The after-tax cash flows associated with the two investments follow:

Year	Project I	Project II
	($100,000)	($100,000)
1	—	63,857
2	134,560	63,857

The company's cost of capital is 10 percent.

REQUIRED:
1. Compute the NPV and the IRR for each investment.
2. Explain why the project with the larger NPV is the correct choice for the company.

E17-9
Computation of
After-Tax Cash Flows
LO 7

Garner, Inc. is considering the possibility of investing in two independent projects. One project is a new information processing system for receiving and the other entails the acquisition of two delivery trucks. The expected annual operating revenues and expenses follow for each project:

Project A (investment in information system)

Revenues	$ 60,000
Cash expenses	(30,000)
Depreciation	(10,000)
Income before taxes	$ 20,000
Taxes	(8,000)
Net income	$ 12,000

Project B (acquisition of two delivery trucks)

Cash expenses	$20,000
Depreciation	10,000

REQUIRED: Compute the after-tax cash flows of each project. The tax rate is 40 percent and includes federal and state assessments.

E17-10
MACRS; NPV
LO 7

A company is planning to buy a set of special tools for its manufacturing operation. The cost of the tools is $12,000. The tools have a three-year life and qualify for the use of the three-year MACRS. The tax rate is 40 percent; the cost of capital is 12 percent.

REQUIRED:
1. Calculate the present value of the tax depreciation shield, assuming that straight-line depreciation with a half-year life is used.
2. Calculate the present value of the tax depreciation shield, assuming that MACRS is used.
3. What is the benefit of using MACRS?

E17-11
Lease or Buy
LO 6, LO 7

A small company has decided that it needs to have regular access to a car for local errands and occasional business trips. The owner of the company is trying to decide between buying or leasing the car. The purchase cost is $18,500. The annual operating costs are estimated at $3,000. If the car is leased, a five-year lease will be acquired. The lease requires a refundable deposit of $500 and annual lease payments of $3,500. Operating costs, in addition to the lease payment, also total $4,500 per year. The company's cost of capital is 10 percent and its tax rate is 40 percent. If the car is purchased, MACRS depreciation will be used.

REQUIRED: Using NPV analysis, determine whether the car should be leased or purchased. Assume MACRS depreciation is used for tax purposes.

E17-12
Discount Rates; Advanced Manufacturing Environment
LO 8

A company is considering two competing investments. The first is for a standard piece of production equipment; the second is for some computer-aided manufacturing (CAM) equipment. The investment and after-tax operating cash flows follow:

Year	Standard Equipment	CAM
0	$(500,000)	$(2,000,000)
1	300,000	100,000
2	200,000	200,000
3	100,000	300,000
4	100,000	400,000
5	100,000	400,000
6	100,000	400,000
7	100,000	500,000
8	100,000	1,000,000
9	100,000	1,000,000
10	100,000	1,000,000

The company uses a discount rate of 18 percent for all of its investments. The company's cost of capital is 10 percent.

REQUIRED:
1. Calculate the net present value for each investment using a discount rate of 18 percent.
2. Calculate the net present value for each investment using a discount rate of 10 percent.
3. Which rate should the company use to compute the net present value? Explain.

E17-13
Quality; Market Share; Advanced Manufacturing Environment
LO 8

Refer to E17-12. Assume that the company's cost of capital is 14 percent.

REQUIRED:
1. Calculate the NPV of each alternative using the 14 percent rate.
2. Now assume that if the standard equipment is purchased, the competitive position of the firm will deteriorate because of lower quality (relative to competitors who did automate). Marketing estimates that the loss in market share will decrease the projected net cash inflows by 50 percent for years 3 through 10. Recalculate the NPV of the standard equipment given this outcome. What is the decision now? Discuss the importance of assessing the effect of intangible benefits.

ROBLEMS

P17-1
Basic NPV Analysis
LO 1, LO 3

Tara Anderson, marketing manager, knew that the acceptance of the new product would depend on the economic feasibility of acquiring the equipment needed to produce the product. The equipment would cost $100,000 and its cash operating expenses would total $20,000 per year. The equipment would last for seven years but would need a major overhaul costing $10,000 at the end of the fifth year. At the end of seven years, the equipment would be sold for $8,000. An increase in working capital totaling $10,000 would also be needed at the beginning of the project. This would be recovered at the end of the seven years.

   The new product (exercise equipment) would sell for $100 per unit and would cost $70 per unit to produce (in addition to the operating expenses of the equipment). Tara expects to sell 1,500 units per year. The cost of capital is 10 percent.

REQUIRED:
1. Prepare a schedule of cash flows for the proposed project. Assume there are no income taxes.
2. Compute the NPV of the project. Should the new product be produced?

P17-2
NPV Analysis
LO 1, LO 3

Uintah Communications Company is considering the production and marketing of a communications system that will increase the efficiency of messaging for small businesses or branch offices of large companies. Each unit hooked into the system is assigned a mailbox number, which can be matched to a telephone extension number, providing access to messages 24 hours a day. Up to 20 units can be hooked into the system, allowing the delivery of the same message to as many as 20 people. Personal codes can be used to make messages confidential. Furthermore, messages can be reviewed, recorded, canceled, replied to, or deleted, all during the same phone call. Indicators wired to the telephone blink whenever new messages are present.

   To produce this product, a $1.1 million investment in new equipment is required. The equipment would last ten years but would need major maintenance costing $100,000 at the end of its sixth year. The salvage value of the equipment at the end of ten years is estimated to be $40,000. If this new system is produced, working capital must also be increased by $50,000. This capital will be restored at the end of the product's life cycle, estimated to be ten years. Revenues from the sale of the product are estimated at $1.5 million per year; cash operating expenses are estimated at $1.26 million per year.

REQUIRED:
1. Prepare a schedule of cash flows for the proposed project. Assume there are no income taxes.
2. Assuming that Uintah's cost of capital is 12 percent, compute the project's NPV. Should the product be produced?

P17-3
Basic IRR Analysis
LO 1, LO 4

Quemado Company was approached by a local furnace company with the proposition of replacing its old heating system with a modern, more efficient unit. The cost of the new system was quoted at $50,000, but it would save $10,000 per year in fuel costs. The estimated life of the new system is ten years, with no salvage value expected. Excited over the possibility of saving $10,000 per year and having a more reliable unit, the president of Quemado has asked for an analysis of the project's economic viability. All capital projects are required to earn at least the firm's cost of capital, which is 10 percent. There are no income taxes.

REQUIRED:
1. Calculate the project's internal rate of return. Should the company acquire the new furnace?
2. Suppose that fuel savings are less than claimed. Calculate the minimum annual cash savings that must be realized for the project to earn a rate equal to the firm's cost of capital.
3. Suppose that the life of the furnace is overestimated by two years. Repeat requirements 1 and 2 under this assumption.

P17-4
NPV; Uncertainty
LO 1, LO 3

Eden Airlines is interested in acquiring a new aircraft to service a new route. The route would be from Dallas to El Paso. The aircraft would fly one round-trip daily, except for scheduled maintenance days. There are 15 maintenance days scheduled each year. The seating capacity of the aircraft is 150. Flights are expected to be fully booked. The average revenue per passenger per flight (one-way) is $200. Annual operating costs of the aircraft follow:

Fuel	$1,400,000
Flight personnel	500,000
Food and beverages	100,000
Maintenance	400,000
Other	100,000
Total	$2,500,000

The aircraft will cost $100,000,000 and has an expected life of 20 years. The company requires a 14 percent return. Assume there are no income taxes.

REQUIRED:
1. Calculate the NPV for the aircraft. Should the company buy it?
2. In discussing the proposal, the marketing manager for the airline believes that the assumption of 100 percent booking is unrealistic. He believes that the booking rate will be somewhere between 70 percent and 90 percent, with the most likely rate being 80 percent. Recalculate the NPV using an 80 percent seating capacity. Should the aircraft be purchased?
3. Calculate the average seating rate that would be needed so that NPV = 0.
4. Suppose that the price per passenger could be increased by 10 percent without any effect on demand. What is the average seating rate now needed to achieve a NPV = 0? What would you now recommend?

P17-5
Review of Basic Capital Investment Procedures
LO 1, LO 2, LO 3, LO 4

Dr. Donna White had just returned from a conference in which she learned of a new procedure for performing root canals, which reduces the time to perform them by 50 percent. Given her patient-load pressures, Dr. White was anxious to try out the new technique. By decreasing the time spent on root canals, she could increase her total revenues by performing more services within a work period. Unfortunately, in order to implement the new procedure, some special equipment costing $20,000 was needed. The equipment had an expected life of four years, with a salvage value of $2,000. Dr. White estimated that her cash revenues would increase by the following amounts:

Year	Revenue Increases
1	$5,600
2	8,000
3	9,800
4	9,800

She also expected additional cash expenses amounting to $1,000 per year. The cost of capital is 12 percent. Assume there are no income taxes.

REQUIRED:
1. Compute the payback period for the new equipment.
2. Compute the accounting rate of return using both original investment and average investment.
3. Compute the NPV and IRR for the project. Should Dr. White purchase the new equipment? Should she be concerned about payback or the accounting rate of return in making this decision?
4. Before finalizing her decision, Dr. White decided to call two dentists who had been using the new procedure for the past six months. The conversations revealed a somewhat less glowing report than she received at the conference. Nearly 25 percent of the patients receiving the procedure returned with complaints about the affected tooth. A traditional rework had to be performed on these patients. Dr. White estimated that the increase in cash revenues would be cut by 33 percent because of the extra time and cost involved in rework. Furthermore, who knew what the effect on patient goodwill would be? Using this information, recompute the NPV and the IRR of the project. What would you now recommend?

P17-6
Replacement

Madison Company is considering replacing its existing mainframe computer with a new model manufactured by a different company. The old computer was acquired three years ago, has a

Decision; Basic NPV Analysis
LO 1, LO 6, LO 7

remaining life of five years, and will have a salvage value of $10,000. The book value is $200,000. Straight-line depreciation with a half-life convention is being used for tax purposes. The cash operating costs of the existing computer, including software, personnel, and other supplies, total $100,000 per year.

The new computer has an initial cost of $500,000 and will have cash operating costs of $50,000 per year. The new computer will have a life of five years and will have a salvage value of $100,000 at the end of the fifth year. MACRS depreciation will be used for tax purposes. If the new computer is purchased, the old one will be sold for $50,000. The company needs to decide whether to keep the old computer or buy the new one. The cost of capital is 12 percent. The tax rate is 40 percent.

REQUIRED: Compute the NPV of each alternative. Should the company keep the old computer or buy the new one?

P17-7
Lease versus Buy
LO 1, LO 6, LO 7

Trasky Company is trying to decide whether it should purchase or lease a new automated machine to be used in the production of a new product. If purchased, the new machine would cost $100,000 and would be used for ten years. The salvage value at the end of ten years is estimated at $20,000. The machine would be depreciated using MACRS over a seven-year period. The annual maintenance and operating costs would be $20,000. Annual revenues are estimated at $55,000.

If the machine is leased, the company would need to pay annual lease payments of $20,700. The first lease payment and a deposit of $5,000 are due immediately. The last lease payment is paid at the beginning of year 10. The deposit is refundable at the end of the tenth year. In addition, under a normal contract, the company must pay for all maintenance and operating costs, although the leasing company does offer a service contract that will provide annual maintenance (on leased machines only). The contract must be paid up front and costs $30,000. Trasky estimates that the contract will reduce its annual maintenance and operating costs by $10,000. Trasky's cost of capital is 14 percent. The tax rate is 40 percent.

REQUIRED:
1. Prepare schedules showing the after-tax cash flows for each alternative. (Prepare schedules for the lease alternative with and without the service contract; assume that the service contract is amortized on a straight-line basis for the ten years.) Include all revenues and costs associated with each alternative.
2. Compute the NPV for each alternative, assuming that Trasky does not purchase the service contract. Should the machine be purchased or leased? For this analysis, was it necessary to include all of the costs and revenues for each alternative? Explain.
3. Compute the NPV for the lease alternative assuming that the service contract is purchased. Does this change your decision about leasing? What revenues and costs could be excluded without affecting the conclusion?

P17-8
Competing Investments; NPV; Basic Analysis
LO 1, LO 6, LO 7

Harold Griggs has decided to start a dry cleaning business. As part of his service, he is planning to have a pickup and delivery service. A premium will be charged for the service, and this premium is expected to cover the extra operating costs. Harold has two options for providing the service. He can buy a delivery truck and hire a driver or he can pay an annual fee to a local agency that will provide the pickup and delivery service. Cost and other data follow:

	Ownership Option	Agency Option
Initial outlay	$25,000	—
Annual premiums	20,000	$20,000
Cash expenses	12,000	8,800

The expected life of the truck is six years, and it will have a salvage value of $1,000. The truck qualifies as five-year property for MACRS purposes. Harold's tax rate is 40 percent. The cost of capital is 12 percent.

REQUIRED: Compute the NPV of each alternative and make a recommendation to Harold.

"I know that it's the thing to do," insisted Pamela Kincaid, vice-president of finance for Colgate Manufacturing. "If we are going to be competitive, we need to build this completely automated plant."

"I'm not so sure," replied Bill Thomas. "The savings from labor reductions and increased productivity are only $4 million per year. The price tag for this factory—and it's a small one—is $45 million. That gives a payback period of more than eleven years. That's a long time to put the company's money at risk."

"Yeah, but you're overlooking the savings that we'll get from the increase in quality," interjected John Simpson, production manager. "With this system, we can decrease our waste and our rework time significantly. Those savings are worth another million dollars per year."

"Another million will only cut the payback to nine years," retorted Bill. "Ron, you're the marketing manager—do you have any insights?"

"Well, there are other factors to consider, such as service quality and market share. I think that increasing our product quality and improving our delivery service will make us a lot more competitive. I know for a fact that two of our competitors have decided against automation. That'll give us a shot at their customers, provided our product is of higher quality and we can deliver it faster. I estimate that it'll increase our net cash benefits by another $6 million."

"Wow! Now that's impressive," Bill exclaimed, nearly convinced. "The payback is now getting down to a reasonable level."

"I agree," said Pamela, "but we do need to be sure that it's a sound investment. I know that estimates for construction of the facility have gone as high as $49.8 million. I also know that the expected residual value, after the 20 years of service we expect to get, is $5 million. Also, you're using before-tax cash flows. We need after-tax cash flows. I think I had better see if this project can cover our 14 percent cost of capital."

"Now wait a minute, Pamela," Bill demanded. "You know that I usually insist on a 20 percent rate of return, especially for a project of this magnitude."

REQUIRED:
1. Compute the NPV of the project using the original savings and investment figures. Do the calculation for discount rates of 14 percent and 20 percent. Assume straight-line depreciation with no half-year convention used for tax purposes. The tax rate is 40 percent (includes state and federal taxes).
2. Compute the NPV of the project using the additional benefits noted by the production and marketing managers. Also, use the original cost estimate of $45 million. Again, do the calculation for both possible discount rates.
3. Compute the NPV of the project using all estimates of cash flows, including the possible initial outlay of $49.8 million. Do the calculation using discount rates of 14 percent and 20 percent.
4. If you were making the decision, what would you do? Explain.

Olnack Products, Inc. is evaluating a new accounting information system. The initial cost of the system is estimated at $430,000 and includes a computer, terminals, software, and installation. There is no expected salvage value. The new system has a useful life of eight years and is projected to produce cash operating savings of $135,000 per year over the old manual system. In addition to the operating savings, the new system will produce a depreciation tax shield absent under the old system. Straight-line depreciation (with half-year convention) will be used for tax purposes. The tax rate is 40 percent and the cost of capital is 16 percent.

REQUIRED:
1. Compute the NPV of the new system. Use the proper class life for depreciation.
2. One year after implementation, the internal audit staff noted the following about the new system: (1) the cost of acquiring the system was $30,000 more than expected due to higher installation costs, and (2) the annual cost savings were $10,000 less than expected because more in-house programming was needed than expected. Using the changes in expected costs and benefits, compute the NPV as if this information had been available one year ago. Did the company make the right decision?
3. Why is a postaudit beneficial to a firm?

Pearson Manufacturing, Inc. produces microwave ovens, electric ranges, and freezers. Because of increasing competition, Pearson is considering making an investment in a computer-aided manu-

Advanced Manufacturing Environment

LO 7, LO 8

facturing (CAM) system. The microwave plant has been selected for initial evaluation. The CAM system for the dishwasher line would replace an existing system (purchased one year ago for $6 million). Although the existing system will be fully depreciated in nine years, it is expected to last another ten years. The CAM system would also have a useful life of ten years.

The existing system is capable of producing 100,000 microwave units per year. Sales and production data using the existing system are provided by the accounting department:

Sales per year (units)	100,000
Selling price	$300
Costs per unit:	
Direct materials	80
Direct labor	90
Volume-related overhead	20
Direct fixed overhead	40*

*These are all cash expenses with the exception of depreciation, which is $6 per unit. The existing equipment is being depreciated using straight-line with no salvage value considered.

The CAM system will cost $34 million to purchase, plus an estimated $20 million in software and implementation. (Assume that all investment outlays occur at the beginning of the first year.) If the CAM equipment is purchased, the old equipment can be sold for $3 million.

The CAM system will require fewer parts for production and will produce with less waste. Because of this, the direct materials cost per unit will be reduced by 25 percent. Automation will also require fewer support activities and, as a consequence, volume-related overhead will be reduced by $4 per unit and direct fixed overhead (other than depreciation) by $17 per unit. Direct labor is reduced by 60 percent. Assume, for simplicity, that the new investment will be depreciated on a pure straight-line basis for tax purposes with no salvage value. Ignore the half-life convention.

The firm's cost of capital is 12 percent but management chooses to use 20 percent as the required rate of return for evaluation of investments. The tax rate is 40 percent.

REQUIRED:

1. Compute the net present value for the old system and the CAM system. Which system would the company choose?
2. Repeat the net present value analysis of requirement 1 using 12 percent as the discount rate.
3. Upon seeing the projected sales for the old system, the marketing manager commented: "Sales of 100,000 units per year cannot be maintained in the current competitive environment for more than one year unless we buy the CAM system. The CAM system will allow us to compete on the basis of quality and lead time. If we keep the old system, our sales will drop by 10,000 units per year." Repeat the net present value analysis using this new information and a 12 percent discount rate.
4. An industrial engineer for Pearson noticed that salvage value for the CAM equipment had not been included in the analysis. He estimated that the equipment could be sold for $4 million at the end of ten years. He also estimated that the equipment of the old system would have no salvage value at the end of ten years. Repeat the net present value analysis using this information, the information in requirement 3, and a 12 percent discount rate.
5. Given the outcomes of the previous four requirements, comment on the importance of providing accurate inputs for assessing investments in CAM manufacturing systems.

P17-12

Inflation and Capital Investment

LO 3, LO 4

Thayn Thompson, divisional manager, has been pushing headquarters to grant approval for the installation of a new flexible manufacturing system. Finally, in the last executive meeting, Thayn was told that if he could show how the new system would increase the firm's value, it would be approved. Thayn gathered the following information:

Year	Old System	Flexible System
Initial investment	—	$1,250,000
Annual operating costs	$350,000	$95,000
Annual depreciation	100,000	?
Tax rate*	34%	34%
Cost of capital	12%	12%
Expected life	10 years	10 years
Salvage value	none	none

*In order to locate its operations in the state, the company was exempted from state income taxes for 20 years. Since the company had only operated in the state for ten years, the state tax rate could be ignored in the analysis.

With the exception of the cost of capital, this information ignores the rate of inflation, which has been 4 percent per year and is expected to continue at this level for the next decade.

REQUIRED:
1. Compute the NPV for each system.
2. Compute the NPV for each system adjusting the future cash flows for the rate of inflation.
3. Comment on the importance of adjusting cash flows for inflationary effects.

 MANAGERIAL DECISION CASES

C17-1
Capital Investment and Ethical Behavior
LO 3

Manny Carson, CMA and controller of the Wakeman Enterprises, had been given permission to acquire a new computer and software for the company's accounting system. The capital investment analysis had shown an NPV of $100,000; however, the initial estimates of acquisition and installation costs had been made on the basis of tentative costs without any formal bids. Manny now has two formal bids, one that would allow the firm to meet or beat the original projected NPV and one that would reduce the projected NPV by $50,000. The second bid involves a system that would increase both the initial cost and the operating cost.

Normally, Manny would take the first bid without hesitation. However, Todd Downing, the owner of the firm presenting the second bid, was a close friend. Manny had called Todd and explained the situation, offering Todd an opportunity to alter his bid and win the job. Todd thanked Manny and then made a counteroffer.

Todd: Listen, Manny, this job at the original price is the key to a successful year for me. The revenues will help me gain approval for the loan I need for renovation and expansion. If I don't get that loan, I see hard times ahead. The financial stats for loan approval are so marginal that reducing the bid price may blow my chances.

Manny: Losing the bid altogether would be even worse, don't you think?

Todd: True. However, I have a suggestion. If you grant me the job, I will have the capability of adding personnel. I know that your son is looking for a job, and I can offer him a good salary and a promising future. Additionally, I'll be able to take you and your wife on that vacation to Hawaii that we have been talking about.

Manny: Well, you have a point. My son is having an awful time finding a job, and he has a wife and three kids to support. My wife is tired of having them live with us. She and I could use a vacation. I doubt that the other bidder would make any fuss if we turned it down. Its offices are out of state, after all.

Todd: Out of state? All the more reason to turn it down. Given the state's economy, it seems almost criminal to take business outside. Those are the kind of business decisions that cause problems for people like your son.

REQUIRED: Evaluate the ethical behavior of Manny. Should Manny have called Todd in the first place? What if Todd had agreed to meet the lower bid price—would there have been any problems? Identify the standards of ethical conduct (listed in Chapter 1) that Manny may be violating, if any.

C17-2
Payback; NPV; IRR;
Effect of Differences
in Sales on Project
Viability
LO 2, LO 3, LO 4

Shaftel Ready Mix is a processor and supplier of concrete, aggregate, and rock products. The company operates in the intermountain Western United States. Currently, Shaftel has 14 cement-processing plants and a labor force of more than 375 employees. With the exception of cement powder, all raw materials (for example, aggregates and sand) are produced internally by the company. The demand for concrete and aggregates has been growing steadily nationally, and in the West, the growth rate has been above the national average. Because of this growth, Shaftel has more than tripled its gross revenues over the past ten years.

Of the intermountain states, Arizona has been experiencing the most growth. Processing plants have been added over the past several years and the company is considering the addition of yet another plant to be located in Scottsdale. A major advantage of another plant in Arizona is the ability to operate year round, a feature not found in states such as Utah and Wyoming.

In setting up the new plant, land would have to be purchased and a small building constructed. Equipment and furniture would not need to be purchased; these items would be transferred from a plant that had been opened in Wyoming during the oil-boom period and closed a few years after the end of that boom. However, the equipment needs some repair and modifications before it can be used. It has a book value of $200,000, and the furniture has a book value of $30,000. Neither has any outside market value. Other costs, such as the installation of a silo, well, electrical hookups, and so on, will be incurred. No salvage value is expected. The summary of the initial investment costs by category is as follows:

Land	$ 20,000
Building	135,000
Equipment:	
Book value	200,000
Modifications	20,000
Furniture (book value)	30,000
Silo	20,000
Well	80,000
Electrical hookups	27,000
General setup	50,000

Estimates concerning the operation of the Scottsdale plant follow:

Life of plant and equipment	10 years
Expected annual sales (in cubic yards)	35,000
Selling price (per cubic yard)	$45.00
Variable costs (per cubic yard):	
Cement	$12.94
Sand/gravel	6.42
Fly ash	1.13
Admixture	1.53
Driver labor	3.24
Mechanics	1.43
Plant operations (batching and cleanup)	1.39
Loader operator	0.50
Truck parts	1.75
Fuel	1.48
Other	3.27
Total variable cost	$35.08
Fixed costs (annual):	
Salaries	$135,000
Insurance	75,000
Telephone	5,000
Depreciation	58,200
Utilities	25,000
Total fixed cost	$298,200

After reviewing these data, Karl Flemming, vice-president of operations, argued against the proposed plant. Karl was concerned because the plant would earn significantly less than the normal 8.3 percent return on sales. All other plants in the company were earning between 7.5 and 8.5 percent on sales. Karl also noted that it would take more than five years to recover the total initial outlay of $582,000. In the past, the company had always insisted that payback be no more than four years. The company's cost of capital is 10 percent. Assume there are no income taxes.

REQUIRED:

1. Prepare a variable-costing income statement for the proposed plant. Compute the ratio of net income to sales. Is Karl correct that the return on sales is significantly lower than the company average?
2. Compute the payback period for the proposed plant. Is Karl right that the payback period is greater than four years? Explain. Suppose that you were told that the equipment being transferred from Wyoming could be sold for its book value. Would this affect your answer?
3. Compute the NPV and the IRR for the proposed plant. Would your answer be affected if you were told that the furniture and equipment could be sold for their book values? If so, repeat the analysis with this effect considered.
4. Compute the cubic yards of cement that must be sold for the new plant to break even. Using this break-even volume, compute the NPV and the IRR. Would the investment be acceptable? If so, explain why an investment that promises to do nothing more than break even can be viewed as acceptable.
5. Compute the volume of cement that must be sold for the IRR to equal the firm's cost of capital. Using this volume, compute the firm's expected annual income. Explain this result.

C17-3
Cash Flows; NPV; Choice of Discount Rate; Advanced Manufacturing Environment
LO 1, LO 6, LO 7, LO 8

Charles Bradshaw, president and owner of Wellington Metal Works, had just returned from a trip to Europe.[10] While there, he had toured several plants using robotic manufacturing. Seeing the efficiency and success of these companies, Charles became convinced that robotic manufacturing is the wave of the future and that Wellington could gain a competitive advantage by adopting the new technology.

Based on this vision, Charles requested an analysis detailing the costs and benefits of robotic manufacturing for the material handling and merchandising equipment group. This group of products consists of such items as cooler shelving, stocking carts, and bakery racks. The products are sold directly to supermarkets.

A committee, consisting of the controller, the marketing manager, and the production manager was given the responsibility of preparing the analysis. As a starting point, the controller provided the following information on expected revenues and expenses for the existing manual system:

		Percentage of Sales
Sales	$ 400,000	100%
Less: Variable expenses[a]	(228,000)	57
Contribution margin	$ 172,000	43
Less: Fixed expenses[b]	(92,000)	23
Income before taxes	$ 80,000	20

[a]Variable cost detail (as a percentage of sales):
Direct materials   16
Direct labor   20
Variable overhead   9
Variable selling   12
[b]Of the total, $20,000 is depreciation; the rest are cash expenses.

Given the current competitive environment, the marketing manager thought that this level of profitability would likely not change for the next decade.

After some investigation into various robotic equipment, the committee settled on an Aide 900 system, a robot that has the capability to weld stainless steel or aluminum. It is capable of being

---

10. This case is based, in part, on David A. Greenberg, "Robotics: One Small Company's Experience," in *Cost Accounting for the 90s* (Montvale, N.J.: National Association of Accountants, 1986), 57–63.

programmed to adjust the path, angle, and speed of the torch. The production manager was excited about the robotic system because it would eliminate the need to hire welders, which was so attractive because the market for welders seemed perpetually tight. By reducing the dependence on welders, better production scheduling and fewer late deliveries would result. Moreover, the robot's production rate is four times that of a person.

It was also discovered that robotic welding is superior in quality to manual welding. As a consequence, some of the costs of poor quality could be reduced. By providing better-quality products and avoiding late deliveries, the marketing manager was convinced that the company would have such a competitive edge that it would increase sales by 50 percent for the affected product group by the end of the fourth year. The marketing manager provided the following projections for the next ten years, the useful life of the robotic equipment:

	Year 1	Year 2	Year 3	Years 4–10
Sales	$400,000	$450,000	$500,000	$600,000

Currently, the company employs four welders, who work 40 hours per week and 50 weeks per year at an average wage of $10 per hour. If the robot is acquired, it will need one operator, who will be paid $10 per hour.

Because of improved quality, the robotic system will also reduce the cost of direct materials by 25 percent, the cost of variable overhead by 33.33 percent, and variable selling expenses by 10 percent. All of these reductions will take place immediately after the robotic system is in place and operating. Fixed costs will be increased by the depreciation associated with the robot. The robot will be depreciated using MACRS (the manual system uses straight-line depreciation without a half-year convention and has a current book value of $200,000). If the robotic system is acquired, the old system will be sold for $40,000.

The robotic system requires the following initial investment:

Purchase price	$380,000
Installation	70,000
Training	30,000
Engineering	40,000

At the end of ten years, the robot will have a salvage value of $20,000. Assume that the company's cost of capital is 12 percent. The tax rate is 40 percent.

REQUIRED:
1. Prepare a schedule of after-tax cash flows for the manual and robotic systems.
2. Using the schedule of cash flows computed in requirement 1, compute the NPV for each system. Should the company invest in the robotic system?
3. In practice, many financial officers tend to use a higher discount rate than is justified by what the firm's cost of capital is. For example, a firm may use a discount rate of 20 percent when its cost of capital is or could be 12 percent. Offer some reasons for this practice. Assume that the annual after-tax cash benefit of adopting the robotic system is $80,000 per year more than the manual system. The initial outlay for the robotic system is $340,000. Compute the NPV using 12 percent and 20 percent. Would the robotic system be acquired if 20 percent is used? Could this conservative approach have a negative impact on a firm's ability to stay competitive?

C17-4
Research Assignment

The capital expenditure approaches that you have studied in this chapter rely on quantitative, financial measures such as payback, net present value, and the internal rate of return. Some have argued that these traditional capital expenditure models should only be a starting point in the analysis. Other criteria such as cycle time (the time it takes to convert materials into a finished good) and flexibility may be important considerations in a capital expenditure decision—yet these factors are not captured by IRR or NPV. In fact, there have been efforts to build formal frameworks that allow explicit consideration of multiple criteria. One of these frameworks is an analytical hierarchy process. This approach is described in the following article:

David E. Stout, Matthew J. Liberatore, and Thomas F. Monahan, "Decision Support Software for Capital Budgeting," *Management Accounting* (July, 1991): 50–53.

REQUIRED: Read the article and write a paper that describes how the method works. In your paper offer a critique of the method. What is your opinion of the approach? Is it better than the traditional models? Or do you think there are ways that the traditional models can capture the effects? Do you think that managers would really use this methodology? Explain.

1. Describe the traditional inventory management model.

2. Describe JIT inventory management.

3. Describe the theory of constraints and explain how it can be used to manage inventory.

CHAPTER

Inventory Management

SCENARIO

ichelle Anderson, president and owner of Anderson Parts, Inc., had just finished reading the report prepared by Henry Jensen, a special consultant attached to the management advisory section of a national public accounting firm. The recommendations in the report were somewhat surprising and Michelle was looking forward to her meeting with him to discuss them. Her thoughts were interrupted by Henry's arrival.

"Have a seat, Henry. I have to confess that your recommendations are intriguing. If you can convince me that they'll work, you'll have more than earned your fee."

"I think I can provide a lot of support for those recommendations. When we first met, you mentioned that your company had lost 20 percent of its market share over the past five years. In your industry, as in many others, much of that loss is because of the gains made by foreign competitors. Foreign producers are offering a higher-quality product at a lower price and with better delivery performance."

"I am aware of that. You remember that in our first meeting I said as much. I was certain at that time that the solution was automation and was prepared to sink millions into that approach. I was convinced that automating would improve quality, lower manufacturing costs, and cut down our lead time for production. Because so much money was involved, I hired you to tell us how to automate and exactly what type of equipment to buy. Instead you tell me that I shouldn't automate—at least not right away—but simplify our purchasing and manufacturing by installing something called a just-in-time system. Do you really believe that this will bring the

benefits I'm seeking? Are you speaking from experience or experiment?"

"Experience. You're certainly not a guinea pig for something we haven't tried before. Case after case has shown us that 80 percent of the competitive benefits from automation can be achieved by implementing JIT—and at a significantly decreased cost. First implement JIT; then you can see where automation will be of the most benefit. The strategy we recommend is first simplify, then automate, and, finally, integrate.[1] Of course, you should realize that JIT and activity-based costing are not an easy fix to all your problems. But these measures should help. I might add that they have helped some firms more than others."

"It sounds promising. But can you be more specific? What benefits have other companies experienced?"

"Well, Michelle, your firm manufactures machine parts. Another firm in your same line of business was having a difficult time competing. It needed 24 weeks to produce one of its products from start to finish while a Japanese competitor produced and delivered the same part in 6 weeks. After installing a JIT system, the American firm was able to produce the part in only 20 days."

"Henry, that's hard to believe. Yet I know that a lot of the business we have lost is because we have such poor delivery performance compared with some of our competitors. You're telling me that we can make dramatic improvements in our lead time with our existing technology?"

"Yes, but that isn't all. Reducing lead time is only one of the benefits. A JIT purchasing and manufacturing system can reduce your inventories— raw materials, work in process, and finished goods—to much lower levels. Do you realize that U.S. industry has as much as 40 percent of its assets tied up in inventory?[2] That's a lot of nonproductive capital. The Lansing plant of General Motors used to carry 60,000 tons of sheet steel in inventory while consuming 900 tons a day. Now it carries 4,000 tons and consumes 1,200 tons a day. Overall, using JIT, GM has cut inventory-related costs from $8 billion to $2 billion. There are other examples. Motorola has reduced inventory by $210 million.[3] A chain saw manufacturer in Oregon has taken $15 million out of inventory through JIT."[4]

"Incredible. But what about quality?"

"JIT cannot work without adopting the concept of total quality control. Defects cannot be tolerated. JIT demands quality. For example, Hewlett-Packard's Fort Collins Division reduced scrap and rework by 60 percent. Xerox reduced its reject rate on outsourced parts from 5,000 parts-per-million one year to 1,300 parts-per-million the next."[5]

1. For a detailed discussion of the strategy, see Stephen M. Hronec, "The Effects of Manufacturing Productivity on Cost Accounting and Management Reporting," *Cost Accounting for the 90s* (Montvale, N.J.: Institute of Management Accountants, 1986): 117–125. See also William G. Stoddard, Stephen G. Schaus, and Nolan W. Rhea, "New Guidelines for Factory Automation," *Material Handling Engineering* (May 1985): 104–107.
2. Ernest Raia, "Just-in-Time USA," *Purchasing* (13 February 1986): 50.
3. Raia, "Just-in-Time USA."
4. Al Furst, "Spreading the Gospel at Fluke," *Electronic Business* (1 April 1986): 82.
5. Both examples are in Raia, "Just-in-Time USA."

Questions to Think About

1. *Why do firms carry inventory?*
2. *What are inventory costs?*
3. *What can be done to minimize inventory costs?*
4. *How does JIT reduce inventories?*
5. *What are the weaknesses of JIT?*
6. *Why is effective management of inventory so important?*

TRADITIONAL INVENTORY MANAGEMENT

Objective 1

Describe the traditional inventory management model.

Managing the levels of inventory is fundamental to establishing a long-term competitive advantage. Quality, product engineering, prices, overtime, excess capacity, ability to respond to customers (due-date performance), lead times, and overall profitability are all affected by inventory levels. In general, firms with higher inventory levels than their competitors tend to be in a worse competitive position. Inventory and how it is managed is strongly related to the ability of firms to obtain the necessary competitive edge to make money now and in the future. Inventory management policy has become a competitive weapon.

How inventory policy can be used to aid in establishing a competitive advantage is the focus of this chapter. First, we review the traditional inventory management model—the model that has been the mainstay of American manufacturing firms for decades. Learning the basics of this model and its underlying conceptual foundation will help us understand where it can still be appropriately applied. Understanding traditional inventory management also provides the necessary background for grasping the advantages of inventory management methods that are used in the advanced manufacturing environment such as JIT and the theory of constraints.

Inventory Costs

In a world of certainty—a world in which the demand for a product or material is known with certainty for a given period of time (usually a year)—two major costs are associated with inventory. If the inventory is a material or good purchased from an outside source, then these inventory-related costs are known as *ordering costs* and *carrying costs*. If the material or good is produced internally, then the costs are called *setup costs* and *carrying costs*.

ordering costs

Ordering costs are the costs of placing and receiving an order. Examples include the costs of processing an order (clerical costs and documents), the cost of insurance for shipment, and unloading costs.

setup costs

Setup costs are the costs of preparing equipment and facilities so they can be used to produce a particular product or component. Examples are wages of idled production workers, the cost of idled production facilities (lost income), and the costs of test runs (labor, materials, and overhead).

carrying costs   Carrying costs are the costs of carrying inventory. Examples include insurance, inventory taxes, obsolescence, the opportunity cost of funds tied up in inventory, handling costs, and storage space.

Ordering costs and setup costs are similar in nature—both represent costs that must be incurred to acquire inventory. They differ only in the nature of the prerequisite activity (filling out and placing an order versus configuring equipment and facilities). Thus, in the discussion that follows, any reference to order costs can be viewed as a reference to setup costs.

stock-out costs   If demand is not known with certainty, a third category of inventory costs—called *stock-out costs*—exists. Stock-out costs are the costs of not having a product available when demanded by a customer. Examples are lost sales (both current and future), the costs of expediting (increased transportation charges, overtime, and so on), and the costs of interrupted production.

Traditional Reasons for Holding Inventory

Maximizing profits requires that inventory-related costs be minimized. But minimizing carrying costs favors ordering or producing in small lot sizes, whereas minimizing ordering costs favors large, infrequent orders (minimization of setup costs favors long, infrequent production runs). Thus, minimizing carrying costs encourages small or no inventories and minimizing ordering or setup costs encourages larger inventories. The need to balance these two sets of costs so that the *total* cost of carrying and ordering can be minimized is one reason organizations choose to carry inventory.

Dealing with uncertainty in demand is a second major reason for holding inventory. Even if the ordering or setup costs were negligible, organizations would still carry inventory because of stock-out costs. If the demand for materials or products is greater than expected, inventory can serve as a buffer, giving organizations the ability to meet delivery dates (thus keeping customers satisfied). Although balancing conflicting costs and dealing with uncertainty are the two most frequently cited reasons for carrying inventories, other reasons also exist.

Inventories of parts and raw materials are often viewed as necessary because of supply uncertainties. That is, inventory buffers of parts and materials are needed to keep production flowing in case of late deliveries or no deliveries (strikes, bad weather, and bankruptcy are examples of uncertain events that can cause an interruption in supply). Unreliable production processes may also create a demand for producing extra inventory. For example, a company may decide to produce more units than needed to meet demand because the production process usually yields a large number of nonconforming units. Similarly, buffers of inventories may be required to continue supplying customers or processes with goods even if a process goes down because of a failed machine. Finally, organizations may acquire larger inventories than normal to take advantage of quantity discounts or to avoid anticipated price increases. Exhibit 18-1 summarizes the reasons

18-1 ···························

Exhibit
Traditional Reasons for
Carrying Inventory

1. To balance ordering or setup costs and carrying costs
2. To satisfy customer demand (for example, meet delivery dates)
3. To avoid shutting down manufacturing facilities because of
    a.   machine failure
    b.   defective parts
    c.   unavailable parts
    d.   late delivery of parts
4. To buffer against unreliable production processes
5. To take advantage of discounts
6. To hedge against future price increases

typically offered for carrying inventory. It's important to realize that these are reasons that are given to *justify* carrying inventories. There are a host of other reasons that can be offered that *encourage* the carrying of inventories. For example, performance measures such as measures of machine and labor efficiency may promote the buildup of inventories.

Economic Order Quantity: The Traditional Inventory Model

In developing an inventory policy, two basic questions must be addressed:

1. How much should be ordered (or produced)?
2. When should the order be placed (or the setup done)?

The first question needs to be addressed before the second can be answered.

Order Quantity and Total Ordering and Carrying Costs Assume that demand is known. In choosing an order quantity or a lot size for production, managers need be concerned only with ordering (or setup) and carrying costs. The total ordering (or setup) and carrying cost can be described by the following equation:

$$TC = \frac{PD}{Q} + \frac{CQ}{2}$$

$$= \text{Ordering cost} + \text{Carrying cost}$$

(18.1)

where TC = *The total ordering (or setup) and carrying cost*
P = The cost of placing and receiving an order (or the cost of setting up a production run)
D = The known annual demand
Q = The number of units ordered each time an order is placed (or the lot size for production)
C = The cost of carrying one unit of stock for one year

The cost of carrying inventory can be computed for any organization that carries inventories, including retail, service, and manufacturing organizations. Of course, the inventory cost model using setup costs and lot size as inputs pertains only to those organizations that produce their own inventories (parts or finished goods). To illustrate the application for a service organization, assume that the following values apply for a part used in the repair of refrigerators (the part is purchased from external suppliers):

$$D = 10,000 \text{ units}$$
$$Q = 1,000 \text{ units}$$
$$P = \$25 \text{ per order}$$
$$C = \$2 \text{ per unit}$$

Dividing D by Q produces the number of orders per year, which is 10 $(\frac{10,000}{1,000})$. Multiplying the number of orders per year by the cost of placing and receiving an order $(\frac{D}{Q} \times P)$ yields the total ordering cost of $250 (10 \times \$25).

The total carrying cost for the year is given by $\frac{CQ}{2}$; this expression is equivalent to multiplying the average inventory on hand $(\frac{Q}{2})$ by the carrying cost per unit (C). For an order of 1,000 units with a carrying cost of $2 per unit, the average inventory is 500 $(\frac{1,000}{2})$ and the carrying cost for the year is $1,000 ($2 $\times$ 500). (Assuming average inventory to be $\frac{Q}{2}$ is equivalent to assuming that inventory is consumed uniformly.)

Applying equation 18.1, the total cost is $1,250 ($250 + $1,000). An order quantity of 1,000 with a total cost of $1,250, however, may not be the best choice. Some other order quantity may produce a lower total cost. The objective is to find the order quantity that minimizes the total cost. This order quantity is called the economic order quantity (EOQ). The EOQ model is an example of a *push inventory system*. In a push system, the acquisition of inventory is initiated in anticipation of future demand—not in reaction to present demand. Fundamental to the analysis is the assessment of D, the future demand.

economic order quantity (EOQ)

Each Christmas season, Mattel brings out a special "Christmas Barbie." In 1994, Mattel overproduced Christmas Barbie, and many of the dolls were left on the toy store shelf on December 26. Determined not to repeat the error in 1995, Mattel's problem turned from too much inventory to too little, and stockouts occurred around the country. Parents scrambled to locate "Christmas Barbie" and a number of disappointed little girls received a certificate to get the doll by April 1996.

Computing the EOQ

Since the EOQ is the quantity that minimizes equation 18.1, a formula for computing this quantity is easily derived:[6]

$$Q = \text{EOQ} = \sqrt{\frac{2DP}{C}} \tag{18.2}$$

Using the data from the preceding example, the EOQ can be computed using equation 18.2:

$$\text{EOQ} = \sqrt{\frac{2 \times 10{,}000 \times 25}{2}}$$
$$= \sqrt{250{,}000}$$
$$= 500$$

Substituting 500 as the value of Q into equation 18.1 yields a total cost of $1,000. The number of orders placed would be 20 ($\frac{10{,}000}{500}$); thus, the total ordering cost is $500 (20 × $25). The average inventory is 250 ($\frac{500}{2}$), with a total carrying cost of $500 (250 × $2). Notice that the carrying cost equals the ordering cost. This is always true

6. $\frac{d(TC)}{dQ} = \frac{C}{2} - \frac{DP}{Q^2} = 0$, which implies that $Q^2 = \frac{2DP}{C}$ and $Q = \left(\frac{2DP}{C}\right)^{1/2}$

for the simple EOQ model described by equation 18.2. Also notice that an order quantity of 500 is less costly than an order quantity of 1,000 ($1,000 versus $1,250).

Reorder Point

reorder point

lead time

The EOQ answers the question of how much to order (or produce). Knowing when to place an order (or setup for production) is also an essential part of any inventory policy. The reorder point is the point in time when a new order should be placed (or setup started). It is a function of the EOQ, the lead time, and the rate at which inventory is depleted. Lead time is the time required to receive the economic order quantity once an order is placed or a setup is initiated.

To avoid stock-out costs and to minimize carrying costs, an order should be placed so that it arrives just as the last item in inventory is used. Knowing the rate of usage and lead time allows us to compute the reorder point (ROP) that accomplishes these objectives:

$$\text{ROP} = \text{Rate of usage} \times \text{Lead time} \qquad (18.3)$$

To illustrate equation 18.3, we will continue to use the refrigerator part example. Assume that the producer uses 50 parts per day and that the lead time is four days. If so, an order should be placed when the inventory level of the refrigerator part drops to 200 units (4 × 50). Exhibit 18-2 provides a graphical illustration. Note that the inventory is depleted just as the order arrives and that the quantity on hand jumps back up to the EOQ level.

Demand Uncertainty and the Reorder Point If the demand for the part or product is not known with certainty, the possibility of stock-out exists. For example, if the refrigerator part was used at a rate of 60 parts a day instead of 50, the firm would use 200 parts after three and one-third days. Since the new order would not arrive until the end of the fourth day, repair activity requiring this part would be idled for two-thirds of a day. To avoid this problem, organizations often choose to carry safety stock. Safety stock is extra inventory carried to serve as insurance against fluctuations in demand. Safety stock is computed by multiplying the lead time by the difference between the maximum rate of usage and the average rate of usage. For example, if the maximum

safety stock

Exhibit
The Reorder Point

Inventory (units)

usage of the refrigerator part is 60 units per day, the average usage is 50 units per day, and the lead time is four days, the safety stock is computed as follows:

Maximum usage	60
Average usage	(50)
Difference	10
Lead time	× 4
Safety stock	40

With the presence of safety stock, the reorder point is computed as follows:

$$\text{ROP} = (\text{Average rate of usage} \times \text{Lead time}) + \text{Safety stock} \qquad (18.4)$$

For the refrigerator part example, the reorder point with safety stock is computed as:

$$\text{ROP} = (50 \times 4) + 40$$
$$= 240 \text{ units}$$

Thus, an order is automatically placed whenever the inventory level drops to 240 units.

A Manufacturing Example The service repair setting involved the purchase of inventory. The same concepts can be applied to settings where inventory is manufactured. To illustrate, consider Benson Company, a large manufacturer of farm implements with several plants throughout the nation. Each plant produces all subassemblies necessary to assemble a particular farm implement. One large plant in the Midwest produces plows. The manager of this midwestern plant is trying to determine the size of the production runs for the blade fabrication area. He is convinced that the current lot size is too large and wants to identify the quantity that should be produced to minimize the sum of the carrying and setup costs. He also wants to avoid stockouts since any stockout would shut down the assembly department.

To help him in his decision, the controller has supplied the following information:

Average demand for blades	320 per day
Maximum demand for blades	340 per day
Annual demand for blades	80,000
Unit carrying cost	$5
Setup cost	$12,500
Lead time	20 days

Based on this information, the economic order quantity and the reorder point are computed in Exhibit 18-3. As the computation illustrates, the blades should be produced in batches of 20,000 and a new setup should be started when the supply of blades drops to 6,800.

EOQ and Inventory Management

The traditional approach to managing inventory has been referred to as a *Just-in-Case system*.[7] In some settings, a just-in-case inventory system is entirely appropriate. For example, hospitals need inventories of medicines, drugs, and other critical supplies on hand at all times so that life-threatening situations can be handled. Using an economic order coupled with safety stock would seem eminently sensible in such an environment. Relying on a critical drug to arrive just in time to save a heart attack victim is simply not

---

7. Eliyahu M. Goldratt and Robert E. Fox, *The Race* (Croton-on-Hudson, N.Y.: North River Press, 1986).

Exhibit
18-3
EOQ and Reorder Point
Illustrated

$$EOQ = \sqrt{\frac{2DP}{C}}$$

$$= \sqrt{\frac{2 \times 80,000 \times 12,500}{5}}$$

$$= \sqrt{400,000,000}$$

$$= 20,000 \text{ blades}$$

Maximum usage	340
Average usage	(320)
Difference	20
Lead time	$\times$ 20
Total safety stock	400

Reorder point = (Average usage $\times$ Lead time) + Safety stock
$$= (320 \times 20) + 400$$
$$= 6,800 \text{ units}$$

practical. Furthermore, many smaller retail stores, manufacturers, and services may not have the buying power to command alternative inventory management systems such as just-in-time purchasing.

As the plow blade example illustrates (Exhibit 18-3), the EOQ model is very useful in identifying the optimal trade-off between inventory carrying costs and setup costs. It also is useful in helping to deal with uncertainty by using safety stock. The historical importance of the EOQ model in many American industries can be better appreciated by understanding the nature of the traditional manufacturing environment. This environment has been characterized by the mass production of a few standardized products that typically have a very high setup cost. The production of the plow blades fits this pattern. The high setup cost encouraged a large batch size: 20,000 units. The annual demand of 80,000 units can be satisfied using only four batches. Thus, production runs for these firms tended to be quite long. Furthermore, diversity was viewed as being costly and was avoided. Producing variations of the product can be quite expensive, especially since additional, special features would usually demand even more expensive and frequent setups—the reason for the standardized products.

JIT INVENTORY MANAGEMENT

Objective 2

Describe JIT inventory management.

The manufacturing environment for many of these traditional, large-batch, high setup cost firms has changed dramatically in the past 10 to 20 years. For one thing, the competitive markets are no longer defined by national boundaries. Advances in transportation and communication have contributed significantly to the creation of global competition. Advances in technology have contributed to shorter life cycles for products, and product diversity has increased. Foreign firms offering higher-quality, lower-cost products *with specialized features* have created tremendous pressures for our domestic large-batch, high setup cost firms to increase both quality and product diversity while simultaneously reducing total costs. These competitive pressures have led many firms to abandon the EOQ model in favor of a JIT approach. JIT has two strategic objectives: to increase profits and to improve a firm's competitive position. These two objectives are achieved by controlling costs (enabling better price competition and increased profits), improving delivery performance, and improving quality. JIT offers increased cost efficiency and simultaneously has the flexibility to respond to customer demands for better quality and more variety. Quality, flexibility, and cost efficiency are foundation principles for world-class competition.

JIT manufacturing and purchasing represent the continual pursuit of productivity through the elimination of waste. *Nonvalue-added* activities are a major source of waste. Nonvalue-added activities are either unnecessary, or necessary but inefficient and improvable. Necessary activities are essential to the business and/or are of value to customers. Eliminating nonvalue-added activities is a major thrust of JIT but it is also a basic objective of any company following the path of continuous improvement—regardless of whether or not JIT is being used. Clearly, JIT is much more than an inventory management system. Inventories, however, are particularly viewed as representing waste. They tie up resources such as cash, space, and labor. They also conceal inefficiencies in production and increase the complexity of a firm's information system. Thus, even though JIT focuses on more than inventory management, control of inventory is an important ancillary benefit. In this chapter, the inventory dimension of JIT is emphasized. In Chapter 4, other benefits and features of JIT were described.

A Pull System

JIT is a manufacturing approach that maintains that goods should be pulled through the system by present demand rather than pushed through the system on a fixed schedule based on anticipated demand. Many fast-food restaurants, like McDonald's, use a pull system to control their finished goods inventory. When a customer orders a hamburger, it is taken from the rack. When the number of hamburgers gets too low, then the cooks make new hamburgers. Customer demand pulls the materials through the system. This same principle is used in manufacturing settings. Each operation produces only what is necessary to satisfy the demand of the succeeding operation. The material or subassembly arrives just in time for production to occur so that demand can be met.

One effect of JIT is to reduce inventories to very low levels. The pursuit of insignificant levels of inventories is vital to the success of JIT. This idea of pursuing insignificant inventories, however, necessarily challenges the traditional reasons for holding inventories (see Exhibit 18-1). These reasons are no longer viewed as valid.

According to the traditional view, inventories solve some underlying problem related to each of the reasons listed in Exhibit 18-1. For example, the problem of resolving the conflict between ordering or setup costs and carrying costs is solved by selecting an inventory level that minimizes the sum of these costs. If demand is greater than expected or if production is reduced by breakdowns and production inefficiencies, then inventories serve as buffers, providing products to customers that may otherwise not have been available. Similarly, inventories can prevent shutdowns caused by late delivery of material, defective parts, and failures of machines used to produce subassemblies. Finally, inventories are often the solution to the problem of buying the best raw materials for the least cost through the use of quantity discounts.

JIT refuses to use inventories as the solution to these problems. In fact, inventories are not only viewed as wasteful but are viewed as being directly associated with the ability of a firm to compete. High inventories signal the existence of problems that need to be addressed. High inventories often mean poor quality, long lead times, and poor due-date performance (among other things). JIT inventory management offers alternative solutions that do not require high inventories.

Setup and Carrying Costs: The JIT Approach

JIT takes a radically different approach to minimizing total carrying and setup costs. The traditional approach accepts the existence of setup costs and then finds the order quantity that best balances the two categories of costs. JIT, on the other hand, does not accept setup costs (or ordering costs) as a given; rather, JIT attempts to drive these costs to zero. If setup costs and ordering costs become insignificant, the only remaining cost to minimize is carrying cost, which is accomplished by reducing inventories to very low levels. This approach explains the push for zero inventories in a JIT system.

Long-term Contracts, Continuous Replenishment, and Electronic Data Interchange Ordering costs are reduced by developing close relationships with suppliers. Negotiating long-term contracts for the supply of outside materials will obviously reduce the number of orders and the associated ordering costs. Retailers have found a way to reduce ordering costs by adopting an arrangement known as *continuous replenishment*. With continuous replenishment a manufacturer assumes the inventory management function for the retailer. The manufacturer tells the retailer when and how much stock to reorder. The retailer reviews the recommendation and approves the order if it makes sense. Wal-Mart and Procter & Gamble, for example use this arrangement.[8] The arrangement has reduced inventories for Wal-Mart, and has also reduced stock-out problems. Additionally, Procter & Gamble's goods are often sold before Wal-Mart has to pay for them. Procter & Gamble, on the other hand, has become a preferred supplier, has more and better shelf space, and has also less demand uncertainty. The ability to project demand better allows Procter & Gamble to produce and deliver continuously in smaller lots—a goal of JIT manufacturing. Similar arrangements can be made between manufacturers and suppliers.

The process of continuous replenishment is facilitated by *electronic data interchange*. Electronic data interchange (EDI) allows suppliers access to a buyer's on-line database. By knowing the buyer's production schedule (in the case of a manufacturer), the supplier can deliver the needed parts where they are needed just in time for their use. EDI involves no paper—no purchase orders or invoices. The supplier uses the production schedule, which is in the database, to determine its own production and delivery schedules. When the parts are shipped, an electronic message is sent from the supplier to the buyer that a shipment is en route. When the parts arrive, a bar code is scanned with an electronic wand and this initiates payment for the goods. Clearly, EDI requires a close working arrangement between the supplier and the buyer—they almost operate as one company rather than two separate companies. General Motors' Saturn plant uses an EDI arrangement with its component suppliers. This has enabled both suppliers and Saturn to reduce overhead.[9]

Reducing Setup Times Reducing setup times requires a company to search for new, more efficient ways to accomplish setup. Fortunately, experience has indicated that dramatic reductions in setup times can be achieved. Upon adopting a JIT system, Harley-Davidson reduced setup times by more than 75 percent on the machines evaluated.[10] In some cases, Harley-Davidson was able to reduce the setup times from hours to minutes. Other companies have experienced similar results. Generally, setup times can be reduced by at least 75 percent.[11]

Due-Date Performance: The JIT Solution

Due-date performance is a measure of a firm's ability to respond to customer needs. In the past, finished goods inventories have been used to ensure that a firm is able to meet a requested delivery date. JIT solves the problem of due-date performance not by building inventory but by dramatically reducing lead times. Shorter lead times increase a firm's ability to meet requested delivery dates and to respond quickly to the demands of

8. Michael Hammer and James Champy, *Reengineering the Corporation* (HarperBusiness, New York, 1993).
9. Hammer and Champy, pp. 90–91.
10. Gene Schwind, "Man Arrives Just in Time to Save Harley-Davidson," *Material Handling Engineering* (August 1984): 28–35.
11. William J. Stoddard and Nolan W. Rhea, "Just-in-Time Manufacturing: The Relentless Pursuit of Productivity," *Material Handling Engineering* (March 1985): 70–76.

(margin notes)

continuous replenishment

electronic data interchange (EDI)

the market. Thus, the firm's competitiveness is improved. JIT cuts lead times by reducing setup times, improving quality, and using cellular manufacturing.

Manufacturing cells reduce travel distance between machines and inventory; they can also have a dramatic effect on lead time. For example, in a traditional manufacturing system, one company took two months to manufacture a valve. By grouping the lathes and drills used to make the valves into U-shaped cells, the lead time was reduced to two or three days. Oregon Cutting Systems, a chain-saw manufacturer, was able to reduce travel distance from 2,620 feet to 173 feet and lead times from twenty-one days to three. Because of the reduced lead time and plans for even further reduction, the company now fills orders directly from the factory rather than from finished goods warehouses.[12] These reductions in lead time are not unique—most companies experience at least a 90 percent reduction in lead times when they implement JIT.[13]

Avoidance of Shutdown and Process Reliability: The JIT Approach

Most shutdowns occur for one of three reasons: machine failure, defective material or subassembly, and unavailability of a raw material or subassembly. Holding inventories is one traditional solution to all three problems.

Those espousing the JIT approach claim that inventories do not solve the problems but cover up or hide them. JIT proponents use the analogy of rocks in a lake. The rocks represent the three problems and the water represents inventories. If the lake is deep (inventories are high), then the rocks are never exposed and managers can pretend they do not exist. By reducing inventories to zero, the rocks are exposed and can no longer be ignored. JIT solves the three problems by emphasizing total preventive maintenance and total quality control and by building the right kind of relationship with suppliers.

total preventive maintenance

Total Preventive Maintenance Zero machine failures is the goal of total preventive maintenance. By paying more attention to preventive maintenance, most machine breakdowns can be avoided. This objective is easier to attain in a JIT environment because of the interdisciplinary labor philosophy. It is not uncommon for a cell worker to be trained in maintenance of the machines he or she operates. Because of the pull-through nature of JIT, it is also not unusual for a cell worker to have idle manufacturing time. Some of this time, then, can be used productively by having the cell workers involved in preventive maintenance.

Total Quality Control The problem of defective parts is solved by striving for zero defects. Because JIT manufacturing does not rely on inventories to replace defective parts or materials, the emphasis on quality for both internally produced and externally purchased materials increases significantly. The outcome is impressive: the number of rejected parts tends to fall by 75 to 90 percent.[14] Decreasing defective parts also diminishes the justification for inventories based on unreliable processes.

Kanban system

The Kanban System To ensure that parts or materials are available when needed, a system called the Kanban system is employed. This is an information system that controls production through the use of markers or cards. The Kanban system is responsible for ensuring that the necessary products (or parts) are produced (or acquired) in the necessary quantities at the necessary time. It is the heart of the JIT inventory management system.

12. Richard Schonberger, "Just-in-Time Production Systems: Replacing Complexity with Simplicity in Manufacturing Management," *Industrial Engineering* (October 1984): 52–63. For an excellent description of the savings realized by Oregon Cutting Systems, read the article by Jack Bailes and Ilene K. Kleinsorge, "Cutting Waste with JIT," *Management Accounting* (May 1992): 28–32.
13. See Stoddard and Rhea, "Just-in-Time Manufacturing," p. 76.
14. Stoddard and Rhea, "Just-in-Time Manufacturing."

A Kanban system uses cards or markers, which are plastic, cardboard, or metal plates measuring 4 inches by 8 inches. The Kanban is usually placed in a vinyl sack and attached to the part or a container holding the needed parts.

A basic Kanban system uses three cards: a *withdrawal Kanban*, a *production Kanban*, and a *vendor Kanban*. The first two control the movement of work among the manufacturing processes, while the third controls movement of parts between the processes and outside suppliers. A withdrawal Kanban specifies the quantity that a subsequent process should withdraw from the preceding process. A production Kanban specifies the quantity that the preceding process should produce. Vendor Kanbans are used to notify suppliers to deliver more parts; they also specify when the parts are needed. The three Kanbans are illustrated in Exhibits 18-4, 18-5, and 18-6, respectively.

How Kanban cards are used to control the work flow can be illustrated with a simple example. Assume that two processes are needed to manufacture a product. The first process (CB Assembly) builds and tests printed circuit boards (using a U-shaped manufacturing cell). The second process (Final Assembly) puts eight circuit boards into a subassembly purchased from an outside supplier. The final product is a personal computer.

Exhibit 18-7 provides the plant layout corresponding to the manufacture of the personal computers. Refer to the exhibit as the steps involved in using Kanbans are outlined.

Consider first the movement of work between the two processing areas. Assume that eight circuit boards are placed in a container and that one such container is located in the CB stores area. Attached to this container is a production Kanban (P-Kanban). A second container with eight circuit boards is located near the Final Assembly line (the withdrawal store) with a withdrawal Kanban (W-Kanban). Now assume that the production schedule calls for the immediate assembly of a computer.

The Kanban setups can be described as follows:

1. A worker from the Final Assembly line goes to the withdrawal store, removes the eight circuit boards and places them into production. The worker also removes the withdrawal Kanban and places it on the withdrawal post.
2. The withdrawal Kanban on the post signals that the Final Assembly unit needs an additional eight circuit boards.
3. A worker from Final Assembly (or a material handler called a *carrier*) removes the withdrawal Kanban from the post and carries it to CB stores.
4. At the CB stores area, the carrier removes the production Kanban from the container of eight circuit boards and places it on the production-ordering post.

withdrawal Kanban
production Kanban
vendor Kanbans

18-4

Exhibit
Withdrawal Kanban

Item No.	15670T07	Preceding Process
Item Name	Circuit Board	CB Assembly
Computer Type	TR6547 PC	
Box Capacity	8	Subsequent Process
Box Type	C	Final Assembly

18-5

Exhibit
Production Kanban

Item No. _____**15670T07**_____   _____Process_____

Item Name _____**Circuit Board**_____   _____**CB Assembly**_____

Computer Type _____**TR6547 PC**_____

Box Capacity _____**8**_____

Box Type _____**C**_____

5. The carrier next attaches the withdrawal Kanban to the container of parts and carries the container back to the Final Assembly area. Assembly of the next computer can begin.
6. The production Kanban on the production-ordering post signals the workers of the CB assembly to begin producing another lot of circuit boards. The production Kanban is removed and accompanies the units as they are produced.
7. When the lot of eight circuit boards is completed, the units are placed in a container in the CB stores area with the production Kanban attached. The cycle is then repeated.

The use of Kanbans ensures that the subsequent process (Final Assembly) withdraws the circuit boards from the preceding process (CB Assembly) in the necessary quantity at the appropriate time. The Kanban system also controls the preceding process by allowing it to produce only the quantities withdrawn by the subsequent process. In this way, inventories are kept at a minimum, and the components arrive just in time to be used.

Essentially, the same steps are followed for a purchased subassembly. The only difference is the use of a vendor Kanban in place of a production Kanban. A vendor Kanban on a vendor post signals to the supplier that another order is needed. As with the circuit boards, the subassemblies must be delivered just in time for use. A JIT

18-6

Exhibit
Vendor Kanban

Item No. _____**15670T08**_____   Name of Receiving Company

Item Name _____**Computer Casing**_____   _____**Electro PC**_____

Box Capacity _____**8**_____   Receiving Gate

Box Type _____**A**_____   _____**75**_____

Time to Deliver _____**8:30 A.M., 12:30 P.M., 2:30 P.M.**_____

Name of Supplier _____**Gerry Supply**_____

························Kanban Process

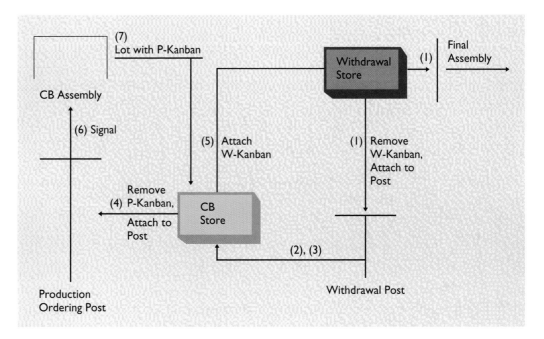

purchasing system requires the supplier to deliver small quantities on a frequent basis. These deliveries could be weekly, daily, or even several times a day. This calls for a close working relationship with suppliers. Long-term contractual agreements tend to ensure supply of materials.

Discounts and Price Increases: JIT Purchasing versus Holding Inventories

Traditionally, inventories are carried so that a firm can take advantage of quantity discounts and hedge against future price increases of the items purchased. The objective is to lower the cost of inventory. JIT achieves the same objective without carrying inventories. The JIT solution is to negotiate long-term contracts with a few chosen suppliers located as close to the production facility as possible and to establish more extensive supplier involvement. Suppliers are not selected on the basis of price alone. Performance—the quality of the component and the ability to deliver as needed—and commitment to JIT purchasing are vital considerations. Other benefits of long-term contracts exist. They stipulate prices and acceptable quality levels. Long-term contracts also reduce dramatically the number of orders placed, which helps to drive down the ordering cost. Another effect of JIT purchasing is to lower the cost of purchased parts by 5 to 20 percent.[15]

JIT's Limitations

JIT is not simply an approach that can be purchased and plugged in with immediate results. Its implementation should be more of an evolutionary process than a revolutionary process. Patience is needed. JIT is often referred to as a program of simplification—yet this does not imply that it is simple or easy to implement. Time is required, for example, to build sound relationships with suppliers. Insisting on immediate changes in delivery times and quality may not be realistic and may cause difficult confrontations

15. Stoddard and Rhea, "Just-in-Time Manufacturing."

between a company and its suppliers. Partnership, not coercion, should be the basis of supplier relationships. To achieve the benefits that are associated with JIT purchasing, a company may be tempted to redefine unilaterally its supplier relationships. Unilaterally redefining supplier relationships by extracting concessions and dictating terms may create supplier resentment and actually may cause suppliers to retaliate. In the long run, suppliers may seek new markets, find ways to charge higher prices (than would exist with a preferred supplier arrangement), or seek regulatory relief. These actions may destroy many of the JIT benefits extracted by the impatient company.

Workers also may be affected by JIT. Studies have shown that sharp reductions in inventory buffers may cause a regimented work flow and high levels of stress among production workers.[16] Some have suggested a deliberate pace of inventory reduction to allow workers to develop a sense of autonomy and to encourage their participation in broader improvement efforts. Forced and dramatic reductions in inventories may indeed reveal problems—but it may cause more problems: lost sales and stressed workers. If the workers perceive JIT as a way of simply squeezing more out of them, then JIT efforts may be doomed. Perhaps a better strategy for JIT implementation is one where inventory reductions follow the process improvements that JIT offers. Implementing JIT is not easy and it requires careful and thorough planning and preparation. Companies should expect some struggle and frustration.

The most glaring deficiency of JIT is the absence of inventory to buffer production interruptions. Current sales are constantly being threatened by an unexpected interruption in production. In fact, if a problem occurs, JIT's approach consists of trying to find and solve the problem before any further production activity occurs. Retailers who use JIT tactics also face the possibility of shortages (JIT retailers order what they need now—not what they expect to sell—the idea is to flow goods through the channel as late as possible, keeping inventories low and decreasing the need for markdowns). If demand increases well beyond the retailer's supply of inventory, the retailer may be unable to make order adjustments quickly enough to avoid lost sales and irked customers. For example, during the Christmas shopping season in 1993, many retailers such as Toys "R" Us and Target Stores, using a JIT approach, lost millions in sales because of their inability to accurately forecast demand for Mighty Morphin Power Rangers.[17] It was estimated that shipments of the Power Ranger action figures would be around 600,000 units (before December 25) compared with an estimated demand of 12 million units. Yet in spite of the downside, retailers seem to be strongly committed to JIT. Apparently, losing sales on surprise hits is less costly than the cost of carrying high levels of inventory.

The JIT manufacturing company is also willing to place current sales at risk to achieve assurance of future sales. This assurance comes from higher quality, quicker response time, and less operating costs. Even so, we must recognize that a sale lost today is a sale lost forever. Installing a JIT system so that it operates with very little interruption is not a short-run project. Thus, losing sales is a real cost of installing a JIT system.

An alternative, and perhaps complementary approach, is the *theory of constraints* (TOC). In principle, TOC can be used in conjunction with JIT manufacturing; after all, JIT manufacturing environments also have constraints. Furthermore, the TOC approach has the very appealing quality of protecting current sales while also striving to increase future sales by increasing quality, lowering response time, and decreasing operating costs.

THEORY OF CONSTRAINTS

Objective 3

Describe the theory of constraints and explain how it can be used to manage inventory.

constraints

Every firm faces limited resources and limited demand for each product. These limitations are called constraints. The theory of constraints recognizes that the performance

---

16. For a more complete discussion of supplier and worker effects of JIT, see Paul L. Zipkin, "Does Manufacturing Need a JIT Revolution?" *Harvard Business Review* (January/February, 1991): 40–50.

17. Joseph Pereira, "Tough Game: The Power Rangers Surprise," *The Wall Street Journal* (21 December 1993): A1, A5.

of any organization is limited by its constraints. The theory of constraints then develops a specific approach to manage constraints to support the objective of continuous improvement. According to TOC, if performance is to be improved, an organization must identify its constraints, exploit the constraints in the short run, and in the longer term, find ways to overcome the constraints.

Basic Concepts

throughput

inventory
operating expenses

TOC focuses on three measures of organizational performance: *throughput, inventory,* and *operating expenses.* Throughput is the rate at which an organization generates money through sales.[18] In operational terms, throughput is the difference between sales revenue and unit-level variable costs such as materials and power. Direct labor is typically viewed as a fixed unit-level expense and is not usually included in the definition. With this understanding, throughput corresponds to contribution margin. Inventory is all the money the organization spends in turning raw materials into throughput. Operating expenses are defined as all the money the organization spends in turning inventories into throughput. Based on these three measures, the objectives of management can be expressed as increasing throughput, minimizing inventory, and decreasing operating expenses.

By increasing throughput, minimizing inventory, and decreasing operating expenses, three financial measures of performance will be affected: net income and return on investment will increase and cash flow will improve. Increasing throughput and decreasing operating expenses have always been emphasized as key elements in improving the three financial measures of performance. The role of minimizing inventory, however, in achieving these improvements has been traditionally regarded as less important than throughput and operating expenses.

The theory of constraints, like JIT, assigns inventory management a much more prominent role than the traditional viewpoint. TOC recognizes that lowering inventory decreases carrying costs and, thus, decreases operating expenses and improves net income. TOC, however, argues that lowering inventory helps produce a competitive edge by having better products, lower prices, and faster response to customer needs.

Better Products Better products mean higher quality. It also means that the company is able to improve products and provide these improved products quickly to the market. The relationship between low inventories and quality has been described in the JIT section. Essentially, low inventories allow defects to be detected more quickly and the cause of the problem assessed. Improving products is also a key competitive element. New or improved products need to reach the market quickly—before competitors can provide similar features. This goal is facilitated with low inventories. Low inventories allow new product changes to be introduced more quickly because the company has fewer old products (in stock or in process) that would need to be scrapped or sold before the new product is introduced.

Lower Prices High inventories mean more productive capacity is needed and thus more investment in equipment and space. Since lead time and high work-in-process inventories are usually correlated, high inventories may often be the cause of overtime. Overtime, of course, increases operating expenses and lowers profitability. Lower inventories reduce carrying costs, per-unit investment costs, and other operating expenses such as overtime and special shipping charges. By lowering investment and operating costs, the unit margin of each product is increased, providing more flexibility in pricing decisions. Lower prices are possible or higher product margins if competitive conditions do not require prices to be lowered.

18. This follows the definition of Eliyahu Goldratt and Robert Fox in *The Race.* Other definitions and basic concepts of the theory of constraints are also based upon the developments of Goldratt and Fox.

Responsiveness Delivering goods on time and producing goods with shorter lead times than the market dictates are important competitive tools. Delivering goods on time is related to a firm's ability to forecast the time required to produce and deliver goods. If a firm has higher inventories than its competitors, then the firm's production lead time is higher than the industry's forecast horizon. High inventories may obscure the actual time required to produce and fill an order. Lower inventories allow actual lead times to be more carefully observed and more accurate delivery dates can be provided. Shortening lead times is also crucial. Shortening lead times is equivalent to lowering work-in-process inventories. A company carrying ten days of work-in-process inventories has an average production lead time of ten days. If the company can reduce lead time from ten to five days, then the company should now be carrying only five days of work-in-process inventories.

As lead times are reduced, it is also possible to reduce finished goods inventories. For example, if the lead time for a product is ten days and the market requires delivery on demand, then the firms must carry, on average, ten days of finished goods inventory (plus some safety stock to cover demand uncertainty). Suppose that the firm is able to reduce lead time to five days. In this case, finished goods inventory should also be reduced to five days. Thus, the level of inventories signal the organization's ability to respond. High levels relative to those of competitors' translate into a competitive disadvantage. TOC thus emphasizes reduction of inventories by reducing lead times.

TOC Steps

The theory of constraints uses five steps to achieve its goal of improving organizational performance:

1. Identify the organization's constraint(s).
2. Exploit the binding constraint(s).
3. Subordinate everything else to the decisions made in step 2.
4. Elevate the binding constraint(s).
5. Repeat the process.

external constraints

internal constraints

loose constraints

binding constraints

Step 1: Identify the Organization's Constraint(s) Constraints can be classified as *external* or *internal*. External constraints are limiting factors imposed on the firm from external sources (such as market demand). Internal constraints are limiting factors found within the firm (such as machine-time availability). Although resources and demands may be limited, certain product mixes may not meet all the demand or use all of the resources available to be used. Constraints whose limited resources are not fully used by a product mix are loose constraints. Binding constraints are those constraints whose available resources are fully utilized. Internal and external constraints are identified. The optimal product mix is identified as the mix that maximizes throughput subject to all the organization's constraints. The optimal mix reveals how much of each constrained resource is used and which of the organization's constraints are binding.

Decisions about product mix can have a significant impact on an organization's profitability. Each mix represents an alternative that carries with it an associated profit level. A manager should choose the alternative that maximizes total profits. The usual approach is to assume that only unit-based variable costs are relevant to the product mix decision. Thus, assuming that nonunit-level costs are the same for different mixes of products, the optimal mix is one that maximizes total contribution margin.

A manager must choose the optimal mix given the constraints faced by the firm. Assume, for example, that Confer Company produces two types of machine parts: X and Y, with unit contribution margins of $300 and $600, respectively. Assuming that Confer can sell all that is produced, some may argue that only part Y should be produced and sold because it has the larger contribution margin. However, this solution is not necessarily the best. The selection of the optimal mix can be significantly affected by the relationships of the constrained resources to the individual products. These relationships affect the quantity of each product that can be produced and, consequently, the total contribution margin that can be earned. This point is most vividly illustrated with one binding, internal resource constraint.

One Binding Internal Constraint Assume that each part must be drilled by a special machine. The firm owns three machines that together provide 120 drilling hours per week. Part X requires 1 hour of drilling, and part Y requires 3 hours of drilling. Assuming no other binding constraints, what is the optimal mix of parts? Since each unit of X requires 1 hour of drilling, 120 units of X can be produced per week ($\frac{120}{1}$). At $300 per unit, Jorgenson can earn a total contribution margin of $36,000 per week. On the other hand, Y requires 3 hours of drilling per unit; therefore, 40 ($\frac{120}{3}$) parts can be produced. At $600 per unit, the total contribution margin is $24,000 per week. Producing only X yields a higher profit level than producing only Y—even though the unit contribution margin for Y is two times larger than that for X.

The contribution margin per unit of each product is not the critical concern. The contribution margin per unit of *scarce resource* is the deciding factor. The product yielding the highest contribution margin per drilling hour should be selected. Part X earns $300 per machine hour ($\frac{\$300}{1}$), while part Y earns only $200 per machine hour ($\frac{\$600}{3}$). Thus, the optimal mix is 120 units of part X and none of part Y, producing a total contribution margin of $36,000 per week. Notice that the mix uses up all 120 machine hours and so the machine-hour constraint is binding.

Internal Binding Constraint and External Binding Constraint The contribution margin per unit of scarce resource can also be used to identify the optimal product mix when an external binding constraint exists. For example, assume the same internal constraint of 120 drilling hours but also assume that Confer can sell at most 30 units of part X and 100 units of part Y. The internal constraint allows Confer to produce 120 units of part X, but this is no longer a feasible choice because only 30 units of X can be sold. Thus, we now have a binding external constraint, one that affects the earlier decision to produce and sell only part X. Since the contribution per unit of scarce resource (machine hour) is $300 for part X and $200 for part Y, it still makes sense to produce as much of X as possible before producing any of Y. Confer should first produce 30 units of X, using 30 machine hours. This leaves 90 machine hours, allowing the production of 30 units of Y. The optimal mix is now 30 units of X and 30 units of Y, producing a total contribution margin of $27,000 per week ($300 × 30 + $600 × 30).

Step 2: Exploit the Binding Constraint(s) One way to make the best use of binding constraints is to ensure that the optimal product mix is produced. Making the best use of binding constraints, however, is more extensive than simply ensuring production of the optimal mix. This step is the heart of TOC's philosophy of short-run constraint management and is directly related to TOC's goal of reducing inventories and improving performance.

In most organizations, there are only a few binding resource constraints. The major binding constraint is defined as the *drummer*. Assume, for example, that there is only one internal binding constraint. By default, this constraint becomes the drummer. The drummer constraint's production rate sets the production rate for the entire plant. Downstream processes fed by the drummer constraint are naturally forced to follow its rate of production. Scheduling for downstream processes is easy. Once a part is finished at the drummer process, the next process begins its operation. Similarly, each subsequent operation begins when the prior operation is finished. Upstream processes that feed the drummer constraint are *scheduled* to produce at the same rate as the drummer constraint. Scheduling at the drummer rate prevents the production of excessive upstream work-in-process inventories.

For upstream scheduling, there are two additional features that TOC uses in managing constraints to lower inventory levels and improve organizational performance: *buffers* and *ropes*. First, an inventory buffer is established in front of the major binding constraint. The inventory buffer is referred to as the *time buffer*. A time buffer is the

time buffer

inventory needed to keep the constrained resource busy for a specified time interval. The purpose of a time buffer is to protect the throughput of the organization from any disruption that can be overcome within the specified time interval. For example, if it takes one day to overcome most interruptions that occur upstream from the drummer constraint, then a two-day buffer should be sufficient to protect throughput from any interruptions. Thus, in scheduling, the operation immediately preceding the drummer constraint should produce the parts needed by the drummer resource two days in advance of their planned usage. Any other preceding operations are scheduled backward in time to produce so that their parts arrive just in time for subsequent operations.

ropes

Ropes are actions taken to tie the rate at which raw material is released into the plant (at the first operation) to the production rate of the constrained resource. The objective of a rope is to ensure that the work-in-process inventory will not exceed the level needed for the time buffer. Thus, the drummer rate is used to limit the rate of raw material release and effectively controls the rate at which the first operation produces. The rate of the first operation then controls the rates of subsequent operations. The TOC inventory system is often called the Drum-Buffer-Rope (DBR) System. Exhibit 18-8 illustrates the DBR structure for a general setting.

Drum-Buffer-Rope (DBR) System

The Confer Company example can be expanded to provide a specific illustration of the DBR system. Assume that there are three sequential processes: grinding, drilling, and polishing. Each of these processes has a limited amount of resources. Demand for each type of machine part produced is also limited (30 for part X and 100 for part Y as indicated earlier). Assume that the only internal binding constraint is drilling and that the optimal mix consists of 30 units of part X and 30 units of part Y (per week). This is the most that the drilling process can handle. The other two processes represent loose constraints and so are capable of producing more per week of each part than the optimal mix calls for. Since the drilling process feeds the polishing process, we can define the drilling constraint as the drummer for the plant. Assume that the demand for each part is uniformly spread out over the week. This means that the production rate should be 6 per day of each part (for a five-day workweek). A two-day time buffer would require 24 completed parts from the grinding process: 12 for part X and 12 for part Y. To ensure that the time buffer does not increase at a rate greater than 6 per day for each part, raw materials should be released to the grinding process such that only 6 of each part can be produced each day (this is the rope—tying the release of materials to the production rate of the drummer constraint). Exhibit 18-9 summarizes the specific DBR details for the Confer Company.

Step 3: Subordinate Everything Else to the Decisions Made in Step 2 The drummer constraint essentially sets the capacity for the entire plant. All remaining departments should be subordinated to the needs of the drummer constraint. This principle requires many companies to change the way they view things. For example, the use of efficiency measures at the departmental level may no longer be appropriate. Consider the Confer Company once again. Encouraging maximum productive efficiency for the grinding department would produce excess work-in-process inventories. For example, assume that the capacity of the grinding department is 80 units per week. Assuming the two-day buffer is in place, the grinding department, would add 20 units per week to the buffer in front of the drilling department. Over a period of a year, the potential exists for building very large work-in-process inventories (1,000 units of the two parts would be added to the buffer over a 50-week period). Polishing, of course, must produce at the rate of drilling because it follows drilling in the sequential production process. Thus, the only concern for polishing is that it can handle the output of drilling.

Step 4: Elevate the Binding Constraint(s) Once actions have been taken to make the best possible use of the existing constraints, the next step is to embark on a program of continuous improvement by reducing the limitations that the binding constraint(s) have on the organization's performance.

Exhibit
Drum-Buffer-Rope
System: General
Description

Raw Materials

Initial
Process

Process
A

ROPE →

Process
B

TIME | BUFFER

**DRUMMER
PROCESS**

Process
C

Final
Process

Finished Goods

Suppose, for example, that Confer Company adds a half shift for the drilling department, increasing the drilling hours from 120 to 180 per week. With 60 additional drilling hours, Confer can increase production of part Y from 30 to 50 units, an additional 20 units per week (recall that part Y uses 3 hours per unit, yielding the 20 additional units $(\frac{60}{3})$). Since part Y has a unit contribution margin of $600, this will increase throughput by $12,000 per week ($600 × 20), assuming that grinding and polishing can handle an increase of 20 units of Y per week. We know, for example, that grinding has 80 hours per week available and that X and Y each uses 1 hour of grinding. Currently, 60 hours are being used. An increase of 20 units is possible.

Now assume that polishing has 160 hours available and that part X uses 2 hours per unit and part Y 1 hour per unit. For the current mix (30 of X and 30 of Y), 90 hours are being used. To increase production of Y by 20 units, 20 more hours are needed—

Exhibit
Drum-Buffer-Rope:
Confer Company

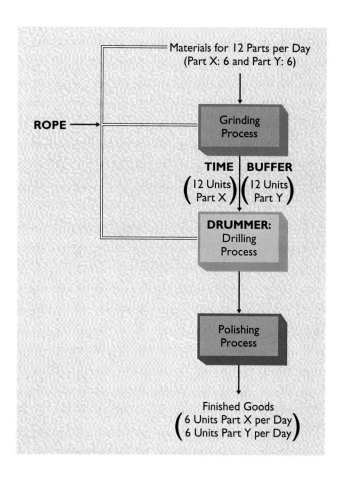

certainly possible. Thus, moving from a mix of 30 units of X and 30 units of Y to a mix of 30 of X and 50 of Y is possible. Is the half shift worth it? This question is answered by comparing the cost of adding the half shift with the increased throughput of $12,000 per week. If the cost of adding the half shift is $50 per hour, then the incremental cost is $3,000 per week and the decision to add the half shift is a good one.

Step 5: Repeat the Process Eventually, the drilling resource constraint will be elevated to a point where the constraint is no longer binding. Suppose, for example, that the company adds a full shift for the drilling operation, increasing the resource availability to 240 hours. Both the drilling and polishing constraints are capable of producing more of part Y, but the grinding process cannot (grinding can produce a maximum of 80 units per week of any combination of X and Y). Thus, the new drummer constraint is grinding. Once the new drummer constraint is identified, then the TOC process is repeated. The objective is to continually improve performance by managing constraints.

SUMMARY OF LEARNING OBJECTIVES

1. Describe the traditional inventory management model.

The traditional approach uses inventories to manage the trade-offs between ordering (setup) costs and carrying costs. The optimal trade-off defines the economic order quantity. Other reasons for inventories are also offered: due-date performance, avoiding shutdowns (protecting sales), hedging against future price in-

creases, and taking advantage of discounts. JIT and TOC, on the other hand, argue that inventories are costly and are used to cover up fundamental problems that need to be corrected so that the organization can become more competitive.

2. Describe JIT inventory management.

JIT uses long-term contracts, continuous replenishment, and EDI to reduce (eliminate) ordering costs. Engineering efforts are made to reduce setup times drastically. Once ordering costs and setup costs are reduced to minimal levels, then it is possible to reduce carrying costs by reducing inventory levels. JIT carries small buffers in front of each operation and uses a Kanban system to regulate production. Production is tied to market demand. If an interruption occurs, throughput tends to be lost because of the small buffers. Yet future throughput tends to increase because efforts are made to improve such things as quality, productivity, and lead time.

3. Describe the theory of constraints and explain how it can be used to manage inventory.

TOC identifies an organization's constraints and exploits them so that throughput is maximized and inventories and operating costs are minimized. Identifying the optimal mix is part of this process. The major binding constraint is identified and is used to set the productive rate for the plant. Release of raw materials into the first process (operation) is regulated by the drummer constraint. A time buffer is located in front of critical constraints. This time buffer is sized so that it protects throughput from any interruptions. As in JIT, the interruptions are used to locate and correct the problem. However, unlike JIT, the time buffer serves to protect throughput. Furthermore, because buffers are located only in front of critical constraints, TOC may actually produce smaller inventories than JIT.

 EY TERMS

Binding constraints *765*
Carrying costs *751*
Constraints *763*
Continuous replenishment *758*
Drum-Buffer-Rope (DBR) System *767*

Economic order quantity (EOQ) *752*
Electronic data interchange (EDI) *758*
External constraints *765*
Internal constraints *765*
Inventory *764*
Kanban system *759*

Lead time *754*
Loose constraints *765*
Operating expenses *764*
Ordering costs *750*
Production Kanban *760*
Reorder point *754*
Ropes *767*
Safety stock *754*

Setup costs *750*
Stock-out costs *751*
Throughput *764*
Time buffer *766*
Total preventive maintenance *759*
Vendor Kanbans *760*
Withdrawal Kanban *760*

 EVIEW PROBLEM

Traditional and JIT inventory management systems also have drummers—factors that determine the production rate of the plant. For a just-in-case system, the drummer is the excess capacity of the first operation. For JIT the drummer is market demand.

REQUIRED:

1. Explain why the drummer of a just-in-case system is identified as excess capacity of the first operation.
2. Explain how market demand drives the JIT production system.
3. Explain how a drummer constraint is used in the TOC approach to inventory management.
4. What are the advantages and disadvantages of the three types of drummers?

Solution

1. In a traditional inventory system, local efficiency measures encourage the manager of the first operation to keep the department's workers busy. Thus, raw materials are released to satisfy this objective. This practice is justified because the inventory may be needed just in case demand is greater than expected, or just in case the first operation has downtime or other problems.

2. In a JIT system, when the final operation delivers its goods to a customer, a backward-rippling effect triggers the release of raw materials into the factory. First, the last process removes the buffer inventory from the withdrawal store and this leads to a P-Kanban being placed on the production post of the preceding operation. This operation then begins production, withdrawing parts it needs from its withdrawal store, leading to a P-Kanban being placed on the production post of its preceding operation. This process repeats itself—all the way back to the first operation.

3. A drummer constraint sets the production rate of the factory to match its own production rate. This is automatically true for succeeding operations. For preceding operations, the rate is controlled by tying the drummer constraint's rate of production to that of the first operation. A time buffer is also set in front of the drummer constraint to protect throughput in the event of interruptions.

4. The excess capacity drummer typically will build excess inventories. This serves to protect current throughput. However, it ties up a lot of capital and tends to cover up problems such as poor quality, bad delivery performance, and inefficient production. Because it is costly and covers up certain critical productive problems, the just-in-case approach may be a threat to

future throughput by damaging a firm's competitive position. JIT reduces inventories dramatically—using only small buffers in front of each operation as a means to regulate production flow and signal when production should occur. JIT has the significant advantage of uncovering problems and eventually correcting them.

However, discovering problems usually means that current throughput will be lost while problems are being corrected. Future throughput tends to be protected because the firm is taking actions to improve its operations. TOC uses time buffers in front of the critical constraints. These buffers are large enough to keep the critical constraints operating while other operations may be down. Once the problem is corrected, the other resource constraints usually have sufficient excess capacity to catch up. Thus, current throughput is protected. Furthermore, future throughput is protected because TOC uses the same approach as JIT—namely, uncovering and correcting problems. TOC can be viewed as an improvement on JIT methods—correcting the lost throughput problem while maintaining the other JIT features.

QUESTIONS FOR WRITING AND DISCUSSION

1. What are ordering costs? Provide examples.
2. What are setup costs? Illustrate with examples.
3. What are carrying costs? Illustrate with examples.
4. What are stock-out costs?
5. Explain why, in the traditional view of inventory, carrying costs increase as ordering costs decrease.
6. Discuss the traditional reasons for carrying inventory.
7. What is the economic order quantity?
8. Suppose that a raw material has a lead time of three days and that the average usage of the material is 12 units per day. What is the reorder point? If the maximum usage is 15 units per day, what is the safety stock?
9. Explain how safety stock is used to deal with demand uncertainty.
10. What approach does JIT take to minimize total inventory costs?
11. Explain how long-term contractual relationships with suppliers can reduce the acquisition cost of raw materials.
12. What is EDI and what relationship does it have to continuous replenishment?
13. One reason for inventory is to prevent shutdowns. How does the JIT approach to inventory management deal with this potential problem?
14. Explain how the Kanban system helps reduce inventories.
15. What is a constraint? an internal constraint? an external constraint?
16. What are loose constraints? binding constraints?
17. Define and discuss the three measures of organizational performance used by the theory of constraints.
18. Explain how lowering inventory produces better products, lower prices, and better responsiveness to customer needs.
19. What are the five steps that TOC uses to improve organizational performance?
20. What is a drum-buffer-rope system?

WARM-UP EXERCISES

This section provides short warm-up exercises based on the examples in the chapter. Each warm-up exercise gives the page number on which the text example can be found. You may want to refer to the text example to see how the exercise can be set up and solved.

W18-1
Inventory Costs
LO 1
p. 752

A local TV repair shop uses 36,000 units of a part each year. It costs $20 to place and receive an order. The shop orders in lots of 400 units. It cost $4 to carry one unit per year in inventory.

REQUIRED:
1. Calculate the total annual ordering cost.
2. Calculate the total annual carrying cost.
3. Calculate the total annual inventory cost.

W18-2
EOQ
LO 1
pp. 752–753

Refer to the data in W18-1. The company wants to know if there is an order size that will reduce its total inventory costs.

REQUIRED:
1. Calculate the EOQ.
2. Calculate the total annual inventory cost using the EOQ inventory policy.
3. How much is saved per year using the EOQ versus an order size of 400 units?

W18-3
Reorder Point
LO 1
pp. 754–755

Suppose that the repair shop referred to in W18-1 uses an average of 50 units of the part per day. The lead time for an order is three days.

REQUIRED:
1. Compute the reorder point.
2. Suppose that the usage of the part can be as much as 60 units per day with the average being 50 units. Calculate the safety stock and the new reorder point.

W18-4
Optimal Mix
LO 3
p. 755–756

Two types of gears are produced: A and B. Gear A has a unit contribution margin of $200 and gear B has a unit contribution margin of $400. Gear A uses 2 hours of grinding time and gear B uses 5 hours of grinding time. There are 200 hours of grinding time available per week. This is the only constraint.

REQUIRED:
1. Is the grinding constraint an internal or an external constraint?
2. Determine the optimal mix. What is the total contribution margin?
3. Suppose that there is an additional demand constraint: Market conditions will allow the sale of only 80 units of each gear. Now what is the optimal mix? the total contribution margin?

E XERCISES

E18-1
Ordering and Carrying Costs
LO 1

Cuzco Company uses 24,000 carburetors each year in its production of snowmobiles. The cost of placing an order is $62.50. The cost of holding one unit of inventory for one year is $3. Currently, Cuzco places six orders of 4,000 carburetors per year.

REQUIRED:
1. Compute the annual ordering cost.
2. Compute the annual carrying cost.
3. Compute the cost of Cuzco's current inventory policy.

E18-2
Economic Order Quantity
LO 1

Refer to the data in E18-1.

REQUIRED:
1. Compute the economic order quantity.
2. Compute the ordering cost and the carrying cost for the EOQ.
3. How much money does using the EOQ policy save the company over the policy of purchasing 2,000 carburetors per order?

E18-3
Economic Order Quantity
LO 1

Quito Mining Company uses 24,000 gallons of sulphuric acid each year. The cost of placing an order is $15, and the carrying cost for 1 gallon of acid is $0.50.

REQUIRED:
1. Compute the economic order quantity for sulphuric acid.
2. Compute the carrying cost and ordering cost for the EOQ.

E18-4
Reorder Point
LO 1

Nissan Company manufactures radios. One part it orders from an outside supplier is a potentiometer. Information pertaining to the potentiometer is as follows:

Economic order quantity	6,000 units
Average daily usage	400 units
Maximum daily usage	600 units
Lead time	4 days

REQUIRED:
1. What is the reorder point, assuming no safety stock is carried?
2. What is the reorder point assuming that safety stock is carried?

| **E18-5** **EOQ with Setup Costs; Reorder Point; Production Scheduling** LO 1 | Gate Manufacturing produces two different types of frames for bicycles. The two frames are for women's and men's bikes, respectively. In order to produce the different frames, equipment must be set up. Each setup configuration corresponds to a particular type of frame. The setup cost per batch of frames is $1,000 for the women's model and $1,200 for the men's model. The cost of carrying women's frames in inventory is $2 per frame per year. The cost of carrying men's frames is $3 per frame per year. During the coming year, the company expects to produce 81,000 frames for women's bikes and 125,000 frames for men's bike. The company hopes to sell an average of 324 women's frames per workday and an average of 500 men's frames per workday. It takes Gate two days to set up the equipment for production of either frame. Once set up, Gate can produce 1,500 frames per workday. There are 250 workdays available per year. |

REQUIRED:
1. Compute the number of frames for women's bikes that should be produced per setup to minimize total setup and carrying costs for this product.
2. Compute the total setup and carrying costs associated with the economic order quantity for women's frames.
3. What is the reorder point for women's frames?
4. Repeat requirements 1 through 3 for the men's frames.
5. Using the economic order batch size, is it possible for Gate to produce the amount that can be sold of each frame? Does scheduling have a role here? Explain. Is this a push- or pull-system approach to inventory management? Explain.

| **E18-6** **Safety Stock** LO 1 | Pinegar Manufacturing produces a component used in its production of answering machines. The time to set up and produce a batch of the components is six days. The average daily usage is 300 components and the maximum daily usage is 350 components. |

REQUIRED: Compute the reorder point assuming that safety stock is carried by Pinegar Manufacturing. How much safety stock does the company carry?

| **E18-7** **Reasons for Carrying Inventory** LO 1, LO 2, LO 3 | The following reasons have been offered for holding inventories: |

a. To balance ordering or setup costs and carrying costs
b. To satisfy customer demand (for example, meet delivery dates)
c. To avoid shutting down manufacturing facilities because of
    (i)   machine failure
    (ii) defective parts
    (iii) unavailable parts
    (iv) late delivery of parts
d. To buffer against unreliable production processes
e. To take advantage of discounts
f. To hedge against future price increases

REQUIRED:
1. Explain how the JIT approach responds to each of these reasons and, consequently, argues for insignificant levels of inventories.
2. The theory of constraints (TOC) criticizes the JIT approach to inventory management, arguing that it fails to protect throughput. Explain what this means and describe how TOC addresses this issue.

| **E18-8** **Kanban Cards** LO 2 | Explain the use of each of the following cards in the Kanban system: |

1. The withdrawal Kanban
2. The production Kanban
3. The vendor Kanban

| **E18-9** **JIT Limitations** LO 2 | Many companies have viewed JIT as a panacea—a knight in shining armor which promises rescue from sluggish profits, poor quality, and productive inefficiency. It is often lauded for its beneficial effects on employee morale and self-esteem. Yet JIT may also cause a company to struggle and may produce a good deal of frustration. In some cases, JIT appears to deliver less than its reputation seems to call for. |

REQUIRED: Discuss some of the limitations and problems that companies may encounter when implementing a JIT system.

E18-10
Product Mix
Decisions; Single
Constraint
LO 3

Marvel Company has the capability of producing three types of rods used in the manufacture of different kinds of hydraulic cylinders. All three rods can be shaped and cut on the same machine. Marvel owns one of these machines which has a total operating capacity of 20,000 hours per year. Information on each of the three rods follows:

	Type I	Type II	Type III
Selling price	$20.00	$30.00	$50.00
Unit variable cost	$10.00	$14.00	$24.00
Machine hours required	0.20	0.50	1.50

The marketing manager has determined that the company can sell all that it can produce of each of the three products.

1. How many of each product should be sold to maximize total contribution margin? What is the total contribution margin for this product mix?
2. Suppose that Marvel can sell no more than 50,000 units of each type at the prices indicated. What product mix would you recommend and what would be the total contribution margin?

E18-11
Drum-Buffer-Rope
System
LO 3

Goicoechea, Inc. manufactures two models of bows: regular and deluxe. They sell all they produce. Bows are produced in three processes: laminating, molding, and finishing. In laminating, limbs are created by laminating layers of wood. In molding, the limbs are heat treated, under pressure, to form a strong resilient limb. In finishing, any protruding glue is removed, and the limbs are cleaned with acetone, dried, and sprayed with final finishes. Recently Goicoechea implemented a TOC approach for its Waco plant. One binding constraint was identified and the optimal product mix was determined. The following diagram reflects the TOC outcome.

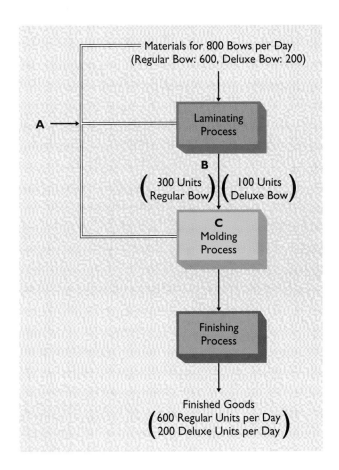

REQUIRED:
1. What is the daily production rate? Which process sets this rate?
2. How many days of buffer inventory is Goicoechea carrying? How is this time buffer determined?
3. Explain what the letters *A*, *B*, and *C* represent. Discuss each of their roles in the TOC system.

 PROBLEMS

P18-1

EOQ and Reorder Point

LO 1

Italia Pizzeria is a popular pizza restaurant near a college campus. Brandon Thayn, an accounting student, works for Italia Pizzeria. After several months at the restaurant, Brandon began to analyze the efficiency of the business, particularly inventory practices. He noticed that the owner had more than fifty items regularly carried in inventory. Of these items, the most expensive to buy and carry was cheese. Cheese was ordered in blocks at $17.50 per block. Annual usage totals 14,000 blocks.

Upon questioning the owner, Brandon discovered that the owner did not use any formal model for ordering cheese. It took five days to receive a new order when placed, which was done whenever the inventory of cheese dropped to 200 blocks. The size of the order was usually 400 blocks. The cost of carrying one block of cheese is 10 percent of its purchase price. It costs $40 to place and receive an order.

Italia Pizzeria stays open seven days a week and operates 50 weeks a year. The restaurant closes for the last two weeks of December.

REQUIRED:
1. Compute the total cost of ordering and carrying the cheese inventory under the current policy.
2. Compute the total cost of ordering and carrying cheese if the restaurant were to change to the economic order quantity. How much would the restaurant save per year by switching policies?
3. If the restaurant uses the economic order quantity, when should it place an order? (Assume that the amount of cheese used per day is the same throughout the year.) How does this compare with the current reorder policy?
4. Suppose that storage space allows a maximum of 600 blocks of cheese. Discuss the inventory policy that should be followed with this restriction.
5. Suppose that the maximum storage is 600 blocks of cheese and that cheese can be held for a maximum of ten days. The owner will not hold cheese any longer in order to ensure the right flavor and quality. Under these conditions, evaluate the owner's current inventory policy.

P18-2

EOQ with Safety Stock

LO 1

Parry Chiropractic Clinic uses an EOQ model to order supplies. Lately, several chiropractors have been complaining about the availability of X-ray film. During the past three months, the clinic has had to place five rush orders because of stockouts. Because of the problem, the supply officer has decided to review the current inventory policy. The following data have been gathered:

Cost of placing and receiving an order	$60
Cost of carrying one package	$1.50
Average usage per day	8 packages
Maximum usage per day	10 packages
Lead time for an order	4 days
Annual demand	2,000 packages

The clinic currently does not carry any safety stock. The clinic operates 250 days each year.

REQUIRED:
1. Compute the economic order quantity and the reorder point. What is the total ordering and carrying cost for the clinic's current inventory policy?
2. Assume that the clinic has decided to carry safety stock. Compute how much should be carried to ensure no stockouts. Compute the total ordering and carrying cost for this policy. Will the reorder point change? If so, what is it?

P18-3

EOQ; Safety Stock;

Geneva Company produces safety goggles for coal miners. Goggles are produced in batches according to model and size. Although the setup and production time varies for each model, the smallest lead time is 6 days. The most popular model, Model SG4, takes 2 days for setup and the production rate is 750 units per day. The expected annual demand for the model is 36,000 units. Demand for the model, however, can reach 45,000 units. The cost of carrying one SG4 unit is $3 per unit. The setup cost is $6,000. Geneva chooses its batch size based on the economic order quantity criterion. Expected annual demand is used to compute the EOQ.

Recently, Geneva has encountered some stiff competition—especially from foreign sources. Some of the foreign competitors have been able to produce and deliver the goggles to retailers in half the time it takes Geneva to produce. For example, a large retailer recently requested a delivery of 12,000 SG4 goggles with the stipulation that they be delivered within 7 working days. Geneva had 3,000 units of SG4 in stock. They informed the potential customer that they could deliver 3,000 units immediately and the other 9,000 units in about 14 working days—with the possibility of interim partial orders being delivered. The customer declined the offer indicating that the total order had to be delivered within 7 working days so that their stores could take advantage of some special local conditions. The customer expressed regret and indicated that they would accept the order from another competitor who could satisfy the time requirements.

REQUIRED:

1. Calculate the optimal batch size for Model SG4 using the EOQ model. Was Geneva's response to the customer right? Would it take the time indicated to produce the number of units wanted by the customer? Explain with supporting computations.
2. Upon learning of the lost order, the marketing manager grumbled about Geneva's inventory policy. "We lost the order because we didn't have sufficient inventory. We need to carry more units in inventory to deal with unexpected orders like these." Do you agree? How much additional inventory would have been needed to meet customer requirements? In the future, should Geneva carry more inventory? Can you think of other solutions?
3. Fenton Gray, the head of industrial engineering, reacted differently to the lost order. "Our problem is more complex than insufficient inventory. I know that our foreign competitors carry much less inventory than we do. What we need to do is decrease the lead time. I have been studying this problem and my staff has found a way to reduce setup time for Model SG4 from 2 days to 1.5 hours. Using this new procedure, setup cost can be reduced to about $94. Also, by rearranging the plant layout for this product—creating what are called manufacturing cells—we can increase the production rate from 750 units per day to about 2,000 units per day. This is done simply by eliminating a lot of move time and waiting time—both nonvalue-added activities."

   Assume that the engineer's estimates are on target. Compute the new optimal batch size (using the EOQ formula). What is the new lead time? Given this new information, would Geneva have been able to meet the customer's time requirements? Assume that there are eight hours available in each workday.
4. Suppose that the setup time and cost are reduced to 0.5 hour and $100, respectively. What is the batch size now? As setup time approaches zero and the setup cost becomes negligible, what does this imply? Assume for example that it takes 5 minutes to setup and costs about $0.864 per setup.

Packer Company produces a product that requires two processes. In the first process, a subassembly is produced (subassembly A); in the second process, this subassembly and a subassembly purchased from outside (subassembly B) are assembled to produce the final product. For simplicity, assume that the assembly of one unit takes the same time as the production of subassembly A. Subassembly A is placed in a container and sent to an area called the subassembly stores (SB stores) area. A production Kanban is attached to this container. A second container, also with one subassembly, is located near the assembly line (called the withdrawal store). This container has attached to it a withdrawal Kanban.

REQUIRED:

1. Explain how withdrawal and production Kanban cards are used to control the work flow between the two processes. How does this approach minimize inventories?
2. Explain how vendor Kanban cards can be used to control the flow of the purchased subassembly. What implications does this have for supplier relationships? What role, if any, do continuous replenishment and EDI play in this process?

P18-5
Product Mix Decision; Single and Multiple Constraints
LO 3

Morning Beverages, Inc. produces two instant breakfast drinks: Rich Instant and Diet Instant. Rich Instant has more ingredients and requires more machine time for grinding and mixing. The manufacturing process is highly mechanized; both products are produced by the same equipment by using different settings. For the coming period, 400,000 machine hours are available. Management is trying to decide on the quantities of each product to produce. The following data are available:

	Rich Instant	Diet Instant
Machine hours per unit	1.00	0.50
Unit selling price	$2.50	$3.00
Unit variable cost	$1.50	$2.25

REQUIRED:
1. Determine the units of each product that should be produced in order to maximize profits. What is the total contribution margin earned by this optimal mix?
2. Because of market conditions, the company can sell no more than 300,000 packages of Rich Instant and 600,000 packages of Diet Instant. Now what is the optimal mix? total contribution margin?

P18-6
Optimal Product Mix Decisions
LO 3

Wilson Company manufactures and sells three components in a factory of three departments. The components are used as replacement parts in jet aircraft. After machining in each department, the components are subjected to stress tests. The nature of the machine processing and of the labor skills required for stress testing is such that neither machines nor test labor can be switched from one department to another.

Wilson's management is attempting to plan its production schedule for the next several months. The planning is complicated by the fact that labor shortages exist in the community and some machines will be down several months for repairs.

Following is information regarding available machine and test time by department and the machine hours and test hours required for each component. These data are valid for at least the next six months.

		Department		
Monthly Capacity		A	B	C
Machine hours available		6,000	6,200	5,400
Test hours available		7,400	9,000	5,500

Component	Input per Unit Produced			
12-L	Test hours	2	3	3
	Machine hours	1	1	2
16-M	Test hours	1	2	—
	Machine hours	1	1	—
40-S	Test hours	2	2	2
	Machine hours	2	2	1

The monthly demand for the next six months will be as follows:

Component	Units Sold
12-L	1,000
14-M	800
40-S	2,000

Inventory levels will not be increased or decreased during the next six months. The unit cost and price data for each component are as follows:

	Component		
	12-L	14-M	40-S
Unit costs:			
Direct material	$ 14	$ 26	$ 34
Test labor	66	38	51
Variable overhead	27	20	25
Fixed overhead	15	10	32
Variable selling	3	2	4
Total unit cost	$125	$ 96	$146
Unit selling price	$203	$136	$184

REQUIRED:

1. Calculate the monthly requirement for machine hours and direct labor hours for producing components 12-L, 14-M, and 40-S to determine whether the factory can meet the monthly sales demand.
2. Determine the quantities of each component that should be produced monthly to maximize profits. Prepare a schedule that shows the contribution to profits of your product mix. (CMA adapted)

P18-7
Identifying and Exploiting Constraints; Constraint Elevation
LO 3

Covey Company produces two metal parts used in industrial equipment (part A and part B). The company has three processes: molding, grinding, and finishing. In molding, molds are created and molten metal is poured into the shell. Grinding removes the gates that allowed the molten metal to flow into the mold's cavities. In finishing, rough edges caused by the grinders are removed by small, handheld pneumatic tools. In molding, the setup time is 1 hour. The other two processes have no setup time required. The demand for part A is 300 units per day and the demand for part B is 500 units per day. The minutes required per unit for each product follow:

	Minutes Required per Unit of Product		
Product	Molding	Grinding	Finishing
Part A	5	10	15
Part B	10	15	20

The company operates one 8-hour shift. The molding process employs 12 workers (who each work 8 hours). Two hours of their time, however, is used for setups (assuming both products are produced). The grinding process has sufficient equipment and workers to provide 12,000 grinding minutes per shift.

The finishing department is labor intensive and employs 35 workers, who each work 8 hours per day. The only significant unit-level variable costs are materials and power. For part A, the variable cost per unit is $40 and for part B, it is $50. Selling prices for A and B are $90 and $110, respectively. Covey's policy is to use two setups per day: an initial setup to produce all that is scheduled for A and a second setup (changeover) to produce all that is scheduled for B. The amount scheduled does not necessarily correspond to each product's daily demand.

REQUIRED:

1. Calculate the time (in minutes) needed each day to meet the daily market demand for part A and part B. What is the major internal constraint facing Covey Company?
2. Describe how Covey should exploit its major binding constraint. Specifically, identify the product mix that will maximize daily throughput.
3. Assume that manufacturing engineering has found a way to reduce the molding setup time from one hour to ten minutes. Explain how this affects the product mix and daily throughput.

P18-8
Theory of Constraints; Internal Constraints
LO 3

Young Company produces two subassemblies used by aircraft manufacturers: sub A and sub B. Sub A is made up of two components, one manufactured internally and one purchased from external suppliers. Sub B is made up of three components, one manufactured internally and two purchased from suppliers. The company has two processes: fabrication and assembly. In fabrication, the internally produced components are made. Each component takes 20 minutes to produce. In assembly, it takes 30 minutes to assemble the components for sub A and 40 minutes to assemble the components for sub B. Young Company operates one shift per day. Each process employs 100 workers who each work eight hours per day.

Sub A earns a unit contribution margin of $20 and sub B earns a unit contribution margin of $24 (calculated as the difference between revenue and the cost of materials and energy). Young can sell all that it produces of either part. There are no other constraints. Young can add a second shift of either process. Although a second shift would work eight hours, there is no mandate that it employ the same number of workers. The labor cost per hour for fabrication is $8 and the labor cost per hour for assembly is $7.

REQUIRED:

1. Identify the constraints facing Young. How many binding constraints are possible? What is Young's optimal product mix? What daily contribution margin is produced by this mix?
2. What is the drummer constraint? How much excess capacity does the other constraint have? Assume that a 1.5-day buffer inventory is needed to deal with any production interruptions. Describe the drummer-buffer-rope concept using the Young data to illustrate the process.
3. Explain why the use of local labor efficiency measures will not work in Young's TOC environment.
4. Suppose Young decides to elevate the binding constraint by adding a second shift of 50 workers (for assembly only). Would elevation of Young's binding constraint improve its system performance? Explain with supporting computations.

P18-9
TOC; Internal and External Constraints
LO 3

Bountiful Manufacturing produces two types of bike frames (X and Y). Frame X passes through four processes: cutting, welding, polishing, and painting. Frame Y uses three of the same processes: cutting, welding, and painting. Each of the four processes employs ten workers who work eight hours each day. Frame X sells for $40 per unit and frame Y sells for $55 per unit. Raw materials is the only unit-level variable expense. The materials cost for frame X is $20 per unit and the materials cost for frame Y is $25 per unit. Bountiful's accounting system has provided the following additional information about its operations and products:

Resource Name	Resource Available	Frame X Resource Usage (per unit)	Frame Y Resource Usage (per unit)
Cutting labor	4,800 minutes	15 minutes	10 minutes
Welding labor	4,800 minutes	15 minutes	30 minutes
Polishing labor	4,800 minutes	15 minutes	—
Painting labor	4,800 minutes	10 minutes	15 minutes
Market demand: Frame X	200 per day	1 unit	—
Market demand: Frame Y	100 per day	—	1 unit

Bountiful's management has determined that any production interruptions can be corrected within two days.

REQUIRED:

1. Assuming that Bountiful can meet daily market demand, compute the potential daily profit. Now compute the minutes needed for each process to meet the daily market demand. Can Bountiful meet daily market demand? If not, where is the bottleneck?
2. Determine the optimal mix and the maximum daily contribution margin (throughput).
3. Explain how a DBR system would work for Bountiful.
4. Suppose that the engineering department has proposed a process design change that will increase the polishing time for frame X from 15 to 23 minutes per unit and decrease its welding time from 15 to 10 minutes per unit. The cost of process redesign would be $10,000. Evaluate this proposed change. What step in the TOC process does this proposal represent?

ⓂANAGERIAL DECISION CASES

C18-1
Ethical Issues

Mac Ericson and Tammy Ferguson met at a IMA conference two months ago and began dating. Mac is the controller for Longley Enterprises and Tammy is a marketing manager for Sharp

Products. Longley is a major supplier for Piura Products, a major competitor of Sharp's. Longley has entered into a long-term agreement to supply certain materials to Piura. Piura has been developing a JIT purchasing and manufacturing system. As part of its development, Piura and Longley have established EDI capabilities. The following conversation took place during a luncheon engagement:

Tammy: Mac, I understand that you have EDI connections with Piura. Is that right?

Mac: Sure. It's part of the partners-in-profits arrangement that we have worked so hard to get. It's working real well. Knowing Piura's production schedule helps us stabilize our own schedule. It has actually cut some of our overhead costs. It has also decreased Piura's costs. I estimate that we both have decreased production costs by about 7 to 10 percent.

Tammy: That's interesting. You know, I have a real chance of getting promoted to VP of marketing . . .

Mac: Hey that's great. When will you know?

Tammy: It all depends on this deal that I am trying to cut with Balboa—if I win the contract, then I think I have it. My main problem is with Piura. If I knew what their production schedule was, I could get a pretty good idea as to how long it would take them to deliver. I could then make sure that we beat their delivery offer—even if we had to work overtime and do all kinds of expediting. I know that how fast we can deliver is very very important to Balboa. Our quality is as good as Piura's, but they tend to beat on us delivery time. My boss would love to kick Piura. They have beat us too many times recently. I am wondering if you would be willing to help me out.

Mac: Tammy, you know that I would help if I could, but Piura's production schedule is confidential information. If word got out that I had leaked that kind of stuff to you, I would be history.

Tammy: Well, no one would ever know. Besides I have already had a chat with Tom Anderson, who is our CEO. Our VP of finance is retiring. He knows about you and your capabilities. I think he would be willing to hire you—especially if he knew that you helped swing this Balboa deal. You could increase your salary by 40 percent.

Mac: I don't know. I have my doubts about the propriety of all this. It might look kind of funny if I take over as VP of finance not long after Piura loses the Balboa deal. But a VP position and a big salary increase are tempting. It's unlikely that I'll ever have a shot at the VP position in my company.

Tammy: Think it over. If you are interested, I'll arrange a dinner with Tom Anderson. He said he'd like to meet you. He knows a little about this. I'm sure that he has the ability to keep it quiet. I don't think there is much risk.

REQUIRED:
1. Based on this information, has Mac violated any of the IMA standards of ethical conduct? Explain.
2. Suppose that Mac decides to provide information in exchange for the VP position. What IMA standards has he violated?

GLOSSARY

A

Absorption costing A product-costing method that assigns all manufacturing costs to a product: direct materials, direct labor, variable overhead, and fixed overhead.

Absorption costing (full-costing) income Income computed by following a functional classification.

Acceptable quality level (AQL) An approach to quality control that permits or allows defects to occur provided they do not exceed a predetermined level.

Accounting rate of return The rate of return obtained by dividing the average accounting net income by the original investment (or by average investment).

Activity A basic unit of work performed within an organization. It also can be defined as an aggregation of actions within an organization useful to managers for purposes of planning, controlling, and decision making.

Activity analysis The process of identifying, describing, and evaluating the activities an organization performs.

Activity attributes Nonfinancial and financial information items that describe individual activities.

Activity-based cost (ABC) system A cost system that first traces costs to activities and then traces costs from activities to products.

Activity-based costing A cost assignment approach that first uses direct and driver tracing to assign costs to activities and then uses drivers to assign costs to cost objects.

Activity-based management (ABM) A system-wide, integrated approach that focuses management's attention on activities with the objective of improving customer value and the profit achieved by providing this value. It includes driver analysis, activity analysis, and performance evaluation, and draws on activity-based costing as a major source of information.

Activity capacity The ability to perform activities.

Activity drivers Factors that measure the demands placed on activities by cost objects which are used to assign the cost of activities to cost objects.

Activity elimination The process of eliminating nonvalue-added activities.

Activity flexible budgeting The prediction of what activity costs will be as activity usage changes.

Activity inputs The resources consumed by an activity in producing its output (they are the factors that enable the activity to be performed).

Activity inventory A listing of the activities performed within an organization.

Activity output The result or product of an activity.

Activity output measure The number of times an activity is performed. It is the quantifiable measure of the output.

Activity rate The average unit cost, obtained by dividing the resource expenditure by the activity's practical capacity.

Activity reduction Decreasing the time and resources required by an activity.

Activity selection The process of choosing among sets of activities caused by competing strategies.

Activity sharing Increasing the efficiency of necessary activities by using economies of scale.

Actual cost system A system that assigns actual costs for direct materials, direct labor, and overhead.

Adjusted cost of goods sold The cost of goods sold after all adjustments for overhead variance are made.

Administrative costs All costs associated with the general administration of the organization that cannot be reasonably assigned to either marketing or production.

Advance pricing agreements Agreements between the Internal Revenue Service and a taxpayer on the acceptability of a transfer price. The agreement is private and is binding on both parties for a specified period of time.

Advanced manufacturing environment An environment characterized by intense competition (worldwide usually), sophisticated technology, total quality control, and continuous improvement.

Aesthetics A quality attribute that is concerned with the appearance of tangible products (for example, style and beauty) as well as the appearance of the facilities, equipment, personnel, and communication materials associated with services.

Allocation Assignment of indirect costs to cost objects.

Annuity A series of future cash flows.

Applied overhead Overhead assigned to production using predetermined rates.

Appraisal costs Costs incurred to determine whether products and services are conforming to requirements.

B

Base period A prior period used to set the benchmark for measuring productivity changes.

Batch-level activities Activities that are performed each time a batch is produced.

Batch-level drivers Output measures for batch-level activities.

Benchmarking An approach that uses best practices as the standard for evaluating activity performance.

Best-fitting line The line that fits a set of data points the best in the sense that the sum of the squared deviations of the data points from the line is the smallest.

Binding constraints Constraints whose resources are fully utilized.

Break-even point The point where total sales revenue equals total costs. The point of zero profits.

Budget committee A committee responsible for setting budgetary policies and goals, reviewing and approving the budget, and resolving any differences that may arise in the budgetary process.

Budget director The individual responsible for coordinating and directing the overall budgeting process.

Budgetary slack The process of padding the budget by overestimating costs and underestimating revenues.

Budgets Plans of action expressed in financial terms.

C

Capital budgeting The process of making capital investment decisions.

Capital investment decisions The process of planning, setting goals and priorities, arranging financing, and identifying criteria for making long-term investments.

Carrying costs The costs of holding inventory.

Cash budget A detailed plan that outlines all sources and uses of cash.

Causal factors Activities or variables that invoke service costs. Generally, it is desirable to use causal factors as the basis for allocating service costs.

Centralized decision making A system in which decisions are made at the top level of an organization and local managers are given the charge to implement them.

Certified Internal Auditor (CIA) A person who has passed a comprehensive examination designed to ensure technical competence and has two years' experience.

Certified Management Accountant (CMA) A person who has passed a rigorous qualifying examination, has met an experience requirement, and participates in continuing education.

Certified Public Accountant (CPA) A person who is permitted (by law) to serve as an external auditor and who must pass a national examination and be licensed by the state in which he or she practices.

Coefficient of correlation The square root of the coefficient of determination, which is used to express not only the degree of correlation between two variables but also the direction of the relationship.

Coefficient of determination The percentage of total variability in a dependent variable (e.g., cost) that is explained by an independent variable (e.g., activity level). It assumes a value between 0 and 1.

Committed fixed expenses Expenses incurred for the acquisition of long-term activity capacity, usually as the result of strategic planning.

Common costs The costs of resources used in the output of two or more services or products.

Common fixed expenses Fixed expenses that cannot be directly traced to individual segments and that are unaffected by the elimination of any one segment.

Comparable uncontrolled price method The transfer price most preferred by the Internal Revenue Service under Section 482. The comparable uncontrolled price is essentially equal to the market price.

Compounding of interest Paying interest on interest.

Constraint set The collection of all constraints that pertain to a particular optimization problem.

Constraints Mathematical expressions that express resource limitations.

Consumption ratio The proportion of an overhead activity consumed by a product.

Contemporary responsibility accounting A control system defined by centering responsibility on processes and teams where activity performance is measured in terms of time, quality, and efficiency.

Continuous budget A moving twelve-month budget with a future month added as the current month expires.

Continuous improvement The process of searching for ways of increasing the overall efficiency and productivity of activities by reducing waste, increasing quality, and reducing costs.

Continuous replenishment A system where a manufacturer assumes the inventory management function for the retailer.

Contribution margin Sales revenue minus total variable cost or price minus unit variable cost.

Contribution margin ratio Contribution margin divided by sales revenue. It is the proportion of each sales dollar available to cover fixed costs and provide for profit.

Control The process of setting standards, receiving feedback on actual performance, and taking corrective action whenever actual performance deviates significantly from planned performance.

Control activities Activities performed by an organization to prevent or detect poor quality (because poor quality may exist).

Control costs Costs incurred from performing control activities.

Control limits The maximum allowable deviation from a standard.

Controllable costs Costs that managers have the power to influence.

Controller The chief accounting officer; supervises all accounting departments.

Controlling The managerial activity of monitoring a plan's implementation and taking corrective action as needed.

Conversion cost The sum of direct labor cost and overhead cost.

Cost The cash or cash equivalent value sacrificed for goods and services that are expected to bring a current or future benefit to the organization.

Cost assignment The process of associating the costs, once measured, with the units produced.

Cost behavior The way in which a cost changes in relation to changes in activity usage.

Cost center A division of a company that is evaluated on the basis of cost.

Cost formula A linear function, $Y = F + VX$, where Y = Total mixed cost, F = Fixed cost, V = Variable cost per unit of activity, and X = Activity level.

Cost measurement The act of determining the dollar amounts of direct materials, direct labor, and overhead used in production.

Cost object Any item, such as products, departments, projects, activities, and so on, for which costs are measured and assigned.

Cost of capital The cost of investment funds, usually viewed as a weighted average of the costs of funds from all sources.

Cost of goods manufactured The total cost of goods completed during the current period.

Cost of goods sold The cost of direct materials, direct labor, and overhead attached to the units sold.

Cost of resource usage The activity rate multiplied by the actual activity usage.

Cost of unused activity The activity rate multiplied by the unused activity.

Cost-plus method A transfer price acceptable to the Internal Revenue Service under Section 482. The cost-plus method is simply a cost-based transfer price.

Cost reconciliation The final section of the production report that compares the costs to account for with the costs accounted for to ensure that they are equal.

Cost-volume-profit graph A graph that depicts the relationships among costs, volume, and profits. It consists of a total revenue line and a total cost line.

Costs of quality Costs incurred because poor quality may exist or because poor quality does exist.

Currency appreciation When one country's currency becomes stronger and can purchase more units of another country's currency.

Currency depreciation When one country's currency becomes weaker and can purchase fewer units of another country's currency.

Currency risk management A company's management of its transaction, economic, and translation exposure due to exchange rate fluctuations.

Currently attainable standards Standards that reflect an efficient operating state; they are rigorous but achievable.

Customer value The difference between what a customer receives (customer realization) and what the customer gives up (customer sacrifice).

Cycle time The length of time required to produce one unit of a product.

D

Decentralization The granting of decision-making freedom to lower operating levels.

Decentralized decision making A system in which decisions are made and implemented by lower-level managers.

Decision making The process of choosing among competing alternatives.

Decision model A specific set of procedures that, when followed, produces a decision.

Decision package A description of service levels, with associated costs, that a decision unit can or would like to offer.

Defective product A product or service that does not conform to specifications.

Degree of operating leverage (DOL) A measure of the sensitivity of profit changes to changes in sales volume. It measures the percentage change in profits resulting from a percentage change in sales.

Dependent variable A variable whose value depends on the value of another variable. For example, Y in the cost formula $Y = F + VX$ depends on the value of X.

Deviation The difference between the cost predicted by a cost formula and the actual cost. It measures the distance of a data point from the cost line.

Direct costs Costs that can be easily and accurately traced to a cost object.

Direct fixed expenses Fixed costs that are directly traceable to a given segment and, consequently, disappear if the segment is eliminated.

Direct labor Labor that is traceable to the goods or services being produced.

Direct labor budget A budget showing the total direct labor hours needed and the associated cost for the number of units in the production budget.

Direct materials Materials that are traceable to the goods or services being produced.

Direct materials budget A budget that outlines the expected usage of materials production and purchases of the direct materials required.

Direct method A method that allocates service costs directly to producing departments. This method ignores any interactions that may exist among support departments.

Direct tracing The process of identifying costs that are specifically or physically associated with a cost object.

Discount factor The factor used to convert a future cash flow to its present value.

Discount rate The rate of return used to compute the present value of future cash flows.

Discounted cash flows Future cash flows expressed in present-value terms.

Discounting The act of finding the present value of future cash flows.

Discounting models Capital investment models that explicitly consider the time value of money in identifying criteria for accepting or rejecting proposed projects.

Discretionary fixed expenses Expenses incurred for the acquisition of short-term capacity or services, usually as the result of yearly planning.

Driver analysis The effort expended to identify those factors that are the root causes of activity costs.

Driver tracing The use of drivers to assign costs to cost objects.

Drivers Factors that cause changes in resource usage, activity usage, costs, and revenues.

Drum-Buffer-Rope (DBR) System The TOC inventory management system that relies on the drum beat of the major constrained resources, time buffers, and ropes to determine inventory levels.

Dumping Predatory pricing in the international market.

Durability The length of time a product functions.

Dysfunctional behavior Individual behavior that conflicts with the goals of the organization.

E

Economic order quantity (EOQ) The amount that should be ordered (or produced) to minimize the total ordering (or setup) and carrying costs.

Economic risk The possibility that a firm's present value of future cash flows can be affected by exchange fluctuations.

Electronic data interchange (EDI) An inventory management method that allows suppliers access to a buyer's on-line data base.

Employee empowerment The authorization of operational personnel to plan, control, and make decisions without explicit authorization from middle and higher-level management.

Ending finished goods inventory budget A budget that describes planned ending inventory of finished goods in units and dollars.

Equivalent units of output Complete units that could have been produced given the total amount of manufacturing effort expended during the period.

Ethical behavior Choosing actions that are "right" and "proper" and "just." Our behavior can be right or wrong, it can be proper or improper, and the decisions we make can be fair or unfair.

Exchange gain A gain on the exchange of one currency for another due to appreciation in the home currency.

Exchange loss A loss on the exchange of one currency for another due to depreciation in the home currency.

Exchange rates The rates at which foreign currency can be exchanged for the domestic currency.

Expected activity level Expected activity output for the coming year.

Expenses Expired costs.

External constraints Limiting factors imposed on the firm from external sources (such as market demand).

External failure costs Costs incurred because products fail to conform to requirements after being sold to outside parties.

F

Facility-level activities Activities that sustain a facility's general manufacturing process.

Facility-level drivers Output measures for facility-level activities.

Failure activities Activities performed by an organization or its customers in response to poor quality (poor quality *does* exist).

Failure costs The costs incurred by an organization because failure activities are performed.

Favorable variances Variances produced whenever the actual amounts are less than the budgeted or standard allowances.

Feasible set of solutions The collection of all feasible solutions.

Feasible solution A product mix that satisfies all constraints.

Features (quality of design) Characteristics of a product that differentiate functionally similar products.

Feedback Information that can be used to evaluate or correct the steps being taken to implement a plan.

FIFO costing method A process-costing method that separates units in beginning inventory from those produced during the current period. Unit costs include only current period costs and production.

Financial accounting information system An accounting information subsystem that is primarily concerned with producing outputs for external users and uses well-specified economic events as inputs and processes that meet certain rules and conventions.

Financial budgets The portions of the master budget that include the cash budget, the budgeted balance sheet, the budgeted statement of cash flows, and the capital budget.

Financial productivity measure A productivity measure in which inputs and outputs are expressed in dollars.

Fitness of use The suitability of a product for carrying out its advertised functions.

Fixed (activity) costs Costs that, *in total*, are constant within the relevant range as the activity output varies.

Fixed overhead spending variance The difference between actual fixed overhead and applied fixed overhead.

Fixed overhead volume variance The difference between budgeted fixed overhead and applied fixed overhead; it is a measure of capacity utilization.

Flexible budget A budget that can specify costs for a range of activity.

Flexible budget variance The sum of price variances and efficiency variances in a performance report comparing actual costs to expected costs predicted by a flexible budget.

Foreign trade zones Areas which are physically on U.S. soil, but considered to be outside U.S. commerce. Goods imported into a foreign trade zone are duty free until they leave the zone.

Forward contract An agreement which requires the buyer to exchange a specified amount of a currency at a specified rate (the forward rate) on a specified future date.

Future value The value that will accumulate by the end of an investment's life if the investment earns a specified compounded return.

G

Goal congruence The alignment of a manager's personal goals with those of the organization.

Goodness of fit The degree of association between Y and X (cost and activity). It is measured by how much of the total variability in Y is explained by X.

H

Half-year convention The assumption that a newly acquired asset is in service for one-half year of its first taxable year regardless of the date the service actually began.

Hedging A way of insuring against gains and losses on foreign currency exchange.

Heterogeneity When there is a greater chance of variation in the performance of services than in the production of products.

Hidden quality costs Opportunity costs resulting from poor quality.

High-low method A method for fitting a line to a set of data points using the high and low points in the data set. For a cost formula, the high and low points represent the high and low activity levels. It is used to break out the fixed and variable components of a mixed cost.

Homogeneous cost pool A collection of overhead costs associated with activities that have the same process and the same level, and can use the same activity driver to assign costs to products.

I

Ideal standards Standards that reflect perfect operating conditions.

Incentives The positive or negative measures taken by an organization to induce a manager to exert effort toward achieving the organization's goals.

Incremental (or baseline) budgeting The practice of taking the prior year's budget and adjusting it upward or downward to determine next year's budget.

Independent projects Projects that, if accepted or rejected, will not affect the cash flows of another project.

Independent variable A variable whose value does not depend on the value of another variable. For example, in the cost formula $Y = F + VX$, the variable X is an independent variable.

Indirect costs Costs that cannot be traced to a cost object.

Input trade-off efficiency The least-cost, technically efficient mix of inputs.

Inseparability The fact that producers of services and buyers of services must usually be in direct contact for an exchange to take place.

Intangibility When buyers of services cannot see, feel, hear, or taste a service before it is bought.

Intercept parameter The fixed cost, representing the point where the cost formula intercepts the vertical axis. In the cost formula $Y = F + VX$, F is the intercept parameter.

Internal constraints Limiting factors found within the firm (such as machine time availability).

Internal failure costs Costs incurred because products and services fail to conform to requirements where lack of conformity is discovered prior to external sale.

Internal rate of return The rate of return that equates the present value of a project's cash inflows with the present value of its cash outflows (i.e., it sets the NPV equal to zero). Also, the rate of return being earned on funds that remain internally invested in a project.

Inventory The money an organization spends in turning raw materials into throughput.

Investment center A division of a company that is evaluated on the basis of return on investment.

J

JIT manufacturing A demand-pull system whose objective is to eliminate waste by producing a product only when it is needed and only in the quantities demanded by customers.

JIT purchasing A purchasing method that requires suppliers to deliver parts and materials just in time to be used in production.

Job-order cost sheet A subsidiary account to the work-in-process account on which the total cost of materials, labor, and overhead for a single job are accumulated.

Job-order costing system A costing system in which costs are collected and assigned to units of production for each individual job.

Joint products Products that are inseparable prior to a split-off point. All manufacturing costs up to the split-off point are joint costs.

Joint venture A type of partnership in which investors co-own the enterprise.

K

Kanban system An information system that controls production on a demand-pull basis through the use of cards or markers.

Keep-or-drop decisions Relevant costing analyses that focus on keeping or dropping a segment of a business.

L

Labor efficiency variance (LEV) The difference between the actual direct labor hours used and the standard direct labor hours allowed multiplied by the standard hourly wage rate.

Labor rate variance (LRV) The difference between the actual hourly rate paid and the standard hourly rate multiplied by the actual hours worked.

Lead time For purchasing, the time to receive an order after it is placed. For manufacturing, the time to produce a product from start to finish.

Life-cycle cost management The management of value-chain activities so that a long-term competitive advantage is created.

Life-cycle costs All costs that are associated with the product for its entire life cycle.

Line positions Positions that have direct responsibility for the basic objectives of an organization.

Linear programming A method that searches among possible solutions until it finds the optimal solution.

Long run A period of time in which all costs are variable.

Loose constraints Constraints whose limited resources are not fully used by a product mix.

M

Make-or-buy decisions Relevant costing analyses that focus on whether a component should be made internally or purchased externally.

Management accounting information system An information system that produces outputs using inputs and processes needed to satisfy specific management objectives.

Manufacturing cells Machines grouped in families, usually in a semicircle, so that they can be used to perform a variety of operations in sequence. Each cell is set up to produce a particular product or product family.

Maquiladoras Manufacturing plants located in Mexico which process imported materials and reexport them to the United States.

Margin The ratio of net operating income to sales.

Margin of safety The units sold or expected to be sold or sales revenue earned or expected to be earned above the break-even volume.

Marketing (selling) costs The costs necessary to market and distribute a product or service.

Markup The percentage applied to a base cost; it includes desired profit and any costs not included in the base cost.

Master budget The collection of all area and activity budgets representing a firm's comprehensive plan of action.

Materials price variance (MPV) The difference between the actual price paid per unit of materials and the standard price allowed per unit multiplied by the actual quantity of materials purchased.

Materials requisition form A source document that records the type, quantity, and unit price of the direct materials issued to each job.

Materials usage variance (MUV) The difference between the direct materials actually used and the direct materials allowed for the actual output multiplied by the standard price.

Maximum transfer price The transfer price that will make the buying division no worse off if an input is acquired internally.

Method of least squares A statistical method to find a line that best fits a set of data. It is used to break out the fixed and variable components of a mixed cost.

Minimum transfer price The transfer price that will make the selling division no worse off if an output is sold internally.

Mixed costs Costs that have both a fixed and a variable component.

Modified accelerated cost recovery system (MACRS) An allowable method for computing depreciation for tax purposes.

Monetary incentives The use of economic rewards to motivate managers.

Multinational corporation (MNC) A corporation for which a significant amount of business is done in more than one country.

Multiple-period quality trend report A graph that plots quality costs (as a percentage of sales) against time.

Multiple regression The use of least squares analysis to determine the parameters in a linear equation involving two or more explanatory variables.

Mutually exclusive projects Projects that, if accepted, preclude the acceptance of competing projects.

Myopic behavior Managerial actions that improve budgetary performance in the short run at the expense of the long-run welfare of the organization.

N

Net income Operating income less income taxes.

Net present value The difference between the present value of a project's cash inflows and the present value of its cash outflows.

Nondiscounting models Capital investment models that identify criteria for accepting or rejecting projects without considering the time value of money.

Noninventoriable (period) costs Costs that are expensed in the period in which they are incurred.

Nonmonetary incentives The use of psychological and social rewards to motivate managers.

Nonproduction costs Costs associated with the functions of selling and administration.

Nonunit-based activity cost drivers Factors, other than the number of units produced, that measure the demands that cost objects place on activities.

Nonvalue-added activities All activities other than those that are absolutely essential to remain in business.

Nonvalue-added costs Costs that are caused either by non-value-added activities or by the inefficient performance of valued-added activities.

Normal activity level The average activity output for a given period.

Normal cost of goods sold The cost of goods sold before adjustment for any overhead variance.

Normal costing systems Costing systems that measure overhead costs on a predetermined basis and use actual costs for direct materials and direct labor.

O

Objective function The function to be optimized, usually a profit function; thus, optimization usually means maximizing profits.

Observable quality costs Quality costs that are available from an organization's accounting records.

Operating assets Assets used to generate operating income, consisting usually of cash, inventories, receivables, property, plant, and equipment.

Operating budgets Budgets associated with the income-producing activities of an organization.

Operating expenses The money an organization spends in turning inventories into throughput.

Operating income Revenues minus expenses from the firm's normal operations. Income taxes are excluded.

Operating leverage The use of fixed costs to extract higher percentage changes in profits as sales activity changes. Leverage is achieved by increasing fixed costs while lowering variable costs.

Operation costing A hybrid costing method which assigns materials cost to a product using a job-order approach and assigns conversion cost using a process approach.

Operational measures Physical or nonfinancial measures of performance.

Operational productivity measure A measure that is expressed in physical terms.

Opportunity cost The benefit sacrificed or foregone when one alternative is chosen over another.

Opportunity cost approach A transfer pricing system that identifies the minimum price that a selling division would be willing to accept and the maximum price that a buying division would be willing to pay.

Optimal solution The feasible solution that produces the best value for the objective function (the largest value if seeking to maximize the objective function; the minimum otherwise).

Ordering costs The costs of placing and receiving an order.

Outsourcing The payment by a company for a business function which was formerly done in-house.

Overapplied overhead The amount by which applied overhead exceeds actual overhead.

Overhead All production costs other than direct materials and direct labor.

Overhead budget A budget that reveals the planned expenditures for all indirect manufacturing items.

Overhead variance The difference between actual overhead and applied overhead.

P

Parallel processing A processing pattern in which two or more sequential processes are required to produce a finished good.

Partial productivity measurement A ratio that measures productive efficiency for one input.

Participative budgeting An approach to budgeting that allows managers who will be held accountable for budgetary performance to participate in the budget's development.

Payback period The time required for a project to return its investment.

Performance The measure of how consistent and well a product functions.

Performance reports Reports that compare the actual data with planned data.

Perishability When services cannot be stored for future use by a consumer.

Perquisites A type of fringe benefit over and above salary which is received by managers.

Physical flow schedule A schedule which reconciles units to account for with units accounted for. The physical units are not adjusted for percent of completion.

Planning Setting objectives and identifying methods to achieve those objectives.

Pool rate The overhead costs for a homogeneous cost pool divided by the practical capacity of the activity driver associated with the pool.

Postaudit A follow-up analysis of an investment decision, comparing actual benefits and costs with expected benefits and costs.

Postpurchase costs The costs of using, maintaining, and disposing of the product.

Practical activity level The activity output produced when the activity is performed efficiently.

Practical capacity The efficient level of activity performance.

Predatory pricing The practice of setting prices below cost for the purpose of injuring competitors and eliminating competition.

Predetermined overhead rate An overhead rate computed using estimated data.

Present value The current value of a future cash flow. It represents the amount that must be invested now if the future cash flow is to be received assuming compounding at a given rate of interest.

Prevention costs Cost incurred to prevent defects in products or services being produced.

Price discrimination The charging of different prices to different customers for essentially the same product.

Price gouging A subjective term referring to the practice of setting an "excessively" high price.

Price (rate) variance The difference between standard price and actual price multiplied by the actual quantity of inputs used.

Price-recovery component The difference between the total profit change and the profit-linked productivity change.

Price standard The price that should be paid per unit of input.

Prime cost The sum of direct materials cost and direct labor cost.

Process-costing system A costing system that accumulates production costs by process or by department for a given period of time.

Process improvement Incremental and constant increases in the efficiency of an existing process.

Process innovation (business reengineering) The performance of a process in a radically new way with the objective of achieving dramatic improvements in response time, quality, and efficiency.

Process value analysis An approach that focuses on processes and activities and emphasizes systemwide performance instead of individual performance.

Producing departments Units within an organization responsible for producing the products or services that are sold to customers.

Product cost A cost assignment method that satisfies a well-specified managerial objective.

Product diversity The situation present when products consume overhead in different proportions.

Product-level (sustaining) activities Activities that are performed to enable the production of each different type of product.

Product-level drivers Output measures for product-level activities.

Product life cycle The time a product exists—from conception to abandonment.

Production budget A budget that shows how many units must be produced to meet sales needs and satisfy ending inventory requirements.

Production costs Those costs associated with the manufacture of goods or the provision of services.

Production Kanban A card or marker that specifies the quantity that the Kanban system should produce.

Production report A document that summarizes the manufacturing activity that takes place in a process department for a given period of time.

Productivity The efficient production of output, using the least quantity of inputs possible.

Productivity measurement The assessment of productivity changes.

Profile measurement A series or vector of separate and distinct partial operational measures.

Profit center A division of a company that is evaluated on the basis of operating income or profit.

Profit-linked productivity measurement An assessment of the amount of profit change—from the base period to the current period—attributable to productivity changes.

Profit-volume graph A graphical portrayal of the relationship between profits and sales activity.

Pseudoparticipation A budgetary system in which top management solicits inputs from lower-level managers and then ignores those inputs. Thus, in reality, budgets are dictated from above.

Q

Quality of conformance Conforming to the design requirements of the product.

Quality product (service) A product which meets or exceeds customer expectations.

Quantity standard The quantity of input allowed per unit of output.

R

Reciprocal method A method that simultaneously allocates service costs to all user departments. It gives full consideration to interactions among support departments.

Relevant costs Future costs that change across alternatives.

Relevant range The range over which an assumed cost relationship is valid for the normal operations of a firm.

Reliability The probability that the product or service will perform its intended function for a specified length of time.

Reorder point The point in time at which a new order (or setup) should be initiated.

Required activities The activities that are necessary to comply with legal mandates.

Required rate of return The minimum rate of return that a project must earn in order to be acceptable. Usually corresponds to the cost of capital.

Resale price method A transfer price acceptable to the Internal Revenue Service under Section 482. The resale price method computes a transfer price equal to the sales price received by the reseller less an appropriate markup.

Residual income The difference between operating income and the minimum required dollar return on a company's operating assets.

Resource drivers Factors that measure the demands placed on resources by activities which are used to assign the cost of resources to activities.

Resource spending The cost of acquiring capacity to perform an activity.

Resource usage The amount of activity capacity used in producing an organization's output.

Resources Economic elements that are consumed in performing activities.

Resources supplied as used and needed Resources acquired from outside sources, where the terms of acquisition do not require any long-term commitment for any given amount of the resource.

Resources supplied in advance of usage Resources acquired by the use of either an explicit or an implicit contract to obtain a given quantity of resource, regardless of whether the quantity of the resource available is fully used or not.

Responsibility accounting A system that measures the results of each responsibility center according to the information managers need to operate their center.

Responsibility center A segment of the business whose manager is accountable for specified sets of activities.

Return on investment (ROI) The ratio of operating income to average operating assets.

Revenue center A segment of the business that is evaluated on the basis of sales.

Ropes Actions taken to tie the rate at which raw material is released into the plant (at the first operation) to the production rate of the constrained resource.

S

Safety stock Extra inventory carried to serve as insurance against fluctuations in demand.

Sales budget A budget that describes expected sales in units and dollars for the coming period.

Sales mix The relative combination of products (or services) being sold by an organization.

Scattergraph A plot of (X, Y) data points. For cost analysis, X is activity usage and Y is the associated cost at that activity level.

Scatterplot method A method to fit a line to a set of data using two points that are selected by judgment. It is used to break out the fixed and variable components of a mixed cost.

Segment A subunit of a company of sufficient importance to warrant the production of performance reports.

Segment margin The contribution a segment makes to cover common fixed costs and provide for profit after direct fixed costs and variable costs are deducted from the segment's sales revenue.

Segmented reporting The preparation of financial performance reports for each segment of importance within a firm.

Sell or process further Relevant costing analysis that focuses on whether a product should be processed beyond the split-off point.

Selling and administrative expenses budget A budget that outlines planned expenditures for nonmanufacturing activities.

Sensitivity analysis The "what if" process of altering certain key variables to assess the effect on the original outcome.

Sequential (or step) method A method that allocates service costs to user departments in a sequential manner. It gives partial consideration to interactions among support departments.

Sequential processing A processing pattern in which units pass from one process to another in a set order.

Service A task or activity performed for a customer or an activity performed by a customer using an organization's products or facilities.

Serviceability The ease of maintaining and/or repairing a product.

Setup costs The costs of preparing equipment and facilities so that they can be used for production.

Short run A period of time in which at least one cost is fixed.

Simplex method An algorithm that identifies the optimal solution for a linear programming problem.

Slope parameter The variable cost per unit of activity usage, represented by V in the cost formula $Y = F + VX$.

Special-order decisions Relevant costing analyses that focus on whether a specially priced order should be accepted or rejected.

Split-off point The point at which products become distinguishable after passing through a common process.

Spot rate The exchange rate of one currency for another for immediate delivery.

Staff positions Positions that are supportive in nature and have only indirect responsibility for an organization's basic objectives.

Standard cost per unit The per-unit cost that should be achieved given materials, labor, and overhead standards.

Standard cost sheet A listing of the standard costs and standard quantities of direct materials, direct labor, and overhead that should apply to a single product.

Standard hours allowed The direct labor hours that should have been used to produce the actual output (Unit labor standard × Actual output).

Standard quantity of materials allowed The quantity of materials that should have been used to produce the actual output (Unit materials standard × Actual output).

Static budget A budget for a particular level of activity.

Step-cost function A cost function in which cost is defined for ranges of activity usage rather than point values. The function has the property of displaying constant cost over a range of activity usage and then changing to a different cost level as a new range of activity usage is undertaken.

Step-fixed cost A step-cost function in which cost remains constant over wide ranges of activity usage.

Step-variable cost A step-cost function in which cost remains constant over relatively narrow ranges of activity.

Stock option The right to purchase a certain amount of stock at a fixed price.

Stock-out costs The costs of insufficient inventory.

Strategic decision making Selecting strategies that yield a long-term competitive advantage.

Strategic plan The long-term plan for future activities and operations, usually involving at least five years.

Sunk cost A cost for which the outlay has already been made and that cannot be affected by a future decision.

Supplies Those materials necessary for production that do not become part of the finished product or which are not used in providing a service.

Support departments Units within an organization that provide essential support services for producing departments.

T

Tactical decision making Choosing among alternatives with an immediate or limited end in view.

Taguchi loss function A function that assumes any variation from the target value of a quality characteristic causes hidden quality costs.

Tangible products Goods that are produced by converting raw materials through the use of labor and capital inputs such as plant, land, and machinery.

Target cost The difference between the sales price needed to achieve a projected market share and the desired per-unit profit.

Target costing A method of determining the cost of a product or service based on the price (target price) that customers are willing to pay.

Tariff The tax on imports levied by the federal government.

Technical efficiency The point at which, for any mix of inputs that will produce a given output, no more of any one input is used than is absolutely necessary.

Theoretical activity level The activity output possible if the activity is performed with perfect efficiency.

Throughput The rate at which an organization generates money through sales.

Time buffer The inventory needed to keep the constrained resource busy for a specified time interval.

Time ticket A source document by which direct labor costs are assigned to individual jobs.

Total budget variance The difference between the actual cost of an input and its planned cost.

Total preventive maintenance A program of preventive maintenance that has zero machine failures as its standard.

Total product The complete range of tangible and intangible benefits that a customer receives from a purchased product.

Total productive efficiency The point at which technical and price efficiency are achieved.

Total productivity measurement An assessment of productive efficiency for all inputs combined.

Total quality management An approach to quality in which manufacturers strive to create an environment that will enable workers to manufacture perfect (zero-defect) products.

Traceability The ability to assign a cost directly to a cost object in an economically feasible way using a causal relationship.

Tracing Assigning costs to a cost object using an observable measure of the cost object's resource consumption.

Traditional responsibility accounting A control system defined by centering responsibility on organizational units and individuals with traditional budgets and standard costing used to evaluate and monitor performance.

Transaction risk The possibility that future cash transactions will be affected by changing exchange rates.

Transfer price The price charged for goods transferred from one division to another.

Transfer pricing problem The problem of finding a transfer pricing system that simultaneously satisfies the three objectives of accurate performance evaluation, goal congruence, and autonomy.

Transferred-in costs Costs transferred from a prior process to a subsequent process.

Translation (or accounting) risk The degree to which a firm's financial statements are exposed to exchange rate fluctuation.

Treasurer The person responsible for the finance function. Specifically, the treasurer raises capital and manages cash and investments.

Turnover The ratio of sales to average operating assets.

U

Underapplied overhead The amount by which actual overhead exceeds applied overhead.

Unfavorable variances Variances produced whenever the actual input amounts are greater than the budgeted or standard allowances.

Unit-level activities Activities that are performed each time a unit is produced.

Unit-level activity drivers Output measures for unit-level activities.

Unused capacity The difference between the acquired activity capacity and the actual activity usage.

Usage (efficiency) variance The difference between standard quantities and actual quantities multiplied by standard price.

V

Value-added activities Activities that are necessary to achieve corporate objectives and remain in business.

Value-added costs Costs caused by value-added activities.

Value-added standard The optimal output level for an activity.

Value chain The set of activities required to design, develop, produce, market, and deliver products and services to customers.

Variable budgets *See* Flexible budget.

Variable cost ratio Variable costs divided by sales revenues. It is the proportion of each sales dollar needed to cover variable costs.

Variable costing A product-costing method that assigns only variable manufacturing costs to production: direct materials, direct labor, and variable overhead. Fixed overhead is treated as a period cost.

Variable costs Costs that, in total, vary in direct proportion to changes in a cost driver.

Variable overhead efficiency variance The difference between the actual direct labor hours used and the standard hours allowed multiplied by the standard variable overhead rate.

Variable overhead spending variance The difference between the actual variable overhead and the budgeted variable overhead based on actual hours used to produce the actual output.

Velocity The number of units that can be produced in a given period of time (e.g., output per hour).

Vendor Kanbans Cards or markers that signal to a supplier the quantity of materials that need to be delivered and the time of delivery.

W

Weighted average costing method A process-costing method that combines beginning inventory costs with current-period costs to compute unit costs. Costs and output from the current period and the previous period are averaged to compute unit costs.

What-if analysis *See* Sensitivity analysis.

Whole-life cost The life cycle cost of a product plus costs that consumers incur, including operation, support, maintenance, and disposal.

Withdrawal Kanban A marker or card that specifies the quantity that a subsequent process should withdraw from a preceding process.

Work in process All partially completed units found in production at a given point in time.

Work-in-process file A file that is the collection of all job cost sheets.

Z

Zero-base budgeting An alternative approach to budgeting in which the prior year's budgeted level is not taken for granted. Instead, the existing operations are analyzed, and continuance of the activity or operation must be justified on the basis of its need or usefulness to the organization.

Zero defects A quality performance standard that requires all products and services to be produced and delivered according to specifications.

COMPANY INDEX

(Service companies are in italics)

CHECK FIGURES

P2-1	4. Unit cost, stereo = $41 (using activity drivers)
P2-7	2. Unit cost = $163
P2-8	1. DM = $240,000
P2-9	3. Income = $400,000
P2-10	2. 1.56 employees
	4. Prime cost = $1.00; Conversion cost = $0.81
	6. Income = $428
C2-1	2. Income = $184,360
	3. Y = $515,000 + 126.57X
P3-1	2. Resource spending decreases by $45,000
	3. Cost of unused machining activity = $5,000
P3-2	3. Charge = $106
	4. Charge = $98.40
P3-3	3. Y = $10,800 + $6X
	4. Y = $4,510 + $13.38X
P3-4	1. Unit variable cost = $210
P3-5	2. Y = $8,750 + $1.125X
	3. Y = $6,877.50 + $1.21X
P3-6	2. $R^2 = 0.91$
	3. Unused capacity cost = $3,000
P3-7	1. F = $(10,006)
P3-8	1. $R^2 = 0.93$
	2. $R^2 = 0.013$
C3-1	2. Forecast = $2,150,000
P4-1	1. Unit cost (duffel bags) = $4.00
	2. Unit cost = $0.50
	3. Unit cost (duffel bags) = $2.00
P4-2	1. Overhead cost per unit = $2.00
	3. Engine A = $5.30 per unit
P4-3	1. Basic = $87.50 per unit
	3. Basic = $84.40 per unit
P4-5	1. $524.17 per day
	3. High severity = $766.67 per day
P4-6	1. X12, unit gross margin = $5.25
	2. X12, unit gross margin = $8.30
P4-8	1. Modern = $32 per unit
	2. Modern = $25 per unit
P4-9	1. Category I unit ordering cost = $0.075
	2. Reduction in resource spending = $2,450,000
C4-1	3. Revised profit per ton (LLHC) = $(35.41)

P5-1	1. Dept. 2 = $5.60/machine hour
	2. Dept. 1 = $7,000 underapplied overhead
	4. Unit cost = $153.16
P5-2	1. Unit cost = $2,025
	3. Unit cost = $1,657.50
P5-3	1. Job #18 total cost = $12,374
P5-4	2. Job #3 total cost = $46,578
	4. Profit = $18,951
P5-5	1. Unit bid price SS = $18.75
	2. Unit bid price TT = $101.01
P5-6	2. Overhead per unit, hairsetter = $2.99
P5-7	1. Cassette Dept. = $8/Mhr
	2. Total cost = $679
P5-8	1. $9/DLH
	3. Cost on 6/20/98 = $7
P5-9	1. Pottery Dept. = $1.40/DLH
	2. Total cost = $615.75
	3. Total price = $355.31
P5-10	1. Price this year = $176.40
	2. Purchasing rate = $3 per purchase order
	3. Price = $141.40
	4. Total cost = $41.55
C5-2	1. Total cost = $26
	2. Gross margin (4-surface) = $22.33
C5-3	1. Unit cost = $7.16
	3. Actual unit cost = $7.54
	4. Total price = $2,980.25
P6-1	1. Total equivalent units = 12,980
P6-2	Cost/equivalent unit = $5.9139
P6-3	1. (b) Equivalent units conversion = 521,000
	2. Total unit cost = $0.4017
	3. EWIP = $11,136
P6-4	Total unit cost = $7.851
P6-5	Cost Transferred Out = $333,959
P6-6	Cost Transferred Out = $210,420
P6-7	Cost Transferred Out = $44,258
P6-8	Cost of EWIP = $6,123
P6-9	1. (c) Unit cost = $5.71
	3. (c) Unit cost = $11.05
P6-10	1. (d) Cost of EWIP = $10,144
	3. (d) Cost of EWIP = $23,419
P6-11	1. Unit cost = $122.30
	2. Cost of EWIP = $585
P6-12	1. Unit cost = $119.13
	2. Cost of EWIP = $591
P6-13	3. Packaging unit conversion cost = $3.05
	4. Molding EWIP = $1,260
P6-14	2. Molding total unit cost = $11.437
	3. Assembly Transferred Out = $11,754
P6-15	Unit cost = $18.015
C6-2	1. Unit cost = $70.71
	2. Unit cost Econo Model = $48.75
P7-1	1. Reno = $266,500
	2. Las Vegas = $144,470
P7-2	1. Midwest total = $413,360
	2. Midwest total = $407,750
	3. Midwest total = $410,638

P7-3	1. (a) Bid price = $2,034.08
	1. (b) Bid price = $2,118.33
P7-4	1. (a) Bid price = $2,161.38
P7-5	1. $0.17 per mile
	2. Truck = $12,020
P7-6	1. (b) Cooking = $195,980
	2. Fixed overhead rate (Packaging) = $3.09/DLH
	5. (a) Price = $178,386
P7-7	1. $0.10 per kilowatt hour
	2. $0.126 per kilowatt hour
P7-8	1. PD1 = $261,750
	2. PD1 = $247,924
P7-9	1. Yuma = $26,072
	2. El Gato share of Purchasing = $7,500
P7-10	1. Dept. B = $2,000,000
	2. Bid price per unit TT = $101.45
C7-2	1. 206L-1 profit per hour = $62.37
	2. Loss = $131,538
	3. Revenue = $623,171
	4. Revised price 206L-1 = $566.19 per hour
P8-1	2. February production = 29,000
	3. March No. 326 = $180,000
	5. March Total = $373,000
	7. Unit cost = $77.41
	10. January ending balance = $33,800
P8-2	1. Cash = $13,550
	2. September ending balance = $12,005
P8-4	Total cash available = $546,106
P8-5	Total sales revenue = $32,736,000
P8-6	2. Total cost variance = $984 F
P8-7	Quarter 4 production = 80,000 units
	Ending Finished Goods = $3,329,000
	Quarter 2 Ending Cash balance = $3,128,000
P8-8	1. Total Variance = $162,240 F
P8-10	October net income = $16,930
P8-11	2. Total budgeted costs = $3,060,700
P8-12	May materials payments = $1,156,000
C8-2	1. Total cash needs = $24,264
P9-1	1. MUV = 3,000 F
	2. LRV = $4,000 U
	3. LEV = $4,000 F
P9-2	1. Unit prime cost = $8.62
	4. MUV, pads = $550 U
P9-3	2. 0.384 hours per unit
	3. Unit cost = $19.29
P9-4	1. MPV = $39,000 F
	2. LEV = $12,000 U
	4. Volume variance = $12,000 F
P9-5	1. Standard cost, regular = $25.40
	2. MPV = $5,600 F
	3. LEV (small) = $1,600 U
P9-6	1. FOH Spending Variance = $10,000 U
	2. VOH Spending Variance = $8,000 U
P9-7	2. Investigate liquid variances
	3. Investigate labor efficiency variance
P9-8	1 (c) $30,000 U
	1 (d) Volume Variance = $15,000 U
	1 (e) Efficiency Variance = $15,000 U

P9-10	1. 60,000 units
	3. Planned labor variance = $18,480
P9-11	1. SQ/unit = 0.6 lbs; SP = $5.00; SH/unit = 0.2
	3. LRV = $660 U
	4. 2,400 hours
C9-2	3. Cost per bag = $0.7294
P10-2	2. Potential reduction: $7.10 per unit
	3. Target cost to expand = $8
P10-3	2. Unused Capacity Variance = $25,000 F
	3. Standard, Eng. = 20,400 hours
P10-4	1. $340
	2. Novalue-added cost = $115 per unit
P10-6	2. Return on sales (B) = 22.5%
	3. $575,000 for A
P10-7	2. $10 per unit
	3. $15 per unit
P10-8	1. 0.30
P10-10	2. Unit cost = $15.07
	3. Volume Variance = $120,000
P10-12	4. Potential reduction of conversion cost = $16.67
P11-2	2. Prevention = 4.3%
	4. Profit improvement = $1,600,000
P11-3	1. 8.7 quarters to regain profitability
	3. After 9.8 quarters, price should be reduced
P11-4	1. Loss = $2,000,000
	2. Breakeven = $50,000,000
	3. Breakeven = $17,054,264
P11-5	1. Savings = $550,000 for the year
P11-8	2. Increase = $28,000
	3. Price recovery = $(7,500)
P11-9	2. $28,000
	3. $10,000
	4. $18,000
P11-10	12. Profit change = $2,225,000 increase
P11-11	2. Profit change = $1,665 decrease
	3. Profit change = $13,335 increase
P11-12	2. Setting A provides a $240,000 increase
	3. A = $197,784
P12-1	1. Company contribution margin = $600,000
	5. Company contribution margin = $750,000
P12-2	2. Western division increased CM = $30,000
	3. Price = $61
P12-3	1. 10.33%
	4. Margin = 9.13%
	5. Without: 14.09%
P12-4	1. Parts increased profit = $400,000
	2. Parts decreased profit = $500,000
P12-5	1. Minimum = $26
	2. $28.50
P12-6	3. Chemical reduced costs = $50,000
P12-7	2. Transfer price = $285
	4. $276.75
P12-8	1. Maximum = $2.35
P12-9	1. Transfer price = $18.69 per seat
P12-11	1. Meyers bonus pool = $41,700
C12-1	1. ROI if iron is produced = 15.79%

P13-3	1. 162,705 francs
	2. $74,677 (total from both customers)
P13-4	Comparable uncontrolled price = $12.75
P13-5	1. Canada $410
C13-2	2. Allowable cost without adjustment = $6
	3. Maximum = $12
P14-1	1. Net income = $323,400
	2. Net income = $323,400
P14-2	1. Net income = $239,280
P14-3	1. Net loss = $150,000
	2. Net income = $270,375
P14-4	1. Net income with D = $76,250
P14-5	1. Difference = $6,000
	2. Variable income = $(29,000)
P14-6	1. Net income = $4,850,000
	2. 1998 net income = $6,250,000
	3. 1996 difference = $1,400,000
P14-7	1. Month 1 Absorption unit cost = $9.60
	2. Month 3 difference = $20,000
	3. Month 2 difference = 0
P14-8	1. Napkin segment margin = $194,500
P14-9	2. Year 2 net income = $15,000
P14-10	2. 1997 net loss = $3,400
	3. 1998 difference = $6,500,000
P14-11	1. Variable unit cost = $17.50
	2. Net income = $65,000
	3. Net income = $42,000
P14-12	1. Net loss = $350,000
P14-13	1. Fixed overhead rate = $12/DLH
	2. Absorption net loss = $177,500
	3. Wall clocks segment margin = $80,000
	4. Southwest segment margin = $255,200
C14-2	1. Net loss = $3,500
	2. Contribution margin = $1,890
P15-1	1. CM ratio = .5
	2. Net income = $388,540
	3. $270,000
	5. $850,000
	6. Operating leverage = 8.06
P15-2	1. 41,805 Wars; 33,444 Dragons
	2. Contribution margin ratio = .469
	3. 56,399 Wars; 24,171 Dragons
P15-3	1. Advertising = $105,000
	2. (a) Price = $0.45
	3. Increase in income = $50,000
P15-4	1. Average number of residential customers = 1,182
P15-5	1. Contribution margin ratio = .48
	2. $375,000
	3. $501,689
P15-6	2. $333,513
	3. Increase prices by 11.6%
P15-7	1. Grade I = 224 units; Grade II = 524 units
	2. Grade I = 168 units; Grade II = 392 units
P15-8	1. $450,000
	3. Operating leverage = 4.0
P15-9	1. Trim kits CM ratio = .375
	3. Door handles = 16,222; Trim kits = 32,444
	4. Net income = $99,000

P15-10	1. Break even units = 21,429
	2. $318,000
	3. Break even units = 23,810
P15-11	1. Moline unit contribution = $48
	2. Operating income $3,628,800
	3. Operating income $4,094,400
P15-12	1. $18,025,000
C15-1	1. Manual Process = 5,000 cases
C15-2	1. Net loss = $268,000
	2. CM per Nutcracker performance = $29,150
	3. Sleeping Beauty 14; Nutcracker 28; Others 7 each
	4. Increase in CM = $72,020
	5. Net loss = $135,980
P16-1	1. Difference = $12,000
P16-2	1. Difference = $692
	2. $1.384 additional income/pound
P16-3	1. Net income = $6,100
	2. Net income = $16,558
P16-4	1. Kevin's profits increase by $4,000
P16-5	1. Net loss = $70,900
P16-6	1. First year buy total = $35,800,000
P16-7	1. Tissue CM/Mhr = $1.50
	2. Maximum profit = $275,000
P16-8	1. Net loss = $58,000
	2. Net loss without T-gauge = $18,000
P16-9	2. Total contribution margin = $113,250
	3. Optimum output Product 402 = 400 units
P16-10	1. Drop B and Make relevant costs = $48,000
	2. Make relevant costs = $54,360
	3. Drop B and Make relevant costs = $60,824
P16-11	1. Tackle boxes contribution/hour = $26.40
P16-12	1. (a) 2" cost per ton = $220
C16-2	Total avoidable costs = $492,000
P17-1	2. NPV = $14,724
P17-2	2. NPV = $184,520
P17-3	2. CF = $8,176
	3. IRR is between 10% and 12%
P17-4	1. NPV = $22,525,500
	2. NPV = $(5,291,100)
	3. Seats = 126 (one way)
	4. Seating rate = 77%
P17-5	1. 2.65 years
	4. NPV = $(2,254)
P17-6	1. Buy NPV = $(315,812)
P17-7	2. NPV (purchase) = $38,559
	3. NPV = $39,592
P17-8	1. NPV = $4,059
P17-9	1. NPV (14%) = $(23,441,400)
	2. MPV (20%) = $(8,832,000)
	3. NPV (14%) = $211,008
P17-10	1. NPV = $26,634
	2. NPV = $(22,108)
P17-11	1. NPV (new) = $7,663
	3. NPV = $13,680
P17-12	1. NPV (flexible) = $(1,314,892)
	2. NPV (old) = $(1,379, 872)
C17-2	1. Net income = $51,000
	2. Payback = 3.28 years

	4. Breakeven = 29,859 cubic yards; NPV = $(6,651)
	5. Income = $1,082
C17-3	2. NPV (Robotics) = $775,911
	3. NPV (12%) = $112,000
P18-1	1. Total cost = $1,750
	2. Savings = $350
P18-2	1. Total cost = $600
	2. ROP = 40
P18-3	1. Time required = 14 days
	3. Lead time = 7.5 hours
	4. Batch size = 144 units
P18-5	1. 800,000 packages of diet instant
	2. 600,000 packages of diet instant and 100,000 of rich
P18-6	2. Contribution margin (total) = $226,500
P18-7	1. Molding
	2. Contribution margin = $30,000 per day
	3. 104 units of A and 500 units of B
P18-8	1. Sub A = 1,600 units; Sub B = 0
	2. Drummer = Assembly
	4. Daily contribution margin increases by $16,000
P18-9	1. Welding is a bottleneck
	2. Daily contribution = $5,800
	4. Daily contribution increases by $990